CW01021801

You are holding a reproduction of an original work that is in the public domain in the United States of America, and possibly other countries.You may freely copy and distribute this work as no entity (individual or corporate) has a copyright on the body of the work.This book may contain prior copyright references, and library stamps (as most of these works were scanned from library copies).These have been scanned and retained as part of the historical artifact.

This book may have occasional imperfections such as missing or blurred pages, poor pictures, errant marks, etc. that were either part of the original artifact, or were introduced by the scanning process. We believe this work is culturally important, and despite the imperfections, have elected to bring it back into print as part of our continuing commitment to the preservation of printed works worldwide. We appreciate your understanding of the imperfections in the preservation process, and hope you enjoy this valuable book.

SVNT MELIORA MIHI

RICHARDVS HOOKER Exoniensis scholaris
sociusq; Collegij Corp: Christi Oxon: deinde Londi:
Templi interioris in Sacris magister Rectorq;
huius Ecclesiæ, scripsit octo libros Politiæ
Ecclesiasticæ Anglicanæ, quorum tres desi:
derantur: Obijt Añ: Dñi M.DC.III. Ætat:
suæ L.
Posuit hoc pijssimo viro monumentum Añ:
Dñi M.DC.XXXV. Guli: Cowper Armiger,
in Christo Iesu quem genuit per Euangelium.
1 Corinth: 4. 15.

OF THE
LAWES
of
ECCLESIASTICAL
Politie.

Eight Bookes

By RICHARD HOOKER.

LONDON
Printed for R. Scot, T. Basset,
J. Wright & R. Chiswell.

THE
WORKS

Of that Learned and Judicious Divine,

Mr. Richard Hooker,

IN

EIGHT BOOKS

Of the LAWS of

Ecclefiaftical Polity,

Compleated out of his own MANUSCRIPTS.

Dedicated to the King's moſt excellent Majeſty,

CHARLES II.

By whoſe ROYAL FATHER (near his Martyrdom) the former five Books (then only extant) were commended to his Dear Children, as an excellent means to ſatisfy private Scruples, and ſettle the publick Peace of this CHURCH and KINGDOM.

To which are added, Several other Treatiſes by the ſame Author.

All Reviſed and Corrected in numberleſs Places of the former Editions, by a diligent Hand.

There is alſo prefix'd before the Book,
The LIFE of the AUTHOR, written by ISAAC WALTON.

To this Edition is added a large Alphabetical INDEX.

LONDON,

Printed for *John Walthoe, George Conyers, James Knapton, Robert Knaplock, J.* and *B. Sprint, Dan. Midwinter, Bernard Lintot, Benj. Cowſe, William Taylor, W.* and *J. Innys, John Osborne, Ranew Robinſon, Sam. Tooke, Tho. Wotton.* M.DCC.XXIII.

To the King's moſt excellent Majeſty

CHARLES II.

By the grace of God,

King of *Great Britain, France,* and *Ireland,*

Defender of the Faith, &c.

Moſt Gracious Sovereign,

ALTHO I know how little leiſure *great kings* have to read large books, or indeed any, ſave only *God*'s, (the ſtudy, belief, and obedience of which, is preciſely commanded, even to *kings, Deut.* 17. 18, 19. and from which, whatever wholly *diverts* them, will hazard to *damn* them ; there being no affairs of ſo great importance, as their ſerving *God,* and *ſaving their own ſouls* ; nor any *precepts* ſo wiſe, juſt, holy, and ſafe, as thoſe of the *divine oracles* ; nor any *empire* ſo glorious, as that by which *kings,* being *ſubject to God's law,* have *dominion* over *themſelves,* and ſo beſt deſerve and exerciſe it over their *ſubjects* :)

Yet having lived to ſee the wonderful and happy *reſtoration* of *your majeſty* to *your* rightful kingdoms, and of this *reformed church* to its juſt rights, primitive order, and priſtine conſtitution, by *your majeſty's* prudent care, and unparallel'd bounty, I know not what to preſent more worthy of *your majeſty's* acceptance, and my duty, than theſe *elaborate* and *ſeaſonable works* of the famous and prudent Mr. *Richard Hooker,* now augmented, and I hope completed with the *three laſt books,* ſo much deſired and ſo long concealed.

The publiſhing of which *volume* ſo *intire,* and thus *preſenting* it to *your majeſty,* ſeems to be a *bleſſing* and *honour* reſerved by *God's* providence, to add a further luſtre to *your majeſty's* glorious name, and *happy reign,*

A 2   whoſe

Works In Eight Books Of The Laws Of Ecclesiastical Polity

whoſe tranſcendent favour, juſtice, merit, and munificence to the _long afflicted church_ of _England_, is a ſubject no leſs worthy of _admiration_ than _gratitude_ to all poſterity. And of all things, next _God's_ Grace, not to be abuſed or turned into wantonneſs by any of _your majeſty's_ clergy, who are highly obliged, beyond all other _ſubjects_ to piety, loyalty and induſtry.

I ſhall need nothing more to ingratiate this _incomparable piece_ to _your majeſty's_ acceptance, and all the _Engliſh world's_, than thoſe _high commendations_ it hath ever had, as from all prudent, peaceable and impartial _readers_, ſo eſpecially from _your majeſty's_ royal _father_, who a few days before he was _crowned with martyrdom_, commended to _his deareſt children_, the diligent reading of Mr. _Hooker's Eccleſiaſtical Polity_, even next the _bible_; as an excellent means to ſettle them in the _truth of religion_, and in the _peace of this church_, as much _chriſtian_, and as well _reformed_ as any under _heaven_: as if _God_ had reſerved this _ſignal honour_ to be done by the beſt of _kings_, and _greateſt ſufferers_ for this _church_, to _him_ who was one of the beſt _writers_, and ableſt _defenders_ of it.

To this _completed edition_, is added ſuch particular accounts as could be got of the _author's perſon, education, temper, manners, fortunes, life_ and _death_, which is now done with much _exactneſs_ and _proportion_: that hereby _your majeſty_, and all the _world_, may ſee what ſort of men are fitteſt for _church-work_ (which like the building of _Solomon's_ temple, is beſt carried on with moſt _evenneſs_ of judgment, and leaſt _noiſe_ of paſſion;) alſo what manner of _man_ he was, to whom we all owe this _noble work_, and _durable defence_.

Which is indeed at once (as the tongues of _eloquent princes_ are to themſelves, and their _ſubjects_) both a _treaſury_, and an _armory_, to inrich their friends, and defend them againſt the enemies of the _church_ of _England_: a rare compoſition of _unpaſſionate reaſon_, and _unpartial religion_; the mature product of a _judicious ſcholar_, a _loyal ſubject_, an _humble preacher_, and a moſt _eloquent writer_: the very _abſtract_ and _quinteſſence_ of _laws human_ and _divine_; a _ſummary_ of the grounds, rules

‡   and

and proportions of *true polity* in *church* and *ſtate*: upon which clear, ſolid and ſafe *foundations*, the good order, peace and government of this *church* was antiently ſettled, and on which, while it ſtands firm, it will be *flouriſhing*. All other popular and ſpecious *pretenſions*, being found by late ſad experiences, to be as *novel* and *unfit*, ſo *factious* and *fallacious*, yea, dangerous and deſtructive to the *peace*, and *proſperity* of this *church* and *kingdom*, whoſe inſeparable *happineſs* and *intereſts* are bound up in *monarchy* and *epiſcopacy*.

The politick and viſible managing of both which, *God* hath now graciouſly reſtored and committed to *your majeſty's* ſovereign *wiſdom*, and *authority*, after the many and long *tragedies* ſuffered from thoſe *club-maſters* and *tub-miniſters*, who ſought not fairly to obtain *reformation* of what might ſeem amiſs, but violently and wholly to overthrow the antient and goodly *fabrick* of this *church* and *kingdom*. For finding themſelves not able in many years to *anſwer this one book*, long ago written in defence of the truth, order, government, authority, and liberty, in things indifferent, of this *reformed church*, agreeable to *right reaſon* and *true religion* (which makes this well-temper'd piece, a file capable to break the *teeth* of any that venture to bite it) they conſpired at laſt to betake themſelves to *arms*, to kindle thoſe horrid fires of *civil wars*, which this wiſe *author* foreſaw, and foretold, in his admirable *preface*, would follow thoſe *ſparks* and that *ſmoak* which he ſaw riſe in his *days*: ſo that from *impertinent diſputes*, ſeconded with *ſcurrilous pamphlets*, they fled to *tumults*, *ſedition*, *rebellion*, *ſacrilege*, *parricide* yea, *regicide*; *counſels*, *weapons*, and *practices* certainly, no way becoming the hearts and hands of *chriſtian ſubjects*, nor ever ſanctified by *Chriſt* for his ſervice, or his *church's* good.

What now remains, but *your majeſty's* perfecting and preſerving that in this *church*, which you have with much prudence and tenderneſs ſo *happily* begun and proſecuted, with more *zeal* than the eſtabliſhment of *your* own *throne*. The ſtill *crazy church* of *England*, together with this *book*, its great and impregnable *ſhield*,

do

do further need, and humbly implore *your majesty's* royal protection under *God:* nor can *your majesty* by any generous instance and perseverance, most worthy of a *christian king*, more express that pious and grateful sense which *God* and all good men expect from *your majesty*, as some retribution for his many *miraculous mercies* to your self, than in a wise, speedy, and happy setling of our *religious peace*; with the least *grievance*, and most *satisfaction* to all *your good subjects: sacred order* and *uniformity* being the *center* and *circumference* of our *civil tranquillity*; *sedition* naturally rising out of *schism*, and *rebellion* out of *faction*. The only cure and antidote against both, are good *laws* and *canons*, first wisely made, with all *christian moderation*, and *seasonable charity*; next, duly executed with justice and impartiality: which sober severity is indeed the *greatest charity* to the publick. Whose verity, unity, sanctity, and solemnity in religious concernments, being once duly *established*, must not be shaken, or sacrificed to any private varieties and extravagancies. Where the internals of doctrine, morality, mysteries, and evangelical duties, being, as they are in the *church of England*, sound and sacred, the externals of decent forms, circumstances, rites and ceremonies, being subordinate and servient to the main, cannot be either evil or unsafe, neither offensive to *God* nor good *christians*.

For the attaining of which *blessed ends* of piety and peace, that the sacred *sun* and *shield* of the *divine grace* and *power* directing and protecting, may ever shine upon *your majesty's* person and family, counsels and power, is the humble prayer of

Your sacred majesty's

most loyal subject,

and devoted servant,

JOH. EXON.

TO THE

READER.

I Think it neceſſary to inform my reader, that doctor Gauden (the late biſhop of Worceſter) hath alſo lately wrote and publiſh'd the life of maſter Hooker. And tho this be not writ by deſign to oppoſe what he hath truly written ; yet I am put upon a neceſſity to ſay, That in it there be many material miſtakes, and more omiſſions. I conceive ſome of his miſtakes did proceed from a belief in maſter Thomas Fuller, who had too haſtily publiſhed what he hath ſince moſt ingenuouſly retracted. And for the biſhop's omiſſions, I ſuppoſe his more weighty buſineſs and want of time, made him paſs over many things without that due examination, which my better leiſure, my diligence, and my accidental advantages, have made known unto me.

And now for my ſelf, I can ſay, I hope, or rather know, there are no material miſtakes in what I here preſent to you that ſhall become my reader. Little things that I have received by tradition (to which there may be too much or too little faith given) I will not at this diſtance of time undertake to juſtify: for, tho I have uſed great diligence, and compared relations and circumſtances, and probable reſults and expreſſions ; yet I will not impoſe my belief upon my reader ; I ſhall rather leave him at liberty : but, if there ſhall appear any material omiſſion, I deſire every lover of truth and the memory of maſter Hooker, that it may be made known unto me. And, to incline him to it, I here promiſe to acknowledge and rectify any ſuch miſtake in a ſecond impreſſion, which the printer ſays he hopes for ; and by this means my weak (but faithful) endeavours may become a better monument, and in ſome degree more worthy the memory of this venerable man.

I confeſs, that when I conſider the great learning and virtue of maſter Hooker, and what ſatisfaction and advantages many eminent ſcholars and admirers of him have had by his labours ; I do not a little wonder that in ſixty years no man did undertake to tell poſterity of the excellencies of his life and learning, and the accidents of both ; and ſometimes wonder more at my ſelf, that I have been perſuaded to it : and indeed I do not eaſily pronounce my own pardon, nor expect that my reader ſhall, unleſs my introduction ſhall prove my apology, to which I refer him.

A Copy

A copy of a letter writ to Mr .Walton, by doctor King, lord bishop of Chichester.

Honest ISAAC,

THO a familiarity of forty years continuance, and the constant experience of your love, even in the worst times, be sufficient to indear our friendship; yet I must confess my affection much improved, not only by evidences of private respect to those very many that know and love you, but by your new demonstration of a publick spirit, testified in a diligent, true and useful collection of so many material passages as you have now afforded me in the life of venerable Mr. *Hooker*; of which, since desired by such a friend as your self, I shall not deny to give the testimony of what I know concerning him and his learned books; but shall first here take a fair occasion to tell you, that you have been happy in chusing to write the lives of three such persons, as posterity hath just cause to honour; which they will do the more for the true relation of them by your happy pen: of all which I shall give you my unfeigned censure.

I shall begin with my most dear and incomparable friend doctor *Donne*, late dean of saint *Paul's* church, who not only trusted me as his executor, but three days before his death delivered into my hands those excellent sermons of his which are now made publick: professing before doctor *Winniff*, doctor *Montford*, and I think your self, then present at his bedside, that it was by my restless importunity that he had prepared them for the press; together with which (as his best legacy) he gave me all his sermon-notes, and his other papers, containing an extract of near fifteen hundred authors. How these were got out of my hands, you, who were the messenger for them, and how lost both to me and your self, is not now seasonable to complain: but since they did miscarry, I am glad that the general demonstration of his worth was so fairly preserved, and represented to the world by your pen in the history of his life; indeed so well, that beside others, the best critick of our later time (Mr. *John Hales* of *Eaton* college) affirmeth to me, *He had not seen a life written with more advantage to the subject, or more reputation to the writer, than that of doctor* Donne's.

After the performance of this task for doctor *Donne*, you undertook the like office for our friend sir *Henry Wotton*, betwixt which two there was a friendship begun in *Oxford*, continued in their various travels, and more confirmed in the religious friendship of age: and doubtless this excellent person had writ the life of doctor *Donne*, if death had not prevented him; by which means, his and your pre-collections for that work, fell to the happy manage of your pen; a work, which you would have declined, if imperious persuasions had not been stronger than your modest resolutions against it. And I am thus far glad, that the first life was so imposed upon you, because it gave an unavoidable cause of writing the second; if not, 'tis too probable we had wanted both, which had been a prejudice to all lovers of honour and ingenious learning. And let me not leave my friend sir *Henry* without this testimony added to yours, that he was a man of as florid a wit, and elegant a pen, as any former, or ours, which in that kind is a most excellent age, has ever produced.

And now having made this voluntary observation of our two deceased friends, I proceed to satisfy your desire concerning what I know and believe of the ever-memorable Mr. *Hooker*, who was *schismaticorum malleus*, so great a champion for the church of *England's* rights, against the factious torrent of separatists that then ran high against church-discipline, and in his unanswerable books continues still to be so against the unquiet discipline of their schism, which now under other names carry on their design; and who (as the proper heirs of their irrational zeal) would again rake into the scarce-closed wounds of a newly bleeding state and church.

And first, though I dare not say I knew Mr. *Hooker*; yet, as our ecclesiastical history reports to the honour of *Ignatius*, that he lived in the time of saint *John*, and had seen him in his childhood; so I also joy, that in my minority I have often seen Mr. *Hooker* with my father, then lord bishop of *London*; from whom, and others at that time, I have

heard

heard moft of the material paffages which you relate in the hiftory of his life ; and from my father received fuch a character of his learning, humility, and other virtues, that like jewels of unvaluable price, they ftill caft fuch a luftre as envy or the ruft of time fhall never darken. From my father I have alfo heard all the circumftances of the plot to defame him ; and how fir *Edwin Sandys* outwitted his accufers, and gained their confeffion ; and could give an account of each particular of that plot, but that I judge it fitter to be forgotten, and rot in the fame grave with the malicious authors. I may not omit to declare, that my father's knowledge of Mr. *Hooker* was occafioned by the learned doctor *John Spencer*, who after the death of Mr. *Hooker*, was fo careful to preferve his unvaluable fixth, feventh and eighth books of *ECCLESIASTICAL POLITY*, and his other writings, that he procured *Henry Jackfon*, then of *Corpus-Chrifti* college, to tranfcribe for him all Mr. *Hooker's* remainnig written papers, many of which were imperfect ; for his ftudy had been rifled or worfe ufed by Mr. *Chark*, and another of principles too like his. But as thefe papers were, they were endeavoured to be compleated by his dear friend doctor *Spencer*, who bequeathed them as a precious legacy to my father ; after whofe death they refted in my hand, till doctor *Abbot*, then arch-bifhop of *Canterbury*, commanded them out of my cuftody, authorizing doctor *John Barkham* (his lordfhip's chaplain) to require and bring them to him to *Lambeth* : at which time I have heard they were put into the bifhop's library, and that they remained there till the martyrdom of arch-bifhop *Laud*, and were then by the brethren of that faction given with the library to *Hugh Peters*, as a reward for his remarkable fervice in thofe fad times of the church's confufion : and tho they could hardly fall into a fouler hand, yet there wanted not other endeavours to corrupt and make them fpeak that language, for which the faction then fought ; which was, *to fubject the fovereign power to the people*. I need not ftrive to vindicate Mr. *Hooker* in this particular : his known loyalty to his prince whilft he lived, the forrow expreffed by king *James* for his death ; the value our late fovereign (of ever bleffed memory) put upon his works, and now the fingular character of his worth given by you in the paffages of his life, (efpecially in your appendix to it) do fufficiently clear him from that imputation. And I am glad you mention how much value *Robert Stapleton*, pope *Clement* the eighth, and other eminent men of the romifh perfuafion, have put upon his books, having been told the fame in my youth by perfons of worth that have travelled *Italy*. Laftly, I muft again congratulate this undertaking of yours, as now more proper to you than any other perfon, by reafon of your long knowledge and alliance to the worthy family of the *Cranmers* (my old friends alfo) who have been men of noted wifdom, efpecially Mr. *George Cranmer*, whofe prudence added to that of fir *Edwin Sandys*, proved very ufeful in the compleating of Mr. *Hooker's* matchlefs books ; one of their letters I herewith fend you to make ufe of, if you think fit. And let me fay further, you merit much from many of Mr. *Hooker's* beft friends then living ; namely, from the ever-renowned arch-bifhop *Whitgift*, of whofe incomparable worth, with the character of the times, you have given us a more fhort and fignificant account than I have received from any other pen. You have done much for fir *Henry Savile*, his contemporary and familiar friend ; amongft the furviving monuments of whofe learning (give me leave to tell you fo) two are omitted ; his edition of *Euclid*, but efpecially his tranflation of king *James his apology for the oath of allegiance*, into elegant latin : which flying in that drefs as far as *Rome*, was by the pope and conclave fent unto *Francifcus Suarez* to *Salamanca* (he then refiding there as prefident of that college) with a command to anfwer it. When he had perfected the work (which he calls *Defenfio fidei catholicæ*) it was tranfmitted to *Rome* for a view of the inquifitors ; who according to their cuftom blotted out what they pleafed, and (as Mr. *Hooker* hath been ufed fince his death) added whatfoever might advance the pope's fupremacy, or carry on their own intereft, commonly coupling together *deponere & occidere*, the depofing and killing of princes : which cruel and unchriftian language Mr. *John Saltkeld* (his amanuenfis, when he wrote at *Salamanca*, but fince a convert, living long in my father's houfe) often profeffed, the good old man (whofe piety and charity Mr. *Saltkell* magnified much) not only difavowed, but detefted. Not to trouble you further, your reader (if, according to your defire, my approbation of your work carries any weight) will find many juft reafons to thank you for it ; and for this circumftance here mentioned (not known to many) may happily apprehend one to thank him, who is,

Chichefter,
Novemb.
12. 16.

S I R,

Your ever faithful and affectionate old friend,

Henry Chichefter

THE

LIFE

OF

Mr. Richard Hooker.

The INTRODUCTION.

I HAVE been perfuaded by a friend, that I ought to obey, to write The life of RICHARD HOOKER, the happy author of five (if not more) of the eight learned books of The laws of ecclefiaftical polity. And tho I have undertaken it, yet it hath been with fome unwillingnefs, forefeeing that it muft prove to me, and efpecially at this time of my age, a work of much labour to enquire, confider, research, and determine what is needful to be known concerning him. For I knew him not in his life, and muft therefore not only look back to his death (now fixty four years paft) but almoft fifty years beyond that, even to his childhood and youth; and gather thence fuch obfervations and prognofticks, as may at leaft adorn, if not prove neceffary for the compleating what I have undertaken.

This trouble I forefee, and forefee alfo that it is impoffible to efcape cenfures; againft which I will not hope my well-meaning and diligence can protect me (for I confider the age in which I live) and fhall therefore but intreat of my reader a fufpenfion of them, till I have made known unto him fome reafons which, I my felf would not fain be- lieve; do make me in fome meafure fit for this undertaking: and if thefe reafons fhall not acquit me from all cenfures, they may at leaft abate of their feverity; and this is all I can probably hope for.

My reafons follow.

About forty years paft (for I am now in the feventieth of my age) I began a happy affinity with William Cranmer, (now with God) grand nephew unto the great archbifhop of that name; a family of noted prudence and refolution. With him and two of his fifters I had an entire and free friendfhip: one of them was the wife of doctor Spencer, a bofom-friend, and fometime com-pupil with Mr. Hooker in Corpus-Chrifti college in Oxford, and after prefident of the fame. I name them here; for that I fhall have occafion to mention them in this following difcourfe; as alfo George Cranmer their bro- ther, of whofe ufeful abilities my reader may have a more authentick teftimony than my pen can purchafe for him, by that of our learned Camden and others.

This William Cranmer, and his two fore-named fifters, had fome affinity, and a moft familiar friendfhip with Mr. Hooker; and had had fome part of their education with him in his houfe, when he was parfon of Bifhop's-bourn near Canterbury; in which city

a 2   their

their good father then lived. They had (I say) a great part of their education with him, as my self, since that time, a happy cohabitation with them ; and having some years before read part of Mr. Hooker*'s works with great liking and satisfaction, my affection to them made me a diligent inquisitor into many things that concerned him ; as namely, of his person, his nature, the management of his time, his wife, his family, and the fortune of him and his. Which inquiry hath given me much advantage in the knowledge of what is now under my consideration, and intended for the satisfaction of my reader.*

I had also a friendship with the reverend doctor Usher, *the late learned archbishop of* Armagh ; *and with doctor* Morton, *the late learned and charitable bishop of* Durham ; *as also with the learned* John Hales *of* Eaton college : *and with them also (who loved the very name of Mr.* Hooker*) I have had many discourses concerning him ; and from them, and many others that have now put off mortality, I might have had more information, if I could then have admitted a thought of any fitness for what by persuasion I have now undertaken. But, tho that full harvest be irrecoverably lost, yet my memory hath preserved some gleanings, and my diligence made such additions to them, as I hope will prove useful to the compleating of what I intend. In the discovery of which I shall be faithful, and with this assurance put a period to my introduction.*

The LIFE.

IT is not to be doubted, but that *Richard Hooker* was born within the precincts, or in the city of *Exeter*. A city which may justly boast that it was the birth-place of him and sir *Thomas Bodley* ; as indeed the county may, in which it stands, that it hath furnished this nation with bishop *Jewel*, sir *Francis Drake*, sir *Walter Raleigh*, and many others memorable for their valour and learning. He was born about the year of our redemption one thousand five hundred fifty and three ; and of parents that were not so remarkable for their extraction or riches, as for their virtue and industry, and God's blessing upon both : by which they were enabled to educate their children in some degree of learning, of which our *Richard Hooker* may appear to be one fair testimony, and that nature is not so partial as always to give the great blessings of wisdom and learning, and with them the greater blessings of vertue and government, to those only that are of a more high and honourable birth.

His complexion (if we may guess by him at the age of forty) was sanguine, with a mixture of choler ; and yet his motion was slow, even in his youth, so was his speech, never expressing an earnestness in either of them, but a gravity suitable to the aged. And it is observed (so far as inquiry is able to look back at this distance of time) that at his being a school-boy, he was an early questionist, quietly inquisitive, *Why this was, and that was not, to be remembred ? Why this was granted, and that denyed ?* This being mixt with a remarkable modesty, and a sweet serene quietness of nature ; and with them a quick apprehension of many perplext parts of learning, imposed then upon him as a scholar, made his master and others to believe him to have an inward blessed divine light, and therefore to consider him to a little wonder. For in that, children were less pregnant, less confident, and more malleable, than in this wiser, but not better age.

This meekness and conjuncture of knowledge, with modesty in his conversation, being observed by his school-master, caused him to persuade his parents (who intended him for an apprentice) to continue him at school till he could find out some means, by persuading his rich uncle, or some other charitable person, to ease them of a part of their care and charge : assuring them, that their son was so enriched with the blessings of nature and grace, that God seemed to single him out as a special instrument of his glory. And the good man told them also, that he would double his diligence in instructing him,

and

and would neither expect nor receive any other reward, than the content of so hopeful and happy an employment.

This was not unwelcome news, and especially to his mother, to whom he was a dutiful and dear child; and all parties were so pleased with this proposal, that it was resolved *so it should be.* And in the mean time his parents and master laid a foundation for his future happiness, by instilling into his soul the *seeds of piety;* those conscientious principles of *loving and fearing God; of an early belief, that he knows the very secrets of our souls; that he punisheth our vices and rewards our innocence; that we should be free from hypocrisy, and appear to man what we are to God, because first or last the crafty man is catch'd in his own snare.* These seeds of piety were so seasonably planted, and so continually water'd with the daily dew of God's blessed Spirit, that his infant vertues grew into such holy habits, as did make him grow daily into more and more favour, both with God and man; which, with the great learning that he did attain to, hath made *Richard Hooker* honoured in this, and will continue him to be so to succeeding generations.

This good school-master, whose name I am not able to recover, (and am sorry, for that I would have given him a better memorial in this humble monument, dedicated to the memory of his scholar) was very sollicitous with *John Hooker,* then chamberlain of *Exeter,* and uncle to our *Richard,* to take his nephew into his care, and to maintain him for one year in the university, and in the mean time to use his endeavours to procure an admission for him into some college: still urging and assuring him that his charge would not continue long; for the lad's learning and manners were both so remarkable, that they must of necessity be taken notice of; and that God would provide him some second patron, that would free him and his parents from their future care and charge.

These reasons, with the affectionate rhetorick of his good master, and God's blessing upon both, procured from his uncle a faithful promise that he would take him into his care and charge before the expiration of the year following, which was performed.

This promise was made about the fourth year of the reign of queen *Mary;* and the learned *John Jewel* (after bishop of *Salisbury*) having been in the first of this queen's reign expelled out of *Corpus-Christi* college in *Oxford,* (of which he was a fellow) for adhering to the truth of those principles of religion, to which he had assented in the days of her brother and predecessor, *Edward* the sixth; and he having now a just cause to fear a more heavy punishment than expulsion, was forc'd by forsaking this, to seek safety in another nation, and with that safety the enjoyment of that doctrine and worship for which he suffered.

But the cloud of that persecution and fear ending with the life of queen *Mary,* the affairs of the church and state did then look more clear and comfortable; so that he, and many others of the same judgment, made a happy return into *England* about the first of queen *Elizabeth;* in which year this *John Jewel* was sent a commissioner or visitor of the churches of the western parts of this kingdom, and especially of those in *Devonshire,* in which county he was born; and then, and there he contracted a friendship with *John Hooker,* the uncle of our *Richard.*

In the third year of her reign, this *John Jewel* was made bishop of *Salisbury;* and there being always observed in him a willingness to do good and oblige his friends, and now a power added to it, *John Hooker* gave him a visit in *Salisbury, and besought him for charity's sake to look favourably upon a poor nephew of his, whom nature had fitted for a scholar; but the estate of his parents was so narrow, that they were unable to give him the advantage of learning; and that the bishop would therefore become his patron, and prevent him from being a tradesman; for he was a boy of remarkable hopes.* And tho the bishop knew men do not usually look with an indifferent eye upon their own children and relations, yet he assented so far to *John Hooker,* that he appointed the boy and his school-master should attend him about *easter* next following at that place; which was done accordingly: and then, after some questions and observations of the boy's learning, and gravity, and behaviour, the bishop gave the school-master a reward, and took order for an annual pension for the boy's parents, promising also to take him into his care for a future preferment; which was performed.

For, about the fourteenth year of his age, which was *Anno* 1567, he was by the bishop appointed to remove to *Oxford,* and there to attend doctor *Cole,* then president of *Corpus-Christi* college: which he did, and doctor *Cole* had (according to a promise made to the bishop) provided for him both a tutor (which was said to be the learned doctor *John Reynolds*) and a clerk's place in that college: which place, tho it were not a full maintenance, yet with the contribution of his uncle, and the continued pension of his patron, the good bishop, gave him a comfortable subsistence. And in this condition

Admitted into *Corpus-Christi* college, *Oxon.*

Bishop *Jewel* his patron.

dition he continued unto the eighteenth year of his age, ftill increaſing in learning and prudence, and ſo much in humility and piety, that he ſeemed to be filled with the Holy Ghoſt, and even like ſaint *John Baptiſt*, to be ſanctified from his mother's womb, who did often bleſs the day in which ſhe bare him.

About this time of his age, he fell into a dangerous ſickneſs, which laſted two months: all which time, his mother having notice of it, did in her hourly prayers as earneſtly beg his life of God, as the mother of ſaint *Auguſtine* did, that he might become a true chriſtian: and their prayers were both ſo heard, as to be granted. Which Mr. *Hooker* would often mention with much joy, *and pray that he might never live to occaſion any ſorrow to ſo good a mother, whom he would often ſay, he loved ſo dearly, that he would endeavour to be good, even as much for her ſake, as for his own.*

As ſoon as he was perfectly recovered from his ſickneſs, he took a journey from *Oxford* to *Exeter*, to ſatisfy and ſee his good mother, being accompanied with a country-man and companion of his own college, and both on foot; which was then either more in faſhion, or want of mony, or their humility made it ſo: but on foot they went, and took *Salisbury* in their way, purpoſely to ſee the good biſhop, who made Mr. *Hooker* and his companion dine with him at his own table; which Mr. *Hooker* boaſted of with much joy and gratitude when he ſaw his mother and friends: and at the biſhop's parting with him, the biſhop gave him good council, and his benediction, but forgot to give him money; which when the biſhop had confidered, he ſent a ſervant in all haſte to call *Richard* back to him: and at *Richard*'s return, the biſhop ſaid to him, ' *Richard*, I ' ſent for you back to lend you a horſe which hath carried me many a mile, and I thank ' God with much eaſe.' And preſently delivered into his hand a walking-ſtaff, with which he profeſſed he had travelled thro many parts of *Germany*. And he ſaid, ' *Ri-* ' *chard*, I do not give, but lend you my horſe; be ſure you be honeſt, and bring my horſe ' back to me at your return this way to *Oxford*. And I do now give you ten groats to ' bear your charges to *Exeter*; and here is ten groats more, which I charge you to deliver ' to your mother, and tell her, I ſend her a biſhop's benediction with it, and beg the con- ' tinuance of her prayers for me. And if you bring my horſe back to me, I will give you ' ten groats more to carry you on foot to the college: And ſo God bleſs you good ' *Richard*.'

And this, you may believe, was performed by both parties. But alas! the next news that followed Mr. *Hooker* to *Oxford* was, that his learned and charitable patron had changed this for a better life. Which may be believed, for that as he lived; ſo he died, in devout meditation and prayer; and in both ſo zealously, that it became a religious queſtion, *whether his laſt ejaculations, or his ſoul, did firſt enter into heaven?*

And now Mr. *Hooker* became a man of ſorrow and fear: of ſorrow, for the loſs of ſo dear and comfortable a patron; and of fear for his future ſubſiſtence. But Mr. *Cole* raiſed his ſpirits from this dejection, by bidding him go chearfully to his ſtudies, and aſſuring him, that he ſhould neither want food nor rayment, (which was the utmoſt of his hopes) for he would become his patron.

And ſo he was for about nine months, or not much longer; for about that time this following accident did befal Mr. *Hooker*.

Edwin Sandys (then biſhop of *London*, and after arch-biſhop of *York*) had alſo been in the days of queen *Mary* forced, by forſaking this, to ſeek ſafety in another nation; where for many years, biſhop *Jewel* and he were companions at bed and board in *Germany*; and where, in this their exile, they did often eat the bread of ſorrow, and by that means they there began ſuch a friendſhip, as time did not blot out, but laſted till the death of biſhop *Jewel*, which was one thouſand five hundred ſeventy and one. A little before which time the two biſhops meeting, *Jewel* began a ſtory of his *Richard Hooker*, and in it gave ſuch a character of his learning and manners, that tho biſhop *Sandys* was educated in *Cambridge*, where he had obliged, and had many friends; yet his reſolution was, that his ſon *Edwin* ſhould be ſent to *Corpus-Chriſti* college in *Oxford*, and by all means be pupil to Mr. *Hooker*, tho his ſon *Edwin* was then almoſt of the ſame age: for the biſhop ſaid, ' I will have a tutor for my ſon, that ſhall teach him learning by in- ' ſtruction, and virtue by example; and my greateſt care ſhall be of the laſt; and (God ' willing) this *Richard Hooker* ſhall be the man, into whoſe hands I will commit my *Ed-* ' *win*.' And the biſhop did ſo about twelve months after this reſolution.

And doubtleſs, as to theſe two, a better choice could not be made: for Mr. *Hooker* was now in the nineteenth year of his age; had ſpent five in the univerſity; and had by a conſtant unwearied diligence, attained unto a perfection in all the learned languages: by the help of which, an excellent tutor, and his unintermitted ſtudy, he had made the ſubtilty of all the arts eaſy and familiar to himſelf, and uſeful for the diſcovery

of

of such learning as lay hid from common searches. So that by these added to his great reason, and his industry added to both, he did not only know more of causes and effects; but what he knew, he knew better than other men. And with this knowledge he had a most blessed and clear method of demonstrating what he knew, to the great advantage of all his pupils, (which in time were many) but especially to his two first, his dear *Edwin Sandys*, and his as dear *George Cranmer*, of which there will be a fair testimony in the ensuing relation.

This for his learning. And for his behaviour, amongst other testimonies, this still remains of him, that in four years he was but twice absent from the chappel prayers; and that his behaviour there was such as shewed an awful reverence of that God which he then worshipped and prayed to; giving all outward testimonies that his affections were set on heavenly things. This was his behaviour towards God; and for that to man, it is observable, that he was never known to be angry, or passionate, or extreme in any of his desires; never heard to repine or dispute with providence, but by a quiet gentle submission and resignation of his will to the wisdom of his creator, bore the burden of the day with patience; never heard to utter an uncomely word; and by this and a grave behaviour, which is a divine charm, he begot an early reverence unto his person, even from those that at other times, and in other companies, took a liberty to cast off that strictness of behaviour and discourse that is required in a collegiate life. And when he took any liberty to be pleasant, his wit was never blemished with scoffing, or the utterance of any conceit that bordered upon, or might beget a thought of loosenes in his hearers. Thus innocent and exemplary was his behaviour in his college; and thus this good man continued till death; still increasing in learning, in patience and piety.

In this nineteenth year of his age, he was chosen, *December* 24. 1573. to be one of the twenty scholars of the foundation; being elected and admitted as born in *Devon-shire*; (out of which county a certain number are to be elected in vacancies by the founders statutes.) And now he was much encouraged; for now he was perfectly incorporated into this beloved college, which was then noted for an eminent library, strict students, and remarkable scholars. And indeed it may glory, that it had bishop *Jewel*, doctor *John Reynolds*, and doctor *Thomas Jackson*, of that foundation. The first, famous by his learned apology for the church of *England*, and his defence of it against *Harding*. The second, for the learned and wise manage of a publick dispute with *John Hart*, of the romish persuasion, about the head and faith of the church, then printed by consent of both parties. And the third, for his most excellent exposition of the creed, and for his other treatises; all such as have given greatest satisfaction to men of the greatest learning. Nor was this man more eminent for his learning, than for his strict and pious life, testifyed by his abundant love and charity to all men.

In the year 1576. *February* 23. Mr. *Hooker's* grace was given him for inceptor of arts; doctor *Herbert Westphaling*, a man of noted learning, being then vice-chancellor; and the act following he was compleated master, which was *anno* 1577. his patron doctor *Cole* being that year vice-chancellor, and his dear friend *Henry Savil* of *Merton* college, then one of the proctors. It was that *Henry Savil*, that was after sir *Henry Savil*, warden of *Merton* college, and provost of *Eaton*: he which founded in *Oxford* two famous lectures, and endowed them with liberal maintenance. It was that sir *Henry Savil* that translated and enlightned the history of *Cornelius Tacitus*, with a most excellent comment; and enriched the world by his laborious and chargeable collecting the scattered pieces of saint *Chrysostom*, and the publication of them in one entire body in *Greek*; in which language he was a most judicious critick. It was this sir *Henry Savil* that had the happines to be a contemporary, and a most familiar friend to our *Richard Hooker*, and let posterity know it.

And in this year of 1577. he was chosen fellow of the college: happy also in being the contemporary and friend of doctor *John Reynolds*, of whom I have lately spoken, and of doctor *Spencer*; both which were after, and successively, made presidents of his college: men of great learning and merit, and famous in their generations.

Nor was Mr. *Hooker* more happy in his contemporaries of his time and college, than in the pupilage and friendship of his *Edwin Sandys* and *George Cranmer*, of whom my reader may note, that this *Edwin Sandys* was after sir *Edwin Sandys*, and as famous for his *Speculum Europæ*, as his brother *George* for making posterity beholden to his pen by a learned relation and comment on his dangerous and remarkable travels; and for his harmonious translation of the psalms of *David*, the book of *Job*, and other poetical parts of holy writ, into most high and elegant verse. And for *Cranmer*, his other pupil, I shall refer my reader to the printed testimonies of our learned master *Camben*, the lord *Tottenes*, *Fines Morison*, and others.

This

This *Cranmer*, whose christen name was *George*, was a gentleman of singular hope, the eldest son of *Thomas Cranmer*, son of *Edmund Cranmer*, the arch-bishop's brother : he spent much of his youth in *Corpus-Christi* college in *Oxford*, where he continued master of arts for many years before he removed, and then betook himself to travel, accompanying that worthy gentleman sir *Edwin Sandys* into *France*, *Germany* and *Italy*, for the space of three years; and after their happy return, he betook himself to an employment under secretary *Davison*: after whose fall, he went in place of secretary with Sir *Henry Killegrew* in his embassage into *France*; and after his death he was sought after by the most noble lord *Mountjoy*, with whom he went into *Ireland*, where he remained, until in a battel against the rebels near *Carlingford*, an unfortunate wound put an end both to his life, and the great hopes that were conceived of him.

Betwixt Mr. *Hooker*, and these his two pupils, there was a sacred friendship; a friendship made up of religious principles, which increased daily by a similitude of inclinations to the same recreations and studies; a friendship elemented in youth, and in an university, free from self-ends, which the friendships of age usually are not. In this sweet, this blessed, this spiritual amity, they went on for many years: and, as the holy prophet saith, *so they took sweet counsel together, and walked in the house of God as friends.* By which means they improved it to such a degree of amity, as bordered upon heaven; a friendship so sacred, that when it ended in this world, it began in the next, where it shall have no end.

And, tho this world cannot give any degree of pleasure equal to such a friendship; yet obedience to parents, and a desire to know the affairs, and manners, and laws, and learning of other nations, that they might thereby become the more serviceable unto their own, made them put off their gowns, and leave Mr. *Hooker* to his college: where he was daily more assiduous in his studies, still inriching his quiet and capacious soul with the precious learning of the philosophers, casuists, and schoolmen; and with them the foundation and reason of all laws, both sacred and civil; and with such other learning as lay most remote from the track of common studies. And as he was diligent in these, so he seemed restless in searching the scope and intention of God's Spirit revealed to mankind in the sacred scripture: for the understanding of which, he seemed to be assisted by the same Spirit with which they were written; he that regardeth truth in the inward parts, making him to understand wisdom secretly. And the good man would often say, ' The scripture was not writ to beget pride and disputations, and op-' position to government; but moderation, and charity, and humility, and obedience, ' and peace, and piety in mankind; of which no good man did ever repent himself upon ' his death-bed.' And that this was really his judgment, did appear in his future writings, and in all the actions of his life. Nor was this excellent man a stranger to the more light and airy parts of learning, as musick and poetry; all which he had digested, and made useful; and of all which, the reader will have a fair testimony in what follows.

Thus he continued his studies in all quietness for the space of three or more years; about which time he entred into sacred orders, and was made both deacon and priest: and not long after, in obedience to the college statutes, he was to preach either at saint *Peter's Oxford*, or at saint *Paul's-cross London*; and the last fell to his allotment.

In order to which sermon, to *London* he came, and immediately to the *Shunamites* house : which is a house so called, for that, besides the stipend paid the preacher, there is provision made also for his lodging and diet two days before, and one day after his sermon. This house was then kept by *John Churchman*, sometimes a draper of good note in *Watling-street*, upon whom, after many years of plenty, poverty had at last come like an armed man, and brought him into a necessitous condition; which tho it be a punishment, is not always an argument of God's disfavour, for he was a vertuous man : I shall not yet give the like testimony of his wife, but leave the reader to judge by what follows. But to this Mr. *Hooker* came so wet, so weary and weather-beaten, that he was never known to express more passion, than against a friend that disswaded him from footing it to *London*, and for hiring him no easier an horse, (supposing the horse trotted when he did not) and at this time also, such a faintness and fear possest him, that he would not be perswaded two days quietness, or any other means could be used to make him able to preach his Sunday's sermon; but a warm bed, and rest, and drink proper for a cold, given him by mistress *Churchman*, and her diligent attendance added unto it, enabled him to perform the office of the day, which was in or about the year one thousand five hundred eighty and one.

And in this first publick appearance to the world, he was not so happy as to be free from exceptions against a point of doctrine delivered in his sermon, which was, *that in God there were two wills; an antecedent, and a consequent will: his first will,*

†

that

that all mankind fhould be faved ; but his fecond will was, that thofe only fhould be fa-ved that did live anfwerable to that degree of grace which he had offered or afforded them. This feemed to crofs a late opinion of Mr. *Calvin*'s, and then taken for granted by ma-ny that had not a capacity to examine it, as it had been by him, and hath been fince by doctor *Jackfon*, doctor *Hammond*, and others of great learning, who believe that a con-ry opinion trenches upon the honour and juftice of our merciful God. How he juftify'd this, I will not undertake to declare ; but it was not excepted againft (as Mr. *Hooker* declares in an occafional anfwer to Mr. *Travers*) by *John Elmer*, then bifhop of *Lon-don*, at this time one of his auditors, and at laft one of his advocates too, when Mr. *Hooker* was accufed for it.

But the juftifying of this doctrine did not prove of fo bad confequence, as the kind-nefs of Mrs. *Churchman*'s curing him of his late diftemper and cold ; for that was fo gratefully apprehended by Mr. *Hooker*, that he thought himfelf bound in confcience to believe all that fhe faid : fo that the good man came to be perfuaded by her, ' that ' he was a man of a tender conftitution ; and, that it was beft for him to have a wife, ' that might prove a nurfe to him ; fuch a one as might both prolong his life, and make it ' more comfortable : and fuch a one fhe could and would provide for him, if he thought fit ' to marry.' And he not confidering, that *the children of this world are wifer in their generation than the children of light* ; but like a true *Nathanael* who feared no guile, becaufe he meant none ; did give her fuch a power as *Eleazar* was trufted with, when he was fent to chufe a wife for *Ifaac* ; for even fo he trufted her to chufe for him, pro-mifing upon a fair fummons to return to *London*, and accept of her choice ; and he did fo in that, or the year following. Now, the wife provided for him, was her daughter *Joan*, who brought him neither beauty nor portion ; and for her conditions, they were too like that wife's, which is by *Solomon* compared to a dripping houfe : fo that he had no reafon to *rejoice in the wife of his youth*, but rather to lay with the holy prophet, *Wo is me that I am conftrained to have my habitation in the tents of* Kedar !

This choice of Mr. *Hooker*'s (if it were his choice) may be wondred at : but let us confider that the prophet *Ezekiel* fays, *there is a wheel within a wheel* ; a fecret fa-cred wheel of providence (efpecially in marriages) guided by his hand that *allows not the race to the fwift*, nor *bread to the wife*, nor good wives to good men : and he that can bring good out of evil (for mortals are blind to fuch reafons) only knows why this blefling was denied to patient *Job*, and (as fome think) to meek *Mofes*, and to our as meek and patient Mr. *Hooker*. But fo it was ; and let the reader ceafe to wonder, for affliction is a divine diet ; which tho it be unpleafing to mankind, yet almighty God hath often, very often impofed it as good, tho bitter phyfick to thofe children whofe fouls are deareft to him.

And by this means the good man was drawn from the tranquillity of his college ; from that garden of piety, of pleafure, of peace, and a fweet converfation, into the thorny wildernefs of a bufy world ; into thofe corroding cares that attend a married prieft, and a country parfonage ; which was *Draiton Beauchamp* in *Buckinghamfhire*, (not far from *Ailsbury*, and in the diocefs of *Lincoln*) to which he was prefented by *John Cheny* Efquire (then patron of it) the ninth of *December* 1584. where he be-haved himfelf fo, as to give no occafion of evil, but (as faint *Paul* advifeth a minifter of God) *in much patience, in afflictions, in anguifhes, in neceffities, in poverty, and no doubt in long-fuffering* ; yet troubling no man with his difcontents and wants.

And in this mean condition he continued about a year ; in which time his two pupils, *Edwin Sandys*, and *George Cranmer*, were returned from travel, and took a journey to *Draiton* to fee their tutor ; where they found him with a book in his hand (it was the odes of *Horace*) he being then tending his fmall allotment of fheep in a common field ; which he told his pupils he was forced to do, for that his fervant was then gone home to dine, and affift his wife to do fome neceffary houfhold bufinefs. When his fer-vant returned and releafed him, his two pupils attended him unto his houfe, where their beft entertainment was his quiet company, which was prefently denyed them ; for *Richard* was called to rock the cradle : and their welcome was fo like this, that they ftaid but next morning, which was time enough to difcover and pity their tutor's con-dition : and having in that time remembred and paraphrafed on many of the innocent recreations of their younger days, and by other fuch like diverfions, given him as much prefent pleafure as their acceptable company and difcourfe could afford him, they were for-ced to leave him to the company of his wife, and feek themfelves a quieter lodging. But at their parting from him, Mr. *Cranmer* faid, ' Good tutor, I am forry your lot is faln ' in no better ground, as to your parfonage ; and more forry your wife proves not a ' more comfortable companion, after you have wearied your thoughts in your reftlefs

b　' ftudies.

' studies.' To whom the good man replied, ' My dear *George*, if faints have ufually a ' double fhare in the miferies of this life, I that am none, ought not to repine at what my ' wife creator hath appointed for me ; but labour, as indeed I do daily, to fubmit to his ' will, and poffefs my foul in patience and peace.'

Made mafter of the Temple. At their return to *London*, *Edwin Sandys* acquaints his father (then bifhop of *London*, and after arch-bifhop of *York*) with his tutor's fad condition, and follicits for his removal to fome benefice that might give him a more comfortable fubfiftence : which his father did moft willingly grant him, when it fhould next fall into his power. And not long after this time, which was in the year one thoufand five hundred eighty and five,

* He was dead, and the place void in the month of Auguft, anno 1584. J. S. * Mr. *Alvey* (mafter of the *Temple*) died, who was *a man of a ftrict life, of great learning, and of fo venerable behaviour, as to gain fuch a degree of love and reverence from all men that knew him, that he was generally known by the name of father* Alvey. At the *Temple* reading, next after the death of this father *Alvey*, the arch-bifhop of *York* being then at dinner with the judges, the reader and benchers of that fociety, he met there with a condolement for the death of father *Alvey*, an high commendation of his faint-like life, and of his great merit both to God and man : and as they bewailed his death, fo they wifht for a like pattern of virtue and learning to fucceed him. And here came in a fair occafion for the arch-bifhop to commend Mr. *Hooker* to father *Alvey's* place, which he did with fo effectual an earneftnefs, and that feconded with fo many other teftimonies of his worth, that Mr. *Hooker* was fent for from *Draiton Beauchamp* to *London*, and there the mafterfhip of the *Temple* propofed unto him by the bifhop, as a greater freedom from his country cares, the advantage of a better fociety, and a more liberal penfion than his parfonage did afford him. But thefe reafons were not powerful enough to incline him to a willing acceptance of it : his wifh was rather to gain a better country living, where he might be free from noife, (fo he expreft the defire of his heart) and eat that bread which he might more properly call his own, in privacy and quietnefs. But, notwithftanding this averfenefs, he was at laft perfuaded to accept of the bifhop's propofal ; and was by † patent for life made mafter of the *Temple* the 17 of *March* 1585. he being then in the 34th year of his age.

† This you may find in the *Temple*-records. *Will. Ermftead* was mafter of the *Temple* at the diffolution of the priory, and died 2 *Eliz*. Richard Alvey, *Bat. Divinity, Pat.* 13. Feb. 2 Eliz. *Magifter five cuftos domûs & ecclefia novi templi*; died 27 Eliz. *Richard Hooker* fucceeded that year by patent, *in terminis*, as *Alvey* had it; and he left it, 33 *Eliz.* That year doctor *Balgey* fucceeded Rich. *Hooker.*

But before any mention was made of Mr. *Hooker* for this place, two other divines

Endeavours for Travers to be mafter of the Temple. J. S. were nominated to fucceed *Alvey*; whereof Mr. *Walter Travers*, a difciplinarian in his judgment and practice, and preacher here in the afternoons, was chief, and recommended by *Alvey* himfelf on his death-bed, to be mafter after him : and no marvel, for *Alvey's* and *Travers's* principles did fomewhat correfpond. And many gentlemen of the houfe defired him ; which defire the lord treafurer *Burghley* was privy to, and by their requeft, and his own inclination towards him being a good preacher, he moved the queen to allow of him : for the difpofal of the place was in her : But arch-bifhop *Whitgift* knew the man, and his hot temper and principles, from the time he was fellow of *Trinity*-college, and had obferved his fteps ever after : he knew how turbulently he had carried himfelf at the college, how he had difowned the *English* eftablifhed church, and epifcopacy, and went to *Geneva*, and afterwards to *Antwerp*, to be ordained minifter, as he was by *Villers* and *Cartwright*, and others the heads of a congregation there : and fo came back again more confirmed for the difcipline. And know-

Oppofed by the archbifh. ing alfo how much the doctrine and converfe of the mafter, to be placed here, would influence the gentlemen, and their influence and authority prevail in all parts of the realm, where their habitations and eftates were, that careful prelate made it his endeavour to ftop *Travers's* coming in : and had a learned man in his view, and of principles more conformable and agreeable to the church, namely, one doctor *Bond*, the queen's chaplain, and well known to her. She well underftanding the importance of this place, and knowing by the arch-bifhop what *Travers* was, by a letter he timely writ to her majefty upon the vacancy, gave particular order to the treafurer to difcourfe with the archbifhop about it.

The lord treafurer hereupon, in a letter, confulted with the faid archbifhop, and mentioned *Travers* to him, as one defired by many of the houfe. But the archbifhop in his anfwer, plainly fignified to his lordfhip, that he judged him altogether unfit, for the reafons mentioned before ; and that he had recommended to the queen doctor *Bond*, as a very fit perfon. But however, fhe declined him, fearing his bodily ftrength to perform the duty of the place, as fhe did *Travers* for other caufes. And by laying both afide, fhe avoided giving difguft to either of thofe great men. This doctor *Bond* feems to be that doctor *Nicolas Bond* that afterwards was prefident of *Magdalen* college, *Oxon*, and that was much abufed by *Martin Mar-prelate.*

Thefe

These particulars I have collected from a letter of the archbishop to the queen, and other letters that passed between the archbishop and the lord treasurer about this affair, while the mastership was vacant. The passages whereof taken *verbatim* out of their said letters, may deserve here to be specified for the satisfaction of the readers.

And first, in the month of *August*, upon the death of the former master, the arch‑bishop wrote this following letter unto the queen.

‘ **I** T may please your majesty to be advertised, that the mastership of the *Temple* is va‑ *The arch‑*
‘ cant by the death of Mr. *Alvey*. The living is not great, yet doth it require a lear‑ *bishop to the*
‘ ned, discreet, and wise man, in respect of the company there : who being well directed *queen, concer‑*
‘ and taught, may do much good elsewhere in the commonwealth, as otherwise also they *cancy of the*
‘ may do much harm. And because I hear there is suit made to your highness for one *Temple.*
‘ Mr. *Travers*, I thought it my duty to signify unto your majesty, that the said *Travers*
‘ hath been, and is one of the chief and principal authors of dissension in this church, a
‘ contemner of the book of prayers, and of other orders by authority established ; an
‘ earnest seeker of innovation ; and either in no degree of the ministry at all, or else
‘ ordered beyond the seas, not according to the form in this church of *England* used.
‘ Whose placing in that room, especially by your majesty, would greatly animate the
‘ rest of that faction, and do very much harm in sundry respects.
‘ Your majesty hath a chaplain of your own, doctor *Bond*, a man in my opinion very
‘ fit for that office, and willing also to take pains therein, if it shall please your high‑
‘ ness to bestow it upon him. Which I refer to your own most gracious disposition : be‑
‘ seeching almighty God long to bless, prosper, and preserve your majesty to his glory,
‘ and all our comforts.

Your majesty's most faithful

servant and chaplain,

From *Croydon*, the ⸻ of
August, 1584.

Jo. Cantuar.

Next, in a letter of the archbishop to the lord treasurer, dated from *Lambeth*, *Sept.* *The archb.*
14. 1584. he hath these words : ‘ I beseech your lordship to help such an one to the *to the lord*
‘ mastership of the *Temple* as is known to be conformable to the laws and orders esta‑ *treasurer.*
‘ blished ; and a defender, not a depraver of the present state and government. He that
‘ now readeth there is nothing less, as I of my own knowledge and experience can
‘ testify. Doctor *Bond* is desirous of it, and I know not a fitter man.

The lord treasurer in a letter to the archbishop, dated from *Oatlands* (where the *The lord*
queen now was) *Sept.* 17. 1584. thus wrote. ‘ The queen hath asked me what I *treasurer to*
‘ thought of *Travers* to be master of the *Temple*. Whereunto I answered, that at the *the archbish.*
‘ request of doctor *Alvey* in his sickness, and a number of honest gentlemen of the *Tem‑*
‘ *ple*, I had yielded my allowance of him to the place, so as he would shew himself con‑
‘ formable to the orders of the church. Whereunto I was informed, that he would so
‘ be. But her majesty told me, that your grace did not so allow of him. Which, I
‘ said, might be for some things supposed to be written by him in a book, intituled,
‘ *De disciplina ecclesiastica*. Whereupon her majesty commanded me to write to your
‘ grace, to know your opinion, which I pray your grace to signify unto her, as God
‘ shall move you. Surely it were great pity, that any impediment should be occasion to
‘ the contrary ; for he is well learned, very honest, and well allowed, and loved of the
‘ generality of that house. Mr. *Bond* told me, that your grace liked well of him ; and
‘ so do I also, as of one well learned and honest ; but, as I told him, if he came not to the
‘ place with some applause of the company, he shall be weary thereof. And yet I com‑
‘ mended him unto her majesty, if *Travers* should not have it. But her majesty thinks
‘ him not fit for that place, because of his infirmities. Thus wishing your grace assistance
‘ of God's Spirit, to govern your charge unblameable,

From the court at *Oatlands*,
the 27 *Sept.* 1584.

Your grace's to command,

Will. Burghley.

Part of the archbishop's letter in answer to this, was to this tenour.

The archb.
in answer to
the letter of
the lord
treasurer.

‘ Mr. *Travers,* whom your lordship names in your letter, is to no man better
‘ known, I think, than to my self; I did elect him fellow of *Trinity*-College, being be-
‘ fore rejected by doctor *Beaumont* for his intolerable stomach; whereof I had also after-
‘ wards such experience, that I was forced by due punishment so to weary him, till he
‘ was fain to travel, and depart from the college to *Geneva,* otherwise he should have
‘ been expelled for his want of conformity towards the orders of the house, and for
‘ his pertinacy. Neither was there ever any under our government, in whom I found
‘ less submission and humility than in him. Nevertheless, if time and years have now
‘ altered that disposition, (which I cannot believe, seeing yet no token thereof, but rather
‘ the contrary) I will be as ready to do him good as any friend he hath. Otherwise I
‘ cannot in duty but do my endeavour to keep him from that place, where he may do so
‘ much harm, and do little or no good at all. For howsoever some commend him to
‘ your lordship and others, yet I think that the greater and better number of both the
‘ temples have not so good an opinion of him. Sure I am, that divers grave, and of
‘ the best affected of them, have shewed their misliking of him to me; not only out of
‘ respect of his disorderliness in the manner of the communion, and contempt of the
‘ prayers, but also of his negligence in reading; whose lectures, by their report, are
‘ so barren of matter, that his hearers take no commodity thereby.
     ‘ The book *de disciplina ecclesiastica,* by common opinion, hath been reputed of his
‘ penning, since the first publishing of it. And by divers arguments I am moved to make
‘ no doubt thereof. The drift of which book is wholly against this state and government.
‘ Wherein also, among other things, he condemneth the taking and paying of first-fruits,
‘ tenths, &c. And therefore, unless he will testify his conformity by subscription, as
‘ all others do, which now enter into ecclesiastical livings; and make proof unto me,
‘ that he is a minister ordered according to the laws of this church of *England,* as I verily
‘ believe he is not, because he forsook his place in the college upon that account, I can
‘ by no means yield my consent to the placing him there, or elsewhere, in any *function*
‘ of this church.’

    And here I shall make a stop; and, that the reader may the better judge of what fol-
lows, give him a character of the times, and temper of the people of this nation, when Mr.
Hooker had his admission into this place; a place which he accepted rather than desired:
and yet here he promised himself a virtuous quietness, that blessed tranquillity which he
always prayed and laboured for; that so he might in peace bring forth the fruits of peace,
and glorify God by uninterrupted prayers and praises: for this he always thirsted; and
yet this was denied him. For his admission into this place was the very beginning of
those oppositions and anxieties, which till then this good man was a stranger to, and of
which the reader may guess by what follows.
    In this character of the times, I shall, by the reader's favour, and for his information,
look so far back as to the beginning of the reign of queen *Elizabeth;* a time in which
*the many pretended titles to the crown, the frequent treasons, the doubts of her suc-
cessor, the late civil war, and the sharp persecution that had raged to the effusion of so
much blood in the reign of queen* Mary, were fresh in the memory of all men; and these
begot fears in the most pious and wisest of this nation, lest the like days should return a-
gain to them or their present posterity. The apprehension of which dangers begot an
earnest desire of a settlement in the church and state; believing there was no other probable way to make them sit quietly under their own *vines* and *fig-trees,* and enjoy the
desired fruit of their labours. But *time,* and *peace,* and *plenty,* begot *self-ends;* and
those begot *animosities, envy, opposition,* and *unthankfulness* for those blessings for
which they lately thirsted, being then the very utmost of their desires, and even beyond
their hopes.
    This was the temper of the times in the beginning and progress of her reign; and thus
it continued too long: for those very people that had enjoyed the desires of their hearts
in a reformation from the church of *Rome,* became at last so like the grave, as never to
be satisfied; but were still thirsting for more and more, neglecting to pay that obedience to
government, and perform those vows to God, which they made in their days of adversi-
ties and fears: so that in short time there appeared three several interests, each of them
fearless and restless in the prosecution of their designs; they may for distinction be called,
the *active romanists,* the *restless nonconformists* (of which there were many sorts) and
the passive *peaceable protestant.* The counsels of the first considered and resolved on in
Rome: the second in *Scotland,* in *Geneva,* and in divers selected, secret, dangerous
                                                  conventicles,

conventicles, both there, and within the bofom of our own nation : the third pleaded
and defended their caufe by eftablifh'd laws, both ecclefiaftical and civil ; and if they
were active, it was to prevent the other two from deftroying what was by thofe known
laws happily eftablifh'd to them and their pofterity.

I fhall forbear to mention the very many and as dangerous plots of the *romanifts* againft
the church and ftate : becaufe, what is principally intended in this digreffion, is an account of the opinions and activity of the nonconformifts ; againft whofe judgment and
practice Mr. *Hooker* became at laft, but moft unwillingly, to be ingaged in a book-war ;
a war which he maintained not as againft an enemy, but with the fpirit of meeknefs and
reafon.

In which number of nonconformifts, though fome might be fincere and well-meaning
men, whofe indifcreet zeal might be fo like charity, as thereby to cover a multitude of
errors, yet of this party there were many that were poffeft with an high degree of
fpiritual wickednefs ; I mean with an innate reftlefs radical pride and malice ; I mean
not thofe leffer fins that are more vifible and more properly carnal, and fins againft a
man's felf, as gluttony and drunkennefs, and the like (from which good Lord deliver
us!) but fins of an higher nature ; becaufe more unlike the nature of God, which is
love, and *mercy*, and *peace* ; and more like the devil, (who is not a glutton, nor can be
drunk, and yet is a devil) thofe wickedneffes of malice, and revenge, and oppofition,
and a complacence in working and beholding confufion (which are more properly his
work, who is the enemy and difturber of mankind ; and greater fins, tho many will not
believe it) men whom a furious zeal and prejudice had blinded, and made incapable of
hearing reafon, or adhering to the ways of peace ; men whom pride and felf-conceit had
made to overvalue their own wifdom, and become pertinacious, and to hold foolifh and
unmannerly difputes againft thofe men which they ought to reverence, and thofe laws
which they ought to obey ; men that laboured and joyed to *fpeak evil of government*,
and then to be the authors of confufion (of confufion as it is confufion) whom company, and converfation, and cuftom had blinded, and made infenfible that thefe were errors ; and at laft became fo reftlefs, and fo hardned in their opinions, that like thofe
which perifh'd in the gain-faying of *Core*, fo thefe died without repenting thefe fpiritual
wickedneffes, of which *Coppinger* and *Hacket*, and their adherents, are too fad teftimonies.

And in thefe times, which tended thus to confufion, there were alfo many others that
pretended to tendernefs of confcience, refufing to fubmit to ceremonies, or to take an
oath before a lawful magiftrate : and yet thefe very men did in their fecret conventicles,
covenant and fwear to each other, to be affiduous and faithful in ufing their beft endeavours to fet up a church-government that they had not agreed on. To which end, there
were many felect parties that wandered up and down, and were active in fowing difcontents and fedition, by venomous and fecret murmurings, and a difperfion of fcurrilous
pamphlets and libels againft the church and ftate ; but efpecially againft the bifhops : by
which means, together with very bold, and as indifcreet fermons, the common people
became fo phanatick, as faint *Peter* obferved there were in his time, *fome that wrefted the
fcripture to their own deftruction :* fo by thefe men, and this means, many came to believe the *bifhops to be antichrift*, and the only obftructors of God's difcipline ; and many
of them were at laft given over to fuch defperate delufions, as to find out a text in the *revelation of faint John*, that *antichrift was to be overcome by the fword*, which they were
very ready to take into their hands. So that thofe very men, that began with tender
meek petitions, proceeded to print publick *admonitions* ; and then to *fatirical remon-
ftrances* ; and at laft (having like *David* number'd who was not, and who was, for their
caufe) they got a fuppofed certainty of fo great a party, that they durft threaten *firft the
bifhops*, and not long after, both *the queen and parliament* ; to all which they were fecretly encouraged by the earl of *Leicefter*, then in great favour with her majefty, and the
reputed cherifher and and patron-general of thefe pretenders to tendernefs of confcience ;
whom he ufed as a facrilegious fnare to further his defign, which was by their means to
bring fuch an odium upon the *bifhops*, as to procure an alienation of their lands, and a
large proportion of them for himfelf : which avaritious defire had fo blinded his reafon,
that his ambition and greedy hopes had almoft flattered him into prefent poffeffion
of *Lambeth*-houfe.

And to thefe ftrange and dangerous undertakings, the nonconformifts of this nation
were much encouraged and heightned by a correfpondence and confederacy with that
brotherhood in *Scotland* ; fo that here they became fo bold, that one * told the queen o-
penly in a fermon, *fhe was like an untamed heifer, that would not be ruled by God's
people, but obftructed his difcipline*. And in *Scotland* they were more confident, for
there

*Nonconfor-
mifts repre-
fented.*

* *Mr. Dering.*

* See bishop Spotswood's history of the church of Scotland.

there * they declared her an atheist, and grew to such an height as not to be accountable for any thing spoken against her; *no nor for treason against their own king, if spoken in the pulpit :* shewing at last such a disobedience even to him, that his mother being in *England*, and then in distress, and in prison, and in danger of death, the church denied the king their prayers for her; and at another time, when he had appointed a day of feasting, their church declared for a general fast, in opposition to his authority.

To this height they were grown in both nations, and by these means there was distilled into the minds of the common people such other venomous and turbulent principles, as were inconsistent with the safety of the church and state, and these, vented so daringly, that beside the loss of life and limbs, the church and state were both forced to use such other severities as will not admit of an excuse, if it had not been to prevent confusion, and the perillous consequences of it; which, without such prevention, would in a short time have brought unavoidable ruin and misery to this numerous nation.

These errors and animosities were so remarkable, that they begot wonder in an ingenious *Italian*, who being about this time come newly into this nation, writ scoffingly to a friend in his own country; *That the common people of* England *were wiser than the wisest of his nation; for here the very women and shop-keepers were able to judge of predestination, and determine what laws were fit to be made concerning church government; then, what were fit to be obeyed or abolished. That they were more able (or at least thought so) to raise and determine perplexed cases of conscience, than the most learned colleges in* Italy. *That men of the slightest learning, and the most ignorant of the common people were mad for a new, or* super, *or re-reformation of religion; and that in this* they appeared like that man, who would never cease to whet, and whet his knife, till there was no steel left to make it useful. And he concluded his letter with this observation, *that those very men that were most busy in oppositions, and disputations, and controversies, and finding out the faults of their governours, had usually the least of humility and mortification, or of the power of godliness.*

And to heighten all these discontents and dangers, there was also sprung up a generation of godless men; men that had so long given way to their own lusts and delusions; and had so often, and so highly opposed the blessed motions of his blessed Spirit, and the inward light of their own consciences, that they had thereby sinned themselves to a belief of what they would, but were not able to believe; into a belief, which is repugnant even to human nature (for the heathens believe there are many gods) but these have sinned themselves into a belief, that there is no God: and so finding nothing in themselves, but what is worse than nothing, began to wish what they were not able to hope for, *that they should be like the beasts that perish*; and, in wicked company (which is the atheists sanctuary) were so bold as to say so: tho the worst of mankind, when he is left alone at midnight, may wish, but cannot then think it. Into this wretched, this reprobate condition, many had then sinned themselves.

And now, when the church was pestered with them, and with all these other irregularities; when her lands were in danger of alienation, her power at least neglected, and her peace torn to pieces by several schisms, and such heresies as do usually attend that sin; when the common people seemed ambitious of doing those very things which were attended with most dangers, that thereby they might be punished, and then applauded and pitied; when they called the spirit of opposition a tender conscience, and complained of persecution, because they wanted power to persecute others; when the giddy multitude raged, and became restless to find out misery for themselves and others; and the rabble would herd themselves together, and endeavour to govern and act in spite of authority: in this extremity, fear, and danger of the church and state, when to suppress the growing evils of both, they needed a man of prudence and piety, and of an high and fearless fortitude; they were blest in all by *John Whitgift* his being made archbishop of *Canterbury*; of whom ingenious sir *Henry Wotton* (that knew him well) hath left this true character, *that he was a man of a reverend and sacred memory; and of the primitive temper : a man of such a temper, as when the church by lowliness of spirit did flourish in highest examples of virtue.*

And tho I dare not undertake to add his character, yet I shall neither do right to this discourse, nor to my reader, if I forbear to give him a further and short account of the life and manners of this excellent man; and it shall be short, for I long to end this digression, that I may lead my reader back to Mr. *Hooker*, where we left him at the *Temple.*

‡

John Whitgift was born in the county of *Lincoln*, of a family that was antient, and noted to be prudent and affable, and genteel by nature. He was educated in *Cambridge* ; much of his learning was acquir'd in *Pembroke-hall*, where Mr. *Bradford* the martyr was his tutor: from thence he was removed to *Peter-house* ; from thence to be master of *Pembroke-hall* ; and from thence to the mastership of *Trinity-college*. About which time the queen made him her chaplain ; and not long after prebend of *Ely*, and then dean of *Lincoln* ; and having for many years past looked upon him with much reverence and favour, gave him a fair testimony of both, by giving him the bishoprick of *Worcester*, and (which was not a usual favour) forgiving him his first-fruits ; then by constituting him vice-president of the principality of *Wales*. And having for several years experimented his wisdom, his justice and moderation in the manage of her affairs, in both these places, she in the twenty-sixth of her reign made him archbishop of *Canterbury* ; and, not long after, of her privy-council ; and trusted him to manage all her ecclesiastical affairs and preferments. In all which removes, he was like the ark, which left a blessing upon the place where it rested ; and in all his imployments, was like *Jehoida* that did good unto *Israel*.

Some account of *Whitgift*, archbishop of *Canterbury*.

These were the steps of this bishop's ascension to this place of dignity and cares ; in which place (to speak Mr. *Camden's* very words in his *annals*) *he devoutly consecrated both his whole life to God, and his painful labours to the good of his church.* And yet in this place he met with many oppositions in the regulation of church-affairs, which were much disorder'd at his entrance, by reason of the age and remisness * of bishop *Grindal* (his immediate predecessor) the activity of the nonconformists, and their chief assistant the earl of *Leicester* ; and indeed, by too many others of the like sacrilegious principles. With these he was to encounter ; and tho he wanted neither courage nor a good cause, yet he foresaw, that without a great measure of the queen's favour, it was impossible to stand in the breach that was made into the lands and immunities of the church, or to maintain the remaining rights of it. And therefore by justifiable sacred insinuations, such as saint *Paul* to *Agrippa*, (*Agrippa, believest thou ? I know thou believest*) he wrought himself into so great a degree of favour with her, as by his pious use of it, hath got both of them a greater degree of fame in this world, and of glory in that into which they are now entred.

* Or rather by reason of his suspension and sequestration, which he lay under (together with the queen's displeasure) for some years, when the ecclesiastick affairs were managed by certain civilians. *J. S:*

His merits to the queen, and her favours to him were such, that *she called him her little black husband, and called his servants her servants :* and she saw so visible and blessed a sincerity shine in all his cares and endeavours for the church's, and for her good, that she was supposed to trust him with the very secrets of her soul, and to make him her confessor : of which she gave many fair testimonies ; and of which one was, That *she would never eat flesh in lent, without obtaining a licence from her little black husband* ; and would often say, *She pitied him because she trusted him, and had eased herself by laying the burden of all her clergy-cares upon his shoulders, which she was certain he managed with prudence and piety.*

I shall not keep my self within the promised rules of brevity in this account of his interest with her majesty, and his care of the church's rights, if in this digression I should enlarge to particulars ; and therefore my desire is, that one example may serve for a testimony of both. And that the reader may the better understand it, he may take notice, that not many years before his being made archbishop, there passed an act or acts of parliament intending the better preservation of church lands, by recalling a power which was vested in others to sell or lease them, by lodging and trusting the future care and protection of them only in the crown : and amongst many that made a bad use of this power or trust of the queen's, the earl of *Leicester* was one ; and the good bishop having by his interest with her majesty put a stop to the earl's sacrilegious designs, they two fell to an open opposition before her ; after which they both quitted the room, not friends in appearance. But the bishop made a sudden and a seasonable return to her majesty, (for he found her alone) and spake to her with great humility and reverence, and to this purpose :

' I beseech your majesty to hear me with patience, and to believe that your's and
' the church's safety are dearer to me than my life ; but my conscience dearer than
' both : and therefore give me leave to do my duty, and tell you, that princes are de-
' puted nursing fathers of the church, and owe it a protection ; and therefore God for-
' bid that you should be so much as passive in her ruin, when you may prevent it ; or
' that I should behold it without horror and detestation, or should forbear to tell your
' majesty of the sin and danger. And tho you and my self are born in an age of frail-
' ties,

His speech to the queen.

ǂ

' ties, when the primitive piety and care of the church's lands and immunities are much
' decayed ; yet (madam) let me beg that you will but first confider, and then you
' will believe there are fuch fins as prophanenefs and facrilege ; for if there were not,
' they could not have names in holy writ ; and particularly in the new teftament.
' And I befeech you to confider, that tho our Saviour faid, *He judged no man* ; and
' to teftify it, would not judge nor divide the inheritance betwixt the two brethren,
' nor would judge the woman taken in adultery ; yet, in this point of the church's
' rights, he was fo zealous, that he made himfelf both the accufer and the judge, and
' the executioner to punifh thefe things ; witneffed, in that he himfelf made the whip
' to drive the prophaners out of the temple ; overthrew the tables of the money-changers,
' and drove them out of it. And confider, that it was faint *Paul* that faid to thofe
' chriftians of his time that were offended with idolatry, yet, *Thou that abborreft*
' *idols, doft thou commit facrilege ?* fuppofing, I think, facrilege to be the greater
' fin. This may occafion your majefty to confider, that there is fuch a fin as facri-
' lege ; and to incline you to prevent the curfe that will follow it, I befeech you
' alfo to confider, that *Conftantine* the firft chriftian emperor, and *Helena* his mother ;
' that king *Edgar*, and *Edward the Confeffor*, and indeed many others of your prede-
' ceffors, and many private chriftians, have alfo given to God, and to his church,
' much land, and many immunities, which they might have given to thofe of their
' own families, and did not ; but gave them as an abfolute right and facrifice to
' God : and with thefe immunities and lands they have intailed a curfe upon
' the alienators of them ; God prevent your majefty from being liable to that
' curfe.
   ' And, to make you that are trufted with their prefervation, the better to under-
' ftand the danger of it ; I befeech you forget not, that, befides thefe curfes, the
' church's land and power have been alfo endeavour'd to be preferved, as far as human
' reafon and the law of this nation have been able to preferve them, by an immediate
' and moft facred obligation on the confciences of the princes of this realm. For
' they that confult *magna charta*, fhall find, that as all your predeceffors were at
' their coronation, fo you alfo were fworn before all the nobility and bifhops then pre-
' fent, and in the prefence of God, and in his ftead to him that anointed you, *to*
' *maintain the church-lands, and the rights belonging to it* ; and this teftified openly
' at the holy altar, by laying your hands on the bible then lying upon it. And not
' only *magna charta*, but many modern ftatutes have denounced a curfe upon thofe
' that break *magna charta*. And now what account can be given for the breach of
' this oath at the laft great day, either by your majefty, or by me, if it be wilful-
' ly, or but negligently violated, I know not.
   ' And therefore, good madam, let not the late lord's exceptions againft the failings
' of fome few clergy-men prevail with you to punifh pofterity, for the errors of this
' prefent age ; let particular men fuffer for their particular errors, but let God and his
' church have their right : and tho I pretend not to prophefy, yet I beg pofterity to
' take notice of what is already become vifible in many families ; *That church-land*,
' *added to an antient inheritance, hath proved like a moth fretting a garment, and fe-*
' *cretly confumed both : or like the eagle that ftole a coal from the altar, and there-*
' *by fet her neft on fire, which confumed both her young eagles, and her felf that ftole it.*
' And, tho I fhall forbear to fpeak reproachfully of your father ; yet, I beg you to
' take notice, that a part of the church's rights, added to the vaft treafure left him
' by his father, hath been conceived to bring an unavoidable confumption upon both,
' notwithftanding all his diligence to preferve it.
   ' And confider, that after the violation of thofe laws, to which he had fworn in *mag-*
' *na charta*, God did fo far deny him his reftraining grace, that he fell into greater fins
' than I am willing to mention. *Madam, religion is the foundation and cement of*
' *human focieties :* and, when they that ferve at God's altar, fhall be expofed to po-
' verty, then religion it felf will be expofed to fcorn, and become contemptible ; as
' you may already obferve in too many poor vicaridges in this nation. And there-
' fore, as you are by a late act or acts entrufted with a great power to preferve or
' wafte the church's lands ; yet, difpofe of them for Jefus fake as the donors intended :
' let neither falfhood nor flattery beguile you to do otherwife ; and put a ftop (I be-
' feech you) to the approaching ruins of God's church, as you expect comfort at
' the laft great day ; *for kings muft be judged.* Pardon this affectionate plainnefs, my
' moft dear fovereign, and let me beg to be ftill continued in your favour ; and the
' Lord ftill continue you in his.'

The

The queen's patience hearing this affectionate speech, her future care to preserve the church's rights, which till then had been neglected, may appear a fair testimony, that he made her's and the church's good the chiefest of his cares, and that she also thought so. And of this there were such daily testimonies given, as begot betwixt them so mutual a joy and confidence, that they seemed born to believe and do good to each other: she not doubting his piety to be more than all his opposers, which were many, and those powerful too ; nor his prudence equal to the chiefest of her council, who were then as remarkable for active wisdom, as those dangerous times did require, or this nation did ever enjoy. And in this condition he continued twenty years, in which time he saw some flowings, but many more ebbings of her favour towards all men that opposed him, especially the earl of *Leicester :* so that God seemed still to keep him in her favour, that he might preserve the remaining church-lands and immunities from sacrilegious alienations. And this good man deserved all the honour and power with which she trusted him ; for he was a pious man, and naturally of noble and grateful principles : he eased her of all her church-cares by his wise manage of them ; he gave her faithful and prudent counsels in all the extremities and dangers of her temporal affairs, which were very many ; he lived to be the chief comfort of her life in her declining age ; to be then most frequently with her, and her assistant at her private devotions ; to be the greatest comfort of her soul upon her death-bed, to be present at the expiration of her last breath ; and to behold the closing of those eyes that had long looked upon him with reverence and affection. And let this also be added, that he was the chief mourner at her sad funeral ; nor let this be forgotten, that within a few hours after her death, he was the happy proclaimer that king *James* (her peaceful successor) was heir to the crown.

Let me beg of my reader, that he allow me to say a little, and but a little, more of this good bishop ; and I shall then presently lead him back to Mr. *Hooker :* and, because I would hasten, I will mention but one part of the bishop's charity and humility ; but this of both. He built a large alms-house near to his own palace at *Croyden* in *Surrey,* and endowed it with maintenance for a master and twenty eight poor men and women ; which he visited so often, that he knew their names and dispositions ; and was so truly humble, that he called them brothers and sisters : and whensoever the queen descended to that lowliness to dine with him at his palace in *Lambeth,* (which was very often) he would usually the next day shew the like lowliness to his poor brothers and sisters at *Croyden,* and dine with them at his hospital ; at which time, you may believe there was joy at the table.

And at this place he built also a fair free-school, with a good accommodation and maintenance for the master and scholars. Which gave just occasion for *Boyse Sisi,* then embassador for the *French* king, and resident here, at the bishop's death, to say, ' The ' bishop had published many learned books ; but a free-school to train up youth, and ' 'an hospital to lodge and maintain aged and poor people, were the best evidences of ' christian learning that a bishop could leave to posterity.' This good bishop lived to see king *James* settled in peace, and then fell sick at *Lambeth ;* of which the king having notice, went to visit him, and found him in his bed in a declining condition, and very weak ; and after some short discourse, the king assured him, *He had a great affection for him, and high value for his prudence and virtues, which were so useful for the church, that he would earnestly beg his life of God.* To which he replied, *Pro ecclesia Dei, pro ecclesia Dei :* which were the last words he ever spake ; therein testifying, That as in his life, so at his death, his chiefest care was of God's church.

This *John Whitgift* was made archbishop in the year one thousand five hundred eighty and three. In which busy place, he continued twenty years and some months ; and in which time, you may believe he had many trials of his courage and patience ; but his motto was, *Vincit, qui patitur ;* i. e. *He conquers that endures.* And he made it good. Many of his many tryals were occasion'd by the then powerful earl of *Leicester,* who did still (but secretly) raise and cherish a faction of non-conformists to oppose him ; especially one *Thomas Cartwright,* a man of noted learning ; sometime contemporary with the bishop in *Cambridge,* and of the same college, of which Dr. *Whitgift,* before he was bishop, was master : in which place there began some emulations, (the particulars I forbear) and at last open and high oppositions betwixt them, and in which you may believe Mr. *Cartwright* was most faulty, if his expulsion out of the university can incline you to it,

And

And in this discontent, long before the earl's death (which was one thousand five hundred eighty and eight) Mr. *Cartwright* appeared a chief cherisher of a party that were for the *Geneva* church-government; and to effect it, he ran himself into many dangers both of liberty and life; appearing to justify himself and his party in many remonstrances (especially that called the *Admonition to the parliament.*) Which last he caused to be printed; to which the doctor made an answer, and *Cartwright* replied upon him; and then the doctor having rejoined to his reply, (however Mr *Cartwright* would not be satisfied) he wrote no more, but left the reader to be judge which *J. S.* had maintained their cause with most charity and reason. [And to posterity he left such a learned and most useful book, as does abundantly establish the reformation and constitution of our church, and vindicate it against all the cavils of the innovators.]

After some years the doctor being preferred to the see, first of *Worcester*, and then of *Canterbury*, Mr. *Cartwright*, after his share of trouble and imprisonment (for setting up new presbyteries in divers places, against the establish'd order) having received from the archbishop many personal favours, retired himself to a more private living, which was at *Warwick*, where he became master of an hospital, and lived quietly, and grew rich; and where the archbishop gave him a licence to preach, upon promise not to meddle with controversies, but incline his hearers to piety and moderation: and this promise he kept during his life, which ended one thousand six hundred and two, the archbishop surviving him but one year, each ending his days in perfect charity with the other.

J. S.   ['Tis true, the archbishop treated *Cartwright* with such a civility as gained much upon him, and made him declare unto his patron, the earl of *Leicester*, how much the archbishop's human carriage had endeared him to him; and withal shewed his desire that he might have liberty sometimes to have access to him; professing that he would seek to persuade all with whom he had concern and converse, to keep up an union with the church of *England*. This, I say, is certain; but it is not so certain, that the archbishop gave *Cartwright* a licence to preach. It appears, that in the year 1585, he refused to grant him, however sollicited by *Leicester*'s own letter to do it: and notwithstanding *Cartwright*'s promises, he required more space of time to be satisfied of his conformity. For the elucidation whereof, and some further light into this matter, let both these letters be read and consider'd; the former, of the earl to the archbishop; the latter, of the archbishop to the earl.

My good lord,

The earl of
Leicester to the
archbishop,
concerning
Mr. Cart-
wright.

'I Most heartily thank you for your favourable and courteous usage of Mr. *Cartwright*, who hath so exceeding kindly taken it also, as, I assure your grace, he ' cannot speak enough of it. I trust it shall do a great deal of good. And he protesteth ' and professeth to me, to take no other course, but to the drawing of all men to ' the unity of the church; and that your grace hath so dealt with him, as no man ' shall so command him, and dispose of him, as you shall: and doth mean to let this ' opinion publickly be known, even in the pulpit; (if your grace so permit him) what ' he himself will, and would all others should do, for obedience to the laws establish-' ed. And if any little scruple be, it is not great, and easy to be reformed by your ' grace; whom I do most heartily entreat to continue your favour and countenance to-' wards him, with such access sometimes as your leisure may permit. For I perceive ' he doth much desire and crave it, *&c.* Thus, my good lord, praying to God to ' bless his church, and to make his servants constant and faithful, I bid your grace ' farewel.

Your grace's very assured friend,

At the court, this
14th of *July.*

Rob. Leicester.

To which letter the archbishop returned this answer.

My singular good lord,

The archbi-
shop to the
earl.

'M R. *Cartwright* shall be welcome to me at all times, and using himself quietly, ' as becomes him, and as I hope he will, he shall find me willing to do him ' any good; but to grant unto him, as yet, my licence to preach, without longer

tryal,

' tryal, I cannot ; especially seeing he protesteth himself to be of the same mind he was
' at the writing of his book, for the matter thereof, tho not for the manner ; my self
' also, I thank God, not altered in any point by me set down, to the contrary ;
' and knowing many things [in his book] to be very dangerous. Wherefore, not-
' withstanding, I am content and ready to be at peace with him, so long as he
' liveth peaceably ; yet doth my conscience and duty forbid me to give unto him
' any further publick approbation, until I be better persuaded of his conformity.
' And so being bold to use my accustomed plainness with your good lord-
' ship, I commit you to the tuition of almighty God; this 17th of *July*,
' 1585.]

And now after this long digression made for the information of my reader concerning what follows, I bring him back to venerable Mr. *Hooker*, where we left him
in the *Temple*, and where we shall find him as deeply engaged in a controversy with
Walter Travers, a friend and favourite of Mr. *Cartwright*'s, as doctor *Whitgift* had
ever been with Mr. *Cartwright* himself, and of which I shall proceed to give this following account.

And first this ; That tho the pens of Mr. *Cartwright* and doctor *Whitgift* were now at
rest, and had been a great while, yet there was sprung up a new generation of restless
men, that by company and clamours became possest of a faith which they ought to have
kept to themselves, but could not : men that were become positive in asserting, *That a
papist cannot be saved*: insomuch, that about this time, at the execution of the queen
of *Scots*, the bishop that preached her funeral sermon (which was doctor *Howland*, then
bishop of *Peterborough*) was reviled for not being positive for her damnation. And besides this boldness of their becoming God's, so far as to set limits to his mercies ;
there was not only *Martin Mar-prelate*, but other venomous books daily printed
and dispersed ; books that were so absurd and scurrilous, that the graver divines disdained them an answer. And yet these were grown in high esteem with the common
people, till *Tom Nash* appeared against them all, who was a man of a sharp wit, and the
master of a scoffing satirical merry pen, which he employ'd to discover the absurdities of
those blind malicious senseless pamphlets, and sermons as senseless as they : *Nash* his answers being like his books, which bore these titles, *An almond for parrot* ; *A fig for my
god-son* ; *Come crack me this nut*, and the like : so that his merry wit made such a
discovery of their absurdities, as (which is strange) he put a greater stop to these
malicious pamphlets, than a much wiser man had been able.

And now the reader is to take notice, That at the death of father *Alvey*, who was The contro-
master of the *Temple*, this *Walter Travers* was lecturer there for the evening ser- versy be-
mons, which he preached with great approbation, especially of the younger gentlemen tween Hooker
of that society ; and for the most part approved by Mr. *Hooker* himself, in the midst and Travers.
of their oppositions. For he continued lecturer a part of his time ; Mr. *Travers* being
indeed a man of competent learning, of a blameless life. But
he had taken orders by the presbyters in *Antwerp*, and if in any thing he was trans-
ported, it was in an extreme desire to set up that government in this nation : for the
promoting of which he had a correspondence with *Theodore Beza* at *Geneva*, and others
in *Scotland* ; and was one of the chiefest assistants to Mr. *Cartwright* in that design.

Mr. *Travers* had also a particular hope to set up this government in the *Temple*, and
to that end used his endeavours to be master of it ; and his being disappointed by
Mr. *Hooker*'s admittance, proved some occasion of his opposition of Mr. *Hooker*'s sermons publickly in the pulpit. Many of which were concerning the doctrine, discipline
and ceremonies of this church : and Mr. *Hooker* again publickly justified his doctrine
against the other's exceptions. Insomuch, that as saint *Paul* withstood saint *Peter* to
his face, so did they. For as one hath pleasantly exprefs'd it, *The forenoon sermons
speak Canterbury, and the afternoons Geneva*.

In these sermons there was little of bitterness, but each party brought all the reasons
he was able, to prove his adversary's opinions erroneous. And thus it continued for
a time, till the oppositions became so high, and the consequences so dangerous, especially in that place, that the prudent archbishop put a stop to Mr. *Travers* his preaching, by a positive prohibition ; [and that chiefly because of his foreign ordination.]
Against which Mr. *Travers* appealed, and petitioned her majesty and her privy council
to have it recalled, where he met with many assisting powerful friends ; but they were
not able to prevail with or against the archbishop, whom the queen had intrusted with
all church-power ; and he had received so fair a testimony of Mr. *Hooker*'s principles,

and

and of his learning and moderation, that he withstood all sollicitations. But the denying this petition of Mr. *Travers* was unpleasant to divers of his party, and the reasona-
bleness of it became at last to be so magnified by them and many others, as never to be
answered : so that intending the bishops and Mr. *Hooker's* disgrace, they procured it to
be privately printed and scattered abroad ; and then Mr. *Hooker* was forced to appear as
publickly, and print an answer to it, which he did, and dedicated it to the archbishop ;
and it proved so full an answer, to have in it so much of clear reason, and writ with so
much meekness and majesty of style, that the bishop began to wonder at the man, to
rejoice that he had appeared in his cause, and disdained not earnestly to beg his friendship ;
even a familiar friendship with a man of so much quiet learning and humility.

To enumerate the many particular points, in which Mr. *Hooker* and Mr. *Travers* dissented (all or most of which I have seen written) would prove at least tedious : and
therefore I shall impose upon my reader no more than two, which shall immediately follow, and by which he may judge of the rest.

Mr. *Travers* excepted against Mr. *Hooker*, for that in one of his sermons he declared,
' That the assurance of what we believe by the word of God, is not to us so certain as
' that which we perceive by sense.' And Mr. *Hooker* confesseth he said so, and endeavours to justify it by the reasons following.

I.   ' First, I taught, that the things which God promises in his word, are not surer to
' us than what we touch, handle or see ; but are we so sure and certain of them ? If
' we be, why doth God so often prove his promises to us as he doth, by arguments drawn
' from our sensible experience ? For we must be surer of the proof, than of the things
' proved ; otherwise it is no proof. For example, How is it that many men looking on
' the moon at the same time, every one knoweth it to be the moon as certainly as the
' other doth ? But many believing one and the same promise, have not all one and the
' same fulness of persuasion. For how falleth it out, that men being assured of any
' thing by sense, can be no surer of it than they are ; whenas the strongest in faith that
' liveth upon the earth, hath always need to labour, strive and pray, that his assurance
' concerning heavenly and spiritual things, may grow, increase and be augmented ? '

The sermon that gave him the cause of this his justification, makes the case more
plain, by declaring, *that there is besides this certainty of evidence, a certainty of ad-*
herence. In which, having most excellently demonstrated what the *certainty of adhe-*
rence is, he makes this comfortable use of it : ' comfortable (he says) as to weak be-
' lievers, who suppose themselves to be faithless, not to believe, when notwithstanding
' they have their adherence. The Holy Spirit hath his private operations, and worketh
' secretly in them, and effectually too, tho they want the inward testimony of it.'

Tell this to a man that hath a mind too much dejected by a sad sense of his sin ; to
one that by a too severe judging of himself, concludes that he wants faith, because he
wants the comfortable assurance of it ; and his answer will be, ' Do not perswade me a-
' gainst my knowledge, against what I find and feel in my self : I do not, I know I do not
' believe.' (Mr. *Hooker's* own words follow) ' Well then, to favour such men a little in
' their weakness, let that be granted which they do imagine ; be it, that they adhere
' not to God's promises, but are faithless, and without belief : but are they not grieved
' for their unbelief ? They confess they are : do they not wish it might, and also strive
' that it may be otherwise ? We know they do. Whence cometh this, but from a secret
' love and liking, that they have of those things believed ? for no man can love those
' things which in his own opinion are not : and, if they think those things to be, which
' they shew they love, when they desire to believe them ; then must it be, that by de-
' siring to believe, they prove themselves true believers : for, without faith no man thin-
' keth that things believed are : which argument all the subtilties of infernal powers
' will never be able to dissolve.' This is an abridgment of part of the reasons he gives for
his justification of this his opinion, for which he was excepted against by Mr.
Travers.

II.   Mr. *Hooker* was also accused by Mr. *Travers*, for that he in one of his sermons had
declared, ' That he doubted not but that God was merciful to save many of our fore-
' fathers living heretofore in popish superstition, for as much as they sinned ignorantly : '
and Mr. *Hooker* in his answer professeth it to be his judgment, and declares his reasons for
this charitable opinion to be as followeth.

But first (because *Travers's* argument against this charitable opinion of *Hooker* was,
That they could not be saved, because they sought to be justified by the merit of their
works,

works, and fo overthrow the foundation of faith) he ftates the queftion about juftification and works, and how the foundation of faith is overthrown ; and then he proceeds
to difcover that way which natural men and fome others have miftaken to be the way,
by which they hope to attain true and everlafting happinefs : and having difcovered the
miftaken, he proceeds to direct to that true way, by which, and no other, everlafting
life and bleffednefs is attainable.   And thefe two ways he demonftrates thus (they be
his own words that follow) ' That, the way of nature ; this, the way of grace : the
' end of that way falvation merited, prefuppofing the righteoufnefs of mens works :
' their righteoufnefs, a natural ability to do them ; that ability, the goodnefs of God
' which created them in fuch perfection.   But the end of this way, falvation beftowed
' upon men as a gift : prefuppofing not their righteoufnefs, but the forgivenefs of their
' unrighteoufnefs, juftification ; their juftification not their natural ability to do good,
' but their hearty forrow for not doing, and unfeigned belief in him, for whofe fake
' not doers are accepted, which is their vocation ; their vocation, the election of God,
' taking them out of the number of loft children ; their election, a Mediator in whom
' to be elect : this mediation, inexplicable mercy ; this mercy, fuppofing their mifery
' for whom he vouchfafed to die, and make himfelf a Mediator.'
    And he alfo declareth, ' There is no meritorious caufe for our juftification, but Chrift ;
' no effectual, but his mercy : ' and fays alfo, ' We deny the grace of our Lord Jefus
' Chrift ; we abufe, difannul, and annihilate the benefit of his paffion, if by a proud ima-
' gination we believe we can merit everlafting life, or can be worthy of it.'   This
belief (he declareth) is to deftroy the very effence of our juftification, and he makes all
opinions that border upon this, to be very dangerous.   ' Yet neverthelefs (and for
' this he was accufed) confidering how many virtuous and juft men, how many faints
' and martyrs have had their dangerous opinions, amongft which this was one, that
' they hoped to make God fome part of amends, by voluntary punifhments which they
' laid upon themfelves : becaufe by this, or the like erroneous opinions which do by
' confequent overthrow the merits of Chrift ; fhall man be fo bold as to write on their
' graves, *Such men are damned, there is for them no falvation ?* ' Saint *Auftin* fays,
Errare poffum, hæreticus effe nolo.   And except we put a difference betwixt them that
err ignorantly, and them that obftinately perfift in it, how is it poffible that any man
fhould hope to be faved ? Give me a pope or a cardinal, whom great afflictions have
made to know himfelf, whofe heart God hath touched with true forrow for all his fins,
and filled with a love of Chrift and his gofpel ; whofe eyes are willingly open to fee
the truth, and his mouth ready to renounce all error, this one opinion of merit excepted, which he thinketh God will require at his hands ; and becaufe he wanteth,
trembleth, and is difcouraged, and yet can fay, *Lord, cleanfe me from all my fecret
fins :* fhall I think becaufe of this, or a like error, fuch men touch not fo much as the
hem of Chrift's garment ? If they do, wherefore fhould I doubt, but that virtue may
proceed from Chrift to fave them ? No, I will not be afraid to fay to fuch a one, ' You
' err in your opinion, but be of good comfort, you have to do with a merciful God,
' who will make the beft of that little which you hold well ; and not with a captious
' fophifter, who gathereth the worft out of every thing in which you are miftaken.'
    But it will be faid, ' The admittance of merit in any degree, overthroweth the foun-
' dation, excludeth from the hope of mercy, from all poffibility of falvation.'   And
now Mr. *Hooker*'s own words follow.
    ' What tho they hold the truth fincerely in all other parts of chriftian faith ? al-
' tho they have in fome meafure all the virtues and graces of the Spirit ? altho they
' have all other tokens of God's children in them ?   altho they be far from having any
' proud opinion, that they fhall be faved by the worthinefs of their deeds ?   altho the
' only thing that troubleth and molefteth them, be a little too much dejection, fome-
' what too great a fire arifing from an erroneous conceit, that God will require a wor-
' thinefs in them, which they are grieved to find wanting in themfelves ? altho they
' be not obftinate in this opinion ? altho they be willing, and would be glad to forfake
' it, if any one reafon were brought fufficient to difprove it ? altho the only caufe why
' they do not forfake it e'er they die, be their ignorance of that means by which it
' might be difproved ? altho the caufe why the ignorance in this point is not removed,
' be the want of knowledge in fuch as fhould be able, and are not, to remove it ?   Let
' me die (fays Mr. *Hooker*) if it be ever proved, that fimply an error doth exclude a
' pope or cardinal in fuch a cafe utterly from hope of life.'   Surely, I muft confefs,
that if it be an error to think that God may be merciful to fave men, even when
they err, my greateft comfort is, my error : were it not for the love I bear to this error,
I would never wifh to fpeak or to live.

I was

I was willing to take notice of thefe two points, as fuppofing them to be very material; and that as they are thus contracted, they may prove ufeful to my reader; as alfo for that the anfwers be arguments of Mr. *Hooker's* great and clear reafon, and equal charity. Other exceptions were alfo made againft him, as, ' That he prayed before, and ' not after his fermons ; that in his prayers he named bifhops; that he kneeled, both ' when he prayed, and when he received the facrament ; and (fays Mr. *Hooker* in his ' defence) other exceptions fo like thefe, as but to name, I fhould have thought a ' greater fault than to commit them.'

And 'tis not unworthy the noting, that in the manage of fo great a controverfy, a fharper reproof than this, and one like it, did never fall from the happy pen of this humble man. That like it, was upon a like occafion of exceptions, to which his anfwer was, *Your next argument confifts of railing and of reafons ; to your railing I fay nothing, to your reafons I fay what follows.* And I am glad of this fair occafion, to teftify the dove-like temper of this meek, this matchlefs man : doubtlefs, if almighty God had bleft the diffenters from the ceremonies and difcipline of this church, with a like meafure of wifdom and humility, inftead of their pertinacious zeal ; then obedience and truth had kiffed each other, then peace and piety had flourifhed in our nation, and this church and ftate had been bleft like *Jerufalem*, that is, at unity with it-felf : but that can never be expected, till God fhall blefs the common people with a belief, *that fchifm is a fin, and that there may be offences taken which are not given ; and that laws are not made for private men to difpute, but to obey.*

J. S.
The articles of falfe doctrine objected by *Travers* to *Hooker.*

[Before we pafs from thefe unhappy difcerptations between *Hooker* and *Travers,* as we have heard two articles of pretended falfe doctrine objected by the one to the other, fo it is pity the reft fhould be wholly loft, and for ever buried in filence : therefore, for the making this confiderable part of the reverend man's life and hiftory compleat, and to retrieve whatfoever may be gotten of the pen and mind of fo learned and judicious a perfon, take this further account, not only of two, but of all the articles that his beforementioned adverfary had marfhalled up againft him, collected from a fermon or fermons he had heard him preach at the *Temple* ; together with his endeavoured confutation of them : and likewife *Hooker's* own vindication of himfelf to each of thofe articles. Thefe articles feem to have been delivered by *Travers* to the lord treafurer. The fame lord delivered them to *Hooker,* to confider of, and to make his reply to. And of thefe articles the archbifhop alfo was privy, and briefly declared his judgment and determination of. I fhall fet all down exactly from an authentick manufcript.

Doctrines delivered by Mr. *Hooker,* as they were fet down and fhewed by Mr. *Travers, Mar.* 30. 1585. under this title :

A fhort note of fundry unfound points of doctrine, at divers times delivered by Mr. Hooker *in his publick fermons.*

1. The church of *Rome* is a true church of Chrift, and a church fanctified by profeffion of that truth which God hath revealed unto us by his Son ; tho not a pure and perfect church.

2. The fathers which lived and died in popifh fuperftition were faved, becaufe they finned ignorantly.

3. They which are of the church of *Rome* may be faved by fuch a faith as they have in Chrift, and a general repentance of all their fins.

4. The church of *Rome* holdeth all men finners, even the bleffed virgin, tho fome of them think otherwife of her.

5. The church of *Rome* teacheth Chrift's righteoufnefs to be the only meritorious caufe of taking away fin.

6. The *Galatians* which joined with faith in Chrift, circumcifion, as neceffary unto falvation, notwithftanding be faved.

7. Neither the church of *Rome,* nor the *Galatians,* deny the foundation directly, but only by confequent ; and therefore may be faved. Or elfe neither the *Lutherans,* nor whofoever hold any error (for every error by confequent denieth the foundation) may be faved.

8. An additament taketh not away that whereunto it is added, but confirmeth it. As he that faith of any, that he is a righteous man, faith, that he is a man : except it be privative ; as when he faith, he is a dead man, then he denieth him to be a man : and

of

of this fort of [privative] additaments neither are works, which are added to Chrift by the church of *Rome*; nor circumcifion, added to him by the *Galatians*.

9. The *Galatians* cafe is harder than the cafe of the church of *Rome*; for they added to Chrift, circumcifion, which God had forbidden and abolifhed: but that which the church of *Rome* addeth are works, which God hath commanded.

10. No one fequel urged by the apoftle againft the *Galatians*, for joining circumcifion with Chrift, but may be as well enforced againft the *lutherans* holding ubiquity.

11. A bifhop or cardinal of the church of *Rome*, yea, the pope himfelf denying all other errors of popery, notwithftaning his opinion of juftification by works, may be faved.

12. Predeftination is not of the abfolute will of God, but conditional.

13. The doings of the wicked are not of the will of God pofitive, but only permiffive.

14. The reprobates are not rejected, but for the evil works which God did forefee they would commit.

15. The affurance of things which we believe by the word, is not fo fure, as of thofe which we perceive by fenfe.

Here follows an account, given in by Mr. Hooker *himfelf, of what he preached March* 28. 1585. *and then of what* Travers *in his lectures excepted thereunto: and laftly, of* Hooker's *reply, and vindication of himfelf and his fermons.*

'I Doubted not but that God was merciful to thoufands of our fathers, which lived 'in popifh fuperftition: for that they finned ignorantly. But we have the light of 'the truth. *Hooker's own relation of his affertions, and vindication of them againft Travers.*

'Which doctrine was withftood, becaufe

Travers his own anfwer.

Salvation belongeth to the church of Chrift. We may not think, that they could be capable of it, which lived in the errors held and maintained in the church of Rome, that feat of antichrift. Wherefore to his people God fpeaketh in this fort, Go out of Babylon, my people, go out of her, that you be not partaker of her fins, and that you tafte not of her plagues. The Galatians thinking that they could not be faved by Chrift, except they were circumcifed, did thereby exclude themfelves from falvation. Chrift did profit them nothing. So they which join their own works with Chrift.

we are commanded to depart out of *Baby-* 'lon, elfe we fhall be partakers of thofe 'plagues there denounced againft fuch as 'repent not of their fuperftitions: which 'they cannot who know them not.

'I anfwered, that there were thoufands 'in our days who hate fin, defiring to 'walk according to the will of God; and 'yet committing fin, which they know 'not to be fin. I think, that they 'that defire forgivenefs of fecret fins, 'which they know not to be fins, and 'that are forry for fins, that they know 'not to be fins, [fuch] do repent.

'It is replied, that without faith there is no repentance. Our fathers defiring mercy, 'did but as divers pagans; and had no true repentance.

'They thought they could not be faved by Chrift, without works, as the *Galatians* 'did: and fo they denied the foundation of faith.

'I anfwered, altho the propofition were true, that he who thinketh that he cannot 'be faved by Chrift without works, overthroweth the foundation; yet we may per-'fuade our felves, that our forefathers might be faved. 1. Becaufe many of them were 'ignorant of the dogmatical pofitions of the church of *Rome*. 2. Albeit they had 'divers pofitions of that church, yet it followeth not that they had this. 3. Altho 'they did generally hold this pofition, yet God might be merciful unto them. No ex-'ception hath been taken againft any one of thefe affertions. 4. I add, that albeit all 'thofe of whom we fpeak, did not only hold this generally, but as the fcholars of *Rome* 'hold this pofition now, of joining works with Chrift, whether doth that pofition o-'verthrow the foundation directly, or only by confequence? If it doth overthrow the 'foundation directly, &c. To make all plain, thefe points are to be handled. *Firft*, 'what is meant by the foundation. *Secondly*, what it is to deny the foundation direct-'ly. *Thirdly*, whether the elect may be fo deceived, that they may come to this, to 'deny

‘ deny the foundation directly. *Fourthly*, whether the *Galatians* did directly deny
‘ it. *Fifthly*, whether the church of *Rome*, by joining works with Chrift in the mat-
‘ ter of falvation, do directly deny it.

‘ I. To the firft I anfwer, The foundation is, that which *Peter*, *Nathaniel*, and
‘ the *Samaritan* confeffed ; and that which the apoftles exprefly affirm, *Acts* 4. *There
‘ is none other name under heaven given among men, whereby we muft be faved.* It is,
‘ in fine, this, *Salvation is by Chrift only.* This word *only*, what doth it exclude ?
‘ as when we fay, this judge fhall *only* determine this matter : this *only* doth not
‘ exclude all other things, befides the perfon of the judge ; as neceffary witneffes, the
‘ equity of the caufe, &c. but all perfons : and not all perfons from being prefent, but
‘ from determining the caufe. So when we fay, Salvation *only* is by Chrift, we do
‘ not exclude all other things. For then how could we fay, that faith were neceffary ?
‘ We exclude therefore, not thofe means, whereby the benefits of Chrift are applied
‘ to us, but all other perfons, from working any thing for our redemption.

‘ II. To the fecond point, We are faid to deny the foundation directly, when plain-
‘ ly and exprefly we deny, that Chrift only doth fave. By confequence we deny the
‘ foundation, when any fuch thing is defended whereby it may be inferred, that Chrift
‘ doth not *only* fave.

‘ III. To the third, The elect of God cannot fo err, that they fhould deny directly
‘ the foundation. For that Chrift doth keep them from that extremity. And there
‘ is no falvation to fuch as deny the foundation directly. Therefore it is faid, that they
‘ fhall worfhip the beaft, whofe names are not found in the book of life. Antichrift
‘ may prevail much againft them, (*viz.* the elect) and they may receive the fign of the
‘ beaft in the fame degree, but not fo that they fhould directly deny the foundation.

‘ IV. To the fourth, Albeit the *Galatians* fell into error, yet not fo that they loft
‘ falvation. If they had died before they had known the doctrine of *Paul*, being be-
‘ fore deceived by thofe that they thought did teach the truth ; what ? do you think
‘ fhould they have been damned ? This we are taught, that fuch errors as are damning
‘ fhall not take hold, but on thofe that love not the truth. The *Galatians* had embra-
‘ ced the truth, and for it had fuffered many things, &c. There came among them
‘ feducers, that required circumcifion. They being moved with a religious fear,
‘ thought it to be the word of God, that they fhould be circumcifed. The beft of them
‘ might be brought into that opinion ; and dying before they could be otherwife in-
‘ ftructed, they may not for that be excluded from falvation. Circumcifion being
‘ joined with Chrift, doth only by confequence overthrow the foundation. To hold
‘ the foundation with an additament is not to deny the foundation, unlefs the addi-
‘ tament be a privative. He is a juft man, therefore a man : but this followeth not ;
‘ he is a dead man, therefore he is a man. In the 15*th* chapter of the *Acts* they are
‘ called *credentes* (*i. e.* fuch as believed) that taught the neceffity of circumcifion.
‘ That name could not have been given unto them, if directly they had denyed the
‘ foundation. That which the apoftle doth urge againft the *Galatians*, in refpect of
‘ circumcifion, may be urged againft the *lutherans*, in refpect of their confubftan-
‘ tiation. But they do not directly deny the foundation. So neither did the *Galatians*
‘ directly deny it.

‘ V. *Laftly*, Whether doth the church of *Rome* directly deny the foundation, by join-
‘ ing Chrift and works. There is great difference between the papifts and the *Galatians* :
‘ for circumcifion, which the *Galatians* joined with Chrift, was forbidden, and taken
‘ away by Chrift ; but works are commanded, which the church of *Rome* doth join
‘ with Chrift. So that there is greater repugnancy to join circumcifion with Chrift,
‘ than to join works with him. But let them be equal. As the *Galatians* only by
‘ confequent denied the foundation, fo do the papifts, *Zanchy, Calvin, Mornay* ; I
‘ need not go fo far as fome of thefe. But this I think, if the pope, or any of the
‘ cardinals, fhould forfake all other their corruptions, and yield up their fouls, hold-
‘ ing the foundation again but by a flender thread, and did but as it were touch the hem
‘ of Chrift’s garment, being that which the church of *Rome* doth in this point of doc-
‘ trine, they may obtain mercy. For they have to deal with God, who is no captious
‘ fophifter, and will not examine them in quiddities, but accept them, if they plainly
‘ hold the foundation.

‘ This

' This error is my only comfort, as touching the salvation of our fathers : I follow
' Mr. *Martyr.* I know *Ignorantia non excusat in toto,* but *in tanto.* It maketh not
' a fault to be no fault, but that which is a fault to be a less one.'

At length, thus did the archbishop of *Canterbury* discreetly and warily correct and
moderate these articles between them both.

I. Papists, living and dying papists, may notwithstanding be saved. The reason ; _{The arch-}
ignorance excused them. As the apostle alledgeth, 1 *Tim.* 1. 13. *I obtained mercy, be-* _{bishop's judg-}
cause I did it ignorantly. _{ment of these controversy;}

The archbishop's judgment.

Not papists, but our fathers. Nor they all, but many of them. Nor living and
dying papists, but living in popish superstitions. Nor simply might, but might, by the
mercy of God, be saved. Ignorance did not excuse the fault, to make it no fault :
but the less their fault was, in respect of ignorance, the more hope we have, that God
was merciful to them.

II. Papists hold the foundation of faith : so that they may be saved, notwithstanding
their opinion of merit.

Archbishop. And papists overthrow the foundation of faith, both by their doctrine
of merit, and otherwise many ways. So that if they have, as their errors deserve,
I do not see how they should be saved.

III. General repentance may serve to their salvation, tho they confess not their error
of merit.

Archbishop. General repentance will not serve any but the faithful man. Nor
him, for any sin ; but for such sins only as he doth not mark, nor know to be
sin.

IV. The church of *Rome* is within the new covenant.

Archbishop. The church of *Rome* is not as the assemblies of *Turks, Jews,* and
painims.

V. The *Galatians* joining the law with Christ might have been saved, before they
received the epistle.

Archbishop. Of the *Galatians,* before they were told of their error, what letteth
us to think, as of our fathers, before the church of *Rome* was admonished of her defection from the truth ?

And this also may be worthy of noting, That these exceptions of Mr. *Travers,* a-
gainst Mr. *Hooker,* were the cause of his transcribing several of his sermons, which we
now see printed with his books ; of his answer to Mr. *Travers* his supplication ; and
of his most learned and useful discourse of justification, of faith, and works : and by their
transcription, they fell into the hands of others, that have preserved them from being
lost, as too many of his other matchless writings have been : and from these I have
gathered many observations in this discourse of his life.

After the publication of his answer to the petition of Mr. *Travers,* Mr. *Hooker*
grew daily into greater repute with the most learned and wise of the nation ; but it had
a contrary effect in very many of the *Temple* that were zealous for Mr. *Travers,* and
for his church-discipline ; insomuch, that tho Mr. *Travers* left the place, yet the seeds
of discontent could not be rooted out of that society, by the great reason, and as great
meekness of this humble man : for tho the chief benchers gave him much reverence
and encouragement, yet he there met with many neglects and oppositions by those of

Mr. *Travers*'s judgment; infomuch that it turned to his extreme grief: and that he might unbeguile and win them, he defigned to write a deliberate fober treatife of the church's power to make canons for the ufe of ceremonies, and by law to impofe an obedience to them, as upon her children; and this he propofed to do in eight books of *the laws of ecclefiaftical polity*; intending therein to fhew fuch arguments, as fhould force an affent from all men, if reafon, delivered in fweet language, and void of any provocation, were able to do it: and that he might prevent all prejudice, he wrote before it a large *preface* or *epiftle* to the diffenting brethren, wherein there were fuch bowels of love, and fuch a commixture of that love with reafon, as was never exceeded but in holy writ; and particularly, by that of faint *Paul* to his dear brother and fellow-labourer *Philemon*; than which none ever was more like this epiftle of Mr. *Hooker's*. So that his dear friend and companion in his ftudies, doctor *Spencer*, might, after his death, juftly fay, ' What admirable height of learning, and depth of judgment, dwelt ' in the lowly mind of this truly humble man; great in all wife mens eyes, except his ' own! With what gravity and majefty of fpeech his tongue and pen uttered heavenly ' myfteries; whofe eyes, in the humility of his heart, were always caft down to the ' ground! How all things that proceeded from him, were breathed as from the Spirit of ' love; as if he, like the bird of the Holy Ghoft, the dove, had wanted gall! Let thofe ' that knew him not in his perfon, judge by thefe living images of his foul, his writings.'

The foundation of thefe books was laid in the *Temple*; but he found it no fit place, to finifh what he had there defigned; and therefore follicited the archbifhop for a remove, to whom he fpake to this purpofe; ' My lord, when I loft the freedom of my cell, ' which was my college, yet I found fome degree of it in my quiet country parfonage: ' but I am weary of the noife and oppofitions of this place; and indeed, God and na- ' ture did not intend me for contentions, but for ftudy and quietnefs. And, my lord, ' my particular contefts here with Mr. *Travers*, have proved the more unpleafant to me, ' becaufe I believe him to be a good man; and that belief hath occafioned me to examine ' mine own confcience concerning his opinions; and, to fatisfy that, I have confulted ' the holy fcripture, and other laws, both human and divine, whether the confcience of ' him, and others of his judgment, ought to be fo far complied with by us, as to alter our ' frame of church government, our manner of God's worfhip, our praifing and praying ' to him, and our eftablifhed ceremonies, as often as their tender confciences fhall re- ' quire us. And, in this examination, I have not only fatisfyed my felf; but have begun ' a treatife, in which I intend the fatisfaction of others, by a demonftration of the rea- ' fonablenefs of our laws of *ecclefiaftical polity*; and therein laid a hopeful foundation ' for the church's peace; and fo as not to provoke your adverfary Mr. *Cartwright*, nor ' Mr. *Travers*, whom I take to be mine (but not mine enemy) God knows this to be ' my meaning. To which end, I have fearched many books, and fpent many thoughtful ' hours; and, I hope, not in vain; for I write to reafonable men. But, my lord, I fhall ' never be able to finifh what I have begun, unlefs I be removed into fome quiet country ' parfonage, where I may fee God's bleffings fpring out of my mother earth, and eat ' mine own bread in peace and privacy. A place where I may, without difturbance, me- ' ditate my approaching mortality, and that great account, which all flefh muft, at the ' laft great day, give to the God of all fpirits.

' This is my defign; and as thefe are the defires of my heart, fo they fhall, by God's ' affiftance, be the conftant endeavours of the uncertain remainder of my life. And ' therefore if your grace can think me and my poor labours worthy fuch a favour, let ' me beg it, that I may perfect what I have begun: which is a bleffing I cannot hope for ' in this place.'

About the time of this requeft to the bifhop, the parfonage or rectory of *Bofcum*, in the diocefs of *Sarum*, and fix miles from that city, became void. The bifhop of *Sarum* is patron of it; but in the vacancy of that fee (which was three years betwixt the death of bifhop *Pierce*, and bifhop *Caldwell's* admiffion into it) the difpofal of that, and all benefices belonging to it, during the time of this faid vacancy, came to be dif-pofed of by the archbifhop of *Canterbury*; and he prefented *Richard Hooker* to it in the year 1591. And *Richard Hooker* was alfo in this faid year inftituted (*July* 17.) to be a minor prebend of *Salisbury*, the corps to it being *Nether-Havin*, about ten miles from that city; which prebend was of no great value, but intended chiefly to make him capable of a better preferment in that church. In this *Bofcum* he continued till he had finifhed four of his eight propofed books of the laws of *eccle-fiaftical polity*, and thefe were enter'd into the regifter-book in *Stationers-hall*, the

9th of *March* 1592. but not printed till the Year 1594. and then with the beforementioned large and affectionate preface, which he directs *to them that seek (as they term
it) the reformation of the laws and orders ecclesiastical in the church of* England; of
which books I shall yet say nothing more, but that he continued his laborious diligence
to finish the remaining four during his life (of all which more properly hereafter) but at
Boscum he finish'd and publish'd but only the first four, being then in the 39th year
of his age.

He left *Boscum* in the year 1595. by a surrender of it into the hands of bishop
Caldwell, and he presented *Benjamin Russel*, who was instituted into it, the 23d of
June in the same year.

The parsonage of *Bishops-bourne* in Kent, three miles from *Canterbury*, is in that
arch-bishop's gift; but in the latter-end of the year 1594. doctor *William Redman*,
the rector of it, was made bishop of *Norwich*; by which means the power of presenting to it was *pro ea vice* in the queen; and she presented *Richard Hooker*, whom
she loved well, to this good living of *Bourne*, the 7th of *July* 1595. in which living he
continued till his death, without any addition of dignity or profit.

And now having brought our *Richard Hooker* from his birth-place to this, where
he found a grave, I shall only give some account of his books, and of his behaviour
in this parsonage of *Bourne*, and then give a rest both to my self and my reader.

His first four books and large epistle have been declared to be printed at his being at
Boscum, anno 1594. Next, I am to tell, that at the end of these four books, there is
printed this advertisement to the reader; ' I have for some causes thought it at this
' time more fit to let go these first four books by themselves, than to stay both them
' and the rest, till the whole might together be published. Such generalities of the
' cause in question as are here handled, it will be perhaps not amiss to consider apart,
' by way of introduction unto the books that are to follow concerning particulars: in
' the mean time the reader is requested to mend the printers errors, as noted under-
' neath. '

And I am next to declare, that his fifth book (which is larger than his first four)
was first also printed by it self, *anno* 1597, and dedicated to his patron (for till then
he chose none) the archbishop.   These books were read with an admiration of their
excellency in this, and their just fame spread it self into foreign nations.   And I have
been told, more than forty years past, that cardinal *Allen*, or learned doctor *Stapleton*
(both englishmen, and in *Italy* when Mr. *Hooker*'s four books were first printed) meeting with this general fame of them, were desirous to read an author, that both the reformed and the learned of their own church did so much magnify; and therefore caused
them to be sent for: and, after reading of them, boasted to the pope (which then was
Clement the eighth) *That tho he had lately said, he never met with an* English
book, whose writer deserved the name of an author; yet there now appear'd a wonder to
them, and it would be so to his holiness, if it were in *Latin*; for *a poor obscure* English
*priest had writ four such books of laws, and church-polity, and in a style that ex-
prest so grave and such humble majesty, with clear demonstration of reason, that
in all their readings they had not met with any that exceeded him.* And this begot
in the pope an earnest desire that doctor *Stapleton* should bring the said four books, and
looking on the *English*, read a part of them to him in *Latin*, which doctor *Stapleton*
did, to the end of the first book; at the conclusion of which, the pope spake to this
purpose; ' There is no learning that this man hath not searched into, nothing
' too hard for his understanding.   This man indeed deserves the name of an
' author; his books will get reverence by age, for there is in them such seeds of
' eternity, that if the rest be like this, they shall last till the last fire shall con-
' sume all learning. '

Nor was this high, the only testimony and commendations given to his books; for
at the first coming of king *James* into this kingdom, he inquired of the archbishop
Whitgift for his friend Mr. *Hooker*, that wrote the books of church-polity; to which
the answer was, that he died a year before queen *Elizabeth*, who received the sad news
of his death with very much sorrow; to which the king replied, ' And I receive it
' with no less, that I shall want the desired happiness of seeing and discoursing with that

' man,

'man, from whofe books I have received fuch fatisfaction : indeed, my lord, I have
'received more fatisfaction in reading a leaf, or paragraph in Mr. *Hooker,* tho it were
'but about the fafhion of churches, or church mufick, or the like, but efpecially of
'the facraments, than I have had in the reading particular large treatifes written but of
'one of thofe fubjects by others, tho very learned men : and, I obferve, there is in
'Mr. *Hooker* no affected language ; but a grave, comprehenfive, clear manifeftation of
'reafon ; and that backt with the authority of the *fcripture,* the *fathers* and *fchool-*
'*men,* and with all *law* both *facred* and *civil.* And tho many others write well, yet
'in the next age they will be forgotten ; but doubtlefs there is in every page of Mr.
'*Hooker's* book, the picture of a divine foul, fuch pictures of *truth* and *reafon,* and
'drawn in fo facred colours, that they fhall never fade, but give an immortal memory
'to the author.' And it is fo truly true, that the king thought what he fpake ; that, as
the moft learned of the nation have and ftill do mention Mr. *Hooker* with reverence, fo
he alfo did never mention him but with the epithet of *learned,* or *judicious,* or *reve-*
rend, or *venerable* Mr. *Hooker.*

Nor did his fon, our late king *Charles* the firft, ever mention him but with the fame
reverence, enjoining his fon, our now gracious king, to be ftudious in Mr. *Hooker's*
* In his an-
nals of *Eliz.*
1599. books. And our learned antiquary Mr. *Cambden** mentioning the death, the modefty,
and other virtues of Mr. *Hooker,* and magnifying his books, wifh'd, *that for the honour*
of this, and benefit of other nations, they were turned into the univerfal language.
Which work tho undertaken by many, yet they have been weary and forfaken it ; but
the reader may now expect it, having been long fince begun, and lately finifh'd, by
the happy pen of doctor *Earl,* now lord bifhop of *Salisbury,* of whom I may juftly fay
(and let it not offend him, becaufe it is fuch a truth as ought not to be concealed from
pofterity, or thofe that now live and yet know him not) that fince Mr. *Hooker* died,
none have lived whom God hath bleft with more innocent wifdom, more fanctified
learning, or a more pious, peaceable, primitive temper : fo that this excellent perfon
feems to be only like himfelf and our venerable *Richard Hooker* ; and only fit to make
the learned of all nations happy in knowing what hath been too long confined to the
language of our little ifland.

There might be many more and juft occafions taken to fpeak of his books, which
none ever did or can commend too much ; but I decline them, and haften to an account
of his chriftian behaviour and death at *Bourne;* in which place he continu'd his cuftomary rules of mortification and felf-denial ; was much in fafting, frequent in meditation
and prayers, enjoying thofe bleffed returns, which only men of ftrict lives feel and
know, and of which men of loofe and godlefs lives cannot be made fenfible ; for fpiritual
things are fpiritually difcerned.

At his entrance into this place, his friendfhip was much fought for by doctor *Ha-*
drian Saravia, then one of the prebendaries of *Canterbury,* a *German* by birth, and
fometimes a paftor both in *Flanders* and *Holland,* where he had ftudied and well confidered the controverted points concerning epifcopacy and facrilege, and in *England*
had a juft occafion to declare his judgment concerning both, unto his brethren minifters
of the *Low-Countries,* which was excepted againft by *Theodore Beza* and others ; a-
gainft whofe exceptions he rejoined, and thereby became the happy author of many
learned tracts writ in *Latin,* efpecially of three ; one of the *degrees of minifters,* and *of*
the bifhops fuperiority above the presbytery; a fecond againft *facrilege;* and a third
of *chriftian obedience to princes* ; the laft being occafioned by *Gretzerus* the jefuit.
And it is obfervable, that when in a time of church tumults, *Beza* gave his reafons to
the chancellor of *Scotland,* for the abrogation of epifcopacy in that nation, partly by
letters, and more fully in a treatife of a three-fold epifcopacy (which he calls *divine,*
human and *fatanical*) this doctor *Saravia* had, by the help of bifhop *Whitgift,* made
fuch an early difcovery of their intentions, that he had almoft as foon anfwered that
treatife as it became publick ; and therein difcovered how *Beza's* opinion did contradict that of *Calvin's* and his adherents ; leaving them to interfere with themfelves
in point of epifcopacy. But of thefe tracts it will not concern me to fay more, than
that they were moft of them dedicated to his and the church of *England's* watchful patron *John Whitgift,* the archbifhop ; and printed about the year in which Mr.
Hooker alfo appeared firft to the world, in the publication of his four books of ecclefiaftical polity.

This

This friendship being sought for by this learned doctor, you may believe was not denied by Mr. *Hooker*, who was by fortune so like him as to be engaged against Mr. *Travers*, Mr. *Cartwright*, and others of their judgment in a controversy too like doctor *Saravia's*; so that inthis year of 1595, and in this place of *Bishops-bourne*, these two excellent persons began a holy friendship, increasing daily to so high and mutual affections, that their two wills seemed to be but one and the same; and designs both for the glory of God, and peace of the church; still assisting and improving each others virtues, and the desired comforts of a peaceable piety; which I have willingly mentioned, because it gives a foundation to some things that follow.

This parsonage of *Bourne*, is from *Canterbury* three miles, and near to the common road that leads from that city to *Dover*; in which parsonage Mr. *Hooker* had not been twelve months, but his books, and the innocency and sanctity of his life became so remarkable, that many turned out of the road, and others (scholars especially) went purposely to see the man, whose life and learning were so much admired; and alas, as our Saviour said of saint *John* the baptist, *What went they out to see? a man clothed in purple and fine linen?* no indeed; but *an obscure harmless man; a man in poor clothes, his loins usually girt in a coarse gown or canonical coat; of a mean stature, and stooping, and yet more lowly in the thoughts of his soul; his body worn out, not with age, but study and holy mortifications; his face full of heat-pimples, begot by his unactivity and sedentary life.* And to this true character of his person, let me add this of his disposition and behaviour; God and nature blessed him with so blessed a bashfulness, that as in his younger days, his pupils might easily look him out of countenance; so neither then, nor in his age, *did he ever willingly look any man in the face; and was of so mild and humble a nature, that his poor parish-clerk and he did never talk but with both their hats on, or both off at the same time.* And to this may be added, that tho he was not pur-blind, yet he was short or weak-sighted; and where he fixt his eyes at the beginning of his sermon, there they continued till it was ended; and the reader has a liberty to believe that his modesty and dim-sight were some of the reasons why he trusted mistress *Churchman* to chuse a wife for him.

This parish-clerk lived till the third or fourth year of the late long parliament; betwixt which time and Mr. *Hooker's* death, there had come many to see the place of his burial, and the monument dedicated to his memory by sir *William Cooper* (who still lives;) and the poor clerk had many rewards for shewing Mr. *Hooker's* grave-place, and his said monument, and did always hear Mr. *Hooker* mentioned with commendations and reverence; to all which he added his own knowledge and observations of his humility and holiness: in all which discourses, the poor man was still more confirmed in his opinion of Mr. *Hooker's* virtues and learning. But it so fell out, that about the said third or fourth year of the long parliament, the present parson of *Bourne* was sequestred (you may guess why) and a *Genevian* minister put into his good living. This, and other like sequestrations, made the clerk express himself in a wonder, and say, *They had sequestred so many good men, that he doubted if his good master Mr.* Hooker *had lived till now, they would have sequestred him too.*

It was not long before this intruding minister had made a party in and about the said parish, that were desirous to receive the sacrament as in *Geneva*; to which end, the day was appointed for a select company, and forms and stools set about the altar or communion table for them to sit and eat and drink; but when they went about this work, there was a want of some joint-stools, which the minister sent the clerk to fetch, and then to fetch cushions. When the clerk saw them begin to sit down, he began to wonder; but the minister bad him *cease wondring; and lock the church door*: to whom he replied, *Pray take you the keys, and lock me out, I will never come more into this church; for all men will say my master* Hooker *was a good man, and a good scholar, and I am sure it was not used to be thus in his days:* and report says, the old man went presently home and died; I do not say died immediately, but within a few days after.

But let us leave this grateful clerk in his quiet grave, and return to Mr. *Hooker* himself, continuing our observations of his christian behaviour in this place, where he gave a holy valediction to all the pleasures and allurements of earth; possessing his soul in a virtuous

His holy behaviour at *Bishops-bourne.*

virtuous quietnefs, which he maintained by conftant ftudy, prayers and meditations: his ufe was to preach once every funday, and he or his curate to catechize after the fecond leffon in the evening prayer: his fermons were neither long nor earneft, but uttered with a grave zeal, and an humble voice: his eyes always fix'd on one place, to prevent his imagination from wandering; infomuch that he feemed to ftudy as he fpake; the defign of his fermons (as indeed of all his difcourfes) was to fhew reafons for what he fpake: and with thefe reafons fuch a kind of rhetorick, as did rather convince and perfuade, than frighten men into piety. Studying not fo much for matter (which he never wanted) as for apt illuftrations to inform and teach his unlearned hearers by familiar examples, and then make them better by convincing applications; never labouring by hard words, and then by needlefs diftinctions and fubdiftinctions to amufe his hearers, and get glory to himfelf; but glory only to God. Which intention he would often fay, was difcernable in a preacher, *as an artificial from a natural beauty.*

He never failed the funday before every *ember* week, to give notice of it to his parifhioners, perfuading both to faft, and then to double their devotions, for a learned and pious clergy, but efpecially for the laft; faying often, *that the life of a pious clergy-man was vifible rhetorick, and fo convincing, that the moft godlefs men (tho they would not deny themfelves the enjoyment of their prefent lufts) did yet fecretly wifh themfelves like thofe of the ftricteft lives.* And to what he perfuaded others, he added his own example of fafting and prayer; and did ufually every *ember* week, take from the parifh-clerk the key of the church-door, into which place he retired every day, and lock'd himfelf up for many hours; and did the like moft *fridays*, and other days of fafting.

He would by no means omit the cuftomary time of proceffion, perfuading all both rich and poor, if they defired the prefervation of love, and their parifh rights and liberties, to accompany him in his perambulation; and moft did fo: in which perambulation, he would ufually exprefs more pleafant difcourfe than at other times, and would then always drop fome loving and facetious obfervations to be remembred againft the next year, efpecially by the boys and young people; ftill inclining them, and all his prefent parifhioners, to meeknefs and mutual kindneffes and love; becaufe *love thinks not evil, but covers a multitude of infirmities.*

He was diligent to inquire who of his parifh were fick, or any way diftreffed, and would often vifit them unfent for; fuppofing that the fitteft time to difcover thofe errors, to which health and profperity had blinded them. And having by pious reafons and prayers moulded them into holy refolutions for the time to come, he would incline them to confeffion, and bewailing their fins, with purpofe to forfake them, and then to receive the communion, both as ftrengthning of thofe holy refolutions, and as a feal betwixt God and them of his mercies to their fouls, in cafe that prefent ficknefs did put a period to their lives.

And as he was thus watchful and charitable to the fick, fo he was as diligent to prevent law-fuits, ftill urging his parifhioners and neighbours, to bear with each others infirmities, and live in love, becaufe (as faint *John* fays) *he that lives in love, lives in God, for God is love.* And to maintain this holy fire of love, conftantly burning on the altar of a pure heart, his advice was to watch and pray, and always keep themfelves fit to receive the communion, and then to receive it often; for it was both a confirming, and a ftrengthning of their graces. This was his advice, and at his entrance or departure out of any houfe, he would ufually fpeak to the whole family, and blefs them by name, infomuch, that as he feemed in his youth to be taught of God, fo he feemed in this place to teach his precepts, as *Enoch* did by walking with him, in all holinefs and humility; making each day a ftep towards a bleffed eternity. And tho in this weak and declining age of the world, fuch examples are become barren, and almoft incredible; yet let his memory be bleft with this true recordation, becaufe he that praifes *Richard Hooker*, praifes God, who hath given fuch gifts to men; and let this humble and affectionate relation of him, become fuch a pattern as may invite pofterity to imitate his virtues.

This

This was his conſtant behaviour at *Bourne* ; thus as *Enoch*, ſo he walked with God ; thus did he tread in the footſteps of primitive piety ; and yet, as that great example of meekneſs and purity, even our bleſſed *Jeſus*, was not free from falſe accuſations, no more was this diſciple of his, this moſt humble, moſt innocent holy man. His was a ſlander parallel to that of chaſt *Suſanna*'s by the wicked elders ; or that againſt ſaint *Athanaſius*, as it is recorded in his life (for that holy man had heretical enemies) and which this age calls *trepanning*. The particulars need not a repetition, and that it was falſe, needs no other teſtimony than the publick puniſhment of his accuſers, and their open confeſſion of his innocency. 'Twas ſaid, that the accuſation was contrived by a diſſenting brother, one that endured not church ceremonies, hating him for his books ſake, which he was not able to anſwer ; and his name hath been told me : but I have not ſo much confidence in the relation, as to make my pen fix a ſcandal on him to poſterity ; I ſhall rather leave it doubtful till the great day of revelation. But this is certain, that he lay under the great charge, and the anxiety of this accuſation, and kept it ſecret to himſelf for many months: and, being a helpleſs man, had lain longer under this heavy burden, but that the protector of the innocent gave ſuch an acci-dental occaſion as forced him to make it known to his two dear friends, *Edwin San-dys* and *George Cranmer*, who were ſo ſenſible of their tutor's ſufferings, that they gave themſelves no reſt, till by their diſquiſitions and diligence they had found out the fraud, and brought him the welcome news, that his accuſers did confeſs they had wrong-ed him, and begged his pardon. To which the good man's reply was to this purpoſe, *the Lord forgive them* ; and *the Lord bleſs you for this comfortable news. Now I have a juſt occaſion to ſay with* Solomon, *Friends are born for the days of adverſity, and ſuch you have proved to me : and to my God I ſay, as did the mother of ſaint* John baptiſt, Thus hath the Lord dealt with me, in the day wherein he looked upon me, to take away my reproach among men. *And, o my God, neither my life, nor my repu-tation, are ſafe in mine own keeping, but in thine, who didſt take care of me, when I yet hanged on my mother's breaſt. Bleſſed are they that put their truſt in thee, o Lord ; for when falſe witneſſes were riſen up againſt me ; when ſhame was ready to cover my face ; when I was bowed down with an horrible dread, and went mourning all the day long ; when my nights were reſtleſs, and my ſleeps broken with a fear worſe than death ; when my ſoul thirſted for a deliverance, as the hart pan-teth after the rivers of waters ; then thou, Lord, didſt hear my complaints, pity my condition, and art now become my deliverer ; and as long as I live I will hold up my hands in this manner, and magnify thy mercies, who didſt not give me over as a prey to mine enemies. O bleſſed are they that put their truſt in thee ; and no proſperity ſhall make me forget thoſe days of ſorrow, or to perform thoſe vows that I have made to thee in the days of my fears and affliction ; for with ſuch ſacrifices thou, o God, art well pleaſed ; and I will pay them.*

Thus did the joy and gratitude of this good man's heart break forth ; and 'tis obſer-vable, that as the invitation to this ſlander was his meek behaviour and dove-like ſim-plicity, for which he was remarkable ; ſo his chriſtian charity ought to be imitated : for, tho the ſpirit of revenge is ſo pleaſing to mankind, that it is never conquered but by a ſupernatural grace, being indeed ſo deeply rooted in human nature, that to pre-vent the exceſſes of it (for men would not know moderation) almighty God allows not any degree of it to any man, but ſays, *vengeance is mine :* and, tho this be ſaid by God himſelf, yet this revenge is ſo pleaſing, that man is hardly perſuaded to ſubmit the manage of it to the time, and juſtice, and wiſdom of his creator, but would haſten to be his own executioner of it. And yet neverthelefs, if any man ever did wholly decline, and leave this pleaſing paſſion to the time and meaſure of God alone, it was this *Richard Hooker* of whom I write : for when his ſlanderers were to ſuffer, he la-boured to procure their pardon ; and, when that was denied him, his reply was, *that however he would faſt and pray, that God would give them repentance and patience to undergo their puniſhment.* And his prayers were ſo far returned into his own boſom, that the firſt was granted, if we may believe a penitent behaviour, and an open confeſ-ſion. And it is obſervable, that after this time he would often ſay to doctor *Sa-ravia,* ' O with what quietneſs, did I enjoy my ſoul after I was free from the fears ' of my ſlander ! And how much more after a conflict and victory over my deſires of ' revenge ! '

In

✳

His ficknefs
and death.

In the year one thoufand fix hundred, and of his age forty fix, he fell into a long and
fharp ficknefs, occafioned by a cold taken in his paffage betwixt *London* and *Gravefend,*
from the malignity of which he was never recovered ; for till his death he was not
free from thoughtful days, and reftlefs nights ; but a fubmiffion to his will, that makes
the fick man's bed eafy by giving reft to his foul, made his very languifhment comfortable : and yet all this time he was follicitous in his ftudy, and faid often to doctor
Saravia (who faw him daily, and was the chief comfort of his life) ' That he did
' not beg a long life of God, for any other reafon, but to live to finifh his three remain-
' ing books of POLITY : and then, Lord, let thy fervant depart in peace ;' which
was his ufual expreffion. And God heard his prayers, tho he denied the benefit of
them as compleated by himfelf ; and 'tis thought he haftned his own death, by haftning to give life to his books. But this is certain, that the nearer he was to his death,
the more he grew in *humility,* in *holy thoughts* and *refolutions.*

About a month before his death, this good man, that never knew, or at leaft, never
confidered the pleafures of the palate, became firft to lofe his appetite, then to have an
averfenefs to all food ; infomuch, that he feemed to live fome intermitted weeks by the
fmell of meat only ; and yet ftill ftudied and writ. And now his guardian angel feemed to foretel him, that his years were paft away as a fhadow, bidding him prepare to
follow the generation of his fathers, for the day of his diffolution drew near ; for which
his vigorous foul appeared to thirft.

In this time of his ficknefs, and not many days before his death, his houfe was rob-
bed ; of which he having notice, his queftion was, *Are my books and written papers
fafe* ? Being anfwered, *that they were* ; his reply was, *Then it matters not, for no
other lofs can trouble me.*

About one day before his death, doctor *Saravia,* who knew the very fecrets of his
foul (for they were fuppofed to be confeffors to each other) came to him, and after a
conference of the benefit, the neceffity, and fafety of the church's abfolution, it was
refolved the doctor fhould give him both that and the facrament the day following. To
which end the doctor came, and after a fhort retirement and privacy, they returned to the
company ; and then the doctor gave him and fome of thofe friends that were with him,
the bleffed facrament of the body and blood of our Lord Jefus. Which being performed, the doctor thought he faw a reverend gaiety and joy in his face ; but it lafted not
long ; for his bodily infirmities did return fuddenly, and became more vifible ; infomuch, that the doctor apprehended death ready to feize him : yet, after fome amendment, left him at night, with a promife to return early the day following ; which he
did, and then found him better in appearance, deep in contemplation, and not inclinable to difcourfe ; which gave the doctor occafion to require his prefent thoughts : to
which he replyed, ' That he was meditating the number and nature of angels, and their
' bleffed obedience and order, without which peace could not be in heaven : and oh !
' that it might be fo on earth !' After which words, he faid, ' I have lived to fee this
' world is made up of perturbations, and I have been long preparing to leave it, and
' gathering comfort for the dreadful hour of making my account with God, which I
' now apprehend to be near : and tho I have by his grace loved him in my youth,
' and feared him in mine age, and laboured to have a confcience void of offence to him
' and to all men ; yet if thou, o Lord, be extreme to mark what I have done amifs,
' who can abide it ? and therefore, where I have failed, Lord fhew mercy to me ; for
' I plead not my righteoufnefs, but the forgivenefs of my unrighteoufnefs, for his merits,
' who died to purchafe a pardon for penitent finners. And fince I owe thee a death,
' Lord, let it not be terrible ; and then take thine own time. I fubmit to it. Let not mine,
' o Lord, but let thy will be done !' With which expreffion he fell into a dangerous flumber, dangerous as to his recovery ; yet recover he did, but it was
to fpeak only thefe few words, ' Good doctor, God hath heard my daily petitions ;
' for I am at peace with all men, and he is at peace with me ; and from which
' bleffed affurance I feel that inward joy, which this world can neither give nor take
' from me.' More he would have fpoken, but his fpirits failed him ; and, after a fhort
conflict betwixt nature and death, a quiet figh put a period to his laft breath, and
fo he fell afleep.

And here I draw his curtain, till with the moſt glorious company of the patriarchs and apoſtles, the moſt noble army of martyrs and confeſſors, this moſt learned, moſt humble, holy man, ſhall alſo awake to receive an eternal tranquillity, and with it a greater degree of glory than common chriſtians ſhall be made partakers of. In the mean time, *Bleſs, O Lord, Lord bleſs his brethren, the clergy of this nation, with ardent deſires, and effectual endeavours to attain, if not to his great learning, yet to his remarkable meekneſs, his godly ſimplicity, and his chriſtian moderation : for theſe are praiſeworthy ; theſe bring peace at the laſt. And let the labours of his life, his moſt excellent writings, be bleſt with what he deſigned when he undertook them ; which was glory to thee, O God on high, peace in thy church, and good will to mankind.*

Amen, amen.

ē   An

AN
APPENDIX
TO THE
LIFE
OF
Mr. Richard Hooker.

HAVING by a long and laborious search satisfied my self, and I hope my reader, by imparting to him the true relation of Mr. *Hooker*'s life; I am desirous also to acquaint him with some observations that relate to it, and which could not properly fall to be spoken till after his death, of which my reader may expect a brief and true account in the following appendix.

And first, it is not to be doubted but he died in the forty seventh, if not in the forty sixth year of his age; which I mention, because many have believed him to be more aged; but I have so examined it, as to be confident I mistake not: and for the year of his death, Mr. *Camden*, who in his annals of queen *Elizabeth* 1599. mentions him with a high commendation of his life and learning, declares him to die in the year 1599. and yet in that inscription of his monument set up at the charge of sir *William Cooper* in *Bourne* church, where Mr. *Hooker* was buried, his death is said to be *an.* 1603. but doubtless both mistaken; for I have it attested under the hand of *William Somner* the archbishop's register for the province of *Canterbury*, that *Richard Hooker*'s Will bears date *October* the 26th, in *anno* 1600. and that it was proved the third of *December* following. And this attested also, that at his death he left four daughters, *Alice, Cicily, Jane,* and *Margaret*, that he gave to each of them a hundred pounds; that he left *Joan* his wife his sole executrix; and that by his inventory his estate (a great part of it being in books) came to 1092 *l.* 9 *s.* 2 *d.* which was much more than he thought himself worth; and, which was not got by his care, much less by the good huswifery of his wife, but saved by his trusty servant *Thomas Lane*, that was wiser than his master in getting money for him, and more frugal than his mistress in keeping it: of which will I shall say no more, but that his dear friend *Thomas*, the father of *George Cranmer*, of whom I have spoken, and shall have occasion to say more, was one of the witnesses to it.

One of his elder daughters was married to one *Chalinor*, sometime a school-master in *Chichester*, and both dead long since. *Margaret* his youngest daughter was married unto

Ezekiel

Ezekiel Clark, batchelor in divinity, and rector of saint *Nicholas* in *Harbledown* near *Canterbury*, who died about 16 years paft, and had a fon *Ezekiel*, now living, and in facred orders, being at this time rector of *Waldron* in *Suffex* ; fhe left alfo a daughter, with both whom I have fpoken not many months paft, and find her to be a widow in a condition that wants not, but far from abounding : and thefe two attefted unto me, that *Richard Hooker* their grandfather had a fifter, by name *Elizabeth Harvey*, that lived to the age of 121 years, and died in the month of *September*, 1663.

For his other two daughters, I can learn little certainty, but have heard they both died before they were marriageable ; and for his wife, fhe was fo unlike *Jephtha's* daughter, that fhe ftaid not a comely time to bewail her widowhood ; nor lived long enough to repent her fecond marriage, for which doubtlefs fhe would have found caufe, if there had been but four months betwixt Mr. *Hooker's* and her death. But fhe is dead, and let her other infirmities be buried with her.

Thus much briefly for his age, the year of his death, his eftate, his wife, and his children. I am next to fpeak of his books, concerning which I fhall have a neceffity of being longer, or fhall neither do right to my felf or my reader, which is chiefly intended in this appendix.

I have declared in his life that he propofed eight books, and that his firft four were printed *anno* 1594, and his fifth book firft printed, and alone, *anno* 1597 ; and that he lived to finifh the remaining three of the propofed eight : but, whether we have the laft three as finifh'd by himfelf, is a juft and material queftion ; concerning which I do declare, that I have been told almoft forty years paft, by one that very well knew Mr. *Hooker*, and the affairs of his family, that a month after the death of Mr. *Hooker*, bifhop *Whitgift*, then archbifhop of *Canterbury*, fent one of his chaplains to enquire of Mrs. *Hooker*, for the three remaining books of polity, writ by her husband ; of which fhe would not or could not give any account : and I have been told, that about three months after the bifhop procured her to be fent for to *London*, and then by his procurement fhe was to be examined, by fome of her majefty's council, concerning the difpofal of thofe books : but by way of preparation for the next day's examination, the bifhop invited her to *Lambeth*, and, after fome friendly queftions, fhe confeffed to him, *that one Mr.* Chark *and another minifter that dwelt near* Canterbury, *came to her, and defired that they might go into her husband's ftudy, and look upon fome of his writings ; and that there they two burnt and tore many of them, affuring her that they were writings not fit to be feen, and that fhe knew nothing more concerning them.* Her lodging was then in *King-ftreet* in *Weftminfter*, where fhe was found next morning dead in her bed, and her new husband fufpected and queftioned for it ; but was declared innocent of her death.

And I declare alfo, that doctor *John Spencer* (mentioned in the life of Mr. *Hooker*) who was of Mr. *Hooker's* college, and of his time there ; and betwixt whom there was fo friendly a friendfhip, that they continually advifed together in all their ftudies, and particularly in what concerned thefe books of polity : this doctor *Spencer*, the three firft books being loft, had delivered into his hands (I think by bifhop *Whitgift*) the imperfect books, or firft rough draughts of them, to be made as perfect as they might be, by him, who both knew Mr. *Hooker's* hand-writing, and was beft acquainted with his intentions. And a fair teftimony of this may appear by an epiftle firft and ufually printed before Mr. *Hooker's* five books (but omitted, I know not why, in the laft impreffion of the eight printed together in *anno* 1662. in which the publifhers feem to impofe the three doubful, as the undoubted books of Mr. *Hooker*) with thefe two letters *J. S.* at the end of the faid epiftle, which was meant for this *John Spencer* ; in which epiftle the reader may find thefe very words, which may give fome authority to what I have here written.

' And tho Mr. *Hooker* haftned his own death by haftning to give life to his books,
' yet he held out with his eyes to behold thefe *Benjamins*, thefe fons of his right hand,
' tho to him they proved *Benonies*, fons of pain and forrow : but, fome evil difpofed
' minds, whether of malice or covetoufnefs, or wicked blind zeal, it is uncertain, as
' foon as they were born, and their father dead, fmothered them, and, by conveying
' the perfect copies, left unto us nothing but the old imperfect mangled draughts dif-
' membred into pieces ; no favour, no grace, not the fhadow of themfelves remaining
' in them. Had the father lived to behold them thus defaced, he might rightly have
' named them *Benonies*, the fons of forrow ; but being the learned will not fuffer them to
' die and be buried, it is intended the world fhall fee them as they are : the learned will
' find in them fome fhadows and refemblances of their father's face. God grant, that as
' they were with their brethren dedicated to the church for meffengers of peace ; fo, in the
          ' ftrength

‘ ſtrength of that little breath of life that remaineth in them, they may proſper in their
‘ work, and that by ſatisfying the doubts of ſuch as are willing to learn, they may
‘ help to give an end to the calamities of theſe our civil wars!

J. S.

And next the reader may note, that this epiſtle of doctor *Spencer*'s was writ, and
firſt printed within four years after the death of Mr. *Hooker*; in which time, all diligent
ſearch had been made for the perfect copies; and then granted not recoverable, and
therefore endeavoured to be compleated out of Mr. *Hooker*'s rough draughts, as is expreſs'd by the ſaid doctor *Spencer*, ſince whoſe death it is now fifty years.

And I do profeſs by the faith of a chriſtian, that doctor *Spencer*'s wife (who was my
aunt, and ſiſter to *George Cranmer* of whom I have ſpoken) told me forty years ſince,
in theſe, or in words to this purpoſe, ‘ That her husband had made up or finiſh'd
‘ Mr. *Hooker*'s laſt three books; and that upon her husband's death-bed, or in his laſt
‘ ſickneſs, he gave them into her hand, with a charge they ſhould not be ſeen by
‘ any man, but be by her delivered into the hands of the then archbiſhop of *Canter-*
‘ *bury,* which was doctor *Abbot,* or unto doctor *King* biſhop of *London*; and that ſhe
‘ did as he enjoyned her.

I do conceive, that from doctor *Spencer*'s and no other copy, there have been divers
tranſcripts, and were to be found in ſeveral places, as namely in ſir *Thomas Bodley*'s library, in that of doctor *Andrews,* late biſhop of *Winton,* in the late lord *Conway*'s,
in the archbiſhop of *Canterbury*'s, and in the biſhop of *Armagh*'s, and in many others;
and moſt of theſe pretended to be the author's own hand, being much diſagreeing, being indeed altered and diminiſh'd as men have thought fitteſt to make Mr. *Hooker*'s
judgment ſuit with their fancies, or give authority to their corrupt deſigns. And for
proof of a part of this, take theſe following teſtimonies.

Doctor *Barnard,* ſometime chaplain to doctor *Uſher* late lord archbiſhop of *Armagh,*
hath declared in a late book called *Clavi Trabales,* printed by *Richard Hodgkinſon,*
anno 1661, that in his ſearch and examination of the ſaid biſhop's manuſcripts, he there
found the three written books, which were the ſuppoſed ſixth, ſeventh and eighth of
Mr. *Hooker*'s books of eccleſiaſtical polity; and, that in the ſaid three books (now
printed as Mr. *Hooker*'s) there are ſo many omiſſions, that they amount to many para-
graphs, and which cauſe many incoherencies; the omiſſions are by him ſet down at
large in the ſaid printed book, to which I refer the reader for the whole; but think fit
in this place to inſert this following ſhort part of them.

‘ *Firſt,* As there could be in natural bodies no motion of any thing, unleſs there
‘ were ſome firſt which moved all things and continued unmoveable; even ſo in poli-
‘ tick ſocieties, there muſt be ſome unpuniſhable, or elſe no man ſhall ſuffer puniſhment:
‘ for, ſith puniſhments proceed always from ſuperiors, to whom the adminiſtration of
‘ juſtice belongeth, which adminiſtration muſt have neceſſarily a fountain that deriveth
‘ it to all others, and receiveth not from any, becauſe otherwiſe the courſe of juſtice
‘ ſhould go infinitely in a circle, every ſuperior having his ſuperior without end, which
‘ cannot be; therefore, a well-ſpring, it followeth, there is a ſupreme head of juſtice
‘ whereunto all are ſubject, but it ſelf in ſubjection to none. Which kind of prehemi-
‘ nency if ſome ought to have in a kingdom, who but the king ſhall have it? Kings
‘ therefore, or no man, can have lawful power to judge.

‘ If private men offend, there is the magiſtrate over them which judgeth; if magi-
‘ ſtrates, they have their prince; if princes, there is heaven a tribunal, before which
‘ they ſhall appear: on earth they are not accountable to any.' Here, ſays the doctor,
it breaks off abruptly.

And I have theſe words alſo atteſted under the hand of Mr. *Fabian Phillips,* a man of
note for his uſeful books. ‘ I will make oath if I ſhall be required, that doctor *Sander-*
‘ *ſon* the late biſhop of *Lincoln* did a little before his death affirm to me he had ſeen a
‘ manuſcript, affirmed to him to be the hand-writing of Mr. *Richard Hooker,* in which
‘ there was no mention made of the king or ſupreme governors being accountable to the
‘ people; this I will make oath that that good man atteſted to me.

Fabian Phillips.

So

‡

So that there appear to be both omissions and additions in the said last three printed books ; and this may probably be one reason why doctor *Sanderson*, the said learned bishop (whose writings are so highly and justly valued) gave a strict charge near the time of his death, or in his last will, ' That nothing of his that was not already print-' ed, should be printed after his death.

It is well known how high a value our learned king *James* put upon the books writ by Mr. *Hooker*, as also that our late king *Charles* (the martyr for the church) valued them the second of all books, testified by his commending them to the reading of his son *Charles*, that now is our gracious king ; and you may suppose that this *Charles* the first was not a stranger to the pretended three books, because in a discourse with the lord *Say*, when the said lord required the king to grant the truth of his argument, be-cause it was the judgment of Mr. *Hooker*, (quoting him in one of the three written books,) the king replied, ' They were not allowed to be Mr. *Hooker*'s books ; *but* ' *however* he would allow them to be Mr. *Hooker*'s, and consent to what his lordship ' proposed to prove out of those doubtful books, if he would but consent to the judg-' ment of Mr. *Hooker* in the other five that were the undoubted books of ' Mr. *Hooker*.'

In this relation concerning these three doubtful books of Mr. *Hooker*'s, my purpose was to enquire, then set down what I observed and know, which I have done, not as an engaged person, but indifferently ; and now leave my reader to give sentence, for their legitimation, as to himself, but so as to leave others the same liberty of believing, or disbelieving them to be Mr. *Hooker*'s : and 'tis observable, that as Mr. *Hooker* advised with doctor *Spencer*, in the design and manage of these books, so also, and chiefly with his dear pupil *George Cranmer* (whose sister was the wife of doctor *Spencer*) of which this following letter may be a testimony ; and doth also give authority to some things mentioned both in this appendix, and in the life of Mr. *Hooker* ; and is therefore added.

George

George Cranmer's

L E T T E R

UNTO

Mr. Richard Hooker,

February 1598.

WHAT posterity is like to judge of these matters concerning church-discipline, we may the better conjecture, if we call to mind what our own age, within few years, upon better experience, hath already judged concerning the same. It may be remembred, that at first the greatest part of the learned in the land were either eagerly affected, or favourably inclin'd that way. The books then written, for the most part, favoured the disciplinary style : it sounded every where in pulpits, and in common phrase of mens speech : the contrary part began to fear they had taken a wrong course ; many which impugned the discipline, yet so impugned it, not as not being the better form of government, but as not being so convenient for our state, in regard of dangerous innovations thereby like to grow ; * one man alone there was to speak of, (whom let no suspicion of flattery deprive of his deserved commendation) who in the defiance of the one part, and courage of the other, stood in the gap, and gave others respite to prepare themselves to the defence, which by the sudden eagerness and violence of their adversaries had otherwise been prevented ; wherein God hath made good unto him his own impress, *Vincit qui patitur :* for what contumelious indignities he hath at their hands sustained, the world is witness ; and what reward of honour above his adversaries God hath bestowed upon him, themselves (tho nothing glad thereof) must needs confess. Now of late years the heat of men towards the discipline is greatly decayed, their judgments begin to sway on the other side : the learned have weighed it and found it light ; wise men conceive some fear, lest it prove not only not the best kind of government, but the very bane and destruction of all government. The cause of this change in mens opinions may be drawn from the general nature of error, disguised and clothed with the name of truth ; which is mightily and violently to possess men at first, but afterwards, the weakness thereof being by time discovered, to lose that reputation which before it had gained. As by the outside of an house the passers by are oftentimes deceived, till they see the conveniency of the rooms within ; so by the very name of discipline and reformation, men were drawn at first to cast a fancy towards it, but now they have not contented themselves only to pass by and behold afar-off the fore front of this reformed house ; they have entred in, even at the special request of master-workmen, and chief builders thereof ; they have perused the rooms, the lights, the conveniencies ; they find them not answerable to that report which was made of them, nor to that opinion which upon report they had conceived : so as now the discipline which at first triumphed over all, being unmasked, beginneth to droop and hang down her head.

*[margin: * John Whitgift, the arch-bishop.]*

This

This caufe of change in opinion concerning the difcipline, is proper to the learned, or to fuch as by them have been inftructed. Another caufe there is more open, and more apparent to the view of all, namely, the courfe of practice, which the reformers have had with us from the beginning. The firft degree was only fome fmall difference about cap and furplice, but not fuch as either bred divifion in the church, or tended to the ruin of the government eftablifhed. This was peaceable; the next degree more ftirring. *Admonitions* were directed to the parliament in peremptory fort againft our whole form of regiment; in defence of them, volumes were publifhed in *Englifh*, and in *Latin*; yet this was no more than writing. Devices were fet on foot to erect the practice of the difcipline without authority: yet herein fome regard of modefty, fome moderation was ufed. Behold, at length it brake forth into open outrage, firft in writing by *Martin*, in whofe kind of dealing thefe things may be obferved. 1. That whereas *T. C.* and others his great mafters had always before fet out the difcipline as a queen, and as the daughter of God; he contrariwife, to make her more acceptable to the people, brought her forth as a vice upon the ftage. 2. This conceit of his was grounded (as may be fuppofed) upon this rare polity, that feeing the difcipline was by writing refuted, in parliament rejected, in fecret corners hunted out and decried, it was imagined that by open railing (which to the vulgar is commonly moft plaufible) the ftate ecclefiaftical might have been drawn into fuch contempt and hatred, as the overthrow thereof fhould have been moft grateful to all men, and in manner defired of the common people. 3. It may be noted (and this I know my felf to be true) how fome of them, altho they could not for fhame approve fo leud an action, yet were content to lay hold on it to the advancement of their caufe, acknowledging therein the fecret judgments of God againft the bifhops, and hoping that fome good might be wrought thereby for his church, as indeed there was, tho not according to their conftruction. For, 4. Contrary to their expectation, that railing fpirit did not only not further, but extremely difgrace and prejudice the caufe, when it was once perceived from how low degrees of contradiction, at firft, to what outrage of contumely and flander they were at length proceeded, and were alfo likely further to proceed.

Hacket and *Coppinger.*

A further degree of outrage was in fact; certain * prophets did arife, who deeming it not poffible that God fhould fuffer that to be undone, which they did fo fiercely defire to have done, namely, that his holy faints, the favourers and fathers of the difcipline, fhould be enlarged, and deliver'd from perfecution; and feeing no means of deliverance ordinary, were fain to perfuade themfelves that God muft needs raife fome extraordinary means; and being perfuaded of none fo well as of themfelves, they forthwith muft needs be the inftruments of this great work. Hereupon they framed unto themfelves an affured hope, that upon their preaching out of a peafe-cart, all the multitude would have prefently joined unto them, and in amazement of mind have asked them, *Viri fratres, quid agimus?* whereunto it is likely they would have returned an anfwer far unlike to that of faint *Peter, Such and fuch are men unworthy to govern, pluck them down; fuch and fuch are the dear children of God, let them be advanced.* Of two of thefe men, it is meet to fpeak with all commiferation, yet fo that others by their example may receive inftruction, and withal fome light may appear, what ftirring affections the difcipline is like to infpire, if it light upon apt and prepared minds.

Now if any man doubt of what fociety they were, or if the reformers difclaim them, pretending that by them they were condemned, let thefe points be confidered. 1. *Whofe affociates were they before they entred into this frantick paffion? whofe fermons did they frequent? whom did they admire?* 2. *Even when they were entring into it, whofe advice did they require?* And when they were in, *whofe approbation? whom advertifed they of their purpofe? whofe affiftance by prayers did they requeft?* But we deal injurioufly with them to lay this to their charge; for they reprov'd and condemn'd it. How? did they difclofe it to the magiftrate, that it might be fuppreffed? or were they not rather content to ftand aloof off, and fee the end of it, and loth to quench the fpirit? No doubt thefe mad practitioners were of their fociety, with whom before, and in the practice of their madnefs, they had moft affinity. Hereof, read doctor *Bancroft's* book.

A third inducement may be to diflike of the difcipline, if we confider not only how far the reformers themfelves have proceeded, but what others upon their foundation have built. Here come the *brownifts* in the firft rank, their lineal defcendants, who have feized upon a number of ftrange opinions; whereof, altho their anceftors, the reformers, were never actually poffeffed, yet by right and intereft from them derived, the *brownifts* and *barrowifts* have taken poffeffion of them: for if the pofitions of

the

the reformers be true, I cannot fee how the main and general conclufions of *brownifm* fhould be falfe; for upon thefe two points, as I conceive, they ftand.

1. That becaufe we have no church, they are to fever themfelves from us.
2. That without civil authority, they are to erect a church of their own.

And if the former of thefe be true, the latter, I fuppofe, will follow: for if above all things, men be to regard their falvation; and if out of the church there be no falvation, it followeth, that if we have no church, we have no means of falvation: and therefore feparation from us, in that refpect, is both lawful and neceffary: as alfo, that men fo feparated from the falfe and counterfeit church, or to affociate themfelves unto fome church; not to ours; to the popifh much lefs; therefore to one of their own making. Now the ground of all thefe inferences being this [*That in our church, there is no means of falvation*] is out of the reformers principles moft clearly to be proved. For wherefoever any matter of faith unto falvation neceffary is denyed, there can be no means of falvation: but in the church of *England*, the difcipline by them accounted a matter of faith, and neceffary to falvation, is not only denyed, but impugned, and the profeffors thereof oppreffed. *Ergo*.

Again (but this reafon perhaps is weak) every true church of Chrift acknowledgeth the whole gofpel of Chrift: the difcipline, in their opinion, is a part of the gofpel, and yet by our church refifted. *Ergo*.

Again, the difcipline is effentially united to the church: by which term *effentially*, they muft mean either an effential part, or an effential property. Both which ways it muft needs be, that where that effential difcipline is not, neither is there any church. If therefore between them and the *brownifts*, there fhould be appointed a folemn difputation, whereof with us they have been oftentimes fo earneft challengers; it doth not yet appear what other anfwer they could poffibly frame to thefe and the like arguments, wherewith they might be preffed, but fairly to deny the conclufion (for all the premifes are their own) or rather ingenuoufly to reverfe their own principles before faid, whereon fo foul abfurdities have been fo firmly built.

What further proofs you can bring out of their high words, magnifying the difcipline, I leave to your better remembrance: but above all points, I am defirous this one fhould be ftrongly inforced againft them, becaufe it wringeth them moft of all, and is of all others (for ought I fee) the moft unanfwerable; you may notwithftanding fay, that you would be heartily glad thefe their pofitions might fo be folved, as the *brownifts* might not appear to have iffued out of their loins; but until that be done, they muft give us leave to think, *that they have caft the feed whereout thefe tares are grown*.

Another fort of men there are, which have been content to run on with the reformers for a time, and to make them poor inftruments of their own defigns. Thefe are a fort of godlefs politicks, who perceiving the plot of difcipline to confift of thefe two parts, the overthrow of epifcopal, and erection of presbyterial authority; and that this latter can take no place till the former be removed, are content to join with them in the deftructive part of difcipline, bearing them in hand, that in the other alfo, they fhall find them as ready. But when time fhall come, it may be they would be as loth to be yoked with that kind of regiment, as now they are willing to be releafed from this. Thefe mens ends in all their actions, is diftraction; their pretence and colour, reformation. Thofe things which under this colour they have effected to their own good, are, 1. By maintaining a contrary faction, they have kept the clergy always in awe; and thereby made them more pliable and willing to buy their peace. 2. By maintaining an opinion of equality among minifters, they have made way to their own purpofes for devouring cathedral churches, and bifhops livings. 3. By exclaiming againft abufes in the church, they have carried their own corrupt dealings in the civil ftate more covertly; for fuch is the nature of the multitude, they are not able to apprehend many things at once, fo as being poffeffed with a diflike or liking of any one thing, many other, in the mean time, may efcape them without being perceived. 4. They have fought to difgrace the clergy, in entertaining a conceit in mens minds, and confirming it by continual practice, that men of learning, and efpecially of the clergy, which are employed in the chiefeft kind of learning, are not to be admitted, or fparingly admitted to matters of ftate; contrary to the practice of all well-governed common-wealths, and of our own, till thefe late years.

A third fort of men there are, tho not defcended from the reformers, yet in part raifed and greatly ftrenghned by them, namely, the curfed crew of atheifts. This alfo is one of thofe points which I am defirous you fhould handle moft effectually, and ftrain your felf therein to all points of motion and affection; as in that of the *brownifts*, to all ftrength and finews of reafon. This is a fort moft damnable, and yet by the general fufpicion of the world at this day moft common. The caufes of it, which are in the parties themfelves, altho you handle in the beginning of the fifth book, yet here again they may be touched; but the occafions of help and furtherance, which by the reformers have been yielded unto them, are, as I conceive, two, *fenfelefs preaching, and difgracing of the miniftry* : for how fhould not men dare to impugn that, which neither by force of reafon, nor by authority of perfons is maintained? But in the parties themfelves, thefe two caufes I conceive of *atheifm*, 1. More abundance of wit than judgment, and of witty than judicious learning, whereby *they are more inclined to contradict any thing, than willing to be informed of the truth.* They are not therefore men of found learning for the moft, but fmatterers; neither is their kind of difpute fo much by force of argument as by fcoffing: which humour of fcoffing, and turning matters moft ferious into merriment, is now become fo common, as we are not to marvel what the prophet means by the *feat of fcorners*, nor what the apoftles by fore-telling of *fcorners to come* : our own age hath verified their fpeech unto us; which alfo may be an argument againft thefe fcoffers and atheifts themfelves, feeing it hath been fo many ages ago foretold, that fuch men the latter days of the world fhould afford, which could not be done by any other fpirit, fave that whereunto *things future and prefent are alike.* And even for the main queftion of the refurrection, whereat they ftick fo mightily, was it not plainly foretold, that men fhould in the latter times fay, *Where is the promife of his coming?* Againft the creation, the ark, and divers other points, exceptions are faid to be taken; the ground whereof is fuperfluity of wit, without ground of learning and judgment.

A fecond caufe of *atheifm*, is *fenfuality*, which maketh men defirous to remove all ftops and impediments of their wicked life; amongft which, becaufe religion is the chiefeft, fo as neither in this life without fhame they can perfift therein, nor (if that be true) without torment in the life to come; they whet their wits to annihilate the joys of heaven, wherein they fee (if any fuch be) they can have no part; and likewife the pains of hell, wherein their portion muft needs be very great. They labour therefore, not that they may not deferve thofe pains, but that deferving them, there may be no fuch pains to feize upon them. But what conceit can be imagined more bafe, than that man fhould ftrive to perfuade himfelf, even againft the fecret inftinct (no doubt) of his own mind, that his foul is as the foul of a beaft, mortal and corruptible with the body? Againft which barbarous opinion, their own atheifm is a very ftrong argument; *for were not the foul a nature feparable from the body, how could it enter into difcourfe of things merely fpiritual, and nothing at all pertaining to the body? Surely, the foul were not able to conceive any thing of heaven, no not fo much as to difpute againft heaven and againft God, if there were not in it fomewhat heavenly and derived from God.*

The laft which have received ftrength and encouragement from the reformers, are papifts; againft whom, altho they are moft bitter enemies, yet unwittingly they have given them great advantage. For what can any enemy rather defire, than the breach and diffention of thofe which are confederates againft him? Wherein they are to remember, that if our communion with papifts in fome few ceremonies do fo much ftrengthen them, as is pretended; how much more doth this divifion and rent among our felves; efpecially feeing it is maintained to be, not in light matters only, but even in matter of faith and falvation? Which over-reaching fpeech of theirs, becaufe it is fo open to advantage for the *barrowift* and the papift, we are to wifh and hope for, that they will acknowledge it to have been fpoken rather in heat of affection, than with foundnefs of judgment; and that thro their exceeding love to that creature of difcipline which themfelves have bred, nourifhed and maintained, their mouth in commendation of her did foon overflow.

From hence you may proceed (but the means of connexion I leave to your felf) to another difcourfe, which I think very meet to be handled, either here or elfewhere at large; the parts whereof may be thefe.

1. That in this caufe between them and us, men are to fever the proper and effential points in controverfy, from thofe which are accidental. The moft effential and proper are thefe two; overthrow of *epifcopal, erection of prefbyterial authority.* But in thefe two points whofoever joineth with them, is accounted of their number; whofoever in all other points agreeth with them, yet thinketh the *authority of bifhops* not unlawful, and of *elders* not neceffary, may juftly be fevered from their retinue. Thofe things therefore which either in the perfons, or in the laws and orders themfelves are faulty, may be complained of, acknowledged, and amended; yet they no whit the nearer their main purpofe. For what if all errors by them fuppofed in our *liturgy* were

‡　　　　　　　　　　　　　　　　　　　　　　　　　amended,

amended, even according to their own hearts defire ; if *non-refidents, pluralities,* and the like, were utterly taken away ; are their *lay-elders* therefore prefently authorized, or their *fovereign ecclefiaftical jurifdiction* eftablifhed ?

But even in their complaining againft the outward and accidental matters in church-government, they are many ways faulty. 1. In their end which they propofe to them-felves : for in declaiming againft abufes, their meaning is not to have them redreffed, but by difgracing the prefent ftate, to make way for their own difcipline. As therefore in *Venice,* if any fenator fhould difcourfe againft the power of their fenate, as being ei-ther too fovereign or too weak in government, with purpofe to draw their authority to a moderation, it might well be fuffered ; but not fo, if it fhould appear he fpake with purpofe to induce another ftate by depraving the prefent : fo in all caufes belonging either to church or commonwealth, we are to have regard what mind the complaining part doth bear, whether of amendment or innovation ; and accordingly, either to fuffer or fupprefs it. Their objection therefore is frivolous, *Why may not men fpeak againft abufes?* Yes ; but with defire to cure the part affected, and not to deftroy the whole. 2. A fecond fault is in their manner of complaining, not only becaufe it is for the moft part in bitter and reproachful terms, but alfo it is to the common people, *who are judges incompetent and infufficient, both to determine any thing amifs ; and for want of skill and authority to amend it.* Which alfo difcovereth their intent and purpofe to be rather deftructive than corrective. 3. Thirdly, thofe very exceptions which they take, are frivolous and impertinent. Some things indeed they accufe as impious, which if they may appear to be fuch, God forbid they fhould be maintained.

Againft the reft it is only alledged, that they are idle ceremonies without ufe, and that better and more profitable might be devifed ; wherein they are doubly deceived : for nei-ther is it a fufficient plea to fay, this muft give place, becaufe a better may be devifed ; becaufe in our judgments of better and worfe, we oftentimes conceive amifs, when we compare thofe things which are in device, with thofe which are in practice : *for the imperfections of the one are hid, till by time and tryal they be difcovered* ; the others are already manifeft and open to all. But laft of all, (which is a point in my opinion of great regard, and which I am defirous to have enlarged) they do not fee that for the moft part when they ftrike at the *ftate ecclefiaftical,* they fecretly wound the *civil ftate* : for perfonal faults, *what can be faid againft the church, which may not alfo agree to the com-monwealth ?* In both, ftatefmen have always been, and will be always, men, fome-times blinded with error, moft commonly perverted by paffions ; many unworthy have been and are advanced in both, many worthy not regarded. And as for abufes which they pretend to be in the laws themfelves, when they inveigh againft *non-refidence,* do they take it a matter lawful or expedient in the *civil ftate,* for a man to have a great and gainful office in the *North,* and himfelf continually remaining in the *South ? He that hath an office, let him attend his office.* When they condemn *plurality of livings fpi-ritual* to the pit of hell ; what think they of *infinity of temporal promotions ?* By the *great philofopher, Pol. lib.* 2. *cap.* 9. it is forbidden as a thing moft dangerous to common-wealths, that by the fame man many great offices fhould be exercifed. When they deride our ceremonies as vain and frivolous, were it hard to apply their excep-tions even to thofe civil ceremonies, which at the *coronation,* in *parliament,* and all *courts of juftice* are ufed ? Were it hard to argue even againft *circumcifion,* the or-dinance of *God,* as being a cruel ceremony ? againft the *paffover,* as being ridiculous, fhould be girt, a ftaff in their hand, to eat a *lamb ?*

To conclude, you may exhort the *clergy,* (or, what if you direct your conclufion not ~~to the *clergy* in general, but only to~~ the learned in or of both *univerfities ?*) you may exhort them to a due confideration of all things, and to a right efteem and valuing of each thing in that degree wherein it ought to ftand : *for it oftentimes falleth out, that what men have either devifed themfelves, or greatly delighted in, the price and the excellency thereof they do admire above defert.* The chiefeft labour of a *chriftian* fhould be to know ; of a *minifter,* to *preach Chrift crucified :* in regard whereof, not only worldly things, but things otherwife precious, even the *difcipline* it felf, is vile and bafe. Where-as now, by the heat of contention and violence of affection, the zeal of men towards the one, hath greatly decayed their love to the other. Hereunto therefore they are to be exhorted, to *preach Chrift crucified,* the *mortification of the flefh,* the *renewing of the fpirit* ; not thofe things which in time of ftrife feem precious, but (paffions being allayed) are vain and childifh.

GEORGE CRANMER.

This *Epitaph* was long fince prefented to the world in memory of Mr. *Hooker*, by fir *William Cooper* ; who alfo
built him a fair monument in *Bourne-Church*, and ac-
knowledges him to have been his *fpiritual father*.

THOUGH nothing can be fpoke worthy his fame,
 Or the remembrance of that precious name,
Judicious Hooker ; though this coft be fpent
On him that hath a lafting monument
In his own Books ; yet ought we to exprefs,
If not his worth, yet our refpectfulnefs.
Church-ceremonies he maintain'd : then why
Without all ceremony fhould he dye?
Was it becaufe his life and death fhould be
Both equal patterns of humility?
Or, that perhaps this only glorious one
Was above all, to ask, why had he none?
Yet he that lay fo long obfcurely low,
Doth now preferr'd to greater honours go.
Ambitious men, learn hence to be more wife;
Humility is the true way to rife:
And God in me this leffon did infpire,
To bid this humble man, friend fit up higher.

W. C.

To

To the moſt reverend father in G o D, my very
good lord, the lord arch-biſhop of

CANTERBURY his grace,

PRIMATE and METROPOLITAN

OF ALL

ENGLAND.

Moſt reverend in Chriſt,

THE long continued, and more than ordinary
favour, which hitherto your grace hath been
pleaſed to ſhew towards me, may juſtly claim
at my hands ſome thankful acknowledgment thereof. In
which conſideration, as alſo for that I embrace willingly the antient received courſe, and conveniency of that
diſcipline, which teacheth inferior degrees and orders in
the church of God, to ſubmit their writings to the ſame
authority, from which their allowable dealings whatſoever, in ſuch affairs, muſt receive approbation; I nothing
fear but that your accuſtomed clemency will take in
good worth the offer of theſe my ſimple and mean labours, beſtowed for the neceſſary juſtification of laws
heretofore made queſtionable, becauſe, as I take it, they
were not perfectly underſtood: for ſurely, I cannot find
any great cauſe of juſt complaint, that good laws have ſo
much been wanting unto us, as we to them. To ſeek
refor-

The cauſe of writing this gene-ral diſ-courſe.

reformation of evil laws, is a commendable endeavour; but for us the more neceſſary, is a ſpeedy redreſs of our ſelves. We have on all ſides loſt much of our firſt fervency towards God; and therefore concerning our own degenerated ways, we have reaſon to exhort with ſaint *Gre-* *gory*, "Ὅπερ ἦμεν γινώμεϑα, *Let us return again unto that which we ſometimes were.* But touching the exchange of laws in practice, with laws in device, which, they ſay, are better for the ſtate of the church, if they might take place; the farther we examine them, the greater cauſe we find to conclude μένωμεν ὅπερ ἐσμὲν, *altho we continue the ſame we are, the harm is not great.* The fervent reprehenders of things eſtabliſhed by publick authority, are always confident and bold-ſpirited men. But their confidence for the moſt part riſeth from too much credit given to their own wits, for which cauſe they are ſeldom free from error. The errors which we ſeek to reform in this kind of men, are ſuch as both received at your own hands their firſt wound, and from that time to this preſent, have been proceeded in with that moderation, which uſeth by patience to ſuppreſs boldneſs, and to make them conquer that ſuffer. Wherein conſidering the nature and kind of theſe controverſies, the dangerous ſequels whereunto they were likely to grow, and how many ways we have been thereby taught wiſdom, I may boldly aver concerning the firſt, that as the weightieſt conflicts the church hath had, were thoſe which touched the head, the perſon of our Saviour Chriſt; and the next of importance, thoſe queſtions which are at this day between us and the church of *Rome*, about the actions of the body of the church of God; ſo theſe which have laſtly ſprung up from complements, rites, and ceremonies of church actions, are in truth, for the greateſt part, ſuch ſilly things, that very eaſineſs doth make them hard to be diſputed of in ſerious manner. Which alſo may ſeem to be the cauſe, why divers of the reverend prelacy, and other moſt judicious men, have eſpecially beſtowed their pains about the matter of juriſdiction. Notwithſtanding, led by your grace's example, my ſelf have thought it convenient to wade through the whole cauſe, following

that

that method which searcheth the truth by the causes of
truth. Now, if any marvel how a thing in it self so
weak, could import any great danger, they must consider
not so much how small the spark is that flyeth up, as how
apt things about it are to take fire. Bodies politick being subject, as much as natural, to dissolution, by divers
means; there are undoubtedly more estates overthrown
thro diseases bred within themselves, than thro violence from abroad; because our manner is always to cast
a more doubtful and a more suspicious eye towards that,
over which we know we have least power: and therefore
the fear of external dangers, causeth forces at home to be
the more united. It is to all sorts a kind of bridle, it maketh virtuous minds watchful, it holdeth contrary dispositions in suspence, and it setteth those wits on work in better things, which could be else imployed in worse; whereas on the other side, domestical evils, for that we think
we can master them at all times, are often permitted to
run on forward, till it be too late to recall them. In the
mean while the commonwealth is not only thro unsoundness so far impaired, as those evils chance to prevail; but farther also, thro opposition arising between
the unsound parts and the found, where each endeavoureth to draw evermore contrary ways, till destruction
in the end bring the whole to ruin.

To reckon up how many causes there are, by force
whereof divisions may grow in a common-wealth, is not
here necessary. Such as rise from variety in matter of
religion, are not only the farthest spread, because in religion all men presume themselves interessed alike; but
they are also for the most part, hotlier prosecuted and
pursued than other strifes; for as much as coldness, which
in other contentions may be thought to proceed from
moderation, is not in these so favourably construed. The
part which, in this present quarrel, striveth against the
current and stream of laws, was a long while nothing
feared; the wisest contented not to call to mind how errors have their effect, many times not proportioned to that
little appearance of reason, whereupon they would seem
built, but rather to the vehement affection or fancy which

i3

is caft towards them, and proceedeth from other caufes.
For there are divers motives drawing men to favour
mightily thofe opinions, wherein their perfuafions are
but weakly fettled; and if the paffions of the mind be
ftrong, they eafily fophifticate the underftanding; they
make it apt to believe upon very flender warrant, and to
imagine infallible truth, where fcarce any probable fhew
appeareth.

Thus were thofe poor feduced creatures, *Hacquet* and
his other two adherents, whom I can neither fpeak or
think of, but with much commiferation and pity. Thus
were they trained by fair ways firft, accounting their own
extraordinary love to his difcipline, a token of God's
more than ordinary love towards them. From hence
they grew to a ftrong conceit, that God which had mov'd
them to love his difcipline, more than the common fort
of men did, might have a purpofe by their means to bring
a wonderful work to pafs, beyond all mens expectation,
for the advancement of the throne of difcipline, by fome
tragical execution, with the particularities whereof it
was not fafe for their friends to be made acquainted; of
whom they did therefore but covertly demand, what they
thought of extraordinary motions of the fpirit in thefe
days; and withal requeft to be commended unto God
by their prayers, whatfoever fhould be undertaken by
men of God, in mere zeal to his glory, and the good of
his diftreffed church. With this unufual and ftrange
courfe they went on forward, till God, in whofe heavieft
worldly judgments, I nothing doubt, but that there may
lie hidden mercy, gave them over to their own inventions,
and left them made, in the end, an example for
headftrong and inconfiderate zeal, no lefs fearful than
Achitophel, for proud and irreligious wifdom. If a fpark
of error have thus prevailed, falling even where the
wood was green and fartheft off, to all mens thinking,
from any inclination unto furious attempts; muft not
the peril thereof be greater in men whofe minds are of
themfelves as dry fewel, apt beforehand unto tumults,
feditions and broils? But by this we fee in a caufe of
religion, to how defperate adventures men will ftrain

†   them-

themſelves for relief of their own part, having law and authority againſt them.

Furthermore, let not any man think, that in ſuch diviſions, either part can free it ſelf from inconveniencies, ſuſtained not only thro a kind of truce; which virtue on both ſides, doth make with vice, during war between truth and error; but alſo, in that there are hereby ſo fit occaſions miniſtred for men to purchaſe to themſelves well-willers by the colour under which they oftentimes proſecute quarrels of envy or inveterate malice, and eſpecially becauſe contentions were as yet never able to prevent two evils: the one a mutual exchange of unſeemly and unjuſt diſgraces, offered by men, whoſe tongues and paſſions are out of rule; the other, a common hazard of both, to be made a prey by ſuch as ſtudy how to work upon all occurrents, with moſt advantage in private. I deny not therefore, but that our antagoniſts in theſe controverſies, may peradventure have met with ſome, not unlike to *Ithacius*, who mightily bending himſelf by all means againſt the hereſy of *Priſcillian*, (the hatred of which one evil, was all the virtue he had) became ſo wiſe in the end, That every man, careful of virtuous converſation, ſtudious of ſcripture, and given unto any abſtinence in diet, was ſet down in his kalendar of ſuſpected priſcillianiſts, for whom it ſhould be expedient to approve their ſoundneſs of faith, by a more licentious and looſe behaviour. Such proctors and patrons the truth might ſpare; yet is not their groſſneſs ſo intolerable, as on the contrary ſide, the ſcurrillous and more than ſatyrical immodeſty of martiniſm; the firſt publiſhed ſchedules whereof, being brought to the hands of a grave and a very honourable knight, with ſignification given, that the book would refreſh his ſpirits, he took it, ſaw what the title was, read over an unſavory ſentence or two, and delivered back the libel with this anſwer, *I am ſorry you are of the mind to be ſolaced with theſe ſports, and ſorrier you have herein thought mine affection to be like your own.* But as theſe ſores on all hands lie open, ſo the deepeſt wounds of the church of God, have been more ſoftly and cloſely given. It being perceived, that the plot of

Sulp. Sever.
Epiſt. Hiſt.
Ecclef.

g diſci-

diſcipline, did not only bend it ſelf to reform ceremonies, but ſeek farther to erect a popular authority of elders, and to take away epiſcopal juriſdiction, together
with all other ornaments and means, whereby any difference or inequality is upheld in the eccleſiaſtical order;
towards this deſtructive part, they have found many helping hands, divers altho peradventure not willing to
be yoked with elderſhips, yet contented (for what intent
God doth know) to uphold oppoſition againſt biſhops,
not without greater hurt to the courſe of their whole
proceedings in the buſineſs of God and her majeſty's ſervice, than otherwiſe much more weighty adverſaries had
been able by their own power to have brought to paſs.
Men are naturally better contented to have their commendable actions ſuppreſt, than the contrary much divulged. And becauſe the wits of the multitude are
ſuch, that many things they cannot lay hold on at once,
but being poſſeſt with ſome notable either diſlike or liking
of any one thing whatſoever, ſundry other in the mean
time may eſcape them unperceived: therefore, if men
deſirous to have their virtues noted, do in this reſpect
grieve at the fame of others, whoſe glory obſcureth and
darkneth theirs, it cannot be choſen, but that when the
ears of the people are thus continually beaten with the ex-
clamations againſt abuſes in the church; theſe tunes
come always moſt acceptable to them, whoſe odious and
corrupt dealings in ſecular affairs, both paſs by that mean
the more covertly, and whatſoever happen, do alſo the
leaſt feel the ſcourge of vulgar imputation, which notwithſtanding they moſt deſerve. All this conſidered, as
behoveth the ſequel of duty on our part, is only that
which our Lord and Saviour requireth, harmleſs diſcretion, the wiſdom of ſerpents, tempered with the innocent meekneſs of doves: for this world will teach them
wiſdom that have capacity to apprehend it. Our wiſdom in this caſe muſt be ſuch, as doth not propoſe to it
ſelf τὸ ἴδιον, our own particular, the partial and immoderate deſire whereof, poiſoneth whereſoever it taketh
place: but the ſcope and mark which we are to aim
at is τὸ κοινὸν, the publick and common good of all; for
the

the eaſier procurement whereof, our diligence muſt ſearch
out all helps and furtherances of direction, which ſcriptures, councils, fathers, hiſtories, the laws and practices of all churches, the mutual conference of all mens
collections and obſervations may afford : our induſtry
muſt even anatomize every particle of that body, which
we are to uphold ſound ; and becauſe, be it never ſo true
which we teach the world to believe, yet if once their affections begin to be alienated, a ſmall thing perſuadeth
them to change their opinions, it behoveth, that we vigi-
lantly note and prevent by all means thoſe evils, whereby
the hearts of men are loſt ; which evils for the moſt part
being perſonal, do arm in ſuch ſort the adverſaries of God
and his church againſt us, that if thro our too much
neglect and ſecurity the ſame ſhould run on, ſoon might
we feel our eſtate brought to thoſe lamentable terms,
whereof this hard and heavy ſentence was by one of the
antients uttered upon like occaſions : *Dolens dico, gemens de-* Leg. Caroli
nuncio, ſacerdotium quod apud nos intus cecidit, foris diu ſtare Mag. fol.
non poterit. But the gracious providence of Almighty God ⁴²¹·
hath, I truſt, put theſe thorns of contradiction in our ſides,
leſt that ſhould ſteal upon the church in a ſlumber, which
now, I doubt not, but thro his aſſiſtance, may be turned
away from us, bending thereunto our ſelves with conſtancy,
conſtancy in labour to do all men good, conſtancy in
prayer unto God for all men ; her eſpecially, whoſe ſacred
power, matched with incomparable goodneſs of nature,
hath hitherto been God's moſt happy inſtrument, by
him miraculouſly kept for works of ſo miraculous preſervation and ſafety unto others ; that as, *By the ſword of* Judg. 7. 16.
God and Gideon, was ſometime the cry of the people of
Iſrael, ſo it might deſervedly be at this day the joyful
ſong of innumerable multitudes, yea, the emblem of ſome
eſtates and dominions in the world, and (which muſt be
eternally confeſs'd even with tears of thankfulneſs) the
true inſcription, ſtyle, or title of all churches as yet ſtanding within this realm, *By the goodneſs of Almighty God and
his ſervant* Elizabeth, *we are.* That God, who is able
to make mortality immortal, give her ſuch future continuance as may be no leſs glorious unto all poſterity, than

the

the days of her regiment paſt have been happy unto our ſelves ; and for his moſt dear anointed's ſake, grant them all proſperity, whoſe labours, cares, and counſels, unfeignedly are referred to her endleſs welfare, thro his unſpeakable mercy, unto whom we all owe everlaſting praiſe. In which deſire I will here reſt, humbly beſeeching your Grace to pardon my great boldneſs, and God to multiply his bleſſings upon them that fear his name.

Your Grace's in all Duty,

Richard Hooker.

A

A

PREFACE

To them that feek (as they term it) the

Reformation of the Laws

AND

ORDERS ECCLESIASTICAL

IN THE

Church of ENGLAND.

THOUGH for no other caufe, yet for this, that pofterity may know we *The caufe and* have not loofly thro filence, permitted things to pafs away as in a dream; *occafion of* there fhall be for mens information extant thus much concerning the prefent *handling thefe* flate of the church of God, eftablifhed amongft us, and their careful endea- *what might be* vour which would have upheld the fame. At your hands, beloved in our *wifhed in* Lord and Saviour Jefus Chrift, (for in him the love which we bear unto all that would *whofe fakes* but feem to be born of him, it is not the fea of your gall and bitternefs that fhall ever *fo much pains* drown) I have no great caufe to look for other, than the felf-fame portion and lot, *is taken.* which your manner hath been hitherto to lay on them that concur not in opinion and fentence with you. But our hope is that the God of peace fhall (notwithftanding man's nature, too impatient of contumelious malediction) enable us quietly, and even gladly to fuffer all things for that work fake, which we covet to perform. The won- derful zeal and fervour wherewith ye have withftood the received orders of this church, was the firft thing which caufed me to enter into confideration, Whether (as all your publifh'd books and writings peremptorily maintain) every chriftian man fearing God, ftand bound to joyn with you for the furtherance of that which ye term The Lord's difcipline. Wherein I muft plainly confefs unto you, that before I examined your fundry declarations in that behalf, it could not fettle in my head to think, but that undoubtedly

fuch

*such numbers of otherwise right well-affected and most religiously enclined minds, had
some marvellous reasonable inducements which led them with so great earnestness that
way. But when once, as near as my slender ability would serve, I had with travel
and care performed that part of the apostle's advice and counsel in such cases, whereby
he willeth to* try all things, *and was come at the length so far, that there remained only the other clause to be satisfied, wherein he concludeth, that* what good is, must be
held : *there was in my poor understanding no remedy, but to set down this as my final
resolute persuasion.* Surely, the present form of church government, which the laws
of this land have established, is such, as no law of God, nor reason of man hath hitherto been alledged of force sufficient to prove they do ill, who to the uttermost of their
power withstand the alteration thereof. *Contrariwise,* The other, which instead of it,
we are required to accept, is only by error and misconceit named the ordinance of Jesus Christ, no one proof as yet brought forth, whereby it may clearly appear to be so in
very deed. *The explication of which two things, I have here thought good to offer into
your own hands ; heartily beseeching you, even by the meekness of Jesus Christ, whom I
trust ye love, that as ye tender the peace and quietness of this church, if there be in
you that gracious humility which hath ever been the crown and glory of a christianly
disposed mind ; if your own souls, hearts, and consciences, (the sound integrity whereof can but hardly stand with the refusal of truth in personal respects) be, as I doubt*

Jam. 2. 1. *not but they are, things most dear and precious unto you ;* let not the faith which ye
have in our Lord Jesus Christ be blemished with partialities; *regard not who it is which
speaketh, but weigh only what is spoken. Think not that ye read the words of one who
bendeth himself as an adversary against the truth, which ye have already embraced, but
the words of one, who desireth even to embrace together with you the self-same truth,
if it be the truth ; and for that cause (for no other, God he knoweth) hath undertaken
the burthensome labour of this painful kind of conference. For the plainer access whereunto, let it be lawful for me to rip up the very bottom, how, and by whom your discipline was planted, at such time as this age we live in, began to make first trial
thereof.*

The first esta-
blishment of
new disci-
pline by Mr.
Calvin's in-
dustry, in the
church of
Geneva ; and
the beginning
of strife about
it amongst
our selves. 2. *A founder it had, whom, for my own part, I think incomparably the wisest
man that ever the* French *church did enjoy, since the hour it enjoyed him. His
bringing up was in the study of the civil law. Divine knowledge he gathered not
by hearing or reading so much, as by teaching others. For tho thousands were
debtors to him, as touching knowledge in that kind, yet he to none but only to God,
the author of that most blessed fountain* The book of life, *and of the admirable dexterity of wit, together with the helps of other learning which were his guides ; till
being occasioned to leave* France, *he fell at the length upon* Geneva. *Which city the bishop and clergy thereof had a little before (as some affirm) forsaken, being of likelihood frighted with the people's sudden attempt for abolishment of popish religion,
the event of which enterprize, they thought it not safe for themselves to wait for
in that place. At the coming of* Calvin *thither, the form of their civil regiment was
popular, as it continueth at this day : neither king, nor duke, nor nobleman of any
authority or power over them, but officers chosen by the people out of themselves,
to order all things with publick consent. For spiritual government, they had no
laws at all agreed upon, but did what the pastors of their souls, by persuasion,
could win them unto.* Calvin *being admitted one of their preachers and a divinity reader amongst them, considered how dangerous it was, that the whole estate of
that church should still hang on so slender a thread, as the liking of an ignorant multitude is, if it have power to change whatsoever it self listeth. Wherefore, taking
unto him two of the other ministers, for more countenance of the action (albeit the
rest were all against it) they moved, and in the end persuaded, with much ado, the
people to bind themselves by solemn oath, first, never to admit the papacy amongst
them again ; and secondly, to live in obedience unto such orders concerning the exercise of their religion, and the form of their ecclesiastical government, as those their
true and faithful ministers of God's word had agreeably to scripture set down for
that end and purpose. When these things began to be put in ure, the people also
(what causes moving them thereunto, themselves best know) began to repent them of
that they had done, and irefully to champ upon the bit they had taken into their
mouths, the rather, for that they grew by means of this innovation into a dislike
with some churches near about them, the benefit of whose good friendship, their
state could not well lack. It was the manner of those times, (whether thro mens
desire,*

*desire, to enjoy alone the glory of their own enterprises, or else because the quick-
ness of their occasions required present dispatch ;) So it was, that every particular church did that within it self, which some few of their own thought good, by
whom the rest were all directed. Such number of churches then being, tho free
within themselves, yet small common conference before-hand might have eased them
of much after trouble. But a great inconvenience it bred, that every later ende-
voured to be certain degrees more removed from conformity with the church of Rome,
than the rest before had been ; whereupon grew marvellous great dissimilitudes, and
by reason thereof, jealousies, heart-burnings, jars, and discords amongst them. Which
notwithstanding might have easily been prevented; if the orders which each church
did think fit and convenient for it self, had not so peremptorily been established under that high commanding form, which rendred them unto the people, as things everlastingly required by the law of that Lord of lords, against whose statutes there is no
exception to be taken. For by this mean it came to pass, that one church could not but
accuse and condemn another of disobedience to the will of Christ, in those things
where manifest difference was between them ; whereas the self-same orders allowed,
but yet established in more wary and suspense manner, as being to stand in force till
God should give the opportunity of some general conference, what might be best for
them afterwards to do : this, I say, had both prevented all occasion of just dislike
which others might take, and reserved a greater liberty unto the authors themselves,
of entring into further consultation afterwards. Which, tho never so necessary, they
could not easily now admit, without some fear of derogation from their credit : and
therefore that which once they had done, they became for ever after resolute to maintain. Calvin therefore, and the other two his associates, stiffly refusing to administer
the holy communion to such as would not quietly, without contradiction and murmur,
submit themselves unto the orders which their solemn oath had bound them to obey,
were, in that quarrel, banished the town. A few years after (such was the levity of
that people) the places of one or two of their ministers being faln void, they were
not before so willing to be rid of their learned pastor, as now importunate to obtain him again from them who had given him entertainment, and which were loth
to part with him, had not unresistible earnestness been used. One of the town-mi-
nisters, that saw in what manner the people were bent for the revocation of Calvin,
gave him notice of their affection in this sort.* The senate of two hundred being as-   *Epist. Cal. 24.*
sembled, they all crave *Calvin.* The next day a general convocation, they cry in like
sort again all, we will have *Calvin,* that good and learned man, Christ's minister. This,
*saith he, when I understood, I could not chuse but praise God ; nor was I able to judge
otherwise, than that this was the Lord's doing, and that it was marvellous in our eyes ;
and that* the stone which the builders refused, was now made the head of the corner.   *Luk. 20. 17.*
The other two whom they had thrown out (together with Calvin) *they were content
should enjoy their exile. Many causes might lead them to be more desirous of him.
First, his yielding unto them in one thing, might happily put them in hope, that time
would breed the like easiness of condescending further unto them. For in his absence
he had persuaded them, with whom he was able to prevail, that albeit himself did
better like of common bread to be used in the eucharist, yet the other they rather
should accept, than cause any trouble in the church about it. Again, they saw that
the name of* Calvin *waxed every day greater abroad, and that together with his fame,
their infamy was spread, who had so rashly and childishly ejected him. Besides it was
not unlikely, but that his credit in the world, might many ways stand the poor town in
great stead : as the truth is, their ministers foreign estimation hitherto hath been the
best stake in their hedge. But whatsoever secret respects were likely to move them,
for contenting of their minds,* Calvin *returned (as it had been another* Tully) *to his
old home. He ripely considered how gross a thing it were for men of his quality, wise
and grave men, to live with such a multitude, and to be tenants at will under them ;
as their ministers, both himself and others, had been. For the remedy of which inconvenience, he gave them plainly to understand, that if he did become their teacher
again, they must be content to admit a complete form of discipline, which both they
and also their pastors, should now be solemnly sworn to observe for ever after : of
which discipline, the main and principal parts were these. A standing ecclesiastical
court to be established ; perpetual judges in that court to be their ministers ; others of
the people annually chosen (twice so many in number as they) to be judges together
with them in the same court. These two sorts, to have the care of all mens manners,
power of determining of all kind of ecclesiastical causes, and authority to convent, to*

controul, to punish, as far as with excommunication, whomsoever they should think worthy, none either small or great excepted. This device I see not how the wisest at that time living, could have bettered, if we duly consider what the present state of Geneva did then require. For their bishop and his clergy being (as it is said) departed from them by moon-light ; or howsoever, being departed, to chuse in his room any other bishop, had been a thing altogether impossible. And for their ministers to seek, that themselves alone might have coercive power over the whole church, would perhaps have been hardly construed at that time. But when so frank an offer was made, that for every one minister, there should be two of the people to sit and give voice in the ecclesiastical consistory, what inconvenience could they easily find which themselves might not be able always to remedy ? Howbeit (as evermore the simpler sort are, even when they see no apparent cause, jealous, notwithstanding, over the secret intents and purposes of wiser men) this proposition of his did somewhat trouble them. Of the ministers themselves, which had staid behind in the city when Calvin was gone, some upon knowledge of the people's earnest intent to recal him to his place again, had beforehand written their letters of submission, and assured him of their allegiance for ever after, if it should like him to hearken unto that publick suit. But yet misdoubting what might happen, if this discipline did go forward, they objected against it the example of other reformed churches, living quietly and orderly without it. Some of the chiefest place and countenance amongst the laity, professed with greater stomach their judgments, that such a discipline was little better than popish tyranny, disguised and tendered unto them under a new form. This sort, it may be, had some fear that the filling up of the seats in the consistory with so great a number of laymen, was but to please the minds of the people, to the end they might think their own sway somewhat ; but when things came to tryal of practice, their pastors learning would be at all times of force to over-persuade simple men, who knowing the time of their own presidentship to be but short, would always stand in fear of their ministers perpetual authority. And among the ministers themselves, one being so far in estimation above the rest, the voices of the rest were likely to be given for the most part respectively with a kind of secret dependency and awe : so that in shew, a marvellous indifferently composed senate ecclesiastical was to govern ; but in effect one only man should, as the spirit and soul of the residue, do all in all. But what did these vain surmises boot ? Brought they were now to so strait an issue, that of two things, they must chuse one : namely, whether they would to their endless disgrace, with ridiculous lightness, dismiss him, whose restitution they had in so important a manner desir'd, or else condescend unto that demand, wherein he was resolute, either to have it or to leave them. They thought it better to be somewhat hardly yoked at home, than for ever abroad discredited. Wherefore, in the end, those orders were on all sides assented unto, with no less alacrity of mind, than cities unable to hold out longer are wont to shew when they take conditions, such as liketh him to offer them, which hath them in the narrow straits of advantage. Not many years An. Do. 1541. were overpassed, before these twice-sworn men adventured to give their last and hottest assault to the fortress of the same discipline, childishly granting by common consent of their whole senate, and that under their town-seal, a relaxation to one Bertelier, whom the eldership had excommunicated : further also decreeing, with strange absurdity, that to the same senate, it should belong to give final judgment in matter of excommunication, and to absolve whom it pleased them : clean contrary to their own former deeds and oaths. The report of which decree, being forthwith brought unto Calvin ; Before (saith he) this decree take place, either my blood or banishment shall sign it. Again, two days before the communion should be celebrated, this speech was publickly to like effect : Kill me if ever this hand do reach forth the things that are holy, to them whom the church hath judged despisers. Whereupon, for fear of tumult, the forenamed Bertelier was by his friends advised for that time, not to use the liberty granted him by the senate, nor to present himself in the church, till they saw somewhat further what would ensue. After the communion quietly ministered, and some likelihood of peaceable ending of these troubles, without any more ado ; that very day in the afternoon, besides all mens expectation, concluding his ordinary sermon, he telleth them, That because he neither had learned nor taught to strive with such as are in authority ; Therefore (saith he) the case so standing, as now it doth, let me use these words of the apostle unto you, I commend you unto God, and the word of his grace ; and so bad them heartily adieu. It sometimes cometh to pass, that the readiest way which a wise man hath to conquer, is to fly. This voluntary and unex-

t

pected

pected mention of sudden departure, caused presently the senate (for according to their wonted manner, they still continued only constant in unconstancy) to gather themselves together, and for a time to suspend their own decree, leaving things to proceed as before, till they had heard the judgment of four Helvetian cities, concerning the matter which was in strife. This to have done at the first, before they gave assent unto any order, had shewed some wit and discretion in them; but now to do it, was as much as to say in effect, that they would play their parts on a stage. Calvin *therefore dispatcheth with all expedition his letters unto some principal pastor in every of those cities, craving earnestly at their hands, to respect this cause as a thing whereupon the whole state of religion and piety in that church did so much depend, that God and all good men were now inevitably certain to be trampled under foot, unless those four cities, by their good means, might be brought to give sentence with the ministers of* Geneva, *when the cause should be brought before them; yea, so to give it, that two things it might effectually contain: the one an absolute approbation of the discipline of* Geneva, *as consonant unto the word of God, without any cautions, qualifications, ifs, or ands; the other, an earnest admonition not to innovate or change the same. His vehement request herein, as touching both points, was satisfied. For albeit the said* Helvetian *churches did never as yet observe that discipline, nevertheless the senate of* Geneva *having required their judgment concerning these three questions;* First, after what manner, by God's commandment, according to the scripture, and unspotted religion, excommunication is to be exercised? Secondly, Epist. 166. whether it may not be exercised some other way, than by the consistory? Thirdly, what the use of their churches was to do in this case? *Answer was returned from the said churches,* That they had heard already of those consistorial laws, and did acknowledge them to be godly ordinances, *drawing towards* the prescript of the word of God; for which cause that they did not think it good for the church of *Geneva,* by innovation to change the same, but rather to keep them as they were. *Which answer, altho not answering unto the former demands, but respecting what Mr.* Calvin *had judged requisite for them to answer, was notwithstanding accepted without any further reply; in as much as they plainly saw, that when stomach doth strive with wit, the match is not equal; and so the heat of their former contentions began to slake. The present inhabitants of* Geneva, *I hope, will not take it in evil part; that the faultiness of their people heretofore, is by us so far forth laid open, as their own learned guides and pastors have thought necessary to discover it unto the world. For out of their books and writings it is, that I have collected this whole narration, to the end it might thereby appear in what sort amongst them, that discipline was planted, for which so much contention is raised amongst our selves. The reason which moved* Calvin *herein to be so earnest, was, as* Beza *himself testifieth,* For that he saw how Quod eam urbem vide- needful these bridles were to be put in the jaws of that city. That which by wis-ret omnino dom he saw to be requisite for that people, was by as great wisdom compassed. But his frænis in *wise are men, and the truth is truth. That which* Calvin *did for establishment of*digere. *his discipline, seemeth more commendable than that which he taught for the countenancing of it established. Nature worketh in us all a love to our own counsels: the contradiction of others is a fan to inflame that love. Our love set on fire to maintain that which once we have done, sharpneth the wit to dispute, to argue, and by all means to reason for it. Wherefore a marvel it were, if a man of so great capacity, having such incitements to make him desirous of all kind of furtherances unto his cause, could espy in the whole scripture of God, nothing which might breed at the least a probable opinion of likelihood, that divine authority it self was the same way somewhat inclinable. And all which the wit even of* Calvin *was able from thence to draw, by sifting the very utmost sentence and syllable, is no more than, that certain speeches there are, which to him did seem to intimate, that all christian churches ought to have their elderships endowed with power of excommunication; and that a part of those elderships every where, should be chosen out from amongst the laity, after that form which himself had framed* Geneva *unto. But what argument are ye able to shew, whereby it was ever proved by* Calvin, *that any one sentence of scripture doth necessarily inforce these things, or the rest wherein your opinion concurreth with his against the orders of your own church? We should be injurious unto virtue it self, if we did derogate from them whom their industry hath made great. Two things of principal moment there are which have deservedly procured him honour throughout the world: the one his exceeding pains in composing the institution of christian religion; the other, his no less industrious travels for exposition*

h   *of*

*of holy scripture, according to the same institutions.   In which two things, who-
soever they were that after him bestowed their labour, he gained the advantage of
prejudice against them, if they gainsayed; and of glory above them, if they consen-
ted. His writings, published after the question about that discipline was once begun,
omit not any the least occasion of extolling the use and singular necessity thereof. Of
what account the master of sentences was in the church of* Rome, *the same, and more
amongst the preachers of reformed churches,* Calvin *had purchased: so that the perfectest divines were judged they, which were skilfullest in* Calvin's *writings; his
books almost the very canon to judge both doctrine and discipline by. French churches
both under others abroad, and at home in their own country, all cast according to that
mould which* Calvin *had made. The church of* Scotland *in erecting the fabrick of their
reformation, took the self-same pattern; till at length the discipline which was at
the first so weak, that without the staff of their approbation, who were not subject
unto it themselves, it had not brought others under subjection, began now to challenge
universal obedience, and to enter into open conflict with those very churches, which
in desperate extremity had been relievers of it. To one of those churches which
lived in most peaceable sort, and abounded as well with men for their learning in o-
ther professions singular, as also with divines, whose equals were not elsewhere to
be found, a church ordered by* Gualter's *discipline, and not by that which* Geneva *ado-
reth; unto this church of* Heidelburgh, *there cometh one who craving leave to dispute publickly, defendeth with open disdain of their government, that to a minister
with his eldership, power is given by the law of* God *to excommunicate whomsoever,
yea, even kings and princes themselves. Here were the seeds sown of that controversy which sprang up between* Beza *and* Erastus, *about the matter of excommunication; whether there ought to be in all churches an eldership having power to excommunicate, and a part of that eldership to be of necessity certain, chosen out from a-
mongst the laity for that purpose. In which disputation they have, as to me it seemeth,
divided very equally the truth between them:* Beza *most truly maintaining the necessity of excommunication;* Erastus *as truly, the non-necessity of lay-elders to be ministers thereof. Amongst our selves, there was in king* Edward's *days some question
moved, by reason of a few mens scrupulosity, touching certain things. And beyond
seas, of them which fled in the days of queen* Mary; *some contenting themselves a-
broad, with the use of their own service-book, at home authorized before their departure out of their realm; others liking better the common-prayer book of the church
of* Geneva *translated; those smaller contentions before begun, were by this mean
somewhat increased. Under the happy reign of her majesty which now is, the
greatest matter a while contended for, was the wearing of the cap and surplice, till
there came admonitions directed unto the high court of parliament, by men who con-
cealing their names, thought it glory enough to discover their minds and affections,
which now were universally bent even against all the orders and laws, wherein this
church is found unconformable to the platform of* Geneva. *Concerning the defender
of which admonitions, all that I mean to say, is but this :   There will come a time,
when three words uttered with charity and meekness, shall receive a far more blessed
reward, than three thousand volumes written with disdainful sharpness of wit. But
the manner of mens writings must not alienate our hearts from the truth, if it appear
they have the truth; as the followers of the same defender do think he hath : and
in that persuasion they follow him, no otherwise than himself doth* Calvin, Beza, *and
others; with the like persuasion that they in this cause had the truth. We being as
fully persuaded otherwise, it resteth, that some kind of tryal be used to find out which
part is in error,*

By what
means so ma-
ny of the peo-
ple are trained
unto the liking
of that disci-
pline.
1 Cor. 10. 13.
& 11. 13.
Luk. 12. 56,
57.
Acts 17. 11.
Rom. 14. 5.

3. *The first mean whereby nature teacheth men to judge good from evil, as well in
laws as in other things, is the force of their own discretion. Hereunto therefore
saint* Paul *referreth oftentimes his own speech, to be considered of by them that heard
him.   I speak as to them which have understanding, judge ye what I say. Again afterward, Judge in your selves, is it comely that a woman pray uncovered? The exercise of this kind of judgment, our Saviour requireth in the Jews. In them of* Be-
roea *the scripture commendeth it. Finally, whatsoever we do, if our own secret judgment consent not unto it as fit and good to be done, the doing of it to us is sin, altho the
thing it self be allowable. Saint* Paul's *rule therefore generally is, Let every man in
his own mind be fully persuaded of that thing which he either alloweth or doth. Some
things are so familiar and plain, that truth from falshood, and good from evil, is most
easily discerned in them, even by men of no deep capacity. And of that nature, for the
most part, are things absolutely unto all mens salvation necessary, either to be held or*
                                                            denied,

denied, either to be done or avoided. For which cause saint Augustine acknowledgeth, that they are not only set down, but also plainly set down in scripture ; so that he which heareth or readeth, may without any great difficulty understand. Other things also there are belonging (tho in a lower degree of importance) unto the offices of christian men : which because they are more obscure, more intricate and hard to be judged of, therefore God hath appointed some to spend their whole time principally in the study of things divine, to the end, that in these more doubtful cases, their understanding might be a light to direct others. If the understanding power or faculty of the soul be (saith the grand physician) like unto bodily sight, not of equal sharpness in all ; what can be more convenient than that, even as the dark-sighted man is directed by the clear about things visible ; so likewise in matters of deeper discourse, the wise in heart doth shew the simple where his way lieth ? In our doubtful cases of law, what man is there, who seeth not how requisite it is, that professors of skill in that faculty be our directors ? so it is in all other kinds of knowledge. And even in this kind likewise the Lord* himself hath appointed, That the priest's lips should preserve knowledge, and that* other men should seek the truth at his mouth, because he is the messenger of the Lord of hosts. Gregory Nazianzen, offended at the peoples too great presumption in controlling* the judgment of them, to whom in such cases they should have rather submitted their own, seeketh by earnest intreaty to stay them within their bounds. Presume not ye that are sheep, to make your selves guides of them that should guide you ; neither seek ye to overslip the fold which they about you have pitched. It sufficeth for your part, if ye can well frame your selves to be ordered. Take not upon you to judge your selves, nor to make them subject to your laws, who should be a law to you ; for God is not a god of sedition and confusion, but of order and peace. But ye will say, that if the* guides of the people be blind, the common sort of men must not close up their own eyes, and be led by the conduct of such ; if the priest be partial in the law, the flock must* not therefore depart from the ways of sincere truth, and in simplicity yield to be followers of him for his place sake and office over them. Which thing, tho in it self most true, is in your defence notwithstanding weak ; because the matter wherein ye think that ye see and imagine that your ways are sincere, is of far deeper consideration than any one amongst five hundred of you conceiveth. Let the vulgar sort among you know, that there is not the least branch of the cause, wherein they are so resolute, but to the tryal of it a great deal more appertaineth, than their conceit doth reach unto. I write not this in disgrace of the simplest that way given, but I would gladly they knew the nature of that cause wherein they think themselves thorowly instructed, and are not ; by means whereof they daily run themselves, without feeling their own hazard, upon the* dint of the apostle's sentence against evil-speakers, as touching things wherein they are* ignorant. If it be granted a thing unlawful for private men, not called unto publick consultation, to dispute which is the best state of civil policy (with a desire of* bringing in some other kind, than that under which they already live, for of such disputes, I take it, his meaning was ;) if it be a thing confest, that of such questions they cannot determine without rashness, in as much as a great part of them consisteth in special circumstances, and for one kind as many reasons may be brought as for another ; is there any reason in the world, why they should better judge what kind of regiment ecclesiastical is the fittest ? For in the civil state more insight, and in those affairs more experience, a great deal, must needs be granted them, than in this they can possibly have. When they which write in defence of your discipline, and commend it unto the highest, not in the least cunning manner, are forced notwithstanding to acknowledge, that with whom the truth is, they know not, they are not certain ; what* certainty or knowledge can the multitude have thereof ? Weigh what doth move the* common sort so much to favour this innovation, and it shall soon appear unto you, that* the force of particular reasons, which for your several opinions are alledged, is a thing* whereof the multitude never did, nor could so consider as to be therewith wholly carried ; but certain general inducements are used to make saleable your cause in gross ; and when once men have cast a fancy towards it, any slight declaration of specialities will serve to lead forward mens inclinable and prepared minds. The method of winning the peoples affection unto a general liking of the cause (for so ye term it) hath been this. First, in the hearing of the multitude, the faults especially of higher callings are ripped up with marvellous exceeding severity and sharpness of reproof ; which being oftentimes done, begetteth a great good opinion of integrity, zeal, and holiness, to such constant reprovers of sin, as by likelihood would never be so much offended at that which is evil, unless themselves were singularly good. The next thing*

Galen. de opt. docen. gen.

Mal. 2. 7.

Greg. Nazian.: orat. qua se excusat.

Matth. 10. 14.

Mal. 2. 9.

Jude ver. 10. 2 Pet. 2. 12.

Calvin. instit. lib. 4. cap. 20. sect. 8.

The author of the petition directed to her majesty, pag. 3.

h 2   here-

hereunto is, to impute all faults and corruptions wherewith the world aboundeth, unto the kind of ecclesiastical government established. Wherein as before by reproving faults they purchased unto themselves, with the multitude, a name to be vertuous ; so by finding out this kind of cause, they obtain to be judged wise above others : whereas in truth unto the form even of jewish government, which the Lord himself (they all confess) did establish, with like shew of reason they might impute those faults which the prophets condemn in the governours of that common-wealth ; as to the English *kind of regiment ecclesiastical (whereof also God himself, tho in another sort, is author) the stains and blemishes found in our state ; which springing from the root of human frailty and corruption, not only are, but have been always more or less, yea, and (for any thing we know to the contrary) will be till the world's end complained of, what form of government soever take place. Having gotten thus much sway in the hearts of men, a third step is to propose their own form of church-government, as the only sovereign remedy of all evils ; and to adorn it with all the glorious titles that may be. And the nature, as of men that have sick bodies, so likewise of the people in the crazedness of their minds, possess with dislike and discontentment at things present, is to imagine, that any thing (the virtue whereof they hear commended) would help them ; but that most, which they least have tried. The fourth degree of inducements is by fashioning the very notions and conceits of mens minds in such sort, that when they read the scripture, they may think that every thing soundeth towards the advancement of that discipline, and to the utter disgrace of the contrary.* Pythagoras, *by bringing up his scholars in speculative knowledge of numbers, made their conceits therein so strong, that when they came to the contemplation of things natural, they imagined that in every particular thing, they even beheld, as it were with their eyes, how the elements of number gave essence and being to the works of nature. A thing in reason impossible, which notwithstanding, thro their mis-fashioned pre-conceit, appeared unto them no less certain, than if nature had written it in the very foreheads of all the creatures of God. When they of the family of love have it once in their heads, that Christ doth not signify any one person, but a quality whereof many are partakers ; that to be raised, is nothing else but to be regenerated, or endued with the said quality ; and that when separation of them, which have it, from them which have it not, is here made, this is judgment : how plainly do they imagine, that the scripture every where speaketh in the favour of that sect ? And assuredly, the very cause which maketh the simple and ignorant to think they even see how the word of God runneth currently on your side, is, that their minds are forestalled, and their conceits perverted beforehand, by being taught, that an elder doth signify a layman, admitted only to the office of rule or government in the church ; a doctor, one which may only teach, and neither preach nor administer the sacraments ; a deacon, one which hath the charge of the alms-box, and of nothing else : that the scepter, the rod, the throne and kingdom of Christ, are a form of regiment, only by pastors, elders, doctors, and deacons ; that by mystical resemblance, mount* Sion *and* Jerusalem *are the churches which admit ;* Samaria *and* Babylon, *the churches which oppugn the said form of regiment. And in like sort, they are taught to apply all things spoken of repairing the walls and decayed parts of the city and temple of God, by* Esdras, Nehemias, *and the rest ; as if purposely the Holy Ghost had therein meant to fore-signify, what the authors of admonitions to the parliament, of supplications to the council, of petitions to her majesty, and of such other-like writs, should either do or suffer in behalf of this their cause. From hence they proceed to an higher point, which is the persuading of men credulous and over-capable of such pleasing errors, that it is the special illumination of the Holy Ghost, whereby they discern those things in the word, which others reading, yet discern them not.*

1 John 4. 1. Dearly beloved, *saith saint* John, *give not credit unto every spirit. There are but two ways whereby the Spirit leadeth men into all truth ; the one extraordinary, the other common ; the one belonging but unto some few, the other extending it self unto all that are of God ; the one, that which we call by a special divine excellency, revelation ; the other reason. If the Spirit by such revelation, have discovered unto them the secrets of that discipline out of scripture, they must profess themselves to be all (even men, women, and children) prophets : or if reason be the hand which the Spirit hath led them by ; forasmuch as persuasions grounded upon reason, are either weaker or stronger, according to the force of those reasons whereupon the same are*

grounded,

grounded, they must every of them, from the greatest to the least, be able for every several article, to shew some special reason, as strong as their persuasion therein is earnest: otherwise how can it be, but that some other sinews there are, from which that overplus of strength in persuasion doth arise? Most sure it is, that when mens affections do frame their opinions, they are in defence of error more earnest a great deal, than (for the most part) sound believers in the maintenance of truth, apprehended according to the nature of that evidence which scripture yieldeth: which being in some things plain, as in the principles of christian doctrine; in some things, as in these matters of discipline, more dark and doubtful, frameth correspondently that inward assent which God's most gracious Spirit worketh by it, as by his effectual instrument. It is not therefore the fervent earnestness of their persuasion, but the soundness of those reasons whereupon the same is built, which must declare their opinions in these things to have been wrought by the Holy Ghost, and not by the fraud of that evil spirit which is even in his illusions strong. After that the fancy of the common sort hath once thorowly apprehended the Spirit to be author of their persuasions concerning discipline; then is instilled into their hearts, that the same Spirit, leading men into this opinion, doth thereby seal them to be God's children; and that as the state of the times now standeth, the most special token to know them that are God's own from others, is an earnest affection that way. This hath bred high terms of separation between such, and the rest of the world; whereby the one sort are named the brethren, the godly, and so forth; the other, worldlings, time-servers, pleasers of men, not of God, with such like. From hence they are easily drawn on to think it exceeding necessary, for fear of quenching that good Spirit, to use all means whereby the same may be both strengthened in themselves, and made manifest unto others. This maketh them diligent hearers of such as are known that way to incline: this maketh them eager to take and seek all occasions of secret conference with such: this maketh them glad to use such as counsellors and directors in all their dealings, which are of weight, as contracts, testaments, and the like: this maketh them, through an unweariable desire of receiving instruction from the masters of that company, to cast off the care of those very affairs which do most concern their estate, and to think that they are like unto Mary, commendable for making choice of the better part. Finally, this is it which maketh them willing to charge, yea, oftentimes even to over-charge themselves, for such mens sustenance and relief, lest their zeal to the cause should any way be unwitnessed. For what is it, which poor beguiled souls will not do through so powerful incitements? In which respect it is also noted, that most labour hath been bestowed to win and retain towards this cause, them whose judgments are commonly weakest by reason of their sex. And although not women loaden with sins, as the apostle saint Paul speaketh, but (as we verily esteem of them for the most part) women propense and inclinable to holiness, be otherwise edified in good things, rather than carried away as captives into any kind of sin and evil, by such as enter into their houses with purpose to plant there a zeal and a love towards this kind of discipline; yet some occasion is hereby ministred for men to think, that if the cause which is thus furthered, did gain by the soundness of proof, whereupon it doth build it self, it would not most busily endeavour to prevail, where least ability of judgment is: and therefore that this so eminent industry in making proselytes more of that sex than of the other, groweth, for that they are deemed apter to serve as instruments and helps in the cause. After they are through the eagerness of their affection, that maketh them, which way soever they take, diligent in drawing their husbands, children, servants, friends and allies, the same way: after thro that natural inclination unto pity, which breedeth in them a greater readiness than in men, to be bountiful towards their preachers, who suffer want: after thro sundry opportunities, which they especially have, to procure encouragements for their brethren: finally, after thro a singular delight which they take, in giving very large and particular intelligence, how all near about them stand affected, as concerning the same cause. But be they women, or be they men, if once they have tasted of that cup, let any man of contrary opinion open his mouth to persuade them, they close up their ears, his reasons they weigh not, all is answered with rehearsal of the words of John, We are of God; he that knoweth God heareth us: as for the rest, ye are of the world; for this world's pomp and vanity it is that ye speak, and the world whose ye are, heareth you. Which cloak sitteth no less fit on the back of their

cause,

1 Thess. 1. 11.

2 Tim. 3. 6.

i John 4. 6.

cause, than of the anabaptists; when the dignity, authority, and honour of God's magistrates is upheld against them. Shew these eagerly-affected men their inability to judge of such matters ; their answer is, God hath chosen the simple. Convince them of folly, and that so plainly, that very children upbraid them with it ; they have their bucklers of like defence : Christ's own apostle was accounted mad : the best men evermore by the sentence of the world, have been judged to be out of their right minds. When instruction doth them no good, let them feel but the least degree of most mercifully tempered severity, they fasten on the head of the Lord's vicegerents here on earth, whatsoever they any where find uttered against the cruelty of blood-thirsty men ; and to themselves they draw all the sentences which scripture hath in the favour of innocency persecuted for the truth ; yea, they are of their due and deserved sufferings no less proud, than those antient disturbers, to whom saint Augustine *writeth, saying ;* Martyrs, *rightly so named, are they not which suffer for their disorder, and for the ungodly breach they have made of christian unity ; but which for righteousness sake are persecuted.* For *Agar also suffered persecution at the hands of* Sarah ; *wherein, she which did impose was holy, and she unrighteous which did bear the burden. In like sort, with the thieves was the Lord himself crucified, but they who were matcht in the pain which they suffered, were in the cause of their sufferings disjoin'd. If that must needs be the true church which doth endure persecution, and not that which persecuteth, let them ask of the apostle, what church* Sarah *did represent, when she held her maid in affliction. For even our mother which is free, the heavenly* Jerusalem, *that is to say, the true church of God, was, as he doth affirm, prefigured in that very woman, by whom the bond-maid was so sharply handled. Altho if all things be throughly scanned, she did in truth more persecute* Sarah *by proud resistance, than* Sarah *her by severity of punishment. These are the paths wherein ye have walked, that are of the ordinary sort of men ; these are the very steps ye have trodden, and the manifest degrees whereby ye are of your guides and directors trained up in that school : a custom of inuring your ears with reproof of faults, especially in your governours ; and use to attribute those faults to the kind of spiritual regiment, under which ye live ; boldness in warranting the force of their discipline, for the cure of all such evil ; a slight of framing your conceits to imagine, that scripture every where favoureth that discipline ; persuasion that the cause why ye find it in scripture, is the illumination of the Spirit ; that the same Spirit is a seal unto you of your nearness unto God; that ye are by all means to nourish and witness it in your selves, and to strengthen on every side your minds against whatsoever might be of force to withdraw you from it.*

4. *Wherefore to come unto you, whose judgment is a lanthorn of direction for all the rest ; you that frame thus the people's hearts, not altogether (as I willingly persuade my self) of a politick intent or purpose, but your selves being first overborn with the weight of greater mens judgments ; on your shoulders is laid the burden of upholding the cause by argument. For which purpose, sentences out of the word of God ye alledge divers ; but so, that when the same are discust, thus it always in a manner falleth out, that what things by virtue thereof ye urge upon us as altogether necessary, are found to be thence collected only by poor and marvellous slight conjectures. I need not give instance in any one sentence so alledged, for that I think the instance in any alledged otherwise a thing not easy to be given. A very strange thing sure it were, that such a discipline as ye speak of, should be taught by* Christ *and his apostles in the word of God, and no church ever have found it out, nor received it till this present time. Contrariwise, the government against which ye bend your selves, has been observed every where throughout all generations and ages of the christian world, no church ever perceiving the word of God to be against it. We require you to find out but one church upon the face of the whole earth, that hath been ordered by your discipline, or hath not been ordered by ours, that is to say, by episcopal regiment, sithence the time that the blessed apostles were here conversant. Many things out of antiquity ye bring, as if the purest times of the church had observed the self-same orders which you require ; and as though your desire were, that the churches of old should be patterns for us to follow, and even glasses wherein we might see the practice of that, which by you is gathered out of scripture. But the truth is, ye mean nothing less. All this is done for fashion-sake only ; for ye complain of it as of an injury, that men should be willed to seek for examples and patterns of government in any of those times*

that

Marginal notes (left column):

1 Cor. 27.
Acts 16. 24.
Sap. 5. 4.
We fools thought his life madness.
Merc. Trif ad Æsculap.
Οἱ ἐν γνώσει ὄντες ὑμῖν τοῖς σπλάγχνοις ἀξιόχρεων, ὅτε δὲ μᾶλλοι ἀυτοὶς μεμψάμενοι ᾗ δοκῶσι, ᾗ γᾶλλα δριμύτερον. vide
Lactant. de justit. lib. 5. cap. 16.
August. epist. 50.

What hath caused so many of the learneder sort to approve the same discipline.

T. C. lib. 1. p. 97.

bat have been before. Ye plainly hold, that from the very apostles times till this present age, wherein your selves imagine ye have found out a right pattern of sound discipline, there never was any time safe to be followed; which thing ye thus endeavour to prove. Out of Egesippus, ye say that Eusebius writeth, how altho as Eusab. 3. l. 32. *long as the apostles lived, the church did remain a pure virgin; yet after the death of the apostles, and after they were once gone, whom God vouchsafed to make hearers of the divine wisdom with their own ears, the placing of wicked errors began to come into the church. Clement also in a certain place, to confirm, that there was corrup-* Lib. strom. *tion of doctrine immediately after the apostles times, alledgeth the proverb, that there* somewhat af- *are few sons like their fathers. Socrates saith of the churches of Rome and Alexandria,* ning. *the most famous churches in the apostles times, that about the year 430, the Roman* L. 7. cap. 1 L. *and Alexandrian bishops, leaving the sacred function, were degenerate to a secular rule or dominion. Hereupon ye conclude, that it is not safe to fetch our government from any other than the apostles times. Wherein by the way it may be noted, that in proposing the apostles times as a pattern for the church to follow, tho the desire of you all be one, the drift and purpose of you all is not one. The chiefest thing which lay-reformers yawn for, is, that the clergy may through conformity in state and condition, be apostolical, poor as the apostles of Christ were poor. In which one circumstance, if they imagine so great perfection, they must think that church which hath such store of mendicant fryers, a church in that respect most happy. Were it for the glory of God, and the good of his church, indeed, that the clergy should be left even as bare as the apostles, when they had neither staff nor scrip; that God, which should lay upon them the condition of his apostles, would, I hope, endue them with the self-same affection which was in that holy apostle, whose words concerning his own right-virtuous contentment of heart, as well how to want, as how to* Phil. 4. 12. *abound, are a most fit episcopal emprese. The church of Christ is a body mystical. A body cannot stand, unless the parts thereof be proportionable. Let it therefore be required on both parts, at the hands of the clergy, to be in meanness of state like the apostles; at the hands of the laity, to be as they were who lived under the apostles. And in this reformation there will be, though little wisdom, yet some indifferency. But your reformation, which are of the clergy (if yet it displease you not that I should say ye are of the clergy) seemeth to aim at a broader mark. Ye think, that he which will perfectly reform, must bring the form of church-discipline unto the state which then it was at. A thing neither possible, nor certain, nor absolutely convenient. Concerning the first, what was used in the apostles times, the scripture fully declareth not; so that making their times the rule and canon of church polity, ye make a rule, which being not possible to be fully known, is as impossible to be kept. Again, sith the later, even of the apostles own times, had that which in the former was not thought upon; in this general proposing of the apostles times, there is no certainty which should be followed, especially seeing that ye give us great cause to doubt how far ye allow those times. For albeit the lovers of antichristian building were not, ye say, as then set up, yet the foundations thereof were secretly, and under the ground, laid in the apostles times: so that all other times ye plainly reject; and the apostles own times ye approve with marvellous great suspicion, leaving it intricate and doubtful, wherein we are to keep our selves unto the pattern of their times. Thirdly, whereas it is the error of the common multitude, to consider only what hath been of old, and if the same were well, to see whether still it continue; if not, to condemn that presently which is, and never to search upon what ground or consideration the charge might grow: such rudeness cannot be in you so well born with, whom learning and judgment hath enabled much more soundly to discern how far the times of the church, and the orders thereof, may alter without offence. True it is, the anti-enter* (a), *the better ceremonies of religion are: howbeit, not absolutely true, and without exception; but true, only so far forth as those different ages do agree in the state of those things, for which, at the first those rites, orders, and ceremonies, were instituted. In the apostles times, that was harmless, which being now revived, would be scandalous; as their* (b) *Oscula sancta.*

(a) Antiquitas ceremoniis atque sanis tantum sanctitatis tribuere consuevit, quantum adstruxerit vetustatis. *Arn.* p. 746.

(b) Rom. 16. 16. 2 Cor. 13. 12. 1 Thes. 5. 24. 1 Pet. 5. 14. *In their meetings to serve God, their manner was, in the end to salute one another with a kiss; using these words, peace be with you. For which cause, Tertullian doth call it, signaculum orationis, the seal of prayer,* lib. de orat.

Those

(c) Epift. Jud. ver. 12. *Concerning which feafts, faint* Chryfoftom *faith,* Statis diebus menfas faciebant communes, & peractâ fynaxi poft facramentorum communionem inibant convivium, divitibus quidem cibos afferentibus, pauperibus autem & qui nihil habebant etiam vocatis. *In* 1 Cor. 11. hom. 27. *Of the fame feafts in like fort* Tertullian. Cœna noftra de nomine rationem fui oftendit : vocatur enim ἀγάπη, id quod eft penes Græcos dilectio. Quantifcunque fumptibus conftet, lucrum eft pietatis nomine facere fumptum, *Apol. cap.* 39.

Thofe (c) *feafts of charity, which being infti-tuted by the apoftles, were retained in the church long after, are not now thought any where needful. What man is there of underftanding, unto whom it is not manifeft, how the way of providing for the clergy by tythes, the de-vice of alms-houfes for the poor, the forting out of the people into their feveral parifhes; together with fundry other things which the* apoftles *times could not have, (being now eftablifhed) are much more convenient and fit for the church of Chrift, than if the fame fhould be taken away for confor-mity's fake with the antienteft and firft times? The orders therefore which were obferved in the apoftles times, are not to be urged as a rule univerfally, either fufficient or neceffary. If they be, neverthelefs on your part it ftill remaineth to be better proved, that the form of difcipline, which ye intitle apoftolical, was in the apoftles time exercifed. For at this very thing ye fail, even touching that which ye make moft account of, as being matter of fubftance in difci-pline, I mean, the power of your lay-elders, and the difference of your doctors from the paftors in all churches. So that in fum we may be bold to conclude, that befides thefe laft times, which for infolency, pride, and egregious contempt of all good order, are the worft; there are none wherein ye can truly affirm, that the compleat form of your difcipline, or the fubftance thereof was practifed. The evidence therefore of antiquity failing you, ye fly to the judgments of fuch learned men, as feem by their writings, to be of opinion, that all chriftian churches fhould receive your difcipline, and abandon ours. Wherein, as ye heap up the names of a number of men, not unworthy to be had in honour; fo there are a number, whom when ye mention, altho it ferve ye to purpofe with the ignorant and vulgar fort, who meafure by tale and not by weight; yet furely, they who know what quality and value the men are of, will think ye draw very near the dregs. But were they all of as great account as the beft and chiefeft among them, with us notwithftanding neither are they, neither ought they to be of fuch reckoning, that their opinion or conjecture fhould caufe the laws of the church of* England *to give place; much lefs, when they neither do all agree in that opinion, and of them which are at agreement, the moft part through a courteous inducement, have followed one man as their guide; finally, that one therein not unlikely to have fwerved. If any one chance to fay, it is probable that in the apoftles times there were lay-elders, or not to miflike the con-tinuance of them in the church; or to affirm, that bifhops at the firft were a name, but not a power diftinct from presbyters; or to fpeak any thing in praife of thofe churches which are without epifcopal regiment; or to reprove the fault of fuch as abufe that calling; all thefe ye regifter for men, perfuaded as you are, that every chriftian church ftandeth bound by the law of God to put down bi-fhops, and in their rooms to erect an elderfhip fo authorifed as you would have it for the government of each parifh. Deceived greatly they are therefore, who think that all they whofe names are cited amongft the favourers of this caufe, are on any fuch verdict agreed. Yet touching fome material points of your dif-cipline, a kind of agreement we grant there is amongft many divines of reformed churches abroad. For firft, to do as the church of* Geneva *did, the learned in fome other churches muft needs be the more willing, who having ufed in like man-ner not the flow and tedious help of proceeding by publick authority, but the peo-ple's more quick endeavour for alteration; in fuch an exigent I fee not well, how they could have ftaid to deliberate about any other regiment, than that which already was devifed to their hands; that which in like cafe had been ta-ken, that which was eafieft to be eftablifhed without delay, that which was like-lieft to content the people by reafon of fome kind of fway which it giveth them. When therefore the example of one church was thus, at the firft almoft through a kind of conftraint or neceffity, followed by many, their concurrence in perfua-fion about fome material points belonging to the fame polity is not ftrange. For we are not to marvel greatly, if they which have all done the fame thing, do* Galen. Claf. 1. *eafily embrace the fame opinion as concerning their own doings. Befides, mark* lib. de cujuf- *I befeech you, that which* Galen *in matter of philofophy noteth; for the like* que anim. Peccat notitiâ *falleth out, even in queftions of higher knowledge. It fareth many times with* atqꝫ medela.   *mens* men opinions, as with rumors and reports. That which a credible person telleth, is easily thought probable by such as are well persuaded of him : but if two or three, or four, agree all in the same tale, they judge it then to be out of controversie, and so are many times overtaken for want of due consideration ; either some common cause leading them all into error, or one man's oversight deceiving many thro their too much credulity and easiness of belief. Though ten persons be brought to give testimony in any cause, yet if the knowledge they have of the thing whereunto they come as witnesses, appear to have grown from some one amongst them, and to have spread it self from hand to hand, they all are in force but as one testimony. Nor is it otherwise here, where the daughter churches do speak their mother's dialect ; here, where so many sing one song, by reason that he is the guide of the quire, concerning whose deserved authority, amongst even the gravest divines, we have already spoken at large. Will ye ask what should move Petition to queen Mary, pag. 14. those many learned, to be followers of one man's judgment ; no necessity of argument forcing them thereunto ? your demand is answered by your selves. Loth ye are to think that they whom ye judge to have attained as sound knowledge in all points of doctrine, as any since the apostles time, should mistake in discipline. Such is naturally our affection, that whom in great things we mightily admire, in them we are not persuaded willingly that any thing should be amiss. The reason whereof is, for that as dead flies Ecclef. 10. 1. putrefy the ointment of the apothecary, so a little folly him that is in estimation for wisdom. This in every profession hath too much authorized the judgment of a few. This with Germans hath caused Luther, and with many other churches, Calvin, to prevail in all things. Yet are we not able to define, whether the wisdom of that God (who setteth before us in holy scripture, so many admirable patterns of Vertue, and no one of them, without somewhat noted, wherein they were culpable ; to the end, that to him alone it might always be acknowledged, thou only art holy, thou only art just ;) might not permit those worthy vessels of his glory, to be in some things blemished with the stain of humane frailty, even for this cause, lest we should esteem of any man above that which behoveth.

5. Notwithstanding, as tho ye were able to say a great deal more than hitherto your Their calling for tryal by disputation. books have revealed to the world, earnest challengers ye are of tryal by some publick disputation ; wherein, if the thing ye crave, be no more than only leave to dispute openly about those matters that are in question, the schools in universities (for any thing I know) are open unto you. They have their yearly acts and commencements, besides other disputations, both ordinary and upon occasion, wherein the several parts of our own ecclesiastical discipline are oftentimes offered unto that kind of examination. The learnedst of you have been of late years noted seldom or never absent from thence, at the time of those great assemblies ; and the favour of proposing there in convenient sort whatsoever ye can object (which thing my self have known them to grant of scholastical courtesie unto strangers) neither hath (as I think) nor ever will (I presume) be denied you. If your suit be to have some great extraordinary confluence, in expectation whereof the laws that already are, should sleep and have no power over you ; till in the hearing of thousands, ye all did acknowledge your error, and renounce the further prosecution of your cause ; haply, they whose authority is required unto the satisfying of your demand, do think it both dangerous to admit such concourse of divided minds, and unmeet that laws, which being once solemnly established, are to exact obedience of all men ; and to constrain thereunto, should so far stoop as to hold themselves in suspence from taking any effect upon you till some disputer can persuade you to be obedient. A law is the deed of the whole body politick, whereof if ye judge your selves to be any part, then is the law even your deed also. And were it reason, in things of this quality, to give men audience, pleading for the overthrow of that which their own very deed hath ratified? Laws that have been approved, may be (no man doubteth) again repealed, and to that end also disputed against, by the authors thereof themselves : but this is when the whole doth deliberate what laws each part shall observe, and not when a part refuseth the laws which the whole hath orderly agreed upon. Notwithstanding, forasmuch as the cause we maintain, is (God be thanked) such as needeth not to shun any tryal, might it please them on whose approbation the matter dependeth, to condescend so far unto you in this behalf, I wish heartily that proof were made even by solemn conference in orderly and quiet sort, whether you would your selves be satisfy'd, or else could by satisfying others, draw them to your party. Provided always, first, in as much as ye go about to destroy a thing which is in force, and to draw in that which hath not as yet been received ; to impose on us that which we think

i not

not our felves bound unto, and to overthrow thofe things whereof we are poffeffed; that therefore ye are not to claim in any conference other than the plaintiff's or opponent's part, which muft confift altogether in proof and confirmation of two things; the one, that our orders by you condemned we ought to abolifh; the other, that your's we are bound to accept in the ftead thereof. Secondly, Becaufe the queftions in controverfy between us, are many, if once we defcend unto particulars; that for the eafier and more orderly proceeding therein, the moft general be firft difcuffed, nor any queftion left off, nor in each queftion the profecution of any one argument given over, and another taken in hand, till the iffue whereunto, by replies and anfwers, both parts are come, be collected, read, and acknowledged, as well on the one fide as on the other, to be the plain conclufion which they are grown unto. Thirdly, For avoiding the manifold inconveniences whereunto ordinary and extemporal difputes are fubject; as alfo becaufe, if ye fhould fingly difpute one by one, as every man's own wit did beft ferve, it might be conceived by the reft, that haply fome other would have done more; the chiefeft of you do all agree in this action, that whom ye fhall then chufe for your fpeaker, by him that which is publickly brought into difputation, be acknowledged by all your confents, not to be his allegation, but yours; fuch as ye all are agreed upon, and have required him to deliver in all your names; the true copy whereof being taken by a notary, that reafonable time be allowed for return of anfwer unto you in the like form. Fourthly, Whereas a number of conferences have been had in other caufes with the lefs effectual fuccefs, by reafon of partial and untrue reports, publifhed afterwards unto the world; that to prevent this evil, there be at the firft a folemn declaration made on both parts of their agreement, to have that very book and no other fet abroad, wherein their prefent authorized notaries do write thofe things fully and only; which being written, and there read, are by their own open teftimony acknowledged to be their own. Other circumftances hereunto belonging, whether for the choice of time, place, and language, or for prevention of impertinent and needlefs fpeech, or to any end and purpofe elfe, they may be thought on when occafion ferveth. In this fort, to broach my private conceit for the ordering of a publick action I fhould be loth, (albeit I do it not otherwife than under correction of them, whofe gravity and wifdom ought in fuch cafes to over-rule) but that fo venturous boldnefs, I fee, is a thing now general; and am thereby of good hope, that where all men are licenfed to offend, no man will fhew himfelf a fharp accufer.

No end of contention, without fubmiffion of both parts unto fome definitive fentence.

6. *What fuccefs God may give unto any fuch kind of conference or difputation, we cannot tell: but of this we are right fure, that nature, fcripture, and experience it felf, have all taught the world to feek for the ending of contentions, by fubmitting it felf unto fome judicial and definitive fentence, whereunto neither part that contendeth may under any pretence or colour refufe to ftand. This muft needs be effectual and ftrong; as for other means without this, they feldom prevail. I would therefore know, whether for the ending of thefe irkfome ftrifes, wherein you and your followers do ftand thus formally divided againft the authorized guides of this church, and the reft of the people fubject unto their charge; whether, I fay, ye be content to refer your caufe to any other higher judgment than your own, or elfe intend to perfift, and proceed as ye have begun, till your felves can be perfuaded to condemn your felves? If your determination be this, we can be but forry that ye fhould deferve to be reckoned with. fuch, of whom God himfelf* **Rom. 3. 17.** *pronounceth,* The way of peace they have not known. *Ways of peaceable conclufion there are but thefe two certain, the one a fentence of judicial decifion given by authority thereto appointed within our felves; the other, the like kind of fentence given by a more univerfal authority. The former of which two ways, God himfelf in the law prefcribeth, and his Spirit it was which directed the very firft chriftian churches in the world to ufe the latter. The ordinance of God* **Deut. 17. 8.** *in the law was this.* If there arife a matter too hard for thee in judgment, between blood and blood, between plea, &c. then fhalt thou arife, and go up unto the place which the Lord thy God fhall chufe; and thou fhalt come unto the priefts of the Levites, and unto the judge that fhall be in thofe days, and ask, and they fhall fhew thee the fentence of judgment; and thou fhalt do according to that thing which they of that place which the Lord hath chofen, fhew thee; and thou fhalt obferve to do according to all that they inform thee: according to the law which they fhall teach thee, and according to the judgment which they fhall tell thee.

fhalt

shalt thou do ; thou shalt not decline from the thing which they shall shew thee, to the right hand, nor to the left. And that man that will do presumptuously, not harkning unto the priest (that standeth before the Lord thy God to minister there) or unto the judge, that man shall die, and thou shalt take away evil from *Israel*. *When there grew in the church of Christ a question,* Whether the gentiles be- Acts 15. lieving might be saved, altho they were not circumcised after the manner of *Moses,* nor did observe the rest of those legal rites and ceremonies whereunto the Jews were bound ; *after great dissention and disputation about it, their conclusion in the end was, to have it determined by sentence at* Jerusalem, *which was accordingly done in a council there assembled for the same purpose. Are ye able to alledge any just and sufficient cause, wherefore absolutely ye should not condescend in this controversy, to have your judgments over-ruled by some such definitive sentence ; whether it fall out to be given with, or against you, that so these tedious contentions may cease ? Ye will perhaps make answer, That being persuaded already, as touching the truth of your cause, ye are not to hearken unto any sentence, no not tho angels should define otherwise, as the blessed apostle's own example teacheth : again, That men, yea councils, may err ; and that, unless the judgment given do satisfy your minds, unless it be such as ye can by no further argument oppugn ; in a word, unless you perceive and acknowledge it your selves consonant with God's word ; to stand unto it, not allowing it, were to sin against your own consciences. But consider, I beseech you, first, as touching the apostle, how that wherein he was so resolute and peremptory, our Lord Jesus Christ made manifest unto him, even by intuitive revelation, wherein there was no possibility of error : that which you are persuaded of, ye have it no otherwise than by your own only probable collection ; and therefore such bold asseverations as in him were admirable, should in your mouths but argue rashness. God was not ignorant, that the priests and judges, whose sentence in matters of controversy he ordained should stand, both might and oftentimes would be deceived in their judgment. Howbeit, better it was in the eye of his understanding, that sometime an erroneous sentence definitive should prevail, till the same authority perceiving such oversight, might afterwards correct or reverse it, than that strifes should have respite to grow, and not come speedily unto some end. Neither wish we, that men should do any thing which in their hearts they are persuaded they ought not to do ; but this persuasion ought (we say) to be fully settled in their hearts, that in litigious and controversed causes of such quality, the will of God is to have them to do whatsoever the sentence of judicial and final decision shall determine ; yea, tho it seem in their private opinion to swerve utterly from that which is right ; as, no doubt, many times the sentence amongst the Jews, did seem unto one part or other contending : and yet in this case, God did then allow them to do that which in their private judgment it seemed (yea, and perhaps truly seemed) that the law did disallow. For if God be not the author of confusion but of peace, then can he not be the author of our refusal, but of our contentment to stand unto some definitive sentence ; without which, almost impossible it is, that either we should avoid confusion, or ever hope to avoid peace. To small purpose had the council of* Jerusalem *been assembled, if once their determination being set down, men might afterwards have defended their former opinions. When therefore they had given their definitive sentence, all controversy was at an end. Things were disputed before they came to be determined. Men afterwards were not to dispute any longer, but to obey. The sentence of judgment finished their strife, which their disputes before judgment could not do. This was ground sufficient for any reasonable man's conscience to build the duty of obedience upon, whatsoever his own opinion were as touching the matter before in question. So full of wilfulness and self-liking is our nature, that without some definitive sentence, which being given, may stand, and a necessity of silence on both sides afterward imposed ; small hope there is, that strifes thus far prosecuted, will in short time quietly end. Now it were in vain to ask you, Whether you could be content that the sentence of any court already erected, should be so far authorized, as that among the Jews established by God himself, for the determining of all controversies.* That man which will do presumptuously, not hearkening unto the priest that standeth before the Lord to minister there, nor unto the judge, let him die. *Ye have given us already to understand what your opinion is in part, concerning her sacred majesty's court of high commission ; the nature whereof is the same with that amongst the Jews, albeit the power be not so*

Pref. tract.
de excom.
presbyt.

great. *The other way happily may like you better, because master* Beza *in his last book, save one, written about these matters, professeth himself to be now weary of such combats and encounters, whether by word or writing, insomuch as he findeth that controversies thereby are made but brawls; and therefore wisheth, that in some common lawful assembly of churches, all these strifes may at once be decided. Shall there be then in the mean while no doings? Yes. There are the weightier*

Matth. 23. 23. *matters of the law,* judgment, and mercy, and fidelity. *These things we ought to do; and these things, while we contend about less, we leave undone. Happier are they, whom the Lord, when he cometh, shall find doing in these things, than disputing about doctors, elders, and deacons. Or if there be no remedy, but somewhat needs ye must do, which may tend to the setting forward of your discipline, do that which wise men, who think some statute of the realm more fit to be repealed than to stand in force, are accustomed to do, before they come to parliament, where the place of enacting is; that is to say, spend the time in re-examining more duly your cause, and in more throughly considering of that which ye labour to overthrow. As for the orders which are established, sith equity and reason, the law of nature, God and man, do all favour that which is in being, till orderly judgment of decision be given against it, it is but justice to exact of you, and perverseness in you it should be to deny thereunto your willing obedience. Not that I judge it a thing allowable for men to observe those laws, which in their hearts, they are stedfastly persuaded to be against the law of God; but your persuasion in this case, ye are all bound for the time to suspend; and in otherwise doing, ye offend against God, by troubling his church without any just or necessary cause. Be it that there are some reasons inducing you to think hardly of your laws; are those reasons demonstrative, are they necessary, or but mere probabilities only? An argument necessary and demonstrative is such, as being proposed unto any man, and understood, the mind cannot chuse but inwardly assent. Any one such reason dischargeth, I grant, the conscience, and setteth it at full liberty. For the publick approbation given by the body of the whole church, unto those things which are established, doth make it but probable, that they are good; and therefore unto a necessary proof, that they are not good, it must give place. But if the skilfullest among you can shew, that all the books ye have hitherto written, be able to afford any one argument of this nature, let the instance be given. As for probabilities, What thing was there ever set down so agreeable with sound reason, but some probable shew against it might be made? It is meet, that when publick things are received, and have taken place, general obedience thereunto should cease to be exacted, in case this or that private*

T. C. lib. 3. *person, led with some probable conceit, should make open protestation, I Peter, or*
p. 171. John *disallow them, and pronounce them naught. In which case your answer will be, that concerning the laws of our church, they are not only condemned in the opinion of* a private man, *but of thousands, yea, and even of those amongst which divers are in publick charge and authority. As tho when publick consent of the whole hath established any thing, every man's judgment being thereunto compared, were not private, howsoever his calling be to some kind of publick charge. So that of peace and quietness there is not any way possible, unless the probable voice of every intire society or body politick, over-rule all private of like nature in the same body. Which thing effectually proveth, that God being author of peace, and not of confusion in the church, must needs be author of those mens peaceable resolutions, who concerning these things, have determined with themselves, to think and do as the church they are of decreeth, till they see necessary cause enforcing them to the contrary.*

The matter
contained in
these eight
books.

7. *Nor is mine own intent any other, in these several books of discourse, than to make it appear unto you, that for the ecclesiastical laws of this land, we are led by great reason to observe them, and ye by no necessity bound to impugn them. It is no part of my secret meaning, to draw you hereby into hatred, or to set upon the face of this cause any fairer gloss, than the naked truth doth afford; but my whole endeavour is to resolve the conscience, and to shew, as near as I can, what in this controversy the heart is to think, if it will follow the light of sound and sincere judgment, without either cloud of prejudice, or mist of passionate affection. Wherefore, seeing that laws and ordinances in particular, whether such as we observe, or such as your selves would have established; when the mind doth sift and examine them, it must needs have often recourse to a number of doubts and ques-*

tions,

tions, about the nature, kinds, and qualities of laws in general; whereof, unless it be throughly informed, there will appear no certainty to stay our persuasion upon: I have for that cause set down in the first place, an introduction on both sides needful to be considered; declaring therein, what law is, how different kinds of laws there are, and what force they are of, according unto each kind. This done, because ye suppose the laws, for which ye strive are found in scripture; but those not, for which we strive; and upon this surmise, are drawn to hold it, as the very main pillar of your whole cause, That scripture ought to be the only rule of all our actions; and consequently, that the church-orders which we observe, being not commanded in scripture, are offensive and displeasant unto God; I have spent the second book in sifting of this point, which standeth with you for the first and chiefest principle whereon ye build. Whereunto the next in degree is, That as God will have always a church upon earth, while the world doth continue, and that church stand in need of government; of which government, it behoveth himself to be both the author and teacher; so it cannot stand with duty, that man should ever presume in any wise to change and alter the same; and therefore, that in scripture there must of necessity be found some particular form of ecclesiastical polity, the laws whereof admit not any kind of alteration. The first three books being thus ended, the fourth proceedeth from the general grounds and foundations of your cause, unto your general accusations against us, as having in the orders of our church (for so you pretend) corrupted the right form of church-polity with manifold popish rites and ceremonies, which certain reformed churches have banished from amongst them, and have thereby given us such example as (you think) we ought to follow. This your assertion hath herein drawn us to make search, whether these be just exceptions against the customs of our church, when ye plead, that they are the same which the church of Rome hath, or that they are not the same which some other reformed churches have devised. Of those four books which remain, and are bestowed about the specialities of that cause which lieth in controversy, the first examineth the causes by you alledged, wherefore the publick duties of christian religion, as our prayers, our sacraments, and the rest, should not be ordered in such sort as with us they are; nor that power whereby the persons of men are consecrated unto the ministry, be disposed of in such manner as the laws of this church do allow. The second and third, are concerning the power of jurisdiction; the one, whether laymen, such as your governing elders are, ought in all congregations for ever to be invested with that power? The other, whether bishops may have that power over other pastors, and therewithal, that honour which with us they have? And because, besides the power of order, which all consecrated persons have, and the power of jurisdiction, which neither they all, nor they only have, there is a third power, a power of ecclesiastical dominion, communicable, as we think, unto persons not ecclesiastical, and most fit to be restrained unto the prince our sovereign commander over the whole body politick; the eighth book we have allotted unto this question, and have sifted therein your objections against those preeminences royal which thereunto appertain. Thus have I laid before you the brief of these my travels, and presented under your view, the limbs of that cause litigious between us, the whole intire body whereof, being thus compact, it shall be no troublesome thing for any man to find each particular controversy's resting-place, and the coherence it hath with those things, either on which it dependeth, or which depend on it.

8. The case so standing therefore, my brethren, as it doth; the wisdom of governours ye must not blame, in that they, further also forecasting the manifold strange and dangerous innovations, which are more than likely to follow, if your discipline should take place, have for that cause thought it hitherto a part of their duty to withstand your endeavours that way; the rather, for that they have seen already some small beginnings of the fruits thereof, in them, who concurring with you in judgment about the necessity of that discipline, have adventured without more ado, to separate themselves from the rest of the church, and to put your speculations in execution. These mens hastiness the warier sort of you doth not commend; ye wish they had held themselves longer in, and not so dangerously flown abroad before the feathers of the cause had been grown; their error with merciful terms ye reprove, naming them in great commiseration of mind, your poor brethren. They on the contrary side, more bitterly accuse you as their false brethren; and against you they plead,

How just cause there is to fear the manifold dangerous events, likely to ensue upon this intended reformation, if it did take place.

1 Pet. 2. 2.

plead, *saying, From your breasts it is, that we have sucked those things, which when ye delivered unto us, ye termed that heavenly, sincere and wholesom milk of God's word; howsoever ye now abhor as poison, that which the virtue thereof hath wrought, and brought forth in us. Ye sometime our companions, guides, and* Psal. 55. 23. *familiars, with whom we have had most sweet consultations, are now become our professed adversaries, because we think the statute-congregations in England, to be no true christian churches; because we have severed our selves from them; and because without their leave or licence, that are in civil authority, we have secretly framed our own churches according to the platform of the word of God; for of that point between you and us, there is no controversy. Alas, what would ye have us to do? At such time as ye were content to accept us in the number of your own, your teaching we heard, we read your writings: and tho we would, yet able we are not to forget, with what zeal ye have ever profest, that in the English congregations (for so many of them as be ordered according unto their own laws) the very publick service of God is fraught, as touching matter, with heaps of intolerable pollutions, and as concerning form, borrowed from the shop of antichrist; hateful both ways in the eyes of the most Holy; the kind of their government, by bishops and arch-* Pref. against doctor Bauer. *bishops, antichristian; that discipline which Christ hath essentially tied, that is to say, so united unto his church, that we cannot account it really to be his church which hath not in it the same discipline, that very discipline no less there despised, than in the highest throne of antichrist. All such parts of the word of God, as do any way concern that discipline, no less unsoundly taught and interpreted by all authorized English pastors, than by antichrist's factors themselves: at baptism, crossing; at the supper of the lord, kneeling; at both, a number of other the most notorious badges of antichristian recognizance usual. Being moved with these and the like your effectual discourses, whereunto we gave most attentive ear, till they entred, even into our souls, and were as fire within our bosoms; we thought we might hereof be bold to conclude, that sith no such antichristian synagogue may be accounted a true church of Christ, ye by accusing all congregations, ordered according to the laws of England as antichristian, did mean to condemn those congregations, as not being any of them worthy the name of a true christian church. Ye tell us now, it is not your meaning. But what meant your often threatnings of them, who professing themselves the inhabitants of mount Sion, were too loth to depart wholly as they should out of Babylon? whereat our hearts being fearfully troubled, we durst not, we durst not continue longer so near her confines, lest her plagues might suddenly overtake us, before we did cease to be partakers with her sins; for so we could not chuse but acknowledge with grief, that we were, when they doing evil, we by our presence in their assemblies seemed to like thereof; or at leastwise, not so earnestly to dislike, as became men heartily zealous of God's glory. For adventuring to erect the discipline of Christ, without the leave of the christian magistrate, haply ye may condemn us as fools, in that we hazard thereby our estates and persons further than you, which are that way more wise, think necessary: but of any offence or sin therein committed against God, with what conscience can you accuse us, when your own positions are, that the things we observe, should every of them be dearer unto us, than ten thousand lives; that they are the peremptory commandments of God; that no mortal man can dispense with them; and that the magistrate grievously sinneth, in not constraining thereunto? Will ye blame any man for doing that of his own accord, which all men should be compelled to do, that are not willing of themselves? When God commandeth, shall we answer, that we will obey, if so be Cæsar will grant us leave? Is discipline an ecclesiastical matter, or a civil? If an ecclesiastical, it must of necessity belong to the duty of the minister; and the minister (ye say) holdeth all his authority of doing whatsoever belongeth unto the spiritual charge of the house of God, even immediately from God himself, without dependency upon any magistrate. Whereupon it followeth, as we suppose, that the hearts of the people being willing to be under the scepter of Christ, the minister of God, into whose hands the Lord himself hath put that scepter, is without all excuse, if thereby he guide them not. Nor do we find, that hitherto greatly ye have disliked those churches abroad, where the people with direction of their godly ministers, have even against the will of the magistrate, brought in either the doctrine or discipline of Jesus Christ. For which cause we must now think the very same thing of you, which our Saviour did sometime utter concerning false-hearted* Matth. 23, 3. *scribes and pharisees,* They say, and do not: *Thus the foolish barrowist deriveth his schism by way of conclusion, as to him it seemeth, directly and plainly out*

of

of your principles. Him therefore we leave to be satisfied by you, from whom he hath sprung. And if such, by your own acknowledgment, be persons dangerous, altho as yet the alterations which they have made, are of small and tender growth; the changes likely to ensue, throughout all states and vocations within this land, in case your desire should take place, must be thought upon. First, concerning the supream power of the highest, they are no small prerogatives, which now thereunto belonging, the form of your discipline will constrain it to resign; as in the last book of this treatise we have shewed at large. Again, it may justly be feared, whether our English nobility, when the matter came in tryal, would contentedly suffer themselves to be always at the call, and to stand to the sentence of a number of mean persons, assisted with the presence of their poor teacher; a man (sometime it hapneth) tho better able to speak, yet little or no whit apter to judg, than the rest: from whom, be their dealings never so absurd (unless it be by way of complaint to a synod) no appeal may be made unto any one of higher power; in as much as the order of your discipline admitteth no standing inequality of courts, no spiritual judg to have any ordinary superior on earth, but as many supremacies as there are parishes and several congregations. Neither is it altogether without cause, that so many do fear the overthrow of all learning, as a threatened sequel of this your intended discipline. For if the world's preservation depend upon the multitude of Sap. 6. 14. *the wise; and of that sort, the number hereafter be not likely to wax over-great, when (that therewith the son of* Syrach *professeth himself at the heart grieved)* Ecclus. 26. 29. *men of understanding are already so little set by; how should their minds whom the love of so precious a jewel filleth with secret jealousy, even in regard of the least things which may any way hinder the flourishing estate thereof, chuse but misdoubt lest this discipline which always you match with divine doctrine, as her natural and true sister, be found unto all kinds of knowledge a step-mother; seeing that the greatest worldly hopes, which are proposed unto the chiefest kind of learning, ye seek utterly to extirpate as weeds; and have grounded your platform on such propositions, as do after a sort undermine those most renowned habitations, where, thro the goodness of almighty God, all commendable arts and sciences are with exceeding great industry hitherto (and so may they for ever continue!) studied, proceeded in, and profest? To charge you, as purposely bent to the overthrow of that, wherein so many of you have attained no small perfection, were injurious. Only therefore, I wish, that your selves did well consider how opposite certain of your positions are unto the state of collegiate societies, wherein the two universities consist. Those degrees which their statutes bind them to take are by your laws taken away; your selves who have sought them, ye so excuse; as that ye would have men to think ye judge them not allowable, but tolerable only, and to be born with, for some help which ye find in them unto the furtherance of your purposes, till the corrupt estate of the church may be better reformed. Your laws forbidding ecclesiastical persons utterly the exercise of civil power, must needs deprive the heads and masters in the same colleges of all such authority as now they exercise, either at home, by punishing the faults of those, who not as children to their parents by the law of nature, but altogether by civil authority, are subject unto them; or abroad, by keeping courts amongst their tenants. Your laws making permanent inequality amongst ministers a thing repugnant to the word of God, enforce those colleges, the seniors whereof are all, or any part of them, ministers under the government of a master in the same vocation, to chuse as oft as they meet together a new president. For if so ye judge it necessary to do in synods, for the avoiding of permanent inequality amongst ministers, the same cause must needs, even in these collegiate assemblies, enforce the like: except peradventure ye mean to avoid all such absurdities, by dissolving those corporations, and by bringing the universities unto the form of the school of* Geneva. *Which thing men the rather are inclined to look for, inasmuch as the ministry, whereinto their founders, with singular providence, have by the same statutes appointed them necessarily to* Humb. motion to the L. p. 50. *enter at a certain time, your laws bind them much more necessarily to forbear, till some parish abroad call for them. Your opinion concerning the law civil is, that the knowledge thereof might be spared, as a thing which this land doth not need. Professors in that kind being few, ye are the bolder to spurn at them, and not to dissemble your minds, as concerning their removal: in whose studies, altho my self have not been much conversant, nevertheless, exceeding great cause I see there is to wish, that thereunto more incouragement were given, as well for the singular treasures of wisdom therein contained, as also for the great use*

we

we have thereof, both in decifion of certain kinds of caufes arifing daily within our-felves, and efpecially for commerce with nations abroad, whereunto that know-ledge is moft requifite. The reafons wherewith ye would perfuade, that fcripture is the only rule to frame all our actions by, are in every refpect as effectual for proof, that the fame is the only law whereby to determine all our civil controverfies. And then what doth let, but that as thofe men may have their defire, who frankly broach it already, that the work of reformation will never be perfect, till the law of Jefus Chrift be received alone ; fo pleaders and counfellors may bring their books

Acts 19. 19.

of the common law, and beftow them as the ftudents of curious and needlefs arts did theirs in the apoftles time ? I leave them to fcan, how far thofe words of yours

Humb. moti-on, page 74.

may reach, wherein ye declare, that whereas now many houfes lie wafte thro inordi-nate fuits of law, this one thing will fhew the excellency of difcipline for the wealth of the realm, and quiet of fubjects ; that the church is to cenfure fuch a party, who is apparently troublefome and contentious, and without REASONABLE CAUSE, upon a meer will and ftomach, doth vex and moleft his brother, and trouble the country. *For mine own part, I do not fee but that it might very well agree with your principles, if your difcipline were fully planted, even to fend out your writs of* Surceafe *unto all courts of* England *befides, for the moft things handled in them.*

Counterp. page 108.

A great deal further I might proceed, and defcend lower ; but forafmuch as againft all thefe and the like difficulties, your anfwer is, that we ought to fearch what things are confonant to God's will, not which be moft for our own eafe ; and there-fore that your difcipline being (for fuch is your error) the abfolute commandment of almighty God, it muft be received, altho the world by receiving it, fhould be clean turned upfide down : Herein lieth the greateft danger of all. For whereas the name of divine authority is ufed to countenance thefe things, which are not the commandments of God, but your own erroneous collections ; on him ye muft father whatfoever ye fhall afterwards be led, either to do in withftanding the adverfaries of your caufe, or to think in maintenance of your doings. And what this may be, God doth know. In fuch kinds of error, the mind once imagining it felf to feek the execution of God's will, laboureth forthwith to remove both things and perfons, which any way hinder it from taking place ; and in fuch cafes, if any ftrange or new thing feem requifite to be done, a ftrange and new opinion, concerning the law-fulnefs thereof, is withal received and broached under countenance of divine au-thority. One example herein may ferve for many, to fhew, that falfe opinions touching the will of God to have things done, are wont to bring forth mighty and violent practices againft the hindrances of them ; and thofe practices new opinions more pernicious than the firft, yea, moft extreamly fometimes oppofite to that which the firft did feem to intend, where the people took upon them the reformation of the church, by cafting out popifh fuperftition ; they having received from their paftors a general

Mat. 15. 13.

inftruction, that whatfoever the heavenly father hath not planted, muft be rooted out ; proceeded in fome foreign places fo far, that down went oratories, and the very tem-ples of God themfelves. For as they chanced to take the compafs of their commiffion ftricter or larger, fo their dealings were accordingly more or lefs moderate. A-mongft others, there fprang up prefently one kind of men, with whofe zeal and for-wardnefs the reft being compared, were thought to be marvellous cold and dull. Thefe grounding themfelves on rules more general ; that whatfoever the law of Chrift commandeth not, thereof antichrift is the author ; and that whatfoever antichrift, or his adherents did in the world, the true profeffors of Chrift are to undo ; found out many things more than others had done, the extirpation whereof was in their conceit, as necejary as of any thing before removed. Hereupon they fecretly made their dole-

Guy de Bres cont. l' erreur des anabapti-ftes, page 4.

ful complaints every where as they went, that albeit the world did begin to profefs fome diflike of that which was evil in the kingdom of darknefs, yet fruits worthy of a true repentance were not feen ; and that if Men did repent as they ought, they muft endeavour to purge the truth of all manner of evil, to the end there might fol-low a new world afterwards, wherein righteoufnefs only fhould dwell. Private repentance, they faid, muft appear by every man's fafhioning his own life, contrary un-to the cuftom and orders of this prefent world, both in greater things and in lefs. To this purpofe, they had always in their mouths thofe greater things, charity, faith, the true fear of God, the crofs, the mortification of the flefh. All their exhortati-ons were to fet light of the things in this world, to account riches and honours vanity, and in token thereof, not only to feek neither, but if men were poffeffors of both, even to caft away the one, and refign the other, that all men might fee their

Page 5.

unfeigned converfion unto Chrift. They were follicitors of men to fafts, to often medi-

tations

tations of heavenly things, and as it were conferences in secret with God by prayers, page 16.
not framed according to the frozen manner of the world, but expressing such fervent page 118,119.
desire as might even force God to hearken unto them. Where they found men in diet,
attire, furniture of house, or any other way, observers of civility and decent order,
such they reproved as being carnally and earthly-minded. Every word otherwise page 116,126.
than severely and sadly uttered, seemed to pierce like a sword thorow them. If any
man were pleasant, their manner was presently with sighs to repeat those words of page 124.
our Saviour Christ, Wo be to you which now laugh, for ye shall lament. *So great* Luke 6. 11.
was their delight to be always in trouble, that such as did quietly lead their lives,
they judged of all other men to be in most dangerous case. They so much affected to page 117.
cross the ordinary custom in every thing, that when other mens use was to put on better
attire, they would be sure to shew themselves openly abroad in worse. The ordinary
names of the days in the week, they thought it a kind of profaneness to use, and
therefore accustomed themselves to make no other distinction, than by numbers, the
first, second, third day. From this they proceeded unto publick reformation, first
ecclesiastical, and then civil. Touching the former, they boldly avouched, that them- page 40.
selves only had the truth, which thing upon peril of their lives they would
at all times defend; and that since the apostles lived, the same was never be-
fore in all points sincerely taught. Wherefore, that things might again be
brought to that antient integrity which Jesus Christ by his word requireth, they
began to controul the ministers of the gospel, for attributing so much force and
virtue unto the scriptures of God read; whereas the truth was, that when the
word is said to engender faith in the heart, and to convert the soul of man, or to
work any such spiritual divine effect, these speeches are not thereunto applicable
as it is read or preached, but as it is ingrafted in us by the power of the Holy
Ghost, opening the eyes of our understanding, and so revealing the mysteries of
God; according to that which Jeremy *promised before should be, saying,* I will put Jer. 31. 34.
my law in their inward parts, and I will write it in their hearts. *The book of*
God they notwithstanding for the most part so admired, that other disputation page 25.
against their opinions than only by allegation of scripture they would not hear;
besides it, they thought no other writings in the world should be studied; inso- page 27.
much, as one of their great prophets exhorting them to cast away all respects
unto humane writings, so far to his motion they condescended, that as many as had
any books, save the holy bible in their custody, they brought and set them publickly
on fire. When they and their bibles were alone together, what strange fantastical
opinion soever at any time entred into their heads, their use was to think the Spirit
taught it them. Their phrensies concerning our Saviour's incarnation, the state of
souls departed, and such like, are things needless to be rehearsed. And for as
much as they were of the same suit with those of whom the apostle speaketh, saying,
They are still learning, but never attain to the knowledge of truth, *it was no mar-* 1 Tim. 3. 7.
vel to see them every day broach some new thing, not heard of before. Which restless
levity they did interpret to be their growing to spiritual perfection, and a pro-
ceeding from faith to faith. The differences amongst them grew by this mean in a page 65.
manner infinite; so that scarcely was there found any one of them, the forge of
whose brain was not possest with some special mystery. Whereupon altho their mutual page 66.
contentions were most fiercely prosecuted amongst themselves, yet when they came to page 135.
defend the cause common to them all against the adversaries of their faction, they
had ways to lick one another whole, the founder in his own persuasion excusing
THE DEAR BRETHREN, *which were not so far enlightned, and professing* page 25.
a charitable hope of the mercy of God towards them, notwithstanding their swer-
ving from him in some things. Their own ministers they highly magnified, as men page 71.
whose vocation was from God; the rest their manner was to term disdainfully
scribes and pharisees, to account their calling an human creature, and to detain the page 124.
people, as much as might be, from hearing them. As touching sacraments, baptism
administred in the church of Rome, *they judged to be but an execrable mockery, and* page 764.
no baptism; both because the ministers thereof in the papacy are wicked idolaters,
leud persons, thieves and murderers, cursed creatures, ignorant beasts; and also for
that to baptize, is a proper action belonging unto none but the church of Christ,
whereas Rome is antichrist's synagogue. The custom of using god-fathers and god-mothers page 748.
at christnings, they scorned. Baptism of infants, altho confest by themselves to page 512.
have been continued even sithence the very apostles own times, yet they altogether page 518.
condemned; partly, because sundry errors are of no less antiquity; and partly,

k
for

Page 711. *for that there is no commandment in the gospel of Christ, which saith,* baptize infants ; *but he contrariwise in saying,* Go preach and baptize, *doth appoint, that*
Page 716. *the minister of baptism shall in that action first administer doctrine, and then baptism ;*
Page 688. *as also in saying,* Whosoever doth believe and is baptized, *he appointeth, that the*
party to whom baptism is administred, shall first believe, and then be baptized ;
to the end, that believing may go before this sacrament in the receiver, no other-
wise than preaching in the giver ; sith equally in both, the law of Christ declareth,
not only what things are required, but also in what order they are required. The
Page 58. *eucharist they received (pretending our Lord and Saviour's example) after supper.*
And for avoiding all those impieties which have been grounded upon the mystical
Page 112. *words of Christ,* This is my body, this is my blood ; *they thought it not safe to men-*
tion either body or blood in that sacrament, but rather to abrogate both, and to
use no words but these, Take, eat, declare the death of our Lord ; Drink, shew
forth our Lord's death. *In rites and ceremonies their profession was hatred of all*
conformity with the church of Rome : for which cause, they would rather endure
any torment, than observe the solemn festivals which others did, in as much as
antichrist (they said) was the first inventer of them. The pretended end of their
civil reformation was, That Christ might have dominion over all ; that all crowns
and scepters might be thrown down at his feet ; that no other might reign over chris-
tian men, but he ; no regiment keep them in awe, but his discipline ; amongst them
no sword at all be carried besides his, the sword of spiritual excommunication. For
Page 841. *this cause they laboured with all their might, in over-turning the seats of magis-*
tracy, because Christ hath said, Kings of nations ; *in abolishing the execution*
Page 855. *of justice, because Christ hath said,* Resist not evil ; *in forbidding oaths, the*
Page 849. *necessary means of judicial tryal, because Christ hath said,* Swear not at all :
finally, in bringing in community of goods, because Christ by his apostles hath
given the world such example, to the end that men might excel one another,
not in wealth, the pillar of secular authority, but in virtue. These men at the
Page 40. *first were only pitied in their error, and not much withstood by any ; the great hu-*
mility, zeal, and devotion which appeared to be in them, was in all mens opi-
nion a pledge of their harmless meaning. The hardest that men of sound under-
Lactant. de *standing conceived of them, was but this,* O quam honesta voluntate miseri errant ?
justit. lib. 5. With how good a meaning these poor souls do evil ? *Luther made request unto*
cap. 19. *Frederick duke of* Saxony, *that within his dominion they might be favourably dealt*
Page 6. *with and spared, for that (their error exempted) they seemed otherwise right good*
men. By means of which merciful toleration they gathered strength, much more
than was safe for the state of the commonwealth wherein they lived. They had
their secret corner-meetings and assemblies in the night, the people flocked unto
Page 420. *them by thousands. The means whereby they both allured and retained so great*
multitudes, were most effectual ; first, a wonderful shew of zeal towards God,
Page 55. *wherewith they seemed to be even wrapt in every thing they spake : secondly,*
an hatred of sin, and a singular love of integrity, which men did think to be
much more than ordinary in them, by reason of the custom which they had to fill
the ears of the people with invectives against their authorized guides, as well
spiritual as civil : thirdly, the bountiful relief wherewith they eased the broken
estate of such needy creatures, as were in that respect the more apt to be drawn
away : fourthly, a tender compassion which they were thought to take upon the
miseries of the common sort, over whose heads their manner was even to pour
down showers of tears in complaining, that no respect was had unto them, that
Page 6. *their goods were devoured by wicked cormorants, their persons had in contempt,*
Page 7. *all liberty, both temporal and spiritual, taken from them ; that it was high time for God*
now to hear their groans, and to send them deliverance. Lastly, a cunning slight
which they had to stroke and smooth up the minds of their followers, as well by
appropriating unto them all the favourable titles, the good words, and the gra-
cious promises in scripture ; as also by casting the contrary always on the heads of
such as were severed from that retinue. Whereupon, the peoples common accla-
mation unto such deceivers was ; These are verily the men of God, these are his
Page 7. true and sincere prophets. *If any such prophet or man of God did suffer by order of*
law condign and deserved punishment, were it for felony, rebellion, murder, or
what else, the people (so strangely were their hearts inchanted) as tho blessed
Page 17. *saint* Stephen *had been again martyred, did lament, that God took away his most*
dear servants from them. In all these things being fully persuaded, that what

they

*they did, it was obedience to the will of God, and that all men should do the
like; there remained, after speculation, practice, whereby the whole world thereunto (if it were possible) might be framed. This they saw could not be done,* Page 6.
*but with mighty opposition and resistance; against which, to strengthen themselves,
they secretly entred into a league of association. And peradventure considering,
that altho they were many, yet long wars in time would in time waste them out;
they began to think, whether it might not be, that God would have them do for
their speedy and mighty encrease, the same which sometime God's own chosen people,
the people of Israel did. Glad and fain they were to have it so; which very desire was it self apt to breed both an opinion of possibility, and a willingness to
gather arguments of likelihood, that so God himself would have it. Nothing more
clear unto their seeming, than that a new Jerusalem being often spoken of in
scripture, they undoubtedly were themselves that new Jerusalem, and the old
did by way of a certain figurative resemblance signify what they should both be,
and do. Here they drew in a sea of matter, by amplifying all things unto their
own company, which are any where spoken concerning divine favours and benefits
bestowed upon the old common-wealth of Israel; concluding, that as Israel was delivered out of Egypt, so they spiritually out of Egypt of this world's servile
thraldom unto sin and superstition: as Israel was to root out the idolatrous nations, and to plant instead of them, a people which feared God; so the same
Lord's good will and pleasure was now, that these new Israelites should under the
conduct of other Joshuas, Sampsons, and Gideons, perform a work no less miraculous in casting out violently the wicked from the earth, and establishing the
kingdom of Christ with perfect liberty: and therefore, as the cause why the children of Israel took unto one man many wives, might be, lest the casualties of
war should any way hinder the promise of God concerning their multitude, from
taking effect in them; so it was not unlike that, for the necessary propagation of
Christ's kingdom under the gospel, the Lord was content to allow as much. Now
whatsoever they did in such sort collect out of scripture, when they came to justify or persuade it unto others, all was the heavenly Father's appointment, his commandment, his will and charge. Which thing is the very point, in regard
whereof I have gather'd this declaration. For my purpose herein is to shew, that
when the minds of men are once erroneously persuaded, that it is the will of God
to have those things done which they fancy; then opinions are as thorns in their
sides, never suffering them to take rest, till they have brought their speculations
into practice. The lets and impediments of which practice, their restless desire
and study to remove, leadeth them every day forth by the hand into other more
dangerous opinions, sometimes quite and clean contrary to their first pretended
meanings. So as what will grow out of such errors as go masked under the
cloak of divine authority, impossible it is, that ever the wit of man should imagine, till time have brought forth the fruits of them: for which cause, it behoveth
wisdom to fear the sequels thereof, even beyond all apparent cause of fear.
These men, in whose mouths at the first, sounded nothing but only mortification of
the flesh, were come at length, to think they might lawfully have their six or seven
wives apiece. They which at the first thought judgment and justice it self to be
merciless cruelty; accounted, at the length, their own hands sanctified with being
imbrued in christian blood. They who at the first were wont to beat down all
dominion, and to urge against poor constables, kings of nations; had, at the length,
both consuls and kings of their own erection amongst themselves. Finally, They
which could not brook at the first, that any man should seek, no not by law, the
recovery of goods injuriously taken or with-held from him; were grown at the last
to think they could not offer unto God more acceptable sacrifice, than by turning
their adversaries clean out of house and home, and by enriching themselves with
all kind of spoil and pillage. Which thing being laid to their charge, they had in* Page 42.
*a readiness their answer, That now the time was come, when according to our
Saviour's promise, the meek ones must inherit the earth; and that their title* Matth. 5. 5.
*hereunto was the same which the righteous Israelites had unto the goods of the
wicked Egyptians. Wherefore sith the world hath had in these men so fresh* Exod. 11. 2.
*experience, how dangerous such active errors are, it must not offend you, tho
touching the sequel of your present mis-persuasions, much more be doubted than your
own intents and purposes do haply aim at. And yet your words already are* Mart. in his
third libel,
page 18,
somewhat, when ye affirm, that your pastors, doctors, elders, and deacons, ought

to be in this church of England, whether her majesty and our state will or no; when for the animating of your confederates, ye publish the musters which ye have made of your own bands, and proclaim them to amount to I know not how many thousands; when ye threaten, that sith neither your suits to the parliament, nor supplications to our convocation-house; neither your defences by writing, nor challenges of disputation in behalf of that cause, are able to prevail, we must blame our selves, if to bring in discipline, some such means hereafter be used, as shall cause all our hearts to ake. That things doubtful are to be construed in the better part, is a principle not safe to be followed in matters concerning the publick state of a common-weal. But howsoever these and the like speeches be accounted as arrows idly shot at random, without either eye had to any mark, or regard to their lighting-place; hath not your longing desire for the practice of your discipline, brought the matter already unto this demurrer amongst you; whether the people and their godly pastors, that way affected, ought not to make separation from the rest, and to begin the exercise of discipline, without the licence of civil powers, which licence they have sought for, and are not heard? Upon which question, as ye have now divided your selves, the warier sort of you taking the one part, and the forwarder in zeal, the other; so in case these earnest ones should prevail, what other sequel can any wise man imagine but this, that having first resolved that attempts for discipline without superiors are lawful, it will follow in the next place to be disputed, what may be attempted against superiors, which will not have the scepter of that discipline to rule over them? Yea, even by you which have staid your selves from running headlong with the other sort, somewhat notwithstanding there hath been done without the leave or liking of your lawful superiors, for the exercise of a part of your discipline amongst the clergy thereunto addicted. And lest examination of principal parties therein should bring those things to light, which might hinder and let your proceedings; behold, for a bar against that impediment, one opinion ye have newly added unto the rest, even upon this occasion, an opinion to exempt you from taking oaths which may turn to the molestation of your brethren in that cause. The next neighbour opinion whereunto, when occasion requireth, may follow for dispensation with oaths already taken, if they afterwards be found to import a necessity of detecting ought which may bring such good men into trouble or damage, whatsoever the cause be. O merciful God, what man's wit is there able to sound the depth of those dangerous and fearful evils, whereunto our weak and impotent nature is inclinable to sink it self, rather than to shew an acknowledgment of error in that which once we have unadvisedly taken upon us to defend, against the stream, as it were, of a contrary publick resolution! Wherefore, if we any thing respect their error, who being persuaded, even as ye are, have gone further upon that persuasion than ye allow; if we regard the present state of the highest governour placed over us, if the quality and disposition of our nobles, if the orders and laws of our famous universities, if the profession of the civil, or the practice of the common law amongst us, if the mischiefs whereinto, even before our eyes, so many others have fain headlong from no less plausible and fair beginnings than yours are: there is in every of these considerations most just cause to fear, lest our hastiness to imbrace a thing of so perillous consequence, should cause posterity to feel those evils, which as yet are more easy for us to prevent, than they would be for them to remedy.

9. The best and safest way for you therefore, my dear brethren, is, to call your deeds past to a new reckoning, to re-examine the cause ye have taken in hand, and to try it even point by point, argument by argument, with all the diligent exactness ye can, to lay aside the gall of that bitterness wherein your minds have hitherto over-abounded, and with meekness to search the truth. Think ye are men; deem it not impossible for you to err; sift impartially your own hearts, whether it be force of reason, or vehemency of affection, which hath bred, and still doth feed these opinions in you. If truth do any where manifest it self, seek not to smother it with glozing delusion, acknowledge the greatness thereof, and think it your best victory, when the same doth prevail over you.

That ye have been earnest in speaking or writing again and again the contrary way, should be no blemish or discredit at all unto you. Amongst so many, so huge volumes, as the infinite pains of saint Augustine have brought forth, what one hath *gotten him greater love, commendation, and honour, than the book wherein he carefully collecteth his own over-sights, and sincerely condemneth them? Many speeches there are of* Job's, *whereby his wisdom and other vertues may appear; but the glory of an ingenious mind he hath purchased by these words only,* Behold, Job 39 - 34, I will lay mine hand on my mouth; I have spoken once, yet will I not therefore maintain argument; yea, twice, howbeit for that cause further I will not proceed. *Far more comfort it were for us (so small is the joy we take in these strifes) to labour under the same yoke, as men that look for the same eternal reward of their labours, to be enjoined with you in bands of indissoluble love and amity, to live as if our persons being many, our souls were but one, rather than in such dismembred sort, to spend our few and wretched days in a tedious prosecuting of wearisome contentions; the end whereof, if they have not some speedy end, will be heavy, even on both sides. Brought already we are, even to that estate which* Gregory Nazianzen *mournfully describeth, saying,* My mind leadeth me *(sith there is* Greg. Naz. in *no other remedy)* to fly and convoy my self into some corner out of sight, where Apol. I may scape from this cloudy tempest of maliciousness, whereby all parts are entred into a deadly war amongst themselves, and that little remnant of love which was, is now consumed to nothing. The only godliness we glory in, is to find out somewhat whereby we may judge others to be ungodly. Each others faults we observe, as matter of exprobation, and not of grief. By these means we are grown hateful in the eyes of the heathens themselves, and (which woundeth us the more deeply) able we are not to deny, but that we have deserved their hatred: with the better sort of our own our fame and credit is clean lost. The less we are to marvel, if they judge vilely of us, who altho we did well, would hardly allow thereof. On our backs they also build that are lewd, and what we object one against another, the same they use, to the utter scorn and disgrace of us all. This we have gained by our mutual home-dissentions: this we are worthily rewarded with, which are more forward to strive, than becometh men of vertuous and mild disposition. *But our trust in the Almighty is, that with us contentions are now at the highest float, and that the day will come (for what cause of despair is there?) when the passions of former enmity being allayed, we shall with ten times redoubled tokens of our unfeignedly reconciled love, shew our selves each towards other the same which* Joseph, *and the brethren of* Joseph *were at the time of their interview in Ægypt. Our comfortable expectation and most thirsty desire whereof, what man soever amongst you shall any way help to satisfy, (as we truly hope, there is no one amongst you, but some way or other will)* the blessings of the God of peace, both in this world, and in the world to come, be upon him more than the stars of the firmament in number.

What

What things are handled in the following

B O O K S.

B O O K I.

Concerning laws in general.

B O O K II.

Of the use of divine law contained in scripture ; whether that be the only law which ought to serve for our direction in all things, without exception ?

B O O K III.

Of laws concerning ecclesiastical polity : whether the form thereof be in scripture so set down, that no addition or change is lawful ?

B O O K IV.

Of general exceptions taken against the laws of our polity, as being popish, and banished out of certain reformed churches.

B O O K V.

Of our laws which concern the publick religious duties of the church, and the manner of bestowing that power of order, which enableth men in sundry degrees and callings to execute the same.

BOOK

BOOK VI.

BOOK VII.

BOOK VIII.

O F

OF THE

LAWS

OF

Ecclesiastical Polity.

BOOK I.

Concerning laws, and their several kinds in general.

The matter contained in this first book.

HE that goeth about to persuade a multitude, that they are not so well *The cause of writing this general dis-* governed as they ought to be, shall never want attentive and favou- *course.* rable hearers ; because they know the manifold defects whereunto every kind of regiment is subject : but the secret lets and difficulties, which in publick proceedings are innumerable and inevitable, they have not ordinarily the judgment to consider. And because such as openly reprove supposed disorders of state, are taken for principal friends to the common benefit of all, and for men that carry singular freedom of mind ; under this fair and plausible colour, whatsoever they utter, passeth for good and current. That which wanteth in the weight of their speech, is supplied by the aptness of mens minds to accept and believe it. Whereas on the other side, if we maintain things that are established, we have not only to strive with a number of

B   heavy

heavy prejudices, deeply rooted in the hearts of men, who think that herein we serve the time, and speak in favour of the present state, because thereby we either hold or seek preferment ; but also to bear such exceptions as minds, so averted before-hand, usually take against that which they are loth should be poured into them. Albeit therefore, much of that we are to speak in this present cause, may seem to a number perhaps tedious, perhaps obscure, dark and intricate, (for many talk of the truth, which never sounded the depth from whence it springeth ; and therefore when they are led thereunto, they are soon weary, as men drawn from those beaten paths wherewith they have been inured ;) yet this may not so far prevail, as to cut off that which the matter it self requireth, howsoever the nice humour of some be therewith pleased, or no. They unto whom we shall seem tedious, are in no wise injured by us, because it is in their own hands to spare that labour which they are not willing to endure. And if any complain of obscurity, they must, consider, that in these matters it cometh no otherwise to pass, than in sundry the works both of art, and also of nature, where that which hath greatest force in the very things we see, is notwithstanding it self oftentimes not seen. The statelines of houses, the goodliness of trees, when we behold them, delighteth the eye ; but that foundation which beareth up the one, that root which ministreth unto the other nourishment and life, is in the bosom of the earth concealed ; and if there be occasion at any time to search into it, such labour is then more necessary than pleasant, both to them which undertake it, and for the lookers on. In like manner, the use and benefit of good laws, all that live under them may enjoy with delight and comfort, albeit the grounds and first original causes from whence they have sprung, be unknown, as to the greatest part of men they are. But when they who withdraw their obedience, pretend, that the laws which they should obey, are corrupt and vicious ; for better examination of their quality, it behoveth the very foundation and root, the highest well-spring and fountain of them to be discovered. Which because we are not oftentimes accustomed to do, when we do do it, the pains we take are more needful a great deal than acceptable, and the matters which we handle, seem by reason of newness (till the mind grow better acquainted with them) dark, intricate and unfamiliar. For as much help whereof, as may be in this case, I have endeavoured throughout the body of this whole discourse, that every former part might give strength unto all that follow, and every latter bring some light unto all before. So that if the judgments of men do, but hold themselves in suspence, as touching these first more general meditations, till in order they have perused the rest that ensue ; what may seem dark at the first, will afterwards be found more plain, even as the latter particular decisions will appear, I doubt not, more strong, when the other have been read before. The laws of the church, whereby for so many ages together we have been guided in the exercise of christian religion, and the service of the true God, our rites, customs, and orders of ecclesiastical government, are called in question. We are accused as men that will not have Christ Jesus to rule over them ; but have wilfully cast his statutes behind their backs, hating to be reformed and made subject unto the scepter of his discipline. Behold therefore, we offer the laws whereby we live unto the general tryal and judgment of the whole world ; heartily beseeching almighty God, whom we desire to serve according to his own will, that both we and others (all kind of partial affection being laid clean aside) may have eyes to see, and hearts to embrace the things that in his sight are most acceptable. And because the point, about which we strive, is the quality of our laws, our first entrance hereinto cannot better be made, than with consideration of the nature of law in general, and of that law which giveth life unto all the rest which are commendable, just and good, namely, the law whereby the Eternal himself doth work. Proceeding from hence to the law, first of nature, then of scripture, we shall have the easier access unto those things which come after to be debated, concerning the particular cause and question which we have in hand.

Of that law which God from before the beginning hath set for himself to do all things by.   2. All things that are, have some operation not violent or casual : neither doth any thing ever begin to exercise the same, without some fore-conceived end for which it worketh. And the end which it worketh for, is not obtained, unless the work be also fit to obtain it by ; for unto every end, every operation will not serve. That which doth assign unto each thing the kind, that which doth moderate the force and power, that which doth appoint the form and measure of working, the same we term a *law.* So that no certain end could ever be attained, unless the actions whereby it is attained, were regular ; that is to say, made suitable, fit, and correspondent unto their end, by some canon, rule or law. Which thing doth first take place in the works, even of God himself. All things therefore do work after a sort according to law ; all other

things

things according to a law, whereof some superior, unto whom they are subject, is author; only the works and operations of God, have him both for their worker, and for the law whereby they are wrought. The being of God is a kind of law to his working; for that perfection which God is, giveth perfection to that he doth. Those natural, necessary, and internal operations of God, the *generation* of the Son, the *proceeding* of the Spirit, are without the compass of my present intent; which is to touch only such operations as have their beginning and being by a voluntary purpose, wherewith God hath eternally decreed, when, and how they should be; which eternal decree is that we term an *eternal law.* Dangerous it were for the feeble brain of man, to wade far into the doings of the most High; whom altho to know be life, and joy to make mention of his name; yet our foundest knowledge is, to know that we know him not as indeed he is, neither can know him: and our safest eloquence concerning him, is our silence, when we confess without confession, that his glory is inexplicable, his greatness above our capacity and reach. He is above, and we upon earth; therefore it behoveth our words to be wary and few. Our God is one, or rather very oneness, and mere unity, having nothing but it self in it self, and not consisting (as all things do besides God) of many things; in which essential unity of God, a trinity-personal nevertheless subsisteth, after a manner far exceeding the possibility of man's conceit. The works which outwardly are of God, they are in such sort of him being one, that each person hath in them somewhat peculiar and proper: for being three, and they all subsisting in the essence of one deity, from the Father, by the Son, thro the Spirit, all things are. That which the Son doth hear of the Father, and which the Spirit doth receive of the Father and the Son, the same we have at the hands of the Spirit, as being the last, and therefore the nearest unto us in order, altho in power the same with the second and the first. The wise and learned among the very heathens themselves, have all acknowledg'd some first cause, whereupon originally the being of all things dependeth. Neither have they otherwise spoken of that cause than as an agent, which knowing *what* and *why* it worketh, observeth in working a most exact *order* or *law.* Thus much is signify'd by that which *Homer* mentioneth, (*a*) Διὸς δ᾽ ἐτελείετο βωλή. Thus much acknowledg'd by *Mercurius Trismegistus,* (*b*) Τὸν πάντα κόσμον ἐποίησεν ὁ δημιουργός, ὰ χερσίν, ἀλλὰ λόγῳ. Thus much confess'd by *Anaxagoras* and *Plato,* terming the maker of the world an *intellectual worker.* Finally, the *Stoicks,* altho imagining the first cause of all things to be fire, held nevertheless, that the same fire having art, did (*c*) Ὁδῷ βαδίζειν ἐπὶ γνώσιν κόσμου. They all confess therefore, in the working of that first cause, that *counsel* is us'd, *reason* follow'd, a *way* observ'd, that is to say, constant *order* and *law* is kept, whereof it self must needs be author unto it self: otherwise it should have some worthier and higher to direct it, and by a certain so could not it self be the first; being the first, it can have no other than it self to be the author of that law which it willingly worketh by. God therefore is a law both to himself, and to all other things besides. To himself he is a law in all those things whereof our Saviour speaks, saying, *My Father worketh as yet, so I.* God worketh nothing without cause. All those things which are done by him, have some end for which they are done; and the end for which they are done, is a reason of his will to do them. His will had not inclined to create woman, but that he saw it could not be well if she were not created. *Non est bonum, It is not good man should be alone;* therefore let us make an helper for him. That and nothing else is done by God, which to leave undone were not so good. If therefore it be demanded, why God having power and ability infinite, the effects notwithstanding of that power are all so limited as we see they are? the reason hereof is, the end which he hath propos'd, and the law whereby his wisdom hath stinted the effects of his power in such sort, that it doth not work infinitely, but correspondently unto that end for which it worketh, even all things, χιλίους, in most decent and comely sort, all things in *measure, number,* and *weight.* The general end of God's eternal working, is the exercise of his most glorious and most abundant virtue: which abundance doth shew it self in variety, and for that cause this variety is oftentimes in scripture express'd by the name of *riches. The Lord hath made all things for his own sake.* Not that any thing is made to be beneficial unto him, but all things for him to shew beneficence and grace in them. The particular drift of every act proceeding externally from God, we are not able to discern, and therefore cannot always give the proper and certain reason of his works. Howbeit, undoubtedly, a proper and certain reason there is of every finite work of God, in as much as there is a law imposed upon it; which if there were not, it should be infinite even as the worker himself is. They err therefore, who think that of the will of God to do this or that, there is no reason besides his will. Many times no reason known to us; but that there is no reason thereof, I judge it most unreasonable to imagine, in as much

Margin notes: Joh. 16. 13, 14, 15. (a) *Jupiter's* counsel was accomplished. (b) The Creator made the whole world, not with hands, but by reason. Stob. *in Eclog. Phys.* (c) Proceed by a certain and a set way in the making of the world. John 5. 17. Gen. 2. 18. Sap. 8. 1. Sap. 11. 17. Ephes. 1. 17. Phil. 4. 17. Col. 2. 3. Prov. 16. 4.

as he worketh all things, κατὰ τὴν βελὴν τᢒ θελήματᢒ ἀυτᢒ, not only according to his own will, but *the counſel of his own will.* And whatſoever is done with counſel or wiſe reſolution, hath of neceſſity ſome reaſon why it ſhould be done, albeit that reaſon be to us in ſome things ſo ſecret, that it forceth the wit of man to ſtand, as the bleſſed apoſtle himſelf doth, amazed thereat, *O the depth of the riches, both of the wiſdom and knowledge of God! How unſearchable are his judgments,* &c. That law eternal which God himſelf hath made to himſelf, and thereby worketh all things, whereof he is the cauſe and author; that law, in the admirable frame whereof ſhineth with moſt perfect beauty, the countenance of that wiſdom which hath teſtified concerning her ſelf, *The Lord poſſeſſed me in the beginning of his way, even before his works of old I was ſet up:* That law, which hath been the pattern to make, and is the card to guide the world by; that law, which hath been of God, and with God everlaſtingly; that law, the author and obſerver whereof is, one only God, to be bleſſed for ever; how ſhould either men or angels be able perfectly to behold? The book of this law we are neither able nor worthy to open and look into. That little whereof, which we darkly apprehend, we admire; the reſt, with religious ignorance, we humbly and meekly adore. Seeing therefore, that according to this law he worketh, *of whom, thro whom, and for whom, are all things;* altho there ſeem unto us confuſion and diſorder in the affairs of this preſent world: *Tamen quoniam bonus mundum rector temperat; recte fieri cuncta ne dubites.* Let no man doubt but that every thing is well done, becauſe the world is ruled by ſo good a guide, as tranſgreſſeth not his own law; than which, nothing can be more abſolute, perfect and juſt. The law whereby he worketh, is eternal, and therefore can have no ſhew or colour of mutability. For which cauſe, a part of that law being open'd in the promiſes which God hath made (becauſe his promiſes are nothing elſe but declarations, what God will do for the good of men) touching thoſe promiſes the apoſtle hath witneſſed, that God may as poſſibly deny himſelf, and not be God, as fail to perform them. And concerning the counſel of God, he termeth it likewiſe a thing *unchangeable*; the counſel of God, and that law of God, whereof now we ſpeak, being one. Nor is the freedom of the will of God any whit abated, let, or hindred, by means of this; becauſe the impoſition of this law upon himſelf, is his own free and voluntary act. This law therefore, we may name eternal, being *that order which God before all ages hath ſet down with himſelf, for himſelf to do all things by.*

The law which natural agents have given them to obſerve, and their neceſſary manner of keeping it. 3. I am not ignorant, that by *law eternal,* the learned for the moſt part do underſtand the order, not which God hath eternally purpoſed himſelf in all his works to obſerve, but rather that, which with himſelf he hath ſet down as expedient to be kept by all his creatures, according to the ſeveral conditions wherewith he hath endued them. They who thus are accuſtomed to ſpeak, apply the name of *law* unto that only rule of working, which ſuperior authority impoſeth; whereas we, ſomewhat more enlarging the ſenſe thereof, term any kind of rule or canon, whereby actions are framed, a law. Now that law, which as it is laid up in the boſom of God, they call *eternal,* receiveth according unto the different kind of things which are ſubject unto it, different and ſundry kinds of names. That part of it which ordereth natural agents, we call uſually *nature's law;* that which angels do clearly behold, and without any ſwerving obſerve, is a *law celeſtial and heavenly;* the *law of reaſon,* that which bindeth creatures reaſonable in this world, and with which by reaſon they moſt plainly perceive themſelves bound; that which bindeth them, and is not known but by ſpecial revelation from God, *divine law. Human law,* that which out of the law, either of reaſon or of God, men probably gathering to be expedient, they make it a law. All things therefore, which are as they ought to be, are conformed unto this *ſecond law eternal;* and even thoſe things, which to this *eternal law* are not conformable, are notwithſtanding in ſome ſort ordered by the *firſt eternal law.* For what good or evil is there under the ſun; what action correſpondent or repugnant unto the law which God hath impoſed upon his creatures, but in, or upon it, God doth work according to the law which himſelf hath eternally purpoſed to keep; that is to ſay, the *firſt eternal law?* So that a twofold law eternal being thus made, it is not hard to conceive how they both take place in (*d*) all things. Wherefore to come

Epheſ. 1. 11.
Prov. 8. 23.
Rom. 11. 36.
Boet. lib. 4. de
conſol. philoſ.
2 Tim. 2. 13.
Heb. 6. 17.

(*d*) Id omne quod in rebus creatis fit, eſt materia legis æternæ. Th. l. 1, 2. q. 93. art. 4, 5, 6. Nullo modo aliquid legibus ſummi creatoris ordinationique ſubtrahitur, à quo pax univerſitatis adminiſtratur. *Auguſt. de civit. Dei,* lib. 19. c. 22. Immo & peccatum, quatenus à Deo juſto permittitur, cadit in legem æternam. Etiam legi æterna ſubjicitur peccatum; quatenus voluntaria legis tranſgreſſio pœnale quoddam incommodum anime inferit, juxta illud Auguſtini, Juſſiſti Domine, & ſic eſt, ut pœnâ ſua ſibi ſit omnis animus inordinatus. *Conſol.* lib. 1. cap. 12. Nec male Scholaſtici. Quemadmodum, inquiunt, videmus res naturales contingentes, hoc ipſo quod à fine particulari ſuo, atque adeo à lege æterna exorbitant, in eandem legem æternam incidere, quatenus conſequuntur alium finem à lege etiam æternâ ipſis in caſu particulari conſtitutum: ſic veriſimile eſt, homines etiam cum peccant, & deſciſcunt à lege æternâ ut præcipiente, reincidere in ordinem æternæ legis ut punientis.

to the law of nature, albeit thereby we sometimes mean that manner of working which God hath set for each created thing to keep ; yet forasmuch as those things are termed most properly *natural agents*, which keep the law of their kind unwittingly, as the heavens and elements of the world, which can do no otherwise than they do ; and forasmuch as we give unto intellectual natures, the name of *voluntary agents*, that so we may distinguish them from the other ; expedient it will be, that we sever the law of nature observed by the one, from that which the other is tied unto. Touching the former, their strict keeping of one tenure, statute, and law, is spoken of by all, but hath in it more than men have as yet attained to know, or perhaps ever shall attain, seeing the travel of wading herein is given of God to the sons of men ; that perceiving how much the least thing in the world hath in it, more than the wisest are able to reach unto, they may by this means learn humility. *Moses*, in describing the work of creation, attributeth speech unto God : *God said, Let there be light : Let there be a firmament : Let the waters under the heavens be gathered together into one place : Let the earth bring forth : Let there be lights in the firmament of heaven.* Was this only the intent of *Moses*, to signify the infinite greatness of God's power, by the easiness of his accomplishing such effects, without travel, pain, or labour ? Surely, it seemeth that *Moses* had herein, besides this, a further purpose ; namely, first to teach that God did not work as a necessary, but a voluntary agent, intending before-hand, and decreeing with himself, that which did outwardly proceed from him. Secondly, to shew that God did then institute a law natural to be observ'd by creatures ; and therefore according to the manner of laws, the institution thereof is describ'd, as being establish'd by solemn injunction : his commanding those things to be which are, and to be in such sort as they are, to keep that tenure and course which they do, importeth the establishment of nature's law. The world's first creation, and the preservation since of things created, what is it, but only so far forth a manifestation by execution, what the eternal law of God is concerning things natural ? And as it cometh to pass in a kingdom rightly order'd, that after a law is once publish'd, it presently takes effect far and wide, all states framing themselves thereunto ; even so let us think it fareth in the natural course of the world : since the time that God did first proclaim the edicts of his law upon it, heaven and earth have hearkned unto his voice, and their labour hath been to do his will : *He made a law for the rain* ; he gave his *decree unto the sea, that the waters should not pass his commandment.* Now, if nature should intermit her course, and leave altogether, tho it were but for a while, the observation of her own laws ; if those principal and mother elements of the world, whereof all things in this lower world are made, should lose the qualities which now they have ; if the frame of that heavenly arch erected over our heads, should loosen and dissolve it self ; if celestial spheres should forget their wonted motions, and by irregular volubility turn themselves any way as it might happen ; if the prince of the lights of Psal. 19. 5. / heaven, which now as a giant doth run his unwearied course, should, as it were, thro a languishing faintness, begin to stand and to rest himself ; if the moon should wander from her beaten way, the times and seasons of the year blend themselves, by disorder'd and confus'd mixture, the winds breathe out their last gasp, the clouds yield no rain, the earth be defeated of heavenly influence, the fruits of the earth pine away, as children at the wither'd breasts of their mother, no longer able to yield them relief ; what would become of man himself, whom these things do now all serve ? See we not plainly, that obedience of creatures unto the law of nature, is the stay of the whole world ? notwithstanding, with nature it cometh sometimes to pass as with art. Let *Phidias* have rude and obstinate stuff to carve, tho his art do that it should, his work will lack that beauty which otherwise in fitter matter it might have had. He that striketh an instrument with skill, may cause notwithstanding a very unpleasant sound, if the string whereon he striketh chance to be uncapable of harmony. In the matter whereof things natural consist, that of *Theophrastus* takes place, Πολλὰ τὰ ἐχ ἰσανάλυ ὶ ὃ ἀγλιδρισν τὸ ὢ· Theophrast. in Metaph. *Much of it is oftentimes such, as will by no means yield to receive that impression which were best and most perfect.* Which defect in the matter of things natural, they who gave themselves unto the contemplation of nature amongst the heathen, observ'd often : But the true original cause thereof, divine malediction, laid for the sin of man upon these creatures, which God had made for the use of man, this being an article of that saving truth which God hath reveal'd unto his church, was above the reach of their merely natural capacity and understanding. But however, these swervings are now and then incident into the course of nature ; nevertheless so constantly the laws of nature are by natural agents observ'd, that no man denieth, but those things which nature worketh, are wrought either always, or for the most part, after one and the same

manner.

Arist. Rhet. 1. cap. 59. manner. If here it be demanded, what this is which keepeth nature in obedience to her own law, we muſt have recourſe to that higher law, whereof we have already ſpoken ; and becauſe all other laws do thereon depend, from thence we muſt borrow ſo much as ſhall need for brief reſolution in this point. Altho we are not of opinion therefore, as ſome are, that nature in working hath before her certain exemplary draughts or patterns, which ſubſiſting in the boſom of the Higheſt, and being thence diſcovered, ſhe fixeth her eye upon them, as travellers by ſea upon the pole-ſtar of the world, and that according thereunto ſhe guideth her hand to work by imitation :

Τὰ̀ σεγϕυ-μένω μάϕεσι ἕκαστον ἐν-πκερῖ ϕ̀ δἰ τὸ μᾶιϕ̀ε ϕ̀ δἰε τὸ μᾶιϕ. ἡ ἀγασνων ἐκ ἰδάσιν, δὰ περϕσνων ϕυλϕσιν εἰ-δ́ναι, ϕ̀ δ̓ ὰ μὲν ϕσῶι ἐ γιχίσανοι. altho we rather embrace the oracle of *Hippocrates, That each thing, both in ſmall and in great, fulfilleth the taſk which deſtiny hath ſet down* ; and concerning the manner of executing and fulfilling the ſame, *What they do they know not, yet is it in ſhew and appearance, as tho they did know what they do ; and the truth is, they do not diſcern the things which they look on :* nevertheleſs, for as much as the works of nature are no leſs exact, than if ſhe did both behold and ſtudy how to expreſs ſome abſolute ſhape or mirror always preſent before her ; yea, ſuch her dexterity and ſkill appeareth, that no intellectual creature in the world were able by capacity, to do that which nature doth without capacity and knowledge ; it cannot be, but nature hath ſome director of in-finite knowledge to guide her in all her ways. Who is the guide of nature, but only

Acts 17. 28. the God of nature ? *In him we live, move, and are.* Thoſe things which nature is ſaid to do, are by divine art performed, uſing nature as an inſtrument ; nor is there any ſuch art or knowledge divine in nature her ſelf working, but in the guide of nature's work. Whereas therefore things natural, which are not in the number of voluntary agents (for of ſuch only we now ſpeak, and of no other) do ſo neceſſarily obſerve their

(e) Form in o-ther creatures is a thing pro-portionable unto the ſoul in living crea-tures. Senſi-ble it is not, nor otherwiſe diſcernible than only by effects. Ac-cording to the diverſity of inward forms, things of the world are dif-tinguiſh'd into their kinds. certain laws, that as long as they keep thoſe (e) forms which give them their being, they cannot poſſibly be apt or inclinable to do otherwiſe than they do ; ſeeing the kinds of their operations are both conſtantly and exactly framed, according to the ſeveral ends for which they ſerve, they themſelves in the mean while, tho doing that which is fit, yet knowing neither what they do, nor why ; it followeth, that all which they do in this ſort, proceedeth originally from ſome ſuch agent, as knoweth, appointeth, holdeth up, and even actually frameth the ſame. The manner of this divine efficiency being far above us, we are no more able to conceive by our reaſon, than creatures un-reaſonable by their ſenſe, are able to apprehend after what manner we diſpoſe and order the courſe of our affairs. Only thus much is diſcerned, that the natural generation and proceſs of all things, receiveth order of proceeding from the ſettled ſtability of di-vine underſtanding. This appointeth unto them their kinds of working ; the diſpoſi-tion whereof, in the purity of God's own knowledge and will, is rightly termed by the name of *providence.* The ſame being referred unto the things themſelves, here diſpoſed by it, was wont by the antients to be called *natural deſtiny.* That law, the performance whereof we behold in things natural, is as it were an authentical, or an original draught, written in the boſom of God himſelf; whoſe ſpirit being to exe-cute the ſame, uſeth every particular nature, every mere natural agent, only as an in-ſtrument created at the beginning, and ever ſince the beginning uſed to work his own will and pleaſure withal. Nature therefore is nothing elſe but God's inſtrument ; in

Vide Tho. in *Compend. Theol. cap.* 3. *Omne quod mo-vetur ab aliquo, eſt quaſi inſtru-mentum quad-dam primi mo-ventis. Ridi-culum eſt autem etiam apud in-doctos ponere, inſtrumentum moveri non ab aliquo princi-pali agente.* the courſe whereof, *Dionyſius* perceiving ſome ſudden diſturbance, is ſaid to have cryed out, *Aut Deus naturæ patitur, aut mundi machina diſſolvitur :* either God doth ſuffer impediment, and is by a greater than himſelf hindred; or if that be impoſſible, then hath he determined to make a preſent diſſolution of the world; the execution of that law beginning now to ſtand ſtill, without which the world cannot ſtand. This workman, whoſe ſervitor nature is, being in truth but only one, the heathens imagining to be more, gave him in the ſky the name of *Jupiter* ; in the air the name of *Juno* ; in the water the name of *Neptune* ; in the earth the name of *Veſta,* and ſometimes of *Ceres* ; the name of *Apollo* in the ſun ; in the moon the name of *Diana* ; the name of *Æolus,* and divers others in the winds ; and to conclude, even ſo many guides of nature they dreamed of, as they ſaw there were kinds of things natural in the world. Theſe they honoured, as having power to work or ceaſe accordingly as men deſerv'd of them : but unto us, there is one only guide of all agents natural, and he both the creator and the worker of all in all, alone to be bleſſed, adored, and honoured by all for ever. That which hitherto hath been ſpoken, concerneth natural agents conſidered in themſelves : but we muſt further remember alſo (which thing to touch, in a word, ſhall ſuffice) that as in this reſpect they have their law, which law directeth them in the means whereby they tend to their own perfection ; ſo likewiſe another law there is, which toucheth them as they are ſociable parts united into one body : a law which bind-eth them each to ſerve unto others good, and all to prefer the good of the whole,

before

before whatsoever their own particular, as we plainly see they do, when things natural in that regard, forget their ordinary natural wont: that which is heavy, mounting
sometimes upwards of its own accord, and forsaking the center of the earth, which
to it self is most natural, even as if it did bear it self commanded to let go the good
it privately wisheth, and to relieve the present distress of nature in common.

4. But now that we may lift up our eyes (as it were) from the foot-stool to the
throne of God, and leaving these natural, consider a little the state of heavenly and
divine creatures: touching angels, which are spirits immaterial and intellectual, the
glorious inhabitants of those sacred palaces, where nothing but light and blessed immortality, no shadow of matter for tears, discontentments, griefs, and uncomfortable
passions to work upon, but all joy, tranquillity, and peace, even for ever and ever,
doth dwell; as in number and order they are huge, mighty, and royal armies, so
likewise in perfection of obedience unto that law, which the highest, whom they adore,
love and imitate, hath imposed upon them. Such observants they are thereof, that our
Saviour himself being to set down the perfect *idea* of that which we are to pray and
wish for on earth, did not teach to pray or wish for more, than only that here it might
be with us, as with them it is in heaven. God which moveth mere natural agents as
an efficient only, doth otherwise move intellectual creatures, and especially his holy
angels: for beholding the face of God, in admiration of so great excellency, they all
adore him; and being wrapt with the love of his beauty, they cleave inseparably for
ever unto him. Desire to resemble him in goodness, maketh them unweariable and
even unsatiable in their longing, to do by all means all manner of good unto all the
creatures of God, but especially unto the children of men; in the countenance of
whose nature looking downward, they behold themselves beneath themselves; even as
upward in God, beneath whom themselves are, they see that character which is no
where but in themselves and us resembled. Thus far even the painims have approached;
thus far have they seen into the doings of the angels of God; *Orpheus* confessing,
that the fiery throne of God is attended on by those most industrious angels, careful
how all things are performed amongst men; and the mirror of human wisdom plainly
teaching, that God moveth angels, even as that thing doth stir man's heart, which is
thereunto presented amiable. Angelical actions may therefore be reduced unto these
three general kinds. First, most delectable love arising from the visible apprehension
of the purity, glory and beauty of God invisible, saving unto spirits that are
pure: Secondly, adoration grounded upon the evidence of the greatness of God, on
whom they see how all things depend: Thirdly, imitation, bred by the presence of
his exemplary goodness, who ceaseth not before them daily to fill heaven and earth
with the rich treasures of most free and undeserved grace. Of angels, we are not to
consider only what they are and do, in regard of their own being, but that also which
concerneth them as they are linked into a kind of corporation amongst themselves, and
of society or fellowship with men. Consider angels, each of them severally in himself; and their law is that which the Prophet *David* mentioneth, *all ye his angels
praise him*. Consider the angels of God associated; and their law is that which dis-
poseth them as an army, one in order and degree above another. Consider finally the
angels, as having with us that communion which the apostle to the *Hebrews* noteth;
and in regard whereof, angels have not disdained to profess themselves our *fellow-servants*. From hence there springeth up a third law, which bindeth them to works of
ministerial employment; every of which their several functions are by them performed with joy. A part of the angels of God notwithstanding (we know) have fain,
and that their fall hath been thro the voluntary breach of that law, which did require
at their hands continuance in the exercise of their high and admirable virtue. Impossible it was, that ever their will should change or incline to remit any part of their
duty, without some object having force to avert their conceit from God, and to
draw it another way; and that before they attained that high perfection of bliss, wherein now the elect angels are, without possibility of falling. Of any thing more than of
God, they could not by any means like, as long as whatsoever they knew besides God,
they apprehended it not in it self, without dependency upon God; because so long,
God must needs seem infinitely better than any thing which they so could apprehend.
Things beneath them, could not in such sort be presented unto their eyes, but that
therein they must needs see always, how those things did depend on God. It seemeth
therefore, that there was no other way for angels to sin, but by reflex of their understanding upon themselves; when being held with admiration of their own sublimity
and honour, the memory of their subordination unto God, and their dependency on
him was drowned in this conceit; whereupon their adoration, love and imitation of
                                                                        God,

The law
which angels
do work by.
Psal. 104. 4.
Heb. 1. 7.
Eph. 3. 10.
Dan. 7. 10.
Mat. 26. 53.
Heb. 12. 22.
Luke 2. 13.
Mat. 6. 10.
& 18. 10.
Ps. 91. 11, 12,
Luke 15. 7.
Heb. 1. 14;
Acts 10. 3.
Dan. 9. 23.
Mat. 18. 10.
Dan. 4. 10.
Τὸ ᾗ Ṡρῶρος
μεμηνότα-
εσγὰ᾽ χ τζᾶ
μίρῳ, οἶε μᾶ-
γᾶλα, οἶε μᾶ-
μιλάθεσγῖτ -
ἄς πρᾶῷῶ τε-
λᾶῖτωι. Arist.
Metaph. 12.
cap. 7.
Job 38. 7.
Mat. 18. 10.
Psal. 148. 2.
Heb. 1. 6.
Isa. 6. 3.

This is inti-
mated where-
soever we find
them termed
the sons of
God, as Job
1. 6. & 38. 7.
2 Pet. 2. 4.
Jude ver. 6.
Psal. 148. 2.
Luke 2. 13.
Mat. 26. 53.
Psal. 148. 2.
Heb. 12. 22,
Apoc. 22. 9.

Joh. 8. 44.
1 Pet. 5. 8.
Apoc. 9. 11.
Gen. 3. 15.
1 Chro. 11. 1.
Job 1. 7.
& 2. 1.
John 13. 27.
Acts 5. 3.
Apoc. 20. 8.

God, could not chufe but be alfo interrupted. The fall of angels therefore was pride; fince their fall, their practices have been clean contrary unto thofe before mentioned: for being difperfed, fome in the air, fome on the earth, fome in the water, fome amongft the minerals, dens and caves that are under the earth; they have, by all means, laboured to effect an univerfal rebellion againft the laws, and, as far as in them lieth, utter deftruction of the works of God. Thefe wicked fpirits the heathens honoured inftead of Gods, both generally under the name of *Dii inferi.* Gods infernal; and particularly, fome in oracles, fome in idols, fome as houfhold Gods, fome as nymphs: in a word, no foul and wicked fpirit which was not one way or other honoured of men as God, till fuch time as light appeared in the world, and diffolved the works of the devil. Thus much therefore may fuffice for angels, the next unto whom in degree are men.

The law whereby man is in his actions directed to the imitation of God.

5. God alone excepted, who actually and everlaftingly is, whatfoever he may be, and which cannot hereafter be, that which now he is not; all other things befides, are fomewhat in poffibility, which as yet they are not in Act. And for this caufe there is in all things an appetite or defire, whereby they incline to fomething which they may be; and when they are it, they fhall be perfecter than now they are. All which perfections are contained under the general name of *goodnefs.* And becaufe there is not in the world any thing whereby another may not fome way be made the per-

Πάσα ἢ ἐπιτὴν ἔχει ἡ τας. Arif. de An. lib. 1. cap. 4.

fecter, therefore all things that are, are good. Again, fith there can be no goodnefs defired, which proceedeth not from God himfelf, as from the fupreme caufe of all things; and every effect doth after a fort contain, at leaftwife refemble the caufe from which it proceedeth: all things in the world are faid in fome fort to feek the higheft, and to covet more or lefs the participation of God himfelf; yet this doth no where fo much appear, as it doth in man, becaufe there are fo many kinds of perfections which man feeketh. The firft degree of goodnefs is, that general perfection which all things do feek, in defiring the continuance of their being; all things therefore coveting, as much as may be, to be like unto God in being ever, that which cannot hereunto attain perfonally, doth feek to continue it felf another way; that is, by off-fpring and propagation. The next degree of goodnefs is, that which each thing coveteth, by affecting refemblance with God, in the conftancy and excellency of thofe operations which belong unto their kind. The immutability of God they ftrive unto, by working either always, or for the moft part, after one and the fame manner; his abfolute exactnefs they imitate, by tending unto that which is moft exquifite in every

Ἐν ταῖς φύσιν δεῖ τὸ βέλτιον, ἐὰν ἐνδέχηται, ὑπάρχειν μᾶλλον ἢ φύσις ἀεὶ ποιεῖ τῶν ἐνδεχομένων τὸ βέλτιον. Arif. 2. de Cœl. cap. 5. Mat. 5. 48. Sap. 7. 27. Ἡ ἢ τοῦ ἀγαθοῦ κίνησις ἐπιποθὴ ἔχει, ὑψίνικα, ὑπάρχοι τι μᾶλλον τῶν ἀνθρώπων, ἡ λόγος, ἢ λόγου μᾶλλον μετέχειν, μηχανεῖ εἰ τὰς τ' ἀρετὰς.

particular. Hence have rifen a number of axioms in philofophy, fhewing, *how the works of nature do always aim at that which cannot be bettered.* Thefe two kinds of goodnefs rehearfed, are fo nearly united to the things themfelves which defire them, that we fcarcely perceive the appetite to ftir in reaching forth her hand towards them. But the defire of thofe perfections which grow externally, is more apparent, efpecially of fuch as are not exprefly defired, unlefs they be firft known, or fuch as are not for any other caufe, than for knowledge it felf, defired. Concerning perfections in this kind, that by proceeding in the knowledge of truth, and by growing in the exercife of virtue, man, amongft the creatures of this inferior world, afpireth to the greateft conformity with God. This is not only known unto us, whom he himfelf hath fo inftructed, but even they do acknowledge, who amongft men are not judged the neareft unto him. With *Plato,* what one thing more ufual, than to excite men unto love of wifdom, by fhewing, how much wife men are thereby exalted above men; how knowledge doth raife them up into heaven; how it maketh them, tho not gods, yet as gods, high, admirable and divine? And *Mercurius Trifmegiftus* fpeaking of the virtues of a righteous foul, *fuch fpirits* (faith he) *are never cloyed with praifing and fpeaking well of all men, with doing good unto every one by word and deed, becaufe they ftudy to frame themfelves according to* THE PATTERN *of the Father of fpirits.*

Mens firft beginning to grow to the knowledge of that law which they are to obferve. vide Ifai. 7. 16.

6. In the matter of knowledge, there is between the angels of God, and the children of men, this difference: angels already have full and compleat knowledge in the higheft degree that can be imparted unto them: men, if we view them in their fpring, are at the firft without underftanding or knowledge at all. Neverthelefs, from this utter vacuity they grow by degrees, till they come at length to be even as the angels themfelves are. That which agreeth to the one now, the other fhall attain unto in the end; they are not fo far disjoined and fevered, but that they come at length to meet. The foul of man being therefore at the firft as a book, wherein nothing is, and yet all things may be imprinted; we are to fearch by what fteps and degrees it rifeth unto perfection of knowledge. Unto that which hath been already
ready

ready set down, concerning natural agents, this we must add, that albeit therein we have comprised as well creatures living, as void of life, if they be in degree of nature beneath men; nevertheless, a difference we must observe between those natural agents that work altogether unwittingly, and those which have, though weak, yet some under-standing what they do, as fishes, fowls, and beasts have. Beasts are in sensible capa-city as ripe even as men themselves, perhaps more ripe. For as stones, though in dig-nity of nature inferior unto plants, yet exceed them in firmness of strength, or dura-bility of being; and plants, tho beneath the excellency of creatures endued with sense, yet exceed them in the faculty of vegetation, and of fertility: so beasts, though otherwise behind men, may notwithstanding in actions of sense and fancy go beyond them; because the endeavours of nature, when it hath an higher perfection to seek, are in lower the more remiss, not esteeming thereof so much as those things do, which have no better proposed unto them. The soul of man therefore, being capable of a more divine perfection, hath (besides the faculties of growing unto sensible knowledge, which is common unto us with beasts) a further hability, whereof in them there is no shew at all, the ability of reaching * higher than unto sensible things.
Till we grow to some ripeness of years, the soul of man doth only store it self with conceits of things of inferior or more open quality, which afterwards do serve as instruments unto that which is greater; in the mean while, above the reach of meaner creatures it ascendeth not. When once it comprehendeth any thing above this, as the differences of time, affirmations, negations, and contradiction in speech, we then count it to have some use of natural reason: whereunto, if afterwards there might be added the right helps of true art and learning (which helps, I must plainly confess, this age of the world, carrying the name of a learned age, doth neither much know, nor greatly regard) there would undoubtedly be almost as great difference in maturity of judgment between men therewith inured, and that which now men are, as between men that are now, and innocents. Which speech, if any condemn, as being over hy-perbolical, let them consider but this one thing: no art is at the first finding out so perfect as industry may after make it; yet the very first man that to any purpose knew the way we speak of and followed it, hath alone thereby performed more, very near, in all parts of natural knowledge, than sithence in any one part thereof the whole world besides hath done. In the poverty of that other new devised aid, two things there are notwithstanding singular. Of marvellous quick dispatch it is, and doth shew them that it as much almost in three days as if it had dwelt threescore years with them. Again, because the curiosity of man's wit doth many times with peril wade farther in the search of things than were convenient; the same is thereby restrained unto such generalities as every where offering themselves are apparent unto men of the weakest conceit that need be: so as following the rules and precepts thereof, we may find it to be an art which teacheth the way of speedy discourse, and restraineth the mind of man that it may not wax over-wise. Education and instruction are the means, the one by use, the other by precept, to make our natural faculty of reason both the better and the sooner able to judge rightly between truth and error, good and evil. But at what time a man may be said to have attained so far forth the use of reason as sufficeth to make him capable of those laws whereby he is then bound to guide his actions; this is a great deal more easy for common sense to discern, than for any man by skill and learning to deter-mine; even as it is not in philosophers, who best know the nature both of fire and gold, to teach what degree of the one will serve to purify the other, so well as the artizan (which doth this by fire) discerneth by sense when the fire hath that degree of heat which sufficeth for his purpose.

7. By reason man attaineth unto the knowledge of things that are, and are not sensi-ble; it resteth therefore, that we search how man attaineth unto the knowledge of such things unsensible, as are to be known that they may be done. Seeing then that nothing can move unless there be some end, the desire whereof provoketh unto motion; how should that divine power of the soul, that *spirit of our mind*, as the apostle termeth it, ever stir it self unto action, unless it have also the like spur? The end for which we are moved to work, is sometimes the goodness which we conceive of the very work-ing it self, without any further respect at all; and the cause that procureth action is the mere desire of action, no other good besides being thereby intended. Of certain turbulent wits it is said, *Illis quieta movere magna merces videbatur*: they thought the very disturbance of things established an hire sufficient to set them on work. Some-times that which we do is referred to a further end, without the desire whereof we would leave the same undone; as in their actions that gave alms, to purchase thereby the praise of men. Man in perfection of nature being made according to the likeness

of

C

of his Maker, refembleth him alfo in the manner of working ; fo that whatfoever we work as men, the fame we do wittingly work and freely : neither are we according to the manner of natural agents any way fo tied, but that it is in our power to leave the things we do undone. The good which either is gotten by doing, or which confifteth in the very doing it felf, caufeth not action, unlefs apprehending it as good we fo like and defire it. That we do unto any fuch end, the fame we chufe and prefer before the leaving of it undone. Choice there is not, unlefs the thing we take be fo in our power that we might have refufed and left it. If fire confume the ftubble, it chufeth not fo to do, becaufe the nature thereof is fuch that it can do no other. To chufe, is to will one thing before another ; and to will, is to bend our fouls to the having or doing of that which they fee to be good. Goodnefs is feen with the eye of the underftanding, and the light of that eye is reafon. So that two principal fountains there are of human action, *knowledge* and *will* ; which will, in things tending towards any end, is Deut. 30. 19. termed *choice*. Concerning knowledge ; *Behold,* faith *Mofes, I have fet before you this day, good and evil, life and death.* Concerning will, he addeth immediately, *Chufe life* ; that is to fay, the things that tend unto life, them chufe. But of one thing we muft have fpecial care, as being a matter of no fmall moment, and that is, how the will properly and ftrictly taken, as it is of things which are referred unto the end that man defireth, differeth greatly from that inferior natural defire which we call appetite. The object of appetite is whatfoever fenfible good may be wifhed for ; the object of will is that good which reafon doth lead us to feek. Affections, as joy, and grief, and fear, and anger, with fuch like, being as it were the fundry fafhions and forms of appetite, can neither rife at the conceit of a thing indifferent, nor yet chufe but rife at the fight of fome things. Wherefore it is not altogether in our power whether we will be ftirred with affections, or no. Whereas actions which iffue from the difpofition of the will, are in the power thereof to be performed or ftayed. Finally, appetite is the will's folliciter, and the will is appetite's comptroller ; what we covet according to the one, by the other we often reject. Neither is any other defire termed properly will, but that where reafon and underftanding, or the fhew of reafon, prefcribeth the thing defired. It may be therefore a queftion, whether thofe operations of men are to be counted voluntary, wherein that good which is fenfible provoketh appetite, and appetite caufeth action, reafon being never called to counfel ; as when we eat or drink, and betake our felves unto reft, and fuch like. The truth is, that fuch actions in men having attained to the ufe of reafon, are voluntary : for as the authority of higher powers, hath force even in thofe things which are done without their privity, and are of fo mean reckoning that to acquaint them therewith it needeth not ; in like fort, voluntarily we are faid to do that alfo, which the will, if it lifted, might hinder from being done, altho about the doing thereof we do not exprefly ufe our reafon or underftanding, and fo immediately apply our wills thereunto. In cafes therefore of fuch facility, the will muft yield her affent, as it were with a kind of filence, by not diffenting ; in which refpect her force is not fo apparent as in exprefs mandates or prohibitions, efpecially upon advice and confultation going before. Where underftanding therefore needeth, in thofe things reafon is the director of man's will, by difcovering in action what is good. For the laws of well-doing are the dictates of right reafon. Children which are not as yet come unto thofe years whereat they may have ; again, innocents which are excluded by natural defect from ever having ; thirdly, mad-men, which for the prefent cannot poffibly have the ufe of right reafon to guide O mihi prate-
ritos referas fi
Jupiter annos !
Ἐι ἦ τις ἐπὶ
κακιαν ὁρ-
μᾷ, οἴεμπε
μβὶ οὐχ ὡς ἐπὶ
κακὸν ἀλ-
τῶν ἐτίχοτε
ἀλλ᾿ ὡς ἐπ᾿
ἀγαθὸν.
Paulo poſt ;
᾿Αδύνατον ἢ
ὁρμᾷ ἐπὶ
ᾧ μὴ βελ-
ίμεον Γἴμεν
αὐτῷ, ᾿Εἰ ἐλ-
ντὲι ἀγαθῷ,
ἐπὶ οἴφε
μείζονο-
τεχνὶ. Alcin.
de Dog. Plat. themfelves, have for their guide the reafon that guideth other men, which are tutors over them to feek and to procure their good for them. In the reft there is that light of reafon, whereby good may be known from evil ; and which difcovering the fame rightly is termed right. The will, notwithftanding, doth not incline to have or do that which reafon teacheth to be good, unlefs the fame do alfo teach it to be poffible. For albeit the appetite, being more general, may wifh any thing which feemeth good, be it never fo impoffible ; yet for fuch things the reafonable will of man doth never feek. Let reafon teach impoffibility in any thing, and the will of man doth let it go ; a thing impoffible it doth not affect, the impoffibility thereof being manifeft. There is in the will of man naturally that freedom, whereby it is apt to take or refufe any particular object whatfoever being prefented unto it. Whereupon it followeth, that there is no particular object fo good but it may have the fhew of fome difficulty or unpleafant quality annexed to it, in refpect whereof, the will may fhrink and decline it ; contrarywife (for fo things are blended) there is no particular evil which hath not fome appearance of goodnefs whereby to infinuate it felf. For evil, as evil, cannot be defired ; if that be defired which is evil, the caufe is the goodnefs which is or feemeth to be

joined

joined with it. Goodnefs doth not move by being, but by being apparent ; and therefore many things are negleded which are moft precious, only becaufe the value of them
lieth hid. Senfible goodnefs is moft apparent, near, and prefent, which caufeth the
appetite to be therewith ftrongly provoked. Now purfuit and refufal in the will do
follow, the one the affirmation, the other the negation of goodnefs, which the underftanding apprehendeth, grounding it felf upon fenfe, unlefs fome higher reafon do
chance to teach the contrary. And if reafon have taught it rightly to be good, yet
not fo apparently that the mind receiveth it with utter impoffibility of being otherwife,
ftill there is place left for the will to take or leave. Whereas therefore amongft fo many things as are to be done, there are fo few, the goodnefs whereof reafon in fuch fort
doth or eafily can difcover, we are not to marvel at the choice of evil even then when
the contrary is probably known. Hereby it cometh to pafs, that cuftom inuring the
mind by long practice, and fo leaving there a fenfible impreffion, prevaileth more than
reafonable perfuafion what way foever. Reafon therefore may rightly difcern the thing
which is good, and yet the will of man not incline it felf thereunto as oft as the prejudice of fenfible experience doth over-fway. Nor let any man think, that this doth
make any thing for the juft excufe of iniquity : for there was never fin committed
wherein a lefs good was not preferred before a greater, and that wilfully ; which cannot be done without the fingular difgrace of nature, and the utter difturbance of that
divine order, whereby the pre-eminence of chiefeft acceptation is by the beft things
worthily challenged. There is not that good which concerneth us, but it hath evidence
enough for it felf if reafon were diligent to fearch it out. Thro the negled thereof,
abufed we are with the fhew of that which is not ; fometimes the fubtilty of fatan in-
veigling us, as it did *Eve* (*a*); fometimes the haftinefs of our wills preventing the more
confiderate advice of found reafon, as in the (*b*) apoftles, when they no fooner faw
what they liked not, but they forthwith were defirous of fire from heaven ; fometimes the very cuftom of evil making the heart obdurate againft whatfoever inftrudions
to the contrary, as in them over whom our Saviour fpake weeping, (*c*) *O Jerufalem,
how often, and thou wouldft not ?* Still therefore that wherewith we ftand blameable
and can no way excufe it, is, that in doing evil we prefer a lefs good before a greater, the
greatnefs whereof is by reafon inveftigable and may be known. The fearch of knowledge is a thing painful ; and the painfulnefs of knowledge is that which maketh the
will fo hardly inclinable thereunto. The root hereof is divine malediction ; whereby
the * inftruments being weakned wherewithal the foul (efpecially in reafoning) doth
work, it preferreth reft in ignorance before wearifom labour to know. For a fpur of
diligence therefore, we have a natural thirft after knowledge ingrafted in us. But by
reafon of that original weaknefs in the inftruments, without which the underftanding part
is not able in this world by difcourfe to work, the very conceit of painfulnefs is as a
bridle to ftay us. For which caufe the apoftle, who knew right well that the wearinefs of the flefh is a heavy clog to the will, ftriketh mightily upon this key, *Awake
thou that fleepeft, caft off all which preffeth down ; watch, labour, ftrive to go forward, and to grow in knowledge.*

8. Wherefore to return to our former intent of difcovering the natural way, whereby rules have been found out concerning that goodnefs wherewith the will of man
ought to be moved in human actions ; as every thing naturally and neceffarily doth
defire the utmoft good and greateft perfection, whereof nature hath made it capable,
even fo man. Our felicity therefore being the object and accomplifhment of our defire, we cannot chufe but wifh and covet it. All particular things which are fubject unto action, the will doth fo far forth incline unto, as reafon judgeth them the better for
us, and confequently the more available to our blifs. If reafon err, we fall into evil,
and are fo far forth deprived of the general perfection we feek. Seeing therefore, that
for the framing of mens actions, the knowledge of good from evil is neceffary, it only refteth, that we fearch how this may be had. Neither muft we fuppofe that there
needeth one rule to know the good, and another the evil by. For he that knoweth
what is ftrait, doth even thereby difcern what is crooked, becaufe the abfence of
ftraitnefs in bodies capable thereof is crookednefs. Goodnefs in actions is like unto
ftraitnefs ; wherefore that which is done well, we term right. For as the ftrait way
is moft acceptable to him that travelleth, becaufe by it he cometh fooneft to his journey's end ; fo in action, that which doth lie the eveneft between us and the end we
defire, muft needs be the fitteft for our ufe. Befides which fitnefs for ufe, there is alfo
in rectitude, beauty ; as contrariwife in obliquity, deformity. And that which is
good in the actions of men, doth not only delight as profitable, but as amiable alfo.
In which confideration the *Grecians* moft divinely have given to the active perfection of

men,

(a) 2 Cor. 11. 3.
(b) Luke 9. 54.
(c) Mat. 23. 37.
* Sap. 9. 15.
A corruptible
body is heavy
unto the foul,
and the earth-
ly manfion
keepeth down
the mind that
is full of cares.
And hardly
can we dif-
cern the
things that
are upon
earth, and
with great
labour find
we out the
things which
are before us.
Who can then
feek out the
things that
are in heav'n ?
Ephef. 5. 14.
Heb. 12, 1, 12.
1 Cor. 16. 13.
Prov. 2. 4.
Luke 13. 24.

Of the natu-
ral way of
finding out
laws by rea-
fon, to guide
the will unto
that which is
good.

Τῷ ἀθλικαὶ
αὐτὸ ἦ τὸ
κρἀτιστον
ρνάσκρμοτ
κρπὴς ἦ κα-
ἀμφαὶν ὁ χα-
ναεχ. Arift. de
An. lib. 1.

Καλος;2-
δια.

(a) *H εἰω' ἢ
ὡς ἔπι τὸ
πολὺ ἀσπάῦτος
ἀποβαίνει.
Arist. Rhet.
l. 1. c. 39.
(b) Non potest
error contingo-
re ubi omnes
idem opinan-
tur. Monticat.
in 1. Polit.
Quicquid in
omnibus indi-
viduis unius
speciei com-
muniter inest,
id causam
communem ha-
beat oportet,
qua est eorum
individuorum
species & na-
tura. Idem.
Quod à tota
aliqua specie
fit, universalis
particularis;
natura fit in-
stinctu. Ficio.
de Christ. Rel.
Si proficere
cupis, primò
firmè id ve-
rum puta quod
sana mens om-
nium homi-
num attesta-
tur. Cusa in
Compend.
cap. 1.
Non licet na-
turale univer-
saleque homi-
num judicium
falsum anum-
que existimare.
Telesf.
'Ο ἢ πᾶσι
δοκεῖ, τοῦτο
εἶναι φάμὲν.
'Ο ἢ ἀναιρῶν
ταύτην τὴν
πίστιν οὐ-
πάνυ πιστὰ
ἐρεῖ. Arist.Eth.
lib. 10. cap. 2.
(c) Rom. 2.
14.

'Ἀνιόντων ζη-
τοῦντας λόγον,
ἀναιροῦσι λό-
γον. Theoph.
in Metaph.

men, a name expressing both beauty and goodness; because goodness in ordinary speech is for the most part apply'd only to that which is beneficial. But we in the name of goodness, do here imply both. And of discerning goodness, there are but these two ways; the one, the knowledge of the causes whereby it is made such; the other, the observation of those signs and tokens, which being annexed always unto goodness, argue, that where they are found, there also goodness is, altho we know not the cause by force whereof it is there. The former of these is the most sure and infallible way, but so hard that all shun it, and had rather walk as men do in the dark by hap-hazard, than tread so long and intricate mazes for knowledge sake. As therefore physicians are many times forced to leave such methods of curing as themselves know to be the fittest, and being over-ruled by their patients impatiency are fain to try the best they can, in taking that way of cure which the cured will yield unto; in like sort, considering how the case doth stand with this present age full of tongue and weak of brain, behold we yield to the stream thereof: into the causes of goodness we will not make any curious or deep inquiry; to touch them now and then it shall be sufficient, when they are so near at hand that easily they may be conceived without any far removed discourse: that way we are contented to prove, which being the worse in it self, is notwithstanding now by reason of common imbecillity, the fitter and likelier to be brooked. Signs and tokens to know good by are of sundry kinds; some more certain, and some less. The most certain token of evident goodness is, if the general persuasion of all men do so account it. And therefore a common received error is never utterly overthrown, till such times as we go from signs unto causes, and shew some manifest root or fountain thereof common unto all, whereby it may clearly appear how it hath come to pass that so many have been overseen. In which case surmises and slight probabilities will not serve, because the universal consent of men is the perfectest and strongest in this kind, which comprehendeth only the signs and tokens of goodness. Things casual do vary, and that which a man doth but chance to think well of, cannot still have the like hap. Wherefore altho we know not the cause, yet thus much we may know, that some necessary cause there is, whensoever the judgments of all men generally, or for the most part, run one and the same way, especially in matters of that discourse: for of things necessarily and naturally done, there is no more affirmed but this, (a) *They keep either always, or for the most part, one tenure.* The general and perpetual voice of men is as the sentence of God himself: (b) for that which all men have at all times learned, nature her self must needs have taught; and God being the author of nature, her voice is but his instrument. By her, from him, we receive whatsoever in such sort we learn. Infinite duties there are, the goodness whereof is by this rule sufficiently manifested, altho we had no other warrant besides to approve them. The apostle St. *Paul* having speech concerning the heathen, saith of them, (c) *They are a law unto themselves.* His meaning is, that by force of the light of reason wherewith God illuminateth every one which cometh into the world, men being enabled to know truth from falshood, and good from evil, do thereby learn in many things what the will of God is; which will himself not revealing by any extraordinary means unto them, but they by natural discourse attaining the knowledge thereof, seem the makers of those laws which indeed are his, and they but only the finders of them out. A law therefore generally taken is a directive rule unto goodness of operation. The rule of divine operations outward, is the definitive appointment of God's own wisdom set down within himself. The rule of natural agents that work by simple necessity, is the determination of the wisdom of God, known to God himself the principal director of them, but not to them that are directed to execute the same. The rule of natural agents which work after a sort of their own accord, as the beasts do, is the judgment of common sense or fancy concerning the sensible goodness of those objects wherewith they are moved. The rule of ghostly or immaterial natures, as spirits and angels, is their intuitive intellectual judgment concerning the amiable beauty and high goodness of that object which with unspeakable joy and delight doth set them on work. The rule of voluntary agents on earth, is the sentence that reason giveth concerning the goodness of those things which they are to do. And the sentences which reason giveth are some more, some less general, before it come to define in particular actions what is good. The main principles of reason are in themselves apparent: for to make nothing evident of it self unto man's understanding, were to take away all possibility of knowing any thing. And herein that of *Theophrastus* is true, *They that seek a reason of all things do utterly overthrow reason.* In every kind of knowledge some such grounds there are, as that being proposed the mind doth presently embrace them as free from all possibility of error, clear and manifest without proof. In which kind of axioms or principles more general, are such as this, *That the greater good is to be chosen before the less.* If therefore it should be demanded, what reason there is why the will of man, which doth neceffarily fhun, harm, and covet whatfoever is pleafant and fweet, fhould be commanded to count the pleafures of fin evil; and notwithftanding the bitter accidents wherewith virtuous actions are compaft, yet ftill to rejoiced and delight in them : furely this could never ftand with reafon; but that wifdom thus prefcribing groundeth her laws upon an infallible rule of comparifon, which is, that finall difficulties, when exceeding great good is fure to enfue, and on the fide momentany benefits when the hurt which they draw after them is unfpeakable; are not at all to be refpected.   This rule is the ground whereupon the wifdom of the apoftle buildeth a law enjoining patience unto himfelf, *The prefent lightnefs of our affliction worketh unto us,* 2 Cor. 4. 17. *even with abundance upon abundance, an eternal weight of glory; while we look not on the things which are feen, but on the things which are not feen: for the things which are feen, are temporal; but the things which are not feen, are eternal:* therefore chriftianity to be embraced, whatfoever calamities in thofe times it was accompanied withal.   On the fame ground our Saviour proveth the law moft reafonable, that forbids thofe crimes which men for gain fake fall into.   For a man to win the world, if it be with the lofs of his foul, what benefit or good is it ?   Axioms lefs general, yet fo manifeft that they need no farther proof, are fuch as thefe, *God to be worfhipped; parents to be honoured; others* Mat. 16. 26, *to be ufed by us, as we our felves would be by them.*   Such things, as foon as they are alledged, all men acknowledge to be good; they require no proof or further difcourfe to be affured of their goodnefs.   Notwithstanding whatfoever fuch principle there is, it was at the firft found out by difcourfe, and drawn from out of the very bowels of heaven and earth.   For we are to note, that things in the world are to us difcernable, not only fo far forth as ferveth for our vital prefervation, but further alfo in a twofold higher refpect.   For firft, if all other ufes were utterly taken away; yet the mind of man being by nature fpeculative and delighted with contemplation in it felf, they were to be known even for meer knowledge and underftanding's fake.   Yea further befides this, the knowledge of every the leaft thing in the world, hath in it a fecond peculiar benefit unto us, in as much as it ferveth to minifter rules, canons, and laws for men to direct thofe actions by, which we properly term human.   This did the very heathens themfelves obfcurely infinuate, by making *Themis,* which we call *jus* or right, to be the daughter of heaven and earth.   We know things either as they are in themfelves, or as they are in mutual relation one to another.   The knowledge of that which man is in reference unto himfelf, and other things in relation unto man, I may juftly term the mother of all thofe principles, which are as it were edicts, ftatutes and decrees in that law of nature, whereby human actions are framed.   Firft therefore, having obferved that the beft things where they are not hindred, do ftill produce the beft operations; (for which caufe, where many things are to concur unto one effect, the beft is in all congruity of reafon to guide the refidue, that it prevailing moft, the work principally done by it may have greateft perfection;) when hereupon we come to obferve in our felves of what excellency our fouls are; in comparifon of our bodies, and the diviner part in relation unto the bafer of our fouls; feeing that all thefe concur in producing human actions, it cannot be well, unlefs the chiefeft do command and direct the reft.   The foul then ought to conduct the body; *Arift. Polit. 1.* and the fpirit of our minds, the foul.   This is therefore the firft law, whereby the higheft power of the mind requireth general obedience at the hands of all the reft concurring *cap. 5.* with it unto action.   Touching the feveral grand mandates, which being impofed by the underftanding faculty of the mind muft be obeyed by the will of man, they are by the fame method found out, whether they import our duty towards God or towards man.   Touching the one, I may not here ftand to open, by what degrees of difcourfe the minds, even of mere natural men have attained to know; not only that there is a God; but alfo what power, force; wifdom, and other properties that God hath, and how all things depend on him.   This being therefore prefuppofed; from that known relation which God hath unto us (a) as unto children, and unto all good things as unto effects; (b) Ὀσ̀λέ whereof himfelf is the (b) principal caufe, thefe axioms and laws natural concerning our ἐν τε Νόντι duty have arifen: (c) *That in all things we go about, his aid is by prayer to be craved:* ἀνθρώπ. (d) *That he cannot have fufficient honour done unto him; but the uttermoft of that we* (b) Ὅτι ο̈β can do to honour him, we muft;* which is in effect the fame that we read (e) *Thou* Ὀσ̀ε Ἀυτ̀ *fhalt love the Lord thy God with all thy heart, with all thy foul, and with all thy* τὸ αἴνιο αὐ *mind;* which law our Saviour doth term (f) *the firft, and the great commandment.* δύχ ιν.   Arift. Touching the next, which, as our Saviour addeth, is like unto this (he meaneth in am- *Metaph. lib. 1.* plitude and largenefs, in as much as it is the root out of which all laws of duty to men- (c) Ἀλλ᾽ ἡ ward have grown, as out of the former all offices of religion towards God) the like na- Σαλεςλ τίντα ἡ μην

Plat. in Tim. (d) Arift.

‹‹ Ἰσ̀ ἰστο ὁ κ̀ί Θεαχλ ενεχριτεν μαθϊχομν, οθι τὠσν ὀριθ῀ ὣμηκρα ἡ μηχὰλυ πεδίγμαϊφον θεὶσ ἀεὶ ωι. χεδων. Plat. in Tim.   ‹‹ Ἰηλ. lih. δ. cap. ult.   (ε) Deut. δὲ 5.   (γ) Mat. 22. 38.

tural inducement hath brought men to know that it is their duty no lefs to love others than themfelves. For feeing thofe things which are equal muft needs all have one meafure; if I cannot but wifh to receive all good, even as much at every man's hand as any man can wifh unto his own foul, how fhould I look to have any part of my defire herein fatisfied, unlefs my felf be careful to fatisfy the like defire which is undoubtedly in other men, we all being of one and the fame nature? To have any thing offered them repugnant to this defire, muft needs in all refpects grieve them as much as me: fo that if I do harm, I muft look to fuffer; there being no reafon that others fhould fhew greater meafure of love to me, than they have by me fhewed unto them. My defire therefore to be loved of my equals in nature as much as poffible may be, impofeth upon me a natural duty of bearing to them-ward fully the like affection. From which relation of equality between our felves, and them that are as our felves, what feveral Rules and canons natural reafon hath drawn for direction of life no man is ignorant; as namely, (g) *That becaufe we would take no harm, we muft therefore do none; that fith we would not be in any thing extremely dealt with, we muft ourfelves avoid all extremity in our dealings; that from all violence and wrong we are utterly to abftain,* with fuch like; which further to wade in would be tedious, and to our prefent purpofe not altogether fo neceffary, feeing that on thefe two general heads already mentioned all other fpecialities are dependent. Wherefore the natural meafure whereby to judge our doings, is the fentence of reafon determining and fetting down what is good to be done. Which fentence is either mandatory, fhewing what muft be done; or elfe permiffive, declaring only what may be done; or thirdly, admonitory, opening what is the moft convenient for us to do. The firft taketh place where the comparifon doth ftand altogether between doing and not doing of one thing, which in it felf is abfolutely good or evil; as it had been for *Jofeph* to yield or not to yield to the impotent defire of his leud miftrefs, the one evil, the other good fimply. The fecond is when of divers things evil, all being not evitable, we are permitted to take one; which one, faving only in cafe of fo great urgency, were not otherwife to be taken; as in the matter of divorce amongft the Jews. The laft, when of divers things good, one is principal and moft eminent; as in their act who fold their poffeffions and laid the price at the apoftles feet; which poffeffions they might have retained unto themfelves without fin: again, in the apoftle St. *Paul's* own choice, to maintain himfelf by his own labour; whereas in living by the church's maintenance, as others did, there had been no offence committed. In goodnefs therefore there is a latitude or extent, whereby it cometh to pafs that even of good actions fome are better than other fome; whereas otherwife one man could not excel another, but all fhould be either abfolutely good, as hitting jump that indivifible point or centre wherein goodnefs confifteth; or elfe miffing it, they fhould be excluded out of the number of well-doers. Degrees of well-doing there could be none, except perhaps in the feldomnefs and oftennefs of doing well. But the nature of goodnefs being thus ample, a law is properly that which reafon in fuch fort defineth to be good that it muft be done. And the law of reafon or human nature is that which men by difcourfe of natural reafon have rightly found out themfelves to be all for ever bound unto in their actions. Laws of reafon have thefe marks to be known by: fuch as keep them refemble moft lively in their voluntary actions that very manner of working which nature her felf doth neceffarily obferve in the courfe of the whole world. The works of nature are all behoveful, beautiful, without fuperfluity or defect; even fo theirs, if they be framed according to that which the law of reafon teacheth. Secondly, thofe laws are inveftigable by reafon, without the help of revelation, fupernatural and divine. Finally, in fuch fort they are inveftigable, that the knowledge of them is general, the world hath always been acquainted with them; according to that which one in *Sophocles* obferveth, concerning a branch of this law: *it is no child of to day's, or yefterday's birth, but hath been no man knoweth how long fithence.* It is not agreed upon by one, or two, or few, but by all. Which we may not fo underftand, as if every particular man in the whole world did know and confefs whatfoever the law of reafon doth contain: but this law is fuch, that being propofed, no man can reject it as unreafonable and unjuft. Again, there is nothing in it, but any man (having natural perfection of wit, and ripenefs of judgment) may by labour and travel find out. And to conclude, the general principles thereof are fuch, as it is not eafy to find men ignorant of them. Law rational therefore, which men commonly ufe to call the law of nature, meaning thereby the law which human nature knoweth it felf in reafon univerfally bound unto, which alfo for that caufe may be termed, moft fitly, the law of reafon; this law, I fay, comprehendeth all thofe things which men by the light of their natural underftanding evidently know, or at leaftwife may know, to be befeeming or unbefeeming, virtuous or vicious, good or evil for them to do. Now, altho

Marginal notes:

(g) *Quod quis in fe approbat, in alio reprobare non poffe.* lib. in arenam C. de inof. teft. *Quod quifque juris in alium ftatuerit, ipfum quoque eodem uti debere.* lib. quod quifque. *Ab omni penitus injuria atque vi abftinendum.* lib. 1. fect. 1. Quod vi aut clam. Mat. 22. 40. On thefe two commandments hangeth the whole law. Gen. 39. 9. Mark 10. 4. Acts 4. 37. & 5. 4. 2 Theff. 3. 8.

Οὐ γάρ τι νῦν τε κἀχθὲς, ἀλλ' ἀεὶ ποτε ζῇ ταῦτα, κ' οὐδεὶς οἶδεν ἐξ ὅτου 'φάνη. Soph. Antig.

altho it be true, which some have said, that whatsoever is done amiss, the law of nature and reason thereby is transgress'd, because even those offences which are by their special qualities breaches of supernatural laws, do also, for that they are generally evil, violate in general that principle of reason, which willeth universally to fly from evil; yet do we not therefore so far extend the law of reason, as to contain in it all manner of laws whereunto reasonable creatures are bound, but (as hath been shewn) we restrain it to those only duties, which all men by force of natural wit, either do, or might understand to be such duties as concern all men. *Certain half-waking men there are* (as *St. Augustine noteth) who neither altogether asleep in folly, nor yet throughly awake in the light of true understanding, have thought that there is not at all any thing just and righteous in it self; but look wherewith nations are inured, the same they take to be right and just. Whereupon their conclusion is, that seeing each sort of people hath a different kind of right from other, and that which is right of its own nature, must be every where one and the same; therefore in it self there is nothing right. These good folks* (saith he, *that I may not trouble their wits with the rehearsal of too many things) have not looked so far into the world as to perceive that, do as thou wouldst be done unto, is a sentence which all nations under heaven are agreed upon. Refer this sentence to the love of God, and it extinguisheth all heinous crimes: refer it to the love of thy neighbour, and all grievous wrongs it banisheth out of the world.* Wherefore, as touching the law of reason, this was (it seemeth) St. *Augustine's* judgment; namely, that there are in it some things which stand as principles universally agreed upon; and that out of those principles which are in themselves evident, the greatest moral duties we owe towards God and man may without any great difficulty be concluded: if then it be here demanded by what means it should come to pass (the greatest part of the law moral being so easy for all men to know) that so many thousands of men notwithstanding have been ignorant, even of principal moral duties, not imagining the breach of them to be sin: I deny not but leud and wicked custom, beginning perhaps at the first among few, afterwards spreading into greater multitudes, and so continuing from time to time, may be of force even in plain things, to smother the light of natural understanding, because men will not bend their wits to examine whether things wherewith they have been accustomed be good or evil. For example sake, that grosser kind of heathenish idolatry, whereby they worshipped the very works of their own hands, was an absurdity to reason so palpable, that the prophet *David* comparing idols and idolaters together, maketh almost no odds between them, but the one in a manner as much without wit and sense as the other; *they that make them are like unto them, and so are all that trust in them.* That wherein an idolater doth seem so absurd and foolish, is by the wiseman thus express'd, *He is not ashamed to speak unto that which hath no life: he talketh on him that is weak, for health: he prayeth for life unto him which is dead: of him which hath no experience, he requireth help: for his journey he sueth to him which is not able to go: for gain, and work, and success in his affairs, he seeketh furtherance of him that hath no manner of power.* The cause of which senseless stupidity, is afterwards imputed to custom: *When a father mourneth grievously for his son that was taken away suddenly, he made an image for him that was once dead, whom now he worshipped as a god, ordaining to his servants ceremonies and sacrifices.* Thus by process of time this wicked custom prevailed, and was kept as a law; the authority of rulers, the ambition of craftsmen, and such like means, thrusting forward the ignorant, and encreasing their superstition. Unto this which the wiseman hath spoken, somewhat besides may be added. For whatsoever we have hitherto taught, or shall hereafter, concerning the force of man's natural understanding, this we always desire withal to be understood, that there is no kind of faculty or power in man or any other creature, which can rightly perform the functions allotted to it, without perpetual aid and concurrence of that supreme cause of all things. The benefit whereof as oft as we cause God in his justice to withdraw, there can no other thing follow than that which the apostle noteth, even men endued with the light of reason to walk notwithstanding *in the vanity of their mind, having their cogitations darkned, and being strangers from the life of God, thro the ignorance which is in them, because of the hardness of their hearts.* And this cause is mentioned by the prophet *Isaiah*, speaking of the ignorance of idolaters, who see not how the manifest law of reason condemneth their gross iniquity and sin; they have not in them, saith he, so much wit as to think, *shall I bow to the stock of a tree? All knowledge and understanding is taken from them; for God hath shut their eyes that they cannot see.* That which we say in this case of idolatry serveth for all other things, wherein the like kind of general blindness hath prevailed against the manifest laws of reason. Within the compass of which laws we do not only comprehend whatsoever may be

Th. 1, 2. q. 94. art. 3. Omnia peccata sunt in universam contra rationem & natura legem. Aug. de civit. Dei, l. 12. cap. 1. Omne vitium natura nocet, ac per hoc contra naturam est. De doct. chr. lib. 3. cap. 14.

Psal. 135. 18.

Wisd. 13. 17.

Wisd. 14. 15.

Ephes. 4. 17.

Isa. 44. 18, 19.

be eafily known to belong to the duty of all men, but even whatfoever may poffibly be known to be of that quality, fo that the fame be by neceffary confequence deduced out of clear and manifeft principles. For if once we defcend unto probable collections what is convenient for men, we are then in the territory where free and arbitrary determinations, the territory where human laws take place, which laws are after to be confidered.

The benefit of keeping that law which reafon teacheth.

9. Now the due obfervation of this law which reafon teacheth us, cannot but be effectual unto their great good who obferve the fame. For we fee the whole world and each part thereof fo compacted, that as long as each thing performeth only that work which is natural unto it, it thereby preferveth both other things and alfo it felf. Contrariwife, let any principal thing, as the fun, the moon, any one of the heavens or elements, but once ceafe, or fail, or fwerve, and who doth not eafily conceive that the fequel thereof would be ruin both to it felf and whatfoever dependeth on it ? And is it poffible, that man being not only the nobleft creatuie in the world, but even a very world in himfelf, his tranfgreffing the law of his nature fhould draw no manner of harm after it ? Yes, *Tribulation and anguifh unto every foul that doth evil.* Good doth follow unto all things by obferving the courfe of their nature, and on the contrary fide evil by not obferving it ; but not unto natural agents that good which we call *reward*, not that evil which we properly term *punifhment.* The reafon whereof is, becaufe amongft creatures in this world, only man's obfervation of the law of his nature is righteoufnefs, only man's tranfgreffion fin. And the reafon of this is, the difference in his manner of obferving or tranfgreffing the law of his nature. He doth not otherwife than voluntarily the one, or the other. What we do againft our wills, or conftrainedly, we are not properly faid to do it, becaufe the motive caufe of doing it is not in our felves, but carrieth us (as if the wind fhould drive a feather in the air) we no whit furthering that whereby we are driven. In fuch cafes therefore, the evil which is done moveth compaffion. Men are pitied for it, as being rather miferable in fuch refpect than culpable. Some things are likewife done by man, tho not thro outward force and impulfion, tho not againft, yet without their wills ; as in alienation of mind, or any the like inevitable utter abfence of wit and judgment. For which caufe, no man did ever think the hurtful actions of furious men and innocents to be punifhable. Again, fome things we do neither againft nor without, and yet not fimply and merely with our wills, but with our wills in fuch fort moved, that albeit there be no impoffibility but that we might, neverthelefs we are not fo eafily able to do otherwife. In this confideration, one evil deed is made more pardonable than another. Finally, that which we do being evil, is notwithftanding by fo much more pardonable, by how much the exigence of fo doing, or the difficulty of doing otherwife, is greater ; unlefs this neceffity or difficulty have originally rifen from our felves. It is no excufe therefore unto him, who being drunk committeth inceft, and alledgeth that his wits were not his own ; in as much as himfelf might have chofen, whether his wits fhould by that means have been taken from him. Now rewards and punifhments do always prefuppofe fomething willingly done well or ill ; without which refpect, tho we may fometimes receive good or harm, yet then the one is only a benefit and not a reward, the other fimply an hurt not a punifhment.

Voluntate fublatâ, omnem actium parem efſe. lib. fœdiffimam, de adult. *Bonam voluntatem plerumque pro facto reputari.* l. fi quis in teſtament.

From the fundry difpofitions of man's will, which is the root of all his actions, there groweth variety in the fequel of rewards and punifhments, which are by thefe and the like rules meafured : *Take away the will, and all acts are equal : That which we do not, and would do, is commonly accepted as done.* By thefe and the like rules, mens actions are determin'd of and judged, whether they be in their own nature rewardable or punifhable. Rewards and punifhments are not received, but at the hands of fuch as being above us have power to examine and judge our deeds. How men come to have this authority one over another in external actions, we fhall more diligently examine in that which followeth. But for this prefent, fo much all do acknowledge, that fince every

Divus caſte adeunto, pietatem adhibento. Qui fecus faxis, Deus ipfe vindex erit.

man's heart and confcience doth in good or evil, even fecretly committed and known to none but it felf, either like or difallow it felf, and accordingly either rejoice, very nature exulting, as it were, in certain hope of reward, or elfe grieve, as it were, in a fenfe of future punifhment ; neither of which can in this cafe be looked for from any other, faving only from him who difcerneth and judgeth the very fecrets of all hearts : therefore he is the only rewarder and revenger of all fuch actions ; altho not of fuch actions only, but of all, whereby the law of nature is broken whereof himfelf is author. For which caufe, the *Roman laws,* called *the laws of the twelve tables,* requiring offices of inward affection which the eye of man cannot reach unto, threaten the neglecters of them with none but divine punifhment.

10. That

10. That which hitherto we have set down, is (I hope) sufficient to shew their bru- tishness, which imagine that religion and virtue are only as men will account of them ; that we might make as much account, if we would, of the contrary, without any harm unto our selves, and that in nature they are as indifferent one as the other. We see then how nature it self teacheth laws and statutes to live by. The laws, which have been hitherto mention'd, do bind men absolutely, even as they are men, altho they have never any settled fellowship, never any solemn agreement amongst themselves what to do, or not to do. But forasmuch as we are not by our selves sufficient to furnish our selves with competent store of things needful for such a life as our nature doth desire, a life fit for the dignity of man ; therefore to supply those defects and imperfections which are in us living single and solely by our selves, we are naturally induc'd to seek communion and fellowship with others. This was the cause of mens uniting themselves at the first in po- litick societies, which societies could not be without government, nor government with- out a distinct kind of law from that which hath been already declar'd. Two foundations there are which bear up publick societies ; the one a natural inclination, whereby all men desire sociable life and fellowship ; the other an order expresly or secretly agreed upon, touching the manner of their union in living together. The latter is that which we call the law of a commonweal, the very soul of a politick body, the parts whereof are by law animated, held together, and set on work in such actions as the common good re- quireth. Laws politick, ordain'd for external order and regiment amongst men, are ne- ver framed as they should be, unless presuming the will of man to be inwardly obstinate, rebellious, and averse from all obedience unto the sacred laws of his nature : in a word, unless presuming man to be, in regard of his depraved mind, little better than a wild beast, they do accordingly provide notwithstanding so to frame his outward actions that they be no hindrance unto the common good for which societies are instituted ; unless they do this, they are not perfect. It resteth therefore, that we consider how nature findeth out such laws of government as serve to direct even nature depraved to a right end. All men desire to lead in this world an happy life : that life is led most happily, wherein all virtue is exercised without impediment or let. The apostle, in exhorting men to content- ment, altho they have in this world no more than very bare food and raiment, giveth us thereby to understand, that those are even the lowest of things necessary ; that if we should be stripped of all those things without which we might possibly be, yet these must be left ; that destitution in these is such an impediment, as till it be removed suffereth not the mind of man to admit any other care. For this cause, first God assign'd *Adam* main- tenance of life, and then appointed him a law to observe : for this cause after men began to grow to a number, the first thing we read they gave themselves unto, was the tilling of the earth and the feeding of cattle. Having by this means whereon to live, the princi- pal actions of their life afterward are noted by the exercise of their religion. True it is, that the kingdom of God must be the first thing in our purposes and desires. But in as much as a righteous life presupposeth life ; in as much as to live virtuously it is impos- sible except we live ; therefore the first impediment which naturally we endeavour to re- move, is penury and want of things without which we cannot live. Unto life many im- plements are necessary ; more if we seek (as all men naturally do) such a life as hath in it joy, comfort, delight and pleasure. To this end we see how quickly sundry arts me- chanical were found out in the very prime of the world. As things of greatest necessity are always first provided for, so things of greatest dignity are most accounted of by all such as judge rightly. Altho therefore riches be a thing which every man wisheth, yet no man of judgment can esteem it better to be rich, than wise, virtuous, and religious. If we be both, or either of these, it is not because we are so born : for into the world we come as empty of the one as of the other, as naked in mind as we are in body. Both which necessities of man had at the first no other helps and supplies than only domestical ; such as that which the prophet implieth, saying, *can a mother forget her child ?* such as that which the apostle mentioneth, saying, *he that careth not for his own is worse than an infidel :* such as that concerning *Abraham, Abraham will command his sons* and *his houshold after him, that they keep the way of the Lord.* But neither that which we learn of our selves, nor that which others teach us can prevail, where wickedness and malice have taken deep root. If therefore, when there was but as yet one only fa- mily in the world, no means of instruction, human or divine, could prevent effusion of blood, how could it be chosen but that when families were multiplied and encreased upon earth ; after separation, each providing for it self, envy, strife, contention, and violence, must grow amongst them ? For hath not nature furnished man with wit and valour, as it were, with armour, which may be used as well unto extreme evil as good ? Yea, were they not used by the rest of the world unto evil ? unto the contrary only by *Seth,*

D   *Enoch,*

Marginal notes:
How reason doth lead men unto the ma- king of human laws, whereby politick socie- ties are go- verried, and to agreement a- bout laws, whereby the fellowship or communion of independent society stand- eth. Ἔςι γὰ ὁ μαγ-]υϊῆαι ἢ πάνlις φύσει κοινόν δίκαιον κỳ ἄδικον, κỳ ὃ μηδεμία κοι- νωνία πρὸς ἀλλήλυς ἤ μηδ᾽ ἀντι-Θήκη. Arist. Rhet.1.

1 Tim. 6, 8.

Gen. 1. 29. & 2. 17. & 4. 2. & 4. 16.

Matth. 6. 33.

Gen. 4. 10, 21, 22.

Isa. 49. 15.
1 Tim. 5, 8.
Gen. 18. 19.

Gen. 4. 8.

Gen. 6. 5.

Gen. 5.
Enoch, and thofe few the reft in that line? We all make complaint of the iniquity of our times, not unjuftly, for the days are evil: but compare them with thofe times wherein there were no civil focieties, with thofe times wherein there was as yet no manner of publick regiment eftablifhed, with thofe times wherein there were not above eight righ-
2 Pet. 2. 5.
teous perfons living upon the face of the earth; and we have furely good caufe to think that God hath blefled us exceedingly, and hath made us behold moft happy days. To take away all fuch mutual grievances, injuries and wrongs, there was no way but only by growing unto compofition and agreement amongft themfelves, by ordaining fome kind of government publick, and by yielding themfelves fubject thereunto; that unto whom they granted authority to rule and govern, by them the peace, tranquillity, and happy eftate of the reft might be procured. Men always knew, that when force and injury was offer'd, they might be defenders of themfelves; they knew that howfoever men may feek their own commodity, yet if this were done with injury unto others it was not to be fuffered, but by all men, and by all good means to be withftood: finally, they knew that no man might in reafon take upon him to determine his own right, and according to his own determination proceed in maintenance thereof, in as much as every man is towards himfelf, and them whom he greatly affecteth, partial; and therefore that ftrifes and troubles would be endlefs, except they gave their common confent all to be ordered by fome whom they fhould agree upon. Without which confent there were no reafon that one man fhould take upon him to be lord or judge over another; becaufe, altho there be, according to the opinion of fome very great and judicious men, a kind of natural right in
Ariſt. Polit. lib. 3, & 4.
the noble, wife, and virtuous, to govern them which are of fervile difpofition; neverthelefs, for manifeftation of this their right, and mens more peaceable contentment on both fides, the affent of them who are to be governed feemeth neceffary. To fathers within their private families, nature hath given a fupreme power; for which caufe we fee throughout the world, even from the foundation thereof, all men have ever been taken as lords and lawful kings in their own houfes. Howbeit, over a whole grand multitude, having no fuch dependency upon any one, and confifting of fo many families, as every politick fociety in the world doth, impoffible it is that any fhould have complete lawful power but by confent of men, or immediate appointment of God; becaufe not having the natural fuperiority of fathers, their power muft needs be either ufurp'd, and then unlawful; or if lawful, then either granted or confented unto by them over whom they exercife the fame, or elfe given extraordinarily from God unto whom all the world is fubject.
Ariſt. Polit. lib. 1, cap. 3. Vide & Platonem in 3. de legibus.
It is no improbable opinion therefore, which the arch-philofopher was of, that as the chiefeft perfon in every houfhold was always as it were a king, fo when numbers of houfholds join'd themfelves in civil focieties together, kings were the firft kind of governours amongft them. Which is alfo (as it feemeth) the reafon why the name of *father* continu'd ftill in them, who of fathers were made rulers; as alfo the antient cuftom of governours to do as *Melchifedec*, and being kings to exercife the office of priefts, which fathers did at the firft, grew perhaps by the fame occafion: howbeit, this is not the only kind of regiment that hath been receiv'd in the world. The inconveniencies of one kind have caufed fundry other to be devifed. So that, in a word, all publick regiment, of what kind foever, feemeth evidently to have rifen from deliberate advice, confultation, and compofition between men, judging it convenient and behoveful; there being no impoffibility in nature confider'd by it felf, but that men might have liv'd without any publick regiment. Howbeit, the corruption of our nature being prefuppofed, we may not deny, but that the law of nature doth now require of neceffity fome kind of regiment; fo that to bring things unto the firft courfe they were in, and utterly to take away all kind of publick government in the world, were apparently to overturn the whole world. The cafe of man's nature ftanding therefore as it doth, fome kind of regiment the law of nature doth require; yet the kinds thereof being many, nature tieth not to any one, but leaveth the choice as a thing arbitrary. At the firft, when fome certain kind of regiment was once approv'd, it may be that nothing was then further thought upon for the manner of governing, but all permitted unto their wifdom and difcretion which were to
(*a*) Cum praemeretur initio multitudo ab iis qui majores opeshabebant, ad unum aliquem confugiebant virtute
rule; (*a*) till by experience they found this for all parts very inconvenient, fo as the thing which they had devifed for a remedy did indeed but increafe the fore which it fhould have cured. They faw that to live by one man's will, became the caufe of all mens mifery. This conftrained them to come unto laws, wherein all men might fee their duties beforehand, and know the penalties of tranfgreffing them. (*b*) If things be fimply good or

praeftantem, qui cum prohiberet injuriâ tenuiores, aequitate conftituendâ fummos cum infimis pari jure retinebat. Cum id minus contingeret, leges funt inventae. *Cic.* Offic. lib. 2. τὸ χρῆσαι πηδᾶν ἣ φίλως ἀνθρώποις, καὶ ταῖς ἐνεργείαις χάριν ἐπιδίδοται, ταῦτα καὶ τέλος ἥμμια ἐ προεσάντται τῆς ἀνθρώπινε εἰ γεγραμμένοι πόμω ποιεῖν, ἀλλ᾽ ἐανὸς ἀγαθὸν ἣ κατ᾽ ῥύμω ποιεῖ(). *Ariſt.* Rhet. ad Alex. (*b*) *Tanta eſt enim vis voluptatum, ut & ignorantia protulit in occaſionem, & conſcientiam corrumpat in diſſimulationem.* Tertul. lib. de ſpectacul.

evil, and withal univerſally ſo acknowledged, there needs no new law to be made for ſuch things. The firſt kind therefore of things appointed by laws human containeth whatſoever being in it ſelf naturally good or evil, is notwithſtanding more ſecret than that it can be diſcerned by every man's preſent conceit, without ſome deeper diſcourſe and judgment. In which diſcourſe, becauſe there is difficulty and poſſibility many ways to err, unleſs ſuch things were ſet down by laws, many would be ignorant of their duties, which now are not ; and many that know what they ſhould do would nevertheleſs diſſemble it, and to excuſe themſelves pretend ignorance and ſimplicity, which now they cannot. And becauſe the greateſt part of men are ſuch as prefer their own private good before all things, even that good which is ſenſual before whatſoever is moſt divine ; and for that the labour of doing good, together with the pleaſure ariſing from the contrary, doth make men for the moſt part ſlower to the one and proner to the other, than that duty preſcribed them by law can prevail ſufficiently with them ; therefore unto laws that men do make for the benefit of men, it hath ſeemed always needful to add rewards, which may more allure unto good, than any hardneſs deterreth from it ; and puniſhments which may more deter from evil, than any ſweetneſs thereto allureth. Wherein as the generality is natural, *virtue rewardable, and vice puniſhable* ; ſo the particular determination of the reward or puniſhment belongeth unto them by whom laws are made. Theft is naturally puniſhable, but the kind of puniſhment is poſitive ; and ſuch lawful as men ſhall think with diſcretion convenient by law to appoint. In laws, that which is natural bindeth univerſally ; that which is poſitive, not ſo. To let go thoſe poſitive kind of laws which men impoſe upon themſelves, as by vow unto God, contract with men, or ſuch like ; ſomewhat it will make unto our purpoſe, a little more fully to conſider what things are incident unto the making of the poſitive laws for the government of them that live united in publick ſociety. Laws do not only teach what is good, but they enjoin it, they have in them a certain conſtraining force ; and to conſtrain men unto any thing inconvenient, doth ſeem unreaſonable. Moſt requiſite therefore it is, that to deviſe laws which all men ſhall be forc'd to obey, none but wiſe men be admitted. Laws are matters of principal conſequence ; men of common capacity, and but ordinary judgment, are not able (for how ſhould they ?) to diſcern what things are fitteſt for each kind and ſtate of regiment. We cannot be ignorant how much our obedience unto laws dependeth upon this point. Let a man, tho never ſo juſtly, oppoſe himſelf unto them that are diſordered in their ways; and what one among them commonly doth not ſtomach at ſuch contradiction, ſtorm at reproof, and hate ſuch as would reform them ? Notwithſtanding, even they which brook it worſt that men ſhould tell them of their duties, when they are told the ſame by a law, think very well and reaſonably of it. For why ? they preſume that the law doth ſpeak with all indifferency ; that the law hath no ſide reſpect to their perſons ; that the law is as it were an oracle proceeding from wiſdom and underſtanding. Howbeit, laws do not take their conſtraining force from the quality of ſuch as deviſe them, but from that power which doth give them the ſtrength of laws. That which we ſpake before, concerning the power of government, muſt here be apply'd unto the power of making laws whereby to govern, which power God hath over all : and by the natural law, whereunto he hath made all ſubject, the lawful power of making laws, to command whole politick ſocieties of men, belongeth ſo properly unto the ſame entire ſocieties, that for any prince or potentate of what kind ſoever upon earth to exerciſe the ſame of himſelf, and not either by expreſs commiſſion immediately and perſonally received from God, or elſe by authority derived at the firſt from their conſent upon whoſe perſons they impoſe laws, it is no better than mere tyranny. Laws they are not therefore which publick approbation hath not made ſo. But approbation not only they give who perſonally declare their aſſent, by voice, ſign, or act ; but alſo when others do it in their names, by right, originally at the leaſt, derived from them. As in parliaments, councils, and the like aſſemblies, altho we be not perſonally our ſelves preſent, notwithſtanding our aſſent is by reaſon of other agents there in our behalf. And what we do by others, no reaſon but that it ſhould ſtand as our deed, no leſs effectually to bind us than if our ſelves had done it in perſon. In many things aſſent is given, they that give it not imagining they do ſo, becauſe the manner of their aſſenting is not apparent. As for example, when an abſolute monarch commandeth his ſubjects that which ſeemeth good in his own diſcretion ; hath not his edict the force of a law whether they approve or diſlike it ? Again, that which hath been receiv'd long ſithence, and is by cuſtom now eſtabliſh'd, we keep as a law which we may not tranſgreſs ; yet, what conſent was ever thereunto ſought or requir'd at our hands ? Of this point therefore we are to note, that ſith men naturally have no full and perfect power to command whole politick multitudes of men ; therefore, utterly without our conſent, we could in ſuch ſort be at no man's commandment living. And to be commanded we do conſent, when that ſociety whereof we are part, hath at any time before confented, without revoking the fame after by the like univerfal agreement. Wherefore, as any man's deed paft is good as long as himfelf continueth ; fo the act of a publick fociety of men done five hundred years fithence, ftandeth as theirs who prefently are of the fame focieties, becaufe corporations are immortal ; we were then alive in our predeceffors, and they in their fucceffors do live ftill. Laws therefore human of what kind foever, are available by confent. If here it be demanded, how it comes to pafs that this being common unto all laws which are made, there fhould be found even in good laws fo great variety as there is ? we muft note the reafon hereof to be, the fundry particular ends whereunto the different difpofition of that fubject or matter for which laws are provided, caufeth them to have a fpecial refpect in making laws. A law

Arift. Polit. lib. 2. cap. ult. there is mentioned amongft the *Grecians,* whereof *Pittacus* is reported to have been author ; and by that law it was agreed, that he which being overcome with drink did then ftrike any man, fhould fuffer punifhment double as much as if he had done the fame being fober. No man could ever have thought this reafonable, that had intended thereby only to punifh the injury committed according to the gravity of the fact : for who knoweth not, that harm advifedly done is naturally lefs pardonable, and therefore worthy of fharper punifhment ? But forafmuch as none did fo ufually this way offend as men in that cafe, which they wittingly fell into, even becaufe they would be fo much the more freely out-ragious ; it was for their publick good, where fuch diforder was grown, to frame a pofi-tive law for remedy thereof accordingly. To this appertain thofe known laws of making laws ; as that law-makers muft have an eye to that place where, and to the men amongft whom ; that one kind of laws cannot ferve for all kind of regiment ; that where the multitude beareth fway, laws that fhall tend to the prefervation of that ftate muft make common fmaller offices to go by lot, for fear of ftrife and divifion likely to arife; by rea-fon that ordinary qualities fufficing for difcharge of fuch offices, they could not but by many be defired, and fo with danger contended for, and not miffed without grudge and difcontentment ; whereas at an uncertain lot, none can find themfelves grieved, on whomfoever it lighteth. Contrariwife the greateft, whereof but few are capable to pafs by popular election, that neither the people may envy fuch as have thofe honours, inaf-much as themfelves beftow them, and that the chiefeft may be kindled with defire to exer-cife all parts of rare and beneficial virtue ; knowing they fhall not lofe their labour by growing in fame and eftimation amongft the people. If the helm of chief government be in the hands of a few of the wealthieft, that then laws providing for continuance there-of muft make the punifhment of contumely and wrong offer'd unto any of the common fort, fharp and grievous ; that fo the evil may be prevented whereby the rich are moft likely to bring themfelves into hatred with the people, who are not wont to take fo great offence when they are excluded from honors and offices, as when their perfons are contume-lioufly trodden upon. In other kinds of regiment, the like is obferv'd concerning the diffe-rence of pofitive laws, which to be every where the fame, is impoffible, and againft their na-

Staundf. Pre-face to the pleas of the crown. ture. Now as the learned in the laws of this land obferve, that our ftatutes fometimes are only the affirmation or ratification of that which by common law was held before ; fo here it is not to be omitted, that generally all laws human which are made for the or-dering of politick focieties, be either fuch as eftablifh fome duty, whereunto all men by the law of reafon did before ftand bound ; or elfe fuch as make that a duty now, which before was none : the one fort we may for diftinction fake call *mixedly*, and the other *merely human*. That which plain or neceffary reafon bindeth men unto, may be in fundry confiderations expedient to be ratified by human law. For example, if confufion of blood in marriage, the liberty of having many wives at once, or any other the like corrupt and unreafonable cuftom doth happen to have prevail'd far, and to have gotten the upper hand of right reafon with the greateft part ; fo that no way is left to rectify fuch foul diforder

Jud. ver. 10. Ὃι πολλοὶ ἀ-νάγκη μᾶλλον ἢ λόγῳ πει-θόμενοι κὶ ζημίαις ἢ τῷ καλῷ. *Arift.* Eth. lib. 10. cap. 10, without prefcribing by law the fame things which reafon neceffarily doth enforce, but is not perceived that fo it doth ; or if many be grown unto that which the apoftle did lament in fome, concerning whom he writeth, faying, that *even what things they natu-rally know, in thofe very things, as beafts void of reafon, they corrupted themfelves :* or if there be no fuch fpecial accident, yet forafmuch as the common fort are led by the fway of their fenfual defires, and therefore do more fhun fin for the fenfible evils which fol-low it amongft men than for any kind of fentence which reafon doth pronounce againft it : this very thing is caufe fufficient, why duties belonging unto each kind of virtue, albeit the law of reafon teach them, fhould notwithftanding be prefcrib'd even by human law. Which law in this cafe we term *mixt*, becaufe the matter whereunto it bind-eth, is the fame which reafon neceffarily doth require at our hands, and from the law of reafon it differeth in the manner of binding only. For whereas men before ftood bound in confcience to do as the law of reafon teacheth ; they are now by virtue of

human

human law become constrainable, and if they outwardly transgress, punishable. As for laws which are *merely human*, the matter of them is any thing which reason doth but probably teach to be fit and convenient; so that till such time as law hath passed a-mongst men about it, of it self it bindeth no man. One example whereof may be this, lands are by human law in some places, after the owner's decease, divided unto all his children; in some, all descend to the eldest son. If the law of reason did necessarily re-quire but the one of these two to be done, they which by law have received the other, should be subject to that heavy sentence which denounceth against all that decree wicked, Isaiah 10. 1. unjust and unreasonable things, *wo*. Whereas now, which soever be received, there is no law of reason transgress'd; because there is probable reason why either of them may be expedient; and for either of them more than probable reason there is not to be found laws, whether mixtly or merely human, are made by politick societies; some only, as those societies are civilly united; some, as they are spiritually join'd, and make such a body as we call the church. Of laws human in this latter kind, we are to speak in the third book following. Let it therefore suffice thus far to have touched the force where-with almighty God hath graciously endued our nature, and thereby enabled the same to find out both those laws which all men generally are for ever bound to observe; and also such as are most fit for their behoof, who lead their lives in any ordered state of go-vernment. Now besides that law which simply concerneth men, as men; and that which belongeth unto them, as they are men linked with others in some form of politick society, there is a third kind of law which toucheth all such several bodies politick, so far forth as one of them hath publick commerce with another. And this third is, *the law of nations*. Between men and beasts there is no possibility of sociable communion; because the well-spring of that communion is a natural delight which man hath to trans-fuse from himself into others, and to receive from others into himself, especially those things wherein the excellency of his kind doth most consist. The chiefest instrument of Arist. Polit. 1; human communion therefore is speech, because thereby we impart mutually one to another cap. 2. the conceits of our reasonable understanding. And for that cause, seeing beasts are not hereof capable, for as much as with them we can use no such conference, they being in degree, altho above other creatures on earth, to whom nature hath deny'd sense, yet lower than to be sociable companions of man, to whom nature hath given reason; it is of *Adam* said, that amongst the beasts *he found not for himself any meet companion*. Ci-Gen. 2. 20; vil society doth more content the nature of man than any private kind of solitary li-ving; because in society this good of mutual participation is so much larger than other-wise. Herewith notwithstanding we are not satisfy'd, but we covet (if it might be) to have a kind of society and fellowship even with all mankind. Which thing *Socrates* in-Cic. Tusc. 5. tending to signify, professed himself a citizen not of this or that common-wealth, but of the & 1. de Legib. world. And an effect of that very natural desire in us, (a manifest token that we wish, after a sort, an universal fellowship with all men) appeareth by the wonderful delight men have, some to visit foreign countries, some to discover nations not heard of in former ages, we all to know the affairs and dealings of other people, yet to be in league of amity with them: and this not only for traffick's sake, or to the end that when many are confederated, each may make other the more strong; but for such cause also as moved the queen of *Sheba* to visit *Solomon*; and in a word, because nature doth pre-1 Kings 10. 1. sume, that how many men there are in the world, so many gods, as it were, there 2 Chron. 9. 1. are; or at leastwise such they should be towards men. Touching laws which are to Math. 15. 42. serve men in this behalf; even as those laws of reason, which (man retaining his origi-Luke 11. 31. nal integrity) had been sufficient to direct each particular person in all his affairs and duties, are not sufficient, but require the access of other laws now, that man and his off-spring are grown thus corrupt and sinful: again, as those laws, of polity and regi-ment, which would have served men living in publick society together with that harmless disposition which then they should have had, are not able now to serve, when mens iniquity is so hardly restrained within any tolerable bounds; in like manner, the national laws of natural commerce between societies of that former and better quality might have been other than now, when nations are so prone to offer violence, injury and wrong. Hereupon hath grown in every of these three kinds, that distinction between *primary* and *secondary* laws; the one grounded upon sincere, the other built upon depraved na-ture. Primary laws of nations are such as concern embassage, such as belong to the courteous entertainment of foreigners and strangers, such as serve for commodious traf-fick, and the like. Secondary laws in the same kind, are such as this present unquiet world is most familiarly acquainted with; I mean laws of arms, which yet are much better known than kept. But what matter the law of nations doth contain, I omit to search. The strength and virtue of that law is such, that no particular nation can law-

fully

fully prejudice the fame by any their feveral laws and ordinances, more than a man, by his private refolutions, the law of the whole commonwealth or ftate wherein he liveth. For as civil law being the act of the whole body politick, doth therefore over-rule each feveral part of the fame body ; fo there is no reafon that any one commonwealth of it felf fhould, to the prejudice of another, annihilate that whereupon the whole world hath agreed. For which caufe, the *Lacedæmonians* forbidding all accefs of ftrangers into their coafts, are in that refpect both by *Jofephus* and *Theodoret* defervedly blamed, as being enemies to that hofpitality which for common humanity's fake all the nations on earth fhould embrace. Now as there is great caufe of communion, and confequently of laws, for the maintenance of communion amongft nations ; fo amongft nations chriftian, the like in regard even of chriftianity hath been always judged needful. And in this kind of correfpondence amongft nations the force of general councils doth ftand. For as one and the fame law divine, whereof in the next place we are to fpeak, is unto all chriftian churches a rule for the chiefeft things ; by means whereof they all in that refpect make one church, as having all but *one Lord, one faith, and one baptifm :* fo the urgent neceffity of mutual communion for prefervation of our unity in thefe things, as alfo for order in fome other things convenient to be every where uniformly kept, maketh it requifite that the church of God here on earth have her laws of fpiritual commerce between chriftian nations ; laws, by virtue whereof all churches may enjoy freely the ufe of thofe reverend, religious, and facred confultations, which are termed councils general ; a thing whereof God's own bleffed Spirit was the author ; a thing practifed by the holy apoftles themfelves ; a thing always afterwards kept and obferv'd thro-out the world ; a thing never otherwife than moft highly efteemed of, till pride, ambition, and tyranny began by factious and vile endeavours, to abufe that divine intention unto the furtherance of wicked purpofes. But as the juft authority of civil courts and parliaments is not therefore to be abolifhed, becaufe fometimes there is cunning ufed to frame them according to the private intents of men over-potent in the commonwealth; fo the grievous abufe which hath been of councils, fhould rather caufe men to ftudy how fo gracious a thing may again be reduc'd to that firft perfection, than in regard of ftains and blemifhes fithence growing, be held for ever in extreme difgrace. To fpeak of this matter as the caufe requireth, would require very long difcourfe. All I will prefently fay is this, whether it be for the finding out of any thing whereunto divine law bindeth us, but yet in fuch fort, that men are not thereof on all fides refolv'd ; or for the fetting down of fome uniform judgment to ftand touching fuch things, as being neither way matters of neceffity, are notwithstanding offenfive and fcandalous, when there is open oppofition about them ; be it for the ending of ftrifes, touching matters of chriftian belief, wherein the one part may feem to have probable caufe of diffenting from the other ; or be it concerning matters of polity, order and regiment in the church ; I nothing doubt but that chriftian men fhould much better frame themfelves to thofe heavenly precepts which our Lord and Saviour with fo great inftancy gave, as concerning peace and unity, if we did all concur in defire to have the ufe of antient councils again renew'd, rather than thefe proceedings continued, which either make all contentions endlefs, or bring them to one only determination, and that of all other the worft, which is by fword. It followeth therefore, that a new foundation being laid, we now adjoin hereunto that which cometh in the next place to be fpoken of ; namely, wherefore God hath himfelf by fcripture, made known fuch laws as ferve for direction of men.

11. All things (God only excepted) befides the nature which they have in themfelves, receive externally fome perfection from other things, as hath been fhewed. Infomuch, as there is in the whole world no one thing great or fmall, but either in refpect of knowledge or of ufe, it may unto our perfection add fomewhat. And whatfoever fuch perfection there is which our nature may acquire, the fame we properly term our good, our *fovereign good* or *bleffednefs* ; that wherein the higheft degree of all our perfection confifteth, that which being once attained unto there can reft nothing further to be defired ; and therefore with it our fouls are fully content and fatisfied, in that they have they rejoice, and thirft for no more. Wherefore of good things defired, fome are fuch, that for themfelves we covet them not, but only becaufe they ferve as inftruments unto that for which we are to feek : of this fort are riches. Another kind there is, which altho we defire for it felf, as health, and virtue, and knowledge ; neverthelefs, they are not the laft mark whereat we aim, but have their further end whereunto they are referred : fo as in them we are not fatisfy'd, as having attained the utmoft we may, but our defires do ftill proceed. Thefe things are link'd, and as it were chain'd one to another. We labour to eat, and we eat to live, and we live to do good, and the good which we do, is as feed fown with reference unto a future harveft : but we muft come at length to fome paufe. For if every thing

were

Margin notes:

Jofeph. lib. 1. contra Appion.
Theod. lib. 9. de fanand. Græc. affect.

Ephef. 4. 5.

Acts 15. 28.

John 14. 27.

Wherefore God hath by fcripture further made known fuch fupernatural laws, as do ferve for mens direction.

Gal. 6. 8. *He that foweth to the Spirit, fhall of the Spirit reap life everlafting.*

were to be defir'd for fome other, without any ftint, there could be no certain end propos'd unto our actions, we fhould go on we know not whither; yea, whatfoever we do were in vain, or rather nothing at all were poffible to be done. For as to take away the firft efficient of our being were to annihilate utterly our perfons; fo we cannot remove the laft final caufe of our working, but we fhall caufe whatfoever we work to ceafe. Therefore fomething there muft be defir'd for it felf fimply, and for no other: that is, fimply for it felf defirable, unto the nature whereof it is oppofite and repugnant to be defir'd with relation to any other. The ox and the afs defire their food, neither propofe they unto themfelves any end wherefore; fo that of them this is defir'd for it felf. But why? By reafon of their imperfection, which cannot otherwife defire it; whereas that which is defired fimply for it felf, the excellency thereof is fuch as permitteth it not in any fort to be refer'd unto a further end. Now that which man doth defire, with reference to a further end, the fame he defireth in fuch meafure as is unto that end convenient; but what he coveteth as good in it felf, towards that, his defire is ever infinite. So that unlefs the laft good of all, which is defir'd altogether for it felf, be alfo infinite, we do evil in making it our end; even as they who plac'd their felicity in wealth, or honour, or pleafure, or any thing here attain'd, becaufe in defiring any thing as our final perfection which is not fo, we do amifs. Nothing may be infinitely defir'd, but that good which indeed is infinite: for the better, the more defirable; that therefore moft defirable wherein there is infinity of goodnefs: fo that if any thing defirable may be infinite, that muft needs be the higheft of all things that are defir'd. No good is infinite but only God; therefore he is our felicity and blifs. Moreover, defire tendeth unto union with that it defireth. If then in him we be bleffed, it is by force of participation and conjunction with him. Again, it is not the poffeffion of any good thing can make them happy which have it, unlefs they enjoy the things wherewith they are poffeffed. Then are we happy therefore, when fully we enjoy God as an object wherein the powers of our fouls are fatisfy'd even with everlafting delight: fo that altho we be men, yet by being unto God united, we live as it were the life of God. Happinefs therefore is that eftate whereby we attain, fo far as poffibly may be attained, the full poffeffion of that which fimply for it felf is to be defir'd, and containeth in it after an eminent fort the contentation of our defires, the higheft degree of all our perfection. Of fuch perfection capable we are not in this life. For while we are in the world, we are fubject unto fundry * imperfections, grief of body, defects of mind; yea, the beft things we do are painful, and the exercife of them grievous, being continued without intermiffion; fo as in thofe very actions whereby we are efpecially perfected in this life, we are not able to perfift; forced we are with very wearinefs, and that often, to interrupt them: which tedioufnefs cannot fall into thofe operations that are in the ftate of blifs, when our union with God is compleat. Compleat union with him muft be according unto every power and faculty of our minds, apt to receive fo glorious an object. Capable we are of God, both by underftanding and will: by underftanding, as he is that fovereign truth which comprehends the rich treafures of all wifdom: by will, as he is that fea of goodnefs whereof whofo tafteth fhall thirft no more. As the will doth now work upon that object by defire, which is as it were a motion towards the end as yet unobtained, fo likewife upon the fame hereafter received it fhall work alfo by love. *Appetitus inhiantes fit amor fruentis*, faith St. *Auguftine: The longing difpofition of them that thirft, is changed into the fweet affection of them that tafte, and are replenifhed.* Whereas we now love the thing that is good, but good efpecially in refpect of benefit unto us; we fhall then love the thing that is good, only or principally for the goodnefs of beauty in it felf; the foul being in this fort as it is active, perfected by love of that infinite good, fhall, as it is receptive, be alfo perfected with thofe fupernatural paffions of joy, peace, and delight; all this endlefs and everlafting. Which perpetuity, in regard whereof our bleffednefs is termed *a crown which withereth not*, doth neither depend on the nature of the thing it felf, nor proceed from any natural neceffity that our fouls fhould fo exercife themfelves for ever in beholding and loving God, but from the will of God, which doth both freely perfect our nature in fo high a degree, and continue it fo perfected. Under man, no creature in the world is capable of felicity and blifs: firft, becaufe their chiefeft perfection confifteth in that which is beft for them, but not in that which is fimply beft, as ours doth. Secondly, becaufe whatfoever external perfection they tend unto, it is not better than themfelves, as ours is. How juft occafion have we therefore, even in this refpect, with the prophet to admire the goodnefs of God? Lord, what is man, that thou fhouldft exalt him above the works of thy hands, fo far as to make thy felf the inheritance of his reft, and the fubftance of his felicity? Now, if men had not naturally this defire to be hap-

py,

Marginal notes:

Vide *Arift.* Ethic. lib. 10. c. 10. & Metaph. l. 12. cap. 6. & cap. 4. & cap. 30.

* Μέσον δ' Ἀρχίλοχω τὸ ὄνομα τῦ ἀγαδῦ ἐν ἀνθρώποις, τὸ ὄργον δλημαῖ. Τὸ μὴ λίαν ἐχκὸν, ἐνδεὲς τὸ ἀγαδὸν ἐςί. Τὸ γ᾽ ὑπερβάλλον ἀγαδὸν, μεῖων τῦ καλῦ τὸ ὑπάρχον. Ἀδύνατον ἐν τὸ ἀγαδὸν ἐγνωκέναι καδαρώτερον ἢ κακίαν, κέγω ᾗ χεῖρον ἴςω τῷ ἀγαδῷ τῇ εἰς τῶν ναὶ βαλόντι δεῖ ᾗ χειρόνων τῦ ἀγαδῦ, ἐν ἀδυνάτον ἐςιν αὐτὸ ἐν τῷ κόσμῳ εἶναι· ὁ γὸ κόσμῳ πληρωμὰ ἐςι κακίας, ὁ ᾗ διὸς ἀγαδῦ, ἢ τὸ ἀγαδὸν διὸς. *Merc. Trif.*

Aug. de Trin. lib. 9. c. ult.

Mat. 25, *The juft fhall go into life everlafting.*

Mat. 22, *They fhall be as the angels of God.*

2 Tim. 4. 8. 1 Pet. 1. 4.

Pfalm 8.

py, how were it possible that all men should have it? all men have. Therefore this desire in man is natural. It is not in our power not to do the same; how should it then be in our power to do it coldly or remissly? So that our desire being natural, is also in that degree of earnestness whereunto nothing can be added. And is it probable that God should frame the hearts of all men so desirous of that which no man may obtain? It is an axiom of nature, that natural desire cannot utterly be frustrate. This desire of ours being natural should be frustrate, if that which may satisfy the same were a thing impossible for man to aspire unto. Man doth seek a triple perfection; first, a sensual, consisting in those things which very life it self requireth either as necessary supplements, or as beauties and ornaments thereof; then an intellectual, consisting in those things which none underneath man is either capable of or acquainted with; lastly, a spiritual and divine, consisting in those things whereunto we tend by supernatural means here, but cannot here attain unto them. They who make the first of these three the scope of their whole life, are said by the apostle to have no god but only their belly, to be earthly-minded men. Unto the second they bend themselves, who seek especially to excel in all such knowledge and virtue as doth most commend men. To this branch belongeth the law of moral and civil perfection. That there is somewhat higher than either of these two, no other proof doth need than the very process of man's desire, which being natural should be frustrate, if there were not some further thing wherein it might rest at the length contented, which in the former it cannot do. For man doth not seem to rest satisfied, either with fruition of that wherewith his life is preserved, or with performance of such actions as advance him most deservedly in estimation; but doth further covet, yea, oftentimes manifestly pursue with great sedulity and earnestness that which cannot stand him in any stead for vital use; that which exceedeth the reach of sense, yea somewhat above capacity of reason, somewhat divine and heavenly, which with hidden exultation it rather surmiseth than conceiveth; somewhat it seeketh, and what that is directly, it knoweth not; yet very intentive desire thereof doth so incite it, that all other known delights and pleasures are laid aside, they give place to the search of this but only suspected desire. If the soul of man did serve only to give him being in this life, then things appertaining unto this life would content him, as we see they do other creatures; which creatures enjoying what they live by, seek no further, but in this contentation do shew a kind of acknowledgment that there is no higher good which doth any way belong unto them. With us it is otherwise. For altho the beauties, riches, honours, sciences, virtues and perfections of all men living, were in the present possession of one; yet somewhat beyond and above all this, there would still be sought and earnestly thirsted for. So that nature, even in this life, doth plainly claim and call for a more divine perfection than either of these two that have been mentioned. This last and highest estate of perfection whereof we speak, is received of men in the nature of (a) reward. Rewards do always presuppose such duties performed as are rewardable. Our natural means therefore unto blessedness, are our works; nor is it possible that nature should ever find any other way to salvation, than only this. But examine the works which we do, and since the first foundation of the world what one can say, My ways are pure? Seeing then all flesh is guilty of that for which God hath threatned eternally to punish, what possibility is there this way to be saved? There resteth therefore either no way unto salvation, or if any, then surely a way which is supernatural, a way which could never have entred into the heart of man as much as once to conceive or imagine, if God himself had not revealed it extraordinarily. For which cause, we term it the mystery or secret way of salvation. And therefore St. *Ambrose* in this matter appealeth justly from man to God, (b) *Cœli mysterium doceat me Deus qui condidit, non homo qui seipsum ignoravit : Let God himself that made me, let not man that knows not himself, be my instructer concerning the mystical way to heaven.* (c) *When men of excellent wit* (saith *Lactantius*) *had wholly betaken themselves unto study, after farewel bidden unto all kind as well of private as publick action, they spared no labour that might be spent in the search of truth; holding it a thing of much more price, to seek and to find out the reason of all affairs, as well divine as human, than to stick fast in the toil of piling up*

Comment. in Prœm. 2. *Metaph.*

Phil. 3. 19.

(a) Mat. 5. 12. Rejoice and be glad, for great is your reward in heaven.
Aug. de Doct. Christ. cap. 6. Summa merces est ut ipso perfruamur.

(b) Ambros. contra Sym.

(c) Magno & excellenti ingenio viri, cum se doctrinæ penitus dedidissent, quicquid laboris poterat impendi (contemptis omnibus & privatis & publicis actionibus) ad inquirenda veritatis studium contulerunt, existimantes multò esse præclarius humanarum divinarumque rerum investigare ac scire rationem, quàm struendis opibus aut cumulandis honoribus inhærere. Sed neque adepti sunt id quod volebant, & operam simul atque industriam perdiderunt : quia veritas id est arcanum summi Dei qui fecit omnia, ingenio ac propriis sensibus non potest comprehendi. Alioqui nihil inter Deum hominemque distaret, si consilia & dispositiones illius majestati æterna cogitatio assequeretur humana. Quod quia fieri non potuit ut homini per seipsum ratio divina notesceret, non est passus hominem Deus Inmen sapientia requirentem diutius aberrare, ac sine ulla laboris effectu vagari per tenebras inextricabiles. Aperuit oculos ejus aliquando, & notionem veritatis munus suum fecit, ut & humanam sapientiam nullam esse monstraret, & erranti ac vago viam consequenda immortalitatis ostenderet. Lactant. lib. 1. cap. 1.

riches, and gathering together heaps of honours. Howbeit, they did both fail of their purpose, and got not so much as to quit their charges; because truth, which is the secret of the most high God, whose proper handywork all things are, cannot be compassed with that wit and those senses which are our own. For God and man should be very near neighbours, if man's cogitations were able to take a survey of the counsels and appointments of that Majesty everlasting. Which being utterly impossible, that the eye of man by it self should look into the bosom of divine reason; God did not suffer him, being desirous of the light of wisdom, to stray any longer up and down, and with bootless expence of travel to wander in darkness that had no passage to get out by. His eyes at the length God did open, and bestow upon him the knowledge of the truth by way of donative, to the end that man might both be clearly convicted of folly; and being thro error out of the way, have the path that leadeth unto immortality laid plain before him.
Thus far *Lactantius Firmianus*, to shew, that God himself is the teacher of the truth, whereby is made known the supernatural way of salvation and law for them to live in that shall be saved. In the natural path of everlasting life the first beginning is that ability of doing good, which God in the day of man's creation endued him with; from hence obedience unto the will of his Creator, absolute righteousness and integrity in all his actions; and last of all, the justice of God rewarding the worthiness of his deserts with the crown of eternal glory. Had *Adam* continued in his first estate, this had been the way of life unto him and all his posterity.

Whereas I confess notwithstanding, with the (*d*) wittiest of the school-divines, that if we speak of strict justice, God could no way have been bound to require man's labours in so large and ample a manner as human felicity doth import; in as much as the dignity of this exceedeth so far the others value. But be it that God of his great

(*d*) Scot. lib. 4. Sent. dist. 49. 6. *Loquendo de strictâ justitiâ Deus nulli nostrum propter quæcunque merita est debitor perfectionis reddendæ tam intensæ, propter immoderatum excessum illius perfectionis ultra illa merita. Sed esto quod ex liberalitate sua determinasset merita conferre alicui tam perfectum tanquam præmium tali quidem justitiâ qualis decet eum, scilicet supererogantis in præmiis: tamen non sequitur ex hoc necessario, quod per illam justitiam sit reddenda perfectio perennis tanquam præmium, imo abundans fieret retributio in beatitudine unius momenti.*

liberality had determined in lieu of man's endeavours to bestow the same, by the rule of that justice which best beseemeth him, namely, the justice of one that requireth nothing mincingly, but all with pressed, and heaped, and even over-enlarged measure; yet could it never hereupon necessarily be gathered, that such justice should add to the nature of that reward the property of everlasting continuance; sith possession of bliss, tho it should be but for a moment, were an abundant retribution. But we are not now to enter into this consideration, how gracious and bountiful our good God might still appear in so rewarding the sons of men, albeit they should exactly perform whatsoever duty their nature bindeth them unto. Howsoever God did propose this reward, we that were to be rewarded must have done that which is required at our hands; we failing in the one, it were in nature an impossibility that the other should be looked for. The light of nature is never able to find out any way of obtaining the reward of bliss, but by performing exactly the duties and works of righteousness. From salvation therefore and life, all flesh being excluded this way, behold how the wisdom of God hath revealed a way mystical and supernatural, a way directing unto the same end of life by a course which groundeth it self upon the guiltiness of sin, and thro sin desert of condemnation and death. For in this way, the first thing is the tender compassion of God respecting us drowned and swallowed up in misery; the next is redemption out of the same by the precious death and merit of a mighty Saviour, which hath witnessed of himself, saying, *I am the way,* the way that leadeth us from misery into bliss. This supernatural way had God in himself prepared before all worlds. The way of supernatural duty which to us he hath prescrib'd, our Saviour in the gospel of saint *John* doth note, terming it by an excellency. The work of God: *This is the work of God, that ye believe in him whom he hath sent.* Not that God doth require nothing unto happiness at the hands of men saving only a naked belief (for hope and charity we may not exclude;) but that without belief all other things are as nothing, and it is the ground of those other divine virtues. Concerning faith, the principal object whereof is that eternal verity which hath discovered the treasures of hidden wisdom in Christ; concerning hope, the highest object whereof is that everlasting goodness which in Christ doth quicken the dead; concerning charity, the final object whereof is that incomprehensible beauty which shineth in the countenance of Christ the Son of the living God: concerning these virtues, the first of which beginning here with a weak apprehension of things not seen, endeth with the intuitive vision of God in the world to come; the second beginning here with a trembling expectation of things far remov'd, and as yet but only heard of, endeth with real and actual fruition of that which no tongue can express; the third beginning here with a weak inclination of heart towards him, unto whom we are not able to approach, endeth

John 14. 6.

John 6. 29.

E with

with endleſs union; the myſtery whereof is higher than the reach of the thoughts of men concerning that faith, hope, and charity, without which there can be no ſalvation; was there ever any mention made ſaving only in that law which God himſelf hath from heaven reveal'd? There is not in the world a ſyllable muttered with certain truth concerning any of theſe three, more than hath been ſupernaturally receiv'd from the mouth of the eternal God. Laws therefore concerning theſe things are ſupernatural, both in reſpect of the manner of delivering them, which is divine; and alſo in regard of the things delivered, which are ſuch as have not in nature any cauſe from which they flow, but were by the voluntary appointment of God ordained, beſides the courſe of nature, to rectify nature's obliquity withal.

The cauſe why ſo many natural or rational laws are ſet down in holy ſcripture.

* *Jus naturale eſt quod in lege & evangelio continetur,* p. 1. d. 1.

12. When ſupernatural duties are neceſſarily exacted, natural are not rejected as needleſs. The law of God therefore is, tho principally deliver'd for inſtruction in the one, yet fraught with precepts of the other alſo. The ſcripture is fraught even with laws of nature, inſomuch that * *Gratian* defining natural right (whereby is meant the right which exacteth thoſe general duties that concern men naturally even as they are men) termeth natural right, that which the books of the law and the goſpel do contain. Neither is it vain that the ſcripture aboundeth with ſo great ſtore of laws in this kind: for they are either ſuch as we of our ſelves could not eaſily have found out, and then the benefit is not ſmall to have them readily ſet down to our hands; or if they be ſo clear and manifeſt that no man endu'd with reaſon can lightly be ignorant of them, yet the Spirit, as it were, borrowing them from the ſchool of nature, as ſerving to prove things leſs manifeſt, and to induce a perſuaſion of ſomewhat which were in it ſelf more hard and dark, unleſs it ſhould in ſuch ſort be clear'd, the very applying of them unto caſes particular is not without moſt ſingular uſe and profit many ways for mens inſtruction. Beſides, be they plain of themſelves, or obſcure, the evidence of God's own teſtimony, added to the natural aſſent of reaſon concerning the certainty of them, doth not a little comfort and confirm the ſame. Wherefore, inaſmuch as our actions are converſant about things beſet with many circumſtances, which cauſe men of ſundry wits to be alſo of ſundry judgments concerning that which ought to be done; requiſite it cannot but ſeem the rule of divine law ſhould herein help our imbecility, that we might the more infallibly underſtand what is good, and what evil. The firſt principles of the law of nature are eaſy; hard it were to find men ignorant of them.

* Joſeph. lib. ſecundo contra Appium. *Lacedæmonii quomodo non ſunt ob inhoſpitalitatem reprehendi, fædumque neglectum nuptiarum? Elianſes vero & Thebani ob coitum cum maſculis planè impudentem & contra naturam, quem rectè & utiliter exercere putabant? Cumque hæc omnino perpetrarunt, etiam ſuis legibus miſcuere.* Vid. Th.12. q.49.4,5,6. *Lex natura ſic corrupta fuit apud Germanos, ut latrocinium non reputarent peccatum.* Auguſt. (aut quiſquis author eſt) lib. de quæſt. nov. & vet. teſt. *Quis neſciat quid bonæ vitæ conveniat, aut ignoret quia quod ſibi fieri non vult, aliis minimè debeat facere? At verò ubi naturalis lex evanuit oppreſſa conſuetudine delinquendi, tunc oportuit manifeſtari ſcriptis, ut Dei judicium omnes audirent: Non quod penitus obliterata eſt, ſed quia maximâ ejus authoritate carebat, idololatriæ ſtudebatur, timor Dei in terris erat, fornicatio operabatur, circa rem proximi avida erat concupiſcentia. Data ergo lex eſt, ut quæ ſciebantur authoritatem haberent, & quæ latere cœperant, manifeſtarentur.*

But concerning the duty which nature's law doth require at the hands of men in a number of things particular, ſo * far hath the natural underſtanding even of ſundry whole nations been darkned, that they have not diſcerned, no, not groſs iniquity to be ſin. Again, being ſo prone as we are to fawn upon our ſelves, and to be ignorant as much as may be of our own deformities, without the feeling ſenſe whereof we are moſt wretched; even ſo much the more, becauſe not knowing them, we cannot ſo much as deſire to have them taken away; how ſhould our feſtered ſores be cur'd, but that God hath delivered a law as ſharp as the two-edged ſword, piercing the very cloſeſt and moſt unſearchable corners of the heart, which the law of nature can hardly, human laws by no means poſſibly reach unto? Hereby we know even ſecret concupiſcence to be ſin, and are made fearful to offend, tho it be but in a wandring cogitation. Finally, of thoſe things which are for direction of all the parts of our life needful, and not impoſſible to be diſcerned by the light of nature it ſelf; are there not many which few mens natural capacity, and ſome which no man's hath been able to find out? They are, ſaith St. *Auguſtine,* but a few, and they endued with great ripeneſs of wit and judgment, free from all ſuch affairs as might trouble their meditations, inſtructed in the ſharpeſt and the ſubtileſt points of learning, who have, and that very hardly, been able to find out but only the immortality of the ſoul. The reſurrection of the fleſh what man did ever at any time dream of, having not heard it otherwiſe than from the ſchool of nature? Whereby it appeareth, how much we are bound to yield unto our Creator, the father of all mercy, eternal thanks, for that he hath delivered his law unto the world; a law wherein ſo many things are laid open, clear, and manifeſt; as a light, which otherwiſe would have been buried in darkneſs, not without the hazard, or rather not with the hazard, but with the certain loſs of infinite thouſands of ſouls, moſt undoubtedly now ſaved. We ſee therefore that our ſovereign good is deſired naturally; that God, the author of that natural deſire, had appointed natural means whereby to fulfil it; that man

having

having utterly disabled his nature unto those means, hath had other revealed from God, and hath received from heaven a law to teach him how that which is defired naturally muft now fupernaturally be attained. Finally, we fee, that becaufe thofe latter exclude not the former quite and clean as unneceffary, therefore together with fuch fupernatural duties as could not poffibly have been otherwife known to the world, the fame law that teacheth them, teacheth alfo with them fuch natural duties as could not by light of nature eafily have been known.

13. In the firft age of the world God gave laws unto our fathers, and by reafon of the number of their days their memories ferved inftead of books; whereof the manifold imperfections and defects being known to God, he mercifully relieved the fame, by often putting them in mind of that whereof it behoved them to be fpecially mindful. In which refpect, we fee how many times one thing hath been iterated unto fundry, even of the beft and wifeft amongft them. After that the lives of men were fhortned, means more durable to preferve the laws of God from oblivion and corruption grew in ufe, not without precife direction from God himfelf. Firft therefore of *Mofes* it is faid, that he *wrote all the words of God*; not by his own private motion and device: for God taketh this act to himfelf, *I have written*. Furthermore, were not the prophets following commanded alfo to do the like? Unto the holy evangelift faint *John*, how often exprefs charge is given, *fcribe, write thefe things*? Concerning the reft of our Lord's difciples, the words of faint *Auguftine* are, *Quicquid ille de fuis factis & dictis nos legere voluit, hoc fcribendum illis tanquam fuis manibus imperavit*. Now, altho we do not deny it to be a matter merely accidental, unto the law of God to be written; altho writing be not that which addeth authority and ftrength thereunto; finally, tho his laws do require at our hands the fame obedience, howfoever they be delivered; his providence notwithftanding, which hath made principal choice of this way to deliver them, who feeth not what caufe we have to admire and magnify? The fingular benefit that hath grown unto the world by receiving the laws of God, even by his own appointment committed unto writing, we are not able to efteem as the value thereof deferveth. When the queftion therefore is, whether we be now to feek for any revealed law of God otherwhere than only in the facred fcripture; whether we do now ftand bound in the fight of God to yield to traditions urged by the church of *Rome* the fame obedience and reverence we do to his written law, honouring equally, and adoring both as divine? Our anfwer is, No. They that fo earneftly plead for the authority of tradition, as if nothing were more fafely convey'd than that which fpreadeth it felf by report, and defcendeth by relation of former generations unto the ages that fucceed, are not all of them (furely a miracle it were if they fhould be) fo fimple, as thus to perfuade themfelves; howfoever, if the fimple were fo perfuaded, they could be content perhaps very well to enjoy the benefit, as they account it, of that common error. What hazard the truth is in, when it paffeth thro the hands of report, how maimed and deformed it becometh, they are not, they cannot poffibly be ignorant. Let them that are indeed, of this mind, confider but only that little of things divine which the * heathen have in fuch fort received. How miferable had the ftate of the church of God been long e'en this, if, wanting the facred fcripture, we had no record of his laws but only the memory of man receiving the fame by report and relation his predeceffors? By fcripture, it hath in the wifdom of God feemed meet to deliver unto the world much, but perfonally expedient to be practifed of certain men; many deep and profound points of doctrine, as being the main original ground whereupon the precepts of duty depend; many prophecies, the clear performance whereof might confirm the world in belief of things unfeen; many hiftories to ferve as looking-glaffes to behold the mercy, the truth, the righteoufnefs of God towards all that faithfully ferve, obey and honour him; yea, many entire meditations of piety, to be as patterns and precedents in cafes of like nature; many things needful for explication, many for application unto particular occafions, fuch as the providence of God from time to time hath taken, to have the feveral books of his holy ordinance written. Be it then, that together with the principal neceffary laws of God there are fundry other things written, whereof we might haply be ignorant, and yet be fav'd: what? fhall we hereupon think them needlefs? fhall we efteem them as riotous branches, wherewith we fometimes behold moft pleafant vines overgrown? Surely, no more than we judge our hands or our eyes fuperfluous, or what part foever; which if our bodies did want, we might, notwithftanding any fuch defect, retain ftill the complete being of men. As therefore a complete man is neither deftitute of any part neceffary, and hath fome parts whereof tho the want could not deprive him of his effence, yet to have them ftandeth him in fingular ftead in refpect of the fpecial ufes for which they ferve; in like fort, all thofe writings which contain in them the law of God all thofe venerable books

The benefit of having divine laws written:

Exod. 14. 4:

Hof. 8. 11.

Apoc. 1. 11. & 14. 13.

Aug. lib. 1. de Conf. Evan: cap. ult.

* I mean thofe hiftorical matters concerning the anthors ftate of the firft world, the deluge, the fons of *Noah*; the children of *Ifrael's* deliverance out of *Egypt*, the life and doings of *Mofes* their captain, with certain truth whereof delivered in holy fcripture, is of the heathen which had them only by report, fo intermingled with fabulous vanities, that the moft which remaineth in them to be feen, is the fhew of dark and obfcure fteps, where fome part of the truth hath gone.

of scripture, all those sacred tomes and volumes of holy writ, they are with such absolute perfection framed, that in them there neither wanteth any thing, the lack whereof might deprive us of life, nor any thing in such wise aboundeth, that as being superfluous, unfruitful, and altogether needless, we should think it no loss or danger at all, if we did want it.

The sufficiency of scripture unto the end for which it was instituted. *Utrum cognitio supernaturalis necessaria viatori, sit sufficienter tradita in sacrâ scriptura ?* This question proposed by *Scotus,* is affirmatively concluded.

14. Altho the scripture of God therefore be stored with infinite variety of matter in all kinds, altho it abound with all sorts of laws, yet the principal intent of scripture is to deliver the laws of duties supernatural. Oftentimes it hath been in very solemn manner disputed, whether all things necessary unto salvation be necessarily set down in the holy scriptures or no. If we define that necessary unto salvation, whereby the way to salvation is in any sort made more plain, apparent and easy to be known ; then is there no part of true philosophy, no art of account, no kind of science, rightly so call'd, but the scripture must contain it. If only those things be necessary, as surely none else are, without the knowledge and practice whereof, it is not the will and pleasure of God to make any ordinary grant of salvation ; it may be notwithstanding, and oftentimes hath been demanded, how the books of holy scripture contain in them all necessary things, when of things necessary the very chief is to know what books we are bound to esteem holy : which point is confess'd impossible for the scripture it self to teach. Whereunto we may answer with truth, that there is not in the world any art or science, which proposing unto it self an end (as every one doth some end or other) hath been therefore thought defective, if it have not delivered simply whatsoever is needful to the same end ; but all kinds of knowledge have their certain bounds and limits ; each of them presupposeth many necessary things learned in other sciences and known beforehand. He that should take upon him to teach men how to be eloquent in pleading causes, must needs deliver unto them whatsoever precepts are requisite unto that end ; otherwise he doth not the thing which he taketh upon him. Seeing then no man can plead eloquently, unless he be able first to speak ; it followeth, that ability of speech is in this case a thing most necessary. Notwithstanding every man would think it ridiculous, that he which undertaketh by writing to instruct an orator, should therefore deliver all the precepts of grammar ; because his profession is to deliver precepts necessary unto eloquent speech ; yet so, that they which are to receive them be taught before-hand so much of that which is thereunto necessary as comprehendeth the skill of speaking : in like sort, albeit scripture do profess to contain in it all things that are necessary unto salvation ; yet the meaning cannot be simply of all things which are necessary, but all things that are necessary in some certain kind or form ; as all things which are necessary, and either could not all, or could not easily be known by the light of natural discourse ; all things which are necessary to be known that we may be saved ; but known with presupposal of knowledge concerning certain principles whereof it receiveth us already persuaded, and then instructeth us in all the residue that are necessary. In the number of these principles, one is the sacred authority of scripture. Being therefore persuaded by other means that these scriptures are the oracles of God, themselves do then teach us the rest, and lay before us all the duties which God requireth at our hands as necessary unto salvation. Further, there hath been some doubt likewise, whether *containing in scripture* do import express setting down in plain terms, or else *comprehending* in such sort that, by reason, we may from thence conclude all things which are necessary. Against the former of these two constructions, instance hath sundry ways been given. For our belief in the Trinity, the co-eternity of the Son of God with his Father, the proceeding of the Spirit from the Father and the Son, the duty of baptizing infants : these, with such other principal points, the necessity whereof is by none denied, are notwithstanding in scripture no where to be found by express literal mention, only deduced they are out of scripture by collection. This kind of comprehension in scripture being therefore received, still there is no doubt, how far we are to proceed by collection, before the full and complete measure of things necessary be made up. For let us not think, that as long as the world doth endure, the wit of man shall be able to found the bottom of that which may be concluded out of the scripture ; especially, if things contained by collection do so far extend, as to draw in whatsoever may be at any time out of scripture but probably and conjecturally surmized. But let necessary collection be made requisite, and we may boldly deny, that of all those things which at this day are with so great necessity urged upon this church, under the name of reformed church-discipline, there is any one which their books hitherto have made manifest to be contained in the scripture. Let them, if they can, alledge but one properly belonging to their cause, and not common to them and us, and shew the deduction thereof out of scripture to be necessary. It hath been already shewed, how all things necessary unto salvation, in such sort as before we have maintained, must needs be pos-

†   sible

sible for men to know; and that many things are in such sort necessary, the knowledge whereof is by the light of nature impossible to be attained. Whereupon it followeth, that either all flesh is excluded from possibility of salvation, which to think were most barbarous; or else, that God hath by supernatural means revealed the way of life so far forth as doth suffice. For this cause, God hath so many times and ways spoken to the sons of men: neither hath he by speech only, but by writing also, instructed and taught his church. The cause of writing hath been, to the end that things by him revealed unto the world, might have the longer continuance, and the greater certainty of assurance; by how much that which standeth on record, hath in both those respects preheminence above that which passeth from hand to hand, and hath no pens but the tongues, no book but the ears of men to record it. The several books of scripture having had each some several occasion and particular purpose which caused them to be written, the contents thereof are according to the exigence of that special end whereunto they are intended. Hereupon it groweth that every book of holy scripture doth take out of all kinds of truth, (a) natural, (b) historical, (c) foreign, (d) supernatural, so much as the matter (a) Ephes. 5. handled requireth. Now for as much as there have been reasons alledged sufficient to con- 19. clude that all things necessary unto salvation must be made known, and that God himself (b) 1 Tim. 3. 8. hath therefore revealed his will, because otherwise men could not have known so much (c) Tit. 1. 12. as is necessary; his surceasing to speak to the world, since the publishing of the gospel (d) 1 Pet. 1. 4. · of Jesus Christ and the delivery of the same in writing, is unto us a manifest token that the way of salvation is now sufficiently opened, and that we need no other means for our full instruction than God hath already furnished us withal. The main drift of the whole new testament is that which saint *John* setteth down as the purpose of his own history; *These things are written, that ye might believe that Jesus is Christ, the son of God,* Joh. 10. 31. *and that in believing, ye might have life thro his name.* The drift of the old, that which the apostle mentioned to *Timothy, The holy scriptures are able to make thee wise* 2 Tim. 3. 15. *unto salvation.* So that the general end both of old and new is one; the difference between them consisting in this, that the old did make wise by teaching salvation thro Christ that should come; the new, by teaching that Christ the Saviour is come; and that Jesus whom the *Jews* did crucify, and whom God did raise again from the dead, is he. When the apostle therefore affirmeth unto *Timothy,* that the old was able to make him wise to salvation, it was not his meaning, that the old alone can do this unto us which live sithence the publication of the new: for he speaketh with presuppofal of the doctrine of Christ, known also unto *Timothy;* and therefore first it is said, *continue thou in those* 2 Tim. 3. 14. *things which thou hast learned, and art persuaded, knowing of whom thou hast been taught them.* Again, those scriptures he granteth were able to make him wise to salvation; but he addeth, *thro the faith which is in Christ.* Wherefore without the Verse 15. doctrine of the new testament, teaching that Christ hath wrought the redemption of the world; which redemption the old did foreshew he should work; it is not the former alone which can on our behalf perform so much as the apostle doth avouch, who presupposeth this, when he magnifieth that so highly. And as his words concerning the books of antient scripture do not take place but with presuppofal of the gospel of Christ embraced; so our own words also, when we extol the complete sufficiency of the whole entire body of the scripture, must in like sort be understood with this caution, that the benefit of nature's light be not thought excluded as unnecessary, because the necessity of a diviner light is magnified. There is in scripture therefore no defect, but that any man, what place or calling soever he hold in the church of God, may have thereby the light of his natural understanding so perfected, that the one being relieved by the other, there can want no part of needful instruction unto any good work which God himself requireth, be it natural or supernatural, belonging simply unto men, as men; or unto men, as they are united in whatsoever kind of society. It sufficeth therefore, that nature and scripture do serve in such full sort, that they both jointly, and not severally either of them, be so complete, that unto everlasting felicity we need not the knowledge of any thing more than these two may easily furnish our minds with on all sides. And therefore they which add traditions, as a part of supernatural necessary truth, have not the truth, but are in error. For they only plead, that whatsoever God revealeth as necessary for all christian men to do or believe, the same we ought to embrace whether we have received it by writing or otherwise, which no man denieth; when that which they should confirm, who claim so great reverence unto traditions, is, that the same traditions are necessarily to be acknowledged divine and holy. For we do not reject them only because they are not in the scripture, but because they are neither in scripture, nor can otherwise sufficiently by any reason be proved to be of God. That which is of God, and may be evidently proved to be so, we deny not but it hath in his kind, altho unwritten, yet the self-same

force

Whitakerus adverſus Bellarmin. quæſt. 6. cap. 6.

force and authority with the written laws of God. It is by ours acknowledged, *that the apoſtles did in every church, inſtitute and ordain, ſome rites and cuſtoms, ſerving for the ſeemlineſs of church-regiment ; which rites and cuſtoms they have not committed unto writing.* Thoſe rites and cuſtoms being known to be apoſtolical, and having the nature of things changeable, were no leſs to be accounted of in the church, than other things of the like degree ; that is to ſay, capable in like ſort of alteration, altho ſet down in the apoſtles writings. For both being known to be apoſtolical, it is not the manner of delivering them unto the church, but the author from whom they proceed, which doth give them their force and credit.

Of laws poſitive contained in ſcripture; the mutability of certain of them, and the general uſe of ſcripture.

15. Laws being impoſed either by each man upon himſelf, or by a publick ſociety upon the particulars thereof ; or by all the nations of men upon every ſeveral ſociety ; or by the Lord himſelf upon any or every of theſe ; there is not amongſt theſe four kinds any one, but containeth ſundry both natural and poſitive laws. Impoſſible it is, but that they ſhould fall into a number of groſs errors, who only take ſuch laws for poſitive as have been made or invented of men ; and holding this poſition, hold alſo, that all poſitive and none but poſitive laws are mutable. Laws natural do always bind ; laws poſitive not ſo, but only after they have been expreſly and wittingly impoſed. Laws poſitive there are in every of thoſe kinds before-mentioned. As in the firſt kind, the promiſes which we have paſs'd unto men, and the vows we have made unto God ; for theſe are laws which we tie our ſelves unto, and till we have ſo tied our ſelves they bind us not. Laws poſitive in the ſecond kind, are ſuch as the civil conſtitutions, which are peculiar unto each particular commonweal. In the third kind, the law of heraldry in war is poſitive : and in the laſt, all the judicials which God gave unto the people of *Iſrael* to obſerve. And altho no laws but poſitive be mutable, yet all are not mutable which be poſitive. Poſitive laws are either permanent, or elſe changeable, according as the matter it ſelf is concerning which they were firſt made. Whether God or man be the maker of them, alteration they ſo far forth admit, as the matter doth exact. Laws that concern ſupernatural duties, are all poſitive ; and either concern men ſupernaturally, as men, or elſe as parts of a ſupernatural ſociety ; which ſociety we call the church. To concern men as men ſupernaturally, is to concern them as duties, which belong of neceſſity to all, and yet could not have been known by any to belong unto them unleſs God had opened them himſelf ; in as much as they do not depend upon any natural ground at all out of which they may be deduced, but are appointed of God to ſupply the defect of thoſe natural ways of ſalvation, by which we are not now able to attain thereunto. The church being a ſupernatural ſociety, doth differ from natural ſocieties in this, that the perſons unto whom we aſſociate our ſelves in the one, are men, ſimply conſidered as men ; but they to whom we be joined in the other are God, angels, and holy men. Again, the church being both a ſociety, and a ſociety ſupernatural ; altho as it is a ſociety, it have the ſelf-ſame original grounds which other politick ſocieties have, namely, the natural inclination which all men have unto ſociable life, and conſent to ſome certain bond of aſſociation : which bond is the law that appointeth what kind of order they ſhall be aſſociated in ; yet unto the church, as it is a ſociety ſupernatural, this is peculiar ; that part of the bond of their aſſociation which belongs to the church of God, muſt be a law ſupernatural which God himſelf hath revealed concerning that kind of worſhip which his people ſhall do unto him. The ſubſtance of the ſervice of God therefore, ſo far forth as it hath in it any thing more than the law of reaſon doth teach, may not be invented of men, as it is amongſt the heathens ; but muſt be received from God himſelf, as always it hath been in the church, ſaving only when the church hath been forgetful of her duty. Wherefore to end with a general rule concerning all the laws which God hath tied men unto : thoſe laws divine that belong, whether naturally or ſupernaturally, either to men as men, or to men as they live in politick ſociety, or to men as they are of that politick ſociety which is the church, without any further reſpect had unto any ſuch variable accident, as the eſtate of men, and of ſocieties of men, and of the church it ſelf in this world, is ſubject unto ; all laws that ſo belong unto men, they belong for

Iſa. 29. 13. Their fear towards me was taught by the precept of men.

ever, yea, altho they be poſitive laws, unleſs being poſitive, God himſelf which made them, alter them. The reaſon is, becauſe the ſubject or matter of laws in general, is thus far forth conſtant : which matter is, that for the ordering whereof laws were inſtituted, and being inſtituted are not changeable without cauſe, neither can they have cauſe of change, when that which gave them their firſt inſtitution remaineth for ever one and the ſame. On the other ſide, laws that were made for men or ſocieties or churches in regard of their being ſuch, as they do not always continue, but may perhaps be clean otherwiſe awhile after, and ſo may require to be otherwiſe ordered than before ; the laws of God himſelf, which are of this nature, no man endued with common ſenſe will ever deny to be be of a different conſtitution from the former, in reſpect of the ones conſtancy and the mutability of the other. And this doth ſeem to have been the very cauſe why ſaint *John* doth ſo peculiarly term the doctrine that teacheth ſalvation by Jeſus Chriſt, *evangelium æternum, an eternal goſpel*; becauſe there can be no reaſon wherefore the publiſhing thereof ſhould be taken away, and any other inſtead of it proclaimed, as long as the world doth continue: whereas the whole law of rites and ceremonies, altho delivered with ſo great ſolemnity, is notwithſtanding clean abrogated, in as much as it had but temporary cauſe of God's ordaining it. But that we may at the length conclude this firſt general introduction unto the nature and original birth, as of all other laws, ſo likewiſe of thoſe which the ſacred ſcripture containeth, concerning the author whereof, even infidels have confeſſed, that he can neither err nor deceive; albeit, about things eaſy and manifeſt unto all men by common ſenſe there needeth no higher conſultation, becauſe as a man whoſe wiſdom is in weighty affairs admired, would take it in ſome diſdain to have his counſel ſolemnly asked about a toy; ſo the meanneſs of ſome things is ſuch, that to ſearch the ſcripture of God for the ordering of them were to derogate from the reverend authority and dignity of the ſcripture, no leſs than they do by whom ſcriptures are in ordinary talk very idly applied unto vain and childiſh trifles: yet better it were to be ſuperſtitious, than profane; to take from thence our direction even in all things great or ſmall, than to wade thro matters of principal weight and moment, without ever caring what the law of God hath either for or againſt our deſigns. Concerning the cuſtom of the very *Paynims*, thus much *Strabo* witneſſeth: (*a*) *Men that are civil do lead their lives after one common law appointing them what to do. For that otherwiſe a multitude ſhould with harmony amongſt themſelves concur in the doing of one thing, (for this is civilly to live) or that they ſhould in any ſort manage community of life, it is not poſſible. Now laws or ſtatutes are of two ſorts. For they are either received from gods, or elſe from men. And our antient predeceſſors did ſurely moſt honour and reverence that which was from the gods. For which cauſe, conſultation with oracles was a thing very uſual and frequent in their times.* Did they make ſo much account of the voice of their gods, which in truth were no gods; and ſhall we neglect the precious benefit of conference with thoſe oracles of the true and living God, whereof ſo great ſtore is left to the church, and whereunto there is ſo free, ſo plain, and ſo eaſy acceſs for all men? (*b*) *By thy commandments* (this was *David's* confeſſion unto God) *thou haſt made me wiſer than mine enemies. Again, I have had more underſtanding than all my teachers, becauſe thy teſtimonies are my meditations.* What pains would not they have beſtowed in the ſtudy of theſe books, who travelled ſea and land to gain the treaſure of ſome few days talk with men whoſe wiſdom the world did make any reckoning of? (*c*) That little which ſome of the heathens did chance to hear concerning ſuch matter as the ſacred ſcripture plentifully containeth, they did in wonderful ſort affect; their ſpeeches, as oft as they make mention thereof, are ſtrange, and ſuch as themſelves could not utter as they did other things, but ſtill acknowledged that their wits, which did every where elſe conquer hardneſs, were with profoundneſs here over-matched. Wherefore ſeeing that God hath endued us with ſenſe, to the end that we might perceive ſuch things as this preſent life doth need; and with reaſon, leſt that which ſenſe cannot reach unto, being both now and alſo in regard of a future eſtate hereafter neceſſary to be known, ſhould lie obſcure; finally, with the heavenly ſupport of propheticall revelation, which doth open thoſe hidden myſteries that reaſon could never have been able to find out, or to have known the neceſſity of them unto our everlaſting good: uſe we the precious gifts of God unto his glory and honour that gave them, ſeeking by all means to know what the will of our God is; what righteous before him; in his ſight what holy, perfect and good, that we may truly and faithfully do it.

16. Thus far therefore we have endeavoured in part to open, of what nature and force laws are, according unto their ſeveral kinds: the law which God with himſelf hath eternally ſet down to follow in his own works: the law which he hath made for his creatures to keep: the law of natural and neceſſary agents: the law which angels in heaven obey: the law whereunto by the light of reaſon, men find themſelves bound, in that they are men: the law which they make by compoſition of multitudes and politick ſocieties of men to be guided by: the law which belongeth unto each nation: the law that concerneth the fellowſhip of all: and laſtly, the law which God himſelf hath ſupernaturally revealed. It might peradventure have been more popular, and more plauſible to vulgar ears, if this firſt diſcourſe had been ſpent in extolling the force of laws, in ſhewing the great neceſſity of them when they are good, and in aggravating their offence, by whom publick laws are injuriouſly traduced. But for as much as with ſuch kind of matter, the paſſions of men are rather ſtirred one way or other, than their knowledge

any

Apoc. 14 6.
Ἐρχόμενα ἀεα ?
Θεὶς ἀπλᾶν
ᾗ ἀπελθεῖν ἐν
ᾗ ἑξῆς ᾗ ἐν
λόγῳ, ᾗ ἔτε
αὐτὸς μαθήσα-
ται, ἔτε ἄλλοι
τας, ἔτε ἄλλοι
ἰξανταλᾷ, ἐπὶ
χν φαιλασίαι,
ὅτι χν λόγοι,
ἐν χν ϛημαίαν
ϛηματὶ, ἰδ'
ὑπὰς ἰδ' ὁταρ.
Plat. in fine
2 Polit.

(a) Πολλι-
καὶ ᵬɩɛ αου
ϛεϛϛϛμ]ᶲ
αοιᵬ ϛων.
Ἄλλοι χὶ ἐν
οἷωτε τᵬς
σολλῆς ἐν
χν τουᵬ αυ-
ᾔς ἡμῶᶲμι-
τως ἀλλήλος
ἄτῳ ᵬδ' τὶ
ϛαᴸῳᶲϛαι-
ᾗ ἄλλαι αᵬὶ
ᵬᶲμᵬ δυν
ᶮᶲϛϛ. Τ ᵬ γ
φεϛϛαϛϛσα
ᴚᵬᵬⱮ, ᶰ ⱱᵬ
ᵬϛα δωι, ᶰ
ϛϛα ἀνϛω-
ᶹⱳ. ᶁᵬ ᶾ ᵬ
ᶮ αϛχαῖα το
Ɱαϛἀⱱ τᵬ
ϛᵬⱱ ᵬ δωⱱ
Ɱⱱⱱⱱϛ, ᴚᶴ
μⱱⱱμⱱⱱ, ᴚᶴ
διὰ τϛτο ᵬ ᵬ
χⱱⱮⱱⱮϛ-
μⱱⱱᶴ λῶ τϛτα
ϛωⱱ́ς. Strab.
Geogr. lib. 16.
(b) Pſal. 119.
98.

(c) Vide Or-
phei Carmina.
Ὁτᶴ ᶾ δ ϛϛ
ϛαⱮⱱϛαⱱⱱ
ϛϛϛ τᵬⱱᶲ
2 ϛϛϛᶲⱱⱱᶛ
ᶲⱱⱱᶴ. Philo
de Moſ.

A concluſion,
ſhewing how
all this belong-
eth to the
cauſe in queſ-
tion.

any way set forward unto the tryal of that whereof there is doubt made; I have therefore turned aside from that beaten path, and chosen, tho a less easy, yet a more profitable way, in regard of the end we propose. Lest therefore any man should marvel whereunto all these things tend, the drift and purpose of all is this, even to shew in what

Jam. 1. 17.

manner, as every good and perfect gift, so this very gift of good and perfect laws is derived from the father of lights, to teach men a reason why just and reasonable laws are of so great force, of so great use in the world; and to inform their minds with some method of reducing the laws, whereof there is present controversy, unto their first original causes, that so it may be in every particular ordinance thereby the better discerned, whether the same be reasonable, just and righteous, or no. Is there any thing which can either be thorowly understood or soundly judged of, till the very first causes and principles from

Arist. Phys. l. 1. cap. 1.

which originally it springeth be made manifest? If all parts of knowledge have been thought by wise men to be then most orderly delivered and proceeded in, when they are drawn to their first original; seeing that our whole question concerneth the quality of ecclesiastical laws, let it not seem a labour superfluous, that in the entrance thereunto, all these several kinds of laws have been considered; in as much as they all concur as principles, they all have their forcible operations therein, altho not all in like apparent and manifest manner: by means whereof it cometh to pass, that the force which they have, is not observed of many. Easier a great deal it is for men by law to be taught what they ought to do, than instructed how to judge as they should do of law; the one being a thing which belongeth generally unto all; the other, such as none but the wiser and more

Arist. Ethic. 10. τὸ κρῖναι ὀρθῶς, μέγιστον. Intelligit de legum qualitate judicium.

judicious sort can perform. Yea, the wisest are always touching this point the readiest to acknowledge, that soundly to judge of a law is the weightiest thing which any man can take upon him. But if we will give judgment of the laws under which we live; first, let that law eternal be always before our eyes, as being of principal force and moment to breed in religious minds a dutiful estimation of all laws, the use and benefit whereof we see; because there can be no doubt, but that laws apparently good, are (as it were) things copied out of the very tables of that high everlasting law, even as the book of

Prov. 8. 15.

that law hath said concerning it self, *By me kings reign, and by me princes decree justice.* Not as if men did behold that book, and accordingly frame their laws; but because it worketh in them, because it discovereth, and (as it were) readeth it self to the world by them, when the laws which they make are righteous. Furthermore, altho we perceive not the goodness of laws made; nevertheless, sith things in themselves may have that which we peradventure discern not; should not this breed a fear into our hearts how we speak or judge in the worst part concerning that, the unadvised disgrace whereof may be no mean dishonour to him towards whom we profess all submission and awe? Surely there must be very manifest iniquity in laws, against which we shall be able to justify our contumelious invectives. The chiefest root whereof, when we use them without cause, is ignorance how laws inferior are derived from that supreme or highest law. The first that receive impression from thence are natural agents. The law of whose operations might be haply thought less pertinent, when the question is about laws for human actions, but that in those very actions which most spiritually and supernaturally concern men, the rules and actions of natural operations have their force. What can be more immediate to our salvation, than our persuasion concerning the law of Christ towards his church? What greater assurance of love towards his church, than the knowledge of that mystical union, whereby the church is become as near unto Christ as any one part of his flesh is unto other? That the church being in such sort his, he must needs protect it; what proof more strong, than if a manifest law so require, which law it is not possible for Christ to violate? And what other law doth the apostle for this alledge, but such as is

Ephes. 5. 29.

both common unto Christ with us, and unto us with other things natural; *No man hateth his own flesh, but doth love and cherish it?* The axioms of that law therefore, whereby natural agents are guided, have their use in the moral, yea even in the spiritual actions of men, and consequently in all laws belonging unto men howsoever. Neither are the angels themselves so far severed from us in their kind and manner of working, but that between the law of their heavenly operations and the actions of men in this our state of mortality, such correspondence there is as maketh it expedient to know in some sort the

Apoc. 19. 10.

one for the others more perfect direction. Would angels acknowledge themselves fellow-servants with the sons of men, but that both having one Lord, there must be some kind of law which is one and the same to both, whereunto their obedience being perfecter, is to our weaker both a pattern and a spur? Or would the apostles, speaking of that

1 Pet. 1. 12. Ephes. 3. 10. 1 Tim. 5. 21.

which belongeth unto saints as they are linked together in the bond of spiritual society, so often make mention how angels are therewith delighted, if in things publickly done by the church we are not somewhat to respect what the angels of heaven do? Yea, so

far

far hath the apostle saint *Paul* proceeded, as to signify that even about the outward orders of the church, which serve but for comeliness, some regard is to be had of angels, who best like us when we are most like unto them in all parts of decent demeanour.   So that the law of angels we cannot judge altogether impertinent unto the affairs of the church of God.   Our largeness of speech how men do find out what things reason bindeth them of necessity to observe, and what it guideth them to chuse in things which are left as arbitrary ; the care we have had to declare the different nature of laws which severally concern all men, from such as belong unto men either civilly or spiritually associated ; such as pertain to the fellowship which nations, or which christian nations have amongst themselves ; and in the last place, such as concerning every or any of these, God himself hath revealed by his holy word ; all serveth but to make manifest, that as the actions of men are of sundry distinct kinds, so the laws thereof must accordingly be distinguish'd. There are in men operations, some natural, some rational, some supernatural, some politick, some finally ecclesiastical : which if we measure not each by his own proper law, whereas the things themselves are so different, there will be in our understanding and judgment of them, confusion.   As that first error sheweth whereon our opposites in this cause have grounded themselves : for as they rightly maintain, that God must be glorified in all things, and that the actions of men cannot tend unto his glory unless they be framed after his law ; so it is their error to think that the only law which God hath appointed unto men in that behalf is the sacred scripture.   By that which we work natu- Psal. 148. 7. rally, as when we breathe, sleep, move, we set forth the glory of God as natural agents 8, 9. do, albeit we have no express purpose to make that our end, nor any advised determination therein to follow a law, but do that we do (for the most part) not as much as thinking thereon.   In reasonable and moral actions another law taketh place ; a law, by the ob- Rom. 1. 21. servation whereof we glorify God in such sort, as no creature else under man is able to do ; because other creatures have not judgment to examine the quality of that which is done by them, and therefore in that they do they neither can accuse nor approve them- Rom. 2. 15. selves.   Men do both as the apostle teacheth ; yea, those men which have no written law of God to shew what is good or evil, carry written in their hearts the universal law of mankind, the law of reason, whereby they judge as by a rule which God has given unto all men for that purpose. The law of reason doth somewhat direct men how to honour God as their creator ; but how to glorify God in such sort as is required, to the end he may be an everlasting saviour, this we are taught by divine law, which law both ascertaineth the truth, and supplieth unto us the want of that other law.   So that in moral actions, divine law helpeth exceedingly the law of reason to guide man's life ; but in supernatural, it alone guideth.   Proceed we further, let us place man in some publick society with others, whether civil or spiritual ; and in this case there is no remedy, but we must add yet a farther law.   For altho, even here likewise, the laws of nature and reason be of necessary use ; yet somewhat over and besides them is necessary, namely, human and positive law, together with that law which is of commerce between grand societies, the law of nations, and of nations christian.   For which cause, the law of God hath likewise said, *Let every soul be subject to the higher powers.*   The publick power of all so- Rom. 13. 1. cieties is above every soul contained in the same societies.   And the principal use of that power is to give laws unto all that are under it ; which laws in such case we must obey, unless there be reason shewed which may necessarily inforce, that the law of reason or of God doth enjoin the contrary : because except our own private and but probable resolutions be by the law of publick determinations over-rul'd, we take away all possibility of sociable life in the world.   A plainer example whereof than our selves we cannot have. How cometh it to pass, that we are at this present day so rent with mutual contentions, and that the church is so much troubled about the polity of the church ?   No doubt, if men had been willing to learn how many laws their actions in this life are subject unto, and what the true force of each law is, all these controversies might have died the very day they were first brought forth.   It is both commonly said, and truly, that the best men otherwise are not always the best in regard of society.   The reason whereof is, for that the law of mens actions is one, if they be respected only as men ; and another, when they are considered as parts of a politick body.   Many men there are, than whom Παλλοὶ γὰ ἐν nothing is more commendable when they are singled ; and yet in society with others, ιδία τοῖς οἰκεί- none less fit to answer the duties which are looked for at their hands.   Yea, I am persua- οις οἱ τῇ ἀρετῇ ded, that of them, with whom in this cause we strive, there are whose betters among ̓βασι, ἢ ἢ ταῖς men would be hardly found if they did not live amongst men, but in some wilderness by πρὸς ἑτέρου themselves.   The cause of which their disposition so unframable unto societies wherein Arist. Ethic. they live is, for that they discern not aright what place and force these several kinds of lib. 5. cap. 3. laws ought to have in all their actions.   Is their question either concerning the regiment

f   of

of the church in general, or about conformity between one church and another, or of ceremonies, offices, powers, jurisdictions in our own church? of all these things, they judge by that rule which they frame to themselves with some shew of probability; and what seemeth in that sort convenient, the same they think themselves bound to practise; the same by all means they labour mightily to uphold; whatsoever any law of man to the contrary hath determined, they weigh it not. Thus by following the law of private reason, where the law of publick should take place, they breed disturbance. For the better inuring therefore of men's minds with the true distinction of laws, and of their several force, according to the different kind and quality of our actions, it shall not per-adventure be amiss to shew in some one example, how they shall take place. To seek no **Job 34. 3.** further, let but that be considered, than which there is not any thing more familiar unto **Psal. 145. 15,** us, our food. What things are food, and what are not, we judge naturally by sense; **16.** neither need we any other law to be our director in that behalf than the self-same which is common unto us with beasts. But when we come to consider of food, as of a benefit which God of his bounteous goodness has provided for all things living; the law of rea-son doth here require the duty of thankfulness at our hands towards him, at whose hands we have it. And lest appetite in the use of food should lead us beyond that which is meet, we owe in this case obedience to that law of reason, which teacheth mediocrity in meats and drinks. The same things divine law teacheth also, as at large we have shewed it doth all parts of moral duty, whereunto we all of necessity stand bound, in regard of the life to come. But of certain kinds of food the Jews sometimes had, and we our-selves likewise have a mystical, religious and supernatural use; they of their paschal lamb and oblations; we of our bread and wine in the eucharist: which use none but divine law could institute. Now as we live in civil society, the state of the commonwealth wherein we live both may and doth require certain laws concerning food; which laws, saving only that we are members of the commonwealth where they are of force, we should need to respect as rules of action; whereas now in their place and kind they must be respected and obeyed. Yea, the self-same matter is also a subject wherein sometime ecclesiastical laws have place; so that unless we will be authors of confusion in the church, our private discretion, which otherwise might guide us a contrary way, must here submit it self to be that way guided, which the publick judgment of the church hath thought **'Οτι ὁ καλὸν** better. In which case, that of *Zonaras* concerning fasts may be remembered. *Fastings* **τὸ καλὸν, ὅταν** *are good, but let good things be done in good and convenient manner. He that transgres-* **μὴ καλῶς γί-** *seth in his fasting the orders of the holy fathers, the positive laws of the church of* **νηται. Zonar.** **in can. apost.** *Christ, must be plainly told, that good things do lose the grace of their goodness, when* **66.** *in good sort they are not performed.* And as here men's private fancies must give place to the higher judgment of that church, which is in authority a mother over them; so the very actions of whole churches have, in regard of commerce and fellowship with o-ther churches, been subject to laws concerning food, the contrary unto which laws had else been thought more convenient for them to observe; as by that order of abstinence **Acts 15. 20.** from things strangled and blood may appear; an order grounded upon that fellowship which the churches of the *Gentiles* had with the *Jews*. Thus we see howeven one and the self-same thing is under divers considerations conveyed thro many laws; and that to measure by any one kind of law all the actions of men, were to confound the admirable order wherein God hath disposed all laws, each as in nature, so in degree, distinct from other. Wherefore that here we may briefly end: Of law there can be no less acknowledged than that her seat is the bosom of God, her voice the harmony of the world: all things in heaven and earth do her homage, the very least as feeling her care, and the greatest as not exempted from her power: both angels, and men, and creatures of what condition soever, tho each in different sort and manner, yet all with uniform consent admiring her as the mother of their peace and joy.

O F

OF THE

L A W S

OF

Ecclesiastical Polity.

BOOK II.

Concerning their first position who urge reformation in the church of England ; *namely, that scripture is the only rule of all things, which in this life may be done by men.*

The matter contained in this second book.

1. AN answer to their first proof brought out of scripture, Prov. 2. 9.
2. To their second, 1 Cor. 10. 31.
3. To their third, 1 Tim. 4. 5.
4. To their fourth, Rom. 14. 23.
5. To their proofs out of fathers, who dispute negatively from the authority of holy scripture.
6. To their proof, by the scripture's custom of disputing from divine authority negatively.
7. An examination of their opinion concerning the force of arguments taken from human authority for the ordering of mens actions and persuasions.
8. A declaration what the truth is in this matter.

AS that which in the title hath been proposed for the matter whereof we treat is only the ecclesiastical law whereby we are governed ; so neither is it my purpose to maintain any other thing than that which therein truth and reason shall approve. For concerning the dealings of men who administer government, and unto whom the execution of that law belongeth, they have their judge who sitteth in heaven, and before whose tribunal-seat they are accountable for whatsoever abuse or corruption, which (being worthily misliked in this church) the want either of care or of conscience in them hath bred. We are no patrons of those things therefore, the best defence whereof is speedy redress and amendment. That which is of God we defend to the uttermost of that ability which he hath given : that which is otherwise, let it wither even in the root from whence it hath sprung. Wherefore all these abuses being severed and set apart, which rise from the corruption of men, and not from the laws themselves ; come we to those things which in the very whole entire form of our church-polity have been (as we persuade our selves) injuriously blamed by them who endeavour to overthrow the same, and instead thereof to establish a much worse ; only thro a strong misconceit they have, that the same is grounded on divine authority. Now, whether it be that thro an earnest longing desire to see things brought to a peaceable end ; I do but imagine the matters whereof we contend to be fewer than indeed they are ; or else for that in truth they are fewer when they come to be discuss'd by reason than otherwise they seem when by heat of contention they are divided into many slips, and of every branch an heap is made :

F 2

sure-

furely, as now we have drawn them together, chufing out thofe things which are requifite to be feverally all difcufs'd, and omitting fuch mean fpecialities as are likely (without
any great labour) to fall afterwards of themfelves : I know no caufe why either the
number or the length of thefe controverfies fhould diminifh our hope of feeing them end
with concord and love on all fides ; which of his infinite love and goodnefs the father
of all peace and unity grant. Unto which fcope that our endeavour may the more
directly tend, it feemeth fitteft that firft thofe things be examin'd, which are as feeds
from whence the reft that enfue have grown. And of fuch the moft general is that,
wherewith we are here to make our entrance : a queftion not moved (I think)
any where in other churches, and therefore in ours the more likely to be foon (I truft)
determined; the rather for that it hath grown from no other root than only a defire to
enlarge the neceffary ufe of the word of God; which defire hath begotten an error,
inlarging it further than (as we are perfuaded) foundnefs of truth will bear. For where-
T. C. l. 1. p. 59, 60.
as God hath left fundry kinds of laws unto men, and by all thofe laws the actions of
men are in fome fort directed ; they hold that one only law, the fcripture, muft be the
rule to direct in all things, even fo far as to the *taking up of a rufh or ftraw.* About
which point there fhould not need any queftion to grow, and that which is grown might
prefently end, if they did yield but to thefe two reftraints. The firft is, not to extend
the actions whereof they fpeak, fo low as that inftance doth import of taking up a
ftraw, but rather keep themfelves at the leaft within the compafs of moral actions, actions which have in them vice or virtue. The fecond, not to exact at our hands for
every action the knowledge of fome place of fcripture out of which we ftand bound
to deduce it, as by divers teftimonies they feek to enforce ; but rather as the truth is,
fo to acknowledge, that it fufficeth if fuch actions be framed according to the law of
reafon ; the general axioms, rules and principles of which law, being fo frequent in
holy fcripture, there is no let but in that regard, even out of fcripture fuch duties may
be deduced by fome kind of confequence (as by long circuit of deduction it may be
that even all truth, out of any truth, may be concluded) howbeit no man bound
in fuch fort to deduce all his actions out of fcripture, as if either the place be to him
unknown whereon they may be concluded, or the reference unto that place not
prefently confidered of the action, fhall in that refpect be condemned as unlawful. In
this we diffent, and this we are prefently to examine.

The firft pre-
tended proof
of the firft
pofition out
of fcripture.
Prov. 2. 6.
T. C. l. 1. p.
20. I fay,
that the word
of God con-
taineth what-
foever things
can fall into
any part of
man's life.
For fo Solomon
faith in the fe-
cond chapter
of the Pro-
verbs, My fon,
if thou receive
my words,
&c. then thou
fhalt under-
ftand juftice,
and judgment,
and equity,
and every good
way.
1. In all parts of knowledge, rightly fo termed, things moft general are moft ftrong.
Thus it muft be, inafmuch as the certainty of our perfuafion touching particulars, dependeth altogether upon the credit of thofe generalities out of which they grow. Albeit therefore every caufe admit not fuch infallible evidence of proof, as leaveth no
poffibility of doubt or fcruple behind it ; yet they who claim the general affent of the
whole world unto that which they teach, and do not fear to give very hard and heavy
fentence upon as many as refufe to embrace the fame, muft have fpecial regard that
their firft foundations and grounds be more than flender probabilities. This whole
queftion, which hath been moved about the kind of church-regiment, we could not but
for our own refolution fake endeavour to unrip and fift ; following therein as near as
we might, the conduct of that judicial method which ferveth beft for invention of
truth. By means whereof having found this the head theorem of all their difcourfes,
who plead for the change of ecclefiaftical government in *England*, namely, *that the
fcripture of God is in fuch fort the rule of human actions, that fimply whatfoever we
do, and are not by it directed thereunto, the fame is fin* ; we hold it neceffary that the
proofs hereof be weighed. Be they of weight fufficient or otherwife, it is not ours
to judge and determine ; only what difficulties there are which as yet with-hold our
affent till we be further and better fatisfied, I hope, no indifferent amongft them will
fcorn or refufe to hear. Firft therefore, whereas they alledge, *that wifdom doth teach
men every good way* ; and have thereupon inferred that no way is good in any kind
of action unlefs wifdom do by fcripture lead unto it ; fee they not plainly how they
reftrain the manifold ways which wifdom hath to teach men by, unto one only way of
teaching, which is by fcripture ? The bounds of wifdom are large, and within them
much is contained. Wifdom was *Adam's* inftructor in paradife : wifdom endued
the fathers who lived before the law, with the knowledge of holy things ; by the wif-
Pfal. 115. 95.
dom of the law of God *David* attained to excel others in underftanding, and *Solomon*
likewife to excel *David* by the felf-fame wifdom of God, teaching him many things
befides the law. The ways of well-doing are in number even as many, as are the kinds
of voluntary actions ; fo that whatfoever we do in this world, and may do it ill, we
fhew our felves therein by well-doing to be wife. Now if wifdom did teach men by
fcripture not only all the ways that are right and good in fome certain kind, according

to that of (*a*) St. *Paul*, concerning the use of scripture, but did simply without any manner of exception, restraint, or distinction, teach every way of doing well, there is no art but scripture should teach it, because every art doth teach the way how to do something or other well. To teach men therefore wisdom professeth, and to teach them every good way ; but not every good way by one way of teaching. Whatsoever either men on earth, or the angels of heaven do know, it is as a drop of that unemptiable fountain of wisdom ; which wisdom hath diversly imparted her treasures unto the world. As her ways are of sundry kinds, so her manner of teaching is not merely one and the same. Some things she openeth by the sacred books of scripture ; some things by the glorious works of nature ; with some things she inspireth them from above by spiritual influence ; in some things she leadeth and traineth them only by worldly experience and practice. We may not so in any one special kind admire her that we disgrace her in any other ; but let all her ways be according unto their place and degree adored.

(a) 1 Tim. 3; 16. *The whole scripture is given by inspiration of God, and is profitable to teach, to improve, to correct, and to instruct in righteousness, that the man of God may be absolute, being made perfect unto all good works. He meaneth all and only those* good works which belong unto us as we are men of God, and which unto salvation are necessary. Or if we understand by men of God God's ministers, there is not required in them an universal skill of every good work or way, but an hability to teach whatsoever men are bound to do that they may be saved : and with this kind of knowledge the scripture sufficeth to furnish them as touching matter.

2. That *all things be done to the glory of God*, the blessed apostle (it is true) exhorteth. The glory of God is the admirable excellency of that virtue divine, which being made manifest, causeth men and angels to extol his greatness, and in regard thereof to fear him. By being glorified, it is not meant, that he doth receive any augmentation of glory at our hands ; but his name we glorify, when we testify our acknowledgment of his glory. Which albeit we most effectually do by the virtue of obedience ; nevertheless it may be perhaps a question, whether saint *Paul* did mean that we sin as oft as ever we go about any thing without an express intent and purpose to obey God therein. He faith of himself, *I do in all things please all men, seeking not my own commodity, but rather the good of many, that they may be saved*. Shall it hereupon be thought, that saint *Paul* did not move either hand or foot, but with express intent even thereby to further the common salvation of men ? We move, we sleep, we take the cup at the hand of our friend, a number of things we oftentimes do only to satisfy some natural desire, without present, express and actual reference unto any commandment of God. Unto his glory even these things are done which we naturally perform, and not only that which morally and spiritually we do. For by every effect proceeding from the most concealed instincts of nature, his power is made manifest. But it doth not therefore follow, that of necessity we shall sin unless we expresly intend this in every such particular. But be it a thing which requireth no more than only our general presupposed willingness to please God in all things, or be it a matter wherein we cannot so glorify the name of God as we should without an actual intent to do him in that particular some special obedience ; yet for any thing there is in this sentence alledged to the contrary, God may be glorify'd by obedience, and obey'd by performance of his will, and his will be performed with an actual intelligent desire to fulfil that law which maketh known what his will is, altho no special clause or sentence of scripture be in every such action set before mens eyes to warrant it. For scripture is not the only law whereby God hath opened his will touching all things that may be done ; but there are other kinds of laws which notify the will of God, as in the former book hath been proved at large : nor is there any law of God, whereunto he doth not account our obedience his glory. *Do therefore all things unto the glory of God*, (faith the apostle) *be inoffensive both to the Jews and Grecians, and the church of God ; even as I please all men in all things, not seeking my own commodity, but many as, that they may be saved*. In the least thing done disobediently towards God, or offensively against the good of men, whose benefit we ought to seek for as for our own, we plainly shew that we do not acknowledge God to be such as indeed he is, and consequently that we glorify him not. This the blessed apostle teacheth ; but doth any apostle teach that we cannot glorify God otherwise than only in doing what we find that God in scripture commandeth us to do ? The churches dispersed amongst the heathen in the east part of the world are by the apostle saint *Peter* exhorted to have their *conversation honest among the gentiles, that they which speak evil of them as of evil-doers, might by the good works which they should see, glorify God in the day of visitation*. As long as that which christians did was good, and no way subject unto just reproof, their virtuous conversation was a mean to work the heathens conversion unto Christ. Seeing therefore this had been a thing altogether impossible, but that infidels themselves did discern in matters of life and conversation, when believers did well and when otherwise ; when they glorified their heavenly father, and when not : it followeth, that some things wherein

God

The second proof out of scripture.
T. C. l. 1. p. 16. Saint *Paul* faith, *that whether we eat or drink, or whatsoever we do, we must do it to the glory of God. But no man can glorify God in any thing but by obedience, and there is no obedience but in respect of the commandment and word of God, therefore it followeth that the word of God directeth a man in all his actions.*

1 Pet. 2. 12.

God is glorified, may be some other way known than only by the sacred scripture; of which scripture the gentiles being utterly ignorant, did notwithstanding judge rightly of the quality of christian mens actions. Most certain it is, that nothing but only sin doth dishonour God. So that to glorify him in all things, is to do nothing whereby the name of God may be blasphemed; nothing whereby the salvation of Jew or Grecian, or any in the church of Christ, may be let or hindred; nothing whereby his law is transgressed. But the question is, whether only scripture do shew whatsoever God is glorified in?

3. And tho meats and drinks be said to be sanctified by the word of God, and by prayer, yet neither is this a reason sufficient to prove, that by scripture we must of necessity be directed in every light and common thing which is incident unto any part of man's life. Only it sheweth that unto us the word, that is to say, the gospel of Christ, having not delivered any such difference of things clean and unclean, as the law of Moses did unto the Jews, there is no cause but that we may use indifferently all things as long as we do not (like swine) take the benefit of them without a thankful acknowledgment of his liberality and goodness by whose providence they are enjoyed. And therefore the apostle gave warning before-hand to take heed of such as should enjoin to *abstain from meats, which God hath created to be received with thanksgiving, by them which believe and know the truth. For every creature of God is good, and nothing to be refused, if it be received with thanksgiving, because it is sanctified by the word of God and prayer.* The gospel, by not making many things unclean, as the law did, hath sanctified those things generally to all, which particularly each man unto himself must sanctify by a reverend and holy use. Which will hardly be drawn so far as to serve their purpose, who have imagined the word in such sort to sanctify all things, that neither food can be tasted, nor raiment put on, nor in the world any thing done, but this deed must needs be sin in them which do not first know it appointed unto them by scripture before they do it.

4. But to come unto that which of all other things in scripture is most stood upon; that place of St. *Paul,* they say, is of all other most clear, where *speaking of those things which are called indifferent,* in the end he concludeth, *That whatsoever is not of faith, is sin; but faith is not but in respect of the word of God; therefore whatsoever is not done by the word of God, is sin.* Whereunto we answer, that albeit the name of faith being properly and strictly taken, it must needs have reference unto some uttered word as the object of belief; nevertheless, sith the ground of credit is the credibility of things credited; and things are made credible, either by the known condition and quality of the utterer, or by the manifest likelihood of truth which they have in themselves; hereupon it riseth, that whatsoever we are persuaded of, the same we are generally said to believe. In which generality the object of faith may not so narrowly be restrained, as if the same did extend no further than only to the scriptures of God. *Tho* (saith our Saviour) *ye believe not me, believe my works, that ye may know and believe that the Father is in me, and I in him.* The other disciples said unto Thomas, *We have seen the Lord;* but his answer unto them was, *Except I see in his hands the print of the nails, and put my finger into them, I will not believe.* Can there be any thing more plain, than that which by these two sentences appeareth; namely, That there may be a certain belief grounded upon other assurance than scripture; any thing more clear, than that we are said not only to believe the things which we know by another's relation, but even whatsoever we are certainly persuaded of, whether it be by reason or by sense? Forasmuch therefore as (a) it is granted that saint *Paul* doth mean nothing else by faith, but only *a full persuasion that that which we do is well done;* against which kind of faith or persuasion, as saint *Paul* doth count it sin to enterprize any thing, (b) so likewise some of the very heathen have taught, as *Tully, That nothing ought to be done whereof thou doubtest, whether it be right or wrong;* whereby it appeareth that even those which had no knowledge of the word of God, did see much of the equity of this which the apostle requireth of a christian man; I hope we shall not seem altogether unnecessarily to doubt of the soundness of their opinion, who think simply that nothing but only the word of God can give us assurance in any thing we are to do, and resolve us that we do well. For might not the *Jews* have been fully persuaded that they did well to think (if they had so thought) that in Christ God the Father was, altho the only ground of this their faith had been the wonderful works they saw him do? Might not, yea, did not *Thomas* fully in the end persuade himself, that he did

Rom. i. 34.

1 Cor. 10. 31.
Rom. 2. 23.

The third scripture proof, 1 *Tim.* 4. 5. and that which saint *Paul* said of meats and drinks, that they are sanctified unto us by the word of God, the same is to be understood of all things else whatsoever we have the use of. *T.C. l. 1. p. 16.* 1 Tim. 4.

The fourth scripture proof, *Rom.* 14. 23. *T.C.* l. 1. p. 27.

Psal. 19. 8.
Apoc. 3. 14.
2 Cor. 1. 18.

John 10. 38.
John 20. 25.

(a) And if any will say, that saint *Paul* meaneth there a πληροφορία and full persuasion that that which is well done, I grant it: But from whence can that spring but from faith? How can we persuade and assure our selves that we do

well, but whereas we have the word of God for our warrant? T. C. l. 1. p. 27.　(b) What also that some even of those heathen men have taught, that nothing ought to be done, whereof thou doubtest whether it be right or wrong? Whereby it appeareth, that even those which had no knowledge of the word of God, did see much of the equity of this which the apostle requireth of a christian man: and that the chiefest difference is, that where they sent men for the difference of good and evil to the light of reason, in such things the apostle sendeth them to the school of Christ in his word, which only is able thro faith to give them assurance and resolution in their doings. T. C. l. 1. p. 60.

well

well to think that body which now was raifed, to be the fame which had been crucified? That which gave *Thomas* this affurance was his fenfe; *Thomas, becaufe thou haft feen, thou believeft,* faith our Saviour. What fcripture had *Tully* for his affurance? Yet I nothing doubt, but that they who alledge him, think he did well to fet down in writing a thing fo confonant unto truth. Finally, we all believe that the fcriptures of God are facred, and that they have proceeded from God; our felves we affure that we do right well in fo believing. We have for this point a demonftration found and infallible. But it is not the word of God which doth or poffibly can affure us, that we do well to think it his word. For if any one book of fcripture did give teftimony to all; yet ftill that fcripture which giveth credit to the reft, would require another fcripture to give credit unto it; neither could we ever come unto any paufe whereon to reft our affurance this way: fo that unlefs befide fcripture, there were fomething which might affure us that we do well, we could not think we do well; no, not in being affur'd that fcripture is a facred and holy rule of well-doing. On which determination we might be contented to ftay our felves without further proceeding herein, but that we are drawn on into a larger fpeech by reafon of their fo great earneftnefs, who beat more and more upon thefe laft alledged words, as being of all other moft pregnant. Whereas therefore they ftill argue, That *wherefoever faith is wanting, there is fin*; and, *in every action not* T.C.l.2.p.58. *commanded, faith is wanting*; ergo, *in every action not commanded, there is fin:* I would demand of them; firft, forafmuch as the nature of things indifferent is neither to be commanded nor forbidden, but left free and arbitrary; how there can be any thing indifferent, if for want of faith fin be committed, when any thing not commanded is done? So that of neceffity they muft add fomewhat, and at leaftwife thus fet it down: In every action not commanded of God, or permitted with approbation, faith is wanting, and for want of faith there is fin. The next thing we are to enquire is, What thofe things be which God permitteth with approbation, and how we may know them to be fo permitted. When there are unto one end fundry means; as for example, for the fuftenance of our bodies many kinds of food, many forts of raiment to clothe our nakednefs, and fo in other things of like condition: here the end it felf being neceffary, but not fo any one mean thereunto; neceffary that our bodies fhould be both fed and clothed, howbeit no one kind of food or raiment neceffary; therefore we hold thefe things free in their own nature and indifferent. The choice is left to our own difcretion, except a principal bond of fome higher duty remove the indifferency that fuch things have in themfelves. Their indifferency is removed, if either we take away our own liberty, as *Ananias* did, for whom to have fold or held his poffeffions it was indifferent, till his fo- Acts 5. lemn vow and promife unto God had ftrictly bound him one only way; or if God himfelf have precifely abridged the fame, by reftraining us unto, or by barring us from fome one or more things of many, which otherwife were in themfelves altogether indifferent. Many fafhions of prieftly attire there were, whereof *Aaron* and his fons might have had Exod.28.c.43. their free choice without fin, but that God exprefly tied them unto one. All meats in- Levit. 11. different unto the *Jew*, were it not that God by name excepted fome, as fwines flefh. Impoffible therefore it is that we fhould otherwife think, than that what things God doth neither command nor forbid, the fame he permitteth them with approbation either to be done or left undone. *All things are lawful unto me,* faith the apoftle, 1 Cor. 6. 12. fpeaking, as it feemeth, in the perfon of the chriftian Gentile for maintenance of liberty in things indifferent; whereunto his anfwer is, that neverthelefs, *all things are not expedient*; in things indifferent there is a choice, they are not always equally expedient. Now in things, altho not commanded of God, yet lawful becaufe they are permitted, the queftion is, What light fhall fhew us the conveniency which one hath above another? For anfwer, their final determination is, That *whereas the heathen did fend men for the difference of good and evil to the light of reafon, in fuch things the apoftle fendeth us to the fchool of Chrift in his word, which only is able thro faith to give us affurance and refolution in our doings.* Which word *only,* is utterly without poffibility of ever being proved. For what if it were true concerning things indifferent, that unlefs the word of the Lord had determined of the free ufe of them, there could have been no lawful ufe of them at all; which notwithftanding is untrue; becaufe it is not the fcriptures fetting down fuch things as indifferent, but their not fetting down as neceffary that doth make them to be indifferent; yet this to our prefent purpofe ferveth nothing at all. We enquire not now, whether any thing be free to be ufed which fcripture hath not fet down as free; but concerning things known and acknowledged to be indifferent, whether particularly in chufing any one of them before another, we fin, if any thing but fcripture direct us into this our choice. When many meats are fet before me, all are indifferent, none unlawful; I take one as moft convenient. If fcripture require me fo

to

to do, then is not the thing indifferent, becaufe I muſt do what ſcripture requireth. They are all indifferent; I might take any; ſcripture doth not require of me to make any ſpecial choice of one; I do notwithſtanding make choice of one, my diſcretion teaching me ſo to do. A hard caſe, that hereupon I ſhould be juſtly condemned of ſin. Nor let any man think that following the judgment of natural diſcretion in ſuch caſes, we can have no aſſurance that we pleaſe God. For to the author and God of our nature, how ſhall any operation proceeding in natural ſort, be in that reſpect unacceptable? The nature which himſelf hath given to work by, he cannot but be delighted with, when we exerciſe the ſame any way, without commandment of his to the contrary. My deſire is to make this cauſe ſo manifeſt, that if it were poſſible, no doubt or ſcruple concerning the ſame might remain in any man's cogitation. Some truths there are, the verity whereof time doth alter: as it is now true that Chriſt is riſen from the dead; which thing was not true at ſuch time as Chriſt was living on earth, and had not ſuffered. It would be known therefore, whether this which they teach concerning the ſinful ſtain of all actions not commanded of God, be a truth that doth now appertain unto us only, or a perpetual truth, in ſuch ſort that from the firſt beginning of the world unto the laſt conſummation thereof it neither hath been, nor can be otherwiſe. I ſee not how they can reſtrain this unto any particular time, how they can think it true now, and not always true, that in every action not commanded there is for want of faith ſin. Then let them caſt back their eyes unto former generations of men, and mark what was done in the prime of the world. *Seth, Enoch, Noah, Sem, Abraham, Job,* and the reſt that lived before any ſyllable of the law of God was written, did they not ſin as much as we do in every action not commanded? That which God is unto us by his ſacred

Job 4. 19. word, the ſame he was unto them by ſuch like means, as *Eliphaz* in *Job* deſcribeth. If therefore we ſin in every action which the ſcripture commandeth us not; it followeth that they did the like in all ſuch actions as were not by revelation from heaven exacted at their hands. Unleſs God from heaven did by viſion ſtill ſhew them what to do, they might do nothing, not eat, not drink, not ſleep, not move. Yea, but even as in darkneſs, candle-light may ſerve to guide mens ſteps, which to uſe in the day were madneſs; ſo when God hath once delivered his law in writing, it may be they are of opinion, that then it muſt needs be ſin for men to do any thing which was not there commanded for them to do, whatſoever they might do before. Let this be granted, and it ſhall hereupon plainly enſue, either that the light of ſcripture once ſhining in the world, all other light of nature is therewith in ſuch ſort drowned, that now we need it not, nei-

Ariſt. Pol. 1. ther may we longer uſe it; or if it ſtand us in any ſtead, yet as *Ariſtotle* ſpeaketh of men whom nature hath framed for the ſtate of ſervitude, ſaying, *They have reaſon ſo far forth as to conceive when others direct them,* but little or none in directing themſelves by themſelves; ſo likewiſe our natural capacity and judgment muſt ſerve us only for the right underſtanding of that which the ſacred ſcripture teacheth. Had the prophets who ſucceeded *Moſes,* or the bleſſed apoſtles which followed them, been ſettled in this perſuaſion, never would they have taken ſo great pains in gathering togethe rnatural arguments, thereby to teach the faithful their duties. To uſe unto them any other motive than *Scriptum eſt, Thus it is written,* had been to teach them other grounds of their actions than ſcripture; which, I grant, they alledge commonly, but not only. Only ſcripture they ſhould have alledged, had they been thus perſuaded, that ſo far forth we do ſin as we do any thing otherwiſe directed than by ſcripture. Saint *Auguſtine*

Auguſt. Fp. 18. was reſolute in points of chriſtianity to credit none, how godly and learned ſoever he were, unleſs he confirmed his ſentence by the ſcriptures, *or by ſome reaſon not contrary to them.* Let them therefore with ſaint *Auguſtine* reject and condemn that which is not grounded either on the ſcripture, or on ſome reaſon not contrary to ſcripture, and we are ready to give them our hands in token of friendly conſent with them.

The firſt aſſertion endeavoured to be proved by the uſe of taking arguments negatively from the authority of ſcripture; which kind of diſputing is uſual in the fathers.   5. But againſt this it may be objected, and is, That the fathers do nothing more uſually in their books, than draw arguments from the ſcripture negatively in reproof of that which is evil; *ſcriptures teach it not, avoid it therefore.* Theſe diſputes with the fathers are ordinary, neither is it hard to ſhew that the prophets themſelves have ſo reaſoned. Which arguments being found good, it ſhould ſeem that it cannot be unſound or evil to hold ſtill the ſame aſſertion, againſt which hitherto we have diſputed. For if it ſtand with reaſon thus to argue, ſuch a thing is not taught us in ſcripture, therefore we may not receive or allow it; how ſhould it ſeem unreaſonable to think that whatſoever we may lawfully do, the ſcripture by commanding it muſt make it lawful? But how far ſuch arguments do reach, it ſhall the better appear by conſidering the matter wherein they have been urged. Firſt therefore this we conſtantly deny, that of ſo many teſtimonies as they are able to produce for the ſtrength of negative arguments,

any

any one doth generally (which is the point in queſtion) condemn either all opinions as falſe, or all actions as unlawful which the ſcripture teacheth us not. The moſt that can be collected out of them is only, that in ſome caſes a negative argument taken from ſcripture is ſtrong, whereof no man endued with judgment can doubt. But doth the ſtrength of ſome negative argument prove this kind of negative argument ſtrong, by force whereof all things are denied which ſcripture affirmeth not, or all things which ſcripture preſcribeth not condemned? The queſtion between us is concerning matter of action, what things are lawful or unlawful for men to do. The ſentences alledged out of the fathers, are as peremptory, and as large in every reſpect for matter of opinion, as of action. Which argueth that in truth they never meant any otherwiſe to tie the one than the other unto ſcripture, both being thereunto equally tied, as far as each is required in the ſame kind of neceſſity unto ſalvation. If therefore it be not unlawful to know, and with full perſuaſion to believe much more than ſcripture alone doth teach; if it be againſt all ſenſe and reaſon to condemn the knowledge of ſo many arts and ſciences as are otherwiſe learned than in holy ſcripture, notwithſtanding the manifeſt ſpeeches of antient catholick fathers, which ſeem to cloſe up within the boſom thereof all manner of good and lawful knowledge; wherefore ſhould their words be thought more effectual to ſhew that we may not in deeds and practice, than they are to prove that in ſpeculation and knowledge we ought not to go any farther than the ſcripture; which ſcripture being given to teach matters of belief, no leſs than of action, the fathers muſt needs be, and are even as plain againſt credit beſides the relation, as againſt practice without the injunction of the ſcripture. Saint *Auguſtine* hath ſaid, *Whether it* *Aug. cont.liter. Petil. l. 3, c. 6.* *be queſtion of Chriſt, or whether it be queſtion of his church, or of what thing ſoever the queſtion be; I ſay not, if we, but if an angel from heaven ſhall tell us any thing beſide that you have received in the ſcripture under the law and the goſpel, let him be ac-* *Tertul. de prae-* *curſed.* In like ſort *Tertullian, We may not give our ſelves this liberty to bring in* *ſcript. adverſ.* *any thing of our will, nor chuſe any thing that other men bring in of their will; we have the apoſtles themſelves for authors, which themſelves brought nothing of their own will; but the diſcipline which they received of Chriſt, they deliver'd faithfully unto the people;* in which place the name of diſcipline importeth not,

> T. C. l. 2. p. 81. *Auguſtine* ſaith, *Whether it be queſtion of Chriſt, or whether it be queſtion of his church,* &c. And left the anſwer ſhould reſtrain the general ſaying of *Auguſtine,* unto the doctrine of the goſpel, ſo that he would thereby ſhut out the diſcipline; even *Tertullian* himſelf, before he was embrued with the hereſy of *Montanus,* giveth teſtimony unto the diſcipline in theſe words, *We may not give our ſelves,* &c.

as they who alledge it would fain have it conſtrued, but as any man (who noteth the circumſtance of the place, and the occaſion of uttering the words) will eaſily acknowledge, even the ſelf-ſame thing it ſignifieth which the name of doctrine doth; and as well might the one as the other there have been uſed. To help them farther, doth not ſaint *Jerom,* after the ſelf-ſame manner, diſpute, *We believe it not, becauſe we read it* *Hierom. contra Helvid.* *not;* yea, we ought not ſo much as to *know the things which the book of the law containeth not,* ſaith ſaint *Hilary.* Shall we hereupon then conclude, that we may not *Hilar. in Pſal. 132.* take knowledge of, or give credit unto any thing which ſenſe, or experience, or report, or art doth propoſe, unleſs we find the ſame in ſcripture? No, it is too plain that ſo far to extend their ſpeeches, is to wreſt them againſt their true intent and meaning. To urge any thing upon the church, requiring thereunto that religious aſſent of chriſtian belief, wherewith the words of the holy prophets are received; to urge any thing as part of that ſupernatural and celeſtially revealed truth which God hath taught, and not to ſhew it in ſcripture, this did the antient fathers evermore think unlawful, impious, execrable. And thus as their ſpeeches were meant, ſo by us they muſt be reſtrained. T. C. l. 1. p. 8. As for thoſe alledged words of *Cyprian, The chriſtian religion ſhall find, that out of* Let him hear what *Cyprian* *this ſcripture rules of all doctrines have ſprung, and that from hence doth ſpring,* ſaith, The *and hither doth return whatſoever the eccleſiaſtical diſcipline doth contain:* ſurely this chriſtian re place would never have been brought forth in this cauſe, if it had been but once read ligion (ſaith he) ſhall find, over in the author himſelf out of whom it is cited. For the words are uttered concern- that, &c. ing that one principal commandment of love; in the honour whereof he ſpeaketh after this ſort: *Surely this commandment containeth the law, and the prophets, and in this* *Verè hoc man* *one word is the abridgment of all the volumes of ſcripture: this nature, and reaſon* *datum legem* *and the authority of thy word, O Lord, doth proclaim; this we have heard out of thy* *complectitur &* *mouth; herein the perfection of all religion doth conſiſt. This is the firſt command-* *prophetas, &* *ment and the laſt: this being written in the book of life, is* (as it were) *an everlaſting* *in hoc verbo omnium ſcripturarum volu-*

mina coarctantur. Hoc natura, hoc ratio, hoc, Domine, verbi tui clamat authoritas, hoc ex ore tuo audivimus, hic invenit conſummationem omnis religio. Primum eſt hoc mandatum & ultimum, hoc in libro vitae conſcriptum indeficientem, & homiliibus, & angelis exhibet lectionem. Legat hoc unum verbum & in hoc mandato meditetur chriſtiana religio, & inveniet ex hac ſcriptura omnium doctrinarum regulas amanaſſe, & hinc naſci & huc recurri quicquid eccleſiaſtica continet diſciplina, & in omnibus irritum eſſe & frivolum quicquid dilectio non confirmat.

leſſon

lesson both to men and angels. *Let christian religion read this one word, and meditate upon this commandment, and out of this scripture it shall find the rules of all learning to have sprung, and from hence to have risen, and hither to return, whatsoever the ecclesiastical discipline containeth ; and that in all things it is vain and bootless which charity confirmeth not.* Was this a sentence (trow you) of so great force to prove that scripture is the only rule of all the actions of men ? Might they not hereby even as well prove, that one commandment of scripture is the only rule of all things, and so exclude the rest of the scripture, as now they do all means besides scripture ? But thus it fareth, when too much desire of contradiction causeth our speech rather to pass by number than to stay for weight. Well, but *Tertullian* doth in this case speak yet more plainly : *The scripture* (saith he) *denieth what it noteth not* ; which are indeed the words of *Tertullian.* But what ? the scripture reckoneth up the kings of *Israel,* and amongst those kings *David* ; the scripture reckoneth up the sons of *David,* and amongst those sons *Solomon.* To prove that amongst the kings of *Israel,* there was no *David* but only one ; no *Solomon* but one in the sons of *David, Tertullian*'s argument will fitly prove. For inasmuch as the scripture did propose to reckon up all ; if there were more, it would have named them. In this case the *scripture doth deny the thing it noteth not.* Howbeit I could not but think that man to do me some piece of manifest injury, which would hereby fasten upon me a general opinion, as if I did think the scripture to deny the very reign of king *Henry* the eighth, because it no where noteth that any such king did reign. *Tertullian*'s speech is probable concerning such matter as he there speaketh of. *There was,* saith *Tertullian, no second* Lamech *like to him that had two wives ; the scripture denieth what it noteth not.* As therefore it noteth one such to have been in that age of the world ; so had there been moe, it would by likelihood as well have noted many as one. What infer we now hereupon ? *There was no second* Lamech ; *the scripture denieth what it noteth not.* Were it consonant unto reason to divorce these two sentences, the former of which doth shew how the latter is restrained, and not marking the former, to conclude by the latter of them, that simply whatsoever any man at this day doth think true is by the scripture denied, unless it be there affirmed to be true ? I wonder that a case so weak and feeble hath been so much persisted in. But to come unto those their sentences wherein matters of action are more apparently touched, the name of *Tertullian* is as before, so here again pretended ; who writing unto his wife two books, and exhorting her in the one to live a widow, in case God before her should take him unto his mercy ; and in the other, if she did marry, yet not to join her self to an infidel, as in those times some widows christian had done for the advancement of their estate in this present world, he urgeth very earnestly saint *Paul*'s words, *only in the Lord :* whereupon he demandeth of them that think they may do the contrary, what scripture they can shew where God hath dispensed and granted licence to do against that which the blessed apostle so strictly doth enjoin ? And because in defence it might perhaps be replied, seeing God doth will that couples which are married when both are infidels, if either party chance to be after converted unto christianity, this should not make separation between them as long as the unconverted was willing to retain the other on whom the grace of Christ had shined ; wherefore then should that let the making of marriage, which doth not dissolve marriage being made ? After great reasons shewed why God doth in converts, being married, allow continuance with infidels, and yet disallow that the faithful when they are free, should enter into bonds of wedlock with such, concludeth in the end concerning those women that so marry, *They that please not the Lord, do even thereby offend the Lord ; they do even thereby throw themselves into evil* ; that is to say, while they please him not by marrying in him, they do that whereby they incur his displeasure ; they make an offer of themselves into the service of that enemy with whose servants they link themselves in so near a bond. What one syllable is there in all this, prejudicial any way to that which we hold ? For the words of *Tertullian,* as they are by them alledged, are two ways misunderstood ; both in the former part, where that is extended generally to *all* things in the neuter gender, which he speaketh in the feminine gender of womens persons ; and in the latter, where *received with hurt,* is put instead of *wilful incurring that which is evil.* And so in some, *Tertullian* doth neither mean nor say as is pretended, *Whatsoever pleaseth not the Lord, displeaseth him, and with hurt is received* ; but, *those women that please not the* Lord *by their kind of marrying, do even thereby offend the Lord, they do even thereby throw themselves into evil.* Somewhat more

Tertul. lib. de Monog.

T.C. l. 2. p. 81. And in another place Tertullian saith, that the scripture denieth that which it noteth not.

T.C. l. 2. p. 80. And that in indifferent things it is not enough that they be not against the word, but that they be according to the word, it may appear by other places, where he saith, that whatsoever pleaseth not the Lord, displeaseth him, and with hurt is received. Lib. 2, ad uxorem.

Quæ Domino non placent, utiq; Dominum offendunt, utiq; malo se inferunt.

more shew there is in a second place of *Tertullian*, which notwithstanding when we have examined, it will be found as the rest are. The *Roman* emperor's custom was at certain solemn times to bestow on his soldiers a donative; which donative they received, wearing garlands upon their heads. There were, in the time of the emperors *Severus* and *Antoninus*, many who, being soldiers, had been converted unto Christ, and notwithstanding continued still in that military course of life: in which number, one man there was amongst all the rest, who at such a time coming to the tribune of the army to receive his donative, came, but with a garland n his hand, and not in such sort as others did. The tribune, offended hereat, demanded what this great singularity would mean: to whom the soldier, *Christianus sum, I am a christian.* Many there were so besides him, which yet did otherwise at that time; whereupon grew a question, whether a christian soldier might herein do as the unchristian did and wear as they wore. Many of them which were very found in christian belief, did rather commend the zeal of this man than approve his action. *Tertullian* was at the same time a *Montanist*, and an enemy unto the church for condemning that prophetical spirit which *Montanus* and his followers did boast they had receiv'd; as if in them Christ had performed his last promise; as if to them he had sent the Spirit that should be their perfecter and final instructer in the mysteries of christian truth. Which exulceration of mind made him apt to take all occasions of contradiction. Wherefore in honour of that action, and to gall their minds who did not so much commend it, he wrote his book *de Corona Militis,* not dissembling the stomach wherewith he wrote it. For the first man he commended as one more constant than the rest of his brethren, *who presumed,* faith he, *that they might well enough serve two lords.* Afterwards choler somewhat rising within him, he addeth, *It doth even remain that they should also devise how to rid themselves of his martyrdoms, towards the prophecies of whose holy spirit they have already shewn their disdain. They mutter that their good and long peace is now in hazard. I doubt not but some of them send the scriptures before, truss up bag and baggage, make themselves in a readiness that they may fly from city to city; for that is the only point of the gospel which they are careful not to forget. I know even their pastors very well what men they are; in peace lions, harts in time of trouble and fear:* Now these men, faith *Tertullian, They must be answered, where do we find it written in scripture,* that a christian man may not wear a garland? And as mens speeches uttered in heat of distempered affection, have oftentimes much more eagerness than weight, so he that shall mark the proofs alledged, and the answers to things objected in that book, will now and then perhaps espy the like imbecillity. Such is that argument whereby they that wore on their heads garlands are charged as transgressors of nature's law, and guilty of sacrilege against God the lord of nature, inasmuch as flowers in such sort worn, can neither be smelt nor seen well by those that wear them; and God made flowers sweet and beautiful, that being seen and smelt unto they might so delight. Neither doth *Tertullian* bewray this weakness in striking only, but also in repelling their strokes with whom he contended. They ask, faith he, *What scripture is there which doth teach that we should not be crowned? And what scripture is there which doth teach that we should?* for in requiring on the contrary part the aid of scripture, they do give sentence beforehand that their part ought also by scripture to be aided. Which answer is of no great force. There is no necessity, that if I confess, I ought not to do that which the scripture forbiddeth me, I should thereby acknowledge my self bound to do nothing which the scripture commandeth me not. For many inducements besides scripture may lead me to that, which if scripture be against, they all give place and are of no value, yet otherwise are strong and effectual to persuade. Which thing himself well enough understanding, and being not ignorant that scripture in many things doth neither command nor fordid, but use silence, his resolution in fine is, that in the church a number of things are strictly observed, whereof no law of scripture maketh mention one way or other; that of things once received and confirmed by use, long usage is a law sufficient; that in civil affairs, when there is no other law, custom it self doth stand for law; that inasmuch as law doth stand upon reason, to alledge reason serveth as well as to cite scripture; that whatsoever is reasonable, the same is lawful, whosoever is the author of it; that the authority of custom is great; finally, that the custom of christians was then, and had been a long time, not to wear garlands, and therefore that undoubtedly they did offend who presumed

G 2

to

T. C. l. 1. p. 81. And to come yet nearer, where he disputeth against the wearing of crown or garland (which is indifferent in it self) to those which objecting asked, where the scripture faith, that a man might not wear a crown? he answereth, by asking where the scripture faith that they may wear? And unto them replying that it is permitted, which is not forbidden; he answereth, that it is forbidden, which is not permitted. Whereby appeareth, that the argument of the scriptures negatively, holdeth not only in the doctrine and ecclesiastical discipline, but even in matters arbitrary and variable by the advice of the church. Where it is not enough that they be not forbidden, unless there be some word which doth permit the use of them: it is not enough that the scripture speaketh not against them, unless it speak for them: and finally, where it displeaseth the Lord which pleaseth him not, we must of necessity have the word of his mouth to declare his pleasure.

Tert. de Coroni Milit.

to violate such a custom by not observing that thing, the very inveterate observation whereof was a law sufficient to bind all men to observe it, unless they could shew some higher law, some law of scripture to the contrary. This presupposed, it may stand then very well with strength and soundness of reason, even thus to answer, *Whereas they ask what scripture forbiddeth them to wear a garland; we are in this case rather to demand, what scripture commandeth them? They cannot here alledge, that that is permitted which is not forbidden them: no, that is forbidden them which is not permitted.* For long received custom forbidding them to do as they did (if so be it did forbid them) there was no excuse in the world to justify their act, unless in the scripture they could shew some law that did license them thus to break a received custom. Now whereas in all the books of *Tertullian* besides, there is not so much found as in that one, to prove not only that we may do, but that we ought to do sundry things which the scripture commandeth not; out of that very book these sentences are brought, to make us believe that *Tertullian* was of a clean contrary mind. We cannot therefore hereupon yield; we cannot grant, that hereby is made manifest the argument of scripture negative to be of force, not only in doctrine and ecclesiastical discipline, but even in matters arbitrary. For *Tertullian* doth plainly hold even in that book, that neither the matter which he entreateth of was arbitrary, but necessary, inasmuch as the received custom of the church did tie and bind them not to wear garlands as the heathens did; yea, and further also he reckoneth up particularly a number of things whereof he expresly concludeth, *Harum & aliarum ejusmodi disciplinarum si legem expostules scripturarum, nullam invenies*; which is as much as if he had said in express words, many things there are which concern the discipline of the church and the duties of men, which to abrogate and take away, the scripture negatively urged may not in any case persuade us, but they must be observed, yea altho no scripture be found which requireth any such thing. *Tertullian* therefore undoubtedly doth not in this book shew himself to be of the same mind with them, by whom his name is pretended.

The first assertion endeavoured to be confirmed by the scripture's custom of disputing from divine authority negatively, 1 *John* 1. 5. *God is light, and there is in him no darkness at all.* Heb. 6. 18. *It is impossible that God should lye.* Numb. 23. 19. *God is not as man, that he should lye.* T.C.l.2. p.48. It is not hard to shew that the prophets have reasoned negatively: as when in the person of the Lord the prophet saith, *Whereof I have not spoken,* Jer. 19. 5. *And which never entered into my heart,* Jer. 7. 31, 32. and where he condemneth them, *because they have not asked counsel at the mouth of the Lord,* Isai. 30. 2. And it may be shewed, that the same kind of argument hath been used in things which are not of the substance of salvation or damnation, and whereof there was no commandment to the contrary (as in the former there was, *Levit.* 18. 21. and 20. 3. *Deut.* 17. 16.) In *Joshua* the children of *Israel* are charged by the prophet that they asked not counsel at the mouth of the Lord, when they entred into covenant with the *Gibeonites, Joshua* 19. 14. and yet that covenant was not made contrary unto any commandment of God. Moreover, we read that when *David* had taken this counsel, to build a temple unto the Lord, albeit the Lord had revealed before in his word, that there should be such a standing place, where the ark of the covenant and the service should have a certain abiding; and albeit there was no word of God which forbad *David* to build the temple: yet the Lord (with commendation of his good affection and zeal he had to the advancement of his glory) concludeth against *David*'s resolution to build the temple, with this reason; namely, that he had given no commandment of this who should build it. 1 *Chron.* 17. 6.

6. But sith the sacred scriptures themselves afford oftentimes such arguments as are taken from divine authority both one way and other; *The Lord hath commanded, therefore it must be:* and again, in like sort, *he hath not, therefore it must not be;* some certainty concerning this point seemeth requisite to be set down. God himself can neither possibly err, nor lead into error. For this cause his testimonies, whatsoever he affirmeth, are always truth and most infallible certainty. Yea, further, because the things that proceed from him are perfect without any manner of defect or maim; it cannot be but that the words of his mouth are absolute, and lack nothing which they should have for performance of that thing whereunto they tend. Whereupon it followeth, that the end being known whereunto he directeth his speech, the argument negatively is evermore strong and forcible concerning those things that are apparently requisite unto the same end. As for example, God intending to set down sundry times that which in angels is most excellent, hath not any where spoken so highly of them as he hath of our Lord and Saviour Jesus Christ; therefore they are not in dignity equal unto him. It is the apostle saint *Paul's* argument. The purpose of God was to teach his people, both unto whom they should offer sacrifice, and what sacrifice was to be offered. To burn their sons in fire unto *Baal* he did not command them, he spake no such thing, neither came it into his mind; therefore this they ought not to have done. Which argument the prophet *Jeremy* useth more than once, as being so effectual and strong, that altho the thing he reproveth were not only not commanded, but forbidden them and that expresly; yet the prophet chuseth rather to charge them with the fault of making a law unto themselves, than the crime of transgressing a law which God had made. For when the Lord hath once himself precisely set down a form of executing that wherein we are to serve him; the fault appeareth greater to do that which we are not, than not to do that which we are commanded. In this we seem to charge the law of God with hardness only, in that with foolishness: in this we shew our selves weak and unapt to be doers of his will, in that we take upon us to be

con-

Levit. 18. 21. &
20. 3.
Deut. 28. 10.

controllers of his wifdom : in this we fail to perform the thing which God feeth meet, convenient and good ; in that we prefume to fee what is meet and convenient better than God himfelf. In thofe actions therefore, the whole form whereof God hath of purpofe fet down to be obferved, we may not otherwife do than exactly as he hath prefcribed : in fuch things negative arguments are ftrong. Again, with a negative argument *David* is preffed concerning the purpofe he had to build a temple unto the Lord : *Thus* 1 Chron.17. 6. *faith the Lord, thou fhalt not build me an houfe to dwell in. Wherefoever I have walked with all* Ifrael, *fpake I one word to any of the judges of* Ifrael, *whom I commanded to feed my people, faying, why have ye not built me an houfe ?* The Jews urged with a negative argument touching the aid which they fought at the hands of the king of *Egypt* ; *Wo to thofe rebellious children* (faith the Lord) *which walk forth to go down* Ifaiah 30. 1. *into* Egypt, *and have not asked counfel at my mouth, to ftrengthen themfelves with the ftrength of* Pharaoh. Finally, the league of *Jofhua* with the *Gibeonites* is likewife with a negative argument touched. It was not as it fhould be : and why ? the Lord gave them not that advice : *They fought not counfel at the mouth of the Lord.* By the Jofh. 9. 14. virtue of which examples, if any man fhould fuppofe the force of negative arguments approved, when they are taken from fcripture, in fuch fort as we in this queftion are preffed therewith, they greatly deceive themfelves. For unto which of all thefe was it faid, that they had done amifs in purpofing to do, or in doing any thing at all which the fcripture commanded them not ? Our queftion is, whether all be fin which is done without direction by fcripture, and not whether the *Ifraelites* did at any time amifs by following their own minds without asking counfel of God. No, it was that people's fingular privilege, a favour which God vouchfafed them above the reft of the world, that in the affairs of their eftate, which were not determinable one way or other by the fcripture, himfelf gave them extraordinary direction and counfel as oft as they fought it at his hands. Thus God did firft by fpeech unto *Mofes* ; after by *Urim* and *Thummim* unto priefts ; laftly, by dreams and vifions unto prophets, from whom in fuch cafes they were to receive the anfwer of God. Concerning *Jofhua* therefore, thus fpake the Lord unto *Mofes*, faying, *He fhall ftand before* Eleazer *the prieft, who fhall ask counfel for* Num. 27. 21. *him by the judgment of* Urim *before the Lord* ; whereof had *Jofhua* been mindful, the fraud of the *Gibeonites* could not fo fmoothly have pafs'd unefpied till there was no help. The Jews had prophets to have refolved them from the mouth of God himfelf whether *Egyptian* aids fhould profit them, yea or no ; but they thought themfelves wife enough, and him unworthy to be of their counfel. In this refpect therefore was their reproof, tho fharp, yet juft, albeit there had been no charge precifely given them that they fhould always take heed of *Egypt*. But as for *David*, to think that he did evil in determining to build God a temple, becaufe there was in fcripture no commandment that he fhould build it, were very injurious ; the purpofe of his heart was religious and godly, the act moft worthy of honour and renown ; neither could *Nathan* chufe but admire his virtuous intent, exhort him to go forward, and befeech God to profper him therein. But God faw the endlefs troubles which *David* fhould be fubject unto during the whole time of his regiment, and therefore gave charge to defer fo good a work till the days of tranquillity and peace, wherein it might without interruption be performed. *David* fuppofed that it could not ftand with the duty which he owed unto God to fet himfelf in an houfe of cedar-trees, and to behold the ark of the Lord's covenant unfettled. This opinion the 1 Chron. 17. Lord abateth, by caufing *Nathan* to fhew him plainly that it fhould be no more imputed unto him for a fault than it had been unto the judges of *Ifrael* before him, his cafe being the fame which theirs was, their times not more unquiet than his, nor more unfit for fuch an action. Wherefore concerning the force of negative arguments fo taken from the authority of fcripture, as by us they are denied, there is in all this lefs than nothing. And touching that which unto this purpofe is borrowed from the controverfy fometimes handled between Mr. *Harding* (a) and the worthieft divine that (a) T. C. l. 2. *Chriftendom* hath bred for the fpace of fome hundreds of years, who being brought up p. 50. Mr. together in one univerfity, it fell out in them which was fpoken of two others, (b) proacheth the *They learned in the fame, that which in contrary camps they did practife.* Of thefe bifhop of Sa- two the one objecting, that with us arguments taken from authority negatively, are lisbury with over common ; the bifhop's anfwer hereunto is, that *this kind of argument is thought* reafoning ;

unto whom
the bifhop anfwereth, the argument of authority negatively is taken to be good, whenfoever proof is taken of God's word, and is ufed not only by us, but alfo by many of the catholick fathers. A little after he fheweth the reafon why the argument of authority of the fcripture negatively is good ; namely, for that the word of God is perfect. In another place unto Mr. *Harding*, cafting him in the teeth with negative arguments, he alledgeth places out of *Irenæus*, *Chryfoftom*, *Leo*, which reafoned negatively of the authority of the fcriptures. The places which he alledgeth be very full and plain in generality, without any fuch reftraints as the anfwerer imagined, as they are there to be feen. (b) *Vell. Paterc. Jugurtha ac Marius fub eodem Africano militantes; in iifdem caftris didicere quæ poftea in contrariis fecerent. Art.* 1. *Divif.* 29.

†   to

to be good, whenſoever proof is taken of God's word ; and is uſed not only by us, but
also by ſaint Paul, and by many of the catholick fathers. Saint Paul ſaith, God ſaid
not unto Abraham, in thy ſeeds all the nations of the earth ſhall be bleſſed; but, in thy
ſeed, which is Chriſt ; and thereof he thought he made a good argument. Likewiſe, ſaith
Origen, the bread which the Lord gave unto his diſciples, ſaying unto them, take and eat,
he deferred not, nor commanded to be reſerved till the next day. Such arguments Origen
and other learned fathers thought to ſtand for good, whatſoever miſliking Mr. Harding
hath found in them. This kind of proof is thought to hold in God's commandments, for
that they be full and perfect : and God hath ſpecially charged us, that we ſhould neither
put to them nor take from them ; and therefore it ſeemeth good unto them that have learned
of Chriſt, Unus eſt magiſter veſter Chriſtus, and have heard the voice of God the father
from heaven, Ipſum audite. But unto them that add to the word of God what them
liſteth, and make God's will ſubject unto their will, and break God's commandments
for their own traditions ſake, unto them it ſeemeth not good. Again, the Engliſh apology alledging the example of the Greeks, how they have neither private maſſes, nor
mangled ſacraments, nor purgatories, nor pardons ; it pleaſeth Mr. Harding to jeſt out
the matter, to uſe the help of his wits where ſtrength of truth failed him, and to anſwer with ſcoffing at negatives. The biſhop's defence in this caſe is, The antient learned
fathers having to deal with politick hereticks, that in defence of their errors, avouched
the judgment of all the old biſhops and doctors that had been before them, and the general conſent of the primitive and whole univerſal church, and that with as good regard of truth, and as faithfully as you do now ; the better to diſcover the ſhameleſs
boldneſs and nakedneſs of their doctrine, were oftentimes likewiſe forced to uſe the negative, and ſo to drive the ſame hereticks, as we do you, to prove their affirmatives,
which thing to do it was never poſſible. The antient father Irenæus thus ſtayed himſelf, as we do, by the negative, Hoc neque prophetæ prædicaverunt, neque dominus
docuit, neque apoſtoli tradiderunt ; This thing neither did the prophets publiſh, nor
our Lord teach, nor the apoſtles deliver. By a like negative, Chryſoſtom ſaith,
This tree neither Paul planted, nor Apollos watered, nor God increaſed. In like ſort
Leo ſaith, What needeth it to believe that thing that neither the law hath taught, nor
the prophets have ſpoken, nor the goſpel hath preached, nor the apoſtles have delivered ?
And again, how are the new devices brought in that our fathers never knew ? Saint
Auguſtine, having reckoned up a great number of the biſhops of Rome, by a general negative, ſaith thus, In all this order of ſucceſſion of biſhops, there is not one biſhop found
that was a Donatiſt. Saint Gregory being himſelf a biſhop of Rome, and writing againſt
the title of univerſal biſhop, ſaith thus, None of all my predeceſſors ever conſented
to uſe this ungodly title ; no biſhop of Rome ever took upon him this name of ſingula-
rity. By ſuch negatives, Mr. Harding, we reprove the vanity and novelty of your
religion ; we tell you none of the catholick, antient, learned fathers, either Greek or
Latin, ever uſed either your private maſs, or your half communion, or your barbarous
unknown prayers. Paul never planted them, Apollos never watered them, God never
increaſed them ; they are of your ſelves, they are not of God. In all this there is not a
ſyllable which any way croſſeth us. For concerning arguments negative, taken from
human authority, they are here proved to be in ſome caſes very ſtrong and forcible. They
are not in our eſtimation idle reproofs, when the authors of needleſs innovations are oppoſed with ſuch negatives, as that of Leo, How are theſe new devices brought in which
our fathers never knew ? When their grave and reverend ſuperiors do reckon up unto
them, as Auguſtine did to the Donatiſts, large catalogues of fathers wondred at for their
wiſdom, piety and learning, amongſt whom for ſo many ages before us no one did ever
ſo think of the church's affairs as now the world doth begin to be perſuaded ; ſurely by
us they are not taught to take exception hereat, becauſe ſuch arguments are negative.
Much leſs when the like are taken from the ſacred authority of ſcripture, if the matter
it ſelf do bear them. For in truth the queſtion is not, whether an argument from ſcripture negatively may be good, but whether it be ſo generally good, that in all actions
men may urge it ? The fathers, I grant, do uſe very general and large terms, even as
Hiero the king did in ſpeaking of Archimedes, From henceforward whatſoever Archimedes ſpeaketh, it muſt be believed. His meaning was not that Archimedes could ſimply
in nothing be deceived, but that he had in ſuch ſort approved his ſkill, that he ſeemed
worthy of credit for ever after in matters appertaining unto the ſcience he was ſkilful in.
In ſpeaking thus largely it is preſumed, that mens ſpeeches will be taken according to
the matter whereof they ſpeak. Let any man therefore that carrieth indifferency of
judgment, peruſe the biſhop's ſpeeches, and conſider well of thoſe negatives concerning
ſcripture, which he produceth out of Irenæus, Chryſoſtom and Leo, which three are
choſen

Margin notes (left column):
Gal. 3.
Orig. in Levit. Hom. 5.
Matth. 23.
Matth. 17.
Defenſ. par. 5. c. 15. diviſ. 1.
Lib. 1. cap. 1.
De incomp. nat. Dei, hom. 3.
Epiſt. 93. c. 11.
Epiſt. 97. c. 3.
Epiſt. 165.
Lib. 4. Ep. 32.

chosen from among the residue, because the sentences of the others (even as one of theirs also) do make for defence of negative arguments taken from human authority, and not from divine only.   They mention no more restraint in the one than in the other ; yet I think themselves will not hereby judge, that the fathers took both to be strong, without restraint unto any special kind of matter wherein they held such argument forcible. Nor doth the bishop either say or prove any more, than that an argument in some kinds of matter may be good, altho taken negatively from scripture.

7. An earnest desire to draw all things unto the determination of bare and naked scripture, hath caused here much pains to be taken in abating the estimation and credit of man. Which if we labour to maintain as far as truth and reason will bear, let not any think that we travel about a matter not greatly needful : for the scope of all their pleading against man's authority, is to overthrow such orders, laws and constitutions in the church, as depending thereupon, if they should therefore be taken away, would peradventure leave neither face nor memory of church to continue long in the world, the world especially being such as now it is.   That which they have in this case spoken, I would for brevity sake let pass ; but that the drift of their speech being so dangerous, their words are not to be neglected.   Wherefore to say that simply an argument taken from man's authority doth hold no way, neither affirmatively nor negatively, is hard.   By a man's authority we here understand the force which his word hath for the assurance of another's mind that buildeth upon it ; as the apostle somewhat did upon their report of the house of *Chloe*; and the *Samaritans* in a matter of far greater moment upon the report of a simple woman : for so it is said in saint *John's* gospel, *Many of the Samaritans of that city believed in him for the saying of the woman, which testified, he hath told me all things that ever I did.*   The strength of man's authority is affirmatively such, that the weightiest affairs in the world depend thereon.   In judgment and justice are not hereupon proceedings grounded ?   Saith not the law, that *in the mouth of two or three witnesses every word shall be confirmed ?*   This the law of God would not say if there were in a man's testimony no force at all to prove any thing.   And if it be admitted that in matter of fact there is some credit to be given to the testimony of man but not in matter of opinion and judgment, we see the contrary both acknowledged and universally practised also throughout the world.   The sentences of wise and expert men were never but highly esteemed.   Let the title of a man's right be called in question, are we not bold to rely and build upon the judgment of such as are famous for their skill in the laws of this land ?   In matter of state, the weight many times of some one man's authority is thought reason sufficient even to sway over whole nations.   And this is not only with the simple sort ; but the learneder and wiser we are, the more such arguments in such cases prevail with us.   The reason why the simpler sort are moved with authority, is the conscience of their own ignorance ; whereby it cometh to pass, that having learned men in admiration, they rather fear to dislike them than know wherefore they should allow and follow their judgments.   Contrariwise with them that are skilful, authority is much more strong and forcible ; because they only are able to discern how just cause there is why to some mens authority so much should be attributed.   For which cause the name of *Hippocrates* (no doubt) was more effectual to persuade even such men as *Galen* himself than to move a silly empirick ; so that the very self-same argument in this kind, which doth but induce the vulgar sort to like, may constrain the wiser to yield.   And therefore not orators only with the people, but even the very profoundest disputers in all faculties, have hereby often with the best learned prevailed most.   As for arguments taken from human authority, and that negatively, for example sake, if we should think the assembling of the people of God together by the sound of a bell, the presenting of infants at the holy font by such as we commonly call their godfathers, or any other the like received custom to be impious, because some men of whom we think very reverently, have in their books and writings no where mentioned or taught that such things should be in the church, this reasoning were subject unto just reproof ; it were but feeble, weak, and unsound.   Notwithstanding even negatively an argument from human authority may be strong, as namely thus ; the chronicles of *England* mention no more than only six kings bearing the name of *Edward* since the time of the last conquest ; therefore it cannot be there should be more.   So that if the question be of the authority of a man's testimony, we cannot simply avouch either that affirmatively it doth not any way hold, or that it hath only force to induce the simpler sort, and not to constrain men of understanding

Their opinion concerning the force of arguments taken from human authority for the ordering of mens actions or persuasions.

T. C. l. 1. p. 15.   When the question is of the authority of a man, it holdeth neither affirmatively nor negatively.   The reason is because the infirmity of man can never attain to the perfection of any thing wherebyhe might speak all things that are to be spoken of it ; neither yet be free from error in those things which he speaketh or giveth out.   And therefore this argument neither affirmatively nor negatively compelleth the hearer, but only induceth him to some liking or disliking of that for which it is brought, and is rather for an orator to persuade the simpler sort, than for a disputer to inforce him that is learned. 1 Cor. 1. 11. John 4. 39.

Deut. 19. 15.

Matth. 18. 16.

standing

standing and ripe judgment to yield assent; or that negatively it hath in it no strength
at all. For unto every of these the contrary is most plain. Neither doth that which is
alledged concerning the infirmity of men overthrow or disapprove this. Men are blinded with ignorance and error; many things escape them; and in many things they may
be deceived; yea those things which they do know, they may either forget, or upon
sundry indirect considerations let pass; and altho themselves do not err, yet may they
thro malice or vanity even of purpose deceive others. Howbeit, infinite cases there
are wherein all these impediments and lets are so manifestly excluded, that there is no
shew or colour whereby any such exception may be taken, but that the testimony of man
will stand as a ground of infallible assurance. That there is a city of *Rome*, that *Pius
Quintus* and *Gregory* the thirteenth, and others have been popes of *Rome*, I suppose we
are certainly enough persuaded. The ground of our persuasion, who never saw the place
nor persons before named, can be nothing but man's testimony. Will any man here
notwithstanding alledge those mentioned human infirmities as reasons why these things
should be mistrusted or doubted of? yea, that which is more, utterly to infringe the
force and strength of man's testimony were to shake the very fortress of God's truth.
For whatsoever we believe concerning salvation by Christ, altho the scripture be therein
the ground of our belief; yet the authority of man is, if we mark it, the key which
openeth the door of entrance into the knowledge of the scripture. The scripture doth
not teach us the things that are of God, unless we did credit men who have taught us
that the words of scripture do signify those things. Some way therefore, notwithstanding man's infirmity, yet his authority may inforce assent. Upon better advice and deliberation so much is perceived, and at the length confessed, that arguments taken from
the authority of men, may not only so far forth
as hath been declared, but further also be of
some force in human sciences; which force be
it never so small, doth shew that they are not
utterly naught. But in matters divine it is still
maintained stiffly that they have no manner of
force at all. Howbeit, the very self-same reason, which causeth to yield that they are of some
force in the one, will at the length constrain also to acknowledge that they are not in the other
altogether unforcible. For if the natural strength
of man's wit may by experience and study attain unto such ripeness in the knowledge of things
human, that men in this respect may presume
to build somewhat upon their judgment; what

T. C. l. 1. p. 10. Altho that kind of argument of authority of
men is good neither in human nor divine sciences, yet it hath some
small force in human sciences, forasmuch as naturally, and in that
he is a man, he may come to some ripeness of judgment in those
sciences, which in divine matters hath no force at all; as of him
which naturally, and as he is a man, can no more judge of them
than a blind man of colours: yea so far is it from drawing credit
if it be barely spoken without reason and testimony of scripture,
that it carrieth also a suspicion of untruth whatsoever proceedeth
from him; which the apostle did well note, when to signify a thing
corruptly spoken, and against the truth, he saith, That it is spoken
according to man, Rom. 3. He saith not as a wicked and lying
man, but simply as a man: and altho this corruption be reformed
in many, yet for so much as in whom the knowledge of the truth
is most advanced, there remaineth both ignorance and disordered
affections (whereof either of them turneth him from speaking of
the truth) no man's authority, with the church especially, and
those that are called and persuaded of the authority of the word of
God, can bring any assurance unto the conscience.

reason have we to think but that even in matters divine, the like wits furnish with necessary helps, exercised in scripture with like diligence, and assisted with the grace of Almighty God, may grow unto so much perfection of knowledge, that men should have
just cause, when any thing pertinent unto faith and religion is doubted of, the more willingly to incline their minds towards that which the sentence of so grave, wise, and learned in that faculty shall judge most sound? for the controversy is of the weight of such
mens judgments. Let it therefore be suspected; let it be taken as gross, corrupt, repugnant unto the truth, whatsoever, concerning things divine above nature, shall at any
time be spoken as out of the mouths of mere natural men, which have not the eyes wherewith heavenly things are discerned; for this we contend not. But whom God hath endued with principal gifts to aspire unto knowledge by, whose exercises, labours, and
divine studies he hath so blest, that the world for their great and rare skill that way hath
them in singular admiration; may we reject even their judgment likewise, as being utterly of no moment? for my own part, I dare not so lightly esteem of the church, and
of the principal pillars therein. The truth is, that the mind of man desireth evermore
to know the truth according to the most infallible certainty which the nature of things
can yield. The greatest assurance generally with all men, is that which we have by plain
aspect and intuitive beholding. Where we cannot attain unto this, there what appeareth
to betrue by strong and invincible demonstration, such as wherein it is not by any way
possible to be deceived, thereunto the mind doth necessarily assent, neither is it in the
choice thereof to do otherwise. And in case these both do fail, then which way greatest
probability leadeth thither the mind doth evermore incline. Scripture with christian men
being received as the word of God; that for which we have probable, yea that which
we have necessary reason for, yea that which we see with our eyes, is not thought so
sure as that which the scripture of God teacheth; because we hold that his speech revealeth

vealeth there what himself seeth, and therefore the strongest proof of all, and the most necessarily assented unto by us (which do thus receive the scripture) is the scripture. Now it is not required, nor can be exacted at our hands, that we should yield unto any thing other assent than such as doth answer the evidence which is to be had of that we assent unto. For which cause even in matters divine, concerning some things we may lawfully doubt and suspend our judgment, enclining neither to one side or other; as namely, touching the time of the fall both of man and angels; of some things we may very well retain an opinion that they are probable and not unlikely to be true, as when we hold that men have their souls rather by creation than propagation, or that the mother of our Lord lived always in the state of virginity as well after his birth as before (for of these two, the one, her virginity before, is a thing which of necessity we must believe; the other, her continuance in the same state always, hath more likelihood of truth than the contrary;) finally, in all things then are our consciences best resolved, and in a most agreeable sort unto God and nature settled, when they are so far persuaded as those grounds of persuasion which are to be had will bear. Which thing I do so much the rather set down, for that I see how a number of souls are for want of right information in this point oftentimes grievously vexed. When bare and unbuilded conclusions are put into their minds, they finding not themselves to have thereof any great certainty, imagine that this proceedeth only from lack of faith, and that the Spirit of God doth not work in them as it doth in true believers. By this means their hearts are much troubled, they fall into anguish and perplexity; whereas the truth is, that how bold and confident soever we may be in words, when it cometh to the point of tryal, such as the evidence is, which the truth hath either in it self or thro proof, such is the heart's assent thereunto; neither can it be stronger, being grounded as it should be. I grant that proof derived from the authority of man's judgment is not able to work that assurance which doth grow by a stronger proof; and therefore altho ten thousand general councils would set down one and the same definitive sentence concerning any point of religion whatsoever, yet one demonstrative reason alledged, or one manifest testimony cited from the mouth of God himself to the contrary, could not chuse but over-weigh them all; inasmuch for them to have been deceived, it is not impossible; it is, that demonstrative reason or testimony divine should deceive. Howbeit, in defect of proof infallible, because the mind doth rather follow probable persuasions than approve the things that have in them no likelihood of truth at all; surely if a question concerning matter of doctrine were proposed, and on the one side no kind of proof appearing, there should on the other be alledged and shewed that so a number of the learnedest divines in the world have ever thought; altho it did not appear what reason or what scripture led them to be of that judgment, yet to their very bare judgment somewhat a reasonable man would attribute, notwithstanding the common imbecillities which are incident unto our nature. And whereas it is thought, that especially with the church, and those that are called and persuaded of the authority of the word of God, man's authority with them especially should not prevail; it must and doth prevail even with them, yea with them especially, as far as equity requireth, and farther we maintain it not. For men to be tied and led by authority, as it were with a kind of captivity of judgment, and tho there be reason to the contrary not to listen unto it, but to follow like beasts the first in the herd, they know not, nor care not whither, this were brutish. Again, that authority of men should prevail with men either against or above reason, is no part of our belief. Companies of learned men, be they never so great and reverend, are to yield unto reason, the weight whereof is no whit prejudiced by the simplicity of his person which doth alledge it; but being found to be sound and good, the bare opinion of men to the contrary must of necessity stoop and give place. *Irenæus* writing against *Marcion*, which held one God author of the old testament, and another of the new, to prove that the apostles preached the same God which was known before to the *Jews*, he copiously alledgeth sundry their sermons and speeches uttered concerning that matter and recoredin scripture. And lest any should be wearied

T. C. l. 2. *p.* 11. Of divers sentences of the fathers themselves (whereby some have likened them to brute beasts without reason, which suffer themselves to be led by the judgment and authority of others, some have preferred the judgment of one simple rude man alledging reason, unto companies of learned men) I will content my self at this time with two or three sentences. *Irenæus* saith, ' Whatsoever is to be shewed in the scripture, cannot be shewed but ' out of the scriptures themselves.' *lib.* 3. *cap.* 12. *Jerom* saith, ' No ' man, be he never so holy or eloquent, hath any authority after the ' apostles.' In *Psal.* 86. *Augustine* saith, ' That he will believe none, ' how godly and learned soever he be, unless he confirm his sentence ' by the scriptures, or by some reason not contrary to them.' *Ep.* 18. And in another place, ' Hear this, the Lord saith; hear not this, *Do-* ' *natus* saith, *Rogatus* saith, *Vincentius* saith, *Hilarius* saith, *Ambrose* ' saith, *Augustine* saith, but hearken unto this, 'The Lord saith.' *Ep.* 8. And again, having to do with an *Arian*, he affirmeth, that neither he ought to bring forth the council of *Nice*, nor the other the council of *Ariminie*, thereby to bring prejudice each to other; neither ought the *Arian* to be holden by the authority of the one, nor himself by the authority of the other, but by the scriptures, which are witnesses proper to neither, but common to both, matter with matter, cause with cause, reason with reason ought to be debated, *Cont. Max. Arian. p.* 14. And in another place against *Paul.* the Donatist, he saith, ' Let not these words be heard between us, I say, ' You say; let us hear this, 'Thus saith the Lord,' And by and by ' speaking of the scriptures, he saith, ' There let us seek the church, ' there let us try the cause.' *De unit. Eccles. cap.* 3. Hereby it is manifest, that the argument of the authority of man affirmatively is nothing worth.

with such store of allegations, in the

end he concludeth, *While we labour for these demonstrations out of scripture, and do summarily declare the things which many ways have been spoken, be contented quietly to hear, and do not think my speech tedious* ; quoniam ostensiones quæ sunt in scripturis, non possunt ostendi nisi ex ipsis scripturis, *because demonstrations that are in scripture may not otherwise be shewed, than by citing them out of the scriptures themselves where they are.* Which words make so little unto the purpose, that they seem, as it were, offended at him which hath called them thus solemnly forth to say nothing. And concerning the verdict of saint *Jerom*, if no man, be he never so well learned, have after the apostles any authority to publish new doctrine as from heaven, and to require the world's assent as unto truth received by prophetical revelation ; doth this prejudice the credit of learned mens judgments in opening that truth, which by being conversant in the apostles writings, they have themselves from thence learned ? saint *Augustine* exhorteth not to hear men, but to hearken to what God speaketh. His purpose is not (I think) that we should stop our ears against his own exhortation, and therefore he cannot mean simply that audience should altogether be denied unto men ; but either that if men speak one thing, and God himself teach another, then he, not they, to be obeyed ; or if they both speak the same thing, yet then also man's speech unworthy of hearing, not simply, but in comparison of that which proceedeth from the mouth of God. Yea, but we doubt what the will of God is. Are we in this case forbidden to hear what men of judgment think it to be ? If not, then this allegation also might very well have been spared. In that antient strife which was between the catholick fathers and *Arians*, *Donatists*, and others of like perverse and froward disposition, as long as to fathers or councils alledged on the one side, the like by the contrary side were opposed, impossible it was that ever the question should by this means grow unto any issue or end. The scripture they both believed ; the scripture they knew could not give sentence on both sides ; by scripture the controversy between them was such as might be determined. In this case what madness was it with such kinds of proofs to nourish their contention, when there were such effectual means to end all controversy that was between them ? Hereby therefore it doth not as yet appear that an argument of authority of man affirmatively is in matters divine nothing worth. Which opinion being once inserted into the minds of the vulgar sort, what it may grow unto God knoweth. Thus much we see, in hath already made thousands so headstrong even in gross and palpable errors, that a man whose capacity will scarce serve him to utter five words in sensible manner, blusheth not in any doubt concerning matter of scripture to think his own bare *yea*, as good as the *nay* of all the wise, grave and learned judgments that are in the whole world : which insolency must be repressed, or it will be the very bane of christian religion. Our Lord's disciples marking what speech he uttered unto them, and at the same time calling to mind a common opinion held by the scribes, between which opinion and the words of their master, it seemed unto them that there was some contradiction, which they could not themselves answer with full satisfaction of their own minds ; the doubt they propose to our Saviour, saying, *Why then say the scribes that Elias must first come ?* They knew that the scribes did err greatly, and that many ways even in matters of their own profession : they notwithstanding thought the judgment of the very scribes in matters divine to be of some value ; some probability they thought there was that *Elias* should come, inasmuch as the scribes said it. Now no truth can contradict any truth. Desirous therefore they were to be taught, how both might stand together ; that which they knew could not be false, because Christ spake it ; and this which to them did seem true, only because the scribes had said it. For the scripture from whence the scribes did gather it, was not then in their heads. We do not find that our Saviour reproved them of error for thinking the judgment of the scribes to be worth the objecting, for esteeming it to be of any moment or value in matters concerning God. We cannot therefore be persuaded that the will of God is, we should so far reject the authority of men as to reckon it nothing. No, it may be a question, whether they that urge us unto this be themselves so persuaded indeed. Men do sometimes bewray that by deeds, which to confess they are hardly drawn. Mark then if this be not general with all men for the most part. When the judgments of learned men are alledged against them, what do they but either elevate their credit, or oppose unto them the judgments of others as learned ? Which thing doth argue that all men acknowledge in them some force and weight, for which they are loth the cause they maintain should be so much weakened as their testimony is available. Again, what reason is there why, alledging testimonies as proofs, men give them some title of credit, honour and estimation, whom they alledge, unless before-hand it be sufficiently known who they are ? What reason hereof but only a common engrafted persuasion, that in some men there may be found such qualities as are able to countervail those exceptions

tions

tions which might be taken againſt them, and that ſuch mens authority is not lightly to be ſhaken off? Shall I add further, that the force of arguments drawn from the authority of ſcripture it ſelf, as ſcriptures commonly are alledged, ſhall (being ſifted) be found to depend upon the ſtrength of this ſo much deſpiſed and debaſed authority of man? Surely it doth, and that oftner than we are aware of. For altho ſcripture be of God, and therefore the proof which is taken from thence muſt needs be of all other moſt invincible; yet this ſtrength it hath not, unleſs it avouch the ſelf-ſame thing for which it is brought. If there be either undeniable appearance that ſo it doth, or reaſon ſuch as cannot deceive, then ſcripture-proof (no doubt) in ſtrength and value exceedeth all. But for the moſt part, even ſuch as are readieſt to cite for one thing five hundred ſentences of holy ſcripture; what warrant have they, that any one of them doth mean the thing for which it is alledged? Is not their ſureſt ground moſt commonly, either ſome probable conjecture of their own, or the judgment of others taking thoſe ſcriptures as they do? Which notwithſtanding to mean otherwiſe than they take them, it is not ſtill altogether impoſſible. So that now and then they ground themſelves on human authority, even when they moſt pretend divine. Thus it fareth even clean throughout the whole controverſy about that diſcipline which is ſo earneſtly urged and laboured for. Scriptures are plentifully alledged to prove that the whole chriſtian world for ever ought to embrace it. Hereupon men term it, the diſcipline of God. Howbeit, examine, ſift, and reſolve their alledged proofs, till you come to the very root from whence they ſpring, the heart whereiń their ſtrength lieth; and it ſhall clearly appear unto any man of judgment, that the moſt which can be inferred upon ſuch plenty of divine teſtimonies is only this, That ſome things which they maintain, as far as ſome men can probably conjecture, do ſeem to have been out of ſcripture not abſurdly gathered. Is this a warrant ſufficient for any man's conſcience to build ſuch proceedings upon, as have been and are put in ure for the eſtabliſhment of that cauſe? But to conclude, I would gladly underſtand how it cometh to paſs, that they which ſo peremptorily do maintain that human authority is nothing worth, are in the cauſe which they favour ſo careful to have the common ſort of men perſuaded, that the wiſeſt, the godlieſt, and the beſt learned in all Chriſtendom are that way given, ſeeing they judge this to make nothing in the world for them? Again, how cometh it to paſs, they cannot abide that authority ſhould be alledged on the other ſide, if there be no force at all in authorities on one ſide or other? Wherefore labour they to ſtrip their adverſaries of ſuch furniture as doth not help? Why take they ſuch needleſs pains to furniſh alſo their own cauſe with the like? If it be void and to no purpoſe that the names of men are ſo frequent in their books, what did move them to bring them in, or doth to ſuffer them there remaining? Ignorant I am not how this is ſolved, They do it but after the truth made manifeſt, firſt by reaſon, or by ſcripture: they do it not, but to controul the enemies of truth, who bear themſelves bold upon humane authority, making not for them, but againſt them rather: Which anſwers are nothing: for in what place, or upon what conſideration ſoever it be, they do it, were it in their own opinion of no force being done, they would undoubtedly refrain to do it.

8. But to the end it may more plainly appear what we are to judge of their ſentences, and of the cauſe it ſelf wherein they are alledged; firſt, it may not well be denied, that all actions of men endued with the uſe of reaſon are generally either good or evil: for altho it be granted that no action is properly termed good or evil unleſs it be voluntary; yet this can be no let to our former aſſertion, That all actions of men endued with the uſe of reaſon are generally either good or evil; becauſe even thoſe things are done voluntarily by us which other creatures do naturally, in as much as we might ſtay our doing of them if we would. Beaſts naturally do take their food and reſt when it offereth it ſelf unto them. If men did ſo too, and could not do otherwiſe of themſelves, there were no place for any ſuch reproof as that of our Saviour Chriſt unto his diſciples, Could ye not watch with me one hour? That which is voluntarily performed in things tending to the end, if it be well done, muſt needs be done with deliberate conſideration of ſome reaſonable cauſe wherefore we rather ſhould do it than not. Whereupon it ſeemeth, that in ſuch actions only thoſe are ſaid to be good or evil which are capable of deliberation: ſo that many things being hourly done by men, wherein they need not uſe with themſelves any manner of conſultation at all, it may perhaps hereby ſeem that well or ill doing belongeth only to our weightier affairs, and to thoſe deeds which are of ſo great importance that they require advice. But thus to determine were perillous, and peradventure unſound alſo. I do rather incline to think, that ſeeing all the unforced actions of men are voluntary, and all voluntary actions tending to the end have choice, and all choice preſuppoſeth the knowledge of ſome cauſe wherefore we make it; where the reaſonable cauſe of ſuch actions ſo

Marginal notes (right column):

T.C. lib. 2. c. 21. If at any time it hapned unto Auguſtine (as it did againſt the Donatiſts and others) to alledge the authority of the antient fathers, which had been before him; yet this was not done before he had laid a ſure foundation of his cauſe in the ſcriptures, and that alſo being provoked by the adverſaries of the truth, who bare themſelves high of ſome council, or of ſome man of name that had favoured that part.

A declaration what the truth is in this matter.

Matth. 26. 40,

readily offereth it felf that it needeth not be fought for, in thofe things tho we do not deliberate, yet they are of their nature apt to be deliberated on, in regard of the will which may encline either way, and would not any one way bend it felf, if there were not fome apparent motive to lead it. Deliberation actual we ufe, where there is doubt what we fhould encline our wills unto. Where no doubt is, deliberation is not excluded as impertinent unto the thing, but as needlefs in regard of the agent, which feeth already what to refolve upon. It hath no apparent abfurdity therefore in it to think that all actions of men endued with the ufe of reafon, are generally either good or evil. Whatfoever is good, the fame is alfo approved of God; and according unto the fundry degrees of goodnefs, the kinds of divine approbation are in like fort multiplied. Some things are good, yet in fo mean a degree of goodnefs, that men are only not difproved nor dif-

Ephef. 5. 29.
Matth. 5. 46.
1 Tim. 5. 8. allowed of God for them. *No man hateth his own flefh. If ye do good unto them that do fo to you, the very publicans themfelves do as much. They are worfe than infidels that have no care to provide for their own.* In actions of this fort, the very light of nature alone may difcover that which is fo far forth in the fight of God allowable. Some things in fuch fort are allowed, that they be alfo required as neceffary unto falvation, by way of direct, immediate and proper neceffity final; fo that without performance of them we cannot by ordinary courfe be faved, nor by any means be excluded from life obferving them. In actions of this kind, our chiefeft direction is from fcripture; for nature is no fufficient teacher what we fhould do that we may attain unto life everlafting. The unfufficiency of the light of nature is by the light of fcripture fo fully and fo perfectly herein fupplied, that further light than this hath added there doth not need unto that end.

Finally, fome things, altho not fo required of neceffity, that to leave them undone excludeth from falvation, are notwithftanding of fo great dignity and acceptation with God, that moft ample reward in heaven is laid up for them. Hereof we have no commandment, either in nature or fcripture, which doth exact them at our hands; yet thofe motives that are in both, which draw moft effectually our minds unto them. In this kind there is not the leaft action, but it doth fomewhat make to the acceffory augmentation of our blifs.

Matth. 10. 42. For which caufe our Saviour doth plainly witnefs, that there fhall not be as much as *a cup of cold water* beftowed *for his fake* without *reward*. Hereupon dependeth whatfoever difference there is between the ftates of faints in glory; hither we refer whatfoever belongeth unto the higheft perfection of man by way of fervice towards God: hereunto

Acts 4. 31.
1 Thef. 2. 7, 9. that fervour and firft love of chriftians did bend it felf, caufing them to *fell their poffeffions,* and *lay down the price at the* bleffed *apoftles feet.* Hereat faint *Paul* undoubtedly did aim, in fo far abridging his own *liberty,* and exceeding that which the bond of neceffary and enjoined duty tied him unto. Wherefore feeing that in all thefe feveral kinds of actions, there can be nothing poffibly evil which God approveth; and that he approveth much more than he doth command; and that his very commandments in fome kind, as namely, his precepts comprehended in the law of nature, may be otherwife known than only by fcripture; and that to do them, howfoever we know them, muft needs be acceptable in his fight; let them with whom we have hither difputed, confider well how it can ftand with reafon to make the bare mandate of facred fcripture the only rule of all good and evil in the actions of mortal men. The teftimonies of God are true, the teftimonies of God are perfect, the teftimonies of God are all fufficient unto that end for which they were given. Therefore accordingly we do receive them, we do not think that in them God hath omitted any thing needful unto his purpofe, and left his intent to be accomplifhed by our devifings. What the fcripture purpofeth, the fame in all points it doth perform. Howbeit that here we fwerve not in judgment, one thing efpecially we muft obferve, namely, that the abfolute perfection of fcripture is feen by relation unto that end whereto it tendeth. And even hereby it cometh to pafs, that firft fuch as imagine the general and main drift of the body of facred fcripture not to be fo large as it is, nor that God did thereby intend to deliver, as in truth he doth, a full inftruction in all things unto falvation neceffary, the knowledge whereof man by nature could not otherwife in this life attain unto; they are by this very mean induced either ftill to look for new revelations from heaven, or elfe dangeroufly to add to the word of God uncertain tradition, that fo the doctrine of man's falvation may be compleat; which doctrine we conftantly hold in all refpects without any fuch thing added to be fo compleat, that we utterly refufe as much as once to acquaint our felves with any thing further. Whatfoever, to make up the doctrine of man's falvation, is added as in fupply of the fcripture's unfufficiency, we reject it. Scripture purpofing this, hath perfectly and fully done it. Again, the fcope and purpofe of God in delivering the holy fcripture, fuch as do take more largely than behoveth, they on the contrary fide racking and ftretching it further

†

than

than by him was meant, are drawn into sundry as great inconveniencies. These pre-
tending the scripture's perfection, infer thereupon, that in scripture all things lawful to *T.C. lib. p. 6:*
be done must needs be contained. We count those things perfect which want nothing *Where this*
requisite for the end whereto they were instituted. As therefore God created every part *doctrine is accused of*
and particle of man exactly perfect, that is to say, in all points sufficient unto that use *bringing men*
for which he appointed it; so the scripture, yea every sentence thereof is perfect, *to despair; it*
and wanteth nothing requisite unto that purpose for which God delivered the same. So *hath wrong.*
that if hereupon we conclude, that because the scripture is perfect, therefore all things *For when doubting is*
lawful to be done are comprehended in the scripture; we may even as well conclude so of *the way to despair, a-*
every sentence, as of the whole sum and body thereof, unless we first of all prove that it *gainst which*
was the drift, scope, and purpose of Almighty God in holy scripture to comprize all *this doctrine*
things which man may practise. But admit this, and mark, I beseech you, what would *offereth the remedy; it*
follow. God in delivering scripture to his church should clean have abrogated amongst *must need be*
them the law of nature, which is an infallible knowledge imprinted in the minds of all the *that it bring-*
children of men, whereby both general principles for directing of human actions are com- *eth comfort and joy to the*
prehended, and conclusions derived from them; upon which conclusions groweth in par- *conscience of man.*
ticularity the choice of good and evil in the daily affairs of this life. Admit this, and what
shall the scripture be but a snare and a torment to weak consciences, filling them with
infinite perplexities, scrupulosities, doubts insoluble, and extreme despairs? Not that the
scripture it self doth cause any such thing (for it tendeth to the clean contrary, and the
fruit thereof is resolute assurance and certainty in that it teacheth) but the necessities of
this life urging men to do that which the light of nature, common discretion, and judgment of it self directeth them unto; on the other side, this doctrine teaching them that
so to do were to sin against their own souls, and that they put forth their hands to iniquity whatsoever they go about, and have not first the sacred scripture of God for direction;
how can it chuse but bring the simple a thousand times to their wits end, how can it chuse
but vex and amaze them? For in every action of common life to find out some sentence
clearly and infallibly setting before our eyes what we ought to do (seem we in scripture
never so expert) would trouble us more than we are aware. In weak and tender minds
we little know what misery this strict opinion would breed, besides the stops it would
make in the whole course of all mens lives and actions; make all things sin which we do
by direction of nature's light, and by the rule of common discretion without thinking at
all upon scripture. Admit this position, and parents shall cause their children to sin as oft
as they cause them to do any thing before they come to years of capacity, and be ripe for
knowledge in the scripture. Admit this, and it shall not be with masters as it was with
him in the gospel; but servants *being commanded to go*, shall stand still till they have their *Luke 7. 8.*
errand warranted unto them by scripture. Which as it standeth with christian duty in
some cases, so in common affairs to require it were most unfit. Two opinions therefore
there are concerning sufficiency of holy scripture, each extremely opposite unto the
other, and both repugnant unto truth. The schools of *Rome* teach scripture to be unsufficient, as if, except traditions were added, it did not contain all revealed and supernatural
truth which absolutely is necessary for the children of men in this life to know, that they
may in the next be saved. Others justly condemning this opinion, grow likewise unto a
dangerous extremity, as if scripture did not only contain all things in that kind necessary,
but all things simply, and in such sort, · that to do any thing according to any other law,
were not only unnecessary, but even opposite unto salvation, unlawful and sinful.
Whatsoever is spoken of God, or things appertaining to God, otherwise than as the
truth is, tho it seem an honour, it is an injury. And as incredible praises given unto
men, do often abate and impair the credit of their deserved commendation; so we must
likewise take great heed, left in attributing unto scripture more than it can have, the
incredibility of that do cause even those things which indeed it hath most abundantly,
to be less reverently esteemed. I therefore leave it to themselves to confider, Whether
they have in this first point overshot themselves or not; which, God doth know, is
quickly done, even when our meaning is most sincere, as I am verily persuaded theirs in
this case was.

OF

OF THE
LAWS
OF
Ecclesiastical Polity.

BOOK III.

Concerning their second affertion, That in fcripture there muft be of neceffity contained a form of church polity, the laws where-of may in no wife be altered.

The matter contained in this third book.

1. WHAT the church is, and in what refpect laws of polity are thereunto neceffarily required:
2. Whether it be neceffary that fome particular form of church polity be fet down in fcripture;
firft the things that belong particularly to any fuch form are not of neceffity to falvation.
3. That matters of church polity are different from matters of faith and falvation; and that they themfelves fo teach, which are our reprovers for fo teaching.
4. That hereby we take not from fcripture any thing, which thereunto with the foundnefs of truth may be
given.
5. Their meaning who firft urged againft the polity of the church of England, that nothing ought to be
eftablifhed in the church more than is commanded by the word of God.
6. How great injury men by fo thinking fhould offer unto all the churches of God.
7. A fhift notwithftanding to maintain it, by interpreting commanded, as the it were meant that greater
things only ought to be found fet down in fcripture particularly, and leffer framed by the general rules of
fcripture.
8. Another device to defend the fame, by expounding commanded, as if it did fignify grounded on fcripture, and were oppofed to things found out by the light of natural reafon only.
9. How laws for the polity of the church may be made by the advice of men, and how thofe being not repugnant to the word of God are approved in his fight.
10. That neither God's being the author of laws, nor yet his committing of them to fcripture, is any reafon
fufficient to prove that they admit no addition or change.
11. Whether Chrift muft needs intend laws unchangeable altogether, or have forbidden any where to make
any other law than himfelf did deliver.

ALBEIT the fubftance of thofe controverfies wherein to we have begun to wade, be rather of outward things appertaining to the church of Chrift, than of any thing wherein the nature and being of the church confift-eth : yet becaufe the fubject or matter which this pofition concerneth, is, *a form of church government, or church polity*; if therefore be-hoveth us fo far forth to confider the nature of the church, as is requi-fite for mens more clear and plain underftanding in what refpect laws of polity or govern-ment are neceffary thereunto. That church of Chrift, which we properly term his body myftical, can be but one ; neither can that one be fenfibly difcerned by any man, in-afmuch as the parts thereof are fome in heaven already with Chrift, and the reft that are on earth, (albeit their natural perfons be vifible) we do not difcern under this property whereby

What the church is, and in what refpect laws of polity are thereunto neceffarily re-quired.

whereby they are truly and infallibly of that body. Only our minds by intellectual conceit are able to apprehend that such a real body there is, a body collective, because it containeth an huge multitude ; a body mystical, because the mystery of their conjunction is removed altogether from sense. Whatsoever we read in scripture concerning the endless love and saving mercy which God sheweth towards his church, the only proper subject thereof is this church. Concerning this flock it is that our Lord and Saviour hath promised, *I give unto them eternal life, and they shall never perish, neither shall any pluck them out of my hands.* They who are of this society have such marks and notes of distinction from all others, as are not objects unto our sense ; only unto God who seeth their hearts and understandeth all their secret cogitations, unto him they are clear and manifest. All men knew *Nathanael* to be an *Israelite.* But our Saviour piercing deeper, giveth further testimony of him than men could have done with such certainty as he did, *Behold indeed an Israelite, in whom there is no guile.* If we profess as *Peter* did, that we love the Lord, and profess it in the hearing of men ; charity is prone to believe all things, and therefore charitable men are likely to think we do, as long as they see no proof to the contrary. But that our love is sound and sincere, that it cometh from *a pure heart, a good conscience, and a faith unfeigned,* who can pronounce, saving only the searcher of all mens hearts, who alone intuitively doth know in this kind who are his ? And as those everlasting promises of love, mercy, and blessedness, belong to the mystical church ; even so on the other side, when we read of any duty which the church of God is bound unto, the church whom this doth concern is a sensible known company. And this visible church in like sort is but one, continued from the first beginning of the world to the last end. Which company being divided into two moieties, the one before, the other since the coming of Christ, that part which since the coming of Christ, partly hath embraced and partly shall hereafter embrace the christian religion, we term as by a more proper name the church of Christ. And therefore the apostle affirmeth plainly of all men christian, that be they Jews or gentiles, bond or free, they are all incorporated into one company, they all make but (*a*) *one body.* The unity of which visible body and church of Christ consisteth in that uniformity which all several persons thereunto belonging have, by reason of that *one Lord,* whose servants they all profess themselves ; that *one faith* which they all acknowledge, that *one baptism* wherewith they are all initiated. The visible church of Jesus Christ is therefore one, in outward profession of those things which supernaturally appertain to the very essence of christianity, and are necessarily required in every particular christian man. *Let all the house of Israel know for certainty,* faith *Peter, that God hath made him both Lord and Christ, even this Jesus whom ye have crucified.* Christians therefore they are not, which *call not him their master and lord.* And from hence it came, that first at *Antioch,* and afterward thro-out the whole world, all that were of the church visible were called christians, even amongst the heathens ; which name unto them was precious and glorious ; but in the estimation of the rest of the world, even Christ Jesus himself was (*b*) execrable ; for whose sake all men were so likewise which did acknowledge him to be their Lord. This himself did foresee, and therefore armed his church to the end they might sustain it without discomfort. *All these things will they do unto you for my name's sake ; yea, the time shall come, that whosoever killeth you will think that he doth God good service. These things I tell you, that when the hour shall come, ye may then call to mind how I told you before-hand of them.* But our naming of Jesus Christ our Lord is not enough to prove us christians, unless we also embrace that faith which Christ hath published unto the world. To shew that the angel of *Pergamus* continued in christianity, behold how the Spirit of Christ speaketh, (*c*) *Thou keepest my name, and thou hast not denied my faith.* Concerning which faith, *the rule thereof,* faith Tertullian (*d*), *is one alone, immoveable, and no way possible to be better framed anew.* What rule that is, he sheweth by rehearsing those few articles of christian belief. And before *Tertullian,* (*e*) *Ireny* ; *The church, tho scattered thro the whole world unto the utmost borders of the earth, hath from the apostles and their disciples received belief.* The parts of which belief he also reciteth in substance the very same with *Tertullian,* and thereupon inferreth, *This faith the church being spread far and wide preserveth, as if one house did contain them : these things it equally embraceth, as tho it had even one soul, one heart, and no more : it publisheth, teacheth and delivereth these things with uniform consent, as if God had given it but one only tongue wherewith to speak. He which amongst the guides of the church is best able to speak, uttereth no more than this ; and less than this, the most simple do not utter, when they make pro-*

John 10. 28.

—— 1. 47.

—— 21. 15.

1 Tim. 1. 5.

(a) Ephef. 2. 16. That he might reconcile both unto God in one body. Ephef. 3. 16. That the gentiles should be inheritors also, and of the same body. Vide T. p. 3. q. 7. art. 3. 1 Cor. 12. 13. Ephef. 4. 5. Acts 2. 36. John 13. 13. Col. 3. 24. & 4. 1.

(b) 1 Cor. 1. 23. Vide & Tacitum lib. Annal. 15. Nero quasitissimis pœnis afficit, quos per flagitia invisos vulgus christianos appellabat. Auctor nominis ejus Christus, qui Tiberio imperitante, per procuratorem Pontium Pilatum supplicio affectus erat. Repressaque in præsens exitiabilis superstitio rursus erumpebat, non modo per Judeam, originem ejus mali, sed per urbem etiam, quo cuncta undique atrocia aut pudenda confluunt celebranturque. John 15. 21. and 16. 2, 4.

(c) Apoc. 2. 13. (d) Tertul: de virgin. veland (e) Iren. adverf. Hæref. lib. 1. cap. 2, &c.

session

feſſion of their faith. Now altho we know the chriſtian faith and allow of it, yet in this reſpect we are but entring ; enter'd we are not into the viſible church before our admittance by the door of baptiſm. Wherefore immediately upon the acknowledgment of chriſtian faith, the eunuch (we ſee) was baptized by *Philip,* *Paul* by *Ananias,* by Acts 8. 38. *Peter* a huge multitude containing three thouſand ſouls ; which being once baptiz'd, were & 22. 16. reckoned in the number of ſouls added to the viſible church. As for thoſe virtues that & 2. 41. belong unto moral righteouſneſs and honeſty of life, we do not mention them, becauſe they are not proper unto chriſtian men, as they are chriſtian, but do concern them as they are men. True it is, the want of theſe virtues excludeth from ſalvation. So doth much more the abſence of inward belief of heart ; ſo doth deſpair and lack of hope ; ſo emptineſs of chriſtian love and charity. But we ſpeak now of the viſible church, whoſe children are ſigned with this mark, *One Lord, one faith, one baptiſm.* In whomſoever theſe things are, the church doth acknowledge them for her children ; them only ſhe holdeth for aliens and ſtrangers, in whom theſe things are not found. For want of theſe it is, that Saracens, Jews, and infidels are excluded out of the bounds of the church. Others we may not deny to be of the viſible church, as long as theſe things are not wanting in them. For apparent it is, that all men are of neceſſity either chriſtians or not chriſtians. If by external profeſſion they be chriſtians, then they are of the viſible church of Chriſt ; and chriſtians by external profeſſion they are all, whoſe mark of recogniſance hath in it thoſe things which we have mention'd, yea, altho they be impious idolaters, wicked hereticks, perſons excommunicable, yea, and caſt out for notorious improbity. Such withal we deny not to be the imps and limbs of ſatan, even as long as they continue ſuch. Is it then poſſible, that the ſelf-ſame men ſhould belong both to the ſynagogue of ſatan, and to the church of Jeſus Chriſt ? Unto that church which is his myſtical body, not poſſible ; becauſe that body conſiſteth of none but only true *Iſraelites,* true ſons of *Abraham,* true ſervants and ſaints of God. Howbeit of the viſible body and church of Jeſus Chriſt, thoſe may be and oftentimes are, in reſpect of the main parts of their outward profeſſion, who in regard of their inward diſpoſition of mind, yea, of external converſation, yea, even of ſome parts of their very profeſſion, are moſt worthily both hateful in the ſight of God himſelf, and in the eyes of the ſounder part of the viſible church moſt execrable. Our Saviour therefore compareth the *kingdom of heaven to* Matth. 13. 47. *a net,* whereunto all which cometh, neither is, nor ſeemeth fiſh : his church he compa- & 13. 24. reth unto a *field,* where *tares* manifeſtly known and ſeen by all men, do grow inter-mingled with *good corn* ; and even ſo ſhall continue till the final conſummation of the world. God hath had ever, and ever ſhall have ſome church viſible upon earth. When the people of God *worſhipped the calf* in the wilderneſs ; when they adored *the* Exod. 2o. *brazen ſerpent* ; when they *ſerved the gods of nations* ; when they *bowed their knees to* Pſ.106.19,20. *Baal* ; when they *burnt incenſe and offered ſacrifice unto idols :* true it is, the wrath Jer. 11. 13. of God was moſt fiercely inflamed againſt them, their prophets juſtly condemned them 2 King 22. 17. as an adulterous ſeed, and a wicked generation of miſcreants, which had forſaken the living Iſa. 57. 3. God ; and of him were likewiſe forſaken, in reſpect of that ſingular mercy wherewith & 60. 15. he kindly and lovingly embraceth his faithful children. Howbeit retaining the law of God, and the holy ſeal of his covenant, the ſheep of his viſible flock they continued Jer. 13. 11. even in the depth of their diſobedience and rebellion. Wherefore not only amongſt them 1Kings 19.18. God always had his church, becauſe he had thouſands which never bowed their knees to *Baal* ; but whoſe knees were bowed unto *Baal,* even they were alſo of the viſible church of God. Nor did the prophet ſo complain, as if that church had been quite and clean extinguiſhed ; but he took it as tho there had not been remaining in the world any beſides himſelf that carried a true and an upright heart towards God, with care to ſerve him according unto his holy will. For lack of diligent obſerving the difference, firſt, between the church of God myſtical and viſible, then between the viſible ſound and corrupted, ſometimes more, ſometimes leſs, the overſights are neither few nor light that have been committed. This deceiveth them, and nothing elſe, who think that in the time of the firſt world the family of *Noah* did contain all that were of the viſible church of God. From whence it grew, and from no other cauſe in the world, that the *African* biſhops in the council of *Carthage,* knowing how the adminiſtration of baptiſm, belong-eth only to the church, and ſuppoſing that hereticks which were apparently ſevered from the ſound believing church could not poſſibly be of the church of Jeſus Chriſt, thought it utterly againſt reaſon, That baptiſm adminiſtred by men of corrupt belief, ſhould be ac-counted as a ſacrament. And therefore in maintenance of rebaptization, their arguments Fortunat. in are built upon the fore-alledged ground, *That hereticks are not at all any part of the* Concil. Car. *church of Chriſt. Our Saviour founded his church on a rock, and not upon hereſy. Power of* Mat. 7. 24. *baptizing he gave to his apoſtles, unto hereticks he gave it not. Wherefore they that are* & 28. 19.

I *without*

without the church, and oppose themselves against Chrift, do but ſcatter the ſheep and flock.

Secundinus in
eodem concil.
Without the church, baptize they cannot. Again, *Are hereticks chriſtians, or are they not?*
Matth. 12. 30.
If they be chriſtians, wherefore remain they not in God's church? If they be no chriſtians, how make they chriſtians? Or to what purpoſe ſhall theſe words of the Lord ſerve? He *which is not with me, is againſt me*; and, *He which gathereth not with me, ſcattereth. Wherefore evident it is, that upon miſ-begotten children and the brood of antichriſt, without rebaptization, the Holy Ghoſt cannot deſcend.* But none in this caſe ſo earneſt as *Cyprian: I know no baptiſm but one, and that in the church only* ; *none without the church, where he that doth caſt out the devil, hath the devil : he doth examine about belief, whoſe lips and words do breathe forth a canker : the faithleſs doth offer the articles of faith* ; *a wicked creature forgiveth wickedneſs* ; *in the name of Chriſt, antichriſt ſigneth* ; *he which is curſed of God, bleſſeth* ; *a dead carrion promiſeth life* ; *a man unpeaceable giveth peace* ; *a blaſphemer calleth upon the name of God* ; *a prophane perſon doth exerciſe prieſthood* ; *a ſacrilegious wretch doth prepare the altar* ; *and in the neck of all theſe that evil alſo cometh, the euchariſt a very biſhop of the devil doth preſume to conſecrate.* All this was true, but not ſufficient to prove that hereticks were in no ſort any part of the viſible church of Chriſt, and conſequently their baptiſm no baptiſm. This opinion therefore was afterwards both condemned by a better adviſed council, and alſo revoked by the chiefeſt of the authors thereof themſelves. What is it but only the ſelf-ſame error and miſconceit, wherewith others being at this day likewiſe
In concilio Ni-
ceno. Vide
Hieron. Dial.
adverſ. Luci-
feria.
poſſeſt, they ask us where our church did lurk, in what cave of the earth it ſlept for ſo many hundreds of years together, before the birth of *Martin Luther ?* As if we were of opinion, that *Luther* did erect a new church of Chriſt. No, the church of Chriſt which was from the beginning, is, and continueth unto the end. Of which church, all parts have not been always equally ſincere and ſound. In the days of *Abia,* it plainly appeareth that *Judah* was by many degrees more free from pollution than *Iſrael* ; as that ſolemn oration ſheweth, wherein he pleadeth for the one againſt the other in this
2 Chron. 13.
wiſe. *O Jeroboam, and all Iſrael, hear you me : have ye not driven away the prieſts of the Lord, the ſons of* Aaron, *and the Levites, and have made your prieſts like the people of nations ? Whoſoever cometh to conſecrate with a young bullock, and ſeven rams, the ſame may be a prieſt of them that are no gods. But we belong unto the Lord our God, and have not forſaken him* ; *and the prieſts, the ſons of* Aaron, *miniſter unto the Lord every morning and every evening, burnt-offerings and ſweet incenſe* ; *and the bread is ſet in order upon the pure table, and the candleſtick of gold with the lamps thereof to burn every evening* ; *for we keep the watch of the Lord our God, but ye have forſaken him.* In ſaint *Paul's* time, the integrity of *Rome* was famous ; *Corinth* many ways reproved ; they of *Galatia* much more out of ſquare. In ſaint *John's* time, *Epheſus* and *Smirna* in far better ſtate than *Thyatira* and *Pergamus* were. We hope therefore, that to reform our ſelves, if at any time we have done amiſs, is not to ſever our ſelves from the church we were of before. In the church we were, and we are ſo ſtill. Other difference between our eſtate before and now we know none, but only ſuch as we ſee in *Judah* ; which having ſometime been idolatrous, became afterwards more ſoundly reli-
Hoſ. 14. 15,
& 17.
gious, by renouncing idolatry and ſuperſtition. *If* Ephraim *be joined to idols,* the counſel of the prophet is, *let him alone. If* Iſrael *play the harlot, let not* Judah *ſin.* If it
Joſh. 24. 15.
ſeem evil unto you, ſaith *Joſhua,* to ſerve the Lord, *chuſe you this day whom you will ſerve* ; *whether the gods whom your fathers ſerved beyond the flood, or the gods of the* Amorites *in whoſe land ye dwell : but I and mine houſe will ſerve the Lord.* The indiſpoſition therefore of the church of *Rome* to reform her ſelf, muſt be no ſtay unto us from performing our duty to God ; even as deſire of retaining conformity with them, could be no excuſe if we did not perform that duty. Notwithſtanding ſo far as lawfully we may, we have held and do hold fellowſhip with them. For even as the apoſtle doth
Rom. 11. 28.
ſay of *Iſrael,* that they are in one reſpect enemies, but in another beloved of God ; in like ſort with *Rome,* we dare not communicate concerning ſundry her groſs and grievous abominations : yet touching thoſe main parts of chriſtian truth wherein they conſtantly ſtill perſiſt, we gladly acknowledge them to be of the family of Jeſus Chriſt ; and our hearty prayer unto God Almighty is, that being conjoined ſo far forth with them, they may at the length (if it be his will) ſo yield to frame and reform themſelves, that no diſtraction remain in any thing, but that we *all may with one heart and one mouth glorify God the father of our Lord and Saviour,* whoſe church we are. As there are which make the church of *Rome* utterly no church at all, by reaſon of ſo many, ſo grievous errors in their doctrines ; ſo we have them amongſt us, who under pretence of imagined corruptions in our diſcipline, do give even as hard a judgment of the church of *England* it ſelf. But whatſoever either the one ſort or the other teach, we muſt acknowledge even here-

t   ticks

ticks themselves to be, tho a maimed part, yet a part of the visible church. If an infidel should pursue to death an heretick professing christianity, only for christian profession sake, could we deny unto him the honour of martyrdom? Yet this honour all men know to be proper unto the church. Hereticks therefore are not utterly cut off from the visible church of Christ. If the fathers do any where, as oftentimes they do, make the true visible church of Christ, and heretical companies opposite; they are to be construed as separating hereticks, not altogether from the company of believers, but from the fellowship of sound believers. For where profest unbelief is, there can be no visible church of Christ; there may be, where found belief wanteth. Infidels being clean without the church, deny directly, and utterly reject the very principles of christianity; which hereticks embrace, and err only by misconstruction. Whereupon their opinions, altho repugnant indeed to the principles of christian faith, are notwithstanding by them held otherwise, and maintained as most consonant thereunto. Wherefore being christians in regard of the general truth of Christ which they openly profess; yet they are by the fathers every where spoken of, as men clean excluded out of the right believing church, by reason of their particular errors, for which all that are of a sound belief must needs condemn them. In this consideration, the answer of *Calvin* unto *Farel*, concerning the children of popish parents, doth seem crazed. *Whereas*, saith he, *you ask our judgment about a matter,* Calvin. Epist. *whereof there is doubt amongst you, whether ministers of our order, professing the pure* 143. *doctrine of the gospel, may lawfully admit unto baptism an infant whose father is a stranger unto our churches, and whose mother hath faln from us unto the papacy, so that both the parents are popish: thus we have thought good to answer; namely, That it is an absurd thing for us to baptize them which cannot be reckoned members of our body. And sith papists children are such, we see not how it should be lawful to minister baptism unto them.* Sounder a great deal is the answer of the ecclesiastical college of *Geneva* unto *Knox*, who having signified unto them, that himself did not think it lawful to baptize bastards, or the children of idolaters (he meaneth papists) or of persons excommunicate, till either the parents had by repentance submitted themselves unto the church, or else their children being grown unto the years of understanding, should come and sue for their own baptism; *for thus thinking*, saith he, *I am thought to be over severe, and that* Epist. 183. *not only by them which are popish, but even in their judgments also who think themselves maintainers of the truth.* Master *Knox's* over-sight herein they controuled. Their sentence was, *Wheresoever the profession of christianity hath not utterly perished and been* Epist. 285. *extinct, infants are beguiled of their right if the common seal be denied them.* Which conclusion in it self is sound, altho it seemeth the ground is but weak whereupon they build it. For the reason which they yield of their sentence, is this; *The promise which God doth make to the faithful concerning their seed, reacheth unto a thousand generations; it resteth not only in the first degree of descent. Infants therefore whose great-grand-fathers have been holy and godly, do in that respect belong to the body of the church, altho the fathers and grandfathers of whom they descend, have been apostates: because the tenure of the grace of God which did adopt them three hundred years ago and more in their antient predecessors, cannot with justice be defeated and broken off by their parents impiety coming between.* By which reason of theirs, altho it seem that all the world may be baptized, in as much as no man living is a thousand descents removed from *Adam* himself; yet we mean not at this time, either to uphold, or to overthrow it; only their alledged conclusion we embrace, so it be construed in this sort: *That for as much as men remain in the visible church, till they utterly renounce the profession of christianity, we may not deny unto infants their right, by withholding from them the publick sign of holy baptism, if they be born where the outward acknowledgment of christianity is not clean gone and extinguished.* For being in such sort born, their parents are within the church, and therefore their birth doth give them interest and right in baptism. Albeit not every error and fault, yet heresies and crimes which are not actually repented of and forsaken, exclude quite and clean from that salvation which belongeth unto the mystical body of Christ; yea, they also make a separation from the visible sound church of Christ; altogether from the visible church neither the one nor the other doth sever. As for the act of excommunication, it neither shutteth out from the mystical, nor clean from the visible, but only from fellowship with the visible in holy duties. With what congruity then doth the church of *Rome* deny, that her enemies whom she holdeth always for hereticks, do at all appertain to the church of Christ; when her own so freely grant, that albeit the pope (as they say) cannot teach heresy nor propound error, he may notwithstanding himself worship idols, think amiss concerning matters of faith, yea, give himself unto acts diabolical, even being pope? How exclude they us from being any part of the church of Christ under the colour and pretence of heresy, when they cannot but grant it

possible,

possible, even for him to be as touching his own personal perswasion heretical, who in their opinion not only is of the church, but holdeth the chiefest place of authority over the same? But of these things we are not now to dispute. That which already we have set down, is for our present purpose sufficient. By the church therefore, in this question, we understand no other than only the visible church. For preservation of christianity there is not any thing more needful, than that such as are of the visible church have mutual fellowship and society one with another. In which consideration, as the main body of the sea being one, yet within divers precincts hath divers names; so the catholick church is in like sort divided into a number of distinct societies, every of which is termed a church within it self. In this sense the church is always a visible society of men; not an assembly, but a society. For altho the name of the church be given unto christian assemblies, altho any number of christian men congregated may be termed by the name of a church, yet assemblies properly are rather things that belong to a church. Men are assembled for performance of publick actions; which actions being ended, the assembly dissolveth it self, and is no longer in being; whereas the church which was

Tertul. Ex-
hort. ad Ca-
stit. Ubi tres,
e. clesia est,
licet laici.

assembled, doth no less continue afterwards, than before. *Where but three are, and they of the laity also,* saith *Tertullian, yet there is a church*; that is to say, a christian assembly. But a church, as now we are to understand it, is a society; that is, a number of men belonging unto some christian fellowship, the place and limits whereof are certain.

Acts 2. 47.

That wherein they have communion, is the publick exercise of such duties as those mentioned in the apostles acts, *instruction, breaking of bread, and prayer*. As therefore they that are of the mystical body of Christ, have those inward graces and virtues wherein they differ from all others which are not of the same body; again, whosoever appertain to the visible body of the church, they have also the notes of external profession, whereby the world knoweth what they are: after the same manner, even the several societies of christian men, unto every of which the name of a church is given, with addition betokening severally, as the church of *Rome, Corinth, Ephesus, England,* and so the rest, must be endued with correspondent general properties belonging unto them as they are publick christian societies. And of such properties common unto all societies christian, it may not be denied that one of the very chiefest is ecclesiastical polity. Which word I therefore the rather use, because the name of government, as commonly men understand it in ordinary speech, doth not comprize the largeness of that whereunto in this question it is applied. For when we speak of government, what doth the greatest part conceive thereby, but only the exercise of superiority peculiar unto rulers and guides of others? To our purpose therefore the name of church-polity will better serve, because it containeth both government, and also whatsoever besides belongeth to the ordering of the church in publick. Neither is any thing in this degree more necessary than church-polity, which is a form of ordering the publick spiritual affairs of the church of God.

Whether it be
necessary that
some particu-
lar form of
church-polity
be set down in
scripture, sith
the things that
belong parti-
cularly unto
any such form,
are not of ne-
cessity to salva-
tion.
Tertul. de ha-
bitu mul. Æ-
muli sint ne-
cesse est, quæ
Dei non sunt.
Rom. 2. 15.
Lact. lib.6.c.8.
Ille legis hujus
inventor, dis-
ceptator, lator.
Cic. 3. de re-
pub.

2. But we must note, that he which affirmeth speech to be necessary among all men throughout the world, doth not thereby import that all men must necessarily speak one kind of language; even so the necessity of polity and regimen in all churches may be held without holding any one certain form to be necessary in them all, nor is it possible that any form of polity, much less of polity ecclesiastical, should be good unless God himself be author of it. *Those things that are not of God* (saith *Tertullian*) *they can have no other than God's adversary for their author.* Be it whatsoever in the church of God, if it be not of God, we hate it. Of God it must be; either as those things sometimes were, which God supernaturally revealed, and so delivered them unto *Moses* for government of the commonwealth of *Israel*; or else as those things which men find out by help of that light which God hath given them unto that end. The very law of nature it self, which no man can deny but God hath instituted, is not of God, unless that be of God whereof God is the author as well this latter way as the former. But forasmuch as no form of church polity is thought by them to be lawful, or to be of God, unless God be so the author of it that it be also set down in scripture; they should tell us plainly, whether their meaning be that it must be there set down in whole, or in part. For if wholly, let them shew what one form of polity ever was so. Their own to be so taken out of scripture they will not affirm; neither deny they that in part,even this which they so much oppugn is also from thence taken. Again, they should tell us, whether only that be taken out of scripture which is actually and particularly there set down; or else that also which the general principles and rules of scripture potentially contain. The one way they cannot so much as pretend, that all the parts of their own discipline are in scripture; and the other way their mouths are stopped, when they would plead against all other forms besides their own; seeing their general principles are such as do not particularly

†   prescribe

prescribe any one, but sundry may equally be consonant unto the general axioms of the scripture. But to give them some larger scope, and not to close them up in these streights: let their allegations be considered, wherewith they earnestly bend themselves against all which deny it necessary that any one compleat form of church-polity should be in scripture. First therefore, whereas it hath been told them that matters of faith, and in general, matters necessary unto salvation, are of a different nature from ceremonies, order, and the kind of church-government ; and that the one is necessary to be expresly contained in the word of God, or else manifestly collected out of the same, the other not so ; that it is necessary not to receive the one, unless there be something in scripture for them ; the other free, if nothing against them may thence be alledged: altho there do not appear any just or reasonable cause to reject or dislike of this ; nevertheless, as it is not easy to speak to the contentation of minds exulcerated in themselves, but that somewhat there will be always which displeaseth ; so herein for two things we are reproved.

*The first is, misdistinguishing, because matters of discipline and church-government are (as they say) matters necessary to salvation and of faith, whereas we put a difference betwixt the one and the other. Our second fault is, injurious dealing with the scripture of God, as if it contained only the principal points of religion, some rude and unfashioned matter of building the church, but had left out that which belongeth unto the form and fashion of it ; as if there were in the scripture no more than only to cover the church's nakedness, and not chains, bracelets, rings, jewels, to adorn her ; sufficient to quench her thirst, to kill her hunger, but not to minister a more liberal and (as it were) a more delicious and dainty diet. In which case our apology shall not need to be very long.

<small>* Two things mislliked ; the one, that we distinguish matters of discipline or church-government from matters of faith, and necessary unto salvation : The other, that we are</small>

<small>injurious to the scripture of God, in abridging the large and rich contents thereof. Their words are these : You which distinguish between these, and say, that matters of faith and necessary unto salvation may not be tolerated in the church, unless they be expresly contained in the word of God, or manifestly gathered ; but that ceremonies, order, discipline, government in the church, may not be received against the word of God, and consequently may be received if there be no word against them, altho there be none for them : you (I say) distinguishing or dividing after this sort, do prove your self an evil divider. As tho matters of discipline and kind of government, were not matters necessary to salvation and of faith. It is no small injury which you do unto the word of God, to pin it in so narrow a room as that it should be able to direct us but in the principal points of our religion ; or as tho the substance of religion, or some rude and unfashioned maner of building of the church were uttered in them ; and those things were left out that should pertain to the form and fashion of it ; or, as if there were in the scriptures only to cover the church's nakedness, and not also chains, and bracelets, and rings, and other jewels to adorn her, and set her out : or that to conclude, there were sufficient to quench her thirst, and kill her hunger, but not to minister unto her a more liberal, and (as it were) a more delicious and dainty diet. These things you seem to say, when you say, that matters necessary to salvation, and of faith, are contained in scripture, especially when you oppose these things to ceremonies, order, discipline, and government. T. C. lib. 1. pag. 26.</small>

3. The mixture of those things by speech which by nature are divided, is the mother of all error. To take away therefore that error which confusion breedeth, distinction is requisite. Rightly to distinguish, is by conceit of mind to sever things different in nature, and to discern wherein they differ. So that if we imagine a difference where there is none, because we distinguish where we should not, it may not be denied that we misdistinguish. The only trial whether we do so yea or no, dependeth upon comparison between our conceit and the nature of things conceived. Touching matters belonging to the church of Christ, this we conceive, that they are not of one suit. Some things are merely of faith, which things it doth suffice that we know and believe ; some things not only to be known but done, because they concern the actions of men. Articles about the Trinity are matters of mere faith, and must be believed. Precepts concerning the works of charity are matters of action ; which to know unless they be practised, is not enough. This being so clear to all mens understandings, I somewhat marvel that they especially should think it absurd to oppose church-government, a plain matter of action, unto matters of faith, who know that themselves divide the gospel into doctrine and discipline. For if matters of discipline be rightly by them distinguished from matters of doctrine, why not matters of government by us as reasonably set against matters of faith ? Do not they under doctrine comprehend the same which we intend by matters of faith ? Do not they under discipline comprise the regimen of the church ? When they blame that in us which themselves follow, they give men great cause to doubt that some other thing than judgment doth guide their speech. What the church of God standeth bound to know or do, the same in part nature teacheth. And because nature can teach them but only in part, neither so fully as is requisite for man's salvation, nor so easily as to make the way plain and expedite enough that many may come to the knowledge of it, and so be saved, therefore in scripture hath God both collected the most necessary things that the school of nature teacheth unto that end, and revealeth also whatsoever we neither could with safety be ignorant of, nor at all be instructed in but by supernatural revelation from him. So that scripture containing all things that are in this kind any way needful for the church, and the principal of the other sort, this is the next thing where-

<small>That matters of discipline are different from matters of faith and salvation ; and that they themselves so teach which are our reprovers.</small>

<small>T. C. lib. 2, pag. 1. We offer to shew the discipline to be a part of the gospel. And again, p. 5. I speak of the discipline as of a part of the discipline be one part of the gospel, what other part can they assign but doctrine to answer in division to the discipline ?</small>

wherewith we are charged as with an error. We teach, that whatsoever is unto salvation termed *necessary* by way of excellency; whatsoever it standeth all men upon to know or do that they may be saved; whatsoever there is whereof it may truly be said, *This not to believe, is eternal death and damnation;* or *This every soul that will live, must duly observe;* of which sort the articles of christian faith, and the sacraments of the church of Christ are: all such things, if scripture did not comprehend, the church of God should not be able to measure out the length and the breadth of that way wherein for ever she is to walk; hereticks and schismaticks never ceasing, some to abridge, some to enlarge, all to pervert and obscure the same. But as for those things that are accessary hereunto, those things that so belong to the way of salvation as to alter them is no otherwise to change that way, than a path is changed by altering only the uppermost face thereof; which be it laid with gravel, or set with grass, or paved with stones, remaineth still the same path; in such things, because discretion may teach the church what is convenient, we hold not the church further tied herein unto scripture, than that against scripture nothing be admitted in the church, lest that path which ought always to be

Matth. 13, 23. kept even, do thereby come to be overgrown with brambles and thorns. If this be

unsound, wherein doth the point of unsoundness lie? Is it not that we make some things necessary, some things accessary and appendent only? For our Lord and Saviour himself doth make that difference, by turning judgment, and mercy, and fidelity, with other things of like nature, *the greater and weightier matters of the law.* Is it then in that we account ceremonies (wherein we do not comprise sacraments, or any other the like substantial duties in the exercise of religion, but only such external rites as are

* The govern- usually annexed unto church actions) is it an oversight that we reckon these things and
ment of the   * matters of government in the number of things accessary, not things necessary in such
church of
Christ granted sort as hath been declared? Let them which therefore think us blameable consider well
by Fenner   their own words. Do they not plainly compare the one unto garments, which cover
himself to be
thought a mat- the body of the church; the other unto rings, bracelets and jewels, that only adorn it?
ter of great   the one to that food which the church doth live by, the other to that which maketh her
moment, yet   diet liberal, dainty and more delicious? Is dainty fare a thing necessary to the sustenance,
not of the sub-
stance of reli- or to the clothing of the body rich attire? If not, how can they urge the necessity of
gion, against that which themselves resemble by things not necessary? or by what construction shall
doctor Bridges,
p. 121. if it be any man living be able to make those comparisons true, holding that distinction untrue,
Fenner which   which putteth a difference between things of external regiment in the church and things
was the author
of that book. necessary unto salvation.

That we do   4. Now as it can be to nature no injury that of her we say the same which diligent
not take from
scripture any beholders of her works have observed; namely that she provideth for all living creatures
thing which   nourishment which may suffice; that she bringeth forth no kind of creature whereto she
may be there-
unto given   is wanting in that which is needful: although we do not so far magnify her exceeding
with sound-   bounty, as to affirm that she bringeth into the world the sons of men adorned with gor-
ness of truth,
Arist. pol. lib. geous attire, or maketh costly buildings to spring up out of the earth for them: so I trust
1. cap. 8. &   that to mention what the scripture of God leaveth unto the church's discretion in some
Plato in Me-
nex.   things, is not in any thing to impair the honour which the church of God yieldeth to the
Arist. lib. 3. de sacred scriptures perfection. Wherein seeing that no more is by us maintained, than on-
anima, c. 45. ly that scripture must needs teach the church whatsoever is in such sort necessary as hath

been set down; and that it is no more disgrace for scripture to have left a number of other things free to be ordered at the discretion of the church, than for nature to have left it to the wit of man to devise his own attire, and not to look for it as the beasts of the field have theirs: if neither this can import, nor any other proof sufficient be brought forth, that we either will at any time or ever did affirm the sacred scripture to comprehend no more than only those bare necessaries; if we acknowledge that as well for particular application to special occasions, as also in other manifold respects, infinite treasures of wisdom are over and besides abundantly to be found in the holy scripture; yea, that scarcely there is any noble part of knowledge worthy the mind of man but from thence it may have some direction and light; yea, that altho there be no necessity it should of purpose prescribe any one particular form of church-government, yet touching the manner of governing in general, the precepts that scripture setteth down are not few, and the examples many which it proposeth for all church-governous, even in particularities to follow; yea, that those things, finally, which are of principal weight in the very particular form of church-polity (altho not that form which they imagine, but that which we against them uphold) are in the self-same scriptures contained; if all this be willingly granted by us, which are accused to pin the word of God in so narrow a room as that it should be able to direct us but in principal points of our religion; or as tho the substance of religion, or some rude and unfashioned matter of building the church were uttered in

†

them,

them, and those things left out that should pertain to the form and fashion of it ; let the cause of the accused be referred to the accusers own conscience, and let that judge whether this accusation be deserved where it hath been laid.

5. But so easy it is for every man living to err, and so hard to wrest from any man's mouth the plain acknowledgment of error, that what hath been once inconsiderably defended, the same is commonly persisted in as long as wit, by whetting it self, is able to find out any shift, be it never so slight, whereby to escape out of the hands of present contradiction. So that it cometh herein to pass with men, unadvisedly faln into error, as with them whose state hath no ground to uphold it, but only the help which by subtil conveyance they draw out of casual events arising from day to day, till at length they be clean spent. They which first gave out, *That nothing ought to be established in the church, which is not commanded by the word of God,* thought this principle plainly warranted by the manifest words of the law, *Ye shall put nothing unto the word which I command you, neither shall ye take out therefrom, that ye may keep the commandments of the Lord your God, which I command you.* Wherefore having an eye to a number of rites and orders in the church of *England,* as marrying with a ring, crossing in the one sacrament, kneeling at the other, observing of festival days more than only that which is called the Lord's day, enjoining abstinence at certain times from some kinds of meat, churching of women after childbirth, degrees taken by divines in universities, sundry church offices, dignities and callings ; for which they found no commandment in the holy scripture, they thought by the one only stroke of that axiom to have cut them off. But that which they took for an oracle, being sifted, was repealed. True it is concerning the word of God, whether it be by misconstruction of the sense, or by falsification of the words, wittingly to endeavour that any thing may seem divine which is not, or any thing not seem which is, were plainly to abuse, and even to falsify divine evidence ; which injury offered but unto men, is most worthily counted heinous. Which point I wish they did well observe, with whom nothing is more familiar than to plead in these causes, *The law of God, the word of the Lord* ; who, notwithstanding, when they come to alledge what word and what law they mean, their common ordinary practice is to quote by-speeches in some historical narration or other, and to urge them as if they were written in most exact form of law. What is to add to the law of God, if this be not ? When that which the word of God doth but deliver historically, we construe without any warrant, as if it were legally meant, and so urge it further than we can prove that it was intended ; do we not add to the laws of God, and make them in number seem more than they are ? It standeth us upon to be careful in this case : for the sentence of God is heavy against them that wittingly shall presume thus to use the scripture.

6. But let that which they do hereby intend be granted them ; let it once stand as consonant to reason, that because we are forbidden to add to the law of God any thing, or to take ought from it ; therefore we may not for matters of the church, make any law more than is already set down in scripture. Who seeth not what sentence it shall enforce us to give against all churches in the world, in as much as there is not one, but hath had many things established in it, which tho the scripture did never command, yet for us to condemn, were rashness ? Let the church of God, even in the time of our Saviour Christ, serve for example unto all the rest. In their domestical celebration of the passover, which supper they divided (as it were) into two courses ; what scripture did give commandment, that between the first and the second, he that was chief should put off the residue of his garments, and keeping on his feast robe only, wash the feet of them that were with him ? What scripture did command them never to lift up their hands unwash'd in prayer unto God ; which custom *Aristæus* (be the credit of the author more or less) sheweth wherefore they did so religiously observe ? What scripture did command the *Jews* every festival day to fast till the sixth hour ? the custom both mentioned by *Josephus* in the history of his own life, and by the words of *Peter* signified. Tedious it were to rip up all such things as were in that church established, yea, by Christ himself and by his apostles observed, tho not commanded any where in scripture.

7. Well, yet a gloss there is in colour that paradox, and notwithstanding all this, still to make it appear in shew not to be altogether unreasonable. And therefore till further reply come, the cause is held by a feeble distinction ; that the commandments of God being either general or special, altho there be no expres word for every thing in specialty, yet there are general commandments for all things, to the end, that even such cases as are not in scripture particularly mentioned, might not be left to any to order at their

mandments are of two sorts ; and that all things lawful in the church are commanded if not by special precepts, yet by general rules in the word. 1 Cor. 10. 32. & 14. 40. & 14. 26. Rom. 14. 6, 7. T. C. l. 1. p. 35.

pleasure,

Marginal notes:

Their meanning who first did plead against the polity of the church of England, urging, that nothing ought to be established in the church, which is not commanded by the word of God ; and what scripture they thought they might ground this assertion upon. Deut. 4. 2. & 12. 32.

Whatsoever I command you; take heed you do it. Thou shalt put nothing thereto, nor take ought therefrom.

The same assertion we cannot hold, without doing wrong unto all churches.

John. 13. Cænatorium; de quo Matth. 22. 12. Ibi de Cænatorio Nuptiali.

Acts 2.

A shift to maintain that nothing ought to be established in the church, which is not commanded in the word of God ; namely, that com-

pleafure, only with caution, that nothing be done againſt the word of God ; and that for this cauſe the apoſtle hath ſet down in ſcripture four general rules, requiring ſuch things alone to be received in the church, as do beſt and neareſt agree with the ſame rules, that ſo all things in the church may be appointed, not only *not againſt*, but *by* and *according* to the word of God. The rules are theſe, *nothing ſcandalous* or offenſive unto any, eſpecially unto the church of God ; *all things* in order and with ſeemlineſs ; *all unto edification* ; finally *all to the glory of God*. Of which kind, how many might be gathered out of the ſcripture, if it were neceſſary to take ſo much pains ? Which rules they that urge, minding thereby to prove that nothing may be done in the church but what ſcripture commandeth, muſt needs hold that they tie the church of Chriſt no otherwiſe than only becauſe we find them there ſet down by the finger of the Holy Ghoſt. So that unleſs the apoſtle by writing had delivered thoſe rules to the church, we ſhould by obſerving them have ſinned, as now by not obſerving them. In the church of the *Jews*, is it not granted, *That the appointment of the hour for daily ſacrifices* ; the building of *ſynagogues* throughout the land to hear the word of God, and to pray in when they came not up to *Jeruſalem* ; the erecting of *pulpits* and *chairs* to teach in ; the order of *burial* ; the *rites of marriage*, with ſuch like, being matters appertaining to the church ; yet are not any where preſcribed in the law, but were by the church's diſcretion inſtituted ? What then ſhall we think ? Did they hereby add to the law, and ſo diſpleaſe God by that which they did ? None ſo hardly perſuaded of them. Doth their law deliver unto them the ſelf-ſame general rules of the apoſtle, that framing thereby their orders, they might in that reſpect clear themſelves from doing amiſs ? Saint *Paul* would then of likelihood have cited them out of the law, which we ſee he doth not. The truth is, they are rules and canons of that law which is written in all mens hearts ; the church had for ever no leſs than now ſtood bound to obſerve them, whether the apoſtle had mentioned them or no. Seeing therefore theſe canons do bind as they are edicts of nature, which the *Jews* obſerving as yet unwritten, and thereby framing ſuch church-orders as in their law were not preſcribed, are notwithſtanding in that reſpect unculpable ; it followeth, that ſundry things may be lawfully done in the church, ſo as they be not done againſt the ſcripture, altho no ſcripture do command them ; but the church only following the light of reaſon, judge them to be in diſcretion meet. Secondly, unto our purpoſe and for the queſtion in hand, whether the commandments of God in ſcripture be general or ſpecial it ſkilleth not : for if being particularly applied, they have in regard of ſuch particulars a force conſtraining us, to take ſome one certain thing of many, and to leave the reſt ; whereby it would come to paſs, that any other particular but that one being eſtabliſhed, the general rules themſelves in that caſe would be broken ; then is it utterly impoſſible that God ſhould leave any thing great or ſmall free for the church to eſtabliſh or not. Thirdly, if ſo be they ſhall grant, as they cannot otherwiſe do, that theſe rules are no ſuch laws as require any one particular thing to be done, but ſerve rather to direct the church in all things which ſhe doth ; ſo that free and lawful it is to deviſe any ceremony, to receive any order, and to authorize any kind of regiment, no ſpecial commandment being thereby violated : and the ſame being thought ſuch by them to whom the judgment thereof appertaineth ; as that it is not ſcandalous, but decent, tending unto edification, and ſetting forth the glory of God ; that is to ſay, agreeable unto the general rules of holy ſcripture ; this doth them no good in the world for the furtherance of their purpoſe. That which ſhould make for them, muſt prove that men ought not to make laws for church regiment, but only keep thoſe laws which in ſcripture they find made. The plain intent of the books of eccleſiaſtical diſcipline is to ſhew that men may not deviſe laws of church government ; but are bound for ever to uſe and to execute only thoſe which God himſelf hath already deviſed and delivered in the ſcripture. The ſelf-ſame drift the admonitioners alſo had, in urging, that nothing ought to be done in the church, according unto any law of man's deviſing, but all according unto that which God in his word hath commanded. Which not remembring, they gather out of ſcripture general rules to be followed in making laws ; and ſo in effect they plainly grant that we our ſelves may lawfully make laws for the church, and are not bound out of ſcripture only to take laws already made, as they meant who firſt alledged that principal whereof we ſpeak. One particular plat-form it is which they reſpected, and which they laboured thereby to force upon all churches ; whereas theſe general rules do not let, but that there may well enough be ſundry. It is the particular order eſtabliſhed in the church of *England*, which thereby they did intend to alter, as being not commanded of God ; whereas unto thoſe general rules they know, we do not defend that we may hold any thing unconformable. Obſcure it is not what

meaning

meaning they had, who firſt gave out that grand axiom; and according unto that mean‑ ing it doth prevail far and wide with the favourers of that part. Demand of them, wherefore they conform not themſelves unto the order of our church? and in every par‑ ticular, their anſwer for the moſt part is, *We find no ſuch thing commanded in the word.* Whereby they plainly require ſome ſpecial commandment for that which is exacted at their hands; neither are they content to have matters of the church examined by ge‑ neral rules and canons. As therefore in controverſies between us and the church of *Rome*, that which they practiſe is many times even according to the very groſſneſs of that which the vulgar ſort conceiveth; when that which they teach to maintain it, is ſo nice and ſubtil that hold can very hardly be taken thereupon: in which caſes we ſhould do the church of God ſmall benefit, by diſputing with them according unto the fineſt points of their dark conveyances, and ſuffering that ſenſe of their doctrine to go uncon‑ trouled, wherein by the common ſort it is ordinarily received and practiſed: ſo con‑ ſidering what diſturbance hath grown in the church amongſt our ſelves, and how the authors thereof do commonly build altogether on this as a ſure foundation, *Nothing ought to be eſtabliſhed in the church, which in the word of God is not commanded*; were it reaſon, that we ſhould ſuffer the ſame to paſs without controulment, in that cur‑ rent meaning whereby every where it prevaileth, and ſtay till ſome ſtrange conſtruction were made thereof, which no man would lightly have thought on, but being driven thereunto for a ſhift?

8. The laſt refuge in maintaining this poſition, is thus to conſtrue it, *Nothing ought to be eſtabliſhed in the church, but that which is commanded in the word of God*; that is to ſay, all church orders muſt be *grounded upon the word of God*; in ſuch ſort grounded upon the word, not that being found out by ſome *ſtar, or light of reaſon, or learning, or other help,* they may be received, ſo they be not againſt the

Another anſwer in defence of the former aſſertion, whereby the meaning thereof is opened in this ſort. All church orders muſt be commanded in the word, that is to ſay, grounded upon the word, and made according, at the leaſtwiſe, unto the general rules of holy ſcripture. As for ſuch things as are found out by any ſtar or light of reaſon, and are in that reſpect received, ſo they be not againſt the word of God, all ſuch things it holdeth unlawfully received. *Ariſt. Polit.* 1.

word of God; but according at leaſtwiſe unto the general rules of ſcripture they muſt be made. Which is in effect as much as to ſay, *We know not what to ſay well in de‑ fence of this poſition; and therefore, leſt we ſhould ſay it is falſe, there is no remedy but to ſay, that in ſome ſenſe or other it may be true, if we could tell how.* Firſt, that *ſcholy* had need of a very favourable reader and a tractable, that ſhould think it plain conſtruction, when to be *commanded in the word* and *grounded upon the word* are made all one. If when a man may live in the ſtate of matrimony, ſeeking that good thereby which nature principally deſireth, he make rather choice of a contrary life, in regard of ſaint *Paul's* judgment; that which he doth, is manifeſtly *grounded* upon the 1 Cor. 7. word of God, yet *not commanded* in his word, becauſe without breach of any com‑ mandment he might do otherwiſe. Secondly, whereas no man in juſtice and reaſon, can be reproved for thoſe actions which are framed according unto that known will of God, whereby they are to be judged; and the will of God which we are to judge our actions by, no ſound divine in the world ever denied to be in part made manifeſt even by the light of nature, and not by ſcripture alone: if the church being directed by the former of theſe two (which God hath given, who gave the other that man might in different ſort be guided by them both) if the church, I ſay, do approve and eſtabliſh that which thereby it judgeth meet, and findeth not repugnant to any word or ſyllable of holy ſcrip‑ ture; who ſhall warrant our preſumptuous boldneſs controlling herein the church of Chriſt? But ſo it is, the name of the light of nature is made hateful with men; the *ſtar of reaſon and learning*, and all other ſuch like helps, beginneth no otherwiſe to be thought of than if it were an unlucky comet; or as if God had ſo accurſed it, that it ſhould never ſhine or give light in things concerning our duty any way towards him, but be eſteemed as that *ſtar* in the *revelation*, called *wormwood*; which being faln from Apoc. 8. 10. heaven, maketh rivers and waters in which it falleth ſo bitter, that men taſting them die thereof. A number there are, who think they cannot admire as they ought the power and authority of the word of God, if in things divine they ſhould attribute any force to man's reaſon. For which cauſe they never uſe reaſon ſo willingly as to diſgrace rea‑ ſon. Their uſual and common diſcourſes are unto this effect. Firſt, *The natural man* 1 Cor. 2. 14. *perceiveth not the things of the Spirit of God; for they are fooliſhneſs unto him: nei‑ ther can he know them, becauſe they are ſpiritually diſcerned.* Secondly, it is not for nothing that ſaint *Paul* giveth charge to beware of *philoſophy*, that is to ſay, ſuch know‑ Col. 2. 8. ledge as men by natural reaſon attain unto. Thirdly, conſider them that have from time to time oppoſed themſelves againſt the goſpel of Chriſt, and moſt troubled the church with hereſy. Have they not always been great admirers of human reaſon? Hath

K   their

their deep and profound skill in secular learning made them the more obedient to the truth, and not armed them rather against it? Fourthly, they that fear God will remember how heavy his sentences are in this case: *I will destroy the wisdom of the wise, and will cast away the understanding of the prudent. Where is the wise? where is the scribe? where is the disputer of this world? hath not God made the wisdom of this world foolishness? Seeing the world by wisdom know not God; in the wisdom of God, it pleased God by the foolishness of preaching to save believers.* Fifthly, The word of God in it self is absolute, exact, and perfect. The word of God is a two-edged sword; as for the weapons of natural reason, they are as the armour of *Saul*, rather cumbersom about the soldier of Christ than needful. They are not of force to do that which the apostles of Christ did by the power of the Holy Ghost: *My preaching therefore,* saith *Paul, hath not been in the inticing speech of man's wisdom, but in plain evidence of the spirit of power; that your faith might not be in the wisdom of men, but in the power of God.* Sixthly, if I believe the gospel, there needeth no reasoning about it to persuade me: if I do not believe, it must be the Spirit of God, and not the reason of man that shall convert my heart unto him. By these and the like disputes, an opinion hath spread it self very far in the world; as if the way to be ripe in faith were to be raw in wit and judgment; as if reason were an enemy unto religion, childish simplicity the mother of ghostly and divine wisdom. The cause why such declamations prevail so greatly, is, for that men suffer themselves in two respects to be deluded. One is, that the wisdom of man being debased, either in comparison with that of God, or in regard of some special thing exceeding the reach and compass thereof, it seemeth to them (not marking so much) as if simply it were condemned. Another, that learning, knowledge, or wisdom, falsly so termed, usurping a name whereof they are not worthy; and being under that name controlled, their reproof is by so much the more easily misapplied, and thro equivocation wrested against those things whereunto so precious names do properly and of right belong. This, duly observed, doth to the former allegations it self make sufficient answer. Howbeit, for all mens plainer

I. and fuller satisfaction; First, concerning the inability of reason, to search out and to judge of things divine, if they be such as those properties of God, and those duties of men towards him, which may be conceived by attentive consideration of heaven and earth; we know that of mere natural men, the apostle testifieth, *How they knew both God, and the law of God.* Other things of God there be, which are neither so found, nor, tho they be shewed, can never be approved without the special operation of God's good grace and Spirit. Of such things sometime spake the apostle saint *Paul,* declaring how Christ had called him to be a witness of his death and resurrection from the dead, according to that which the prophets and *Moses* had foreshewed. *Festus,* a mere natural man, an infidel, a *Roman,* one whose ears were unacquainted with such matter, heard him, but could not reach unto that whereof he spake; the suffering, and the rising of Christ from the dead, he rejected as idle superstitious fancies not worth the hearing. The apostle that knew them by the Spirit, and spake of them with power of the Holy Ghost, seemed in his eyes but learnedly mad. Which example maketh manifest what elsewhere the same apostle teacheth, namely, that nature hath need of grace, whereunto I hope we are not opposite, by holding that grace hath use of nature.

II. Secondly, philosophy we are warranted to take heed of; not that philosophy, which is true and found knowledge attained by natural discourse of reason; but that philosophy, which to bolster hereby or error casteth a fraudulent shew of reason upon things which are indeed unreasonable; and by that mean, as by a stratagem, spoileth the simple which are not able to withstand such cunning. *Take heed lest any spoil you thro philosophy, and vain deceit.* He that exhorteth to beware of an enemy's policy, doth not give counsel to be impolitick; but rather to use all prudent foresight and circumspection, left our simplicity be over-reached by cunning sleights. The way not to be inveigled by them that are so guileful thro skill, is throughly to be instructed in that which maketh skilful against guile, and to be armed with that true and and sincere philosophy,

III. which doth teach against that deceitful and vain, which spoileth. Thirdly, but many great philosophers have been very unsound in belief; and many found in belief, have been also great philosophers. Could secular knowledge bring the one sort unto the love of christian faith? nor christian faith, the other sort out of love with secular knowledge. The harm that hereticks did, they did it unto such as were unable to discern between found and deceitful reasoning; and the remedy against it was ever the skill which the antient fathers had to descry and discover such deceit. Insomuch, that *Cresconius* the heretick complained greatly of St. *Augustine,* as being too full of logical subtilties. Hereby prevaileth only by a counterfeit shew of reason; whereby notwithstanding it

1 Cor. 1. 19

1 Cor. 2. 4.

Rom. 1. 21, 32.

Acts 25. 19.

Acts 26. 24.
1 Cor. 2. 14.

Col. 2. 8.

†   becometh

becometh invincible, unlefs it be convicted of fraud by manifeft remonftrance, clearly true and unable to be withftood. When therefore the apoftle requireth hability to con- Tit. 1. 9, 11; vict hereticks, can we think he judgeth it a thing unlawful, and not rather needful to ufe the principal inftrument of their conviction, the light of reafon? It may not be denied, but that in the fathers writings, there are fundry fharp invectives againft hereticks; even for their very philofophical reafonings; the caufe whereof *Tertullian* confeffeth, Tert.de refur. not to have been any diflike conceived againft the kind of fuch reafonings, but the end. carnis, *We may* (faith he) *even in matters of God, be made wifer by reafons drawn from the publick perfuafions which are grafted in mens minds; fo they be ufed to further the truth, not to bolfter error; fo they make with, not againft that which God hath determined. For there are fome things even known by nature, as the immortality of the foul to many, our God unto all. I will therefore my felf alfo, ufe the fentence of fome fuch as* Plato, *pronouncing every foul immortal. I my felf too will ufe the fecret acknowledgment of the commonalty, bearing record of the God of gods: but when I hear men alledge, that which is dead, is dead; and while thou art alive, be alive; and, after death an end of all, even of death it felf: then will I call to mind, both that the heart of the people with God is accounted duft, and that the very wifdom of the world is pronounced folly. If then an heretick flie alfo unto fuch vicious, popular, and fecular conceits, my anfwer unto him fhall be: Thou heretick, avoid the heathen; altho in this ye be one, that ye both bely God; yet thou that doft this under the name of Chrift, differeth from the heathen, in that thou feemeft to thy felf a chriftian. Leave him therefore his conceits, feeing that neither will he learn thine. Why doft thou, having fight, truft to a blind guide? thou which haft put on Chrift, take rayment of him that is naked? If the apoftle have armed thee, why doft thou borrow a ftranger's fhield? Let him rather learn of thee to acknowledge, than thou of him to renounce the refurrection of the flefh.* In a word, the catholick fathers did good unto all by that knowledge, whereby hereticks hindring the truth in many, might have furthered therewith themfelves, but that obftinately following their own ambitious, or otherwife corrupted affections, inftead of framing their wills to maintain that which reafon taught, they bent their wits to find how reafon might feem to teach that which their wills were fet to maintain. For which caufe the apoftle faith of them juftly, that they are for the moft part Tit. 3. 11. *ἀυτοκατάκριτοι,* men condemned even in, and of themfelves. For tho they be not all perfuaded, that it is truth which they withftand; yet that to be error which they uphold, they might undoubtedly the fooner a great deal attain to know, but that their ftudy is more to defend what once they have ftood in, than to find out fincerely and fimply what truth they ought to perfift in for ever. Fourthly, there is in the world no kind of knowledge, whereby any part of truth is feen, but we juftly account it precious; yea, that IV. principal truth, in comparifon whereof all other knowledge is vile, may receive from it fome kind of light; whether it be that *Egyptian* and *Chaldean* wifdom, mathematical, wherewith *Mofes* and *Daniel* were furnifhed; or that natural, moral, and civil Acts 7. 11 wifdom wherewith *Solomon* excelled all men; or that rational and oratorial wifdom of Dan. 1. 17. the *Grecians,* which the apoftle faint *Paul* brought from *Tarfus;* or that judaical, which 1 Kings 4. 29, he learned in *Jerufalem,* fitting at the feet of *Gamaliel:* to detract from the dignity Acts 22. 3. thereof, were to injure even God himfelf, who being that light which none can approach unto, hath fent out thefe lights whereof we are capable, even as fo many fparkles refembling the bright fountain from which they rife. But there are that bear the title of wife men, and fcribes, and great difputers of the world, and are nothing indeed lefs than what in fhew they moft appear. Thefe being wholly addicted unto their own wills, ufe their wit, their learning, and all the wifdom they have, to maintain that which their obftinate hearts are delighted with, efteeming in the frantick error of their minds, the greateft madnefs in the world to be wifdom, and the higheft wifdom foolifhnefs. Such were both Jews and Grecians which profeffed, the one fort legal, and the other fecular skill, neither enduring to be taught the myftery of Chrift: unto the glory of whofe moft bleffed name, who fo ftudy to ufe both their reafon and all other gifts, as well which nature as which grace hath endued them with; let them never doubt, but that the fame God who is to deftroy and confound utterly that wifdom falfly fo named in others, doth make reckoning of them as of true fcribes; fcribes by wifdom inftruc- Matth. 13. 52. ted to the kingdom of heaven; fcribes againft that kingdom hardned in a vain opinion of wifdom; which in the end being proved folly, muft needs perifh; true underftanding, knowledge, judgment and reafon, continuing for evermore. Fifthly, V. unto the word of God, being in refpect of that end for which God ordained it, perfect, exact, and abfolute in it felf, we do not add reafon as a fupplement of any maim or defect therein, but as a neceffary inftrument, without which we could not reap by the fcriptures perfection that fruit and benefit which it yieldeth. *The word of God is a* Heb. 4. 12. *two-*

two-edged sword, put in the hands of reasonable men ; and reason is as the weapon that slew *Goliah*, if they be as *David* was that use it. Touching the apostles, he which gave them from above such power for miraculous confirmation of that which they taught, endued them also with wisdom from above to teach that which they so did confirm. Our Saviour made choice of twelve simple and unlearned men, that the greater their lack of natural wisdom was, the more admirable that might appear which God supernaturally endued them with from heaven. Such therefore as knew the poor and silly estate wherein they had lived, could not but wonder to hear the wisdom of their speech, and be so much the more attentive unto their teaching. They studied for no tongue they spake withal : of themselves they were rude, and knew not so much as how to premeditate ; the Spirit gave them speech and eloquent utterance. But because with saint *Paul* it was otherwise than with the rest, inasmuch as he never conversed with Christ upon earth as they did ; and his education had been scholastical altogether, which theirs was not ; hereby occasion was taken by certain malignants secretly to undermine his great authority in the church of Christ, as tho the gospel had been taught him by others than by Christ himself, and as if the cause of the gentiles conversion and belief, thro his means, had been the learning and skill which he had by being conversant in their books ; which thing made them so willing to hear him, and him so able to persuade them ; whereas the rest of the apostles prevailed, because God was with them, and by a miracle from heaven confirmed his words in their mouths. They were mighty in deeds : as for him, being absent, his writings had some force ; in presence, his power not like unto theirs. In sum, 2 Cor. 10. 10. concerning his preaching, their very by-word was, λόγꝍ ὑξυθυνημένꝍ, addle speech, *empty talk* ; his writings full of great words, but in the power of miraculous operations ; his presence not like the rest of the apostles. Hereupon it ariseth, that saint *Paul* was so often driven to make his apologies. Hereupon it ariseth, that whatsoever time he had spent in the study of human learning, he maketh earnest protestation to them of *Corinth*, that the gospel which he had preached amongst them did not by other means prevail with them, than with others the same gospel taught by the rest of the apostles of Christ. *My* 2 Cor. 2. 4. *preaching*, saith he, *hath not been in the persuasive speeches of human wisdom, but in demonstration of the Spirit and of power ; that your faith may not be in the wisdom of men, but in the power of God.* What is it which the apostle doth here deny ? Is it denied that his speech amongst them had been persuasive ? No : for of him the sacred history Acts 18. 4, 11. plainly testifieth, that for the space of a year and a half he spake in their synagogue every sabbath, and persuaded both Jews and Grecians. How then is the speech of men made persuasive ? Surely there can be but two ways to bring this to'pass, the one human, the other divine. Either saint *Paul* did only by art and natural industry cause his own speech to be credited ; or else God by miracle did authorize it, and so bring credit thereunto, as to the speech of the rest of the apostles. Of which two, the former he utterly denieth. For why ? if the preaching of the rest had been effectual by miracle, his only by force of his own learning ; so great inequality between him and the other apostles in this thing had been enough to subvert their faith. For might they not with reason have thought, that if he were sent of God as well as they, God would not have furnished them and not him, with the power of the Holy Ghost ? Might not a great part of them, being simple, haply have feared lest their assent had been cunningly gotten unto his doctrine, rather thro the weakness of their own wits than the certainty of that truth which he had taught them ? How unequal had it been, that all believers thro the preaching of other apostles, should have their faith strongly built upon the evidence of God's own miraculous approbation ; and they whom he had converted, should have their persuasion built only upon his skill and wisdom who persuaded them ? As therefore calling from men may authorize us to teach, altho it could not authorize him to teach as other apostles did ; so altho the wisdom of man had not been sufficient to enable him to be such a teacher as the rest of the apostles were, unless God's miracles had strengthned both the one and the other's doctrine ; yet unto our ability, both of teaching and learning the truth of Christ, as we are but

VI.   mere christian men, it is not a little which the wisdom of man may add. Sixthly, yea, whatsoever our hearts be to God and to his truth, believe we or be we as yet faithless, for our conversion or confirmation, the force of natural reason is great. The force whereof unto those effects, is nothing without grace. What then ? to our purpose it is sufficient, that whosoever doth serve, honour and obey God, whosoever believeth in him ; that man would no more do this than innocents and infants do, but for the light of natural reason that shineth in him, and maketh him apt to apprehend those things of God, which being by grace discovered, are effectual to persuade reasonable minds and none other, that honour, obedience and credit, belong aright unto God. No man cometh unto God to offer him sacrifice, to pour out supplications and prayers before him, or to do him any service,

which

which doth not firſt believe him both to be, and to be a rewarder of them who in ſuch Heb. 11. 6.
ſort ſeek unto him. Let men be taught this either by revelation from heaven, or by inſtruction upon earth ; by labour, ſtudy and meditation, or by the only ſecret inſpiration
of the Holy Ghoſt ; whatſoever the mean be they know it by, if the knowledge thereof
were poſſible without diſcourſe of natural reaſon ; why ſhould none be found capable
thereof but only men, nor men till ſuch time as they come unto ripe and full ability to
work by reaſonable underſtanding ? The whole drift of the ſcripture of God, what is it,
but only to teach theology ? Theology, what is it, but the ſcience of things divine ?
What ſcience can be attained unto, without the help of natural diſcourſe and reaſon ?
Judge you of that which I ſpeak, ſaith the apoſtle. In vain it were to ſpeak any 1 Cor. 10. 15.
thing of God, but that by reaſon men are able ſomewhat to judge of that they hear, and
by diſcourſe to diſcern how conſonant it is to truth. Scripture indeed teacheth things a-
bove nature, things which our reaſon by it ſelf could not reach unto. Yet thoſe things
alſo we believe, knowing by reaſon, that the ſcripture is the word of God. In the preſence of *Feſtus* a Roman, and of king *Agrippa* a Jew, ſaint *Paul* omitting the one, who
neither knew the Jews religion, nor the books whereby they were taught it, ſpeaks unto the other of things foreſhewed by *Moſes* and the prophets, and performed in Jeſus
Chriſt, intending thereby to prove himſelf ſo unjuſtly accuſed, that unleſs his judges did
condemn both *Moſes* and the prophets, him they could not chuſe but acquit, who taught
only that fulfilled which they ſo long ſince had foretold. His cauſe was eaſy to be diſcerned ; what was done, their eyes were witneſſes ; what *Moſes* and the prophets did ſpeak,
their books could quickly ſhew : it was no hard thing for him to compare them, which
knew the one, and believed the other. *King* Agrippa, *believeſt thou the prophets ? I* Act. 26. 22.
know thou doſt. The queſtion is, how the books of the prophets came to be credited
of king *Agrippa.* For what with him did authorize the prophets, the like with us doth
cauſe the reſt of the ſcripture of God to be of credit. Becauſe we maintain, that in
ſcripture we are taught all things neceſſary unto ſalvation ; hereupon very childiſhly it
is by ſome demanded, what ſcripture can teach us the ſacred authority of the ſcripture,
upon the knowledge whereof our whole faith and ſalvation dependeth ? as tho there
were any kind of ſcience in the world which leadeth men unto knowledge, without pre-
ſuppoſing a number of things already known. No ſcience doth make known the firſt
principles whereon it buildeth ; but they are always either taken as plain and manifeſt in
themſelves, or as proved and granted already, ſome former knowledge having made them
evident. Scripture teacheth all ſupernatural revealed truth ; without the knowledge whereof ſalvation cannot be attained. The main principle whereupon our belief of all things
therein contained dependeth, is, that the ſcriptures are the oracles of God himſelf.
This in it ſelf we cannot ſay is evident : for then all men that hear it, would acknowledge it in heart, as they do when they hear that every whole is more than any part of that
whole, becauſe this in it ſelf is evident. The other we know, that all do not acknowledge when they hear it. There muſt be therefore ſome former knowledge preſuppoſed,
which doth herein aſſure the hearts of all believers. Scripture teacheth us that ſaving truth
which God hath diſcovered unto the world by revelation ; and it preſumeth us taught
otherwiſe, that it ſelf is divine and ſacred. The queſtion then being, by what means
we are taught this : ſome anſwer, that to learn it we have no other way than only tradition ; as namely, that ſo we believe, becauſe both we from our predeceſſors, and they
from theirs have ſo received. But is this enough ? That which all mens experience teacheth them, may not in any wiſe be denied. And by experience we all know, that the
firſt outward motive leading men ſo to eſteem of the ſcripture, is the authority of God's
church. For when we know the whole church of God hath that opinion of the ſcripture, we judge it even at the firſt an impudent thing for any man bred and brought up in
the church, to be of a contrary mind without cauſe. Afterwards the more we beſtow our
labour in reading or hearing the myſteries thereof, the more we find that the thing it ſelf
doth anſwer our received opinion concerning it. So that the former inducement prevailing ſomewhat with us before, doth now much more prevail, when the very thing
hath miniſtered further reaſon. If infidels or atheiſts chance at any time to call it in queſtion, this giveth us occaſion to ſift what reaſon there is, whereby the teſtimony of the
church concerning ſcripture, and our own perſuaſion, which ſcripture it ſelf hath confirmed,
may be proved a truth infallible. In which caſe the antient fathers being often conſtrained
to ſhew, what warrant they had ſo much to rely upon the ſcriptures, endeavoured ſtill
to maintain the authority of the books of God by arguments, ſuch as unbelievers themſelves muſt needs think reaſonable, if they judged thereof as they ſhould. Neither is it
a thing impoſſible, or greatly hard, even by ſuch kind of proofs, ſo to mani[feſt and clear
that point, that no man living ſhall be able to deny it, without denying ſome apparent
prin-

principle, such as all men acknowledge to be true. Wherefore if I believe the gospel, yet is reason of singular use, for that it confirmeth me in this my belief the more : if I do not as yet believe, nevertheless to bring me into the number of believers, except reason did somewhat help, and were an instrument which God doth use unto such purposes, what should it boot to dispute with infidels or godless persons for their conversion and persuasion in that point ? Neither can I think that when grave and learned men do sometime hold that of this principle there is no proof but by the testimony of the Spirit, which assureth our hearts therein, it is their meaning to exclude utterly all force which any kind of reason may have in that behalf ; but I rather incline to interpret such their speeches, as if they had more expresly set down, that other motives and inducements, be they never so strong and consonant unto reason, are notwithstanding ineffectual of themselves to work faith concerning this principle, if the special grace of the Holy Ghost concur not to the enlightning of our minds. For otherwise, I doubt not but men of wisdom and judgment will grant, that the church in this point especially is furnished with reason to stop the mouths of her impious adversaries ; and that as it were altogether bootless to alledge against them what the Spirit hath taught us, so likewise, that even to our own selves it needeth caution and explication, how the testimony of the Spirit may be discerned, by what means it may be known, left men think that the Spirit of God doth testify those things which the spirit of errour suggesteth. The operations of the Spirit, especially these ordinary which be common · unto all true christian men, are, as we know, things secret and undiscernable even to the very soul where they are, because their nature is of another and an higher kind than that they can be by us perceived in this life. |Wherefore albeit the Spirit lead us into all truth, and direct us in all goodness; yet because these workings of the Spirit in us are so privy and secret, we therefore stand on a plainer ground, when we gather by reason from the quality of things believed or done, that the Spirit of God hath directed us in both, than if we settle our selves to believe or to do any certain particular thing, as being moved thereto by the Spirit. But of this enough.

To go from the books of scripture, to the sense and meaning thereof, because the sentences which are by the apostles recited out of the *Psalms*, to prove the resurrection of Jesus Christ, did not prove it, if so be the prophet *David* meant them of himself. This exposition therefore they plainly disprove, and shew by manifest reason that of *David* the words of *David* could not possibly be meant. Exclude the use of natural reasoning about the sense of holy scripture concerning the articles of our faith, and then that the scripture doth concern the articles of our faith who can assure us ? That which by right exposition buildeth up christian faith, being misconstrued, breedeth error ; between true and false construction, the difference reason must shew. Can christian men perform that which *Peter* requireth at their hands ? Is it possible they should both believe, and be able without the use of reason, to render a reason of their belief, a reason sound and sufficient to answer them that demand it, be they of the same faith with us or enemies thereunto ? May we cause our faith without reason to appear reasonable in the eyes of men ? This being required even of learners in the school of Christ, the duty of their teachers in bringing them unto such ripeness must needs be somewhat more than only to read the sentences of scripture, and then paraphrastically to scholy them, to vary them with sundry forms of speech, without arguing or disputing about any thing which they contain. This method of teaching may commend it self unto the world by that easiness and facility which is in it ; but a law or a pattern it is not, as some do imagine, for all men to follow that will do good in the church of Christ. Our Lord and Saviour himself did hope by disputation to do some good, yea, by disputation not only of, but against the truth, albeit with purpose for the truth. That Christ should be the son of *David*, was truth ; yet against this truth, our Lord in the gospel objecteth ; *If Christ be the son of* David, *how doth* David *call him Lord?* There is as yet no way known how to dispute, or to determine of things disputed, without the use of natural reason. If we please to add unto Christ their example, who followed him as near in all things as they could, the sermon of *Paul* and *Barnabas*, set down in the *Acts*, where the people would have offered unto them sacrifice ; in that sermon what is there, but only natural reason to disprove their act ? *O men, why do ye these things? we are men even subject to the self-same passions with you : we preach unto you to leave these vanities, and to turn to the living God, the God that hath not left himself without witness, in that he hath done good to the world, giving rain and fruitful seasons, filling our hearts with joy and gladness.* Neither did they only use reason in winning such unto a christian belief, as were yet thereto unconverted, but with believers themselves they followed the self-same course. In that great and solemn assembly of believing Jews, how doth *Peter* prove that the gentiles were partakers of the grace of God as well as they, but

by

Acts 13. 36.
& 1 34.

1 Pet. 3. 15.

Matth. 22. 43.

Acts 14. 15.

by reason drawn from those effects which were apparently known amongst them: *God* Acts 14. *which knoweth the hearts, hath borne them witness in giving unto them the Holy Ghost as unto you.* The light therefore, which the star of natural reason and wisdom casteth, is too bright to be obscured by the mist of a word or two uttered to diminish that opinion which justly hath been received concerning the force and virtue thereof, even in matters that touch most nearly the principal duties of men, and the glory of the eternal God. In all which hitherto hath been spoken, touching the force and use of man's reason in things divine, I must crave that I be not so understood or construed, as if any such thing, by virtue thereof, could be done without the aid and assistance of God's most blessed Spirit. The thing we have handled according to the question moved about it; which question is, Whether the light of reason be so pernicious, that in devising laws for the church, men ought not by it to search what may be fit and convenient? For this cause therefore we have endeavoured to make it appear, how in the nature of reason it self there is no impediment, but that the self-same Spirit which revealeth the things that God hath set down in his law, may also be thought to aid and direct men in finding out by the light of reason, what laws are expedient to be made for the guiding of his church, over and besides them that are in scripture. Herein therefore we agree with those men, by whom human laws are defined to be ordinances, which such as have lawful authority given them for that purpose, do probably draw from the laws of nature and God, by discourse of reason aided with the influence of divine grace: and for that cause, it is not said amiss touching ecclesiastical canons, *That by instinct of the Holy Ghost they have been made, and consecrated by the reverend acceptation of the world.* *Violatores,* cap. 25. q. 1.

9. Laws for the church are not made as they should be, unless the makers follow How laws for the regiment of the church may be made by the advice of men following therein the light of reason; and how those laws being not repugnant to the word of God are approved in his sight. such direction as they ought to be guided by, wherein that scripture standeth not the church of God in any stead, or serveth nothing at all to direct, but may be let pass as needless to be consulted with, we judge it prophane, impious, and irreligious to think. For altho it were in vain to make laws which the scripture hath already made, because what we are already there commanded to do, on our parts there resteth nothing but only that it be executed; yet because both in that which we are commanded, it concerneth the duty of the church by law to provide, that the looseness and slackness of men may not cause the commandments of God to be unexecuted; and a number of things there are, for which the scripture hath not provided by any law, but left them unto the careful discretion of the church; we are to search how the church in these cases may be well directed to make that provision by laws, which is most convenient and fit. And what is so in these cases, partly scripture, and partly reason must teach to discern. Scripture comprehending examples and laws; laws, some natural, and some positive; examples neither are there for all cases which require laws to be made; and when they are, they can but direct as precedents only. Natural laws direct in such sort, that in all things we must for ever do according unto them; positive so, that against them, in no case, we may do any thing, as long as the will of God is, that they should remain in force. Howbeit, when scripture doth yield us precedents how far forth they are to be followed: when it giveth natural laws, what particular order is thereunto most agreeable; when positive, which way to make laws unrepugnant unto them; yea, tho all these should want, yet what kind of ordinances would be most for that good of the church which is aimed at, all this must be by reason found out. And therefore, *To refuse the conduct of the light of nature,* saith saint *Augustine, is not folly alone, but accompanied with impiety.* The greatest amongst the school divines, studying how to set down by exact definition, the nature of an human law, (of which nature all the church's constitutions are) found not which way better to do it, than in these words: *Out of the precepts of the law of nature, as out of certain common and undemonstrable principles, man's reason doth necessarily proceed unto certain and more particular determinations : which particular determinations being found out according unto the reason of man, they have the names of human laws, so that such other conditions be therein kept as the making of laws doth require,* that is, if they whose authority is thereunto required, do establish and publish them as laws. And the truth is, that all our controversy in this cause concerning the orders of the church, is, what particulars the church may appoint. That which doth find them out, is the force of man's reason. That which doth guide and direct his reason, is first, the general law of nature; which law of nature and the moral law of scripture, are in the substance of law all one. But because there are also in

Luminis naturalis dictatum repellere, non modo stultum est, sed & impium. August. lib. 4. de Trin. cap. 6.

Tho. Aqu. 12. q. 91. art. 3. *Ex praeceptis legis naturalis, quasi ex quibusdam principiis communibus & indemonstrabilibus, necesse est quod ratio humana procedat ad aliqua magis particulariter disponenda. Et ista particulares dispositiones adinventæ secundum rationem humanam dicuntur leges humanæ, observatis aliis conditionibus quæ pertinent ad rationem legis.*

scripture

scripture a number of laws particular and positive, which being in force may not by any law of man be violated, we are in making laws to have thereunto an especial eye. As for example, it might perhaps seem reasonable unto the church of God, following the general laws concerning the nature of marriage, to ordain in particular that cousin-germans shall not marry. Which law notwithstanding ought not to be received in the church, if there should be in the scripture a law particular to the contrary, forbidding utterly the bonds of marriage to be so far forth abridged. The same *Thomas* therefore, whose definition of human laws we mentioned before, doth add thereunto this caution concerning the rule and canon whereby to make them: *Human laws are measures* in respect of men, whose actions they must direct; howbeit such measures they are, as have also their higher rules to be measured by, *which rules are two, the law of God, and the law of nature*. So that laws human must be made according to the general laws of nature, and without contradiction unto any positive law in scripture; otherwise they are ill made. Unto laws thus made and received by a whole church, they which live within the bosom of that church must not think it a matter indifferent either to yield, or not to yield obedience. Is it a small offence to despise the church of God? *My son, keep thy father's commandment*, saith *Solomon*, *and forget not thy mother's instruction: bind them both always about thine heart*. It doth not stand with the duty which we owe to our heavenly Father, that to the ordinances of our mother the church, we should shew our selves disobedient. Let us not say we keep the commandments of the one, when we break the law of the other: for unless we observe both, we obey neither. And what doth lett, but that we may observe both, when they are not the one to the other in any sort repugnant? For of such laws only we speak, as being made in form and manner already declared, can have in them no contradiction unto the laws of almighty God. Yea, that which is more, the laws thus made, God himself doth in such sort authorize, that to despise them, is to despise in them him. It is a loose and licentious opinion which the anabaptists have embraced, holding that a christian man's liberty is lost, and the soul which Christ hath redeemed unto himself injuriously drawn into servitude under the yoke of human power, if any law be now imposed besides the gospel of Jesus Christ: in obedience whereunto the Spirit of God, and not the constraint of man is to lead us, according to that of the blessed apostle, *Such as are led by the Spirit of God, are the sons of God*, and not such as live in thraldom unto men. Their judgment is therefore, that the church of Christ should admit no law-makers but the evangelists. The author of that which causeth another thing to be, is author of that thing also which thereby is caused. The light of natural understanding, wit and reason, is from God; he it is which thereby doth illuminate every man entring into the world. If there proceed from us any thing afterwards corrupt and naught, the mother thereof is our own darkness, neither doth it proceed from any such cause whereof God is the author. He is the author of all that we think or do, by virtue of that light which himself hath given. And therefore the laws which the very heathens did gather to direct their actions by, so far forth as they proceed from the light of nature, God himself doth acknowledge to have proceeded even from himself, and that he was the writer of them in the tables of their hearts. How much more then is he the author of those laws which have been made by his saints, endued farther with the heavenly grace of his Spirit, and directed as much as might be with such instructions as his sacred word doth yield? Surely, if we have unto those laws that dutiful regard which their dignity doth require, it will not greatly need that we should be exhorted to live in obedience unto them. If they have God himself for their author, contempt which is offered unto them cannot chuse but redound unto him. The safest, and unto God the most acceptable way of framing our lives therefore, is with all humility, lowliness and singleness of heart, to study which way our willing obedience, both unto God and man, may be yielded, even to the utmost of that which is due.

1 2 1.Quæst. 9 5. Art. 3.
1 Cor. 11. 22. Prov. 6. 20.
Rom. 8. 14.
John 1. 5.
Rom. 1. 19. & 2. 15.

That neither God's being the author of laws, nor his committing them to scripture, nor the continuance of the end for which they were instituted, is any reason sufficient to prove that they are unchangeable.

10. Touching the mutability of laws that concern the regiment and polity of the church, changed they are when either altogether abrogated, or in part repealed, or augmented with farther additions. Wherein we are to note, that this question about the changing of laws concerneth only such laws as are positive, and do make that now good or evil, by being commanded or forbidden, which otherwise of it self were not simply, the one or the other. Unto such laws it is expresly sometimes added, how long they are to continue in force. If this be no where express'd, then have we no light to direct our judgments concerning the changeableness or immutability of them, but by considering the nature and quality of such laws. The nature of every law must be judged of by the end for which it was made, and by the aptness of things therein prescribed unto the same end. It may so fall out, that the reason why some laws of God were given, is neither opened, nor possible to be gathered by the wit of man. As why God should forbid *Adam*

Adam that one tree, there was no way for *Adam* ever to have certainly underftood. And at *Adam's* ignorance of this point fatan took advantage, urging the more fecurely a falfe caufe, becaufe the tree was unto *Adam* unknown. Why the Jews were forbidden Deut. 22. 10. to plough their ground with an ox and an afs; why to clothe themfelves with mingled 11. attire of wool and linen, it was both unto them, and to us it remaineth obfcure. Such laws perhaps cannot be abrogated faving only by whom they were made; becaufe the intent of them being known unto none but the author, he alone can judge how long it is requifite they fhould endure. But if the reafon why things were inftituted may be known, and being known, do appear manifeftly to be of perpetual neceffity; then are thofe things alfo perpetual, unlefs they ceafe to be effectual unto that purpofe for which they were at the firft inftituted. Becaufe when a thing doth ceafe to be available unto the end which gave it being, the continuance of it muft then of neceffity appear fuperfluous. And of this we cannot be ignorant, how fometimes that hath done great good, which afterwards when time hath changed the antient courfe of things doth grow to be either very hurtful or not fo greatly profitable and neceffary. If therefore the end for which a law provideth be perpetually neceffary, and the way whereby it provideth perpetually alfo moft apt, no doubt but that every fuch law ought for ever to remain unchangeable. Whether God be the author of laws, by authorifing that power of men whereby they are made, or by delivering them made immediately from himfelf by word only, or in writing alfo, in howfoever; notwithftanding the authority of their maker, the mutability of that end for which they are made, maketh them alfo changeable. The law of ceremonies came from God. *Mofes* had commandment to commit it unto the facred records of fcripture, where it continueth even unto this very day and hour, in force ftill as the Jew furmifeth, becaufe God himfelf was author of it; and for us to abolifh what he hath eftablifhed, were prefumption moft intolerable. But (that which they in the blindnefs of their obdurate hearts are not able to difcern) fith the end for which that law was ordained is now *Quod pro na-* fulfilled, paft and gone; how fhould it but ceafe any longer to be, which hath no longer *ceffitate tem-* any caufe of being in force as before? *That which neceffity of fome fpecial time doth caufe poris ftatuitum to be enjoined, bindeth no longer, than during that time, but doth afterward become efts. ceffante free.* Which thing is alfo plain, even by that law which the apoftles, affembled at the *bet ceffare pa-* council of *Jerufalem*, did from thence deliver unto the church of Chrift; the preface *riter quod urga-* whereof to authorife it was, *To the Holy Ghoft, and to us it hath feemed good :* which *bat. 1. q. 1.* ftyle they did not ufe as matching themfelves in power with the Holy Ghoft, but as tefti- Acts 15. fying the Holy Ghoft to be the author, and themfelves but only utterers of that decree. This law therefore to have proceeded from God as the author thereof, no faithful man will deny. It was of God, not only becaufe God gave them the power whereby they might make laws, but for that it proceeded even from the holy motion and fuggeftion of that fecret divine Spirit whofe fentence they did but only pronounce. Notwithftanding, as the law of ceremonies delivered unto the Jews, fo this very law which the gentiles received from the mouth of the Holy Ghoft, is in like refpect abrogated by deceafe of the end for which it was given. But fuch as do not ftick at this point, fuch as grant that what Counterp. p.8. hath been inftituted upon any fpecial caufe needeth not to be obferved, that caufe ceafing, do notwithftanding herein fail; they judge the laws of God only by the author and main end for which they were made, fo that for us to change that which he hath eftablifhed, they hold it execrable pride and prefumption, if fo be the end and purpofe for which God by that mean provideth be permanent. And upon this they ground thofe ample difputes concerning orders and offices, which being by him appointed for the government of his church, if it be neceffary always that the church of Chrift be governed, then doth the end for which God provided remain ftill; and therefore in thofe means which he by law did eftablifh as being fitteft unto that end, for us to alter any thing is to lift up our felves again ft God, and as it were to countermand him. Wherein they mark not that laws are inftruments to rule by, and that inftruments are not only to be framed according unto the general end for which they are provided, but even according unto that very particular which rifeth out of the matter whereon they have to work. The end wherefore laws were made may be permanent, and thofe laws neverthelefs require fome alteration, if there be any unfitnefs in the means which they prefcribe as tending unto that end and purpofe. As for example, a law that to bridle theft doth punifh thieves with a quadruple reftitution, hath an end which will continue as long as the world it felf continueth. Theft will be always, and will always need to be bridled. But that the mean which this law provideth for that end, namely, the punifhment of quadruple reftitution, that this will be alway fufficient to bridle and reftrain that kind of enormity no man can warrant. Infufficiency of laws doth fometimes come by want of judgment in the makers. Which caufe cannot fall into any law termed properly and immediately divine, as it may and doth into human laws often. But that which hath been once made sufficient, may wax otherwise by alteration of time and place ; that punishment which hath been sometime forcible to bridle fin, may grow afterward too weak and feeble. In a word, we plainly perceive by the difference of those three laws which the Jews received at the hands of God, the moral, ceremonial and judicial, that if the end for which, and the matter according whereunto, God maketh his laws, continue always one and the same, his laws also do the like, for which cause the moral law cannot be altered. Secondly, that whether the matter whereon laws are made continue or continue not, if their end have once ceased, they cease also to be of force ; as in the law ceremonial it fareth. Finally, that albeit the end continue, as in that law of theft specified, and in a great part of those antient judicials it doth ; yet for as much as there is not in all respects the same subject or matter remaining, for which they were first instituted, even this is sufficient cause of change. And therefore laws, tho both ordained of God himself, and the end for which they were ordained continuing, may notwithstanding cease, if by alteration of persons or times they be found unsufficient to attain unto that end. In which respect why may we not presume that God doth even call for such change or alteration as the very condition of things themselves doth make necessary ? They which do therefore plead the authority of the law-maker as an argument wherefore it should not be lawful to change that which he hath instituted, and will have this the cause why all the ordinances of our Saviour are immutable ; they which urge the wisdom of God as a proof, that whatsoever laws he hath made, they ought to stand, unless himself from heaven proclaim them disannulled, because it is not in man to correct the ordinance of God ; may know, if it please them to take notice thereof, that we are far from presuming to think that men can better any thing which God hath done, even as we are from thinking that men should presume to undo some things of men which God doth know they cannot better. God never ordained any thing that could be bettered. Yet many things he hath, that have been changed, and that for the better. That which succeedeth as better now when change is requisite, had been worse when that which now is changed was instituted. Otherwise God had not then left this to chuse that, neither would now reject that to chuse this, were it not for some new grown occasion, making that which hath been better worse. In this case therefore men do not presume to change God's ordinance, but they yield thereunto, requiring it self to be changed. Against this it is objected, that to abrogate or innovate the gospel of Christ, if men or angels should attempt, it were most heinous and cursed sacrilege. And the gospel, as they say, containeth not only doctrine instructing men how they should believe, but also precepts concerning the regiment of the church. Discipline therefore is a part of the gospel, and God being the author of the whole gospel, as well of discipline as of doctrine, it cannot be but that both of them have a common cause. So that as we are to believe for ever the articles of evangelical

We offer to shew the discipline to be a part of the gospel, and therefore to have a common cause ; so that in the repulse of the discipline, the gospel receives a check. *And again :* I speak of the discipline as of a part of the gospel ; and therefore neither under nor above the gospel, but the gospel. *T. C. l. 2. p. 14. Tert. de veland. virg. mart. in 1 Sam 14.*

doctrine, so the precepts of discipline we are in like sort bound for ever to observe. Touching points of doctrine ; as for example, the unity of God, the trinity of persons, salvation by Christ, the resurrection of the body, life everlasting, the judgement to come, and such like, they have been since the first hour that there was a church in the world, and till the last they must be believed : but as for matters of regiment, they are for the most part of another nature. To make new articles of faith and doctrine, no man thinketh it lawful ; new laws of government, what common-wealth or church is there which maketh not either at one time or another ? *The rule of faith,* faith *Tertullian, is but one, and that alone immovable, and impossible to be framed or cast anew.* The law of outward order and polity not so. There is no reason in the world wherefore we should esteem it as necessary always to do, as always to believe the same things ; seeing every man knoweth that the matter of faith is constant, the matter contrariwise of action daily changeable, especially the matter of action belonging unto church-polity. Neither can I find that men of soundest judgement have any otherwise taught, than that articles of belief, and things which all men must of necessity do to the end they may be saved, are either expresly set down in scripture, or else plainly thereby to be gathered. But touching things which belong to discipline and outward polity, the church hath authority to make canons, laws and decrees, even as we read, that in the apostles times it did. Which kind of laws (for as much as they are not in themselves necessary to salvation) may after they are made, be also changed as the difference of times or places shall require. Yea it is not denied, I am sure, by themselves, that certain things in discipline are of that nature, as they may be varied by times, places, persons and other

Acts 15.

the like circumstances. Whereupon I demand, are those changeable points of discipline commanded in the word of God, or no ? If they be not commanded, and yet may be received in the church, how can their former position stand, condemning all things in the church which in the word are not commanded ? If they be commanded, and yet may suffer change ; how can this latter stand, affirming all things immutable which are commanded of God ? Their distinction touching matters of substance and of circumstance, tho true, will not serve. For be they great things, or be they small, if God have commanded them in the gospel, and his commanding them in the gospel do make them unchangeable, there is no reason we should more change the one, than we may the other. If the authority of the maker do prove unchangeableness in the laws which God hath made, then must all laws which he hath made, be necessarily for ever permanent, tho they be but of circumstance only, and not of substance. I therefore conclude, that neither God's being author of laws for government of his church, nor his committing them unto scripture, is any reason sufficient, wherefore all churches should for ever be bound to keep them without change. But of one thing we are here to give them warning by the way : For whereas in this discourse, we have oftentimes profess'd, that many parts of discipline or church-polity are delivered in scripture, they may perhaps imagine that we are driven to confess their discipline to be delivered in scripture ; and that having no other means to avoid it, we are fain to argue for the changeableness of laws ordained even by God himself, as if otherwise theirs of necessity should take place, and that under which we live be abandoned. There is no remedy therefore, but to abate this error in them, and directly to let them know, that if they fall into any such a conceit, they do but a little flatter their own cause. As for us, we think in no respect so highly of it. Our persuasion is, that no age ever had knowledge of it but only ours ; that they which defend it, devised it ; that neither Christ, nor his apostles, at any time taught it, but the contrary. If therefore we did seek to maintain that which most advantageth our own cause, the very best way for us, and the strongest against them, were to hold even as they do, that in scripture there must needs be found some particular form of church-polity which God hath instituted, and which * for that very cause belongeth to all churches, to all times. But with any such partial eye to respect our selves, and by cunning to make those things seem the truest which are the fittest to serve our purpose, is a thing which we neither like nor mean to follow. Wherefore that which we take to be generally true concerning the mutability of laws, the same we have plainly delivered, as being persuaded of nothing more than we are of this ; † That whether it be in matter of speculation or of practice, no untruth can possibly avail the patron and defender long, and that things most truly, are likewise most behovefully spoken.

* Disciplina est christiana ecclesia politia, à Deo ejus rectà administranda causà constituta, ac propterea ex ejus verbo petenda, & ob eandem causam omnium ecclesiarum

communis & omnium temporum. Lib. 3. de ecclef. discip. in anal.   † Ἐοίκασιν ὑκ οἱ ἀληθεῖς δεὶ λόγων, ἃ μόνον πρὸς τὸ νικᾶσαι χρησιμώτατοι εἶναι, ἀλλὰ ἡ πρὸς τ βίον. Συνοδεῖ γὸ ὄψεσι τρῖσοις, τισίωντας. Arist. Ethic. lib. 10. cap. 1.

11. This we hold and grant for truth, that those very laws which of their own nature are changeable, be notwithstanding uncapable of change, if he which gave them, being of authority so to do, forbid absolutely to change them ; neither may they admit alteration against the will of such a law-maker. Albeit therefore we do not find any cause, why of right there should be necessarily an immutable form set down in holy scripture ; nevertheless, if indeed there have been at any time a church-polity so set down, the change whereof the sacred scripture doth forbid, surely for men to alter those laws which God for perpetuity hath established, were presumption most intolerable. To prove therefore, that the will of Christ was to establish laws so permanent and immutable, that in any sort to alter them, cannot but highly offend God ; thus they reason, first, (a) if Moses being but a servant in the house of God, did therein establish laws of government for a perpetuity ; laws, which they that were of the houshold might not alter ; shall we admit into our thoughts, that the Son of God hath in providing for this his houshold, declared himself less faithful than Moses ? Moses delivering unto the Jews such laws as were durable, if those be changeable which Christ hath delivered unto us, we are not able to avoid it, but (that which to think were heinous impiety) we of necessity must confess, even the Son of God himself to have been less faithful than Moses: which argument shall need no touch-stone to try it by, but some other of the like making. Moses erected in the wilderness a tabernacle, which was moveable from place to place ; Solomon a sumptu-

Whether Christ hath forbidden all change of those laws which are set down in scripture.

(a) Heb. 3. 6. Either that commendation of the Son before the servant is a false testimony, or the Son ordained a permanent government in the church. If permanent, then not to be changed. What then do they, that hold it may be changed at the magistrate's pleasure, but advise the magistrate by his positive laws to proclaim, that it is his will, that if there shall be a church within his dominions, he will maim and deform the same ? M. M. p. 16. He that was as faithful as Moses, left as clear instruction for the government of the church : but Christ was as faithful as Moses : ergo. Demonstr. of discip. cap. 1.

ous and stately temple, which was not moveable : therefore *Solomon* was faithfuller than *Moses*, which no man endued with reason will think. And yet by this reason it doth plainly follow : he that will see how faithful the one or other was, must compare the things which they both did, unto the charge which God gave each of them. The apostle in making comparison between our Saviour and *Moses*, attributeth faithfulness unto both, and maketh this difference between them ; *Moses in*, but *Christ over* the house of God ; *Moses* in that house which was *his by charge and commission*, tho to govern it, yet to govern it *as a servant* ; but *Christ* over this house as being *his own entire possession*. Our Lord and Saviour doth make protestation, (*b*) *I have given unto them the words which thou gavest me* ; faithful therefore he was, and concealed not any part of his Father's will. But did any part of that will require the immutability of laws concerning church-polity ? They answer, yea ; for else God should less favour us than the *Jews*. God would not have their churches guided by any laws but his own : and seeing this did so continue even till Christ ; now to ease God of that care, or rather to deprive the church of his patronage, what reason have we ? Surely none, to derogate any thing from the antient love which God hath borne to his church. An heathen philosopher there is, who considering how many things beasts have which men have not, how naked in comparison of them, how impotent, and how much less able we are to shift for our selves a long time after we enter into this world, repiningly concluded hereupon, that nature being a careful mother for them, is towards us a hard-hearted step-dame. No, we may not measure the affection of our gracious God towards his by such differences. For even herein shineth his wisdom, that tho the ways of his providence be many, yet the end which he bringeth all at the length unto, is one and the self same. But if such kind of reasoning were good, might we not even as directly conclude the very same concerning laws of secular regiment ? Their own words are these ; (*c*) *In the antient church of the Jews*, God did command, and Moses *commit unto writing all things pertinent as well to the civil as to the ecclesiastical state*. God gave them law of civil regiment, and would not permit their common-weal to be governed by any other laws than his own. Doth God less regard our temporal estate in this world, or provide for it worse than theirs ? To us notwithstanding, he hath not as to them, delivered any particular form of temporal regiment, unless perhaps we think, as some do, that the grafting of the *Gentiles*, and their incorporating into *Israel* doth import that we ought to be subject unto the rites and laws of their whole polity. We see then how weak such disputes are, and how finally they make to this purpose. That Christ did not mean to set down particular positive laws for all things in such sort as *Moses* did, the very different manner of delivering the laws of *Moses* and the laws of Christ doth plainly shew. *Moses* had commandment to gather the ordinances of God together distinctly, and orderly to set them down according unto their several kinds, for each publick duty and office the laws that belong thereto, as appeareth in the books themselves written of purpose for that end. Contrariwise the laws of Christ, we find rather mentioned by occasion in the writings of the apostles, than any solemn thing directly written to comprehend them in legal sort. Again, the positive laws which *Moses* gave, they were given for the greatest part, with restraint to the land of *Jewry* : *Behold*, saith *Moses*, I have taught you ordinances and laws, *as the Lord my God commanded me, that ye should do so even within the land whither ye go to possess it.* Which laws and ordinances positive, he plainly distinguished afterward from the laws of the two tables which were moral. *The Lord spake unto you out of the midst of the fire ; ye heard the voice of the words, but saw no similitude, only a voice. Then he declared unto you his covenant which he commanded you to do, the ten commandments, and wrote them upon two tables of stone. And the Lord commanded me that same time, that I should teach you ordinances and laws which ye should observe in the land, whither ye go to possess it.* The same difference is again set down in the next chapter following. For rehearsal being made of the ten commandments, it followeth immediately : *These words the Lord spake unto all your multitude in the mount, out of the midst of the fire, the cloud and the darkness, with a great voice, and added no more, and wrote them upon two tables of stone : and delivered them unto me.* But concerning other laws, the people give their consent to receive them at the hands of *Moses. Go thou nearer, and hear all that the Lord our God saith, and declare thou unto us all that the Lord our God saith unto thee, and we will hear it, and do it.* The people's alacrity herein God highly commendeth with most effectual and hearty speech : *I have heard the voice of the words of this people ; they have spoken well. O that there were such an heart in them to fear me, and to keep all my commandments always, that it might go well with them, and with their children for ever ! Go, say unto them, return you to your tents ; but stand thou here with me, and I will* tell

(b) John 17.
Either God hath left a prescript form of government now, or else he is less careful under the new testament, than under the old. *Demonst. of disc. cap. 1.*

(c) Ecclesiast. disc. lib. 1.

Rom. 11. 17.
Ephes. 2. 12.

Deut. 4. 5.

ver. 12, 13, 14.

Deut. 5. 22.

ver. 27.

ver. 28, 29, 30, 31.

†

tell thee all the commandments and the ordinances, and the laws which thou shalt teach them, that they may do them in the land which I have given them to possess. From this latter kind the former are plainly distinguished in many things. They were not both at one time delivered, neither both after one sort, nor to one end. The former uttered by the voice of God himself in the hearing of six hundred thousand men ; the former written with the finger of God ; the former termed by the name of a covenant ; the former given to be kept without either mention of time how long, or of place where. On the other side, the latter given after, and neither written by God himself, nor given unto the whole multitude immediately from God, but unto *Moses*, and from him to them both by word and writing : finally, the latter termed ceremonies, judgments, ordinances, but no where covenants. The observation of the latter restrained unto the land where God would establish them to inhabit. The laws positive are not framed without regard had to the place and persons for the which they are made. If therefore Almighty God, in framing their laws, had an eye unto the nature of that people, and to the country where they were to dwell ; if these peculiar and proper considerations were respected in the making of their laws, and must be also regarded in the positive laws of all other nations besides ; then seeing that nations are not all alike, surely the giving of one kind of positive laws unto one only people without any liberty to alter them, is but a slender proof that therefore one kind should in like sort be given to serve everlastingly for all. But that which most of all maketh for the clearing of this point, is, * That the *Jews* who had laws so particularly determining and so fully instructing them in all affairs what to do, were notwithstanding continually inured with causes exorbitant, and such as their laws had not provided for. And

** T. C. lib. 1. p. 35. Whereas you say, That they (the *Jews*) had nothing, but was determined by the law, and we have many things undetermined and left to the order of the church, I will offer for one that you shall bring that we have left to the order of the church, to shew you that they had twenty which were undecided by the express word of God.*

in this point much more is granted us than we ask, namely, that for one thing which we have left to the order of the church, they had twenty which were undecided by the express word of God ; and that as their ceremonies and sacraments were multiplied above ours, even so grew the number of those cases which were not determined by any express word. So that if we may devise one law, they by this reason might devise twenty ; and if their devising so many were not forbidden, shall their example prove us forbidden to devise as much as one law for the ordering of the church ? We might not devise, no not one, if their example did prove that our Saviour hath utterly forbidden all alteration of his laws, in as much as there can be no law devised, but needs it must either take away from his, or add thereunto more or less, and so make some kind of alteration. But of this so large a grant we are content not to take advantage. Men are oftentimes in a sudden passion more liberal than they would be, if they had leisure to take advice ; and therefore so bountiful words of course and frank speeches we are contented to let pass, without turning them to advantage with too much rigour. It may be they had rather be listned unto, when they commend the kings of *Israel*, which attempted nothing in the government of the church without the express word of God ; and when they urge, that God left nothing in his word undescribed, whether it concerned the worship of God or outward polity, nothing unset down ; and therefore charged them strictly to keep themselves unto that without any alteration. Howbeit seeing it cannot be denied, but that many things there did belong unto the course of their publick affairs wherein they had no express word at all to shew precisely what they should do ; the difference between their condition and ours in these cases will bring some light unto the truth of this present controversy. Before the fact of the son of *Shelomith*, there was no law which did appoint any certain punishment for blasphemers : that wretched creature being therefore apprehended in that impiety was held in ward, till the mind of the Lord was known concerning his case. The like practice is also mentioned upon occasion of a breach of the sabbath-day. They find a poor silly creature gathering sticks in the wilderness ; they bring him unto *Moses* and *Aaron* and all the congregation ; they lay him in hold, because it was not declared what should be done with him, till God had said unto *Moses*, *This man shall die the death.* The law requireth to keep the sabbath-day ; but for the breach of the sabbath what punishment should be inflicted it did not appoint. Such occasions as these, are rare : and for such things as do fall scarce once in many ages of men, it did suffice to take such order as was requisite when they fell. But if the case were such, as being not already determined by law, were notwithstanding likely oftentimes to come into question, it gave occasion of adding laws that were not before. Thus it fell out in the case of those men polluted, and of the daughters of *Zelophehad*, whose causes *Moses* having brought before the Lord, received laws to serve for the like in time to come. The *Jews* to this end had the oracle of God, they had the prophets. And

T. C. in the table to his second book.

T.C. lib. 1. p. 446. If he will needs separate the worship of God from the external polity ; yet as the Lord set forth the one so he left not thing undescribed in the other.

Levit. 24. 14

Numb. 15. 32.

Numb. 9.
Numb. 27.

by

by such means, God himself instructed them from heaven what to do in all things, that did greatly concern their state, and were not already set down in the law. Shall we then hereupon argue even against our own experience and knowledge ? Shall we seek to perfuade men, that of necessity it is with us, as it was with them, that because God is ours in all respects as much as theirs, therefore either no such way of direction hath been at any time ; or if it hath been, it doth still continue in the church ; or if the same do not continue, that yet it must be at the least supplied by some such mean as pleaseth us to account of equal force ? A more dutiful and religious way for us were to admire the wisdom of God, which shineth in the beautiful variety of all things ; but most in the manifold and yet harmonious dissimilitude of those ways, whereby his church upon earth is guided from age to age throughout all generations of men. The *Jews* were necessarily to continue till the coming of Christ in the flesh, and the gathering of nations unto him.

Gen. 18. 18.
Gen. 48. 10.
So much the promise made unto *Abraham* did import. So much the prophecy of *Jacob* at the hour of his death did foreshew. Upon the safety therefore of their very outward state and condition for so long, the after good of the whole world and the salvation of all did depend. Unto their so long safety, for two things it was necessary to provide ; namely, the preservation of their state against foreign resistance, and the continuance of their peace within themselves. Touching the one, as they received the promise of God to be the rock of their defence, against which whoso did violently rush should but bruise and batter themselves ; so likewise they had his commandment in all their affairs that way to seek direction and counsel from him. Mens consultations are always perillous. And it falleth out many times, that after long deliberation those things are by their wit even resolved on, which by tryal are found most opposite to publick safety. It is no impossible thing for states, be they never so well established, yet by over-sight in some one act or treaty between them and their potent opposites, utterly to cast away themselves for ever. Wherefore left it should so fall out to them, upon whom so much did depend, they were not permitted to enter into war, nor conclude any league of peace, nor to wade thro any act of moment between them and foreign states, unless the oracle of God or his prophets were first consulted with. And left domestical disturbance should waste them within themselves, because there was nothing unto this purpose more effectual than if the authority of their laws and governours were such as none might presume to take exception against it, or to shew disobedience unto it, without incurring the hatred and detestation of all men that had any spark of the fear of God ; therefore he gave them even their positive laws from heaven, and as oft as occasion required, chose in like sort rulers also to lead and govern them. Notwithstanding, some desperately impious there were, which adventured to try what harm it could bring upon them if they did attempt to be authors of confusion, and to resist both governours and laws. Against such monsters God maintained his own by fearful execution of extraordinary judgment upon them. By which means it came to pass, that altho they were a people infested and mightily hated of all others throughout the world, altho by nature hard-hearted, querulous, wrathful, and impatient of rest and quietness ; yet was there nothing of force, either one way or other, to work the ruin and subversion of their state till the time before mentioned was expired. Thus we see that there was no cause of dissimilitude in these things between that one only people before Christ, and the kingdoms of the world since. And whereas
T. C. lib. 2.
p. 440.
it is farther alledged, *That albeit in civil matters and things pertaining to this present life, God hath used a greater particularity with them than amongst us, framing laws according to the quality of that people and country ; yet the leaving of us at greater liberty in things civil, is so far from proving the like liberty in things pertaining to the kingdom of heaven, that it rather proves a straiter bond. For even as when the Lord would have his favour more appear by temporal blessings of this life towards the people under the law than towards us, he gave also politick laws most exactly, whereby they might both most easily come into, and most stedfastly remain in possession of those earthly benefits : even so at this time, wherein he would not have his favour so much esteemed by those outward commodities, it is required, that as his care in prescribing laws for that purpose hath somewhat faln, in leaving them to mens consultations, which may be deceived ; so his care for conduct and government of the life to come, should (if it were possible) rise, in leaving less to the order of men than in times past.* These are but weak and feeble disputes for the inference of that conclusion which is intended. For, saving only in such consideration as hath been shewed, there is no cause wherefore we should think God more desirous to manifest his favour by temporal blessings towards them than towards us. Godliness had unto them, and it hath also unto us, the promises both of this life and the life to come. That the care of God hath faln in earthly things, and therefore should rise as much in heavenly ; that more is left unto mens consultations in the one,

one, and therefore less must be granted in the other; that God having used a greater particularity with them than with us for matters pertaining unto this life, is to make us amends by the more exact delivery of laws for government of the life to come. These are proportions, whereof if there be any rule, we must plainly confess that, which truth is, we know it not. God which spake unto them by his prophets, hath unto us by his only begotten Son; those mysteries of grace and salvation which were but darkly disclosed unto them, have unto us more clearly shined. Such differences between them and us, the apostles of Christ have well acquainted us withal. But as for matter belonging unto the outward conduct or government of the church; seeing that even in sense it is manifest, that our Lord and Saviour hath not by positive laws descended so far into particularities with us, as *Moses* with them; neither doth by extraordinary means, oracles and prophets, direct us, as them he did, in those things which rising daily by new occasions, are of necessity to be provided for; doth it not hereupon rather follow, that altho not to them, yet to us there should be freedom and liberty granted to make laws? Yea but the apostle saint *Paul* doth fearfully charge *Timothy, Even in the sight of God who quickneth all, and of Jesus Christ who witnessed that famous confession before* Pontius *Pilate, to keep what was commanded him safe and sound, till the appearance of our Lord Jesus Christ.* This doth exclude all liberty of changing the laws of Christ, whether by abrogation or addition, or howsoever. For in *Timothy* the whole church of Christ receiveth charge concerning her duty. And that charge is to keep the apostle's commandment; and his commandment did contain the law that concerned church-government: and those laws he straitly requireth to be observed without breach or blame till the appearance of our Lord Jesus Christ. In scripture we grant every one man's lesson to be the common instruction of all men, so far forth as their cases are like; and that religiously to keep the apostle's commandments in whatsoever they may concern us, we all stand bound. But touching that commandment which *Timothy* was charged with, we swerve undoubtedly from the apostle's precise meaning, if we extend it so largely that the arms thereof shall reach unto all things which were commanded him by the apostle. The very words themselves do testrain themselves unto some special commandment among many. And therefore it is not said, *Keep the ordinances, laws and constitutions which thou hast received; but* τ̀ηὺἰολὴὐ, *that great commandment which doth principally concern thee and thy calling:* that commandment which Christ did so often inculcate unto *Peter*; that commandment unto the careful discharge whereof they of *Ephesus* are exhorted, *Attend to your selves, and to all the flock wherein the Holy Ghost hath placed you bishops, to feed the church of God, which he hath purchased by his own blood:* finally, that commandment which unto the same *Timothy* is by the same apostle, even in the same form and manner afterwards again urged, *I charge thee in the sight of God and the Lord Jesus Christ, which will judge the quick and dead at his appearance, and in his kingdom, preach the word of God.* When *Timothy* was instituted in that office, then was the credit and trust of this duty committed unto his faithful care. The doctrine of the gospel was then given him, *as the precious talent or treasure of Jesus Christ*; then received he for performance of this duty the special gift of the Holy Ghost. To keep this commandment immaculate and blameless, *was to teach the gospel of Christ without mixture of corrupt and unsound doctrine*; such as a number even in those times intermingled with the mysteries of christian belief. *Till the appearance of Christ to keep it so,* doth not import the time wherein it should be kept, but rather the time whereunto the final reward for keeping it was reserved; according to that of saint *Paul* concerning himself, *I have kept the faith; for the residue there is laid up for me a crown of righteousness, which the Lord, the righteous judge, shall in that day render unto me.* If they that labour in this harvest should respect but the present fruit of their painful travel, a poor encouragement it were unto them to continue therein all the days of their life. But their reward is great in heaven; the crown of righteousness which shall be given them in that day is honourable. The fruit of their industry then shall they reap with full contentment and satisfaction, but not till then. Wherein the greatness of their reward is abundantly sufficient to countervail the tediousness of their expectation. Wherefore till then, they that are in labour must rest in hope. O *Timothy*, keep that which is committed unto thy charge; that great commandment which thou hast received keep till the appearance of our Lord Jesus Christ. In which sense, altho we judge the apostle's words to have been uttered; yet hereunto do we not require them to yield; that think any other construction more sound. If therefore it be rejected, and theirs esteemed more probable which hold, that the last words do import perpetual observation of the apostle's commandment imposed necessarily for ever upon the militant church of Christ; let them withal consider, that then his commandment cannot so largely be taken to comprehend

what-

Margin notes:
1 Tim. 6. 14.
John 18. 37.
John 21. 15.
Acts 20. 28.
2 Tim. 4. 1.
1 Tim. 6. 20. τὴυ παραθλα-θήκηυ.
1 Tim. 4. 14.
2 Tim. 4. 7.

whatfoever the apoſtle did command *Timothy*. For themſelves do not all bind the church unto ſome things, whereof *Timothy* received charge, as namely, unto that precept concerning the choice of widows : ſo as they cannot hereby maintain, that all things poſitively commanded concerning the affairs of the church, were commanded for perpetuity. And we do not deny that certain things were commanded to be, tho poſitive, yet perpetual in the church. They ſhould not therefore urge againſt us places that ſeem to forbid change, but rather ſuch as ſet down ſome meaſure of alteration ; which meaſure, if we have exceeded, then might they therewith charge us juſtly : whereas now they themſelves, both granting and alſo uſing liberty to change, cannot in reaſon diſpute abſolutely againſt all change. Chriſt delivered no inconvenient or unmeet laws. Sundry of ours they hold inconvenient ; therefore ſuch laws they cannot poſſibly hold to be Chriſt's ; being not his, they muſt of neceſſity grant them added unto his. Yet certain of thoſe very laws ſo added, they themſelves do not judge unlawful ; as they plainly confeſs, both in matter of preſcript attire, and of rites appertaining, to burial. Their own proteſtations are, that they plead againſt the inconvenience not the unlawfulneſs of popiſh apparel ; and againſt the inconvenience not the unlawfulneſs of ceremonies in burial. Therefore they hold it a thing not unlawful to add to the laws of Jeſus Chriſt; and ſo conſequently they yield that no law of Chriſt forbiddeth addition unto church laws. The judgment. of *Calvin* being alledged againſt them, to whom of all men they attribute moſt ; whereas his words be plain, that for ceremonies and external diſcipline the church hath power to make laws: the anſwer which hereunto they make, is, That indefinitely the ſpeech is true, and that ſo it was meant by him ; namely, That ſome things belonging unto external

T. C. lib. 3. p. 241. My reaſons do never conclude the unlawfulneſs of theſe ceremonies of burial, but the inconvenience and inexpedience of them. *And in the table.* Of the inconvenience, not of the unlawfulneſs of popiſh apparel and ceremonies in burial. *T. C. lib. 1. p.* 32. Upon the indefinite ſpeaking of Mr. *Calvin*, ſaying, Ceremonies and external diſcipline, without adding all or ſome, you go about ſubtilly to make men believe, that Mr. *Calvin* hath placed the whole external diſcipline in the power and arbitrement of the church. For if all external diſcipline were arbitrary, and in the choice of the church, excommunication alſo (which is a part of it) might be caſt away ; which I think you will not ſay. *And in the very next words before.* Where you will give to underſtand, that ceremonies and external diſcipline are not preſcribed particularly by the word of God, and therefore left to the order of the church : you muſt underſtand, that all external diſcipline is not left to the order of the church, being particularly preferibed in the ſcriptures, no more than all ceremonies are left to the order of the church, as the ſacraments of baptiſm and the ſupper of the Lord.

diſcipline and ceremonies are in the power and arbitrement of the church : but neither was it meant, neither is it true generally, That all external diſcipline, and all ceremonies are left to the order of the church, in as much as the ſacraments of baptiſm and the ſupper of the Lord are ceremonies, which yet the church may not therefore abrogate. Again, excommunication is a part of external diſcipline, which might alſo be caſt away if all external diſcipline were arbitrary and in the choice of the church. By which their anſwer it doth appear, that touching the names of ceremony and external diſcipline, they gladly would have us ſo underſtood, as if we did herein contain a great deal more than we do. The fault which we find with them, is, that they over-much abridge the church of her power in theſe things. Whereupon they recharge us, as if in theſe things we gave the church a liberty which hath no limits or bounds ; as if all things which the name of diſcipline containeth were at the church's free choice. So that we might either have church-governors and government, or want them ; either retain or rejeƈt church-cenſures as we liſt. They wonder at us as at men which think it ſo indifferent what the church doth in matter of ceremonies, that it may be feared leſt we judge the very ſacraments themſelves to be held at the church's pleaſure. No, the name of ceremonies we do not uſe in ſo large a meaning, as to bring ſacraments within the compaſs and reach thereof; altho things belonging unto the outward form and ſeemly adminiſtration of them are contained in that name, even as we uſe it. For the name of ceremonies we uſe as they themſelves do, when they ſpeak after this ſort : *The doƈtrine and diſcipline of the church, as the weightieſt things, ought* *T. C. lib. 3. p.* 171. *eſpecially to be looked unto ; but the ceremonies alſo, as mint and cummin, ought not to be negleƈted.* Beſides, in the matter of external diſcipline or regiment it ſelf, we do not deny but there are ſome things whereto the church is bound till the world's end. So as the queſtion is only, how far the bounds of the church's liberty do reach. We hold, that the power which the church hath lawfully to make laws and orders for it ſelf doth extend unto ſundry things of eccleſiaſtical juriſdiƈtion, and ſuch other matters, whereto their opinion is, that the church's authority and power doth not reach. Whereas therefore in diſputing againſt us about this point, they take their compaſs a great deal wider than the truth of things can afford, producing reaſons and arguments by way of generality, to prove that Chriſt hath ſet down all things belonging any way unto the form of ordering his church, and hath abſolutely forbidden change by addition or diminution, great or ſmall (for ſo their manner of diſputing is :) we are conſtrained to make our defence by ſhewing, that Chriſt hath not deprived his church ſo far of all liberty in making orders and laws for it ſelf, and that they themſelves do not think he hath ſo

done.

done. For are they able to shew that all particular customs, rites and orders of reformed churches, have been appointed by Christ himself? No: they grant, that in matter of circumstance they alter that which they have received; but in things of substance they keep the laws of Christ without change. If we say the same in our own behalf (which surely we may do with a great deal more truth) then must they cancel all that hath been before alledged, and begin to inquire afresh, whether we retain the laws that Christ hath delivered concerning matters of substance, yea or no. For our constant persuasion in this point is as theirs, that we have no where altered the laws of Christ, farther than in such particularities only as have the nature of things changeable according to the difference of times, places, persons, and other the like circumstances. Christ hath commanded prayers to be made, sacraments to be ministred, his church to be carefully taught and guided. Concerning every of these somewhat Christ hath commanded, which must be kept till the world's end. On the contrary side, in every of them somewhat there may be added, as the church shall judge it expedient. So that if they will speak to purpose, all which hitherto hath been disputed of, they must give over, and stand upon such particulars only as they can shew we have either added or abrogated otherwise than we ought in the matter of church-polity. Whatsoever Christ hath commanded for ever to be kept in his church, the same we take not upon us to abrogate; and whatsoever our laws have thereunto added besides, of such quality we hope it is as no law of Christ doth any where condemn. Wherefore, that all may be laid together and gathered into a narrow room: First, so far forth as the church is the mystical body of Christ and his **I.** invisible spouse, it needeth no external polity. That very part of the law divine which teacheth faith and works of righteousness, is it self alone sufficient for the church of God in that respect. But as the church is a visible society and body politick, laws of polity it cannot want. Secondly, Whereas therefore it cometh in the second place to **II.** be inquired, what laws are fittest and best for the church; they who first embraced that rigorous and strict opinion, which depriveth the church of liberty to make any kind of law for her self, inclined (as it should seem) thereunto; for that they imagined all things which the church doth without commandment of holy scripture, subject to that reproof which the scripture it self useth in certain cases, when divine authority ought alone to be followed. Hereupon they thought it enough for the cancelling of any kind of order whatsoever, to say, *The word of God teacheth it not, it is a device of the brain of man, away with it therefore out of the church.* Saint *Augustine* was of another mind, who speaking of fasts on the sunday, saith, *That he which would chuse out that day to fast on, should give thereby no small offence to the church of God, which had received a contrary custom, For in these things, whereof the scripture appointeth no certainty, the use of the people of God, or the ordinances of our fathers, must serve for a law. In which case, if we will dispute, and condemn one sort by another's custom, it will be but matter of endless contention: where, for as much as the labour of reasoning shall hardly beat into mens heads any certain or necessary truth, surely it standeth us upon to take heed, lest with the tempest of strife, the brightness of charity and love be darkned.* If all things must be commanded of God which may be practised of his church, I would know what commandment the *Gileadites* had to erect that altar which is spoken of in the book of *Joshua*. Did not congruity of reason induce them thereunto, and suffice for defence of their fact? I would know what commandment the women of *Israel* had yearly to mourn and lament in the memory of *Jephtha*'s daughter; what commandment the Jews had to celebrate their feast of *Dedication*, never spoken of in the law, yet solemnized even by our Saviour himself; what commandment, finally, they had for the ceremony of odours used about the bodies of the dead, after which custom notwithstanding (sith it was their custom) our Lord was contented that his own most precious body should be intombed. Wherefore to reject all orders of the church which men have established, is to think worse of men in this respect, than either the judgment of wise men alloweth, or the law of God it self will bear. Howbeit, they which had once taken upon them to condemn all things done in the church, and not commanded of God to be done, saw it was necessary for them (continuing in defence of this their opinion) to hold, that needs there must be in scripture set down a complete particular form of church-polity, a form prescribing how all the affairs of the church must be ordered, a form in no respect lawful to be altered by mortal men. For reformation of which oversight and error in them, there were that thought it a part of christian love and charity to instruct them better, and to open unto them the difference between matters of perpetual necessity to all mens salvation, and matters of ecclesiastical polity: the one both fully and plainly taught in holy scripture, the other not necessary to be in such sort there prescribed: the one not capable of any diminution or augmentation at all by

M   men,

Marginal notes: T. C. lib. 1. f. 27. We deny not but certainty things are left to the order of the church, because they are of the nature of those which are varied by times, places, persons, and other circumstances, and so could not at once be set down and established for ever.

Isa. 29. 14. Col. 2. 23.

August. Epist. 86.

Josh. 22.

Judg. 11. 40.
Joh. 10. 22.

Joh. 19. 40.

men, the other apt to admit both. Hereupon the authors of the former opinion were presently seconded by other wittier and better learned, who being loth that the form of church-polity which they sought to bring in, should be otherwise than in the highest degree accounted of, took first an exception against the difference between church-polity and matters of necessity to salvation. Secondly, Against the restraint of scripture, which (they say) receiveth injury at our hands, when we teach that it teacheth not as well matters of polity, as of faith and salvation. Thirdly, Constrained thereby we have been, therefore, both to maintain that distinction as a thing not only true in it self, but by them likewise so acknowledged, tho unawares. Fourthly, And to make manifest that from scripture, we offer not to derogate the least thing that truth thereunto doth claim, in as much as by us it is willingly confess'd, that the scripture of God is a store-house abounding with inestimable treasures of wisdom and knowledge in many kinds, over and above things in this one kind barely necessary ; yea, even that matters of ecclesiastical polity are not therein omitted but taught also, albeit not so taught as those other things before mentioned. For so perfectly are those things taught, that nothing ever can need to be added, nothing ever cease to be necessary : these on the contrary side, as being of a far other nature and quality, not so strictly nor everlastingly commanded in scripture ; but that unto the complete form of church-polity, much may be requisite which the scripture teacheth not ; and much which it hath taught become unrequisite, sometimes because we need not use it, sometimes also because we cannot. In which respect, for mine own part, altho I see that certain reformed churches, the Scotish especially and French, have not that which best agreeth with the sacred scripture, I mean the government that is by bishops, in as much as both those churches are faln under a different kind of regiment ; which to remedy it is for the one altogether too late, and too soon for the other during their present affliction and trouble : this their defect and imperfection I had rather lament in such a case than exaggerate, considering that men oftentimes, without any fault of their own, may be driven to want that kind of polity or regiment which is best ; and to content themselves with that which either the irremediable error of former times, or the necessity of the present hath cast upon them. Fifthly, Now, because that position first mentioned, which holdeth it necessary that all things which the church may lawfully do in her own regiment be commanded in holy scripture, hath by the later defenders thereof been greatly qualified ; who, tho perceiving it to be over extreme, are notwithstanding loth to acknowledge any oversight therein, and therefore labour what they may to salve it up by construction ; we have for the more perspicuity delivered what was thereby meant at the first. Sixthly, How injurious a thing it were unto all the churches of God for men to hold it in that meaning. Seventhly, And how unperfect their interpretations are, who so much labour to help it either by dividing commandments of scripture into two kinds, and so defending, that all things must be commanded if not in special, yet in general precepts. Eighthly, Or by taking it as meant, that in case the church do devise any new order, she ought therein to follow the direction of scripture only, and not any star-light of man's reason. Ninthly, Both which evasions being cut off, we have in the next place declared after what sort the church may lawfully frame to her self laws of polity, and in what reckoning such positive laws both are with God, and should be with men. Tenthly, Furthermore, because to abridge the liberty of the church in this behalf, it hath been made a thing very odious, that when God himself hath devised some certain laws, and committed them to sacred scripture, man by abrogation, addition, or any way, should presume to alter and change them ; it was of necessity to be examined, whether the authority of God in making, or his care in committing those his laws unto scripture, be sufficient arguments to prove that God doth in no case allow they should suffer any such kind of change. Eleventhly, The last refuge for proof, that divine laws of christian church-polity may not be altered, by extinguishment of any old, or addition of new in that kind, is partly a marvellous strange discourse, that Christ (unless he should shew himself not so faithful as *Moses*, or not * so wise as *Lycurgus* and *Solon*) must needs have have set down in holy scripture some certain complete and unchangeable form of polity ; and partly a coloured shew of some evidence, where change of that sort of laws may seem expresly forbidden, altho in truth nothing less be done. I might have added hereunto their more familiar and popular disputes, as, The church is a city, yea, the city of the great King ; and the life of a city is polity. The church is the house of the living God ; and what house can there be without some order for the government of it ? In the royal house of a prince, there

I.
II.
III.
IV.
V.
VI.
VII.
VIII.
IX.
X.
XI.

* *Nisi reip. sua statum omnem constituere, magistratus ordinarit, singulorum munera potestatemque descripserit, quæ judiciorum soríque ratio habenda ? quomodo civium finienda lites ? non solum minus ecclesiæ christianæ providit, quam Moses olim Judaicæ, sed quam à Lycurgo, Solone, Numa, civitatibus suis prospectum sit.* Lib. de ecclesiast. discip.

†   must

muſt be officers for government, ſuch as not any ſervant in the houſe, but the prince whoſe the houſe is, ſhall judge convenient : ſo the houſe of God muſt have orders for the government of it, ſuch as not any of the houſhold, but God himſelf, hath appointed. It cannot ſtand with the love and wiſdom of God to leave ſuch order untaken as is neceſſary for the due government of his church. The numbers, degrees, orders and attire of *Solomon*'s ſervants, did ſhew his wiſdom ; therefore he which is greater than *Solomon* hath not failed to leave in his houſe ſuch orders for government thereof as may ſerve to be as a looking-glaſs for his providence, care and wiſdom, to be ſeen in. That little ſpark of the light of nature which remaineth in us, may ſerve us for the affairs of this life ; but as in all other matters concerning the kingdom of heaven, ſo principally in this which concerneth the very government of that kingdom, needful it is we ſhould be taught of God. *As long as men are perſuaded of any order that it is only of men, they preſume of their own underſtanding, and they think to deviſe another not only as good, but better than that which they have received. By ſeverity of puniſhment this preſumption and curioſity may be reſtrained. But that cannot work ſuch cheerful obedience as is yielded, where the conſcience hath reſpect to God as the author of laws and orders: This was it which countenanced the laws of* Moſes, *made concerning outward polity for the adminiſtration of holy things. The like ſome lawgivers of the heathens did pretend, but falſly ; yet wiſely diſcerning the uſe of this perſuaſion. For the better obedience ſake therefore it was expedient, that God ſhould be author of the polity of his church. But to what iſſue doth all this come ? A man would think that they which hold out with ſuch diſcourſes, were of nothing more fully perſuaded than of this, that the ſcripture hath ſet down a complete form of church polity, univerſal, perpetual, altogether unchangeable.* For ſo it would follow, if the premiſes were found and ſtrong to ſuch effect as is pretended. Notwithſtanding, they which have thus formally maintained argument in defence of the firſt overſight, are by the very evidence of truth themſelves conſtrained to make this in effect their concluſion, that the ſcripture of God hath many things concerning church polity ; that of thoſe many, ſome are of greater weight, ſome of leſs ; that what hath been urged as touching the immutability of laws, it extendeth in truth no farther than only to laws wherein things of greater moment are preſcribed. Now theſe things of greater moment, what are they ? Forſooth, *doctors, paſtors, lay-elders, elderſhips compounded of theſe three : ſynods, conſiſting of many elderſhips, deacons, women-church-ſervants, or widows ; free conſent of the people unto actions of greateſt moment, after they be by churches or ſynods orderly reſolved.* All this form of polity (if yet we may term that a form of building, when men have laid a few rafters together, and thoſe not all of the foundeſt neither) but howſoever, all this form they conclude is preſcribed in ſuch ſort, that to add to it any thing as of like importance (for ſo I think they mean) or to abrogate of it any thing at all, is unlawful. In which reſolution, if they will firmly and conſtantly perſiſt, I ſee not but that concerning the points which hitherto have been diſputed of, they muſt agree, that they have moleſted the church with needleſs oppoſition ; and henceforward, as we ſaid before, betake themſelves wholly unto the tryal of particulars, whether every of thoſe things which they eſteem as principal be either ſo eſteemed of, or at all eſtabliſhed for perpetuity in holy ſcripture ; and whether any particular thing in our church polity be received other than the ſcripture alloweth of, either in greater things, or in ſmaller. The matters wherein church polity is converſant are the publick religious duties of the church, as the adminiſtration of the word and ſacraments, prayers, ſpiritual cenſures, and the like. To theſe the church ſtandeth always bound. Laws of polity, are laws which appoint in what manner theſe duties ſhall be performed. In performance whereof, becauſe all that are of the church cannot jointly and equally work, the firſt thing in polity required, is, a difference of perſons in the church, without which difference thoſe functions cannot in orderly ſort be executed. Hereupon we hold, that God's clergy are a ſtate, which hath been and will be, as long as there is a church upon earth, neceſſarily by the plain word of God himſelf ; a ſtate whereunto the reſt of God's people muſt be ſubject, as touching things that appertain to their ſouls health. For where polity is, it cannot but appoint ſome to be leaders of others, and ſome to be led by others. *If* Luke 6. 39. *the blind lead the blind, they both periſh.* It is with the clergy, if their perſons be reſpected, even as it is with other men ; their quality many times far beneath that which the dignity of their place requireth. Howbeit, according to the order of polity, they being *the lights of the world,* others (tho better and wiſer) muſt that way be ſubject Matth. 5. 14. unto them. Again, foraſmuch as where the clergy are any great multitude, order doth neceſſarily require that by degrees they be diſtinguiſhed ; we hold there have ever been, and ever ought to be in ſuch caſe, at leaſtwiſe, two ſorts of eccleſiaſtical perſons, the

The defence of godly miniſters againſt Dr. Bridges, p. 133.

M 2   one

one subordinate unto the other ; as to the apostles in the beginning, and to the bishops always since, we find plainly both in scripture, and in all ecclesiastical records, other ministers of the word and sacraments have been. Moreover, it cannot enter into any man's conceit to think it lawful, that every man which listeth, should take upon him charge in the church ; and therefore a solemn admittance is of such necessity, that without it there can be no church polity. A number of particularities there are, which make for the more convenient being of these principal and perpetual parts in ecclesiastical polity, but yet are not of such constant use and necessity in God's church. Of this kind are, time and places appointed for the exercise of religion ; specialties belonging to the publick solemnity of the word, the sacraments and prayer ; the enlargement or abridgement of functions ministerial, depending upon those two principals before mentioned : to conclude, even whatsoever doth by way of formality and circumstance concern any publick action of the church. Now altho' that which the scripture hath of things in the former kind be for ever permanent ; yet in the latter, both much of that which the scripture teacheth is not always needful ; and much the church of God shall always need what the scripture teacheth not. So as the form of polity by them set down for perpetuity, is three ways faulty : faulty in omitting some things which in scripture are of that nature, as namely, the difference that ought to be of pastors, when they grow to any great multitude : faulty in requiring doctors, deacons, widows and such like, as things of perpetual necessity by the law of God, which in truth are nothing less : faulty also in urging some things by scripture immutable ; as their lay-elders, which the scripture neither maketh immutable, nor at all teacheth, for any thing either we can as yet find, or they have been hitherto able to prove. But hereof more in the books that follow. As for those marvellous discourses whereby they adventure to argue, that God must needs have done the thing which they imagine was to be done ; I must confess, I have often wondred at their exceeding boldness herein. When the question is, whether God have delivered in scripture (as they affirm he hath) a complete particular immutable form of church polity ; why take they that other both presumptuous and superfluous labour to prove he should have done it ; there being no way in this case to prove the deed of God, saving only by producing that evidence wherein he hath done it ? But if there be no such thing apparent upon record, they do as if one should demand a legacy by force and virtue of some written testament, wherein there being no such thing specified, he pleadeth, that there it must needs be, and bringeth arguments from the love or good will which always the testator bore him ; imagining, that these or the like proofs will convict a testament to have that in it which other men can no where by reading find. In matters which concern the actions of God, the most dutiful way on our part, is to search what God hath done, and with meekness to admire that,· rather than to dispute what he in congruity of reason ought to do. The ways which he hath whereby to do all things for the greatest good of his church, are more in number than we can search ; other in nature than that we should presume to determine, which of many should be the fittest for them to chuse, till such time as we see he hath chosen of many some one ; which one, we then may boldly conclude to be the fittest, because he hath taken it before the rest. When we do otherwise, surely we exceed our bounds ; who, and where we are, we forget. And therefore needful it is, that our pride in such cases be controlled, and our disputes beaten back with those demands of the blessed apostle, *How* Rom. 11. 33. *unsearchable are his judgments, and his ways past finding out ! Who hath known the mind of the Lord, or who was his counsellor ?*

O F

OF THE
L A W S
OF
Ecclesiastical Polity.

BOOK IV.

Concerning their third assertion, That our form of church-polity is corrupted with popish orders, rites and ceremonies, banished out of certain reformed churches, whose example therein we ought to have followed.

The matter contained in this fourth book

1. **H**OW *great use ceremonies have in the church.*
2. *The first thing they blame in the kind of our ceremonies, is, that we have not in them antient apostolical simplicity, but a greater pomp and stateliness.*
3. *The second, that so many of them are the same which the church of* Rome *useth; and the reasons which they bring to prove them for that cause blame-worthy.*
4. *How when they go about to expound what popish ceremonies they mean, they contradict their own arguments against popish ceremonies.*
5. *An answer to the argument, whereby they would prove, that sith we allow the customs of our fathers to be followed, we therefore may not allow such customs as the church of* Rome *hath, because we cannot account of them which are of that church as of our fathers.*
6. *To their allegation, that the course of God's own wisdom doth make against our conformity with the church of* Rome *in such things.*
7. *To the example of the eldest church, which they bring for the same purpose.*
8. *That it is not our best polity (as they pretend it is) for establishment of sound religion, to have in these things no agreement with the church of* Rome *being unsound.*
9. *That neither the papists upbraiding us as furnished out of their store, nor any hope which in that respect they are said to conceive, doth make any more against our ceremonies than the former allegations have done.*
10. *The grief, which they say godly brethren conceive, at such ceremonies as we have common with the church of* Rome.
11. *The third thing, for which they reprove a great part of our ceremonies, is, for that as we have them from the church of* Rome, *so that church had them from the* Jews.
12. *The fourth, for that sundry of them have been (they say) abused unto idolatry, and are by that means become scandalous.*
13. *The fifth, for that we retain them still, notwithstanding the example of certain churches reformed before us, which have cast them out.*
14. *A declaration of the proceedings of the church of* England, *for the establishment of things as they are.*

SUCH was the antient simplicity and softness of spirit, which sometimes prevailed in the world, that they whose words were even as oracles amongst men, seemed evermore loth to give sentence against any thing publickly received in the church of God, except it were wonderfully apparently evil; for that they did not so much incline to that severity which delighteth to reprove the least things it seeth amiss, as to that charity which is unwilling to behold any thing that duty bindeth it to reprove. The state of this present age wherein

How great are ceremonies have in the church.

in

in zeal hath drowned charity, and skill meekneſs, will not now ſuffer any man to mar‑vel, whatſoever he ſhall hear reproved, by whomſoever. Thoſe rites and ceremonies of the church therefore, which are the ſelf-ſame now, that they were when holy and virtuous men maintained them againſt prophane and deriding adverſaries, her own chil‑dren have at this day in deriſion. Whether juſtly or no, it ſhall then appear, when all things are heard which they have to alledge againſt the outward received orders of this church. Which inaſmuch as themſelves do compare unto *mint* and *cummin*, granting them to be no part of thoſe things which in the matter of polity are weightier, we hope that for ſmall things their ſtrife will neither be earneſt nor long. The ſifting of that which is objected againſt the orders of the church in particular, doth not belong unto this place. Here we are to diſcuſs only thoſe general exceptions, which have been taken at any time againſt them. Firſt therefore, to the end that their nature and uſe where‑to they ſerve may plainly appear, and ſo afterwards their quality the better be diſcerned ; we are to note, that in every grand or main publick duty which God requireth at the hands of his church, there is beſides that matter and form wherein the eſſence thereof con‑ſiſteth, a certain outward faſhion whereby the ſame is in decent ſort adminiſtered. The ſubſtance of all religious actions is delivered from God himſelf in few words. For ex‑ample ſake in the ſacraments, *unto the element let the word be added, and they both do make a ſacrament,* ſaith ſaint *Auguſtine.* Baptiſm is given by the element of water, and that preſcript form of words which the church of Chriſt doth uſe ; the ſacrament of the body and blood of Chriſt is adminiſtered in the elements of bread and wine, if thoſe myſtical words be added thereunto. But the due and decent form of adminiſtring thoſe holy ſacraments doth require a great deal more. The end which is aimed at in ſetting down the outward form of all religious actions, is the edification of the church. Now men are edified, when either their underſtanding is taught ſomewhat whereof in ſuch acti‑ons, it behoveth all men to conſider, or when their hearts are moved with any affection ſuitable thereunto ; when their minds are in any ſort ſtirred up unto that reverence, de‑votion, attention and due regard, which in thoſe caſes ſeemeth requiſite. Becauſe there‑fore unto this purpoſe not only ſpeech, but ſundry ſenſible means beſides have alway been thought neceſſary, and eſpecially thoſe means which being object to the eye, the live‑lieſt and the moſt apprehenſive ſenſe of all other, have in that reſpect ſeemed the fitteſt to make a deep and ſtrong impreſſion. From hence have riſen not only a number of prayers, readings, queſtionings exhortings, but even of viſible ſigns alſo, which being uſed in per‑formance of holy actions, are undoubtedly moſt effectual to open ſuch matter as men when they know and remember carefully muſt needs be a great deal the better informed to what effect ſuch duties ſerve. We muſt not think but that there is ſome ground of reaſon even in nature, whereby it cometh to paſs that no nation under heaven either doth or ever did ſome publick actions which are of weight, whether they be civil and temporal, or elſe ſpiritual and ſacred, to paſs without ſome viſible ſolemnity : the very ſtrangeneſs whereof, and difference from that which is common doth cauſe popular eyes to obſerve and to mark the ſame. Words, both becauſe they are common and do not ſo ſtrongly move the phanſy of man, are for the moſt part but ſlightly heard ; and therefore with ſingular wiſdom it hath been provided that the deeds of men which are made in the preſence of witneſſes, ſhould paſs not only with words but alſo with certain ſenſible actions, the memory whereof is far more eaſy and durable than the memory of ſpeech can be. The things which ſo long experience of all ages hath confirmed and made profitable, let not us preſume to condemn as follies and toys, becauſe we ſometimes know not the cauſe and reaſon of them. A wit diſpoſed to ſcorn whatſoever it doth not con‑ceive, might ask wherefore *Abraham* ſhould ſay to his ſervant : *Put thy hand under my thigh and ſwear* ; was it not ſufficient for his ſervant to ſhew the religion of an oath, by naming the lord God of heaven and earth, unleſs that ſtrange ceremony were added ? In contracts, bargains and conveyances, a man's word is a token ſufficient to expreſs his will. *Yet this was the antient manner in* Iſrael *concerning redeeming and exchanging to eſtabliſh all things ; a man did pluck off his ſhoe, and gave it to his neighbour ; and this was a ſure witneſs in* Iſrael. Amongſt the *Romans* in their making of a bond-man free, was it not wondered wherefore ſo great a-do ſhould be made ? The maſter to pre‑ſent his ſlave in ſome court, to take him by the hand, and not only to ſay in the hearing of the publick magiſtrate, I will that this man become free ; but after hteſe ſolemn words uttered to ſtrike him on the cheek, to turn him round, the hair of his head to be ſhaved off, the magiſtrate to touch him thrice with a rod, in the end a cap and a white garment to be given him : to what purpoſe all this circumſtance ? Amongſt the *Hebrews* how ſtrange, and in outward appearance almoſt againſt reaſon, that he which was minded to make himſelf a perpetual ſervant, ſhould not only teſtify ſo much in the preſence of the judge,

Matth. 23. 23.
The doctrine and diſcipline of the church, as the weigh‑tieſt things, ought eſpecial‑ly to be look‑ed unto : but the ceremo‑nies alſo, as *mint* and *cum‑min*, ought not to be neglec‑ted. *T. C. l.* 3. *p.* 171.

Gen 24. 2.

Ruth 4. 7.

Exod. 21. 6.

judge, but for a visible token thereof have also his ear bored thro with an awl? It were an infinite labour to prosecute these things so far as they might be exemplified both in civil and religious actions. For in both they have their necessary use and force. (a) *These sensible things which religion hath allowed, are resemblances framed according to things spiritually understood, whereunto they serve as a hand to lead, and a way to direct.* And whereas it may peradventure be objected, that to add to religious dutys such rites and ceremonies as are significant, is to institute new sacraments ; sure I am they will not say that *Numa Pompilius* did ordain a sacrament, a significant ceremony he did ordain, in commanding the priests (b) *to execute the work of their divine service with their hands as far as to the fingers covered ; thereby signifying that fidelity must be defended, and that mens right hands are the sacred seat thereof.* Again, we are also to put them in mind, that themselves do not hold all significant ceremonies for sacraments, insomuch as imposition of hands they deny to be a sacrament, and yet they give thereunto a forcible signification. For concerning it their words are these, (c) *The party ordained by this ceremony, was put in mind of his separation to the work of the Lord, that remembring himself to be taken as it were with the hand of God from amongst others, this might teach him not to account himself now his own, nor to do what himself listeth ; but to consider that God hath set him about a work, which if he will discharge and accomplish, he may at the hands of God assure himself of reward ; and, if otherwise, of revenge.* Touching significant ceremonies, some of them are sacraments, some as sacraments only. Sacraments are those, which are signs and tokens of some general promised grace, which always really descendeth from God unto the soul that duly receiveth them : other significant tokens are only as sacraments, yet no sacraments : which is not our distinction but theirs. For concerning the apostles imposition of hands, these are their own words, *magnum signum hoc & quasi sacramentum usurparunt* ; they used this sign, or as it were a sacrament.

Concerning rites and ceremonies there may be fault, either in the kind or in the number and multitude of them. The first thing blamed about the kind of ours is, that in many things we have departed from the antient simplicity of Christ and his apostles ; we have embraced more outward statelinss, we have those orders in the exercise of religion, which they who best pleased God and served him most devoutly never had. For it is out of doubt, that the first state of things was best, that in the prime of christian religion faith was soundest, the scriptures of God were then best understood by all men, all parts of godliness did then most abound ; and therefore it must needs follow, that customs, laws and ordinances devised since are not so good for the church of Christ ; but she best way is to cut off later inventions, and to reduce things unto the antient state wherein at the first they were. Which rule or canon we hold to be either uncertain, or at least wise unsufficient, if not both. For in case be it certain, hard it cannot be for them to shew us where we shall find it so exactly set down, that we may say without all controversy, these were the orders of the apostles times, these wholly and only, neither fewer nor more than these. True it is, that many things of this nature be alluded unto, yea many things declared, and many things necessarily collected out of the apostles writings. But is it necessary that all the orders of the church which were then in use should be contained in their books ? Surely no. For if the tenor of their writings be well observed, it shall unto any man easily appear, that no more of them are there touched than were needful to be spoken of sometimes by one occasion, and sometimes by another. Will they allow then of any other records besides ? Well assured I am they are far enough from acknowledging that the church ought to keep any thing as apostolical, which is not found in the apostles writings, in what other records soever it be found. And therefore whereas saint *Augustine* affirmeth, that those things which the whole church of Christ doth hold, may well be thought to be apostolical, altho they be not found written ; this his judgment they utterly condemn. I will not here stand in defence of saint *Augustine's* opinion, which is, that such things are indeed apostolical ; but yet with this exception, unless the decree of some general council have haply caused them to be received : for of positive laws and orders received throughout the whole christian world, saint *Augustine* could imagine no other fountain save these two. But to let pass saint *Augustine*, they who condemn him herein must needs confess it a very uncertain thing what the orders of the church were in the apostles times, seeing the scriptures do not mention them all, and other records thereof besides they utterly reject. So that in tying the church to the orders of the apostles times they tye it to a marvellous uncertain rule ; unless they

therefore here is no sufficient doctrine contained in scripture, whereby we may be saved. For all the commandments of God and of the apostles, are needful for our salvation. *Idem*, p. 118.

re-

(a) *Dionys. p. 121.* ...
(b) *Liv. lib. 1. Manu ad digitos usq; involutâ rem divinam facere, significantes fidem tutandam, sedemq; ejus etiam in dextris sacratam esse.*
(c) *Ecclef. dif. fol. 51.*

Fol. 15.

The first thing they blame in the kind of our ceremonies, is, that we have not in them antient apostolical simplicity, but a greater pomp and statelinss. *Lib. Ecclef. dif. & T.C. l. 3. p. 181.*

Tom. 7. de bapt. contra donatist. lib. 5. cap. 23. T.C. l. 3. p. 182. If this judgment of saint *Augustine* be a good judgment and found ; then there be some things commanded of God, which are not in the scripture ; and require the obfervation of no orders but only thofe which are known to be apoftolica by the apoftles own writings. But then is not this their rule of fuch fufficiency, that w e fhould ufe it as a touch-ftone to try the orders of the church by for ever. Our end ought always to be the fame ; our ways and means thereunto not fo. The glory of God and the good of the church was the thing which the apoftles aimed at, and therefore ought to be the mark whereat we alfo level. But feeing thofe rites and or-ders may be at one time more which at another are lefs available unto that purpofe: what reafon is there in thefe things to urge the ftate of our only age as a pattern for all to follow ? It is not, I am right fure, their meaning that we fhould now affemble our peo-ple to ferve God in clofe and fecret meetings ; or that common brooks or rivers fhould be ufed for places of baptifm; or that the eucharift fhould be miniftered after meat ; or that the cuftom of church-feafting fhould be renewed ; or that all kind of ftanding pro-vifion for the miniftry fhould be utterly taken away, and their eftate made again depen-dent upon the voluntary devotion of men. In thefe things they eafily perceiv e how un-fit that were for the prefent, which was for the firft age convenient enough. The faith, zeal and godlinefs of former times is worthily had in honour ; but doth this prove that the orders of the church of Chrift muft be ftill the felf-fame with theirs, that nothing may be which was not then, or that nothing which then was may lawfully fince have ceafed ? They who recal the church unto that which was at the firft, muft neceffarily fet bounds and limits unto their fpeeches. If any thing have been received repugnant unto that which was firft delivered, the firft things in this cafe muft ftand, the laft give place unto them. But where difference is without repugnancy, that which hath been can be no prejudice to that which is. Let the ftate of the people of God when they were in the houfe of bondage, and their manner of ferving God in a ftrange land, be com-pared with that which *Canaan* and *Jerufalem* did afford: and who feeth not what huge difference there was between them ? In *Egypt* it may be, they were right glad to take fome corner of a poor cottage, and there to ferve God upon their knees, peradventure covered in duft and ftraw fometimes. Neither were they therefore the lefs accepted of God: but he was with them in all their afflictions, and at the length by working of their admirable deliverance, did teftify that they ferved him not in vain. Notwithftanding in the very defart they are no fooner poffeft of fome little thing of their own, but a taber-nacle is required at their hands. Being planted in the land of *Canaan*, and having *David* to be their king, when the Lord had given him reft from all his enemies, it grieved his re-ligious mind to confider the growth of his own eftate and dignity, the affairs of religion continuing ftill in the former manner : *Behold now I dwell in the houfe of cedar-trees,* | 2 Sam. 7. 4.

and the ark of God remaineth ftill within curtains. What he did purpofe, it was the pleafure of God that *Solomon* his fon fhould perform, and perform it in manner futable un-to their prefent, not their antient eftate and condition ; for which caufe *Solomon* writeth unto the king of *Tyrus, The houfe which I build is great and wonderful* ; *for great is our* | 2 Chron. 2. 5. *God above all gods.* Whereby it clearly appeareth, that the orders of the church of God may be acceptable unto him, as well being framed fuitable to the greatnefs and dig-nity of later, as when they keep the reverend fimplicity of antienter times. Such dif-fimilitude herefore between us and the apoftles of Chrift, in the order of fome outward things, is no argument of default.

3. Yea, but we have fram'd our felves to the cuftoms of the church of *Rome* : our orders and ceremonies are papiftical. It is efpied that our church-founders were not fo careful as in this matter they fhould have been, but contented themfelves with fuch dif-cipline as they took from the church of *Rome*. Their error we ought to reform by a-bolifhing all popifh orders. There muft be no communion nor fellowfhip with papifts, neither i ndoctrine, ceremonies, nor government. It is not enough that we are divided from the church of *Rome* by the fingle wall of doctrine, retaining as we do part of their ceremonies and almoft their whole government ; but government or ceremonies whatfo-ever it be which is popifh, away with it. This is the thing they require in us, the utter relinquifhment of all things popifh. Wherein, to the end we may anfwer them according to their plain direct meaning, and not take advantage of doubtful fpeech, whereby controverfies grow always endlefs : their main pofition being this, that nothing fhould be placed in the church, but what God in his word hath commanded, they muft of ne-ceffity hold all for popifh which the church of *Rome* hath over and befides this. By popifh orders, ceremonies and government, they muft therefore mean in every of thefe fo much as the church of *Rome* hath embraced without commandment of God's word : fo that whatfoever fuch thing we have, if the church of *Rome* hath it alfo, it goeth under the name of thofe things that are popifh, yea altho it be lawful, altho agreeable to the word of God. For fo they plainly affirm, faying : *Altho the forms and ceremonies which they* (the church of *Rome*) *ufd were not unlawful, and that they contained nothing which is not*

agree-

Our orders and ceremo-nies blamed, in that fo ma-ny of them are the fame which the church of *Rome* ufeth. *Ecclef. Difcipl. fol. 12. T. C. lib. 1. p 131. T. C. l. 1. p. 20. T. C. l. 1. p. 15.*

T. C. lib. 1. p. 131

†

agreeable to the word of God, yet notwithstanding neither the word of God, nor reason, nor the examples of the eldest churches, both jewish and christian, do permit us to use the same forms and ceremonies, being neither commanded of God, neither such as there may not as good as they, and rather better be established. The question therefore is, whether we may follow the church of *Rome* in those orders, rites and ceremonies, wherein we do not think them blameable, or else ought to devise others, and to have no conformity with them, no not so much as in these things? In this sense and construction therefore as they affirm, so we deny, that whatsoever is popish we ought to abrogate. Their arguments to prove that generally all popish orders and ceremonies ought to be clean abolished, are in sum these: First, *whereas we allow the judgment of saint* Augustine, *that touching* T.C. l.1. p.30. *those things of this kind which are not commanded or forbidden in the scripture, we are to observe the custom of the people of God and the decrees of our forefathers; how can we retain the customs and constitutions of the papists in such things, who were neither the people of God nor our forefathers?* Secondly, *altho the forms and ceremonies of the* T.C. l. 1. p. 131. *church of* Rome *were not unlawful, neither did contain any thing which is not agreeable to the word of God, yet neither the word of God, nor the example of the eldest churches of God, nor reason do permit us to use the same,* they being hereticks and so near about us, *and their orders being neither commanded of God, nor yet such, but that as good or rather better may be established. It is against the word of God to have conformity with the church of* Rome *in such things, as appeareth in that the wisdom of God hath thought it a good way to keep his people from infection of idolatry and superstition by severing them from idolaters in outward ceremonies, and therefore hath forbidden them to do things which are in themselves very lawful to be done. And farther, whereas the Lord was careful to sever them by ceremonies from other nations, yet was he not so careful to sever them from any as from the Egyptians amongst whom they lived, and from those nations which were next neighbours to them, because from them was the greatest fear of infection.* So that following the course which the wisdom of God doth T.C. l. 1. p. 132. teach, *it were more safe for us to conform our indifferent ceremonies to the Turks which are far off, than to the papists which are so near.* Touching *the example of the eldest churches of God, in one council it was decreed, that christians should not deck their* Tom. 1. Braca. 73. *houses with bay-leaves and green boughs, because the pagans did use so to do; and that they should not rest from their labours those days that the pagans did; that they should not keep the first day of every month as they did. Another council decreed that christians* Con. Afric. cap. 27. *should not celebrate feasts on the birth-days of the martyrs, because it was the manner of the heathen.* O, saith Tertullian, *better is the religion of the heathen: for they use* Lib. de idolat. *no solemnity of the christians, neither the Lord's day, neither the pentecost; and if* He seemeth to mean the feast of eafter- *they knew them, they would have nothing to do with them: for they would be afraid lest they should seem christians: but we are not afraid to be called heathens.* The same day, celebra-ted in the memory of our Saviour's resurrection, and for that cause termed the Lord's day. Lib. de anima. Tertullian *would not have christians to sit after they have prayed, because the idolaters did so.* Whereby it appeareth, *that both of particular men and of councils, in making or abolishing of ceremonies, heed had been taken that the christians should not be like that idolaters, no not in those things which of themselves are most indifferent to be used or not used. The same conformity is not less opposite unto reason,* first, inasmuch as contraries must be cured by their contraries; and therefore popery being antichristianity, is not healed but by establishment of orders thereunto opposite. The way to bring a drunken man to sobriety, is to carry him as far from excess of drink as may be. To rectify a crooked stick, we bend it on the contrary side, as far as it was at the first on that side from whence we draw it; and so it cometh in the end to a middle between both, which is perfect straitness. Utter inconformity therefore with the church of Rome in these things, is the best and surest policy which the church can use. While we use their ceremonies, they take occasion to blaspheme, saying that our religion cannot stand by it self, unless it lean upon the staff of their ceremonies. (a) *They hereby conceive great hope* (a) T.C. l. 4. p. 178. *of having the rest of their popery in the end, which hope causeth them to be more frozen in their wickedness.* Neither is it without cause that they have this hope, considering that which Mr. Bucer noteth upon the eighteenth of saint Matthew, that where these things have been left, popery hath returned; but on the other part, in places which have been cleansed of these things, it hath not yet been seen that it hath had any (b) T.C. l. 3. p. 179. entrance. (b) *None make such clamours for these ceremonies, as the papists,* and those whom they suborn; *a manifest token how much they triumph and joy in these things.* They breed *grief of mind in a number that are godly-minded, and have antichristianity in such detestation, that their minds are martyred with the very sight of them in the church.* Such godly brethren we ought not thus to grieve with unprofitable ce- T.C. l. 3. p. 180. remonies, yea ceremonies wherein there is not only no profit, but also danger of great

hurt

hurt that may grow to the church by infection, which popish ceremonies are means to breed. This in effect is the fum and fubftance of that which they bring by way of oppofition againft thofe orders which we have common with the church of *Rome*; thefe are the reafons wherewith they would prove our ceremonies in that refpect worthy of blame.

4. Before we anfwer unto thefe things, we are to cut off that, whereunto they from whom thefe objections proceed, do oftentimes fly for defence and fuccour, when the force and ftrength of their argument is elided. For the ceremonies in ufe amongft us being in no other refpect retained, faving only for that to retain them is to our feeming good and profitable, yea fo profitable and fo good, that if we had either fimply taken them clean away, or elfe removed them fo as to place in their ftead others, we had done worfe; the plain and direct way againft us herein had been only to prove, that all fuch ceremonies as they require to be abolifh'd, are retained by us to the hurt of the church, or with lefs benefit than the abolifhment of them would bring. But forafmuch as they faw how hardly they fhould be able to perform this, they took a more compendious way, traducing the ceremonies of our church under the name of being popifh. The caufe why this way feemed better unto them was, for that the name of popery is more odious than very paganifm amongft divers of the more fimple fort; fo whatfoever they hear named popifh they prefently conceive deep hatred againft it, imagining there can be nothing contained in that name, but needs it muft be exceeding detestable. The ears of the people they have therefore filled with ftrong clamours. *The church of* England *is fraught with popifh ceremonies : they that favour the caufe of reformation, maintain nothing but the fincerity of the gofpel of* Jefus Chrift : *all fuch as withftand them fight for the laws of his fworn enemy, uphold the filthy relicks of antichrift ; and are defenders of that which is* popifh. Thefe are the notes wherewith are drawn from the hearts of the multitude fo many fighs ; with thefe tunes their minds are exafperated againft the lawful guides and governours of their fouls : thefe are the voices that fill them with general difcontentment, as tho the bofom of that famous church wherein they live were more noifom than any dungeon. But when the authors of fo fcandalous incantations are examined and called to account, how can they juftify fuch their dealings ? When they are urged directly to anfwer, whether it be lawful for us to ufe any fuch ceremonies as the church of *Rome* ufeth, altho the fame be not commanded in the word of God ; being driven to fee that the ufe of fome fuch ceremonies muft of neceffity be granted lawful, they go about to make us believe that they are juft of the fame opinion, and that they only think fuch ceremonies are not to be ufed when they are unprofitable, or when as good or better may be eftablifhed. Which anfwer is both idle in regard of us, and alfo repugnant to themfelves. It is, in regard of us, very vain to make this anfwer, becaufe they know that what ceremonies we retain common unto the church of *Rome*, we therefore retain them, for that we judge them to be profitable, and to be fuch that others inftead of them would be worfe. So that when they fay that we ought to abrogate fuch romifh ceremonies as are unprofitable, or elfe might have other more profitable in their ftead, they trifle, and they beat the air about nothing which toucheth us, unlefs they mean that we ought to abrogate all romifh ceremonies, which in their judgment have either no ufe, or lefs ufe than fome other might have. But then muft they fhew fome commiffion, whereby they are authorized to fit as judges, and we required to take their judgment for good in this cafe. Otherwife, their fentences will not be greatly regarded, when they oppofe their me-thinketh unto the orders of the church of *England :* as in the queftion about furplices one of them doth ; *If we look to the colour, black me-thinks is the more decent ; if to the form, a garment down to the foot hath a great deal more comelinefs in it.* If they think that we ought to prove the ceremonies commodious which we have retained, they do in this point very greatly deceive themfelves. For in all right and equity, that which the church hath received and held fo long for good, that which publick approbation hath ratified, muft carry the benefit of prefumption with it to be accounted meet and convenient. They which have ftood up as yefterday to challenge it of defect, muft prove their challenge. If we being defendents do anfwer, that the ceremonies in queftion, are godly, comely, decent, profitable for the church ; their reply is childifh and unorderly to fay, that we demand the thing in queftion, and fhew the po-

That whereas they who blame us in this behalf, when reafon evicteth that all fuch ceremonies are not to be abolifh'd, make anfwer ; That when they condemn popifh ceremonies, their meaning is of ceremonies unprofitable, or ceremonies, inftead whereof as good or better may be devifed : they cannot hereby get out of the briars, but contradict and gainfay themfelves : infafmuch as their ufual manner is to prove that ceremonies uncommanded in the church of God, and yet ufed in the church of Rome, are for this very caufe unprofitable to us, and not fo good as others in their place would be.

T. C. l. 3. p. 171. What an open untruth is it, that this is one of our principles, not to be lawful to ufe the fame ceremonies which the papifts did ; when as I have both before declared the contrary, and even here have exprefly added, that they are not to be ufed when as good or better may be eftablifhed ?

Ecclef. difcip. fol. 100.

T. C. l. 3. p. 176. As for your often repeating that the ceremonies in queftion are godly, comely, and decent : it is your old wont of demanding the thing in queftion, and an undoubted argument of your extreme poverty. T. C. l. 3. p. 174.

verty

verty of our caufe, the goodnefs whereof we are fain to beg that our adverfaries would grant. For on our part this muft be the anfwer, which orderly proceeding doth require. The burthen of proving doth reft on them. In them it is frivolous to fay we ought not to ufe bad ceremonies of the church of *Rome*, and prefume all fuch bad as it pleafeth themfelves to diflike, unlefs we can perfuade them the contrary. Befides, they are herein oppofite alfo to themfelves. For what one thing is fo common with them, as to ufe the cuftom of the church of *Rome* for an argument to prove, that fuch and fuch ceremonies cannot be good and profitable for us, inafmuch as that church ufeth them? Which ufual kind of difputing, fheweth that they do not difallow only thofe *Romifh* ceremonies which are unprofitable, but count all unprofitable which are *Romifh*, that is to fay, which have been devifed by the church of *Rome*, or which are ufed in that church and not prefcribed in the word of God. For this is the only limitation which they can ufe fuitable unto their other pofitions. And therefore the caufe which they yield, why they hold it lawful to retain in *doctrine* and in *difcipline* fome things as good, which yet are common to the church of *Rome*, is, for that thofe good things are perpetual commandments in whofe place no other can come: but ceremonies are changeable. So that their judgment in truth is, that whatfoever by the word of God is not changeable in the church of *Rome*, that church's ufing is a caufe why reformed churches ought to change it, and not to think it good or profitable. And left we feem to father any thing upon them more than is properly their own, let them read even their own words, where they complain, That we *are thus conftrained to be like unto the papifts in any their ceremonies*; yea, they urge that this caufe, altho it were alone, ought to move them to whom that belongeth, to do them away, *forafmuch as they are their ceremonies*; and that the bifhop of *Salifbury* doth juftify this their complaint. The claufe is untrue which they add concerning the bifhop of *Salifbury*, but the fentence doth fhew that we do them no wrong in fetting down the ftate of the

T. C. l. 3. p. 177. And that this complaint of ours is juft, in that we are thus conftrained to be like unto the papifts in any their ceremonies; and that this caufe only ought to move them to whom that belongeth, to do theirs away, forafmuch as they are their ceremonies, the reader may farther fee in the bifhop of Salifbury, who brings divers proofs thereof.

queftion between us thus: Whether we ought to abolifh out of the church of *England* all fuch orders, rites and ceremonies as are eftablifhed in the church of *Rome*, and are not prefcribed in the word of God. For the affirmative whereof we are now to anfwer fuch proofs of theirs as have been before alledged.

5. Let the church of *Rome* be what it will, let them that are of it be the people of God and our fathers in the chriftian faith, or let them be otherwife; hold them for catholicks, or hold them for hereticks, it is not a thing either one way or other in this prefent queftion greatly material. Our conformity with them in fuch things as have been propofed is not proved as yet unlawful by all this. St. *Auguftine* hath faid, yea, and we have allowed his faying, *That the cuftom of the people of God, and the decrees of our forefathers are to be kept, touching thofe things whereof the fcripture hath neither one way nor other given us any charge.* What then? Doth it here therefore follow, that they, being neither the people of God, nor our forefathers, are for that caufe in nothing to be followed? This confequent were good, if fo be it were granted, that only the cuftom of the people of God, and the decrees of our forefathers are in fuch cafe to be obferv'd. But then fhould no other kind of latter laws in the church be good, which were a grofs abfurdity to think. St. *Auguftine's* fpeech therefore doth import, that where we have no divine precept, if yet we have the cuftom of the people of God, or a decree of our forefathers, this is a law, and muft be kept. Notwithftanding it is not denied, but that we lawfully may obferve the pofitive conftitutions of our own churches, altho the fame were but yefterday made by our felves alone. Nor is there any thing in this to prove, that the church of *England* might not by law receive orders, rites or cuftoms from the church of *Rome*, altho they were neither the people of God nor yet our forefathers. How much lefs, when we have received from them nothing but that which they did themfelves receive from fuch as we cannot deny to have been the people of God, yea fuch as either we muft acknowledge for our own forefathers, or elfe difdain the race of Chrift?

That our allowing the cuftoms of our fathers to be followed, is no proof that we may not allow fome cuftoms which the church of Rome hath, altho we do not account of them as of our fathers,

6. The rites and orders wherein we follow the church of *Rome*, are of no other kind than fuch as the church of *Geneva* it felf doth follow them in. We follow the church of *Rome* in more things; yet they in fome things of the fame nature about which our prefent controverfy is: fo that the difference is not in the kind, but in the number of rites only, wherein they and we do follow the church of *Rome*. The ufe of wafer-cakes, the cuftom of godfathers and godmothers in baptifm are things not commanded nor forbidden in the fcripture, things which have been of old, and are retained in the church of *Rome* even at this very hour. Is conformity with *Rome* in fuch things a blemifh unto the church

That the courfe which the wifdom of God doth teach, maketh not againft our conformity with the church of Rome in fuch things.

of

of *England*, and unto churches abroad an ornament ? Let them, if not for the reverence they owe unto this church (in the bowels whereof they have received I truſt that precious and bleſſed vigour, which ſhall quicken them to eternal life) yet at the leaſtwiſe for the ſingular affection which they do bear towards others, take heed how they ſtrike, leſt they wound whom they would not. For undoubtedly it cutteth deeper than they are aware of, when they plead that even ſuch ceremonies of the church of *Rome* as contain in them nothing which is not of it ſelf agreeable to the word of God, ought nevertheleſs to be aboliſhed, and that neither the word of God, nor reaſon, nor the examples of the eldeſt churches do permit the church of *Rome* to be therein followed. Hereticks they are, and they are our neighbours. By us and amongſt us they lead their lives. But what then ? Therefore is no ceremony of theirs lawful for us to uſe ? We muſt yield and will, that none are lawful if God himſelf be a precedent againſt the uſe of any. But how appeareth it

T.C.l.1.p.89. that God is ſo ? Hereby, they ſay, it doth appear, in that *God ſevered his people from*
& 131. *the heathens, but eſpecially from the Egyptians, and ſuch nations as were neareſt neigh-*
Lev. 18. 3. *bours unto them, by forbidding them to do thoſe things which were in themſelves very*
lawful to be done, yea very profitable ſome, and incommodious to be forborn : ſuch things
it pleaſed God to forbid them only becauſe thoſe heathens did them, with whom conformi-
Levit. 19. 27. *ty in the ſame thing might have bred infection.* Thus in *ſhaving, cutting, apparel-*
& 19. 19. *wearing, yea in ſundry kinds of meats alſo, ſwines-fleſh, conies and ſuch like, they were*
Deut. 22. 11. *forbidden to do ſo and ſo, becauſe the gentiles did ſo. And the end why God forbad*
& 14. 7. *them ſuch things was to ſever them, for fear of infection, by a great and an high wall,*
Levit. 11. *from other nations,* as ſaint Paul teacheth. The cauſe of more careful ſeparation from
Epheſ. 2. 14. the neareſt nations was, the greatneſs of danger to be eſpecially by them infected. Now,
papiſts are to us as thoſe nations were unto *Iſrael.* Therefore if the wiſdom of God
be our guide, we cannot allow conformity with them, no not in any ſuch indifferent ceremonies. Our direct anſwer hereunto is, that for any thing here alledged we may ſtill
doubt whether the Lord in ſuch indifferent ceremonies as thoſe whereof we diſpute did
frame his people of ſet purpoſe unto any utter diſſimilitude, either with *Egyptians,* or
with any other nation elſe. And if God did not forbid them all ſuch indifferent ceremonies, then our conformity with the church of *Rome* in ſome ſuch is not hitherto as yet
diſproved, altho *papiſts* were unto us as thoſe *heathens* were unto *Iſrael. After*
Levit. 18. 3. *the doings of the land of Egypt, wherein you dwelt, ye ſhall not do, ſaith the Lord ;*
and after the manner of the land of Canaan, whither I will bring you, ſhall ye not do,
neither walk in their ordinances : do after my judgments, and keep my ordinances to
walk therein : I am the Lord your God. The ſpeech is indefinite, *Ye ſhall not be like*
them : it is not general, *Ye ſhall not be like them in any thing, or like to them in any*
thing indifferent, or like unto them in any indifferent ceremony of theirs. Seeing therefore it is not ſet down how far the bounds of his ſpeech concerning diſſimilitude ſhould
reach, how can any man aſſure us that it extendeth farther than to thoſe things only
wherein the nations there mentioned were idolatrous, or did againſt that which the law
of God commandeth ? Nay, doth it not ſeem a thing very probable, that God doth
purpoſely add, *Do after my judgments,* as giving thereby to underſtand that his meaning in the former ſentence was but to bar ſimilitude in ſuch things as were repugnant unto
the ordinances, laws and ſtatutes which he had given ? *Egyptians* and *Canaanites* are
for example ſake named unto them, becauſe the cuſtoms of the one they had been, and
of the other they ſhould be beſt acquainted with. But that wherein they might not be
like unto either of them, was ſuch peradventure as had been no whit leſs unlawful,
altho thoſe nations had never been. So that there is no neceſſity to think that God for
fear of infection by reaſon of nearneſs, forbad them to be like unto the *Canaanites* or
the *Egyptians* in thoſe things which otherwiſe had been lawful enough. For I would
know what one thing was in thoſe nations, and is here forbidden, being indifferent in it
ſelf, yet forbidden only becauſe they uſed it. In the laws of *Iſrael* we find it written,
Levit. 19. 27. *Ye ſhall not cut round the corners of your heads, neither ſhalt thou tear the tufts of thy*
beard. Theſe things were uſual amongſt thoſe nations, and in themſelves they are indifferent. But are they indifferent, being uſed as ſigns of immoderate and hopeleſs lamentation for the dead ? In this ſenſe it is that the law forbiddeth them. For which cauſe
the very next words following are, *Ye ſhall not cut your fleſh for the dead, nor make any*
print of a mark upon you ; I am the Lord. The like in *Leviticus,* where ſpeech is of
Levit. 21. 5. mourning for the dead, *They ſhall not make bald parts upon their head, nor ſhave off the*
locks of their beard, nor make any cutting in their fleſh. Again in *Deuteronomy, Ye*
Deut. 14. 1. *are the children of the Lord your God ; ye ſhall not cut your ſelves, nor make you*
baldneſs between your eyes for the dead. What is this but in effect the ſame which the
1 Theſſ. 4. 13. apoſtle doth more plainly expreſs, ſaying, *Sorrow not as they do who have no hope ?*

The

The very light of nature it self was able to see herein a fault; that which those nations did use having been also in use with others, the antient *Roman* laws do forbid. That shaving therefore and cutting which the law doth mention, was not a matter in it self indifferent, and forbidden only because it was in use amongst such idolaters as were neighbours to the people of God; but to use it had been a crime, had no other people or nation under heaven should have done it saving only themselves. As for those laws concerning attires, *There shall no garment of linen and woollen come upon thee*; as also those touch- Levit. 19. 19.
ing food and diet, wherein *swines-flesh* together with sundry other meats are forbidden; Deut. 22. 11. the use of these things had been indeed of it self harmless and indifferent: so that hereby it doth appear, how the law of God forbad in some special consideration, such things as were lawful enough in themselves. But yet even here they likewise fail of that they intend. For it doth not appear that the consideration in regard whereof the law forbiddeth Deut 14. 7. these things, was because those nations did use them. Likely enough it is that the *Ca-* Levit. 11.
Levit. 19. 19. *naanites* used to feed as well on sheep as on swines-flesh; and therefore if the forbidding of the latter had no other reason than dissimilitude with that people, they which of their own heads alledge this for reason, can shew I think some reason more than we are able to find why the former was not also forbidden. Might there not be some other mystery in this prohibition than they think of? Yes, some other mystery there was in it by all like- lihood. For what reason is there, which should but induce, and therefore much less in- Deut. 14.
Levit. 11. force us to think that care of dissimilitude between the people of God and the heathen na- tions about them, was any more the cause of forbidding them to put on garments of sun- dry stuff, than of charging them withal not to sow their fields with meslin; or that this was any more the cause of forbidding them to eat swines-flesh, than of charging them withal not to eat the flesh of *eagles, hawks,* and the like? Wherefore altho the church of *Rome* were to us, as to *Israel* the *Egyptians* and *Canaanites* were of old; yet doth it not follow that the wisdom of God without respect doth teach us to erect between us and them a partition-wall of difference in such things indifferent as have been hitherto Ephes. 2. 14. disputed of.

7. Neither is the example of the eldest churches a whit more available to this purpose, That the ex- notwithstanding some fault undoubtedly there is in the very resemblance of idolaters. ample of the Were it not some kind of blemish to be like unto infidels and heathens, it would not so eldest churches
is not herein usually be objected; men would not think it any advantage in the causes of religion to against us. be able therewith justly to charge their adversaries as they do. Wherefore to the end that T.C.l.1. p.131. it may a little more plainly appear what force this hath and how far the same extendeth, The councils we are to note how all men are naturally desirous, that they may seem neither to judge altho they
did not ob- nor to do amiss, because every error and offence is a stain to the beauty of nature, for serve them- which cause it blusheth thereat, but glorieth in the contrary; from whence it riseth, that selves always
in making of they which disgrace or depress the credit of others, do it either in both or in one of these. decrees this To have been in either directed by a weak and unperfect rule, argueth imbecillity and im- rule, yet have
kept this con- perfection. Men being either led by reason, or by imitation of other mens examples; if sideration con- their persons be odious whose example we chuse to follow, as namely, if we frame our tinually in ma-
king of their opinions to that which condemned hereticks think, or direct our actions according to laws, that that which is practised and done by them; it lies as an heavy prejudice against us, unless they would somewhat mightier than their bare example did move us to think or do the same things have christians
differ from with them. Christian men therefore having besides the common light of all men, so great others in their help of heavenly direction from above, together with the lamps of so bright examples as ceremonies. the church of God doth yield, it cannot but worthily seem reproachful for us to leave both the one and the other to become disciples unto the most hateful sort that live, to do as they do, only because we see their example before us, and have a delight to follow it. Thus we may therefore safely conclude, that it is not evil simply to concur with the hea- thens either in opinion or in action: and that conformity with them is only then a dis- grace, when either we follow them in that they think and do amiss, or follow them gene- rally in that they do, without other reason than only the liking we have to the pattern of their example: which liking doth intimate a more universal approbation of them than is allowable. *Faustus* the manichee therefore objecting against the Jews, that they forsook the idols of the gentiles; but their temples, and oblations, and altars, and priesthoods, and all kind of ministry of holy things, they exercised even as the gentiles did, yea more super- stitiously a great deal; against the catholick christians likewise, that between them and the heathens there was in many things little difference; *From them* (saith *Faustus*) *ye have* Tom. 6. cont. *learned to hold that one only God is the author of all; their sacrifices you have turned in-* Faust. manich.
lib. 20. cap. 4. *to feasts of charity, their idols into martyrs, whom ye honour with the like religious of- fices unto theirs; the ghosts of the dead ye appease with wine and delicates, the festi- val days of the nations ye celebrate together with them, and of their kind of life ye* have

have utterly changed nothing. Saint *Auguftine's* defence in behalf of both, is, that touching the matters of action, Jews and catholick chriftians were free from the gentiles faultinefs, even in thofe things which were objected as tokens of their agreement with the gentiles : and concerning their confent in opinion, they did not hold the fame with the gentiles becaufe gentiles had fo taught, but becaufe heaven and earth had fo witneffed the fame to be truth, that neither the one fort could err in being fully perfuaded thereof, nor the other but err in cafe they fhould not confent with them.   In things of their own na-

T. C. l. 1. p. 132. Alfo it was decreed in another council that they fhould not deck their houfes with bay leaves and green boughs. becaufe the pagans did ufe fo ; and that they fhould not reft from their labour thofe days that the pagans did, that they fhould not keep the firft day of every month as they did.

ture indifferent, if either councils, or particular men have at any time with found judgment mifliked conformity between the church of God and infidels, the caufe whereof hath been fomewhat elfe than only affectation of diffimilitude, they faw it neceffary fo to do inrefpect of fome fpecial accident, which the church being not always fubject unto hath not ftill caufe to do the like.   For example, in the dangerous days of tryal, wherein there was no way for the truth of Jefus Chrift to triumph over infidelity but thro the conftancy of his faints, whom yet a natural defire to fave themfelves from the flame might peradventure caufe to join with pagans in external cuftoms, too far ufing the fame as a cloak to conceal themfelves in, and a mift to darken the eyes of infidels withal ; for remedy hereof thofe laws it might be were provided, which forbad that chriftians fhould deck their houfes with boughs as the pagans did ufe to do, or reft thofe feftival days whereon the pagans refted, or celebrate fuch feafts as were tho not heathenifh, yet, fuch as the fimpler fort of hea-

T.C l.1.p.132. Tertul. faith, O, faith he, better is the religion,of the heathen for they ufe no folemnity of the chriftians, neither the Lord's day, neither, &c. but are not a-fraid to be cal-led heathen.
T.C. l.1.p.133. But having fhewed this in general to be the policy of God firft, and of his people after-wards, to put as much dif-ference as can be commodi-oufly between the people of God and o-thers which are not, I fhall not, &c.

thens might be beguiled in fo thinking them.   As for *Tertullian's* judgment concerning the rites and orders of the church, no man, having judgment can be ignorant how juft exceptions may be taken againft it.   His opinion touching the catholick church was as unindifferent, as touching our church the opinion of them that favour this pretended reformation is ; he judged all them who did not montanize to be but carnally minded ; he judged them ftill over-abjectly to fawn upon the heathens, and to curry favour with infidels ; which as the catholick church did well provide that they might not do indeed, fo *Tertullian* over often thro difcontentment carpeth injurioufly at them, as tho they did it even when they were free from fuch meaning.   But if it were fo that either the judgment of thofe councils before alledged, or of *Tertullian* himfelf againft the chriftians, are in no fuch confideration to be underftood as we have mentioned ; if it were fo, that men are condemned as well of the one as of the other, only for ufing the ceremonies of a religion contrary unto their own, and that this caufe is fuch as ought to prevail no lefs with us than with them ; fhall it not follow, that feeing there is ftill between our religion and paganifm the felf-fame contrariety, therefore we are no lefs rebukeable if we now deck our houfes with boughs, or fend new-years gifts unto our friends, or feaft on thofe days which the gentiles then did, or fit after prayer as they were accuftomed ?   For fo they infer upon the premifes, that as great difference as commodioufly may be there fhould be in all outward ceremonies between the people of God, and them which are not his people.   Again, they teach, as hath been declared, that there is not as great a difference as may be between them, except the one do avoid whatfoever rites and ceremonies uncommanded of God the other doth embrace.   So that generally they teach that the very difference of fpiritual condition it felf between the fervants of Chrift and others, requireth fuch difference in ceremonies between them, altho the one be never fo far disjoined in time or place from the other.   But in cafe the people of God and Belial do chance to be neighbours ; then as the danger of infection is greater, fo the fame difference they fay is thereby made more neceffary.   In this refpect as the Jews were fevered from the heathen, fo moft efpecially from the heathen neareft them.   And in the fame refpect we, which ought to differ howfoever from the church of *Rome,* are now, they fay, by reafon of our nearnefs, more bound to differ from them in ceremonies than from *Turks.*   A ftrange kind of fpeech unto chriftian ears, and fuch as, I hope, they themfelves do acknowledge unadvifedly uttered.   *We are not fo much to fear infection from Turks as from papifts.*   What of that ?   we muft remember that by conforming rather our felves in that refpect to *Turks,* we fhould be fpreaders of a worfe infection into others than any we are likely to draw from papifts by our conformity with them in ceremonies.   If they did hate, as *Turks* do, the chriftian, or as *Cananites* did of old the jewifh religion, even in grofs ; the circumftance of local nearnefs in them unto us, might haply inforce in us a duty of greater feparation from them than from thofe other mentioned.   But forafmuch as papifts are fo much in Chrift nearer unto us than *Turks,* is there any reafonable man, trow you, but will judge it meeter that our ceremonies of chriftian religion fhould be popifh, than turkifh or heathenifh ?   efpecially confidering that we

t   were

were not brought to dwell amongſt them (as *Iſrael* in *Canaan*) having not been of them. For even a very part of them we were. And when God did by his good Spirit put it into our hearts, firſt to reform our ſelves (whence grew our ſeparation) and then by all good means to ſeek alſo their reformation ; had we not only cut off their corruptions but alſo eſtranged our ſelves from them in things indifferent, who ſeeth not how greatly prejudicial this might have been to ſo good a cauſe, and what occaſion it had given them to think (to their greater obduration in evil) that thro a froward or wanton deſire of innovation, we did unconſtrainedly thoſe things for which conſcience was pretended ? Howſoever the cauſe doth ſtand, as *Juda* had been rather to chuſe conformity in things indifferent with *Iſrael* when they were neareſt oppoſites, than with the fartheſt removed pagans ; ſo we in like caſes, much rather with papiſts than with *Turks*. I might add farther for a more full and complete anſwer, ſo much concerning the large odds between the caſe of the eldeſt churches in regard of thoſe heathens and ours in reſpect of the church of *Rome*, that very cavillation it ſelf ſhould be ſatisfied, and have no ſhift to fly unto.

8. But that no one thing may detain us over long, I return to their reaſons againſt our conformity with that church. That extreme diſſimilitude which they urge upon us, is now commended as our beſt and ſafeſt policy for eſtabliſhment of ſound religion. The ground of which politick poſition is, That *evils muſt be cured by their contraries* ; and therefore the cure of the church infected with the poiſon of antichriſtianity, muſt be done by that which is thereunto as contrary as may be. A medled eſtate of the orders of the goſpel and the ceremonies of popery, is not the beſt way to baniſh popery. We are contrariwiſe of opinion, that he which will perfectly recover a ſick and reſtore a diſeaſed body unto health, muſt not endeavour ſo much to bring it to a ſtate of ſimple contrariety, as of fit proportion in contrariety unto thoſe evils which are to be cured. He that will take away extreme heat by ſetting the body in extremity of cold, ſhall undoubtedly remove the diſeaſe, but together with it the diſeaſed too. The firſt thing therefore in skilful cures is the knowledge of the part affected ; the next is of the evil which doth affect it ; the laſt is not only of the kind, but alſo of the meaſure of contrary things whereby to remove it. They which meaſure religion by diſlike of the church of *Rome*, think every man ſo much the more ſound, by how much he can make the corruptions thereof to ſeem more large. And therefore ſome there are, namely the *Arians* in reformed churches of *Poland*, which imagine the canker to have eaten ſo far into the very bones and marrow of the church of *Rome*, as if it had not ſo much as a ſound belief, no, not concerning God himſelf ; but that the very belief of the Trinity were a part of antichriſtian corruption ; and that the wonderful providence of God did bring to paſs that the biſhop of the ſee of *Rome* ſhould be famous for his triple crown ; a ſenſible mark whereby the world might know him to be that myſtical beaſt ſpoken of in the Revelation, to be that great and notorious antichriſt in no one reſpect ſo much as in this, that he maintaineth the doctrine of the Trinity. Wiſdom therefore and skill is requiſite to know what parts are ſound in that church, and what corrupted. Neither is it to all men apparent, which complain of unſound parts, with what kind of unſoundneſs every ſuch part is poſſeſſed. They can ſay, that in *doctrine*, in *diſcipline*, in *prayers*, in *ſacraments*, the church of *Rome* hath (as it hath indeed) very foul and groſs corruptions ; the nature whereof notwithſtanding becauſe they have not for the moſt part exact skill and knowledge to diſcern, they think that amiſs many times which is not ; and the ſalve of reformation they mightily call for ; but where and what the ſores are which need it, as they wot full little, ſo they think it not greatly material to ſearch. Such mens contentment muſt be wrought by ſtratagem ; the uſual method of art is not for them. But with thoſe that profeſs more than ordinary and common knowledge of good from evil, with them that are able to put a difference between things naught and things indifferent in the church of *Rome*, we are yet at controverſy about the manner of removing that which is naught : whether it may not be perfectly helped, unleſs that alſo which is indifferent be cut off with it ſo far till no rite or ceremony remain which the church of *Rome* hath, being not found in the word of God. If we think this too extreme, they reply, that to draw men from great exceſs is not amiſs, tho we uſe them unto ſomewhat leſs than is competent ; and that a crooked ſtick is not ſtraitned, unleſs it be bent as far on the clean contrary ſide, that ſo it may ſettle it ſelf at the length in a middle eſtate of evenneſs between both. But how can theſe compariſons ſtand them in any ſtead ? When they urge us to extreme oppoſition

Marginal notes:

That it is not our beſt policy for the eſtabliſhment of ſound religion, to have in theſe things no agreement with the church of *Rome* being unſound.

T.C. l.1.p.131. Common reaſon ſo doth teach that contraries are cured by their contraries. Now chriſtianity and antichriſtianity, the goſpel and popery, be contraries ; and therefore antichriſtianity muſt be cured, not by it ſelf, but by that which is (as much as may be) contrary unto it.

T.C. l.1.p.132. If a man would bring a drunken man to ſobriety, the beſt and neareſt way is to carry him

Footnote:

as far from his exceſs in drink as may be : and if a man could not keep a mean, it were better to fault in preſcribing leſs than he ſhould drink, than to fault in giving him more than we ought. As we ſee, to bring a ſtick which is crooked to be ſtrait, we do not only bow it ſo far until it come to be ſtrait, but we bend it ſo far until we make it to be ſo crooked on the other ſide as it was before of the firſt ſide ; to this end, that at the laſt it may ſtand ſtrait, and as it were in the mid-way, between both the crooks.

againſt

against the church of *Rome*, do they mean we should be drawn unto it only for a time, and afterwards return to a mediocrity? Or was it the purpose of those reformed churches which utterly abolished all popish ceremonies, to come in the end back again to the middle point of evenness and moderation? Then have we conceived amiss of their meaning. For we have always thought their opinion to be, that utter inconformity with the church of *Rome* was not an extremity whereunto we should be drawn for a time; but the very mediocrity it self wherein they meant we should ever continue. Now by these comparisons it seemeth clean contrary, that howsoever they have bent themselves at first to an extreme contrariety against the *Romish* church, yet therein they will continue no longer than only till such time as some more moderate course for establishment of the church may be concluded. Yea, albeit this were not at the first their intent, yet surely now there is great cause to lead them unto it. They have seen that experience of the former policy which may cause the authors of it to hang down their heads. When *Germany* had stricken off that which appeared corrupt in the doctrine of the church of *Rome*, but seemed nevertheless in discipline still to retain therewith very great conformity; *France*, by that rule of policy which hath been before mentioned, took away the popish orders which *Germany* did retain. But process of time hath brought more light into the world; whereby men perceiving that they of the religion in *France* have also retained some orders which were before in the church of *Rome*, and are not commanded in the word of God; there hath arisen a sect in *England*, which following still the very self-same rule of policy seeketh to reform even the *French* reformation, and purge out from thence also dregs of popery. These have not taken as yet such root that they are able to establish any thing. But if they had, what would spring out of their stock, and how far the unquiet wit of man might be carried with rules of such policy, God doth know. The trial which we have lived to see, may somewhat teach us what posterity is to fear. But our Lord, of his infinite mercy, avert whatsoever evil our swervings on the one hand or on the other may threaten unto the state of his church.

9. That the church of *Rome* doth hereby take occasion to blaspheme, and to say our religion is not able to stand of it self, unless it lean upon the staff of their ceremonies, is not a matter of so great moment that it did need to be objected, or doth deserve to receive an answer. The name of blasphemy in this place, is like the shoe of *Hercules* on a child's foot. If the church of *Rome* do use any such kind of silly exprobration, it is no such ugly thing to the ear that we should think the honour and credit of our religion to receive thereby any great wound. They which hereof make so perillous a matter do seem to imagine, that we have erected of late a frame of some new religion; the furniture whereof we should not have borrowed from our enemies, lest they relieving us might afterwards laugh and gibe at our poverty: whereas in truth the ceremonies which we have taken from such as were before us, are not things that belong to this or that sect, but they are the antient rites and customs of the church of Christ; whereof our selves being a part, we have the self-same interest in them which our fathers before us had, from whom the same are descended unto us. Again, in case we had been so much beholden privately unto them, doth the reputation of one church stand by saying unto another, *I need thee not?* If some should be so vain and impotent as to mar a benefit with reproachful upbraiding, where at the least they suppose themselves to have bestowed some good turn; yet surely a wife body's part it were not, to put out his fire because his fond and foolish neighbour from whom he borrowed peradventure wherewith to kindle it, might haply cast him therewith in the teeth, saying, were it not for me thou wouldst freeze, and not be able to heat thy self. As for that other argument derived from the secret affection of papists, with whom our conformity in certain ceremonies is said to put them in great hope that their whole religion in time will have re-entrance, and therefore none are so clamorous amongst us for the observation of these ceremonies as papists, and such as papists suborn to speak for them, whereby it clearly appeareth how much they rejoice, how much they triumph in these things; our answer hereunto is still the same, that the benefit we have by such ceremonies over-weigheth even this also. No man that is not exceeding partial can well deny, but that there is most just cause wherefore we should be offended greatly at the church of *Rome*. Notwithstanding at such times as we are to deliberate for our selves, the freer our minds are from all distempered affections, the sounder and better is our judgment. When we are in a fretting mood at the church of *Rome*, and with that angry disposition enter into any cogitation of the orders and rites of our church, taking particular survey of them, we are sure to have always one eye fixed upon the countenance of our enemies, and according to the blithe or heavy aspect thereof our other eye sheweth some other suitable token either of dislike or approbation towards our own orders. For the rule of our judgment in such case being only

*
that

That we are not to abolish our ceremonies either because papists upbraid us as having taken from them, or for that they are said hereby to conceive I know not what great hopes.

T.C.l.3,p.178.

By using of these ceremonies, the papists take occasion to blaspheme, saying that our religion cannot stand by it self, unless it lean upon the staff of their ceremonies.

T.C.l.3,p.179.

To prove the papists triumph and joy in these things, I alledged farther that there are none which make such clamours for these ceremonies, as the papists and those which they suborn.

that of *Homer*, *This is the thing which our enemies would have* ; what they seem con-Ἴκαν γεθάεται tented with, even for that very cause we reject ; and there is nothing but it pleaseth Πεΐ αμῷ. us much the better, if we espy that it galleth them. Miserable were the state and con-dition of that church, the weighty affairs whereof should be ordered by those delibera-tions wherein such an humour as this were predominant. We have most heartily to thank God therefore, that they amongst us, to whom the first consultations of causes of this kind fell, were men which aiming at another mark, namely, the glory of God and the good of this his church, took that which they judged thereunto necessary, not re-jecting any good or convenient thing, only because the church of *Rome* might perhaps like it. If we have that which is meet and right, altho they be glad, we are not to envy them this their solace ; we do not think it a duty of ours to be in every such thing their tormentors. And whereas it is said, that popery for want of this utter extirpation hath in some places taken root and flourished a-gain, but hath not been able to re-establish it self in any place after provision made against it by utter evacuation of all *Romish* cere-monies, and therefore as long as we hold any thing like unto them, we put them in some more hope than if all were taken away : as

T. C. l. 3. p. 179. Thus they conceiving hope of having the rest of their popery in the end, it causeth them to be more frozen in their wickedness, *&c.* For not the cause but the occasion also ought to be taken away, *&c.* Altho let the reader judge, whether they have cause given to hope, that the tail of popery yet remain-ing, they shall the easilier hale in the whole body after : consider-ing also that Mr. *Bucer* noteth, that where these things have been left, there popery hath returned ; but on the other part, in places which have been cleansed of these dregs, it hath not been seen that it hath had any entrance.

we deny not but this may be true ; so being of two evils to chuse the less, we hold it better that the friends and favourers of the church of *Rome* should be in some kind of hope to have a corrupt religion restored, than both we and they conceive just fear left under colour of rooting out popery the most effectual means to bear up the state of religion be removed, and so a way made either for paganism or for extreme barbarity to enter. If desire of weakning the hope of others should turn us away from the course we have taken ; how much more the care of preventing our own fear, with-hold us from that we are urged unto ? especially seeing that our own fear we know, but we are not so certain what hope the rites and orders of our church have bred in the hearts of others. For it is no sufficient argument therefore to say, that in maintaining and urging these ceremonies, none are so clamorous as papists and they whom papists suborn ; this speech being more hard to justify than the former, and so their proof more doubtful than the thing it self which they prove. He that were cer-tain that this is true, must have marked who they be that speak for ceremonies ; he must have noted, who amongst them doth speak oftnest or is most earnest ; he must have been both acquainted thorowly with the religion of such, and also privy to what con-ferences or compacts are passed in secret between them and others ; which kind of no-tices are not wont to be vulgar and common. Yet they which alledge this, would have it taken as a thing that needeth no proof, a thing which all men know and see. And if so be it were granted them as true, what gain they by it ? Sundry of them that be popish are eager in maintenance of ceremonies. Is it so strange a matter to find a good thing fathered by ill men of a sinister intent and purpose, whose forwardness is not there-fore a bridle to such as favour the same cause with a better and a sincerer meaning ? They that seek, as they say, the removing of all popish orders out of the church, and reckon the state of bishops in the number of those orders, do (I doubt not) presume that the cause which they prosecute is holy. Notwithstanding it is their own ingenuous acknowledgment, that even this very cause which they term so often by an excellency, *The Lord's cause, is gratissima, most acceptable unto some which hope for prey and spoil* Eccles.dis.s.94. *by it, and that our age hath store of such, and that such are the very sectaries of* Dionysius *the famous atheist.* Now if hereupon we should upbraid them with irreligious, as they do us with superstitious favourers ; if we should follow them in their own kind of pleading, and say, that the most clamorous for this pretended reformation are either atheists or else proctors suborned by atheists ; the answer which herein they would make unto us, let them apply unto themselves, and there end. For they must not forbid us to presume our cause in defence of our church-orders to be as good as theirs against them, till the contrary be made manifest to the world.

10. In the mean while sorry we are, that any good and godly mind should be grieved The grief with that which is done. But to remedy their grief, lyeth not so much in us as in them-say, godly selves. They do not wish to be made glad with the hurt of the church : and to remove brethren con-all out of the church whereat they shew themselves to be sorrowful, would be, as we are of such cere-persuaded, hurtful if not pernicious thereunto. Till they be able to persuade the con-monies as we have common

with the church of *Rome. T. C. l. 3. p. 180.* There be numbers which have antichristianity in such detestation, that they cannot without grief of mind behold them. And afterwards, such godly brethren are not easily to be grieved, which they seem to be, when they are thus martyred in their minds for ceremonies, which (to speak the best of them) are unprofitable.

trary,

trary, they muſt and will, I doubt not, find out ſome other good mean to chear up
themſelves. Amongſt which means the example of *Geneva* may ſerve for one. Have
not they the old popiſh cuſtom of uſing godfathers and godmothers in baptiſm? the
old popiſh cuſtom of adminiſtring the bleſſed ſacrament of the holy euchariſt with wafer-cakes? Theſe things then the godly there can digeſt. Wherefore ſhould not the
godly here learn to do the like, both in them and in the reſt of the like nature? Some
farther mean peradventure it might be to aſſuage their grief, if ſo be they did conſider
the revenge they take on them which have been, as they interpret it, the workers of
their continuance in ſo great grief ſo long. For if the maintenance of ceremonies be a
corroſive to ſuch as oppugn them; undoubtedly to ſuch as maintain them it can be no great
pleaſure, when they behold how that which they reverence is oppugned. And therefore they that judge themſelves martyrs when they are grieved, ſhould think withal
what they are whom they grieve. For we are ſtill to put them in mind, that the cauſe
doth make no difference; for that it muſt be preſumed as good at the leaſt on our part
as on theirs, till it be in the end decided who have ſtood for truth and who for error.
So that till then the moſt effectual medicine, and withal the moſt ſound, to eaſe their
grief, muſt not be (in our opinion) the taking away of thoſe things whereat they are
grieved, but the altering of that perſuaſion which they have concerning the ſame. For
this we therefore both pray and labour; the more becauſe we are alſo perſuaded, that it
is but conceit in them to think that thoſe *Romiſh* ceremonies whereof we have hitherto

T.C.l.3.p.171. ſpoken, are like leprous clothes, infectious to the church; or like ſoft and gentle poiſons,
Altho the cor- the venom whereof being inſenſibly pernicious, worketh death and yet is never felt
ruptions in
them ſtrike working. Thus they ſay: but becauſe they ſay it only, and the world hath not as yet
not ſtrait to had ſo great experience of their art in curing the diſeaſes of the church, that the bare
the heart, yet
as gentle poi- authority of their word ſhould perſuade in a cauſe ſo weighty, they may not think much
ſons they con- if it be required at their hands to ſhew; firſt, by what means ſo deadly infection can
fume by little
and little. grow from ſimilitude between us and the church of *Rome* in theſe things indifferent: ſecondly, for that it were infinite, if the church ſhould provide againſt every ſuch evil as
may come to paſs, it is not ſufficient that they ſhew poſſibility of dangerous event, unleſs there appear ſome likelihood alſo of the ſame to follow in us, except we prevent it.
Nor is this enough, unleſs it be moreover made plain, that there is no good and ſufficient
way of prevention but by evacuating clean, and by emptying the church of every ſuch
rite and ceremony as is preſently called in queſtion. Till this be done, their good affection towards the ſafety of the church is acceptable, but the way they preſcribe us to
preſerve it by muſt reſt in ſuſpence. And leſt hereat they take occaſion to turn upon
Jer. 51. 9. us the ſpeech of the prophet *Jeremy* uſed againſt *Babylon*, *Behold we have done our
endeavour to cure the diſeaſes of Babylon, but ſhe thro her wilfulneſs doth reſt uncured:*
let them conſider into what ſtraits the church might drive it ſelf in being guided by this
their counſel. Their axiom is, that the ſound believing church of Jeſus Chriſt may not
be like heretical churches in any of thoſe indifferent things which men make choice of,
and do not take by preſcript appointment of the word of God. In the word of God
the uſe of bread is preſcribed as a thing without which the euchariſt may not be celebrated; but as for the kind of bread, it is not denied to be a thing indifferent. Being
indifferent of it ſelf, we are by this axiom of theirs to avoid the uſe of unleavened
bread in their ſacrament, becauſe ſuch bread the church of *Rome* being heretical uſeth.
But doth not the ſelf-ſame axiom bar us even from leavened bread alſo, which the church
of the *Grecians* uſeth, the opinions whereof are in a number of things the ſame for
which we condemn the church of *Rome*; and in ſome things erroneous, where the
church of *Rome* is acknowledged to be ſound; as namely, in the article of the Holy
Ghoſt's proceeding? And leſt here they ſhould ſay, that becauſe the *Greek* church is
farther off, and the church of *Rome* nearer, we are in that reſpect rather to uſe that
which the church of *Rome* uſeth not; let them imagine a reformed church in the city
of *Venice*, where a *Greek* church and popiſh both are: and when both theſe are equally
near, let them conſider what the third ſhall do. Without leavened or unleavened bread
it can have no ſacrament; the word of God doth tie it to neither; and their axiom
doth exclude it from both. If this conſtrain them, as it muſt, to grant that their axiom
is not to take any place ſave in thoſe things only where the church hath larger ſcope; it
reſteth, that they ſearch out ſome ſtronger reaſon than they have as yet alledged; otherwiſe they conſtrain not us to think that the church is tied unto any ſuch rule or axiom,
not then when ſhe hath the wideſt field to walk in and the greater ſtore of choice.

Their excep-   11. Againſt ſuch ceremonies generally as are the ſame in the church of *England* and
tion againſt of *Rome*, we ſee what hath been hitherto alledged. Albeit therefore we do not find
ſuch ceremo-
nies as we have received from the church of *Rome*, that church having taken them from the *Jews*,

the

the one church's having of such things to be sufficient cause why the other should not have them ; nevertheless in case it may be proved, that amongst the number of rites and orders common unto both, there are particulars the use whereof is utterly unlawful, in regard of some special bad and noisome quality ; there is no doubt but we ought to relinquish such rites and orders, what freedom soever we have to retain the other still.   As therefore we have heard their general exception against all those things, which being not commanded in the word of God were first received in the church of *Rome*, and from thence have been derived into ours, so it followeth that now we proceed unto certain kinds of them, as being excepted against, not only for that they are in the church of *Rome*, but are besides either *jewish* or abused unto idolatry and so grown scandalous.

The church of *Rome*, they say, being ashamed of the simplicity of the gospel, did almost out of all religions take whatsoever had any fair and gorgeous shew, borrowing in that respect from the *Jews* sundry of their abolished ceremonies. Thus by foolish and ridiculous imitation, all their massing furniture almost they took from the law, lest having an altar and a priest they should want vestments for their stage ; so that whatsoever we have in common with the church of *Rome*, if the same be of this kind, we ought to remove it. *Constantine* the emperor, speaking of the keeping of the feast of *Easter*, saith, *That it is an unworthy thing to have any thing common with that most spiteful company of the* Jews. And a little after he saith, *That it is most absurd and against reason, that the* Jews *should vaunt and glory that the christians could not keep those things without their doctrine.* And in another place it is said after this sort ; *It is convenient so to order the matter, that we have nothing common with that nation.* The council of *Laodicea*, which was afterward confirmed by the sixth general council, decreed, *That the christians should not take unleavened bread of the* Jews, *or communicate with their impiety.* For the easier manifestation of truth in this point, two things there are which must be considered ; namely, the causes wherefore the church should decline from *Jewish* ceremonies ; and how far it ought so to do. One cause is, that the *Jews* were the deadliest and spitefullest enemies of christianity that were in the world, and in this respect their orders so far forth to be shunned as we have already set down in handling the matter of heathenish ceremonies. For no enemies being so venomous against Christ as *Jews*, they were of all other most odious, and by that means, least to be used as fit church patterns for imitation. Another cause is, the solemn abrogation of the *Jews* ordinances : which ordinances for us to resume, were to check our Lord himself which hath disannulled them. But how far this second cause doth extend, it is not on all sides fully agreed upon. And touching those things whereunto it reacheth not, altho there be small cause wherefore the church should frame it self to the *Jews* example in respect of their persons which are most hateful ; yet God himself having been the author of their laws, herein they are (notwithstanding the former consideration) still worthy to be honoured, and to be followed above others, as much as the state of things will bear. *Jewish* ordinances had some things natural, and of the perpetuity of those things no man doubteth. That which was positive, we likewise know to have been, by the coming of Christ, partly necessary not to be kept, and partly indifferent to be kept or not. Of the former kind, circumcision and sacrifice were. For this point *Stephen* was accused, and the evidence which his accusers brought against him in judgment was, *This man ceaseth not to speak blasphemous words against this holy place and the law ; for we have heard him say, That this* Jesus *of* Nazareth *shall destroy this place, and shall change the ordinances that* Moses *gave us.* True it is, that this doctrine was then taught, which unbelievers condemning for blasphemy, did therein commit that which they did condemn. The apostles notwithstanding, from whom *Stephen* had received it, did not so teach the abrogation, no not of those things which were necessarily to cease, but that even the *Jews*, being christians, might for a time continue in them. And therefore in *Jerusalem* the first christian bishop not circumcised was *Mark* ; and he not bishop till the days of *Adrian* the emperor, after the overthrow of *Jerusalem* ; there having been fifteen bishops before him which were all of the circumcision. The christian *Jews* did think at the first, not only themselves, but the christian *gentiles* also bound, and that necessarily, to observe the whole law. There went forth certain of the sect of *pharisees* which did believe ; and they coming unto *Antioch* taught, that it was necessary for the *gentiles* to be circumcised and to keep the law of *Moses*. Whereupon there grew dissension, *Paul* and *Barnabas* disputing against them. The determination of the council held at *Jerusalem* concerning this matter, was finally this ; *Touching the* gentiles *which believe, we have written and determined, that they observe no such thing* : their protestation by letters is, *For as much as we have heard, that certain which departed from us, have troubled you with words, and cumbred your minds, saying, Ye must be*

circumcised

[marginal notes:]
Eccles. Disc. fol. 98, and T.C. l.3.p.131.
Many of these popish ceremonies faulty by reason of the pomp in them, where they should be agreeable to the simplicity of the gospel crucified.
T.C. l.1.p.132. Euseb. L.3.c.17. Socra. l. 1. c.9. To. 1. concil. Laud. can. 38.

Acts 6. 13,14.

Vide Niceph. lib. 3. cap. 25. & Sulpit. Sever. p. 149. in edit. Plant.

Acts 15.

Acts 21. 25. Acts 15. 24.

circumcifed and keep the law ; *know, that we gave them no fuch commandment*. *Paul*
therefore continued ftill teaching the *gentiles*, not only that they were not bound to obferve the laws of *Mofes*, but that the obfervation of thofe laws, which were neceffarily
to be abrogated, was in them altogether unlawful. In which point, his doctrine was
mif-reported, as tho he had every where preached this not only concerning the *gentiles*
but alfo touching the *Jews*. Wherefore coming unto *James* and the reft of the clergy
Acts 21. 20. at *Jerufalem*, they told him plainly of it, faying, *Thou feeft, brother, how many
thoufand* Jews *there are which believe, and they are all zealous of the law. Now they
are informed of thee, that thou teacheft all the* Jews *which are amongft the* gentiles, *to
forfake* Mofes, *and fayeft, that they ought not to circumcife their children, neither-to
live after the cuftoms*. And hereupon they give him counfel to make it apparent in the
eyes of all men, that thofe flying reports were untrue, and that himfelf being a *Jew*
kept the law, even as they did. In fome things therefore we fee the apoftles did teach,
that there ought not to be conformity between the chriftian *Jews* and *gentiles*. How
many things this law of inconformity did comprehend, there is no need we fhould ftand
to examine. This general is true, that the *gentiles* were not made conformable unto
Acts 15. 28. the *Jews*, in that which was neceffarily to ceafe at the coming of Chrift. Touching
things pofitive, which might either ceafe or continue as occafion fhould require, the
apoftles, tendring the zeal of the *Jews*, thought it neceffary to bind even the gentiles for
Acts 16. 4. a time to abftain as the *Jews* did *from things offered unto idols, from blood, from things
ftrangled*. Thefe decrees were every where deliver'd unto the gentiles to be ftraitly
obferved and kept. In the other matters the *gentiles* were free, and the *Jews* in
Rom. 14. 10. their own opinion ftill tied : the apoftles doctrine unto the *Jews* was, *condemn not the
gentile* ; unto the gentile, *defpife not the* Jews. The one fort, they warned to take
heed that fcrupulofity did not make them rigorous in giving unadvifed fentence againft
their brethren which were free ; the other, that they did not become fcandalous by a-
bufing their liberty and freedom, to the offence of their weak brethren which were fcrupulous. From hence therefore, two conclufions there are which may evidently be drawn ;
the firft, that whatfoever conformity of pofitive laws the apoftles did bring in between
the churches of *Jews* and gentiles, it was in thofe things only which might either ceafe
or continue a fhorter or a longer time, as occafion did moft require ; the fecond, that they
did not impofe upon the churches of the gentiles any part of the *Jews* ordinances with
bond of neceffary and perpetual obfervation (as we all, both by doctrine and practice,
acknowledge) but only in refpect of the conveniency and fitnefs for the prefent ftate of
the church, as then it ftood. The words of the council's decree, concerning the gentiles,
are, *It feemed good to the Holy Ghoft, and to us, to lay upon you no more burden, faving only
thefe things of neceffity; abftinence from idol-offerings, from things ftrangled, and blood,
and from fornication*. So that in other things pofitive which the coming of Chrift did
not neceffarily extinguifh, the gentiles were left altogether free. Neither ought it to feem
unreafonable, that the gentiles fhould neceffarily be bound and tied to *jewifh* ordinances
fo far forth as that decree importeth. For to the *Jew*, who knew that their difference from
other nations, which were aliens and ftrangers from God, did efpecially confift in this,
that God's people had pofitive ordinances given to them of God himfelf ; it feemeth marvellous hard, that the chriftian gentiles fhould be incorporated into the fame commonwealth with God's own chofen people, and be fubject to no part of his ftatutes, more
Lib. qui Seder
Olam infcri-
bitur. than only the law of nature, which heathens count themfelves bound unto. It was an
opinion conftantly received amongft the *Jews*, that God did deliver unto the fons of
צינו 1
ברנחושם 2
מא 3
שונבית 4
גילי מרו- 5
ויל 6
חעל 7
אנו מי, 8
חתי *Noah* feven precepts : namely, to live in fome form of regiment, under, firft, publick
laws : fecondly, to ferve and call upon the name of God : thirdly, to fhun idolatry :
fourthly, not to fuffer effufion of the blood : fifthly, to abhor all unclean knowledge in
the flefh : fixthly, to commit no rapine : feventhly, and finally, not to eat of any
living creature, whereof the blood was not firft let out. If therefore the gentiles would
be exempted from the law of *Mofes*, yet it might feem hard they fhould alfo caft off
even thofe things pofitive which were obferved before *Mofes*, and which were not of the
fame kind with laws that were neceffarily to ceafe. And peradventure hereupon the
council faw it expedient to determine, that the gentiles fhould according unto the third,
the feventh, and the fifth of thofe precepts, abftain from things facrificed unto idols,
Heb. 13. 4.
1 Cor. 5. 11.
Gal. 5. 19. from things ftrangled, and blood, and from fornication. The reft, the gentiles did of their
own accord obferve, nature leading them thereto. And did not nature alfo teach them
to abftain from fornication ? No doubt it did. Neither can we with reafon think, that
as the former two are pofitive ; fo likewife this, being meant as the apoftle doth otherwife ufually underftand it. But very marriage within a number of degrees being not
Lev. 18. only by the law of *Mofes*, but alfo by the law of the fons of *Noah* (for fo they took
it) an unlawful difcovery of nakednefs ; this difcovery of nakednefs by unlawful marriages,

riages, such as *Moses* in the law reckoneth up, I think it for mine own part more prbbable to have been meant in the words of that canon, than fornication according unto the sense of the law of nature. Words must be taken according to the matter whereof they are uttered. The apostles command to abstain from blood. Construe this according to the law of nature, and it will seem that homicide only is forbidden. But construe it in reference to the law of the *Jews*, about which the question was, and it shall easily appear to have a clean other sense, and in any man's judgment a truer, when we expound it of eating and not of shedding blood : so if we speak of fornication, he that knoweth no law but only the law of nature, must needs make thereof a narrower construction, than he which measureth the same by a law wherein sundry kinds even of conjugal copulation are prohibited as impure, unclean, unhonest. St. *Paul* himself doth term in- 1 Cor. 5. 1. cestuous marriage fornication. If any do rather think, that the christian gentiles themselves, thro the loose and corrupt customs of those times, took simple fornication for no sin, and were in that respect offensive unto believing *Jews*, which by the law had been better taught, our proposing of another conjecture is unto theirs no prejudice. Some things therefore we see there were, wherein the gentiles were forbidden to be like unto the *Jews* ; some things wherein they were commanded not to be unlike. Again, some things also there were, wherein no law of God did let but that they might be either like or unlike, as occasion should require. And unto this purpose *Leo* saith, *Apostolical* Leo in jejun. *ordinance (beloved) knowing that our Lord Jesus Christ came not into this world to* mens. Sept.
fer. 9. *undo the law, hath in such sort distinguished the mysteries of the old testament, that certain of them it hath chosen out to benefit evangelical knowledge withal, and for that purpose appointed that those things which before were* Jewish, *might now be christian customs.* The cause why the apostles did thus conform the christians as much as might be according to the pattern of the *Jews*, was to rein them in by this mean the more, and to make them cleave the better. The church of Christ hath had in no one thing, so many and so contrary occasions of dealing, as about judaism : some having thought the whole *Jewish* law wicked and damnable in it self ; some not condemning it as the former sort absolutely, have notwithstanding judged it, either sooner necessary to be abrogated, or farther unlawful to be observed than truth can bear ; some of scrupulous simplicity urging perpetual and universal observation of the law of *Moses* necessary, as the christian *Jews* at the first in the apostles times ; some as hereticks, holding the same no less even after the contrary determination set down by consent of the church at *Jerusalem* ; finally, some being herein resolute thro mere infidelity and with open profess'd enmity against Christ, as unbelieving *Jews*. To controul slanderers of the law and prophets, such as *marcionites* and *manichees* were, the church in her liturgies hath intermingled with readings out of the new testament lessons taken out of the law and prophets ; Tertul. de whereunto *Tertullian* alluding, saith of the church of Christ, *It intermingleth with* praescript. ad-
vers. haeret. *evangelical and apostolical writings the law and the prophets ; and from thence it* T.C. l. 3. p. 171. *drinketh in that faith which with water it sealeth, clotheth with the Spirit, nourish-* What an abu-
sing also is it *eth with the eucharist, with martyrdom setteth forward.* They would have wondred to affirm, the in those times to hear that any man being not a favourer of heresy, should term this by mangling of way of disdain, *mangling of the gospels and epistles.* They which honour the law as an the gospels
and epistles to image of the wisdom of God himself, are notwithstanding to know that the same had an have been end in Christ. But what ? was the law so abolished with Christ, that after his ascension brought into
the church by the office of priests became immediately wicked, and the very name hateful, as import- godly and ing the exercise of an ungodly function? No, as long as the glory of the temple conti- learned men ? nued until the time of that final desolation was accomplished, the very christian Jews T.C. l. 3. p. 116.
Seeing that the did continue with their sacrifices and other parts of legal service. That very law there- office and fore which our Saviour was to abolish did not *so soon* become unlawful to be observed as function of
priests was af- some imagine ; nor was it afterward unlawful *so far*, that the very name of altar, of ter our Saviour priests, of sacrifice it self, should be banished out of the world. For tho God do now Christ's ascen- hate sacrifice, whether it be heathenish or jewish, so that we cannot have the same sion naught
and ungodly ; things which they had, but with impiety ; yet unless there be some greater let than the the name only evacuation of the law of *Moses*, the names themselves may (I hope) be retained whereby they
were called, without sin, in respect of that proportion, which things established by our Saviour have which did exer- unto them which by him are abrogated. And so thro-out all the writings of the antient cise that un- fathers, we see that the words which were, do continue ; the only difference is, that godly func-
tion, cannot whereas before they had a literal, they now have a metaphorical use ; and are as so many be otherwise notes of remembrance unto us, that what they did signify in the letter, is accomplished taken, than in
the evil part. in the truth. And as no man can deprive the church of this liberty, to use names whereunto the law was accustomed ; so neither are we generally forbidden the use of things which the law hath, tho it neither command us any particularity, as it did the Jews a

†

number,

number, and the weightieſt which it did command them are unto us in the goſpel prohibited. Touching ſuch, as thro ſimplicity of error, did urge univerſal and perpetual obſervation of the law of *Moſes* at the firſt, we have ſpoken already. Againſt jewiſh hereticks and falſe apoſtles teaching afterwards the ſelf-ſame, ſaint *Paul* in every epiſtle commonly either diſputeth or giveth warning. Jews that were zealous for the law, but
withal infidels in reſpect of chriſtianity, and to the name of Jeſus Chriſt moſt ſpiteful
enemies, did, while they flouriſhed, no leſs perſecute the church than heathens ; and after their eſtate was overthrown, they were not that way ſo much to be feared. Howbeit, becauſe they had their ſynagogues in every famous city almoſt throughout the
world, and by that means great opportunity to withdraw from the chriſtian faith, which
to do, they ſpared no labour ; this gave the church occaſion to make ſundry laws againſt
Concil. *Laod.* can. 37, 38.
T.C. l.1.p.132.
T.C. l.3.p.176. them. As, in the council of *Laodicea*, *The feſtival preſents which Jews or hereticks
uſed to ſend, muſt not be received, nor holidays ſolemnized in their company*. Again,
*From the Jews, men ought not to receive their unleavened [bread] nor to communicate
with their impieties*. Which council was afterwards indeed confirmed by the ſixth general council. But what was the true ſenſe or meaning both of the one, and the other ?
Were chriſtians here forbidden to communicate in unleavened bread becauſe the Jews
did ſo, being enemies of the church ? He which attentively ſhall weigh the words,
will ſuſpect that they rather forbid communion with Jews than imitation of them ;
much more, if with theſe two decrees be compared a third in the council of *Conſtanti-*
Concil. Con-
ſtantinop. 6.
cap. 11. *nople : Let no man, either of the clergy or laity eat the unleavened of the Jews, nor
enter into any familiarity with them, nor ſend for them in ſickneſs, nor take phyſick
at their hands, nor as much as go into the bath with them. If any do otherwiſe, being a clergy-man, let him be depoſed ; if being a lay-perſon, let excommunication be
his puniſhment*. If theſe canons were any argument, that they which made them did
utterly condemn ſimilitude between the chriſtians and Jews in things indifferent appertaining unto religion, either becauſe the Jews were enemies unto the church, or elſe for
that their ceremonies were abrogated ; theſe reaſons had been as ſtrong and effectual
againſt their keeping the feaſt of *Eaſter* on the ſame day the Jews kept theirs, and not
according to the cuſtom of the weſt church. For ſo they did from the firſt beginning
till *Conſtantine*'s time. For in theſe two things the eaſt and weſt churches did interchangeably both confront the Jews, and concur with them ; the weſt church uſing unleavened bread as the Jews in their paſſover did, but differing from them in the day
whereon they kept the feaſt of *Eaſter* ; contrariwiſe, the eaſt church celebrating the
feaſt of *Eaſter* on the ſame day with the Jews, but not uſing the ſame kind of bread
which they did. Now if ſo be the eaſt church in uſing leavened bread had done well,
either for that the Jews were enemies to the church, or becauſe jewiſh ceremonies were
abrogated ; how ſhould we think but that *Victor* the biſhop of *Rome* (whom all judicious men do in that behalf diſallow) did well to be ſo vehement and fierce in drawing
them to the like diſſimilitude for the feaſt of *Eaſter* ? Again, if the weſt churches
had in either of thoſe two reſpects affected diſſimilitude with the Jews in the feaſt of
Eaſter, what reaſon had they to draw the eaſtern church here unto them, which reaſon
did not enforce them to frame themſelves unto it in the ceremony of leavened bread ?
Difference in rites ſhould breed no controverſy between one church and another ;
but if controverſy be once bred, it muſt be ended. The feaſt of *Eaſter* being therefore litigious in the days of *Conſtantine*, who honoured of all other churches moſt the
church of *Rome* ; which church was the mother, from whoſe breaſts he had drawn
that food which gave him nouriſhment to eternal life ; ſith agreement was neceſſary,
and yet impoſſible, unleſs the one part were yielded unto ; his deſire was that of the
two, the eaſtern church ſhould rather yield. And to this end he uſeth ſundry perſuaſive
ſpeeches. When *Stephen* biſhop of *Rome*, going about to ſhew what the catholick
church ſhould do, had alledged what the hereticks themſelves did, namely, that they
received ſuch as came unto them, and offered not to baptize them anew ; ſaint *Cyprian*
being of a contrary mind to him about the matter at that time in queſtion, which
was, *Whether hereticks converted ought to be rebaptized, yea or no* ; anſwered the alle-
Cypr. ad pomp.
lib. cont.
epiſt. Stepha-
ni. gation of pope *Stephen* with exceeding great ſtomach, ſaying, *To this degree of wretchedneſs, the church of God and ſpouſe of Chriſt is now come, that her ways ſhe frameth
to the example of hereticks ; that to celebrate the ſacraments, which heavenly inſtruction hath delivered, light it ſelf doth borrow from darkneſs, and chriſtians do
that which antichriſts do*. Now albeit *Conſtantine* have done that to further a better
cauſe, which *Cyprian* did to countenance a worſe, namely, the rebaptization of hereticks ; and have taken advantage at the odiouſneſs of the Jews, as *Cyprian* of hereticks, becauſe the eaſtern church kept their feaſt of *Eaſter* always the fourteenth day of
*
the

the month as the Jews did, what day of the week foever it fell; or howfoever *Conftantine* did take occafion in the handling of that caufe, to fay, * *It is unworthy to have any thing common with that fpiteful nation of the Jews*; fhall every motive or argument ufed in fuch kind of conferences, be made a rule for others ftill to conclude the like by, concerning all things of like nature, when as probable inducements may lead them to the contrary ? Let both this and other allegations fuitable unto it ceafe to bark any longer idly againft that truth, the courfe and paffage whereof it is not in them to hinder.

* Socr. ecclefiaft. hift. l. 5. c.21. Plerique antiquitus 14. die menfis, nullâ ratione diei fabbati habitâ hoc feftum obfervarunt.

Quod dum faciebant cum aliis qui aliam rationem in eodem fefto agendo fequebantur; ufque eo nequaquam diffenferunt, quoad Victor epifcopus Romanus fupra modum iracundiâ inflammatus, omnes in Afiâ qui erant τεσσαρεσκαιδεκατίτας appellati, excommunicaverit. Ob quod factum, Irenæus epifcopus Lugduni in Victorem per epiftolam graviter invectus eft. Eufeb. de vita Conftant. lib. 3. cap. 17. Quid præftabilius, quidve auguftius effe poterat, quam ut hoc feftum per quod fpem immortalitatis nobis oftentatam habemus, uno modo & ratione apud omnes integre fincereque obfervaretur ? Ac primum omnium dignum plane videbatur ut ritum & confuetudinem imitantes Judæorum (qui quoniam fuas ipforum manus immani fcelere polluerunt, merito, ut fcelefti docet, cæco animorum errore tenentur irretiti) iftud feftum fanctiffimum ageremus. In noftra enim fitum eft poteftate ut, illorum more rejecto, veriore ac magis fincero inftituto (quod quidem ufque à prima paffionis die hactenus recoluimus) hujus fefti celebrationem ad pofterorum feculorum memoriam propagemus. Nihil igitur fit nobis cum Judæorum turba, omnium odiofa maxime.

12. But the weightieft exception, and of all the moft worthy to be refpected, is againft fuch kind of ceremonies, as have been fo grofly and fhamefully abufed in the church of *Rome*, that where they remain they are fcandalous, yea, they cannot chufe but be ftumbling-blocks, and grievous caufes of offence. Concerning this point therefore we are firft to note, what properly it is to be fcandalous or offenfive. Secondly, what kind of ceremonies are fuch. And thirdly, when they are neceffarily for remedy thereof to be taken away, and when not. The common conceit of the vulgar fort is, whenfoever they fee any thing which they miflike and are angry at, to think that every fuch thing is fcandalous, and that themfelves in this cafe are the men concerning whom our Saviour fpake in fo fearful a manner, faying, *Whofoever fhall fcandalize or offend any one of thefe little ones which believe in me*, (that is, as they conftrue it, whofoever fhall anger the meaneft and fimpleft artifan which carrieth a good mind, by not removing out of the church fuch rites and ceremonies as difpleafe him) *better he were drowned in the bottom of the fea*. But hard were the cafe of the church of Chrift, if this were to fcandalize. Men are fcandalized when they are moved, led and provoked unto fin. At good things evil men may take occafion to do evil; and fo Chrift himfelf was a rock of offence in *Ifrael*, they taking occafion at his poor eftate and at the ignominy of his crofs to think him unworthy the name of that great and glorious *Meffiah*, whom the prophets defcribe in fuch ample and ftately terms. But that which we therefore term offenfive, becaufe it inviteth men to offend, and by a dumb kind of provocation, encourageth, moveth, or any way leadeth unto fin, muft of neceffity be acknowledged actively fcandalous. Now fome things are fo even by their very effence and nature, fo that wherefoever they be found they are not, neither can be without this force of provocation unto evil ; of which kind, all examples of fin and wickednefs are. Thus *David* was fcandalous, in that bloody act, whereby he caufed the enemies of God to be blafphemous : thus the whole ftate of *Ifrael* was fcandalous, when their publick diforders caufed the name of God to be ill fpoken of amongft the nations. It is of this kind that *Tertullian* meaneth : *Offence or fcandal, if I be not deceived*, faith he, *is when the example not of a good but of an evil thing doth fet men forward unto fin. Good things can fcandalize none, fave only evil minds :* Good things have no fcandalizing nature in them. Yet that which is of its own nature either good, or at leaft not evil, may by fome accident become fcandalous at certain times, and in certain places, and to certain men ; the open ufe thereof, neverthelefs, being otherwife without danger. The very nature of fome rites and ceremonies therefore is fcandalous, as it was in a number of thofe which the *manichees* did ufe, and is in all fuch as the law of God doth forbid. Some are offenfive only thro the agreement of men to ufe them unto evil, and not elfe ; as the moft of thofe things indifferent which the heathens did to the fervice of their falfe gods ; which another, in heart condemning their idolatry, could not do with them in fhew and token of approbation without being guilty of fcandal given. Ceremonies of this kind, are either devifed at the firft unto evil ; as the *eunomian* hereticks in difhonour of the bleffed Trinity brought in the laying on of water but once, to crofs the cuftom of the church which in baptifm did it thrice : or elfe having had a profitable ufe, they are afterward interpreted and wrefted to the contrary ; as thofe hereticks which held the Trinity to be three diftinct, not perfons, but natures, abufed the ceremony of three times laying on water in baptifm, unto the ftrengthning of their herefy. The element of water is in baptifm neceffary ; once to fay it on or twice, is indifferent. For which caufe, *Gregory* making mention thereof, faith, *To dive an infant either thrice or but once in baptifm, can be no way a thing reprovable ; feeing that both in three times wafhing, the Trinity of perfons, and in one the unity of the Godhead*

Their exception againft fuch ceremonies as have been abufed by the church of *Rome*, and are faid in that refpect to be fcandalous.

Matth. 18. 6.

1 Pet. 1. 8.

2 Sam. 11. 14. Rom. 2. 24. Ezek. 36. 20.

Tertul. lib. de virgin. veland.

Epift. ad Leandrum Hifp.

†   head

head may be signified. So that of thefe two ceremonies, neither being hurtful in it felf, both may ferve unto good purpofe, yet one was devifed and the other converted unto evil. Now whereas in the church of *Rome* certain ceremonies are faid to have been fhamefully abufed unto evil, as the ceremony of croffing at baptifm, of kneeling at the euchariſt, of ufing wafer-cakes, and fuch like; the queſtion is, whether for remedy of that evil wherein fuch ceremonies have been fcandalous, and perhaps may be ſtill unto fome even amongſt our felves, whom the prefence and fight of them may confirm in that former error whereto they ferved in times paſt, they are of neceffity to be removed. Are thefe, or any other ceremonies we have common with the church of *Rome* fcanda-lous and wicked in their very nature? This no man objecteth. Are any fuch as have been polluted from their very birth, and inſtituted, even at the firſt, unto that thing which is evil? That which hath been ordained impiously at the firſt, may wear out that impiety in tract of time; and then, what doth let, but that the ufe thereof may ſtand without offence? The names of our months

Hom. 11 de Pafch. *Idololatria confuetudo in tantum homines occa-caverat, ut Solis, Luna, Martis, atque Mercurii, Jovis, Veneris, Sa-turni, & diverfis elementorum ac damonum appellationibus dies voci-tarent, & luci tenebrarum nomen imponerent.* Beda de ratione temp. cap. 4. *Octavus dies idem primus eſt, ad quem reditur, indeque rur-fus hebdomada inchoatur. His nomina à planetis gentilitas indidit, habere fe credentes à Sole fpiritum, à Luna corpus, à Marte fanguinem, à Mercurio ingenium & linguam, à Jove temperantiam, à Venere vo-luptatem, à Saturno tarditatem.* Ifid. Hifp. lib 5. Etymol. cap. 30. *Dies dicti à Diis, quorum nomina Romani quibufdam fyderibus facra-verunt.*

and of our days, we are not ignorant from whence they came, and with what difhonour un-to God they are faid to have been devifed at the firſt. What could be fpoken againſt any thing more effectual to ſtir hatred, than that which fometime the antient fathers in this cafe fpeak? Yet thofe very names are at this day in ufe throughout chriſtendom without hurt or fcandal

to any. Clear and manifeſt it is, that things devifed by hereticks, yea, devifed of a ve-ry heretical purpofe, even againſt religion, and at their firſt devifing worthy to have been withſtood, may in time grow meet to be kept; as that cuſtom, the inventers whereof were the *eunomian* hereticks. So that cuſtoms once eſtabliſhed and confirmed by long ufe being prefently without harm, are not in regard of their corrupt original to be held fcandalous. But concerning thofe our ceremonies which they reckon for moſt popiſh, they are not able to avouch that any of them was otherwife inſtituted than unto good; yea, fo ufed at the firſt. It followeth then, that they all are fuch as having ferved to good purpofe, were afterwards converted unto the contrary. And fith it is not fo much as objected againſt us, that we retain together with them the evil wherewith they have been infected in the church of *Rome*; I would demand. who they are whom we fcanda-lize, by ufing harmlefs things unto that good end for which they were firſt inſtituted. Amongſt our felves that agree in the approbation of this kind of good ufe, no man will fay, that one of us is offenfive or fcandalous unto another. As for the favourers of the church of *Rome*, they know how far we herein differ and diffent from them; which thing neither we conceal, and they by their publick writings alfo profefs daily how much it grieveth them. So that of them there will not many rife up againſt us, as witneffes un-to the indictment of fcandal whereby we might be condemned and caſt, as having ſtrengthned them in that evil wherewith they pollute themfelves in the ufe of the fame ceremonies. And concerning fuch as withſtand the church of *England* herein, and hate it becaufe it doth not fufficiently feem to hate *Rome*; they (I hope) are far enough from being by this mean drawn to any kind of popiſh error. The multitude therefore of them, unto whom we are fcandalous thro the ufe of abufed ceremonies, is not fo apparent, that it can juſtly be faid in general of any one fort of men or other, we caufe them to offend. If it be fo, that now and then fome few are efpied, who having been accuf-tomed heretofore to the rites and ceremonies of the church of *Rome*, are not fo fcoured of their former ruſt as to forfake their antient perfuafion which they have had, howfoever they frame themfelves to outward obedience of laws and orders; becaufe fuch may mif-conſtrue the meaning of our ceremonies, and fo take them, as tho they were in every fort the fame they have been, fhall this be thought a reafon fufficient whereon to conclude that fome law muſt neceffarily be made to aboliſh all fuch ceremonies? They anfwer, that there is no law of God which doth bind us to retain them. And faint *Paul's* rule is, that in thofe things from which without hurt we may lawfully abſtain, we fhould frame the ufage of our liberty, with regard to the weaknefs and imbecillity of our brethren. Where-

1 Cor. 6. 11. fore unto them which ſtood upon their own defence, faying, *All things are lawful unto me*; he replieth, *but all things are not expedient* in regard of others. All things are clean, all meats are lawful; but evil unto that man that eateth offenfively. If for thy meat's fake thy brother be grieved, thou walkeſt no longer according to charity. Def-troy not him with thy meat for whom Chriſt died. Diffolve not for food's fake the work of God. We that are ſtrong, muſt bear the imbecillity of the impotent, and not pleafe our felves. It was a weaknefs in the chriſtian Jews, and a maim of judgment in them,

† tha

that they thought the gentiles polluted by the eating of thofe meats which themfelves were afraid to touch for fear of tranfgrefling the law of *Mofes* ; yea, hereat their hearts did fo much rife, that the apoftle had juft caufe to fear, left they would rather forfake chriftianity than endure any fellowfhip with fuch as made no confcience of that which was unto them abominable.   And for this caufe mention is made of deftroying Rom. 14. the weak by meats, and of diffolving that which was his church, a part of & 15. 1. the living ftones whereof were believing Jews.   Now thofe weak brethren before mentioned are faid to be as the Jews were, and our ceremonies which have been abufed in the church of *Rome*, to be as the fcandalous meats, from which the gentiles are exhorted to abftain in the prefence of Jews for fear of averting them from chriftian faith.   Therefore as charity did bind them to refrain from that for their brethren's fake, which otherwife was lawful enough for them ; fo it bindeth us for our brethren's fake likewife, to abolifh fuch ceremonies, altho we might lawfully elfe retain them.   But between thefe two cafes there are great odds.   For neither are our weak brethren as the Jews, nor the ceremonies which we ufe as the meats which the gentiles ufed.   The Jews were known to be generally weak in that refpect ; whereas contrariwife the imbecillity of ours is not common unto fo many, that we can take any fuch certain notice of them.   It is a chance, if here and there fome one be found ; and therefore feeing we may prefume men commonly otherwife, there is no necefity that our practice fhould frame it felf by that which the apoftle doth prefcribe to the gentiles.   Again, their ufe of meats was not *Vide* Harme- like unto our ceremonies; that being a matter of private action in common life, where nop. *lib.* 1. every man was free to order that which himfelf did ; but this a publick conftitution for *tit.* 1. *fect.* 18. the ordering of the church : and we are not to look that the church fhould change her publick laws and ordinances, made according to that which is judged ordinarily and commonly fitteft for the whole, altho it chance that for fome particular men the fame be found inconvenient, efpecially when there may be other remedy alfo againft the fores of particular inconveniences.   In this cafe therefore, where any private harm doth grow, we are not to reject inftruction, as being an unmeet plaifter to apply unto it ; neither can we fay, that he which appointeth teachers for phyficians in this kind of evil, is, *As* T.C.l.3.p.178. *if a man would fet one to watch a child all day long left he fhould hurt himfelf with a knife, whereas by taking away the knife from him, the danger is avoided and the fervice of the man better imployed.*   For a knife may be taken from a child, without depriving them of the benefit thereof which have years and difcretion to ufe it.   But the ceremonies which children do abufe, if we remove quite and clean, as it is by fome required that we fhould ; then are they not taken from children only, but from others alfo : which is as tho becaufe children may perhaps hurt themfelves with knives, we fhould conclude, that therefore the ufe of knives is to be taken quite and clean even from men alfo. Thofe particular ceremonies which they pretend to be fo fcandalous, we fhall in the next book have occafion more throughly to fift, where other things alfo traduced in the publick duties of the church whereunto each of thefe appertaineth, are together with thefe to be touched, and fuch reafons to be examined as have at any time been brought either againft the one or the other.   In the mean while, againft the conveniency of curing fuch evils T.C.l.3. p.177. by inftruction, ftrange it is, that they fhould object the multitude of other neceffary It is not fo matters wherein preachers may better beftow their time, than in giving men warning convenient, that the mi- not to abufe ceremonies. A wonder it is, that they fhould object this, which have fo ma- nifter having ny years together troubled the church with quarrels concerning thefe things ; and are even fo many ne-ceffary points to this very hour fo earneft in them. that if they write or fpeak publickly but five words, to beftow his one of them is lightly about the dangerous eftate of the church of *England*, in refpect of time in, fhould be driven to abufed ceremonies.   How much happier had it been for this whole church, if they which fpend it in gi- have raifed contention therein, about the abufe of rites and ceremonies, had confidered ving warning of not abufing in due time that there is indeed ftore of matters fitter and better a great deal for teachers them, of to fpend time and labour in?   It is thro their importunate and vehement affeverations, which (altho more than thro any fuch experience which we have had of our own, that we are inforced they were ufed to the beft) to think it poffible for one or other, now and then at leaftwife, in the prime of the re- there is no formation of our church, to have ftumbled at fome kind of ceremonies.   Wherein, for profit. as much as we are contented to take this upon their credit, and to think it may be ; fith alfo, they farther pretend the fame to be fo dangerous a fnare to their fouls that are at any time taken therein ; they muft give our teachers leave, for the faving of thofe fouls (be they never fo few) to intermingle fometime with other more neceffary things, admonition concerning thefe not unneceffary.   Wherein they fhould in reafon more eafily yield this leave, confidering that hereunto we fhall not need to ufe the hundredth part of that time, which themfelves think very needful to beftow in making moft bitter invectives againft the ceremonies of the church.

P   13. But

Our ceremonies excepted against, for that some churches reformed before ours, have cast out those things, which we, notwithstanding their example to the contrary, do retain still.
(a) *T. C. l. 1. p. 133.*
(b) *1 Cor. 16. 1.*
(c) *Can. 20.* The canon of that council which is here cited, doth provide against kneeling at prayer on sundays or for fifty days after easter, on any day, and not at the feast of pentecost only.
(d) *T. C. l. 1. p. 182, 183.*
(e) *Rom. 16. 5, 7.*
(f) *1 Cor. 14. 37.*

Respon. ad Med.

13. But to come to the last point of all; the church of *England* is grievously charged with forgetfulness of her duty, which duty had been to frame herself unto the pattern of their example that went before her in the work of reformation. (a) *For as the churches of Christ ought to be most unlike the synagogue of antichrist in their indifferent ceremonies; so they ought to be most like one unto another, and for preservation of unity, to have as much as possible may be all the same ceremonies. And therefore saint Paul, to establish this order in the church of* Corinth, *that they should make their gatherings for the poor upon the first day of the sabbath (which is our sunday) alledgeth this for a reason,* (b) *That he had so ordained in other churches.* Again, *As children of one father, and servants of one family; so all churches should not only have one diet, in that they have one word, but also wear, as it were, one livery in using the same ceremonies.* Thirdly, (c) *This rule did the great council of* Nice *follow, when it ordained, That where certain at the feast of pentecost did pray kneeling, they should pray standing: the reason whereof is added, which is, That one custom ought to be kept thro-out all churches. It is true, That the diversity of ceremonies ought not to cause the churches to dissent one with another: but yet it maketh most to the avoiding of dissension, that there be amongst them an unity, not only in doctrine, but also in ceremonies.* (d) *And therefore our form of service is to be amended, not only for that it cometh too near that of the papists, but also because it is so different from that of the reformed churches.* Being asked to what churches ours should conform it self? and why other reformed churches should not as well frame themselves to ours? their answer is, *That if there be any ceremonies which we have better than others, they ought to frame themselves to us; if they have better than we, then we ought to frame our selves to them: if the ceremonies be alike commodious, the latter churches should conform themselves to the first, as the younger daughter to the elder.* (e) *For as saint Paul in the members, where all other things are equal, noteth it for a mark of honour above the rest, that one is called before another to the gospel; so is it, for the same cause, amongst the churches.* (f) *And in this respect he pincheth the* Corinths, *that not being the first which received the gospel, yea they would have their several manners from other churches. Moreover, where the ceremonies are alike commodious, the fewer ought to conform themselves unto the more. For as much therefore as all the churches (so far as they know which plead after this manner) of our confession in doctrine, agree in the abrogation of divers things which we retain; our church ought either to shew that they have done evil, or else she is found to be in fault that doth not conform herself in that, which she cannot deny to be well abrogated.* In this axiom, that preservation of peace and unity amongst christian churches should be by all good means procured, we join most willingly and gladly with them. Neither deny we, but that, to the avoiding of dissension, it availeth much, that there be amongst them an unity as well in ceremonies as in doctrine. The only doubt is, about the manner of their unity; how far churches are bound to be uniform in their ceremonies, and what way they ought to take for that purpose. Touching the one, the rule which they have set down, is, That in ceremonies indifferent, all churches ought to be one of them unto another as like as possibly they may be. Which possibly, we cannot otherwise construe, than that it doth require them to be, even as like as they may be without breaking any positive ordinance of God. For the ceremonies whereof we speak, being matter of positive law, they are indifferent, if God have neither himself commanded nor forbidden them, but left them unto the church's discretion: so that if as great uniformity be required as is possible in these things, seeing that the law of God forbiddeth not any one of them; it followeth, that from the greatest unto the least, they must be in every christian church the same, except mere impossibility of so having it be the hindrance. To us this opinion seemeth over extreme and violent: we rather incline to think it a just and reasonable cause for any church, the state whereof is free and independent, if in these things it differ from other churches only for that it doth not judge it so fit and expedient to be framed therein by the pattern of their example, as to be otherwise framed than they. That of *Gregory* unto *Leander*, is a charitable speech, and a peaceable; *In una fide nil officit ecclesiæ sanctæ consuetudo diversa. Where the faith of the holy church is one, a difference in customs of the church doth no harm.* That of saint *Augustine* to *Cassulanus*, is somewhat particular, and toucheth what kind of ceremonies they are, wherein one church may vary from the example of another without hurt. *Let the faith of the whole church, how wide soever it hath spread it self, be always one, altho the unity of belief be famous for variety of certain ordinances, whereby that which is rightly believed suffereth no kind of let or impediment.* Calvin goeth further, *As concerning rites in particular, let the sentence of* Augustine *take place, which leaveth it free unto all churches to receive their own custom. Yea, sometime it profiteth, and is expedient that*

that there be difference, left men should think that religion is tied to outward ceremonies. Always provided, that there be not any emulation, nor that churches delighted with novelty affect to have that which others have not. They which grant it true, That the diverfity of ceremonies in this kind ought not to caufe diffention in churches, muft either acknowledge that they grant in effect nothing by thefe words ; or, if any thing be granted, there muft as much be yielded unto, as we affirm againft their former ftrict affertion. For, if churches be urged by way of duty, to take fuch ceremonies as they like not of, how can diffention be avoided ? Will they fay, that there ought to be no diffention, becaufe fuch as are urged ought to like of that whereunto they are urged ? If they fay this, they fay juft nothing. For how fhould any church like to be urged of duty by fuch as have no authority or power over it, unto thofe things which being indifferent, it is not of duty bound unto them ? Is it their meaning, that there ought to be no diffention, becaufe that which churches are not bound unto, no man ought by way of duty to urge upon them ; and if any man do, he ftandeth in the fight of both God and men moft juftly blameable, as a needlefs difturber of the peace of God's church, and an author of diffention ? In faying this, they both condemn their own practice, when they prefs the church of *England* with fo ftrict a bond of duty in thefe things ; and they overthrow the ground of their practice, which is, That there ought to be in all kind of ceremonies uniformity, unlefs impoffibility hinder it. For proof whereof, it is not enough to alledge what faint *Paul* did about the matter of collections, or what noblemen do in the liveries of their fervants, or what the council of *Nice* did for ftanding in time of prayer on certain days ; becaufe, tho faint *Paul* did will them of the church of *Corinth* (a), every man to lay up fomewhat by him upon the funday, and to referve it in ftore till himfelf did come thither to fend it to the church of *Jerufalem* for relief of the poor there ; fignifying withal, that he had taken the

(a) *T. C. l. 1. p. 133.* And therefore faint *Paul*, to eftablifh this order in the church of *Corinth*, that they fhould make their gatherings for the poor upon the firft day of the fabbath (which is our funday) alledgeth this for a reafon; that he had fo ordained in other churches.

like order with the churches of *Galatia* ; yet the reafon which he yieldeth of this order taken, both in the one place and the other, fheweth the leaft part of his meaning to have been that whereunto his words are writhed. *Concerning collection for the faints* (he meaneth them of *Jerufalem*) *as I have given order to the church of* Galatia, *fo likewife do ye* (faith the apoftle) *that is, in every firft day of the week, let each of you lay afide by himfelf, and referve according to that which God hath bleffed him with ; that when I come, collections be not then to make ; and that when I am come, whom ye fhall chufe, them I may forthwith fend away by letters, to carry your beneficence unto* Jerufalem. Out of which words to conclude the duty of uniformity thro-out all churches, in all manner of indifferent ceremonies will be very hard, and therefore beft to give it over. But perhaps they are by fo much the more loth to forfake this argument, for that it hath, tho nothing elfe, yet the name of fcripture to give it fome kind of countenance more than the pretext of livery-coats afforded them. For neither is it any man's duty to clothe all his children or all his fervants with one weed, nor theirs to clothe themfelves fo, if it were left to their own judgments, as thefe ceremonies are left of God to the judgment of the church. And feeing churches are rather in this cafe like divers families, than like divers fervants of one family, becaufe every church, the ftate whereof is independent upon any other, hath authority to appoint orders for it felf in things indifferent ; therefore of the two we may rather infer, That as one family is not abridged of liberty to be clothed in fryers-grey for that another doth wear clay colour, fo neither are all churches bound to the felf-fame indifferent ceremonies which it liketh fundry to ufe. As for that canon in the council of *Nice*, let them but read it and weigh it well. The antient ufe of the church thro-out all chriftendom was, for fifty days after *eafter* (which fifty days were called *pentecoft*, tho moft commonly the laft day of them, which is *whitfunday*, be fo called) in like fort on all the fundays thro-out the whole year their manner was to ftand at prayer ; whereupon their meetings unto that purpofe on thofe days had the name of ftations given them. Of which cuftom *Tertullian* fpeaketh in this wife ; *It is not with us thought fit either to faft on the Lord's day, or to pray kneeling. The fame immunity from fafting and kneeling we keep all the time which is between the feafts of eafter and pentecoft.* This being therefore an order generally received in the church ; when fome began to be fingular and different from all others, and that in a ceremony which was then judged very convenient for the whole church, even by the whole, thofe few excepted which brake out of the common pale ; the council of *Nice* thought good to enclofe them again with the reft, by a law made in this fort : *Becaufe there are certain which will needs kneel at the time of prayer on the Lord's day, and in the fifty days after eafter ; the holy fynod judging it meet, that a*

T.C.l. 1. p. 133. So that as children of one father, and fervants of one mafter he will have all the churches not only have one diet, in that they have one word, but alfo wear as it were one livery, in ufing the fame ceremonies.

i Cor. 16. 1.

T.C.l. 1. p. 135. This rule did the great council of Nice follow, minico, & per omnem pentecoftem, nec da geniculis adorare, & jejunium folvere,&c. De coro. mili- tis.

         convenient

convenient custom be observed thro-out all churches, hath decreed, That standing we make our prayers to the Lord. Whereby it plainly appeareth, that in things indifferent, what the whole church doth think convenient for the whole, the same if any part do wilfully violate, it may be reformed and inrailed again by that general authority whereunto each particular is subject; and that the spirit of singularity in a few ought to give place unto publick judgment : this doth clearly enough appear, but not that all christian churches are bound in every indifferent ceremony to be uniform ; because where the whole church hath not tied the parts unto one and the same thing, they being therein left each to their own choice, may either do as others do, or else otherwise without any breach of duty at all. Concerning those indifferent things, wherein it hath been heretofore thought good that all christian churches should be uniform, the way which they now conceive to bring this to pass was then never thought on. For till now it hath been judged, that seeing the law of God doth not prescribe all particular ceremonies which the church of Christ may use, and in so great variety of them as may be found out, it is not possible, that the law of nature and reason should direct all churches unto the same things, each deliberating by it self what is most convenient ; the way to establish the same things indifferent thro-out them all must needs be the judgment of some judicial authority drawn into one only sentence, which may be a rule for every particular to follow. And because such authority over all churches, is too much to be granted unto any one mortal man ; there yet remaineth that which hath been always followed as the best, the safest, the most sincere and reasonable way ; namely, the verdict of the whole church orderly taken and set down in the assembly of some general council. But to maintain, That all christian churches ought for unity's sake to be uniform in all ceremonies, and then to teach that the way of bringing this to pass, must be by mutual imitation, so that where we have better ceremonies than others, they shall be bound to follow us, and we them, where theirs are better ; how should we think it agreeable and consonant to reason ? For sith in things of this nature, there is such variety of particular inducements, whereby one church may be led to think that better, which another church led by other inducements judgeth to be worse : (for example, the east church did think it better to keep *easter*-day after the manner of the Jews, the west church better to do otherwise ; the greek church judgeth it worse to use unleavened bread in the eucharist, the latin church leavened ; one church esteemeth it not so good to receive the eucharist sitting as standing, another church not so good standing as sitting ; there being on the one side probable motives, as well as on the other) unless they add somewhat else to define more certainly what ceremonies shall stand for best in such sort, that all churches in the world shall know them to be the best, and so know them that there may not remain any question about this point, we are not a whit the nearer for that they have hitherto said. They themselves, altho resolved in their own judgments what ceremonies are best, foreseeing that such as are addicted unto be not all so clearly and so incomparably best, but others there are, or may be at leastwise, when all things are well considered, as good ; know not which way smoothly to rid their hands of this matter, without providing some more certain rule to be followed for establishment of uniformity in ceremonies, when there are divers kinds of equal goodness :

T.C.l.3.p.183. If the ceremonies be alike commodious, the latter churches should conform themselves to the first, &c. And again, The fewer ought to conform themselves unto the more. and therefore in this case they say, That the latter churches, and the fewer, should conform themselves unto the elder, and the moe. Hereupon they conclude, that for as much as all the reformed churches (so far as they know) which are of our confession in doctrine, have agreed already in the abrogation of divers things which we retain ; our church ought either to shew that they have done evil, or else she is found to be in fault for not conforming her self to those churches, in that which she cannot deny to be in them well abrogated. For the authority of the first churches (and those they account to be the first in this cause which were first reformed) they bring the comparison of younger daughters conforming themselves in attire to the example of their elder sisters ; wherein there is just as much strength of reason, as in the livery-coats before mentioned. Rom. 16. 5. Saint *Paul,* they say, noteth it for a mark of special honour, that *Epænetus* was the first man in all *Achaia* which did embrace the christian faith ; after the same sort he toucheth it also as a special preheminence of *Junius* and *Andronicus,* that in christianity they were 1 Cor. 14. 36. his antients. The *Corinthians* he pincheth with this demand, *Hath the word of God gone from out of you, or hath it lighted on you alone ?* But what of all this ? If any man should think that alacrity and forwardness in good things doth add nothing unto mens commendation ; the two former speeches of saint *Paul* might lead him to reform his judgment. In like sort to take down the stomach of proud conceited men, that glory as tho they were able to set all others to school, there can be nothing more fit than some such words as the apostle's third sentence doth contain ; wherein he teacheth the church

of

of *Corinth* to know, that there was no such great odds between them and the rest of their brethren, that they should think themselves to be gold, and the rest to be but copper. He therefore useth speech unto them to this effect : *Men instructed in the knowledge of Jesus Christ there both were before you, and are besides you in the world ; ye neither are the fountain from which first, nor yet the river into which alone the word hath flowed.* But altho as *Epænetus* was the first man in all *Achaia*, so *Corinth* had been the first church in the whole world that received Christ ; the apostles doth not shew, that in any kind of things indifferent whatsoever this should have made their example a law unto all others. Indeed, the example of sundry churches for approbation of one thing doth sway much ; but yet still as having the force of an example only and not of a law. They are effectual to move any church, unless some greater thing do hinder ; but they bind none, no not tho they be many, saving only when they are the major part of a general assembly, and then their voices being more in number, must over-sway their judgments who are fewer, because in such cases the greater half is the whole. But as they stand out single, each of them by it self, their number can purchase them no such authority, that the rest of the churches being fewer should be therefore bound to follow them, and to relinquish as good ceremonies as theirs for theirs. Whereas therefore it is concluded out of these so weak premises, that the retaining of divers things in the church *of England*, which other reformed churches have cast out, must needs argue that we do not well, unless we can shew that they have done ill ; what needed this wrest to draw out from us an accusation of foreign churches ? It is not proved as yet, that if they have done well, our duty is to follow them ; and to forsake our own course, because it differeth from theirs, altho indeed it be as well for us every way, as theirs for them. And if the proofs alledged for confirmation hereof had been found, yet seeing they lead no further than only to shew, that where we can have no better ceremonies, theirs must be taken ; as they cannot with modesty think themselves to have found out absolutely the best which the wit of men may devise ; so liking their own somewhat better than other mens, even because they are their own, they must in equity allow us to be like unto them in this affection : which if they do, they ease us of that uncourteous burden, whereby we are charged, either to condemn them, or else to follow them. They grant we need not follow them if our own ways already be better. And if our own be but equal, the law of common indulgence alloweth us to think them, at the least, half a thought the better because they are our own ; which we may very well do, and never draw any indictment at all against theirs, but think commendably even of them also.

T.C.l.3.p.181. Our church either to shew that they have done evil, or else she is found to be in fault, that doth not conform her self in that which the cannot deny to be well abrogated.

14. To leave reformed churches therefore, and their actions, for him to judge of in whose sight they are as they are ; and our desire is, that they may even in his sight be found such, as we ought to endeavour by all means that our own may likewise be : some-what we are enforced to speak by way of simple declaration concerning the proceedings of the church of *England* in these affairs, to the end that men whose minds are free from those partial constructions, whereby the only name of difference from some other churches is thought cause sufficient to condemn ours, may the better discern whether that we have done be reasonable, yea or no. The church of *England* being to alter her received laws concerning such orders, rites and ceremonies, as had been in former times an hinderance unto piety and religious service of God, was to enter into consideration first, that the change of laws, especially concerning matter of religion, must be warily proceeded in. Laws, as all other things human, are many times full of imperfection ; and that which is supposed behoveful unto men, proveth oftentimes most pernicious. The wisdom which is learned by tract of time, findeth the laws that have been in for-mer ages established, needful in latter to be abrogated. Besides, that which sometime is expedient doth not always so continue ; and the number of needless laws unabolished doth weaken the force of them that are necessary. But true withal it is, that altera-tion, tho it be from worse to better, hath in it inconveniencies, and those weighty ; unless it be in such laws as have been made upon special occasions, which occasions ceasing, laws of that kind do abrogate themselves. But when we abrogate a law, as being ill made, the whole cause for which it was made still remaining ; do we not herein revoke our very own deed, and upbraid our selves with folly, yea, all that were makers of it, with oversight and with error ? Farther, if it be a law which the custom and continual practice of many ages or years hath confirmed in the minds of men ; to alter it, must needs be troublesome and scandalous. It amazeth them, it causeth them to stand in doubt whether any thing be, in it self, by nature, either good or evil ; and not all things rather such as men at this or that time agree to account of them, when they behold even those things disproved, disannulled, rejected, which use had made in a manner na-tural. What have we to induce men unto the willing obedience and observation of

A declaration of the pro-ceedings of the church of England, for establishment of things as they are.

laws,

laws, but the weight of so many mens judgments as have with deliberate advice assented thereunto ; the weight of that long experience which the world hath had thereof with consent and good liking ? So that to change any such law, must needs with the common sort impair and weaken the force of those grounds whereby all laws are made effectual. Notwithstanding, we do not deny alteration of laws to be sometimes a thing necessary ; as when they are unnatural, or impious, or otherwise hurtful unto the publick community of men, and against that good for which human societies were instituted. When the apostles of our Lord and Saviour were ordained to alter the laws of heathenish religion received throughout the whole world, chosen, I grant, they were (*Paul* excepted) the rest ignorant, poor, simple, unschooled altogether, and unlettered men ; howbeit, extraordinarily endued with ghostly wisdom from above, before they ever undertook this enterprise ; yea, their authority confirmed by miracle, to the end it might plainly appear that they were the Lord's ambassadors, unto whose sovereign power for all flesh to stoop, for all the kingdoms of the earth to yield themselves willingly conformable in whatsoever should be required, it was their duty. In this case therefore, their oppositions in maintenance of publick superstition against apostolick endeavours, as that they might not condemn the ways of their antient predecessors, that they must keep *religiones traditas*, the rights which from age to age had descended, that the ceremonies of religion had been ever accounted by so much holier as elder ; these and the like allegations, in this case, were vain and frivolous. Not to stay longer therefore in speech concerning this point, we will conclude, that as the change of such laws, as have been specified, is necessary, so the evidence that they are such, must be great. If we have neither voice from heaven that so pronounceth of them ; neither sentence of men grounded upon such manifest and clear proof, that they in whole hands it is to alter them, may likewise infallibly even in heart and conscience judge them so ; upon necessity to urge alteration, is to trouble and disturb without necessity. As for arbitrary alterations, when laws of themselves not simply bad or unmeet, are changed for better and more expedient, if the benefit of that which is newly better devised be but small, sith the custom of easiness to alter and change is so evil, no doubt, but to bear a tolerable sore, is better than to venture on a dangerous remedy. Which being generally thought upon as a matter that touched nearly their whole enterprise, whereas change was notwithstanding concluded necessary in regard of the great hurt which the church did receive by a number of things then in use, whereupon a great deal of that which had been was now to be taken away and removed out of the church ; yet sith there are divers ways of abrogating things established, they saw it best to cut off presently such things as might in that sort be extinguished without danger, leaving the rest to be abolished by disusage thro tract of time. And as this was done for the manner of abrogation ; so touching the stint or measure thereof, rites and ceremonies and other external things of like nature being hurtful unto the church, either in respect of their quality, or in regard of their number ; in the former, there could be no doubt or difficulty what should be done ; their deliberation in the latter was more hard. And therefore in as much as they did resolve to remove only such things of that kind as the church might best spare, retaining the residue ; their whole counsel is in this point utterly condemned, as having either proceeded from the blindness of those times, or from negligence, or from desire of honour and glory, or from an erroneous opinion, that such things might be tolerated for a while ; or if it did proceed (as they which would seem most favou-

T.C.l.1,p.19,
It may well
be, their pur-
pose was by
that temper of
popish cere-
monies with
the gospel,
partly the easi-
lier to draw
the papists to
the gospel, &c.
partly to re-
deem peace
thereby.

rable, are content to think it possible) from a purpose, *partly the easilier to draw papists unto the gospel,* by keeping so many orders still the same with theirs, *and partly to redeem peace thereby, the breach whereof they might fear would ensue upon more thorow alteration* ; or howsoever it came to pass, the thing they did is judged evil. But such is the lot of all that deal in publick affairs, whether of church or common-wealth, that which men list to surmise of their doings be it good or ill, they must before-hand patiently arm their minds to endure. Wherefore to let go private surmises, whereby the thing in it self is not made either better or worse ; if just and allowable reasons might lead them to do as they did, then are all these censures frustrate. Touching ceremonies harmless therefore in themselves, and hurtful only in respect of number ; was it amiss to decree, that those things which were least needful and newliest come, should be the first that were taken away ; as in the abrogating of a number of saints days, and of other the like customs, it appeareth they did, till afterwards the form of common-prayer being perfected, articles of sound religion and discipline agreed upon, catechisms framed for the needful instruction of youth, churches purged of things that indeed were burdensome to the people, or to the simple offensive and scandalous, all was brought at the length unto that wherein now we stand ? Or was it amiss, that having this way

eased

eased the church, as they thought of superfluity, they went on till they had plucked up even those things also which had taken a great deal stronger and deeper root, those things, which to abrogate without constraint of manifest harm thereby arising, had been to alter unnecessarily (in their judgments) the antient received custom of the whole church, the universal practice of the people of God, and those very decrees of our fathers, which were not only set down by agreement of general councils, but had accordingly been put in ure, and so continued in use till that very time present ? True it is, that neither councils nor customs, be they never so antient and so general, can let the church from taking away that thing which is hurtful to be retained. Where things have been instituted, which being convenient and good at the first, do afterward in process of time wax otherwise ; we make no doubt but they may be altered, yea, tho councils or customs general have received them. And therefore it is but a needless kind of opposition which they make, who thus dispute, *If in those things which are not expressed* T.C.l.3.p.30. *in the scripture, that is to be observed of the church, which is the custom of the people of God, and decree of our fore-fathers ; then how can these things at any time be varied, which heretofore have been once ordained in such sort ?* Whereto we say, that things so ordained are to be kept, howbeit not necessarily, any longer than till there grow some urgent cause to ordain the contrary. For there is not any positive law of men, whether it be general or particular, received by formal express consent, as in councils ; or by secret approbation, as in custom it cometh to pass ; but the same may be taken away if occasion serve. Even as we all know, that many things generally kept heretofore, are now in like sort generally unkept and abolished every where ; notwithstanding till such things be abolished, what exception can there be taken against the judgment of St. *Augustine*, who saith, *That of things harmless, whatsoever there* August. Epist: *is which the whole church doth observe throughout the world, to argue for any man's* 118. *immunity from observing the same, it were a point of most insolent madness ?* And surely, odious it must needs have been for one christian church to abolish that which all had received and held for the space of many ages, and that without any detriment unto religion so manifest and so great, as might in the eyes of unpartial men appear sufficient to clear them from all blame of rash and inconsiderate proceeding, if in fervor of zeal they had removed such things. Whereas contrariwise, so reasonable moderation herein used, hath freed us from being deservedly subject unto that bitter kind of obloquy, whereby as the church of *Rome* doth under the colour of love towards those things which be harmless, maintain extremely most hurtful corruptions ; so we peradventure might be upbraided, that under colour of hatred towards those things that are corrupt, we are on the other side as extreme even against most harmless ordinances ; and as they are obstinate to retain that, which no man of any conscience is able well to defend, so we might be reckoned fierce and violent to tear away that, which if our own mouths did condemn, our consciences would storm and repine thereat. The *Romans* having T.C.l.1.p.131. banished *Tarquinius* the proud, and taken a solemn oath that they never would permit For indeed it any man more to reign, could not herewith content themselves, or think that tyranny were more was throughly extinguished, till they had driven one of their consuls to depart the conform our city, against whom they found not in the world what to object, saving only that his indifferent ce= name was *Tarquin*, and that the common-wealth could not seem to have recovered the Turks perfect freedom as long as a man of so dangerous a name was left remaining. For the off, than to church of *England* to have done the like, in casting out papal tyranny and superstition, the papists to have shewed greater willingness of accepting the very ceremonies of the *Turk*, which are so Christ's professed enemy, than of the most indifferent things which the church of *Rome* near. approveth ; to have left not so much as the names which the church of *Rome* doth give unto things innocent ; to have rejected whatsoever that church doth make account of, be it never so harmless in it self, and of never so antient continuance, without any other crime to charge it with, than only that it hath been the hap thereof to be used by the church of *Rome*, and not to be commanded in the word of God : this kind of proceeding might happily have pleased some few men, who having begun such a course themselves, must needs be glad to see their example followed by us. But the Almighty which giveth wisdom, and inspireth with right understanding whomsoever it pleaseth him, he foreseeing that which man's wit had never been able to reach unto ; namely, what tragedies the attempt of so extreme alteration would raise in some parts of the christian world, did for the endless good of his church (as we cannot chuse but interpret it) use the bridle of his provident restraining hand to stay those eager affections in some, and to settle their resolution upon a course more calm and moderate : lest as in other most ample and heretofore most flourishing dominions it hath since fall'n out ; so likewise, if in ours it had come to pass, that the adverse part being enraged, and betaking it self to such practices

as men are commonly wont to embrace when they behold things brought to defperate extremities, and no hope left to fee any other end than only the utter oppreffion and clean
extinguifhment of one fide; by this means chriftendom flaming in all parts of greateft importance at once, they all had wanted that comfort and mutual relief, whereby they are
now for the rime fuftained (and not the leaft by this our church which they fo much impeach) till mutual combuftions, bloodfheds and waftes (becaufe no other inducements
will ferve) may enforce them thro very faintnefs, after the experience of fo endlefs
miferies, to enter on all fides at the length into fome fuch confultation as may tend to the
beft re-eftablifhment of the whole church of Jefus Chrift. To the fingular good whereof,
it cannot but ferve as a profitable direction, to teach men what is moft likely to prove
available, when they fhall quietly confider the trial that hath been thus long had of both
kinds of reformation ; as well this moderate kind which the church of *England* hath taken, as that other more extreme and rigorous which certain churches elfewhere have
better liked. In the mean while it may be, that fufpence of judgment and exercife of
charity were fafer and feemlier for chriftian men, than the hot purfuit of thefe controverfies, wherein they that are more fervent to difpute be not always the moft able to determine. But who are on his fide, and who againft him, our Lord in his good time fhall
reveal. And fith thus far we have proceeded in opening the things that have been done,
let not the principal doers themfelves be forgotten. When the ruins of the houfe of God
(that houfe which confifting of religious fouls, is moft immediately the precious temple
of the Holy Ghoft) were become not in his fight alone, but in the eyes of the whole
world fo exceeding great, that very fuperftition began even to feel it felf too far grown ;
the firft that with us made way to repair the decays thereof, by beheading fuperftition,
was king *Henry* the eighth ; the fon and fucceffor of which famous king, as we know,
was *Edward* the faint ; in whom (for fo by the event we may gather) it pleafed God
righteous and juft to let *England* fee, what a bleffing fin and iniquity would not fuffer it
to enjoy. Howbeit, that which the wifeman hath laid concerning *Enoch* (whofe days
were, tho many in refpect of ours, yet fcarce as three to nine in comparifon of theirs
with whom he lived) the fame to that admirable child moft worthily may be applied,
Tho he departed this world foon, yet fulfilled he much time. But what enfued ? that
work which the one in fuch fort had began, and the other fo far proceeded in, was in
fhort fpace fo overthrown, as if almoft it had never been : till fuch time as that God,
whofe property is to fhew his mercies then greateft when they are neareft to be utterly
defpaired of, caufed in the depth of difcomfort and darknefs a moft glorious ftar to arife,
and on her head fettled the crown ; whom himfelf had kept as a lamb from the flaughter
of thofe bloody times, that the experience of his goodnefs in her own deliverance might
caufe her merciful difpofition to take fo much the more delight in faving others whom
the like neceffity fhould prefs. What in this behalf hath been done towards nations
abroad, the parts of chriftendom moft afflicted can beft teftify. That which efpecially
concerneth our felves in the prefent matter we treat of is, the ftate of reformed religion, a thing at her coming to the crown, even raifed, as it were, by miracle from the
dead ; a thing which we fo little hoped to fee, that even they which beheld it done,
fcarcely believed their own fenfes at the firft beholding. Yet being then brought to pafs,
thus many years it hath continued ftanding by no other worldly mean, but that one
only hand which erected it ; that hand, which as no kind of imminent danger could caufe
at the firft to withhold it felf, fo neither have the practices, fo many, fo bloody, following fince, been ever able to make weary. Nor can we fay in this cafe fo juftly, that
Aaron and *Hur*, the ecclefiaftical and civil ftates, have fuftained the hand which did
lift it felf to heaven for them ; as that heaven it felf hath by this hand fuftained them,
no aid or help having thereunto been miniftred for performance of the work of reformation, other than fuch kind of help or aid as the angel in the prophet *Zechariah* fpeaketh
of, faying, *Neither by an army, nor ftrength, but by my fpirit, faith the Lord of*
hofts. Which grace and favour of divine affiftance, having not in one thing or two
fhewed it felf, nor for fome few days or years appeared, but in fuch fort fo long continued, our manifold fins and tranfgreffions ftriving to the contrary ; what can we lefs
thereupon conclude, than that God would at leaftwife by tract of time teach the world,
that the thing which he bleffeth, defendeth, keepeth fo ftrangely, cannot chufe but be
of him ? Wherefore, if any refufe to believe us difputing for the verity of religion eftablifhed, let them believe God himfelf thus miraculoufly working for it, and wifh life,
even for ever and ever, unto that glorious and facred inftrument whereby he worketh.

O F

OF THE
L A W S
OF
Ecclefiaftical Polity.

BOOK V.

Concerning their fourth affertion, That touching feveral publick duties of chriftian religion, there is amongft us much fuperfti- tion retained in them ; and concerning perfons, which for per- formance of thofe Duties are endued with the power of eccle- fiaftical order, our laws and proceedings according thereunto, are many ways herein alfo corrupted.

Q

28. *The form of our liturgy too near the Papists, too far different from that of other reformed churches, as they pretend.*

29. *Attire belonging to the service of God.*

30. *Of gesture in praying, and of different places chosen to that purpose.*

31. *Easiness of praying after our form.*

32. *The length of our service.*

33. *Instead of such prayers as the primitive churches have used, and those that the reformed now use; we have (say they) divers short cuts or shreddings, rather wishes than prayers.*

34. *Lessons intermingled with our prayers.*

35. *The number of our prayers for earthly things, and our oft rehearsing of the Lord's prayer.*

36. *The peoples saying after the minister.*

37. *Our manner of reading the psalms, otherwise than the rest of the scripture.*

38. *Of musick with psalms.*

39. *Of singing or saying psalms, and other parts of common prayer, wherein the people and the minister answer one another by course.*

40. *Of Magnificat, Benedictus, and Nunc Dimittis.*

41. *Of the litany.*

42. *Of Athanasius Creed, and Gloria Patri.*

43. *Of our want of particular thanksgiving.*

44. *In some things the matter of our prayer, as they affirm, is unsound.*

45. *When thou hadst overcome the sharpness of death, thou didst open the kingdom of heaven unto all believers.*

46. *Touching prayer for deliverance from sudden death.*

47. *Prayer for those things which we, for our unworthiness, dare not ask; God, for the worthiness of his Son, would vouchsafe to grant.*

48. *Prayer to be evermore delivered from all adversity.*

49. *Prayer that all men may find mercy, and of the will of God, that all men might be saved.*

50. *Of the name, the author, and the force of sacraments, which force consisteth in this, That God hath ordained them as means to make us partakers of him in Christ, and of life through Christ.*

51. *That God is in Christ by the personal incarnation of the Son, who is very God.*

52. *The mis-interpretations which heresy hath made of the manner how God and man are united in one Christ.*

53. *That by the union of the one with the other nature in Christ, there groweth neither gain nor loss of essential properties to either.*

54. *What Christ hath obtained according to the flesh, by the union of his flesh with deity.*

55. *Of the personal presence of Christ every where, and in what sense it may be granted, he is every where present according to the flesh.*

56. *The union or mutual participation, which is between Christ and the church of Christ, in this present world.*

57. *The necessity of sacraments unto the participation of Christ.*

58. *The substance of baptism, the rites or solemnities thereunto belonging; and that the substance thereof being kept, other things in baptism may give place to necessity.*

59. *The ground in scripture, whereupon a necessity of outward baptism hath been built.*

60. *What kind of necessity in outward baptism hath been gathered by the words of our Saviour Christ; and what the true necessity thereof indeed is.*

61. *What things in baptism have been dispensed with by the fathers, respecting necessity.*

62. *Whether baptism by women be true baptism, good and effectual to them that receive it.*

63. *Of interrogatories in baptism, touching faith, and the purpose of a christian life.*

64. *Interrogatories proposed unto infants in baptism, and answered, as in their names by godfathers.*

65. *Of the cross in baptism.*

66. *Of confirmation after baptism.*

67. *Of the sacrament of the body and blood of Christ.*

68. *Of faults noted in the form of administring that holy sacrament.*

69. *Of festival days, and the natural causes of their convenient institution.*

70. *The manner of celebrating festival days.*

71. *Exceptions against our keeping of other festival days, besides the sabbath.*

72. *Of days appointed, as well for ordinary as for extraordinary fasts in the church of God.*

73. *The celebration of matrimony.*

74. *The churching of women.*

75. *The rites of burial.*

76. *Of the nature of that ministry, which serveth for performance of divine duties in the church of God, and how happiness, not eternal only, but also temporal, doth depend upon it.*

77. *Of power given unto men, to execute that heavenly office, of the gift of the holy ghost in ordination; and whether conveniently the power of order may be sought or sued for.*

78. *Of degrees, whereby the power of order is distinguished, and concerning the attire of ministers.*

79. *Of oblations, foundations, endowments, tythes, all intended for perpetuity of religion; which purpose being chiefly fulfilled by the clergies certain and sufficient maintenance, must needs by alienation of church-livings be made frustrate.*

80. *Of ordination lawful without title, and without any popular election precedent, but in no case without regard of due information what their quality is that enter into holy orders.*

81. *Of the learning that should be in ministers, their residence, and the number of their livings.*

Few

FEW there are of so weak capacity, but publick evils they easily espy; fewer so patient, as not to complain, when the grievous inconveniencies thereof work on the sensible smart. Howbeit, to see wherein the harm which they feel consisteth, the seeds from which it sprang, and the method of curing it, belongeth to and the stay a skill, the study whereof is so full of toil, and the practice so beset with difficulties, that wary and respective men had rather seek quietly their own, and wish that the world may go well, so it be not long of them, than with pain and hazard make themselves advisers for the common good. We which thought it at the very first a sign of cold affection towards the church of God, to prefer private ease before the labour of appeasing publick disturbance, must now of necessity refer events to the gracious providence of almighty God, and in discharge of our duty towards him, proceed with the plain and unpartial defence of a common cause. Wherein our endeavour is not so much to overthrow them with whom we contend, as to yield them just and reasonable causes of those things, which for want of due consideration heretofore they misconceived, accusing laws for mens over-sights, imputing evils grown through personal defects unto that which is not evil, framing unto some sores unwholsome plaisters, and applying otherfome where no sore is. To make therefore our beginning that which to both parts is most acceptable, *We agree*, That pure and unstained religion ought to be the highest of all cares appertaining to publick regiment, as well in regard of that (ᵃ) aid and protection which they who faithfully serve God confess they receive at his merciful hands, as also for the force which religion hath to qualify all sorts of men, and to make them in publick affairs the more serviceable; governors the apter to rule with conscience; inferiors for conscience fake the willinger to obey. It is no peculiar conceit, but a matter of sound consequence, that all duties are by so much the better performed, by how much the men are more religious from whose abilities the same proceed. For if (ᵇ) the course of politick affairs cannot in any good sort go forward without fit instruments, and that which fitteth them be their virtues; Let policy acknowledge it self indebted to religion, godliness being the (ᶜ) chiefest top and well-spring of all true virtues, even as God is of all good things. So natural is the union of religion with justice, that we may boldly deem there is neither, where both are not. For how should they be unfeignedly just, whom religion doth not cause to be such; or they religious, which are not found such by the proof of their just actions? If they which employ their labour and travel about the publick administration of justice, follow it only as a trade, with unquenchable and unconscionable thirst of gain, being not in heart persuaded that (ᵈ) justice is God's own work, and themselves his agents in this business; the sentence of right God's own verdict, and themselves his priests to deliver it; formalities of justice do but serve to smother right, and that which was necessarily ordained for the common good, is through shameful abuse made the cause of common misery. The same piety, which maketh them that are in authority desirous to please and resemble God by justice, inflameth, every way, men of action with zeal to do good (as far as their place will permit) unto all. For that, they know, is most noble and divine. Whereby, if no natural or casual inability cross their desires, they always delighting to inure themselves with actions most beneficial to others, cannot but gather great experience, and through experience the more wisdom; because conscience, and precept, the fear of swerving from that which is right, maketh them diligent observers of circumstances, the loose regard whereof is the nurse of vulgar folly, no less than Solomon's attention thereunto, was of natural farthereances the most effectual to make him eminent above others. For he gave good heed, and pierced every thing to the very ground, and by that means became the author of many parables. Concerning fortitude, sith evils great and unexpected (the true touchstone of constant minds) do cause oftentimes even them to think upon divine power with fearfullest suspicions, which have been otherwise the most secure despisers thereof; how should we look for any constant resolution of mind in such cases, saving only where unfeigned affection to Godward hath bred the most assured confidence to be assisted by his hand? For proof whereof, let but the acts of the ancient Jews be indifferently weighed, from whose magnanimity, in causes of most extreme hazard, those strange and unwonted resolutions have grown, which for all circumstances, no people under the roof of heaven did ever hitherto match. And that which did always animate them was their meer religion. Without which, if so be it were possible that all other ornaments of mind might be had in their full perfection, nevertheless the mind that should possess them, divorced from

[marginal notes:] True religion is the root of all true virtues, and the stay of all well ordered commonweals. (ᵃ) Psal. 144. 2. C. Th. lib. 16. tit. 2. *Gaudere & gloriari ex fide semper volumus, scientes magis religionibus quam officiis & labore corporis vel sudore nostram rempublicam contineri.* (ᵇ) Ἔργα δ᾽ ἰδίων ἐὸ τοῖς φιλέουσι φιλέσσιν & μισέων & μισές. Ἔαν ἄρθ σὺ μισθῷ ᾖ, λίσσω ᾖ ἀνομίαν. Τὸ γ᾽ ἀνομίαον ᾖ ἔστι τὸ τοῖς ἀσεβέσι ἐχθρῶ. Arist. Moral. lib. 1. cap. 1. (ᶜ) Ἀρχὴ δ᾽ ἀγαθὸν τῷ τί εἶναι θεός, ἀγάπης δ᾽ ευ-οτ᾽. Εἰ.᾽ Ευ.᾽ Eth. lo de dec. & praecept. (ᵈ) 2 Chron. 19. 6. *Ἀ̓μαπτῷ δ᾽ ἀνθρωπῶν, ἀλλ᾽ κυρίῳ, ᾧ θεωρεῖ.* cr. Arist. Ethic. lib. 1. cap. 2. Ecclef. 12. 10. Wisd. 17. 13.

piety, could be but a spectacle of commiseration ; even as that body is, which adorned with sundry other admirable beauties, wanted eye-sight, the chiefest grace that nature hath in kind to bestow. They which commend so much the felicity of that innocent world, wherein it is said, that men of their own accord did embrace fidelity and honesty, not for fear of the magistrate, or because revenge was before their eyes, if at any time they should do otherwise, but that which held the people in awe was the shame of ill-doing, the love of equity, and right it self, a bar against all oppressions which greatness of power causeth : They which describe unto us any such estate of happiness amongst men, though they speak not of religion, do notwithstanding declare that which is in truth her only working. For if religion did possess sincerely and sufficiently the hearts of all men, there would need no other restraint from evil. This doth not only give life and perfection to all endeavours wherewith it concurreth ; but what event soever ensues, it breedeth, if not joy and gladness always, yet always patience, satisfaction, and reasonable contentment of mind. Whereupon it hath been set

Psalm 1. 3. down as an axiom of good experience, that all things religiously taken in hand are prosperously ended ; because, whether men in the end have that which religion did allow them to desire, or that which it teacheth them contentedly to suffer, they are in neither

Τὸ ⟨Greek⟩ event unfortunate. But lest any man should here conceive, that it greatly skilleth not of what sort our religion be, in as much as Heathens, Turks and Infidels, impute to religion a great part of the same effects which our selves ascribe hereunto, they having ours in the same detestation that we theirs ; it shall be requisite to observe well, how far forth there may be agreement in the effects of different religions. First, By the bitter strife which riseth oftentimes from small differences in this behalf, and is by so much always greater as the matter is of more importance ; we see a general agreement in the secret opinion of men, that every man ought to embrace the religion which is true ;

Arist. Ethic.
lib. 1. cap.10. and to shun, as hurtful, whatsoever dissenteth from it, but that most, which doth fartheft dissent. The generality of which persuasion argueth, That God hath imprinted it by nature, to the end it might be a spur to our industry in searching and maintaining that religion, from which as to swerve in the least points is error, so the capital enemies thereof God hateth as his deadly foes, aliens, and without repentance, children of endless perdition. Such therefore, touching man's immortal state after this life, are not likely to reap benefit by their religion, but to look for the clean contrary, in regard of so important contrariety between it and the true religion. Nevertheless, in as much as the errors of the most seduced this way have been mixed with some truths, we are not to marvel, that although the one did turn to their endless woe and confusion, yet the other had

Cæf. de Bell.
Gall. lib. 6. many notable effects, as touching the affairs of this present life. There were in these quarters of the world, sixteen hundred years ago, certain speculative men, whose authority disposed the whole religion of those times. By their means it became a received opinion, that the souls of men departing this life, do flit out of one body into some other. Which opinion, though false, yet entwined with a true, that the souls of men do never perish, abated the fear of death in them which were so resolved, and gave them courage unto all adventures. The *Romans* had a vain superstitious custom, in most of their enterprises, to conjecture before hand of the event by certain tokens which they noted in birds, or in the entrails of beasts, or by other the like frivolous divinations. From whence notwithstanding as oft as they could receive any sign which they took to be favourable, it gave them such hope, as if their gods had made them more than half a promise of prosperous success. Which many times was the greatest cause that they did prevail, especially being men, of their own natural inclination, hopeful and strongly conceited, whatsoever they took in hand. But could their fond superstition have farthered so great attempts, without the mixture of a true persuasion concerning the unresistable force of divine power ? Upon the wilful violation of oaths, execrable blasphemy, and like contempts, offered by deriders of religion even unto false gods, fearful tokens of divine revenge have been known to follow. Which occurrents the devouter sort did take for manifest arguments, that the gods whom they worshipped were of power to reward such as sought unto them, and would plague those that feared them

Wisd. 14. 31. not. In this they erred. For (as the *wise man* rightly noteth concerning such) it was not the power of them by whom they sware, but the vengeance of them that sinned, which punished the offences of the ungodly. It was their hurt untruly to attribute so great power unto false gods. Yet the right conceit which they had, that to perjury vengeance is due, was not without good effect as touching the course of their lives, who feared the wilful violation of oaths in that respect. And whereas we read so many of them so much commended, some for their mild and merciful disposition, some for their virtuous severity, some for integrity of life, all these were the fruits of true and infallible

lible

lible principles delivered unto us in the word of God, as the axioms of our religion, which being imprinted by the God of nature in their hearts also, and taking better root in some than in most others, grew, though not from, yet with and amidst the heaps of manifold repugnant errors; which errors of corrupt religion had also their suitable effects in the lives of the self-same parties. Without all controversy, the purer and perfecter our religion is, the worthier effects it hath in them who stedfastly and sincerely embrace it, in others not. They that love the religion which they profess, may have failed in choice, but yet they are sure to reap what benefit the same is able to afford; whereas the best and soundest professed by them that bear it not the like affection, yieldeth them, retaining it in that sort, no benefit. *David* was a *man after God's own heart*, so termed, because his affection was hearty towards God. Beholding the like disposition in them which lived under him, it was his prayer to almighty God, *O keep this for ever in the purpose and thoughts of the heart of this people.* But when, after that *David* had ended his days in peace, they who succeeded him in place, for the most part followed him not in quality; when their kings (some few excepted) to better their worldly estate (as they thought) left their own and their peoples ghostly condition uncar'd for, by woful experience they both did learn, that to forsake the true God of heaven, is to fall into all such evils upon the face of the earth, as men either destitute of grace divine may commit, or unprotected from above, endure. Seeing therefore it doth thus appear that the safety of all estates dependeth upon religion; that religion unfeignedly loved perfecteth men's abilities unto all kinds of virtuous services in the commonwealth; that men's desire in general is to hold no religion but the true; and that whatsoever good effects do grow out of their religion, who embrace instead of the true a false, the roots thereof are certain sparks of the light of truth intermingled with the darkness of error; because no religion can wholly and only consist of untruths, we have reason to think, that all true virtues are to honour true religion as their parent, and all well ordered commonweals to love her as their chiefest stay.

2. They of whom God is altogether unapprehended, are but few in number, and for grossness of wit such, that they hardly and scarcely seem to hold the place of human being. These we should judge to be of all others most miserable, but that a wretcheder sort there are, on whom, whereas nature has bestowed riper capacity, their evil disposition seriously goeth about therewith to apprehend God as being not God. Whereby it cometh to pass, that of these two sorts of men, both godless, the one having utterly no knowledge of God, the other study how to persuade themselves that there is no such thing to be known. The fountain and well-spring of which impiety, is a resolved purpose of mind to reap in this world what sensual profit or pleasure soever the world yieldeth, and not to be barred from any whatsoever means available thereunto. And that this is the very radical cause of their atheism, no man (I think) will doubt, which considereth what pains they take to destroy their principal spurs and motives unto all virtue, the creation of the world, the providence of God, the resurrection of the dead, the joys of the kingdom of heaven, and the endless pains of the wicked, yea, above all things, the authority of the scripture, because on these points it evermore beateth, and the souls immortality, which granted, draweth easily after it the rest as a voluntary train. Is it not wonderful, that base desires should so extinguish in men the sense of their own excellency, as to make them willing that their souls should be like to the souls of beasts, mortal and corruptible with their bodies? Till some admirable or unusual accident happen (as it hath in some) to work the beginning of a better alteration in their minds, disputation about the knowledge of God with such kind of persons commonly prevaileth little. For how should the brightness of wisdom shine, where the windows of the soul are of very set purpose closed? True religion hath many things in it, the only mention whereof galleth and troubleth their minds. Being therefore loth that enquiry into such matters should breed a persuasion in the end contrary unto that they embrace, it is their endeavour to banish, as much as in them lieth, quite and clean from their cogitation whatsoever may sound that way. But it cometh many times to pass (which is their torment) that the thing they shun doth follow them; truth, as it were, even obtruding itself into their knowledge, and not permitting them to be so ignorant as they would be. Whereupon, inasmuch as the nature of man is unwilling to continue doing that wherein it shall always condemn it self, they continuing still obstinate to follow the course which they have begun, are driven to devise all the shifts that wit can invent for the smothering of this light, all that may but with any the least shew of possibility stay their minds from thinking that true, which they heartily wish were false, but cannot think it so without some scruple and

4   fear

Marginal notes:
1 Chr. 29. 17.

The most extreme opposite to true religion, is affected atheism.

Wisd. 2. 21. Such things they imagine, and go astray, because their own wickedness hath blinded them.

Ἔσ' γὸ ὶ ἐ- ναι φθαρτικὰ ἀτ γὰ.
Arist. Eth. lib. 6. cap. 5.

Sufan. ver. 9. They turned away their mind, and cast down their eyes, that they might not see heaven, nor remember just judgments.

Hæc est summa
malitii, nolle
agnoscere quem
ignorare non
possis. Cypr.
de Idol. Va-
nit.
2 Pet. 3. 3.
Jude Verf. 18.

Dan. 3. 29.

(ᵃ) Vos scelera
admissa puni-
sis, apud nos
& cogitare
peccare est;
vos conscii ti-
metis, nos eti-
am conscienti-
am solam, si-
ne qua est non
possumus. Mi-
nu. Fel. in
Octav.
Summum præ-
sidium regni
est justitia ob
apertos tumul-
tus, & religio
ob occultos.
Carda. de Sa-
pien. lib. 3.
(ᵇ) Mach.
Disc. l. 1. c.
11, 12, 13, 14.

fear of the contrary. Now because that judicious learning, for which we commend most worthily the ancient sages of the world, doth not in this case serve the turn, these trenchermates (for such the most of them be) frame to themselves a way more pleasant, a new method they have of turning things that are serious into mockery, an art of contradiction by way of scorn, a learning wherewith we were long sithence forewarn'd that the miserable time whereunto we are fallen should abound. This they study, this they practise, this they grace with a wanton superfluity of wit, too much insulting over the patience of more virtuously disposed minds. For towards these so forlorn creatures we are (it must be confest) too patient. In zeal to the glory of God, *Babylon* hath exceeded *Sion*. We want that decree of *Nebuchodonosor*; the fury of this wicked brood hath the reins too much at liberty; their tongues walk at large; the spit-venom of their poison'd hearts breaketh out to the annoyance of others; what their untamed lust suggesteth, the same their licentious mouths do every where set abroach. With our contentions their irreligious humour also is much strengthned. Nothing pleaseth them better than these manifold oppositions upon the matter of religion, as well for that they have hereby the more opportunity to learn on one side how another may be oppugn'd, and so to weaken the credit of all unto themselves; as also because by this hot pursuit of lower controversies among men professing religion, and agreeing in the principal foundations thereof, they conceive hope that about the higher principles themselves time will cause altercation to grow. For which purpose, when they see occasion, they stick not sometime in other men's persons, yea, sometime without any vizard at all, directly to try what the most religious are able to say in defence of the highest points whereupon all religion dependeth. Now for the most part it so falleth out, touching things which generally are receiv'd, that although in themselves they be most certain; yet because men presume them granted of all, we are hardliest able to bring such proof of their certainty as may satisfy gainsayers, when suddenly and besides expectation they require the same at our hands. Which impreparation and unreadiness when they find in us, they turn it to soothing up of themselves in that cursed fancy, whereby they would fain believe that the hearty devotion of such as indeed fear God, is nothing else but a kind of harmless error, bred and confirm'd in them by the sleights of wiser men. For a politick use of religion they see there is, and by it they would also gather that religion it self is a meer politick device, forged purposely to serve for that use. Men fearing God are thereby a great deal more effectually, than by positive laws, restrain'd from doing evil; in as much as those laws have no farther power than over our outward actions only, whereas unto men's inward cogitations, unto the privy intents and motions of their hearts, religion serveth for a bridle. What more savage, wild and cruel than man, if he see himself able either by fraud to over-reach, or by power to over-bear the laws whereunto he should be subject? Wherefore in so great boldness to offend, it behoveth that the world should be held in awe, not by a vain surmise, but a true apprehension of somewhat, which no man may think himself able to withstand. This is the politick use of religion. In which respect there are, of these wise malignants, (ᵇ) some who have vouchsafed it their marvelous favourable countenance and speech; very gravely affirming, That religion honoured, addeth greatness; and contemned, bringeth ruin unto commonweals: That princes and states which will continue, are above all things to uphold the reverend regard of religion, and to provide for the same by all means in the making of their laws. But when they should define what means are best for that purpose, behold, they extol the wisdom of paganism; they give it out as a mystical precept of great importance, that princes and such as are under them in most authority and credit with the people, should take all occasions of rare events, and from what cause soever the same do proceed, yet wrest them to the strengthening of their religion, and not make it nice for so good a purpose to use, if need be, plain forgeries. Thus while they study to bring to pass that religion may seem but a matter made, they lose themselves in the very maze of their own discourses, as if reason did even purposely forsake them, who of purpose forsake God the author thereof. For surely, a strange kind of madness it is, that those Men, who though they be void of piety, yet because they have wit, cannot chuse but know that treachery, guile and deceit, are things which may for a while, but do not use long to go unespied, should teach, that the greatest honour to a state is perpetuity; and grant that alterations in the service of God, for that they impair the credit of religion, are therefore perilous in commonweals, which have no continuance longer than religion hath all reverence done unto it; and withal acknowledge (for so they do) that when people began to espy the falshood of oracles, whereupon all gentilism was built, their hearts were utterly averted from it; and notwithstanding counfel, princes, in fober earneft for the ftrengthning of their ftates, to maintain religion, and for the maintenance of religion, not to make choice of that which is true, but to authorize that they make choice of by thofe falfe and fraudulent means which in the end muft needs overthrow it. Such are the counfels of men godlefs, when they would fhew themfelves politick devifers, able to create God in man by art.

3. Wherefore to let go this execrable crew, and to come to extremities on the contrary hand; two affections there are, the forces whereof, as they bear the greater or leffer fway in man's heart, frame accordingly to the ftamp and character of his religion, the one zeal, the other fear. Zeal, unlefs it be rightly guided, when it endeavoureth moft bufily to pleafe God, forceth upon him thofe unfeafonable offices which pleafe him not. For which caufe, if they who this way fwerve, be compared with fuch fincere, found and difcreet, as *Abraham* was in matter of religion; the fervice of the one is like unto flattery; the other, like the faithful fedulity of friendfhip. Zeal, except it be ordered aright, when it bendeth it felf unto conflict with all things, either in deed, or but imagined to be oppofite unto religion, ufeth the razor many times with fuch eagernefs, that the very life of religion it felf is thereby hazarded; through hatred of tares, the corn in the field of God is plucked up. So that zeal needeth both ways a fober guide. Fear, on the other fide, if it have not the light of true underftanding concerning God, wherewith to be moderated, breedeth likewife fuperftition. It is therefore dangerous, that in things divine we fhould work too much upon the fpur, either of zeal or fear. Fear is a good folicitor to devotion. Howbeit, fith fear in this kind doth grow from an apprehenfion of deity, endued with irrefiftible power to hurt, and is of all affections (anger excepted) the unapteft to admit any conference with reafon; for which caufe the wife man doth fay of fear, that it is a betrayer of the forces of reafonable underftanding; therefore, except men know beforehand what manner of fervice pleafeth God, while they are fearful they try all things which fancy offereth. Many there are who never think on God, but when they are in extremity of fear; and then becaufe, what to think, or what to do, they are uncertain, perplexity not fuffering them to be idle, they think and do, as it were, in a phrenfy, they know not what. Superftition neither knoweth the right kind, nor obferveth the due meafure of actions belonging to the fervice of God, but is always joined with a wrong opinion touching things divine. Superftition is, when things are either abhorred or obferved with a zealous or fearful, but erroneous relation to God. By means whereof, the fuperftitious do fometimes ferve, though the true God, yet with needlefs offices, and defraud him of duties neceffary; fometimes load others than him, with fuch honours as properly are his. The one, their overfight who mifs in the choice of that wherewith they are affected; the other, theirs who fail in the election of him towards whom they fhew their devotion: This, the crime of idolatry; that, the fault of voluntary, either nicenefs or fuperfluity in religion. The chriftian world it felf being divided into two grand parts, it appeareth by the general view of both, that with matter of herefy the Weft hath been often and much troubled; but the Eaft part never quiet till the deluge of mifery, wherein now they are, overwhelmed them. The chiefeft caufe whereof doth feem to have lien in the reftlefs wits of the *Grecians*, evermore proud of their own curious and fubtle inventions; which when at any time they had contrived, the great facility of their language ferved them readily to make all things fair and plaufible to men's underftandings. Thofe grand heretical impieties therefore, which moft highly and immediately touched God and the glorious Trinity, were all in a manner the monfters of the Eaft. The Weft bred fewer a great deal, and thofe commonly of a lower nature, fuch as more nearly and directly concerned rather men than God; the Latins being always to capital herefies lefs inclined, yet unto grofs fuperftition more. Superftition, fuch as that of the *Pharifees* was, by whom divine things indeed were lefs, becaufe other things were more divinely efteemed of than reafon would; the fuperftition that rifeth voluntarily, and by degrees which are hardly difcerned, mingling it felf with the rites even of divine fervice done to the only true God, muft be confidered of as a creeping and incroaching evil; an evil, the firft beginnings whereof are commonly harmlefs, fo that it proveth only then to be an evil, when fome farther accident doth grow unto it, or it felf come unto farther growth. For in the church of God, fometimes it cometh to pafs, as in over-battle grounds, the fertile difpofition whereof is good; yet becaufe it exceedeth due proportion, it bringeth forth abundantly, through too much ranknefs, things lefs profitable; whereby that which principally it fhould yield, being either prevented in place, or defrauded of nourifhment, faileth. This (if fo large a difcourfe were neceffary) might be exemplified even by heaps of rites and cuftoms, now fuperftitious in the greateft part of the chriftian

world;

Of fuperftition, and the root thereof, either mifguided zeal, or ignorant fear of divine glory.

2 Chron. 20. *Abraham* thy friend.

Wifd. 17. 11.

Mark 7. 9.

world; which in their firſt original beginnings, when the ſtrength of vertuous, devout, or charitable affection bloomed them, no man could juſtly have condemned as evil.

Of the redreſs of ſuperſtition in God's church, and concerning the queſtion of this book.

4. But howſoever ſuperſtition doth grow; that wherein unſounder times have done amiſs, the better ages enſuing muſt rectify as they may. I now come therefore to thoſe accuſations brought againſt us by pretenders of reformation. The firſt in the rank whereof is ſuch, That if ſo be the church of *England* did at this day therewith as juſtly deſerve to be touched, as they in this cauſe have imagined it doth, rather would I exhort all ſorts to ſeek pardon even with tears at the hands of God, than meditate words of defence for our doings, to the end that men might think favourably of them. For as the caſe of this world, eſpecially now, doth ſtand, what other ſtay or ſuccour have we to lean unto, ſaving the teſtimony of our conſcience, and the comfort we take in this, that we ſerve the living God (as near as our wits can reach unto the knowledge thereof) even according to his own will, and do therefore truſt that his mercy ſhall be our ſafeguard againſt thoſe enraged powers abroad, which principally in that reſpect are become our Enemies? But ſith no man can do ill with a good conſcience, the conſolation which we herein ſeem to find, is but a meer deceitful pleaſing of our ſelves in error, which at the length muſt needs turn to our greater grief, if that which we do to pleaſe God moſt, be for the manifold defects thereof offenſive unto him. For ſo it is judged, our prayers, our ſacraments, our faſts, our times and places of publick meeting together for the worſhip and ſervice of God; our marriages, our burials, our functions, elections and ordinations eccleſiaſtical, almoſt whatſoever we do in the exerciſe of our religion according to the laws for that purpoſe eſtabliſhed, all things are ſome way or other thought faulty, all things ſtained with ſuperſtition. Now, although it may be the wiſer ſort of men are not greatly moved hereat, conſidering how ſubject the very beſt things have been always unto cavil, when wits poſſeſſed either with diſdain or diſlike thereof have ſet them up as their mark to ſhoot at: Safe notwithſtanding it were not therefore to neglect the danger which from hence may grow, and that eſpecially in regard of them, who deſiring to ſerve God as they ought, but being not ſo ſkilful as in every point to unwind themſelves where the ſnares of gloſing ſpeech do lye to entangle them, are in mind not a little troubled, when they hear ſo bitter invectives againſt that which this church hath taught them to reverence as holy, to approve as lawful, and to obſerve as behoveful for the exerciſe of chriſtian duty. It ſeemeth therefore, at leaſt for their ſakes, very meet, that ſuch as blame us in this behalf, be directly anſwered; and they which follow us, informed plainly in the reaſons of that we do. On both ſides, the end intended between us is to have laws and ordinances, ſuch as may rightly ſerve to aboliſh ſuperſtition, and to eſtabliſh the ſervice of God with all things thereunto appertaining in ſome perfect form. There is an inward reaſonable, and there is a ſolemn outward ſerviceable worſhip belonging unto God. Of the former kind are all manner of virtuous duties, that each man in reaſon and conſcience to Godward oweth. Solemn and ſerviceable worſhip we name for diſtinction ſake, whatſoever belongeth to the church or publick ſociety of God by way of external adoration. It is the latter of theſe two, whereupon our preſent queſtion groweth. Again, this latter being ordered partly, and as touching principal matters, by none but precepts divine only; partly, and as concerning things of inferior regard, by ordinances as well human as divine: about the ſubſtance of religion, wherein God's only law muſt be kept, there is here no controverſy. The crime now intended againſt us, is, That our laws have not ordered thoſe inferior things as behoveth, and that our cuſtoms are either ſuperſtitious, or otherwiſe amiſs, whether we reſpect the exerciſe of publick duties in religion, or the functions of perſons authorized thereunto.

Four general propoſitions demanding that which may reaſonably be granted concerning matters of outward form in the exerciſe of true religion. And fifthly, of a rule not ſafe nor reaſonable in theſe caſes.

5. It is with teachers of mathematical ſciences uſual, for us in this preſent queſtion neceſſary, to lay down firſt certain reaſonable demands, which in moſt particulars following are to ſerve as principles whereby to work, and therefore muſt be before-hand conſidered. The men whom we labour to inform in the truth, perceive that ſo to proceed is requiſite. For to this end they alſo propoſe, touching cuſtoms and rites indifferent, their general axioms, ſome of them ſubject unto juſt exceptions, and, as we think, more meet by them to be farther conſidered, than aſſented unto by us. As that, *In outward things belonging to the ſervice of God, reformed churches ought by all means to ſhun conformity with the church of* Rome; that, *The firſt reformed ſhould be a pattern whereunto all that come after, ought to conform themſelves;* that, *Sound religion may not uſe the things, which being not commanded of God, have been either deviſed or abuſed unto ſuperſtition.* Theſe and the reſt of the ſame conſort we have in the book going before examined. Other canons they alledge, and rules not unwor-

I

thy

thy of approbation ; as, *That in all such things the glory of God, and the edification or ghostly good of his people must be sought ; that nothing should be undecently or unorderly done.* But forasmuch as all the difficulty is, in discerning what things do glorify God and edify his church, what not ; when we should think them decent and fit, when otherwise : because these rules being too general, come not near enough unto the matter which we have in hand ; and the former principles being nearer the purpose, are too far from truth ; we must propose unto all men certain petitions incident and very material in causes of this nature, such as no man of moderate judgment hath cause to think unjust or unreasonable.

6. The first thing therefore which is of force to cause approbation with good conscience towards such customs and rites as publickly are established, is, when there ariseth from the due consideration of those customs and rites in themselves apparent reason, although not always to prove them better than any other that might possibly be devised, (for who did ever require this in man's ordinances ?) yet competent to shew their conveniency and fitness, in regard of the use for which they would serve. Now touching the nature of religious services, and the manner of their due performance, thus much generally we know to be most clear ; That whereas the greatness and dignity of all manner of actions is measured by the worthiness of the subject from which they proceed, and of the object whereabout they are conversant, we must of necessity in both respects acknowledge, that this present world affordeth not any thing comparable unto the publick duties of religion. For if the best things have the perfectest and best operations ; it will follow, that seeing man is the worthiest creature upon earth ; and every society of men more worthy than any man ; and of societies, that most excellent which we call the church ; there can be in this world no work performed equal to the exercise of true religion, the proper operation of the church of God. Again, forasmuch as religion worketh upon him, who in majesty and power is infinite, as we ought we account not of it, unless we esteem it even according to that very height of excellency which our hearts conceive, when divine sublimity it self is rightly considered. In the powers and faculties of our souls God requireth the uttermost which our unfeigned affection towards him is able to yield : So that if we affect him not far above and before all things, our religion hath not that inward perfection which it should have, neither do we indeed worship him as our God. That which inwardly each man should be, the church outwardly ought to testify. And therefore the duties of our religion which are seen, must be such as that affection which is unseen ought to be. Signs must resemble the things they signify. If religion bear the greatest sway in our hearts, our outward religious duties must shew it as far as the church hath outward ability. Duties of religion performed by whole Societies of men, ought to have in them, according to our power, a sensible excellency, correspondent to the majesty of him whom we worship. Yea, then are the publick duties of religion best ordered, when the militant church doth resemble by sensible means, as it may in such cases, that hidden dignity and glory wherewith the church triumphant in heaven is beautified. Howbeit, even as the very heat of the sun it self, which is the life of the whole world, was to the people of God in the desert a grievous annoiance, for ease whereof his extraordinary providence ordained a cloudy pillar to over-shadow them : So things of general use and benefit (for in this world, what is so perfect that no inconvenience doth ever follow it ?) may by some accident be incommodious to a few. In which case, for such private evils, remedies there are of like condition, though publick ordinances, wherein the common good is respected, be not stirred. Let our first demand be therefore, That in the external form of religion, such things as are apparently, or can be sufficiently proved effectual and generally fit to set forward godliness, either as betokening the greatness of God, or as beseeming the dignity of religion, or as concurring with celestial impressions in the minds of men, may be reverently thought of ; some few, rare, casual, and tolerable, or otherwise curable inconveniences notwithstanding.

7. Neither may we in this case lightly esteem what hath been allowed as fit in the judgment of antiquity, and by the long continued practice of the whole church ; from which unnecessarily to swerve, experience never as yet found it safe. For wisdom's sake we reverence them no less that are young, or not much less than if they were stricken in Years. And therefore of such it is rightly said, *That the ripeness of understanding is gray hair, and the virtues old age.* But because wisdom and youth are seldom joined in one, and the ordinary course of the world is more according to *Job's* Observation, who giveth men advice to seek wisdom *amongst the ancient, and in the length of*

The first proposition touching judgment, what things are convenient in the outward publick ordering of church affairs.

John 4. 24.
Wisd. 6. 10.
1 Chron. 29. 17.

2 Chron. 2. 5.

Ἐκκλησία ἔστι ἀπὸ γεῆς, Germa. ὁ δὲ ἰσσε ωλὴ ου. Defectatio Domini in æthereum fas est ; ecclesia vero est imago cœlestium. Ambros. de interpel. Dav.
Facit in terris operacœlorum. Sidon. Apol. Epist. lib. 6.

The second Proposition.

Wisdom 4. 9.
Job 12. 12.

days

days underſtanding ; therefore if the compariſon do ſtand between man and man, which ſhall hearken unto other, ſith the aged for the moſt part are beſt experienced, leaſt ſubject to raſh and unadviſed Paſſions ; it hath been ever judged reaſonable, That their ſentence in matter of counſel ſhould be better truſted, and more relied upon than other men's. The goodneſs of God having furniſhed men with two chief inſtruments, both neceſſary for this life, hands to execute, and a mind to deviſe great things ; the one is not profitable longer than the vigor of youth doth ſtrengthen it ; nor the other greatly, till age and experience have brought it to perfection. In whom therefore time hath not perfected knowledge, ſuch muſt be contented to follow them in whom it hath. For this cauſe none is more attentively heard, than they whoſe ſpeeches are, as *David*'s were, *I have been young, and now am old*, much I have ſeen and obſerved in the world. Sharp and ſubtile diſcourſes of wit procure many times very great applauſe ; but being laid in the balance with that which the habit of ſound experience plainly delivereth they are over-weighed. God may endue men extraordinarily with underſtanding as it pleaſeth him : But let no man preſuming thereupon neglect the inſtructions, or deſpiſe the ordinances of his elders ; ſith he, whoſe gift wiſdom is, hath

Deut. 32. 7. ſaid, *Ask thy father, and he will ſhew thee ; thine ancients, and they ſhall tell thee.* It is therefore the voice both of God and nature, not of learning only, that, eſpecially

Ariſt. Eth. 6.
cap. 11. in matters of action and policy, *The ſentences and judgments of men experienced, aged and wiſe, yea though they ſpeak without any proof or demonſtration, are no leſs to be hearkned unto, than as being demonſtrations in themſelves ; becauſe ſuch men's long obſervation is as an eye, wherewith they preſently and plainly behold thoſe principles which ſway over all actions.* Whereby we are taught both the cauſe wherefore wiſe men's judgments ſhould be credited, and the means how to uſe their judgments to the increaſe of our own wiſdom. That which ſheweth them to be wiſe, is, the gathering of principles out of their own particular experiments. And the framing of our particular experiments, according to the rule of their principles, ſhall make us ſuch as they are. If therefore even at the firſt, ſo great account ſhould be made of wiſe men's coun-

a Πλὲῖ τὸς ἐκ πολλῶν, ὀλί-γῷ ὑδεὶς οὐ-των. Philo. Πᾶσι λυ-μίτεται τὸ Cῖν τότῳ πυντι-ντὸθται. Synef. Τὸ ἐκ πολλῶν ἐν' ἀποδεί-χτηι ἢ τηπιειν-ται αφοδίνως. Greg. Naz. ἐν Συχ.
b δ πει ὑὶ ἀ-τάδ' πειν τρὸ-πων τὸ ὑ ἀρ-χαιότι[σ]ῷ ὀυμιὸν τῷ ἐϱι-τοτερτῆς τρεπιειμοῦ ἑ ἄπειρο-πίπτει ὑ π'τείϱων δε-ϱϋλλαέην ἢ ὁροδέντη χ'ϱ τε χόϱεν ἢ πολιτ, τεὺϱ̓ꝯ καϑϱ̓ꝯ τὰ ουπ̃. Baſil. de Spirit. Sanct. cap. 7. Ὁ μὲν μικρὸν τὰ εὖ μεπέρ-Caϊτωϱ, ἢ ϕϑ-χ'ꝯ. Ariſt. Ethic. 2. c.9. Modiei nulla fere ratio ha-beri ſolet. Tiraquel de jud. in reb. exig. cap. 10. ſels touching things that are publickly done ; as time ſhall add thereunto continuance and approbation of ſucceeding ages, their credit and authority muſt needs be greater. They which do nothing but that which men of account did before them, are, although they do amiſs, yet the leſs a faulty, becauſe they are not the authors of harm. And doing well, their actions are freed from prejudice and novelty. To the beſt and wiſeſt while they live, the world is continually a froward oppoſite, a curious obſerver of their defects and imperfections ; their virtues it afterwards as much admireth. And for this cauſe many times that which moſt deſerveth approbation, would hardly be able to find favour, if they which propoſe it were not content to profeſs themſelves therein ſcholars and followers of the ancients. For the world will not endure to hear that we are wiſer than they have been which went before. In which conſideration there is cauſe why we ſhould be ſlow and unwilling to change, without very urgent neceſſity, the ancient ordinances, rites, and long approved cuſtoms of our venerable predeceſſors. The love of things ancient doth argue b ſtayedneſs ; but levity and want of experience maketh apt unto innovations. That which wiſdom did firſt begin, and hath been with good men long continued, challengeth allowance of them that ſucceed, altho' it plead for it ſelf nothing. That which is new, if it promiſe not much, doth fear condemnation before trial ; 'till trial, no man doth acquit or truſt it, what good ſoever it pretend and promiſe. So that in this kind, there are few things known to be good, 'till ſuch time as they grow to be ancient. The vain pretence of thoſe glorious names, where they could not be with any truth, neither in reaſon ought to have been ſo much alledged, hath wrought ſuch a prejudice againſt them in the minds of the common ſort, as if they had utterly no force at all ; whereas (eſpecially for theſe obſervances which concern our preſent queſtion) antiquity, cuſtom, and conſent in the church of God, making with that which Law doth eſtabliſh, are themſelves moſt ſufficient reaſons to uphold the ſame, unleſs ſome notable publick inconvenience enforce the contrary. For a ſmall thing in the eye of law is nothing. We are therefore bold to make our ſecond petition this, That in things, the fitneſs whereof is not of it ſelf apparent, nor eaſy to be made ſufficiently manifeſt unto all, yet the judgment of antiquity concurring with that which is received, may induce them to think it not unfit, who are not able to alledge any known weighty inconvenience which it hath, or to take any ſtrong exception againſt it.

2. All

8. All things cannot be of ancient continuance, which are expedient and needful *The third* for the ordering of spiritual affairs: but the church being a body which dieth not, *proposition.* hath always power, as occasion requireth, no less to ordain that which never was, than to ratify what hath been before. To prescribe the order of doing in all things, is a peculiar prerogative which *wisdom* hath, as a queen or soveraign commandress over other vertues. This in every several man's actions of common life appertaineth unto *'Η μἰν ὲριρη-* *moral*; in publick and politick secular affairs, unto *civil* wisdom. In like manner, *ης μεἰ τὰ* to devise any certain form for the outward administration of publick duties in the ser- *ξευς ἀιντε* vice of God, or things belonging thereunto, and to find out the most convenient for *πθεἰω.* Phi-that use, is a point of wisdom *ecclesiastical*. It is not for a Man, which doth know *lo. Pag. 35.* or should know what order is, and what peaceable government requireth, to ask, *Why we should hang our judgment upon our churches sleeve*; and, *why in matters of* T. C. l. 3. *order, more than in matters of doctrine*. The church hath authority to establish that p. 171. for an order at one time, which at another time it may abolish, and in both may do well. But that which in doctrine the church doth now deliver rightly as a truth, no man will say that it may hereafter recal, and as rightly avouch the contrary. Laws touching matter of order are changeable by the power of the church; articles concerning doctrine, not so. We read often in the writings of catholick and holy men touching matters of doctrine, *this we believe, this we hold, this the prophets and evangelists have declared, this the apostles have delivered, this martyrs have sealed with their blood, and confessed in the midst of torments*; *to this we cleave, as to the anchor of our souls*; *against this, tho' an angel from heaven should preach unto us, we would not believe*. But did we ever in any of them read touching matters of meer comeliness, order and decency, neither commanded nor prohibited by any prophet, any evangelist, any apostle, *although the church wherein we live do ordain them to be kept, although they be never so generally observed, though all the churches in the world should command them, though angels from heaven should require our subjection thereto*, I would hold him accursed that *doth obey?* Be it in matter of the one kind or of the other, what scripture doth plainly deliver, to that the first place both of credit and obedience is due; the next whereunto is, whatsoever any man can necessarily conclude by Force of reason; after these, the voice of the church succeedeth. That which the church by her ecclesiastical authority shall probably think and define to be true or good, must in congruity of reason over-rule all other inferior judgments whatsoever. To them which ask, why we thus hang our judgments on the churches sleeve, I answer with *Solomon*, because *a two are better than one*. *Yea simply* (saith *b Basil*) *a Eccles. 4.* *and universally, whether it be in works of nature, or voluntary choice and counsel: I* *b Basil. Ep.* *see not any thing done as it should be, if it be wrought by an agent singling it self* 68. d. 8. c. *from conforts*. The *Jews* had a sentence of good advice, *c take not upon thee to be Que contra.* *judge alone; there is no sole judge but one only*; *say not to others, receive my sen- nis pari uni-tence, when their authority is above thine*. The bare consent of the whole church *verso suo non* should it self in these things stop their mouths, who living under it, dare presume to *congruens.* bark against it. *There is* (saith *d Cassianus*) *no place of audience left for them, by in Cap. Patr.* *whom obedience is not yielded to that which all have agreed upon*. Might we not *d Cassian. de* think it more than wonderful, that nature should in all communities appoint a predo- *c. 6.* minant judgment to sway and over-rule in so many things; or that God himself should allow so much authority and power unto every poor family for the ordering of all which are in it; and the city of the living God, which is his church, be able neither to command, nor yet to forbid any thing which the meanest shall in that respect, and for her sole authorities sake be bound to obey? We cannot hide or dissemble that evil, the grievous inconvenience whereof we feel. Our dislike of them, by whom too much heretofore hath been attributed unto the church, is grown to an error on the contrary hand; so that now from the church of God too much is derogated. By which removal of one extremity with another the world seeking to procure a remedy, hath purchased a meer exchange of the evil which before was felt. Suppose we, that the sacred word of God can at their hands receive due honour, by whose incitement the holy ordinances of the church endure every where open contempt? No, it is not possible they should observe as they ought the one, who from the other withdraw unnecessarily their own or their brethren's obedience. Surely the church of God in this business is neither of capacity, I trust, so weak, nor so unstrengthened, I know, with authority from above; but that her laws may exact obedience at the hands of her own children, and injoin gainsayers silence, giving them roundly to understand, that where our duty is submission, weak oppositions betoken Pride. We therefore crave, thirdly, to have it granted, that where neither

the

the evidence of any law divine, nor the ſtrength of any invincible argument otherwiſe found out by the light of reaſon, nor any notable publick inconvenience doth make againſt that which our own laws eccleſiaſtical have, although but newly, inſtituted, for the ordering of theſe affairs, the very authority of the church it ſelf, at the leaſt in ſuch caſes, may give ſo much credit to our own laws, as to make their ſentence touch- ing fitneſs and conveniency, weightier than any bare or naked conceit to the contrary; eſpecially in them, who can owe no leſs than child-like obedience to her that hath more than motherly power.

The fourth propoſition.

9. There are ancient ordinances, laws (which on all ſides are allowed to be juſt and good, yea divine and apoſtolick conſtitutions) which the church, it may be, doth not always keep, nor always juſtly deſerve blame in that reſpect. For in evils that cannot be removed, without the manifeſt danger of greater to ſucceed in their rooms; wiſdom (of neceſſity) muſt give place to neceſſity. All it can do in thoſe caſes is, to deviſe how that which muſt be endured may be mitigated, and the in- conveniences thereof countervailed as near as may be; that when the beſt things are not poſſible, the beſt may be made of thoſe that are. Nature, than which there is nothing more conſtant, nothing more uniform in all her ways, doth notwithſtanding ſtay her hand, yea, and change her courſe, when that which God by creation did

Numb. 22. 28.

command, he doth at any time by neceſſity countermand. It hath therefore pleaſed himſelf ſometime to unlooſe the very tongues even of dumb creatures, and to teach them to plead this in their own defence, left the cruelty of man ſhould perſiſt to afflict them for not keeping their wonted courſe, when ſome invincible impediment hath hindred. If we leave nature and look into art, the workman hath in his heart a purpoſe, he carrieth in mind the whole form which his work ſhould have; there wanteth not in him ſkill and deſire to bring his labour to the beſt effect, only the matter which he hath to work on is unframable. This neceſſity excuſeth him; ſo that nothing is derogated from his credit, although much of his works perfection be found wanting. Touching actions of common life, there is not any defence more fa- vourably heard than theirs, who alledge ſincerely for themſelves, that they did as ne- ceſſity conſtrained them. For when the mind is rightly ordered and affected as it ſhould be, in caſe ſome external impediment croſſing well adviſed deſires ſhall in- tently draw Men to leave what they principally wiſh, and to take a courſe which they would not if their choice were free; what neceſſity forceth Men unto, the ſame

Neceſſitas, quicquid co- git, defendit. Senec. Con- trov. l. 9.

in this caſe it maintaineth, as long as nothing is committed ſimply in it ſelf evil, nothing abſolutely ſinful or wicked, nothing repugnant to that immutable law, where- by whatſoever is condemned as evil, can never any way be made good. The caſt- ing away of things profitable for the ſuſtenance of Man's Life, is an unthankful abuſe of the fruits of God's good providence towards mankind. Which conſideration, for

Acts 27. 38.

all that, did not hinder St. *Paul* from throwing corn into the Sea, when care of ſaving mens lives made it neceſſary to loſe that which elſe had been better ſaved. Neither was this to do evil, to the end that good might come of it; for of two ſuch evils, being not both evitable, the choice of the leſs is not evil. And evils muſt be in our conſtructions judged inevitable, if there be no apparent ordinary way to avoid them; becauſe, where counſel and advice bear rule, of God's extraordinary power without extraordinary warrant, we cannot preſume. In civil affairs, to declare what ſway neceſſity hath ever been accuſtomed to bear, were labour infinite. The laws of all ſtates and kingdoms in the world have ſcarcely of any thing more common uſe. Should then only the church ſhew it ſelf inhumane and ſtern, abſolutely urging a rigorous obſervation of ſpiritual ordinances without relaxation or exception, what neceſſity ſoever happen? We know the contrary practice to have been commended by

Luke 6. 4.

him, upon the warrant of whoſe judgment the church, moſt of all delighted with merciful and moderate courſes, doth the oftner condeſcend unto like equity, permit-

Cauſa neceſſi- tatis & utili- tatis æquipa- rantur in jure. Ab. Panor. ad c. ut ſuper nu. 15. de. Reb. Eccleſ. non alien.

ting in caſes of neceſſity, that which otherwiſe it diſalloweth and forbiddeth. Caſes of neceſſity being ſometime but urgent, ſometime extream, the conſideration of pub- lick utility is with very good advice judged at the leaſt equivalent with the eaſier kind of neceſſity. Now that which cauſeth numbers to ſtorm againſt ſo neceſſary tolerati- ons, which they ſhould rather let paſs with ſilence, conſidering that in polity as well ecclefiaſtical as civil, there are and will be always evils which no art of man can cure, breaches and leaks more than man's wit hath hands to ſtop; that which maketh odious unto them many things, wherein notwithſtanding the truth is that very juſt regard hath been had of the publick good; That which in a great part of the weightieſt cauſes belonging to this preſent controverſy, hath infnared the judgments both of fundry good, and of ſome well learned men, is the manifeſt truth of certain general principles whereup-

4

on

on the ordinances that ferve for ufual practice in the church of God are grounded. Which principles men knowing to be moft found, and that the ordinary practice accordingly framed is good, whatfoever is over and befides that ordinary, the fame they judge repugnant to thofe true principles. The caufe of which error is ignorance, what reftraints and limitations all fuch principles have in regard of fo manifold varieties, as the matter whereunto they are appliable, doth commonly afford. Thefe varieties are not known but by much experience, from whence to draw the true bounds of all principles, to difcern how far forth they take effect, to fee where and why they fail, to apprehend by what degrees and means they lead to the practice of things in fhow, though not in deed repugnant and contrary one to another, requireth more fharpnefs of wit, more intricate circuitions of difcourfe, more induftry and depth of judgment, than common ability doth yield. So that general rules, till their limits be fully known, (efpecially in matter of publick and ecclefiaftical affairs) are by reafon of the manifold fecret exceptions which lie hidden in them, no other to the eye of man's underftanding, than cloudy mifts caft before the eye of common fenfe. They that walk in darknefs know not whither they go. And even as little is their certainty, whofe opinions generalities only do guide. With grofs and popular capacities nothing doth more prevail than unlimited generalities, becaufe of their plainnefs at the firft fight : Nothing lefs with men of exact judgment, becaufe fuch rules are not fafe to be trufted over far. General laws are like general rules of phyfick, according whereunto as no wife man will defire himfelf to be cured, if there be joined with his difeafe fome fpecial accident, in regard whereof that whereby others in the fame infirmity, but without like accident, recover health; would be to him either hurtful, or at the leaft unprofitable : So we muft not, under a colourable commendation of holy ordinances in the church, and of reafonable caufes whereupon they have been grounded for the common good, imagine that all men's cafes ought to have one meafure. Not without fingular wifdom therefore it hath been provided, That as the ordinary courfe of common affairs is difpofed of by general laws, fo likewife men's rarer innocent neceffities and utilities fhould be with fpecial equity confidered. From hence it is, that fo many privileges, immunities, exceptions and difpenfations have been always with great equity and reafon granted, not to turn the edge of juftice, nor to make void at certain times, and in certain men, through meer voluntary grace or benevolence, that which continually and univerfally fhould be of force (as fome men underftand it) but in very truth to practife general laws according to their right meaning. We fee in contracts, and other dealings, which daily pafs between man and man, that, to the utter undoing of fome, many things by ftrictnefs of law may be done, which equity and honeft meaning forbiddeth. Not that the law is unjuft, but unperfect; nor equity againft, but above law; binding men's confciences in things which law cannot reach unto. Will any man fay, That the virtue of private equity is oppofite and repugnant to that law, the filence whereof it fupplieth in all fuch private dealing ? No more is publick equity againft the law of publick affairs; albeit the one permit unto fome, in fpecial confiderations, that which the other, agreeably with general Rules of juftice, doth in general fort forbid. For, fith all good laws are the voices of right reafon, which is the inftrument wherewith God will have the world guided; and impoffible it is that right fhould withftand right ; it muft follow, that principles and rules of juftice, be they never fo generally uttered, do no lefs effectually intend, than if they did plainly exprefs an exception of particulars, wherein their literal practice might any way prejudice equity. And becaufe it is natural unto all men to wifh their own extraordinary benefit, when they think they have reafonable inducements fo to do; and no man can be prefumed a competent judge what equity doth require in his own cafe; the likelieft mean whereby the wit of man can provide, that he which ufeth the benefit of any fpecial benignity above the common courfe of others, may enjoy it with good confcience, and not againft the true purpofe of laws which in outward fhew are contrary, muft needs be to arm with authority fome fit both for quality and place to adminifter that, which in every fuch particular fhall appear agreeable with equity : Wherein, as it cannot be denied, but that fometimes the practice of fuch jurifdiction may fwerve through error even in the very beft, and for other refpects where lefs integrity is ; fo the watchfulleft obfervers of inconveniences that way growing, and the readieft to urge them in difgrace of authorized proceedings, do very well know, that the difpofition of thefe things refteth not now in the hands of popes, who live in no worldly awe or fubjection, but is committed to them whom law may at all times bridle, and fuperior power control ; yea, to them alfo in fuch fort, that law it felf hath fet down to what perfons, in what caufes, with what circumftances, almoft every faculty or favour fhall be grant-

ed,

ed, leaving in a manner nothing unto them more than only to deliver what is already given by law. Which maketh it by many degrees lefs reafonable, that under pretence of inconveniences, fo eafily ftopped if any did grow, and fo well prevented that none may, men fhould be altogether barred of the liberty that law with equity and reafon granteth. Thefe things therefore confidered, we laftly require, That it may not feem hard, if in cafes of neceffity, or for common utilities fake, certain profitable ordinances fometimes be releafed, rather than all men always ftrictly bound to the general rigor thereof.

The rule of men's private fpirits not fafe in in thefe Cafes to be followed.

10. Now where the word of God leaveth the church to make choice of her own ordinances, if againft thofe things which have been received with great reafon, or againft that which the ancient practice of the church hath continued time out of mind, or againft fuch ordinances as the power and authority of that church under which we live, hath in it felf devifed for the publick good, or againft the difcretion of the church in mitigating fometimes with favourable equity that rigor which otherwife the literal generality of ecclefiaftical laws hath judged to be more convenient and meet ; if againft all this it fhould be free for men to reprove, to difgrace, to reject at their own liberty what they fee done and practifed according to order fet down ; if in fo great variety of ways as the wit of man is eafily able to find out towards any purpofe, and in fo great liking as all men efpecially have unto thofe inventions , whereby fome one fhall feem to have been more enlightned from above than many thoufands, the church did give every man licenfe to follow what himfelf imagineth that *God's fpirit doth reveal* unto him, or what he fuppofeth that God is likely to have revealed to fome fpecial perfon whofe vertues deferve to be highly efteemed : What other effect could hereupon enfue, but the utter confufion of his church under pretence of being taught, led and guided by his Spirit? the gifts and graces whereof do fo naturally all tend unto common peace, that where fuch fingularity is, they whofe hearts it poffeffeth ought to fufpect it the more ; in as much as if it did come of God, and fhould, for that caufe, prevail with others, the fame God which revealeth it to them, would alfo give them power of confirming it to others, either with miraculous operation, or with ftrong and invincible remonftrance of found reafon, fuch as whereby it might appear that God would indeed have all men's judgments give place unto it ; whereas now the error and unfufficiency of their arguments do make it on the contrary fide againft them a ftrong prefumption, that God hath not moved their hearts to think fuch things as he hath not enabled them to prove. And fo from rules of general direction, it refteth that now we defcend to a more diftinct explication of particulars, wherein thofe rules have their fpecial efficacy.

Places for the publick fervice of God.

11. Solemn duties of publick fervice to be done unto God, muft have their places fet and prepared in fuch fort as befeemeth actions of that regard. *Adam*, even during the fpace of his fmall continuance in Paradife, had [a] where to prefent himfelf before the Lord. *Adam's* fons had out of Paradife in like fort [b] whither to bring their Sacrifices. The patriarchs ufed [c] altars, and [d] mountains, and [e] groves, to the felf-fame purpofe. In the vaft wildernefs, when the people of God had themfelves no fettled habitation , yet a moveable [f] tabernacle they were commanded of God to make. The like charge was given them againft the time they fhould come to fettle themfelves in the land which had been promifed unto their fathers, [g] *Te fhall feek that place which the Lord your God fhall choofe.* When God had chofen *Jerufalem,* and in *Jerufalem* mount [h] *Moriah,* there to have his ftanding habitation made, it was in the chiefeft of *David's* defires to have performed fo good a work. His grief was no lefs that he could not have the honour to build God a temple, than their anger is at this day, who bite afunder their own tongues with very wrath, that they have not as yet the power to pull down the temples which they never built, and to level them with the ground. It was no mean thing which he purpofed. To perform a work fo majeftical and ftately was no fmall charge. Therefore he [k] incited all men unto bountiful contribution, and procured towards it with all his power, gold, filver, brafs, iron, wood, precious ftones in great abundance. Yea moreover, [l] *Becaufe I have* (faith David) *a joy in the houfe of my God, I have of my own gold and filver , befides all that I have prepared for the houfe of the fanctuary, given to the houfe of my God three thoufand talents of gold, even the gold of ophir, feven thoufand talents of fined filver.* After the overthrow of this firft houfe of God, a fecond was inftead thereof erected ; but with fo great odds, that [m] they wept which had feen the former, and beheld how much this latter came behind it, the beauty whereof notwithftanding was fuch , that even this was alfo the wonder of the whole world. Befides which temple, there were both in other parts of the land, and even in *Jerufalem,* by procefs of time, no fmall number of fy-

a Gen. 3. 8.
b Gen. 4. 3.
c Gen. 13. 4.
d 22. 1.
e 21. 33.
f Exod. 26.

g Deut. 12. 5.

h 2 Chron. 3. 1.
i 2 Chron. 6. 7.
Pfal. 132. 5.

k 2 Chron. 25. 9.

l 2 Chron. 29. 3.

m Ezr. 3. 12.
Agge. 2. 4.

nagogues for men to refort unto. Our Saviour himfelf, and after him the apoftles frequented both the one and the other. The church of Chrift which was in *Jerufa-lem*, and held that profeffion which had not the publick allowance and countenance of authority, could not fo long ufe the exercife of chriftian religion but in private only. So that as *Jews* they had accefs to the temple and fynagogues , where God was ferved after the cuftom of the law ; but for that which they did as chriftians, they were of neceffity forced other where to affemble themfelves. And as God gave increafe to his church, they fought out both there and abroad for that purpofe not the fitteft (for fo the times would not fuffer them to do) but the fafeft place they could. In procefs of time, fome whiles by fufferance, fome whiles by fpecial leave and favour, they began to erect themfelves oratories; not in any fumptuous or ftately manner, which neither was poffible by reafon of the poor eftate of the church, and had been perilous in regard of the world's envy towards them. At length, when it pleafed God to raife up kings and emperors favouring fincerely the chriftian truth, that which the church before either could not or durft not do, was with all alacrity performed. Temples were in all places erected, no coft fpared, nothing judged too dear which that way fhould be fpent. The whole world did feem to exult, that it had occafion of pouring out gifts to fo bleffed a purpofe. That chearful devotion which *David* this way did exceedingly delight to behold, and wifh that the fame in the *Jewifh* people might be perpetual, was then in chriftian people every where to be feen. Their actions, 'till this day, always accuftomed to be fpoken of with great honour, are now called openly into queftion. They, and as many as have been followers of their example in that thing ; we efpecially that worfhip God , either in temples which their hands made, or which other men's fithence have framed by the like pattern, are in that refpect charged no lefs than with the fin of *Idolatry*. Our churches (in the foam of that good fpirit which directeth fuch fiery tongues) they term fpitefully the temples of *Baal*, idle fynagogues, abominable fties.

Aas 1. 13. & a. 1. & a. 46.

1 Chron. 19. 17, 18.

12. Wherein the firft thing which moveth them thus to caft up their poifons, are certain folemnities ufeful at the firft erection of churches. Now although the fame fhould be blameworthy, yet this age (thanks be to God) hath reafonably well forborn to incur the danger of any fuch blame. It cannot be laid unto many men's charge at this day living, either that they have been fo curious as to trouble the bifhops with placing the firft ftone in the churches they built, or fo fcrupulous as after the erecting of them to make any great ado for their dedication. In which kind notwithftanding as we do neither allow unmeet, nor purpofe the ftiff defence of any unneceffary cuftom heretofore received ; fo we know no reafon wherefore churches fhould be the worfe, if at the firft erecting of them, at the making of them publick, at the time when they are delivered, as it were, into God's own poffeffion, and when the ufe whereunto they fhall ever ferve is eftablifhed, ceremonies fit to betoken fuch intents, and to accompany fuch actions be ufual, as [a] in the pureft times they have been. When [b] *Conftantine* had finifhed an houfe for the fervice of God at *Jerufalem*, the dedication he judged a matter not unworthy, about the folemn performance whereof the greateft part of the bifhops in *Chriftendom* fhould meet together. Which thing they did at the emperor's motion, each moft willingly fetting forth that action to their power, fome with orations, fome with fermons, fome with the facrifices of prayers unto God for the peace of the world, for the churches fafety, for the emperor's and his children's good. [c] By *Athanafius* the like is recorded concerning a bifhop of *Alexandria*, in a work of the like devout magnificence. So that whether emperors or bifhops in thofe days were church-founders, the folemn dedication of churches they thought not to be a work in it felf either vain or fuperftitious. Can we judge it a thing feemly for any man to go about the building of an houfe to the God of heaven with no other appearance, than if his end were to rear up a kitchen, or parlour, for his own ufe ? Or when a work of fuch nature is finifhed, remaineth there nothing but prefently to ufe it, and fo an end ? It behoveth that the place where God fhall be ferved by the whole church, be a publick place for the avoiding of privy conventicles, which covered with pretence of religion may ferve unto dangerous practices. Yea, though fuch affemblies be had indeed for religion's fake ; hurtful neverthelefs they may eafily prove, as well in regard of their fitnefs to ferve the turn of hereticks, and fuch as privily will fooneft adventure to inftil their poifon into men's minds; as alfo for the occafion which thereby is given to mali-

The folemnity of erecting churches condemned by Bar. p. 130.
The hallowing and dedicating of them fcorned, p. 141.

Durand. rational. lib. 1. cap. 6. & de confecr. d. 1. c. tabernaculum. Greg. Mag. lib. 1c. epift. 12. & lib. 7. epift. 71. & l. 8. epift. 63. [a] Ἐξαίϱετα μάλιϛα πελιτ Gr. [greek] ζαλῶς ἔχον, μάλιϛος ἤ τα ἕτα παάδϰι δι ἐξ ϙϙιϙιον. Καὶ τϙτο ἐχ δ̓ αὐξ, ἀλλὰ ἡ πολλϙις ἱμϊϛι τϙ ἐπ̓ αὐτϙ ἀπὸ τϙϙϙϙ ᵗ αυι- ῖϙν ἡμϙϱας ὑπεϱϙϙϙι ἱπα μϙ ἐξῖπλε τϙ χϙϙι ϙωιϙᵗ τϙ ϙαλϙᵗ, Greg. Nazian. Orat. εἰς ᵗ ϙυϙαϙϙϙ. [b] *Vide* Eufeb. de vita Conftant. l. 4. c. 41, 43, 44, 45.

[e] Athanafius Apol. ad Conftantium.

mali-

malicious perfons, both of fufpecting, and of traducing with more colourable fhew thofe actions, which in themfelves being holy, fhould be fo ordered that no man might probably otherwife think of them. Which confiderations have by fo much the greater weight, for that of thefe inconveniences the church heretofore had fo plain experience, when chriftian men were driven to ufe fecret meetings, becaufe the liberty of publick places was not granted them. There are which hold, that the prefence of a chriftian multitude, and the duties of religion performed amongft them do make the place of their affembly publick ; even as the prefence of the king and his retinue maketh any man's houfe a court. But this I take to be an error, in as much as the only thing which maketh any place publick, is the publick affignment thereof unto fuch duties. As for the multitude there affembled, or the duties which they perform, it doth not appear how either fhould be of force to infufe any fuch prerogative. Nor doth the folemn dedication of churches ferve only to make them publick, but farther alfo to furrender up that right, which otherwife their founders might have in them,

Exod. 40. 34. and to make God himfelf their owner. For which caufe, at the erection and confe-
1 Reg. 8. 11. cration as well of the tabernacle as of the temple, it pleafed the Almighty to give a
Exod. 40. 9. manifeft fign that he took poffeffion of both. Finally, it notifieth in folemn manner
1 Reg. 8. the holy and religious ufe whereunto it is intended fuch houfes fhall be put. Thefe things the wifdom of *Solomon* did not account fuperfluous. He knew how cafily that which was meant fhould be holy and facred, might be drawn from the ufe whereunto it was firft provided ; he knew how bold men are to take even from God himfelf; how
Levit. 16. 2. hardly that houfe would be kept from impious profanation he knew; and right wifely
The place therefore endeavoured by fuch folemnities to leave in the minds of men that impreffion,
named holy. which might fomewhat reftrain their boldnefs, and nourifh a reverend affection towards
Ezr. 6. 16. the houfe of God. For which caufe when the firft houfe was deftroyed, and a new in the ftead thereof erected by the children of *Ifrael* after their return from captivity, they kept the dedication even of this houfe alfo with joy.

The argument which our Saviour ufeth againft prophaners of the temple, he taketh
Mat. 21. 13. from the ufe whereunto it was with folemnity confecrated. And as the prophet *Jeremy*
Jer. 17. 24. forbiddeth the carrying of burdens on the fabbath, becaufe that was a fanctified day : So
Mark 11. 16. becaufe the temple was a place fanctified, our Lord would not fuffer, no not the carriage of a veffel through the temple. Thefe two commandments therefore are in the
Levit. 26. 2. law conjoined, *Ye fhall keep my fabbaths, and reverence my fanctuary.* Out of thofe
1 Cor. 11. 22. the apoftle's words, *Have ye not houfes to eat and drink in ?* albeit temples, fuch as now, were not then erected for the chriftian religion, it hath been neverthelefs not
Pet. Cluniac. abfurdly conceived, that he teacheth what difference fhould be made between houfe and houfe ; that what is fit for the dwelling place of God, and what for man's habitation he fheweth; requireth that chriftian men at their own home take common food, and in the houfe of the Lord none but that food which is heavenly; he inftructeth them, that as in the one place they ufe to refrefh their bodies, fo they may in the other learn to feek the nourifhment of their fouls; and as there they fuftain temporal life, fo here they would learn to make provifion for the eternal. Chrift could not fuffer that the temple fhould ferve for a place of mart, nor the apoftle of Chrift that the church fhould be made an inn. When therefore we fanctify and hallow churches, that which we do is only to teftify, that we make them places of publick refort, that we inveft God himfelf with them, that we fever them from common ufes. In which action, other folemnities than fuch as are decent and fit for that purpofe we approve none. Indeed we condemn not all as unmeet, the like whereunto have either been devifed or ufed haply amongft idolaters. For why fhould conformity with them in matter of opinion be lawful, when they think that which is true, if in action, when they do that which is meet, if it be not lawful to be like unto them ? Are we to forfake any true opinion, becaufe idolaters have maintained it ? Or to fhun any requifite action only becaufe we have in the practice thereof been prevented by idolaters ? It is no impoffible thing, but that fometimes they may judge as rightly what is decent about fuch external affairs of God, as in greater things what is true. Not therefore whatfoever idolaters have either thought or done, but let whatfoever they have either thought or done *idolatroufly, be fo far forth* abhorred. For of that which is good even in evil things, God is author.

Of the names
whereby we 13. Touching the names of angels and faints whereby the moft of our churches are
diftinguifh called, as the cuftom of fo naming them is very ancient, fo neither was the caufe
our churches thereof at the firft, nor is the ufe and continuance with us at this prefent hurtful. That churches were confecrated unto none but the Lord only, the very general name it felf doth fufficiently fhew, in as much as by plain grammatical conftruction, *Church*

　　doth

doth fignify no other thing than *the Lord's houfe*. And becaufe the multitude, as of persons, fo of things particular, caufeth variety of proper names to be devifed for di-ftinction fake, founders of churches did herein that which beft liked their own conceit at the prefent time ; yet each intending, that as oft as thofe buildings came to be mentioned, the name fhould put men in mind of fome memorable thing or perfon. *From Kueia-ρ , Kyre, and by adding letters of afpiration, Chyrch.*

Thus therefore it cometh to pafs that all churches have had their names, fome as memorials of peace, fome of wifdom, fome in memory of the Trinity it felf, fome of Chrift under fundry titles, of the blefled virgin not a few, many of one apoftle, faint, or martyr, many of all. In which refpect their commendable purpofe being not of every one underftood, they have been in latter ages conftrued as though they had fuper-ftitioufly meant, either that thofe places, which were denominated of angels and faints, fhould ferve for the worfhip of fo glorious creatures ; or elfe thofe glorified creatures for defence, protection, and patronage of fuch places. A thing which the ancients do utterly difclaim. To them, faith St. *Auguftine*, we appoint no churches, becaufe they are not to us as gods. Again , *The nations to their gods erected temples, we not temples to our martyrs as unto God, but memorials as unto dead men, whofe fpirits with God are ftill living.* Divers confiderations there are, for which chriftian churches might firft take their names of faints: As either becaufe by the miniftry of faints it pleafed God there to fhew fome rare effect of his power ; or elfe in regard of death, which thofe faints have fuffered for the teftimony of Jefus Chrift, did thereby make the places where they died venerable ; or, thirdly, for that it liked good and virtuous men to give fuch occafion of mentioning them often, to the end that the naming of their perfons might caufe enquiry to be made, and meditation to be had of their virtues. Wherefore, feeing that we cannot juftly account it fuperftition, to give unto churches thofe fore-rehearfed names, as memorials either of holy perfons or things ; if it be plain, that their founders did with fuch meaning name them ; fhall not we in otherwife taking them, offer them injury ? Or if it be obfcure or uncertain what they meant, yet this conftruction being more favourable, charity (I hope) conftraineth no man which ftandeth doubtful of their minds, to lean to the hardeft and worft interpretation that their words can carry. Yea, although it were clear, that they all (for the error of fome is manifeft in this behalf) had therein a fuperftitious intent, wherefore fhould their fault prejudice us, who (as all men know) do ufe by way of mere diftinction the names which they of fuperftition gave ? In the ufe of thofe names whereby we diftinguifh both days and months, are we culpable of fuperftition, becaufe they were who firft invented them ? The fign *Caftor* and *Pollux* fuperftitioufly given unto that fhip, where-in the apoftle failed, polluteth not the evangelift's pen, who thereby doth but diftin-guifh that fhip from others. If to *Daniel* there had been given no other name but only *Beltifbazzar*, given him in honour of the *Babylonian* idol *Belti*, fhould their idolatry, which were the authors of that name, cleave unto every man which had fo termed him by way of perfonal difference only ? Were it not to fatisfy the minds of the fimpler fort of men, thefe nice curiofities are not worthy the labour which we be-ftow to anfwer them.

Vid. Socr. l. 1. c. 16. Ev. lib. 4. c. 30. Hift. trip. 14. c. 18.

V. Aug. l. 8. de civi. Dei c. 27. l. 22. c. 10. Epift. 49. ad Deo gra. The duty which chriftian men performed in keeping Feftival dedications, St. Bafil termeth Aεγ-γγεiας τῆ θεῖ, acknowledging the fame to have been withal μιὸν τῆς μαρτύ-ρος. Bafil in Pfal. 114.

Acts 28. 11.

Dan. 4. 5. Vide Scal. de emendat. temp. l. 6. p. 277.

14. The like unto this, is a fancy which they have againft the fafhion of our churches, as being framed according to the pattern of the *Jewifh* temple. A fault no lefs grievous, if fo be it were true, than if fome king fhould build his manfion-houfe by the model of *Solomon*'s palace. So far forth as our churches and their temple have one end , what fhould let, but that they may lawfully have one form ? The temple was for facrifice, and therefore had rooms to that purpofe, fuch as ours have none. Our churches are places provided, that the people might there affemble themfelves in due and decent manner, according to their feveral degrees and order. Which thing being common unto us with *Jews*, we have in this refpect our churches divided by certain partitions, although not fo many in number as theirs. They had their feveral for hea-then nations, their feveral for the people of their own nation, their feveral for men, their feveral for women, their feveral for their priefts, and for the high-prieft alone their feveral. There being in ours for local diftinction between the clergy and the reft (which yet we do not with any great ftrictnefs or curiofity obferve neither) but one partition, the caufe whereof at the firft (as it feemeth) was, that as many as were capable of the holy myfteries, might there affemble themfelves, and no other creep amongft them : This is now made a matter fo heinous, as if our religion thereby were be-come even plain *Judaifm* ; and as though we retained a moft holy place, whereinto there might not any but the high-prieft alone enter, according to the cuftom of the *Jews*.

Of the fafhi-on of our churches.

15. Some it highly difpleafeth, that fo great expences this way are employed : *The mother of fuch magnificence* (they think) *is but a proud ambitious defire to be* *fpoken*

The fumptu-oufnefs of Churches.

S

spoken of far and wide. Suppose we that God himself delighteth to dwell sumptuously? Or taketh pleasure in chargeable pomp? No; then was the Lord most acceptably served, when his temples were rooms borrowed within the houses of poor men. This was suitable unto the nakedness of Jesus Christ, and the simplicity of his Gospel. What thoughts or cogitations they had which were authors of those things, the use and benefit whereof hath descended unto our selves, as we do not know, so we need not search. It cometh (we grant) many times to pass, that the works of men being the same, their drifts and purposes therein are divers. The charge of *Herod* about the Temple of God, was ambitious; yet *Solomon's* virtuous, *Constantine's* holy. But howsoever their hearts are disposed by whom any such thing is done in the world, shall we think that it baneth the work which they leave behind them, or taketh away from others the use and benefit thereof? Touching God himself, hath he any where revealed, that it is his delight to dwell beggarly? And that he taketh no pleasure to be worshipped, saving only in poor cottages? Even then was the Lord as acceptably honoured of his people as ever, when the stateliest places and things in the whole world were sought out to adorn his temple. This is most suitable, decent, and fit for the greatness of Jesus Christ, for the sublimity of his gospel, except we think of Christ and his gospel, as [b] the officers of *Julian* did. As therefore the Son of *Syrach* giveth verdict concerning those things which God hath wrought, [c] *A man need not say, this is worse than that, this more acceptable to God, that less; for in their season they are all worthy praise:* The like we may also conclude, as touching these two so contrary ways of providing, in meaner or in costlier sort, for the honour of almighty God, *A man need not say, this is worse than that, this more acceptable to God, that less; for with him they are in their season both allowable;* the one, when the state of the church is poor; the other, when God hath enriched it with plenty. When they which had seen the beauty of the first temple built by *Solomon* in the days of his great prosperity and peace, beheld how far it excelled the second, which had not builders of like ability, the tears of their grieved eyes the prophets [d] endeavoured with comforts to wipe away. Whereas if the house of God were by so much the more perfect, by how much the glory thereof is less, they should have done better to rejoice than weep, their prophets better to reprove than comfort. It being objected against the church, in the times of universal persecution, that her service done to God, was not solemnly performed in temples fit for the honour of divine majesty, their most convenient answer was, that [e] *The best temples which we can dedicate to God, are our sanctified souls and bodies.* Whereby it plainly appeareth how the fathers, when they were upbraided with that defect, comforted themselves with the meditation of God's most gracious and merciful nature, who did not therefore the less accept of their hearty affection and zeal, rather than took any great delight, or imagined any high perfection in such their want of external ornaments, which when they wanted, the cause was their only lack of ability: Ability serving, they wanted them not. Before the Emperor *Constantine's* time, under *Severus, Gordian, Philip* and *Galienus,* the state of christian affairs being tolerable, the former buildings, which were but of mean and small estate, contented them not; spacious and ample churches they erected throughout every city. No envy was able to be their hindrance, no practice of satan, or fraud of men, available against their proceedings herein, while they continued as yet worthy to feel the aid of the arm of God extended over them for their safety. These churches *Diocletian* caused by solemn edict to be afterwards overthrown. *Maximinus* with like authority giving them leave to erect them, the hearts of men were even rapt with divine joy, to see those places which tyrannous impiety had laid waste, recovered, as it were, out of mortal calamity, churches *reared up to an height immeasurable, and adorned with far more beauty in their restauration, than their founders before had given them.* Whereby we see, how most christian minds then stood affected, we see how joyful they were to behold the sumptuous statelines of houses built unto God's glory. If we should, over and besides this, alledge the care which was had that all things about the tabernacle of *Moses* might be as beautiful, gorgeous and rich, as art could make them; or what travel and cost was bestowed, that the goodlines of the temple might be a spectacle of admiration to all the world; this, they will say, was figurative, and served by God's appointment but for a time, to shadow out the true everlasting glory of a more divine sanctuary; whereunto

Christ

2

[a] Ἔργον τὸ μέγα, κ. καλὸν τίμιον. τῇ γάρ τοιότῃ ἡ θεωρία Sευ-γμαςὶ. Arist. Eth. l. 4. c. 2. τὰ αἰσθήσει καλά ἢ τοῖσιν καλῶν οἰκόντα: Philo. Jud.
[b] Fotis, thesauri imperialis quæstor, conspicatus sacrorum vasorum pretia; En, inquit, qualibus vasis ministratur Mariæ filio! Theodoret. hist. Ecclef. l. 3. c. 12.
[c] Ecclef. 39. 34.

[a] Agge 2. 5, 10.

[b] Minut. Fel. in Octav.

Eufeb. l. 8. c. 1.

Eufeb. l. 10. c. 2.

Chrift being long fithence entred, it feemeth that all thofe curious exornations fhould rather ceafe.   Which thing we alfo our felves would grant, if the ufe thereof had been meerly and only myftical.   But fith the prophet *David* doth mention a natural conveniency which fuch kind of bounteous expences have, as well for that we do thereby give unto God a teftimony of our chearful affection, which thinketh nothing too dear to be beftowed about the furniture of his fervice, as alfo becaufe it ferveth to the world for a witnefs of his almightinefs, whom we outwardly honour with the chiefeft of outward things, as being of all things himfelf incomparably the greateft. Befides, were it not alfo ftrange, if God fhould have made fuch ftore of glorious crea-tures on earth, and leave them all to be confumed in fecular vanity, allowing none but the bafer fort to be employed in his own fervice?   To fet forth the majefty of kings, his vicegerents in this world, the moft gorgeous and rare treafures which the world hath, are procured.   We think, belike, that he will accept what the meaneft of them would difdain.   If there be great care to build and beautify thefe corruptible fanctu-aries, little or none, that the living temples of the Holy Ghoft, the redeemed fouls of the people of God may be edified ; huge expences upon timber and ftone, but to-wards the relief of the poor fmall devotion ; coft this way infinite, and in the mean while charity cold : We have in fuch cafe juft occafion to make complaint as St. *Je-rom* did, *The walls of the church there are enow contented to build, and to under-fet it with goodly pillars, the marbles are polifhed, the roofs fhine with gold, the altar hath precious ftones to adorn it ; and of Chrift's minifters no choice at all.*   The fame *Jerom*, both in that place and elfewhere, debafeth with like intent the glory of fuch magnificence (a thing whereunto men's affections in thofe times needed no fpur) there-by to extol the neceffity fometimes of charity and alms, fometimes of other the moft principal duties belonging unto chriftian men ; which duties were neither fo highly efteemed as they ought, and being compared with that in queftion, the directeft fen-tence we can give of them both, as unto me it feemeth, is this ; *God who requireth the one as neceffary, accepteth the other alfo as being an honourable work.*

16. Our opinion concerning the force and virtue which fuch places have, is, I truft, without any blemifh or ftain of herefy.   Churches receive, as every thing elfe, their chief perfection from the end whereunto they ferve.   Which end being the publick worfhip of God, they are in this confideration houfes of greater dignity than any pro-vided for meaner purpofes.   For which caufe they feem after a fort even to mourn, as being injured and defrauded of their right, when places not fanctified, as they are, prevent them *unneceffarily* in that preheminence and honour.   Whereby alfo it doth come to pafs, that the fervice of God hath not then it felf *fuch perfection of grace and comelinefs*, as when the dignity of place which it wifheth for, doth concur.   Again, albeit the true worfhip of God be to God in it felf acceptable, who refpecteth not fo much in what place, as with what affection he is ferved ; and therefore *Mofes* in the midft of the fea, *Job* on the dunghil, *Ezekiah's* in bed, *Jeremy* in mire, *Jonas* in the whale, *Daniel* in the den, the children in the furnace, the thief on the crofs, *Pe-ter* and *Paul* in prifon, calling unto God were heard, as St. *Bafil* noteth : Manifeft not-withftanding it is, that the very majefty and holinefs of the place where God is wor-fhipped, hath *in regard of us* great virtue, force and efficacy, for that it ferveth as a fenfible help to ftir up devotion ; and *in that refpect*, no doubt, *bettereth* even our holieft and beft actions in this kind.   As therefore we every where exhort all men to worfhip God ; even fo, for performance of this fervice by the people of God affem-bled, we think not any place *fo good* as the church, neither any exhortation fo fit as that of *David, O worfhip the Lord in the beauty of holinefs.*

17. For of our churches thus it becometh us to efteem, howfoever others, rapt with the pang of a furious zeal, do pour out againft them devout blafphemies, crying, ª *Down with them, down with them, even to the very ground : For to idolatry they have been abufed.   And the places where idols have been worfhipped, are by* ᵇ *the law of God devote to utter deftruction.   For execution of which law, the* ᶜ *kings that were godly, Afa, Jehofaphat, Ezechia, Jofiah, deftroyed all the high places, altars and groves, which had been erected in Juda and Ifrael.   He that faid, Thou fhalt have no other gods before my face, hath likewife faid, Thou fhalt utterly deface and deftroy all thefe fynagogues and places where fuch idols have been worfhipped.   This law containeth the temporal punifhment which God hath fet down, and willeth that men execute for the breach of the other law.   They which fpare them therefore, do but referve, as the hypocrite Saul did, execrable things to worfhip God withal.*   The truth is, that as no man ferveth God, and loveth him not ; fo neither can any man fincere-ly love God, and not extremely abhor that fin which is the higheft degree of treafon

1 Chron. 28. 14.

2 Chron. 2. 5.

Matth. 6. 29.

Malac. 1. 8.

AdNepotian. de vita Cle-rie.

Ad Demetr. Epift. 12. ad Gaudentium.

What holi-nefs and vir-tue we af-cribe to the church, more than other places.

Exhort ad bap. & pœni-tent.

Pfal. 96. 9.

Their pre-tence that would have churches ut-terly raz-d. ª Pfal. 137. 7. ᵇ Deut. 12. 2. ᶜ 2 Chron. 17. 6. 2 Chron. 29. 2 Chron. 3.

againft

a Ifa. 8. 21.
45. 20.
Hof. 14. 4.
Ifa. 41. 24.
b Pfal.115. 8.
81. 13.
c Rom. 1. 24.
c Judic. 6.13.
d Apoc. 21. 8.
Ifa. 2. 21.
e Act. 14. 14.
f Deut. 28.
20.
g Jer. 2. 17.

againſt the ſupreme guide and monarch of the whole world, with whoſe divine authority and power it inveſteth others. By means whereof the ſtate of idolaters is two ways miſerable. Firſt, in that which they worſhip [a] they find no ſuccour: And ſecondly, At his hands whom they ought to ſerve, there is no other thing to be looked for, but the effects of moſt juſt diſpleaſure, the [b] withdrawing of grace, [c] dereliction in this world, and in the world to come [d] confuſion. [e] Paul and Barnabas, when infidels admiring their virtues went about to ſacrifice unto them, rent their garments in token of horror, and as frighted perſons ran crying thorough the preſs of the people, [f] O men, wherefore do ye theſe things? They knew the force of that dreadful [f] curſe whereunto idolatry maketh ſubject. Nor is there cauſe why the guilty ſuſtaining the ſame, ſhould grudge or complain of injuſtice. For, whatſoever befalleth in that reſpect, [g] themſelves have made themſelves worthy to ſuffer it. As for thoſe things either whereon, or elſe wherewith ſuperſtition worketh, polluted they are by ſuch abuſe, and deprived of that dignity which their nature delighteth in. For there is nothing which doth not grieve, and, as it were, even loath it ſelf, whenſoever iniquity cauſeth it to ſerve unto vile purpoſes. Idolatry therefore maketh whatſoever it toucheth the worſe. Howbeit ſith creatures which have no underſtanding, can ſhew no will ; and where no will is, there is no ſin ; and only that which ſinneth, is ſubject to puniſhment ; Which way ſhould any ſuch creature be puniſhable by the law of God? There may be cauſe ſometimes to aboliſh or to extinguiſh them ; but ſurely, never by way of puniſhment to the things themſelves. Yea farther, howſoever the law of Moſes did puniſh idolaters, we find not that God hath appointed for us any definite or certain temporal judgment, which the chriſtian magiſtrate is of neceſſity for ever bound to execute upon offenders in that kind, much leſs upon things that way abuſed as mere inſtruments. For what God did command touching Canaan, the ſame concerneth not us any otherwiſe than only as a fearful pattern of his juſt diſpleaſure and wrath againſt ſinful nations. It teacheth us, how God thought good to plague and afflict them ; it doth not appoint in what form and manner we ought to puniſh the ſin of idolatry in all others. Unleſs they will ſay, that becauſe the Iſraelites were commanded to make no covenant with the people of that land, therefore leagues and truces made, between ſuperſtitious perſons, and ſuch as ſerve God aright, are unlawful altogether ; or, becauſe God commanded the Iſraelites to ſmite the inhabitants of Canaan, and to root them out, that therefore reformed churches are bound to put all others to the edge of the ſword. Now whereas commandment was alſo given to deſtroy all places where the Canaanites had ſerved their gods, and not to convert any one of them to the honour of the true God ; this precept had reference unto a ſpecial intent and purpoſe, which was, that there ſhould be but one only place in the whole land whereunto the people might bring ſuch offerings, gifts and ſacrifices, as their levitical law did require. By which law, ſevere charge was given them in that reſpect, not to convert thoſe places to the worſhip of the living God, where nations before them had ſerved idols. But to ſeek the place which the Lord their God ſhall chuſe out of all their tribes. Beſides, it is reaſon we ſhould likewiſe conſider, how great a difference there is between their proceedings, who erect a new commonwealth, which is to have neither people, nor law, neither regiment nor religion the ſame that was ; and theirs, who only reform a decayed eſtate, by reducing it to that perfection from which it hath ſwerved. In this caſe we are to retain as much, in the other as little of former things as we may. Sith therefore examples have not generally the force of laws which all men ought to keep, but of counſels only and perſuaſions not amiſs to be followed by them whoſe caſe is the like ; ſurely where caſes are ſo unlike as theirs and ours, I ſee not how that which they did ſhould induce, much leſs any way enforce us to the ſame practice, eſpecially conſidering that groves and hill-altars were, while they did remain, both dangerous in regard of the ſecret acceſs, which people ſuperſtitiouſly given, might have always thereunto with eaſe ; neither could they remaining, ſerve with any fitneſs unto better purpoſe : Whereas our temples (their former abuſe being by order of law removed) are not only free from ſuch peril, but withal ſo conveniently framed for the people of God to ſerve and honour him therein ; that no man beholding them, can chuſe but think it exceeding great pity they ſhould be ever any otherwiſe employed. Yea but the cattle of Amalek (you will ſay) were fit for ſacrifice ; and this was the very conceit which ſometime deceived Saul. It was ſo. Nor do I any thing doubt, but that Saul, upon this conceit, might even lawfully have offered to God thoſe reſerved ſpoils, had not the Lord in that particular caſe, given ſpecial charge to the contrary. As therefore notwithſtanding the commandment of Iſrael to deſtroy Canaanites, idolaters may be converted and live : So the temples which have ſerved idolatry

Deut. 12. 2.

Deut. 12.4,5.

latry as inftruments, may he fanctified again and continue, albeit to *Ifrael* commandment have been given that *they* fhould deftroy all idolatrous places *in their land ;* and
to the good kings of *Ifrael* commendation for fulfilling, to the evil for difobeying
the fame commandment, fometimes punifhment, always fharp and fevere reproof hath
even from the Lord himfelf befallen. Thus much it may fuffice to have written in
defence of thofe chriftian oratories, the overthrow and ruin whereof is defired, not
now by Infidels, Pagans or Turks, but by a fpecial refined fect of chriftian believers ;
pretending themfelves exceedingly grieved at our folemnities in erecting churches, at
the names which we fuffer them to hold, at their form and fafhion, at the ftatelinefs,
of them and coftlinefs, at the opinion which we have of them, and at the manifold
fuperftitious abufes whereunto they have been put.

18. Places of publick refort being thus provided for , our repair thither is efpecially for
mutual conference, and as it were commerce to
be had between God and us. Becaufe therefore want ª of the knowledge of God is the
caufe of all iniquity amongft men, as contrariwife the ground of all our happinefs, and the
feed of whatfoever perfect virtue groweth from
us, is a right opinion touching things divine, this

Of publick teaching, or preaching; and the firft kind
thereof, catechifing.

ª *Contraria fortia in quibus homines fibi invicem opponuntur fecundum exercitia & defideria & opiniones, omnia proveniunt ex ignorantia : ficut cæcus ex privatione fui vifus vagatur ubique & la-
ditur. Scientia veritatis tollit hominum inimicitiam & odium.
Hæc promifit fancta Theologia dicens, Habitabit agnus cum lupo.
Et affignat rationem, repleta eft terra fapientia Domini.* Mofes
Ægypt. in Nar. Hannebuch. lib. 3. cap. 12.

kind of knowledge we may juftly fet down for the firft and chiefeft thing which God
imparteth unto his people, and our duty of receiving this at his merciful hands, for the
firft of thofe religious offices wherewith we publickly honour him on earth. For the
inftruction therefore of all forts of men to eternal life it is neceffary, that the facred
and faving truth of God be openly publifhed unto them. Which open publication of
heavenly myfteries, is by an excellency termed *preaching.* For otherwife there is not
any thing *publickly notified,* but we may in that refpect, rightly and properly fay it is
preached. So that when the fchool of God doth ufe it as *a word of art,* we are ac- Luc 8. 39.
cordingly to underftand it with reftraint to fuch fpecial matter as that fchool is ac- 12. 3.
cuftomed to publifh. We find not in the world any people that have lived altogether
without religion. And yet this duty of religion, which provideth that publickly all
forts of men may be inftructed in the fear of God, is to the church of God, and hath
been always fo peculiar, that none of the heathens, how curious foever in fearching out Vide Tertul.
all kinds of outward ceremonies like to ours, could ever once fo much as endeavour adverf. hæc.
to refemble *herein* the churches care for the endlefs good of her children. Ways of
teaching there have been fundry always ufual in God's church. For the firft introdu- The Jews
ction of youth to the knowledge of God, the *Jews* even to this day have their cate- Catech. called
chifms. With religion it fareth as with other fciences , the firft delivery of the Lekach Tob.
elements thereof muft, for like confideration,
ᵇ be framed according to the weak and flender
capacity of young beginners : Unto which
manner of teaching principles in chriftianity,
the apoftle in the fixth to the *Hebrews* is himfelf underftood to allude: For this caufe therefore, as the decalogue of *Mofes* declareth fum-
marily thofe things which we ought to do ;
the prayer of our Lord, whatfoever we fhould
requeft or defire ; fo, either by the apoftles, or at
the leaftwife out of their writings, we have the
fubftance of ᶜ chriftian belief compendioufly

ᵇ *Incipientibus brevius ac fimplicius tradi præcepta magis convenit. Aut enim difficultate inftitutionis tam numerofa atque per-
plexa deterreri folent, aut ea tempore qua præcipue alenda ingenia
atque indulgentia quædam enutrienda funt, afperiorum rerum tractatu atteruntur.* Fab. procem. li 8. *Incipientibus nobis exponere
jura populi Romani, ita videntur poffe tradi commodiffime, fi primo
levi ac fimplici via ; poft deinde diligentiffima atque exactiffima in-
terpretatione fingula tradantur. Alioqui fi ftatim ab initio rudem
adhuc & infirmum animum ftudiofi multitudine ac varietate rerum
onceraverimus, duorum alterum, aut defertorem ftudiorum efficiemus,
aut cum magno labore ejus , fæpe etiam cum diffidentia (quæ plerumque juvenes avertit) ferius ad id perducemus, ad quod leviore
via ductus fine magno labore & fine ullo diffidentia maturius per-
duci potuiffet.* Inftitut. Imper. L. 1. tit. 1.
ᶜ Vide Ruff. in Symb.

drawn into few and fhort articles, to the end that the weaknefs of no man's wit might
either hinder *altogether* the knowledge, or excufe the utter ignorance of needful
things. Such as were trained up in their rudiments , and were fo made fit to be afterward by baptifm received into the church, the fathers ufually in their writings do
term.ᵈ *Hearers* ; as having no further commu-
nion or fellowfhip with the church, than only
this, that they were admitted to hear the principles of chriftian faith made plain unto them.
Catechizing may be in fchools, it may be in
private families ; but when we make it a kind

ᵈ Tert. de pœnitent. *An alius eft tinctis Chriftus ? Alius audientibus ? Audientes optare intinctionem, non præfumere oportet.* Cyprian. Epift. 17. l. 3. *Audientibus vigilantia veftra non defit.*
Rupert. de divin. Offic. lib. 4. cap. 18. *Audiens quifque re-
gulam fidei , Catechumenus dicitur. Catechumenus namque Audi-
tor interpretatur.*

of preaching, we mean always the publick performance thereof in the open hearing of men, becaufe things are preached, not in that they are taught, but in that they
are publifhed.   4

19. Mo-

19. *Moses* and the prophets, Christ and his apostles, were in their times all preachers of God's truth; some by word, some by writing, some by both. This they did partly as faithful *witnesses*, making mere *relation* what God himself had *revealed* unto them; and partly as careful *expounders*, teachers, persuaders thereof. The church in like case *preacheth* still, first publishing by way of *testimony* or relation the truth which from them she hath received, even in such sort as it was received, *written in the sacred volumes of scripture*: Secondly, by way of *explication*, discovering the mysteries which lie hid therein. The church as a witness preacheth his mere revealed truth by reading *publickly* the sacred scripture. So that a second kind of preaching is the reading of holy writ. For thus we may the boldlier speak, being strengthened ᵃ with the examples of so reverend a prelate, as faith, That *Moses*, from the time of ancient generations and ages long since past, had amongst the cities of the very *Gentiles* them that preached him, *in that* he was read every sabbath-day. For so of necessity it must be meant, in as much as we know that the *Jews* have always had their weekly readings of the *law of Moses*; but that they always had in like manner their weekly *sermons upon some part of the law of Moses*, we no where find. Howbeit still we must here remember, that the church, by her publick reading of the book of God, preacheth only *as a witness*. Now the principal thing required in a witness is fidelity. Wherefore as we cannot excuse that church, which either through corrupt translations of scripture delivereth, instead of divine speeches, any thing repugnant unto that which God speaketh; or, through falsified additions proposeth that to the people of God as scripture, which is in truth no scripture: So the blame which in both these respects hath been laid upon the church of *England*, is surely altogether without cause. Touching translations of holy scripture, albeit we may not disallow of their painful travels herein who strictly have tied themselves to the very original letter; yet the judgment of the church, as we see by the practice of all Nations, *Greeks*, *Latins*, *Persians*, *Syrians*, *Æthiopians*, *Arabians*, hath been ever, That the fittest for publick audience are such, as following a middle course between the rigor of literal translators, and the liberty of paraphrasts, do with greatest shortness and plainness deliver the meaning of the Holy Ghost. Which being a labour of so great difficulty, the exact performance thereof we may rather wish than look for. So that, except between the *words of translation* and the *mind of scripture* it self there be *contradiction*, every little difference should not seem an intolerable blemish necessarily to be spunged out.

Whereas therefore the prophet *David* in a certain psalm doth say concerning *Moses* and *Aaron*, that they were obedient to the word of God, and in the self-same place our allowed translation faith, they *were not* obedient, we are for this cause challenged as manifest gainsayers of scripture, even in that which we read for scripture unto the people. But for as much as words are resemblances of that which the mind of the speaker conceiveth, and conceits are images representing that which is spoken of; it followeth, that they who will judge of words, should have recourse to the things themselves from whence they rise. In setting down that miracle, at the sight

whereof *Peter* fell down astonished before the feet of Jesus, and cried, *Depart, Lord, I am a sinner*; the evangelist St. *Luke* faith, the store of the fish which they took was such, that the net took it in *brake*, and the ships which they loaded therewith

sunk: St. *John*, recording the like miracle, faith, That albeit the fishes in number were so many, yet the net with so great a weight was *not broken*. Suppose they had written both of one miracle; although there be in their words a manifest shew of jar; yet none, if we look upon the difference of matter, with regard whereunto they might have both spoken even of one miracle the very same which they spake of divers; the one intending thereby to signify, that the greatness of the burden exceeded the natural ability of the instruments which they had to bear it; the other, that the weakness thereof was supported by a supernatural and miraculous addition of strength. The nets, as touching themselves, *brake*, but through the power of God they *held*.

Are not the words of the prophet *Micheas* touching *Bethleem*, Thou *Bethleem* the least? And doth not the very evangelist translate these words, *Thou Bethleem not the least?* The one regarding the quantity of the place, the other the dignity. *Micheas* attributeth unto it smalness, in respect of circuit; *Matthew*, greatness in regard of honour and estimation, by being the native soil of our Lord and Saviour Christ. Sith therefore speeches which gain-say one another, must of necessity be applied unto one and the self-same subject; sith they must also the one affirm, the other deny the self-same thing; what necessity of contradiction can there be between the letter of the prophet *David*, and our authorized translation thereof, if he un-

der-

derſtanding *Moſes* and *Aaron*, do ſay, *They were not diſobedient* ; we applying our ſpeech to *Pharaoh* and the *Ægyptians*, do ſay of them, *They were not obedient ?* Or (which the matter it ſelf will eaſily enough likewiſe ſuffer) if the *Ægyptians* being meant by both, it be ſo that *they* in regard of their offer to let go the people, when they ſaw the fearful darkneſs, *diſobeyed not* the word of the Lord ; and yet they *did not obey* his word, in as much as the ſheep and cattle at the ſelf-ſame time they with-held. Of both tranſlations the better I willingly acknowledge that which cometh nearer to the very letter of the original verity ; yet ſo, that the other may likewiſe ſafely enough be read, without any peril at all of gain-ſaying as much as the leaſt jot or ſyllable of God's moſt ſacred and precious truth. Which truth, as in this we do not violate, ſo neither is the ſame gainſaid or croſs'd, no not in thoſe very preambles placed before certain readings, wherein the ſteps of the *Latin*-ſervice book have been ſomewhat too nearly followed. As when we ſay, Chriſt ſpake [a] *to his diſciples,* That which the goſpel declareth he ſpake [b] *unto the Pharifees.* For doth the goſpel affirm he ſpake to the Phariſees *only ?* Doth it mean that they, and beſides them no man elſe was at that time ſpoken unto by our Saviour Chriſt ? If not, then is there in this diverſity no contrariety. I ſuppoſe it ſomewhat probable, that St. *John* and St. *Matthew,* which have recorded thoſe ſermons, heard them, and being hearers did think themſelves as well reſpected as the *Phariſees,* in that which their Lord and [c] Maſter taught concerning the paſtoral care he had over his own flock, and his offer of grace made to the whole world ; which things are the matter whereof he treateth in thoſe ſermons. Wherefore as yet there is nothing found, wherein we read for the word of God that which may be condemned as repugnant unto his word. Further-

[a] The goſpel on the ſecond ſunday after Eſter, and on the twentieth after Trinity. John 10. 11.
[b] Matt. 22. 1.

more, ſomewhat they are diſpleaſed, in that we follow not the method of reading which [c] in their judgment is moſt commendable, the me-thod uſed in ſome foreign churches, where ſcriptures are read *before* the time of divine ſer-vice, and without either *choice* or *ſtint* appoint-ed by any determinate order. Neverthelcſs, till ſuch time as they will vouchſafe us ſome juſt and ſufficient reaſon to the contrary, we muſt by their patience, if not allowance, retain the [d] an-cient received cuſtom which we now obſerve.

[c] *T. C. l. 2. p.* 381. Altho' it be very convenient which is uſed in ſome churches, where before preaching time the church aſſembled hath the ſcriptures read ; yet neither is this, nor any other order of bare publick reading in the church neceſſary. h. d.

[d] Aug. de Civ. Dei, l. 22. c. 8. *Paſto ſilentio, ſcripturarum ſunt lecta divina ſolennia.* That for ſeveral times ſeveral pieces of ſcriptures were read as parts of the ſervice of the *Greek* church, the fathers thereof in their ſundry homilies and other writings do all teſtify. The like order in the *Syrian* churches, is clear by the very inſcriptions of chapters throughout their Tranſlation of the New teſtament. See the edition at *Vienna, Paris* and *Antwerp.*

For with us the reading of the ſcripture in the church is a part of our church-liturgy, a ſpecial portion of the ſervice which we do to God, and not an exerciſe to ſpend the time when one doth wait for anothers coming, till the aſſembly of them which ſhall afterwards worſhip him be compleat. Wherefore, as the form of our publick ſervice is not voluntary , ſo neither are the parts thereof left uncertain, but they are all ſet down in ſuch order, and with ſuch choice as hath in the wiſdom of the church ſeemed beſt to concur as well with the ſpecial occaſions, as with the general purpoſe which we have to glorify God.

20. Other publick readings there are of books and writings not canonical, whereby the church doth alſo preach, or openly make known the doctrine of virtuous converſa-tion ; whereupon, beſides thoſe things in regard whereof we are thought to read the ſcriptures of God amiſs, it is thought amiſs that we read in our churches any thing at all beſides the ſcriptures. To exclude the reading of any ſuch profitable inſtruction as the church hath deviſed for the better underſtanding of ſcripture, or for the eaſier train-ing up of the people in holineſs and righteouſ-neſs of life, they [e] plead , that God in the law would have *nothing* brought into the temple, neither beſoms, nor fleſh-hooks, nor trumpets, but thoſe only which were ſanctified ; that for the expounding of darker places, we *ought* to follow the *Jews* [f] polity, who under *Antio-chus,* where they had not the commodity of ſermons, appointed always at their meeting ſomewhat out of the prophets to be read toge-

Of preaching by the pub-lick reading of other pro-fitable in-ſtructions ; and concern-ing books A-pocryphal.

[e] *T. C. l. 1. p.* 196. Neither the homilies, nor the Apo-crypha, are at all to be read in the church. Wherein, firſt, It is good to conſider the order which the Lord kept with his people in times paſt, when he commanded , *Exod.* 30. 29. that no veſſel nor no inſtrument, either beſom or fleſh-hook, or pan ſhould once come into the temple , but thoſe only which are ſanctified and ſet apart for that uſe. And in the book of *Numbers* he will have no other trumpets blown to call the people together, but thoſe only which were ſet apart for that purpoſe, *Numb.* 10. 2.

[f] *T. C. l. 1. p.* 197. Beſides this , the Polity of the church of God in times paſt is to be followed, &c.

ther with the law, and ſo by the one made the other plainer to be underſtood ; That before and after our Saviour's coming, they neither read *Onkelos* nor *Jonathan's* para-phraſe , though having both ; but contented themſelves [g] with the reading only of ſcriptures ; that if in the primitive church there had been any thing read beſides the mo-

[g] Acts 15. 15.
Acts 15. 21.

numents

ᵃ Juſtin. A-
pol. 2. Ori-
gen. Hom. 1.
ſuper Exod.
& in Judic.
ᵇ Concil.
Laod. c. 59.
ᶜ Concil.
Valenſ. 2.
ᵈ Concil.
Colon. par. 2.
numents of the prophets and apoſtles, ᵃ Juſtin Martyr and Origen, who mention
theſe, would have ſpoken of the other likewiſe : That ᵇ the moſt ancient and beſt
councils forbid any thing to be read in churches, ſaving canonical ſcripture only :
That when ᶜ other things were afterwards permitted, ᵈ fault was found with it, it ſucceeded but ill, the bible it ſelf was thereby in time quite and clean thruſt out. Which
arguments, if they be only brought in token of the authors good will and meaning towards the cauſe which they would ſet forward, muſt accordingly be accepted by them
who already are perſuaded the ſame way. But if their drift and purpoſe be to perſuade
others, it would be demanded, by what rule the legal *hallowing* of beſoms and fleſh-
hooks muſt needs exclude all other readings in the church ſave ſcripture. Things ſanctified were thereby in ſuch ſort appropriated unto God, as that they might never afterwards again be made common. For which cauſe, the Lord, to ſign and mark them

ᵉ Exod. 30.
25, 32.
ᶠ Ex. 40. 15.
as his own, ᵉ appointed oil of holy ointment, the like whereunto it was not lawful to
make for ordinary and daily uſes. Thus the ᶠ anointing of *Aaron* and his Sons tied
them to the office of the prieſthood for ever ; the anointing not of thoſe ſilver trumpets

ᵍ Num. 10, 2.
ʰ Exod. 27.
3. & 30. 26,
27, 28.
(which ᵍ *Moſes* as well for ſecular as ſacred uſes was commanded to make, not to ſanctify) but the unction of the ʰ tabernacle, the table, the laver, the altar of God, with
all the inſtruments appertaining thereunto, this made them for ever holy unto him, in
whoſe ſervice they were employed. But what of this ? Doth it hereupon follow,
that all things now in the church, from the greateſt *to the leaſt*, are unholy, which
the Lord hath not himſelf preciſely inſtituted ?

ⁱ T. C. l. 1. p. 127. The Lord would by theſe Rudiments and Pædagogies teach , that he would have nothing
brought into the church, but that which he appointed.
For ſo ⁱ thoſe rudiments, they ſay, do import.
Then is there nothing holy, which the church
by her authority hath appointed ; and conſe-
quently all poſitive Ordinances that ever were made by eccleſiaſtical power touching
ſpiritual affairs, are prophane, they are unholy. I would not wiſh them to undertake
a work ſo deſperate as to prove, that for the people's inſtruction no kind of reading is
good, but only that which the *Jews* deviſed under *Antiochus*, although even that alſo

ᵏ Elias
Theſb. in
verbo patar.
be miſtaken. For, according to ᵏ *Elias* the Levite (out of whom it doth ſeem borrowed) the thing which *Antiochus* forbad, was the publick reading of the law, and
not *ſermons* upon the law. Neither did the *Jews* read a portion of the prophets together with the law to ſerve for an interpretation thereof, becauſe ſermons were not permitted them: But, inſtead of the law, which they might not read openly, they read
of the prophets that, which in likeneſs of matter came neareſt to each ſection of their

ˡ Acts 15. 21.
ᵐ Acts 13. 15.
law. Whereupon, when afterwards the liberty of reading the law ˡ was reſtored, the
ſelf-ſame cuſtom ᵐ as touching the prophets did continue ſtill. If neither the *Jews*
have uſed publickly to read their paraphraſts,

ⁿ T. C. l. 1. p. 197. This practice continued ſtill in the
churches of God after the apoſtles times, as may appear by
the ſecond apology of *Juſtin. Martyr. Idem*, p. 198. It was
decreed in the council of *Laodicea*, that nothing ſhould be
read in the church but the canonical books of the Old and
New Teſtament. Afterwards, as corruptions grew in the
church, the reading of homilies and of martyrs lives was
permitted. But, beſides the evil ſucceſs thereof, that uſe
and cuſtom was controuled, as may appear by the council of
Collen, albeit otherwiſe popiſh. The bringing in of homilies and martyrs lives hath thruſt the bible clean out of the
church, or into a corner.
nor ⁿ the primitive church for a long time any
other writings than ſcripture , except the cauſe
of their not doing it were ſome law of God,
or reaſon forbidding them to do that which we
do, why ſhould the latter ages of the church be
deprived of the liberty the former had ? Are
we bound while the world ſtandeth, to put nothing in practice, but only that which was at
the very firſt? Concerning the council of *Lao-*

The Apoca-
lypſe.
dicea, as it forbiddeth the reading of thoſe things which are not canonical, ſo it maketh ſome things not canonical, which are. Their judgment in this we may not, and
in that we need not follow. We have by thus many years experience found, that exceeding great good, not incumbred with any notable inconvenience, hath grown by
the cuſtom which we now obſerve. As for the harm whereof judicious men have
complained in former times; it came not of this, that other things were read beſides
the Scripture, but that ſo evil choice was made. With us there is never any time beſtowed in divine ſervice without the reading of a great part of the holy ſcripture, which
we account a thing moſt neceſſary. We dare not admit any ſuch form of liturgy, as
either appointeth no ſcripture at all, or very little to be read in the church. And therefore the thruſting of the bible out of the houſe of God, is rather there to be feared

ᵒ T. C. l. 2. p. 381. It is untrue , that *ſimple reading* is
neceſſary in the church. A number of churches which have
no ſuch order of *ſimple reading*, cannot be in this point charged with the breach of God's commandment , which they
might be, if *ſimple reading* were *neceſſary*. [By *ſimple reading*
he meaneth the cuſtom of bare reading more than the
preacher at the ſame time expoundeth unto the people.]
where men eſteem it a matter ᵒ ſo indifferent,
whether the ſame be by ſolemn appointment
read publickly or not read, the bare text except-
ted, which the preacher happily chuſeth out to
expound. But let us here conſider , what the
practice of our fathers before us hath been, and
how far forth the ſame may be followed. We
4
find

find that in ancient times there was publickly read firft the ª fcripture, as namely fomething out of the books of the ᵇ prophets of God which were of old ; fomething out of ᵉ the apoftles writings; and laftly, out of the holy ᵈ evangelifts fome things which touched the perfon of our Lord Jefus Chrift himfelf. The caufe of their reading firft the old teftament, then the new, and always fomewhat out of both, is moft likely to have been that which ᵉ *Juftin Martyr* and St. *Auguftin* obferve in comparing the two teftaments. *The apoftles* (faith the one) *have taught us as themfelves did learn, firft the precepts of the law, and then the gofpels. For what elfe is the law but the gofpel forefhewed? What other the gofpel, than the law fulfilled?* In like fort the other, *What the old teftament hath, the very fame the new containeth; but that which lieth there as under a fhadow, is here brought forth into the open fun. Things there prefigured, are here performed.* Again, *In the old teftament there is a clofe comprehenfion of the new; in the new, an open difcovery of the old.* To be fhort, the method of their publick readings either purpofely did tend, or at the leaft-wife doth fitly ferve, *That from fmaller things the minds of the hearers may go forward to the knowledge of greater, and by degrees climb up from the loweft to the higheft things.* Now befides the fcripture, the books which they called *Ecclefiaftical* were thought not unworthy fometime to be brought into publick audience, and with that name they intituled the books which we term *Apocryphal*. Under the felf-fame name they alfo comprized certain; no otherwife annexed unto the new than the former unto the old teftament, as a book of *Hermes*, epiftles of *Clement*, and the like. According therefore to the phrafe of antiquity, thefe we may term the new, and the other the old ecclefiaftical books or writings. For we being directed by a fentence (I fuppofe) of St. *Jerom*, who faith, that *all writings not canonical are apocryphal*, ufe not now the title *Apocryphal* as the reft of the Fathers ordinarily have done, whofe cuftom is fo to name for the moft part only fuch as might not publickly be read or divulged. *Ruffinus* therefore having rehearfed the felf-fame books of canonical Scripture, which with us are held to be only canonical, addeth immediately, by way of caution, *We muft know that other books there are alfo, which our forefathers have ufed to name not canonical but ecclefiaftical books, as the book of* Wifdom, Ecclefiafticus, Toby, Judith, *the* Maccabees, *in the old teftament ; in the new, the book of* Hermes, *and fuch others : All which books and writings they willed to be read in churches, but not to be alledged as if their authority did bind us to build upon them our faith. Other writings they named* Apocryphal, *which they would not have read in churches. Thefe things delivered unto us from the fathers we have in this place thought good to fet down.* So far *Ruffinus*. He which confidereth notwithftanding what ftore of falfe and forged writings, dangerous unto chriftian belief, and yet bearing ᵉ glorious infcriptions, began foon upon the apoftles times to be admitted into the church, and to be honoured as if they had been indeed apoftolick, fhall eafily perceive what caufe the provincial Synod of ᶠ *Laodicea* might have as then to prevent efpecially the danger of books made newly ecclefiaftical, and, for fear of the fraud of hereticks, to provide that fuch publick readings might be altogether taken out of the canonical fcripture. Which ordinance refpecting but that abufe which grew through the intermingling of leffons human with facred, at fuch time as the one both affected the credit and ufurped the name of the other (as by the canon of ᵍ a later council, providing remedy for the felf-fame evil, and yet allowing the old ecclefiaftical books to be read, it doth more plainly and clearly appear) neither can be conftrued, nor fhould be urged utterly to prejudice our ufe of thofe old ecclefiaftical writings; much lefs of Homilies, which were a third kind of readings ufed in former times, a moft commendable inftitution, as well then ʰ to fupply the cafual, as now the neceffary defect of fermons.

In the heat of general perfecution, whereunto chriftian belief was fubject upon the firft promulgation thereof throughout the world, it much confirmed the courage and conftancy of weaker minds, when publick relation was made unto them after what manner God had been glorified through the fufferings of Martyrs, famous amongft them for holinefs during life, and at the time of their death admirable in all men's eyes through miraculous evidence of grace divine affifting them from above. For which caufe the vir-

T   tues

Marginal notes:

ª *Coimus ad divinarum litterarum commemorationem.* Tertul: Apol. p. 692.

ᵇ *Judaicarum Hiftoriarum libri traditi funt ab apoftolis legendi in ecclefiis.* Orig. in Jof. Hom. 15.

ᵉ Παιδίων κ̅ πάλιν ἢ ἀγρὸς μεθ᾽ ἡμῶν ἐπὶ τὸ αὐτὸ οντελθότε ὠλιτρ, κỵ τα ἀπομνημονεύματα τ̅ Ἀποςόλων ἢ τα συγράμματα τ̅ Προφητῶν ἀναγινώσκε. Juftin. Apol. 2. p. 162. *Factum eft ut ifta die dominica, prophetica lectione jam lecta; ante altare adftante qui lectionem S. Pauli proferret, beatiffimus Antiftes Ambrofius, &c.* Sulpit. Sever. l. 3. de vita St. Mart.

ᵈ Vide Concil. Vaf. 2. habitum an. Dom. 444. tom. Concil. 2. p. 19. Item. Synod. Laod. c. 16. Cypr. l. 2. epift. 5. & l. 4. epift. 5. Amb. l. 1. Offic. c. 8. & epift. 75. & lib. de Helia atque jejunio, cap. 20.

ᵉ Juft. quæft. 101.

Auguft. quæft. 33. in Num.

Walaf. Strab. de rebus ecclefiaft. cap. 22.

Hieron. in prolog. Galeat.

Ruffinus in Symbol. Apoft. apud Cypr.

ᵉ *Vide Gelaf. decret. tom.*

ᶠ *Circa An. Dom. 366.*

ᵍ *Concil. Carthag. 3. c. 47. Præter fcripturas canonicas nihil in ecclefia legatur fub nomine divinarum fcripturarum. An. Dom. 401.*

ʰ *Concil. Vafen. 2. habitum An. Dom. 444. tom. Concil. 2. p. 19. Si Presbyter, aliqua infirmitate prohibente, per feipfum non potuerit prædicare, Sanctorum Patrum Homiliæ a Diaconibus recitentur.*

tues of some being thought expedient to be annually had in remembrance above the
rest, this brought ᵃ in a fourth kind of publick reading, whereby the lives of such saints
and martyrs had at the time of their yearly memorials solemn recognition in the church
of God. The fond imitation of which laudable custom being in latter ages resumed,
where there was neither the like cause to do as the fathers before had done, nor any
care, conscience, or wit, in such as undertook to perform that work, some brainless
men have by great labour and travel brought to pass, that the church is now ashamed
of nothing more than of saints. If therefore Pope ᵇ Gelasius did so long sithence see
those defects of judgment, even then, for which the reading of the acts of martyrs
should be, and was at that time forborn in the church of Rome; we are not to marvel,
that afterwards legends being grown in a manner to be nothing else but heaps of frivolous and scandalous vanities, they have been even with disdain thrown out, the ᶜ very
nests which bred them abhorring them. We are not therefore to except only scripture,
and to make confusedly all the residue of one sute, as if they who abolish legends could
not without incongruity retain in the church either homilies or those ecclesiastical books.
Which books in case my self did think, as some others do, safer and better to be left
publickly unread; nevertheless as in other things of like nature, even so in this, ᵈ my
private judgment I should be loth to oppose against the force of their reverend authority, who rather considering the divine excellency of some things in all, and of all
things in certain of those Apocrypha which we publickly read, have thought it better
to let them stand as a list or marginal border unto the old testament, and tho' with divine, yet as human compositions, to grant at the least unto certain of them publick
audience in the house of God. For in as much as the due estimation of heavenly truth
dependeth wholly upon the known and approved authority of those famous oracles of
God, it greatly behoveth the church to have always most especial care, lest through con-
fused mixture at any time, human usurp the room and title of divine writings. Wherefore albeit for the people's more plain instruction (as the ancient use hath been) we
read in churches certain books besides the scripture, yet as the scripture we read them
not. All men know our professed opinion, touching the difference whereby we sever
them from the scripture. And if any where it be suspected, that some one or other
will haply mistake a thing so manifest in every man's eye, there is no lett, but that
as often as those books are read, and need so requireth, the stile of their difference may
expresly be mentioned, to bar even all possibility of error. It being then known, that
we hold not the Apocrypha for sacred (as we do the holy scripture) but for human
compositions, the subject whereof are sundry divine matters; let there be reason shewed, why to read any part of them publickly, it should be unlawful or hurtful unto the
church of God. I hear it said, that many things in them are very frivolous and unworthy of publick audience; yea, many contrary, plainly contrary to the holy scripture.
Which hitherto is neither sufficiently proved by him who saith it; and if the proofs thereof were strong, yet the very allegation it self is weak. Let us therefore suppose (for I
will not demand to what purpose it is, that against our custom of reading books not
canonical, they bring exceptions of matter in those books which we never read,) suppose (I say) that what faults soever they have observed throughout the passages of
all those books, the same in every respect were such as neither could be construed,
nor ought to be censured otherwise than even as themselves pretend: Yet as men
through too much haste oftentimes forget the errand whereabout they should go; so here
it appeareth, that an eager desire to rake together what might prejudice or any way
hinder the credit of apocryphal books, hath caused the collector's pen so to run as it
were on wheels, that the mind which should guide it had not leisure to think, whether that which might haply serve to with-hold from giving them the authority which
belongeth unto sacred scripture, and to cut them off from the canon, would as effectually serve to shut them altogether out of the church, and to withdraw from granting unto them that publick use wherein they are only held as profitable for instruction.
Is it not acknowledged, that those books are holy, that they are ecclesiastical and sacred,
that to term them divine, as being for their excellency next unto them which are properly so termed, is no way to honour them above desert; yea, even that the whole
church of Christ, as well at the first as sithence, hath most worthily approved their fitness for the publick information of life and manners? Is not thus much, I say, acknowledged, and that by them, who notwithstanding receive not the same for any part
of the canonical scripture; by them who deny not but that they are faulty; by them
who are ready enough to give instances wherein they seem to contain matter scarce
agreeable with holy scripture? So little doth such their supposed faultiness in moderate
men's judgments inforce the removal of them out of the house of God, that still
they are judged to retain worthily those very titles of commendation, than which

there

2

ᵃ Concil.
Carthag. 3.
Can. 13. &
Greg. Turon.
de gloria.
mart. ca. 86.
& Hadria.
epist. ad Ca-
rol. Magn.
ᵇ Gelas. cir-
ca An. Dom.
492. to. Con-
cil. 2. p.461.
ᶜ Concil. Co-
lon. celebrat.
An. D. 1536.
par. 2. cap.6.
Melch. Can.
locor. theol.
lib. 11. Viv.
de trad. disc.
lib. 5.
ᵈ In errorum
barathrum fa-
ciliter ruunt,
qui conceptus
proprios pa-
trum definitio-
nibus antepo-
nunt. c. usque
Relig. d. in
extra.

ᵉ Hieron.
præf. ad li-
bros Salom.
Aug.de præd.
Sanct. l. 1.
c. 14. Præf.
gloss. ord. &
Lyr. ad prol.
Hieron. in
Tob.

T. C. l. 2.
p. 400, 401.

Harm. Con-
fes. sect. 1.
Bel. con art.
6. Lubert.
de princip.
Christ.dogm.
l. 1. c. 5.

there cannot greater be given to writings, the authors whereof are men. As in truth if the scripture it self, ascribing to the persons of men righteousness in regard of their manifold virtues, may not rightly be construed as though it did thereby clear them and make them quite free from all faults, no reason we should judge it absurd to commend their writings as reverend, holy and found, wherein there are so many singular perfections, only for that the exquisite wits of some few peradventure are able dispersedly here and there to find now a word and then a sentence, which may be more probably suspected than easily cleared of error by us which have but conjectural knowledge of their meaning. Against immodest invectives therefore whereby they are charged as being fraught with [a] *outragious lies*, we doubt not but their more allowable censure will prevail, who without so passionate terms of disgrace do note a difference great enough between apocryphal and other writings, a difference such as [b] *Josephus* and *Epiphanius* observe : The one declaring, that amongst the *Jews*, books written after the days of *Artaxerxes* were not of equal credit with them which had gone before, in as much as the *Jews* sithence that time had not the like exact succession of prophets ; the [c] other acknowledging that they are profitable, although denying them to be divine, in such construction and sense as the scripture it self is so termed. With what intent they were first published, those words of the [d] nephew of *Jesus* do plainly enough signify, *After that my grandfather Jesus had given himself to the reading of the law and the prophets, and other books of our fathers, and had gotten therein sufficient judgment, he purposed also to write something pertaining to learning and wisdom, to the intent that they which were desirous to learn, and would give themselves to these things, might profit much more in living according to the law.* Their end in writing, and ours in reading them, is the same. The books of *Judith, Toby, Baruch, Wisdom*, and *Ecclesiasticus* we read, as serving most unto that end. The rest we leave unto men in private. Neither can it be reasonably thought, because upon certain solemn occasions, some lessons are chosen out of those books, and of scripture it self some chapters not appointed to be read at all, that we thereby do offer disgrace to the word of *God*, or lift up the writings of men above it. For in such choice we do not think, but that fitness of speech may be more respected than worthiness. If in that which we use to read, there happen by the way any clause, sentence or speech that soundeth towards error ; should the mixture of a little dross constrain the church to deprive her self of so much gold, rather than to learn how by art and judgment to make separation of the one from the other ? To this effect very fitly, from the counsel that St. *Jerom* giveth *Læta*, of taking heed how she read the *Apocrypha*, as also by the help of other learned men's judgments delivered in like case, we may take direction. But surely the arguments that should bind us not to read them, or any part of them publickly at all, must be stronger than as yet we have heard any.

21. We marvel the less that our reading of books not canonical is so much impugned, when so little is attributed unto the reading of canonical scripture it self, that now it hath grown to be a question, whether the word of God be any ordinary mean to save the souls of men, in that it is either privately studied, or publickly read, and so made known ; or else only as the same is preached, that is to say, *explained by a lively voice*, and applied to the people's use as the *speaker in his wisdom thinketh meet*. For this alone is it which they use to call *preaching*. The publick reading of the *Apocrypha* they condemn altogether as a thing effectual unto evil ; the bare reading in like sort of whatsoever, yea even of scriptures themselves, they mislike as a thing uneffectual to do that good which we are persuaded may grow by it. Our desire is in this present controversy, as in the rest, not to be carried up and down with the waves of uncertain arguments, but rather positively to lead on the minds of the simpler sort by plain and easy degrees, till the very nature of the thing it self do make manifest what is truth. First therefore, because whatsoever is spoken concerning the efficacy or necessity of God's word, the same they tie and restrain only unto sermons, howbeit not sermons read neither (for such they also abhor in the church) but sermons without book, sermons which spend their life in their birth, and may have publick audience but once ; for this cause, to avoid ambiguities wherewith they often entangle themselves, not marking what doth agree to the word of God it self, and what in regard of outward accidents which may befal it, we are to know that the word of God is his heavenly truth touching matters of eternal life, revealed and uttered unto men, unto Prophets and Apostles, by immediate divine inspiration, from them to us by their books and writings. We therefore have no word of God but the scripture. Apostolick sermons were unto such as heard them his word, even as properly as to us their writings are. Howbeit not so our own sermons, the exposi-

[a] The libel of Metaphys. School. art. 34.
[b] Joseph. cont. App. lib. 1.
[c] Epiph. in Ancyrot. Χρήσιμα μ̀ ἀυτὰ ἀναγινώσκει, ἀλλ᾿ εἰς δόγμα φανερὸν οὐ ρῆδ.
[d] Præfat. ad lib. Ecclesi.

Of preaching by sermons ; and whether sermons be the only ordinary way of teaching whereby men are brought to the saving knowledge of God's truth.

tions which our difcourfe of wit doth gather and minifter out of the word of God.
For which caufe, in this prefent queftion we are, when we name the word of God,
always to mean the fcripture only. The end of the word of God is to fave, and
therefore the way for all men to be faved, is by the
knowledge of that truth which the word hath taught. And fith eternal life is a thing
of it felf communicable unto all, it behoveth that the word of God, the neceffary
mean thereunto, be fo likewife. Wherefore the word of life hath been always a
treafure, though precious, yet eafy, as well to attain, as to find; left any man defirous of life fhould perifh through the difficulty of the way. To this end the word of
God no otherwife ferveth, than only in the nature of a doctrinal inftrument. It faveth, becaufe it maketh *wife unto falvation*. Wherefore the ignorant it faveth
not; they which live by the word, muft know it. And being it felf the inftrument
which God hath purpofely framed, thereby to work the knowledge of falvation in the
hearts of men, what caufe is there wherefore it fhould not of it felf be acknowledged a moft apt and a likely mean to leave an *apprehenfion* of things divine in our
underftanding, and in the mind an *affent* thereunto? For touching the one, fith God
who knoweth and difclofeth beft the rich treafures of his own wifdom, hath by delivering his word made choice of the fcriptures as the moft effectual means whereby
thofe treafures might be imparted unto the world, it followeth, that to man's underftanding the fcripture muft needs be even of it felf intended as a full and perfect
difcovery, fufficient to imprint in us the lively character of all things neceffarily required for the attainment of eternal life. And concerning our affent to the myfteries of heavenly truth, feeing that the word of God, for the author's fake, hath credit with all that confefs it (as we all do) to be his word, every propofition of holy
fcripture, every fentence being to us a principle; if the principles of all kinds of
knowledge elfe have that virtue in themfelves, whereby they are able to procure our
affent unto fuch conclufions as the induftry of right difcourfe doth gather from them;
we have no reafon to think the principles of that truth which tendeth unto men's
everlafting happinefs, lefs forcible than any other, when we know that of all other
they are for their certainty the moft infallible. But as every thing of price, fo this
doth require travel. We bring not the knowledge of God with us into the world.
And the lefs our own opportunity or ability is that way, the more we need the help
of other men's judgments to be our direction herein. Nor doth any man ever believe, into whom the doctrine of belief is not inftilled by inftruction, fome way received at the firft from others. Wherein whatfoever fit means there are to notify the
myfteries of the word of God, whether publickly (which we call *preaching*) or in
private howfoever, the word by *every fuch mean* even *ordinarily* doth fave, and not
only by being delivered unto men in fermons. *Sermons* are not *the only preaching*
which doth fave fouls. For, concerning the ufe and fenfe of this word *preaching*,
which they fhut up in fo clofe a prifon, although more than enough have already been
fpoken to redeem the liberty thereof; yet becaufe they infift fo much, and fo proudly
infult thereon, we muft a little inure their ears with hearing how others, whom they
more regard, are in this cafe accuftomed to ufe the felf-fame language with us, whofe
manner of fpeech they deride. [a] *Juftin Martyr* doubteth not to tell the *Grecians*, That
even in certain of their *writings* the very judgment to come i preached; nor the [b] council of *Vaus* to infinuate, that presbyters, abfent through infirmity from the churches,
might be faid to preach by thofe deputies who in their ftead did but read *Homilies*; nor
the [c] council of *Toledo*, to call the ufual publick reading of the *Gofpels* in the church,
preaching; nor [d] others, long before thefe our days to write, that by him who but
readeth a *leffon* in the folemn affembly as part of divine fervice, the very office of preaching is fo far forth executed. Such kind of fpeeches were then familiar, thofe phrafes feemed not to them abfurd; they would have marvelled to hear the [e] outcries which
we do, becaufe we think that the apoftles *in writing*, and others *in reading* to the
church thofe books which the apoftles wrote, are neither untruly nor unfitly faid to
preach. For although men's *tongues* and their *pens* differ, yet to one and the felf-
fame general, if not particular *effect*, they may both ferve. It is no good argument,
St. *Paul* could not *write with his tongue*, therefore neither could he *preach with his
pen*. For preaching is a general end whereunto writing and fpeaking do both ferve.
Men fpeak not with the inftruments of writing, neither write with the inftruments of
fpeech; and yet things *recorded* with one, and *uttered* with the other, may be [f] *preached* well enough with both. By their patience therefore be it fpoken, the apoftles
preached as well when they *wrote*, as when they *fpake* the gofpel of Chrift; and our ufual

pub-

* Paraenet.
ad Gent. p.
17.
b Concil. Va-
fen. 2. c. 2.
c Concil. Tol.
4. c. 11.
d Rupert. de
Divin. Offic.
l. 1. c. 12, 13.
Ifid. de Ec-
clef. Offic.
l. 1. c. 10.
e The Libel
of Schoolp. art.
11.
T. C. lib. 2.
p. 388.
St. Paul's
writing is no
more preach-
ing, than his
pen or his
hand is his
tongue: fee-
ing they can-
not be the
fame, which
cannot be
made by the
fame inftru-
ments.
f Evangeliza
mann & fcri-
ptione. Ra|nol.
de Rom. Ec-
clef. Idolola.
praf. ad Co.
Effex.

publick reading of the word of God for the peoples inftruction is *preaching*.   Not about words would we ever contend, were not their purpofe in fo reftraining the fame, injurious to God's moft facred word and fpirit.   It is on both fides confefs'd, that the word of God outwardly adminiftred (his [a] Spirit inwardly concurring there- [a] John 6. 46.
with) converteth, edifieth and faveth fouls.   Now whereas the external adminiftra- Matth. 16. 17.
tion of his word is as well by reading barely the fcripture, as by explaining the fame 2 Cor. 4. 6.
when fermons thereon be made ; in the one, they deny that the finger of God hath 1 Cor. 12. 3.
ordinarily certain *principal operations*, which we moft ftedfaftly hold and believe that Acts 16. 14.
it hath in both.

22. So worthy a part of divine fervice we fhould greatly wrong, if we did not *What they attribute to*
efteem preaching as the bleffed ordinance of God, fermons as keys to the kingdom of *fermons on-*
heaven, as wings to the foul, as fpurs to the good affections of man, unto the *ly, and what*
found and healthy as food, as phyfick unto difeafed minds.   Wherefore, how highly *we to read ing alfo.*
foever it may pleafe them with words of truth to extol Sermons, they fhall not
herein offend us.   We feek not to derogate from any thing which they can juftly
efteem, but our defire is to uphold the juft eftimation of that from which it feemeth
unto us they derogate more than becometh them.   That which offendeth us is, firft,
the great Difgrace which they offer unto our Cuftom of bare reading the Word of
God, and to his gracious fpirit, the principal virtue whereof thereby manifefting it
felf for the endlefs good of men's fouls, even the virtue which it hath to *convert*,
to *edify*, to *fave* Souls ; this they mightily ftrive to obfcure : And, fecondly, the
fhifts wherewith they maintain their opinion of fermons, whereunto while they labour to appropriate the faving power of the Holy Ghoft, they feparate from all apparent hope of life and falvation, thoufands whom the goodnefs of almighty God
doth not exclude.   Touching therefore the ufe of fcripture, even in that it is openly read, and the ineftimable good which the church of God by that very mean hath
reaped ; there was, we may very well think, fome caufe which moved the apoftle
St. *Paul* to require, that thofe things which any one churches affairs gave particular 1 Thef. 5.
occafion to write, might, for the inftruction of all, be publifhed, and that by *read-* 27.
ing. 1. When the very having of the books of God, was a matter of no fmall Colof. 4. 16.
charge and difficulty, in as much as they could not be had otherwife than only in
written Copies, it was the neceffity not of preaching things agreeable with the word,
but of reading the word it felf at large to the people, which caufed churches throughout the world to have publick care, that the facred oracles of God being procured by
common charge, might, with great fedulity, be kept both entire and fincere.   If
then we admire the providence of God in the fame continuance of fcripture, notwithftanding the violent endeavours of infidels to abolifh, and the fraudulence of hereticks always to deprave the fame, fhall we fet light by that cuftom of reading, from
whence fo precious a benefit hath grown ? 2. The voice and teftimony of the church,
acknowledging fcripture to be the law of the living God, is, for the truth and certainty thereof, no mean evidence.   For if with reafon we may prefume upon things
which a few mens depofitions do teftify, fuppofe we that the minds of men are not
both, at their firft accefs to the fchool of Chrift, exceedingly moved, yea, and for
ever afterwards alfo confirmed much, when they confider the main confent of all the
churches in the whole world witneffing the facred authority of fcriptures, ever fince
the firft publication thereof, even till this prefent day and hour ? And that they all
have always fo teftified, I fee not how we fhould poffibly wifh a proof more palpable, than this manifeft received and every where continued cuftom of reading them
publickly as the fcriptures.   The reading therefore of the word of God, as the ufe
hath ever been in open audience, is the plaineft evidence we have of the churches
affent and *acknowledgment*, that it is his word.   3. A further commodity this cuftom hath, which is to furnifh the very *fimpleft* and *rudeft* fort with fuch infallible
axioms and *precepts* of facred truth, delivered even in the *very letter* of the law of
God, as may ferve them for rules whereby to judge the *better all other doctrines*
and *inftructions* which they *hear*.   For which end and purpofe, I fee not how the John 5. 39
fcripture could be poffibly made familiar unto all, unlefs far more fhould be read in Ifa. 8. 20.
the peoples hearing, than by a fermon can be opened.   For whereas in a manner the
whole book of God is by reading every year publifhed, a fmall part thereof, in comparifon of the whole, may hold very well the readieft interpreter of fcripture occupied many years.   4. Befides, wherefore fhould any man think, but that reading
it felf is one of the ordinary means, whereby it pleafeth God of his gracious goodnefs to inftil that celeftial verity, which being *but fo* received, is neverthelefs effectual

to

to *fave fouls?* Thus much therefore we afcribe to the reading of the word of God, as the manner is in our churches. And becaufe it were odious, if they, on their part, fhould altogether defpife the fame, they yield that reading may fet forward, but

T. C. l. 2. p. 376, 377, 395. not begin the work of falvation: That faith may be nourifhed therewith, but not bred; that herein mens attention to the fcriptures, and the fpeculation of the crea-
Pag. 378. tures of God have like efficacy, both being of power to augment, but neither to
Pag. 383. effect belief without fermons; that if any believe by reading alone, we are to account it a miracle, an extraordinary work of God. Wherein that which they grant, we gladly accept at their hands, and wifh that patiently they would examine how lit-

2 Chron. 34. 18. tle caufe they have to deny that which as yet they grant not. The fcripture witnef-feth, that when the book of the law of God had been fometime miffing, and was after found; the King, which heard it but only read, tare his cloaths, and with tears confeffed, *Great is the wrath of the Lord upon us, becaufe our fathers have not kept*

2 Chron. 34. 3. *his word, to do after all things which are written in this book.* This doth argue, that by bare reading (for of fermons at that time there is no mention) true repen-

Deut. 31. 13. tance may be wrought in the hearts of fuch as fear God, and yet incur his difplea-fure, the deferved effect whereof is eternal death. So that their repentance (although it be not their firft entrance) is, notwithftanding, the firft ftep of their re-entrance into life, and may be in them wrought by the word only read unto them. Befides, it feemeth that God would have no man ftand in doubt, but that the reading of fcripture is effectual, as well to lay even the firft foundation, as to add degrees of farther perfection in the fear of God: And therefore the law faith, *Thou fhalt read this law before all Ifrael, that men, women and children may hear, yea, even that their children, which as yet have not known it, may hear it, and by hear-*

Luke 16. 20. *ing it fo read, may learn to fear the Lord.* Our Lord and Saviour was himfelf of opinion, that they which would not be drawn to amendment of life, by the teftimony which *Mofes* and the prophets have given concerning the miferies that follow finners after death, were not likely to be perfuaded by other means, although God from the very dead fhould have raifed them up preachers. Many hear the books of God, and believe them not. Howbeit, their unbelief, in that cafe, we may not impute unto any weaknefs or infufficiency in the mean which is ufed toward them, but to the wilfull bent of their obftinate hearts againft it. With minds obdurate nothing prevaileth. As well they that preach, as they that read unto fuch, fhall ftill have caufe to complain with the prophets which were of old, *Who will give credit unto our teaching?* But with whom ordinary means will prevail, furely the power of the word of God, even without the help of interpreters in God's church, worketh mightily, not unto their confirmation alone which are converted, but alfo to their converfion which are not. It fhall not boot them who derogate from reading, to excufe it, when they fee no other remedy, as if their intent were only to deny that aliens and ftrangers from the family of God are won, or that belief doth ufe to be wrought at the firft in them without Sermons. For they know it is our cuftom of fimple reading, not for converfion of infidels eftranged from the houfe of God, but for inftruction of men baptized, bred and brought up in the bofom of the church, which they defpife as a thing uneffectual to fave fuch fouls. In fuch they imagine that God hath no ordinary mean to work faith without fermons. The reafon why no man can attain belief by the bare contemplation of heaven and earth, is, for that they neither are fufficient to give us as much as the leaft fpark of light concerning the very principal myfteries of our faith; and whatfoever we may learn by them, the fame we can only attain to know according to the manner of natural fciences, which meer difcourfe of wit and reafon findeth out; whereas the things which we properly believe, be only fuch as are received upon the credit of divine teftimony. Seeing therefore, that he which confidereth the creatures of God, findeth therein both thefe defects, and neither the one nor the other in Scriptures, becaufe he that readeth unto us the Scriptures, delivereth all the myfteries of faith, and not any thing amongft them all more than the mouth of the Lord doth warrant: It followeth in thofe two refpects, that our confideration of creatures, and attention unto fcriptures are not in themfelves, and without fermons, things of like difability to breed or beget Faith. Small caufe alfo there is, why any man fhould greatly wonder as at an extraordinary work, if without fermons, reading be found to effect thus much. For I would know by fome fpecial inftance, what one article of chriftian faith, or what duty required neceffarily unto all mens falvation there is, which the very reading of the word of God is not apt to notify. Effects are mira-

2   culous

culous and ftrange, when they grow by unlikely means. But did we ever hear it accounted for a wonder, that he which doth read, fhould believe and live according
to the will of Almighty God? Reading doth convey to the mind that truth with- Exod. 24. 7.
out addition or diminution, which fcripture hath derived from the Holy Ghoft.
And the end of all fcripture is the fame which St. *John* propofeth in the writing of John 20. 31.
that moft divine Gofpel, namely *faith*, and through faith falvation. Yea, all fcripture is
to this effect in it felf available, as they which wrote it were perfuaded; unlefs we Prov. 1. 2, 3,
fuppofe that the evangelifts, or others, in fpeaking of their own intent to inftruct 4. Rom. 1. 16.
and to fave by writing, had a fecret conceit, which they never opened to any; a 2 Tim. 3. 15.
conceit that no man in the world fhould ever be that way the better for any fentence by them written, till fuch time as the fame might chance to be preached upon, or alledged at the leaft in a fermon. Otherwife, if he which writeth doth that
which is forcible in it felf, how fhould he which readeth, be thought to do that
which in it felf is of no force to work belief, and to fave believers? Now, altho' we
have very juft caufe to ftand in fome jealoufy and fear, left by thus overvaluing their
fermons, they make the price and eftimation of fcripture, otherwife notified, to fall;
neverthelefs fo impatient they are, that being but requefted to let us know what
caufes they leave for mens encouragement to attend to the reading of the fcripture,
if fermons only be the power of God to fave every one which believeth; that which
we move for our better learning and inftruction fake, turneth unto anger and choler
in them, they grow altogether out of quietnefs with it; they anfwer fumingly, that
they are *afhamed to defile their pens with making anfwer to fuch idle queftions*: T. C. l. 2. p. 376.
Yet in this their mood, they caft forth fomewhat, wherewith under pain of greater
difpleafure, we muft reft contented. They tell us, the profit of reading is fingular,
in that it ferveth for a preparative unto fermons, it helpeth prettily towards the nourifhment of faith, which fermons have once ingendred; it is fome ftay to his mind
which readeth the fcripture, when he findeth the fame things there which are taught
in fermons, and thereby perceiveth how God doth concur in opinion with the
preacher; befides, it keepeth fermons in memory, and doth in that refpect, although
not feed the foul of man, yet help the retentive force of that ftomach of the mind
which receiveth ghoftly food at the preachers hands. But the principal caufe of writing
the gofpel was, that it might be preached upon, or interpreted by publick minifters apt
and authorized thereunto. Is it credible that a fuperftitious conceit (for it is no better)
concerning fermons, fhould in fuch fort both darken their eyes, and yet fharpen
their wits withal, that the only true and weighty caufe why fcripture was written, the
caufe which in fcripture is fo often mentioned, the caufe which all men have ever
till this prefent day acknowledged, this they fhould clean exclude, as being no caufe
at all, and load us with fo great ftore of ftrange concealed caufes, which did never
fee light till now? In which number the reft muft needs be of moment, when the
very chiefeft caufe of committing the facred word of God unto books, is furmifed to
have been, left the preacher fhould want a text whereupon to fcholy. Men of learning hold it for a flip in judgment, when offer is made to demonftrate that as proper
to one thing, which reafon findeth common unto more. Whereas therefore they
take from all kind of teachings, that which they attribute to fermons, it had been
their part to yield directly fome ftrong reafon why between *fermons alone* and *faith*,
there fhould be ordinarily that coherence which caufes have with their ufual effects,
why a chriftian mans belief fhould fo naturally grow from fermons, and not poffibly from any other kind of teaching. In belief there being but thefe two operations, *apprehenfion* and *affent*, do only fermons caufe belief, in that no other way
is able to explain the myfteries of God, that the mind may rightly apprehend or conceive them as behoveth? We all know that many things are believed, although
they be intricate, obfcure and dark, although they exceed the reach and capacity of
our wits, yea although in this world they be no way poffible to be underftood.
Many things believed are likewife fo plain, that every common perfon may therein
be unto himfelf a fufficient expounder. Finally, to explain even thofe things which
need and admit explication, many other ufual ways there are befides fermons.
Therefore fermons are not the only ordinary means whereby we firft come to apprehend the myfteries of God. Is it in regard then of fermons only, that apprehending the Gofpel of Chrift, we yield thereunto our unfeigned affent, as to a thing
infallibly true? They which rightly confider after what fort the heart of man hereunto is framed, muft of neceffity acknowledge, that whofo affenteth to the words
of eternal life, doth it in regard of his authority, whofe words they are. This is, in
man's converfion unto God, τὸ ἔσω ἡ ἀρχὴ τῆς κινήσεως, the firft ftep whereat his race
towards

towards heaven beginneth. Unless therefore, clean contrary to our own experience, we shall think it a miracle, if any man acknowledge the divine authority of the scripture, till some sermon have persuaded him thereunto, and that otherwise neither conversation in the bosom of the church, nor religious education, nor the reading of learned mens books, nor information received by conference, nor whatsoever pain and diligence in hearing, studying, meditating day and night on the law, is so far blest of God, as to work this effect in any man; how would they have us to grant, that faith doth not come but only by hearing sermons? Fain they would have us to believe the apostle St. *Paul* himself, to be the author of this their paradox, only because he hath said, that it pleased God by the *foolishness of preaching* to save them which believe; and again, *How shall they call on him in whom they have not believed? How shall they believe in him of whom they have not heard? How shall they hear without a preacher? How shall men preach except they be sent?* To answer therefore both allegations at once; the very substance of what they contain is in few but this. Life and salvation God will have offered unto all; his will is, that *Gentiles* should be saved as well as *Jews.* Salvation belongeth unto none but such *as call upon the name of our Lord Jesus Christ.* Which nations as yet unconverted neither do, nor possibly can do, till they believe. What they are to believe, impossible it is they should know till they hear it. Their hearing requireth our preaching unto them. *Tertullian*, to draw even *Paynims* themselves unto christian belief, willeth the books of the old testament to be searched, which were at that time in *Ptolemy's* library. And if men did not list to travel so far, though it were for their endless good, he addeth, that in *Rome*, and other places, the *Jews* had synagogues, whereunto every one which would might resort; that this kind of liberty they purchased by payment of a standing tribute; that there they did openly read the scriptures; and whosoever *will hear*, (saith *Tertullian*) he *shall find God; whosoever will study to know, shall be also fain to believe.* But sith there is no likelihood that ever voluntarily they will seek instruction at our hands, it remaineth, that, unless we will suffer them to perish, salvation it self must seek them; it behoveth God to send them preach-

* *Apologet. c.* 11. *in fine.* This they did in a tongue, which to all learned men amongst the Heathens, and to a great part of the simplest, was familiarly known; as appeareth by a supplication offered unto the Emperor *Justinian*, wherein the *Jews* made request, that it might be lawful for them to read the *Greek* translations of the seventy interpreters in their synagogues, as their custom before had been. *Authent.* 146. *Col.* 10. *incipit. Æquum sane.*

ers, as he did his elect apostles throughout the world. There is a knowledge which God hath always revealed unto them in the works of nature. This they honour and esteem highly as profound wisdom; howbeit this wisdom saveth them not. That which must save believers, is *the knowledge of the cross of Christ*, the only subject of all our preaching. And in their eyes, what seemeth this but folly? It pleaseth God by *the foolishness of preaching* to save. These words declare how admirable force these mysteries have which the world do deride as follies; they shew that the foolishness of the cross of Christ is the wisdom of true believers; they concern the object of our faith, the matter preached of, and believed in by christian men. we know that the *Grecians* or *Gentiles* did account foolishness; but that they did ever think it a fond or unlikely way to seek mens conversion by sermons, we have not heard. Manifest therefore it is, that the apostle applying the name of *foolishness* in such sort as they did, must needs, by the *foolishness of preaching,* mean the doctrine of Christ, which we learn that we may be saved; but that sermons are the only manner of teaching whereby it pleaseth our Lord to save, he could not mean. In like sort, where the same apostle proveth, that as well the sending of the apostles, as their preaching to the *Gentiles* was necessary, dare we affirm it was ever his meaning, that unto their salvation, who even from their tender infancy never knew any other faith or religion than only christian, no kind of teaching can be available, saving that which was so needful for the first universal conversion of *Gentiles* hating christianity, neither the sending of any sort allowable in the one case, except only of such as had been in the other also most fit and worthy instruments? Belief, in all sorts, doth come by hearkning and attending to the word of life, which word sometime proposeth and preacheth it self to the hearer; sometime they deliver it, whom privately zeal and piety moveth to be instructors of others by conference; sometime of them it is taught, whom the church hath called to the publick either reading thereof, or interpreting. All these tend unto one effect; neither doth that which St. *Paul*, or other apostles teach concerning the necessity of such teachings as theirs was, or of sending such as they were, for that purpose, unto the *Gentiles*, prejudice

I

the

the efficacy of any other way of publick inftruction, or inforce the utter difability of any other mens vocation thought requifite in this church for the faving of fouls, where means more effectual are wanting.   Their only proper and direct proof of the thing in queftion had been to fhew, in what fort, and how far man's falvation doth neceffarily depend upon the knowledge of the word of God; what conditions, properties and qualities there are, whereby fermons are diftinguifhed from other kinds of adminiftring the word unto that purpofe; and what fpecial property or quality that is, which being no where found but in fermons, maketh them effectually to fave fouls, and leaveth all other doctrinal means befides deftitute of vital efficacy.   Thefe pertinent inftructions, whereby they might fatisfy us, and obtain the caufe it felf for which they contend; thefe things which only would ferve, they leave; and (which needeth not) fometime they trouble themfelves with fretting at the ignorance of fuch as withftand them in their opinion; fometime they [a] fall upon their poor brethren [a] T. C. l. 2. which can but read, and againft them they are bitterly eloquent.   If we alledge what p. 373. the fcriptures themfelves do ufually fpeak for the faving force of the word of God, not with reftraint to any one certain kind of delivery, but howfoever the fame fhall chance to be made known, yet by one trick or other, they always [b] reftrain it unto fermons.   Our Lord and Saviour hath faid, [c] *Search the fcriptures, for in them ye think to have eternal life*.   But they tell us he fpake to the *Jews*, which *Jews* before had heard his fermons; and that peradventure it was his mind they fhould fearch, not by reading, nor by hearing them read, but by attending whenfoever the fcriptures fhould happen to be alledged in fermons.   Furthermore, having received apoftolical doctrine, [d] the apoftle St. *Paul* hath taught us to efteem the fame as the fupream rule whereby all other doctrines muft for ever be examined.   Yea, but in as much as the Apoftle doth here fpeak of that he had preached, he flatly maketh (as they ftrangely affirm) his preachings or fermons the rule whereby to examine all. And then, I befeech you, what rule have we whereby to judge or examine any?   For if fermons muft be our rule, becaufe the Apoftles fermons were fo to their hearers; then, fith we are not as they were, hearers of the Apoftles fermons, it refteth that either the fermons which we hear fhould be our rule, or (that being abfurd) there will (which yet hath greater abfurdity) no rule at all be remaining for trial what doctrines now are corrupt, what confonant with heavenly truth.   Again, let the [1 Tim. 3. 16] fame Apoftle acknowledge all fcripture profitable to teach, to improve, to correct, to inftruct in righteoufnefs; ftill notwithftanding we err, if hereby we prefume to gather, that fcripture read will avail unto any one of all thefe ufes; they teach us the meaning of the words to be, that fo much the fcripture can do, if the minifter that way apply it in his fermons, otherwife not.   Finally, they never hear fentence which mentioneth the word or fcripture, but forthwith their gloffes upon it are, the word preached, the fcripture explained, or delivered unto us in fermons.   Sermons they evermore underftand to be that word of God, which alone hath vital operation; the dangerous fequel of which conftruction, I wifh they did more attentively wait.   For, fith fpeech is the very image whereby the mind and foul of the fpeaker conveyeth it felf into the bofom of him which heareth, we cannot chufe but fee great reafon wherefore the word which proceedeth from God, who is himfelf very truth and life, fhould be (as the apoftle to the *Hebrews* noteth) lively and mighty in operation, *fharper than any two-edged fword*.   Now, if in this and the like places, we did conceive that our own fermons are that ftrong and forcible word, fhould we not hereby impart even the moft peculiar glory of the word of God, unto that which is not his word?   For, touching our fermons, that which giveth them their very being, is the wit of man, and therefore they oftentimes accordingly tafte too much of that over-corrupt fountain from which they come.   In our fpeech of moft holy things, our moft frail affections many times are bewrayed.   Wherefore when we read or recite the fcripture, we then deliver to the people properly the word of God.   As for our fermons, be they never fo found and perfect, his word they are not as the fermons of the prophets were; no, they are but ambiguoufly termed his word, becaufe his word is commonly the fubject whereof they treat, and muft be the rule whereby they are framed.   Notwithftanding, by thefe and the like fhifts, they derive unto fermons alone, whatfoever is generally fpoken concerning the word.   Again, what feemeth to have been uttered concerning fermons, or their efficacy or neceffity in regard of divine matter, and muft confequently be verified in fundry other kinds of teaching, if the matter be the fame in all; their ufe is to faften every fuch fpeech unto that one only manner of teaching, which is by fermons, that

Side notes:
[a] T. C. l. 2.
p. 373.
This tail of readers.
The bifhops more than beggarly prefents.
Thofe rafcal minifters.
[b] T. C. l. 2.
p. 37.
[c] John 5. 39.
[d] Gal. 1. 9.
[1 Tim. 3. 16]
Heb. 4. 12.

T. C. l. 2. p. still sermons may be all in all. Thus, because *Solomon* declareth, that the *people de-*
381.
Prov. 29. 18. cay, *or perish, for want of knowledge,* where no prophesying at all is, they gather,
that the hope of life and salvation is cut off, where preachers are not, which prophecy by sermons, how many soever they be in number, that read daily the word of
God, and deliver, though in other sort, the self-same matter which sermons do.
The people which have no way to come to the knowledge of God, no prophesying,
no teaching, perish. But that they should of necessity perish, where any one way of
* T. C. l. 2. knowledge lacketh, is more than the words of *Solomon* import. * Another usual
p. 379. point of their art in this present question, is to make very large and plentiful dis-
John 3. 14.
* 2 Cor. 2. 16. courses how Christ is by sermons [b] lifted up higher and more [c] apparent to the eyes
* 2 Tim. 2. of faith, how the [d] favour of the word is more sweet, being brayed, and more able
15.
[d] Matth. 16. to nourish, being divided by preaching, than by only reading proposed ; how sermons
19. are the keys of the kingdom of heaven, and do open the scriptures, which being but read,
* 1 Cor. 3. 6. remain in comparison still clasped ; how God [e] giveth richer increase of grace to the
ground that is planted and watered by preaching, than by bare and simple reading.
Out of which premises declaring how attainment unto life is easier where sermons
[f] T. C. l. 2. are, they conclude an [f] impossibility thereof where sermons are not. *Alcidamas* the
p. 380. sophister hath many arguments to prove, that voluntary and extemporal far excelleth
No salvation
to be looked premeditated speech. The like whereunto, and in part the same, are brought by
for, where them who commend sermons, as having (which all men, I think, will acknowledge)
no preach-
ing is. sundry [g] peculiar and proper virtues, such as no other way of teaching besides hath.
[g] T. C. l. 2. Aptness to follow particular occasions presently growing, to put life into words by
p. 395. countenance, voice and gesture, to prevail mightily in the sudden affections of men,
this sermons may challenge. Wherein notwithstanding so eminent properties whereof
lessons are haply destitute, yet lessons being free from some inconveniencies whereunto sermons are more subject, they may in this respect no less take, than in other
they must give the hand which betokeneth pre-eminence. For there is nothing
which is not some way excelled, even by that which it doth excel. Sermons therefore and lessons may each excel other in some respects, without any prejudice unto
either, as touching that vital force which they both have in the work of our salvation. To which effect, when we have endeavoured as much as in us doth lie to find
out the strongest causes, wherefore they should imagine that reading is it self so unavailable, the most we can learn at their hands is, that sermons are the ordinance of
T. C. l. 2. God ; the scriptures dark, and the labour of reading easy. First, therefore, as we
p. 396. know that God doth aid with his grace, and by his special providence evermore bless
with happy success those things which himself appointeth ; so his church, we persuade our selves, he hath not in such sort given over to a reprobate sense, that whatsoever it deviseth for the good of the souls of men, the same he doth still accurse and
make frustrate. Or if he always did defeat the ordinances of his church, is not read-
Deut. 31. 13. ing the ordinance of God ? Wherefore then should we think that the force of his
secret grace is accustomed to bless the labour of dividing his word according unto
each mans private discretion in publick sermons, and to withdraw it self from concurring with the publick delivery thereof, by such selected portions of scriptures, as
the whole church hath solemnly appointed to be read for the peoples good, either by
ordinary course, or otherwise, according to the exigence of special occasions ? Read-
[h] De Ecclef. ing (saith [h] *Isidore*) is to the hearers no small edifying. To them whose [i] delight
Offic. l. 1. c.
10. and meditation is in the law, seeing that happiness and bliss belongeth, it is not in
[i] Psal. 1. 2. us to deny them the benefit of heavenly grace. And I hope we may presume, that
a rare thing it is not in the church of God, even for that very word which is read,
[k] Psal. 119. to be both presently their [k] joy, and afterwards their study that hear it. [l] St. *Augu-*
16.
[l] Aug. in. *stin,* speaking of devout men, noteth how they daily frequented the church, how at-
Psal. 66. tentive ear they gave unto the lessons and chapters read, how careful they were to re-
[m] Cyprian. l. member the same, and to muse thereupon by themselves. [m] St. *Cyprian* observeth,
2. Epist. 5.
Lecto personat that reading was not without effect in the hearts of men. Their joy and alacrity
verba sublimia. was to him an argument that there is in this ordinance a blessing, such as ordinarily
Evangelium
Christi legit, a doth accompany the administration of the word of life. It were much if there should
fratribus con- be such a difference between the hearing of sermons preached, and of lessons read in
spicitur, cum the church, that he which presenteth himself at the one, and maketh his prayer with
gaudio frater-
nitatis audi- the prophet [n] *David, Teach me, O Lord, the way of thy statutes, direct me in the*
tur. *path of thy commandments,* might have the ground of usual experience, whereupon
[n] Psal. 119. to build his hope of prevailing with God, and obtaining the grace he seeketh ; they
33, 35. contrariwise not so, who crave the like assistance of his Spirit, when they give ear to the

reading

2

reading of the other. In this therefore preaching and reading are equal, that both are approved as his ordinances, both aſſiſted with his grace. And if his grace do aſſiſt them both to the nouriſhment of faith already bred, we cannot, without ſome very manifeſt cauſe yielded, imagine, that in the breeding or begetting faith, his grace doth cleave to the one, and utterly forſake the other. Touching *hardneſs*, which is the ſecond pretended impediment, as againſt homilies being plain and popular inſtructions it is no bar, ſo neither doth it infringe the efficacy, no not of ſcriptures, although but read. The force of reading, how ſmall ſoever they will have it, muſt of neceſſity be granted ſufficient to notify that which is plain or eaſy to be underſtood. And of things neceſſary to all mens ſalvation, we have been hitherto accuſtomed to hold (eſpecially ſince the publiſhing of the goſpel of Jeſus Chriſt, whereby the ſimpleſt having now a key unto knowledge, which the eunuch in the *Acts* did want, our children may of themſelves by reading underſtand that which he without an interpreter could not) they are in ſcripture plain and eaſy to be underſtood. As for thoſe things which at the firſt are obſcure and dark, when memory hath laid them up for a time, judgment afterwards growing, explaineth them. Scripture therefore is not ſo hard, but that the only reading thereof may give life unto willing hearers. The eaſy performance of which holy labour is in like ſort a very cold objection to prejudice the virtue thereof. For what though an infidel, yea, though a child may be able to read; there is no doubt, but the meaneſt and worſt amongſt the people under the law had been as able as the prieſts themſelves were to offer ſacrifice: Did this make ſacrifice of no effect unto that purpoſe for which it was inſtituted? In religion ſome duties are not commended ſo much by the hardneſs of their execution, as by the worthineſs and dignity of that acceptation wherein they are held with God. We admire the goodneſs of God in nature, when we conſider how he hath provided that things moſt needful to preſerve this life, ſhould be moſt prompt and eaſy for all living creatures to come by. Is it not as evident a ſign of his wonderful providence over us, when the food of eternal life, upon the utter want whereof our endleſs death and deſtruction neceſſarily enſueth, is prepared, and always ſet in ſuch a readineſs, that thoſe very means, than which nothing is more eaſy, may ſuffice to procure the ſame? Surely, if we periſh, it is not the lack of ſcribes and learned expounders that can be our juſt excuſe. The word which ſaveth our ſouls is near us; we need for knowledge but to read and live. The man which readeth the word of God, the word it ſelf doth pronounce bleſſed, if he alſo obſerve the ſame. Now all theſe things being well conſidered, it ſhall be no intricate matter for any man to judge with indifferency on which part the good of the church is moſt conveniently ſought; whether on ours, whoſe opinion is ſuch as hath been ſhewed, or elſe on theirs, who leaving no ordinary way of ſalvation for them unto whom the word of God is but only read, do ſeldom name them but with great diſdain and contempt, who execute that ſervice in the church of Chriſt. By means whereof it hath come to paſs, that churches which cannot enjoy the benefit of uſual preaching, are judged as it were even forſaken of God, forlorn, and without either hope or comfort: Contrariwiſe, thoſe places which every day, for the moſt part, are at ſermons, as the flowing ſea, do both by their emptineſs at times of reading, and by other apparent tokens, ſhew to the voice of the living God, this way ſounding in the ears of men, a great deal leſs reverence than were meet. But if no other evil were known to grow thereby, who can chuſe but think them cruel, which do hear them ſo boldly teach, that if God (as to him there is nothing impoſſible) do haply ſave any ſuch as continue where they have all other means of inſtruction, but are not taught by continual preaching, yet this is miraculous, and more than the fitneſs of ſo poor inſtruments can give any man cauſe to hope for; that ſacraments are not effectual to ſalvation, except men be inſtructed by preaching before they be made partakers of them; yea, that both ſacraments and prayers alſo, where ſermons are not, *do not only not feed, but are ordinarily to further condemnation*; what mans heart doth not riſe at the mention of theſe things? It is true, that the weakneſs of our wits, and the dulneſs of our affections do make us, for the moſt part, even as our Lord's own diſciples were for a certain time, hard and ſlow to believe what is written. For help whereof expoſitions and exhortations are needful, and that in the moſt effectual manner. The principal churches throughout the land, and no ſmall part of the reſt, being in this reſpect by the goodneſs of God ſo abundantly provided for, they which want the like furtherance unto knowledge, wherewith it were greatly to be deſired that they alſo did abound, are yet, we hope, not left in ſo extream deſtitution, that

U 2   juſtly

[marginal notes:]
T. C. l. 2. p. 383, 384, 392.

Acts 8. 31.

Apoc. 1. 3.

T. C. l. 2. p. 363. p. 473.

Pag. 364.
375, 380, 363, 384.

Pag. 392.
Pag. 364.

juftly any man fhould think the ordinary means of eternal life taken from them, becaufe their teaching is in publick for the moft part but by reading. For which caufe
amongft whom there are not thofe helps that others have to fet them forward in the
way of life, fuch to difhearten with fearful fentences, as though their falvation
could hardly be hoped for, is not in our underftanding fo confonant with chriftian
charity. We hold it fafer a great deal, and better to give them [a] encouragement; to
put them in mind, that it is not the deepnefs of their knowledge, but the [b] finglenefs
of their belief which God accepteth: That they which [c] *hunger and thirft after righteoufnefs, fhall be fatisfied:* That no [d] imbecillity of means can prejudice the truth
of the promife of God herein: That the weaker their helps are, the more their need
is to fharpen the edge of their own [e] induftry; and that [f] plainnefs by feeble means,
fhall be able to gain that, which in the plenty of more forcible inftruments, is,
through floth and negligence, loft. As for the men, with whom we have thus far
taken pains to confer about the force of the word of God, either read by it felf, or
opened in fermons, their fpeeches concerning both the one and the other, are in
truth fuch, as might give us very juft caufe to think, that the reckoning is not great
which they make of either. For howfoever they have been driven to devife fome
odd kind of blind ufes whereunto they may anfwer that reading doth ferve, yet the
reading of the word of God in publick, more than their preachers bare text, who
will not judge that they deem needlefs? When if we chance at any time to term it
neceffary, as being a thing which God himfelf did inftitute amongft the *Jews* for
purpofes that touch as well us as them; a thing which the apoftles commend under
the Old, and ordain under the New Teftament; a thing whereof the church of God
hath ever fince the firft beginning, reaped fingular commodity; a thing which without exceeding great detriment no church can omit, they only are the men that ever
we heard of, by whom this hath been croffed and gainfaid; they only the men which
have given their peremptory fentence to the contrary: *It is untrue that fimple reading is neceffary in the church.* And why untrue? *Becaufe, although it be very convenient which is ufed in fome churches, where before preaching-time, the church affembled hath the fcriptures read in fuch order, that the whole canon thereof is oftentimes in one year run through; yet a number of churches which have no fuch order
of fimple reading, cannot be in this point charged with breach of God's commandment, which they might be, if fimple reading were neceffary.* A poor, a cold and an
hungry cavil! fhall we therefore to pleafe them, change the word *neceffary,* and fay,
that it hath been a commendable order, a cuftom very expedient, or an ordinance
moft profitable (whereby they know right well that we mean exceedingly behoveful)
to read the word of God at large in the church, whether it be as our manner is, or
as theirs is, whom they prefer before us? It is not this that will content or fatisfy
their minds. They have againft it a marvellous deep and profound Axiom, that
*Two things to one and the fame end, cannot but very improperly be faid moft profi-
table.* And therefore if preaching be moft profitable to man's falvation, then is not
reading; if reading be, then preaching is not. Are they refolved then at the leaftwife, if preaching be the only ordinary mean whereby it pleafeth God to fave our
fouls, what kind of preaching it is which doth fave? Underftand they, how or in
what refpect there is that force or virtue in preaching? We have reafon wherefore
to make thefe demands; for that, although their pens run all upon preaching and
fermons, yet when themfelves do practife that whereof they write, they change their
dialect, and thofe words they fhun as if there were in them fome fecret fting. It is
not their phrafe to fay they preach, or to give to their own inftructions and exhortations the name of fermons; the pain they take themfelves in this kind, is either opening, or lecturing, or reading, or exercifing, but in no cafe preaching. And in this
prefent queftion, they alfo warily proteft, that what they afcribe to the virtue of
preaching, they ftill mean it of good preaching. Now one of them faith, that a good
fermon muft expound and apply a large portion of the text of fcripture at one time.
Another giveth us to underftand, that found preaching *is not to do as one did at* London, *who fpent moft of his time in invectives againft good men, and told his audience how the magiftrate fhould have an eye to fuch as troubled the peace of the church.*
The beft of them hold it for no good preaching, *when a man endeavoureth to make a
glorious fhew of eloquence and learning, rather than to apply himfelf to the capacity of
the fimple.* But let them exclude and inclofe whom they will with their definitions, we
are not defirous to enter into any contention with them about this, or to abate the
conceit they have of their own ways, fo that when once we are agreed what fermons fhall

Marginal notes: [a] Ecclef. 51. 26, 27. / Matth. 12.20. [b] 1 Tim. 1. 5. / Rom. 14. 1. / 1 Thef. 5. 10. [c] Matth. 5.6. [d] Phil. 1. 6. / 1 Pet. 5. 10. / Matth. 3. 9. [e] 1 Thef. 4. 18. / Heb. 10. 24. / Jude ver. 20. / 1. Pet. 4. 10. [f] Luke 11. 31. / T. C. l. 2. p. 381. / T. C. l. 2. p. 372. / T. C. l. 2. p. 385. / Complaint of the commonalty. / Dr. Somes, painter, p. 21. / T. C. l. 2. p. 385.

currently pass for good, we may at length understand from them, what that is in a good sermon which doth make it the word of life unto such as hear.   If substance of matter, evidence of things, strength and validity of arguments and proofs, or if any other virtue else which words and sentences may contain ; of all this, what is there in the best sermons being uttered, which they lose by being read ? But they utterly deny that the reading either of scriptures, or homilies and sermons, can ever by the ordinary grace of God save any soul.   So that although we had all the Sermons word for word which *James*, *Paul*, *Peter*, and the rest of the apostles made, some one of which sermons was of power to convert thousands of the hearers unto christian faith ; yea, although we had all the instructions, exhortations, consolations which came from the gracious lips of our Lord Jesus Christ himself, and should read them ten thousand times over, to faith and salvation no man could hope hereby to attain.   Whereupon it must of necessity follow, that the vigor and vital efficacy of sermons doth grow from certain accidents, which are not in them, but in their maker : His virtue , his gesture, his countenance, his zeal, the motion of his body, and the inflection of his voice, who first uttereth them as his own, is that which giveth them the form, the nature, the very essence of instruments available to eternal life.   If they like neither that nor this, what remaineth but that their final conclusion be, *sermons we know are the only ordinary means to salvation, but why or how, we cannot tell ?* Wherefore to end this tedious controversy, wherein the too great importunity of our over-eager adversaries hath constrained us much longer to dwell than the barrenness of so poor a cause could have seemed at the first likely either to require or to admit, if they which without partialities and passions are accustomed to weigh all things, and accordingly to give their sentence, shall here sit down to receive our audit, and to cast up the whole reckoning on both sides ; the sum which truth amounteth unto will appear to be but this, that as medicines, provided of nature and applied by art for the benefit of bodily health, take effect sometime under and sometime above the natural proportion of their virtue, according as the mind and fancy of the patient doth more or less concur with them ; so, whether we barely read unto men the scriptures of God ; or by homilies concerning matter of belief and conversation seek to lay before them the duties which they owe unto God and man ; whether we deliver them books to read and consider of in private at their own best leisure, or call them to the hearing of sermons publickly in the house of God ; albeit every of these and the like unto these means do truly and daily effect that in the hearts of men for which they are each and all meant ; yet the operation which they have in common being most sensibly and most generally noted in one kind above the rest, that one hath in some men's opinions drowned altogether the rest, and injuriously brought to pass that they have been thought not less effectual than the other, but without the other uneffectual to save souls.   Whereas the cause why sermons only are observed to prevail so much, while all means else seem to sleep and do nothing, is in truth but that singular affection and attention which the people sheweth every where towards the one, and their cold disposition to the other ; the reason hereof being partly the art which our adversaries use for the credit of their sermons, to bring men out of conceit with all other teaching besides ; partly a custom which men have to let those things carelesly pass by their ears, which they have oftentimes heard before, or know they may hear again whenever it pleaseth themselves ; partly the especial advantages which sermons naturally have to procure attention, both in that they come always new, and because by the hearer it is still presumed, that if they be let slip for the present, what good soever they contain is lost, and that without all hope of recovery.   This is the true cause of odds between sermons and other kinds of wholesome instruction.   As for the difference which hath been hitherto so much defended on the contrary side, making sermons the only ordinary means unto faith and eternal life, sith this hath neither evidence of truth, nor proof sufficient to give it warrant, a cause of such quality may with far better grace and conveniency ask that pardon, which common humanity doth easily grant, than claim in challenging manner that assent, which is as unwilling, when reason guideth it, to be yielded where it is not, as withheld where it is apparently due.   All which notwithstanding, as we could greatly wish that the rigor of this their opinion were allayed and mitigated ; so, because we hold it the part of religious ingenuity to honour virtue in whomsoever, therefore it is our most hearty desire, and shall always be our prayer unto Almighty God, that in the self-same fervent zeal wherewith they seem to affect the good of the souls of men, and to thirst after nothing more than that all men might by all means be directed in the way of life, both they and we may constantly persist to the world's end.   For in this we are not their adversaries, though they in the other hitherto have been ours.

Of prayer.

23. Between the throne of God in heaven, and his church upon earth here militant, if it be so that angels have their continual intercourse, where should we find the same more verified than in those two ghostly exercises, the one doctrine, and the other prayer? For what is the assembling of the church to learn, but the receiving of angels descended from above? What to pray, but the sending of angels upwards? His heavenly inspirations, and our holy desires are as so many angels of intercourse and commerce between God and us. As teaching bringeth us to know that God is our supreme truth; so prayer testifieth that we acknowledge him our sovereign good. Besides, sith on God, as the most High, all inferior causes in the world are dependant; and the higher any cause is, the more it coveteth to impart virtue unto things beneath it, how should any kind of service we do or can do, find greater acceptance than prayer, which sheweth our concurrence with him in desiring that wherewith his very nature doth most delight? Is not the name of prayer usual to signify even all the service that ever we do unto God? And that for no other cause, as I suppose, but to shew that there is in religion no acceptable duty which devout invocation of the name of

a Ose. 14 3.
b Rev. 5. 8.
c Acts 10. 4.

God doth not either presuppose or infer. Prayers are those [a] *calves of men's lips;* those most gracious and sweet [b] odours; those rich presents and gifts, which being [c] carried up into heaven, do best testify our dutiful affection, and are, for the purchasing of all favour at the hands of God, the most undoubted means we can use. On others what more easily, and yet what more fruitfully bestowed than our prayers? If we give counsel, they are the simpler only that need it; if alms, the poorer only are relieved; but by prayer we do good to all. And whereas every other duty besides is but to shew it self as time and opportunity require, for this all times are convenient: When we are

Rom. 1. 9.
1 Thes. 5. 17.
Luke 18. 1.

not able to do any other things for mens behoof, when through maliciousness or unkindness they vouchsafe not to accept any other good at our hands, prayer is that which we always have in our power to bestow, and they never in theirs to refuse. Where-

1 Sam. 12. 23.

fore *God forbid,* saith *Samuel* speaking unto a most unthankful people, a people weary of the benefit of his most virtuous government over them, *God forbid that I should sin against the Lord, and cease to pray for you.* It is the first thing wherewith a righteous life beginneth, and the last wherewith it doth end. The knowledge is small which we have on earth concerning things that are done in heaven. Notwithstanding, thus much we know even of saints in heaven, that they pray. And therefore prayer being a work common to the church as well triumphant as militant, a work common unto men with angels, what should we think, but that so much of our lives as celestial and divine as we spend in the exercise of prayer? For which cause we see that the most

Dan. 9. 20.
Acts 10. 30.

comfortable visitations which God hath sent men from above, have taken especially the times of prayer as their most natural opportunities.

Of publick prayer.
Psal. 55. 18.
Dan. 9. 3.
Acts 10. 9.

24. This holy and religious duty of service towards God concerneth us one way in that we are men, and another way in that we are joined as parts to that visible mystical body, which is his church. As men, we are at our own choice both for time and place and form, according to the exigence of our occasions in private: But the service which we do as members of a publick body, is publick, and for that cause must needs be accounted by so much worthier than the other, as a whole society of such

Mat. 18. 20.
2 Cor. 1. 11.

condition exceedeth the worth of any one. In which consideration unto christian assemblies there are most special promises made. St. *Paul,* though likely to prevail with God as much as any one, did notwithstanding think it much more, both for God's glory, and his own good, if prayers might be made and thanks yielded in his be-

Jonah 4. 11.

half by a number of men. The prince and people of *Nineveh* assembling themselves as a main army of supplicants, it was not in the power of God to withstand them. I speak no otherwise concerning the force of publick prayer in the church of God, than

Apolog. 1. 39.
Ambros. l. de Pœn. *Multi minimi dum congregantur unanimes, sunt magni; & multorum preces impossibile est contemni.*
Psal. 122. 1.

before me *Tertullian* hath done, *We come by troops to the place of assembly, that being banded as it were together, we may be supplicants enough to besiege God with our prayers: These forces are unto him acceptable.* When we publickly make our prayers it cannot be but that we do it with much more comfort than in private, for that the things we ask publickly are approved as needful and good in the judgment of all, we hear them sought for and desired with common consent. Again, thus much help and furtherance is more yielded, in that, if so be our zeal and devotion to God-ward be slack, the alacrity and fervour of others serveth as a present spur. *For even prayer it self* (saith St. *Basil*) *when it hath not the comfort of many voices to strengthen it, is not it self.* Finally, the good which we do by publick prayer, is more than in private can be done, for that besides the benefit which is here, is no less procured to our selves, the whole church is much bettered by our good example; and consequently whereas secret neglect of our duty in this kind is but only our own hurt, one man's contempt

2   of

of the common-prayer of the church of God, may be, and oftentimes is most hurt- ‹Καὶ κατὰ ἡ
ful unto many. In which confiderations, the Prophet *David* fo often voweth unto πγοσευχὴ καὶ
God the facrifice of praife and thankfgiving in the congregation; fo earneftly ex- ὁψουσα τῆς
horteth others to fing praifes unto the Lord in his courts, in his fanctuary, before εὐαρδψσίεα
the memorial of his holinefs; and fo much complaineth of his own uncomforta- *Bafil. Epift.*
ble exile, wherein, although he fuftained many moft grievous indignities, and en- 68.
dured the want of fundry both pleafures and honours before enjoyed; yet as if Pfal. 26. 12.
this one were his only grief, and the reft not felt, his fpeeches are all of the hea- 34. 18.
venly benefit of publick affemblies, and the happinefs of fuch as had free accefs there- & 95. 9.
unto. Pfal. 27. 4.

25. A great part of the caufe wherefore religious minds are fo inflamed with the 84. 1.
love of publick devotion, is that virtue, force and efficacy, which by experience they Of the form
find that the very form and reverend folemnity of common-prayer duly ordered, prayer.
hath to help that imbecillity and weaknefs in us, by means whereof we are otherwife of our felves the lefs apt to perform unto God fo heavenly a fervice, with fuch
affection of heart, and difpofition in the powers of our fouls as is requifite. To
this end therefore, all things hereunto appertaining, have been ever thought convenient to be done with the moft folemnity and majefty that the wifeft could devife.
It is not with publick as with private prayer. In this, rather fecrecy is commanded, Matth. 6. 5;
than outward fhew, whereas that being the publick act of a whole fociety, requi- 6.
reth accordingly more care to be had of external appearance. The very affembling
of men therefore unto this fervice, hath been ever folemn. And concerning the
place of affembly, although it ferve for other ufes as well as this, yet feeing that our
Lord himfelf hath to this, as to the chiefeft of all other, plainly fanctified his own
temple, by entitling it *the houfe of prayer,* what pre-eminence of dignity foever Matth. 21.13;
hath been, either by the ordinance, or through the fpecial favour and providence of
God annexed unto his fanctuary, the principal caufe thereof muft needs be in regard of common-prayer. For the honour and furtherance whereof, if it be as the *Chryf. Hom.*
graveft of the ancient fathers ferioufly were perfuaded, and do oftentimes plainly 15. ad Hebræi
teach, affirming, that the houfe of prayer is a court, beautified with the prefence of & 24. in Act.
celeftial powers; that there we ftand, we pray, we found forth hymns unto God,
having his angels intermingled as our affociates; and that with reference hereunto, the
Apoftle doth require fo great care to be had of decency for the angels fake; how can 1 Cor. 11. 10.
we come to the houfe of prayer, and not be moved with the very glory of the
place it felf, fo to frame our affections praying, as doth beft befeem them whofe fuits Pfal. 96. 6.
the Almighty doth there fit to hear, and his Angels attend to further? When this was Power and
ingrafted in the minds of men, there needed no penal ftatutes to draw them unto his fanctu-
publick prayer. The warning-found was no fooner heard, but the churches were ary.
prefently filled; the pavements covered with bodies proftrate, and wafh'd with their
tears of devout joy. And as the place of publick prayer is a circumftance in the out- *Ad dawos po-
ward form thereof, which hath moment to help devotion; fo the perfon much more tim Dominicas
with whom the people of God do join themfelves in this action, as with him that currimus, cor-
ftandeth and fpeaketh in the prefence of God for them. The authority of his place, nimus, miftis
the fervour of his zeal, the piety and gravity of his whole behaviour, muft needs cum fletu gan-
exceedingly both grace and fet forward the fervice he doth. The authority of his mus. Salviati.
calling is a furtherance, becaufe if God hath fo far received him into favour, as to de Prov. l. 7;
impofe upon him by the hands of men, that office of bleffing the people in his
name, and making interceffion to him in theirs; it was in this refpect a comfortable title, Numb. 6. 23;
with his own moft gracious promife, and ratified that promife by manifeft actual per- 2 Chron. 30.
formance thereof, when others before, in like place, have done the fame, is not his 27.
very ordination a feal as it were to us, that the felf-fame divine love which hath
chofen the inftrument to work with, will by that inftrument effect the thing whereunto he ordained it, in bleffing his people, and accepting the prayers which his fervant offereth up unto God for them? It was in this refpect a comfortable title,
which the ancients ufed to give unto God's minifters, terming them ufually *God's
moft beloved,* which were ordained to procure by their prayers, his love and favour
towards all. Again, if there be not zeal and fervency in him which propofeth for Cod. l. 1. tit.
the reft thofe fuits and fupplications which they by their joyful acclamations muft 3. de Epi. &
ratify; if he praife not God with all his might; if he pour not out his foul in 44. fupeo
prayer; if he take not their caufes to heart, and fpeak not as *Mofes, Daniel* and
Ezra did for their people; how fhould there be but in them frozen coldnefs, when
his affections feem benummed from whom theirs fhould take fire? Virtue and god-
lines

linefs of life are required at the hands of the minifter of God, not only in that he is to teach and inftruct the people; who for the moft part are rather led away by the ill example, than directed aright by the wholefome inftruction of them, whofe life fwerveth from the rule of their own doctrine; but alfo much more in regard of this other part of his function; whether we refpect the weaknefs of the people, apt to loath and abhor the fanctuary, when they which perform the fervice thereof, are such which the fons of *Heli* were, or elfe confider the inclination of God himfelf, who requireth the lifting up of pure hands in prayer, and hath given the world plainly to underftand, that the wicked, although they cry, fhall not be heard. They are not fit fupplicants to feek his mercy on the behalf of others, whofe own unrepented fins provoke his juft indignation. *Let thy priefts,* there-fore, O Lord, *be* evermore *cloathed with righteoufnefs, that thy faints may* thereby with more devotion *rejoice and fing!* But of all helps for due performance of this fervice, the greateft is that very fet and ftanding order it felf, which framed with common advice, hath, both for matter and form, prefcribed whatfoever is herein publickly done. No doubt, from God it hath proceeded, and by us it muft be ac-knowledged a work of fingular care and providence, that the church hath evermore held a prefcript form of common-prayer, although not in all things everywhere the fame, yet for the moft part retaining ftill the fame analogy. So that if the li-turgies of all ancient churches throughout the world, be compared amongft them-felves, it may be eafily perceived they had all one original mold, and that the pub-lick prayers of the people of God in churches throughly fettled, did never ufe to be voluntary dictates, proceeding from any man's extemporal wit. To him which con-fidereth the grievous and fcandalous inconveniencies whereunto they make themfelves daily fubject, with whom any blind and fecret corner is judged a fit houfe of com-mon-prayer; the manifold confufions which they fall into, where every man's pri-vate fpirit and gift (as they term it) is the only Bifhop that ordaineth him to this miniftry; the irkfome deformities whereby through endlefs and fenfelefs effufions of indigefted prayers, they oftentimes difgrace in moft unfufferable manner, the wor-thieft part of chriftian duty towards God, who herein are fubject to no certain order, but pray both what and how they lift; to him, I fay, which weigheth duly all thefe things, the reafons cannot be obfcure why God doth in publick prayer fo much refpect the folemnity of places where, the authority and calling of perfons by whom, and the precife appointment even with what words or fentences his name fhould be cal-led on amongft his people.

1 Tim. 2. 8.
John. 9. 31.
Jer. 11. 11.
Ezech. 8. 18.

Pfal. 132. 9.

2 Chron. 6.
20.
Joel 2. 17.
2 Chron. 29.
30.

26. No man hath hitherto been fo impious, as plainly and directly to condemn prayer. The beft ftratagem that Satan hath, who knoweth his kingdom to be no one way more fhaken, than by the publick devout prayers of God's church, is by tradu-cing the form and manner of them, to bring them into contempt, and fo to fhake the force of all mens devotion towards them. From this, and from no other forge, hath proceeded a ftrange conceit, that to ferve God with any fet form of common-prayer, is fuperftitious. As though God himfelf did not frame to his Priefts the very fpeech wherewith they were charged to blefs the people; or as if our Lord, even of purpofe to prevent this fancy of extemporal and voluntary prayers, had not left us of his own framing, one which might both remain as a part of the church liturgy, and ferve as a pattern whereby to frame all other prayers with efficacy, yet without fuperfluity of words. If prayers were no otherwife accepted of God, than being conceived always new, according to the exigence of prefent occafions; if it be right to judge him by our own bellies, and to imagine that he doth loath to have the felf-fame fupplications often iterated, even as we do to be every day fed with-out alteration or change of diet; if prayers be actions which ought to wafte away themfelves in making; if being made to remain that they may be refumed and ufed again as prayers, they be but inftruments of fuperftition; furely, we cannot excufe *Mofes,* who gave fuch occafion of fcandal to the world, by not being con-tented to praife the name of Almighty God, according to the ufual naked fimpli-city of God's Spirit, for that admirable victory given them againft *Pharaoh,* unlefs fo dangerous a precedent were left for the cafting of prayers into certain poetical molds, and for the framing of prayers which might be repeated often, although they never had again the fame occafions which brought them forth at the firft. For that very hymn of *Mofes,* grew afterwards to be a part of the ordinary *Jewifh* li-turgy; nor only that, but fundry other fithence invented. Their books of com-

Of them
which like
not to have
any fet form
of common-
prayer.

Num. 6. 23.

4
mon-

mon-prayer contained partly hymns taken out of the holy fcripture, partly benedictions, thankfgivings, fupplications, penned by fuch as have been, from time to
time, the governors of that fynagogue. Thefe they forted into their feveral times
and places, fome to begin the fervice of God with, and fome to end, fome to go
before, and fome to follow, and fome to be interlaced between the divine readings
of the law and prophets. Unto their cuftom of finifhing the paffover with certain
Pfalms, there is not any thing more probable, than that the holy evangelift doth evidently allude, faying, that after the cup deli-
vered by our faviour unto his apoftles, [a] they
fung, and went forth to the mount of *Olives*.
As the *Jews* had their fongs of *Mofes* and
David, and the reft; fo the church of Chrift
from the very beginning, hath both ufed the

> [a] Matth. 26. 30. *υμνήσαντες*, having fung the pfalms which were ufual at that feaft, thofe pfalms which the *Jews* call the great *Halelujah*, beginning at the 113th, and continuing to the end of the 118th. See *Paul Burgenf. in Pfal.* 112. edit. 1. and *Scaliger de emendat. tempor.*

fame, and befides them other of like nature, the fong of the Virgin *Mary*, the fong
of *Zachary*, the fong of *Simeon*, fuch hymns as the apoftle doth often fpeak of,
faying, [b] *I will pray and fing with the fpirit.* Again, [c] *in Pfalms, Hymns, and*
Songs, making melody unto the Lord, and that heartily. Hymns and Pfalms are
fuch kinds of prayer, as are not wont to be conceived upon a fudden ; but are
framed by meditation before-hand, or elfe by prophetical illumination are in-
fpired, as at that time it appeareth they were, when God, by extraordinary gifts
of the fpirit, enabled men to all parts of fervice neceffary for the edifying of his
church.

> [b] 1 Cot. 14.
> [c] Ephef. 5. 19.

27. Now, albeit the admonitioners did feem at the firft, to allow no prefcript
form of prayer at all, but thought it the beft that their minifter fhould always be left
at liberty to pray as his own difcretion did ferve, yet becaufe this opinion, upon better advice, they afterwards retracted, their defender and his affociates have fithence
propofed to the world a form, fuch as themfelves like, and, to fhew their diflike of
ours, have taken againft it thofe exceptions which, whofoever doth meafure by number, muft needs be greatly out of love with a thing that hath fo many faults ; whofoever by weight, cannot chufe but efteem very highly of that, wherein the wit of fo
fcrupulous adverfaries hath not hitherto obferved any defect, which themfelves can
ferioufly think to be of moment. Grofs errors, and manifeft impiety, they grant we

> Of them who allowing a fet form of prayer, yet allow not ours.

have taken away. Yet [d] many things in it
they fay are amifs ; many inftances they give
of things in our common-prayer, not agreable, as they pretend, with the word of God.
It hath in their eye too great affinity with the
form of the church of *Rome* ; it differeth too
much from that which churches elfewhere reformed, allow and obferve ; or attire dif-
graceth it ; it is not orderly read nor geftured
as befeemeth : It requireth nothing to be done, which a child may not lawfully
do ; it hath a number of fhort cuts or fhreddings, which may be better called wifhes
than prayers ; it intermingleth prayings and readings in fuch manner, as if fupplicants fhould ufe in propofing their fuits unto mortal princes, all the world would
judge them mad ; it is too long, and by that mean abridgeth preaching ; it appointeth the people to fay after the minifter ; it fpendeth time in finging and in reading
the Pfalms by courfe, from fide to fide ; it ufeth the Lord's-Prayer too oft ; the
fongs of *Magnificat, Benedictus* and *Nunc Dimittis*, it might very well fpare ; it
hath the *Litany*, the Creed of *Athanafius*, and *Gloria Patri*, which are fuperfluous;
it craveth earthly things too much ; for deliverance from thofe evils againft which we
pray, it giveth no thanks ; fome things it afketh unfeafonably, when they need not
to be prayed for, as deliverance from thunder and tempeft, when no danger is nigh ;
fome in too abject and diffident manner, as that God would give us that which we
for our unworthinefs dare not afk ; fome which ought not to be defired, as the deliverance from fudden death, riddance from all adverfity, and the extent of faving
mercy towards all men. Thefe, and fuch like, are the imperfections, whereby our
form of common-prayer is thought to fwerve from the word of God. A great favourer of that part, but yet (his error that way excepted) a learned, painful, a right
vertuous and good man, did not fear fometime to undertake, againft popifh de-
tractors, the general maintenance and defence of our whole church-fervice, as having in it nothing repugnant to the word of God. And even they which would

> [d] *T. C.* l. 1. p. 131. afterwards p. 135. Whereas Mr. Doctor affirmeth, that there can be nothing fhewed in the whole book, which is not agreeable unto the word of God : I am very loth, &c. Notwithftanding, my duty of de-
> fending the truth, and love which I have firft towards God, and then towards my country, conftraineth me, being thus provoked, to fpeak a few words more particularly of the form of prayer, that when the blemifhes thereof do ap-
> pear, it may pleafe the queen's majefty, and her honoura-
> ble council, with thofe of the parliament, &c.

X

file away moſt from the largeneſs of that offer, do notwithſtanding in more ſparing terms acknowledge little leſs. For when thoſe oppoſite judgments which never are wont to conſtrue things doubtful to the better, thoſe very tongues which are always prone to aggravate whatſoever hath but the leaſt ſhew whereby it may be ſuſpected to favour of, or to ſound towards any evil, do, by their own voluntary ſentence, clearly free us from groſs errors, and from manifeſt impiety herein; who would not judge us to be diſcharged of all blame, which are confeſs'd to have no great fault, even by their very word and teſtimony, in whoſe eyes no fault of ours hath ever hitherto been accuſtomed to ſeem ſmall? Neverthleſs, what they ſeem to offer us with the one hand, the ſame with the other they pull back again. They grant we err not in palpable manner, we are not openly and notoriouſly impious; yet errors we have, which the ſharp inſight of their wiſeſt men doth eſpy, there is hidden impiety, which the profounder ſort are able enough to diſcloſe. Their ſkilful ears perceive certain harſh and unpleaſant diſcords in the ſound of our common-prayer, ſuch as the rules of divine harmony, ſuch as the laws of God cannot bear.

The form of our liturgy too near the papiſts, too far different from that of other reformed churches, as they pretend.

28. Touching our conformity with the church of *Rome*, as alſo of the difference between ſome reformed churches and ours, that which generally hath been already anſwered, may ſerve for anſwer to that exception, which in theſe two reſpects they take particularly againſt the form of our common-prayer. To ſay, that in nothing they may be followed which are of the church of *Rome*, were violent and extream. Some things they do, in that they are men, in that they are wiſe men, and chriſtian men ſome things, ſome things in that they are men miſled and blinded with error. As far as they follow reaſon and truth, we fear not to tread the ſelf-ſame ſteps wherein they have gone, and to be their followers. Where *Rome* keepeth that which is ancienter and better; others whom we much more affect, leaving it for newer, and changing it for worſe; we had rather follow the perfections of them whom we like not, than in defects reſemble them whom we love.

T. C. l. 1. p. 135. A book of the form of common-prayer tendered to the parliament, p. 46.

For although they profeſs they agree with us touching a *preſcript form of prayer to be uſed in the church*; yet in that very form which they ſay is *agreeable to God's word, and the uſe of reformed churches*, they have by ſpecial proteſtation declared, that their meaning is not, it ſhall be preſcribed as a thing whereunto they will tye their miniſter. *If ſhall not* (they ſay) *be neceſſary for the miniſter daily to repeat all theſe things before-mentioned, but beginning with* ſome like *confeſſion, to proceed to the ſermon; which ended, he either uſeth the prayer for all ſtates before-mentioned, or elſe prayeth as the ſpirit of God ſhall move his heart.* Herein therefore we hold it much better, with the church of *Rome*, to appoint a preſcript form, which every man ſhall be bound to obſerve, than with them to ſet down a kind of direction, a form for men to uſe if they liſt, or otherwiſe to change as pleaſeth themſelves. Furthermore, the church of *Rome* hath rightly alſo conſidered, that publick prayer is a duty entire in it ſelf, a duty requiſite to be performed much oftner than ſermons can poſſibly be made. For which cauſe, as they, ſo we have likewiſe a publick form how to ſerve God both morning and evening, whether ſermons may be had or no. On the contrary ſide, their form of reformed prayer, ſheweth only what ſhall be done *upon the days appointed for the preaching of the word;* with what words the miniſter ſhall begin, *when the hour appointed for ſermon is come;* what ſhall be ſaid or ſung before ſermon, and what after. So that according to this form of theirs, it muſt ſtand for a rule, *no ſermon, no ſervice.* Which over-ſight occaſioned the *French* ſpitefully to term religion, in that ſort exerciſed, a meer preach. Sundry other more particular defects there are, which I willingly forbear to rehearſe; in conſideration whereof, we cannot be induced to prefer their reformed form of prayer before our own, what church ſoever we reſemble therein.

Pag. 22. Pag. 24.

<hr>

ᵏ Attire belonging to the ſervice of God.

ᵇ T. C. l. 1. p. 71. We think the ſurplice eſpecially unmeet for a miniſter of the goſpel to wear, p. 75. It is eaſily ſeen by *Solomon, Eccleſ.* 8, 9. that to wear a white garment, was highly eſteemed in the *Eaſt* parts, and was ordinary to thoſe that were in any eſtimation, as black with us, and therefore was no ſeveral apparel for the miniſters to execute their miniſtry in.

29. The ᵃ attire which the miniſter of God is by order to uſe at times of divine ſervice, being but a matter of meer formality, yet, ſuch as for comelineſs-ſake, hath hitherto been judged by the wiſer ſort of men, not unneceſſary to concur with other ſenſible notes, betokening the different kind or quality of perſons and actions whereto it is tied; as we think not our ſelves the holier becauſe we uſe it, ſo neither ſhould they, with whom no ſuch thing is in uſe, think us therefore unholy, becauſe we ſubmit our ſelves

unto

unto that, which in a matter fo indifferent, the wifdom of authority and law hath thought comely. To folemn actions of royalty and juftice, their fuitable ornaments are a beauty. Are they only in religion a ftain? *Divine religion*, faith St. *Jerom*, (he fpeaketh of the prieftly attire of the law) *hath one kind of habit wherein to minifter before the Lord, another for ordinary ufes belonging unto common life.* *Pelagius* having carped at the curious neatnefs of men's apparel in thofe days, and through the fowrenefs of his difpofition, fpoken fomewhat too hardly thereof, affirming, that the *glory of cloaths and ornaments, was a thing contrary to God and godlinefs;* St. *Jerom*, whofe cuftom is not to pardon over-eafily his adverfaries, if any where they chance to trip, preffeth him, as thereby making all forts of men in the world *God's enemies.* *Is it enmity with God* (faith he) *if I wear my coat fomewhat hand-fome?* If a bifhop, a prieft, deacon, and the reft of the ecclefiaftical order, *come to adminifter the ufual facrifice in a white garment,* are they hereby God's adverfaries? *Clerks, monks, widows, virgins, take heed, it is dangerous for you to be otherwife feen, than in foul and ragged cloaths. Not to fpeak any thing of fecular men, which are proclaimed to have war with God, as oft as ever they put on precious and fhining cloaths.* By which words of *Jerom*, we may take it at the leaft for a probable conjecture, that his meaning was to draw *Pelagius* into hatred, as condemning, by fo general a fpeech, even the neatnefs of that very garment it felf, wherein the clergy did then ufe to adminifter publickly the holy facrament of Chrift's moft bleffed body and blood : For that they did then ufe fome fuch ornament, the words of *Chryfoftom* give plain teftimony, who fpeaking to the clergy of *Antioch*, telleth them, that if they did fuffer notorious malefactors to come to the table of our Lord, and not put them by, it would be as heavily revenged upon them, as if themfelves had fhed his blood ; that for this purpofe, God had called them to the rooms which they held in the church of Chrift ; that this they fhould reckon was their dignity, this their fafety, this their whole crown and glory ; and therefore this they fhould carefully intend, and not when the facrament is adminiftred, imagine themfelves called only *to walk up and down in a white and fhining garment.* Now, whereas thefe fpeeches of *Jerom* and *Chryfoftom,* do feem plainly to allude unto fuch minifterial garments as were then in ufe : To this they anfwer, that by *Jerom* nothing can be gathered, but only that the minifters came to church in handfome holy-day apparel, and that himfelf did not think them bound by the law of God, to go like flovens, but the weed which we mean he defendeth not. That *Chryfoftom* meaneth the fame which we defend, but feemeth rather to reprehend, than allow it as we do. Which anfwer wringeth out of *Jerom* and *Chryfoftom* that which their words will not gladly yield. They both fpeak of the fame perfons, (namely , the Clergy) and of their weed at the fame time when they adminifter the bleffed facrament ; and of the felf-fame

Hierom. in Ezech. 44. Hiero.Adver. Pelag. l. 1. c. 9. T. C. l. 1. p. 77. By a white garment is meant a comely Apparel, and not flovenly.

Chryfoft. ad popul. Antioch. tom. 5. Serm. 80.

T. C. l. 1. p. 75. It is true, *Chryfoftom* maketh mention of a white garment, but not in commendation of it, but rather to the contrary : for he fheweth that the dignity of the miniftry was in taking heed that none unmeet were admitted to the Lord's fupper, not in going about the church with a white garment.

kind of weed, a white garment, fo far as we have wit to conceive ; and for any thing we are able to fee, their manner of fpeech is not fuch as doth argue either the thing it felf to be different whereof they fpeak, or their judgment concerning it different ; although the one do only maintain it againft *Pelagius,* as a thing not therefore unlawful becaufe it was fair or handfom ; and the other make it a matter of fmall commendation in it felf, if they which wear it do nothing elfe but wear the robes which their place requireth. The honefty, dignity, and eftimation of white apparel in the *Eaftern* part of the world , is a token of greater fitnefs for this facred ufe, wherein it were not convenient that any thing bafely thought of fhould be fuffered. Notwithftanding, I am not bent to ftand ftiffly upon thefe probabilities, that in *Jerom's* and *Chryfoftom's* time any fuch attire was made feveral to this purpofe. Yet furely the words of *Solomon* are very impertinent to prove it an ornament, therefore not feveral for the minifters to execute their miniftry in, becaufe men of credit and eftimation wore their ordinary apparel white. For we know that when *Solomon* wrote thofe words, the feveral apparel for the minifters of the law to execute their miniftry in, was fuch. The wife man which feared God from his heart, and honoured the fervice that was done unto him, could not mention fo much as the garment of holinefs, but with effectual fignification of moft fingular reverence and love. Were it not better that the love which men bear to God fhould make the leaft things which are employed in his fervice amiable, than that their over-fcrupulous diflike of fo mean a thing as a veftment, fhould from the very fer-

Eccl. 45. 7.

vice of God withdraw their hearts and affections? I term it rathera mean thing, a thing not much to be repsected, becauſe even they ſo account now of it, whoſe firſt diſputations againſt it were ſuch, as if religion had ſcarcely any thing of greater weight. Their allegations were then, *That if a man were aſſured to gain a thouſand, by doing that which may offend any one brother, or be unto him a cauſe of falling, he ought not to do it ; that this popiſh apparel, the ſurplice eſpecially,hath been by papiſts abominably abuſed; that it hath been a mark, and a very ſacrament of abomination; that remaining, it ſerveth as a monument of idolatry ; and not only* ediſieth not, but as a dangerous and ſcandalous ceremony doth exceeding much harm *to them of whoſe good we are commanded to have regard ; that it cauſeth men to periſh, and make ſhipwrack of conſcience,* for ſo themſelves profeſs they mean, when they ſay the weak are offended herewith ; *that it hardueth papiſts, hindreth the weak from profiting in the knowledge of the goſpel, grieveth godly minds, and giveth them occaſion to think hardly of their miniſters ; that if the magiſtrates may command, or the church appoint rites and ceremonies, yet ſeeing our abſtinence from things in their own nature indifferent, if the weak brother ſhould be offended, is a flat commandment of the Holy Ghoſt, which no authority, either* of church or commonwealth *can make void;* therefore neither may the one, nor the other, lawfully *ordain this* ceremony, *which hath great incommodity , and no profit, great offence, and no edifying ;* that by the law it ſhould have been burnt and conſumed with fire, as a thing infected with leproſy ; that the example of *Ezekiah* beating to powder the brazen ſerpent, and of *Paul* abrogating thoſe abuſed feaſts of charity, *inforceth upon us the duty of aboliſhing altogether* a thing which hath been, and is ſo offenſive : Finally, that God by his prophet hath given an expreſs commandment, which in this caſe toucheth us no leſs than of old it did the *Jews, Te ſhall pollute the covering of the images of ſilver, and the rich ornament of your images of gold, and caſt them away as a ſtained rag ; thou ſhalt ſay to it, Get thee hence.* Theſe and ſuch like were their firſt diſcourſes touching that church-attire, which with us, for the moſt part, is uſual in publick prayer, our eccleſiaſtial laws ſo appointing, as well becauſe it hath been of reaſonable continuance, and by ſpecial choice was taken out of the number of thoſe holy garments, which (over and beſides their myſtical reference) ſerved for comelineſs under the law, and is, in the number of thoſe ceremonies, which may with choice and diſcretion be uſed to that purpoſe in the church of Chriſt; as alſo that it ſuiteth ſo fitly with that lightſome affection of joy, wherein God delighteth when his ſaints praiſe him ; and ſo lively reſembleth the glory of the ſaints in heaven, together with the beauty wherein angels have appeared unto men, that they which are to appear for men in the preſence of God as angels, if they were left to their own choice, and would chuſe any, could not eaſily deviſe a garment of more decency for ſuch a ſervice. As for thoſe fore-rehearſed vehement allegations againſt it, ſhall we give them credit, when the very authors from whom they come, confeſs they believe not their own ſayings ? For when once they began to perceive how many, both of them in the two univerſities, and of others who abroad having eccleſiaſtical charge, do favour mightily their cauſe, and by all means ſet it forward, might, by perſiſting in the extremity of that opinion, hazard greatly their own eſtates, and ſo weaken that part which their places do now give them much opportunity to ſtrengthen ; they asked counſel, as it ſeemed, from ſome abroad, who wiſely conſidered that the body is of far more worth than the rayment. Whereupon, for fear of dangerous inconveniencies, it hath been thought good to add, that ſometimes authority *muſt and may with good conſcience be obeyed, even where commandment is not given upon good ground ; that the duty of preaching is one of the abſolute commandments of God, and therefore ought not to be forſaken for the bare inconveniency of a thing, which in its own nature is indifferent ; that one of the fouleſt ſpots in the ſurplice, is the offence which it giveth in occaſioning the weak to fall, and the wicked to be* confirmed in their wickedneſs ; yet hereby there is no unlawfulneſs proved, but *only an inconveniency,* that ſuch things ſhould be eſtabliſhed, howbeit no ſuch inconveniency neither as may not be born with ; that when God doth flatly command us to abſtain from things in their own nature indifferent, if they offend our weak brethren, his meaning is not we ſhould obey his commandment herein, unleſs we may do it, *and not leave undone that which the Lord hath abſolutely commanded.* Always provided, that whoſoever will enjoy the benefit of this diſpenſation, to wear a ſcandalous badge of idolatry, rather than forſake his paſtoral charge, do (*as occaſion ſerveth*) teach nevertheleſs ſtill *the incommodity of the thing it ſelf, admoniſh the weak brethren that they be not, and pray unto God ſo to ſtrengthen them,*

T. C. l. 1. p. 79.
71.
75.
T. C. l. 2. p. 403. l. 1. p. 73, 76. l. 2. p. 403.
Lib 1. p. 76. Pag. 81.
Pag. 78.
Eſay 30. 22.
Exod. 28. 2. Exod. 39. 27. Pſal. 149. 2. Apoc. 15. 6. Mar. 16. 5.
T. C. l. 1. p. 74. & l. 2. p. 250. Index. l. 3. c. 8. l. 3. p. 262, 263.
Lib. 3. p. 263.
Pag. 263.

I
that

that they may not be offended thereat. So that whereas before, they which had authority to inftitute rites and ceremonies, were denied to have power to inftitute this, it is now confefs'd, that this they may alfo lawfully, but not fo conveniently appoint; they did well before, and as they ought, who had it in utter deteftation and hatred, as a thing abominable; they now do well, which think it may be both born and ufed with a very good confcience; before, he which by wearing it, were he fure to win thoufands unto Chrift, ought not to do it, if there were but one which might be offended; now, though it be with the offence of thoufands, yet it may be done, rather than that fhould be given over, whereby notwithftanding we are not certain we fhall gain one. The examples of *Ezekias* and of *Paul*, the charge which was given to the *Jews* by *Efay*, the ftrict apoftolical prohibition of things indifferent, whenfoever they may be fcandalous, were before fo forcible laws againft our ecclefiaftical attire, as neither church nor common-wealth could poffibly make void; which now one of far lefs authority than either, hath found how to fruftrate, by difpenfing with the breach of inferior commandments, to the end that the greater may be kept. But it booteth them not thus to folder up a broken caufe, whereof their firft and laft difcourfes will fall afunder, do what they can. Let them ingenuoufly confefs that their invectives were too bitter, their arguments too weak, the matter not fo dangerous as they did imagine. If thofe alledged teftimonies of fcripture did indeed concern the matter to fuch effect as was pretended, that which they fhould infer, were unlawfulnefs, becaufe they were cited as prohibitions of that thing which indeed they concern. If they prove not our attire unlawful, becaufe in truth they concern it not, it followeth, that they prove not any thing againft it, and confequently not fo much as uncomelinefs or inconveniency. Unlefs therefore they be able thoroughly to refolve themfelves, that there is no one fentence in all the fcriptures of God, which doth controul the wearing of it in fuch manner, and to fuch purpofe, as the church of *England* alloweth; unlefs they can fully reft and fettle their minds in this moft found perfuafion, that they are not to make themfelves the only competent judges of decency in thefe cafes, and to defpife the folemn judgment of the whole church, preferring before it their own conceit, grounded only upon uncertain fufpicions and fears, whereof, if there were at the firft fome probable caufe, when things were but raw and tender, yet now very tract of time hath it felf worn that out alfo; unlefs, I fay, thus refolved in mind, they hold their paftoral charge with the comfort of a good confcience, no way grudging at that which they do, or doing that which they think themfelves bound of duty to reprove, how fhould it poffibly help or further them in their courfe, to take fuch occafions as they fay are requifite to be taken, and in penfive manner to tell their audience, " *Bre-*
" *thren, our hearts defire is, that we might enjoy the full liberty of the Gofpel, as in*
" *other reformed churches they do elfewhere, upon whom the heavy hand of autho-*
" *rity hath impofed no grievous burthen. But fuch is the mifery of thefe our days,*
" *that fo great happinefs we cannot look to attain unto. Were it fo, that the equity*
" *of the law of* Mofes *could prevail, or the zeal of* Ezechias *be found in the hearts*
" *of thofe guides and governors under whom we live; or the voice of God's own pro-*
" *phets be duly heard; or the examples of the apoftles of Chrift be followed; yea, or*
" *their precepts be anfwered with full and perfect obedience: Thefe abominable rags,*
" *polluted garments, marks and facraments of idolatry, which power, as you fee,*
" *conftraineth us to wear, and confcience to abhor, had long ere this day been moved*
" *both out of fight, and out of memory. But, as now things ftand, behold to what*
" *narrow ftreights we are driven: On the one fide we fear the words of our Saviour*
" *Chrift,* Woe be to them by whom fcandal and offence cometh; *an the other fide,*
" *at the apoftles fpeech we cannot but quake and tremble,* If I preach not the Gofpel,
" *woe be unto me. Being thus hardly befet, we fee not any other remedy, but to*
" *hazard your fouls the one way, that we may the other way endeavour to fave*
" *them. Touching the offence of the weak therefore, we muft adventure it. If*
" *they perifh, they perifh. Our paftoral charge is God's moft abfolute command-*
" *ment. Rather than that fhall be taken from us, we are refolved to take this filth*
" *and put it on, although we judge it to be fo unfit and inconvenient, that as oft as*
" *ever we pray or preach fo arrayed before you, we do as much as in us lieth, to caft*
" *away your fouls that are weak-minded, and to bring you unto endlefs perdition.*
" *But we befeech you, Brethren, have a care of your own fafety, take heed to your*
" *fteps, that ye be not taken in thofe fnares which we lay before you. And our*
" *prayer in your behalf to almighty God is, that the poifon which we offer you, may*
" *never have the power to do you harm."* Advice and counfel is beft fought for at

their

their hands which either have no part at all in the cause whereof they instruct, or else are so far engaged, that themselves are to bear the greatest adventure in the success of their own counsels. The one of which two considerations, maketh men the less respective, and the other the more circumspect. Those good and learned men which gave the first directions to this course, had reason to wish, that their own proceedings at home might be favoured abroad also, and that the good affection of such as inclined towards them might be kept alive. But if themselves had gone under those sails which they require to be hoised up, if they had been themselves to execute their own theory in this church, I doubt not but easily they would have seen, being nearer at hand, that the way was not good which they took of advising men, first to wear the apparel, that thereby they might be free to continue their preaching, and then of requiring them so to preach, as they might be sure they could not continue, except they imagine that laws which permit them not to do as they would, will endure them to speak as they list, even against that which themselves do by constraint of laws; they would have easily seen, that our people being accustomed to think evermore that thing evil, which is publickly under any pretence reproved, and the men themselves worse which reprove it, and use it too, it should be to little purpose for them to salve the wound, by making protestations in disgrace of their own actions, with plain acknowledgment that they are scandalous, or by using fair intreaty with the weak brethren; they would easily have seen how with us it cannot be endured to hear a man openly profess that he putteth fire to his neighbours house, but yet so halloweth the same with prayer, that he hopeth it shall not burn. It had been therefore perhaps safer, and better for ours, to have observed St. *Basil's* advice, both in this, and in all things of like nature : *Let him which approveth not his governors ordinances, either plainly (but privately always) shew his dislike if he have* λόγον ἰαμεὸν, *strong and invincible reason against them, according to the true will and meaning of scripture; or else let him quietly with silence do what is enjoined.* Obedience with profess'd unwillingness to obey, is no better than manifest disobedience.

Basil. Ascet. responf. ad inter. 47.

30. Having thus disputed, whether the surplice be a fit garment to be used in the service of God, the next question whereinto we are drawn is, whether it be a thing allowable or no, that the minister should say service in the chancel, or turn his face at any time from the people, or before service ended, remove from the place where it was begun ? By them which trouble us with these doubts, we would more willingly be resolved of a greater doubt ; whether it be not a kind of taking God's name in vain, to debase religion with such frivolous disputes, a sin to bestow time and labour about them ? Things of so mean regard and quality, although necessary to be ordered, are notwithstanding very unsavory when they come to be disputed of: Because disputation presupposeth some difficulty in the matter which is argued, whereas in things of this nature, they must be either very simple, or very froward, who need to be taught by disputation what is meet. When we make profession of our faith, we stand ; when we acknowledge our sins, or seek unto God for favour, we fall down ; because the gesture of constancy becometh us best in the one, in the other the behaviour of humility. Some parts of our liturgy consist in the reading of the word of God, and the proclaiming of his law, that the people may thereby learn what their duties are towards him ; some consist in words of praise and thanksgiving, whereby we acknowledge unto God, what his blessings are towards us ; some are such, as albeit they serve to singular good purpose, even when there is no communion administred, nevertheless, being devised at the first for that purpose, are at the table of the Lord for that cause also commonly read ; some are uttered as from the people, some as with them unto God, some as from God unto them, all as before his sight whom we fear, and whose presence to offend with any the least unseemliness, we would be surely as loth as they who most reprehend or deride what we do. Now, because the gospels which are weekly read, do all historically declare something which our Lord Jesus Christ himself either spake, did, or suffered in his own person, it hath been the custom of christian men then especially, in token of the greater reverence to stand, to utter certain words of acclamation, and at the name of Jesus to bow. Which harmless ceremonies, as there is *no man constrained to use*; so we know no reason wherefore any man should yet imagine it an unsufferable evil. It sheweth a reverend regard to the Son of God above other messengers, altho' speaking as from God also. And against Infidels, *Jews, Arians,* who derogate from the honour of Jesus Christ, such ceremonies are most profitable. As for any erroneous *estimation,* advancing the Son *above the Father and the holy Ghost,* seeing that the truth of his equality with them, is a mystery so hard for the wits of mortal men to rise un-

Of gesture in praying, and of different places chosen to that purpose.
T. C. L 1. p. 134.

T. C. L 1. p. 203.

Mark 12. 6.

T. C. l. 3. p. 215.

4   to,

to, of all herefies, that which may give him fuperiority above them, is leaft to be feared.　But to let go this, as a matter fcarce worth the fpeaking of, whereas if fault be in thefe things any where juftly found, law hath referred the whole difpofition and redrefs thereof to the ordinary of the place; they which elfewhere complain that difgrace and injury is offered, even to the meaneft parifh minifter, when the magiftrate appointeth him what to wear, and leaveth not fo fmall a matter as that to his own difcretion, being prefumed a man difcreet, and trufted with the care of the peoples fouls, do think the graveft prelates in the land no competent judges to difcern and appoint where it is fit for the minifter to ftand, or which way convenient to look praying.　From their ordinary, therefore, they appeal to themfelves, finding great fault, that we neither reform the thing againft the which they have fo long fince given fentence, nor yet make anfwer unto what they bring, which is, that St. *Luke* declaring how *Peter ftood up in the midft of the difciples*, did thereby deliver an unchangeable rule, that *whatfoever* is done in the church, *ought to be done* in the midft of the church; and therefore not baptifm to be adminiftred in one place, marriage folemnized in another, the fupper of the Lord received in a third, in a fourth fermons, in a fifth prayers to be made; that the cuftom which we ufe is levitical, abfurd, and fuch as hindreth the underftanding of the people; that if it be meet for the minifter, at fome time to look towards the people, if the body of the church be a fit place for fome part of divine fervice, it muft needs follow; that whenfoever his face is turned any other way, or any thing done any other where, it hath abfurdity.　*All thefe reafons*, they fay, have been brought, and were hitherto never anfwered; befides a number of merriments and jefts, unanfwered likewife, wherewith they have pleafantly moved much laughter at our manner of ferving God.　Such is their evil hap to play upon dull fpirited men.　We are ftill perfuaded, that a bare denial is anfwer fufficient to things which meer fancy objecteth; and that the beft apology to words of fcorn and petulancy, is *Ifaac's* apology to his brother *Ifmael*, the apology which patience and filence maketh.　Our anfwer therefore to their reafons is, no; to their fcoffs, nothing.

Marginal notes:
T. C. l. 1. p. ... T. C. l. 1.
p. 124. l. 3.
p. 187.
Acts 1. 15.
T. C. l. 1. p. 134. l. 5. p. 187.

31. When they object that our book requireth nothing to be done, which a child may not do as *lawfully, and as well, as that man wherewith the book contenteth it felf:* Is it their meaning, that the fervice of God ought to be a matter of great difficulty, a labour which requireth great learning, and deep skill, or elfe that the book containing it,

Eafinefs of praying after our form.

T. C. l. 1. p. 133. & l. 3. p. 184. Another fault in the whole fervice or liturgy of *England* is, for that it maintaineth an unpreaching miniftry, in requiring nothing to be done by the minifter, which a child of ten years old cannot do as well, and as lawfully, as that man wherewith the book contenteth it felf.

fhould teach what men are fit to attend upon it, and forbid either men unlearned, or children, to be admitted thereunto?　In fetting down the form of common-prayer, there was no need that the book fhould mention either the learning of a fit, or the unfitnefs of an ignorant minifter, more than that he which defcribeth the manner how to pitch a field, fhould fpeak of moderation and fobriety in diet.　And concerning the duty it felf, although the hardnefs thereof be not fuch as needeth much art, yet furely they feem to be very far carried befides themfelves, to whom the dignity of publick prayer doth not difcover fomewhat more fitnefs in men of gravity and ripe difcretion, than in *children of ten years of age*, for the decent difcharge and performance of that office.　It cannot be that they who fpeak thus, fhould thus judge.　At the board, and in private, it very well becometh childrens innocency to pray, and their elders to fay *Amen*.　Which being a part of their virtuous education, ferveth greatly both to nourifh in them the fear of God, and to put us in continual remembrance of that powerful grace which openeth the mouths of infants to found his praife.　But publick prayer, the fervice of God in the folemn affembly of faints, is a work, though eafy, yet withal fo weighty, and of fuch refpect, that the great facility thereof, is but a flender argument to prove it may be as well and as lawfully committed to children, as to men of years, howfoever their ability of learning be but only to do that in decent order, wherewith the book contenteth it felf.　The book requireth but orderly reading.　As in truth, what fhould any prefcript form of prayer framed to the minifter's hand require, but only fo to be read as behoveth?　We know that there be in the world certain voluntary overfeers of all books, whofe cenfure, in this refpect, would fall as fharp on us, as it hath done on many others, if delivering but a form of prayer, we fhould either exprefs or include any thing, more than doth properly concern prayer.　The minifters greatnefs

or

or meanness of knowledge to do other things, his aptness or insufficiency otherwise than by reading to instruct the flock, standeth in this place as a stranger, with whom our form of common-prayer hath nothing to do. Wherein their exception against easiness, as if that did nourish ignorance, proceedeth altogether out of a needless jealousy. I have often heard it enquired of by many, how it might be brought to pass, that the church should every where have preachers to instruct the people; what impediments there are to hinder it; and which were the speediest way to remove them. In which consultation, the multitude of parishes, the paucity of schools, the manifold discouragements which are offered unto mens inclinations that way, the penury of the ecclesiastical estate, the irrecoverable loss of so many livings of principal value, clean taken away from the church long sithence, by being appropriated, the daily bruises that spiritual promotions use to take by often falling, the want of somewhat in certain statutes which concern the state of the church, the too great facility of many bishops, the stony hardness of too many patrons hearts, not touched with any feeling in this case: Such things oftentimes are debated, and much thought upon by them that enter into any discourse concerning any defect of knowledge in the clergy. But whosoever be found guilty, the communion book hath surely deserved least to be called in question for this fault. If all the clergy were as learned, as themselves are that most complain of ignorance in others, yet our book of prayer might remain the same; and remaining the same it is, I see not how it can be a let unto any man's skill in preaching. Which thing we acknowledge to be God's good gift, howbeit no such necessary element, that every act of religion should be thought imperfect and lame, wherein there is not somewhat exacted that none can discharge but an able preacher.

The length of our service.
T. C. l. 1.
p. 133. & l. 3. p. 184.

Aug. Ep. 121.

Luke 6. 12.

32. Two faults there are which our Lord and Saviour himself especially reproved in prayer; the one, when ostentation did cause it to be open; the other, when superstition made it long. As therefore prayers the one way are faulty, not when soever they be openly made, but when hypocrisy is the cause of open praying: So the length of prayer is likewise a fault, howbeit, not simply, but where error and superstition causeth more than convenient repetition or continuation of speech to be used. It is not, as some do imagine, (saith St. *Augustin*) that long praying is that fault of much speaking in prayer, which our saviour did reprove; for then would not he himself in prayer have continued whole nights. *Use in prayer no vain superfluity of words, as the heathens do, for they imagine that their much speaking will cause them to be heard*: Whereas in truth the thing which God doth regard, is how virtuous their minds are, and not how copious their tongues in prayer; how well they think, and not how long they talk, who come to present their supplications before him. Notwithstanding forasmuch as in publick prayer we are not only to consider what is needful in respect of God, but there is also in men that which we must regard; we somewhat the rather incline to length, lest overquick dispatch of a duty so important, should give the world occasion to deem that the thing it self is but little accounted of, wherein but little time is bestowed. Length thereof is a thing which the gravity and weight of such actions doth require. Beside, this benefit also it hath, that they whom earnest lets and impediments do often hinder from being partakers of the whole, have yet, through the length of divine service, opportunity left them, at the least, for access unto some reasonable part thereof. Again, it should be considered, how it doth come to pass that we are so long. For if that very service of God in the *Jewish* synagogues, which our Lord did approve and sanctify with the presence of his own person, had so large portions of the law and the prophets, together with so many prayers and Psalms read day by day, as do equal in a manner the length of ours, and yet in that respect was never thought to deserve blame, is it now an offence that the like measure of time is bestowed in the like manner? Peradventure the church hath not now the leisure which it had then, or else those things whereupon so much time was then well spent, have sithence that lost their dignity and worth. If the reading of the law, the prophets and psalms be a part of the service of God as needful under Christ as before, and the adding of the new testament as profitable as the ordaining of the old to be read; if therewith, instead of *Jewish* prayers, it be also for the good of the church,

1 Tim. 2. 1.

to annex that variety which the apostle doth commend, seeing that the time which we spend is no more than the orderly performance of these things necessarily required, why are we thought to exceed in length? Words, be they never so few,

are

are too many when they benefit not the hearer. But he which speaketh no more than edifieth, is undefervedly reprehended for much fpeaking. That as *the* T. C. l. 5. p. 184. *Devil under the colour of long prayer drave preaching out of the church* heretofore, *fo we in appointing fo long prayers and readings, whereby the lefs can be fpent in preaching, maintain an unpreaching miniftry*, is neither advifedly not truly fpoken. They reprove long prayer, and yet acknowledge it to be in it felf a thing commenda̓ble ; for fo it muft needs be, if the Devil have ufed it as a colour to hide his malicious practices. When malice would work that which is evil, and in working avoid the fufpicion of any evil intent, the colour wherewith it overcafteth it felf, is always a fair and plaufible pretence of feeking to further that which is good. So that if we both retain that good which Satan hath pretended to feek, and avoid the evil which his purpofe was to effect, have we not better prevented his malice, than if, as he hath under colour of long prayer driven preaching out of the church, fo we fhould take the quarrel of fermons in hand, and revenge their caufe by requital, thrufting prayer in a manner out of doors under colour of long preaching ? In cafe our prayers being made at their full length did neceffarily enforce fermons to be the fhorter, yet neither were this to uphold and maintain an unpreaching miniftry, unlefs we will fay, that thofe ancient fathers, *Chryfoftom*, *Auguftin*, *Leo*, and the reft whofe homilies in that confideration were fhorter for the moft part than our fermons are, did then not preach when their fpeeches were not long. The neceffity of fhortnefs caufed men to cut off impertinent difcourfes, and to comprife much matter in few words. But neither did it maintain inability, nor at all prevent opportunity of preaching, as long as a competent time is granted for that purpofe. *An hour and an half* is , they fay, in reformed churches ordinarily thought reafonable *for their whole Liturgy or fervice.* Neh. 8. 3. Do we then continue, as *Ezra* did in reading the law, from morning till midday ? or, as the Apoftle St. *Paul* did in prayer and preaching, till men through wearinefs be taken up dead at our feet ? The huge length whereof they make fuch Acts 20. 9. complaint is but this, that if our whole form of prayer be read , and befides an hour allowed for a fermon, we fpend ordinarily in both more time than they do by half an hour. Which half hour being fuch a matter as the *age of fome, and the infirmity of other fome, are not able to bear* ; if we have any fenfe of the *common imbecillity*, if any care to preferve men's wits from being broken with the very *bent of fo long attention*, if any love or defire to provide that things moft holy be not with hazard of men's fouls abhorred and loathed, this half hour's tedioufnefs muft be remedied, and that only by cutting off the greateft part of our common-prayer. For no other remedy will ferve to help fo dangerous an inconvenience.

33. The Brethren in *Ægypt* (faith St. *Auguftin, Epift.* 121.) are reported to have many prayers, but every one of them ve-
ry fhort, as if they were darts thrown out with | Inftead of fuch *prayers as the primitive churches have*
a kind of fudden quicknefs, left that vigilant | ufed, and thofe that be reformed now ufe ; we have (they
and erect attention of mind which in prayer is | fay) divers fhort cuts or fhreddings , rather wifhes than
| prayers. T. C. l. 1. p. 138. & l. 3. p. 210, 211.
very neceffary, fhould be wafted or dulled
through continuance, if their prayers were few and long. But that which St. *Auguftin* doth allow , they condemn. Thofe prayers whereunto devout minds have added a piercing kind of brevity, as well in that refpect which we have already mentioned, as alfo thereby the better to exprefs that quick and fpeedy expedition wherewith ardent affections, the very wings of prayer, are delighted to prefent our fuits in heaven, even fooner than our tongues can devife to utter them ; they in their mood of contradiction fpare not openly to deride, and that with fo bafe terms as do very ill befeem Men of their gravity. Such fpeeches are fcandalous, that favour not of God in him that ufeth them, and unto virtuoufly difpofed minds they are grievous corrofives. Our cafe were miferable, if that wherewith we moft endeavour to pleafe God were in his fight fo vile and defpicable, as men's difdainful fpeech would make it.

34. Again, for as much as effectual prayer is joined with a vehement intention of the Leffons in- inferior powers of the foul, which cannot therein long continue without pain, it hath termingled been therefore thought good fo by turns to interpofe ftill fomewhat for the higher part with our of the mind, the underftanding to work upon, that both being kept in continual exercife with variety , neither might feel any great wearinefs, and yet each be a fpur to other. For prayer kindleth our defire to behold God by fpeculation ; and the mind delighted with that contemplative fight of God, taketh every where new inflammations

Y   to to pray, the riches of the mysteries of heavenly wisdom continually stirring up in us correspondent desires towards them. So that he which prayeth in due sort, is thereby made the more attentive to hear; and he which heareth, the more earnest to pray, for the time which we bestow as well in the one as the other. But for what cause soever we do it, this intermingling of lessons with prayers is, [a] in their taste a thing as unsavoury, and as unseemly in their sight, as if the like should be done in suits and supplications before some mighty prince of the world. Our speech to worldly superiors, we frame in such sort as serveth best to inform and persuade the minds of them who otherwise could nor would greatly regard our necessities: Whereas, because we know that God is indeed a King, but a *great* King, who understandeth all things before-hand,

[a] We have no such forms in scripture, as that we should pray in two or three lines, and then after having read a while some other thing, come and pray as much more, and so the twentieth or the thirtieth time, with pauses between. If a man should come to a prince, and having very many things to demand; after he had demanded one thing, would stay a long time, and then demand another, and so the third; the prince might well think, that either he came to ask before he knew what he had need of, or that he had forgotten some piece of his suit, or that he were distracted in his understanding, or some other like cause of the disorder of his supplication. *T. C.* l. 1. p. 138. This kind of reason the prophet in the matter of sacrifices doth use. *T. C.* l. 3. p. 210.

which no other king besides doth; a king which needeth not to be informed what we lack; a king readier to grant, than we to make our requests; therefore in prayer we do not so much respect what precepts art delivereth, touching the method of persuasive utterance in the presence of great men, as what doth most avail to our own edification in piety and godly zeal. If they on the contrary side do think, that the same rules of decency which serve for things done unto terrene powers, should universally decide what is fit in the service of God, if it be their meaning to hold it for a maxim, that the church must deliver her publick supplications unto God, in no other form of speech, than such as decent, if suit should be made to the great *Turk*, or some other monarch, let them apply their own rule unto their own form of common-prayer. Suppose that the people of a whole town, with some chosen men before them, did continually twice or thrice a week, resort to their king, and every time they come, first acknowledge themselves guilty of rebellions and treasons, then sing a song, and after that explain some statute of the land to the standers by, and therein spend, at the least, an hour; this done, turn themselves again to the king, and for every sort of his subjects crave somewhat of him; at the length sing him another song, and so take their leave: Might not the king well think, that either they knew not what they would have, or else that they were distracted in mind, or some other such like cause of the disorder of their supplication? This form of suing unto kings, were absurd: This form of praying unto God, they allow. When God was served with legal sacrifices, such was the miserable and wretched disposition of some mens minds, that the best of every thing they had, being culled out for themselves, if there were in their flocks any poor, starved, or diseased thing, not worth the keeping, they thought it good enough for the altar of God, pretending, (as wise hypocrites do, when they rob God to enrich themselves) that the fatness of calves doth benefit him nothing; to us the best things are most profitable, to him all is one, if the mind of the offerer be good, which is the only thing he respecteth. In reproof of which their devout fraud, the prophet *Malachi* alledgeth, that gifts are offered unto God, not as [b] supplies of his want indeed, but yet as testimonies of that affection wherewith we acknowledge and honour his greatness. For which cause, sith the greater they are whom we honour, the more regard we have to the quality and choice of those presents which we bring them for honours sake; it must needs follow, that if we dare not disgrace our worldly superiors, with offering unto them such refuse as we bring unto God himself, we shew plainly, that our acknowledgment of his greatness is but feigned; in heart we fear him not so much

[b] Μέρη τιμῆς τὰ δῶρα, τὰ περ ἐχίουσι τιμῆς. Καὶ ᾗ τὸ μεῖζον δεῖ τιμᾶσθω δόσις ᾗ τιμῆς σημεῖον. Διὸ ᾗ οἱ φιλοχρήματοι ᾗ οἱ φιλότιμοι ἐφίενται αὐτῶν. Ἀμφοτέροις ᾗ Νόνται. Καὶ ᾗ κτῆμα ἐστι ᾗ ἐφίενται οἱ φιλοχρήματοι, ᾗ τιμᾶ ἔχει ᾗ ἡ φιλότιμοι. Arist. Rhet. lib. 1. cap. 5.

Mal. 1. 8, 14. as we dread them. *If ye offer the blind for a sacrifice, is it not evil? Offer it now unto thy prince; will he be content, or accept thy person, faith the Lord of Hosts? Cursed be the deceiver, which hath in his flock a male, and having made a vow, sacrificeth unto the Lord a corrupt thing: For I am a great king, faith the Lord of Hosts.* Should we hereupon frame a rule, that what form, or speech, or behaviour soever is fit for suiters in a princes court, the same, and no other, beseemeth us in our prayers to almighty God?

35. But in vain we labour to perſuade them that any thing can take away the te- diouſneſs of Prayer, except it be brought to the very ſame both meaſure and form which themſelves aſſign. Whatſoever therefore our Liturgy hath more than theirs, un- der one deviſed pretence or other they cut it off. We have of prayers for earthly things in their opinion too great a number; ſo oft to rehearſe the Lord's prayer in ſo ſmall a time, is, as they think, a loſs of time; the people's praying after the mini- ſter, they ſay, both waſteth time, and alſo ma- keth an unpleaſant ſound; the Pſalms they would not have to be made (as they are) a part of our Common-Prayer, not to be ſung or ſaid by turns, nor ſuch muſick to be uſed with them; thoſe evangelical Hymns they allow not to ſtand in our Liturgy; the Litany, the Creed of Athanaſius, the Sentence of Glory, where- with we uſe to conclude Pſalms, theſe things they cancel, as having been inſtituted in re- gard of occaſions peculiar to the times of old, and as being therefore now ſuperfluous. Touch- ing prayers for things earthly, we ought not to think that the church hath ſet down ſo many of them without cauſe. They peradventure, which find this fault are of the ſame affection with Solomon; ſo that if God ſhould offer to

I can make no geometrical and exact meaſure, but ve- rily I believe there ſhall be found more than a third part of the prayers, which are not pſalms and texts of ſcripture, ſpent in praying for and praying againſt the commodities and incommodities of this life, which is contrary to all the arguments or contents of the prayers of the church ſet down in the ſcripture, and eſpecially of our Saviour Chriſt's prayer, by the which ours ought to be directed. T. C. l. 1. p. 136. What a reaſon is this, we muſt repeat the Lord's prayer oftentimes, therefore oftentimes in half an hour, and one on the neck of another? Our Saviour Chriſt doth not there give a preſcript form of prayer whereunto he bindeth us: but giveth us a rule and ſquare to frame all our prayers by. I know it is neceſſary to pray and pray of- ten. I know alſo that in a few words it is impoſſible for any man to frame ſo pithy a prayer, and I confeſs that the church doth well in concluding their prayers with the Lord's prayer: But I ſtand upon this, That there is no ne- ceſſity laid upon us to uſe theſe very words and no more. T. C. l. 1. p. 219.

grant them whatſoever they ask, they would neither crave riches, nor length of days, nor yet victory over their enemies, but only an underſtanding heart; for which cauſe themſelves having Eagles wings, are offended to ſee others fly ſo near the ground. But the tender kindneſs of the church of God it very well beſeemeth to help the weaker ſort, which are by ſo great odds more in number, although ſome few of the perfecter and ſtronger may be therewith for a time diſpleaſed. Ignorant we are not, that ſuch as reſorted to our Saviour Chriſt being preſent on earth, there came not any unto him with better ſucceſs for the benefit of their ſouls everlaſting happineſs, than they whoſe bodily neceſſities gave them the firſt occaſion to ſeek relief, where they ſaw willingneſs and ability of doing every way good unto all. The graces of the Spirit are much more precious than worldly benefits; our ghoſtly evils of greater importance than any harm which the body feeleth. Therefore our deſires to heaven- ward ſhould both in meaſure and number no leſs exceed, than their glorious object doth every way excel in value. Theſe things are true and plain in the eye of a per- fect judgment. But yet it muſt be withal conſidered, that the greateſt part of the world are they which be fartheſt from perfection. Such being better able by ſenſe to diſcern the wants of this preſent life, than by ſpiritual capacity to apprehend things above ſenſe which tend to their happineſs in the world to come, are in that reſpect the more apt to apply their minds, even with hearty affection and zeal at the leaſt, unto thoſe branches of publick prayer wherein their own particular is moved. And by this mean there ſtealeth upon them a double benefit; firſt, becauſe that good affe- ction which things of ſmaller account have once ſet on work, is by ſo much the more eaſily raiſed higher; and ſecondly, in that the very cuſtom of ſeeking ſo particular aid and relief at the hands of God, doth by a ſecret contradiction withdraw them from endeavouring to help themſelves by thoſe wicked ſhifts, which they know can never have his allowance whoſe aſſiſtance their prayer ſeeketh. Theſe multi- plied petitions of worldy things in prayer have therefore, beſides their direct uſe, a ſervice, whereby the church under-hand, through a kind of heavenly fraud, taketh therewith the ſouls of men as with certain baits. If then their calculation be true (for ſo they reckon) that a full third of our prayers be allotted unto earthly benefits, for which our Saviour in his platform hath appointed but one petition amongſt ſeven, the difference is without any great diſagreement; we reſpecting what men are, and do- ing that which is meet in regard of the common imperfection; our Lord contrari- wiſe propoſing the moſt abſolute proportion that can be in men's deſires, the very higheſt mark whereat we are able to aim.

[a] For which cauſe alſo our cuſtom is both to place it in the front of our prayers as a guide, and to add it in the end of ſome principal limbs or parts, as a complement which fully perfecteth whatſoever may be defe- ctive

[a] Præmiſſa legitima & ordinaria oratione, quaſi fundamento, accidentium jus eſt deſideriorum, jus eſt ſuperſtruendi extrinſecus pe- titiones. Tertul. de Orat.

ctive in the reft. Twice we rehearfe it ordinarily, and oftner as occafion requireth more folemnity or length in the form of divine fervice ; not miftrufting, till thefe new curiofities fprang up, that ever any man would think our labour herein mifſpent, the time waſtefully confumed, and the office it felf made worfe, by fo repeating that which otherwife would more hardly be made familiar to the fimpler fort ; for the good of whofe fouls there is not in chriſtian religion any thing of like continual ufe and force throughout every hour and moment of their whole lives. I mean not only becaufe Prayer, but becaufe this very prayer is of fuch efficacy and neceffity : For that our Saviour did but fet men a bare example how to contrive or devife prayers of their own, and no way bind them to ufe this, is no doubt an error.   Luke 11. 1.   John the Baptiſt's difciples, which had been always brought up in the bofom of God's church from the time of their firſt infancy, till they came to the fchool of John, were not fo brutifh that they could be ignorant how to call upon the name of God : But of their maſter they had received a form of prayer amongſt themfelves, which form none did ufe faving his difciples, fo that by it as by a mark of fpecial difference they were known from others. And of this the apoſtles having taken notice, they requeſt that as John had taught his, fo Chriſt would likewife teach them to pray. Tertullian and St. Auguſtin do for that caufe term it, Orationem legitimam, the prayer which Chriſt's own law hath tied his church to ufe in the fame prefcript form of words wherewith he himfelf did deliver it : And therefore what part of the world foever we fall into, if chriſtian religion have been there received, the ordinary ufe of this very prayer hath with equal continuance accompanied the fame, as one of the principal and moſt material duties of honour done to Jefus Chriſt.   Cypr. in O-rat. Dom.   *Seeing that we have* (faith St. *Cyprian*) *an advocate with the Father for our fins, when we that have finned come to feek for pardon, let us alledge unto God the words which our advocate hath taught. For fith his promife is our plain warrant, that in his name what we ask we fhall receive, muſt we not needs much the rather obtain that for which we fue, if not only his name do countenance, but alfo his Speech prefent our requefts ?* Though men fhould fpeak with the tongues of angels, yet words fo pleafing to the ears of God as thofe which the Son of God himfelf hath compofed, were not poffible for men to frame. He therefore which made us to live, hath alfo taught us to pray, to the end that fpeaking unto the Father in his Son's own prefcript form, without fcholy or glofs of ours, we may be fure that we utter nothing which God will either difallow or deny. Other prayers we ufe many befides this, and this oftner than any other ; although not tied fo to do by any commandment of fcripture, yet moved with fuch confiderations as have been before fet down : The caufelefs diflike whereof which others have conceived , is no fufficient reafon for us as much as once to forbear, in any place, a thing which uttered with true devotion and zeal of heart, affordeth to God himfelf that glory, that aid to the weakeſt fort of men, to the moſt perfect that folid comfort which is unfpeakable.

The people's faying after the miniſter.   36. With our Lord's prayer they would find no fault, fo that they might perfuade us to ufe it before or after fermons only (becaufe fo their manner is) and not (as all

Another fault is, That all the people are appointed in divers places to fay after the miniſter, whereby not only the time is unprofitably waſted, and a confufed noife of the people (one fpeaking after another) caufed, but an opinion bred in their heads, that thofe only be their prayers which they pronounce with their own mouths after the miniſter, otherwife than the order which is left to the church doth bear, 1 Cor. 14. 16. and otherwife than Juſtin Martyr fheweth the cuſtom of the Churches to have been in his time. T. C. l. 1. p. 139. & l. 3. p. 211, 212, 213.

chriſtian people have been of old accuſtomed) infert it fo often into the Liturgy. Twice we appoint that the words which the miniſter firſt pronounceth, the whole congregation fhall repeat after him. As firſt in the publick confeffion of fins, and again in rehearfal of our Lord's prayer prefently after the bleffed facrament of his body and blood received. A thing no way offenfive, no way unfit or unfeemly to be done, although it had been fo appointed oftner than with us it is. But furely, with fo good reafon it ſtandeth in thofe two places , that otherwife to order it were not in all refpects fo well. Could there be any thing devifed better, than that we all, at our firſt accefs unto God by prayer, fhould acknowledge meekly our fins, and that not only in heart but with tongue ; all which are prefent being made ear-witneffes even of every man's diſtinct and deliberate affent unto each particular branch of a common indictment drawn againſt our felves ? How were it poffible that the church fhould any way elfe with fuch cafe and certainty provide that none of her children may, as Adam, diffemble that wretchednefs, the penitent confeffion whereof is fo neceffary a preamble, efpecially to
com-

common-prayer? In like manner, if the church did ever devife a thing fit and convenient, what more than this, that when together we have all received thofe heavenly
myfteries wherein Chrift imparteth himfelf unto us, and giveth vifible teftification
of our bleffed communion with him, we fhould in hatred of all herefies, factions
and fchifms, the paftor as a leader, the people as willing followers of him ftep by
ftep, declare openly our felves united as brethren in one, by offering up with all our
hearts and tongues, that moft effectual fupplication, wherein he unto whom we offer *Τίς ᾖ τῳ*
it, hath himfelf not only comprehended all our neceffities, but in fuch fort alfo *ἰχθεῖν ἀ-*
framed every petition, as might moft naturally ferve for many, and doth, though not *γενέσθαι δύ-
ναίαι ωθʼ ἕ*
always require, yet always import a multitude of fpeakers together? For which caufe *μίαν ἀίνκα*
communicants have ever ufed it, and we at that time, by the form of our very *πρὸς θεὸν ᾗ*
utterance, do fhew we ufe it, yea, every word and fyllable of it, as communicants.' *Bafil. Præf. in
Pfal.*
In the reft, we obferve that cuftom whereunto St. *Paul* alludeth, and whereof the
fathers of the church in their writings, make often mention, to fhew indefinitely *1 Cor. 14. 16.*
what was done, but not univerfally to bind for ever all prayers, unto one only fafhion of utterance. The reafons which we have alledged, induce us to think it ftill
a good work, which they, in their penfive care for the well beftowing of time, account wafte. As for unpleafantnefs of found, if it happen, the good of mens fouls
doth either deceive our ears, that we note it not, or arm them with patience to endure it. We are not fo nice as to caft away a fharp knife, becaufe the edge of it
may fometimes grate. And fuch fubtil opinions, as few but *Utopians* are likely to fall
into, we in this climate do not greatly fear.

37. The complaint which they make about
pfalms and hymns, might as well be over-paft
without any anfwer, as it is without any caufe
brought forth. But our defire is, to content them, if it may be, and to yield them a
juft reafon even of the leaft things, wherein
undefervedly they have but as much as dreamed
or fufpected that we do amifs. They feem

> Our manner of reading the Pfalms otherwife than the
> reft of the fcripture.
>
> They have always the fame profit to be ftudied in, to be
> read, and preached upon, which other fcriptures have, and
> this above the reft, that they are to be fung. But to make
> daily prayers of them, hand over head, or otherwife than
> the prefent eftate wherein we be, doth agree with the matter
> contained in them, is an abufing of them. *T. C.* l. 3. p. 206.

fometimes fo to fpeak, as if it greatly offended them that fuch hymns and pfalms as
are fcripture, fhould in common-prayer be otherwife ufed, than the reft of the fcripture is wont; fometimes difpleafed they are at the artificial mufick which we add
unto pfalms of this kind, or of any nature elfe; fometimes the plaineft and the
moft intelligible rehearfal of them yet they favour not, becaufe it is done by inter-
locution, and with a mutual return of fentences from fide to fide. They are not
ignorant what difference there is between other parts of fcripture and pfalms. The
choice and flower of * all things profitable in
other books, the pfalms do both more briefly
contain, and more movingly alfo exprefs, by

> * ἡ ἀειακηλὰ ᾗ παντέρων ὑμνολογία. Dionyf. Hierar. Ec-
> clef. cap. 3.

reafon of that poetical form wherewith they are written. The ancients, when they
fpeak of the book of pfalms, ufe to fall into large difcourfes, fhewing how this part,
above the reft, doth of purpofe fet forth and celebrate all the confiderations and operations which belong to God; it magnifieth the holy meditations and actions of divine men; it is of things heavenly an univerfal declaration, working in them whofe
hearts God infpireth with the due confideration thereof, an habit or difpofition of
mind whereby they are made fit veffels, both for receipt and for delivery of whatfoever fpiritual perfection. What is there neceffary for man to know, which the
pfalms are not able to teach? They are, to beginners, an eafy and familiar introdu-
duction, a mighty augmentation of all virtue and knowledge, in fuch as are entred
before, a ftrong confirmation to the moft perfect amongft others. Heroical magnanimity, exquifite juftice, grave moderation, exact wifdom, repentance unfeigned, unwearied patience, the myfteries of God, the fufferings of Chrift, the terrors of wrath,
the comforts of grace, the works of providence over this world, and the promifed
joys of that world which is to come, all good neceffarily to be either known, or
done, or had, this one celeftial fountain yieldeth. Let there be any grief or difeafe
incident unto the foul of man, any wound or ficknefs named, for which there is
not in this treafure-houfe a prefent comfortable remedy at all times ready to be
found? Hereof it is, that we covet to make the pfalms efpecially familiar unto
all. This is the very caufe why we iterate the pfalms oftner than any other part of
fcripture befides; the caufe wherefore we inure the people together with their
mini-

minifter, and not the minifter alone, to read them as other parts of fcripture he doth.

38. Touching mufical harmony, whether by inftrument or by voice, it being but of high and low in founds a due proportionable difpofition, fuch notwithftanding is the force thereof, and fo pleafing effects it hath, in that very part of man which is moft divine, that fome have been thereby induced to think, that the foul it felf by Nature is, or hath in it harmony. A thing which delighteth all ages, and befeemeth all States; a thing as feafonable in grief as in joy; as decent being added unto actions of greateft weight and folemnity, as being ufed when men moft fequefter themfelves from action. The reafon hereof is an admirable facility which mufick hath to exprefs and reprefent to the mind, more inwardly than any other fenfible mean, the very ftanding, rifing and falling, the very fteps and inflections every way, the turns and varieties of all paffions, whereunto the mind is fubject; yea, fo to imitate them, that whether it refemble unto us the fame ftate wherein our minds already are, or a clean contrary, we are not more contentedly by the one confirmed, than changed and led away by the other. In harmony, the very image and character even of virtue and vice is perceived, the mind delighted with their refemblances, and brought by having them often iterated into a love of the things themfelves. For which caufe there is nothing more contagious and peftilent, than fome kinds of harmony; than fome, nothing more ftrong and potent unto good. And that there is fuch a difference of one kind from another, we need no proof but our own experience, in as much as we are at the hearing of fome more inclined unto forrow and heavinefs, of fome more mollified and foftened in mind; one kind apter to ftay and fettle us, another to move and ftir our affections: There is that draweth to a marvellous, grave and fober mediocrity; there is alfo that carrieth as it were into extafies, filling the mind with an heavenly joy, and for the time, in a manner, fevering it from the body: So that although we lay altogether afide the confideration of ditty or matter, the very harmony of founds being framed in due fort, and carried from the ear to the fpiritual faculties of our fouls, is by a native puiffance and efficacy, greatly available to bring to a perfect temper whatfoever is there troubled, apt as well to quicken the fpirits, as to allay that which is too eager, foveraign againft melancholy and defpair, forceable to draw forth tears of devotion, if the mind be fuch as can yield them, able both to move and to moderate all affections. The prophet *David* having therefore fingular knowledge, not in poetry alone, but in mufick alfo, judged them both to be things moft neceffary for the houfe of God, left behind him to that purpofe a number of divinely indited poems, and was further the author of adding unto poetry, melody in publick prayer, melody both vocal and inftrumental for the raifing up of mens hearts, and the fweetning of their affections towards God. In which confiderations, the church of Chrift doth likewife at this prefent day, retain it as an ornament to God's fervice, and an help to our own devotion. They which, under pretence of the law ceremonial abrogated, require the abrogation of inftrumental mufick, approving neverthelefs the ufe of vocal melody to remain, muft fhew fome reafon wherefore the one fhould be thought a legal ceremony, and not the other. In church mufick curiofity and oftentation of art, wanton, or light, or unfuitable harmony, fuch as only pleafeth the ear, and doth not naturally ferve to the very kind and degree of thofe impreffions, which the matter that goeth with it leaveth, or is apt to leave in mens minds, doth rather blemifh and difgrace that we do, than add either beauty or furtherance unto it. On the other fide, the faults prevented, the force and efficacy of the thing it felf, when it drowneth not utterly, but fitly fuiteth with matter altogether founding to the praife of God, is in truth moft admirable, and doth much edify, if not the underftanding, becaufe it teacheth not; yet furely the affection, becaufe therein it worketh much. They muft have hearts very dry and tough, from whom the melody of the *Pfalms* doth not fometime draw that wherein a mind religioufly affected delighteth. Be it as *Rabanus Maurus* obferveth, that at the firft, the church in this exercife was more fimple and plain than we are; that their finging was little more than only a melodious kind of pronunciation; that the cuftom which we now ufe, was not inftituted fo much for their caufe which are fpiritual, as to the end that into groffer and heavier minds, whom bare words do not eafily move, the fweetnefs of melody might make fome entrance for good things. St. *Bafil* himfelf acknowledging as much, did not think that from fuch inventions, the leaft jot of

2   eftima-

eſtimation and credit thereby ſhould be derogated : ᵃ *For (ſaith he) whereas the holy ſpi-*
rit ſaw that mankind is unto virtue hardly
drawn, and that righteouſneſs is the leaſt ac-
counted of by reaſon of the proneneſs of our
affections to that which delighteth ; it pleaſed
the wiſdom of the ſame ſpirit, to borrow from
melody that pleaſure, which mingled with hea-
venly myſteries, cauſeth the ſmoothneſs and
ſoftneſs of that which toucheth the ear, to convey, as it were, by ſtealth, the trea-
ſure of good things into man's mind. To this purpoſe were thoſe harmonious tunes
of Pſalms deviſed for us, that they which are either in years but young, or touch-
ing perfection of virtue as yet not grown to ripeneſs, might, when they think they
ſing, learn. O the wiſe conceit of that heavenly teacher, which hath by his skill
found out a way, that doing thoſe things wherein we delight, we may alſo learn that
whereby we profit!

39. And if the prophet *David* did think,
that the very meeting of men together, and
their accompanying one another to the houſe
of God, ſhould make the bond of their love
inſoluble, and tie them in a league of inviolable amity, *Pſal.* 54. 14. How much more
may we judge it reaſonable to hope, that the
like effects may grow in each of the people
towards other, in them all towards their paſtor,
and in their paſtor towards every of them ; between whom there daily and interchangeably

> Of ſinging or ſaying *Pſalms*, and other parts of common-
> prayer, wherein the people and miniſter anſwer one ano-
> ther by courſe. For the ſinging of *Pſalms* by courſe, and
> ſide after ſide, although it be very ancient, yet it is not
> commendable; and ſo much the more to be ſuſpected, for
> that the devil hath gone about to get it ſo great authority,
> partly by deriving it from *Ignatius's* time, and partly in
> making the world believe that this came from heaven, and
> that the angels were heard to ſing after this ſort. Which
> as it is a meer fable , ſo it is confuted by hiſtoriogra-
> phers, whereof ſome aſcribe the beginning of this to
> *Damaſus*, ſome other unto *Flavianus* and *Diodorus*, T. C. l.
> 1. p. 203.

paſs in the hearing of God himſelf, and in the
preſence of his holy angels, ſo many heavenly acclamations, exultations, provocations, petitions, ſongs of comfort, pſalms of praiſe and thanksgiving ? in all which
particulars, as when the paſtor maketh their ſuits, and they, with one voice, teſtify
a general aſſent thereunto ; or when he joyfully beginneth, and they with like alacrity follow, dividing between them the ſentences wherewith they ſtrive, which
ſhall moſt ſhew his own, and ſtir up others zeal, to the glory of that God whoſe
name they magnify ; or when he propoſeth unto God their neceſſities, and they their
own requeſts for relief in every of them ; or when he lifteth up his voice like a
trumpet, to proclaim unto them the laws of God, they adjoining, though not as
Iſrael did, by way of generality a chearful promiſe, ᵇ *All that the Lord hath com-* ᵇ Exod. 19.
manded, we will do ; yet that which God doth no leſs approve, that which favoureth 8. & 24. 3.
more of meekneſs, that which teſtifieth rather a feeling knowledge of our common Deut. 5. 27.
imbecillity, unto the ſeveral branches thereof, ſeveral lowly and humble requeſts for Joſh. 24. 16.
grace at the merciful hands of God, to perform the thing which is commanded ;
or when they wiſh reciprocally each others ghoſtly happineſs ; or when he by exhortation raiſeth them up, and they by proteſtation of their readineſs, declare he ſpeaketh not in vain unto them : Theſe interlocutory forms of ſpeech, what are they
elſe, but moſt effectual, partly teſtifications, and partly inflammations of all piety ?
When, and how this cuſtom of ſinging by courſe, came up in the church, it is not
certainly known. ᶜ *Socrates* maketh *Ignatius*, the biſhop of *Antioch* in *Syria*, the ᶜ Socrat.'Hiſt.
firſt beginner thereof, even under the apoſtles themſelves. But againſt *Socrates* they Eccl. lib. 6.
ſet the authority of ᵈ *Theodoret*, who draweth the original of it from *Antioch*, as ᵈ Theod. lib.
Socrates doth ; howbeit, aſcribing the invention to others, *Flavian* and *Diodore*, 2. cap. 24.
men which conſtantly ſtood in defence of the apoſtolick faith, againſt the biſhop of
that church, *Leontius*, a favourer of the *Arians*. Againſt both *Socrates* and *Theo-*
doret, ᵉ *Platina* is brought as a witneſs, to teſtify that *Damaſus*, biſhop of *Rome*, ᵉ Plat. in vi-
began it in his time. Of the *Latin* church, it may be true which *Platina* ſaith. ta Damaſi.
And therefore the eldeſt of that church which maketh any mention thereof, is
St. *Ambroſe*, ᶠ biſhop of *Milan*, at the ſame
time when *Damaſus* was of *Rome*. Amongſt
the *Grecians*, St. ᵍ *Baſil* having brought it
into his church, before they of *Neocæſarea*
uſed it, *Sabellius* the heretick, and *Marcellus*,
took occaſion thereat to incenſe the churches

> ᶠ Bene mari plerunque comparatur ecclesia, qua primo ingredi-
> entis populi agmine totis veſtibulis undas vomit : deinde in oratione
> totius plebis nunquam undis reſluentibus ſtridet ; tum reſponſoriis
> Pſalmorum, cantu virorum, mulierum, virginum, partulorum
> conſonus undarum fragor reſultat. Hexam. lib. 2. cap. 5.
> ᵍ Baſil. Epiſt. 63.

against him, as being an author of new devices in the service of God. Whereupon, to avoid the opinion of novelty and singularity, he alledgeth for that which he himself did, the example of the churches of *Ægypt, Libya, Thebes, Palestina, the Arabians, Phænicians, Syrians, Mesopotamians,* and, in a manner, all that reverenced the custom of singing *Psalms* together. If the *Syrians* had it then before *Basil, Antioch,* the mother church of those parts, must needs have used it before *Basil,* and consequently before *Damasus.* The question is then, how long before, and whether so long, that *Ignatius,* or as ancient as *Ignatius,* may be probably thought the first inventors. *Ignatius* in *Trajan's* days suffered martyrdom. And of the churches in *Pontus* and *Bithynia,* to *Trajan* the emperor, his own vicegerent there affirmeth, that the only crime he knew of them was, they used to meet together at a certain day, and to praise Christ with hymns, as a God, *secum invicem,* one to another amongst themselves. Which, for any thing we know to the contrary, might be the self-same form which *Philo Judæus* expresseth, declaring how the *Essenes* were accustomed with hymns and psalms to honour God, sometime all exalting their voices together in one, and sometime one part answering another, wherein, as he thought, they swerved not much from the pattern of *Moses* and *Miriam.* Whether *Ignatius* did at any time hear the Angels praising God after that sort or no, what matter is it? If *Ignatius* did not, yet one which must be with us of greater authority, did. *I saw the Lord* (saith the prophet *Isaiah*) *on an high throne, the Seraphims stood upon it,* one cried to another, *saying, Holy, holy, holy, Lord God of hosts, the whole world is full of his glory.* But whosoever were the author, whatsoever the time, whensoever the example of beginning this custom in the church of Christ; sith we are wont to suspect things only before trial, and afterwards either to approve them as good, or if we find them evil, accordingly to judge of them; their counsel must needs seem very unseasonable, who advise men now to suspect that wherewith the world hath had, by their own account, twelve hundred years acquaintance, and upwards, enough to take away suspicion and jealousy. Men know by this time, if ever they will know, whether it be good or evil, which hath been so long retained. As for the devil, which way it should greatly benefit him to have this manner of singing psalms accounted an invention of *Ignatius,* or an imitation of the Angels of heaven, we do not well understand. But we very well see in them who thus plead, a wonderful celerity of discourse. For perceiving at the first but only some cause of suspicion and fear, left it should be evil, they are presently in one and the self-same breath resolved, [a] That *what beginning soever it had, there is no possibility it should be good.* The potent arguments which did thus suddenly break in upon them, and overcome them, are; first, that it is not lawful for the people all jointly to praise God in singing of psalms. Secondly, that they are not any where forbidden by the law of God, to sing every verse of the whole psalm, both with heart and voice, quite and clean throughout. Thirdly, that it cannot be understood what is sung after our manner. Of which three, forasmuch as lawfulness to sing one way, proveth not another way inconvenient; the former two are true allegations, but they lack strength to accomplish their desire; the third so strong, that it might persuade, if the truth thereof were not doubtful. And shall all this inforce us to banish a thing, which all christian churches in the world have received; a thing which so many ages have held; a thing which the most approved counsels and laws have so oftentimes ratified; a thing which was never found to have any inconvenience in it; a thing which always heretofore the best men, and wisest governors of God's people, did think they could never commend enough; a thing which, as *Basil* was persuaded, did both strengthen the meditation of those holy words which were uttered in that sort, and serve also to make attentive, and to raise up the hearts of men; a thing whereunto God's people of old did resort with hope and thirst, that thereby especially their souls might be edified; a thing which filleth the mind with comfort and heavenly delight, stirreth up fragrant desires and affections correspondent unto that which the words contain; allayeth all kind of base and earthly cogitations, banisheth and driveth away those evil secret suggestions, which our invisible enemy is always

Plin. secund.
Epist. lib. 10.
Ep. 97.
Exod. 15. 1.
21.

Isa. 6. 3.

[a] From whencesoever it came, it cannot be good, considering, that when it is granted, that all the people may praise God (as it is in singing of psalms) then this ought not to be restrained unto a few; and where it is lawful, both with heart and voice, to sing the whole psalm, there it is not meet that they should sing but the one half with their heart and voice, and the other with their heart only. For where they may both with heart and voice sing, there the heart is not enough. Therefore, besides the incommodity which cometh this way, in that being tossed after this sort, men cannot understand what is sung, those other two inconveniencies come of this form of singing, and therefore it is banished in all reformed churches. *T. C. l. 1. p. 203.*

ways apt to minister, watereth the heart to the end it may fructify, maketh the vertuous in trouble full of magnanimity and courage, serveth as a most approved remedy against all doleful and heavy accidents which befal men in this present life. To
conclude, so fitly accordeth with the Apostle's own exhortation, *Speak to your selves* Eph. 5. 19.
*in psalms and hymns, and spiritual songs, making melody , and singing to the Lord
in your Hearts* ; that surely, there is more cause to fear lest the want thereof be a
maim, than the use a blemish to the service of God. It is not our meaning, that
what we attribute unto the psalms, should be thought to depend altogether on
that only form of singing or reading them by course , as with us the manner
is ; but the end of our speech is to shew, that because the fathers of the church,
with whom the self-same custom was so many ages ago in use, have uttered all
these things concerning the fruit which the church of God did then reap , observing that and no other form, it may be justly avouched , that we our selves
retaining it , and besides it also the other more newly and not unfruitfully devised, do neither want that good which the latter invention can afford, nor lose any
thing of that for which the ancients so oft and so highly commend the former. Let
novelty therefore in this give over endless contradictions, and let ancient custom
prevail.

40. We have already given cause sufficient
for the great conveniency and use of reading the psalms oftner than other scriptures.
Of reading or singing likewise *Magnificat,
Benedictus* , and *Nunc dimittis* , oftner than
the rest of the psalms, the causes are no whit
less reasonable ; so that if the one may very
well monthly , the other may as well even

Of *Magnificat*, *Benedictus*, and *Nunc dimittis*.

These thanksgivings were made by occasion of certain
particular benefits, and are no more to be used for ordinary prayers, than the *Ave-Maria*. So that both for this
cause, and the other before alledged of the psalms, it is
not convenient to make ordinary prayers of them. *T. C.*
lib. 3. p. 208.

daily be iterated. They are songs which concern us so much more than the songs
of *David*, as the gospel toucheth us more than the law, the new testament than
the old. And if the psalms for the excellency of their use deserve to be oftner repeated than they are, but that the multitude of them permitted not any oftner
repetition, what disorder is it, if these few evangelical hymns, which are in no respect less worthy, and may be by reason of their paucity imprinteth with much more
ease in all men's memories, be for that cause every day rehearsed ? In our own behalf
it is convenient and orderly enough, that both they and we make day by day prayers
and supplications the very same ; why not as fit and convenient to magnify the name of
God day by day with certain the very self-same psalms of praise and thanksgiving ? Either
let them not allow the one, or else cease to reprove the other. For the ancient received use of intermingling hymns and psalms with divine readings, enough hath been
written. And if any may fitly serve unto that purpose, how should it better have been
devised, than that a competent number of the old being first read, these of the new
should succeed in the place where now they are set ? In which place notwithstanding,
there is joined with *Benedictus* the hundred psalm ; with *Magnificat* the ninety eight ;
the sixty seventh with *Nunc dimittis* ; and in every of them the choice left free for the
minister to use indifferently the one for the other. Seeing therefore they pretend
no quarrel at other psalms, which are in like manner appointed also to be daily read,
why do these so much offend and displease their taste? They are the first gratulations
wherewith our Lord and Saviour was joyfully received at his entrance into the world,
by such as in their hearts, arms, and very bowels embraced him ; being prophetical dis-
coveries of Christ already present, whose future coming the other psalms did but fore-
signify ; they are against the obstinate incredulity of the *Jews* the most luculent testimonies that christian religion hath ; yea, the only sacred hymns they are, that christianity hath peculiar unto it self; the other being songs too of praise and thanksgiving, but songs wherewith, as we serve God, so the *Jew* likewise. And whereas
they tell us, these songs were fit for that purpose, when *Simeon* and *Zachary*, and the
blessed Virgin uttered them, but cannot so be to us which have not received like
benefit ; should they not remember how expresly *Hezekiah*, amongst many other 2 Chron. 29;
good things, is commended for this also , That the praises of God were through his 30.
appointment daily set forth, by using in publick divine service, the songs of *David*
and *Asaph* unto that very end ? Either there wanted wise men to give *Hezekiah*
advice, and to inform him of that which in his case was as true as it is in ours ;
namely, that without some inconvenience and disorder, he could not appoint those

Z   *Psalms*

Pſalms to be uſed as ordinary prayers, ſeeing that although they were ſongs of thankſgiving, ſuch as *David* and *Aſaph* had ſpecial occaſion to uſe, yet not ſo the whole church and people afterwards, whom like occaſions did not befal : or elſe *Hezekiah* was perſuaded as we are, that the praiſes of God in the mouths of his ſaints are not ſo reſtrained to their own particular, but that others may both conveniently and fruitfully uſe them ; firſt, becauſe the myſtical communion of all faithful men is ſuch as maketh every one to be intereſſed in thoſe precious bleſſings which any one of them receiveth at God's hands : Secondly, becauſe when any thing is ſpoken to extol the goodneſs of God, whoſe *mercy endureth for ever,* albeit the very particular occaſion whereupon it riſeth do come no more ; yet, the fountain continuing the ſame, and yielding other new effects which are but only in ſome ſort proportionable, a ſmall reſemblance between the benefits, which we and others have received, may ſerve to make the ſame words of praiſe and thankſgiving fit, though not equally in all circumſtances fit for both ; a clear demonſtration whereof we have in all the ancient fathers commentaries and meditations upon the *Pſalms.* Laſt of all, becauſe even when there is not as much as the ſhew of any reſemblance ; nevertheleſs by often uſing their words in ſuch manner, our minds are daily more and more inured with their affections.

Of the litany. 41. The publick eſtate of the church of God amongſt the *Jews* hath had many rare and extraordinary occurrences ; which alſo were occaſions of ſundry [a] open ſolemnities and offices, whereby the people did with general conſent make ſhew of correſpondent affection towards God. The like duties appear uſual in the ancient church of Chriſt, by that which [b] *Tertullian* ſpeaketh of chriſtian women matching themſelves with infidels. *She cannot content the Lord with performance of his diſcipline, that hath at her ſide a vaſſal whom Satan hath made his vice-agent to croſs whatſoever the faithful ſhall do. If her preſence be required at the time of ſtation or ſtanding prayer, he chargeth her at no time but that, to be with him in his baths ; if a faſting day come, he hath on that day a banquet to make ; if there be cauſe for the church to go forth in ſolemn proceſſion, his whole family have ſuch buſineſs come upon them that no one can be ſpared.* Theſe proceſſions, as it ſeemeth, were firſt begun for the interring of holy martyrs, and the viſiting of thoſe places where they were entombed. Which thing, the name it ſelf applied by [c] heathens unto the office of exequies, and partly the ſpeeches of ſome of the ancients delivered concerning [d] chriſtian proceſſions, partly alſo the very droſs which ſuperſtition thereunto added, I mean, the cuſtom of invocating ſaints in proceſſions, heretofore uſual, do ſtrongly inſinuate. And as things invented to one

[a] We pray for the avoiding of thoſe dangers which are nothing near us ; as from lightning and thundring in the midſt of winter ; from ſtorms and tempeſt, when the weather is moſt fair, and the ſeas moſt calm. It is true, that upon ſome urgent calamity a prayer may, and ought to be framed, which may beg either the commodity, for want whereof the church is in diſtreſs, or the turning away of that miſchief which either approacheth, or is already upon it. But to make thoſe prayers, which are for the preſent time and danger, ordinary and daily prayers ; I cannot hitherto ſee any, either ſcripture, or example of the primitive church. And here for the ſimples ſake, I will ſet down after what ſort this abuſe crept into the church. There was one *Mamercus,* Biſhop of *Vienna,* which in the time of great earthquakes which were in *France,* inſtituted certain ſupplications which the *Grecians* (and we of them) call the *Litany,* which concerned that matter : There is no doubt but as other diſcommodities roſe in other countries, they likewiſe had prayers accordingly. Now Pope *Gregory* either made himſelf, or gathered the ſupplications that were made againſt the calamities of every country, and made of them a great *Litany* or ſupplication, as *Platina* calleth it, and gave it to be uſed in all churches : Which thing albeit all churches might do for the time , in reſpect of the caſe of the calamity which the churches ſuffered ; yet there is no cauſe, why it ſhould be perpetual that was ordained but for a time ; and why all lands ſhould pray to be delivered from the incommodities that ſome land hath been troubled with. *T. C. l.* 1. *p.* 137. Exod. 15. 20. Wiſd. 10. 20. 2 Sam. 6. 2. 1 Chron. 13. 5. 2 Chron. 20. 3. Joel 2. 15.
[b] *Tertul. lib.* 2. *ad Uxor.*
[c] *Terent. Andr.*
[d] Hier. Epiſt. 22. ad Euſt. *Martyres tibi quærantur in cubiculo tuo. Nunquam cauſa deerit procedendi , ſi ſemper quando neceſſe eſt, progreſſura ſis.*

[e] Socrat. l. 6.
c. 8. Sozom.
L 8. c. 8.
Theod. l. 16.
L 30. l. 3.
c. 10. Novel.
68. 51.
[f] Baſil. Epiſt.
63. Niceph.
l. 14. c. 3.
Cedren. in
Theodoſ.

purpoſe are by uſe eaſily converted to more, [e] it grew, that ſupplications with this ſolemnity for the appeaſing of God's wrath, and the averting of publick evils, were of the Greek church termed *Litanies, Rogations* of the Latin [f]. To the people of *Vienna* (*Mamercus* being their Biſhop about 450 years after Chriſt) there befel many things, the ſuddenneſs and ſtrangeneſs whereof ſo amazed the hearts of all men, that the city they began to forſake as a place which heaven did threaten with imminent ruin. It beſeemed not the perſon of ſo grave a prelate to be either utterly without counſel, as the reſt were, or in a common perplexity to ſhew himſelf alone ſecure. Wherefore as many as remained he earneſtly exhorteth to prevent portended calamities, uſing thoſe virtuous and holy means wherewith others in like caſe have prevailed with God. To which purpoſe he perfecteth the *Rogations* or *Litanies* before in uſe, and addeth unto them that which the preſent neceſſity required. Their good ſucceſs moved *Sidonius* Biſhop of *Averna,* to uſe the ſame ſo corrected *Rogations,* at ſuch time as he and his people were after afflicted with famine, and beſieged with potent ad-

Sidon. l. 7.
Epiſt. 1.

adverfaries. For, till the empty name of the Empire came to be fettled in *Charles the Great*, the fall of the *Romans* huge dominion, concurring with other univerfal evils, caufed thofe times to be days of much affliction and trouble throughout the world. So that *Rogations*, or *Litanies*, were then the very ftrength, ftay and comfort of God's church. Whereupon, in the year five hundred and fix, it was by the council of *Aurelia* decreed, that the whole church fhould beftow yearly, at the *Concil. tom.* feaft of *Pentecoft*, three days in that kind of proceffionary fervice. About half an ². *F. 513.* hundred years after, to the end that the *Latin* churches, which all obferved this cuftom, might not vary in the order and form of thofe great *Litanies*, which were fo folemnly every where exercifed, it was thought convenient by *Gregory* the firft, and the beft of that name, to draw the flower of them all into one. But this Iron began at length to gather ruft; which thing the fynod of *Colen* faw, and in part redrefs'd within that province; neither denying the neceffary ufe for which fuch *Litanies* ferve, wherein God's clemency and mercy is defired by publick fuit, to the end that plagues, deftructions, calamities, famines, wars, and all other the like ad- *Concil. tom.* verfities, which, for our manifold fins, we have always caufe to fear, may be turned ⁵. *Anno.* away from us, and prevented through his grace; nor yet diffembling the great abufe ¹⁵⁶⁶ whereunto, as fundry other things, fo this had grown by men's improbity and malice; to whom, that which was devifed for the appeafing of God's difpleafure, gave opportunity of committing things which juftly kindled his wrath. For remedy whereof, it was then thought better, that thefe, and all other fupplications and proceffions, fhould be no where ufed, but only within the walls of the houfe of God, the place fanctified unto prayer. And by us not only fuch inconveniencies being remedied, but alfo whatfoever was otherwife amifs in form or matter, it now remaineth a work, the abfolute perfection whereof upbraideth with error, or fomewhat worfe, them whom in all parts it doth not fatisfy. As therefore *Litanies* have been of longer continuance, than that we fhould make either *Gregory* or *Mamercus* the author of them; fo they are of more permanent ufe, than that now the church fhould think it needeth them not. What dangers at any time are imminent, what evils hang over our heads, God doth know, and not we. We find by daily experience, that thofe calamities may be neareft at hand, readieft to break in fuddenly upon us, which we, in regard of times or circumftances, may imagine to be fartheft off. Or if they do not indeed approach, yet fuch miferies as being prefent, all men are apt to bewail with tears, the wife by their prayers fhould rather prevent. Finally, if we, for our felves, had a privilege of immunity, doth not true chriftian charity require, that whatfoever any part of the world, yea, any one of all our brethren elfewhere, doth either fuffer, or fear, the fame we account as our own burthen? What one petition is there found in the whole *Litany*, whereof we fhall ever be able at any time to fay, that no man living needeth the grace or benefit therein craved at God's hands? I am not able to exprefs, how much it doth grieve me, that things of principal excellency fhould be thus bitten at by men, whom God hath endued with graces, both of wit and learning, for better purpofes.

42. We have from the apoftles of our Lord Jefus Chrift, received that brief con- *Of Athana-* feffion of faith, which hath been always a badge of the church, a mark whereby to *fius's Creed,* difcern chriftian men from Infidels and *Jews:* ª *This faith, received from the apo-* *Patri.* *ftles, and their difciples,* (faith *Irenæus*) *though difperfed throughout* ª *Iren. lib. 1.* *the world, doth notwithftanding keep as fafe, as if it dwelt within the walls of fome* *cap. 3.* *one houfe, and as uniformly hold, as if it had but one only heart and foul; this as confonantly it preacheth, teacheth, and delivereth, as if but one tongue did fpeak for all. As one fun fhineth to the whole world; fo there is no faith but this one publifhed, the brightnefs whereof muft enlighten all that come to the knowledge of the truth.* ᵇ *This rule* (faith *Tertullian*) *Chrift did inftitute; the ftream and current of this rule hath gone as far, it hath continued as long as the very promulgation of the Gofpel.* ᶜ Under *Conftantine* the Emperor, about three hundred years and upward after Chrift, *Arius*, a prieft in the church of *Alexandria*, a fubtle-witted, and a marvellous fair-fpoken man, but difcontented that one fhould be placed before him in honour, whofe fuperior he thought

ᵇ Tertul. de Præfer. adverf. Hæret. & adverf. Prax.

ᶜ The like may be faid of the *Gloria Patri*, and the *Athanafian* Creed. It was firft brought into the church, to the end that men thereby fhould make an open profeffion in the church of the divinity of the Son of God, againft the deteftable opinion of *Arius* and his difciples, wherewith at that time marvelloufly fwarmed almoft the whole *Chriftendom*. Now that it hath pleafed the Lord to quench that fire, there is no fuch caufe why thefe things fhould be ufed in the church, at the leaft, why that *Gloria Patri* fhould be fo often repeated. T. C. lib. 1. p. 137.

Z 2 him-

himfelf in defert, became, through envy and ftomach, prone unto contradiction, and bold to broach at the length that Herefy, wherein the Deity of our Lord Jefus Chrift, contained, but not opened in the former Creed, the co-equality and co-eternity of the Son with the Father was denied. Being for this impiety deprived of his place by the bifhop of the fame church, the punifhment which fhould have reformed him, did but increafe his obftinacy, and give him occafion of labouring with greater earneftnefs elfewhere, to intangle unwary minds with the fnares of his damnable opinion. *Arius* in a fhort time had won to himfelf a number both of followers, and of great defenders, whereupon much difquietnefs on all fides enfued. The Emperor, to reduce the church of Chrift unto the unity of found belief, when other means, whereof tryal was firft made, took no effect, gathered that famous affembly of three hundred and eighteen bifhops in the council of *Nice*; where, befides order taken from many things which feemed to need redrefs, there was with common confent, for the fettling of all mens minds, that other confeffion of faith fet down, which we call the *Nicene Creed*, whereunto the *Arians* themfelves which were prefent, fubfcribed alfo; not that they meant fincerely, and indeed to forfake their error; but only to efcape deprivation and exile, which they faw they could not avoid; openly perfifting in their former opinions, when the greater part had concluded againft them, and that with the Emperor's royal affent. Referving therefore themfelves unto future opportunities, and knowing it would not boot them to ftir again in a matter fo compofed, unlefs they could draw the Emperor firft, and by his means the chiefeft bifhops unto their part; till *Conftantine's* death, and fomewhat after, they always profeffed love and zeal to the *Nicene* faith, yet ceafed not in the mean while to ftrengthen that part which in heart they favoured, and to infeft by all means, under colour of other quarrels, their greateft adverfaries in this caufe. Amongft them *Athanafius* efpecially, whom by the fpace of forty fix years, from the time of his confecration to fucceed *Alexander*, Archbifhop in the church of *Alexandria*, till the laft hour of his life in this world, they never fuffered to enjoy the comfort of a peaceable day. The heart of *Conftantine* ftoln from him: *Conftantius, Conftantine's* fucceffor, his fcourge and torment, by all the ways which malice, armed with foveraign authority, could devife and ufe. Under *Julian* no reft given him; and in the days of *Valentinian*, as little. Crimes there were laid to his charge many; the leaft whereof, being juft, had bereaved him of eftimation and credit with men, while the world ftandeth. His judges evermore the felf-fame men, by whom his accufers were fuborned. Yet the iffue always, on their part, fhame, on his, triumph. Thofe bifhops and prelates, who fhould have accounted his caufe theirs, and could not, many of them, but with bleeding hearts, and with watered cheeks, behold a perfon of fo great place and worth, conftrained to endure fo foul indignities, were fure by bewraying their affection towards him, to bring upon themfelves thofe moleftations, whereby, if they would not be drawn to feem his adverfaries, yet others fhould be taught how unfafe it was to continue his friends. Whereupon it came to pafs in the end, that (very few excepted) all became fubject to the fway of time; other odds there was none amongft them, (faving only that fome fell fooner away, fome later, from the foundnefs of belief; fome were leaders in the hoft of impiety, and the reft as common foldiers, either yielding through fear, or brought under with penury, or by flattery enfnared, or elfe beguiled through fimplicity, which is the faireft excufe that well may be made for them. Yea, (that which all men did wonder at) *Ofius*, the ancienteft bifhop that *Chriftendom* then had, the moft forward in defence of the Catholick caufe, and of the contrary part moft feared; that very *Ofius*, with whofe hand the *Nicene* Creed it felf was fet down, and framed for the whole chriftian world to fubfcribe unto, fo far yielded in the end, as even with the fame hand to ratify the *Arians* confeffion, a thing which they neither hoped to fee, nor the other part ever feared, till with amazement they faw it done. Both were perfuaded, that although there had been for *Ofius* no way, but either prefently fubfcribe, or die, his anfwer and choice would

a Mac. 6. 24.

Major centenario, Sulpit. Sever. hift. l. 2.

have been the fame that *Eleazar's* was, *It doth not become our age to diffemble, whereby many young perfons might think that* Ofius *an hundred years old and upward, were now gone to another religion; and fo, through mine hypocrify,* [*for a little time of tranfitory life*] *they might be deceived by me, and I procure malediction and reproach to my old age. For though I were now delivered from the torments of men, yet could I not efcape the hand of the Almighty, neither alive nor dead.* But fuch was the ftream of thofe times, that all men gave place unto it,

I   which

which we cannot but impute partly to their own overfight : For at the firft the Emperor was theirs, the determination of the council of *Nice* was for them ; they had the *Arians* hands to that council.   So that advantages are never changed fo far to the contrary, but by great error.   It plainly appeareth, that the firft thing which weakned them, was their fecurity.   Such as they knew were in heart ftill affected towards *Arianifm*, they fuffered by continual nearnefs to poffefs the minds of the greateft about the Emperor, which themfelves might have done with very good acceptation, and neglected it.   In *Conftantine's* life time, to have fettled *Conftantius* the fame way, had been a duty of good fervice towards God, a mean of peace, and great quietnefs to the church of Chrift ; a labour eafy, and how likely we may conjecture, when after that fo much pains was taken to inftruct and ftrengthen him in the contrary courfe, after that fo much was done by himfelf to the furtherance of herefy, yet being touched in the end voluntarily with remorfe, nothing more grieved him, than the memory of former proceedings in the caufe of religion ; and that which he now forefaw in *Julian*, the next phyfician, into whofe hands the body that was thus diftempered muft fall.   Howbeit, this we may fomewhat excufe, in as much as every man's particular care to his own charge was fuch, as gave them no leifure to heed what others practifed in princes courts.   But of the two fynods of *Arimine* and *Seleucia*, what fhould we think ? *Conftantius*, by the *Arians* fuggeftion, had devifed to affemble all the bifhops of the whole world about this controverfy ; but in two feveral places, the bifhops of the *Weft* at *Arimine* in Italy, the *Eaftern* at *Seleucia* the fame time.   Amongft them of the *Eaft* there was no ftop, they agreed without any great ado, gave their fentence againft herefy, excommunicated fome chief maintainers thereof, and fent the Emperor word what was done.   They had at *Arimine* about four hundred which held the truth, fcarce of the adverfe part four fcore ; but thefe obftinate, and the other weary of contending with them : Whereupon, by both it was refolved to fend to the Emperor fuch as might inform him of the caufe, and declare what hindred their peaceable agreement.   There are chofen for the catholick fide, [a] fuch men as had in them
nothing to be noted but boldnefs, neither gravity, nor learning, nor wifdom.   The *Arians*, for the credit of their faction, take the eldeft, the beft experienced, the moft wary, and the longeft practifed *Veterans* they had amongft them.   The Emperor conjecturing of

[a] *Ex parte noftra leguntur homines adolefcentes, parum docti, parum cauti.   Ab Arianis autem miffi fenes, callidi & ingenio calentes veterano, perfidia imbuti, qui apud Regem facile fuperiores exterunt.* Sulpic. lib. 2.

the reft on either part, by the quality of them whom he faw, fent them fpeedily away, and with them a certain confeffion of faith, [b] ambiguoufly and fubtilly drawn by the *Arians*, whereunto, unlefs they all fubfcribed, they fhould in no cafe be fuffered to depart

[b] *Eifdemque confcripta ab improbis fidem tradit verbis fallentibus involutam, qua Catholicam difciplinam perfidia lente loquetur.* Ib.

from the place where they were.   At length it was perceived, that there had not been in the Catholicks, either at *Arimine*, or at *Seleucia*, fo much forefight, as to provide that true intelligence might pafs between them what was done.   Upon the advantage of which error, their adverfaries abufing each with perfuafion that the other had yielded, furprized both.   The Emperor the more defirous and glad of fuch events, for that, befides all other things wherein they hindred themfelves, the gall and bitternefs of certain mens writings, who fpared him little for honours fake, made him, for their fakes, the lefs inclinable to that truth which he himfelf fhould have honoured and loved.   Only in *Athanafius* there was nothing obferved, throughout the courfe of that long tragedy, other than fuch as very well became a wife man to do, and a righteous to fuffer.   So that this was the plain condition of thofe times.   The whole world againft *Athanafius*, and *Athanafius* againft it : Half an hundred of years fpent in doubtful trial, which of the two, in the end, would prevail, the fide which had all, or elfe the part which had no friend but God and Death ; the one a defender of his innocency, the other a finifher of all his troubles.   Now although thefe contentions were caufe of much evil, yet fome good the church hath reaped by them, in that they occafioned the learned and found in faith to explain fuch things as herefy went about to deprave.   And in this refpect, the Creed of *Athanafius*, firft exhibited unto *Julius*, bifhop of *Rome*, and afterwards (as we may probably gather) fent to the Emperor *Jovinian*, for his more full information concerning that truth which *Arianifm* fo mightily did impugn, was, both in the *Eaft* and the *Weft* churches, accepted as a treafure of ineftimable price, by as many as had not

given

Ταύτω καὶ
ἀναύσιν αἰδέ-
μϕοι ἤ ἐμα-
λογίας ἕλλ⟨⟩ ⟨⟩
ἀσμειαι, ᾗ ⟨⟩
ἰδίας ἴϵσν ἐϵ-
ἀϵιμϖ. Greg.
Nazian. de
Athan.

given up even the very ghoſt of belief. Then was the Creed of *Athanaſius* written, howbeit not then ſo expedient to be publickly uſed, as now in the church of God; becauſe while the heat of diviſion laſteth, truth it ſelf enduring oppoſition, doth not ſo quietly and currently paſs throughout all mens hands, neither can be of that account which afterwards it hath when the world once perceiveth the virtue thereof, not only in it ſelf, but alſo by the conqueſt which God hath given it over hereſy.

That Creed
which in the
book of com-
mon-prayer,
followeth
immediately
after the
reading of
the Goſpel.

That which hereſy did by ſiniſter interpretations go about to pervert, in the firſt and moſt ancient apoſtolical Creed, the ſame being by ſingular dexterity and plainneſs, cleared from thoſe heretical corruptions, partly by this Creed of *Athanaſius*, written about the year three hundred and forty, and partly by that other, ſet down in the ſynod of *Conſtantinople* forty years after, comprehending together with the *Nicene* Creed an addition of other articles which the *Nicene* Creed omitted, becauſe the controverſy then in hand needed no mention to be made of them. Theſe catholick declarations of our belief delivered by them, which were ſo much nearer than we are unto the firſt publication thereof, and continuing needful for all men at all times to know, theſe confeſſions as teſtimonies of our continuance in the ſame faith to this preſent day, we rather uſe than any other gloſs or paraphraſe deviſed by our ſelves, which though it were to the ſame effect

Hilar. Arela.
Epiſt.adAug.

notwithſtanding, could not be of the like authority and credit. For that of *Hilary* unto St. *Auguſtine*, hath been ever, and is likely to be always true. *Your moſt religious wiſdom knoweth, how great their number is of God, whom the very authority of mens names doth keep in that opinion which they hold already,*

1 Cor. 15. 40.
Exod. 33. 18.
Heb. 1. 3.
Matth. 18.
13.

or draw unto that which they have not before held. Touching the hymn of glory, or uſual concluſion to Pſalms, the glory of all things is that wherein their higheſt perfection doth conſiſt; and the glory of God that divine excellency whereby he is eminent above all things, his omnipotent, infinite, and eternal being, which angels and glorified ſaints do intuitively behold; we on earth apprehend principally by faith, in part alſo by that kind of knowledge which groweth from experience of thoſe effects, the greatneſs whereof exceedeth the powers and abilities of all creatures, both in heaven and earth. God is glorified, when ſuch his excellency above all

Joſh. 7. 19.
Pſal. 22. 23.

things is with due admiration acknowledged. Which dutiful acknowledgment of God's excellency, by occaſion of ſpecial effects, being the very proper ſubject, and almoſt the only matter purpoſely treated of in all Pſalms, if that joyful hymn of Glory have any uſe in the church of God, whoſe name we therewith extol and magnify, can we place it more fitly, than where now it ſerveth as a cloſe or concluſion to Pſalms? Neither is the form thereof newly or unneceſſarily invented. *We muſt*

Baſil. Ep. 78.

(ſaith St. Baſil) as we have received, even ſo baptize; and as we baptize, even ſo believe; and as we believe, even ſo give glory. Baptizing, we uſe the name of the Father, of the Son, and of the Holy Ghoſt: Confeſſing the chriſtian faith, we declare our belief in the Father, and in the Son, and in the Holy Ghoſt: Aſcribing Glory unto God, we give it to the Father, and to the Son, and to the Holy Ghoſt. It is ἀπόδειξις τῦ ὀρθᾶ φρονήματ⟨⟩, *the token of a true and ſound underſtanding* for matter of doctrine about the Trinity, when in miniſtring baptiſm, and making confeſſion, and giving glory, there is a conjunction of all three, and no one of the three ſevered from the other two. Againſt the *Arians*, affirming the Father to be greater than the Son in honour, excellency, dignity, majeſty, this form and manner of glorifying God, was not at that time firſt begun, but received long be-

Fœbad. lib.
contr. Arian.

fore, and alledged at that time, as an argument for the truth. *If (ſaith Fœbadius) there be that inequality which they affirm, then do we every day blaſpheme God, when in thankſgivings and offerings of ſacrifice, we acknowledge thoſe things common to the Father and the Son.* The *Arians* therefore, for that they perceived how this did prejudice their cauſe, altered the hymn of glory; whereupon enſued in the

Theod. lib. 1.
cap. 24.
Sozom. lib. 4.
cap. 19.

church of *Antioch*, about the year three hundred forty nine, that jar which *Theodoret* and *Sozomen* mention. *In their Choirs, while they praiſed God together, as the manner was, at the end of the Pſalms which they ſung, it appeared what opinion every man held; foraſmuch as they glorified ſome the Father, and the Son, and the Holy Ghoſt; ſome the Father by the Son, in the Spirit; the one ſort thereby declaring themſelves to embrace the Son's equality with the Father, as the council of Nice had defined; the other ſort againſt the council of Nice his inequality.* *Leontius*, their biſhop, although an enemy to the better part, yet wary and ſubtile, as in a manner all the heads of the *Arians* faction are, could at no time be heard to uſe either form, perhaps, leſt his open contradiction of them whom he favoured

not,

not, might make them the more eager, and by that means the less apt to be privately won; or peradventure for that, though he joined in opinion with that fort of *Arians* who denied the Son to be equal with the Father; yet from them he dissented, which thought the Father and Son, not only unequal, but unlike, as *Aetius* did upon a frivolous and false surmise, that because the apostle hath said, *One God of* **1 Cor. 8. 6.** *whom, one Lord by whom, one Spirit in whom,* his different manner of speech doth **1 Cor. 12. 13,** argue a different nature and being in them, of whom he speaketh. Out of which **4, 13.** blind collection it seemeth, that this their new devised form did first spring. But in truth, even that very form which the *Arians* did then use (saving that they chose it to serve as their special mark of recognisance, and gave it secretly within themselves a sinister construction) hath not otherwise as much as the shew of any thing which soundeth towards impiety. For albeit, if we respect God's glory within it self, it be the equal right and possession of all three, and that without any odds, any difference; yet, touching his manifestation thereof unto us by continual effects, and our perpetual acknowledgment thereof unto him likewise by virtuous offices, doth not every tongue both ways confess, that the brightness of his Glory hath spread it self throughout the world, *by* the ministry of his only begotten Son, and is *in* the manifold Graces of the spirit every way marvellous? Again, that whatsoever we do to his glory, it is done *in* the power of the Holy Ghost, and made acceptable *by* the merit and mediation of Jesus Christ? So that glory to the Father, *and* the Son, or glory to the Father *by* the Son, saving only where evil minds do abuse and pervert holy things, are not else the voices of error and schism, but of sound and sincere religion. It hath been the custom of the church of Christ, to end sometimes prayers, and sermons always, with words of glory; wherein, as long as the blessed Trinity had due honour, and till *Arianism* had made it matter of great sharpness and subtilty of wit, and to be a found believing christian, men were not curious what syllables or particles of speech they used. Upon which confidence and trust notwithstanding, when St. *Basil* began to practise the like indifferency, and to conclude publick prayers, glorifying sometime the Father, with the Son, and the Holy Ghost; sometime the Father, by the Son, in the Spirit; whereas long custom had enured them unto the former kind alone, by means whereof the latter was new and strange in their ears; this needless experiment brought afterwards upon him a necessary labour of excusing himself to his friends, and maintaining his own act against them; who because the light of his candle too much drowned theirs, were glad to lay hold on so colourable matter, and exceeding forward to traduce him, as an author of suspicious innovation. How hath the world forsaken that course which it sometime held? How are the judgments, hearts, and affections of men altered? May we not wonder, that a man of St. *Basil's* authority and quality, an arch-prelate in the house of God, should have his name far and wide called in question, and be driven to his painful apologies, to write in his own defence whole volumes, and yet hardly to obtain with all his endeavour a pardon; the crime laid against him being but only a change of some one or two syllables in their usual church Liturgy? It was thought in him an unpardonable offence to alter any thing, in us as intolerable, that we suffer any thing to remain unaltered. The very Creed of *Athanasius*, and that sacred Hymn of Glory, than which nothing doth sound more heavenly in the ears of faithful men, are now reckoned as superfluities, which we must in any case pare away, left we cloy God with too much service. Is there in that confession of Faith, any thing which doth not at all times edify and instruct the attentive hearer? Or is our faith in the blessed Trinity, a matter needless to be so oftentimes mentioned, and opened in the principal part of that duty which we owe to God, our publick prayer? Hath the church of Christ, from the first beginning, by a secret universal instruction of God's good Spirit, always tied it self to end neither sermon, nor almost any speech of moment which hath concerned matters of God, without some special words of honour and glory to that Trinity which we all adore; and is the like conclusion of Psalms become now at length an eye-sore, or a galling to their ears that hear it? Those flames of *Arianism*, they say, are quenched, which were the cause why the church devised in such sort to confess and praise the glorious Deity of the Son of God. Seeing therefore the sore is whole, why retain we as yet the plaister? When the cause why any thing was ordained doth once cease, the thing it self should cease with it; that the church being eased of unprofitable labours, needful offences may the better be attended. For the doing of things unnecessary, is many times the cause why the most necessary are not done. But in this case so to reason, will not

l   serve ferve their turns. For firſt, the ground whereupon they build is not certainly their own, but with ſpecial limitations: Few things are ſo reſtrained to any one end or purpoſe, that the ſame being extinct, they ſhould forthwith utterly become fruſtrate. Wiſdom may have framed one and the ſame thing, to ſerve commodiouſly for divers ends, and of thoſe ends any one be ſufficient cauſe for continuance, though the reſt have ceaſed; even as the tongue which nature hath given us for an inſtrument of ſpeech, is not idle in dumb perſons, becauſe it alſo ſerveth for taſte. Again, if time have worn out, or any other mean altogether taken away, what was firſt intended; uſes not thought upon before, may afterwards ſpring up, and be reaſonable cauſes of retaining that which other conſiderations did formerly procure to be inſtituted. And it cometh ſometime to paſs, that a thing unneceſſary in it ſelf, as touching the whole direct purpoſe whereunto it was meant, or can be applied, doth notwithſtanding appear convenient to be ſtill held, even without uſe, left by reaſon of that coherence which it hath with ſomewhat moſt neceſſary, the removal of the one ſhould indamage the other. And therefore men which have clean loſt the poſſibility of ſight, keep ſtill their eyes nevertheleſs in the place where nature ſet them. As for theſe two branches whereof our queſtion groweth, Arianiſm was indeed ſome occaſion of the one, but a cauſe of neither, much leſs the only entire cauſe of both. For albeit conflict with Arians brought forth the occaſion of writing that Creed, which long after was made a part of the church Liturgy, as hymns and ſentences of glory were a part thereof before; yet cauſe ſufficient there is, why both ſhould remain in uſe, the one as a moſt divine explication of the chiefeſt articles of our chriſtian belief, the other as an heavenly acclamation of joyful applauſe to his praiſes in whom we believe; neither the one nor the other unworthy to be heard ſounding as they are in the church of Chriſt, whether Arianiſm live or die. Againſt which poiſon likewiſe, if we think that the church, at this day, needeth not thoſe ancient preſervatives which ages before us were ſo glad to uſe, we deceive our ſelves greatly. The weeds of hereſy being grown unto ſuch ripeneſs as that was, do, even in the very cutting down, ſcatter oftentimes thoſe ſeeds, which for a while lie unſeen and buried in the earth, but afterward freſhly ſpring up again, no leſs pernicious than at the firſt. Which thing they very well know, and I doubt not will eaſily confeſs, who live to their great, both toil and grief, where the blaſphemies of Arians, Samoſatenians, Tritheits, Eutychians and Macedonians, are renewed by them, who to hatch their hereſy, have choſen thoſe churches as fitteſt neſts, where Athanaſius's Creed is not heard; by them, I ſay, renewed, who following the courſe of extream reformation, were wont, in the pride of their own proceedings, to glory that whereas Luther did but blow away the Roof, and Zuinglius batter but the walls of popiſh ſuperſtition, the laſt and hardeſt work of all remained, which was to raze up the very ground and foundation of popery, that doctrine concerning the Deity of Chriſt, which Satanaſius (for ſo it pleaſed thoſe impious forſaken miſcreants to ſpeak) hath in this memorable Creed explained. So mani-

Fuibad. contra Ar. feſtly true is that which one of the ancients hath concerning Arianiſm, Mortuis authoribus hujus veneni, ſcelerata tamen eorum doctrina non moritur. The authors of this venom being dead and gone, their wicked doctrine notwithſtanding continueth.

Our want of particular thankſgiving.

As ſuch prayers are needful, whereby we beg releaſe from our diſtreſſes, ſo there ought to be as neceſſary prayers of thankſgiving, when we have received thoſe things at the Lord's hand which we aſked, T. C. l. 1. p. 158. I do not ſimply require a ſolemn and expreſs thankſgiving for ſuch benefits; but only upon a ſuppoſition, which is, that if it be expedient that there ſhould be expreſs prayers againſt ſo many of their earthly miſeries, that then alſo it is meet that upon the deliverance there ſhould be an expreſs thankſgiving. T. C. l. 3. p. 209.

43. Amongſt the heaps of theſe exceſſes and ſuperfluities, there is eſpied the want of a principal part of duty, *There are no thankſgivings for the benefits for which there are petitions in our book of prayer.* This they have thought a point material to be objected. Neither may we take it in evil part to be admoniſhed, what ſpecial duties of thankfulneſs we owe to that merciful God, for whoſe unſpeakable graces the only requital we are able to make, is a true, hearty, and ſincere acknowledgment how precious we eſteem ſuch benefits received, and how infinite in goodneſs the author from whom they come. But that to every petition we make for things needful, there ſhould be ſome anſwerable ſentences of thanks provided, particularly to follow ſuch requeſts obtained; either it is not a matter ſo requiſite as they pretend; or if it be, wherefore have they not then in ſuch order framed their

own

own book of common-prayer? Why hath our Lord and Saviour taught us a form of prayer, containing so many petitions of those things which we want, and not delivered in like sort as many several forms of thankfgiving to serve when any thing we pray for is granted? What answer soever they can reasonably make unto these demands, the same shall discover unto them how causeless a censure it is, that there are not in our book thankfgivings for all the benefits for which there are petitions. For concerning the blessings of God, whether they tend unto this life, or the life to come, there is great cause why we should delight more in giving thanks, than in making requests for them, in as much as the one

The default of the Book, for that there are no forms of thankfgiving for the release from those common calamities from which we have petitions to be delivered. T. C. l. 3. p. 208.

hath pensiveness and fear, the other always joy annexed; the one belongeth unto them that seek, the other unto them that have found happiness; they that pray do but yet sow, they that give thanks, declare they have reaped. Howbeit, because there are so many graces, whereof we stand in continual need, graces for which we may not cease daily and hourly to sue, graces which are in bestowing always, but never come to be fully had in this present life; and therefore, when all things here have an end, endless thanks must have their beginning in a state which bringeth the full and final satisfaction of all such perpetual desires. Again, because our common necessities, and the lack which we all have, as well of ghostly as of earthly favours, is in each kind so easily known; but the gifts of God, according to those degrees and times which he in his secret wisdom seeth meet, are so diversly bestowed, that it seldom appeareth what all receive, what all stand in need of it seldom lieth hid; we are not to marvel, though the church do oftner concur in suits, than in thanks unto God for particular benefits. Nevertheless, left God should be any way unglorified, the greatest part of our daily service, they know, confisteth according to the blessed apostle's own precise rule, in much variety of Psalms and Hymns, for no other purpose, but only that out of so plentiful a treasure, there might be for every man's heart to chuse out his own sacrifice, and to offer unto God by particular secret instinct, what fitteth best the often occasions which any several either party or congregation may seem to have. They that would clean take from us therefore the daily use of the very best means we have to magnify and praise the name of Almighty God for his rich blessings, they that complain of our reading and singing so many Psalms for so good an end; they, I say, that find fault with our store, should of all men be least willing to reprove our scarcity of thankfgiving. But because peradventure they see, it is not either generally fit or possible that churches should frame thankfgivings answerable to each petition, they shorten somewhat the reins of their censure; there are no forms of thankfgiving, they say, for release of those common calamities from which we have petitions to be delivered. *There are prayers set forth to be said in the common calamities and universal scourges of the realm, as plague, famine, &c. And indeed so it ought to be by the word of God. But as such prayers are needful,* whereby we beg release from our distresses, so there ought to be as necessary prayers of thankfgiving, when we have received those things at the Lord's hands which we asked in our prayers. As oft therefore as any publick or universal scourge is removed, as oft as we are delivered from these, either imminent or present calamities, against the storm and tempest whereof we all instantly craved favour from above, let it be a question what we should render unto God for his blessings universally, sensibly and extraordinarily bestowed. A prayer of three or four lines inserted into some part of our church-liturgy? No, we are not perfuaded that when God doth in trouble enjoin us the duty of invocation, and promise us the benefit of deliverance, and profess that the thing he expecteth after at our hands, is to gratify him as our mighty and only Saviour, the church can discharge in manner convenient, a work of so great importance, by fore-ordaining some short collect wherein briefly to mention thanks. Our custom therefore, whensoever so great occasions are incident, is by publick authority to appoint throughout all churches, set and solemn forms as well of supplication and of thankfgiving, the preparations and intended complements whereof may stir up the minds of men in much more effectual sort, than if only there should be added to the book of prayer that which they require. But we err in thinking that they require any such matter. For albeit their words to our understanding be very plain, that in our book *there are prayers set forth*, to be said when *common calamities* are felt, as *plagues, famine,* and such like: Again, that

Ephes. 5. 9. Colos. 3. 16.

T. C. l. 1. P. 138.

A a   *indeed*

indeed *so it ought to be by the word of God:* That likewise *there ought to be as ne-cessary prayers of thanksgiving, when we have received those things:* Finally, that the want of such forms of thanksgiving for the release from those common calami-ties from which we have petitions to be deliver'd, is the *default of the book of com-mon prayer:* Yet all this they mean, but only by way of *supposition, if express pray-ers* against so many earthly miseries were convenient, that then indeed as many ex-press and particular thanksgivings should be likewise necessary. Seeing therefore we know that they hold the one superfluous, they would not have it so understood, as though their minds were that any such addition to the book is needful, whatsoever they say for arguments sake concerning this pretended defect. The truth is, they wave in and out, no way sufficiently grounded, no way resolved what to think, speak, or write, more than only that because they have taken it upon them, they must (no remedy now) be opposite.

In some things the matter of our prayer, as they affirm, unfound.

44. The last supposed fault concerneth some few things, the very matter whereof is thought to be much amiss. In a song of praise to our Lord Jesus Christ we have these words, *When thou hadst overcome the sharpness of death, thou didst open the kingdom of heaven to all believers.* Which maketh some shew of giving coun-tenance to their error, who think that the faithful which departed this life before the coming of Christ, were never till then made partakers of joy, but remained all in that place which they term the *Lake of the Fathers.* In our Liturgy request is made, that we may be preserved *from sudden death.* This seemeth frivolous, be-cause the godly should always be prepared to die. Request is made, that God would give those things which we for our unworthiness dare not ask. *This,* they say, carrieth with it the note of popish servile fear, *and favoureth not of that confidence and reverent familiarity that the of children God have through Christ, with their heavenly father.* Request is made, that we may evermore be defended from all adversity. For this *there is no promise in scripture;* and therefore *it is no prayer of faith, or of the which we can assure our selves that we shall obtain it.* Finally, request is made, that God *would have mercy upon all men.* This is im-possible, because some are vessels of wrath, to whom God will never extend his Mercy.

When thou hadst over-come the sharpness of death, thou didst open the kingdom of Heaven unto all be-lievers.

45. As Christ hath purchased that heavenly kingdom, the last perfection whereof is *glory in the life to come,* grace in this life a preparation thereunto; so the same he hath opened to the world in such sort, that whereas none can possibly without him attain salvation, by him *all that believe* are saved. Now whatsoever he did or suffered, the end thereof was to open the doors of the kingdom of heaven, which our iniquities had shut up. But because by *ascending after that the sharpness of death* was overcome, he took the very *local possession* of glory, and that *to the use of all that are his,* even as himself before had witnessed, *I go to prepare a place for you;* and again, *Whom thou hast given me, O Father, I will that where I*

John 14. 2. & 17. 24.

am, they be also with me, that my glory which thou hast given me, they may be-hold: It appeareth, that *when Christ did ascend,* he then most *liberally opened* the kingdom of Heaven, *to the end,* that with him, and by him, all believers might reign. In what estate the fathers rested which were dead before, it is not here-by either one way or other determined. All that we can rightly gather is, that as touching their souls, what degree of joy or happiness soever it pleased God to be-stow upon them, *his ascension* which succeeded *procured* theirs, and theirs concern-

Hieron. contra Helvid. August. Hær. 84.

ing the body must needs be *not only of,* but after his. As therefore *Helvidius,* against whom St. *Jerome* writeth, abused greatly those words of *Matthew* con-cerning *Joseph,* and the mother of our Saviour Christ, *He knew her not, till she had brought forth her first-born,* thereby gathering against the honour of the blessed Virgin, that a thing denied with special circumstance, doth import an opposite affirmation when once that circumstance is expired: after the self-same manner it should be a weak collection, if whereas we say, that when Christ had *overcome the sharpness of death,* he then *opened the kingdom of Heaven to all believers;* a thing in such sort affirmed with circumstance, were taken as insinuating an opposite denial before that circumstance be accomplished, and consequently, that because when the sharpness of death was overcome, he then opened Heaven *as well to believing Gentiles as Jews,* Heaven till then was no receptacle to the souls of either. Wherefore, be the spirits of the just and righteous before Christ, truly or falsly thought excluded out of Heavenly joy, by that which we in the words alledged before do attribute to Christ's ascension,

there

there is to no such opinion, nor to the favourers thereof, any countenance at all given. We cannot better interpret the meaning of these words, than Pope *Leo* himself expoundeth them, whose speech concerning our Lord's ascension, may serve instead of a marginal gloss, *Christ's exaltation is our promotion; and whither the glory of the head is already gone before, thither the hope of the body also is to follow. For at this day, we have not only the possession of paradise assured unto us, but in Christ we have entred the highest of the heavens.* His *opening the kingdom of heaven,* and his entrance thereunto, was not only to his own use, but for the benefit of all believers.

46. Our good or evil estate after death, dependeth most upon the quality of our lives. Yet somewhat there is, why a virtuous mind should rather wish to depart this world with a kind of treatable dissolution, than to be suddenly cut off in a moment; rather to be taken, than snatch'd away from the face of the earth. Death is that which all men suffer, but not all men with one mind, neither all men in one manner. For being of necessity a thing common, it is through the manifold persuasions, dispositions, and occasions of men, with equal deserts both of praise and dispraise, shunned by some, by others desired. So that absolutely we cannot discommend, we cannot absolutely approve either willingness to live, or forwardness to die. And concerning the ways of death, albeit the choice thereof be only in his hands, who alone hath the power of all flesh, and unto whose appointment we ought with patience meekly to submit our selves (for to be agents voluntarily in our own destruction, is against both God and nature) yet there is no doubt, but in so great variety our desires will and may lawfully prefer one kind before another. Is there any man of worth and virtue, although not instructed in the school of Christ, or ever taught what the soundness of Religion meaneth, that had not rather end the days of this transitory life as *Cyrus* in *Xenophon,* or in *Plato Socrates* are described, than to sink down with them of whom *Elihu* hath said *Momento moriuntur,* there is scarce an instant between their flourishing and their not being? But let us which know what it is to die as *Absalon,* or *Ananias* and *Saphira* died; let us beg of God, that when the hour of our rest is come, the patterns of our dissolution may be *Jacob, Moses, Joshua, David;* who leisurably ending their lives in peace, prayed for the mercies of God to come upon their posterity; replenished the hearts of the nearest unto them, with words of memorable consolation; strengthned men in the fear of God, gave them wholesome instructions of life, and confirmed them in true religion; in sum, taught the world no less vertuously how to die, than they had done before how to live. To such as judge things according to the sense of natural men, and ascend no higher, suddenness, because it shortneth their grief, should in reason be most acceptable. That which causeth bitterness in death, is the languishing attendance and expectation thereof ere it come. And therefore tyrants use what art they can to increase the slowness of death. Quick riddance out of life, is often both requested and bestowed as a benefit. Commonly therefore it is, for vertuous considerations, that wisdom so far prevaileth with men, as to make them desirous of slow and deliberate death, against the stream of their sensual inclination, content to endure the longer grief and bodily pain, that the soul may have time to call it self to a just account of all things past, by means whereof repentance is perfected, there is wherein to exercise patience, the joys of the kingdom of heaven have leisure to present themselves, the pleasures of sin and this world's vanities are censured with uncorrupt judgment, charity is free to make advised choice of the soil wherein her last seed may most fruitfully be bestowed, the mind is at liberty to have due regard of that disposition of worldly things, which it can never afterwards alter; and because the nearer we draw unto God, the more we are oftentimes enlightned with the shining beams of his glorious presence, as being then even almost in sight, a leisurable departure may in that case bring forth for the good of such as are present, that which shall cause them for ever after from the bottom of their hearts to pray, *O let us die the death of the righteous, and let our last end be like theirs.* All which benefits and opportunities are by sudden death prevented. And besides, for as much as death howsoever is a general effect of the wrath of God against sin, and the suddenness thereof a thing which hapneth but to few; the world in this respect feareth it the more, as being subject to doubtful constructions, which as no man willingly would incur, so they whose happy estate after life is of all mens the most certain, should especially wish that no such accident in their death may give uncharitable minds occasion of rash, sinister,

Lyr. super Gen. 19. Th. p. 3. q.

Leo. Ser. 1. de Ascens.

Touching prayer for deliverance from sudden death.

Job 34. 20.

Heb. 11. 21. Deut. 33. Josh. 24. 1 Kings 2.

Cypr. de Mortal.

ſter, and ſuſpicious verdicts whereunto they are over-prone. So that whether evil men or good be reſpected, whether we regard our ſelves or others, to be preſerved *from ſudden death*, is a bleſſing of God. And our prayer againſt it importeth a two-fold deſire ; firſt, that death when it cometh may give us ſome convenient reſpite ; or ſecondly, if that be denied us of God, yet we may have wiſdom to provide always beforehand ; that thoſe evils overtake us not, which death unexpected doth uſe to bring upon careleſs men ; and that although it be ſudden in it ſelf, nevertheleſs in regard of our prepared minds, it may not be ſudden.

47. But is it credible that the very acknowledg-ment of our own unworthineſs to obtain, and in that reſpect our profeſſed fearfulneſs to ask any thing, otherwiſe than only for his ſake to whom God can deny nothing, that this ſhould be termed baſeneſs, abjection of mind, or ſer-vility, is it credible ? That which we for our unworthineſs are afraid to crave, our prayer is, that God for the worthineſs of his Son would notwithſtanding vouchſafe to grant. May it pleaſe them to ſhew us which of theſe words it is that carrieth the note of popiſh and ſervile fear ? In reference to other creatures of this inferior world, man's worth and excellency is admired. Com-pared with God, the trueſt inſcription wherewith we can circle ſo baſe a coin is that of *David, Univerſa vanitas eſt omnis homo* ; whoſoever hath the name of a mortal man, there is in him whatſoever the name of vanity doth comprehend. And there-fore what we ſay of our own unworthineſs, there is no doubt but truth will ratify ; alledged in prayer, it both becometh and behoveth ſaints. For as humility is in ſui-ters a decent virtue ; ſo the teſtification thereof by ſuch effectual acknowledgments, not only argueth a ſound apprehenſion of his ſuper-eminent glory and majeſty before whom we ſtand, but putteth alſo into his hands a kind of pledge or bond for ſecurity againſt our unthankfulneſs, the very natural root whereof is always either ignorance, diſſimulation, or pride. Ignorance, when we know not the author from whom our good cometh : diſſimulation, when our hands are more open than our eyes upon that we receive : pride, when we think our ſelves worthy of that which mere grace and undeſerved mercy beſtoweth. In prayer therefore, to abate ſo vain imaginations with the *true conceit of unworthineſs*, is rather to prevent than commit a fault. It being no error thus to think, no fault thus to ſpeak of our ſelves when we pray ; is it a fault, that the conſideration of our unworthineſs maketh us fearful to open our mouths by way of ſuit ? While *Job* had proſperity and lived in honour, men feared him for his authorities ſake, and in token of their fear, when they ſaw him, *they hid themſelves*. Between *Elihu* and the reſt of *Job*'s familiars, the greateſt diſparity was but in years. And he, though riper than they in judg-ment, doing them reverence in regard of age, ſtood long * *doubtful* and very loth to adven-ture upon ſpeech in his elders hearing. If ſo ſmall inequality between man and man make their modeſty a commendable virtue, who reſpecting ſuperiors, *as ſupe-riors*, can neither ſpeak nor ſtand before them without fear ; that the publican ap-proacheth not more boldly to God ; that when Chriſt in mercy draweth near to *Pe-ter*, he in humility and fear craveth diſtance : That being to ſtand, to ſpeak, to ſue in the preſence of ſo great majeſty, we are afraid, let no man blame us. In which conſiderati-on notwithſtanding, becauſe to fly altogether from God, to deſpair that creatures unworthy ſhall be able to obtain any thing at his hands, and under that pretence to ſurceaſe from prayers as bootleſs or fruitleſs offices, were to him no leſs injurious than pernicious to our own ſouls ; even that which we tremble to do, we do, we ask thoſe things which we dare not ask. The know-ledge of our own unworthineſs is not without belief in the merits of Chriſt. With that true fear which the one cauſeth, there is coupled true boldneſs ; and encourage-ment drawn from the other. The very ſilence which our unworthineſs putteth us unto, doth it ſelf make requeſt for us, and that in the confidence of his grace. Look-ing inward we are ſtricken dumb ; looking upward, we ſpeak and prevail. O happy mixture, wherein things contrary do ſo qualify and correct the one the danger of the others exceſs, that neither boldneſs can make us preſume, as long as we are kept under

with

Prayer that thoſe things which we for our unworthineſs dare not ask, God, for the worthineſs of his Son, would vouchſafe to grant.
This requeſt carrieth with it ſtill the note of the popiſh ſervile fear, and favoureth not of that confidence and reve-rent familiarity that the children of God have, through Chriſt, with their Heavenly father. *T. C. l.* 1. *p.* 136.

Pſal. 39. 5.

[Greek text] *Phil. de Sa-crif. Abel. & Cain.*

Job 29. 8. Amongſt the parts of honour *Ariſtotle* reckon-eth [Greek] and [Greek]. *Rhet. l.* 1. *c.* 5.

* Job 32. 6.

The Publican did indeed not lift up his eyes. So that if by his example we ſhould ſay, we dare ask nothing, we ought alſo to ask nothing ; otherwiſe inſtead of teaching true humility, we open a ſchool to hypocriſy, which the Lord deteſteth. *T. C. l.* 3. *p.* 203.

with the senfe of our own wretchedneſs; nor, while we truſt in the mercy of God through Jeſus Chriſt, fear be able to tyrannize over us! As therefore our fear excludeth not that boldneſs which becometh faints; ſo if our familiarity with God do not favour of this fear, it draweth too near that irreverent confidence wherewith true humility can never ſtand.

Rom. 5. 2, 8,
15.
Heb. 10. 19.

48. Touching continual deliverance in the world from all adverſity, their conceit is that we ought not to ask it of God by prayer, for as much as in ſcripture there is no promiſe that we ſhall be evermore free from vexations, calamities, and troubles. Minds religiouſly affected are wont in every thing of weight and moment, which they do or ſee, to examine

Prayer to be evermore delivered from all adverſity.

For as much as there is no promiſe in the ſcripture, that we ſhould be free from all adverſity, and that evermore; it ſeemeth that this prayer might have been better conceived, being no prayer of faith, or of the which we can aſſure our ſelves that we ſhall obtain it. *T. C. l.* 1. p. 136.

according unto rules of piety, what dependency it hath on God, what reference to themſelves, what coherence with any of thoſe duties whereunto all things in the world ſhould lead, and accordingly they frame the inward diſpoſition of their minds, ſometime to admire God, ſometime to bleſs him and give him thanks, ſometime to exult in his love, ſometime to implore his mercy. All which different elevations of ſpirit unto God are contained in the name of prayer. Every good and holy deſire, though it lack the form, hath notwithſtanding in it ſelf the ſubſtance, and with him the force of a prayer, who regardeth the very moanings, groans and ſighs of the heart of man. Petitionary prayer belongeth only to ſuch as are in themſelves impotent and ſtand in need of relief from others. We thereby declare unto God what our own deſire is, that he by his power ſhould effect. It preſuppoſeth therefore in us, firſt, the want of that which we pray for: Secondly, a feeling of that want: Thirdly, an earneſt willingneſs of mind to be eaſed therein: Fourthly, a declaration of this our deſire in the ſight of God; not as if he ſhould be otherwiſe ignorant of our neceſſities, but becauſe we this way ſhew we honour him as our God, and are verily perſuaded that no good thing can come to paſs which he by his omnipotent power effecteth not. Now becauſe there is no man's prayer acceptable whoſe perſon is odious, neither any man's perſon gracious without faith; it is of neceſſity required that they which pray, do believe. The prayers which our Lord and Saviour made were for his own worthineſs accepted; ours God accepteth not but with this condition, if they be joined with belief in Chriſt. The prayers of the juſt are accepted always, but not always thoſe things granted for which they pray. For in prayer, if faith and aſſurance to obtain were both one and the ſame thing, ſeeing that the effect of not obtaining is a plain teſtimony that they which pray were not ſure they ſhould obtain, it would follow, that their prayer being without certainty of the event, was alſo made unto God without faith, and conſequently that God abhorred it. Which to think of ſo many prayers of ſaints as we find have failed in particular requeſts, how abſurd were it? His faithful people have this comfort, that whatſoever they rightly ask, the ſame (no doubt, but) they ſhall receive, ſo far as may ſtand with the glory of God and their own everlaſting good; unto either of which two, it is no virtuous man's purpoſe to ſeek, or deſire to obtain any thing prejudicial; and therefore that clauſe which our Lord and Saviour in the prayer of his agony did expreſs, we in petitions of like nature do always imply; *Pater, ſi poſſibile eſt,* if it may ſtand with thy will and pleaſure. Or if not, but that there be ſecret impediments and cauſes, in regard whereof the thing we pray for is denied us; yet the prayer it ſelf which we make is a pleaſing ſacrifice to God, who both accepteth and rewardeth it ſome other way. So that ſinners, in very truth, are denied when they ſeem to prevail in their ſupplications, becauſe it is not for their ſakes, or to their good that their ſuits takes place; the faithful contrariwiſe, becauſe it is for their good oftentimes that their petitions do not take place, prevail even then when they moſt ſeem denied. *Our Lord God in anger hath granted ſome impenitent men's requeſts; as on the other ſide the apoſtles ſuit he hath of favour and mercy not granted* (faith St. *Auguſtin.*) To think we may pray unto God for nothing but what he hath promiſed in holy ſcripture we ſhall obtain, is perhaps an error. For of prayer there are two uſes. It ſerveth as a mean to procure thoſe things which God hath promiſed to grant when we ask; and it ſerveth as a mean to expreſs our lawful deſires alſo towards that, which whether we ſhall have or no we know not, till we ſee the event. Things in themſelves unholy

Oratio, quæ non fit per Chriſtum, non ſolum non poteſt delere peccatum, ſed etiam ipſa fit peccatum. Aug. Enar. 1. in Pſal. 108.

Numb. 11. 33.
1 Sam. 8. 7.
Job 1. 12. &
2. 6.
Luke 8. 32.
2 Cor. 12. 7.
8, 9.
Aug. Ep. 121.
Ad Probam
viduam.

holy or unseemly, we may not ask; we may whatsoever being not forbidden, either nature or grace shall reasonably move us to wish, as importing the good of men; albeit God himself have no where by promise assured us of that particular which our prayer craveth. To pray for that which is in it self, and of its own nature, apparently a thing impossible, were not convenient. Wherefore, though men do, without offence, wish daily that the affairs which with evil success are past, might have fallen out much better; yet to pray that they may have been any other than they are, this being a manifest impossibility in it self, the rules of religion do not permit. Whereas contrariwise, when things of their own nature contingent and mutable, are by the secret determination of God appointed one way, though we the other way make our prayers, and consequently ask those things of God, which are by this supposition impossible, we notwithstanding do not hereby in prayer transgress our lawful bounds. That Christ, as the only begotten Son of God, having no superior, and therefore owing honour unto none, neither standing in any need, should either give thanks, or make petition unto God, were most absurd. As man, what could beseem him better, whether we respect his affection to Godward, or his own necessity, or his charity and love towards men? Some things he knew should come to pass, and notwithstanding prayed for them, because he also knew that the necessary means to effect them were his prayers. As in the

Psal. 2. 8. *Psalm* it is said, *Ask of me, and I will give thee the heathen for thine inheritance, and the ends of the earth for thy possession.* Wherefore, that which here God pro-

John 17. 1, 2. miseth his Son, the same in the seventeenth of *John* he prayeth for, *Father, the hour is come, glorify thy Son, that thy Son also may glorify thee, according as thou hast given him power over all flesh.* But had Christ the like promise concerning the effect of every particular for which he prayed? That which was not effected, could

Matth. 26. 39. Mark 14. 36. 'Luke 22. 42. Neither did our Saviour Christ pray without promise; for as other the children of God, to whose condition he had humbled himself have, so had he a promise of deliverance, so far as the glory of God in that accomplishment of his vocation would suffer. *T. C. l. 3. p. 200.*

not be promised. And we know in what sort he prayed for removal of that bitter cup, which cup he tasted, notwithstanding his prayer. To shift off this example, they answer first, *That as other children of God, so Christ had a promise of deliverance, as far as the glory of God in the accomplishment of his vocation*

would suffer. And if we our selves have not also in that sort the promise of God to be evermore delivered from all adversity, what meaneth the sacred scripture to

Deut. 30. 9. speak in so large terms, *Be obedient, and the Lord thy God will make thee plenteous in every work of thy hand, in the fruit of thy body, and in the fruit of thy cattle, and in the fruit of the land for thy wealth.* Again, *Keep his laws, and thou shalt be blest above all people, the Lord shall take from thee all infirmities.* The

Deut. 7. 15. Psal. 1. 4. man whose delight is in the law of God, *whatsoever he doth, it shall prosper.* For the ungodly there are *great plagues* remaining; but whosoever putteth his trust in

Psal. 32. 11, 17. the Lord, mercy embraceth him *on every side.* Not only that mercy which keepeth from being overlaid or opprest'd, but mercy which saveth from being touched with grievous miseries, mercy which turneth away the course of *the great water floods,*

T. C. l. 3. p. 201. and permitteth them not to *come near.* Nevertheless, because the prayer of Christ did concern but one calamity, they are still bold to deny the lawfulness of our prayer for deliverance out of all, yea, though we pray with the same exception that he did, *If such deliverance may stand with the pleasure of Almighty God, and not otherwise.* For they have, secondly, found out a rule, that prayer ought only to be made for deliverance *from this or that particular adversity, whereof we know not,*

We ought not to desire to be free from all adversity, if it be his will, considering that he hath already declared his will therein. T. C. l. 3. p. 201. but upon the event, what the pleasure of God is. Which quite overthroweth that other principle, wherein they require unto every prayer which is of faith, an assurance to obtain the thing we pray for. At the first to pray against all adversity was unlawful, because we cannot assure our selves that this will be granted. Now we have licence to pray against any particular adversity, and the reason given, because we know not but upon the event what God will do. If we know not what God will do, it followeth, that for any assurance we have, he may do otherwise than we pray, and we may faithfully pray for that which we cannot assuredly presume that God will grant. Seeing therefore neither of these two answers will serve the turn, they have a third; which is, that to pray in such sort, is but misspent labour, because God hath already revealed his will touching this request; and we know that the suit we make is denied, before we make it. Which neither is

2   true,

true, and if it were, was Christ ignorant what God had determined touching those things which himself should suffer? To say, *He knew not what we ght* T. C. l. 3. *of sufferances his heavenly Father had measured unto him*, is somewhat hard; har- *p. 201.* der, that although *he knew them*, notwithstanding for the present time *they were forgotten through the force of those unspeakable pangs, which he then was in.* The one against the plain express words of the holy Evangelist, *He knew all* John 18. 4. *things that should come upon him*; the other less credible, if any thing ma y be of less credit than what the scripture it self gainsayeth. Doth any of them w hich wrote his sufferings, make report that memory failed him? Is there in his w ords and speeches any sign of defect that way? Did not himself declare b efore whatsoever was to happen in the course of that whole tragedy? Can we g ather by any thing after taken from his own mouth, either in the place of publick judgment, or upon the altar of the cross, that through the bruising of his body some part of the treasures of his soul were scattered and slipt from him? If that which was perfect both before and after did fail at this only middle instant, there must appear some manifest cause how it came to pass. True it is, that the pangs of his heaviness and grief were unspeakable; and as true, that because the minds of the afflicted do never think they have fully conceived the weight or measure of their own woe, they use their affection as a whetstone both to wit and memory; these as Nurses, do feed grief, so that the weaker his conceit had been touching that which he was to suffer, the more it must needs in that hour have helped to the mitigation of his anguish. But his anguish we see was then at the very highest whereunto it could possibly rise; which argueth his deep apprehension, even to the last drop of gall which that cup contained, and of every circumstance wherein there was any force to augment heaviness; but above all, things, the resolute determination of God and his own unchangeable purpose, which he at that time could not forget. To what intent then was his prayer, which plainly testifieth so great willingness to avoid death? Will, whether it be in God or man, belongeth to the essence or nature of both. The nature therefore of God being one, there are not in God divers wills, although the God-head be in divers persons, because the power of willing is a natural, not a personal propriety. Contrariwise, the Person of our Saviour Christ being but one, there are in him two wills; because two natures, the nature of God, and the nature of man, which both do imply this faculty and power. So that in Christ there is a divine, and there is an human will, otherwise he were not both God and man. Hereupon the church hath of old condemned *Monothelites* as Hereticks, for holding that Christ had but one will. The works and operations of our Saviour's human will were all subject to the will of God, and framed according to his law, *I desire to do thy will, O God, and thy law is within mine heart.* Now as Psal. 40. , man's will, so the will of Christ hath two several kinds of operation, the one natural or necessary, whereby it desireth simply whatsoever is good in it self, and shunneth as generally all things which hurt; the other deliberate, when we therefore embrace things as good, because the eye of understanding judgeth them good to that end which we simply desire. Thus in it self we desire health, physick only for health's sake. And in this sort special reason often times causeth the will by choice to prefer one good thing before another, to leave one for another's sake, to forego meaner for the attainment of higher desires, which our Saviour likewise did. These different inclinations of the will considered, the reason is easy, how in Christ there might grow desires seeming, but not indeed opposite, either the one of them unto the other, or either of them to the will of God. For let the manner of his speech be weighed, *My soul is* John 12. 27, *now troubled, and what shall I say? Father, save me out of this hour. But yet for this very cause I am come unto this hour.* His purpose herein was most effectually to propose to the view of the whole world two contrary objects, the like whereunto in force and efficacy were never presented in that manner to any, but only to the soul of Christ. There was presented before his eyes in that fearful hour, on the one side God's heavy indignation and wrath towards Mankind as yet unappeased, death as yet in full strength, hell as yet never mastered by any that came within the confines and bounds thereof, somewhat also peradventure more than is either possible or needful for the wit of

man

4.

ª Matth. 27. 46. *Non potuit divinitas humanitatem & se-*
cundum aliquid deseruisse, & secundum aliquid non deseruisse?
Subtraxit protectionem, sed non separavit unionem. Sic ergo dere-
liquit ut non adjuvaret, sed non dereliquit ut recederet. Sic ergo
humanitas à divinitate in passione derelicta est. Quam tamen
mortem quia non pro sua iniquitate, sed pro nostra redemptione susti-
nuit, quare sit derelicta requirit, non quasi adversus Deum, de pœ-
na murmurans, sed nobis innocentiam suam in pœna demonstrans.
Hug. de sacra. lib. 2. part. 1. cap. 10. *Deus meus, utquid*
dereliquisti me? Vox est nec ignorantia, nec diffidentia, nec quere-
lœ, sed admirationis tantum, quœ aliis investiganda causa ardorem
& diligentiam acuat.

man to find out; finally, himself flesh and blood ª left alone to enter into conflict with all these: On the other side, a world to be saved by one, a pacification of wrath through the dignity of that sacrifice which should be offered, a conquest over death through the power of that Deity which would not suffer the tabernacle thereof to see corruption, and an utter disappointment of all the forces of infernal powers, through the purity of that soul which they should have in their hands and not be able to touch. Let no man marvel that in this case the soul of Christ was much troubled. For what could such apprehensions breed, but (as their nature is) inexplicable passions of mind, desires abhorring what they embrace, and embracing what they abhor? In which agony, *how should the tongue go about to express what the soul endured?* When the griefs of *Job* were exceeding great, his words accordingly to open them were many; howbeit, still unto his seeming they were undiscovered: *Though my talk (saith Job) be this day in bitterness, yet my plague is greater than my groaning.* But here to what purpose should words serve, when nature hath more to declare than groans and strong cries, more than streams of bloody sweats, more than his doubled and tripled prayers can express, who thrice putting forth his hand to receive the cup, besides which there was no other cause of his coming into the world, he thrice pulleth it back again, and as often even with tears of blood craveth, *If it be possible, O Father, or if not, even what thine own good pleasure is*; for whose sake the passion, that hath in it a bitter and a bloody conflict even with wrath and death and hell, is most welcome. Whereas therefore we find in God a will resolved that Christ shall suffer; and in the human will of Christ two actual desires; the one avoiding, and the other accepting death; is that desire which first declareth it self by prayer, against that wherewith he concludeth prayer, or either of them against his mind to whom prayer in this case seeketh? We may judge of these diversities in the will, by the like in the understanding. For as the intellectual part doth not cross it self, by conceiving man to be just and unjust, when it meaneth not the same man, nor by imagining the same man learned and unlearned, if learned in one skill, and in another kind of learning unskilful, because the parts of every true opposition do always both concern the same subject, and have reference to the same thing, sith otherwise they are but in shew opposite, and not in truth: So the will about one and the same thing may in contrary respects have contrary inclinations, and that without contrariety. The minister of justice may, for publick example to others, virtuously will the execution of that party whose pardon another for consanguinities sake as virtuously may desire. Consider death in it self, and nature teacheth Christ to shun it. Consider death as a mean to procure the salvation of the world, and mercy worketh in Christ all willingness of mind towards it. Therefore in these two desires there can be no repugnant opposition. Again, compare them with the will of God, and if any opposition be, it must be only between his appointment of Christ's death and the former desire which wisheth deliverance from death. But neither is this desire opposite to the will of God. The will of God was, that Christ should suffer the pains of death. Not so his will, as if the torment of innocency did in it self please and delight God, but such was his will, in regard of the end whereunto it was necessary, that Christ should suffer. The death of Christ in it self therefore, God willeth not, which to the end we might thereby obtain life, he both alloweth and appointeth. In like manner, the Son of man endureth willingly to that purpose those grievous pains, which simply not to have shunned had been against nature, and by consequent against God. I take it therefore to be an error, that Christ either knew not what himself was to suffer, or else had forgotten the things he knew. The root of which error was an over-restrained consideration of prayer, as though it had no other lawful use but only to serve for a chosen mean, whereby the will resolveth to seek that which the understanding certainly knoweth it shall obtain: Whereas prayers in truth, both ours are, and his were, as well sometime a presentation of mere desires, as a mean of procuring desired effects at the hands of God. We are therefore

Job 23. 2.

Isa. 53. 10.
John 10. 15.

2   fore

fore taught by his example, that the presence of dolorous and dreadful objects, even in minds most perfect, may as clouds over-cast all sensible joy; that no assurance touching future victories can make present conflicts so sweet and easy, but nature will shun and shrink from them; nature will desire ease and deliverance from oppressive burthens; that the contrary determination of God is oftentimes against the effect of this desire, yet not against the affection it self, because it is naturally in us; that in such case our prayers cannot serve us as means to obtain the thing we desire; that notwithstanding they are unto God most acceptable sacrifices, because they testify we desire nothing but at his hands, and our desires we submit with contentment to be over-ruled by his will; and in general they are not repugnant unto the natural will of God, which wisheth to the works of his own hands, in that they are his own handy-work, all happiness; although perhaps for some special cause in our own particular, a contrary determination have seemed more convenient; finally, that thus to propose our desires which cannot take such effects as we specify, shall notwithstanding otherwise procure us heavenly grace, even as this very prayer of Christ obtained angels to be sent him as comforters *Luke 22. 43.* in his agony. And, according to this example, we are not afraid to present unto God our prayers for those things, which that he will perform unto us we have no sure nor certain knowledge. St. *Paul's* prayer for the church of *Co-* *2 Cor. 13. 7.* *rinth* was, that they might not do any evil, although he knew that no man liveth which sinneth not, although he knew that in this life we always must pray, *Forgive us our sins.* It is our frailty, that in many things we all do amiss; but a *We may not* virtue, that we would do amiss in nothing; and a testimony of that virtue, when we *pray in this* pray that what occasion of sin soever do offer it self, we may be strengthened *free from all* from above to withstand it. They pray in vain to have sin pardoned, which seek *sin, because* not also to prevent sin by prayer, even every particular sin, by prayer against all *ways pray,* sin; except men can name some transgression wherewith we ought to have truce. *Forgive us our* For in very deed, altho' we cannot be free from all sin collectively, in such sort *l. 3. p. 200.* that no part thereof shall be found inherent in us, yet distributively, at the least, all great and grievous actual offences, as they offer themselves one by one, both may and ought to be by all means avoided. So that in this sense, to be preserved from all sin, is not impossible. Finally, concerning deliverance it self from all adversity, we use not to say men are in adversity whensoever they feel any small hindrance of their welfare in this world, but when some notable affliction or cross, some great calamity or trouble befalleth them. Tribulation hath in it divers circumstances, the mind sundry faculties to apprehend them: It offereth sometime it self to the lower powers of the soul, as a most unpleasant spectacle; to the higher sometimes, as drawing after it a train of dangerous inconveniences; sometime as bringing with it remedies for the curing of sundry evils, as God's instrument of revenge and fury sometimes; sometime as a rod of his just, yet moderate ire and displeasure; sometime as matter for them that spitefully hate us to exercise their profound malice; sometime as a furnace of trial for virtue to shew it self, and through conflict to obtain glory. Which different contemplations of adversity, do work for the most part their answerable effects. Adversity either apprehended by sense as a thing offensive and grievous to nature, "or by reason conceived as a snare, an occasion of many men's falling from God, a sequel of God's indignation and wrath, a thing which Satan desireth and would be glad to behold; tribulation thus considered being present causeth sorrow, and being imminent breedeth fear. For moderation of which two affections, growing from the very natural bitterness and gall of adversity, the scripture much al- *Psal. 119. 71.* ledgeth contrary fruits, which affliction likewise hath, whensoever it falleth on them *2 Tim. 3. 12.* that are tractable, the grace of God's holy Spirit concurring therewith. But when the *against perse-* apostle St. *Paul* teacheth, that *every one which will live godly in Christ Jesus, must* *cution, is* *suffer persecution,* and, *by many tribulations we must enter into the kingdom of hea-* *that word* *ven;* because in a forest of many wolves, sheep cannot chuse but feed in continual *which faith,* danger of life; or when [a] St. *James* exhorteth to *account it a matter of exceeding joy,* *one which* *when we fall into divers temptations,* because, *by the trial of faith, patience is* *will live god-* brought forth; was it, suppose we, their meaning to frustrate our Lord's admonition, *ly in Christ* *Pray that ye enter not into temptation?* When himself pronounceth them blessed that *suffer perse-* should for his name's sake be subject to all kinds of ignominy and opprobrious maledi- *cution. T. C.* ction, was it his purpose that no man should ever pray with *David,* [b] *Lord, remove* *l. 3. p. 200.* *from me shame and contempt?* In those tribulations, saith St. *Augustine,* [c] *which may* [b] *Psal 119. 22.* *hurt as well as profit, we must say with the prophet, What we should ask as we ought* [c] *Aug. Epist.*

We may not pray in this life, to be free from all sin, because we must always pray, Forgive us our sins. T. C. l. 3. p. 200.

To pray against persecution, is contrary to that word which faith, That every one which will live godly in Christ Jesus, must suffer persecution. T. C. l. 3. p. 200.

121. cap. 14.

we know not; yet becaufe they are tough, becaufe they are grievous, becaufe the fenfe of our weaknefs flieth them, we pray according to the general defire of the will of man, that God would turn them away from us: owing in the mean while this devotion to the Lord our God; that if he remove them not, yet we do not therefore imagine our felves in his fight defpifed, but rather with godly fufferance of evils expect greater good at his merciful hands. For thus is virtue in weaknefs perfected. To the flefh (as the apoftle himfelf granteth) all affliction is naturally grievous. Therefore nature which caufeth to fear, teacheth to pray againft all adverfity. Profperity in regard of our corrupt inclination to abufe the bleffings of Almighty God, doth prove for the moft part a thing dangerous to the fouls of men. Very eafe it felf is death to the wicked, *and the profperity of fools flayeth them:* Their table is a fnare, and their felicity their utter overthrow. Few men there are which long profper and fin not. Howbeit, even as thefe ill effects, although they be very ufual and common, are no bar to the hearty prayers whereby moft virtuous minds wifh peace and profperity always where they love, becaufe they confider that this in it felf is a thing naturally defired: So becaufe all adverfity is in it felf againft nature, what fhould hinder to pray againft it, although the providence of God turn it often unto the great good of many men? Such prayers of the church to be delivered from all adverfity are no more repugnant to any reafonable difpofitions of men's minds towards death, much lefs to that bleffed patience and meek contentment which faints by heavenly infpiration have, to endure what crofs or calamity foever it pleafeth God to lay upon them, than our Lord and Saviour's own prayer before his paffion was repugnant unto his moft gracious refolution to die for the fins of the whole world.

49. In praying for deliverance from all adverfity, we feek that which nature doth wifh to it felf; but by intreating for mercy towards all, we declare that affection wherewith chriftian charity thirfteth after the good of the whole world, we difcharge that duty which the * apoftle himfelf doth impofe on the church of Chrift, as a *commendable* office, a facrifice *acceptable* in God's fight, a fervice according to his heart, whofe *defire* is to have all men faved: A work moft fuitable with his purpofe, who gave himfelf to be the price of redemption *for all,* and a forcible mean to *procure the converfion* of all fuch as are not yet acquainted with the myfteries of that truth which muft fave their fouls. Againft it, there is but the bare fhew of this one impediment, that all men's falvation, and many men's eternal condemnation or death, are things the one repugnant to the other; that both cannot be brought to pafs; that we know there are veffels of wrath, to whom God will never extend mercy, and therefore that wittingly we afk an impoffible thing to be had. The truth is, that as life and death, mercy and wrath are matters of mere underftanding or knowledge, all men's falvation, and fome men's endlefs perdition are things fo oppofite, that whofoever doth affirm the one, muft neceffarily deny the other; God himfelf cannot effect both, or determine that both fhall be. There is in the knowledge both of God and man this certainty, that life and death have divided between them the whole body of mankind. What portion either of the two hath, God himfelf knoweth; for us he hath left no fufficient means to comprehend, and that caufe neither given any leave to fearch in particular who are infallibly the heirs of the kingdom of God, who caft-aways. Howbeit, concerning the ftate of all men with whom we live (for only of them our prayers are meant) we may till the worlds end, *for the prefent,* always prefume, That *as far as in us there is power to difcern* what others are; and as far as any duty of ours dependeth upon the notice of their condition in refpect of God, the fafeft Axioms for charity to reft it felf upon, are thefe, *He which believeth already is;* and, *he which believeth not as yet, may be the child of God.* It becometh not us, *during life, altogether to condemn any man, feeing that* (for any thing we know) *there is hope of every man's forgivenefs; the poffibility of whofe repentance is not yet cut off by death.* And therefore charity which *hopeth all things,* prayeth alfo for all men. Wherefore to let go perfonal knowledge touching veffels of wrath and mercy, what they are inwardly in the fight of God it fkilleth not; for us there is caufe fufficient in all men, whereupon to ground our prayers unto God in their behalf. For whatfoever the mind of man apprehendeth as good, the will of charity and love is to have it enlarged in the very uttermoft extent, that all may enjoy it to whom it can any way add perfection. Becaufe therefore, the farther a good thing doth reach the nobler and worthier we reckon it; our prayers for all men's good, no lefs than for our own, the apoftle with very fit terms commendeth as being καλὸν, a work commendable

Marginal notes:

Prov. 1. 32.

Prayer, that all men may find mercy, and of the will of God that all men might be faved.

*1 Tim. 2. 3.

Sidon. Apol. lib. 6. Epift.

1 Cor. 14. 7.

dable

dable for the largeness of the affection from whence it springeth; even as theirs which have requested at God's hands the salvation of many with the loss of of their own souls; drowning, as it were, and over-whelming themselves in the abundance of their love towards others, is proposed as being in regard of the rarenefs of such affections *ὑπερβολὴ*, more than excellent. But this extraordinary height of desire after other men's salvation, is no common mark. The other is a duty which belongeth unto all, and prevaileth with God daily. For as it is in it self good, so God accepteth and taketh it in very good part at the hands of faithful Men. Our prayers for all men do include both them that shall find mercy, and them also that shall find none. For them that shall, no man will doubt but our prayers are both accepted and granted. Touching them for whom we crave that mercy which is not to be obtained, let us not think that our Saviour did misinstruct his Disciples, willing them to pray for the peace even of such as should be incapable of so great a blessing; or that the prayers of the prophet *Jeremy* offended God, because the answer of God was a resolute denial of favour to them for whom supplication was made. And if any man doubt how God should accept such prayers in case they be opposite to his will, or not grant them if they be according unto that which himself willeth, our answer is, that such suits God accepteth in that they are conformable unto his *general inclination*, which is that all men might be saved; yet always he granteth them not, for as much as there is in God sometimes a more private *occasioned will* which determineth the contrary. So that the other being the rule of our actions, and not this; our requests for things opposite to this will of God are not therefore the less gracious in his sight. There is no doubt but we ought in all things to frame our wills to the will of God, and that otherwise in whatsoever we do we sin. For of our selves, being so apt to err, the only way which we have to strengthen our paths is, by following the rule of his will, whose footsteps naturally are right. If the eye, the hand, or the foot, do that which the will commandeth, though they serve as instruments to sin, yet is sin the commanders fault and not theirs, because nature hath absolutely, and without exception, made them subjects to the will of man, which is lord over them. As the body is subject to the will of man, so man's will to the will of God; for so it behoveth that the better should guide and command the worse. But because the subjection of the body to the will is by natural necessity, the subjection of the will unto God voluntary; we therefore stand in need of direction after what sort our wills and desires may be rightly conformed to his, Which is not done, by willing always the self-same thing that God intendeth. For it may chance, that his purpose is sometime the speedy death of them, whose long continuance in life if we should not wish, we were unnatural. When the object or matter therefore of our desires is (as in this case) a thing both good of it self, and not forbidden of God; when the end for which we desire it is virtuous and apparently most holy; when the root from which our affection towards it proceedeth is charity; piety that which we do in declaring our desire by prayer; yea, over and besides all this, sith we know, that to pray for all men living is but to shew the same affection which towards every of them our Lord Jesus Christ hath born, who knowing only as God who are his, did as man taste death for the good of all men; surely, to that will of God which ought to be, and is the known rule of all our actions, we do not herein oppose our selves, although his secret determination haply be against us; which if we did understand, as we do not; yet to rest contented with that which God will have done, is as much as he requireth at the hands of men. And concerning our selves, what we earnestly crave in this case, the same, as all things else that are of like condition, we meekly submit unto his most gracious will and pleasure. Finally, as we have cause sufficient why to think the practice of our church allowable in this behalf, so neither is ours the first which hath been of that mind. For to end with the words of *Prosper, This law of supplication for all men* (saith he) *the devout zeal of all priests, and of all faithful men, doth hold with such full agreement, that there is not any part of all the world, where christian people do not use to pray in the same manner. The church every where maketh prayers unto God, and such as already in Christ are regenerate; but for all infidels and enemies of the cross of Jesus Christ, for all idolaters, for all that persecute Christ in his followers, for Jews*

Rom. 9. 3, & *10. 1.*

Matth. 10. 11, *12.*

Jer. 15. 1.

Propterea nihil contrarietatis erat, si Christus homo secundum affectum pietatis quam in humanitate sua assumpserat, aliquid volebat, quod tamen secundum voluntatem divinam, in qua cum Patre omnia disponebat, futurum non esse praescilebat; quia & hoc ad veram humanitatem pertinebat, ut pietate moveretur, & hoc ad veram divinitatem, ut à sua dispositione non moveretur. Hug. de Quat. Christi Volunt.

Prosp. de Voc. cat. Gen. l. 1. c. 4. inter opera Am- bros.

to whose blindness the light of the gospel doth not yet shine; for hereticks and schismaticks, who from the unity of faith and charity are estranged. And for such, what doth the church ask of God but this, that leaving their errors, they may be converted unto him, that faith and charity may be given them, and that out of the darkness of ignorance, they may come to the knowledge of his truth? which because they cannot themselves do in their own behalf, as long as the sway of evil custom over-beareth them, and the chains of Satan detain them bound, neither are they able to break through those errors wherein they are so determinately settled, that they pay unto falsity the whole sum of whatsoever love is owing unto God's truth. Our Lord merciful and just requireth to have all men prayed for; that when we behold innumerable multitudes drawn up from the depth of so bottomless evils, we may not doubt, but (in part) God hath done the thing requested; nor despair, but that being thankful for them, towards whom already he hath shewed mercy, the rest which are not as yet enlightned, shall, before they pass out of life, be made partakers of the like grace. Or if the grace of him which saveth (for so we see it falleth out) over-pass some, so that the prayer of the church for them be not received, this we may leave to the hidden judgments of God's righteousness, and acknowledge that in this secret there is a gulf, which while we live we shall never found.

Of the name, the author, and the force of sacraments; which force consisteth in this, That God hath ordained them as means to make us partakers of him in Christ, and of life through Christ.

* Gal. 4. 26. Isai. 54. 3.

50. Instruction and prayer, whereof we have hitherto spoken, are duties which serve as elements, parts or principals to the rest that follow, in which number the sacraments of the church are chief. The church is to us that very * mother of our new birth, in whose bowels we are all bred, at whose breasts we receive nourishment. As many therefore as are apparently to our judgment born of God, they have the seed of their regeneration by the ministry of the church, which useth to that end and purpose not only the word, but the sacraments, both having generative force and virtue. As oft as we mention a sacrament properly understood (for in the writings of the ancient fathers, all articles which are peculiar to christian faith, all duties of religion containing that which sense or natural reason cannot of it self discern, are most commonly named sacraments) our restraint of the word to some few principal divine ceremonies, importeth in every such ceremony two things, the substance of the ceremony it self which is visible, and besides that somewhat else more secret, in reference whereunto we conceive that ceremony to be a sacrament. For we all admire and honour the holy sacraments, not respecting so much the service which we do unto God in receiving them, as the dignity of that sacred and secret gift which we thereby receive from God. Seeing that sacraments therefore consist altogether in relation to some such gift or grace supernatural, as only God can bestow, how should any but the church administer those ceremonies as sacraments, which are not thought to be sacraments by any but by the church? There is in sacraments to be observed their force and their form of administration. Upon their force, their necessity dependeth. So that how they are necessary we cannot discern till we see how effectual they are. When sacraments are said to be visible signs of invisible grace, we thereby conceive how grace is indeed the very end for which these heavenly mysteries were instituted; and besides sundry other properties observed in them, the matter whereof they consist is such as signifieth, figureth, and representeth their end. But still their efficacy resteth obscure to our understanding, except we search somewhat more distinctly what grace in particular that is whereunto they are referred, and what manner of operation they have towards it. The use of sacraments is but only in this life, yet so, that here they concern a far better life than this, and are for that cause accompanied with grace which worketh salvation. Sacraments are powerful instruments of God to eternal life. For as our natural life consisteth in the union of the body with the soul, so our life supernatural in the union of the soul with God.

Oportebat Deum carnem fieri, ut in seipso conmet-cordiam concibularet Terrenorum pariter æterum pariter largens.
And for as much as there is no union of God with man, without that mean between both, which is both; it seemeth requisite, that we must first consider how God is in Christ, then how Christ is in us, and how the sacraments do serve to make us partakers of Christ. In other things we may be more brief, but the weight of these requireth largeness.

atque cælestium, cum utriusque partis in se connectens pignora, & Deum pariter homini, & hominem Deo copularet. Tertul. de Trinit.

51. The

51. The Lord our God is but one God. In which indivisible unity notwithstanding we adore the Father, as being altogether of himself; we glorify that consubstantial Word which is the Son ; we bless and magnify that co-essential Spirit eternally proceeding from both, which is the Holy Ghost. Seeing therefore the Father is
of none, the Son is of the Father, and the Spirit is of both, they are by these their
several properties really distinguishable each from other. For the substance of God,
with this property *to be of none*, doth make the person of the Father; the very
self-same substance in number with this property *to be of the Father*, maketh the
person of the Son; the same substance having added unto it the property of *pro-*
ceeding from the other two, maketh the person of the Holy Ghost. So that in
every person there is implied both the substance of God, which is one; and also
that property which causeth the same person

really and truly to differ from the other two.
Every person hath his own subsistence which
no other besides hath, although there be
others besides that of the same substance.
As no man but *Peter* can be the person
which *Peter* is, yet *Paul* hath the self-same nature which *Peter* hath. Again,
Angels have every of them the nature of pure and indivisible spirits, but every Angel
is not that Angel which appeared in a dream to *Joseph*. Now when God became
man, lest we should err in applying this to the person of the Father, or of the Spirit, St. *Peter's* confession unto Christ was, *Thou art the Son of the Living God*;
and St. *John's* exposition thereof was made plain, that it is the word which was made
Flesh. *The Father and the Holy Ghost*
(saith *Damascen*) *have no communion with*
the incarnation of the word, otherwise than
only by approbation and assent. Notwith-
standing, forasmuch as the word and deity are one subject, we must beware we exclude not the nature of God from incarnation, and so make the Son of God
incarnate not to be very God. For undoubt-
edly, even the nature of God it self in the
only person of the Son is incarnate, and hath
taken to it self flesh. Wherefore, Incarnation
may neither be granted to any person but only one, nor yet denied to that nature which is
common unto all three. Concerning the cause of which incomprehensible mystery,
for as much as it seemeth a thing unconsonant that the world should honour any
other as the Saviour, but him whom it honoureth as the creator of the world, and
in the wisdom of God it hath not been thought convenient to admit any way of
saving man but by man himself, though nothing should be spoken of the love and
mercy of God towards man, which this way are become such a spectacle as neither
men nor angels can behold without a kind of heavenly astonishment, we may hereby perceive there is cause sufficient why divine nature should assume humane, that
so God might be in Christ reconciling to himself the world. And if some cause
be likewise required, why rather to this end and purpose the Son, than either the
Father or the Holy Ghost should be made man, could we which are born the children of wrath, be adopted the Sons of God, through grace, any other than the
natural Son of God being mediator between God and us? It became therefore him,
by whom all things are, to be the way of salvation to all, that the institution and
restitution of the world might be both wrought by one hand. The world's salvation was without the incarnation of the Son of God a thing impossible; not simply impossible, but impossible, it being presupposed, that the will of God was no
otherwise to have it saved, than by the death of his own Son. Wherefore taking
to himself our flesh, and by his incarnation making it his own flesh, he had now
of his own, although from us, what to offer unto God for us. And as Christ took
manhood, that by it he might be capable of death, whereunto he humbled himself;
so because manhood is the proper subject of compassion and feeling pity, which
maketh the scepter of Christ's regency even in the kingdom of Heaven be amiable,
he which without our nature could not on earth suffer for the sins of the world, doth
now also by means thereof, both make intercession to God for sinners, and exercise
dominion over all men with a true, a natural, and a sensible touch of mercy.

52. It

Side notes (right margin):
That God is in Christ by the personal incarnation of the Son, who is very God.
Ma. 9. 6.
Jer. 23. 6.
Rom. 9. 5.
Joh. 16. 15.
& 5. 21.
Col. 2. 9.
1 John 5. 20.
Matth. 16.
16.
John 1. 14.
Ignat. Epist.
ad Magnes.
2 Cor. 5.
19.
4 Heb. 2. 10.
Heb. 4. 15.

The misin-
terpretations
which here-
by hath made
of the man-
ner, how God
and man are
united in one
Christ.
52. It is not in man's ability either to express perfectly, or conceive the manner how this was brought to pass. But the strength of our faith is tried by those things wherein our wits and capacities are not strong. Howbeit, because this divine mystery is more true than plain, divers, having framed the same to their own conceits and fancies, are found in their expositions thereof more plain than true: In so much, that by the space of five hundred years after Christ, the church was almost troubled with nothing else, saving only with care and travel to preserve this article from the

An. Dom. 325.
sinister construction of hereticks. Whose first mists when the light of the *Nicene* council had dispelled, it was not long e're *Macedonius* transferred unto God's most holy spirit the same blasphemy wherewith *Arius* had already dishonoured his co-eternally begotten Son; not long e're *Apollinarius* began to pare away from Christ's humanity. In refutation of which impieties, when the fathers of the church, *Atha-nasius*, *Basil*, and the two *Gregories*, had by their painful travels, sufficiently clear-ed the truth; no less for the deity of the Holy Ghost, than for the compleat huma-nity of Christ, there followed hereupon a final conclusion, whereby those contro-versies, as also the rest which *Paulus Samosatenus*, *Sabellius*, *Photinus*, *Ætius*, *Eunomius*, together with the whole swarm of pestilent *Demi-Arians* had from time to time stirred up since the council of *Nice*, were both privately, first at *Rome* in a smaller synod, and then at *Constantinople*, in a general famous assembly, brought to

An. Dom. 381.
a peaceable and quiet end; sevenscore bishops and ten agreeing in that confession, which by them set down, remaineth at this present hour a part of our church-liturgy, a memorial of their fidelity and zeal, a soveraign preservative of God's peo-ple from the venomous infection of heresy. Thus in Christ the verity of God, and the compleat substance of man, were with full agreement established throughout the world, till such time as the heresy of *Nestorius* broached it self, *dividing Christ into two per-sons, the Son of God, and the Son of man, the one a person begotten of God before all worlds, the other also a person born of the virgin* Mary, *and in special favour chosen to be made entire to the Son of God above all* men, *so that whosoever will honour God, must together honour Christ, with whose person God hath vouchsafed to join himself in so high a degree of gracious respect and favour.* But that the self-same person which verily is man, should properly be God also, and that by reason not of two persons linked in amity, but of two natures human and divine, conjoined in one and the same person, the God of glory may be said as well to have suffered death, as to have raised the dead from their graves; the son of man as well to have made as to have redeemed the world, *Nestorius* in no case would admit. That which deceived him was want of heed to the first begin-

John 1. 14.
ning of that admirable combination of God with man. *The word* (saith St. *John*) *was made flesh, and dwelt in us.* The evangelist useth the plural number, men for manhood, *us* for the nature whereof we consist, even as the apostle denying the assumption of *angelical nature*, saith likewise in the plural number, he took not

Heb. 2. 16.
angels, but the seed of *Abraham*. It pleased not the *word* or wisdom of God, to take to it self some one person amongst men, for then should that one have been advanced, which was assumed, and no more; but wisdom, to the end she might save many, built her house of that *nature* which is common unto all, she made not *this or that* man her habitation, but dwelt *in us.* The seeds of herbs and plants at the first, are not in act, but in possibility that which they afterwards grow to be. If the Son of God had taken to himself a man now made and already perfected, it would of necessity follow, that there are in Christ two persons, the one assuming, and the other assumed; whereas the Son of God did not assume a man's person into his own, but man's nature to his own person; and therefore took *Semen*, the seed of *Abraham*, the very first original element of our nature, before it was come to have any personal human subsistence. The flesh and the conjunction of the flesh with God, began both at one instant; his making and taking to himself our flesh, was but one act, so that in Christ there is no personal subsistence but one, and that from everlasting. By taking only the nature of man, he still continueth one person, and changeth but the manner of his subsisting, which was before in the meer glory of the Son of God, and is now in the habit of our flesh. For as much therefore as Christ hath no personal subsistence but one, whereby we acknowledge him to have been eternally the Son of God, we must of necessity apply to the person of the Son

4   of

of God, even that which is spoken of Christ according to his human nature. For example, according to the flesh, he was born of the virgin *Mary*, baptized of *John* in the River *Jordan*, by *Pilate* adjudged to die, and executed by the *Jews*. We cannot say properly, that the Virgin bore, or *John* did baptize, or *Pilate* condemn, or the *Jews* crucify the nature of man, because these all are personal attributes; his person is the subject which receiveth them, his nature that which maketh his person capable or apt to receive. If we should say, that the person of a man in our Saviour Christ was the subject of these things, this were plainly to intrap our selves in the very snare of the *Nestorian* heresy, between whom and the church of God there was no difference, saving only that *Nestorius* imagined in Christ as well a personal human subsistence, as a divine; the church acknowledging a substance both divine and human, but no other personal subsistence than divine, because the Son of God took not to himself a man's person, but the nature only of a man. Christ is a person both divine and human, howbeit not therefore two persons in one; neither both these in one sense, but a person divine, because he is personally the Son of God; human, because he hath really the nature of the children of men. In Christ therefore God and man, *There is* (saith *Paschasius*) *a twofold substance, not a two-* Pasch. lib. de Spir. Sanct. *fold person, because one person distinguisheth another, whereas one nature cannot in another become extinct.* For the personal being which the Son of God already had, suffered not the substance to be personal which he took, although together with the nature which he had, the nature also which he took, continueth. Whereupon it followeth against *Nestorius*, that no person was born of the Virgin but the Son of God, no person but the Son of God baptized, the Son of God condemned, the Son of God and no other person crucified; which one only point of christian belief, *The infinite worth of the Son of God*, is the very ground of all things believed concerning life and salvation, by that which Christ either did or suffered as man in our behalf. But forasmuch as St. *Cyril*, the chiefest of those two hundred bishops assembled in the council of *Ephesus*, where the heresy of *Nestorius* was condemned, An. Dom. 431. had in his writings against the *Arians* avouched, that the word or wisdom of God hath but one nature which is eternal, and whereunto he assumed flesh, (for the *Arians* were of opinion, that besides God's own eternal wisdom, there is a wisdom which God created before all things, to the end he might thereby create all things else; and that this created wisdom was the word which took flesh.) Again, forasmuch as the same *Cyril* had given instance in the body and the soul of man, no farther than only to enforce by example against *Nestorius*, that a visible and invisible, a mortal and an immortal substance, may united make *one person*; the words of *Cyril* were in process of time so taken, as though it had been his drift to reach, that even as in us the body and the soul, so in Christ God and man make but *one nature*. Of which error, six hundred and thirty fathers in the council of *Chal-* An. Dom. 451. *cedon* condemned *Eutyches*. For as *Nestorius* teaching rightly, that God and man are distinct natures, did thereupon mis-infer, that in Christ those natures can by no conjunction make one person; so *Eutyches*, of sound belief as touching their true personal copulation, became unsound, by denying the difference which still continueth between the one and the other nature. We must therefore keep warily a middle course, shunning both that distraction of persons, wherein *Nestorius* went awry; and also this latter confusion of natures, which deceived *Eutyches*. These 'Ἀχώριϛον ἀσύγχιτον ἢ ὁπερ ϛι ἐκεῖν Οὐίας φύσεις διαιρεῖον θεαλογεῖν, θεὸς τῆς σεμνῆς τῷ κἂν τῆς Θεο- δωρ. Dial. 'Ἀτρεπῆς. natures, from the moment of their first combination, have been and are for ever inseparable. For even when his soul forsook the tabernacle of his body, his deity forsook neither body nor soul. If it had, then could we not truly hold, either that the person of Christ was buried, or that the person of Christ did raise up himself from the dead. For the body separated from the word, can in no true sense be termed the person of Christ; nor is it true to say, that the Son of God in raising up that body, did raise up himself, if the body were not both with him, and of him, even during the time it lay in the sepulchre. The like is also to be said of the soul, otherwise we are plainly and inevitably *Nestorians*. The very person of Christ therefore for ever one and the self-same, was only, touching the bodily substance, con- That by the union of the one with the other nature in Christ, there grow-eth neither gain nor loss of essential properties to either. cluded within the grave, his soul only from thence severed; but by personal union his deity still inseparably joined with both.

53. The sequel of which conjunction of natures in the person of Christ, is no abolishment of natural properties appertaining to either substance, no transition or transmigration thereof out of one substance into another: Finally, no such mutual infusion, as really causeth the same natural operations or properties to be made com-

mon

2

mon unto both substances; but whatsoever is natural to deity, the same remaineth in Christ uncommunicated unto his manhood, and whatsoever natural to manhood, his deity thereof is uncapable. The true properties and operations of his deity are, to know that which is not possible for created natures to comprehend; to be simply the highest cause of all things, the well-spring of immortality and life; to have neither end nor beginning of days; to be every where present, and inclosed no where; to be subject to no alteration nor passion; to produce of it self those effects which cannot proceed but from infinite majesty and power. The true properties and operations of his manhood are such as *Iræneus* reckoneth up, *If Christ* (saith he) *had not taken flesh from the very earth, he would not have coveted those earthly nourishments, wherewith bodies which be taken from thence are fed. This was the nature which felt hunger after long fasting, was desirous of rest after travel, testified compassion and love by tears, groaned in heaviness, and with extremity of grief even melted away it self into bloody sweats.* To Christ we ascribe both working of wonders, and suffering of pains; we use concerning him speeches as well of humility, as of divine glory; but the one we apply unto that nature which he took of the Virgin *Mary*, the other to that which was in the beginning. We may not therefore imagine, that the properties of the weaker nature have vanished with the presence of the more glorious, and have been therein swallowed up as in a gulf. We dare not in this point give ear to them who over-boldly affirm, [a] *That the nature which Christ took weak and feeble from us, by being mingled with deity, became the same which deity is; that the assumption of our substance unto his, was like the blending of a drop of vinegar with the huge ocean, wherein although it continue still, yet not with those properties which severed it hath; because sithence the instant of their conjunction, all distinction of the one from the other is extinct, and whatsoever we can now conceive of the Son of God, is nothing else but meer deity:* Which words are so plain and direct for *Eutyches*, that I stand in doubt, they are not his whose name they carry. Sure I am they are far from truth, and must of necessity give place to the better advised sentences of other men. *He which in himself was appointed* (saith Hilary) *a mediator to save his church, and for performance of that mystery of mediation between God and man, is become God and man, doth now being but one, consist of both those natures united; neither hath he, through the union of both, incurred the damage or loss of either; lest by being born a man, we should think he hath given over to be God; or that, because he continued God, therefore he cannot be man also; whereas the true belief which maketh a man happy, proclaimeth jointly God and man, confesseth the word and flesh together.* Cyril more plainly, *His two natures have knit themselves the one to the other, and are in that nearness as uncapable of confusion as of distraction. Their coherence hath not taken away the difference between them; flesh is not become God, but doth still continue flesh, although it be now the flesh of God. Yea, of each substance* (saith *Leo*) *the properties are all preserved and kept safe.* These two natures are as causes and original grounds of all things which Christ hath done. Wherefore some things he doth as God, because his deity alone is the well-spring from which they flow; some things as man, because they issue from his meer human nature; some things jointly as both God and man, because both natures concur as principles thereunto. For albeit the properties of each nature do cleave only to that nature whereof they are properties; and therefore Christ cannot naturally be as God the same which he naturally is as man, yet both natures may very well concur unto one effect, and Christ in that respect be truly said to work both as God and man, one and the self-same thing. Let us therefore set it down for a rule or principle so necessary, as nothing more, to the plain deciding of all doubts and questions about the union of natures in Christ, that of both natures there is a co-operation often, an association always, but never any mutual participation, whereby the properties of the one are infused into the other. Which rule must serve for the better understanding of that which [b] *Damascene* hath

touch-

ταῦτα πάντα σύμβολα σαρκὸς ἦ ἀπὸ γῆς εἰλημμένης. *Irem. l. 3. Adverf. Hæref.*

Christ did all these ἀνθρώπινα σώματ[ος] νόμφ. *Greg. Naz-anz. Orat. 2. de Filio.* Τὴς μὲν παντὸς λόγῳ τῇ ἐν Μαρίᾳ ἀνθρώπου, τοῦ δ᾽ ἀναγμένου ᾖ διαπρεπῆς τῇ ἐν ἀρχῇ ὄντι λόγῳ. *Theod. Dial.* Ἀνθρωπῇ[ος].

[a] *Greg. Nyff. Epift. ad Theophil. Alexandr.*

Hilar. de Trin. lib. 9.

Cypr. Epift. ad Neft. Salva propriætate utriusque naturæ, suscepta est a Majestate humilitas, a virtute infirmitas, ab æternitate mortalitas. Leo. Epift. ad Flav.

[b] Οὐ τὴς ἑτέρου φύσεως ἀντιδόσεως. ἐνεργεῖ ἑκάτερον τῶν ἑτέρα τὰ ἴδια. *Damasc. de Orthod. Fid. l. 3. c. 4. Verum est duarum in Christo naturarum alteram suas alteri proprietates impertire, enunciando videlicet, idque non in abstracto sed in concreto solum, divinas homini non humanitati, humanas non deitati sed Deo tribui. Cujus hæc est ratio, quia, cum suppositum prædicationis sit ejusmodi, ut utramque naturam in se contineat, sive ab una sive ab altera denominetur, nihil refert.*

touching crofs and circulary fpeeches, wherein thêre are attributed to God fuch things as belong to manhood, and to man fuch as properly concern the deity of Chrift Jefus, the caufe whereof is the affociation of natures in one fubjeƈt. A kind of mutual commutation there is, whereby thefe concrete names, *God* and *man*, when we fpeak of Chrift, do take interchangeably one anothers room; fo that for truth of fpeech, it skilleth not whether we fay, that the Son of God hath created the world, and the Son of man by his death hath faved it; or elfe, that the Son of man did cre-ate, and the Son of God die to fave the world. Howbeit, as oft as we attribute to God what the manhood of Chrift claimeth, or to man what his deity hath right un-to, we underftand by the name of God, and the name of man, neither the one nor the other nature, but the whole perfon of Chrift, in whom both natures are. When the apoftle faith of the *Jews*, that they crucified the Lord of Glory; and when the Son of man, being on earth, affirmeth, that the Son of man was in heaven at the fame inftant; there is in thefe two fpeeches that mutual circulation before-menti-oned. In the one, there is attributed to God, or the Lord of Glory, death, where- 1 Cor. 2. 8. of divine nature is not capable; in the other ubiquity unto man, which human na-ture admitteth not. Therefore by the Lord of Glory, we muft needs underftand the John 3. 13. whole perfon of Chrift, who being Lord of Glory, was indeed crucified, but not in that nature for which he is termed the Lord of Glory. In like manner, by the Son of man, the whole perfon of Chrift muft neceffarily be meant, who being man up-on earth, filled heaven with his glorious prefence, but not according to that nàture for which the title of man is given him. Without this caution, the fathers, whofe belief was fincere, and their meaning moft found, fhall feem in their writings, one to deny what another conftantly doth affirm. *Theodoret* difputeth with great ear-neftnefs, that God cannot be faid to fuffer. But he thereby meaneth Chrift's divine nature againft *Apollinarius*, which held even deity it felf paffible. *Cyril* on the Θεοτόκος τῷ υἱῷ other fide againft *Neftorius* as much contendeth, that whofoever will deny *very God* σταυρωδέωτι σι τῆς 'αθανάτας to have fuffered death, doth forfake the Faith. Which notwithftanding to hold, the Greg. Nyſſ. dé Seɕator. were herely, if the name of God in this affertion did not import, as it doth, the Apollinar. E- perfon of Chrift, who being verily God, fuffered death, but in the flefh, and not in piſt. ad Flav. that fubftance for which the name of God is given him.

54. If then both natures do remain with their properties in Chrift thus diftinƈt, as hath been fhewed, we are for our better underftanding, what either nature re-ceiveth from other, to note, that Chrift is by three degrees a receiver; firft, in that he is the Son of God: Secondly, in that his human nature hath had the honour of union with deity beftowed upon it: Thirdly, in that by means thereof fundry emi-

What Chrift hath obtain-ed according to the flefh, by the union of his flefh with deity.

nent graces have flowed as effeƈts from deity into that nature which is coupled with it. On Chrift therefore is beftowed the gift of eternal generation, the gift of union, and the gift of unƈtion. By the gift of eternal generation, Chrift hath received of the Fa-ther one, and in number the a felf-fame fub-ftance, which the Father hath of himfelf un-received from any other. For every b *begin-ning is a father* unto that which cometh of it, and every *off-spring is a fon* unto that out of which it groweth. Seeing therefore the Father alone is c originally that deity which Chrift d originally is not (for Chrift is God e by being of God; light f by if-fuing out of light;) it followeth hereup-on, that whatfoever Chrift hath g com-mon unto him with his heavenly Father, the fame of neceffity muft be given him, but naturally and h eternally given; not be-ftowed by way of benevolence and favour, as the other gifts both are. And therefore i where the Fathers give it out for a rule, that whatfoever Chrift is faid in fcripture to have received, the fame we ought to apply only to the manhood of Chrift: Their affer-

* *Nativitas Dei non poteſt non eam ex qua profeƈta eſt tenere na=turam. Neque nim aliud quam Deus fubfiſtit, qui non aliunde quam ex Deo Deus fubfiſtit.* Hilar. de Trin. lib. 5. *Cum fit gloria, fempiternitate, virtute, regno, poteſtate hoc quod Pater eſt, omnia tamen hæc non fine auƈtore ficut pater, fed ex patre tanquam filius fine initio & æqualis habet.* Ruffin in Symb. Apoſt. cap. 9. *Filium aliunde non deduco, fed de fubſtantia Patris omnem a paire confecutum poteſtatem.* Tertul. contra Prax.

b Ephef. 1. 15. πᾶσα σοφία, quicquid alteri quovis modo dat effe.

c Jam. 1. 17. *Pater luminum υἱῷ τε ἡ πνευματι δ'ωλωνότι* Pachym. in Dionyf. de cœl. Hierav. cap. 1. *Pater eſt principium totius divinitatis, quia ipfe a nullo eſt. Non enim habet de quo procedat, fed ab eo & Filius.eſt genitus & Spiritus fanƈus procedit.* Aug. de Trinit. lib. 4. cap. 20. *Hinc Chriſtus deitatis loco no-men ubique patris ufurpat, quia pater nimirum eſt πηγαῖος θεότης* gatio. Tertul. contra. Prax.

e *Quod enim Deus eſt, ex Deo eſt.* Hilar. de Trin. lib. 5. *Nihil nifi natum habet filius.* Hilar. lib. 4.

f 'Απαύγασμα δόξης. Heb. 1. 3. 'Εςι ςαίρξεια ε τῆ παντο-κράτορ@ δόξης, εἰλικρινὴς, ἀπαύγασμα φωτὸς αϊδίε. Sap. 7. 25, 26.

g *Nihil in fe ʤorfum ac diffimile habent natus & generans.* Hilar. de Synod. adverf. Aria. *In Trinitate alius atque alius, non aliud atque aliud.* Vincent. Lyr. cap. 19.

h *Ubi author æternus eſt, ibi & nativitatis æternitas eſt: Quia ficut nativitas ab authore eſt, ita & ab æterno authore æterna nati-vitas eſt.* Hilar. de Trin. lib. 12. *Sicut naturam præſtat filio fine initio Generatio: Ita Spiritus fanƈo præſtat eſſentiam fine ini-tio Proceſſio.* Aug. de Trin. lib. 5. cap. 15.

i 'Οσα λέγεν ὁ γεγραπ ὁτι ἔλαβεν ὅτι ὔἱος ἡ ἀνθέλθη, διὰ τὴν ἀνθρωπότητα αὐτε λέγει, ὃυ τὴν θεότητα. Theod. fol. 42. & ad Greg. Nazianz. Orat. 2. de Fol. ibid. 44.

C c

tion is true of all things which Chrift hath received by grace; but to that which he hath received of the Father by eternal nativity or birth, it reacheth not. Touching union of deity with manhood, it is by grace, becaufe there can be no greater grace fhewed towards men, than that God fhould vouchfafe to unite unto man's nature the perfon of his only begotten Son. Becaufe *the Father loveth the Son* as man, he hath by uniting deity with manhood, *given all things into his hands.* It hath pleafed the Father, that in him *all fulnefs fhould dwell.* The *name* which he hath *above all names* is given him. *As the Father hath life in himfelf,* the *Son in himfelf hath life alfo by* the gift of the Father. The gift whereby God hath made Chrift a fountain of life, is that *conjunction of the nature of God with the nature of man,* in the perfon of Chrift, *which gift* (faith Chrift to the woman of *Samaria*) if thou didft know, and in *that refpect* underftand *who it is* which asketh water of thee, thou wouldeft ask of him, that he might give thee living water. The union therefore of the flefh with deity, is to that flefh a gift of principal grace and favour. For by virtue of this grace, man is really made God, a creature is exalted above the dignity of all creatures, and hath all creatures elfe under it. This admirable union of God with man can inforce in that higher nature no alteration, becaufe unto God there is nothing more natural, than not to be fubject to any [a] change. Neither is it a thing impoffible, that the Word being made Flefh, fhould be that which it was not before, as touching the manner of fubfiftence, and yet continue in all qualities or properties of nature the fame it was, becaufe the incarnation of the Son of God confifteth *merely in the union* of natures, which union doth add perfection to the weaker, to the nobler [b] no alteration at all. If therefore it be demanded what the perfon of the Son of God hath attained by affuming manhood; furely, the whole fum of all is this, to be as we are, truly, really, and naturally man, by means whereof he is made capable of meaner offices than otherwife his perfon could have admitted; the only gain he thereby purchafed for himfelf, was to be capable of lofs and detriment for the good of others. But may it rightly be faid concerning the incarnation of Jefus Chrift, that as our nature hath in no refpect changed his, fo from his to ours as little alteration hath enfued? The very caufe of his taking upon him our nature, was to change it, to better the quality, and to advance the condition thereof, although in no fort to abolifh the fubftance which he took; nor to infufe into it the natural forces and properties of his deity. As therefore we have fhewed, how the Son of God by his incarnation hath changed the manner of that perfonal fubfiftence which before was folitary, and is now in the affociation of flefh, no alteration thereby accruing to the nature of God; fo neither are the *properties of man's nature* in the perfon of Chrift, by force and virtue of the fame conjunction fo much altered, as not to ftay within thofe limits which our fubftance is bordered withal; nor the *ftate and quality* of our fubftance fo unaltered, but that there are in it many glorious effects proceeding from fo near copulation with deity. God from us can receive nothing, we by him have obtained much. For albeit, the natural properties of deity be not communicable to man's nature, the fupernatural gifts, graces, and effects thereof are. The honour which our flefh hath by being the flefh of the Son of God, is in many refpects great. If we refpect but that which is common unto us with him, the glory provided for him and his in the kingdom of heaven, his right and title thereunto, even in that he is man, differeth from other mens, becaufe he is that man of whom God is himfelf a part. We have right to the fame inheritance with Chrift; but not the fame right which he hath; his being fuch as we cannot reach, and ours fuch as he cannot ftoop unto. Furthermore, to be the way, the truth, and the life; to be the wifdom, righteoufnefs, fanctification, refurrection; to be the peace of the whole world, the hope of the righteous, the heir of all things; to be that fupream head whereunto all power, both in heaven and in earth is given; thefe are not honours common unto Chrift with other men; they are titles above the dignity and worth of any which were but a meer man, yet true of Chrift, even in that he is man; but man with whom deity is perfonally joined, and unto whom it hath added thofe excellencies which make

[a] 'Ωσπερ τῶ ανθρωπων κοινον ἐςι το θνητον, ἱουτω δ᾽ ἁγιας Τριαδ῀ κοινον το ἀτρεπτον τε κ᾽ ἀναλλοιωτον. *Theod. Dial.* 'Ατρεπτ῀.

[b] *Periculum ftatus fui deo nullum eft.* Tertul. de Car. Chr. *Majeftati Filii Dei corporea Nativitas nihil contulit, nihil abftulit,* Leo de Nativit. Ser. 8. Μινω ὁ ὑπ᾽ ἀρ᾽ δεχᾶς, θεδε μὲνω, κ᾽ τλὸ ὑμῶν ἐν ἑαυτῶ μεασχεμ ἀζων ὑμαςξιν. *Theophil. in formam fervi tranfiffe non eft naturam perdidiffe Dei.* Hilar. de Trin. lib. 12.

make him more than worthy thereof. Finally, Sith God hath deified our nature, though not by turning it into himself, yet by making it his own inseparable habitation, we cannot now conceive, how God should without man, either [a] exercise divine power, or receive the glory of divine praise. For man is in [b] both an associate of deity. But to come to the grace of unction : Did the parts of our nature, the soul and body of Christ receive by the influence of deity wherewith they were match'd, no ability of operations, no virtue, or quality above nature? Surely, as the sword which is made fiery, doth not only cut by reason of the sharpness which simply it hath, but also burn by means of that heat which it hath from fire ; so, there is no doubt but the deity of Christ hath enabled that nature which it took of man, to do more than man in this world hath power to comprehend ; for as much as (the bare essential properties of deity excepted) he hath imparted unto it all things, and hath replenished it with all such perfections, as the same is any where apt to receive, at the least, according to the exigence of that œconomy or service for which it pleased him in love, and mercy to be made man. For as the parts, degrees, and offices of that mystical administration did require, which he voluntarily undertook, the beams of deity did in operation always accordingly either restrain or enlarge themselves. From hence we may somewhat conjecture, how the powers of that soul are illuminated, which being so inward unto God, cannot chuse but be privy unto all things which God worketh, and must therefore of necessity be endued with know- [Matth.27.46.] ledge so far forth [c] universal, though not with infinite knowledge peculiar to deity [c Col. 2. 3.] it self. The soul of Christ that saw in this life the face of God, was here, through so visible presence of deity, filled with all manner [d] of graces and virtues in that un- [d Isa. 11. 2.] matchable degree of perfection, for which, of him we read it written, *That God with the oil of gladness anointed [e] him [f] above his [g] fellows.* And as God hath in [e Isa. 61. 1.] Christ unspeakably glorified the nobler, so likewise the meaner part of our nature, [Luke 4. 18.] the very bodily substance of man. Where also that must again be remembered which [f Heb. 1. 9.] we noted before, concerning the degrees of the influence of deity proportionable [g 2 Cor. 1.] unto his own purposes, intents and counsels. For in this respect his body which [1 John 2. 20,] by natural condition was corruptible, wanted the gift of everlasting immunity from [27.] death, passion and dissolution, till God which gave it to be slain for sin, had for righteousness sake restored it to life, with certainty of endless continuance. Yea, in this respect the very glorified body of Christ retained in it the [h] scars and marks of [h John 20.] former mortality. But shall we say, that in heaven his glorious body, by virtue of [27.] the same cause, hath now power to present it self in all places, and to be every where at once present? We nothing doubt but God hath many ways, above the reach of our capacities, exalted that body which it hath pleased him to make his own, that body wherewith he hath saved the world, that body which hath been, and is the root of eternal life; the instrument wherewith deity worketh, the sacrifice which taketh away sin, the price which hath ransomed souls from death, the leader of the whole army of bodies that shall rise again. For though it had a beginning from us, yet God hath given it vital efficacy, heaven hath endowed it with celestial power, that virtue it hath from above, in regard whereof all the angels of heaven adore it. Notwithstanding a body still it continueth, a body consubstantial with our bodies, a body of the same both nature and measure which it had on earth. To gather therefore into one sum, all that hitherto hath been spoken touching this point, there are but four things which concur to make compleat the whole state of our Lord Jesus Christ; his deity, his manhood, the conjunction of both, and the distinction of the one from the other being joined in one. Four principal heresies there are, which have in those things withstood the truth. *Arians,* by bending themselves against the deity of Christ ; *Apollinarians,* by maiming and misinterpreting that which belongeth to his human nature ; *Nestorians,* by renting Christ asunder, and dividing him into two persons ; the followers of *Eutyches,* by confounding in his person those natures which they should distinguish. Against these there have been four most famous ancient general councils ; the council of *Nice,* to define against *Arians* ; against *Apollinarians* the council of *Constantinople* ; the coun-

cil

cil of *Ephefus* againſt *Neſtorians*; againſt *Eutychians* the *Chalcedon* council. In four words, ἀληθῶς, τελέως, ἀδιαιρέτως, ἀσυγχύτως, *truly, perfectly, indiviſibly, diſtinctly*: The firſt apply to his being God; and the ſecond to his being man; the third to his being of both one; and the fourth to his ſtill continuing in that one both; we may fully, by way of abridgment, comprize whatſoever antiquity hath at large handled, either in declaration of chriſtian belief, or in refutation of the aforeſaid hereſies. Within the compaſs of which four heads, I may truly affirm, that all hereſies which touch but the perſon of Jeſus Chriſt, (whether they have riſen in theſe later days, or in any age heretofore,) may be with great facility brought to confine themſelves. We conclude therefore, that to ſave the world it was of neceſſity the Son of God ſhould be thus incarnate, and that God ſhould ſo be in Chriſt, as hath been declared.

55. Having thus far proceeded in ſpeech concerning the perſon of Jeſus Chriſt, his two natures, their conjunction, that which he either is or doth in reſpect of both, and that which the one receiveth from the other; ſith God in Chriſt is generally the medicine whereby we are every one particularly cured: In as much as Chriſt's incarnation and paſſion can be available to no man's good which is not made partaker of Chriſt, neither can we participate of him without his preſence; we are briefly to conſider how Chriſt is preſent, to the end it may thereby better appear how we are made partakers of Chriſt, both otherwiſe, and in the ſacraments themſelves. All things are in ſuch ſort divided into finite and infinite, that no one ſubſtance, nature or quality, can be poſſibly capable of both. The world, and all things in the world are ſtinted; all effects that proceed from them; all the powers and abilities whereby they work; whatſoever they do, whatſoever they may, and whatſoever they are, is limited. Which limitation of each creature is both the perfection and alſo the preſervation thereof. Meaſure is that which perfecteth all things, becauſe every thing is for ſome end; neither can that thing be available to any end which is not proportionable thereunto; and to proportion, as well exceſſes as defects are oppoſite. Again, foraſmuch as nothing doth periſh, but only through exceſs or defect of that, the due proportioned meaſure whereof doth give perfection, it followeth, that meaſure is likewiſe the preſervation of all things. Out of which premiſes we may conclude, not only that nothing created can poſſibly be unlimited, or can receive any ſuch accident, quality or property, as may really make it infinite (for then ſhould it ceaſe to be a creature) but alſo that every creatures limitation is according to his own kind; and therefore, as oft as we note in them any thing above their kind, it argueth that the ſame is not properly theirs, but groweth in them from a cauſe more powerful than they are. Such as the ſubſtance of each

thing is, ſuch is alſo the preſence thereof. Impoſſible it is, that God ſhould withdraw his preſence from any thing, becauſe the very ſubſtance of God is infinite. He filleth heaven and earth, although he take up no room in either, becauſe his ſubſtance is immaterial, pure, and of us in this world ſo incomprehenſible, that albeit no part of us be ever abſent from him who is preſent whole unto every particular thing, yet his preſence with us we no way diſcern further than only that God is preſent; which partly by reaſon, and more perfectly by faith, we know to be firm and certain. Seeing therefore that preſence every where is the ſequel of an infinite and incomprehenſible ſubſtance (for what can be every where, but that which can no where be comprehended?) to enquire whether Chriſt be every where, is to enquire of a natural property, a property that cleaveth to the deity of Chriſt. Which deity being common unto him with none but only the Father and the Holy Ghoſt, it followeth, that nothing of Chriſt which is limited, that nothing created, that neither the ſoul nor the body of Chriſt, and conſequently not Chriſt as man, or Chriſt according to his human nature, can poſſibly be every where preſent, becauſe thoſe phraſes of limitation and reſtraint do either point out the principal ſubject whereunto every ſuch attribute adhereth, or elſe they intimate the radical cauſe out of which it groweth. For example, when we ſay that Chriſt as man, or according to his human nature, ſuffered death; we ſhew what nature was the proper ſubject of mortality: When we ſay, that as God, or according to his deity, he conquered death, we declare his deity to have been the cauſe by force and virtue whereof he raiſed himſelf from the grave. But neither is the manhood of Chriſt that ſubject whereunto univerſal preſence agreeth, neither is it the cauſe

I   original

original by force whereof his perfon is enabled to be every where prefent. Wherefore Chrift is effentially prefent with all things in that he is very God, but not prefent with all things as Man, becaufe Manhood and the parts thereof can neither be the caufe nor the true fubject of fuch prefence. Notwithftanding, fomewhat more plainly to fhew a true immediate reafon wherefore the Manhood of Chrift can neither be every where prefent, nor caufe the Perfon of Chrift fo to be; we acknowledge that of St. *Augu-*
ftin concerning Chrift moft true, *In that he* $\qquad$ *Quod ad verbum attinet, Creator eft; quod ad hominem, crea-*
is perfonally the word, he created all things; $\qquad$ *tura eft.* Aug. Epift. 57. *Deus qui femper eft, & femper erat,*
in that he is naturally man, he himfelf is crea- $\qquad$ *fit creatura.* Leo. de Nativ. *Multi timore trepidant ne Chri-*
ted of God; and it doth not appear that any $\qquad$ *ftum effe Creaturam dicere compellantur; not proclamamus non*
one creature hath power to be prefent with all $\qquad$ *effe periculum dicere, Chriftum effe creaturam.* Hier. in Epift. ad Eph. 2.
Creatures. Whereupon neverthelefs it will not follow, that Chrift cannot therefore be thus prefent becaufe he is himfelf a creature; for as much as only infinite prefence is that which cannot poffibly ftand with the effence or being of any creature; as for prefence with all things that are, fith the whole race, mafs and body of them is finite, Chrift by being a *creature* is not *in that refpect* excluded from poffibility of prefence with them. That which excludeth him therefore, as Man, from fo great largenefs of prefence, is only his being *Man*, a creature *of this particular kind*, whereunto the God of Nature hath fet thofe bounds of reftraint and limitation, beyond which to attribute unto it any thing more than a creature *of that fort* can admit, were to give it another nature, to make it a creature of fome other kind than in truth it is. Furthermore, if Chrift, in that he is man, be every where prefent, feeing this cometh not by the nature of manhood it felf, there is no other way how it fhould grow, but either by the grace of union with deity, or by the grace of unction received from deity. It hath been already fufficiently proved, that by force of union the properties of both natures are imparted *to the Perfon only* in whom they are, and not what belongeth to the one nature really conveyed or tranflated into the other; it hath been likewife proved, that natures united in Chrift continue the very fame which they are where they are not united. And concerning the grace of unction, wherein are contained the gifts and virtues which Chrift as man hath above men, they make him really and habitually a man more excellent than we are, they take not from him the nature and fubftance that we have, they caufe not his foul nor body to be of another kind than ours is. Supernatural endowments are an advancement, they are no extinguifhment of that nature whereto they are given. The fubftance of the body of Chrift hath no prefence, neither can have, but only local. It was not therefore every where feen, nor did every where fuffer death, every where it could not be entombed, it is not every where now, being exalted into heaven. There is no proof in the world ftrong enough to enforce that Chrift had a true body, but by the true and natural properties of his body. Amongft which properties, definite or local prefence is chief. *How is it true of Chrift* (faith *Tertullian*) *that he died, was buried,* Tertul. de *and rofe again, if Chrift had not that very flefh, the nature whereof is capable of* Car. Chr. *thefe things, flefh mingled with blood, fupported with bones, woven with finews, embroidered with veins?* If his majeftical body have now any fuch new property, by force whereof it may every where really even *in fubftance* prefent it felf, or may at once be in many places; then hath the majefty of his eftate extinguifhed the verity of his nature. *Make then no doubt or queftion of it* (faith St. *Au-* Aug. Epift. *guftin*) *but that the man Chrift Jefus is now in that very place, from whence he* 3). *fhall come in the fame form and fubftance of flefh which he carried thither, and from which he hath not taken nature, but given thereunto immortality. According to this form he fpreadeth not out himfelf into all places: For it behoveth us to take great heed, left while we go about to maintain the glorious Deity of him which is man, we leave him not the true bodily fubftance of a man.* According to St. *Auguftin's* opinion therefore, that majeftical body which we make to be every where prefent, doth thereby ceafe to have the fubftance of a true body. To conclude, we hold it in regard of the fore-alledged proofs, a moft infallible truth, that Chrift, as man, is not every where prefent. There are which think it as infallibly true, That Chrift is every where prefent as man, which peradventure in fome fenfe may be well enough granted. His human fubftance in it felf is naturally abfent from the Earth; his foul and body not on earth, but in heaven only: Yet becaufe this fubftance is infeparably joined to that perfonal Word, which by his very divine effence is prefent with all things; the nature which cannot have in it felf univer-

fal prefence, hath it *after a fort*, by being *no where fevered* from that which every where is prefent. For in as much as that infinite word is not divifible into parts, it could not in part, but muft needs be wholly incarnate ; and confequently wherefoever the word is, it hath with it manhood, elfe fhould the word be in part, or fomewhere God only and not man, which is impoffible. For the *perfon of Chrift is whole*, perfect God and perfect man, wherefoever ; altho' the parts of his manhood, being finite, and his deity infinite, we cannot fay that the *whole of Chrift* is fimply every where, as we may fay that his deity is, and that his perfon is by force of deity. For, *fomewhat of the perfon of Chrift* is not every where in that fort ; namely his manhood, the *only conjunction* whereof with deity is extended as far as deity, the *actual pofition* reftrained and tied to a certain place ; yet prefence *by way of conjunction* is in fome fort prefence. Again, as the manhood of Chrift may after a fort be every where faid to be prefent, becaufe that perfon is every where prefent from whofe divine fubftance manhood is no where fevered ; fo the fame univerfality of prefence may likewife feem in another refpect appliable thereunto, namely, by co-operation with deity, and that *in all things*. The light created of God in the beginning, did firft by it felf illuminate the world ; but after that the fun and moon were created, the world fithence hath by them always enjoyed the fame. And that deity of Chrift, which before our Lord's incarnation wrought all things without man, doth now work nothing wherein the nature which it hath affumed is either abfent from it or idle. Chrift, as man, hath all power both in heaven and earth given him. He hath as man, not as God only, fupreme dominion over quick and dead ; for fo much his afcenfion into heaven and his feffion at the right hand of God do import. The Son of God which did firft humble himfelf by taking our flefh upon him, defcended afterwards much lower, and became according to the flefh obedient fo far as to fuffer death, even the death of the crofs for all men, becaufe fuch was his Father's will. The former was an humiliation of deity, the latter an humiliation of manhood ; for which caufe there followed upon the latter an exaltation of that which was humbled : For with power he created the world, but reftored it by obedience. In which obedience, as according to his manhood he had glorified God on earth ; fo God hath glorified in heaven that nature which yielded him obedience ; and hath given unto Chrift, even in that he is man, fuch fulnefs of power over the whole world, that he which before fulfilled in the ftate of humility and patience whatfoever God did require, doth now reign in glory till the time that all things be reftored. He which came down from heaven, and defcended into the loweft parts of the earth, is afcended far above all heavens ; that fitting at the right hand of God, he might from thence fill all things with the gracious and happy fruits of his faving prefence. Afcenfion into heaven is a plain local tranflation of Chrift according to his manhood, from the lower to the higher parts of the world. Seffion at the right hand of God is the actual exercife of that regency and dominion wherein the manhood of Chrift is joined, and matched with the deity of the Son of God. Not that his manhood was before without the poffeffion of the fame power, but becaufe the full ufe thereof was fufpended, till that humility which had been before as a vail to hide and conceal majefty, were laid afide. After his rifing again from the dead, then did God fet him at his right hand in heavenly places, far above all principality, and power, and might, and domination, and every name that is named, not in this world only, but alfo in that which is to come; and hath put all things under his feet, and hath appointed him over all the head to the church, which is his body, the fulnefs of him that filleth all in all. The fcepter of which fpiritual regiment over us in this prefent world is at the length to be yielded up into the hands of the Father which gave it ; that is to fay, the ufe and exercife thereof fhall ceafe, there being no longer on earth any militant church to govern. This government therefore he exercifeth both as God and as man ; as God, by effential prefence with all things ; as man, by co-operation with that which effentially is prefent. Touching the manner how he worketh as man in all things ; the principal powers of the foul of man are the will and underftanding, the one of which two in Chrift affenteth unto all things, and from the other nothing which deity doth work is hid ; fo that by knowledge and affent the foul of Chrift is prefent with all things which the deity of Chrift worketh. And even the body of Chrift it felf, although the definite limitation thereof be moft fenfible, doth notwithftanding admit in fome fort a kind of infinite and unlimited prefence likewife. For his body being a part of that nature, which whole na-

Matth. 28.
Rom. 14. 8.

Phil. 2. 9.
Heb. 2. 9.
Rev. 5. 12.

Luke 21. 27.

Acts 3. 21.
Ephef. 4. 9.

Ephef. 1. 20.

Pfal. 8. 6.
Heb. 2. 8.
1 Cor. 15.

nature is presently joined unto deity; wheresoever deity is, it followeth, that his bodily substance hath every where a presence of true conjunction with deity. And for as much as it is, by virtue of that conjunction, made the body of the Son of God, by whom also it was made a sacrifice for the sins of the whole world, this giveth it a *presence of force and efficacy* throughout all generations of men. Albeit therefore nothing be *actually* infinite *in substance* but God only in that he is God; nevertheless, as every number is infinite by possibility of addition, and every line by possibility of extension infinite; so there is no stint which can be set to the value or merit of the sacrificed body of Christ, it hath no measured certainty of limits, bounds of efficacy unto life it knoweth none, but is also it self infinite in possibility of application. Which things indifferently every way considered, that gracious promise of our Lord and Saviour Jesus Christ concerning presence with his to the very end of the world, I see no cause but that we may well and safely interpret he doth perform, both as God, by essential presence of deity, and as man, in that order, sense and meaning, which hath been shewed.

56. We have hitherto spoken of the person and of the presence of Christ. Participation is that mutual inward hold which Christ hath of us and we of him, in such sort that each possesseth other by way of special interest, property, and inherent copulation. For plainer explication whereof, we may from that which hath been before sufficiently proved, assume to our purpose these two principles, *That every original cause imparteth it self unto those things which come of it; and whatsoever taketh being from any other, the same is after a sort in that which giveth it being.* It followeth hereupon, that the Son of God being light of light, must needs be also light in light. The persons of the Godhead, by reason of the unity of their substance, do as necessarily remain one within another, as they are of necessity to be distinguished one from another, because two are the issue of one, and one the off-spring of the other two; only of three, one not growing out of any other. And sith they all are but one God in number, one indivisible essence or substance, their distinction cannot possibly admit separation. For how should that subsist solitarily by it self, which hath no substance, but individually the very same whereby others subsist with it? seeing that the multiplication of substances in particular is necessarily required to make those things subsist a-part, which have the self-same general nature, and the persons of that Trinity are not three particular substances to whom one general nature is common, but three that subsist by one substance which it self is particular; yet they all three have it, and their several ways of having it are that which maketh their personal distinction. The Father therefore is in the Son, and the Son in him; they both in the Spirit, and the Spirit in both them: So that the Father's off-spring, which is the Son, remaineth eternally in the Father; the Father eternally also in the Son, not severed or divided by reason of the sole and single unity of their substance. The Son in the Father, as light in that light out of which it floweth without separation; the Father in the Son, as light in that light which it causeth and leaveth not. And because in this respect his eternal Being is of the Father, which eternal Being is his life, therefore he by the Father liveth. Again, sith all things do accordingly love their off-spring as themselves are more or less contained in it, he which is thus the only begotten, must needs be in this degree the only beloved of the Father. He therefore which is in the Father by eternal derivation of being and life from him, must needs be in him through an eternal affection of love. His incarnation causeth him also as man to be now in the Father, and the Father to be in him. For in that he is man, he receiveth life from the Father as from the fountain of that ever-living Deity, which in the person of the Word hath combined it self with manhood, and doth thereunto impart such life as to no other creature besides him is communicated. In which consideration likewise, the love of the Father towards him is more than it can be towards any other; neither can any attain unto that perfection of love which he beareth towards his heavenly Father. Wherefore God is not so in any, nor any so in God as Christ; whether we consider him as the personal Word of God; or as the natural Son of man. All other things that are of God, have God in them, and he them in himself likewise. Yet because their substance and his wholly differeth, their coherence

rence

The union or mutual participation which is between Christ and the church of Christ, in this present world.

In the bosom of the father, *John* 1. 18. *alium esse Patrem, & alium Filium; non divisione alium, sed distinctione,* Tertul. contra Prax. *pluralem deduit incertores generatio, nec in divisionem cadit, ubi qui nascitur mequaquam à generante separatur,* Ruffin. in Symbol. *Ecce dico alium; Nec in numerum.*

Luke 3. 22. John 3. 34. 35. & 5. 20. & 10. 17. & 14. 31. & 15. 10.

rence and communion either with him or amongst themselves, is in no sort like unto that before-mention'd. God hath his influence into the very essence of all things, without which influence of deity supporting them, their utter annihilation could not chuse but follow. Of him all things have both received their first being, and their continuance to be that which they are. All things are therefore partakers of God, they are his off-spring, his influence is in them, and the personal wisdom of God is for that very cause said to excel in nimbleness or agility, to pierce into all intellectual, pure and subtil parts, to go through all, and to reach unto every thing which is. Otherwise, how can the same wisdom be that which supporteth, beareth up, and sustaineth all? Whatsoever God doth work, the hands of all three persons are jointly and equally in it, according to *the order of that connection* whereby they each depend upon other. And therefore albeit in that respect the Father be first, the Son next, the Spirit last, and consequently nearest unto every effect which groweth from all three; nevertheless, they all being of one essence, are likewise all of one efficacy. Dare any man, unless he be ignorant altogether how inseparable the persons of the Trinity are, persuade himself that every of them may have their sole and several possessions, or that we being not partakers of all, can have fellowship with any one? The Father as goodness, the Son as wisdom, the Holy Ghost as power, do all concur in every particular, outwardly issuing from that one only glorious Deity which they all are. For that which moveth God to work is goodness; and that which ordereth his work is wisdom; and that which perfecteth his work is power. All things which God in their times and seasons hath brought forth, were eternally and before all times in God, as a work unbegun is in the artificer which afterward bringeth it unto effect. Therefore whatsoever we do behold now in this present world, it was enwrapped within the bowels of divine mercy, written in the book of eternal wisdom, and held in the hands of omnipotent Power, the first foundations of the world being as yet unlaid. So that all things which God hath made are in that respect the off-spring of God, they are in him as effects in their highest cause; he likewise actually is in them, the assistance and influence of his Deity is their life. Let hereunto saving efficacy be added, and it bringeth forth a special off-spring amongst Men, containing them to whom God hath himself given the gracious and amiable name of sons. We are by nature the sons of *Adam*. When God created *Adam*, he created us; and as many as are descended from *Adam*, have in themselves the root out of which they spring. The sons of God have God's own natural Son as a second *Adam* from heaven, whose race and progeny they are by spiritual and heavenly birth. God therefore loving eternally his Son, he must needs eternally in him have loved and preferred before all others, them which are spiritually sithence descended and sprung out of him. These were in God as in their Saviour, and not as in their Creator only. It was the purpose of his *saving* goodness, his *saving* wisdom, his *saving* power, which inclined it self towards them. They which thus were in God eternally by their intended admission to life, have by vocation or adoption God actually now in them, as the artificer is in the work which his hand doth presently frame. Life, as all other gifts and benefits, groweth originally from the Father, and cometh not to us but by the Son; nor by the Son to any of us in particular, but through the Spirit. For this cause the Apostle wisheth to the Church of *Corinth, The grace of our Lord Jesus Christ, and the love of God, and the fellowship of the Holy Ghost.* Which three St. *Peter* comprehendeth in one, *the participation of divine nature.* We are therefore in God through Christ eternally, according to that intent and purpose whereby we were chosen to be made his in this present world, before the world it self was made: We are in God, through the knowledge which is had of us, and the love which is born towards us from everlasting. But in God we actually are no longer than only from the time of our actual adoption into the body of his true church, into the fellowship of his children. For his church he knoweth and loveth; so that they which are in the church, are thereby known to be in him. Our being in Christ by eternal fore-knowledge saveth us not without our actual and real adoption into the fellowship of his saints in this present world. For in him we actually are by our actual incorporation into that society which hath him for their head; and doth make together with him one body, (he and they in that respect having one name) for which cause by virtue of this mystical conjunction, we are of him, and in him, even as tho' our very flesh and bones should be made continuate with his. We are in Christ, because he know-

Wisd. 7. 25.
Heb. 1. 3.

John 14. 23.

Acts 17. 28,
29.
John 1. 4.
& 1. 10.
Isai. 40. 26.
1 John 3. 1.

1 Cor. 15. 47.

Ephes. 1. 3, 4.

1 John 5. 11.
Rom. 8. 10.
2 Cor. 13. 13.
2 Pet. 1. 4.

Col. 2. 10.

1 Cor. 12. 12.

Ephes. 5. 30.

knoweth and loveth us, even as parts of himself. No man actually is in him, but they in whom he actually is. For *he which hath not the Son of God, hath not life : I am the vine, and ye are the branches : He which abideth in me, and I in him, the same bringeth forth much fruit* ; but the branch severed from the vine withereth. We are therefore adopted sons of God to eternal life by participation of the only begotten Son of God, whose life is the well-spring and cause of ours. It is too cold an interpretation whereby some Men expound our being in Christ to import nothing else, but only that the self same nature which maketh us to be Men, is in him, and maketh him man as we are. For what man in the world is there, which hath not so far forth communion with Jesus Christ ? It is not this that can sustain the weight of such sentences as speak of the mystery of our coherence with Jesus Christ. The church is in Christ, as *Eve* was in *Adam.* Yea, by grace we are every of us in Christ and in his church, as by nature we were in those our first parents. God made *Eve* of the Rib of *Adam* ; and his church he frameth out of the very flesh, the very wounded and bleeding side of the Son of man. His body crucified and his blood shed for the life of the world, are the true elements of that heavenly Being, which maketh us such as himself is of whom we come. For which cause the words of *Adam* may be fitly words of Christ concerning his church, *flesh of my flesh, and bone of my bones* ; a true nature extract out of my own body. So that in him, even according to his manhood, we, according to our heavenly being, are as branches in that root out of which they grow. To all things he is life, and to men light, *as the Son of God* ; to the church, both life and light eternal, by being made the Son of man for us, and by being in us a Saviour, whether we respect him as God or as Man. *Adam* is in us as an original cause of nature, and of that corruption of nature which causeth death ; Christ as the cause original of restoration to life. The person of *Adam* is not in us, but his nature, and the corruption of his nature deriveth into all men by propagation ; Christ having *Adam's* nature, as we have, but incorrupt, deriveth not nature but incorruption, and that immediately from his own person, into all that belong unto him. As therefore we are really partakers of the body of sin and death received from *Adam* ; so except we be truly partakers of Christ, and as really possessed of his spirit, all we speak of eternal life is but a dream. That which quickneth us is the spirit of the second *Adam,* and his flesh that wherewith he quickneth. That which in him made our nature uncorrupt, was the union of his deity with our nature. And in that respect the sentence of death and condemnation, which only taketh hold upon sinful flesh, could no way possibly extend unto him. This caused his voluntary death for others to prevail with God, and to have the force of an expiatory sacrifice. The blood of Christ, as the apostle witnesseth, doth therefore take away sin, because *through the eternal Spirit he offered himself unto God without spot.* That which sanctified our nature in Christ, that which made it a sacrifice available to take away sin, is the same which quickneth it, raised it out of the grave after death, and exalted it unto glory. Seeing therefore that Christ is in us as a quickning spirit, the first degree of communion with Christ must needs consist in the participation of his Spirit, which *Cyprian* in that respect well termeth *Germaniſſimam Societatem*, the highest and truest society that can be between man and him, which is both God and man in one. These things St. *Cyril* duly considering, reproveth their speeches which taught that only the deity of Christ is the vine whereupon we by faith do depend as branches, and that neither his flesh nor our bodies are comprised in this resemblance. For doth any man doubt, but that even from the flesh of Christ our very bodies do receive that life which shall make them glorious at the latter day ; and for which they are already accounted parts of his blessed body ? Our corruptible bodies could never live the life they shall live, were it not that here they are joined with his body which is incorruptible, and that his is in ours as a cause of immortality, a cause by removing through the death and merit of his own flesh that which hindered the life of ours. Christ is therefore, both as God and as man, that true vine whereof we both spiritually and corporally are branches. The mixture of his bodily substance with ours is a thing which the ancient fathers [a] disclaim. Yet the mixture of his flesh with ours they [b] speak of, to signify what our very bodies, through mystical conjunction,

Marginal references:
John 15. 9.
1 John 5. 12.
John 15.5, 6.
John 14. 19.
Ephes 5. 23.
John 14. 20.
& 15. 4.
1 Cor. 15.48.
John 1.
& 6. 57.
Heb. 5. 9.
1 Cor. 15 45.
22.
Heb. 9. 14.
Cypr. de Cœna Dom. cap. 6.
Cyril. in Joan. lib. 10. cap. 13.

[a] *Noſtra quippe & ipſius conjunctio nec miſcet perſonas nec unit ſubſtantias, ſed affectus conſociat & conſæderat voluntates.* Cypr. de Cœn. Dom.
[b] *Quomodo dicunt carnem in corruptionem devenire, & non percipere vitam, quæ à corpore Domini & ſanguine alitur ?* Iren. lib. 4. adverſ. Hæreſ. cap. 34.

   re-

a *Unde confiderandum eft non folum 光σι feu conformitate affe-*
ctionum, Chriftum in nobis effe ; verum etiam participatione Natu-
rali (id eft reali & vera :) quemadmodum fi quis igne liquefactam
ceram alii cera fimiliter liquefacta ita mifcuerit, ut unum quid ex
utrifque factum videatur ; fic communicatione Corporis & Sangui-
nis Chrifti ipfe in nobis eft , & nos in ipfo. Cyril. in Joan. lib.
10. cap. 13.

receive from that vital efficacy which we know
to be in his ; and from bodily mixtures they
borrow divers fimilitudes, rather to declare the
truth, than the manner of a coherence between
his facred, and the fanctified bodies of faints.
Thus much no chriftian man will deny, that
when Chrift fanctified his own flesh, giving as
God, and taking as man the Holy Ghoft, he did not this for himfelf only, but for
our fakes, that the grace of fanctification and life, which was firft received in him,
might pafs from him to his whole race, as malediction came from *Adam* unto all
mankind. Howbeit, becaufe the work of his fpirit to thofe effects is in us prevented
by fin and death, poffeffing us before ; it is of neceffity, that as well our prefent
fanctification unto newnefs of life, as the future reftoration of our bodies, fhould
prefuppofe a participation of the grace, efficacy, merit, or virtue of his body and
blood ; without which foundation firft laid, there is no place for thofe other operations
of the fpirit of Chrift to enfue. So that Chrift imparteth plainly himfelf by degrees.

a Eph. 1. 23.
Ecclefia com-
plementum
ejus qui implet
omnia in om-
nibus. τὸ
πλήρωμα τῦ
πάντα ἐν πᾶσι
πληρμένε.

It pleafeth him in mercy to account himfelf incompleat and maimed b without us.
But moft affured we are, that we all receive of his fulnefs, becaufe he is in us as a
moving and working caufe ; from which many bleffed effects are really found to enfue, and that in fundry both kinds and degrees, all tending to eternal happinefs. It
muft be confefs'd, that of Chrift working as a creator and a governor of the world
by providence and univerfal prefence all are partakers ; not all partakers of that grace whereby he inhabi-
teth whom he faveth. Again, as he dwelleth not by grace in all, fo neither doth he

b Aug. Ep.
57.

equally work in all them in whom he dwelleth. c *Whence is it* (faith St. *Auguftin)*
that fome be holier than others are , but becaufe God doth dwell in fome more plenti-
fully than in others ? And becaufe the divine fubftance of Chrift is equally in all,
his human fubftance equally diftant from all ; it appeareth that the participation of
Chrift, wherein there are many degrees and differences, muft needs confift in fuch effects, as being derived from both natures of Chrift really into us, are made our own ;
and we by having them in us, are truly faid to have him from whom they come ; Chrift
alfo more or lefs, to inhabit and impart himfelf, as the graces are fewer or more,
greater or fmaller, which really flow into us from Chrift. Chrift is whole with the
whole church, and whole with every part of the church, as touching his perfon, which
can no way divide it felf, or be poffefs'd by degrees and portions. But the participation of Chrift importeth, befides the prefence of Chrift's perfon, and befides the myftical copulation thereof with the parts and members of his whole church, a true actual influence of grace whereby the life which we live according to godlinefs is his ;
and from him we receive thofe perfections wherein our eternal happinefs confifteth.

Gal. 2. 20.
Ifai. 53. 5.
Ephef. 1. 7.

Thus we participate Chrift, partly by imputation ; as when thofe things which he did
and fuffered for us are imputed unto us for righteoufnefs : Partly by habitual and real
infufion, as when grace is inwardly beftowed while we are on earth, and afterwards

Rom. 8. 9.
Gal. 4. 6.

more fully both our fouls and bodies made like unto his in Glory. The firft thing of
his fo infufed into our hearts in this life is the Spirit of Chrift ; whereupon, becaufe
the reft of what kind foever, do all both neceffarily depend and infallibly alfo enfue ;

1 John 3. 9.
Ephef. 1. 14.
Rom. 8. 23.

therefore the apoftles term it, fometime the feed of God, fometime the pledge of our
heavenly inheritance, fometime the handfel or earneft of that which is to come. From
whence it is, that they which belong to the myftical body of our Saviour Chrift,
and be in number as the ftars of heaven, divided fucceffively, by reafon of their mor-

1 Cor. 12. 27.
Ephef. 4. 15.
Rom. 12. 5.
Ephef. 4. 15.

tal condition, into may generations, are notwithftanding coupled every one to Chrift
their head, and all unto every particular perfon amongft themfelves, in as much as
the fame fpirit which anointed the bleffed Soul of our Saviour Chrift, doth fo for-
malize, unite and actuate his whole race, as if both he and they were fo many
limbs compacted into one body, by being quickned all with one and the fame foul.
That wherein we are partakers of Jefus Chrift by imputation, agreeth equally unto all
that have it. For it confifteth in fuch acts and deeds of his, as could not have longer
continuance than while they were in doing, nor at that very time belong unto any
other, but to him from whom they come ; and therefore how men, either then, or
before, or fithence, fhould be made partakers of them , there can be no way imagined, but only by imputation. Again, a deed muft either not be imputed to any, but
reft altogether in him whofe it is ; or if at all it be imputed, they which have it by
imputation, muft have it fuch as it is, whole. So that degrees being neither in the
perfonal prefence of Chrift, nor in the participation of thofe effects which are ours by
im-

imputation only; it refteth that we wholly apply them to the participation of Chrift's infufed grace; although, even in this kind alfo, the firft beginning of life, the feed of God, the firft fruits of Chrift's fpirit, be without latitude. For we have hereby only the being of the fons of God, in which number how far foever one may feem to excel another, yet touching this that all are fons, they are all equals, fome haply better fons than the reft are, but none any more a fon than another.

Thus therefore we fee, how the Father is in the Son, and the Son in the Father; how they both are in all things, and all things in them; what communion Chrift hath with his church, how his church, and every member thereof is in him by original derivation, and he perfonally in them, by way of myftical affociation, wrought through the gift of the Holy Ghoft, which they that are his receive from him, and together with the fame, what benefit foever the vital force of his body and blood may yield; yea, by fteps and degrees they receive the compleat meafure of all fuch divine grace as doth fanctify and fave throughout, till the day of their final exaltation, to a ftate of fellowfhip in glory with him, whofe partakers they are now in thofe things that tend to glory. As for any mixture of the fubftance of his flefh with ours, the participation which we have of Chrift includeth no fuch kind of grofs furmife.

57. It greatly offendeth that fome, when they labour to fhew the ufe of the holy The necefli-facraments, affign unto them no end, but only to teach the mind by other fenfes ty of Sacra-ments unto that which the word doth teach by hearing. Whereupon, how eafily neglect and the partici-carelefs regard of fo heavenly myfteries may follow, we fee in part by fome experi- pation of Chrift. ence had of thofe men with whom that opinion is moft ftrong. For where the word of God may be heard, which teacheth with much more expedition and more full explication any thing we have to learn, if all the benefit we reap by facraments be inftruction, they which at all times have opportunity of ufing the better mean to that purpofe, will furely hold the worfe in lefs eftimation. And unto infants, which are not capable of inftruction, who would not think it a meer fuperfluity that any facrament is adminiftred, if to adminifter the facraments be but to teach receivers what God doth for them? There is of facraments therefore, undoubtedly, fome other more excellent and heavenly ufe. Sacraments, by reafon of their mix'd nature, are more diverfly interpreted and difputed of than any other parts of religion befides; for that in fo great ftore of properties belonging to the felf-fame thing, as every man's wit hath taken hold of fome efpecial confideration above the reft, fo they have accordingly feemed one to crofs another, as touching their feveral opinions about the neceffity of facraments; whereas in truth their difagreement is not great. For, let refpect be had to the duty which every communicant doth undertake, and we may well-determine concerning the ufe of facraments, that they ferve as bonds of obedience to God, ftrict obligations to the mutual exercife of chriftian charity, provocations to godlinefs, prefervations from fin, memorials of the principal benefits of Chrift; refpect the time of their inftitution, and it thereby appeareth, that God hath annexed them for ever unto the new teftament, as other rites were before with the old; regard the weaknefs which is in us, and they are warrants for the more fecurity of our belief; compare the receivers of them with fuch as receive them not, and facraments are marks of diftinction to feparate God's own from ftrangers; fo that in all thefe refpects, they are found to be moft neceffary. But their chiefeft force and virtue confifteth not herein, fo much as in that they are heavenly ceremonies which God hath fanctified and ordained to be adminiftred in his church: Firft, As marks whereby to know when God doth impart the vital or faving grace of Chrift unto all that are capable thereof; and fecondly, as means conditional, which God requireth in them unto whom he imparteth Grace. For fith God in himfelf is invifible, and cannot by us be difcerned working, therefore when it feemeth good in the eyes of his heavenly wifdom, that men for fome fpecial intent and purpofe fhould take notice of his glorious prefence, he giveth them fome plain and fenfible token whereby to know what they cannot fee. For *Mofes* to fee God and live, was impoffible; yet *Mofes* Exod. 3. 2. by fire knew where the glory of God extraordinarily was prefent. The angel by John 5. 4. whom God endued the waters of the pool called *Bethefda*, with fupernatural virtue to heal, was not feen of any; yet the time of the angels prefence known by the troubled motions of the waters themfelves. The apoftles by fiery tongues, which Acts 2. 3. they faw, were admonifhed when the Spirit, which they could not behold, was upon them. In like manner it is with us. Chrift and his holy Spirit, with all their

blefled

blessed effects, though entring into the soul of man, we are not able to apprehend or express how, do notwithstanding give notice of the times when they use to make their access, because it pleaseth Almighty God to communicate by sensible means, those blessings which are incomprehensible. Seeing therefore that grace is a consequent of sacraments, a thing which accompanieth them as their end, a benefit which they have received from God himself, the author of sacraments, and not from any other natural or supernatural quality in them; it may be hereby both understood, that sacraments are necessary, and that the manner of their necessity to life supernatural, is not in all respects as food unto natural Life, because they contain in themselves no vital force or efficacy; they are not physical, but moral instruments of salvation, duties of service and worship; which unless we perform as the author of grace requireth, they are unprofitable. For, all receive not the grace of God, which receive the sacraments of his grace. Neither is it ordinarily his will, to bestow the grace of sacraments on any, but by the sacraments; which grace also, they that receive by sacraments or with sacraments, receive it from him, and not from them. For of sacraments, the very same is true, which *Solomon*'s wisdom observeth in the brazen serpent, *He that turned towards it, was not healed by the thing he saw, but by thee, O saviour of all.* This is therefore the necessity of sacraments. That saving grace which Christ originally is, or hath for the general good of his whole church, by sacraments he severally deriveth into every member thereof. Sacraments serve as the instruments of God, to that end and purpose: Moral instruments, the use whereof is in our own hands, the effect in his; for the use, we have his express commandment; for the effect, his conditional promise: So that without our obedience to the one, there is of the other no apparent assurance; as contrariwise, where the signs and sacraments of his grace are not either through contempt unreceived, or received with contempt, we are not to doubt, but that they really give what they promise, and are what they signify. For we take not baptism nor the eucharist for bare resemblances or memorials of things absent, neither for naked signs and testimonies assuring us of grace received before, but (as they are indeed and in verity) for means effectual, whereby God, when we take the sacraments, delivereth into our hands that grace available unto eternal life, which grace the sacraments *b* represent or signify. There have grown in the doctrine concerning sacraments, many difficulties for want of distinct explication, what kind or degree of grace doth belong unto each sacrament. For by this it hath come to pass, that the true immediate cause why baptism and why the supper of our Lord is necessary, few do rightly and distinctly consider. It cannot be denied but sundry the same effects and benefits which grow unto men by the one sacrament, may rightly be attributed unto the other. Yet then doth baptism challenge to it self but the inchoation of those graces, the consummation whereof dependeth on mysteries ensuing. We receive Christ Jesus in baptism once, as the first beginner; in the eucharist often, as being by continual degrees the finisher of our life. By baptism therefore we receive Christ Jesus, and from him that saving grace which is proper unto baptism; by the other sacrament we receive him also; imparting therein himself and that grace which the eucharist properly bestoweth. So that each sacrament having both that which is general or common, and that also which is peculiar unto it self, we may hereby gather, that the participation of Christ, which properly belongeth to any one sacrament, is not otherwise to be obtained, but by the sacrament whereunto it is proper.

The substance of baptism; the rites or solemnities thereunto belonging, and that the substance thereof being kept, other things in baptism may give place to necessity.

58. Now even as the soul doth organize the body, and give unto every member thereof that substance, quantity, and shape, which nature seeth most expedient; so the inward Grace of sacraments may teach what serveth best for their outward form; a thing in no part of christian religion, much less here to be neglected. Grace intended by sacraments, was a cause of the choice, and is a reason of the fitness of the elements themselves. Furthermore, seeing that the grace which here we receive, doth no way depend upon the natural force of that which we presently behold, it was of necessity,

---

a Wis. 16. 17. *Spiritus Sancti munus est gratiam implere mysterii.* Ambr. in Luc. cap. 3. *Sanctificatis elementis effectum non propria ipsorum natura prebet, sed virtus divine potentiae operatur.* Cyp. de Chrism.

b *Dum homini bonum invisibile redditur, foris ei ejusdem significatio per species visibiles adhibetur, ut foris excitetur & intus reparetur. In ipsa vasa specie virtus exprimitur medicina.* Hugo de Sacram. lib. 1. cap. 3. *Si ergo vasa sunt spiritualis gratiae sacramenta, non ex suo sanant, quia vasa aegrotum non curant, sed medicina.* Idem, lib. 1. cap. 4.

neceffity, that words of expreſs declaration taken from the very mouth of our Lord himſelf, ſhould be added unto viſible elements, that the one might infallibly teach what the other do moſt aſſuredly bring to paſs.   In writing and ſpeaking of the bleſſed ſacrament, we [a] uſe for the moſt part under the name of their ſubſtance, not only to compriſe that whereof they outwardly and ſenſibly conſiſt, but alſo the ſecret grace which they ſignify and exhibit.   This is the reaſon wherefore commonly in [b] definitions, whether they be framed larger to augment, or ſtricter to abridge the number of ſacraments, we find grace expreſly mentioned as their true eſſential form, elements as the matter whereunto that form doth adjoin it ſelf.   But if that be ſeparated which is ſecret, and that conſidered alone which is ſeen, as of neceſſity it muſt in all thoſe ſpeeches that make diſtinction of ſacraments from ſacramental grace, the name of a ſacrament in ſuch ſpeeches can imply no more than what the outward ſubſtance thereof doth comprehend.   And to make compleat the outward ſubſtance of a ſacrament, there is required an outward form, which form ſacramental elements receive from ſacramental words.   Hereupon it groweth, that [c] many times there are three things ſaid to make up the ſubſtance of a ſacrament ; namely, the grace which is thereby offered, the element which ſhadoweth or ſignifieth grace, and the word which expreſſeth what is done by the element.   So that whether we conſider the outward by it ſelf, or both the outward and inward ſubſtance of any ſacraments, there are in the one reſpect but two eſſential parts, and in the other but three that concur to give ſacraments their full being.   Furthermore, becauſe definitions are to expreſs but the moſt immediate and neareſt parts of nature, whereas other principles farther off, altho' not ſpecified in defining, are notwithſtanding in nature implied and preſuppoſed, we muſt note, that in as much as ſacraments are actions religious and myſtical, which nature they have not unleſs they proceed from a ſerious meaning ; and what every man's private mind is, as we cannot know, ſo neither are we bound to examine ; Therefore always in theſe caſes the known intent of the church generally doth ſuffice ; and where the contrary is not [d] manifeſt, we may preſume that he which outwardly doth the work, hath inwardly the purpoſe of the church of God.   Concerning all other orders, rites, prayers, leſſons, ſermons, actions, and their circumſtances whatſoever, they are to the outward ſubſtance of baptiſm but things acceſſory, which the wiſdom of the church of Chriſt is to order according to the exigence of that which is principal.   Again, conſidering that ſuch ordinances have been made to adorn the ſacrament, [e] not the ſacrament to depend upon them ; ſeeing alſo, that they are not of the ſubſtance of baptiſm, and that baptiſm is far more neceſſary than any ſuch incident rite or ſolemnity ordained for the better adminiſtration thereof ; [f] if the caſe be ſuch as permitteth not baptiſm to have the decent complements of baptiſm, better it were to enjoy the body without his furniture, than to wait for this till the opportunity of that for which we deſire it be loſt.   Which premiſes ſtanding, it ſeemeth to have been no abſurd collection, that in caſes of neceſſity, which will not ſuffer delay till baptiſm be adminiſtred with uſual ſolemnities, (to ſpeak the leaſt) it may be tolerably given without them, rather than any man without it ſhould be ſuffered to depart this life.

59.   They which deny that any ſuch caſe of neceſſity can fall, in regard whereof the church ſhould tolerate baptiſm without the decent rites and ſolemnities thereunto belonging, pretend that ſuch tolerations have riſen from a falſe interpretation which certain men have made of the ſcripture, grounding a neceſſity of external bap-

The grounds in ſcripture whereupon a neceſſity of outward baptiſm hath been built.

[a] Euchariſtia duabus ex rebus conſtat, terrena & cæleſti. Iren. Adverſ. Hæreſ. lib. 4. cap. 34.   Arcanorum rerum ſymbola non nudis ſignis, ſed ſignis ſimul & rebus conſtant, Helvet. Conſeſ. Prior. Art. 2.

[b] Sacramentum eſt , cum res geſta viſibilis longe aliud inviſibile intus operatur, Iſid. Etym. lib. 1.   Sacramentum eſt per quod ſub tegumento rerum viſibilium divina virtus ſalutem ſecretius operatur, Greg. Mag.   Sacramentum eſt ſignum ſignificans efficaciter effectum Dei gratuitum , Occa. Sent. 4. d. 1.   Sacramentum proprie non eſt ſignum cujuſlibet rei ſacræ , ſed tantum rei ſacræ ſanctificantis homines, Tho. 12. q. 101. 4. & q. 102. 5.   Sacramentum eſt ſignum paſſionis Chriſti gratia & gloria.   Ideo eſt commemoratio præteriti, demonſtratio præſentis , & prognoſticon futuri, Tho. 3. q. 60. 3.   Sacramenta ſunt ſigna & ſymbola viſibilia verum internarum & inviſibilium , per quæ , ſeu per media, Deus virtute Spiritus Sancti in nobis agit, Conf. Belg. Art. 33.   Item, Bohem. Conf. cap. 11.

[c] Sacramenta conſtant verbo, ſignis, & rebus ſignificatis.   Conſeſ. Helvet. Poſt. c. 10.

[d] Si aliquid Miniſtri agere intendant, puta ſacris illudere ſti. ſteriis, vel aliud quod Eccleſia non conſentiat , nihil agitur : ſed ſide enim ſpiritualis poteſtas exercei quidem poteſt , ſine Eccleſia intentione non poteſt.   Lancel. Inſt. Jur. Can. lib. 2. Tit. 2. 5.   Hoc tamen.

[e] Acceſſorium non regulat Principale, ſed ab eo regulatur. 42.; De Regul. Jur. in Sext. lib. 3. ff. quod juſſu.

[f] Etſi nihil facile mutandum eſt ex ſolennibus , tamen ubi æquitas evidens poſcit , ſubveniendum eſt.   Lib. 183. de Reg. Jur.

T. C. l. 1. p. 143. Private baptism first rose upon a false interpretation of the place of St. *John* Ch. 3. 5. *Unless a man be born again of water, and of the spirit,* &c. where certain do interpret the word *water,* for the material and elemental water, when as our Saviour Christ taketh water there by a borrowed speech, for the Spirit of God, the effect whereof it shadoweth out. For even as in another place, *Mat* 3. 11. *By fire and the spirit,* he meaneth nothing but the Spirit of God, which purgeth and purifieth as the fire doth: So in this place, by water and the spirit, he meaneth nothing else but the Spirit of God, which cleanseth the filth of Sin, and cooleth the boiling heat of an unquiet Conscience; as water washeth the thing which is foul, and quencheth the heat of the fire.

baptism upon the words of our Saviour Christ: *Unless a man be born again of water and of the spirit, he cannot enter into the kingdom of heaven.* For by water and the Spirit, we are in that place to understand (as they imagine) no more than if the spirit alone had been mentioned, and water not spoken of. Which they think is plain, because elsewhere it is not improbable that *the Holy Ghost and fire* do but signify the Holy Ghost in operation resembling fire. Whereupon they conclude, that seeing fire in one place may be,

therefore water in another place is but a metaphor; Spirit, the interpretation thereof; and so the words do only mean, *That unless a man be born again of the spirit, he cannot enter into the kingdom of heaven.* I hold for a most infallible rule in expositions of sacred scripture, that where a literal construction will stand, the farthest from the letter is commonly the worst. There is nothing more dangerous than this licentious and deluding art, which changeth the meaning of words, as Alchimy doth or would do the substance of metals, maketh of any thing what it listeth, and bringeth in the end all truth to nothing. Or howsoever such voluntary exercise of wit might be born with otherwise; yet in places which usually serve, as this doth concerning regeneration by water and the Holy Ghost, to be alledged for grounds and principles, less is permitted. To hide the general consent of antiquity, agreeing in the literal interpretation, they cunningly affirm, that certain have taken those words as meant of material water, when they know that of all the ancients there is not one to be named that ever did otherwise either expound or alledge the place, than

[a] Minime sunt mutanda, qua interpretationem certam semper habuerunt. D. lib. 1. tit. 2. lib. 23.

as implying external baptism. Shall that which hath always [a] received this and no other construction, be now disguised with the toy of novelty? Must we needs at the only shew of a critical conceit, without any more deliberation, utterly condemn them of error, which will not admit that fire in the words of *John* is quenched with the name of the Holy Ghost; or, with the name of the Spirit, water dried up in the words of Christ? When the letter of the law hath two things plainly and expresly specified, water and the spirit; water as a duty required on our parts, the spirit as a gift which God bestoweth; there is danger in presuming so to interpret it, as if the clause which concerneth our selves were more than needeth. We may by such rare Expositions attain perhaps in the end to be thought witty, but

[b] Acts 1. 3. John baptized with water, but you shall within few days be baptized with the Holy Ghost.
[c] Acts 2. 3.

with ill advice. Finally, if at [b] the time when that baptism which was meant by *John* came to be really and truly performed by Christ himself, we find the apostles that had been, as we are, before baptized, new baptized with the Holy Ghost; and in this their later baptism as well a [c] visible descent of fire, as a secret miraculous infusion of the Spirit; if on us he accomplish likewise the heavenly work of our new birth, not with the spirit alone, but with water thereunto adjoined; sith the faithfullest expounders of his words are his own deeds, let that which his hand hath manifestly wrought, declare what his speech did doubtfully utter.

What kind of necessity in outward baptism hath been gathered by the words of our Saviour Christ; and what the true necessity thereof indeed is.

T. C. l. 1. p. 143. Secondly, This error (of private baptism) came by a false and unnecessary conclusion drawn from that place. For although the scripture should say, that none can be saved, but those which have the Spirit of God, and are baptized with material and elemental water; yet it ought to be understood of those which can conveniently and orderly be brought to baptism; as the scripture, saying, That whoso doth not believe the gospel, is condemned already, *Joh.* 3. 18. meaneth this sentence of those which can hear the gospel, and have discretion to understand it when they hear it; and cannot here shut under this condemnation, either those that be born deaf and so remain, or little infants, or natural fools that have not wit to conceive what is preached.

[d] Ἀναγκαῖον λέγω ᾧ ἄνευ οὐκ ἐνδέχεται ζῆν ὡς συναιτίῳ· ἢ ὧν ἄνευ τὸ ἀγαθὸν μὴ ἐνδέχεται ἢ εἶναι ἢ γίνεσθαι, ἢ τὸ κακὸν ἀποβαλεῖν, ἢ στερηθῆναι. *Necessarium id dicitur, sine quo ut con-causa fieri non potest ut vivatur: Et ea sine quibus fieri nequit ut bonum aut fit aut fiat; vel malum aliquod amoveatur, aut non adsit.* Arist. Metaph. 5. cap. 5.   [e] Joh. 3. 5.

60. To this they add, that as we err by following a wrong construction of the place before alledged; so our second oversight is, that we hereupon infer a necessity over rigorous and extreme. The true necessity of baptism, a few propositions considered will soon decide. All things which either are known [d] causes or set means, whereby any great good is usually procured, or men delivered from grievous evil, the same we must needs confess necessary. And if regeneration were not in this very sense a thing necessary to eternal life, would Christ himself have taught *Nicodemus,* that to see the kingdom of God is [e] impossible, saving only for those men which are born from above? His words following in the next sentence are a proof sufficient, that to our regeneration his spirit is no less

4

[a] ne-

a Verse 5. necessary, than regeneration it self necessary unto life. Thirdly, unless as the spirit is a necessary inward cause, so water were a necessary outward mean to our regeneration, what construction should we give unto those words wherein we are said to
be new born, and that ἐξ ὕδατος, even of water ? Why are we taught, that [b] with [b] Ephes. 5.
water God doth purify and cleanse his church? Wherefore do the apostles of Christ [26].
term baptism [c] a bath of regeneration ? What purpose had they in giving men advice
to receive outward baptism, and in persuading them, it did avail [d] to remission of [c] Tit. 3. 5.
fins ? If outward baptism were a cause in it self possessed of that power, either natu- [d] Acts 2. 38.
ral or supernatural, without the present operation whereof no such effect could pos- [e] *Fideles sala-*
sibly grow ; it must then follow, that seeing effects do never prevent the necessary *tem ex istis*
causes out of which they spring, no man could ever receive grace before bap- *elementis non*
tism : Which being apparently both known, and also confess'd to be otherwise in *quaerunt, eti-*
many particulars, although in the rest we make not baptism a cause of grace ; yet *quaerunt. Non*
the grace which is given them with their [e] baptism, doth so far forth depend on the *enim ista tri-*
very outward sacrament, that God will have it embraced, not only as a sign or *ista tribuitur.*
token what we receive, but also as an instrument or mean whereby we receive Hugo de Sa-
grace, because baptism is a sacrament which God hath instituted in his church, to the cram. lib. 1.
end that they which receive the same might
thereby be [f] incorporated into Christ ; and so
through his most precious merit obtain, as well
that saving grace of imputation which taketh
away [g] all former guiltiness, as also that [h] infused divine virtue of the Holy Ghost which
giveth to the powers of the foul their first
disposition towards future newness of life.
There are that elevate too much the ordinary
and immediate means of life, relying wholly
upon the bare conceit of that eternal election,
which notwithstanding includeth a subordination of means, without which we are not
actually brought to enjoy what God secretly
did intend ; and therefore to build upon God's
election, if we keep not our selves to the
ways which he hath appointed for men to
walk in, is but a self-deceiving vanity.   When

[f] *Susceptus a Christo, Christumque suscipiens, non idem sit post lavacrum qui ante Baptismum fuit ; sed corpus regenerati sit caro crucifixi.* Leo. Serm. 4. de Pas. Dom.
[g] *Caro abluitur ut anima emaculetur,* Tert. de Carn. Resur. *Homo per aquam Baptismi licet a foris idem esse videatur, intus tamen alter efficitur ; cum peccato natus, sine peccato renascitur ; prioribus perit, succedentibus proficit ; deterioribus exuitur, in meliora innovatur ; persona tingitur, & natura mutatur.* Euseb. Emis. de Epiphan. Homil. 3. Τριφύλα γεννησιν ηικειν εἶδεν ὁ λόγος, ἢ ἐκ σώματος, ἢ ἐκ βαπτίσματος, ἢ ἐξ ἀναστάσεως. Αὐτη μεν ἡ βαπτίσματος χάρισις σώμασις, ὁ κόσμος καταλλάσσεται δὲ πάλαι, ἢ ἢ τῷ ναῷ ἐφεστην αμαρτιας ἐξ ὕδατις ἔχωμεν. Greg. Homil. de Sanct. Bapt.
[h] *Unde genitalis auxilio superioris ævi labe detersa in expiatum pectus ac purum desuper se lumen infundit.* Cypr. Epist. ad Donat. Οὐ μόνον τῶν παλαιῶν ἁμαρτημάτων οἱ πῶτοι τ᾽ ἀσεσιν, ἀλλὰ ἢ τ᾽ ἐκπιὼν τῶν ὑπαγγελμάτων ἐστίδησιν ἀγαθῶν, ἢ τῷ διαπτονται δωκύτε ἢ τ᾽ ἀνασασεως καταικται παινωνὲς, ἢ τ᾽ ἐν ποδιμαζεῖ δωρεαῖς τ᾽ ἱστορίαν χαιζέται. Theod. Epit. Divin. Dogmat.   *Baptizari, est purgari a sordibus peccatorum, & donari varia Dei gratia ad vitam novam & innocentem.* Confess. Helvet. cap. 20.

the apostle saw men called to the participation of Jesus Christ, after the gospel of
God embraced, and the sacrament of life received, he feareth not [i] then to put them [i] Eph. 1. 1.
in the number of elect saints ; he [k] then accounteth them delivered from death and [k] Eph. 5. 8.
clean purged from all sin.   Till then, notwithstanding their pre-ordination unto life,
which none could know of saving God ; what were they in the Apostles own [l] ac- [l] Eph. 2. 3,
count, but children of wrath, as well as others, plain aliens, altogether without [12] [12]
hope, strangers, utterly without God in this present world ? So that by sacraments,
and other sensible tokens of grace, we may boldly gather, that he whose mercy
vouchsafeth now to bestow the means, hath also long sithence intended us that
whereunto they lead.   But let us never think it safe to presume of our own last
end by bare conjectural collections of his first intent and purpose, the means failing
that should come between.   Predestination bringeth not to life without the grace of
external [m] vocation, wherein our baptism is implied: For as we are not naturally [m] Rom. 8.30,
men without birth, so neither are we christian men in the eye of the church of
God but by new birth ; nor according to the manifest ordinary course of divine
dispensation new born, but by that baptism which both declareth and maketh us
christians.   In which respect, we justly hold it to be the door of our actual entrance into God's house, the first apparent
[n] beginning of life, a seal perhaps to the
[o] grace of election before received ; but to
our sanctification here, a step that hath not
any before it.   There were of the old *Valentinian* hereticks some which had knowledge
in such admiration, that to it they ascribed all,
and so despised the sacraments of Christ, pretending that as ignorance had made us
subject to all misery, so the full redemption of the inward man, and the work

[n] Ἀρχή μοι ζωῆς τὸ βάπτισμα. Basil. de Spir. Sanct. cap. 10.
[o] *T. C. l. 3. p. 134.* He which is not a christian before he come to receive baptism, cannot be made a christian by baptism ; which is only the seal of the grace of God before received.

of

[a] Iren. contra Hæref. l. 1. c. 18.

[b] Hic sceleftiffimi illi provocant quæftiones. Adeo dicunt, Baptifmus non eft neceffarius quibus fides fatis eft. Tert. de Baptif. Huic nulla proderit fides, qui, cum poffit, non percipit facramentum. Bern. Epift. 70. ad Hugon.

[c] 2 Kings 5. 14.
[d] Num. 21.8.
[e] Mark 16.16.

[f] Inftitutio Sacramentorum quantum ad Deum Authorem, difpenfationis eft ; quantum vero ad hominem obedientem, neceffitatis. Quoniam in poteftate Dei eft præter ifta hominem falvare, fed in poteftate hominis non eft fine iftis ad falutem pervenire. Hugo. de Sacra. lib. 1. cap. 5.

[f] Pelagius afferere arrepta impietate præfumit non propter vitam, fed propter regnum Cælorum Baptifmum parvulis conferendum. Eufeb. Emiff. Hom. 5. de pafch.

[h] Benignius leges interpretanda funt, quo voluntas earum confervetur. L. Benign. D. de legib. & Senatufc.
[i] T.C. lib. 1. p. 143.

[k] Bern. Epift. 70. ad Hugonem.

of our reftoration muft needs belong unto [a] knowledge only. They draw very near unto this error who fixing wholly their minds on the known neceffity of faith, [b] imagine that nothing but faith is neceffary for the attainment of all grace. Yet is it a branch of belief, that facraments are in their place no lefs required than belief it felf. For when our Lord and Saviour promifeth eternal life, is it any otherwife than as he promifed reftitution of health unto *Naaman* the *Syrian*, namely, with this condition, [c] *Wafh, and be clean ?* or as to them which were ftung of ferpents, health by [d] beholding the brazen ferpent ? If Chrift himfelf which giveth falvation, do [e] require baptifm ; it is not for us that look for falvation to found and examine him, whether unbaptized men may be faved ; but ferioufly to [f] do that which is required, and religioufly to fear the danger which may grow by the want thereof. Had Chrift only declared his will to have all men baptized, and not acquainted us with any caufe why baptifm is neceffary, our ignorance in the reafon of that he enjoyneth, might perhaps have hindred fomewhat the forwardnefs of our obedience thereunto : Whereas now being taught that baptifm is neceffary to take away fin, how have we the fear of God in our hearts, if care of delivering men's fouls from fin do not move us to ufe all means for their baptifm ? [g] *Pelagius* which denied utterly the guilt of original fin, and in that refpect the neceffity of baptifm, did notwithftanding both baptize infants, and acknowledge their baptifm neceffary for entrance into the kingdom of God. Now the law of Chrift, which in thefe confiderations maketh baptifm neceffary, muft be conftrued and underftood according to rules of [h] natural equity. Which rules, if they themfelves did not follow in expounding the law of God, would they never be able to prove, that [i] the fcripture faying, *Whofo believeth not the gofpel of Chrift, is condemned already*, meaneth this fentence of thofe which can hear the gofpel, and have difcretion when they hear, to underftand it ; neither ought it to be applied unto infants, deaf men and fools. That which teacheth them thus to interpret the law of Chrift, is natural equity. And (becaufe equity fo teacheth) it is on all parts gladly confefs'd, *that there may be in divers cafes* life by vertue of inward baptifm, even where outward is not found. So that if any queftion be made, it is but about the bounds and limits of this poffibility. For example, to think that a man whofe baptifm the crown of martyrdom preventeth, doth lofe in that cafe the happinefs which fo many thoufands enjoy, that only have had the grace to believe, and not the honour to feal the teftimony thereof with death, were almoft barbarous. Again, when [k] fome certain opinionative men in St. *Bernard*'s time began privately to hold that, becaufe our Lord hath faid, *unlefs a man be born again of water*, therefore life, without either actual baptifm or martyrdom inftead of baptifm, cannot poffibly be obtained at the hands of God ; *Bernard* confidering, that the fame equity which had moved them to think the neceffity of baptifm no bar againft the happy eftate of unbaptized martyrs, is as forcible for the warrant of their falvation, in whom, although there be not the fufferings of holy martyrs, there are the virtues which fanctified thofe fufferings, and made them precious in God's fight, profeffed himfelf an enemy to that feverity and ftrictnefs which admitteth no exception but of martyrs only. For, faith he, if a man defirous of baptifm be fuddenly cut off by death, in whom there wanted neither found faith, devout hope, nor fincere charity (God be merciful unto me, and pardon me if I err) but verily of fuch a ones falvation, in whom there is no other defect befides his faultlefs lack of baptifm, defpair I cannot, nor induce my mind to think his faith void, his hope confounded, and his charity faln to nothing, only becaufe he hath not that which not contempt but impoffibility withholdeth. *Tell me, I befeech you,* (faith *Ambrofe*) *what there is in any of us more than to will, and to feek for our own good. Thy fervant* Valentinian, *O Lord, did both.* (For *Valentinian* the emperor died before his purpofe to receive baptifm could take effect.) *And is it poffible, that he which had purpofely thy fpirit given him to defire grace, fhould not receive thy grace which that fpirit did defire ? Doth it move you that the outward accuftomed*

I

fo-

solemnities were not done? As though converts that suffer martyrdom before bap-
tism, did thereby forfeit their right to the crown of eternal glory in the kingdom of
heaven. If the blood of martyrs in that case be their baptism, surely his religious
desire of baptism standeth him in the same stead. It hath been therefore constantly
held as well touching other believers, as [a] mar-
tyrs, that baptism, taken away by necessity, is
supplied by desire of baptism, because with
equity this opinion doth best stand. Touching
infants which die unbaptized, sith they neither
have the sacrament itself, nor any sense or
conceit thereof, the judgment of many hath gone hard against them. But yet seeing grace is not absolutely tied unto sacraments; and besides, such is the lenity of
God, that unto things altogether impossible he bindeth no man; but where we
cannot do what is enjoined us, accepteth our will to do instead of the deed it self;
Again, for as much as there is in their christian parents, and in the church of God, a
presumed desire, that the sacrament of baptism might be given them; yea, a purpose also that it shall be given; remorse of equity hath moved divers of the
[b] school-divines in these considerations, ingenuously to grant, that God, all merciful to such as are not in themselves able to desire baptism, imputeth the secret desire
that others have in their behalf, and accepteth the same as theirs, rather than casteth
away their souls for that which no man is able to help. And of the will of God to
impart his grace unto infants without baptism in that case, the very circumstance of
their natural birth may serve as a just argument; whereupon it is not to be misliked,
that men in charitable presumption do gather a great likelihood of their salvation,
to whom the benefit of christian parentage being given, the rest that should follow
is prevented by some such casualty, as man hath himself no power to avoid. For,
we are plainly taught of God, [c] that the seed of faithful parentage is holy from the
very birth. Which albeit we may not so understand, as if the children of believing parents were without sin; or grace from baptized parents derived by propagation; or God, by covenant and promise, tied to save any in mere regard of their parents
belief: Yet seeing that to all professors of the name of Christ, this pre-eminence a-
bove infidels is freely given; the fruit of their bodies bringeth into the world with
it a present interest and right to those means wherewith the ordinance of Christ is
that his church shall be sanctified, it is not to be thought that he which, as it
were, from heaven hath nominated and designed them unto holiness by special privilege of their very birth, will himself deprive them of regeneration and inward grace, only because necessity depriveth them of outward sacraments. In which
case, it were the part of charity to hope, and to make men rather partial than cruel
judges, if we had not those fair appearances which here we have. Wherefore a necessity there is of receiving, and a necessity of administring the sacrament of baptism; the one peradventure not so absolute as some have thought, but out of all
peradventure the other more strait and narrow than that the church, which is by
office a mother unto such as crave at her hands the sacred mystery of their new
birth, should repel them, and see them die unsatisfied of these their ghostly desires, rather than give them their souls [d] rights with omission of those things which
serve but only for the more convenient and orderly administration thereof. For
as on the one side we grant, that those sentences of holy scripture which make sacraments most necessary to eternal life, are no prejudice to their salvation that want
them by some inevitable necessity and without any fault of their own; so it ought,
in reason, to be likewise acknowledged, that for as much as our Lord himself maketh baptism necessary, necessary whether we respect the good received by baptism, or the testimony thereby yielded unto God of that humility and meek obedience, which reposing wholly it self on the absolute authority of his commandment, and on the truth of his heavenly promise, doubteth not but from creatures
despicable in their own condition and substance in other grace of inestimable value; or rather not from them, but from him, yet by them, as by his appointed
means; howsoever he, by the secret ways of his own incomprehensible mercy, may
be thought to save without baptism, this cleareth not the church from guiltiness of
blood, if through her superfluous scrupulosity, lets and impediments of less regard
should cause a grace of so great moment to be withheld, wherein our merciless
strictness may be our own harm, though not theirs towards whom we shew it; and
we for the hardness of our hearts may perish, albeit they through Gods unspeakable mercy do live. God which did not afflict that innocent whose circumcision

Notes in margin:

[a] *Qui ad tolerandam omnem pro Dei gloria injuriam semel di-*
tavit animum in Martyrium, mihi videtur implesse. Summi ergo
meriti est semel sirisse sententiam, atque ideo, ut dixi, ratio prin-
cipatum obtinet passionis, & si sors perpetiendi deneget facultatem,
pertulit tamen cuncta quæ voluit pati. Joseph. lib. de Imper.
Ration.

[b] *Gerf. Serm.*
in Nativit.
Beatæ Mar.
Cajetan. in 3.
Tho. 9. 68.
Art. 1. & 2.
Biel. in 4.
Sentend. 4.q.2.
Tilman. Sege-
berg. de Sacr.
cap. 1. Eli-
sius Neapol. in
Clyp. Adverf.
Heref. cap. de
Baptif.
[c] *1 Cor. 7. 12.*

[d] *T. C. l. 3.*
p. 218. It is
in question,
whether
there be any
such necessi-
ty of bap-
tism, as that
for the mini-
string there-
of, the com-
mon decent
orders should
be broken.

Exod. 4. 14. *Mofes* had over-long deferred, took revenge upon *Mofes* himfelf for the injury which was done through fo great neglect; giving us thereby to underftand, that they whom God's own mercy faveth without us, are on our parts notwithftanding, and as much as in us lieth, even deftroyed, when under unfufficient pretences we defraud them of fuch ordinary outward helps as we fhould exhibit. We have for baptifm no day fet, as the *Jews* had for circumcifion; neither have we by the law of God, * In omnibus obligationibus in quibus dies non poritur, præfenti die debetur. Lib. 14. D. de Reg. Jur. but only by the churches difcretion, a place thereunto appointed. Baptifm therefore even in the meaning of the law of Chrift, belongeth unto infants capable thereof from the * very inftant of their birth. Which if they have not howfoever, rather than lofe it, by being put off becaufe the time, the place, or fome fuch like circumftance doth not folemnly enough concur, the church, as much as in her lieth, wilfully cafteth away their fouls.

What things in baptifm have been difpens'd with by the fathers, refpecting neceffity.

b *T. C. l.* 1. *p.* 146. The authors themfelves of that error, that they cannot be faved which are not baptized, did never feek a remedy of the mifchief in women's or private baptifm. *T. C. l.* 5. *p.* 219. What plainer teftimony can there be than that of *Auguftin*? which noteth the ufe of the church to have been, to come to the church with their children in danger of death, and that when fome had opinion that their children could not be faved if they were not baptized, *Cont. Lit. Parm.* lib. 2. cap. 13. I would alfo know of him what he will anfwer to that which is noted of a chriftian *Jew* defperately fick of the palfey, that was with his bed carried to the place of baptifm, *Socr.* lib. 7. c. 4. What will he anfwer to this, That thofe which were baptized in their beds, were thereby made unapt to have any place amongft the clergy (as they call them) doth it not leave a note of infamy in thofe which had procured that baptifm fhould be adminiftred in private houfes? *Eufeb.* lib. 6. cap. 43. What unto the emperors decree, which upon authority of the ancient laws, and of the apoftles, forbiddeth, That the holy things fhould be adminiftred in any man's houfe? *Juft. Novel.* 57.
c *Leo Epift.* 4. *ad Epifc. Sicil.*

61. The ancients it may be were too fevere, and made the neceffity of baptifm more abfolute than reafon would, as touching infants. But will b any man fay, that they, notwithftanding their too much rigor herein, did not in that refpect fuftain and tolerate defects of local, or of perfonal folemnities belonging to the facrament of baptifm? The apoftles themfelves did neither ufe nor appoint for baptifm any certain time. The church for general baptifm heretofore made choice of two chief days in the year; the feaft of *Eafter*, and the feaft of *Pentecoft*. Which cuftom when certain churches in *Sicily* began to violate without caufe, they were by c *Leo* bifhop of *Rome* advifed, rather to conform themfelves to the reft of the world in things fo reafonable, than to offend mens minds through needlefs fingularity: Howbeit, always providing, that neverthelefs in apparent peril of death, danger of fiege, ftraits of perfecution, fear of fhipwrack, and the like exigents, no refpect of time fhould caufe this fingular defence of true

d *Vict. Ep. ad Theoph. Alexand. in Pontif. Damaf.* fafety to be denied unto any. This of *Leo* did but confirm that fentence which d *Victor* had many years before given, extending the fame exception as well unto places as times. That which St. *Auguftine* fpeaketh of Women hafting to bring their children to the church when they faw danger, is a weak proof *That when neceffity did not leave them fo much time*, it was not then permitted them neither to make a church of their own home. Which anfwer difchargeth likewife their example of a fick *Jew* carried in a bed to the place of baptifm, and not baptized at home in private. The caufe why fuch kind of baptifm barred men afterwards from entring into holy orders, the reafon wherefore it was objected againft *Novatian*, in what refpect, and how far forth it did difable, may be gathered by the twelfth Canon fet down in the council of *Neocæfarea* after this manner. *A man which hath been baptized in ficknefs, is not after to be ordained prieft.* For it may be thought, *That fuch do rather at that time, becaufe they fee no other remedy, than of a voluntary mind, lay hold on the Chriftian Faith, unlefs their true and fincere meaning be made afterwards the more manifeft, or elfe the fcarcity of others inforce the church to admit them.* They bring in *Juftinian's* imperial conftitution, but to what purpofe? Seeing it only forbiddeth men to have the myfteries of God adminiftred in their private chapels, left under that pretence hereticks fhould do fecretly thofe things which were unlawful. In which confideration he therefore commandeth, that if they would ufe thofe private oratories otherwife than only for their private prayers, the bifhop fhould appoint them a clerk, whom they might entertain for that purpofe. This is plain by later conftitutions made in the time of Leo Conft. 4. *Leo*: It *was thought good* (faith the Emperor) *in their judgment which have gone before, that in private Chappels none fhould celebrate the holy communion but priefts belonging unto greater churches. Which order they took as it feemeth for the cuftody of Religion, left men fhould fecretly receive from hereticks, inftead of the food,* Idem,Conft.15. *the bane of their fouls, pollution in the place of expiation.* Again, *Whereas a facred canon of the fixth reverend fynod requireth baptifm, as others have likewife the holy facrifices and myfteries, to be celebrated only in temples hallowed for publick ufe, use, and not in private oratories ; which strict decrees appear to have been made heretofore in regard of hereticks which entred closely into such mens houses as favoured their opinions, whom, under colour of performing with them such religious offices, they drew from the soundness of true religion: Now that perverse opinions, through the grace of almighty God, are extinct and gone, the cause of former restraints being taken away, we see no reason but that private oratories may henceforward enjoy that liberty, which to have granted them heretofore, had not been safe.* In sum, all these things alledged are nothing, nor will it ever be prov'd while the world doth continue, but that the practice of the church in cases of extream necessity, hath made for private baptism always more than against it. Yea, *baptism by any man, in the case of necessity,* was the voice of the whole world heretofore. Neither is *Tertullian, Epiphanius, Augustin,* or any other of the ancients against it. The boldness of such, as pretending *Tecla*'s example, took openly upon them both baptism, and all other publick functions of priesthood, *Tertullian* severely controuleth, saying, [b] *To give baptism is in truth the bishop's right. After him it belongeth unto priests and deacons ; but not to them without authority from him received. For so the honour of the church requireth, which being kept, preserveth peace. Were it not in this respect, the laity might do the same ; all sorts might give, even as all sorts receive.* But because emulation is the mother of schisms, *Let it content thee* (which art of the order of lay-men) *to do it in necessity, when the state of time, or place, or person thereunto compelleth. For then is their boldness privileged that help, when the circumstance of other mens dangers craveth it.* What he granteth generally to lay-persons of the house of God, the same we cannot suppose he denieth to any sort or sex contain'd under that name, unless himself did restrain the limits of his own speech ; especially seeing that *Tertullian*'s rule of interpretation is elsewhere, *Specialties are signified under that which is general, because they are therein comprehended.* All which *Tertullian* doth [c] deny is, that women may be called to bear, or publickly take upon them to execute offices of ecclesiastical order, whereof none but men are capable. As for *Epiphanius,* he striketh on the very self-same anvil with *Tertullian.* And in necessity, if St. *Augustin* alloweth as much unto lay-men as *Tertullian* doth, his not mentioning of women, is but a slender proof that his meaning was to exclude women. Finally, the council of *Carthage* likewise, although it make no express submission, may be very well presumed willing to stoop, as other positive ordinances do, to the countermands of necessity. Judge therefore what the ancients would have thought, if in their days it had been heard, which is published in ours, [d] *That because The substance of the sacrament doth chiefly depend on the institution of God, which is the form, and as it were the life of the sacrament ; therefore first, If the whole institution be not kept, it is no sacrament ;* and secondly, if baptism be private, his institution is broken, in as much as *according to the orders which he hath set for baptism, it should be done in the congregation ;* from whose ordinance in this point *we ought not to swerve, although we know that infants should be assuredly damned without baptism.* O Sir, you that would spurn thus at such, as in case of so dreadful extremity should lie prostrate before your feet ; you that would turn away your face from them at the hour of their most need ; you that would dam up your ears, and harden your hearts as iron against the unresistible cries of supplicants, calling upon you for mercy with terms of such invocation, as that most dreadful perplexity might minister, if God by miracle did open the mouths of infants to express their supposed necessity, should first imagine your self in their case, and them in yours. This done, let their suppli-

[a] *T. C. lib. 1. pag. 145.* To allow of womens baptising, is not only contrary to the learned writers now, but also contrary to all learned antiquity, and contrary to the practice of the church whilst there was any tolerable estate. *Tertul. de Virgin. veland. & lib. de Baptis. Epipha. lib. 1. & lib. 2. cont. Hæres.* St. *Augustin,* although he seem to allow of a lay-man's baptism in time of necessity, *Cont. Epist. Parmen. lib. 2. cap. 13.* yet there he mentioneth not womens baptism ; and in the fourth council of *Carthage,* cap. 100. it is simply, without exception decreed, that a woman ought not to baptize.

[b] *Subjectum est veneratis speciale. In ipso significatur, quia in ipso continetur.* Tertul. de Veland. Virg. *Posito genere, supponitur species.* Aug. in lib. 2. cap. de Transact.

[c] *Non permittitur mulieri in ecclesia loqui, sed nec docere, nec tingere, nec offerre, nec ullius virilis muneris nedum sacerdotalis officii sortem sibi vindicare.* Tertul. de Velandis Virg.

[d] *T. C. lib. 1. pag. 144.* The substance of the sacrament dependeth chiefly of the institution and word of God, which is the form, and, as it were, the life of the sacrament. *T. C.* lib. 8. pag. 144. Although part of the institution be observed, yet if the whole institution be not, it is no sacrament. *T. C.* lib. 1. pag. 146. The orders which God hath set, are, that it should be done in the congregation, and by the minister. *T. C.* lib. 1. pag. 146. And I will further say, that although the infants which die without baptism, should be assuredly damned (which is most false) yet ought not the orders which God hath set in his church, to be broken after this sort.

Supplications proceed out of your mouth, and your anſwer out of theirs. Would
Noſtro peccato
alterius ſaluti
conſulere non
debemus. Aug.
lib. cont.
Mead. cap.
17.
Mat. 9. 13.
you then contentedly hear, *My Son, the rites and ſolemnities of baptiſm muſt be
kept ; we may not do ill, that good may come of it ; neither are ſouls to be delivered
from eternal death and condemnation, by breaking orders which Chriſt hath ſet :*
Would you in their caſe your ſelf be ſhaken off with theſe anſwers, and not rather
embrace, incloſed with both your arms, a ſentence, which now is no Goſpel
unto you, *I will have mercy and not ſacrifice?* To acknowledge Chriſt's inſtitution
the ground of both ſacraments, I ſuppoſe no chriſtian man will refuſe : For it giveth
them their very nature, it appointeth the matter whereof they conſiſt, the form of
their adminiſtration it teacheth ; and it bleſſeth them with that Grace whereby to us
they are both pledges and inſtruments of life. Nevertheleſs, ſeeing Chriſt's inſtitution containeth, beſides that which maketh compleat the eſſence of nature, other
things that only are parts, as it were, of the furniture of ſacraments ; the difference between theſe two muſt unfold that which the general terms of indefinite
ſpeech would confound. If the place appointed for baptiſm be a part of Chriſt's inſtitution, it is but his inſtitution as ſacrifice, baptiſm his inſtitution as mercy : In this
caſe, he which requireth both mercy and ſacrifice, rejecteth his own inſtitution of
ſacrifice, where the offering of ſacrifice would hinder mercy from being ſhewed.
Matth. 25.
23.
External Circumſtances, even in the holieſt and higheſt actions, are but the *leſſer
things of the law*, whereunto thoſe actions themſelves being compared, are the
greater ; and therefore as the greater are of ſuch importance, that they muſt be done ;
ſo in that extremity before ſuppoſed, if our account of the leſſer which are not to
be omitted, ſhould cauſe omiſſion of that which is more to be accounted of, were
not this our ſtrict obedience to Chriſt's inſtitution touching mint and cummin, a diſobedience to his inſtitution concerning love ? But ſith no inſtitution of Chriſt hath ſo
ſtrictly tied baptiſm to publick aſſemblies, as it hath done all men unto baptiſm ;
away with theſe mercileſs and bloody ſentences, let them never be found ſtanding in
the book and writings of a chriſtian man ; they ſavour not of Chriſt, nor of his
moſt gracious and meek ſpirit, but under colour of exact obedience, they nouriſh
cruelty, and hardneſs of heart.

*Whether baptiſm by women, be true baptiſm, good and
effectual to them that receive it.*

ᵃ T. C. l. 1. p. 144. On this point, whether he be a
miniſter, or no, dependeth not only the dignity, but alſo
the being of the ſacrament. So that I take the baptiſm of
women to be no more the holy ſacrament of baptiſm, than
any other daily or ordinary waſhing of the child.

62. To leave private baptiſm therefore, and
to come unto baptiſm by women, which they
ſay ᵃ is no more a ſacrament, than any other
ordinary waſhing or bathing of a man's body :
The reaſon whereupon they ground their opinion herein is ſuch, as making baptiſm by women void, becauſe women are no miniſters in
the church of God, muſt needs generally an-
nihilate the baptiſm of all unto whom their conceit ſhall apply this exception, whether it be in regard of Sex, of quality, of inſufficiency, or whatſoever. For if want
of calling do fruſtrate baptiſm, they that baptize without calling do nothing, be they
women or men. To make women teachers in the houſe of God, were a groſs ab-
ᵇ 1 Tim. 2.
12.
ᶜ 1 Tim. 14.
34.
ſurdity, ſeeing the apoſtle hath ſaid, ᵇ *I permit not a woman to teach.* And again,
ᶜ *Let your women in churches be ſilent.* Thoſe extraordinary gifts of ſpeaking with
Tongues and propheſying, which God at that time did not only beſtow upon men,
but on women alſo, made it the harder to hold them confined within private bounds.
Whereupon the apoſtle's ordinance was neceſſary againſt womens publick admiſſion
to teach. And becauſe, when law hath begun ſome one thing or other well, it
giveth good occaſion either to draw by judicious expoſition out of the very law it
ſelf, or to annex to the law by authority and juriſdiction things of like conveniency,
Clem. Conſt.
Apoſtol. lib. 2.
cap. 9.
therefore *Clement* extendeth this apoſtolick conſtitution to baptiſm. For (ſaith
he) *if we have denied them leave to teach, how ſhould any man diſpenſe with nature, and make them miniſters of holy things ; ſeeing this unskilfulneſs is a part
of the Grecians impiety, which for the ſervice of women-goddeſſes have women-
prieſts?* I ſomewhat marvel, that men which would not willingly be thought to
ſpeak or write but with good conſcience, dare hereupon openly avouch *Clement*
T. C. l. 1. p.
144.
for a witneſs, *That as, when the church began not only to decline, but to fall away
from the ſincerity of Religion, it borrowed a number of other profanations of the
heathens ; ſo it borrowed this, and would needs have women-prieſts, as the heathens had ; and that this was one occaſion of bringing baptiſm by women into the
church of God.* Is it not plain in their own eyes, that firſt by an evidence which
forbiddeth women to be miniſters of baptiſm, they endeavour to ſhew how women
were admitted unto that function in the wane and declination of chriſtian piety ?
Second-

Secondly, That by an evidence rejecting the heathens, and condemning them of impiety, they would prove such affection towards heathens, as ordereth the affairs of the church by the pattern of their example: And thirdly, that out of an evidence which nameth the heathens, as being in some part a reason why the church had no women-priests, they gather the heathens to have been one of the first occasions why it had. So that throughout every branch of this testimony their issue is yea; and their evidence directly no. But to women's baptism in private by occasion of urgent necessity, the reasons that only concern ordinary baptism in publick, are no just prejudice; neither can we by force thereof, disprove the practice of those churches which (necessity requiring) allow baptism in private to be administred by women. We may not from laws that prohibit any thing with restraint, conclude absolute and unlimited prohibitions: Although we deny not, but *Licita prohibentur, ne fi permitterentur, eorum occasione perveniatur ad illicita.* they which utterly forbid such baptism, may have perhaps wherewith to justify their orders against it. For, even things lawful are well prohibited, when there is fear left they make the way too unlawful more easy. And it may be the liberty of baptism by women at such times, doth sometimes embolden the rasher sort to do it *neque tamen.* where no such necessity is. But whether of permission besides law, or in presumption against law they do it, is it thereby altogether frustrate, void, and as though it *Just.deAsuth. Tut.lib. Officium. D. de rei Vind.* were never given? They which have not at the first their right baptism, must of necessity be rebaptized, because the law of Christ tieth all men to receive bap- *Ephes. 4. 5.* tism. Iteration of baptism once given hath been always thought a manifest contempt of that ancient apostolick Aphorism, *One Lord, one Faith, one Baptism:* Baptism not only one, in as much as it hath every where the same substance, and offereth unto all men the same grace, but one also, for that it ought not to be received by any one man above once. We serve that Lord which is but one, because no other can be joined with him: We embrace that Faith which is but one, because it admitteth no innovation: That baptism we receive which is but one, because it cannot be admitted often. For how should we practise iteration of baptism; and yet teach, that we are by baptism born anew: That by baptism we are admitted unto the heavenly society of saints; that those things be really and effectually done by baptism, which are no more possible to be often done, *¹* than a man can naturally be often born, or civilly be often adopted into any one stock and family? This also is the cause, why they that present us unto baptism, are entituled for ever after our parents in God, and the reason why there we receive new names, in token that by baptism we are made new creatures. As Christ hath therefore died and risen from the dead but once, so that sacrament which both extinguisheth in him our former sin, and beginneth in us a new condition of life, is by one only actual administration for ever available; according to that in the *Nicene* Creed, *I believe one* *August. de Bap.* *baptism for remission of sins.* And because second baptism was ever abhorred in the *lib. 2. cap.14.* church of God, as a kind of incestuous birth, they that iterate baptism, are driven *Tert. de Bapt.* under some pretence or other, to make the former baptism void. *Tertullian,* the *Cypr. Epist.71.* first that proposed to the church; *Agrippinus,* the first in the church that accepted, and against the use of the church *Novatianus* the first that publickly began to practise re-baptization, did it therefore upon these two grounds; a true persuasion that baptism is necessary; and a false, that the baptism which others administred, was no baptism. *Novatianus* his conceit was, that none can administer true baptism, but the true church of Jesus Christ; that he and his followers alone were the church; and for the rest, he accounted them wicked and prophane persons, such as by baptism could cleanse no man, unless they first did purify themselves, and reform the faults wherewith he charged them. At which time St. *Cyprian,* with the *Euseb. lib. 7.* greatest part of *African* bishops, because they likewise thought that none but only *cap. 1, 2, 3.* the true church of God can baptize, and were of nothing more certainly persua- *Cypr. Epist.70, 71, 72, 75,* ded, than that hereticks are as rotten branches cut off from the life and body of *74, 75, 76.* the true church, gathered hereby that the church of God both may with good consideration, and ought to reverse that baptism which is given by hereticks. These held and practised their own opinion, yet with great protestations often made, that they neither loved a whit the less, nor thought in any respect the worse of them that were of a contrary mind. In requital of which ingenuous moderation, the

¹ *Una est Nativitas de terra, alia de cælo; una de carne, alia de Spiritu; una de æternitate, alia de mortalitate; una de masculo & femina, alia de Deo & Ecclesia. Sed ipsæ duæ singulares sunt. Quomodo enim uterus non potest repeti, sic nec Baptismus iterari.* Prosp Senten. 331. *Eja fratres lacteum genitalis fontis ad laticem convolate, ut semper vobis aqua sufficiat, hoc ante omnia scientes quia hanc nec effundere licet nec rursus haurire.* Zeno. Invit. ad Font.

the reſt that withſtood them, did it in a peaceable ſort, with very good regard had of them, as of men in error, but not hereſy. The biſhop of *Rome* againſt their novelties upheld, as beſeemed him, the ancient and true apoſtolick cuſtoms, till they which unadviſedly before had erred, became in a manner all [a] reconciled friends unto truth, and ſaw that hereſy in the miniſters of bap- tiſm could no way evacuate the force there- of: [b] Such hereſy alone excepted, as by rea- ſon of unſoundneſs in the higheſt articles of chriſtian Faith, preſumed to change, and by changing to maim the ſubſtance, the form of baptiſm. In which reſpect, the church did neither ſimply diſannul, nor abſolutely ratify baptiſm by hereticks. For the baptiſm which *Novatianiſts* gave ſtood firm; whereas they whom [f] *Samoſatenians* had baptized were re-baptized. It was likewiſe ordered in the council of *Arles*, [d] that if any *Arian* did reconcile himſelf to the church, they ſhould admit him without new baptiſm, unleſs by examination they found him not baptized in the name of the Trinity. *Dionyſius*, biſhop of *Alexandria*, [e] maketh report, how there lived under him a man of good reputation, and of very ancient continuance in that church, who being preſent at the rites of baptiſm, and obſerving with better conſideration than ever before, what was there done, came, and with weeping ſubmiſſion craved of his biſhop not to deny him baptiſm, the due of all which profeſs Chriſt, ſeeing it had been ſo long ſithence his evil hap to be deceived by the fraud of hereticks, and at their hands (which till now he never throughly and duly weighed) to take a baptiſm full fraught with blaſphemous impieties; a baptiſm in nothing like unto which the true church of Chriſt uſeth. The biſhop was greatly moved thereat, yet durſt not adventure to re-baptize, but did the beſt he could to put him in good com- fort, uſing much perſuaſion with him not to trouble himſelf with things that were paſt and gone, nor after ſo long continuance in the fellowſhip of God's people, to call now in queſtion his firſt entrance. The poor man that ſaw himſelf in this ſort anſwered, but not ſatisfied, ſpent afterwards his life in continual perplexity, where- of the biſhop remained fearful to give releaſe; perhaps too fearful, if the baptiſm were ſuch as his own declaration importeth. For that, the ſubſtance whereof was rotten at the very firſt, is never by tract of time able to recover ſoundneſs. And where true baptiſm was not before given, the caſe of re-baptization is clear. But by this it appeareth, that baptiſm is not void in regard of hereſy; and therefore much leſs through any other moral defect in the miniſter thereof. Under which ſe- cond pretence, *Donatiſts* notwithſtanding took upon them to make fruſtrate the churches baptiſm, and themſelves to re-baptize their own fry. For whereas ſome forty years after the martyrdom of bleſſed *Cyprian*, the Emperor *Diocletian* began to perſecute the church of Chriſt; and for the ſpeedier aboliſhment of their reli- gion to burn up their ſacred books; there were in the church it ſelf Traditors, content to deliver up the books of God by compoſition, to the end their own lives might be ſpared. Which men growing thereby odious to the reſt, whoſe con- ſtancy was greater; it fortuned that after, when one *Cecilian* was ordained bi- ſhop in the church of *Carthage*, whom others endeavoured in vain to defeat by excepting againſt him as a Traditor, they whoſe accuſations could not prevail, deſ- perately joined themſelves in one, and made a biſhop of their own crue, account- ing from that day forward, their faction the only true and ſincere church. The firſt biſhop on that part was *Majorinus*, whoſe ſucceſſor *Donatus*, being the firſt that wrote in defence of their ſchiſm, the birds that were hatched before by others, have their names from him. *Arians* and *Donatiſts* began both about one time. Which hereſies according to the different ſtrength of their own ſinews wrought as hope of ſucceſs led them; the one with the choiceſt wits, the other with the multitude, ſo far that after long and troubleſome experience, the perfecteſt view men could take of both, was hardly able to induce any certain determinate reſolution, whether error may do more by the curious ſubtilty of ſharp diſcourſe, or elſe by the mere appearance of zeal and devout affection; the latter of which two aids gave *Donatiſts*, beyond all mens expectation, as great a ſway as ever any ſchiſm or hereſy had within that reach of the chriſtian world, where it bred and grew : The rather perhaps, becauſe the church, which neither greatly

Side notes (left margin):

[k] *Illi ipſi Epiſcopi qui rebaptizandos Hæreticos cum Cypriano ſtatuerant, ad antiquam conſuetudinem revoluti novum emiſere de- cretum.* Hieron. cont. Lucifer. Vide & Auguſt. contr. Creſ- con. lib. 3. cap. 2, 3. & Epiſt. 48.

[b] *Dixiſti fieri non poſſe ut in falſo Baptiſmate inquinatus abluat, immundus emundet, ſupplantator erigat, perditus liberet, reus veni- am tribuat, damnatus abſolvat. Bene hæc omnia poterunt ad ſolos Hæreticos pertinere, qui falſaverunt Symbolum, dum alter dixerit duos Deos, cum Deus unus ſit, alter Patrem vult in perſona Filii cognoſci, alter carnem ſubducens Filio Dei per quam Deo reconcilia- tus eſt mundus: Et cæteri hujuſmodi, qui a Sacramentis Catholicis alieni noſcuntur.* Optat. lib. 1.

[c] Synod. Ni- cæ. cap. 19.
[d] Synod. Arelat. cap. 8.

[e] Euſeb. Ec- cleſ. Hiſt. lib. 7. cap. 8.

Circa. An. 300.

greatly feared them, and besides had necessary cause to bend it self against others that aimed directly at a far higher mark, the deity of Christ, was contented to let *Donatists* have their course by the space of threescore years and above ; even from ten years before *Constantine*, till the time that *Optatus* Bishop of *Milevis* published his Books against *Parmenian.* During which term, and the space of that schism's con- *Circa An. 370.* tinuance afterwards, they had, besides many other secular and worldly means to help them forward, these special Advantages. First, the very occasion of their breach with the church of God, a just hatred and dislike of traditors, seemed plausible ; they easily persuaded their hearers, that such men could not be holy, as held communion and fellowship with them that betray'd Religion. Again ; when to dazzle the eyes of the simple, and to prove that it can be no church which is not holy, they had in shew and found of words the glorious pretence of the creed apostolick, *I believe the holy catholick church* ; we need not think it any strange thing, that with the multitude they gained credit. And avouching that such as are not of the true church can administer no true Baptism, they had for this point whole volumes of St. *Cyprian's* own writing, together with the judgments of divers *African* Synods, whose sentence was the same with his. Whereupon the fathers were likewise, in defence of their just cause, very greatly prejudiced ; both for that they could not enforce the duty of mens communion with a church, confess'd to be in many things blame-worthy, unless they should oftentimes seem to speak as half-defenders of the faults themselves, or at the least not so vehement accusers thereof as their adversaries : And to withstand iteration of baptism, the other branch of the *Donatists* heresy, was impossible, without manifest and profess'd rejection of *Cyprian*, whom the world universally did, in his life-time, admire as the greatest among prelates, and now honour as not the lowest in the kingdom of heaven. So true we find it, by experience of all ages in the church of God, that the teacher's error is the people's trial, harder and heavier by so much to bear, as he is in worth and regard greater that mis-persuadeth them. Altho' there was odds between *Cyprian's* cause and theirs, he differing from others of sounder understanding in that point, but not dividing himself from the body of the church by schism, as did the *Donatists.* For which cause, saith *Vincentius, Of one and the same opinion we judge (which may seem strange)* *Vincent. Lirin.* *the authors catholick and the followers heretical ; we acquit the masters, and con-* *adver. Haref.* *demn the scholars : They are heirs of heaven which have written those books, the* *cap. 11.* *defenders whereof are trodden down to the pit of hell.* The invectives of catholick writers therefore against them are sharp ; the words of imperial edicts, by *Honorius* *Vide C. Theod.* and *Theodosius* made to bridle them, very bitter ; the punishments severe, in revenge *lib. 16. tit. 6.* of their folly. Howbeit, for fear (as we may conjecture) left much should be de- *l. Adversari-* rogated from the baptism of the church, and baptism by *Donatists* be more esteem- *lus, circa An.* ed of than was meet ; if on the one side, that which hereticks had done ill, should *405.* stand as good ; on the other side, that be reversed which the catholick church had well and religiously done ; divers better minded than advised men, thought it fittest to meet with this inconvenience, by re-baptizing *Donatists*, as well as they re-baptized catholicks. For stay whereof, the same Emperors saw it meet to give *Si quis C. Ne.* their law a double edge, whereby it might equally on both sides cut off not only *sanct. Baptif.* hereticks, which re-baptized whom they could pervert ; but also catholick and chri- *circa An. 413.* stian priests, which did the like unto such as before had taken baptism at the hands of hereticks, and were afterwards reconciled to the church of God. *Donatists* were therefore, in process of time, though with much ado, wearied, and at length worn out by the constancy of that truth which teacheth, that evil ministers of good things are as torches, a light to others, a waste to none but themselves only ; and that the foulness of their hands can neither any whit impair the virtue, nor stain the glory of the mysteries of Christ. Now that which was done amiss by virtuous and good men, (as *Cyprian*, carried aside with hatred against heresy, and was secondly followed by *Donatists*, whom envy and rancor, covered with shew of godliness, made obstinate to cancel whatsoever the church did in the sacrament of baptism) hath of later days, in another respect far different from both the former, been brought freshly again into practice. For the Anabaptist re-baptizeth, because in his estimation the baptism of the church is frustrate, for that we give it unto infants which have not faith ; whereas, according unto Christ's institution, as they conceive it, true baptism should always presuppose actual belief in receivers, and is otherwise no baptism. Of these three errors, there is not any but hath been able at the least to alledge in defence of it self many fair proba-

2   bilities.

bllities. Notwithstanding, sith the church of God hath hitherto always constantly maintained, that to re-baptize them which are known to have received true baptism, is unlawful; that if baptism seriously be administred in the same element, and with the same form of words which Christ's institution teacheth, there is no other defect in the world that can make it frustrate, or deprive it of the nature of a true sacrament: And lastly, That baptism is only then to be re-administred, when the first delivery thereof is void, in regard of the fore-alledged imperfections, and no other: Shall we now in the case of baptism, which having (both for matter and form) the substance of Christ's institution, is by a fourth sort of men voided for the only defect of ecclesiastical authority in the minister, think it enough that they blow away the force thereof with the bare strength of their very breath, by saying, *We take such baptism to be no more the sacrament of baptism, than any other ordinary bathing to be a sacrament?* It behoveth generally all sorts of men to keep themselves within the limits of their own vocation. And seeing God, from whom mens several degrees and pre-eminences do proceed, hath appointed them in his church, at whose hands his pleasure is that we should receive both baptism and all other publick medicinable helps of soul, perhaps thereby the more to settle our hearts in the love of our ghostly superiors; they have small cause to hope that with him their voluntary services will be accepted, who thrust themselves into functions, either above their capacity, or besides their place, and over-boldly intermeddle with duties, whereof no charge was ever given them. They that in any thing exceed the compass of their own order, do as much as in them lieth to dissolve that order which is the harmony of God's church. Suppose therefore, that in these and the like considerations, the Law did utterly prohibit baptism to be administred by any other than persons thereunto solemnly consecrated, what necessity soever happen; are not many things firm, being done, although in part done otherwise than positive rigor and strictness did require? Nature, as much as is possible, inclineth unto validities and preservations: Dissolutions and nullities of things done, are not only not favoured, but hated, when either urged without cause, or extended beyond their reach. If therefore at any time it come to pass, that in teaching publickly or privately in delivering this blessed sacrament of regeneration, some unsanctified hand, contrary to Christ's supposed ordinance, do intrude it self to execute that whereunto the laws of God and his church have deputed others; which of these two opinions seemeth more agreeable with equity, ours that disallow what is done amiss, yet make not the force of the word

Marginal notes left column:
Numb. 16. 10.
Levit. 1c. 1.
1 Sam. 13. 11.
2 Sam. 6. 6.
2 Chron. 26. 16.
Heb. 5. 4.

Seq. 306.
Lugdunensis ex literis decret. de Matrim. contract. Damaf. Burch. Reg. 109. *Prohibita fieri, β flant,non tenent. In prohibitionibus autem circa res favorabiles, contrarium obtinet.*

and sacraments, much less their nature and very substance, to depend on the minister's authority and calling; or else [a] theirs, which defeat, disannul, and annihilate both, in respect of that one only personal defect; there being not any law of God which saith, That if the minister be incompetent, his word shall be no word, his baptism no baptism? He which teacheth and is not sent, loseth the reward, but yet retaineth the name of a teacher: His usurped actions have in him the same nature which they have in others, although they yield not him the same comfort. And if these two cases be peers, the case of doctrine and the case of baptism both alike; sith no defect in their vocation that teach the truth is able to take away the benefit thereof from him which heareth, wherefore should the want of a lawful calling in them that baptise make baptism to be vain? [b] They grant, that the matter and the form in sacraments are the only parts of substance, and that if these two be retained, albeit other things besides be used which are inconvenient, the sacrament notwithstanding is administred, but

Footnote a: [a] T. C. lib. 1. pag. 144. As St. Paul faith, *That a man cannot preach, which is not sent;* Rom. 10. 15. No, not although he speak the words of the Scripture, and interpret them: So I cannot see how a Man can baptise, unless he be sent to that end; although he pour water, and rehearse the words which are to be rehearsed in the Ministry of Baptism.

Footnote b: [b] T. C. lib. 1. pag. 165. If either the Matter of the Sacrament, or the Form of it, which is the Institution, (which things are only substantial parts) were wanting, there should then have been no Sacrament at all ministred. But they being retained, and yet other things used which are not convenient, the Sacrament is ministred, but not sincerely.

not sincerely. Why persist they not in this opinion; when by these fair speeches they have put us in hope of agreement? Wherefore sup they up their words again, interlacing such frivolous interpretations and glosses as disgrace their sentence? What should move them, having named the matter and the form of the sacrament, to give us presently warning, [c] that they mean by the form of

Footnote c: [c] T. C. lib. 3. pag. 113.

the

I

the facrament the inftitution? Which expofition darkneth whatfoever was before plain. For whereas, in common underftanding, that form which added to the element, doth make a facrament, and is of the outward fubftance thereof, containeth only the words of ufual application, they fet it down (left common dictionaries fhould deceive us) that the form doth fignify in their language, the inftitution; which inftitution in truth comprehendeth both form and matter. Such are their fumbling fhifts to inclofe the minifter's vocation within the compafs of fome effential part of the facrament. A thing that can never ftand with found and fincere conftruction. For what if the * minifter be *no circumftance, but a fub-* ordinate efficient caufe in the work of baptifm?* What if the minifter's vocation

* T. C. lib. 3. pag. 121.

be a matter *b of perpetual neceffity, and not a ceremony variable as times and occafions require? What if his calling be a principal part of the inftitution of Chrift?* Doth it therefore follow, that the minifter's authority is *c of the fubftance of the facrament,* and as incident into the nature thereof, as the matter and the form it felf, yea, more incident? For whereas in cafe of neceffity, the greateft amongft them profeffeth the change of the element of water lawful, and others which like not fo well this opinion, could be better content that voluntarily the words of Chrift's inftitution were altered, and men baptized in the name of Chrift, without either

* T. C. lib. 3. pag. 135. The minifter is of the fubftance of the facrament, confidering that it is a principal part of Chrift's inftitution. Beza, Epift. 2. *Deft aqua, & tamen baptifmus alicujus differri cum adificatione non poffit, nec debeat; ego certe quouis alio liquore non minus rite quam aqua baptizarim.*
*b T. C. lib. 3. pag. 138. Shew me why the breach of the inftitution in the form fhould make the facrament unavailable, and not the breach of this part (which concerneth the minifter) T. C. ibid. Howfoever fome learned and godly give fome liberty in the change of the elements of the holy facrament; yet I do not fee how that can ftand. Idem, pag. 155. I would rather judge him baptized, who is baptized into the name of Chrift, without adding the Father and the Holy Ghoft, when the element of water is added, than when the other words being duly kept, fome other liquor is ufed.

mention made of the Father or of the Holy Ghoft; neverthelefs, in denying that baptifm adminiftred by private perfons, ought to be reckoned of as a facrament, they both agree. It may therefore pleafe them both to confider, that baptifm is an action in part moral, in part ecclefiaftical, and in part myftical: Moral, as being a duty which men perform towards God: Ecclefiaftical, in that it belongeth unto God's church as a publick duty: Finally, myftical, if we refpect what God doth thereby intend to work. The greateft moral perfection of baptifm confifteth in mens devout obedience to the law of God, which law requireth both the outward act or thing done, and alfo that religious affection which God doth fo much regard, that without it whatfoever we do is hateful in his fight; who therefore is faid to refpect *Adverbs* more than *Verbs,* becaufe the end of his law in appointing what we fhall do, is our own perfection: Which perfection confifteth chiefly in the vertuous difpofition of the mind, and approveth it felf to him not by doing, but by doing well. Wherein appeareth alfo the difference between human and divine laws; the one of which two are content with *Opus operatum,* the other require *Opus operantis;* the one do but claim the deed, the other efpecially the mind. So that according to laws which principally refpect the heart of men, works of religion being not religioufly performed, cannot morally be perfect. Baptifm as an ecclefiaftical work, is for the manner of performance ordered by divers ecclefiaftical laws, providing that as the facrament it felf is a gift of no mean worth, fo the miniftry thereof might in all circumftances appear to be a function of no fmall regard. All that belongeth to the myftical perfection of baptifm outwardly, is the element, the word, and the ferious application of both unto him which receiveth both; whereunto if we add that fecret reference which this action hath to life and remiffion of Sins, by virtue of Chrift's own compact folemnly made with his church, to accomplifh fully the facrament of baptifm, there is not any thing more required. Now put the queftion, whether baptifm adminiftred to infants, without any fpiritual calling, be unto them both a true facrament, and an effectual inftrument of grace, or elfe an act of no more account than the ordinary wafhings are: The fum of all that can be faid to defeat fuch baptifm is, that thofe things which have no being can work nothing; and that baptifm, without the power of ordination, is as a judgment without fufficient jurifdiction, void, fruftrate, and of no effect. But to this we anfwer, that the fruit of baptifm dependeth only upon the covenant which God hath made: That God by covenant requireth in the elder fort, faith and baptifm; in children, the facrament of baptifm alone, whereunto he hath alfo given them right by fpecial privilege of

birth

birth within the bosom of the holy church: That infants therefore which have received baptism compleat, as touching the myftical perfection thereof, are by virtue of his own covenant and promife cleanfed from all fin ; for as much as all other laws, concerning that which in baptifm is either moral or ecclefiaftical, do bind the church which giveth baptifm, and not the infant which receiveth it of the church. So that if any thing be therein amifs, the harm which groweth by violation of holy ordinances, muft altogether reft where the bonds of fuch ordinances hold. For, that in actions of this nature it fareth not as in jurifdictions, may fomewhat appear by the very opinion which men have of them. The nullity of that which a judge doth by way of authority, without authority, is known to all men, and agreed upon with full confent of the whole world ; every man receiveth it as a general edict of nature; whereas the nullity of baptifm, in regard of the like defect, is only a few mens new ungrounded, and as yet unapproved imagination. Which difference of generality in mens perfuafions on the one fide, and their paucity whofe conceit leadeth them the other way, hath rifen from a difference eafy to obferve in the things themfelves. The exercife of unauthorized jurifdiction is a grievance unto them that are under it, whereas they that without authority prefume to baptize, offer nothing but that which to all men is good and acceptable. Sacraments are food, and the minifters thereof as parents, or as nurfes, at whofe hands when there is neceffity, but no poffibility of receiving it, if that which they are not prefent to do in right of their office, be of pity and compaffion done by others; fhall this be thought to turn celeftial bread into gravel, or the medicine of fouls into poifon? Jurifdiction is a yoke which law hath impofed on the necks of men in fuch fort, that they muft endure it for the good of others, how contrary foever it be to their own particular appetites and inclinations. Jurifdiction bridleth men againft their wills; that which a judge doth, prevails by virtue of his very power ; and therefore not without great reafon, except the law hath given him authority, whatfoever he doth, vanifheth. Baptifm, on the other fide, being a favour which it pleafeth God to beftow, a benefit of foul to us that receive it, and a grace which they that deliver are but as meer veffels, either appointed by others, or offered of their own accord to this fervice ; of which two, if they be the one, it is but their own honour ; their own offence to be the other ; can it poffibly ftand

^a *Factum alterius alii nocere non debet.* Ulp. l. de pupillo, fect. Si Plurimum. Item, Alphen. l. Pater familias. De Hære. Inftit. *Maleficia tenent Authores fuos, non alios.* L. Sancimus 21. C. de Pœn.

with [a] equity and right, that the faultinefs of their prefumption in giving baptifm, fhould be able to prejudice us, who by taking baptifm have no way offended? I know there are many fentences found in the books and writings of the ancient fathers, to prove both ecclefiaftical and alfo moral defects in the minifter of baptifm, a bar to the heavenly benefit thereof. Which fentences we always

^b Auguft. Epift. 23.

fo underftand, as [b] *Auguftin* underftood in a cafe like nature, the words of St. *Cyprian.* When infants baptized were, after their parents revolt, carried by them in arms to the ftews of idols, thofe wretched creatures, as St. *Cyprian* thought, were not only their own ruin, but their childrens alfo : *Their children,* whom this their apoftafy prophaned, *did lofe what chriftian baptifm had given them being newly born.* They loft (faith St. *Auguftin*) *the Grace of baptifm, if we confider to what their parents impiety did tend;* although the mercy of God preferved them, and will alfo in that dreadful day of account give them favourable audience, pleading in their own behalf, *The harm of other mens perfidioufnefs, it lay not in us to avoid.* After the fame manner, whatfoever we read written, if it found to the prejudice of baptifm, through any either moral or ecclefiaftical defect therein, we conftrue it as equity and reafon teacheth, with reftraint to the offender only; which doth,

T. C. lib. 3. pag. 136. *Auguftine* ftandeth in doubt, whether baptifm by a lay-man be available, or no. *Cont. Lit. Parm.* lib. 2. cap. 13. Where by all likelihood he was out of doubt, that that which was miniftred by a woman, whofe unaptnefs herein is double to that of a lay-man, was of no effect.

as far as concerneth himfelf and them which wittingly concur with him, make the facrament of God fruitlefs. St. *Auguftin's* doubtfulnefs, whether baptifm by a lay-man may ftand or ought to be re-adminiftred, fhould not be mentioned by them which prefume to define peremptorily of that wherein he was content to profefs himfelf unrefolved. Albeit, in very truth, his opinion is plain enough; but the manner of delivering his judgment being modeft, they make of a virtue an imbecillity, and impute his calmnefs of fpeech to an irrefolution of mind. His difputation in that place is againft *Parmenian,* which held that a bifhop or a prieft, if they fall into any herefy,

4

do

do thereby lofe the power which they had before to baptize ; and that therefore baptifm by hereticks is meerly void. For anfwer whereof, he firft denieth
that herefy can more deprive men of power to baptize others, than it is of force
to take from them their own baptifm : And in the fecond place he farther addeth,
that if hereticks did lofe the power which before was given them by ordination, and
did therefore unlawfully ufurp, as often as they took upon them to give the facrament of baptifm, it followeth not, that baptifm by them adminiftred without authority is no baptifm. For then what fhould we think of baptifm by lay-men, to
whom authority was never given ? I doubt (faith St. *Auguftin*) whether any man
which carrieth a virtuous and godly mind will affirm, that the baptifm which lay-
men do in cafe of neceffity adminifter, fhould be iterated : *For to do it unneceffa-*   T. c. l. 1.
rily, is to execute another man's office ; neceffity urging, to do it is then either no P. 116.
fault at all (much lefs fo grievous a crime, that it fhould deferve to be termed by The facri-
the name of facrilege,) *or , if any, a very pardonable fault.* But *fuppofe it even* lege of pri-
of very purpofe ufurped, and given unto any man, by every man that lifteth ; yet cially, in ad-
that which is given cannot poffibly be denied to have been given, how truly foever miniftring
we may fay it hath not been given lawfully. Unlawful ufurpation, a penitent affe- the holy fa-
ction muft redrefs. If not, the thing that was given fhall remain to the hurt and baptifm.
detriment of him which unlawfully either adminiftred or received the fame ; y.t fo,
that in this refpect it ought not to be reputed as if it had not at all been given.
Whereby we may plainly perceive, that St. *Auguftin* was not himfelf uncertain
what to think, but doubtful whether any well-minded men in the whole world
could think otherwife than he did. Their argument taken from a ftollen feal, may
return to the place out of which they had it, for
it helpeth their caufe nothing. That which men   T. c. lib. 3. pag. 139. As by the feal which the prince
give or grant to others, muft appear to have   hath fet apart to feal his grants with, when it is ftollen and
proceeded of their own accord. This being   fet to by him that hath no authority, there groweth no
manifeft, their gifts and grants are thereby   affurance to the party that hath it : So if it were poffible
made effectual, both to bar themfelves from   to be the feal of God, which a woman fhould fet to, yet
renovation, and to affecure the right they have   for that fhe hath ftollen it, and put it to, not only with-
given. Wherein, for further prevention of   out, but contrary to the commandment of God ; I
mifchiefs that otherwife might grow by the   fee not how any can take any affurance by reafon thereof.
malice, treachery and fraud of men, it is both equal and meet, that the ftrength of
mens deeds, and the inftruments which declare the fame, fhould ftrictly depend upon divers folemnities, whereof there cannot be the like reafon in things that pafs
between God and us ; becaufe fith we need not doubt, left the treafures of his heavenly grace fhould, without his confent, be pafs'd by forged conveyances ; nor left
he fhould deny at any time his own acts, and feek to revoke what hath been confented unto before : As there is no fuch fear of danger through deceit and falfe-
hood in this cafe, fo neither hath the circumftance of mens perfons that weight
in baptifm, which for good and juft confiderations in the cuftody of feals of office it ought to have. The grace of baptifm cometh by donation from God
alone. That God hath committed the miniftry of baptifm unto fpecial men, it
is for orders fake in his church, and not to the end that their authority might
give being, or add more force to the facrament it felf. That infants have right to
the facrament in baptifm, we all acknowledge. Charge them we cannot as guileful and wrongful poffeffors of that, whereunto they have right by the manifeft
will of the donor, and are not parties unto any defect or diforder in the manner
of receiving the fame. And if any fuch diforder be, we have fufficiently before declared, that *delictum cum capite femper ambulat*, mens own faults are their
own harms. Wherefore, to countervail this and the like mifchofen refemblances
with that which more truly and plainly agreeth ; the ordinance of God concerning their vocation that minifter baptifm, wherein the myftery of our regeneration
is wrought, hath thereunto the fame analogy, which laws of wedlock have to our
firft nativity and birth : So that if nature do effect procreation , notwithftanding
the wicked violation and breach even of natures law made, that the entrance of
all mankind into this prefent world might be without blemifh ; may we not
juftly prefume that grace doth accomplifh the other, although there be faultinefs
in them that tranfgrefs the order which our Lord Jefus Chrift hath eftablifhed in
his church ? Some light may be borrowed from circumcifion, for explication
of what is true in this queftion of baptifm. Seeing then, that even they which
                               F f 2   con-

Exod. 4. 24. *T. C.* lib. 1. pag. 144. I say, that the un-
lawfulness of that fact doth appear sufficiently, in that she
did it before her husband *Moses*, which was a prophet of
the Lord, to whom that office of circumcision did appertain. Besides, that she did cut off the fore-skin of the
infant, not of mind to obey the commandment of God, or
for the salvation of the child, but in a choler only, to the
end that her husband might be eased and have release:
Which mind appeareth in her, both by her words, and by
casting away in anger the fore-skin which she had cut off.
And if it be said, that the event declared, that the act
pleased God, because that *Moses* forthwith waxed better,
and was recovered of his sickness; I have shewed before,
that if we measure things by the event, we shall oftentimes
justify the wicked, and take the righteousness of the righteous from them.

condemn *Zipporah* the wife of *Moses*, for
taking upon her to circumcise her son, a thing
necessary at that time for her to do, and as
I think very hard to reprove in her, considering how *Moses*, because himself had not done
it sooner, was therefore stricken by the hand
of God, neither could in that extremity perform the office; whereupon, for the stay of
God's indignation there was no choice, but
the action must needs fall into her hands;
whose fact therein, whether we interpret as
some have done, that being a *Midianite*, and
as yet not so thoroughly acquainted with the
Jewish rites, it much discontented her to see
her self, through her husband's oversight, in a matter of his own religion, brought
unto these perplexities and streights, that either she must now endure him perishing
before her eyes, or else wound the flesh of her own child; which she could not do
but with some indignation, shewed in that she fumingly both threw down the fore-
skin at his feet, and upbraided him with the cruelty of his religion: Or, if we better like to follow their more judicious exposition, which are not inclinable to think
that *Moses* was matched like *Socrates*, nor that circumcision could now in *Eleazar*
be strange unto her, having had *Gersom*, her eldest son before circumcised; nor that

* *Mala pati-*
mur irascimur,
sed compati-
mur. Boet. de
Consol.

any occasion of choler could arise from a spectacle of such misery, as doth * naturally move compassion and not wrath; nor that *Zipporah* was so impious, as
in the visible presence of God's deserved anger to storm at the ordinance and law
of God; nor that the words of the history it self can inforce any such affection: But do only declare how after the act performed she touched the feet of
Moses, saying, b *Sponsus tu mihi es sangui-*

b Where the usual translation hath, *Exod.* 4. 25. She
cut away the fore-skin of her son, and cast it at his feet,
and said, thou art indeed a bloody husband unto me. So
he departed from him. Then she said, O bloody husband,
because of the circumcision. The words, as they lie in
the original, are rather thus to be interpreted: And she
cut off the fore-skin of her son. Which being done, she
touched his feet, (the feet of *Moses*) and said, thou art to
me an husband of blood, (in the plural number, thereby
signifying effusion of blood.) And the Lord withdrew from
him at the very time, when she said, a husband of blood,
in regard of circumcision.

num, Thou art unto me an husband of blood ;
which might be very well, the one done, and
the other spoken, even out of the flowing
abundance of commiseration and love to signify, with hands laid under his feet, that her
tender affection towards him had caused her
thus to forget womanhood, to lay all motherly affection aside, and to redeem her husband out of the hands of death, with effusion
of blood: The sequel thereof, take it which
way you will, is a plain argument that God was satisfied with that she did; as
may appear by his own testimony, declaring how there followed in the person of
Moses, present release of his grievous punishment, upon her speedy discharge of that
duty which by him neglected had offended God; even as after execution of ju-
Psal. 106. 30. stice by the hands of *Phineas*, the plague was immediately taken away, which former impunity of sin had caused. In which so manifest and plain cases, not to
make that a reason of the event, which God himself hath set down as a reason,
were falsly to accuse whom he doth justify, and without any cause to traduce what
we should allow ; yet seeing they which will

T. C. l. 3. p. 142. Seeing they only are bidden in the
scripture to administer the sacraments, which are bidden to
preach the word, and that the publick ministers have only
this charge of the word ; and seeing that the administration of both these are so linked together, that the denial of
licence to do one, is a denial to do the other ; as of the
contrary part, licence to one, is licence to the other ; considering also that to minister the sacraments, is an honour
in the church which none can take unto him, but he which
is called unto it, as was *Aaron*: And further, for as much
as the baptizing by private persons, and by women especially, confirmeth the dangerous error of the condemnation
of young children which die without baptism: Last of all,
seeing we have the consent of the godly learned of all
times against the baptism by women, and of the reformed
churches now, against the baptism by private men ; we conclude, that the administration of this sacrament by private
persons, and especially by women, is meerly both unlawful
and void.

have it a breach of the law of God for her to
circumcise in that necessity, are not able to
deny but circumcision being in that very manner performed, was to the innocent child
which received it, true circumcision; why
should that defect, whereby circumcision was
so little weakened, be to baptism a deadly
wound? These premises therefore remaining,
as hitherto they have been laid, because the
commandment of our Saviour Christ, which
committeth jointly to publick ministers both
doctrine and baptism, doth no more, by link-
ing them together, import, that the nature of
the sacrament dependeth on the minister's authority and power to preach the word, than
the

the force and virtue of the word doth on licence to give the facrament ; and confidering that the work of external miniftry in baptifm is only a pre-eminence of
honour, which they that take to themfelves, and are not thereunto called, as
Aaron was, do but themfelves in their own perfons, by means of fuch ufurpation, incur the juft blame of difobedience to the law of God; farther alfo, in as
much as it ftandeth in no reafon, that errors grounded on a wrong interpretation
of other mens deeds, fhould make fruftrate whatfoever is mifconceived, and that
baptifm by women fhould ceafe to be baptifm, as oft as any man will thereby
gather that children which die unbaptized are damned; which opinion, if the act
of baptifm adminiftred in fuch manner, did inforce, it might be fufficient caufe of
difliking the fame, but none of defeating or making it altogether void : Laft
of all, whereas general and full confent of the godly learned in all ages doth make
for validity of baptifm; yea, albeit adminiftred in private, and even by women;
which kind of baptifm, in cafe of neceffity, divers reformed churches do both allow and defend; fome others which do not defend, tolerate; few, in comparifon,
and they without any juft caufe, do utterly difannul and annihilate: Surely, howfoever through defect on either fide, the facrament may be without fruit, as well in
fome cafes to him which receiveth, as to him which giveth it; yet no difability of
either part can fo far make it fruftrate and without effect, as to deprive it of the
very nature of true baptifm, having all things elfe which the ordinance of Chrift requireth. Whereupon we may confequently infer, that the adminiftration of this
facrament by private perfons, be it lawful or unlawful, appeareth not as yet to be
meerly void.

63. All that are of the race of Chrift, the fcripture nameth them *Children of the* Interrogato-
promife which God hath made. . The promife of eternal life is the feed of the ries in bap-
church of God. And becaufe there is no attainment of life, but through the only tifm touch-
begotten Son of God, nor by him otherwife than being fuch as the Creed Apofto- and the pur-
lick defcribeth; it followeth that the articles thereof are principles neceffary for all pofe of a
men to fubfcribe unto, whom by baptifm the church receiveth into Chrift's fchool. life.
All points of chriftian doctrine are either demonftrable conclufions, or demonftra-
tive principles. Conclufions have ftrong and invincible proofs, as well in the fchool
of Jefus Chrift, as elfewhere. And principles are grounds which require no proof
in any kind of fcience, becaufe it fufficeth, if either their certainty be evident in
it felf, or evident by the light of fome higher knowledge; and in it felf fuch as
no man's knowledge is ever able to overthrow. Now the principles whereupon
we do build our fouls, have their evidence where they had their original; and as received from thence, we adore them, we hold them in reverend admiration, we neither argue nor difpute about them, we give unto them that affent which the oracles
of God require. We are not therefore afhamed of the Gofpel of our Lord Jefus
Chrift, becaufe mifcreants in fcorn have upbraided us, that the higheft point of our
wifdom is belief. That which is true, and neither can be difcerned by fenfe, nor
concluded by meer natural principles, muft
have principles of revealed truth whereupon   *Apoſtata maledictum.* 'Ουδὲν δοιὲ τὸ πίσυπιο ἢ ὑμῖσεχᵗ
to build it felf, and an habit of faith in us,   ἒπ ςϱίας. *Naz. Orat. 1. contr. Julia.*
wherein principles of that kind are appre-   ᵃ Τοῖς ϛουῶ, δοιὲ λέγω, ὑπὸ ᵕᵍδαλαψιν κπτῆς φλϛϣς τᵃ
hended. ᵃ The myfteries of our religion are   ἱμέτιϛϱ. *Juſt. Mart. Expoſ. Fid.*
above the reach of our underftanding, above
difcourfe of man's reafon, above all that any creature can comprehend. Therefore
the firft thing required of him which ftandeth for admiffion into Chrift's family, is
belief. Which belief confifteth not fo much in knowledge, as in acknowledgment
of all things that heavenly wifdom revealeth; the affection of faith is above her
reach, her love to God-ward above the comprehenfion which fhe hath of God. And
becaufe only for believers all things may be done, he which is goodnefs it felf,
loveth them above all. Deferve we then the love of God, becaufe we believe in
the Son of God? What more oppofite than faith and pride? When God had created
all things, he looked upon them and loved them, becaufe they were all as himfelf
had made them. So the true reafon wherefore Chrift doth love believers is, be-
caufe their belief is the gift of God, a gift than which flefh and blood in this   Matth. 16.
world cannot poffibly receive a greater, And as to love them of whom we   17.
receive good things is duty, becaufe they fatisfy our defires in that which elfe   John 1. 12.
we fhould want; fo to love them on whom we beftow, is nature, becaufe in them

                                                                                                                        WC

I

we behold the effects of our own virtue. Seeing therefore no religion enjoyeth sacraments, the signs of God's love, unless it have also that faith whereupon the sacraments are built ; could there be any thing more convenient, than that our first admittance to the actual receipt of his grace in the sacrament of baptism should be consecrated with profession of belief? which is to the kingdom of God as a key, the want whereof excludeth infidels both from that and from all other saving grace. We find by experience, that although faith be an intellectual habit of the mind, and have her seat in the understanding ; yet an evil moral disposition, obstinately wedded to the love of darkness, dampeth the very light of heavenly illumination, and permitteth not the mind to see what doth shine before it. Men are *lovers of pleasure, more than lovers of God*. Their assent to his saving truth is many times with-held from it, not that the truth is too weak to persuade, but because the stream of corrupt affection carrieth them a clean contrary way. That the mind therefore may abide in the light of faith, there must abide in the will as constant a resolution to have no fellowship at all with the vanities and works of darkness. Two Covenants there are which christian men (saith *Isidore*) do make in baptism, the one concerning relinquishment of Satan, the other touching obedience to the faith of Christ. In like sort St. *Ambrose*, *He which is baptized, forsaketh the intellectual Pharaoh, the prince of this world*, saying, *abrenuncio ; Thee, O Satan, and thy angels, thy works and thy mandates, I forsake utterly.* Tertullian having speech of wicked spirits ; *These* (saith he) *are the angels which we in baptism renounce.* The declaration of [a] *Justin* the martyr concerning baptism, sheweth how such as the church in those days did baptize, made profession of christian belief, and undertook to live accordingly. Neither do I think it a matter easy for any man to prove, that ever baptism did use to be administred without interrogatories of these two kinds. Whereunto [b] St. *Peter* (as it may be thought) alluding, hath said, *That the baptism which saveth us*, is not (as legal purifications were) a cleansing of the flesh from outward impurity, but ἐπερώτημα, *an interrogative tryal of a good conscience towards God.*

Spiritus sanctus habitator ejus templi non efficitur, quod antistitem non habet veram fidem. Jerom. adv. Lucif. c. 4.

*Isid. de Offic. Ecclef. lib. 2. cap. 24.
Ambros. Hexam. l. 1. c. 4.
Tertul. de Spectac.*

[a] ʽΌτσι ἀν πεισθῶσι ἢ πιστ...[Greek footnote text] Justin. Apol.

[b] 1 Pet. 3. 21.

[c] 64. Now the fault which they find with us concerning interrogatories is, our moving of these questions unto infants which cannot answer them, and the answering of them by others as in their names. The anabaptist hath many pretences to scorn at the baptism of children : First, Because the scriptures, he saith, do no where give commandment to baptize infants : Secondly, For that, as there is no commandment, so neither any manifest example shewing it to have been done either by Christ or his apostles. Thirdly, In as much as the word preached and the sacraments must go together, they which are not capable of the one, are not fit receivers of the other. Last of all, sith the order of baptism, continued from the first beginning, hath in it those things which are unfit to be applied to sucking children, it followeth in their conceit, That the baptism of such is no baptism, but plain mockery. They with whom we contend are no enemics to the baptism of infants ; it is not their desire that the church should hazard so many souls, by letting them run on till they come to ripeness of understanding, that so they may be converted, and then baptized, as infidels heretofore have been : They bear not towards God so unthankful minds, as not to acknowledge it even amongst the greatest of his endless mercies, That by making us his own possession so soon, many advantages, which satan otherwise might take, are prevented, and (which should be esteemed a part of no small happiness) the first thing whereof we have occasion to take notice, is, How much hath been done already to our great good, though altogether without our knowledge. The baptism of infants they esteem as an ordinance which Christ hath instituted, even in special love and favour to his own people : They deny not the practice thereof accordingly to have been kept, as derived from the hands, and continued from the days of the apostles themselves unto this present ; only it pleaseth them not, That to infants there

[c] Interrogatories proposed unto infants in baptism, and answered as in their names by Godfathers. They prophane holy baptism in toying foolishly ; for that they ask Questions of an infant which cannot answer, and speak unto them, as was wont to be spoken unto men, and unto such as being converted, answered for themselves and were baptized. Which is but a mockery of God, and therefore against the holy scriptures, Gal. 6. 7. Admonition to the Parliament. The same defended in T. C. l. 1. p. 168.

should

fhould be interrogatories propofed in baptifm. This they condemn as foolifh, toy-ifh, and prophane mockery. But are they able to fhew, that ever the church of Chrift had any publick form of baptifm without interrogatories ; or that the church did ever ufe at the folemn baptifm of infants, to omit thofe queftions as needlefs in this cafe ? *Boniface*, a bifhop in St. *Auguftin's* time, knowing that the church did univerfally ufe this cuftom of baptizing infants with interrogatories, was defirous to learn from St. *Auguftin* the true caufe and reafon thereof. *If* (faith he) *I fhould fet before thee a young infant, and fhould ask of thee, whether that infant when he cometh unto riper age, will be honeft and juft, or no ; thou would'ft anfwer (I know) that to tell in thefe things what fhall come to pafs, is not in the power of mor-tal men. If I fhould ask, what good or evil fuch an infant thinketh ? Thine anfwer hereunto muft needs be again with the like uncertainty. If thou neither canft promife for the time to come, nor for the prefent pronounce any thing in this cafe ; how is it, that when fuch are brought unto baptifm, their parents there undertake what the child fhall afterwards do ? Yea, they are not doubtful to fay, It doth that which is impoffible to be done by infants. At the leaft, there is no man precifely able to affirm it done. Vouchfafe me hereunto fome fhort anfwer, fuch as not only may prefs me with the bare authority of cuftom, but alfo inftruct me in the caufe thereof.* Touching which difficulty, whether it may truly be faid for infants at the time of their baptifm, that they do believe, the effect of St. *Auguftin's* anfwer is Yea ; but with this diftinction, a prefent actual habit of faith there is not in them ; there is delivered unto them that facrament, a part of the due celebration whereof confifteth in anfwering to the articles of faith ; becaufe the habit of faith, which afterwards doth come with years, is but a farther building up of the fame edifice, *the firft foundation whereof was laid by the facrament of baptifm.* For that which there we profeffed without any underftand-ing, when we afterwards come to acknowledge, do we any thing elfe but only bring unto ripenefs the very feed that was fown before ? We are then believers, becaufe then we begin to be that, which procefs of time doth make perfect. And till we come to actual belief, the very facrament of faith is a fhield as ftrong, as after this the faith of the facrament againft all contrary infernal powers : Which whofoever doth think impoffible, is undoubtedly farther off from chriftian belief, though he be baptized, than are thefe innocents which at their baptifm, albeit they have no conceit or cogitation of faith, are notwithftanding pure and free from all oppofite cogitations ; whereas the other is not free. If therefore, without any fear or fcruple, we may account them and term them believers only for their outward profeffion fake, which inwardly are farther from faith than infants ; why not infants much more at the time of their folemn initiation by bap-tifm, the facrament of faith, whereunto they not only conceive nothing oppofite, but have alfo that grace given them, which is the firft and moft effectual caufe out of which our belief groweth ? In fum, the whole church is a multitude of believers, all honoured with that title ; even hypocrites, for their profeffion fake, as well as faints, becaufe of their inward fin-cere perfuafion, and *Infants, as being in the firft degree of their ghoftly motion towards the actual habit of faith :* The firft fort are faithful in the eye of the world ; the fecond faithful in the fight of God ; the laft, in the ready direct way to become both, if all things after be fuitable to thefe their prefent beginnings. *This* (faith St. *Auguftin*) *would not haply content fuch perfons as are uncapable or unquiet ; but to them which having knowledge, are not troublefome, it may fuffice. Wherein I have not for eafe of my felf objected againft you that cuftom only, than which nothing is more firm ; but of a cuftom moft profitable, I have done that little which I could, to yield you a reafonable caufe.* Were St. *Au-guftin* now living, there are which would tell him for his better inftruction, that to [a] fay of a child, It is elect, and to fay, It doth believe, are all one : For which caufe, fith no man is able precifely to affirm the one of any infant in particular, it followeth, that precifely and abfolutely we ought not to fay the other. Which precife and ab-folute

Aug. Ep. 23.

Sicut credere refpondetur, ita etiam fide-les vocatur ; non rem ipfa mente annuen-do, fed ipfius rei facramen-tum percipien-do. Aug.

Multum mirabilis res eft, quemadmodum querundam nondum cognofcentium Deum fit inhabitator Deus ; & quorundam cognofcen-tium, non fit. Nec illi enim ad templum Dei pertinent, qui cog-nofcentes Deum, non ficut Deum glorificaverunt : Et ad templum Dei pertinent parvuli, fanctificati facramento Chrifti, regenerati Spiritu fancto, qui per ætatem nondum poffunt cognofcere Deum, Unde quem potuerunt illi noffe nec habere, ifti potuerunt habere æu-taquam noffe. Aug. Epift. 57.

[a] *T. C. lib.* 1. *pag.* 169. If children could have faith, yet they that prefent the child cannot precifely tell whether that particular child hath faith, or no. We are to think chari-tably, and to hope it is one of the church ; but it can be no more precifely faid that it hath faith, than it may be faid precifely elected.

folute terms are needlefs in this cafe. We fpeak of infants, as the rule of piety alloweth both to fpeak and think. They that can take to themfelves, in ordinary talk, a charitable kind of liberty to name men of their own fort God's dear children (notwithftanding the large reign of hypocrify) fhould not methinks be fo ftrict and rigorous againft the church, for prefuming as it doth of a chriftian innocent. For, when we know how Chrift in general hath faid, that *of fuch is the kingdom of heaven*, which kingdom is the inheritance of God's elect ; and do withal behold, how his providence hath called them unto the firft beginnings of eternal life, and prefented them at the well-fpring of new-birth, wherein original fin is purged ; befides which fin, there is no hindrance of their falvation known to us, as themfelves will grant : Hard it were, that having fo many fair inducements whereupon to ground, we fhould not be thought to utter (at the leaft) a truth as probable and allowable, in terming any fuch particular infant an elect babe, as in prefuming the like of others, whofe fafety neverthelefs we are not abfolutely able to warrant. If any troubled with thefe fcruples be, only for inftruction fake, defirous to know yet fome farther reafon, why interrogatories fhould be miniftred to infants in baptifm, and be anfwer'd unto by others as in their names ; they may confider, That baptifm implieth a covenant or league between God and Man ; wherein, as God doth beftow prefently remiffion of fins and the Holy Ghoft, binding alfo himfelf to add (in procefs of time) what grace foever fhall be farther neceffary for the attainment of everlafting life ; fo every baptized foul receiving the fame grace at the hands of God, tieth likewife it felf for ever to the obfervation of his law, no lefs than the *Jews* by circumcifion bound themfelves to the law of *Mofes*. The law of Chrift requiring therefore faith and newnefs of life in all men, by virtue of the covenant which they make in baptifm ; is it toyifh, that the church in baptifm exacteth at every man's hands an exprefs profeffion of faith, and an irrevocable promife of obedience by way of [a] folemn ftipulation ? That infants may contract and covenant with God, the [b] law is plain. Neither is the reafon of the law obfcure : For fith it tendeth (we cannot fufficiently exprefs how much) to their own good, and doth no way hurt or endanger them to begin the race of their lives herewith ; they are, as equity requireth, admitted hereunto, and in favour of their tender years, fuch formal complements of ftipulation being requifite as are impoffible by themfelves in their own perfons to be performed, leave is given that they may fufficiently [c] difcharge them by others. Albeit therefore neither deaf nor dumb men, neither furious perfons nor children, can receive any civil ftipulation ; yet this kind of ghoftly ftipulation they may through his indulgence, who refpecting the fingular benefit thereof, accepteth children brought unto him for that end, entreth into articles of covenant with them, and in tender commiferation granteth, that other mens profeffions and promifes in baptifm made for them, fhall avail no lefs than if they had been themfelves able to have made their own. None more fit to undertake this office in their behalf, than fuch as prefent them unto baptifm. A wrong conceit that none may receive the facrament of baptifm, but they whofe parents (at the leaft the one of them) are by the foundnefs of their religion, and by their virtuous demeanor, known to be men of God, hath caufed fome to repel children, whofoever bring them, if their parents be mif-perfuaded in religion, or for other mif-deferts excommunicated : Some likewife for that caufe to withhold baptifm, unlefs the father (albeit no fuch exception can juftly be taken againft him) do notwithftanding make profeffion of his faith, and avouch the child to be his own. Thus, whereas God hath appointed them minifters of holy things, they make themfelves inquifitors of mens perfons a great deal farther than need is. They fhould confider, that God hath ordained baptifm in favour of mankind. To reftrain favours is an odious thing ; to enlarge them, acceptable both to God and man. Whereas therefore the civil law gave divers immunities to them that were fathers of three children, and had them living ; thofe

2 John 2.

Gal. 3. 5.

[a] *Stipulatio eft verborum conceptio, quibus is qui interrogatur, daturum facturumve fe quod interrogatus eft, refpondet. L. 5. Sect. 1. ff. de Oblig. & Act. In hac re olim talia verba tradita fuerunt. Spondes? Spondeo. Promittis? Promitto. Fide promittis? Fide promitto. Fide jubes? Fide jubeo. Dabis? Dabo. Facies? Faciam. Inftit. de verb. oblig. L. 3. tit. 15.*

[b] *Gen. 17. 14.*

[c] *Accommodat illis mater Ecclefia aliorum pedes ut veniant, aliorum cor ut credant, aliorum linguam ut fateantur ; ut quoniam quod agri funt alio peccante pragravantur, fic cum fani fiant alio pro eis confitente falventur. Aug. Serm. 10. de Verb. Apoft.*

T. C. l. 1. p. 172.

immunities they held, although their children were all dead, if war had confumed them, becaufe it feemed in that cafe not againft reafon to repute them by a courteous conftruction of law as live men, in that the honour of their fervice done to the commonwealth would remain always.   Can it hurt us, in exhibiting the graces which God doth beftow on men ; or can it prejudice his glory, if the felf-fame equity guide and direct our hands? When God made his covenant with fuch as had *Abraham* to their father, was only *Abraham's* immediate iffue, or only his lineal pofterity according to the flefh, included in that covenant? Were not profelytes as well as *Jews* always taken for the fons of *Abraham*? Yea, becaufe the very heads of families are fathers in fome fort, as touching providence and care for the meaneft that belong unto them, the fervants which *Abraham* had bought with money were as capable of circumcifion, being newly born, as any natural child that *Abraham* himfelf begat.   Be it then, that baptifm belongeth to none but fuch as either believe prefently, or elfe, being infants, are the children of believing parents, in cafe the church do bring children to the holy font, whofe natural parents are either unknown, or known to be fuch as the church accurfeth, but yet forgetteth not in that feverity to take compaffion upon their off-fpring, (for it is the church which doth offer them to baptifm by the miniftry of prefenters) were it not againft both equity and duty to refufe the mother of believers her felf, and not to take her in this cafe for a faithful parent?   It is not the virtue of our fathers, nor the faith of any other that can give us the true holinefs which we have by virtue of our new-birth.   Yet even through the common faith and fpirit of God's church (a thing which no quality of parents can prejudice) I fay, through the faith of the church of God, undertaking the motherly care of our fouls, fo far forth we may be, and are in our infancy fanctified, as to be thereby made fufficiently capable of baptifm, and to be interefted in the rites of our new birth for their pieties fake that offer us thereunto.   *It cometh fometime to pafs* (faith St. *Auguftin*) *that the children of bond-flaves are brought to baptifm by their Lord; fometime the parents being dead, the friends alive undertake that office; fometime ftrangers or virgins confecrated unto God, which neither have, nor can have children of their own, take up infants in the open ftreets, and fo offer them unto baptifm, whom the cruelty of unnatural parents cafteth out, and leaveth to the adventure of uncertain pity.*   As therefore he which did the part of a neighbour, was a neighbour to that wounded man whom the parable of the gofpel defcribeth; fo they are fathers, although ftrangers, that bring infants to him which maketh them the fons of God.   In the phrafe of fome kind of men, they ufe to be termed witneffes, as if they came but to fee and teftify what is done. It favoureth more of piety to give them their old accuftomed name of fathers and mothers in God, whereby they are well put in mind what affection they ought to bear towards thofe innocents, for whofe religious education the church accepteth them as pledges.   This therefore is their own duty : But becaufe the anfwer which they make to the ufual demands of ftipulation propofed in baptifm is not their own; the church doth beft to receive it of them, in that form which beft fheweth whofe the act is.   That which a guardian doth in the name of his guard or pupil, ftandeth by natural equity forcible for his benefit, though it be done without his knowledge.   And fhall we judge it a thing unreafonable, or in any refpect unfit, that infants by words which others utter fhould, though unwittingly, yet truly and forcibly bind themfelves to that whereby their eftate is fo affuredly bettered? Herewith *Neftorius* * the heretick was charged, as having fall'n from this firft profeffion, and broken the promife which he made to God in the arms of others.   Of fuch as profaned themfelves, being chriftians, with irreligious delight in the enfigns of idolatry, heathenifh fpectacles, fhows and ftage-plays, *Tertullian*, to ftrike them the more deep, claimeth the promife which they made in baptifm.   Why were they dumb, being thus challenged? Wherefore ftood they not up to anfwer it in their own defence, that fuch profeffions and promifes made in their names were frivolous; that all which others undertook for them was but mockery and profanation? That which no heretick, no wicked liver, no impious

Margin notes:

Hi enim qui pro Rep. ceciderunt, in perpetuum per gloriam vivere intelliguntur. Inftit. lib. 2. tit. 25. fect. 1.

Offeruntur quippe parvuli ad percipiendam fpiritualem gratiam, non tam ab eis quorum geftantur manibus, quamvis & ab ipfis fi & ipfi boni & fideles fint, quam ab univerfa focietate fanctorum atque fidelium. Aug. in Epift. 23.

Ἀξιοῦται ᾗ δέλα τῶν βασιλευσ, ἵω' ἀγαθὰν τὰ θεϊκὰ τῇ νεων ἐσὶ περιϊψίνων ἀντὶ τῇ Βασιλικον. *Juftin. Rejp. ad Orthod.*

Si Ariana aut Sabelliana herefeos adfertor effes, & non tua ipfius fymbolo tecum uterer; convincerem te tamen teftimoniorum fuorum auctoritate.   Quid tandem fi fic apud te agerem? quid diceres? quid refponderes? nonne obfecro illud, in eo te baptifatum, in eo te renatum effe? Et vero, in negotio quamvis improbo non importuna defenfio, & quae non abfurde caufam erroris diceret, fi pertinaciam non feiares errori.   Nunc autem cum in Catholica urbe natus, Catholica Fide inftitutus, Catholica Baptifmate regeneratus fis, nunquid agere tecum quafi cum Ariano aut Sabelliano poffim? Quod utinam fuiffes.   Minus dolerem in malis editum quam de bonis lapfum, minus fidem non habitam quam amiffam.   Non iniquum autem, Heretice, non iniquum aut grave aliquid poftulo. Hoc fac in Catholica Fide editus, quod fueras pro perverfitate factuarus. Caffia. de incarn. lib. 6. cap. 5.

Tertul. lib. de Spectac.

impious defpifer of God, no mifcreant or malefactor, which had himfelf been baptized, was ever fo defperate as to difgorge in contempt of fo fruitfully received
cuftoms, is now their voice that reftore, as they fay, *The ancient purity of re-*
ligion.

Of the crofs in baptifm.

65. In baptifm many things of very ancient continuance are now quite and clean
aboliſhed; for that the virtue and grace of this facrament had been therewith over-
fhadowed, as fruit with too great abundance of leaves. Notwithftanding to them
which think it always imperfect reformation that doth but fhear and not flea,
our retaining certain of thofe formal rites, efpecially the dangerous fign of the crofs,
hath feemed almoft an impardonable overfight. *The crofs* (they fay) *fith it is but*
a meer invention of man, fhould not therefore at all have been added to the fa-
crament of baptifm. To fign children's foreheads with a·crofs, in token that
hereafter they fhall not be afhamed to make profeffion of the faith of Chriſt, is
to bring into the church a new word, whereas there ought to be no doctor
heard in the church but our Saviour Chriſt. That reafon which moved the fa-
thers to ufe, fhould move us not to ufe the fign of the crofs. They lived with
heathens that had the crofs of Chriſt in contempt,·we with fuch as adore the
crofs; and therefore we ought to abandon it, even as, in like confideration, Ezekias *did of old the brazen Serpent.* Thefe are the caufes of difpleafure conceived againſt the crofs; a ceremony, the ufe whereof hath been profitable, although we obferve it not as the ordinance of God but of man. For (faith *Ter-*

Tertul. de Coron. Mili-tis.

tullian) *if of this and the·like cuſtoms thou fhouldſt require fome commandment*
to be fhewed thee out of fcriptures, there is none found. What reafon there is to
juftify tradition, ufe or cuftom in this behalf, *either thou mayſt of thy felf per-*
ceive, or elfe learn of fome other that doth. Left therefore the name of tradition fhould be offenfive to any, confidering how far by fome it hath been and

[a] *Traditiones non fcriptas, fi doctrinam refpiciant, cum doctrina fcripta connexive debere dicimus. Quod ad rituales & Ecclefiaſti-cas attinet, ordinis & adificationis Ecclefiarum in his femper ha-benda ratio eſt; inutiles autem & noxias, nempe ineptas & fuper-ſtitiofas patronis fuis relinquamus.* Goulart. Genevenf. Annot. in Epiſt. Cypr. 74.

and reafonable caufe to alter them,
and in grofs to be fhaken off, becaufe

is abufed, we mean by [a] traditions, ordinances made in the prime of chriſtian religion, eftabliſhed with that authority which
Chriſt hath left to his church for matters indifferent; and in that confideration requifite to be obferved, till like authority fee juſt
the inventors of them were men. Such as

[b] *T.C. l. 1. p. 171.* They fhould not have been fo bold as to have brought it into the holy facrament of baptifm; and fo mingle the ceremonies and inventions of men with the facraments and inſtitutions of God.

fay, they allow no [b] invention of men to be
mingled with the outward adminiſtration of
facraments; and under that pretence, condemn
our ufing the fign of the crofs, have belike
fome fpecial difpenfation themfelves to violate

their own rules. For neither can they indeed decently, nor do they ever bap-
tife any without manifeſt breach of this their profound Axiom, *That men's inven-*
tions fhould not be mingled with facraments and inſtitutions of God. They feem
to like very well in baptifm the cuſtom of godfathers, *becaufe fo generally the*

T.C. l. 1. p. 170.

churches have received it. Which cuſtom, being of God no more inſtituted than
the other (howfoever they pretend the other hurtful and this profitable) it followeth, that even in their own opinion, if their words do fhew their minds, there is
no neceffity of ftripping facraments out of all fuch attire of ceremonies as man's wifdom hath at any time cloathed them withal; and confequently, that either they muſt
reform their fpeech as over-general, or elfe condemn their own practice as unlawful. Ceremonies have more in weight than in fight; they work by commonnefs of
ufe much, although in the feveral acts of their ufage we fcarcely difcern any good
they do. And becaufe the ufe which they have for the moſt part, is not perfectly

T. C. I 1. p. 170. The profitable fignification of the crofs maketh the thing a great deal worfe, and bringeth in a new word into the Church; whereas there ought to be no doctor heard in the church, but only our Saviour Chriſt. For although it be the word of God, that we fhould not be afhamed of the crofs of Chriſt, yet is it not the word of God, that we fhould be kept in remembrance of that, by two lines drawn acrofs one over another in a child's fore-head.

underſtood, fuperſtition is apt to impute unto
them greater virtue than indeed they have.
For prevention whereof when we ufe this ceremony, we always plainly exprefs the end
whereunto it ferveth, namely, for a fign of
remembrance to put us in mind of our duty. But
by this mean, they fay, we make it a great deal
worfe. For why? Seeing God hath no where commanded to draw two lines in token of the duty
which

which we owe to Chrift, our practice with this expofition publisheth a new gospel, and causeth another word to have place in the church of Chrift, where no voice ought to be heard but his.   By which good reafon the authors of thofe grave admonitions to the parliament are well holpen up, which held, *That sitting at communions betokeneth reft and full accomplishment of legal ceremonies in our Saviour Chrift.* For although it be the word of God that fuch ceremonies are expired ; yet feeing it is not the word of God, that men to fignify fo much fhould fit at the table of our Lord, thefe have their doom as well as others, *Guilty of a new devifed Gofpel in the church of Chrift.* Which ftrange imagination is begotten of a fpecial diflike they have to hear, that ceremonies now in ufe fhould be thought fignificant ; whereas, in truth, fuch as are not fignificant, muft needs be vain.   Ceremonies deftitute of fignification , are no better than the idle geftures of men, whofe broken wits are not mafters of what they do.   For if we look but into fecular and civil complements, what other caufe can there poffibly be given, why to omit them, where of courfe they are looked for ?   For where they are not fo due, to ufe them bringeth mens fecret intents oftentimes into great jealoufy : I would know, I fay, what reafon we are able to yield, why things fo light in their own nature fhould weigh in the opinions of men fo much, faving only in regard of that which they ufe to fignify or betoken ?   Doth not our Lord Jefus Chrift himfelf impute the omiffion of fome courteous ceremonies, even in domeftical entertainment, to a colder degree of loving affection, and take the contrary in better part, not fo much refpecting what was lefs done, as what was fignified by the one than by the other ?   For to that very end he referreth in part thofe gracious expoftulations : *Simon , feeft thou this woman? fince I entred into thine houfe, thou gaveft me no water for my feet ; but fhe hath wafhed my feet with tears, and wiped them with the hairs of her head : Thou gaveft me no kifs, but this woman fince the time I came in, hath not ceafed to kifs my feet : Mine head with oil thou didft not anoint, but this woman hath anointed my feet with ointment.*   Wherefore as the ufual dumb ceremonies of common life are in requeft or diflike according to that they import ; even fo religion, having likewife her filent rites, the chiefeft rule whereby to judge of their quality, is that which they mean or betoken.   For if they fignify good things, (as fomewhat they muft of neceffity fignify, becaufe it is of their very nature to be figns of intimation, prefenting both themfelves unto outward fenfe, and befides themfelves, fome other thing to the underftanding of beholders) unlefs they be either greatly mifchofen to fignify the fame, or elfe applied where that which they fignify agreeth not, there is no caufe of exception againft them, as againft evil and unlawful ceremonies ; much lefs of excepting againft them only in that they are not without fenfe.   And if every religious ceremony which hath been invented of men to fignify any thing that God himfelf alloweth, were the publication of another Gofpel in the church of Chrift ; feeing that no chriftian church in the world is, or can be, without continual ufe of fome ceremonies which men have inftituted, and that to fignify good things (unlefs they be vain and frivolous ceremonies ;) it would follow, that the world hath no chriftian church which doth not daily proclaim new gofpels ; a fequel, the manifeft abfurdity whereof argueth the rawnefs of that fuppofal out of which it groweth.   Now the [a] caufe why antiquity did the more, *in actions of common life,* honour the ceremony of the crofs, might be for that they lived with infidels.   But that which they did in the facrament of baptifm, was for the felf fame good of believers, which is thereby intended ftill.   The crofs is for us an admonition no lefs neceffary than for them, to glory in the fervice of Jefus Chrift, and not to hang down our heads as men afhamed thereof, although it procure us reproach and oblo-

Luke 7. 44.

[a] *T. C.* l. 1. p. 170.   It is known to all that have read the ecclefiaftical hiftories, that the heathens did object to chriftians in times paft, in reproach, that the God which they believed on, was hanged upon a Crofs.   And they thought good to teftify, that they were not afhamed therefore of the Son of God, by the often ufing of the fign of the Crofs.   Which carefulnefs and good mind to keep amongft them an open profeffion of Chrift crucified, although it be to be commended, yet is not this means fo.   For they might otherwife have kept it, and with lefs danger, than by this ufe of croffing.   And as it was brought in upon no good ground, fo the Lord laft a mark of his curfe of it, and whereby it might be perceived to come out of the forge of mens brain, in that it began forthwith, while it was yet in the fwadling-cloute, to be fuperftitioufly abufed.   The chriftians had fuch a fuperftition in it, that they would do nothing without croffing.   But if it were granted, that upon this confideration which I have before-mentioned , the ancient chriftians did well ; yet it followeth not, that we fhould fo do.   For we live not among thofe nations which do caft us in the teeth, or reproach us with the Crofs of Chrift.   Now that we live amongft papifts that do not contemn the Crofs of Chrift, but which efteem more of the wooden Crofs, than of the true Crofs, which is his fufferings ; we ought now to do clean contrariwife to the old chriftians, and abolifh all ufe of thefe croffes.   For contrary difeafes muft have contrary remedies.   If therefore the old chriftians to deliver the Crofs of Chrift from contempt, did often ufe the Crofs ; the chriftians now, to take away the fuperftitious eftimation of it, ought to take away the ufe of it.

quy at the hands of this wretched world. Shame is a kind of fear to incur difgrace and ignominy. Now whereas some things are worthy of reproach, some
things ignominious only through a false opinion which men have conceived of
them, nature, that generally feareth opprobrious reprehension, must by reason and
religion be [a] taught what it should be ashamed of, and what not. But be we never so well instructed what our duty is in this behalf, without some present admonition at the very instant of practice, what we know, is many times not called to
mind, till that be done whereupon our just confusion ensueth. To supply the absence of such as that way might do us good, when they see us in danger of sliding,
there are [b] judicious and wise men which think we may greatly relieve our selves,
by a bare imagined presence of some whose authority we fear, and would be loth to
offend, if indeed they were present with us. Witnesses at hand are a bridle unto
many offences. Let the mind have always some whom it feareth, some whose authority may keep even secret thoughts under awe. Take *Cato*, or if he be too harsh
and rugged, chuse some other of a softer metal, whose gravity of life and speech
thou lovest, his mind and countenance carry with thee, set him always before thine
eyes, either as a watch or as a pattern. That which is crooked we cannot streigh-
ten but by some such level. If men of so good experience and insight in the maims
of our weak flesh, have thought these fancied remembrances available to awaken
shamefacedness, that so the boldness of sin may be staid e're it look abroad; surely the
wisdom of the church of Christ, which hath to that use converted the ceremony of
the cross in baptism, it is no christian man's part to despise; especially seeing that by
this mean, where nature doth earnestly import aid, religion yieldeth her that ready
assistance than which there can be no help more forcible, serving only to relieve memory, and to bring to our cogitation that which should most make ashamed of
Sin. The mind while we are in this present
life, [c] whether it contemplate, meditate, deliberate, or howsoever exercise it self, worketh
nothing without continual recourse unto imagination, the only store-house of wit, and peculiar chair of memory. On this anvil it ceaseth not day and night to strike, by means
whereof as the pulse declareth how the heart doth work, so the very [d] thoughts and
cogitations of man's mind, be they good or bad, do no where sooner bewray themselves, than through the crevises of that wall wherewith nature hath compassed the
cells and closets of fancy. In the forehead nothing more plain to be seen than the
fear of contumely and disgrace. For which cause the scripture (as with great probability it may be thought) describeth them marked of God in the forehead, whom
his mercy hath undertaken to keep from final confusion and shame. Not that God
doth set any corporal mark on his chosen, but to note that he giveth his elect security of preservation from reproach, the fear whereof doth use to shew it self in that
part. Shall I say, that the sign of the cross (as we use it) is in some sort a mean
to work our [e] preservation from reproach ? Surely the mind which as yet hath not
hardned it self in sin, is seldom provoked thereunto in any gross and grievous manner, but nature's secret suggestion objecteth against it ignominy as a bar. Which
conceit being entred into that palace of man's fancy, the gates whereof have imprinted in them that holy sign which bringeth forthwith to mind whatsoever Christ
hath wrought, and we vowed against sin, it cometh hereby to pass that christian
men never want a most effectual, though a silent teacher, to avoid whatsoever may
deservedly procure shame. So that in things which we should be ashamed of, we are
by the cross admonished faithfully of our duty, at the very moment when admonition doth most need. Other things there are which deserve honour, and yet do purchase many times our disgrace in this present world; as of old the very truth of
religion it self, till God by his own out-stretched arm made the glory thereof to
shine over all the earth. Whereupon St. *Cyprian* exhorting to martyrdom in times
of heathenish persecution and cruelty, thought it not vain to alledge unto them,
with other arguments, the very ceremony of that cross whereof we speak. Never
let that hand offer sacrifice to idols which hath already received the body of our
Saviour Christ, and shall hereafter the crown of his glory; *Arm your foreheads* unto all boldness, that the *sign of God* may be kept safe. Again, when it pleased
God that the fury of their enemies being bridled, the church had some little rest
and

[a] Ephes. 5.
12.
Rom. 6. 21.

[b] Sen. Epist.
11. l. 1.

[c] Τὸ νοεῖν ἢ φαντασία τὶς ἢ ἐκ ἄνευ φαντασίας. Arist. de
Anim. lib. 1. cap. 1. Ἡ μὲν διανοητικὴ φαντασία ἢ ἐν τοῖς λοβι-
ζοις ζῴοις ὑπάρχει, ἡ ἢ βουλευτικὴ ἐν τοῖς λογιστικοῖς, Lib. 3.
cap. 11. Τὰ μὲν οὖν εἴδη τὸ νοητικὸν ἐν τοῖς φαντάσμασι νοεῖ,
ἢ ὡς ἐν ἐκείνοις ὥρισαι αὐτῷ τὸ διωκτὸν, ἢ φευκτὸν, ἢ ἐκτὸς
τῆς αἰσθήσεως ὂν, ὅταν ἐπὶ τῶν φαντασμάτων ᾖ, κινεῖται. Lib. 3.
cap. 8.

[d] Fons homi-
nis tristitia,
Hilaritatis,
clementiæ, fe-
veritatis in-
dex est. Plin.
L. 11.
Ezek. 9. 4.
Apoc. 7. 3.
& 9. 4.
Ἐφρὼ σφραγίσαν-
τας ἢ δι' αἰσ-
χυνθέντας.
Arist. Eth. 4.
c. 9.

[e] Caro signa-
tur ut & ani-
ma muniatur,
Tertul. de
Resur. Car.

Cypr. Epist.56.
ad Thiharita-
nos.

and quietnefs, (if fo fmall a liberty but only to breath between troubles, may be termed quietnefs and reft) to fuch as fell not away from Chrift through former perfecutions, he giveth due and deferved praife in the felf-fame manner. *You that were ready to endure imprifonment, and were refolute to fuffer death; you that have couragioufly withflood the world, ye have made your felves both a glorious fpectacle for God to behold, and a worthy example for the reft of your brethren to follow. Thofe mouths which had fanctified themfelves with food coming down from heaven, loathed, after Chrift's own body and blood, to tafte the poyfoned and contagious fcraps of idols; thofe foreheads which the fign of God had purified, kept themfelves to be crowned by him, the touch of the garlands of Satan they abhorred.* Cypr. de Lapf.

Thus was the memory of that fign which they had in baptifm, a kind of bar or prevention to keep them even from apoftafy, whereunto the frailty of flefh and blood, overmuch fearing to endure fhame, might peradventure the more eafily otherwife have drawn them.

Erant enim fupplices coronarii. Tert. lib. de Coro. Mil. In the fervice of idols, the doors of their temples, the facrifices, the altars, the priefts, and the fupplicants that were prefent, wore garlands.

We have not now, through the gracious goodnefs of Almighty God, thofe extream conflicts which our fathers had with blafphemous contumelies every where offered to the name of Chrift, by fuch as profeffed themfelves infidels and unbelievers. Howbeit, unlefs we be ftrangers to the age wherein we live, or elfe in fome partial refpect diffemblers of that we hourly both hear and fee, there is not the fimpleft of us but knoweth with what difdain and fcorn Chrift is difhonoured far and wide. Is there any burden in the world more heavy to bear than contempt? Is there any contempt that grieveth as theirs doth, whofe quality no way making them lefs worthy than others are of reputation, only the fervice which they do to Chrift in the daily exercife of religion treadeth them down? Doth any contumely which we fuftain for religion's fake pierce fo deeply, as that which would feem of meer confcience religioufly fpightful? When they that honour God are defpifed; when the chiefeft fervice of honour that man can do unto him, is the caufe why they are defpifed; when they which pretend to honour him, and that with greateft fincerity, do with more than heathenifh petulancy trample under foot almoft whatfoever either we, or the whole church of God, by the fpace of fo many ages, have been accuftomed unto, for the comelier and better exercife of our religion according to the foundeft rules that wifdom directed by the word of God, and by long experience confirmed, hath been able with common advice, with much deliberation and exceeding great diligence, to comprehend; when no man fighting under Chrift's banner can be always exempted from feeing or fuftaining thofe indignities, the fting whereof not to feel, or feeling not to be moved thereat, is a thing impoffible to flefh and blood: If this be any object for patience to work on, the ftricteft bond that thereunto tieth us, is our vowed obedience to Chrift; the folemneft vow that we ever made to obey Chrift, and to fuffer willingly all reproaches for his fake, was made in baptifm: And amongft other memorials to keep us mindful of that vow, we cannot think that the fign which our new baptized foreheads did there receive, is either unfit or unforcible, the reafons hitherto alledged being weighed with indifferent balance. It is not (you will fay) the crofs in our fore-heads, but in our hearts the faith of Chrift that armeth us with patience, conftancy and courage. Which as we grant to be moft true, fo neither dare we defpife, no not the meaneft helps that ferve, though it be but in the very loweft degree of furtherance towards the higheft fervices that God doth require at our hands. And if any man deny that fuch ceremonies are available, at the leaft as memorials of duty; or do think that himfelf hath no need to be fo put in mind what our duties are; it is but reafonable, that in the one the publick experience of the world over-weigh fome few mens perfuafion; and in the other, the rare perfection of a few condefcend unto common imbecillity. Seeing therefore that to fear fhame, which doth worthily follow fin, and to bear undeferved reproach conftantly, is the general duty of all men profeffing chriftianity; feeing alfo that our weaknefs, while we are in this prefent world, doth need towards fpiritual duties the help even of corporal furtherance; and that by reafon of natural intercourfe between the higheft and the loweft powers of man's mind in all actions, his fancy or imagination carrying in it that fpecial note of remembrance, than which there is nothing more forcible, where either too weak or too ftrong a conceit of infamy and difgrace might do great harm, ftandeth always ready to put forth a kind of neceffary helping hand;

[b] "Εϛιν ᾗ ἀγαϑὸν ᾗ τὸ φυλακϑικὸν ᾖ τούτων ᾗ ᾧ ἀκολυϑεῖ τὸ τοιαῦτα ᾗ τὰ κωλυτικὰ ᾖ τὰ ἐναντίων ᾗ τὰ φϑαρτικά. Arift. Rhet. l. 1. cap. 6.
[b] *Ozias Rex lepra varietate in fronte maculatus eft , ut parte corporis notatus offenfo Domino ubi fignantur qui Dominum promerentur.* Cypr. de unit. Ecclef. cap. 16.

hand; we are in that refpect to acknowledge the [a] good and profitable ufe of this ceremony, and not to think it fuperfluous that Chrift hath his mark applied [b] unto that part where bafhfulnefs appeareth, in token that they which are chriftians fhould be at no time afhamed of his ignominy. But to prevent fome inconveniencies which might enfue, if the over ordinary ufe thereof (as it fareth with fuch rites when they are too common) fhould caufe it to be of lefs obfervation or regard where it moft availeth; we neither omit it in that place, nor altogether make it fo vulgar, as the cuftom heretofore hath been. Although to condemn the whole church of God when it moft flourifhed in zeal and piety, to mark that age with the brand of error and fuperftition only becaufe they had this ceremony more in ufe than we now think needful; boldly to affirm that this their practice grew fo foon through a fearful malediction of God upon the ceremony of the crofs, as if we knew that his purpofe was thereby to make it manifeft in all men's eyes how execrable thofe things are in his fight which have proceeded from human invention, is, as we take it, a cenfure of greater zeal than knowledge. Men whofe judgments in thefe cafes are grown more moderate, although they retain not as we do the ufe of this ceremony, perceive notwithftanding very well fuch cenfures to be out of fquare; and do therefore

[c] Goulart. Annot. in Cypr. lib. ad. Demetr. cap. 19. *Quamvis veteres Chriftiani externo figno crucis ufi funt , id tamen fuit fine fuperftitione, & doctrina de Chrifti merito ab errore qui poftea irrepfit pios fervavit immunes.*
[d] *Idem Annot. in Cypr. Epift. 56. c. 7.*

not only [c] acquit the fathers from fuperftition therein, but alfo think it fufficient to anfwer in excufe of themfelves, [d] *This ceremony which was but a thing indifferent even of old, we judge not at this day a matter neceffary for all chriftian men to obferve.* As for their laft upfhot of all towards this mark, they are of opinion that if the ancient chriftians, to deliver the crofs of Chrift from contempt, did well and with good confideration ufe often the fign of the crofs in teftimony of their faith and profeffion before infidels, which upbraided them with Chrift's fufferings; now that we live with fuch as contrariwife adore the fign of the crofs (becaufe contrary difeafes fhould always have contrary remedies) we ought to take away all ufe thereof. In which conceit they both ways greatly feduce themfelves: firft, for that they imagin the fathers to have had no ufe of the crofs but with reference unto infidels, which mif-perfuafion we have before difcovered at large; and fecondly, by reafon that they think there is not any other way befides univerfal extirpation to reform fuperftitious abufes of the crofs. Wherein, becaufe there are that ftand very much upon the example of *Ezechias*, as if his *breaking to pieces that ferpent* of brafs ₁Kings 18.3. whereunto the children of *Ifrael* had *burnt incenfe*, did enforce the utter abolition of this ceremony; the fact of that virtuous prince is by fo much the more attentively to be confidered. Our lives in this world are partly guided by rules, and partly directed by examples. To conclude out of general rules and axioms by difcourfe of wit our duties in every particular action, is both troublefome, and many times fo full of difficulty, that it maketh deliberations hard and tedious to the wifeft men. Whereupon we naturally incline to obferve examples, to mark what others have done before us, and in favour of our own eafe rather to follow them than to enter into new confultation, if in regard of their virtue and wifdom we may but probably think they have waded without error. So that the willingnefs of men to be led by example of others, both difcovereth and helpeth the imbecillity of our judgment. Becaufe it doth the one, therefore infolent and proud wits would always feem to be their own guides; and becaufe it doth the other, we fee how hardly the vulgar fort is drawn unto any thing for which there are not as well examples as reafons alledged. Reafons proving that which is more particular by things more general and farther from fenfe, are with the fimpler fort of men lefs trufted, for that they doubt of their own judment in thofe things; but of examples which prove unto them one doubtful particular by another, more familiarly and fenfibly known, they eafily perceive in themfelves fome better ability to judge. The force of examples therefore is great, when in matter of action, being doubtful what to do, we are informed what others have commendably done whofe deliberations were like. But whofoever doth perfuade by example, muft as well refpect the fitnefs as the goodnefs of that he alledgeth. To *Ezechias* God himfelf in this fact giveth teftimony of well-doing. So that nothing is here queftionable, but only whether the example alledged be pertinent, pregnant and ftrong. The ferpent fpoken of was firft erected for the extra-

I   ordi-

ordinary and miraculous cure of the *Israelites* in the desart.   Thus use having presently an end, when the cause for which God ordained it was once removed, the thing it self they notwithstanding kept for a monument of God's mercy ; as in like consideration they did the pot of manna, the rod of *Aaron*, and the sword which *David* took from *Goliah*.   In process of time they made of a monument of divine power a plain idol, they burnt incense before it contrary to the law of God, and did it the services of honour due unto God only.   Which gross and grievous abuse continued till *Ezechias*, restoring the purity of sound Religion, destroyed utterly that which had been so long and so generally a snare unto them.   It is not amiss which the canon law hereupon concludeth, namely, *That if our predecessors have done* Dist. à. 3.cap. *some things which at that time might be without fault , and afterwards be turned to* Quia. *error and superstition ; we are taught by* Ezechias *breaking the brazen Serpent, that posterity may destroy them without any delay, and with great authority*.   But may it be simply and without exception hereby gathered, that posterity is bound to destroy whatsoever hath been either at the first invented, or but afterwards turned to like superstition and error ? No, it cannot be.   The serpent therefore, and the sign of the cross, although seeming equal in this point, that superstition hath abused both ; yet being herein also unequal, that neither they have been both subject to the like degree of abuse, nor were in hardness of redress alike, it may be, that even as the one for abuse was religiously taken away, so now, when religion hath taken away abuse from the other, we should by utter abolition thereof deserve hardly his commendation, whose example there is offered us no such necessary cause to follow.   For by the words of *Ezechias* in terming the serpent but *a lump of brass*, to shew that the best thing in it now was the metal or matter whereof it consisteth, we may probably conjecture, that the people whose error is therein controuled, had the self-same opinion of it which the heathens had of idols.   They thought that the power of deity was with it ; and when they saw it dissolved, haply they might, to comfort themselves, imagine as *Olympius* the sophister did beholding the dissipation of idols, *shapes and* Sozom. lib.7. *counterfeits they were, fashioned of matter subject unto corruption, therefore to grind* cap. 15. *them to dust was easy ; but those celestial powers which dwelt and resided in them, are ascended into heaven*.   Some difference there is between these opinions of palpable idolatry, and that which the schools in speculation have bolted out concerning the cross.   Notwithstanding, for as much as the church of *Rome* hath hitherto practised, and doth profess the same adoration to the sign of the cross, and neither less nor other than is due unto Christ himself, howsoever they varnish and qualify their sentence, pretending that the cross which to outward sense presenteth visibly it self alone, is not by them apprehended alone, but hath in their secret surmise or conceit a reference to the person of our Lord Jesus Christ ; so that the honour which they jointly do to both, respecteth principally his person, and the cross but only for his person's sake ; the people not accustomed to trouble their wits with so nice and subtil differences in the exercise of religion, are apparently no less ensnared by adoring the cross, than the *Jews* by burning incense to the brazen serpent.   It is by *Thomas* ingenuously Tho. p. 3. granted, that because unto reasonable creatures a kind of reverence is due for the q. 25. art. 3. excellency which is in them, and whereby they resemble God, therefore if reasona- Resp. ad ble creatures, angels or men, should receive at our hands holy and divine honour, tert. as the sign of the cross doth at theirs, to pretend that we honour not them alone, but we honour God with them , would not serve the turn, neither would this be able to prevent the error of men, or cause them always to respect God in their adorations, and not to finish their intents in the object next before them.   But unto this he addeth, that no such error can grow by adoring in that sort a dead image which every man knoweth to be void of excellency in it self, and therefore will easily conceive that the honour done unto it hath an higher reference.   Howbeit, seeing that we have by over-true experience been taught how often, especially in these cases, the light even of common understanding faileth, surely their usual adoration of the cross is not hereby freed.   For in actions of this kind we are more to respect what the greatest part of men is commonly prone to conceive, than what some few men's wits may devise in construction of their own particular meanings.   Plain it is , that a false opinion of some personal divine excellency to be in those things which either nature or art hath framed, causeth always religious adoration.   And as plain, that the like adoration applied unto things sensible, argueth to vulgar capacities, yea leaveth imprinted in them the very same opinion of deity from whence all idolatrous worship groweth.   Yea, the meaner and baser a thing worshipped is in it felf, the more they incline to think that every man which doth adore it, knoweth there is in it, or with it, a prefence of divine power. Be it therefore true, that croffes purpofely framed or ufed for receipt of divine honour, be even as fcandalous as the brazen ferpent it felf, where they are in fuch fort adored; fhould we hereupon think our felves in the fight of God, and in confcience charged to abolifh utterly the very ceremony of the crofs, neither meant at the firft nor now converted unto any fuch offenfive purpofe? Did the *Jews*, which could never be perfuaded to admit in the city of *Jerufalem* that [a] image of *Cæfar* which the *Romans* were accuftomed to [b] adore, make any fcruple of ' *Cæfar's* image in the coin which they knew very well that men were not wont to worfhip? Between the crofs which fuperftition honoureth as Chrift, and that ceremony of the crofs which ferveth only for a fign of remembrance, there is as plain and as great a difference as between thofe brazen images which *Solomon* made to bear up the ciftern of the temple, and (fith both were of like fhape, but of unlike ufe) that which the *Ifraelites* in the wildernefs did adore; or between the altars which *Jofias* deftroyed, becaufe they were inftruments of mere idolatry, and that which the tribe of *Reuben* with others erected near to the river *Jordan*; for which alfo they grew at the firft into fome diflike, and were by the reft of their brethren fufpected, yea hardly charged with open breach of the law of God, accufed of backwardnefs in religion, upbraided bitterly with the fact of *Peor* and the odious example of *Achan*; as if the building of their altar in that place had given manifeft fhew of no better than intended apoftacy, till by a true declaration made in their own defence, it appeared that fuch as mifliked, mifunderftood their enterprize, in as much as they had no intent to build any altar for facrifice, which God would have no where offered faving in *Jerufalem* only, but to a far other end and purpofe, which being opened fatisfied all parties, and fo delivered them from caufelefs blame. In this particular, fuppofe the worft; imagine that the immaterial ceremony of the crofs had been the fubject of as grofs pollution as any heathenifh or prophane idol. If we think the example of *Ezechias* a proof, that things which error and fuperftition hath abufed, may in no confideration be tolerated, although we prefently find them not fubject to fo vile abufe, the plain example of *Ezechias* proveth the contrary. The temples and idols, which under *Solomon* had been of very purpofe framed for the honour of foreign gods, *Ezechias* deftroyed not; becaufe they ftood as forlorn things, and did now no harm, although formerly they had done harm. *Jofias* for fome inconvenience afterwards razed them up. Yet to both there is one commendation given even from God himfelf, that touching matter of religion, they walked in the fteps of *David*, and did no way difpleafe God. Perhaps it feemeth that by force and virtue of this example, although in bare deteftation and hatred of idolatry, all things which have been at any time worfhipped, are not neceffarily to be taken out of the world, neverthelefs for remedy and prevention of fo great offences, wifdom fhould judge it the fafeft courfe, to remove altogether from the eyes of men that which may put them in mind of evil. Some kinds of evil no doubt there are, very quick in working on thofe affections that moft eafily take fire, which evils fhould in that refpect, no oftner than need requireth, be brought in prefence of weak minds. But neither is the crofs any fuch evil, nor yet the brazen ferpent it felf fo ftrongly poifoned, that our eyes, ears and thoughts, ought to fhun them both for fear of fome deadly harm to enfue the only reprefentation thereof, by gefture, fhape, found, or fuch like fignificant means. And for mine own part, I moft affuredly perfuade my felf, that had *Ezechias* (till the days of whofe moft virtuous reign they ceafed not continually to burn incenfe to the brazen ferpent) had he found the ferpent, though fometime adored, yet at that time recovered from the evil of fo grofs abufe, and reduced to the fame that was before in the time of *David*, at which time they efteemed it only as a memorial, fign or monument of God's miraculous goodnefs towards them, even as we in no other fort efteem the ceremony of the crofs; the due confideration of an ufe fo harmlefs, common to both, might no lefs have wrought their equal prefervation, than different occafions have procured notwithftanding the one's extinguifhment, the other's lawful continuance. In all perfuafions, which ground themfelves upon example, we are not fo much to refpect what is done, as the caufes and fecret inducements leading thereunto. The queftion being therefore, whether the ceremony fuppofed to have

been

[a] *Jofeph. Antiq. lib.* 17. *cap.* 8. & *lib.* 18. *cap.* 3. & *de Bell. lib.* 2. *cap.* 8.

[b] Their eagles their enfigns, and the images of their princes, they carried with them in all their armies, and had always a kind of chapel wherein they placed and adored them as their gods. *Dio. lib.* 40. *Herodian. lib.* 4.

' *Matth.* 22. 20.

2 Chron. 4. 3.
Exod. 32. 4.
2 Chron. 34. 7.
Jofh. 22. 10.

1 Kings 11. 7.
2 Kings 23. 13.
2 Kings 18. 3. 6. & 22. 2.

been fometimes fcandalous and offenfive, ought for that caufe to be now removed, there is no reafon we fhould forthwith yield our felves to be carried away with example, no not of them whofe acts the higheft judgment approveth for having reformed in that manner any publick evil ; but before we either attempt any thing or refolve, the ftate and condition as well of our own affairs, as theirs whofe example preffeth us, is advifedly to be examined ; becaufe fome things are of their own nature fcandalous, and cannot chufe but breed offence, as thofe finks of execrable filth which *Jofias* did overwhelm ; fome things, albeit not by nature, and of themfelves, are not-   2 Kings 23. withftanding fo generally turned to evil, by reafon of an evil corrupt habit grown,   7. and through long continuance, incurably fettled in the minds of the greateft part, that no redrefs can be well hoped for, without removal of that wherein they have ruined themfelves ; which plainly was the ftate of the *Jewifh* people, and the caufe why *Ezechias* did with fuch fudden indignation deftroy what he faw worfhipped ; finally, fome things are, as the fign of the crofs, though fubject either almoft or altogether to as great abufe, yet curable with more facility and eafe. And to fpeak as the truth is, our very nature doth hardly yield to deftroy that which may be fruitfully kept, and without any great difficulty clean fcoured from the ruft of evil, which by fome accident hath grown into it. Wherefore to that which they build in this queftion upon the example of *Ezechias,* let this fuffice. When heathens defpifed chriftian religion, becaufe of the fufferings of Jefus Chrift, the fathers, to teftify how little fuch contumelies and contempts prevailed with them, chofe rather the fign of the crofs, than any other outward mark, whereby the world might moft eafily difcern always what they were. On the contrary fide now, whereas they which do all profefs the chriftian religion, are divided amongft themfelves ; and the fault of the one part is, that in zeal to the fufferings of Chrift they admire too much, and over-fuperftitiously adore the vifible fign of his crofs ; if you afk what we that miflike them fhould do, we are here advifed to cure one contrary by another. Which art or method is not yet fo current as they imagine. For if, as their practice for the moft part fheweth, it be their meaning that the fcope and drift of reformation, when things are faulty, fhould be to fettle the church in the contrary ; it ftandeth them upon to beware of this rule, becaufe feeing vices have not only virtues, but other vices alfo in nature oppofite unto them, it may be dangerous in thefe cafes to feek but that which we find contrary to prefent evils. For in fores and ficknefles of the mind, we are not fimply to meafure good by diftance from evil, becaufe one vice may in fome refpect be more oppofite to another, than either of them to that virtue which holdeth the mean between them both. Liberality and covetoufnefs, the one a virtue and the other a vice, are not fo contrary as the vices of covetoufnefs and prodigality. Religion and fuperftition have more affiance, though the one be light, and the other darknefs, than fuperftition and prophanenefs, which both are vicious extremities. By means whereof it cometh alfo to pafs, that the mean, which is virtue, feemeth in the eyes of each extream an extremity ; the liberal hearted man is by the opinion of the prodigal miferable, and by the judgment of the miferable lavifh : Impiety for the moft part upbraideth religion as fuperftitious, which fuperftition often accufeth as impious ; both fo conceiving thereof, becaufe it doth feem more to participate each extream, than one extream doth another, and is by confequent lefs contrary to either of them, than they mutually between themfelves. Now, if he that feeketh to reform covetoufnefs or fuperftition, fhould but labour to induce the contrary, it were but to draw men out of lime into cole-duft : So that their courfe, which will remedy the fuperftitious abufe of things profitable in the church, is not ftill to abolifh utterly the ufe thereof, becaufe not ufing at all is moft oppofite to ill ufing ; but rather, if it may be, to bring them back to a right perfect and religious ufage, which albeit quite contrary to the prefent fore, is notwithftanding the better, and by many degrees the founder way of recovery : And unto this effect, that very precedent it felf which they propofe, may be beft followed. For as the fathers, when the crofs of Chrift was in utter contempt, did not fuperftitioufly adore the fame, but rather declare that they fo efteemed it as was meet ; in like manner where we find the crofs to have that honour which is due to Chrift, is it not as lawful for us to retain it in that eftimation which it ought to have, and in that ufe which it had of old without offence, as by taking it clean away, to feem followers of their example, which cure wilfully by abfcifion that which they might both preferve and heal ? Touching therefore the fign and ceremony of the crofs, we no way find our felves bound to relinquifh it ; neither becaufe the firft inventors thereof were but mortal men ; nor left the fenfe and fignification we give unto it fhould burden us as authors of a new gofpel in the houfe of God ; nor in refpect of fome caufe which the fathers had more than we have to ufe the fame; nor finally, for any fuch offence or fcandal as heretofore it hath been fubject unto by error, now reformed in the minds of men.

Of confirma-
tion after
baptifm.
ᵃ Cara manus
impofitione
adumbratur,ut
& anima fpi-
ritu illumine-
tur. Tertul.
de refur. Car.

66. The ancient cuftom of the church was, after they had baptized, to add there-unto impofition of hands with effectual prayer for the ᵃ illumination of God's moft holy Spirit, to confirm and perfect that which the grace of the fame Spirit had already begun in baptifm. For our means to obtain the graces which God doth beftow, are our prayers. Our prayers to that intent are available, as well for others as for our felves. To pray for others, is to blefs them for whom we pray ; becaufe prayer pro-cureth the blefsing of God upon them, efpecially the prayer of fuch as God either moft refpecteth for their piety and zeal that way, or elfe regardeth for that their place and calling bindeth them above others unto this duty, as it doth both natural and fpiritual fathers. With prayers of fpiritual and perfonal benediction the manner hath been in all ages to ufe *impofition of hands*, as a ceremony betokening our re-ftrained defires to the party whom we prefent unto God by prayer. Thus when

Gen. 48. 14.

Ifrael blefsed *Ephraim* and *Manaffes*, *Jofeph's* Sons, he impofed upon them his hands and prayed ; *God, in whofe fight my fathers, Abraham and Ifaac, did walk ; God which hath fed me all my life long unto this day, and the angel which hath delivered me from all evil, blefs thefe children.* The prophets which healed difeafes by prayer,

2 Kings 5. 11.

ufed therein the felf-fame ceremony. And therefore when *Elizæus* willed *Naaman* to wafh himfelf feven times in *Jordan* for cure of his foul difeafe, it much offended him ; *I thought* (faith he) *with my felf, furely the man will come forth, and ftand, and call upon the name of the Lord his God, and put his hand on the place, to the*

Num. 27. 18.

end he may fo heal the leprofy. In confecrations and ordinations of men unto rooms of divine calling, the like was ufually done from the time of *Mofes* to Chrift. Their

Matth. 9. 18.
Mark 5. 23.
8. 22.

fuits that came unto Chrift for help were alfo tendred oftentimes, and are expreffed in fuch forms or phrafes of fpeech, as fhew that he was himfelf an obferver of the fame cuftom. He which with impofition of hands and prayer did fo great works of mercy for reftoration of bodily health, was worthily judged as able to effect the in-fufion of heavenly grace into them, whofe age was not yet depraved with that ma-

Matth. 19. 13.
Mark 10. 13.
Luke 18. 15.

lice which might be fuppofed a bar to the goodnefs of God towards them. *They brought him* therefore *young children to put his hands upon them and pray.* After the afcenfion of our Lord and Saviour Jefus Chrift, that which he had begun conti-nued in the daily practice of his apoftles, whofe prayer and impofition of hands were a mean whereby thoufands became partakers of the wonderful gifts of God. The church had received from Chrift a promife, that fuch as believed in him thefe figns

Mark 16. 17.

and tokens fhould follow them, *To caft out devils, to fpeak with tongues, to drive away ferpents, to be free from the harm which any deadly poifon could work, and to cure difeafes by impofition of hands.* Which power, common at the firft in a man-ner unto all believers, all believers had not power to derive or communicate unto all other men; but whofoever was the inftrument of God to inftruct, convert, and

Acts 19. 6.
Acts 8. 17,
18.

baptize them, the gift of miraculous operations by the power of the Holy Ghoft they had not, but only at the apoftles own hands. For which caufe *Simon Magus* per-ceiving that power to be in none but them, and prefuming that they which had it might fell it, fought to purchafe it of them with money. And, as miraculous gra-

Iren. lib. 2.
cap. 57.

ces of the fpirit continued after the apoftles times, For (faith *Irenæus*) *they which are truly his difciples do in his name, and through grace received from him, fuch works for the benefit of other men, as every of them is by him enabled to work: Some caft out devils, in fo much as they which are delivered from wicked fpirits have been thereby won unto Chrift, and do conftantly perfevere in the church and fociety of faithful men: Some excel in the knowledge of things to come, in the grace of vifion from God, and the gift of prophetical prediction: Some by laying on their hands reftore them to health, which are grievoufly afflicted with ficknefs ; yea, there are that of dead have been made alive, and have afterwards many years converfed with us. What fhould I fay? The gifts are innumerable wherewith God hath inriched his church throughout the world, and by virtue whereof, in the name of Chrift crucified under* Pontius Pilate, *the church every day doth many wonders for the good of nations, neither fraudulently, ᶜnor in any refpect of lucre and gain to her felf, but as freely beftowing*, as God *on her hath beftowed his divine graces* : So it no where appeareth, that ever any did by prayer and impofition of hands, fithence the apoftles times, make others partakers of the like miraculous gifts and graces, as long as it pleafed

God

o

God to continue the same in his church, but only bishops, the apostles successors for a time, even in that power. St. *Augustin* acknowledgeth, that such gifts were not permitted to last always, left men should wax cold with the commonness of that, the strangeness whereof at the first inflamed them. Which words of St. *Augustin*, de- ‹Augustin. de Vera Relig. cap. 25.› claring how the vulgar use of these miracles was then expired, are no prejudice to the like extraordinary graces, more rarely observed in some, either then or of latter days. Now whereas the successors of the apostles had but only for a time such power, as by prayer and imposition of hands to bestow the Holy Ghost; the reason wherefore confirmation, nevertheless, by prayer and laying on of hands hath hitherto always continued, is for other very special benefits which the church thereby enjoyeth. The fathers every where impute unto it that gift or grace of the Holy Ghost, not which maketh us first christian men, but when we are made such, assisteth us in all virtue, armeth us against temptation and sin. For, after baptism administred, ‹Tertul. de Baptis.› *there followeth* (saith *Tertullian*) *imposition of hands, with invocation and invitation of the Holy Ghost, which willingly cometh down from the Father, to rest upon the purified and blessed bodies, as it were acknowledging the waters of baptism a fit seat.* St. *Cyprian* in more particular manner alluding to that effect of the spirit, which ‹Cypr. Epist 1. ad Donat. c. 2.› here especially was respected, *How great* (saith he) *is that power and force wherewith the mind is here* (he meaneth in baptism) *enabled, being not only withdrawn from that pernicious hold which the world before had of it, nor only so purified and made clean, that no stain or blemish of the enemies invasion doth remain ; but over and besides* (namely, through prayer and imposition of hands) *becometh yet greater, yet mightier in strength, so far as to reign with a kind of imperial dominion over the whole band of that roaming and spoiling adversary.* As much is signified by *Eusebius Emissenus*, saying, *The Holy Ghost which descendeth with saving influence* ‹Euseb. Emiss. Ser. de Pente.› *upon the waters of baptism, doth there give that fulness which sufficeth for innocency, and afterwards exhibiteth in confirmation an augmentation of further grace.* The fathers therefore being thus persuaded, held confirmation as an ordinance apostolick, ‹Aug. de Trin lib. 15. cap. 26. Heb. 6. 2.› always profitable in God's church, although not always accompanied with equal largeness of those external effects which gave it countenance at the first. The cause of severing confirmation from baptism (for most commonly they went together) was sometimes in the minister, which being of inferior degree, might baptize, but not confirm, as in their case it came to pass whom *Peter* and *John* did confirm, whereas ‹Acts 8. 12, 15. Hier. adversf. Lucif. cap. 4.› *Philip* had before baptized them ; and in theirs of whom St. *Jerome* hath said, *I deny not but the custom of the churches is, that the bishop should go abroad, and imposing his hands, pray for the gift of the Holy Ghost on them whom presbyters and deacons far off, in lesser cities, have already baptized.* Which ancient custom of the church St. *Cyprian* groundeth upon the example of *Peter* and *John*, in the eighth of the *Acts* before alledged. *The faithful in* Samaria (saith he) *had already* ‹Cypr. Epist. 73. ad Jubaianum.› *obtained baptism ; only that which was wanting,* Peter *and* John *supplied by prayer and imposition of hands, to the end the Holy Ghost might be poured upon them. Which also is done among st our selves, when they which be already baptized, are brought to the prelates of the church to obtain by our prayer and imposition of hands the Holy Ghost.* By this it appeareth, that when the ministers of baptism were persons of inferior degree, the bishops did after confirm whom such had before baptized. Sometimes they which by force of their ecclesiastical calling might do as well the one as the other, were notwithstanding men whom heresy had disjoin'd from the fellowship of true believers. Whereupon when any man by them baptized and confirmed, came afterwards to see and renounce their error, there grew in some churches very hot contention about the manner of admitting such into the bosom of the true church, as hath been declared already in the question of rebaptization. But the generally received custom was only to admit them with imposition of hands and prayer. Of which custom while some imagined the reason to be, for that hereticks might give remission of sins by baptism, but not the spirit by imposition of hands, because themselves had not God's spirit, and that therefore their baptism might stand, but confirmation must be given again : the imbecillity of this ground gave *Cyprian* occasion to oppose himself against the practice of the church herein, labouring many ways to prove, that hereticks could do neither ; and consequently that their baptism in all respects was as frustrate as their chrism ; for the manner of those times was in confirming to use anointing. On the other side, against *Luciferians*, which ratified only the baptism of hereticks, but disannulled their confirmations and consecrations, under pretence of the reason which hath been before specified, *Hereticks cannot give the Holy Ghost*, St. *Jerome* proveth at large, that if baptism by hereticks be granted

avail-

available to remiffion of fins, which no man receiveth without the fpirit, it muft needs follow, that the reafon taken from difability of beftowing the Holy Ghoft, was no reafon wherefore the church fhould admit converts with any new impofition of hands. Notwithftanding, becaufe it might be objected, that if the gift of the Holy Ghoft do always join it felf with true baptifm, the church which thinketh the bifhops confirmation after other mens baptifm needful for the obtaining of the Holy Ghoft, fhould hold an error ; St. *Jerome* hereunto maketh anfwer, that the caufe of this ob- fervation is not any abfolute impoffibility of receiving the Holy Ghoft by the facra- ment of baptifm, unlefs a bifhop add after it the impofition of hands, but rather a certain congruity and fitnefs to honour prelacy with fuch pre-eminences, becaufe the fafety of the church dependeth upon the dignity of her chief fuperiors, to whom if fome eminent offices of power above others fhould not be given, there would be in the church as many fchifms as priefts. By which anfwer it appeareth his opinion was, that the Holy Ghoft is received in baptifm ; that confirmation is only a facra- mental complement ; that the reafon why bifhops alone did ordinarily confirm, was not becaufe the benefit, grace and dignity thereof is greater than of baptifm ; but rather for that by the facrament of baptifm men being admitted into God's church, it was both reafonable and convenient, that if he baptize them not unto whom the chiefeft authority and charge of their fouls belongeth, yet for honour's fake, and in

Heb. 7. 7.   token of his fpiritual fuperiority over them, becaufe *to blefs* is an act of authority, the performance of this annexed ceremony fhould be fought for at his hands. Now what effect their impofition of hands hath, either after baptifm adminiftred by here- ticks, or otherwife, St. *Jerome* in that place hath made no mention, becaufe all men underftood that in converts it tendeth to the fruits of repentance, and craveth in be-

Pfal. 51. 10, half of the penitent fuch grace as *David* after his fall defired at the hands of God ;
11, 12.   in others, the fruit and benefit thereof is that which hath been before fhewed. Fi- nally, Sometime the caufe of fevering confirmation from baptifm, was in the parties that received baptifm being infants, at which age they might be very well admitted to live in the family ; but becaufe to fight in the army of God, to difcharge the du- ties of a chriftian man, to bring forth the fruits, and to do the works of the Holy Ghoft, their time of ability was not yet come, (fo that baptifm were not deferred y there could, by ftay of their confirmation, no harm enfue, but rather good. For by this means it came to pafs, that children in expectation thereof were feafoned with the principles of true religion, before malice and corrupt examples depraved their minds, a good foundation was laid betimes for direction of the courfe of their whole lives, the feed of the church of God was preferved fincere and found, the prelates and fathers of God's family, to whom the cure of their fouls belongeth, faw by tryal and examination of them, a part of their own heavy burden difcharged, reaped comfort by beholding the firft beginnings of true godlinefs in tender years, glorified him whofe praife they found in the mouths of infants, and neglected not fo fit op- portunity of giving every one fatherly encouragement and exhortation. Whereunto impofition of hands and prayer being added, our warrant for the good effect thereof is the fame which patriarchs, prophets, priefts, apoftles, fathers and men of God have had for fuch their particular invocations and benedictions, as no man, I fuppofe, pro- feffing truth of religion, will eafily think to have been without fruit. No, there is no caufe we fhould doubt of the benefit, but furely great caufe to make complaint of the deep neglect of this chriftian duty almoft with all them, to whom by right of their place and calling the fame belongeth. Let them not take it in evil part, the thing

a *T. C.* lib. is true, their fmall regard hereunto hath done harm in the church of God. That
1. pag. 199.   which a error rafhly uttereth in difgrace of good things, may peradventure be fpunged
'Tell me why
there fhould

be any fuch confirmation in the church, being brought in by the feigned decretal epiftles of the popes (this is retracted by the fame *T. C.* lib. 3. pag. 232. That it is ancienter than the feigned decretal Epiftles, I yield unto) and no one tittle thereof be- ing once found in the fcripture, and feeing that it hath been fo horribly abufed, and not neceffary ; why ought it not to be utterly abolifhed ? And thirdly, this confirmation hath many dangerous points in it. The firft ftep of popery in this confirmati- on, is the laying on of hands upon the head of the child, whereby the opinion that it is a facrament, is confirmed ; efpecially when as the prayer doth fay, that it is done according to the example of the apoftles, which is a manifeft untruth, and taken indeed from the popifh confirmation. The fecond is, for that the bifhop, as he is called, muft be the only minifter of it ; whereby the popifh opinion, which efteemeth it above baptifm, is confirmed. For whilft baptifm may be miniftred of the minifter, and not confirmation, but only of the bifhop ; there is a great caufe of fufpicion given to think, that bap- tifm is not fo precious a thing as confirmation, feeing this was one of the principal reafons whereby that wicked opinion was eftablifhed in popery. I do not here fpeak of the inconvenience that men are conftrained with charges to bring their children oftentimes half a fcore miles for that, which if it were needful might be as well done at home in their own pa- rifhe's. The third is, for that the book faith, a caufe of ufing confirmation is, that by impofition of hands and prayer, the children may receive ftrength and defence againft all temptations, whereas there is no promife, that by the laying on of hands upon children, any fuch gift fhall be given ; and it maintaineth the popifh diftinction, that the fpirit of God is given at baptifm unto remiffion of Sins ; and in confirmation, unto ftrength.

out,

ons, when the print of those evils which are grown through neglect will remain behind. Thus much therefore generally spoken, may serve for answer unto their demands that require us to tell them *Why there should be any such confirmation in the church,* seeing we are not ignorant how earnestly they have protested against it ; and how directly (although untruly, for so they are content to acknowledge) it hath by some of them been said, *to be first brought in by the feigned decretal epistles of the popes* ; or, why it should not be *utterly abolished, seeing that no one tittle thereof can be once found in the whole scripture,* except the Epistle to the *Hebrews* be scripture.   And again, Heb. 6. 3. seeing that how free soever it be now from abuse, if we look back to the times past, which wise men do always more respect than the present, it hath been abused, and is found at the length no such profitable ceremony, as the whole filly church of Christ for the space of these sixteen hundred years hath through want of experience imagined. Last of all, seeing also besides the cruelty which is shewed towards poor country people, who are fain sometimes to let their ploughs stand still, and with incredible wearisom toil of their feeble bodies to wander over mountains and through woods, it may be, now and then little less than a whole half score of miles for a bishop's blessing, *which if it were needful, might as well be done at home in their own parishes, rather* than they to purchase it with so great loss and so intolerable pain ; there are, they say, in confirmation, besides this, three terrible points.   The first is, *laying on of hands, with pretence that the same is done to the example of the apostles,* which is not only, as they suppose, *a manifest untruth* ; (for all the world doth know that the apostles did never after Baptism lay hands on any, and therefore St. *Luke* which saith they did was much deceived:) but farther also, we thereby teach men to think *impo- Act. 8. 15, 17. sition of hands a sacrament,* belike because it is a principle engrafted by common light of nature in the minds of men, that all things done by apostolick example must needs be sacraments.   The second high point of danger is, *that by tying confirmation to the bishop alone, there is great cause of suspicion given to think that baptism is not so precious a thing as confirmation :* For will any man think that a velvet coat is of more price than a linnen coif, knowing the one to be an ordinary garment, the other an ornament which only serjeants at law do wear ?   Finally, to draw to an end of perils, the last and the weightiest hazard is, where the book it self doth say, that children by imposition of hands and prayer may receive strength against all temptation :   Which speech, as a two-edged sword, doth both ways dangerously wound ; partly because it ascribeth grace to imposition of hands, whereby we are able no more to assure our selves in the warrant of any promise from God, that his heavenly grace shall be given, than the apostle was that himself should obtain grace by the bowing of his knees to God ; and partly because by using the very word *strength* in this matter, a word so Ephes. 3. 14. apt to spread infection, we maintain with popish evangelists an old forlorn *distinction* John 10. 22. of the Holy Ghost bestowed upon Christ's apostles before his ascension into heaven, and Act 1. 8. augmented upon them afterwards ; a distinction of grace infused into christian men by degrees ; planted in them at the first by baptism, after cherished, watered, and (be it spoken without offence) strengthened as by other virtuous offices which piety and true religion teacheth, even so by this very special benediction whereof we speak, the rite or ceremony of confirmation.

67. The grace which we have by the holy eucharist, doth not begin but continue *Of the sacra-* life. No man therefore receiveth this sacrament before baptism, because no dead *ment of the* thing is capable of nourishment. That which groweth must of necessity first live. If *body and* our bodies did not daily waste, food to restore them were a thing superfluous. And *Christ.* it may be that the grace of baptism would serve to eternal life, were it not that the state of our spiritual being is daily so much hindred and impaired after baptism. In that life therefore, where neither body nor soul can decay, our souls shall as little require this sacrament, as our bodies corporal nourishment. But as long as the days of our warfare last, during the time that we are both subject to diminution and capable of augmentation in grace, the words of our Lord and Saviour Christ will remain forcible, *except ye eat the flesh of the son of man, and drink his blood, ye have no life in* John 6. 53. *you.* Life being therefore proposed unto all men as their end, they which by baptism have laid the foundation, and attained the first beginning of a new life, have here their nourishment and food prescribed for continuance of life in them. Such as will live the life of God, must eat the flesh and drink the blood of the son of man ; because this is a part of that diet, which if we want we cannot live. Whereas therefore in our infancy we are incorporated into Christ, and by baptism receive the grace of his spirit without any sense or feeling of the gift which God bestoweth ; in the eucharist we so receive the gift of God, that we know by grace what the grace is which God

giveth us; the degrees of our own increase in holiness and virtue we see, and can judge of them; we understand that the strength of our life begun in Christ, is Christ; that his flesh is meat, and his blood drink, not by surmised imagination, but truly, even so truly, that through faith we perceive in the body and blood sacramentally presented the very taste of eternal life; the grace of the sacrament is here as the food which we eat and drink. This was it that some did exceedingly fear lest *Zwinglius* and *Oecolampadius* would bring to pass, that men should account of this sacrament but only as of a shadow, destitute, empty and void of Christ. But seeing that by opening the several opinions which have been held, they are grown, for ought I can see, on all sides at the length to a general agreement concerning that which alone is material, namely, the real participation of Christ, and of life in his body and blood by means of this sacrament; wherefore should the world continue still distracted, and rent with so manifold contentions, when there remaineth now no controversy, saving only about the subject where Christ is? Yea, even in this point no side denieth, but that the soul of man is the receptacle of Christ's presence. Whereby the question is yet driven to a narrow issue, nor doth any thing rest doubtful but this, whether when the sacrament is administred, Christ be whole within man only, or else his body and blood be also externally seated in the very consecrated elements themselves. Which opinion they that defend, are driven either to consubstantiate and incorporate Christ with elements sacramental, or to transubstantiate and change their substance into his; and so the one to hold him really, but invisibly, moulded up with the substance of those elements; the other to hide him under the only visible shew of bread and wine, the substance whereof, as they imagine, is abolished, and his succeeded in the same room. All things considered, and compared with that success which truth hath hitherto had by so bitter conflicts with errors in this point, shall I wish that men would more give themselves to meditate with silence what we have by the sacrament, and less to dispute of the manner how? If any man suppose that this were too great stupidity and dulness, let us see whether the apostles of our Lord themselves have not done the like. It appeareth by many examples, that they of their own disposition were very scrupulous and inquisitive, yea in other cases of less importance, and less difficulty, always apt to move questions. How cometh it to pass, that so few words of so high a mystery being uttered, they receive with gladness the gift of Christ, and make no shew of doubt or scruple? The reason hereof is not dark to them which have any thing at all observed how the powers of the mind are wont to stir, when that which we infinitely long for presenteth it self above and besides expectation. Curious and intricate speculations do hinder, they abate, they quench such inflamed motions of delight and joy as divine graces use to raise, when extraordinarily they are present. The mind therefore feeling present joy, is always marvellous unwilling to admit any other cogitation, and in that case casteth off those disputes whereunto the intellectual part at other times easily draweth. A manifest effect whereof may be noted, if we compare with our Lord's disciples in the twentieth of *John*, the people that are said in the sixth of *John* to have gone after him to *Capernaum*. These leaving him on the one side of the sea of *Tiberias*, and finding him again as soon as themselves by ship were arrived on the contrary side, whither they knew that by ship he came not, and by land the journey was longer than according to the time he could have to travel, as they wondered, so they

John 6. 26. asked also, *Rabbi, when camest thou hither?* The disciples, when Christ appeared to them in far more strange and miraculous manner, moved no question, but rejoiced greatly in what they saw. For why? The one sort beheld only that in Christ which they knew was more than natural, but yet their affection was not rapt therewith through any great extraordinary gladness; the other, when they looked on Christ, were not ignorant that they saw the well-spring of their own everlasting felicity; the one, because they enjoyed not, disputed; the other disputed not, because they enjoyed. If then the presence of Christ with them did so much move, judge what their thoughts and affections were at the time of this new presentation of Christ, not before their eyes but within their souls. They had learned before, that his flesh and blood are the true cause of eternal life; that this they are not by the bare force of their own substance, but through the dignity and worth of his Person, which offered them up by way of sacrifice for the life of the whole world, and doth make them still effectual thereunto: Finally, that to us they are life in particular, by being particularly received. Thus much they knew, although as yet they understood not perfectly to what effect or issue the same would come, till at the length being assembled for no other cause which they could imagine, but to have eaten the passover only that

4

Moses

Moses appointed, when they saw their Lord and Master, with hands and eyes lifted up to heaven, first bless and consecrate, for the endless good of all generations till the world's end, the chosen elements of bread and wine; which elements, made for ever the instruments of life by virtue of his divine benediction, they being the first that were commanded to receive from him, the first which were warranted by his promise, that not only unto them at the present time, but to whomsoever they and their successors after them did duly administer the same, those mysteries should serve as conducts of life, and conveyances of his body and blood unto them; was it possible they should hear that voice, *Take, eat, this is my body; drink ye all of this, this is my blood?* Possible, that doing what was required, and believing what was promised, the same should have present effect in them, and not fill them with a kind of fearful admiration at the heaven which they saw in themselves? They had at that time a sea of comfort and joy to wade in, and we by that which they did are taught that this heavenly food is given for the satisfying of our empty souls, and not for the exercising of our curious and subtil wits. If we doubt what those admirable words may import, let him be our teacher for the meaning of Christ, to whom Christ was himself a school-master; let our Lord's apostle be his interpreter, content we our selves with his explication; my body, *the communion of my body*: My blood, *the communion of my blood.* Is there any thing more expedite, clear and easy, than that as Christ is termed our life, because through him we obtain life; so the parts of this sacrament are his body and blood, for that they are so to us; who receiving them, receive that by them which they are termed? The bread and cup are his body and blood, because they are causes instrumental upon the receipt whereof the participation of his body and blood ensueth. For that which produceth any certain effect, is not vainly nor improperly said to be that very effect whereunto it tendeth. Every cause is in the effect which groweth from it. Our souls and bodies quickned to eternal life are effects; the cause whereof is the person of Christ: his body and blood are the true well-spring out of which this life floweth. So that his body and blood are in that very subject whereunto they minister life: Not only by effect or operation, even as the influence of the heavens is in plants, beasts, men, and in every thing which they quicken; but also by a far more divine and mystical kind of union, which maketh us one with him, even as He and the Father are one. The real presence of Christ's most blessed body and blood is not therefore to be sought for in the sacrament, but in the worthy receiver of the sacrament. And with this the very order of our Saviour's words agreeth, first, *take and eat*; then, *this is my body which was broken for you:* First, *drink ye all of this*; then followeth, *this is my blood of the new testament, which is shed for many for the remission of Sins.* I see not which way it should be gathered by the words of Christ when and where the bread is his body, or the cup his blood; but only in the very heart and soul of him which receiveth them. As for the sacraments, they really exhibit, but for ought we can gather out of that which is written of them, they are not really, nor do really contain in themselves that grace which with them, or by them, it pleaseth God to bestow. If on all sides it be confess'd, that the grace of baptism is poured into the soul of man; that by water we receive it, although it be neither seated in the water, nor the water changed into it; what should induce men to think, that the grace of the eucharist must needs be in the eucharist before it can be in us that receive it? The fruit of the eucharist is the participation of the body and blood of Christ. There is no sentence of holy scripture which saith, that we cannot by this sacrament be made partakers of his body and blood, except they be first contained in the sacrament, or the sacrament converted into them. *This is my body,* and, *this is my blood,* being words of promise, sith we all agree, that by the sacrament Christ doth really and truly in us perform his promise, why do we vainly trouble our selves with so fierce contentions, whether by consubstantiation, or else by transubstantiation the sacrament it self be first possessed with Christ, or no? A thing which no way can either further or hinder us, howsoever it stand, because our participation of Christ in this sacrament dependeth on the co-operation of his omnipotent power which maketh it his body and blood to us; whether with change or without alteration of the element, such as they imagine, we need not greatly to care or enquire. Take therefore that wherein all agree, and then consider by it self what cause why the rest in question should not rather be left as superfluous than urged as necessary. It is on all sides plainly confess'd, first, that this sacrament is a true and a real participation of Christ, who thereby imparteth himself, even his whole en-

I   tire

Mark 14. 22.

tire perſon, *as a myſtical head*, unto every ſoul that receiveth him, and that every ſuch receiver doth thereby incorporate or unite himſelf unto Chriſt *as a myſtical member* of him, yea of them alſo whom he acknowledgeth to be his own.   Secondly, that to whom *the perſon of Chriſt* is thus communicated, to them he giveth by the ſame ſacrament his Holy Spirit to ſanctify them, as it ſanctifieth him which is their head.   Thirdly, that what *merit, force, or virtue ſoever there is in his ſacred body and blood*, we freely, fully and wholly have it by this ſacrament.   Fourthly, that *the effect thereof in us, is a real tranſmutation of our ſouls and bodies* from ſin to righteouſneſs, from death and corruption to immortality and life.   Fifthly, that becauſe the ſacrament being of it ſelf but a corruptible and earthly creature, muſt needs be thought an unlikely inſtrument to work ſo admirable effects in man, we are therefore to reſt out ſelves altogether upon *the ſtrength of his glorious power*, who is able and will bring to paſs, that the bread and cup which he giveth us ſhall be truly the thing he promiſeth.   It ſeemeth therefore much amiſs, that againſt them whom they term ſacramentaries ſo many invective diſcourſes are made, all running upon two points, that the euchariſt is not a bare ſign or figure only, and that the efficacy of his body and blood is not all we receive in this ſacrament.   For no man, having read their books and writings which are thus traduced, can be ignorant that both theſe aſſertions they plainly confeſs to be moſt true.   They do not ſo interpret the words of Chriſt, as if the name of his body did import but the figure of his body; and to be, were only to ſignify his blood.   They grant that theſe holy myſteries received in due manner, do inſtrumentally both make us partakers of the grace of that body and blood which were given for the life of the world, and beſides alſo impart unto us, even in true and real, though myſtical manner, the very perſon of our Lord himſelf, whole, perfect and entire, as hath been ſhewed.   Now whereas all three opinions do thus far accord in one, that ſtrong conceit which two of the three have embraced, as touching a literal, corporal and oral manducation of the very ſubſtance of his fleſh and blood, is ſurely an opinion no where delivered in holy ſcripture, whereby they ſhould think themſelves bound to believe it; and (to ſpeak with the ſofteſt terms we can uſe) greatly prejudiced in that when ſome others did ſo conceive of eating his fleſh, our Saviour to abate that error in them, gave them directly to underſtand how his fleſh ſo eaten could profit them nothing, becauſe the words which he ſpake were ſpirit; that is to ſay, they had a reference to a myſtical participation; which myſtical participation giveth life.   Wherein there is ſmall appearance of likelihood, that his meaning would be only to make them *Marcionites* by inverſion, and to teach them, that as *Marcion* did think Chriſt ſeemed to be man but was not; ſo they contrariwiſe ſhould believe that Chriſt in truth would ſo give them as they thought his fleſh to eat; but yet, left the horror thereof ſhould offend them, he would not ſeem to do that he did.   When they which have this opinion of Chriſt in that bleſſed ſacrament, go about to explain themſelves, and to open after what manner things are brought to paſs, the one ſort lay the union of Chriſt's Deity with his Manhood, as their firſt foundation and ground: From thence they infer a power which the body of Chriſt hath, thereby to preſent it ſelf in all places; out of which ubiquity of his body they gather the preſence thereof with that ſanctified bread and wine of our Lord's Table: The conjunction of his body and blood with thoſe elements, they uſe as an argument to ſhew how the bread may as well in that reſpect be termed his body, becauſe his body is therewith joined, as the Son of God may be named man, by reaſon that God and man in the perſon of Chriſt are united.   To this they add, how the words of Chriſt commanding us to eat, muſt needs import, that as he hath coupled the ſubſtance of his fleſh and the ſubſtance of bread together, ſo we together ſhould receive both: Which labyrinth, as the other ſort doth juſtly ſhun, ſo the way which they take to the ſame inn, is ſomewhat more ſhort, but no whit more certain.   For through God's omnipotent power they imagine that tranſubſtantiation followeth upon the words of conſecration; and upon tranſubſtantiation the participation of Chriſt's both body and blood, in the only ſhape of ſacramental elements.   So that they all three do plead God's omnipotency: Sacramentaries, to that alteration which the reſt confeſs he accompliſheth; the patrons of tranſubſtantiation, over and beſides that, to the change of one ſubſtance into another; the followers of conſubſtantiation, to the kneading of both ſubſtances, as it were, into one lump.   Touching the ſentence of antiquity in this cauſe; firſt, for as much as they knew that the force of this ſacrament doth neceſſarily preſuppoſe the verity of Chriſt's both body and blood, they uſed oftentimes the ſame as an argument to prove, that Chriſt has as truly the

ſub-

2

substance of man as of God, because here we receive Christ, and those graces which flow from him, in that he is man. So that if he have no such being, neither can the sacrament have any such meaning as we all confess it hath. Thus [a] *Tertullian*, thus [b] *Irenæus*, thus [c] *Theodoret* disputeth. Again, as evident it is how they teach that Christ is personally there present, yea present both a part of Christ be corporally absent from thence, that [d] Christ assisting this heavenly banquet with his personal and true presence, [e] doth by his own divine power add to the natural substance thereof supernatural efficacy, which [f] addition to the nature of those consecrated elements changeth them, and maketh them that unto us which otherwise they could not be, that to us they are thereby made such instruments, [g] as mystically yet truly, invisibly yet really work our communion or fellowship with the person of Jesus Christ, as well in that he is Man as God, our participation also in the fruit, grace and efficacy of his body and blood; whereupon there ensueth a kind of transubstantiation in us, a true [h] change, both of soul and body, an alteration from death to life. In a word, it appeareth not, that of all the ancient fathers of the church any one did ever conceive or imagine other than only a mystical participation of Christ's both body and blood in the sacrament; neither are their speeches concerning the change of the elements themselves into the body and blood of Christ such, that a man can thereby in conscience assure himself it was their meaning to persuade the world either of a corporal consubstantiation of Christ with those sanctified and blessed elements before we receive them; or of the like transubstantiation of them into the body and blood of Christ. Which both to our mystical communion with Christ are so unnecessary, that the fathers, who plainly hold but this mystical communion, cannot easily be thought to have meant any other change of sacramental elements, than that which the same spiritual communion did require them to hold. These things considered, how should that mind which, loving truth and seeking comfort out of holy mysteries, hath not perhaps the leisure, perhaps not the wit nor capacity to tread out so endless Mazes as the intricate disputes of this cause have led men into, how should a virtuously disposed mind better resolve with it self than thus? *Variety of judgments and opinions argueth obscurity in those things whereabout they differ. But that which all parts receive for truth, that which every one having sifted, is by no one denied or doubted of, must needs be matter of infallible certainty. Whereas therefore there are but three expositions made of,* This is my body; *The first,* This is in it self before participation *really and truly the natural substance of my body, by reason of the coexistence which my omnipotent body hath with the sanctified element of bread, which is the* Lutherans *interpretation. The second,* This is in it self and before participation *the very true and natural substance of my body, by force of that deity, which with the words of consecration abolisheth the substance of bread, and substituteth in the place thereof my body, which is the popish construction. The last,* This hallowed food, through concurrence of divine pow-

I i

er,

[a] *Acceptum panem & distributum discipulis, Corpus suum illum fecit, Hoc est Corpus meum dicendo, id est figura corporis mei. Figura autem non fuisset, nisi veritatis esset Corpus, cum vacua res quod est phantasma, Figuram capere non possit.* Tertul. contra Marc. lib. 4. cap. 40.

[b] *Secundum hæc* (that is to say, If it should be true which Hereticks have taught, denying that Christ took upon him the very nature of man) *nec Dominus sanguine suo redemit nos, neque Calix Eucharistiæ communicatio sanguinis ejus erit, nec panis quem frangimus communicatio corporis ejus est. Sanguis enim non est, nisi à venis & carnibus & à reliqua quæ est secundum hominem substantia.* Iren. lib. 5. cap. 1.

[c] *Ἐν τοίνυν τῷ ὄντι σώματι & αἵματι ἐπὶ τὰ δἰ α μυστήρια, σῶμα ἄρα ἐστὶ & τὸ τοῦ Δεσπότου τὸ σῶμα, ἐκ οἷς Δεσπότ & εἶπεν μεταβληθὲν, ἀλλὰ Θείας ἀξίαν ἀπαλαῦον.* Theod. Dialog. Ἀσύγχυτ .

[d] *Sacramenta quidem, quantum in se est, sine propria virtute esse non possunt, nec ullo modo se absentat majestas mysteriis.* Cypr. de Cœn. cap. 7.

[e] *Sacramento visibili ineffabiliter divina se inde fundit essentia, ut esset Religioni circa sacramenta Devotio,* Idem cap. 6. *Invisibilis Sacerdos visibiles creaturas in substantiam corporis & sanguinis sui verbo suo secreta potestate convertit. In spiritualibus Sacramentis verbi præcipit virtus & servit effectus.* Euseb. Emissen. Hom. 5. de Pasch.

[f] *Τὰ σύμβολα τῷ Δεσποτικῷ σώματός τε & αἵματός ἄλλα μὲν εἰσὶ πρὸ & ἱερατικῆς ἐπικλήσεως, μετὰ δὲ τὴν ἐπίκλησιν μεταβάλλεται, & ἕτερα γίνεται. ἀλλ᾽ ἐκ ἐκείνως ἐξίσταται φύσεως. Μένει γὰρ ἐπὶ τῆς προτέρας οὐσίας & τῷ σχήματι & τῷ εἴδει, & ὁρατὰ ἐστι & ἁπτά, διὰ & νοεῖσθαι βούλεται, τοῦτ᾽ ἐστι ὅπερ & ἐγένετο, & πιστεύεται & προσκυνεῖται ὡς ἐκεῖνα οἷς & ἀπὸ μετάγοντι.* Theodor. Et quæ à Domino dictum est, hoc facite in meam commemorationem, Hæc est caro mea, & hic est sanguis meus, quotiescunque his verbis & hac fide actum est, panis iste supersubstantialis, & calix benedictione solenni sacratus, ad totius hominis vitam salutemque proficit. Cypr. de Cœn. cap. 3. *Immortalis alimonia datur, à communibus cibis differens, corporalis substantia retinens speciem, sed virtutis divina invisibili efficientia probans adesse præsentiam.* Ibid. cap. 2.

[g] *Sensibilibus Sacramentis inest vitæ æternæ effectus, & non tam corporali quam spirituali transitione Christo unimur. Ipse enim & panis & caro, & sanguis, idem cibus, & substantia & vita factus est Ecclesiæ suæ quam corpus suum appellat; dans ei participationem spiritus,* Ibid. cap. 5. *Nostra & ipsius conjunctio nec miscet personas, nec unit substantias, sed effectus conscias & confœderat voluntates.* Ibid. cap. 6. *Mansio nostra in ipso est manducatio, & potus quasi quædam incorporatio,* Ibid. cap. 9. *Ille est in Patre per Naturam divinitatis, nos in eo per corporalem ejus Nativitatem, ille rursus in nobis per Sacramentorum mysterium.* Hilar. de Trin. lib. 8.

[h] *Panis hic azymus cibus verus & sincerus per speciem & sacramentum nos tactu sanctificat, fide illuminat, veritate Christo conformat.* Cypr. de Cœn. cap. 6. *Non aliud agit participatio corporis & sanguinis Christi, quam ut in id quod sumimus transeamus, & in quo mortui & sepulti & corresuscitati sumus, ipsum per omnia & spiritu & carne gestemus,* Leo de Pasch. Serm. 14. *Quemadmodum qui est à terra panis percipiens Dei vocationem* (id est facta invocatione divini numinis) *jam non communis panis est, sed Eucharistia ex duabus rebus constans, terrena & cælesti; Sic & corpora nostra percipientia Eucharistiam, jam non sunt corruptibilia spem resurrectionis habentia,* Iren. lib. 4. cap. 34. *Quoniam salutaris caro verbo Dei quod naturaliter vita est conjuncta, vivifica effecta est; Quando eam comedimus, tunc vitam habemus in nobis, illi carni conjuncti, quæ vita effecta est.* Cyril. in Johan. lib. 4. cap. 14.

er, is in verity and truth, unto faithful receivers, instrumentally a cause of that my-stical participation, whereby as I make my self wholly theirs, so I give them in hand an actual possession of all such saving grace as my sacrificed body can yield, and as their souls do presently need. This is to them, and in them, my body. *Of these three rehearsed interpretations, the last hath in it nothing but what the rest do all approve and acknowledge to be most true ; nothing but that which the words of Christ are on all sides confess'd to inforce, nothing but that which the church of God hath always thought necessary ; nothing but that which alone is sufficient for every christian man to believe concerning the use and force of this sacrament : Finally, nothing but that wherewith the writings of all antiquity are consonant, and all christian confessions agreeable. And as truth, in what kind soever, is by no kind of truth gainsaid : So the mind which resteth it self on this, is never troubled with those perplexities which the other do find, by means of so great contradiction between their opinions, and true principles of reason grounded upon experience, nature and sense. Which albeit, with boysterous courage and breath, they seem oftentimes to blow away ; yet whoso observeth how again they labour and sweat by subtilty of wit to make some shew of agreement between their peculiar conceits and the general edicts of nature, must needs perceive they struggle with that which they cannot fully master. Besides, sith of that which is proper to themselves, their discourses are hungry and unpleasant, full of tedious and irksome labour, heartless, and hitherto without fruit ; on the other side, read we them or hear we others, be they of our own or of ancienter times, to what part soever they be thought to incline, touching that whereof there is controversy ; yet in this, where they all speak but one thing, their discourses are heavenly, their words sweet as the hony-comb, their tongues melodiously tuned instruments, their sentences meer consolation and joy : Are we not hereby almost even with voice from heaven admonished which we may safeliest cleave unto ? He which hath said of the one sacrament,* wash and be clean, *hath said concerning the other likewise,* eat and live. *If therefore without any such particular and solemn warrant as this is, that poor distressed woman coming unto Christ for health, could so constantly resolve her self,* may I but touch the skirt of his garment, I shall be whole, *what moveth us to argue of the manner how life should come by bread ? Our duty being here but to take what is offered, and most assuredly to rest persuaded of this, that can we but eat, we are safe. When I behold with mine eyes some small and scarce discernable grain or seed, whereof nature maketh a promise that a tree shall come ; and when afterwards of that tree any skilful artificer undertaketh to frame some exquisite and curious work, I look for the event, I move no question about performance either of the one, or of the other. Shall I simply credit nature in things natural ? Shall I in things artificial rely my self on art, never offering to make doubt ? And in that which is above both art and nature refuse to believe the author of both, except he acquaint me with his ways, and lay the secret of his skill before me ? Where God himself doth speak those things which, either for height and sublimity of the matter, or else for secrecy of performance, we are not able to reach unto, as we may be ignorant without danger, so it can be no disgrace to confess we are ignorant. Such as love piety will, as much as in them lieth, know all things that God commandeth, but especially the duties of service which they owe to God. As for his dark and hidden works, they prefer, as becometh them in such cases, simplicity of faith before that knowledge, which curiously sifting what it should adore, and disputing too boldly of that which the wit of man cannot search, chilleth for the most part all warmth of zeal, and bringeth soundness of belief many times into great hazard. Let it therefore be sufficient for me, presenting my self at the Lord's table, to know what there I receive from him ; without searching or enquiring of the manner how Christ performeth his promise : Let disputes and questions, enemies to piety, abatements of true devotion, and hitherto in this cause but over-patiently heard, let them take their rest : Let curious and sharp-witted men beat their heads about what questions themselves will ; the very letter of the word of Christ giveth plain security, that these mysteries do, as nails, fasten us to his very cross, that by them we draw out, as touching efficacy, force and virtue, even the blood of his goared side: In the wounds of our redeemer we there dip our tongues, we are died red both within and without ; our hunger is satisfied, and our thirst for ever quenched ; they are things wonderful which he feeleth, great which he seeth, and unheard of which he uttereth, whose soul is possess'd of this paschal lamb, and made joyful in the strength of this new wine : This bread hath in it more than the substance which our eyes behold, this cup hallowed with solemn benediction availeth to the endless life and welfare both of soul and body ; in that it serveth as well for a medicine to heal our infirmities and purge our sins, as for a sacrifice of*

2   thanks-

thanksgiving: with touching it sanctifieth, it enlightneth with belief, it truly conformeth us unto the image of Jesus Christ. What these elements are in themselves, it skilleth not; it is enough, that to me which take them they are the body and blood of Christ; his promise in witness hereof sufficeth; his word he knoweth which way to accomplish; why should any cogitation possess the mind of a faithful communicant but this? O my God, thou art true; O my soul, thou art happy! Thus therefore we see, that howsoever men's opinions do otherwise vary; nevertheless touching baptism and the supper of our Lord, we may with one consent of the whole christian world conclude they are necessary, the one to initiate or begin, the other to consummate or make perfect our life in Christ.

68. In administring the sacrament of the body and blood of Christ, the supposed faults of the Church of *England* are not greatly material, and therefore it shall suffice to touch them in few words. *The first is, That we do not use in a generality once for all to say to communicants,* take eat, and drink; *but unto every particular person,* eat thou, drink thou, *which is according to the popish manner, and not the form that our Saviour did use. Our second over-sight is, by gesture. For in kneeling there hath been superstition; sitting agreeth better to the action of a supper; and our Saviour using that which was most fit, did himself not kneel. A third accusation is, for not examining all communicants, whose knowledge in the mystery of the gospel should that way be made manifest; a thing every where, they say, used in the apostles times, because all things necessary were used; and this in their opinion is necessary, yea it is commanded, in as much as the Levites are commanded to prepare the people for the passover; and examination is a part of their preparation, our Lord's supper in place of the passover. The fourth thing misliked is, that against the apostle's prohibition, to have any familiarity at all with notorious offenders, papists being not of the church, are admitted to our very communion, before they have by their religious and gospel-like behaviour purged themselves of that suspicion of Popery which their former life hath caused. They are dogs, swine, unclean beasts, foreigners and strangers from the church of God; and therefore ought not to be admitted, though they offer themselves. We are, fifthly, condemned, in as much as when there hath been store of people to hear sermons and service in the church, we suffer the communion to be ministred to a few. It is not enough, that our book of Common-Prayer hath godly exhortations to move all thereunto which are present. For it should not suffer a few to communicate, it should by ecclesiastical discipline and civil punishment provide that such as would withdraw themselves, might be brought to communicate, according both to the* ᵃ *law of God and the ancient church canons. In the sixth and last place cometh the enormity of imparting this sacrament privately unto the sick.* Thus far accused, we answer briefly to the first ᵇ, that seeing God by sacraments doth apply in particular unto every man's person the grace which himself hath provided for the benefit of all mankind, there is no cause why administring the

ᵃ Numb. 9. 13. Can. 9. Apost. Concil. 2. Brac. cap. 85.
ᵇ T. C. l. 3. p. 166. Besides that it is good to leave the popish form in those things, which we may so conveniently do, it is best to come as near the manner of celebration of the supper which our Saviour Christ did use, as may be. And if it be a good argument to prove that therefore we must rather say, Take thou, than Take ye, because the sacrament is an application of the benefits of Christ, it behoveth that the preacher should direct his admonitions particularly one after another, unto all those which bear his sermon, which is a thing absurd.

sacraments we should forbear to express that in forms of speech, which he by his word and gospel teacheth all to believe. In the one sacrament, *I baptize thee,* displeaseth not. If *eat thou,* in the other offend them, their fancies are no rules for churches to follow. Whether Christ at his last supper did speak generally once to all, or to every one particular, is a thing uncertain. His words are recorded in that form which serveth best for the setting down with historical brevity what was spoken; they are no manifest proof that he spake but once unto all which did then communicate, much less that we in speaking unto every communicante severally do amiss, although it were clear that we herein do otherwise than Christ did. Our imitation of him consisteth not in tying scrupulously our selves unto his syllables, but rather in speaking by the heavenly direction of that inspired divine wisdom, which teacheth divers ways to one end; and doth therein controul their boldness, by whom any profitable way is censured as reproveable, only under colour of some small difference from great examples going before. To do throughout every the like circumstance the same which Christ did in this action, were by following his footsteps in that sort to err more from the purpose he aimed at, than we now do by not following them with so nice and severe strictness. They little weigh with themselves how dull, how heavy, and almost how with-

out fenfe, the greateft part of the common multitude every where is, who think
it either unmeet or unneceſſary to put them, even man by man, efpecially at
that time, in mind whereabout they are. It is true, that in fermons we do not
ufe to repeat our fentences feverally to every particular hearer ; a ftrange madneſs
it were if we fhould. The foftneſs of wax may induce a wife man to fet his
ftamp or image therein; it perfuadeth no man, that becaufe wool hath the like
quality, it may therefore receive the like impreſſion. So the reafon taken from
the ufe of facraments, in that they are inftruments of grace unto every particular
man, may with good congruity lead the church to frame accordingly her words
in adminiftration of facraments, becaufe they eafily admit this form; which being in fermons a thing impoſſible, without apparent ridiculous abfurdity, agreement of facraments with fermons in that which is alledged as a reafonable proof of
conveniency for the one, proveth not the fame allegation impertinent, becaufe it

T.C. l. 1.
p. 165. kneel-
ing carrieth
a fhew of
worfhip. Sit-
ting agreeth
better with
the action of
the fupper.
Chrift and
his apoftles
kneeled not.

doth not enforce the other to be adminiftred in like fort. For equal principles
do then avail unto equal conclufions, when the matter whereunto we apply them
is equal, and not elfe. Our kneeling at communions is the gefture of piety. If we
did there prefent our felves but to make fome fhew or dumb refemblance of a
fpiritual feaft, it may be that fitting were the fitter ceremony ; but coming as receivers of ineftimable grace at the hands of God, what doth better befeem our bodies at that hour, than to be fenfible witneſſes of minds unfeignedly humbled? Our
Lord himfelf did that which cuftom and long ufage had made fit ; we, that which
fitneſs and great decency hath made ufual. The trial of our felves, before we eat
of this bread, and drink of this cup, is by exprefs commandment every man's precife duty. As for neceſſity of calling others unto account befides our felves, albeit
we be not thereunto drawn by any great ftrength which is in their arguments who
firft prefs us with it as a thing neceſſary, by. af-

* T.C. l. 1. p. 164. All things neceſſary were ufed in
the churches of God in the apoftles times ; but examination
was a neceſſary thing, therefore ufed. In the Book of Chronicles, 2 Chron. 35. 6. the Levites were commanded to prepare the people to the receiving of the paſſover, in place
whereof we have the Lord's fupper. Now examination being a part of the preparation, it followeth that here is
commandment of the examination.

firming, * that the apoftles did ufe it, and then
prove the apoftles to have ufed it, by affirming
it to be neceſſary : Again, albeit we greatly
mufe how they can avouch that God did command the Levites to prepare their brethren
againft the feaft of the paſſover, and that the
examination of them was a part of their pre-
paration, when the place alledged to this purpofe doth but charge the Levite, faying,
Make ready Laahhechem for your brethren, to the end they may do according to
the word of the Lord by Mofes. Wherefore in the felf fame place it followeth,
how lambs and kids, and fheep, and bullocks were delivered unto the Levites, and
that thus the fervice was made ready : It followeth likewife, how the Levites having
in fuch fort provided for the people, they made provifion for themfelves, And for the
Priefts, the fons of Aaron: So that confidently from hence to conclude the neceffity of examination, argueth their wonderful great forwardnefs in framing all things to
ferve their turn ; neverthelefs, the examination of communicants when need requireth, for the profitable ufe it may have in fuch cafes, we reject not. Our fault in ad-

1 Cor. 5. 11.
T. C. l. 1.
p. 167.

mitting popifh communicants, is it in that we are forbidden to eat, and therefore
much more to communicate with notorious malefactors? The name of a papift is not
given unto any man for being a notorious malefactor. And the crime wherewith we
are charged, is fuffering papifts to communicate ; fo that, be their life and converfation whatfoever in the fight of man, their popifh opinions are in this cafe laid as
bars and exceptions againft them ; yea, thofe opinions which they have held in former times, although they now both profefs by word, and offer to fhew by fact the

b Although they would receive the communion, yet they
ought to be kept back, until fuch time as by their religious
and gofpel-like behaviour, they have purged themfelves of
that fufpicion of popery which their former life and converfation hath caufed to be conceived. T.C. l. 1. p. 167.

contrary. All this doth not juftify us, which
ought not (they fay) to admit them in any
wife, till their gofpel-like behaviour have removed all fufpicion of popery from them, becaufe papifts are dogs, fwine, beafts, fo-
reigners and ftrangers from the houfe of God ; in a word, they are not of the church.
What the terms of gofpel-like behaviour may include, is obfcure and doubtful : but of
the vifible church of Chrift in this prefent world, from which they feparate all papifts,
we are thus perfuaded. Church is a word which art hath devifed, thereby to fever
and diftingufh that fociety of men which profeſſeth the true religion, from the
reft which profefs it not. There have been in the world from the very firft foundation

dation thereof but three religions, *Paganism*, which lived in the blindness of corrupt and depraved nature; *Judaism*, embracing the law which reformed heathenish impiety, and taught salvation to be looked for through one whom God in the last days would send and exalt to be Lord of all; finally, *Christian Belief*, which yieldeth obedience to the gospel of Jesus Christ, and acknowledgeth him the saviour whom God did promise. Seeing then that the church is a name, which art hath given to *professors of true religion*, as they which will define a man are to pass by those qualities wherein one man doth excel another, and to take only those essential properties whereby a man doth differ from creatures of other kinds; so he that will teach what the church is, shall never rightly perform the work whereabout he goeth, till in matter of religion he touch that difference which severeth the churches religion from theirs who are not the church. Religion being therefore a matter partly of contemplation, partly of action; we must define the church, which is a religious society, by such differences as do properly explain the essence of such things, that is to say, by the object or matter whereabout the contemplations and actions of the church are properly conversant. For so all knowledges and all virtues are defined. Whereupon, because the only object which separateth ours from other religions, is Jesus Christ, in whom none but the church doth believe, and whom none but the church doth worship; we find that accordingly the apostles do every where distinguish hereby the church from *Infidels* and from *Jews, accounting them which call upon the name of our Lord Jesus Christ to be his church.* If we go lower, we shall but add unto this certain casual and variable accidents which are not properly of the being, but make only for the happier and better being of the church of God, either indeed, or in mens opinions and conceits. This is the error of all popish definitions that hitherto have been brought. They define not the church by that which the church essentially is, but by that wherein they imagine their own more perfect than the rest are. Touching parts of eminency and perfection, parts likewise of imperfection and defect in the church of God, they are infinite, their degrees and differences no way possible to be drawn unto any certain account. There is not the least contention and variance, but it blemisheth somewhat the unity that ought to be in the church of Christ, which notwithstanding may have not only without offence or breach of concord, her manifold varieties in rites and ceremonies of religion, but also her strifes and contentions many times, and that about matters of no small importance; yea, her schisms, factions, and such other evils, whereunto the body of the church is subject, found and sick remaining both of the same body, as long as both parts retain by outward profession that vital substance of truth, which maketh christian religion to differ from theirs which acknowledge not our Lord Jesus Christ, the blessed Saviour of mankind, give no credit to his glorious gospel, and have his sacraments, the seals of eternal life, in derision. Now the privilege of the visible church of God (for of that we speak) is to be herein like the ark of *Noah*, that, for any thing we know to the contrary, all without it are lost sheep; yet in this was the ark of *Noah* priviledged above the church, that whereas none of them which were in the one could perish, numbers in the other are cast away, because to eternal life our profession is not enough. Many things exclude from the kingdom of God, although from the the church they separate not. In the church there arise sundry grievous storms, by means whereof whole kingdoms and nations professing Christ, both have been heretofore, and are at this present day divided about Christ. During which divisions and contentions amongst men, albeit each part do justify it self, yet the one of necessity must needs err, if there be any contradiction between them, be it great or little; and what side soever it be that hath the truth, the same we must also acknowledge alone to hold *with the true church in that point*, and consequently reject the other as an enemy, *in that case fallen away from the true church*. Wherefore of hypocrites and dissemblers, whose profession at the first was but only from the teeth outward, when they afterwards took occasion to oppugn certain principal articles of faith, the apostles which defended the truth against them, pronounce them gone out from the fellowship of sound and sincere believers; when as yet the christian religion they had not utterly cast off. In like sense and meaning throughout all ages, hereticks have justly been hated, as branches cut off from the body of the true vine; yet only so far forth cut off as their heresies have extended. Both heresy, and many other crimes which wholly sever from God, do sever from the church of God in part only. The mystery of piety, saith the apostle, is without peradventure great, *God hath been manifested in the flesh, hath been justified in the spirit,*

Rom. 15. 5.
1 Cor. 1. 10.

1 John 2. 19

1 Tim. 3. 16.

spirit, hath been seen of angels, hath been preached to nations, hath been believed on in the world, hath been taken up into glory. The church a pillar and foundation of his truth, which no where is known or profess'd, but only within the church, and they all of the church that profess it. In the mean while it cannot be denied, that many profess this, who are not therefore cleared simply from all either faults or errors, which make separation between us and the well-spring of our happiness. Idolatry severed of old the *Israelites*; iniquity, those Scribes and Pharisees from God, who notwithstanding were a part of the seed of *Abraham*, a part of that very seed which God did himself acknowledge to be his church. The church of God may therefore contain both them which indeed are not his, yet must be reputed his by us that know not their inward thoughts, and them whose apparent wickedness testifieth even in the sight of the whole world that

Matth. 13.
14 47.

God abhorreth them. For to this and no other purpose are meant those parables, which our Saviour in the gospel hath concerning mixture of vice with virtue, light with darkness, truth with error, as well and openly known and seen, as a cunningly cloaked mixture. That which separateth therefore utterly, that which cutteth off clean from the visible church of Christ, is plain apostasy, direct denial, utter rejection of the whole christian faith, as far as the same is professedly different from infidelity. Hereticks, as touching those points of doctrine wherein they fail: Schismaticks, as touching the quarrels for which, or the duties wherein they divide themselves from their brethren: Loose, licentious, and wicked persons, as touching their several offences or crimes, have all forsaken the true church of God; the church which is found and sincere in the doctrine that they corrupt; the church which keepeth the bond of unity, which they violate; the church that walketh in the laws of righteousness, which they transgress: This very true church of Christ they have left, howbeit not altogether left, nor forsaken simply the church; upon the main foundations whereof they continue built, notwithstanding these breaches whereby they are rent in the top asunder. Now because for redress of professed errors and open schisms it is, and must be the churches care that all may in outward conformity be one; as the laudable polity of former ages, even so our own to that end and purpose hath established divers laws, the moderate severity whereof is a mean both to stay the rest, and to reclaim such as heretofore have been led away. But seeing that the offices which laws require are always definite, and when that they require is done, they go no farther, whereupon sundry ill-affected persons, to save themselves from danger of laws, pretend obedience, albeit inwardly they carry still the same hearts which they did before; by means whereof it falleth out, that receiving unworthily the blessed sacrament at our hands, they eat and drink their own damnation: It is for remedy of this mischief * here determined, that whom the law of the realm doth punish, unless they communicate, such if they offer to obey law, the church notwithstanding should not admit without probation before had of their gospel-like behaviour. Wherein they first set no time, how long this supposed probation must continue; again, they nominate no certain judgment, the verdict whereof shall approve mens behaviour to be gospel like; and, that which is most material, whereas they seek to make it more hard for dissemblers to be received into the church, than law and polity as yet hath done, they make it in truth more easy for such kind of persons to wind themselves out of the law, and to continue the same they were. The law requireth at their hands that duty which in conscience doth touch them nearest, because the greatest difference

* *T. C.* lib. 1. pag 167. If the place of the fifth to the *Corinthians*, do forbid that we should have any familiarity with notorious offenders, it doth more forbid that they should be received to the communion: And therefore papists being such, as which are notoriously known to hold heretical opinions, ought not to be admitted, much less compelled to the supper. For seeing that our Saviour Christ did institute his supper amongst his disciples, and those only which were, as St. *Paul* speaketh, within; it is evident, that the papists being without, and foreigners and strangers from the church of God, ought not to be received if they would offer themselves: And that minister that shall give the supper of the Lord to him which is known to be a papist, and which hath never made any clear renouncing of popery with which he hath been defiled, doth profane the Table of the Lord, and doth give the meat that is prepared for the children, unto dogs, and he bringeth into the pasture which is provided for the sheep, swine and unclean beasts, contrary to the faith and trust that ought to be in a steward of the Lord's House, as he is. For albeit that I doubt not but many of those which are now papists, pertain to the election of God, which God also in his good time will call to the knowledge of his truth: Yet notwithstanding they ought to be unto the minister, and unto the church, touching the ministring of sacraments, as strangers, and as unclean beasts. The ministring of the holy sacraments unto them, is a declaration and seal of God's favour and reconciliation with them, and a plain preaching, partly, that they be washed already from their sin, partly that they are of the houshold of God, and such as the Lord will feed to eternal life; which is not lawful to be done unto those which are not of the houshold of faith. And therefore I conclude, that the compelling of papists unto the communion, and the dismissing and letting of them go, when as they be to be punished for their stubbornness in popery (with this condition, if they will receive the communion) is very unlawful; when as, although they would receive it, yet they ought to be kept back till such time as by their religious and gospel-like behaviour, &c.

ference between us and them is the sacrament of the body and blood of Christ, whose name in the service of our communion we celebrate with due honour, which they in the error of their mass prophane. As therefore on our part to hear mass, were an open departure from that sincere profession wherein we stand; so if they on the other side receive our communion, they give us the strongest pledge of fidelity that man can demand. What their hearts are, God doth know. But if they which mind treachery to God and man, should once apprehend this advantage given them, whereby they may satisfy law in pretending themselves conformable, (for what can law with reason or justice require more?) and yet be sure the church will accept no such offer till their gospel-like behaviour be allowed, after that our own simplicity hath once thus fairly eased them from the sting of law; it is to be thought they will learn the mystery of gospel-like behaviour when leisure serveth them. And so while without any cause we fear to prophane sacraments, we shall not only defeat the purpose of most wholesome laws, but lose or wilfully hazard those souls, from whom the likeliest means of full and perfect recovery are by our indiscretion with-held. For neither doth God thus bind us to dive into men's consciences, nor can their fraud and deceit hurt any man but themselves. To him they seem such as they are, but of us they must be taken for such as they seem. In the eye of God they are against Christ, that are not truly and sincerely with him; in our eyes they must be received as with Christ, that are not to outward shew against him, The case of impenitent and notorious sinners is not like unto theirs, whose only imperfection is error severed from pertinacy. Error in appearance, content to submit it self to better instruction: Error so far already cured, as to crave at our hands that sacrament, the hatred and utter refusal whereof, was the weightiest point wherein heretofore they swerved and went astray. In this case therefore they cannot reasonably charge us with remiss dealing, or with carelessness, to whom we impart the mysteries of Christ; but they have given us manifest occasion to think it requisite that we earnestly advise rather, and exhort them to consider as they ought, their sundry-oversights; first, in equalling undistinctly crimes with errors, as touching force to make uncapable of this sacrament: Secondly, in suffering indignation at the faults of the church of *Rome* to blind and with-hold their judgments from seeing that which withal they should acknowledge, concerning so much nevertheless still due to the same church, as to be held and reputed a part of the house of God, a limb of the visible church of Christ: Thirdly, in imposing upon the church a burthen to enter farther into men's hearts, and to make a deeper search of their consciences, than any law of God, or reason of man inforceth: Fourthly and lastly, in repelling, under colour of longer tryal, such from the mysteries of heavenly grace, as are both capable thereof by the laws of God, for any thing we hear to the contrary; and should in divers considerations be cherished according to the merciful examples and precepts whereby the gospel of Christ hath taught us towards such to shew compassion, to receive them with lenity and all meekness; if any thing be shaken in them, to strengthen it; not to quench with delays and jealousies that feeble smoak of conformity which seemeth to breath from them; but to build wheresoever there is any foundation; to add perfection unto slender beginnings; and that as by other offices of piety, even so by this very food of life which Christ hath left in his church, not only for preservation of strength, but also for relief of weakness. But to return to our own selves, in whom the next thing severely reproved is the paucity of communicants. If they require at convenient frequency, we wish *T. C. l. 1.* the same, knowing how acceptable unto God such service is, when multitudes chear- *p. 147.* fully concur unto it; if they encourage men thereunto, we also (themselves ac- *2 Chr. 30. 13.* knowledge it) are not utterly forgetful to do the like; if they require some publick *Psal. 122. 1.* coaction for remedy of that, wherein by milder and softer means little good is done, they know our laws and statutes provided in that behalf, whereunto whatsoever convenient help may be added more by the wisdom of man, what cause have we given the world to think that we are not ready to hearken to it, and to use any good means of sweet compulsion to have this high and heavenly banquet largely furnished? Only we cannot so far yield as to judge it convenient, that the holy desire of a com- *Luke 14. 23.* petent number should be unsatisfied, because the greater part is careless and undisposed to join with them. Men should not (they say) be permitted a few by themselves to communicate when so many are gone away, because this sacrament is a token of our conjunction with our brethren; and therefore by communicating apart from them, we make an apparent shew of distraction. I ask then, on which side unity is broken, whether on theirs that depart, or on theirs who being left behind, do communicate ? Firſt, in the one it is not denied but that they may have reaſonable cauſes of departure, and that then even they are delivered from juſt blame. Of ſuch kind of cauſes two are allowed, namely, danger of impairing health, and neceſſary buſineſs requiring our preſence otherwhere. And may not a third cauſe, which is unfitneſs at the preſent time, detain us as lawfully back as either of theſe two? True it is, that we cannot hereby altogether excuſe our ſelves, for that we ought to prevent this, and do not. But if we have committed a fault in not preparing our minds before, ſhall we therefore aggravate the ſame with a worſe; the crime of unworthy participation? He that abſtaineth doth want for the time that grace and comfort which religious communicants have, but he that eateth and drinketh unworthily, receiveth death; that which is life to others, turneth in him to poiſon. Notwithſtanding, whatſoever be the cauſe for which men abſtain, were it reaſon that the fault of one part ſhould any way abridge their benefit that are not faulty? There is in all the ſcripture of God no one ſyllable which doth condemn communicating amongſt a few, when the reſt are departed from them. As for the laſt thing, which is our imparting this ſacrament privately to the ſick, whereas there have been of old (they grant) two kinds of neceſſity wherein this ſacrament might be privately adminiſtred; of which two, the one being erroneouſly imagined, and the other (they ſay) continuing no longer in uſe, there remaineth unto us no neceſſity at all for which that cuſtom ſhould be retained. The falſly ſurmiſed neceſſity is that whereby ſome have thought all ſuch excluded from poſſibility of ſalvation, as did depart this life, and never were made partakers of the holy euchariſt. The other cauſe of neceſſity was, when men which had fain in time of perſecution, and had afterwards repented them, but were not as yet received again unto the fellowſhip of this communion, did at the hour of death requeſt it, that ſo they might reſt with greater quietneſs and comfort of mind, being thereby aſſured of departure in unity of Chriſt's church; which virtuous deſire the fathers did think it great impiety not to ſatiſfy. This was *Serapion*'s caſe of neceſſity. *Serapion*, a faithful aged perſon, and always of very upright life, till fear of perſecution in the end cauſed him to ſhrink back, after long ſorrow for his ſcandalous offence, and ſuit oftentimes made to be pardoned of the church, fell at length into grievous ſickneſs, and being ready to yield up the ghoſt, was then more inſtant than ever before to receive the ſacrament. Which ſacrament was neceſſary in this caſe, not that *Serapion* had been deprived of everlaſting life without it, but that his end was thereby to him made the more comfortable. And do we think, that all caſes of ſuch neceſſity are clean vaniſhed? Suppoſe that ſome have by miſ-perſuaſion lived in ſchiſm, withdrawn themſelves from holy and publick aſſemblies, hated the prayers, and loathed the ſacraments of the church, falſly preſuming them to be fraught with impious and antichriſtian corruptions: Which error the God of mercy and truth opening at the length their eyes to ſee, they do not only repent them of the evil which they have done, but alſo in token thereof deſire to receive comfort by that whereunto they have offered diſgrace (which may be the caſe of many poor ſeduced Souls, even at this day.) God forbid we ſhould think that the church doth ſin, in permitting the wounds of ſuch to be ſupplied with that oil, which this gracious ſacrament doth yield, and their bruiſed minds not only need but beg. There is nothing which the ſoul of man doth deſire in that laſt hour ſo much, as comfort againſt the natural terrors of death, and other ſcruples of conſcience which commonly do then moſt trouble and perplex the weak; towards whom the very law of God doth exact at our hands all the helps that chriſtian lenity and indulgence can afford. Our general conſolation departing this life is, the hope of that glorious and bleſſed reſurrection which the apoſtle St. *Paul* [b] nameth Ἐξανάϛασιν, [c] to note that as all men ſhould have their Ἀνάϛασιν, and be raiſed again from the dead, ſo the juſt ſhall be taken up and exalted above the reſt, whom the power of God doth but raiſe, and not exalt. This life, and this reſurrection of our Lord Jeſus Chriſt is for all men, as touching the ſufficiency of that he hath done; but that which maketh us partakers thereof, is our particular communion with Chriſt; and this ſacrament a principal mean, as well to ſtrengthen the bond, as to multiply in us the fruits of the ſame communion. For which cauſe St. *Cyprian* [d] termeth it a joyful ſolemnity of expedite and ſpeedy reſurrection; *Ignatius* [e], a medicine which procureth immortality and preventeth death; *Irenæus* [f], the nouriſhment of our bodies to eternal life, and their preſervative from corruption. Now becauſe that ſacrament,

[margin:] *T. C. l. 1. p. 146.*

[margin:] [a] 1 Cor. 15. 21. [b] Phil. 3. 11. [c] ... ἤ ἐκ τῆς ἐπαναϛάσεως. *Theophyl.* Παιρ. Ἦς δὲ ἀνθρωπινᾶ ἀνιϛανται, μᾶλλον δ᾽ ἐϛι καὶ ἐξαίρετᾶ τῶν δικαίων ἡ ἀνάϛασις. Am- mon. *Vide* 1 Theſ. 4. 17. [d] Maturata Reſurrectionis letabunda ſolemnia. Cypr. de Cœn. Dom. cap. 10. [e] Φάρμακον ἀθαναϛίας ἀντίδοτος μὴ Θανεῖν. Ignat. Epiſt. ad Epheſ. Iren. lib. 4. cap. 34. [f] Etſi nihil facile mutandum eſt ex ſolemnibus, tamen ubi equitas evident poſcit, ſubveniendum eſt, l. 138. ff. de Reg. Jur.

which

which at all times we may receive unto this effect, is then most acceptable and most fruitful, when any special extraordinary occasion, nearly and presently urging, kindleth our desires towards it, their severity who cleave unto that alone which is generally fit to be done, and so make all mens conditions alike, may add much affliction to divers troubled and grieved minds, of whose particular estate particular respect being had, according to the charitable order of the church wherein we live, there insueth unto God that glory which his righteous saints comforted in their greatest distresses do yield; and unto them which have their reasonable petitions satisfied, the same contentment, tranquillity and joy, that others before them, by means of like satisfaction, have reaped, and wherein we all are or should be desirous finally to take our leave of the world, whensoever our own uncertain time of most assured departure shall come.   Concerning therefore both prayers and sacraments, together with our usual and received form of administring the same in the church of *England*, let thus much suffice.

69. As the substance of God alone is infinite, and hath no kind of limitation, so likewise his continuance is from everlasting to everlasting, and knoweth neither beginning nor end.   Which demonstrable conclusion being presupposed, it followeth necessarily, that besides him, all things are finite both in substance and in continuance.   If in substance all things be finite, it cannot be but that there are bounds without the compass whereof their substance doth not extend; if in continuance also limited, they all have, it cannot be denied, their set and their certain terms, before which they had no being at all.   This is the reason why first we do most admire those things which are greatest; and secondly, those things which are ancientest; because the one are least distant from the infinite substance, the other from the infinite continuance of God.   Out of this we gather, that only God hath true immortality or eternity, that is to say, continuance wherein there groweth no difference by addition of hereafter unto now, whereas the noblest and perfectest of all things besides have continually, through continuance, the time of former continuance lengthen'd; so that they could not heretofore be said to have continued so long as now, neither now so long as hereafter.   God's own eternity is the hand which leadeth angels in the course of their perpetuity; their perpetuity the hand that draweth out celestial motion; the line of which motion, and the thread of time, are spun together.   Now as nature bringeth forth time with motion, so we by motion have learned how to divide time, and by the smaller parts of time both to measure the greater, and to know how long all things else endure.   For time, considered in it self, is but the flux of that very instant wherein the motion of the heaven began; being coupled with other things, it is the quantity of their continuance measured by the distance of two instants: As the time of a man, is a man's continuance from the instant of his first breath, till the instant of his last gasp.   Hereupon some have defined time to be the measure of the motion of heaven; because the first thing which time doth measure, is that motion wherewith it began, and by the help whereof it measureth other things, as when the prophet *David* saith, that a man's continuance doth not commonly exceed threescore and ten years, he useth the help both of motion and number to measure time.   They which make time an effect of motion, and motion to be in nature before time, ought to have considered with themselves, that albeit we should deny, as *Melissus* did, all motion, we might notwithstanding acknowledge time, because time doth but signify the quantity of continuance, which continuance may be in things that rest and are never moved.   Besides, we may also consider in rest both that which is past, and that which is present, and that which is future; yea, farther, even length and shortness in every of these, although we never had conceit of motion.   But to define, without motion, how long, or how short such continuance is, were impossible.   So that herein we must of necessity use the benefit of years, days, hours, minutes, which all grow from celestial motion.   Again, for as much as that motion is circular whereby we make our divisions of time, and the compass of that circuit such that the heavens, which are therein continually moved and keep in their motions uniform celerity, must needs touch often the same points, they cannot chuse but bring unto us by equal distances frequent returns of the same times.   Furthermore, whereas time is nothing but a meer quantity of that continuance which all things have that are not as God is, without beginning, that which is proper unto all quantities, agreeth also to this kind; so that time doth but measure other things, and neither worketh in them any real effect, nor is it self ever capable of any.   And therefore when commonly we use to say, that time doth eat or fret out all things; that time is the wisest thing in the world, because it

Of festival days, and the natural causes of their convenient institution.

K k   bringeth bringth forth all knowledge; and that nothing is more foolish than time, which never holdeth any thing long, but whatsoever one day learneth, the same another day forgetteth again; that some men see prosperous and happy days, and that some mens days are miserable : In all these, and the like speeches, that which is uttered of the time, is not verified of time it self, but agreeth unto those things which are in time, and do by means of so near conjunction, either lay their burden upon the back, or set their crown upon the head of time. Yea, the very opportunities which we ascribe to time, do in truth cleave to the things themselves wherewith the time is joined.

Χρόν@ ἔςτ
ἐν ᾧ καιρὸς,
ᾗ καιρὸς ἐν ᾧ
χ-   ἐ ᾿ρ᾿
λ᾿᾿. Hippoc.
lib. qui præ-
ceptiones in-
scribitur.

As for time, it neither causeth things, nor opportunities of things, although it comprise and contain both. All things whatsoever having their time, the works of God have always that time which is seasonablest and fittest for them. His works are some ordinary, some more rare; all worthy of observation, but not all of like necessity to be often remembred; they all have their times, but they all do not add the same estimation and glory to the times wherein they are. For as God by being every where, yet doth not give unto all places one and the same degree of holiness; so neither one and the same dignity to all times, by working in all. For if all either places or times, were in respect of God alike, wherefore was it said unto *Moses* by

Exod. 3. 5. particular designation, *This very place wherein thou standest is holy ground?* Why doth the prophet *David* chuse out all the days of the year but one, whereof he speak-

Psal. 118. 24. eth by way of principal admiration, *This is the day the Lord hath made?* No doubt, as God's extraordinary presence hath hallowed and sanctified certain places, so they are his extrordinary works that have truly and worthily advanced certain times; for which cause they ought to be with all men that honour God more holy than other days. The wise man therefore compareth herein not unfitly the times of God with the persons of men. If any should ask how it comes to pass that one day doth excel another, seeing the light of all the days in the year proceedeth from one sun ; to this

Ecclus. 33. 7. he answereth, *That the knowledge of the Lord hath parted them asunder, he hath by them disposed the times and solemn feasts, some he hath chosen out and sanctified, some he hath put among the days to number : But as Adam and all other men are of one substance, all created of the earth : But the Lord hath divided them by great knowledge, and made their ways divers; some he hath blessed and exalted, some he hath sanctified and appropriated unto himself, some he hath cursed, humbled and put them out of their dignity.* So that the cause being natural and necessary for which there should be a difference in days, the solemn observation whereof declareth religious thankfulness towards him whose works of principal reckoning we thereby admire and honour, it cometh next to be considered, what kinds of duties and services they are wherewith such times should be kept holy.

The manner
of celebra-
ting festival
days.

70. The sanctification of days and times is a token of that thankfulness, and a pattern of that publick honour which we owe to God for admirable benefits, whereof it doth not suffice that we keep a secret kalendar, taking thereby our private occasions as we lift our selves to think how much God hath done for all men ; but the days which are chosen out to serve as publick memorials of such his mercies, ought to be cloathed with those outward robes of holiness, whereby their difference from other days may be made sensible. But because time in it self, as hath been already proved, can receive no alteration; the hallowing of festival days must consist in the shape or countenance which we put upon the affairs that are incident into those days. *This is the day which the Lord hath made,* saith the prophet *David, Let us rejoyce and be glad in it.* So that generally

* Grande videlicet officium, focos & choros in publicum educere,
vicatim epulari, civitatem taberna halitu obolefacere, vino lutum
cogere, catervatim curfitare ad injurias, ad impudicitias, ad libi-
dinis illecebras. Siccine exprimitur publicum gaudium per publicum
dedecus ? Tert. Apol. cap. 35. Dies festos Majestati altissime
dedicatos nullis voluminis voluptatibus occupari. C. l. 12. tit. 12.
l. 1. Ἀντὶ † πλανωμέτων ᾗ αἰχυρχας ᾗ αἰχεςσημωσύνης
ἑορταζόντας πανηγύρεις, ᾗ μεθύω ἔχουσαι ᾗ κῶμον ᾗ
χλωία, ἀλλ᾿ ὑμνευσι Θεὸν ᾗ ἱερῶν λόγων ἀκρόασιν, ᾗ μετ᾿
ἀχλω ἀξιωάτοις κοσμμηθέντα δεχιζύσιν. Theod. ad Grac. Insi-
del. Ser. 9. Τὰς ᾿ν αὐ τῆς εὐσεβοῖς ἔτι ἱνατῆ τι εἶναι ᾗ φιλά-
Ϛρωπο, Philo lib. de Abraha.

offices and duties of * religious joy are that wherein the hallowing of festival times consisteth. The most natural testimonies of our rejoicing in God, are first his praises set forth with chearful alacrity of mind. Secondly, our comfort and delight expressed by a charitable largeness of somewhat more than common bounty. Thirdly, sequestration from ordinary labours, the toils and cares whereof are not meet to be companions of such gladness. Festival solemnity therefore is nothing but the due mixture, as it were, of these three elements, praise, bounty, and rest. Touching praise, for as much as the *Jews,* who alone knew the way how to magnify God aright, did commonly (as appeared by their wicked Lives) more of custom and for fashion sake execute the services of their religion,

than

than with hearty and true devotion (which God especially requireth) he therefore protesteth against their sabbaths and solemn days, as being therewith much offended. Isa. 1. 13. Plentiful and liberal expence is required in them that abound, partly as a sign of their own joy in the goodness of God towards them, and partly as a mean whereby to refresh those poor and needy, who being especially at these times made partakers of Deut. 16. 14. relaxation and joy with others, do the more religiously bless God, whose great mer- Nehem. 8. 9. cies were a cause thereof, and the more contentedly endure the burthen of that hard estate wherein they continue. Rest is the end of all motion, and the last perfection of all things that labour. Labours in us are journeys, and even in them which feel no weariness by any work, yet they are but ways whereby to come unto that which bringeth not happiness till it do bring rest. For as long as any thing which we desire is unattained, we rest not. Let us not here take rest for idleness. They are idle, whom the painfulness of action causeth to avoid those labours whereunto both God and nature bindeth them; they rest, which either cease from their work when they have brought it unto perfection, or else give over a meaner labour, because a worthier and better is to be undertaken. God hath created nothing to be idle or ill employed. As therefore man doth consist of different and distinct parts, every part endued with manifold abilities, which all have their several ends and actions thereunto referred; so there is in this great variety of duties which belong to men that dependency and order, by means whereof the lower sustaining always the more excellent, and the higher perfecting the more base, they are in their times and seasons continued with most exquisite correspondence. Labours of bodily and daily toil, purchase freedom for actions of religious joy, which benefit these actions requite with the gift of desired rest; a thing most natural and fit to accompany the solemn festival duties of honour which are done to God. For if those principal works of God, the memory whereof we use to celebrate at such times, be but certain tastes and sayes, as it were, of that final benefit wherein our perfect felicity and bliss lieth folded up, seeing that the presence of the one doth direct our cogitations, thoughts and desires towards the other, it giveth surely a kind of life, and addeth inwardly no small delight to those so comfortable expectations, when the very outward countenance of that we presently do, representeth after a sort that also whereunto we tend; as festival rest doth that celestial estate whereof the very heathens themselves, which had not the means whereby to apprehend much, did notwithstanding imagine that it needs must consist in rest, and have therefore taught that above the highest moveable sphere there is nothing which feeleth alteration, motion or change, but all things immutable, unsubject to passion, blest with eternal continuance in a life of the highest perfection, and of that compleat abundant sufficiency within it self, which no possibility of want, maim, or defect can touch. Besides, whereas ordinary labours are both in themselves painful, and base in comparison of festival services done to God, doth not the natural difference between them shew that the one, as it were by way of submission and homage, should surrender themselves to the other, wherewith they can neither easily concur, because painfulness and joy are opposite, nor decently, because while the mind hath just occasion to make her abode in the house of gladness, the weed of ordinary toil and travel becometh her not? Wherefore even nature hath taught the heathens, and God the *Jews*, and Christ us, first, that festival solemnities are a part of the publick exercise of religion; secondly, that praise, liberality, and rest, are as natural elements whereof solemnities consist. But these things the heathens converted to the honour of their false Gods: And, as they failed in the end it self; so neither could they discern rightly what form and measure religion therein should observe. Whereupon when the *Israelites* impiously followed so corrupt example, they are in every degree noted to have done amiss; their hymns or songs of praise were idolatry; their bounty, excess, and their rest wantonness. Therefore the law of God which appointed them days of solemnity, taught them likewise in what manner the same should be celebrated. According to the pattern of which institution, *David* establishing, the state of religion ordained praise to be given unto God in the sabbaths, months, and appointed times, as their custom had been always 1 Chron. 23. before the Lord. Now, besides the times which God himself in the law of *Moses* 30. particularly specified, there were through the wisdom of the church, certain others devised by occasion of like occurrents to those whereupon the former had risen; as namely, that which *Mordecai* and *Esther* did first celebrate in memory of the Lord's most Esther 9. 27. wonderful protection, when *Haman* had laid his inevitable plot, to man's thinking, for the utter extirpation of the *Jews*, even in one day. This they call the feast of

lots, becaufe *Haman* had caft their life and their death, as it were, upon the hazard of a lot. To this may be added that other alfo of *dedication*, mentioned in the tenth of St. *John's* gofpel, the inftitution whereof is declared in the hiftory of the *Maccabees.* But forafmuch as their law by the coming of Chrift is changed, and we thereunto no way bound, St. *Paul*, although it were not his purpofe to favour invectives againft the fpecial fanctification of days and times to the fervice of God, and to the honour of Jefus Chrift, doth notwithftanding bend his forces againft that opinion which impofed on the *Gentiles* the yoke of *Jewifh* legal obfervations, as if the whole world ought for ever, and that upon pain of condemnation, to keep and obferve the fame. Such as in this perfuafion hallowed thofe *Jewifh* fabbaths, the apoftle fharply reproveth, faying, *Te obferve days, and months, and times, and years ; I am in fear of you, left I have beftowed upon you labour in vain.* Howbeit, fo far off was *Tertullian* from imagining how any man could poffibly hereupon call in queftion on fuch days as the church of Chrift doth obferve, that the obfervation of thefe days he ufeth for an argument whereby to prove, it could not be the apoftle's intent and meaning to condemn fimply all obferving of fuch times. Generally therefore touching feafts in the church of Chrift, they have that profitable ufe whereof St. *Auguftin* fpeaketh, *By feftival folemnities and fet-days, we dedicate and fanctify to God the memory of his benefits, left unthankful forgetfulnefs thereof fhould creep upon us in courfe of time.* And concerning particulars, their fabbath the church hath changed into our Lord's day ; that as the one did continually bring to mind the former world finifhed by creation ; fo the other might keep us in perpetual remembrance of a far better world, begun by him which came to reftore all things, to make both heaven and earth new. For which caufe they honoured the laft day, we the firft in every feven throughout the year. The reft of the days and times which we celebrate, have relation all to one head. We begin therefore our ecclefiaftical year with the glorious annunciation of his birth by angelical embaffage. There being hereunto added his bleffed nativity it felf ; the myftery of his legal circumcifion ; the teftification of his true incarnation by the purification of her which brought him into the world, his refurrection, his afcenfion into heaven, the admirable fending down of his fpirit upon his chofen, and (which confequently enfued) the notice of that incomprehenfible trinity thereby given to the church of God. Again, forafmuch as we know that Chrift hath not only been manifefted great into himfelf, but great in other his faints alfo, the days of whofe departure out of the world are to the church of Chrift as the birth and coronation days of Kings or Emperors ; therefore efpecial choice being made of the very flower of all occafions, in this kind there are annual felected times to meditate of Chrift glorified in them which had the honour to fuffer for his fake, before they had age and ability to know him ; glorified in them, which knowing him as *Stephen*, had the fight of that before death, whereinto fo acceptable death did lead ; glorified in thofe fages of the *Eaft*, that came from far to adore him, and were conducted by ftrange light ; glorified in the fecond *Elias* of the world, fent before him to prepare his way ; glorified in thofe apoftles whom it pleafed him to ufe as founders of his kingdom here ; glorified in the angels, as in *Michael* ; glorified in all thofe happy fouls, that are already poffeffed of heaven. Over and befides which number not great, the reft be but four other days heretofore annexed to the feaft of *Eafter* and *Pentecoft*, by reafon of general baptifm ufual at thofe two feafts ; which alfo is the caufe why they had not, as other days, any proper name given them. Their firft inftitution was therefore through neceffity, and their prefent continuance is now for the greater honour of the principals whereupon they ftill attend. If it be then demanded, whether we obferve thefe times, as being thereunto bound by force of divine law, or elfe by the only pofitive ordinances of the church ? I anfwer to this, that the very law of nature it felf, which all men confefs to be God's law, requireth in general no lefs the fanctification of times, than of places, perfons, and things, unto God's honour. For which caufe it hath pleafed him heretofore, as of the reft, fo of times likewife, to exact fome parts by way of perpetual homage, never to be difpenfed withal, nor remitted : Again, to require fome other parts of time with as ftrict exaction, but for lefs continuance ; and of the reft which were left arbitrary, to accept what the church fhall in due confideration confecrate voluntarily unto like religious ufes. Of the firft kind, amongft the *Jews*, was the fabbath-day ; of the fecond, thofe feafts which are appointed by the law of *Mofes* ; the feaft of dedication, invented by the church, ftandeth in the number of the laft kind. The moral law requiring
there-

John 10. 22.

1 Mac. 4. 54.

Gal. 4. 10.

Si omnem in totum devotionem temporum & dierum & menfium & annorum erafit apoftolus, cur Pafcha celebramus annuo circulo in menfa primo? Cur quinquaginta exinde diebus in omni exultatione decurrimus? Lib. adverf. Pfych. Aug. de Civit. Dei, lib. 16. cap. 4.

Luke 1. 26.
Luke 2. 21.

therefore a feventh part throughout the age of the whole world to be that way employed, although with us the day be changed, in regard of a new revolution begun by our Saviour Chrift; yet the fame proportion of time continueth which was before, becaufe in reference to the benefit of creation, and now much more of renovation thereunto added by him which was prince of the world to come, we are bound to account the fanctification of one day in feven a duty which God's immutable law doth exact for ever. The reft, they fay, we ought to abolifh, becaufe the continuance of them doth nourifh wicked fuperftition in the minds of men; befides, they are all abufed by papifts, the enemies of God; yea, certain of them, as *Eafter* and *Pentecoft*, even by the *Jews*.

71. Touching *Jews*, their *Eafter* and *Pentecoft* have with ours as much affinity as *Philip* the apoftle with *Philip* the *Macedonian* King. As for imitation of papifts, and the breeding of fuperftition, they are now become fuch common guefts, that no man can think it difcourteous to let them go as they came. The next is a rare obfervation and ftrange; you fhall find, if you mark it (as it doth deferve to be noted well) that many thoufands there are, who if

they have virtuoufly during thofe times behaved themfelves, if their devotion and zeal in prayer have been fervent, their attention to the word of God fuch as all chriftian men fhould yield, imagine that herein they have performed a good duty; which notwithftanding to think is a very dangerous error, in as much as the apoftle St. *Paul* hath taught that we ought not to keep our *Eafter* as the *Jews* did for certain days; but in the unleavened bread of fincerity and of truth to feaft continually: Whereas the reftraint of *Eafter* to a certain number of days, caufeth us to reft for a fhort fpace in that near confideration of our duties, which fhould be extended throughout the courfe of our whole lives, and fo pulleth out of our mind the doctrine of Chrift's gofpel e're we be aware. The doctrine of the gofpel, which here they mean, or fhould mean, is, that Chrift

> *T. C. l. 1. p. 151.* If they had been never abufed neither by the papifts, nor by the *Jews*, as they have been, and are daily; yet fuch making of holidays is never without fome great danger of bringing in fome evil and corrupt opinions into the minds of men. I will ufe an example in one, and that the chief of holidays, and moft generally and of longeft time obferved in the church, which is the feaft of *Eafter*, which was kept of fome more days, of fome fewer. How many thoufands are there, I will not fay of the ignorant papifts, but of thofe alfo which profefs the gofpel, which when they have celebrated thofe days with diligent heed taken unto their life, and with fome earneft devotion in praying, and hearing the word of God, do not by and by think that they have well celebrated the feaft of *Eafter*; and yet have they thus notably deceived themfelves: For St. *Paul* teacheth, 1 *Cor.* 5. 8. That the celebrating of the feaft of the chriftians *Eafter* is not, as the *Jews* was, for certain days; but fheweth that we muft keep this feaft all the days of our life in the unleavened bread of fincerity and of truth. By which we fee, that the obferving of the feaft of *Eafter* for certain days in the year, doth pull out of our minds, e're ever we be aware, the doctrine of the gofpel, and caufeth us to reft in that near confideration of our duties, for the fpace of a few days, which fhould be extended to all our life.

having finifhed the law, there is no *Jewifh* pafchal folemnity, nor abftinence from fowre bread now required at our hands; there is no leaven which we are bound to caft out, but malice, fin and wickednefs; no bread but the food of fincere truth wherewith we are tied to celebrate our paffover. And feeing no time of fin is granted us, neither any intermiffion of found belief, it followeth, that this kind of feafting ought to endure always. But how are ftanding feftival folemnities againft this? That which the gofpel of Chrift requireth, is the perpetuity of virtuous duties; not perpetuity of exercife or action; but difpofition perpetual, and practice as oft as times and opportunities require. Juft, valiant, liberal, temperate, and holy men are they, which can whenfoever they will, and will whenfoever they ought, execute what their feveral perfections import. If vertues did always ceafe to be when they ceafe to work, there fhould be nothing more pernicious to virtue than fleep: Neither were it poffible that men, as *Zachary* and *Elizabeth*, fhould in all the commandments of God walk unreproveable; or that the chain of our converfation fhould contain fo many links of divine vertues, as the apoftles in divers places have reckoned up, if in the exercife of each virtue perpetual continuance were exacted at our hands. Seeing therefore all things are done in time, and many offices are not poffible at one and the fame time to be difcharged; duties of all forts muft have neceffarily their feveral fucceffions and feafons; in which refpect the fchoolmen have well and foundly determined, that God's affirmative laws and precepts, the laws that enjoin any actual duty, as prayer, alms, and the like, do bind us *ad femper velle*, but not *ad femper agere*; we are tied to iterate and refume them when need is, howbeit not to continue them without any intermiffion. Feafts, whether God himfelf hath ordained them, or the church by that authority which God hath given, they are of religion fuch publick fervices as neither can nor ought to be continued otherwife than only by iteration. Which iteration is a moft effectual mean to bring unto full maturity and growth thofe feeds of godli-

nefs

nefs, that thefe very men themfelves do grant to be fown in the hearts of many thoufands, during the while that fuch feafts are prefent. The conftant habit of well doing is not gotten without the cuftom of doing well, neither can virtue be made perfect but by the manifold works of virtue often practifed. Before the powers of our
minds be brought unto fome perfection, our firft effays and offers towards virtue
muft needs be raw; yet commendable, becaufe they tend unto ripenefs. For which
caufe the wifdom of God hath commanded, efpecially this circumftance amongft
others in folemn feafts, that to children and novices in religion they minifter the firft
occafion to afk and enquire of God. Whereupon, if there follow but fo much piety
as hath been mentioned, let the church learn to further imbecillity with prayer; *Pre-*
ferve, Lord, thefe good and gracious beginnings, that they fuddenly dry not up like the
morning dew, but may profper and grow as the trees which rivers of waters keep al-
ways flourifhing. Let all mens acclamations be, *Grace, Grace unto it,* as to that
firft laid corner ftone in *Zerubbabel's* buildings. For who hath defpifed the day of
thofe things which are fmall? Or how dare we take upon us to condemn that very
thing which voluntarily we grant maketh us of nothing fomewhat; feeing all we
pretend againft it, is only, that as yet this fomewhat is not much? The days of folemnity which are but few, cannot chufe but foon finifh that outward exercife of
godlinefs which properly appertaineth to fuch times; howbeit, mens inward difpofition to virtue, they both augment for the prefent, and by their often returns, bring
alfo the fame at the length unto that perfection which we moft defire. So that although by their neceffary fhort continuance, they abridge the prefent exercife of piety in fome kind; yet becaufe by repetition they enlarge, ftrengthen and confirm the
habits of all virtue, it remaineth, that we honour, obferve and keep them as ordinances many ways fingularly profitable in God's church. This exception being taken
againft holidays, for that they reftrain the praifes of God unto certain times, another
followeth condemning reftraint of men from their ordinary trades and labours at
thofe times.

a *T. C. l. 1.*
p. 152. I con-
fefs that it is
in the power
of the church
to appoint fo
many days in
the week, or
in the year
(in the which
the congre-
gation fhall
affemble to
hear the
word of God,
and receive
the facra-
ments, and
offer up
prayers unto
God) as it
fhall think
good, accord-
ing to thofe
rules which
are before al-
ledged.

a It is not (they fay) in the power of the church to command reft,
becaufe God hath left it to all men at liberty, that if they think good to beftow fix
whole days in labour, they may; neither is it more lawful for the church to abridge
any man of that liberty which God hath granted, than to take away the yoke which
God hath laid upon them, and to countermand what he doth exprefly enjoin. They
deny not, but in times of publick calamity, that men may the better affemble themfelves to faft and pray, the church, becaufe it hath received commandment from
God to proclaim a prohibition from ordinary works, ftandeth bound to do it, as the
Jews afflicted did in *Babylon.* But without fome exprefs commandment from God
there is no power, they fay, under heaven, which may prefume by any degree to
reftrain the liberty that God hath given. Which opinion, albeit applied here no
farther than to this prefent cafe, fhaketh univerfally the fabrick of government,
tendeth to anarchy and meer confufion, diffolveth families, diffipateth colleges, corporations, armies, overthroweth kingdoms, churches, and whatfoever is now through
the providence of God by authority and power upheld. For whereas God hath fore-
prized things of the greateft weight, and hath therein precifely defined, as well that
which every man muft perform, as that which no man may attempt, leaving all
forts of men in the reft, either to be guided by their own good difcretion, if they

But that it hath power to make fo many holidays as we have, wherein men are commanded to ceafe from their
daily vocations of plowing and exercifing their handicrafts, that I deny to be in the power of the church. For proof
whereof, I will take the fourth commandment, and no other interpretation of it, than Mr. Doctor alloweth of, which is,
that God licenfeth and leaveth it at the liberty of every man to work fix days in the week, fo that he reft the feventh
day. Seeing therefore that the Lord hath left it to all men at liberty, that they might labour, if they think good, fix
days; I fay, the church, nor no man, can take this liberty away from them, and drive them to a neceffary reft of the
body. And if it be lawful to abridge the liberty of the church in this point; and inftead that the Lord faith, fix days
thou mayeft labour, if thou wilt, to fay, thou fhalt not labour fix days; I do not fee, why the church may not as well,
whereas the Lord faith, *Thou fhalt reft the feventh day,* command that thou fhalt not reft the feventh day. For if the church
may reftrain the liberty which God hath given them, it may take away the yoke alfo which God hath put upon them.
And whereas you fay, that notwithftanding this fourth commandment, the *Jews* had certain other feafts which they obferved; indeed, the Lord which gave this general law, might make as many exceptions as he thought good, and fo long
as he thought good. But it followeth not, becaufe the Lord did it, that therefore the church may do it, unlefs it hath
commandment and authority from God fo to do. As when there is any general plague or judgment of God either upon the
church, or coming towards it, the Lord commandeth in fuch a cafe, *Joel* 2. 15. that they fhould fanctify a general
faft, and proclaim *Ghnaffarah,* which fignifieth a prohibition, or forbidding of ordinary works; and is the fame *Hebrew*
word wherewith thofe faft days are noted in the law, wherein they fhould reft. The reafon of which commandment of
the Lord was, that as they abftained that day as much as might be conveniently, from meats; fo they might abftain from
their daily works, to the end they might beftow the whole day in hearing the word of God, and humbling themfelves in
the congregation, confeffing their faults, and defiring the Lord to turn away from his fierce wrath. In this cafe the
church having commandment to make a holiday, may, and ought to do it, as the church which was in *Babylon* did during
the time of their captivity; but where it is deftitute of a commandment, it may not prefume by any decree to reftrain
that liberty which the Lord hath given.

4

be

be free from fubjection to others, or elfe to be ordered by fuch commandments and laws as proceed from thofe fuperiors under whom they live; the patrons of liberty have here made folemn proclamation that all fuch laws and commandments are void, in as much as every man is left to the freedom of his own mind in fuch things as are not either exacted or prohibited by the law of God. And becaufe only in thefe things the pofitive precepts of men have place; which precepts cannot poffibly be given without fome abridgment of their liberty to whom they are given; therefore if the father command the fon, or the husband the wife, or the lord the fervant, or the leader the foldier, or the prince the fubject, to go or ftand, fleep or wake, at fuch times as God himfelf in particular commandeth neither; they are to ftand in defence of the freedom which God hath granted, and to do as themfelves lift, knowing that men may as lawfully command them things utterly forbidden by the law of God, as tie them to any thing which the law of God leaveth free. The plain contradictory whereunto is infallibly certain. Thofe things which the law of God leaveth arbitrary and at liberty, are all fuch fubject to the pofitive laws of men; which laws for the common benefit abridge particular men's liberty in fuch things, as far as the rules of equity will fuffer. This we muft either maintain, or elfe over-turn the world, and make every man his own commander. Seeing then that labour and reft upon any one day of the fix throughout the year, are granted free by the law of God, how exempt we them from the force and power of ecclefiaftical law, except we deprive the world of power to make any ordinance or law at all? Befides, is it probable that God fhould not only allow, but command concurrency of reft with extraordinary occafions of doleful events befalling (peradventure) fome one certain church, or not extending unto many, and not as much as permit or licence the like, when piety, triumphant with joy and gladnefs, maketh folemn commemoration of God's moft rare and unwonted mercies, *fuch efpecially as the whole race of mankind* doth or might participate? Of vacation from labour in times of forrow the only caufe is, for that the general publick prayers of the whole church, and our own private bufinefs, cannot both be followed at once; whereas of reft in the famous folemnities of publick joy, there is both this confideration the fame, and alfo farther a kind of natural repugnancy, which maketh labours (as hath been proved) much more unfit to accompany feftival praifes of God, than offices of humiliation and grief. Again, if we fift what they bring for proof and approbation of reft with fafting, doth it not in all refpects as fully warrant, and as ftrictly command reft whenfoever the church hath equal reafon by feafts and gladfome folemnities to teftify publick thankfulnefs towards God? I would know fome caufe why thofe words of the prophet *Joel, Sanctify a faft, call a fo- lemn affembly*, which words were uttered to the *Jews* in mifery and great diftrefs, fhould more bind the church to do at all times after the like in their like perplexities, than the words of *Mofes* to the fame people in a time of joyful deliverance from mifery, *Remember this day*, may warrant any annual celebration of benefits no lefs importing the good of men; and alfo juftify, as touching the manner and form thereof, what circumftance foever we imitate only in refpect of natural fitnefs or decency, without any *Jewifh* regard to ceremonies, fuch as were properly theirs, and are not by us expedient to be continued. According to the rule of which general directions taken from the law of God, no lefs in the one than the other, the practice of the church commended unto us in holy fcripture, doth not only make for the juftification of black and difmal days (as one of the fathers termeth them) but plainly offereth it felf to be followed by fuch ordinances (if occafion require) as that which *Mordecai* did fometimes devife, *Efther* what lay in her power helped forward, and the reft of the *Jews* eftablifhed for perpetuity; namely, That the fourteenth and fifteenth days of the month *Adar* fhould be every year kept throughout all generations, as days of feafting and joy, wherein they would reft from bodily labour, and what by gifts of charity beftowed upon the poor, what by other liberal figns of amity and love, all teftify their thankful minds towards God, which almoft beyond poffibility had delivered them all, when they all were as men dead. But this decree, they fay, was divine, not ecclefiaftical, as may appear in that there is another decree in another book of fcripture, which decree is plain not to have proceeded from the church's authority, but

from

Joel. 2. 15,

Exod. 1:.

Efth. 9.

a *T. C. lib. 3. pag. 193.* The example out of *Efther* is no fufficient warrant for thefe feafts in queftion. For firft, as in other cafes, fo in this cafe of days, the eftate of chriftiant under the gofpel ought not to be fo ceremonious, as was theirs under the law. Secondly, that which was done there, was done by a fpecial direction of the fpirit of God, either through the miniftry of the prophets which they had, or by fome other extraordinary means, which is not to be followed by us. This may appear by another place, *Zach. 8.* where the *Jews* changed their fafts into feafts, only by the mouth of the Lord, through the miniftry of the prophet. For further proof whereof, firft, I take the 28th Verfe, where it appeareth, that this was an order to endure always, even as long as the other feaft days which were inftituted by the Lord himfelf. So that what abufes foever were of that feaft, yet as a perpetual decree of God it ought to have remained; whereas our churches can make no fuch decree, which may not upon change of times, and other circumftances, be altered. For the other proof hereof I take the laft Verfe: For the prophet contenteth not himfelf with that, that he had rehearfed the decree, as he doth fometimes the decree of prophane kings, but addeth precifely, that as foon as ever the decree was made, it was regifter'd in this book of *Efther,* which is one of the books of canonical fcripture, declaring thereby in what efteem they had it. If it had been of no further authority than our decrees, or than a canon of one of the councils, it had been prefumption to have brought it into the library of the Holy Ghoft. The fum of my anfwer is, That this decree was divine, and not ecclefiaftical only.

from the mouth of the [a] prophet only; and as a poor fimple man fometime was fully perfuaded, that if *Pontus Pilate* had not been a faint, the apoftles would never have fuffered his name to ftand in the Creed; fo thefe men have a ftrong opinion, that becaufe the book of *Efther* is canonical, the decree of *Efther* cannot be poffibly ecclefiaftical. If it were, they ask how the *Jews* could bind themfelves always to keep it, feeing ecclefiaftical laws are mutable? As though the purpofes of men might never intend conftancy in that, the nature whereof is fubject to alteration. Doth the fcripture it felf make mention of any divine commandment? Is the fcripture witnefs of more, than only that *Mordecai* was the author of this cuftom, that by letters written to his brethren the *Jews* throughout all provinces under *Darius* the King of *Perfia,* he gave them charge to celebrate yearly thofe two days, for perpetual remembrance of God's miraculous deliverance and mercy; that the *Jews* hereupon undertook to do it, and made it with general confent an order for perpetuity; that *Efther,* fecondly, by her letters confirmed the fame which *Mordecai* had before decreed; and that finally, the ordinance was written to remain for ever upon record? Did not the *Jews* in provinces abroad obferve at the firft the fourteenth day, the *Jews* in *Sufis* the fifteenth? Were they not all reduced to an uniform order by means of thofe two decrees, and fo every where three days kept; the firft with fafting, in memory of danger; the reft, in token of deliverance, as feftival and joyful days? Was not the firft of thefe three afterwards, the day of forrow and heavinefs, abrogated, when the fame church faw it meet that a better day, a day in memory of like deliverance out of the bloody hands a Mac.15.36. of *Nicanor,* fhould fucceed in the room thereof? But for as much as there is no end of anfwering fruitlefs oppofitions, let it fuffice men of fober minds to know, that the law both of God and nature alloweth generally, days of reft and feftival folemnity to be obferved by way of thankful and joyful remembrance, if fuch miraculous favours be fhewed towards mankind as require the fame; that fuch graces God hath 1 Mac.4.55. beftowed upon his church, as well in latter as in former times; that in fome particulars, when they have fallen out, himfelf hath demanded his own honour, and in the reft hath left it to the wifdom of the church, directed by thofe precedents, and enlightned by other means, always to judge when the like is requifite. About queftions therefore concerning days and times, our manner is not to ftand at bay with the church of God, demanding wherefore the memory of b *Paul* fhould be rather kept than the memory of c *Daniel* : We are content to imagine, it may be perhaps true, that the leaft in the kingdom of Chrift is greater than the greateft of all the prophets of God that have gone before : We never yet faw caufe to defpair, but that the d fimpleft of the people might be taught the right conftruction of as great myfteries as the e name of a faint's day doth comprehend, although the times of the year go on in their wonted courfe : We had rather glorify and blefs God for the fruit we daily behold reaped by fuch ordinances, as his gracious fpirit maketh the ripe wifdom of this national church to bring forth, than vainly boaft of our own peculiar and private inventions, as if the skill of f profitable regiment had left her publick habitation, to dwell in retired manner with fome few men of one livery: We make not our childifh g appeals, fometimes from our own to foreign churches, fometimes from both unto churches ancienter than both are, in

b *Commemoratio Apoftolica paffionis, totius Chriftianitatis magiftra à cunctis jure celebratur.* Cod. l. 3. tit. 12. l. 7.
c *T. C. l. 1. p. 153.* For fo much as the old people did never keep any feaft or holiday for remembrance, either of *Mofes,* &c.
d *T. C. l. 1. p. 153.* The people, when it is called St. *Paul's* day, or the bleffed virgin *Mary's* day, can underftand nothing thereby, but that they are inftituted to the honour of St. *Paul,* or the virgin *Mary,* unlefs they be otherwife taught. And if you fay, let them fo be taught, I have anfwered, that the teaching in this land cannot by any order which is yet taken, come to the moft part of thofe which have drunk this poifon, &c.
e *Scilicet ignorant nos nec Chriftum unquam relinquere, qui pro totius fervandorum mundi falute paffus eft, nec alium quemplam colere poffe. Nam hunc quidem tanquam Filium Dei adoramus, Martyres verò tanquam Difcipulos & Imitatores Domini digne propter infuperabilem in Regem ipforum ac Praeceptorem benevolentiam diligimus, quorum & nos confortes & difcipulos fieri optamus.* Eufeb. Hift. Ecclef. lib. 4. c. 15.
f *T. C. lib. 1. p. 153.* As for all the Commodities, &c.
g *T. C. lib. 1. pag. 154.*

4

in effect always from all others its our own selves; but, as becometh them that follow with all humility the ways of peace, we honour, reverence and obey, in the very next degree unto God, the voice of the church of God wherein we live. They, whose wits are too glorious to fall to so low an ebb, they which have risen and swoln so high that the walls of ordinary rivers are unable to keep them in; they whose wanton contentions in the cause whereof we have spoken, do make all where they go a sea, even they, at their highest float, are constrained both to see and [a] grant, that what their fancy will not yield to like, their judgment cannot with reason condemn. Such is evermore the final victory of all truth, that they which had not the hearts to love her, acknowledge that to hate her they have no cause. Touching those festival days therefore which we now observe, their number being no way felt [b] discommodious to the commonwealth, and their grounds such as hitherto have been shewed; what remaineth, but to keep them throughout all generations holy, severed by manifest notes of differences from other times, adorned with that which most may betoken true, virtuous, and celestial joy? To which intent, because surcease from labour is necessary, yet not so necessary, no not on the sabbath or seventh day it self, but that rather occasions in men's particular affairs, subject to manifest detriment unless they be presently followed, may with very good conscience draw them sometime aside from the ordinary rule, considering the favourable dispensation which our Lord and Saviour groundeth on this axiom, *Man was not made for the sabbath, but the sabbath ordained* **Mark 2. 27.** *for man,* so far forth as concerneth ceremonies annexed to the principal sanctification thereof, howsoever the rigour of the law of *Moses* may be thought to import the contrary; if we regard with what severity the violation of sabbaths hath been sometime punished, a thing perhaps the more requisite at that instant, both because the *Jews*, by reason of their long abode in a place of continual servile toil, could not suddenly be wained and drawn unto contrary offices, without some strong impression of terrour; and also for that there is nothing more needful, than to punish with extremity the first transgressions of those laws that require a more exact observation for many ages to come; therefore as the *Jews*, superstitiously addicted to their sabbaths rest for a long time, not without danger to themselves and [c] obloquy to their very law, did afterwards perceive and amend wisely their former error, not doubting that bodily labours are made by [d] necessity venial, though otherwise especially on that day rest be more convenient: So at all times the voluntary scandalous contempt of that rest from labour, wherewith publickly God is served, we cannot too [e] severely correct and bridle. The emperor [f] *Constantine* having with over-great facility licensed sundays labour in country villages, under that pretence, whereof there may justly no doubt sometime consideration be had, namely, lest any thing which God by his providence hath bestowed should miscarry not being taken in due time; *Leo*, which afterwards saw that this ground would not bear so general and large indulgence as had been granted, doth by a contrary edict both reverse and severely censure his predecessors remissness, saying, *We ordain, according to the true meaning of the Ho-* **Leo Constit.** *ly Ghost and of the apostles thereby directed, that on the sacred day, wherein* **54.** *our own integrity was restored, all do rest and surcease labour; that neither husbandman, nor other, on that day put their hands to forbidden works. For if the* Jews *did so much reverence their sabbath, which was but a shadow of ours, are not we which inhabit the light and truth of grace bound to honour that day which the Lord himself hath honoured, and hath therein delivered us both from dishonour and from death? Are we not bound to keep it singular and inviolable, well contenting our selves with so liberal a grant of the rest, and not encroaching upon that one day which God hath chosen to his own honour?* Were

[a] T. C. l. 1. p. 154. We condemn not the church of *England*, neither in this, nor in other things, which are meet to be reformed. For it is one thing to mislike, another thing to condemn; and it is one thing to condemn something in the church, and another thing to condemn the church for it.

[b] Πολλὰς μὲν θυσίας, πολλὰς ἢ ἐξ ἱερομηνίας ἔπαυσεν· τό τε ῷ πλείστας τῷ ἔτει εἰς αὐτὰς εἶναι... De Claudio dictum apud Dion. l. 60.

[c] Hi vacare consueti sunt septima die, & neque arma portare in prædictis diebus, neque terræ culturam contingere, neque alterius cujusspiam curam habere patiuntur, sed in templis extendentes manus adorare usque ad vesperam soliti sunt. Ingrediente verò in civitatem Ptolemæo Lago cum exercitu & multis hominibus, cum custodire debuerint civitatem, ipsis stultitiam observantibus provincia quidem dominum suscepit amarissimum, Lex verò manifestata est, malam habere solennitatem. Agatharchid. apud Joseph. lib. 1. contra Appion. Vide & Dion. lib. 37.

[d] 1 Mac. 2. 40.

[e] Neh. 13. 15.

[f] Cod. l. 3. tit 12. l. 3.

it not wretchlefs neglect of religion to make that very day common, and to think we
may do with it as with the reft? Imperial laws which had fuch care of hallowing,
efpecially our Lord's day, did not omit to provide that other feftival times might be
kept with vacation from labour, whether they were days appointed on the fudden, as extraordinary occafions fell out, or days which were celebrated yearly
for politick and civil confiderations; or finally, fuch days as chriftian religion
hath ordained in God's church. The joy that fetteth afide labour, difperfeth
thofe things which labour gathereth. For gladnefs doth always rife from a kind
of fruition and happinefs, which happinefs banifheth the cogitation of all want,
it needeth nothing but only the beftowing of that it hath, in as much as the
greateft felicity that felicity hath, is to fpread and enlarge it felf: It cometh
hereby to pafs, that the firft effect of joyfulnefs is to reft, becaufe it feeketh no
more; the next, becaufe it aboundeth, to give. The root of both, is the glorious prefence of that joy of mind, which arifeth from the manifold confiderations of God's unfpeakable mercy, into which confiderations we are led by occafion of facred times. For how could the *Jewifh* congregations of old be put
in mind by their weekly fabbaths, what the world reaped through his goodnefs,
which did of nothing create the world; by their yearly paffover, what farewel
they took of the land of *Egypt*; by their *Pentecoft*, what ordinances, laws and
ftatutes their fathers received at the hands of God; by their feaft of taberna-
cles, with what protection they journeyed from place to place, through fo many
fears and hazards, during the tedious time of forty years travil in the wildernefs; by their annual folemnity of lots, how near the whole feed of *Ifrael* was
unto utter extirpation, when it pleafed that great God which guideth all
things in heaven and earth, fo to change the counfels and purpofes of men,
that the fame hand which had figned a decree, in the opinion both of
them that granted, and of them that procured it, irrevocable, for the general maffacre of man, woman and child, became the buckler of their prefervation, that no hair of their heads might be touched; the fame days which had
been fet for the pouring out of fo much innocent blood, were made the days of
their execution whofe malice had contrived the plot thereof; and the felf-fame
perfons that fhould have endured whatfoever violence and rage could offer, were
employed in the juft revenge of cruelty, to give unto blood-thirfty men the
tafte of their own cup. Or how can the church of Chrift now endure to be fo
much called on, and preached unto, by that
which every [a] dominical day throughout the
year, that which year by year fo many feftival times, [b] if not commanded by the apoftles themfelves, whofe care at that time was
of greater things, yet inftituted either by
fuch [c] univerfal authority as no man, or at
the leaft fuch as we with no reafon may
defpife, do as fometime the holy angels did
from heaven fing, [d] *Glory be unto God on
high, peace on earth, towards men good
will*; (for this in effect is the very fong

T. C. l. 3. tit.
12. Dies fefti.

[a] Matth. 28. 1. Mark 16. 1. Luke 24. 1. John 20. 1.
1 Cor. 16. 2. Apoc. 1. 10.

[b] *Apoftolis propofitum fuit, non ut leges de feftis diebus celebran-
dis fancirent; fed ut recte vivendi rationis & pietatis nobis authores
effent.* Socra. Hift. lib. 5. cap. 21.

[c] *Quæ toto terrarum orbe fervantur, vel ab ipfis Apoftolis vel
conciliis generalibus quorum eft faluberrima in ecclefia authoritas,
ftatuta effe intelligere licet; ficuti quod Domini Paffio & Refur-
rectio, & in Cœlum Afcenfus, & Adventus Spiritus Sancti, an-
niverfaria folennitate celebrantur.* Auguft. Epift. 118.

[d] Luke 2. 14.

that all chriftian feafts do apply as their feveral occafions require) how fhould
the days and times continually thus inculcate what God hath done, and we refufe to agnize the benefit of fuch remembrances; that very benefit which caufed
Mofes to acknowledge thofe guides of day and night, the fun and moon which
enlighten the world, not more profitable to nature by giving all things life, than
they are to the church of God by occafion of the ufe they have in regard of
the appointed feftival times? that which the head of all philofophers hath faid
of women, If they be good, the half of the common-wealth is happy wherein
they are; the fame we may fitly apply to times; well to celebrate thefe
religious and facred days, is to fpend the flower of our time happily. They are
the fplendor and outward dignity of our religion, forcible witneffes of ancient truth,
provocations to the exercifes of all piety, fhadows of our endlefs felicity in heaven,
on earth everlafting records and memorials; wherein they which cannot be drawn
to hearken unto that we teach, may only by looking upon that we do, in a manner read whatfoever we believe.

I

72. The matching of contrary things together is a kind of illuſtration to both. Having therefore ſpoken thus much of feſtival days, the next that offer themſelves to hand are the days of penſive humiliation and ſorrow. Faſtings are either of men's own free and voluntary accord, as their particular devotion doth move them thereunto; or elſe they are publickly enjoined in the church, and required at the hands of all men. There are which altogether diſallow not the former kind; and the latter they greatly commend, ſo that it be upon extraordinary occaſions only, and after one certain manner exerciſed. But yearly or weekly faſts, ſuch as ours in the church of *England,* they allow no farther than as the temporal ſtate of the land doth require the ſame, for the maintenance of ſea-faring men and preſervation of cattle; becauſe the decay of the one, and the waſte of the other, could not well be prevented but by a politick order appointing ſome ſuch uſual change of diet as ours is. We are therefore the rather to make it manifeſt in all men's eyes, that ſet times of faſting, appointed in ſpiritual conſiderations to be kept by all ſorts of men., took not their beginning either from *Montanus,* or any other whoſe hereſies may prejudice the credit and due eſtimation thereof, but have their ground in the law of nature, are allowable in God's ſight, were in all ages heretofore, and may till the world's end be obſerved, not without ſingular uſe and benefit. Much hurt hath grown to the church of God through a falſe imagination that faſting ſtandeth men in no ſtead for any ſpiritual reſpect, but only to take down the frankneſs of nature, and to tame the wildneſs of fleſh. Whereupon the world being bold to ſurfeit,

Of days appointed as well for ordinary, as for extraordinary faſts in the church of God.

T. C. lib. 1. *pag.* 30. I will not enter now to diſcuſs, whether it were well done to faſt in all places according to the cuſtom of the place. You oppoſe *Ambroſe* and *Auguſtin,* I could oppoſe *Ignatius* and *Tertullian;* whereof the one faith, it is *nefas,* a deteſtable thing to faſt upon the Lord's day; the other, that it is to kill the Lord, *Tertul. de Coron. Mil. Ignatius, Epiſt. ad Philippen.* And although *Ambroſe* and *Auguſtin,* being private men at *Rome,* would have ſo done; yet it followeth not, that if they had been citizens and miniſters there, they would have done it. And if they had done ſo, yet it followeth not, but that they would have ſpoken againſt that appointment of days, and ſ 10 7.olas of faſting, whereof *Euſebius* faith, that *Montanus* was the firſt Author. I ſpeak of that which they ought to have done. For otherwiſe I know; they both thought corruptly of faſting; when as the one faith, It was a remedy or reward tb faſt other days, but in *Lent* not to faſt was ſin; and the other asketh, What ſalvation we can obtain, if we blot not out our ſins by faſting, ſeeing that the ſcripture faith, That faſting and alms doth deliver from ſin; and therefore calleth them new teachers, that ſhut out the merit of faſting. *Auguſ. de Temp.* 62. *Serm. Ambr. lib.* 10. *Epiſt.*

doth now bluſh to faſt, ſuppoſing that men when they faſt, do rather bewray a diſeaſe than exerciſe a virtue. I much wonder what they who are thus perſuaded do think, what conceit they have concerning the faſts of the patriarchs, the prophets, the apoſtles, our Lord Jeſus Chriſt himſelf. The affections of joy and grief are ſo knit unto all the actions of man's life, that whatſoever we can do, or may be done unto us, the ſequel thereof is continually the one or the other affection. Wherefore conſidering that they which grieve and joy as they ought, cannot poſſibly otherwiſe live than as they ſhould, the church of Chriſt, the moſt abſolute and perfect ſchool of all virtue, hath by the ſpecial direction of God's good Spirit, hitherto always inured men from their infancy, partly with days of feſtival exerciſe for the framing of the one affection, and partly with times of a contrary ſort for the perfecting of the other. Howbeit, over and beſides this, we muſt note, that as reſtfting, ſo faſting likewiſe attendeth ſometimes no leſs upon the actions of the higher than upon the affections of the lower part of the mind. Faſting, faith *Tertullian,* is a work of reverence towards God. The end thereof, ſometimes elevation of mind; ſometimes the purpoſe thereof clean contrary. The cauſe why *Moſes* in the mount did ſo long faſt, was mere divine ſpeculation; the cauſe why *David,* [a] humiliation. Our life is [b] a mixture of good with evil. When we are partakers of good things, we joy; neither can we but grieve at the contrary. If that befal us which maketh glad, our feſtival ſolemnities declare our rejoicing to be in him whoſe mere undeſerved mercy is the

[a] Tertul. de jejun. *Neque enim cibi tempus in periculo: Semper inedia mæroris ſequela eſt.*

[b] Μ.σθ.ις ά' ιωολαΣίϳω + αχγαϳοr κ̣ ά.μιγ̄ λύτα̣ ια.ρθr απ' ιεγκὺ κ̣ϳαΣαίνοιs θȝι ϯ γ.λῶ, α.λλ' ιγκακιγται κ̣ α.μφοῖr ιΙ γ̄ ειαπs ι μτηρ το α.σ.θ̣αίϊων γιͱ@ λυπαῖs κ̣ ιδὸναιs κ̣ α.χ-θ̣σιν α.ι̣δ.και ημεφινεῖs, παρ.αιιπεʓε ϳ κ̣ α.μφιτοιθ@ ουτοιs, α.-δικόϳαι πατι κ̣ γ.αλε.θ.ιδοιται ϯ ψυχϳlῶ ιϳγ.αιθ.ιται. Philo. l. de Abrah.

author of all happineſs; if any thing be either imminent or preſent which we ſhun, our watchings, faſtings, cries and tears, are unfeigned teſtimonies that our ſelves we condemn as the only cauſes of our own miſery, and do all acknowledge him no leſs inclinable than uſeth to ſave. And becauſe as the memory of the one, though paſt, reneweth gladneſs; ſo the other, called again to mind, doth make the wound of our juſt remorſe to bleed anew; which wound needeth often touching the more, for that we are generally more apt to kalendar ſaints than ſinners days; therefore there is in the church a care not to iterate the one alone, but to have frequent repetition of the other. Never to ſeek after God ſaving only

when

when either the crib or the whip doth conftrain, were brutifh fervility, and a great derogation to the worth of that which is moft predominant in man, if fometimes it had not a kind of voluntarily acceſs to God, and of conference, as it were, with God, all thefe inferior confiderations laid afide. In which fe-queftration, for as much as higher cogitations do naturally drown and bury all inferior cares, the mind may as well forget natural both food and fleep, by being carried above it ſelf with ferious and heavenly meditation, as by being caft down with heavineſs, drowned and ſwallowed up of ſorrow. Albeit therefore, concerning *Jewiſh* abftinence from certain kinds of meats as being unclean, the apoftle doth teach, that *the kingdom of heaven is not meat nor drink*, that *food commendeth us not unto God*, whether we take it, or abftain from it; that if we eat, we are not thereby the more acceptable in his fight; nor the leſs, if we eat not: His purpofe notwithftanding was far from any intent to derogate from that fafting, which is no fuch fcrupulous abftinence as only refufeth fome kinds of meats and drinks, left they make them unclean that tafte them; but an abftinence where-by we either interrupt, or otherwife abridge the care of our bodily fuftenance, to fhew by this kind of outward exercife the ferious intention of our minds fixed on heavenlier and better defires, the earneft hunger and thirft whereof depriveth the body of thofe ufual contentments, which otherwife are not denied unto it. Thefe being in nature the firft caufes that induce fafting, the next thing which fol-loweth to be confidered, is the ancient practice thereof amongft the *Jews*. Touch-ing whofe private voluntary fafts the precept which our Saviour gave them was, *When ye faft, look not ſowre, as hypocrites: For they disfigure their faces, that they might ſeem to men to faſt. Verily I ſay unto you, they have their reward. When thou fafteſt, anoint thy head, and waſh thy face, that thou ſeem not unto men to faſt, but unto thy Father which is in ſecret, and thy Father which ſeeth in ſecret, will reward thee openly.* Our Lord and Saviour would not teach the man-ner of doing, much leſs propofe a reward for doing that which were not both holy and acceptable in God's fight. The *Pharifees* weekly bound themfelves unto double fafts, neither are they for this reproved. Often fafting, which was a virtue in *John's* difciples, could not in them of it ſelf be a vice; and therefore not the oftenneſs of their fafting, but their hypocrify therein was blamed. Of publick en-joined fafts [a], upon caufes extraordinary, the examples in fcripture are fo fat frequent, that they need no particular rehearfal. Publick ex-traordinary faftings were fometimes for [b] one only day, fometimes for [c] three, fometimes for [d] feven. Touching fafts not appointed for any fuch extraordinary caufes, but either year-ly, or monthly, or weekly obferved and kept: Firft, upon the [e] ninth day of that month, the tenth whereof was the feaft of expiation, they were commanded of God that every foul, year by year, fhould afflict it ſelf. Their yearly fafts every fourth month, in regard of the city of *Jerufalem* entered by the enemy; every fifth, for the memory of the overthrow of their temple; every feventh, for the treacherous deftruction and death of *Gedaliah*, the very laft ftay which they had to lean unto in their great-eft mifery; every tenth, in remembrance of the time when fiege began firft to be laid againft them. All thefe not commanded by God himfelf, but ordained by a publick conftitution of their own, the prophet [f] *Zachary* expreſly toucheth. That St. *Jerome*, following the tradition of the *Hebrews*, doth make the firft a memo-rial of the breaking of thofe two tables, when *Mofes* defcended from mount *Si-nai*; the fecond, a memorial as well of God's indignation, condemning them to forty years travel in the defart, as of his wrath in permitting *Chaldeans* to wafte, burn and deftroy their city; the laft a memorial of heavy tidings, brought out of *Jewry* to *Ezekiel* and the reft, which lived as captives in foreign parts; the difference is not of any moment, confidering that each time of forrow is naturally evermore a regifter of all fuch grievous events as have hapned either in, or near about the fame time. To thefe I might add [g] fundry other fafts, about twenty in number, ordain-ed amongft them by like occafions, and obferved in like manner, befides their weekly abftinence, *Mondays* and *Thurfdays*, throughout the whole year. When men fafted, it was not always after one and the fame fort; but either by depriving them-felves

John 4. 34.

Rom. 14. 17.

Matth. 6. 16.

[a] 2 Chron. 20. Jerem. 36. Ezra 8. 1 Sam. 7.
[b] Jud. 20. 26. [c] 2 Mac. 13. 12. [d] 2 Mac. 13. 12. [e] 1 Sam. 31. 13. 1 Chron. 10. 12.
[f] Levit. 23. Levit. 16. *Philo de bujus feſti jejunio ita lo-quitur. Ὁυ σιτίον ἣ ποτὸν ἴξιτι προσενέγκαδαι, ἐγ-δικριτὶ ὅπως διανοίαις μηδενὸς ἐσοχλᾶντῶ μηδὲ ἐμποδίζοντῶ σωμα-τικᾶ πάθεσι ὁπόια φιλᾶ συμβαίνειν ἐκ πλησμονῆς, ἑορτάζωσιν ἱλασκόμενοι ἣ πατέρα τᾶ παντὸς ἱεραῖς εὐχαῖς. ἣ ἂν ἀμνηστίαν ἠδὺ πάλαιαῖ ἁμαρτημάτων, κτῆσιν ἣ ἀπόλαυσιν νέων ἀγαθῶν εἰώθασιν αἰτεῖσθαι.* Pag. 447.

g Zach. 8. 16.

Exod. 32.
Numb. 14.

a Vide Riber.
lib. 5. c. 21.
Dan. 10. 2, 3.

4

selves wholly of all food, during the time that their fasts continued; or by abating both the quantity and kind of diet. We have of the one, a plain example in the *Ninevites* fasting, and as plain a precedent for the other in the prophet *Daniel*; *I was* (saith he) *in heaviness for three weeks of days; I eat no pleasant bread, neither tasted flesh nor wine.* Their tables, when they gave themselves to fasting, had not that usual furniture of such dishes as do cherish blood with blood; but [a] for food, they had bread; for suppage, salt; and for sawce, herbs. Whereunto the apostle may be thought to allude, saying, *One believeth he may eat all things, another which is weak* (and maketh a conscience of keeping those customs which the *Jews* observe) *eateth herbs.* This austere repast they took in the evening after abstinence the whole day : For to forfeit a noon's meal, and then to recompence themselves at night, was not their use. Nor did they ever accustom themselves on sabbaths, or festival days to fast. And yet it may be a question, whether in some sort they did not always fast the sabbath. Their fastings were partly in token of penitency, humiliation, grief and sorrow, partly in sign of devotion and reverence towards God. Which second consideration (I dare not peremptorily and boldly affirm any thing) might induce to abstain till noon, as their manner was on fasting days to do till night. May it not very well be thought, that hereunto the sacred [b] scripture doth give some secret kind of testimony? *Josephus* is plain, that the sixth hour (the day they divided into twelve) was wont on the sabbath always to call them home unto meat. Neither is it improbable, but that the [c] heathens did therefore so often upbraid them with fasting on that day. Besides, they which found so great fault with our Lord's disciples, for rubbing a few ears of corn in their hands on the sabbath day, are not unlikely to have aimed also at the same mark. For neither was the bodily pain so great, that it should offend them in that respect, and the very manner of defence which our Saviour there useth, is more direct and literal to justify the breach of the *Jewish* custom in fasting, than in working at that time. Finally, the apostles afterwards themselves, when God first gave them the gift of tongues, whereas some in disdain and spight termed grace drunkenness, it being then the day of *Pentecost*, and but only a fourth part of the day spent, they use this as an argument against the other cavil, [d] *These men,* saith *Peter, are not drunk, as you suppose, since as yet the third hour of the day is not over-past.* Howbeit, leaving this in suspence, as a thing not altogether certainly known, and to come from *Jews* to *Christians,* we find that of private voluntary fastings, the apostle St. *Paul* speaketh more than once. And (saith *Tertullian*) they are sometime commanded throughout the church, *Ex aliqua sollicitudinis Ecclesiastica causa,* the care and fear of the church so requiring. It doth not appear, Col. 4. 4. that the apostles ordained any set and certain days to be generally kept of all. Notwithstanding, forasmuch as Christ hath fore-signified, that when himself should be taken from them, his absence would soon make them apt to fast, it seemeth, that even as the first festival day appointed to be kept of the church, was the day of our Lord's return from the dead, so the first sorrowful and mournful day, was that which we now observe in memory of his departure out of this world. And because there could be no abatement of grief till they saw him raised, whose death was the occasion of their heaviness; therefore the day he lay in the Sepulchre, hath been also kept and observed as a weeping day. The custom of fasting these two days before *Easter,* is undoubtedly most ancient; insomuch that *Ignatius* not thinking him a Ignat. Epist. Catholick Christian man which did not abhor, and (as the state of the church was ad Philip. then) avoid fasting on the *Jews* sabbath, doth notwithstanding except for ever, that one Sabbath or *Saturday* which falleth out to be the *Easter* Eve, as with us it always doth, and did sometimes also with them which kept at that time their *Easter* the fourteenth day of *March,* as the custom of the *Jews* was. It came afterwards to be an order, that even as the day of Christ's resurrection, so the other two, in memory of his death and burial, were weekly. But this, when St. *Ambrose* lived, had not as yet taken place throughout all churches, no not in *Milan,* where himself was bishop. And for that cause he saith, that although at *Rome* he observed the *Saturday's*

[a] *Puram & sine animalibus cœnam.* Apul. in Asclep. in fine. *Pastum & potum pura nosse, non ventris scilicet sed animæ causa.* Tertul. de Pœnit. Vide Phil. lib. de vita contempl. Rom. 14. 2. Hieron. lib. 2. contr. Jovinian. Judith 8. 6. R. Mos. in Misne Tora. lib. 3. Qui est de tempor. cap. de Sab. & cap. de Jejun.

[b] Nehem. 8. 3. 12. *Hora sexta qua sabbatis nostris ad prandium vocare solet, supervenit.* Joseph. lib. de vita sua.

[c] *Sabbata Judæorum à Mose in omne ævum jejunio dicata.* Justin. lib. 36. *Ne Judæus quidem, mi Tiberi, tam libenter Sabbati jejunium servat, quàm ego hodie servavi.* Sueton. in Octav. c. 76.

[d] Acts 2. 15.

1 Cor. 7. 5.
2 Cor. 6. 5.
& 11. 27.
Col. 4. 4.

day's faſt, becauſe ſuch was then the cuſtom in *Rome*, neverthelefs in his own church at home he did otherwiſe. The churches which did not obſerve that day, had another inſtead thereof; which was the *Wedneſday*, for that when they judged it meet to have weekly a day of humiliation, beſides that whereon our Saviour ſuffered death, it ſeemed beſt to make their choice of that day eſpecially, whereon the *Jews* are thought to have firſt contrived their treaſon, together with *Judas*, againſt Chriſt. So that the inſtituting and ordaining both of theſe, and of all other times of like exerciſe, is as the church ſhall judge expedient for mens good. And concerning every chriſtian man's duty herein, ſurely that which *Auguſtin* and *Ambroſe* are before alledged to have done, is ſuch as all men favouring equity muſt needs allow and follow, if they affect peace. As for their ſpecified errors, I will not in this place diſpute, whether voluntary faſting with a virtuous purpoſe of mind, be any medicinable remedy of evil, or a duty acceptable unto God, and in the world to come, even rewardable as other offices are which proceed from chriſtian piety; whether wilfully to break and deſpiſe the wholeſome laws of the church herein; be a thing which offendeth God; whether truly it may not be ſaid, that penitent both weeping and faſting are means to blot out ſin, means whereby through God's unſpeakable and undeſerved mercy, we obtain or procure our ſelves pardon; which attainment unto any gracious benefit by him beſtowed, the phraſe of antiquity uſeth to expreſs by the name of merit; but if either St. *Auguſtin*, or St. *Ambroſe*, have taught any wrong opinion, ſeeing they which reprove them are not altogether free from error, I hope they will think it no error in us ſo to cenſure mens ſmaller faults, that their virtues be not thereby generally prejudiced. And if in churches abroad, where we are not ſubject to power or juriſdiction, diſcretion ſhould teach us for peace and quietneſs ſake, to frame our ſelves to other men's example, is it meet that at home where our freedom is leſs, our boldneſs ſhould be more? Is it our duty to oppugn, in the churches whereof we are miniſters, the rites and cuſtoms which in foreign churches piety and modeſty did teach us as ſtrangers not to oppugn, but to keep without ſhew of contradiction or diſlike? Why oppoſe they the name of a miniſter in this caſe, unto the ſtate of a private man? Doth their order exempt them from obedience to laws? That which their office and place requireth, is to ſhew themſelves paterns of reverend ſubjection, not authors and maſters of contempt towards ordinances; the ſtrength whereof, when they ſeek to weaken, they do but in truth diſcover to the world their own imbecillities, which a great deal wiſelier they might conceal. But the practice of the church of Chriſt we ſhall by ſo much the better both underſtand and love, if to that which hitherto hath been ſpoken there be ſomewhat added for more particular declaration, how hereticks have partly abuſed faſts, and partly bent themſelves againſt the lawful uſe thereof in the church of God.

'Εἰ τις κυρια-
ακὴ ἢ σάββα-
τον νηστευ-
ελὰν ἑνὸς
σαββάτε, ἑ-
τὸς χριστοκ-
τόνος ὑπάρ-
χει. *Epiſt.*
ad Philip.
* *Vide Irenæ.*
lib. 1. *cap.* 20.
21, 22, 23, 24,
25. *Epiph Hæ-*
ref. 20. 21, 22,
23, 24, 27, 28,
& 41, 42.
Vide Canon.
Apoſt. 55. Whereas therefore *Ignatius* hath ſaid, if any keep *Sundays* or *Saturdays* faſts (one only *Saturday* in the year excepted) that man is no better than a murtherer of Chriſt; the cauſe of ſuch his earneſtneſs at that time, was the impiety of certain hereticks, which thought * that this world being corruptible, could not be made but by a very evil author. And therefore as the *Jews* did, by the feſtival ſolemnity of their ſabbath, rejoice in the God that created the world, as in the author of all goodneſs; ſo thoſe hereticks, in hatred of the maker of the world, ſorrowed, wept and faſted on that day, as being the birth-day of all evil. And as chriſtian men of ſound belief, did ſolemnize the *Sunday* in joyful memory of Chriſt's reſurrection, ſo likewiſe at the ſelf-ſame time ſuch hereticks as denied his reſurrection, did the contrary to them which held it; when the one ſort rejoiced, the other faſted. Againſt thoſe hereticks which have urged perpetual abſtinence from certain meats, as being in their very nature unclean, the church hath ſtill bent her ſelf as an enemy; St. *Paul* giving charge to take heed of them, which under any ſuch opinion ſhould utterly forbid the uſe of meats or drinks. The apoſtles themſelves forbad ſome, as the order taken at *Jeruſalem* declareth. But the cauſe of their ſo doing we all know. Again, when *Tertullian*, together with ſuch as were his followers, began to montanize, and pretending to perfect the ſeverity of chriſtian diſcipline, brought in ſundry unaccuſtomed days of faſting, continued their faſts a great deal longer, and made them more rigorous than the uſe of the church had been; the minds of men being ſomewhat moved at ſo great, and ſo ſudden novelty, the cauſe was preſently enquired into. After notice taken how the *Montaniſts* held theſe additions to be ſupplements of the goſpel, whereunto the ſpirit of prophecy did now mean to put, as it were, the laſt hand, and was therefore newly deſcended upon *Montanus*, whoſe orders all chriſtian men

were

were no lefs to obey, than the laws of the apoftles themfelves; this abftinence the church abhorred likewife, and that juftly. Whereupon *Tertullian* proclaiming even open war to the church, maintained *Montanifm*, wrote a book in defence of the new faft, and intituled the fame, *A treatife of fafting againft the opinion of the carnal fort.* In which treatife neverthelefs, becaufe fo much is found and good, as doth either generally concern the ufe, or in particular declare the cuftom of the churches fafting in thofe times, men are not to reject whatfoever is alledged out of that book, for confirmation of the truth. His error difclofeth it felf in thofe places, where he defendeth his fafts to be duties neceffary for the whole church of Chrift to obferve as commanded by the Holy Ghoft, and that with the fame authority from whence all other apoftolical ordinances came, both being the laws of God himfelf, without any other diftinction or difference, faving only, that he which before had declared his will by *Paul* and *Peter*, did now farther reveal the fame by *Montanus* alfo. *Againft us ye pretend,* faith *Tertullian, that the publick orders which chriftianity is bound to keep, were delivered at the firft, and that no new thing is to be added thereunto. Stand, if you can, upon this point; for behold, I challenge you for fafting more than at* Eafter *your felves. But in fine ye anfwer, that thefe things are to be done as eftablifhed by the voluntary appointment of men, and not by virtue or force of any divine commandment. Well then (*he addeth*) ye have removed your firft footing, and gone beyond that which was delivered, by doing more than was at the firft impofed upon you. You fay, you muft do that which your own judgments have allowed: We require your obedience to that which God himfelf doth inftitute. Is it not ftrange, that men to their own will fhould yield that, which to God's commandment they will not grant? Shall the pleafure of men prevail more with you, than the power of God himfelf?* Thefe places of *Tertullian* for fafting have worthily been put to filence. And as worthily *Aerius* condemned for oppofition againft fafting. The one endeavoured to bring in fuch fafts as the church ought not to receive; the other, to overthrow fuch as already it had received and did obferve: The one was plaufible unto many, by feeming to hate carnal loofenefs and riotous excefs much more than the reft of the world did; the other drew hearers, by pretending the maintenance of chriftian liberty: The one thought his caufe very ftrongly upheld, by making invective declamations with a pale and withered countenance againft the church, by filling the ears of his ftarved hearers with fpeech fuitable to fuch mens humours, and by telling them, no doubt, to their marvellous contentment and liking; *Our new prophecies are refufed, they are defpifed. Is it becaufe* Montanus *doth preach fome other God, or diffolve the Gofpel of Jefus Chrift, or overthrow any canon of faith and hope? No, our crime is, we teach that men ought to faft more often than marry; the beft feaft-maker is with them the perfecteft faint, they are affuredly mere fpirit; and therefore thefe our corporal devotions pleafe them not.* Thus the one for *Montanus* and his fuperftition: The other in a clean contrary tune againft the religion of the church; *Thefe fet-fafts away with them, for they are* Jewifh, *and bring men under the yoke of fervitude: If I will faft, let me chufe my time, that chriftian liberty be not abridged.* Hereupon their glory was to faft, efpecially upon the *Sunday,* becaufe the order of the church was on that day not to faft. *On church fafting days, and efpecially the week before* Eafter, *when with us* (faith *Epiphanius*) *cuftom admitteth nothing but lying down upon the earth, abftinence from flefhly delights and pleafures, forrowfulnefs, dry and unfavoury diet, prayer, watching, fafting, all the medicines which holy affections can minifter; they are up betimes to take in of the ftrongeft for the belly, and when their veins are well fwoln, they make themfelves mirth with laughter at this our fervice, wherein we are perfuaded we pleafe God.* By this of *Epiphanius* it doth appear, not only what faftings the church of Chrift in thofe times ufed, but alfo what other parts of difcipline were together therewith in force, according to the ancient ufe and cuftom of bringing all men at certain times to a due confideration and an open humiliation of themfelves. Two kinds there were of publick penitency; the one belonging to notorious offenders, whofe open wickednefs had been fcandalous; the other appertaining to the whole church, and unto every feveral perfon whom the fame containeth. It will be anfwered, that touching this latter kind, it may be exercifed well enough by men in private. No doubt but penitency is as prayer, a thing acceptable unto God, be it in publick or in fecret. Howbeit, as in the one, if men were wholly left to their own voluntary meditations in their clofets, and not drawn by laws and orders unto the open affemblies of the church, that there they may join with others in prayer; it may be foon

Epiph. Heref. 75.

con-

conjectured what christian devotion that way would come unto in a short time : Even so in the other, we are by sufficient experience taught, how little it booteth to tell men of washing away their sins with tears of repentance, and so to leave them altogether unto themselves. O Lord, what heaps of grievous transgressions have we committed, the best and perfectest, the most righteous amongst us all ; and yet clean pass them over unsorrowed for, and unrepented of, only because the church hath forgotten utterly how to bestow her wonted times of discipline, wherein the publick example of all was unto every particular person a most effectual means to put them often in mind, and even in a manner to draw them to that which now we all quite and clean forget, as if penitency was no part of a christian man's duty. Again, besides our private offences, which ought not thus loosely to be overslipt ; suppose we the body and corporation of the church so just, that at no time it needeth to shew it self openly cast down, in regard of those faults and transgressions, which though they do not properly belong unto any one, had notwithstanding a special sacrifice appointed for them in the law of *Moses*; and being common to the whole society which containeth all, must needs so far concern every man in particular, as at some time in solemn manner to require acknowledgment with more than daily and ordinary testifications of grief. There could not hereunto a fitter preamble be devised, than that memorable commination set down in the book of common prayer, if our practice in the rest were suitable. The head already so well drawn, doth but wish a proportionable body. And by the preface to that very part of the *English* Liturgy it may appear, how at the first setting down thereof no less was intended. For so we are to interpret the meaning of those words, wherein *restitution of the primitive church discipline is greatly wished for,* touching the manner of publick penance in time of *Lent.* Wherewith some being not much acquainted, but having framed in their minds the conceit of a new discipline far unlike to that of old, they make themselves believe, it is undoubtedly this their discipline which at the first was so much desired. They have long pretended, that the whole scripture is plain for them. If now the communion book make for them too (I well think the one doth as much as the other) it may be hoped, that being found such a well-wisher unto their cause, they will more favour it than they have done. Having therefore hitherto spoken both of festival days, and so much of solemn fasts, as may reasonably serve to shew the ground thereof in the law of nature ; the practice partly appointed, and partly allowed of God in the *Jewish* church ; the like continued in the church of Christ ; together with the sinister oppositions, either of hereticks erroneously abusing the same, or of others thereat quarrelling without cause, we will only collect the chiefest points as well of resemblance as of difference between them, and so end. First, in this they agree, that because nature is the general root of both, therefore both have been always common to the church with infidels and heathen men. Secondly, they also herein accord, that as oft as joy is the cause of the one, and grief the well-spring of

^{Con. Laod. c.} the other, they are incompatible. A third degree of affinity between them is, that ^{51. 52. Vetat Natalitia} neither being acceptable to God of it self, but both tokens of that which is accepta- ^{Martyrum in} ble, their approbation with him must necessarily depend on that which they ought to ^{Quadragesima celebrari.} import and signify : So that if herein the mind dispose not itself aright, whether we ^{a Isa. 1. 13.} ^a rest or ^b fast, we offend. A fourth thing common unto them, is, that the greatest ^{b Isa. 58. 3.} part of the world hath always grosly and palpably offended in both ; infidels, because they did all in relation to false gods ; godless, sensual and careless minds, for that there is in them no constant, true and sincere affection towards those things which are pretended by such exercise ; yea, certain flattering oversights there are, wherewith sundry, and they not of the worst sort, may be easily in these cases led away, even through abundance of love and liking to that which must be embraced by all means, but with caution, in as much as the very admiration of saints, whether we celebrate their glory, or follow them in humility ; whether we laugh or weep, mourn or rejoyce with them, is (as in all things the affection of love) apt to deceive ; and ^{c 1 Tim. 4. 8.} doth therefore need the more to be directed by a watchful guide, seeing there is ma- ^{d Ecclef. 12.} nifestly both ways, even in them whom we honour, that which we are to observe ^{13.} ^{Isa. 58. 6, 7.} and shun. The best have not still been sufficiently mindful, that God's very angels ^{Rom. 14. 17.} in heaven, are but angels ; and that bodily exercise, considered ^c in it self, is no ^{James 1. 27.} ^{Heb. 12. 14.} great matter. Finally, seeing that both are ordinances well devised for the good of ^{Ephef. 2. 4.} man, and yet not man created purposely for them as for ^d other offices of virtue, ^{e Eufeb. Ec- clef. Hist. lib.} whereunto God's immutable law for ever tieth ; it is but equity to wish or admonish ^{5. c. 23.} that where, by uniform order , they are not as yet received , the example of ^e *Victor's*

extre-

extremity in the one, and of ᵃ *John's* difciple's curiofity in the other, be not follow- ᵃ Matth. 9.
14.
Col. 2. 16.
ed; yea, where they are appointed by law, that notwithftanding we avoid judaifm :
And, as in feftival days, mens neceflities for matter of labour, fo in times of fafting,
regard be had to their imbecillities, left they fhould fuffer harm, doing good. Thus
therefore we fee how thefe two cuftoms are in divers refpects equal. But of fafting,
the ufe and exercife, though lefs pleafant, is by fo much more requifite than the
other, as grief of neceflity is a more familiar gueft than the contrary paflion of mind,
albeit gladnefs to all men be naturally more welcome. For firft, we our felves do
many more things amifs than well, and the fruit of our own ill doing is remorfe,
becaufe nature is confcious to it felf that it fhould do the contrary. Again, forafmuch as the world ᴄᵥ̈ᵉᵣ-aboundeth with malice, and few are delighted in doing good
to other men, there is no man fo feldom croft as pleafured at the the hands of others;
whereupon it cannot be chofen but every man's woes muft double, in that refpect,
the number and meafure of his delights. Befides, concerning the very choice which Matth. 6. 4.
Ecclef. 7. 4.
oftentimes we are to make, our corrupt inclination well confidered, there is caufe
why our Saviour fhould account them the happieft that do moft mourn, and why
Solomon might judge it better to frequent mourning than feafting-houfes : not better
fimply and in it felf (for then would nature that way incline) but in regard of us
and our common weaknefs better. *Job* was not ignorant that his childrens banquets, Job 1. 5.
though tending to amity, needed facrifice. Neither doth any of us all need to be 'Εν μιϟ δ'
μάϊνομ φ ᷤ
λουκίϟῳ τᷤ
ἡδῆ᷆ καὶ τᷤ᷄
ᾗ δορῦῳ, ἡ ᷄δ
ἀδ᷍ αϟι ϟει-
ρουϟι ᵃυ᷆ι.
Arif. Eth. 2.
ᶜᵃᵖ. 13.
taught that in things which delight we eafily fwerve from mediocrity, and are not ea-
fily led by a right direct line. On the other fide, the fores and difeafes of mind
which inordinate pleafure breedeth, are by dolour and grief cured. For which caufe
as all offences ufe to feduce by pleafing, fo all punifhments endeavour by vexing to
reform tranfgreflions. We are of our own accord apt enough to give entertainment
to things delectable, but patiently to lack what flefh and blood doth defire, and by
virtue to forbear what by nature we covet; this no man attaineth unto but with labour and long practice. From hence it arifeth that in former Ages, abftinence and
fafting more than ordinary, was always a fpecial branch of their praife in whom it
could be obferved and known, were they fuch as continually gave themfelves to au- Ecclef. 9. 7.
Pfal. 35. 13.
ftere life; or men that took often occafions in private vertuous refpects, to lay *So-*
lomon's counfel afide, *Eat thy bread with joy,* and to be followers of *David's* example, which faith, *I humbled my foul with fafting*; or but they who otherwife worthy
of no great commendation, have made of hunger, fome their gain, fome their phyfick, fome their art, that by maftering fenfual appetites without conftraint, they might
grow able to endure hardnefs whenfoever need fhould require: For the body accuftomed to emptinefs, pineth not away fo foon as having ftill ufed to fill it felf. Many fingular effects there are which fhould make fafting even in publick confiderations
the rather to be accepted. For I prefume we are not altogether without experience,
how great their advantage is in martial enterprizes, that lead armies of men trained
in a fchool of abftinence. It is therefore noted at this day in fome, that patience of
hunger and thirft hath given them many victories; in others, that becaufe if they
want, there is no man able to rule them, nor they in plenty to moderate themfelves,
he which can either bring them to hunger or over-charge them, is fure to make
them their own overthrow. What nation foever doth feel thefe dangerous inconveniencies, may know that floth and fulnefs in peaceable times at home, is the caufe
thereof, and the remedy a ftrict obfervation of that part of chriftian difcipline, which
teacheth men in practice of ghoftly warfare againft themfelves, thofe things that afterwards may help them, juftly affaulting or ftanding in lawful defence of themfelves
againft others. The very purpofe of the church of God, both in the number and in
the order of her fafts, hath been not only to preferve thereby throughout all ages
the remembrance of miferies heretofore fuftained, and of the caufes in our felves
out of which they have rifen, that men confidering the one might fear the other the
more, but farther alfo to temper the mind, left contrary affections coming in place,
fhould make it too profufe and diffolute; in which refpect it feemeth that fafts have
been fet as ufhers of feftival days, for preventing of thofe diforders as much as might
be; wherein notwithftanding, the world always will deferve, as it hath done, Valde abfur-
dum eft nimia,
faturitate velle
blame; becaufe fuch evils being not poffible to be rooted out, the moft we can do, honorare mar-
is in keeping them low, and (which is chiefly the fruit we look for) to create in tyrem, quem
fcias Deo fla-
the minds of them a love towards a frugal and fevere life, to undermine the palaces
of wantonnefs; to plant parfimony as nature, where riotoufnefs hath been ftudied; cuiffe jejuniis.
to harden whom pleafure would melt; and to help the tumours which always ful- Hier. Epift.

 nefs ad Euft.

nefs breedeth; that children, as it were in the wool of their infancy, dyed with hardnefs, may never afterwards change colour; that the poor, whofe perpetual fafts are
neceffity, may with better contentment endure the hunger which virtue caufeth
others fo often to chufe; and by advice of religion it felf fo far to efteem above the
contrary, that they which for the moft part do lead fenfual and eafy lives; they which,

Pfal. 73.5.   as the prophet *David* defcribeth them, *are not plagued like other men*, may, by the
publick fpectacle of all, be ftill put in mind what themfelves are; finally, that every
man may be every man's daily guide and example, as well by fafting to declare humility, as by praife to exprefs joy in the fight of God, although it have herein befallen the church, as fometimes *David*, fo that the fpeech of the one may be

Pfal. 69. 10.   truly the voice of the other, *My foul fafted, and even that was alfo turned to my
reproof.*

The celebra-   73. In this world there can be no fociety durable otherwife than only by propa-
tion of ma-   gation. Albeit therefore fingle life be a thing more angelical and divine, yet fith the
trimony.   replenifhing firft of earth with bleffed inhabitants, and then of heaven with faints
T. C. l. 1.
p. 199.   everlaftingly praifing God, did depend upon conjunction of man and woman, he which
made all things compleat and perfect, faw it could not be good to leave man without
an helper unto the fore-alledged end. In things which fome farther end doth caufe
to be defired, choice feeketh rather proportion than abfolute perfection of goodnefs.
So that woman being created for man's fake to be his helper, in regard of the end
beforementioned; namely, the having, and bringing up of children, whereunto it
was not poffible they could concur, unlefs there were fubalternation between them,
which fubalternation is naturally grounded upon inequality, becaufe things equal in
every refpect are never willingly directed one by another: Woman therefore was even
in her firft eftate framed by nature, not only after in time, but inferior in excellency
alfo unto man, howbeit in fo due and fweet proportion, as being prefented before
our eyes, might be fooner perceived than defined. And even herein doth lie the
reafon why that kind of love which is the perfecteft ground of wedlock, is feldom
able to yield any reafon of it felf. Now, that which is born of man muft be nourifhed with far more travel, as being of greater price in nature, and of flower pace to
perfection, than the Off-fpring of any other creature befides. Man and woman being therefore to join themfelves for fuch a purpofe, they were of neceffity to be
linked with fome ftrait and infoluble knot. The bond of wedlock hath been always, more or lefs, efteemed of as a thing religious and facred. The title which the

a Τὰς ἱερὰς   very heathens themfelves do hereunto oftentimes give a is, *Holy*. Thofe rites and
γάμους. Dionyf.   orders which were inftituted in the folemnization of marriage, the *Hebrews* term
ant. lib. 2.
b Kiddufchin   by the name of conjugal b *Sanctification*. Amongft our felves, becaufe fundry
in Rituali   things appertaining unto the publick order of matrimony, are called in queftion by
Heb. de bene-
dictione nupti-   fuch as know not from whence thofe cuftoms did firft grow, to fhew briefly fome
arum.   true and fufficient reafon of them, fhall not be fuperfluous; although we do not
Ecclef. 3. 1.   hereby intend to yield fo far unto enemies of all church orders faving their own,
Joel 2. 16.
1 Cor. 7. 5.   as though every thing were unlawful, the true caufe and reafon whereof at the firft
might hardly perhaps be now rendered. Wherefore, to begin with the times
wherein the liberty of marriage is reftrained; *There is*, faith *Solomon*, *a time for all
things, a time to laugh, and a time to mourn.* That duties belonging unto marriage, and offices appertaining to penance, are things unfuitable, and unfit to be
matched together, the prophets and apoftles themfelves do witnefs. Upon which
ground, as we might right well think it marvellous abfurd to fee in a church
a wedding on the day of a publick faft, fo likewife in the felf-fame confideration
our predeceffors thought it not amifs to take away the common liberty of marriages, during the time which was appointed for preparation unto, and for exercife
of general humiliation by fafting and praying, weeping for fins. As for the delivering up of the woman, either by her father, or by fome other, we muft note that

c *Mulieres antiquo jure tutela perpetua continebat; Recedebant*   in ancient times c all women which had not
vero à tutoris poteftate quæ in manum conveniffent. Boet. in To-   husbands nor fathers to govern them, had their
pic. Cic.   tutors, without whofe authority there was no
act which they did warrantable; and for this
b *Nullam ne privatam quidem rem fœminas fine auctore agere*   caufe, they were in marriage delivered unto
majores noftri voluerunt. Liv. l. 4. The reafon yielded by   their husbands by others. Which cuftom re-
Tully is this, *Propter infirmitatem confilii.* Cic. pro Mur. Vide   tained, hath ftill this ufe, that it putteth wo-
leg. Saxon. tit. 6. & 17.   men in mind of a duty whereunto the very imbe-
cillity of their nature and fex doth bind them; namely, to be always directed, guided
and

I

and ordered by others, although our positive laws do not tie them now as pupils.
The custom of laying down money, seemeth to have been derived from the *Saxons*,
whose manner was to buy their wives. But seeing there is not any great cause
wherefore the memory of that custom should remain, it skilleth not much, although
we suffer it to lie dead, even as we see it in a manner already worn out. The ring
hath been always used as an especial pledge of faith and fidelity; nothing more fit to
serve as a token of our purposed endless continuance in that which we never ought
to revoke. This is the cause wherefore the Heathens themselves did in such cases use
the ring, whereunto *Tertullian* alluding, saith, that in ancient times, [a] *No woman
was permitted to wear gold, saving only upon one finger, which her husband had
fastned unto himself, with that ring which was usually given for assurance of future
marriage.* The cause why the christians use it, as some of the fathers think, is [b] either to testify mutual love, or rather to serve for a pledge of conjunction in heart and
mind agreed upon between them. But what right and custom is there so harmless,
wherein the wit of man bending it self to derision, may not easily find out somewhat to scorn and jest at? He that should have beheld the *Jews*, when they stood
with [c] a four cornered garment, spread over the heads of espoused couples, while
their espousals were in making: He that should have beheld their [d] praying over a
cup, and their delivering the same at the marriage-feast, with set forms of benediction, as the order amongst them was, might, being lewdly affected, take thereat as
just occasion of scornful cavil, as at the use of the ring in wedlock amongst christians. But of all things the most hardly taken is the uttering of these words, *With
my body I thee worship*; in which words when once they are understood, there will
appear as little cause as in the rest, for any wise man to be offended. First therefore, inasmuch as unlawful copulation doth pollute and [e] dishonour both parties, this
protestation that we do worship and honour another with our bodies, may import
a denial of all such lets and impediments to our knowledge, as might cause any
stain, blemish, or disgrace that way; which kind of construction being probable,
would easily approve that speech to a peaceable and quiet mind. Secondly, in that
the apostle doth so expresly affirm that parties married have not any longer entire
power over themselves, but each hath interest in others person, it cannot be thought
an absurd construction to say, that worshipping with the body, is the imparting of
that interest in the body unto another, which none before had, save only our
selves [f]. But if this were the natural meaning, the words should perhaps be as requisite to be used on the one side, as on the other; and therefore a third sense there
is, which I rather rely upon. Apparent it is, that the ancient difference between a
lawful wife and a concubine, was only in the different purpose of man betaking himself to the one or the other. If his purpose were only fellowship, there grew to the
woman by this means no worship at all, but the contrary. In pressing that his intent was to add by his person honour and worship unto hers, he took her plainly
and clearly to wife. This is it which the civil law doth mean, when it maketh a
wife to differ from a concubine in [g] dignity; a wife to be taken where [h] conjugal
honour and affection do go before. The worship that grew unto her being taken
with declaration of this intent was, that her children became by this means legiti-
mate and free; her self was made a mother over his family. Last of all, she received
such advancement of state, as things annexed unto his person might augment her
with; yea, a right of participation was thereby given her both in him, and even all
things which were his. This doth somewhat the more plainly appear, by adding
also that other clause, *With all my worldly goods I thee endow*. The former branch
having granted the principal, the latter granteth that which is annexed thereunto. To
end the publick solemnity of marriage with receiving the blessed sacrament, is a
custom so religious and so holy, that if the church of *England* be blameable in this
respect, it is not for suffering it to be so much, but rather for not providing that it
may be more put in use. The laws of *Romulus* concerning marriage, are therefore
extolled above the rest amongst the Heathens which were before, in that they established the use of certain special solemnities, whereby the minds of men were drawn
to make the greater conscience of wedlock, and to esteem the bond thereof a thing
which could not be without impiety dissolved. If there be any thing in christian religion strong and effectual to like purpose, it is the sacrament of the holy Eucharist;
in regard of the force whereof, *Tertullian* breaketh out into these words, concerning matrimony therewith sealed, *Unde sufficiam ad enarrandam fœlicitatem ejus ma-
trimonii quod ecclesia conciliat, & confirmat oblatio? I know not which way I should*

M m 2

[marginal notes:]
[a] *Aurum mul-
la norat præter
unico digito
quem sponsus
oppignorasset
pronubo annu-
lo.* Tertul.
Apol. cap. 6.
[b] *Isidor. de
Eccles. Offic.* l.
2. c. 19.
[c] *Elias Thesb. in
dict. Elnupha,*
[d] *In Ritual. de
benedict. nup-
tiarum.*

[e] *Rom.* 1. 24.
1 *Cor.* 7. 4.

[f] *L. penult.
D. de concub.*

[g] *L. item le-
gato sect. pe-
nult. D. de
leg.* 3.
[h] *L. Donatio-
nes D. de do-
nationibus.*

[right-margin Greek notes:]
Οὗτ@ ἡ τε-
λυτὴ τῆς τε
γυναικὸς ἡ-
μαρτί᾽, οἷα
μα διΐδει
ἰχόμεν ἱλι-
ξς' δωσεω-
χῆν τῶτε ἂνε
γὰρ τῶδε ἄνε
τ῀῀ το γαμα-
μεσόντ@ ζων
τεῖσιν· ὡς
τὴς ἀνδ᾽εχε
ἀς ἀναγαλ᾽υ
τι ἀναγαμω
φησι χθύαα-
τει ὶ γυναι-
τοι κᾶρτίες,
*Dionyf. Hal.
Antiq. lib.* 2.
be *Tertul. lib.* 2.
ad uxorem.

be able to *shew the happiness of that wedlock, the knot whereof the church doth fasten, and the sacrament of the church confirm.* Touching marriage therefore let thus much be sufficient.

Churching of women.
T. C. l. 1.
p. 350.

74. The fruit of marriage is birth, and the companion of birth, travaile; the grief whereof being so extream, and the danger always so great, dare we open our mouths against the things that are holy, and presume to censure it as a fault in the church of Christ, that women after their deliverance do publickly shew their thankful minds unto God? But behold what reason there is against it! *Forsooth, if there should be solemn and express giving of thanks in the church for every benefit, either equal or greater than this which any singular person in the church doth receive; we should not only have no preaching of the word, nor ministring of the sacraments, but we should not have so much leisure as to do any corporal or bodily work, but should be like those Massilian Hereticks which do nothing else but pray.* Surely better a great deal to be like unto those hereticks which do nothing else but pray, than those which do nothing else but quarrel. Their heads it might haply trouble somewhat more than as yet they are aware of, to find out so many benefits greater than this, or equivalent thereunto, for which if so be our laws did require solemn and express thanksgivings in the church, the same were like to prove a thing so greatly cumbersome as is pretended. But if there be such store of mercies, even inestimable, poured every day upon thousands (as indeed the earth is full of the blessings of the Lord, which are day by day renewed without number and above measure) shall it not be lawful to cause solemn thanks to be given unto God for any benefit, than which greater, or whereunto equal are received, no law binding men in regard thereof to perform the like duty? Suppose that some bond there be that tieth us at certain times to mention publickly the names of sundry our benefactors. Some of them, it may be, are such, that a day would scarcely serve to reckon up together with them the catalogue of so many men besides, as we are either more or equally beholden unto. Because no law requireth this impossible labour at our hands, shall we therefore condemn that law whereby the other being possible and also dutiful, is enjoined us? So much we owe to the Lord of Heaven, that we can never sufficiently praise him; nor give him thanks for half those benefits for which this sacrifice were most due. Howbeit, God forbid we should cease performing this duty when publick order doth draw us unto it, when it may be so easily done, when it hath been so long executed by devout and virtuous people. God forbid, that being so many ways provoked in this case unto so good a duty, we should omit it, only because there are other cases of like nature, wherein we cannot so conveniently, or at least wise do not perform the same most virtuous office of piety. Wherein we trust that as the action it self pleaseth God, so the order and manner thereof is not such as may justly offend any. It is but an overflowing of gall, which causeth the woman's absence from the church during the time of her lying-in to be traduced and interpreted, as though she were so long judged unholy, and were thereby shut out or sequestred from the house of God, according to the ancient *Levitical* law. Whereas the canon law it self doth not so hold, but directly professeth the contrary [a], she is not barred from thence in such sort as they interpret it, nor in respect of any unholiness forbidden entrance into the church, although her abstaining from publick assemblies, and her abode in separation for the time be most convenient. [b] To scoff at the manner of attire, than which there could be nothing devised for such a time more grave and decent, to make it a token of some folly committed, for which they are loth to shew their faces, argueth that great divines are sometime more merry than wise. As for the women themselves, God accepting the service which they faithfully offer unto him, it is no great disgrace, though they suffer pleasant witted men a little to intermingle with zeal, scorn. The name of *oblations* applied not only here to those smaller and petit payments which yet are a part of the minister's right, but also generally given unto all such allowances as serve for their needful maintenance, is both ancient and convenient. For as the life of the clergy is spent in the service of God, so it is sustained with his revenue.

[a] Dist. 5. cap. Hæc quæ. *In lege præcipiebatur ut mulier si masculum pareret, 40. si fæminam, 80. diebus à templi cessaret ingressu. Nunc autem statim post partum ecclesiam ingredi non prohibetur.*

[b] Leo Const. 17. *Quod profecto non tam propter muliebrem immunditiem, quam ob alias causas in intima legis ratione reconditas, & veteri prohibitum esse lege, & gratia tempus traditionis loco suscepisse puto. Existimo siquidem sacram legem id præscripsisse, quo protervam eorum qui intemperanter viverent concupiscentiam castigaret; quemadmodum & alia multa per alia præcepta ordinantur & præscribuntur, quo indomitus quorundam in mulieres stimulus retundatur. Quin & hæc providentiæ quæ legem constituit voluntas est, ut partus à depravatione liberi sint. Quia enim quicquid natura supervacaneum est, idem corruptioum est & inutile, quod hic sanguis superfluus sit, quæ illi obnoxia essent in immunditie, ad id temporis vivere illa Lex jubet, quo ipso etiam naminis sono lascivi concupiscentia ad temperantiam redigatur, ne ex inutili & corrupta materia ipsum animans coagmentetur.*

revenue. Nothing therefore more proper than to give the name of *Oblations* to such payments, in token that we offer unto him whatsoever his ministers receive.

75. But to leave this, there is a duty which the church doth owe to the faithful departed, wherein for as much as the church of *England* is said to do those things which are, though not unlawful, yet inconvenient ; because it appointeth a prescript form of service at burials, suffereth mourning apparel to be worn, and permitteth funeral sermons ; a word or two concerning this point will be necessary, although it be needless to dwell long upon it.   The end of funeral duties is first, to shew that love towards the party deceased which nature requireth ; then to do him that honour which is fit both generally for man, and particularly for the quality of his person : Last of all, to testify the care which the church hath to comfort the living, and the hope which we all have concerning the resurrection of the dead.   For signification of love towards them that are departed, mourning is not denied to be a thing convenient ; as in truth the scripture every where doth approve lamentation unto this end.   The *Jews* by our Saviour's tears therefore gathered in this case, that his love towards *Lazarus* was great.   And that as mourning at such times is fit, so likewise that there may be a kind of attire suitable to a sorrowful affection, and convenient for mourners to wear, how plainly doth *David's* example shew, who being in heaviness, went up the mount with his head covered, and all the people that were with him in like sort ?   White garments being fit to use at marriage feasts, and such other times of joy ; whereunto *Solomon* alluding, when he requireth continual chearfulness of mind, speaketh in this sort, *Let thy garments be always white :*   What doth hinder the contrary from being now as convenient in grief, as this heretofore in gladness hath been ?   *If there be no sorrow,* they say, *it is hypocritical to pretend it ; and if there be, to provoke it by wearing such attire, is dangerous.*   Nay, if there be, to shew it, is natural ; and if there be not, yet the signs are meet to shew what should be, especially sith it doth not come oftentimes to pass, that men are fain to have their mourning gowns pulled off their backs, for fear of killing themselves with sorrow that way nourished.   The honour generally due unto all men, maketh a decent interring of them to be convenient, even for very humanity's sake.   And therefore, so much as is mentioned in the burial of the widow's son, the *carrying of him forth upon a bier,* and the accompanying of him to the earth, hath been used even amongst infidels ; all men accounting it a very extreme destitution not to have at the least this honour done them.   Some man's estate may require a great deal more, according as the fashion of the country where he dieth doth afford.   And unto this pertained the ancient use of the *Jews,* to embalm the corps with sweet odors, and to adorn the sepulchres of certain.   In regard of the quality of men, it hath been judged fit to commend them unto the world at their death, amongst the heathen in funeral orations, amongst the *Jews* in sacred poems ; and why not in funeral sermons also amongst christians ?   Us it sufficeth, that the known benefit hereof doth countervail millions of such inconveniences as are therein surmised, although they were not surmised only, but found therein.   The life and the death of saints is precious in God's sight.   Let it not seem odious in our eyes, if both the one and the other be spoken of, then especially, when the present occasion doth make men's minds the more capable of such speech.   The care, no doubt, of the living, both to live and to die well, must needs be somewhat increased, when they know that their departure shall not be folded up in silence, that the ears of many be made acquainted with it.   Moreover, when they hear how mercifully God hath dealt with their brethren in their last need, besides the praise which they give to God, and the joy which they have or should have by reason of their fellowship and communion with saints, is not their hope also much confirmed against the day of their own dissolution ?   Again, the sound of these things doth not so pass the ears of them that are most loose and dissolute in life, but it causeth them one time or other to wish, *O that I might die the death of the righteous, and that my end might be like his !*   Thus much peculiar good there doth grow at those times by speech concerning the dead, besides the benefit of publick instruction common unto funeral with other sermons.   For the comfort of them whose minds are through natural affection pensive in such cases, no man can justly mislike the custom which the *Jews* had to end their burials with funeral banquets, in reference whereunto the prophet *Jeremy* spake, concerning the people whom God hath appointed unto a grievous manner of destruction, saying, *That men should not give the cup of consolation to drink for their father, or for their mother ;* because it should not be now with them as in

peace.

Of the rites of burial.
T. C. l. 3. p. 236.

John 11. 36.

2 Sam. 15.30.

Eccles. 9. 8.

Luke 7. 12.

Psal. 79. 3.
John 19. 40.
Matth. 23.
27.

2 Sam. 1. 19.

Jer. 16. 7.

peaceable times with others, who bringing their anceſtors unto the grave with weep-
Prov. 31. 6. ing eyes, have notwithſtanding means wherewith to be re-comforted. *Give wine*,
faith *Solomon*, *unto them that have grief of heart*. Surely, he that miniſtreth unto
1 Chron. 19.2.
Job. 2. 11. them comfortable ſpeech, doth much more than give them wine. But the greateſt
thing of all other about this duty of chriſtian burial, is an outward teſtification of
the hope which we have touching the reſurrection of the dead. For which purpoſe
let any man of reaſonable judgment examine, whether it be more convenient for a
company of men, as it were, in a dumb ſhow, to bring a corpſe to the place of burial, there to leave it covered with the earth and ſo end, or elſe have the Exequies devoutly performed with ſolemn recital of ſuch lectures, pſalms and prayers, as are purpoſely framed for the ſtirring up of men's minds unto a careful conſideration of their
eſtate both here and hereafter. Whereas therefore it is objected, that neither the people of God under the law, nor the church in the apoſtles times did uſe any form of
ſervice in burial of the dead; and therefore that this order is taken up without any
good example or precedent followed therein: Firſt, while the world doth ſtand they
ſhall never be able to prove, that all things which either the one or the other did uſe at
burial, are ſet down in holy ſcripture, which doth not any where of purpoſe deliver
the whole manner and form thereof, but toucheth only ſometime one thing, and
ſometime another which was in uſe, as ſpecial occaſions require any of them to
to be either mentioned or inſinuated. Again, if it might be proved that no ſuch
thing was uſual amongſt them, hath Chriſt ſo deprived his church of Judgment, that
what rites and orders ſoever the latter ages thereof have deviſed, the ſame muſt needs
be inconvenient? Furthermore, that the *Jews* before our Saviour's coming had
any ſuch form of ſervice, although in ſcripture it be not affirmed; yet neither is it
there denied (for the forbidding of prieſts to be preſent at burials, letteth not but that
others might diſcharge that duty, ſeeing all were not prieſts which had rooms of publick function in their ſynagogues) and if any man be of opinion that they had no ſuch
form of ſervice; thus much there is to make the contrary more probable. The *Jews*
at this day have, as appeareth in their form of funeral prayers, and in certain of their
funeral ſermons publiſhed; neither are they ſo affected towards chriſtians, as to borrow that order from us; beſides that the form thereof is ſuch as hath in it ſundry
things which the very words of the ſcripture it ſelf do ſeem to allude unto, as namely, after departure from the ſepulchre unto the houſe whence the dead was brought, it
ſheweth the manner of their burial-feaſt, and a conſolatory form of Prayer, appointed
for the maſter of the Synagogue thereat to utter; albeit I may not deny, but it hath
alſo ſome things which are not perhaps ſo ancient as the law and the prophets. But
whatſoever the *Jews* cuſtom was before the days of our Saviour Chriſt, hath it once at
any time been heard of, that either church or chriſtian man of ſound belief did ever
judge this a thing unmeet, undecent, unfit for chriſtianity, till theſe miſerable days,
wherein under the colour of removing ſuperſtitious abuſes, the moſt effectual means
both to teſtify and to ſtrengthen true religion, are plucked at, and in ſome places
even pulled up by the very roots? Take away this which was ordained to ſhew at
burials the peculiar hope of the church of God concerning the dead, and in the
manner of thoſe dumb funerals what one thing is there, whereby the world may
perceive we are chriſtian men?

Of the nature of that miniſtry, which ſerveth for per-   76. I come now unto that function which
formance of divine duties in the church of God; and how   undertaketh the publick miniſtry of holy things
happineſs, not eternal only, but alſo temporal, doth de- according to the laws of chriſtian religion.
pend upon it.   And becauſe the nature of things, conſiſting
as this doth in action, is known by the object
whereabout they are converſant, and by the end or ſcope whereunto they are referred,
we muſt know that the object of this function is both God and Men; God, in that he
is publickly worſhipped of his church; and Men, in that they are capable of happineſs by means which chriſtian diſcipline appointeth. So that the ſum of our whole
labour in this kind, is to honour God and to ſave men. For whether we ſeverally
take, and conſider men one by one, or elſe gather them into one ſociety and body, as
it hath been before declared, that every man's religion is in him the well-ſpring of
all other ſound and ſincere virtues, from whence both here in ſome ſort, and hereafter more abundantly their full joy and felicity ariſeth; becauſe while they live they
are bleſſed of God, and when they die their works follow them: ſo at this preſent
we muſt again call to mind how the very worldly peace and proſperity, the ſecular
happineſs, the temporal and natural good eſtate both of all men, and of all domini-
4   ons

ons, hangeth chiefly upon religion, and doth evermore give plain teftimony, that as well in this as in other confiderations the prieft is a pillar of that commonwealth, wherein he faithfully ferveth God.   For if thefe affertions be true, firft, that nothing can be enjoyed in this prefent world againft his will which hath made all things : fecondly, that albeit God doth fometime permit the impious to *have*, yet impiety permitteth them not to *enjoy*, no not temporal bleffings on earth : thirdly, that God hath appointed thofe bleffings to attend as hand-maids upon religion : and fourthly, that without the work of the miniftry, religion by no means can poffibly continue, the ufe and benefit of that facred function even towards all men's worldly happinefs muft needs be granted.   Now the ª firft being a Theorem both underftood and confefs'd by all, to labour in proof thereof were fuperfluous. The fecond perhaps may be called in queftion, except it be perfectly underftood.   By good things temporal therefore we mean length of days, health of body, ftore of friends and well-willers, quietnefs, profperous fuccefs of thofe things we take in hand ; riches with fit opportunities to ufe them during life, reputation following us both alive and dead ; children, or fuch as inftead of children we wifh to leave fucceffors and partakers of our happinefs.   Thefe things are naturally every man's defire, becaufe they are good. And on whom God beftoweth the fame, them we confefs he gracioufly bleffeth.   Of earthly bleffings the meaneft is wealth, reputation the chiefeft.   For which caufe we efteem the gain of honour an ample recompence for the lofs of all other worldly benefits.   But for as much as in all this there is no certain perpetuity of goodnefs, nature hath taught to affect thefe things, not for their own fake, but with reference and relation to fomewhat independently good, as is the exercife of virtue and fpeculation of truth.   None, whofe defires are rightly ordered, would wifh to live, to breath, and move, without performance of thofe actions which are befeeming man's excellency.   Wherefore having not how to employ it, we wax weary even of life it felf.   Health is precious, becaufe ficknefs doth breed that pain which difableth action.   Again, why do men delight fo much in the multitude of friends, but for that the actions of life, being many, do need many helping hands to further them? Between troublefome and quiet days we fhould make no difference, if the one did not hinder and interrupt, the other uphold our liberty of action.   Furthermore, if thofe things we do, fucceed, it rejoiceth us not fo much for the benefit we thereby reap, as in that it probably argueth our actions to have been orderly and well-guided. As for riches, to him which hath and doth nothing with them, they are a contumely.   Honour is commonly prefumed a fign of more than ordinary virtue and merit, by means whereof when ambitious minds thirft after it, their endeavours are teftimonies how much it is in the eye of nature to poffefs that body , the very fhadow whereof is fet at fo high a rate.   Finally, fuch is the pleafure and comfort which we take in doing, that when life forfaketh us, ftill our defires to continue action and to work, though not by our felves, yet by them whom we leave behind us, caufeth us providently to refign into other men's hand the helps we have gathered for that purpofe, devifing alfo the beft we can to make them perpetual.   It appeareth therefore, how all the parts of temporal felicity are only good in relation to that which ufeth them as inftruments, and that they are no fuch good as wherein a right defire doth ever ftay or reft it felf.   Now temporal bleffings are enjoyed of thofe which have them, know them, *efteem them according to that they are in their own nature*. Wherefore of the wicked whom God doth hate, his ufual and ordinary fpeeches are, That *Blood-thirfty and deceitful men fhall not live out half their days* ; that God Pfal. 55. 23. fhall caufe a peftilence to cleave unto the wicked, and fhall ftrike them with confuming grief, with fevers, burning difeafes, and fores which are paft cure ; that when the im- Deut. 28. 22. pious are fallen, all men fhall tread them down, and none fhew countenance of love towards them, as much as by pitying them in their mifery ; that the fins of the ungodly fhall bereave them of peace ; that all counfels, complots and practices againft God fhall come to nothing ; that the lot and inheritance of the unjuft is beggary ; that the name of unrighteous perfons fhall putrify, and the pofterity of robbers Prov. 10. ftarve. If any think that iniquity and peace, fin and profperity can dwell together, they err, becaufe they diftinguifh not aright between the matter, and that which giveth it the form of happinefs, between poffeffion and fruition, between the having and enjoying

ª *Si creatura Dei, meritò & difpenfatio Dei fumus : Quis enim magis diligit , quam ille qui fecit ? Quis autem ordinatius regit quam is qui & facit & diligit ? Quis verò fapientius & fortius ordinare & regere facta poteft, quam qui & facienda providit & provifa perfecit ? Quapropter omnem poteftatem à Deo effe omnemque ordinationem, & qui non legerunt fentiunt , & qui legerunt cognofcunt.* Paul. Orof. Hift. adverf. Pagan. l. 2.   Οὗ τοι τὰ χρηματ᾽ ἴδια κέκτηνται βροτοὶ τὰ ᾿Θεῶν δ᾽ ἐχοντεσ ἐπιμελούμεθα. Eurip. Phœnif.

joying

joying of good things. The impious cannot enjoy that they have, partly becaufe they receive it not as at God's hands, which only confideration maketh temporal bleſſings comfortable ; and partly becaufe through error, placing it above things of far more price and worth, they turn that to poifon which might be food, they make their proſperity their own ſnare ; in the neſt of their higheſt growth they lay foolifhly thofe eggs out of which their woful over-throw is afterwards hatch'd. Hereby it cometh to paſs, that. wife and judicious men obferving the vain behaviour of fuch as are rifen to unwonted greatneſs, have thereby been able to prognofticate ;their ruin. So that in very truth no impious or wicked man doth profper on earth, but either fooner or later the world may perceive eafily, how at fuch time as others thought them moſt fortu-

Prov. 16. 18.
Ante ruinam
elatio.
φιλῖῖν ὁ Srὸς
αυῖῖα τὰ
ὑπῷλητα
κωλύοντ. ὁ ϗ̃
ἰὰ φερἴκεεν
ἄλλον μἰγα ἤ
ἰαυῖῖν. Herod.
l. 7.nate, they had but only the good eftate which fat oxen have above lean ; when they appeared to grow, their climbing was towards ruin. The grofs and beftial conceit of them which want underftanding is, only that the fulleft bellies are happieſt. Therefore the greateſt felicity they wiſh to the commonwealth wherein they live, is that it may but abound and ftand, that they which are riotous may have to pour out without ſtint ; that the poor may ſleep, and the rich feed them ; that nothing unpleafant may be commanded, nothing forbidden men which themſelves have a luſt to follow ; that kings may provide for the eafe of their fubjects, and not be too curious about their manners ; that wantonneſs, exceſs, and lewdneſs of life may be left free ; and that no fault may be capital, befides diſlike of things ſettled in fo good terms. But be it far from the juſt to dwell either in or near to the tents of thefe fo miferable felicities. Now whereas we thirdly affirm, that religion and the fear of God, as well induceth fecular profperity as everlaſting bliſs in the world to come, this alfo is true. For otherwife godlineſs could not be faid to have the promifes of both lives ; to be that ample revenue wherein there is alway ſufficiency ; and to carry with it a general difcharge of want, even fo general, that *David* himſelf ſhould proteſt, *he never faw the juſt forfaken.* Howbeit, to this we muſt add certain ſpecial limitations ; as firſt, that we do not forget how crazed and difeafed minds (whereof our heavenly phyfician muſt judge) receive oftentimes moſt benefit by being deprived of thofe things which are to others beneficially given, as appeareth in that which the wife man hath noted concerning them whofe lives God mercifully doth abridge, left wickednefs ſhould alter their underſtanding ; again, that the meafure of our outward profperity be taken in proportion with that which every man's eſtate in this prefent life requireth. External abilities are inſtruments of action. It contenteth wife artificers to have their inſtruments proportionable to their work, rather fit for ufe, than huge and goodly to pleafe the eye. Seeing then the actions of a ſervant do not need that which may be neceſſary for men of calling and place in the world, neither men of inferior condition many things which greater perfonages can hardly want, furely they are bleſſed in worldly

ᵃ Ἐπὶ τἠν' ἀριθῖθ' ἰπῖα' τῖις γα ſόφερην. Eurip. Phœnif.

ᵇ Ταπεινοτέρων ἠ λογιμὸς ἰσως, ἀλλ' ἐν ἀσφαλεσίραν, ἴσων ἀπέχων κ̃ ὕψυς κ̃ πτῶμαῖϬ. Greg. Naz̃ian. Apol. 3. They may ſeem haply be the moſt dejëct, but they are the wifeſt for their own fafety, which fear climbing no leſs than falling. Ariſ. polit. l. 4. c. 11.refpects, that have wherewith to perform ᵃ ſufficiently what their ſtation and place asketh, though they have no more. For by reafon of man's imbecillity and proneneſs to elation of mind, ᵇ too high a flow of profperity is dangerous, too low an ebb again as dangerous, for that the virtue of patience is rare, and the hand

of neceſſity ſtronger than ordinary virtue is able to withſtand. *Solomon's* difcreet and moderate defire we all know ; *Give me, O Lord, neither riches nor penury.* Men over-high exalted either in honour or in power, or in nobility, or in wealth ; they likewife that are as much on the contrary hand funk either with beggary, or through dejection, or by bafeneſs, do not eafily give ear to reafon ; but the one exceeding apt unto outrages, and the other unto petty mifchiefs. For greatneſs delighteth to ſhew it felf by effects of power, and bafeneſs to help it felf with ſhifts of malice. For which caufe, a moderate, indifferent temper, between fulneſs of bread and emptineſs, hath been evermore thought and found (all circumſtances duly confidered) the fafeſt and happieſt for all eſtates, even for kings and princes themſelves. Again, we are not to look that thefe things ſhould always concur, no not in them which are accounted happy, neither that the courfe of men's lives, or of publick affairs ſhould continually be drawn out as an even thred (for that the nature of things will not ſuffer) but a juſt furvey being made, as thofe particular men are worthily reputed good, whofe virtues be great and their faults tolerable ; fo him we may regiſter for a man fortunate, and that for a profperous and happy State, which having flouriſhed doth not afterwards feel any tragical alteration, fuch as might caufe them to be a ſpectacle

of

of misery to others. Besides, whereas true felicity consisteth in the highest operations of that nobler part of man, which sheweth sometime greatest perfection, not in using the benefits which delight nature, but in suffering what nature can hardliest endure; there is no cause why either the loss of good, if it tend to the purchase of better, or why any misery, the issue whereof is their greater praise and honour that have sustained it, should be thought to impeach that temporal happiness wherewith religion, we say, is accompanied, but yet in such measure as the several degrees of men may require by a competent estimation, and unless the contrary do more advance, as it hath done those most heroical saints whom afflictions have made glorious. In a word, not to whom no calamity falleth, but whom neither misery nor prosperity is able to move from a right mind, them we may truly pronounce fortunate; and whatsoever doth outwardly happen without that precedent improbity, for which it appeareth in the eyes of sound and unpartial judges to have proceeded from divine revenge, it passeth in the number of human casualties whereunto we are all alike subject. No misery is reckoned more than common or human, if God so dispose that we pass thorough it and come safe to shore; even as contrariwise, men do not use to think those flourishing days happy, which do end with tears. It standeth therefore with these cautions firm and true, yea, ratified by all men's unfeigned confessions drawn from the very heart of experience, that whether we compare men of note in the world with others of like degree and state, or else the same men with themselves, whether we confer one dominion with another, or else the different times of one and the same Dominion, the manifest odds between their very outward condition, as long as they stedfastly were observed to honour God, and their success being fallen from him, are remonstrances more than sufficient how all our welfare even on earth dependeth wholly upon our religion. Heathens were ignorant of true religion. Yet such as that little was which they knew, it much impaired or bettered always their worldly affairs, as their love and zeal towards it did wain or grow. Of the *Jews*, did not even their most malicious and mortal adversaries all acknowledge, that to strive against them it was in vain, as long as their amity with God continued, that nothing could weaken them but apostasy? In the whole course of their own proceedings did they ever find it otherwise, but that during their faith and fidelity towards God, every man of them was in war as a thousand strong, and as much as a grand senate for counsel in peaceable deliberations? contrariwise, that if they swerved, as they often did, their wonted courage and magnanimity forsook them utterly, their soldiers and military men trembled at the sight of the naked sword; when they entred into mutual conference and sate in counsel for their own good, that which children might have seen, their gravest senators could not discern; their prophets saw darkness instead of visions; the wise and prudent were as men bewitch'd, even that which they knew (being such as might stand them in stead) they had not the grace to utter, or if any thing were well proposed, it took no place, it entred not into the minds of the rest to approve and follow it, but as men confounded with strange and unusual amazements of spirit they attempted tumultuously they saw not what; and by the issues of all attempts they found no certain conclusion but this, *God and Heaven are strong against us in all we do.* The cause whereof was secret fear which took heart and courage from them; and the cause of their fear, an inward guiltiness that they all had offered God such apparent wrongs as were not pardonable. But it may be the case is now altogether changed, and that in christian religion there is not the like force towards temporal felicity. Search the ancient records of time, look what hath happened by the space of these sixteen hundred years, see if all things to this effect be not luculent and clear, yea all things so manifest, that for evidence and proof herein, we need not by uncertain dark conjectures surmise any to have been plagued of God for contempt, or blest in the course of faithful obedience towards true religion, more than only them, whom we find in that respect on the one side, guilty by their own confessions, and happy on the other side by all mens acknowledgments; who beholding the prosperous estate of such as are good and virtuous, impute boldly the same to God's most especial favour, but cannot in like manner pronounce, that whom he afflicteth above others, with them he hath cause to be more offended. For virtue is always plain to be seen, rareness causeth it to be observed, and goodness to be honoured with admiration. As for iniquity and sin, it lyeth many times hid; and because we be all offenders, it becometh us not to incline towards hard and severe sentences touching others, unless their notorious wickedness did sen-

sibly

fibly before proclaim that which afterwards came to pafs. Wherefore the fum of every chriftian man's duty is, to labour by all means towards that which other men feeing in us may juftify; and what we our felves muft accufe if we fall into it, that by all means we can to avoid; confidering efpecially, that as hitherto upon the church there never yet fell tempeftuous ftorm, the vapours whereof were not firft noted to rife from coldnefs in affection, and from backwardnefs in duties of fervice towards God, fo if that which the tears of antiquity have uttered concerning this point fhould be here fet down, it were affuredly enough to foften and to mollify an heart of fteel. On the contrary part, although we confefs with St. *Auguftin* moft willingly, that the chiefeft happinefs for which we have fome chriftian kings in fo great admiration above the reft, is not becaufe of their long reigh; their calm and quiet departure out of this prefent life; the fettled eftablifhment of their own flefh and blood fucceeding them in royalty and power; the glorious overthrow of foreign enemies, or the wife prevention of inward danger, and of feeret attempts at home; all which folaces and comforts of this our unquiet life it pleafeth God oftentimes to beftow on them which have no fociety or part in the joys of heaven, giving thereby to underftand, that thefe in comparifon are toys and trifles, far under the value and price of that which is to be looked for at his hands: But in truth the reafon wherefore we moft extol their felicity is, if fo be they have virtuoufly reigned, if honour hath not filled their hearts with pride, if the exercife of their power hath been fervice and attendance upon the majefty of the moft high, if they have feared him as their own inferiors and fubjects have feared them, if they have loved neither pomp nor pleafure more than heaven, if revenge hath flowly proceeded from them, and mercy willingly offered it felf, if fo they have tempered rigor with lenity, that neither extream feverity might utterly cut them off in whom there was manifeft hope of amendment, nor yet the eafinefs of pardoning offences embolden offenders; if, knowing that whatfoever they do, their potency may bear it out, they have been fo much the more careful not to do any thing but that which is commendable in the beft, rather than ufual with greateft perfonages; if the true knowledge of themfelves hath humbled them in God's fight, no lefs than God in the eyes of men hath raifed them up; I fay, albeit we reckon fuch to be the happieft of them that are mightieft in the world, and albeit thofe things alone are happinefs, neverthelefs, confidering what force there is even in outward bleffings, to comfort the minds of the beft difpofed, and to give them the greater joy when religion and peace, heavenly and earthly happinefs are wreathed in one crown, as to the worthieft of chriftian princes it hath by the providence of the almighty hitherto befallen; let it not feem to any man a needlefs and fuperfluous wafte of labour, that there hath been thus much fpoken, to declare how in them efpecially it hath been fo obferved, and withal univerfally noted, even from the higheft to the very meaneft, how this particular benefit, this fingular grace and preheminence religion hath, that either it guardeth as an heavenly fhield from all calamities, or elfe conducteth us fafe through them, and permitteth them not to be miferies; it either giveth honours, promotions and wealth, or elfe more benefit by wanting them, than if we had them at will; it either filleth our houfes with plenty of all good things, or maketh a fallad of green herbs more fweet than all the facrifices of the ungodly. Our fourth propofition before fet down was, that religion without the help of fpiritual miniftery, is unable to plant it felf, the fruits thereof not poffible to grow of their own accord. Which laft affertion is herein as the firft, that it needeth no farther confirmation: If it did, I could eafily declare how all things which ate of God, he hath by wonderful art and wifdom fodered as it were together with the glue of mutual affiftance, appointing the loweft to receive from the neareft to themfelves, what the influence of the higheft yieldeth. And therefore the church being the moft abfolute of all his works, was in reafon to be alfo ordered with like harmony, that what he worketh, might no lefs in grace than in nature be effected by hands and inftruments duly fubordinated unto the power of his own fpirit. A thing both needful for the humility of man, which would not willingly be debtor to any but to himfelf; and of no fmall effect to nourifh that divine love, which now maketh each embrace other, not as men, but as angels of God. Minifterial actions tending immediately unto God's honour, and man's happinefs, are either as contemplation, which helpeth forward the principal work of the miniftry, or elfe they are parts of that principal work of adminiftration it felf, which work confifteth in doing the fervice of God's houfe, and in applying unto men the foxereign medicines of Grace already fpoken of the more largely, to the end it might

Luke 12. 42.
1 Cor. 4. 1.
Tit. 1. 7.

1 Pet. 4. 10.
Ephef. 3. 2.

might thereby appear, that we [a] owe to the guides of our souls, even as much as [a] καὶ σεαυτόν μοι προσοφείλεις. Epist. ad Philem. our souls are worth, although the debt of our temporal blessings should be stricken off.

77. The ministry of things divine is a function, which as God did himself institute, so neither may men undertake the same but by authority and power given them in lawful manner.   That God, which is no way deficient or wanting unto man in necessaries, and hath therefore given us the light of his heavenly truth, because without that inestimable benefit we must needs have wandered in darkness to our endless perdition and woe, hath in the like abundance of mercies ordained certain to attend upon the due execution of requisite parts and offices therein prescribed for the good of the whole world, which men thereunto assigned do hold their authority from him, whether they be such as himself immediately, or as the church in his name investeth; it being neither possible for all, nor for every man without distinction convenient to take upon him a charge of so great importance.   They are therefore ministers of God, not only by way of subordination, as princes and civil magistrates, whose execution of judgment and justice the supream hand of divine providence doth uphold; but ministers of God, as from whom their authority is derived, and not from men.   For in that they are Christ's ambassadors and his labourers, who should give them their commission, but he whose most inward affairs they manage? Is not God alone the father of spirits? Are not souls the purchase of Jesus Christ? What angel in heaven could have said to man, as our Lord did unto *Peter, Feed my sheep? preach? baptize? do this in remembrance of me? whose sins ye retain, they are retained, and their offences in heaven pardoned, whose faults you shall on earth forgive?* What think we? Are these terrestrial sounds, or else are they voices uttered out of the clouds above? The power of the ministry of God translateth out of darkness into glory; it raiseth men from the earth, and bringeth God himself from heaven; by blessing visible elements, it maketh them invisible grace; it giveth daily the Holy Ghost, it hath to dispose of that flesh which was given for the life of the world, and that blood which was poured out to redeem souls; when it poureth malediction upon the heads of the wicked, they perish; when it revoketh the same, they revive. O wretched blindness, if we admire not so great power; more wretched if we consider it aright, and notwithstanding imagine that any but God can bestow it! To whom Christ hath imparted power, both over that mystical body which is the society of souls, and over that natural which is himself for the knitting of both in one, (a work which antiquity doth call the making of Christ's body) the same power is in such not amiss both termed a kind of mark or character, and acknowledged to be indeleble.   Ministerial power is a mark of separation, because it severeth them that have it from other men, and maketh them a special *order,* consecrated unto the service of the most high, in things wherewith others may not meddle. Their difference therefore from other men, is in that they are a distinct *order.*   So *Tertullian* calleth them.   And St. *Paul* himself dividing the body of the church of Christ into two moyeties, nameth the one part δεώτος, which is as much as to say the order of the laity, the opposite part whereunto we in like sort term the order of God's clergy, and the spiritual power which he hath given them, the power of their *order,* so far forth as the same consisteth in the bare execution of holy things, called properly the affairs of God.   For of the power of their jurisdiction over men's persons we are to speak in the books following.   They which have once received this power, may not think to put it off and on like a cloak, as the weather serveth, to take it, reject and resume it as oft as themselves list; of which prophane and impious contempt these latter times have yielded, as of other kinds of iniquity and apostasy, strange examples.   But let them know, which put their hands unto this plough, that once consecrated unto God, they are made his peculiar inheritance for ever. Suspensions may stop, and degradations utterly cut off the use or exercise of power before given; but voluntarily it is not in the power of man to separate and pull asunder what God by his authority coupleth.   So that although there may be through misdesert degradation, as there may be cause of just separation after matrimony; yet if (as sometimes it doth) restitution to former dignity, or reconciliation after breach doth happen, neither doth the one nor the other ever iterate the first knot.   Much less is it necessary, which some have urged, concerning the re-ordination of such, as others in times more corrupt did consecrate heretofore.   Which error already quelled by St. *Jerome,* doth not now require any other refutation.   Examples I grant there are which make for restraint of those men from admittance again into rooms of spi-

Of power given unto men to execute that heavenly office, of the gift of the Holy Ghost in ordination; and whether conveniently the power of order may be sought or sued for.

Tertul. de Adhort. Castit.

Heb. 2. 17.

Matth. 19.

ritual

ritual function, whose fall by herefy , or want of conſtancy in profeſſing the chriſtian faith, hath been once a diſgrace to their calling.　Nevertheleſs, as there is no
law which bindeth, ſo there is no cauſe that ſhould always lead to ſhew one and
the ſame ſeverity towards perſons culpable.　Goodneſs of nature it ſelf more inclineth to clemency than rigour.　And we in other men's offences do behold the plain
image of our own imbecillity.　Beſides alſo them that wander out of the way [a] it

[a] In 12 tabu-
lis cautum,eſt,
ut idem juris
eſſet ſananti-
bus quod forti-
bus, id eſt bo-
nis & qui
nunquam defe-
cerunt à popu-
lo Romæn.
Feſt. in ver.
Samnites.
[b] Ruffin. Hiſt.
Ecclef.l.t. 28.

cannot be unexpedient to win with all hopes of favour, left ſtrictneſs uſed towards
ſuch as reclaim themſelves, ſhould make others more obſtinate in error.　Wherefore
[b] after that the Church of *Alexandria* had ſomewhat recovered it ſelf from the tem-
peſts and ſtorms of *Arianiſm*, being in conſultation about the re-eſtabliſhment of that
which by long diſturbance had been greatly decayed and hindred, the ferventer ſort
gave quick ſentence, that touching them which were of the clergy, and had ſtained
themſelves with hereſy, there ſhould be none ſo received into the church again as
to continue in the order of the clergy.　The reſt, which conſidered how many men's
caſes it did concern, thought it much more ſafe and conſonant to bend ſomewhat
down towards them which were fallen ; to ſhew ſeverity upon a few of the chiefeſt
leaders, and to offer to the reſt a friendly reconciliation without any other demand
ſaving only the abjuration of their error ; as in the goſpel that waſtful young man,
which returned home to his father's houſe, was with joy both admitted and honoured, his elder brother hardly thought of for repining thereat ; neither commended ſo much for his own fidelity and virtue , as blamed for not embracing him freely,
whoſe unexpected recovery ought to have blotted out all remembrance of miſde-
meanors and faults paſt.　But of this ſufficient.　A thing much ſtumbled at in the
manner of giving orders, is our uſing thoſe memorable words of our Lord and Saviour Chriſt, *Receive the Holy Ghoſt.*　The Holy Ghoſt , they ſay, we cannot give,

[c] Papiſticus
quidam ritus,
ſtult-quidem
ab illis & ſine
ullo ſcripturæ
fundamento
inſtitutus, &
diſciplina no-
ſtra autoribus
(pace illorum
dixerim) non
magno præmum
judicio accep-
tus, minore
adhuc in Ec-
cleſia noſtra
retinetur. Ec-
cleſiaſt. di-
ſcip. p. 53.
[d] Eccleſ.diſcip.
fol.52. p.2. l.1.

and therefore we [c] *fooliſhly* bid men receive it.　Wiſe men, for their authorities
ſake, muſt have leave to befool them whom they are able to make wiſe by better inſtruction.　Notwithſtanding, if it may pleaſe their wiſdom, as well to hear
what fools can ſay, as to controul that which they do, thus we have heard ſome
wiſe men teach, namely, that the [c] *Holy Ghoſt* may be uſed to ſignify not the perſon alone, but the gift of the Holy Ghoſt, and we know that ſpiritual gifts are not
only abilities to do things miraculous, as to ſpeak with tongues which were never
taught us, to cure diſeaſes without art, and ſuch like ; but alſo that the very authority and power which is given men in the church to be miniſters of holy
things, is contained within the number of thoſe gifts whereof the Holy
Ghoſt is author; and therefore he which giveth this power may ſay, without ab-
ſurdity or folly, *Receive the Holy Ghoſt*, ſuch power as the Spirit of Chriſt hath
endued his church withal, ſuch power as neither prince nor potentate, king nor
Cæſar on earth can give.　So that if men alone had deviſed this form of ſpeech,
thereby to expreſs the heavenly well-ſpring of that power which eccleſiaſtical ordinations do beſtow, it is not ſo fooliſh but that wiſe men might bear with it.　If then our
Lord and Saviour himſelf have uſed the ſelf ſame form of words, and that in the ſelf
ſame kind of action, although there be but the leaſt ſhew of probability, yea or any
poſſibility that his meaning might be the ſame which ours is, it ſhould teach ſober
and grave men not to be too venturous in condemning that of folly, which is not
impoſſible to have in it more profoundneſs of wiſdom than fleſh and blood ſhould
preſume to controul.　Our Saviour after his reſurrection from the dead gave his

Matth.28.18.
apoſtles their commiſſion, ſaying, *All power is given me in heaven and in earth: go
therefore and teach all nations, baptizing them in the name of the Father, and the
Son, and the Holy Ghoſt, teaching them to obſerve all things whatſoever I have
commanded you.*　In ſum, *As my Father ſent me, ſo ſend I you.*　Whereunto St. *John*

John 20. 27.
doth add farther, that *having thus ſpoken, he breathed on them and ſaid, Receive the
Holy Ghoſt.*　By which words he muſt of likelihood underſtand ſome gift of the ſpirit which was preſently at that time beſtowed upon them, as both the ſpeech of actual
delivery in ſaying *Receive*, and the viſible ſign thereof, his breathing, did ſhew.　Abſurd it were to imagine our Saviour did both to the ear , and alſo to the very eye expreſs a real donation, and they at that time receive nothing.　It reſteth then that we
ſearch what ſpecial grace they did at that time receive.　Touching miraculous power of
the ſpirit moſt apparent it is, that as then they received it not, but the promiſe there-

Luke 24. 49.
of was to be ſhortly after performed.　The words of St. *Luke* concerning that
power are therefore ſet down with ſignification of the time to come, *Behold I
will ſend* the promiſe of my Father upon you, but tarry you in the city of *Je-
ruſa-*

4

rusalem, until ye be endued with power from on high. Wherefore undoubtedly it was some other effect of the Spirit, the Holy Ghost in some other kind which our Saviour did then bestow. What other likelier than that which himself doth mention, as it should seem of purpose to take away all ambiguous constructions, and to declare that the Holy Ghost which he then gave, was an holy and a ghostly authority, authority over the souls of men, authority a part whereof consisteth in power to remit and retain sins? Receive the Holy Ghost, *Whose sins soever ye remit,* John 20. 23. *they are remitted; whose sins ye retain, they are retained.* Whereas therefore the other evangelists had set down, that Christ did before his suffering promise to give his apostles the keys of the kingdom of heaven, and being risen from the dead promised moreover at that time a miraculous power of the Holy Ghost; St. *John* addeth, that he also invested them even then with the power of the Holy Ghost for castigation and relaxation of sin, wherein was fully accomplished that which the promise of the keys did import. Seeing therefore that the same power is now given, why should the same form of words expressing it be thought foolish? The cause why we breathe not as Christ did on them unto whom he imparted power is, for that neither spirit nor spiritual authority may be thought to proceed from us, who are but delegates or assignes to give men possession of his graces. Now besides that the power and authority delivered with those words is it self χάρισμα, a gracious donation which the Spirit of God doth bestow, we may most assuredly persuade our selves, that the hand which imposeth upon us the function of our ministry, doth under the *Etsi necessame* form of words so tye it self thereunto, that he which receiveth the burden is *rium est trepi,* thereby for ever warranted to have the spirit with him and in him for his assistance, *dare de merito,* aid, countenance and support in whatsoever he faithfully doth to discharge duty. *religiosum est tamen gaudero* Knowing therefore that when we take ordination, we also receive the presence of *de dono: quoni-* the Holy Ghost, partly to guide, direct and strengthen us in all our ways, and part- *am qui mihi oneris est autor,* ly to assume unto it self for the more authority those actions that appertain to our *ipse fiet admi-* place and calling, can our ears admit such a speech uttered in the reverend per- *nistrationis ad-* formance of that solemnity; or can we at any time renew the memory and enter, *jutor; & no* into serious cogitations thereof, but with much admiration and joy? Remove what *gratiae sue-* these foolish words do imply, and what hath the ministry of God besides wherein *mus, dabit vir-* to glory? Whereas now, forasmuch as the Holy Ghost, which our saviour in his *tutem qui con-* first ordinations gave, doth no less concur with spiritual vocations throughout all *tulit dignita-* ages, than the Spirit which God derived from *Moses* to them that assisted him in *ser. 1. in an-* his government, did descend from them to their successors in like authority and *niver. die A.* place, we have for the least and meanest duties, performed by virtue of ministerial power, that to dignify, grace and authorize them, which no other offices on earth can challenge. Whether we preach, pray, baptize, communicate, condemn, give *Τὸ πνεῦμα* absolution, or whatsoever; as disposers of God's mysteries, our words, judgments, *τὸ ἅγιον· δι τὸ* acts and deeds are not ours but the Holy Ghost's. Enough if unfeignedly and in *ἡμᾶς εἰς τ̔̔ὸ* heart we did believe it, enough to banish whatsoever may justly be thought corrupt *ταῦτα ἱερ* either in bestowing, or in using, or in esteeming the same otherwise than is meet. *Nazian.Num.* For prophanely to bestow, or loosely to use, or vilely to esteem of the Holy Ghost, *Auth. libr: de* we all in shew and profession abhor. Now because the ministry is an office of dig- *discipl. Eccle-* nity and honour; some are doubtful whether any man may seek for it without of- *siasti* fence; or, to speak more properly, doubtful they are not, but rather bold to accuse our discipline in this respect, as not only permitting, but requiring also ambitious suits, or other oblique ways or means whereby to obtain it. Against this they plead, that our Saviour did stay till his father sent him, and the apostles till he them; that the ancient bishops in the church of Christ were examples and patterns of the same modesty. Whereupon in the end they infer, *Let us therefore at the length amend that custom of repairing from all parts unto the bishop at the day of ordination, and of seeking to obey orders; let the custom of bringing commendatory letters be removed; let men keep themselves at home, expecting there the voice of God, and the authority of such as may call them to undertake charge.* Thus severely they censure and controul ambition, if it be ambition which they take upon them to reprehend. For of that there is cause to doubt. Ambition, as we understand it, hath been accounted a vice which seeketh after honours inordinately. Ambitious minds esteeming it their greatest happiness to be admired, reverenced, and adored above others, use all means lawful and unlawful which may bring them to high rooms. But as for the power of order considered by it self, and as in this case it must be considered, such reputation it hath in the eye of this present world, that they which affect

affect it, rather need encouragement to bear contempt, than deserve blame as men that carry aspiring minds. The work whereunto this power serveth is commended, and the desire thereof allowed by the apostle for good. Nevertheless because the burden thereof is heavy, and the charge great, it cometh many times to pass, that the minds even of virtuous men are drawn into clean contrary affections, some in humility declining that, by reason of hardness, which others in regard of goodness only do with fervent alacrity covet. So that there is not the least degree in this service,

1 Tim. 3. 1.

but it may be both in ª reverence shunned, and of very devotion longed for. If then the desire thereof may be holy, religious and good, may not the profession of that desire be so likewise? We are not to think it so long good as it is dissembled, and evil if once we begin to open it. And allowing that it may be opened without ambition, what offence, I beseech you, is there in opening it there where it may be furthered and satisfied, in case they to whom it appertaineth think meet? In vain are those desires allowed, the accomplishment whereof it is not lawful for men to seek. Power therefore of ecclesiastical order may be desired, the desire thereof may be professed, they which profess themselves that way inclined, may endeavour to bring their desires to effect, and in all this no necessity of evil. Is it the bringing of testimonial Letters, wherein so great obliquity consisteth? What more simple, more plain, more harmless, more agreeable with the law of common humanity, than that men where they are not known, use for their easier access the credit of such as can best give testimony of them? Letters of any other construction our church discipline alloweth not; and these to allow, is neither to require ambitious suings, nor to approve any indirect or unlawful act. The prophet *Esay* receiving his message at the hands of God, and his charge by heavenly vision, heard the voice

Esay 6. 8, 9.

of the Lord, saying, *Whom shall I send, who shall go for us?* Whereunto he recordeth his own answer, *Then I said, here Lord I am, send me.* Which in effect is 'the rule and canon whereby touching this point the very order of the church is framed.

The appointment of times for solemn ordination, is but the publick demand of the church in the name of the Lord himself, *Whom shall I send, who shall go for us?* The confluence of men, whose inclinations are bent that way, is but the answer thereunto, whereby the labours of sundry being offered, the church hath freedom to take whom her agents in such case think meet and requisite. As for the example of our Saviour Christ, who took not to himself this honour to be made our High-

Heb. 5. 5.

priest, but received the same from him which said, *Thou art a priest for ever after the order of Melchisedeck,* his waiting and not attempting to execute the office till God saw convenient time, may serve in reproof of usurped honours, for as much as we ought not of our own accord to assume dignities, whereunto we are not called as Christ was. But yet it should be withal considered, that a proud usurpation without any orderly calling is one thing, and another the bare declaration of willingness to obtain admittance; which willingness of mind, I suppose, did not want in him,

Heb. 6. 9.

whose answer was to the voice of his heavenly calling, *Behold I am come to do thy will.* And had it been for him, as it is for us, expedient to receive his commission signed with the hands of men, to seek it might better have beseemed his humility, than it doth our boldness to reprehend them of pride and ambition, that make no worse kind of suits than by letters of information. Himself in calling his apostles prevented all cogitations of theirs that way, to the end it might truly be said of them, *Ye chose not me, but I of my own voluntary motion made choice of you.* Which kind of undesired nomination to ecclesiastical places befel divers of the most famous amongst the ancient fathers of the church in a clean contrary consideration. For our Saviour's election respected not any merit or worth, but took them which were farthest off from likelihood of fitness; that afterwards their supernatural ability and performance, beyond hope, might cause the greater admiration; whereas in the other, meer admiration of their singular and rare virtues was the reason why honours were inforced upon them, which they of meekness and modesty did what they could to avoid. But did they ever judge it a thing unlawful to wish or desire the office, the only charge and bare function of their ministry? Towards which labour, what doth the blessed apostle else but encourage, saying, *He which desireth it, is desirous of a good work?* What doth he else by such sentences but stir, kindle and inflame ambition; if I may term that desire ambition,

2

which

which coveteth more to testify love by painfulness in God's service, than to reap any other benefit? Although of the very honour it self, and of other emoluments annexed to such labours for more encouragement of man's industry, we are not so to conceive neither, as if no affection can be cast towards them without offence. Only as the wise man giveth counsel, *Seek not to be made a judge, lest thou be not able* Ecclus. 7. 6. *to take away iniquity, and lest thou fearing the person of the mighty, shouldest commit an offence against thine uprightness;* so it always behoveth men to take good heed, lest affection to that which hath in it as well difficulty as goodness, sophisticate the true and sincere judgment which before-hand they ought to have of their own ability, for want whereof many forward minds have found instead of contentment, repentance. But for as much as hardness of things in themselves most excellent, cooleth the fervency of men's desires, unless there be somewhat naturally acceptable to incite labour (for both the method of speculative knowledge doth, by things which we sensibly perceive, conduct to that which is in nature more certain, though less sensible, and the method of virtuous actions is also, to train beginners at the first by things acceptable unto the taste of natural appetite, till our minds at the length be settled to embrace things precious in the eye of reason, merely and wholly for their own sakes) howsoever inordinate desires do hereby take occasion to abuse the polity of God and nature, either affecting without worth, or procuring by unseemly means that which was instituted, and should be reserved for better minds to obtain by more approved courses. In which consideration the emperors *Anthemius* and *Leo* did worthily oppose against such ambitious practices, that ancient and famous constitution, wherein they have these sentences: *Let not a prelate be ordained for reward, or upon request, who should be so far sequestred from all ambition, that they which advance him might be fain to search where he hideth himself, to entreat him drawing back, and to follow him till importunity have made him yield. Let nothing promote him but his excuses to avoid the burden. They are unworthy of that vocation, which are not thereunto brought unwillingly;* notwithstanding, we ought not therefore with the odious name of ambition to traduce and draw into hatred every poor request or suit, wherein men may seem to affect honour; seeing that ambition and modesty do not always so much differ in the mark they shoot at, as in the manner of their prosecutions. Yea, even in this may be certain also, if we still imagine them least ambitious, which most forbear to stir either hand or foot towards their own preferments. For there are that make an idol of their great sufficiency, and because they surmise the place should be happy that might enjoy them, they walk every where like grave pageants, observing whether men do not wonder why so small account is made of so rare worthiness; and in case any other man's advancement be mentioned, they either smile or blush at the marvellous folly of the world, which seeth not where dignities should offer themselves. Seeing therefore that suits after spiritual functions may be as ambitiously forborn as prosecuted, it remaineth that the · Μέσος εἰμὶ *evenest line of moderation between both is, neither to follow them without con-* τις ᾦ τι ἀ- *science;* nor of *pride* to withdraw our selves utterly from them. γαν πολυα- τῶν ὦ ὦ λί- ας ἐνιῶτι ,

ᾦ μὴ τελους ἱππωθίἡαν αγχεσνίαις διωλέτης@, ᦙ η φδιστων τελους διμολεσότης@. Greg. Nazian. Apologet.

b 78. It pleaseth Almighty God to chuse to himself, for discharge of the c legal ministry, one only tribe out of twelve others, the tribe of *Levi*; not all unto every divine service, but *Aaron* and his sons to one charge, the rest of that sanctified tribe to another. With what

b Of degrees whereby the power of order is distinguished; and concerning the attire of ministers.

c Περὶ διατήρησιν η φυλακὴν ὁσιότητ@ η δ'οσιόσίαν η λατρῇ χῶν ἀ. φεῖς ἡ τοῦ ᾦ διο ἡμῶν ἀναβκεσν'ᦙ. Philo. p. 271.

solemnities they were admitted into their Functions, in what manner *Aaron* and his successors the high-priests ascended every sabbath and festival day, offered and ministred in the temple; with what sin-offering once every year they reconciled first themselves and their own house, afterwards the people unto God; how they confessed all the iniquities of the children of *Israel*, laid all their trespasses upon the head of a sacred goat, and so carried them out of the city; how they purged the holy place from all uncleanness, with what reverence they entred within the veil, presented themselves before the mercy-seat, and consulted with the oracle of God; what service the other priests did continually in the holy place, how they ministred about the Lamps, morning and evening; how every sabbath they placed on the table of the Lord those twelves loaves with pure incense, in perpetual remembrance of that

a   mercy

mercy which the Fathers, the twelve tribes had found by the providence of God for their food, when hunger caufed them to leave their natural foil and to feek for fuftenance in *Egypt* ; how they employed themfelves in facrifice day by day ; finally, what offices the *Levites* difcharged, and what duties the reft did execute, it were a labour too long to enter into it, if I fhould collect that which fcriptures and other ancient records do mention. Befides thefe, there were indifferently out of all tribes from time to time fome called of God as prophets, forefhewing them things to come, and giving them counfel in fuch particulars as they could not be directed in by the law ; fome chofen men to read, ftudy and interpret the law of God, as the fons or fcholars of the old prophets, in whofe room afterwards fcribes and expounders of the law fucceeded. And becaufe where fo great variety is, if there fhould be equality, confufion would follow, the *Levites* were in all their fervice at the appointment and direction of the fons of *Aaron*, or priefts ; they fubject to the principal guides and leaders of their own order ; and they all in obedience under the high-prieft. Which difference doth alfo manifeft it felf in the very titles that men for honours fake gave unto them, terming *Aaron* and his fucceffors, high or great ; the ancients over the companies of priefts, arch-priefts ; prophets, fathers ; fcribes and interpreters of the law, mafters. Touching the miniftry of the gofpel of Jefus Chrift, the whole body of the church being divided into laity and clergy, the clergy are either presbyters or deacons. I rather term the one fort presbyters than [a] priefts, becaufe in a matter of fo fmall moment I would not willingly offend their ears to whom the name of priefthood is odious, though without caufe. For as things are diftinguifhed one from another by thofe true effential forms, which being really and actually in them, do not only give them the very laft and higheft degree of their natural perfection, but are alfo the knot, foundation and root whereupon all other inferior perfections depend ; fo if they that firft do impofe names, did always underftand exactly the nature of that which they nominate, it may be that then by hearing the terms of vulgar fpeech, we fhould ftill be taught what the things themfelves moft properly are. But becaufe words have fo many artificers by whom they are made, and the things whereunto we apply them are fraught with fo many varieties, it is not always apparent what the firft inventors refpected, much lefs what every man's inward conceit is which ufeth thefe words. For any thing my felf can difcern herein, I fuppofe that they which have bent their ftudy to fearch more diligently fuch matters, do for the moft part find that names advifedly given, had either regard unto that which is naturally moft proper ; or if perhaps to fome other fpeciality, to that which is fenfibly moft eminent in the thing fignified ; and concerning popular ufe of words, that which the wifdom of their inventors did intend thereby, is not commonly thought of, but by the name the thing altogether conceived in grofs ; as may appear in that if you afk of the common fort what any certain word, for example, what a prieft doth fignify ; their manner is not to anfwer, a prieft is a clergyman which offereth facrifice to God, but they fhew fome particular perfon whom they ufe to call by that name. And if we lift to defcend to grammar, we are told by mafters in thofe fchools, that the word *Prieft* hath his right place [b] ἐπὶ τῇ ψιλῶς περισωτζ. ᾖ δεραπείας τῷ Θεῷ, in him whofe meer function or charge is the fervice of God. Howbeit, becaufe the moft eminent part both of heathenifh and *Jewifh* fervice did confift in facrifice, when learned men declare what the word *Prieft* doth properly fignify, *according to the mind of the firft impofer* of that name, their ordinary [c] fchools do well expound it to imply facrifice. Seeing then that facrifice is now no part of the church-miniftry, how fhould the name of priefthood be thereunto rightly applied? Surely even as St. *Paul* applieth the name of [d] *flefh* unto that very fubftance of fifhes, which hath a proportionable correfpondence to flefh, although it be in nature another thing. Whereupon, when philofophers will fpeak warily, they [e] make a difference between flefh in one fort of living creatures, and that other fubftance in the reft which hath but a kind of analogy to flefh : the apoftle contrariwife, having matter of greater im-

[a] *T. C. l. 1. p.* 198. For fo much as the common and ufual fpeech of *England* is to note by the word *Prieft*, not a minifter of the gofpel, but a *Sacrificer*, which the minifter of the gofpel is not, therefore we ought not to call the minifters of the gofpel *Priefts*. And that this is the *Englifh* fpeech, it appeareth by all the *Englifh* Tranflations, which tranflate always ἱερεῖς, which were facrificers, *Priefts*, and do not on the other fide, for any that ever I read, tranflate πρεσβύτερ, a *Prieft*. Seeing therefore a prieft with us, and in our tongue, doth fignify both by the papifts judgment, in refpect of their abominable Mafs, and alfo by the judgment of the proteftants, in refpect of the beafts which were offered in the Law, a *facrificing office*, which the minifter of the gofpel neither doth nor can execute ; it is manifeft that it cannot be without great offence fo ufed.

[b] *Etym. magn.*

[c] Ἱησύχιος, Σουΐδας.

[d] *Hefy. Chriftus homo dicitur, quia natus eft ; Propheta, quia futura revelavit ; Sacerdos, quia pro nobis hoftiam fe obtulit.* Iid. Orig. l. 7. c. 2.

[e] 1 Cor. 15. 39.

importance whereof to speak, nameth indifferently both flesh. The fathers of the church of Christ with like security of speech call usually the ministry of the gospel *priesthood*, in regard of that which the gospel hath *proportionable* to ancient sacrifices; namely, the *communion* of the blessed body and blood of Christ, although it hath properly now no sacrifice. As for the people, when they hear the name, it draweth no more their minds to any cogitation of sacrifice, than the name of a senator or of an alderman causeth them to think upon old age, or to imagine that every one so termed must needs be ancient, because years were respected in the first nomination of both. Wherefore, to pass by the name, let them use what dialect they will, whether we call it a priesthood, a presbytership, or a ministry, it skilleth not : Although in truth the word *presbyter* doth seem more fit, and in propriety of speech more agreable than *priest* with the drift of the whole gospel of Jesus Christ. For what are they that embrace the gospel but sons of God : What are churches but his families ? Seeing therefore we receive the adoption and state of sons by their ministry, whom God hath chosen out for that purpose; seeing also that when we are the sons of God, our continuance is still under their care which were our progenitors, what better title could there be given them than the reverend name of *presbyters* or fatherly guides? The Holy Ghost throughout the body of the New Testament, making so much mention of them, doth not any where call them priests. The prophet *Esay*, I grant, doth, but in such sort as the ancient fathers, by way of analogy. *A presbyter*, according to the proper meaning of the New Testament, *is he unto whom our Saviour Christ hath communicated the power of spiritual procreation.* Out of twelve patriarchs issued the whole multitude of *Israel* according to the flesh. And, according to the mystery of heavenly birth, our Lord's apostles we all acknowledge to be the patriarchs of his whole church. St. *John* therefore beheld sitting about the throne of God in heaven four and twenty presbyters, the one half fathers of the old, the other of the new *Jerusalem*. In which respect the apostles likewise gave themselves the same title, albeit that name were not proper, but common unto them with others. For of presbyters, some were greater, some less in power, and that by our Saviour's own appointment; the greater they which received fulness of spiritual power, the less they to whom less was granted. The apostles peculiar charge was to publish the gospel of Christ unto all nations, and to deliver them his ordinances received by *immediate revelation from himself.* Which preheminence excepted, to all other offices and duties incident unto their order, it was in them to ordain and consecrate whomsoever they thought meet, even as our Saviour did himself assign seventy other of his own disciples inferior presbyters, whose commission to preach and baptize was the same which the apostles had. Whereas therefore we find that the very first sermon which the apostles did publickly make, was the conversion of above three thousand souls, unto whom there were every day more and more added, they having no open place permitted them for the exercise of christian religion, think we that twelve were sufficient to teach and administer sacraments in so many private places, as so great a multitude of people did require? This harvest our Saviour (no doubt) foreseeing, provided accordingly labourers for it before-hand. By which means it came to pass, that the growth of that church, being so great, and so sudden, they had notwithstanding in a readiness presbyters enough to furnish it. And therefore the history doth make no mention by what occasion presbyters were instituted in *Jerusalem*, only we read of things which they did, and how the like were made afterwards elsewhere. To these two degrees appointed of our Lord and Saviour Christ, his apostles soon after annexed deacons. Deacons therefore must know, saith *Cyprian*, that our Lord himself did elect apostles; but deacons, after his ascension into heaven, the apostles ordained. Deacons were stewards of the church, unto whom at the first was committed the distribution of church-goods, the care of providing therewith for the poor, and the charge to see that all things of expence might be religiously and faithfully dealt in. A part also of their office was attendance upon their presbyters at the time of divine service. For which cause *Ignatius*, to set forth the dignity of their calling, saith, that they are in such case to the bishop, as if angelical powers did serve him. These only being the uses for which deacons were first made, if the church have sithence extended their ministry further than the circuit of their labour at the first was drawn, we are not herein to think the ordinance of scripture violated, except there appear some prohibition which hath abridged the church of that liberty. Which I note chiefly, in regard of them to whom it seemeth a thing so monstrous that deacons should

Ἔχει δ' ἐν-
εἶναι τι τὸ ἐ-
ξωτερικὸν τὸ
πᾶλαι, πίτηρον
ἢ μέχρι ἐς
πᾶς εἰλικρινὲς τὸ
Arist. de Anim.
l. 2. c. 11.

Esay 66. 21.

Rev. 4. 4.
Rev. 21. 14.
Matth.19.28.
1 Pet. 5. 1.

'Οι ἀπόστολοι
διεπεμφθή-
σαν τοῖς ἀποστο-
λαῖς. Dionys.
Areop. p. 119.
Acts 2. 41,
47.

Cypr. Ep. 9.
l. 3. *ad Roga-*
tianum.

Ignat. Epist.
ad Tral.

sometime be licensed to preach, whose institution was at the first to another end.
To charge them for this as men not contented with their own vocations, and as
breakers into that which appertaineth unto others, is very hard. For when they are
thereunto once admitted, it is part of their own vocation, it appertaineth now unto
them as well as others; neither is it intrusion for them to do it, being in such sort
called, but rather in us it were temerity to blame them for doing it. Suppose we
the office of teaching to be so repugnant unto the office of deaconship, that they
cannot concur in one and the same person? What was there done in the church by
deacons, which the apostles did not first discharge, being teachers? Yea, but the
apostles found the burden of teaching so heavy, that they judged it meet to cut off
that other charge, and to have deacons which might undertake it. Be it so. The
multitude of christians increasing in *Jerusalem*, and waxing great, it was too much
for the apostles to teach, and to minister unto tables also. The former was not to
be slacked, that this latter might be followed. Therefore unto this they appointed
others. Whereupon we may rightly ground this axiom, that when the subject
wherein one man's labours of sundry kinds are employed, doth wax so great, that
the same men are no longer able to manage it sufficiently as before, the most natural way to help this is, by dividing their charge into slipes, and ordaining of under-
officers; as our Saviour under twelve apostles, seventy presbyters; and the apostles
by his example seven deacons to be under both. Neither ought it to seem less reasonable, that when the same men are sufficient both to continue in that which they
do, and also to undertake somewhat more, a combination be admitted in this case,
as well as division in the former. We may not therefore disallow it in the church of
Geneva, that *Calvin* and *Beza* were made both pastors and readers in divinity, being men so able to discharge both. To say they did not content themselves with
their pastoral vocations, but brake into that which belongeth to others; to alledge

Rom. 12. 8. against them, *He that exhorteth on exhortation*, as against us, *He that distributeth
in simplicity*, is alledged in great dislike of granting license for deacons to preach,
were very hard. The ancient custom of the church was to yield the poor much relief, especially widows. But as poor people are always querulous and apt to think
themselves less respected than they should be, we see that when the apostles did what
they could without hindrance to their weightier business, yet there were which
grudged that others had too much, and they too little, the *Grecian* widows shorter
commons than the *Hebrews*. By means whereof the apostle saw it meet to ordain
deacons. Now tract of time having clean worn out those first occasions for which
the deaconship was then most necessary, it might the better be afterwards extended
to other services, and so remain, as at this present day, a degree in the clergy of
God which the apostles of Christ did institute. That the first seven deacons were

Epiph. l. 1. c. chosen out of the seventy disciples, is an error in *Epiphanius*. For to draw men
21. from places of weightier, unto rooms of meaner labour, had not been fit. The apostles, to the end they might follow teaching with more freedom, committed the ministry of tables unto deacons. And shall we think they judged it expedient to chuse
so many out of those seventy to be ministers unto tables, when Christ himself had
before made them teachers? It appeareth therefore, how long these three degrees of
ecclesiastical order have continued in the church of Christ; the highest and largest,
that which the apostles; the next that which presbyters; and the lowest that which
deacons had. Touching prophets, they were such men as having otherwise learned
the gospel, had from above bestowed upon them a special gift of expounding

Acts 21. 10. scriptures, and of foreshewing things to come. Of this sort *Agabus* was, and be-
Acts 11. 27. sides him in *Jerusalem* sundry others, who notwithstanding are not therefore to be
reckoned with the clergy, because no mans gifts or qualities can make him a minister of holy things, unless ordination do give him power. And we no where find
prophets to have been made by ordination; but all whom the church did ordain,
were either to serve as presbyters or as deacons. Evangelists were presbyters of principal sufficiency, whom the apostles sent abroad, and used as agents in ecclesiastical
affairs wheresoever they saw need. They whom we find to have been named in scrip-

a Acts 9. 18. ture evangelists, a *Ananias*, b *Apollos*, c *Timothy*, and others, were thus employed.
b Acts 18. 24. And concerning evangelists afterwards in *Trajan's* days, the history ecclesiastical mo-
c 2 Tim. 4. 5, teth, that many of the apostles disciples and scholars which were then alive, and
9. did with singular love of wisdom affect the heavenly word of God, to shew their
1 Tim. 3. 15. willing minds in executing that which Christ first of all requireth at the hands of
5. 14. 2. 8.
Euseb. Eccles.
Hist. l. 3. c.   I   men,
34.

men, they fold their poffeffions, gave them to the poor, and betaking themfelves to travel, undertook the labour of evangelifts, that is, they painfully preached Chrift, and delivered the gofpel to them, who as yet had never heard the doctrine of faith. Finally, whom the apoftle nameth paftors and teachers, what other were they than presbyters alfo, howbeit fettled in fome charge, and thereby differing from evange- lifts? I befeech them therefore which have hitherto troubled the church with quefti- ons about degrees and offices of ecclefiaftical calling, becaufe they principally ground themfelves upon two places, that all partiality laid afide, they would fincerely weigh and examine whether they have not mif-interpreted both places, and all by furmifing incompatible offices, where nothing is meant but fundry graces, gifts and abilities which Chrift beftowed.   To them of *Corinth,* his words are thefe, *God placed in* 1Cor. 12. 28. *the church firft of all, fome apoftles; fecondly, prophets; thirdly, teachers; after them powers, then gifts of cures, aids, governments, kinds of languages. Are all apoftles? Are all prophets? Are all teachers? Is there power in all? Have all grace to cure? Do all fpeak with tongues? Can all interpret? But be you defirous of the better graces.*   They which plainly difcern firft, that fome *one general* thing · there is, which the apoftle doth here divide into all thefe branches, and do fecondly conceive that general to be the church offices, befides a number of other difficulties, can by no means poffibly deny but that many of thefe might concur in one man, and peradventure in fome one all: Which mixture notwithftanding, their form of difcipline doth moft fhun.   On the other fide, admit that *communicants of fpecial infufed grace,* for the benefit of members knit into one body, the church of Chrift, are here fpoken of, which was in truth the plain drift of that whole difcourfe; and fee if every thing do not anfwer in due place with that fitnefs, which fheweth eafily what is likelieft to have been meant.   For why are *apoftles* the firft, but becaufe unto them was granted the revelation of all truth from Chrift immediately? Why *pro- phets* the fecond, but becaufe they had of fome things knowledge in the fame man- ner? *Teachers* the next, becaufe whatfoever was known to them, it came by hear- ing; yet God withal made them able to inftruct, which every one could not do that was taught? After gifts of education, there follow general abilities to work things above nature, grace to cure men of bodily difeafes, fupplies againft occurrent de- fects and impediments, dexterities to govern and direct by counfel; finally, aptnefs to fpeak or interpret foreign tongues.   Which graces, not poured out equally, but diverfly forted and given, were a caufe why not only they all did furnifh up the whole body, but each benefit and help other.   Again, the fame apoftle other-where Ephef. 4. 7. in like fort, *To every one of us is given grace, according to the meafure of the gift* Pfal. 68. 18. *of Chrift. Wherefore he faith, when he afcended up on high, he led captivity cap- tive, and gave gifts unto men, He therefore gave fome apoftles, and fome prophets, and fome evangelifts, and fome paftors and teachers, for the gathering together of faints, for the work of the miniftry, for the edification of the body of Chrift.*   In this place none but gifts of inftruction are exprefs'd.   And becaufe of *teachers* fome were *evangelifts,* which neither had any part of their knowledge by revelation, as the *prophets,* and yet in ability to teach were far beyond other *paftors,* they are, as ha- ving received one way lefs than *prophets,* and another way more than *teachers,* fet accordingly between both.   For the apoftle doth in neither place refpect what any of them were by office or power given them through ordination, but what by grace they all had obtained through miraculous infufion of the Holy Ghoft.   For in chri- ftian religion, this being the ground of our whole belief, that the promifes which God of old had made his prophets concerning the wonderful gifts and graces of the Holy Ghoft, wherewith the reign of the true *Meffias* fhould be made glorious, were immediately after our Lord's afcenfion performed, there is no one thing whereof the apoftles did take more often occafion to fpeak.   Out of men thus endued with gifts of the fpirit upon their converfion to the chriftian faith, the church had her minifters chofen, unto whom was given ecclefiaftical power by ordination.   Now becaufe the apoftle in reckoning degrees and varieties of grace, doth mention *paftors* and *teachers,* although he mention them not in refpect of their ordination to exercife the miniftry, but as examples of men efpecially enriched with the gifts of the Holy Ghoft, divers learned and fkilful men have fo taken it, as if thofe places did intend to teach what orders of ecclefiaftical perfons there ought to be in the church of Chrift; which thing we are not to learn from thence, but out of other parts of holy · fcripture, whereby it clearly appeareth that churches apoftolick did know but three degrees in the power of ecclefiaftical order; at the firft *apoftles, presbyters* and *dea-*

cons;

tont; afterwards inftead of *apoftles*, *bifhops*, concerning whofe order we are to fpeak in the feventh book. There is an error which beguileth many, who do much intangle both themfelves and others, by not diftinguifhing *fervices*, *offices* and *orders* ecclefiaftical. The firft of which three, and in part the fecond, may be executed by the laity; whereas none have, or can have the third, but the clergy. Catechifts, exorcifts, readers, fingers, and the reft of like fort, if the nature only of their labours and pains be confidered, may in that refpect feem clergy-men, even as the fathers for that caufe term them ufually clerks; as alfo in regard of the end whereunto they were trained up, which was to be ordered when years and experience fhould make them able. Notwithftanding, in as much as they no way differed from others of the laity longer than during that work of fervice, which at any time they might give over, being thereunto but admitted, not tied by irrevocable ordination, we find them always exactly fevered from that body whereof thofe three before rehearfed orders alone are natural parts. Touching *widows*, of whom fome men are perfuaded, that if fuch as St. *Paul* defcribeth may be gotten, we ought to retain them in the church

T. C. l. r.
p. 191.
1 Tim. 5. 9. for ever, certain mean fervices there were of attendance; as about women at the time of their baptifm, about the bodies of the fick and dead, about the neceffities of travellers, wayfaring men, and fuch like, wherein the church did commonly ufe them when need required, becaufe they lived of the alms of the church, and were fitteft for fuch purpofes; St. *Paul* doth therefore, to avoid fcandal, require that none but women well experienced and virtuoufly given, neither any under threefcore years of age, fhould be admitted of that number. Widows were never in the church fo highly efteemed as virgins. But feeing neither of them did or could receive ordination, to make them ecclefiaftical perfons were abfurd. The ancienteft therefore of the fathers mention thofe three degrees of ecclefiaftical order fpecified, and no more.

Tertul. de
Perfecut. *When your captains* (faith *Tertullian*) *that is to fay, the deacons, presbyters and*
Optat. l. 1. *bifhops fly, who fhall teach the laity that they muft be conftant? Again, What fhould I mention laymen* (faith *Optatus*) *yea, or divers of the miniftry it felf? To what purpofe deacons, which are in the third, or presbyters in the fecond degree of priefthood, when the very heads and princes of all, even certain of the bifhops themfelves were content to redeem life with the lofs of heaven?* Heaps of allegations in a cafe fo evident and plain are needlefs. I may fecurely therefore conclude, that there are at this day in the church of *England*, no other than the fame degrees of ecclefiaftical orders, namely, *bifhops*, *presbyters* and *deacons*, which had their beginning from Chrift and his bleffed apoftles themfelves. As for *deans*, *prebendaries*, *parfons*, *vicars*, *curates*, *arch-deacons*, *chancellors*, *officials*, *commiffaries*, and fuch other like names, which being not found in holy fcripture, we have been thereby through fome mens error, thought to allow of ecclefiaftical degrees not known, nor ever heard of in the better ages of former times; all thefe are in truth but titles of office, whereunto partly ecclefiaftical perfons, and partly others, are in fundry forms and conditions admitted, as the ftate of the church doth need; degrees of order ftill continuing the fame they were from the firft beginning. Now what habit or attire doth befeem each order to ufe in the courfe of common life, both for the gravity of his place, and for example fake to other men, is a matter frivolous to be difputed of.

Of oblations,
foundations,
endowments,
tithes, all in-
tended for
perpetuity of
religion, A fmall meafure of wifdom may ferve to teach them how they fhould cut their coats. But feeing all well ordered polities have ever judged it meet and fit by certain fpecial diftinct ornaments to fever each fort of men from other when they are in publick, to the end that all may receive fuch compliments of civil honour as are due to their rooms and callings, even when their perfons are not known, it argueth a difproportioned mind in them, whom fo decent orders difpleafe.

which pur-
pofe being
chiefly ful-
filled by the
Clergies cer-
tain and fuf-
ficient main-
tenance, muft
needs by ali-
enation of
church-liv-
ings be made
fruftrate. 79. We might fomewhat marvel what the apoftle St. *Paul* fhould mean, to fay, that *covetoufnefs is idolatry*, if the daily practice of men did not fhew, that whereas nature requireth God to be honoured with wealth, we honour for the moft part wealth as God. Fain we would teach our felves to believe, that for worldly goods it fufficeth frugally and honeftly to ufe them to our own benefit, without detriment and hurt to others; or if we go a degree farther, and perhaps convert fome fmall contemptible portion thereof to charitable ufes, the whole duty which we owe unto God herein is fully fatisfied. But forafmuch as we cannot rightly honour God, unlefs both our fouls and bodies be fometime employed meerly in his fervice; again, fith we know that religion requireth at our hands the taking away of fo great a part of the time of our lives quite and clean from our own bufinefs, and the beftowing of the fame in his;

2
fuppofe.

suppose we that nothing of our wealth and subſtance is immediately due to God, but all our own to beſtow and ſpend as our ſelves think meet? Are not our riches as well his, as the days of our life are his? Wherefore, unleſs with part we acknowledge his ſupreme dominion by whoſe benevolence we have the whole, how give we honour to whom honour belongeth; or how hath God the things that are God's? I would know what nation in the world did ever honour God, and not think it a point of their duty to do him honour with their very goods. So that this we may boldly ſet down as a principle clear in nature, an axiom that ought not to be call'd in que-ſtion, a truth manifeſt and infallible, that men are eternally bound to honour God with their ſubſtance, in token of thankful acknowledgment that all they have is from him. To honour him with our worldly goods, not only by ſpending them in law-ful manner, and by uſing them without offence, but alſo by alienating from our ſelves ſome reaſonable part or portion thereof, and by offering up the ſame to him as a ſign that we gladly confeſs his ſole and ſovereign dominion over all, is a duty which all men are bound unto, and a part of that very worſhip of God, which, as the law of God and nature it ſelf requireth, ſo we are the rather to think all men no leſs ſtrictly bound thereunto than to any other natural duty, inaſmuch as the hearts of men do ſo cleave to theſe earthly things, ſo much admire them for the ſway they have in the world, impute them ſo generally either to nature or to chance and fortune, ſo little think upon the grace and providence from which they come, that unleſs by a kind of continual tribute we did acknowledge God's dominion, it may be doubted that in ſhort time men would learn to forget whoſe tenants they are, and imagine that the world is their own abſolute, free and independant inheri-tance. Now concerning the kind or quality of gifts which God receiveth in that ſort, we are to conſider them, partly as firſt they proceed from us, and partly as afterwards they are to ſerve for divine uſes. In that they are teſtimonies of our affection towards God, there is no doubt but ſuch they ſhould be as beſeemeth moſt his glory to whom we offer them. In this reſpect the fatneſs of *Abel's* ſacrifice is commended; the flower of all men's increaſe aſſigned to God by *Solomon*; the gifts and donations of the people rejected as oft as their cold affection to Godward made their pre-ſents to be little worth. Somewhat the heathens ſaw touching that which was here-in fit, and therefore they unto their gods did not think they might conſecrate any thing which was *impure* or *unſound*, or *already given*, or elſe *not truly their own to* *give*. Again, in regard of uſe, for as much as we know that God hath himſelf no need of worldly commodities, but taketh them becauſe it is our good to be ſo ex-erciſed, and with no other intent accepteth them, but to have them uſed for the end-leſs continuance of religion; there is no place left of doubt or controverſy, but that we in the choice of our gifts, are to level at the ſame mark, and to frame our ſelves to his kown intents and purpoſes. Whether we give unto God therefore that which himſelf by commandment requireth, or that which the publick conſent of the church thinketh good to allot, or that which every man's private devotion doth beſt like, in as much as the gift which we offer proceedeth not only as a teſtimony of our affection towards God, but alſo as a means to uphold religion, the exerciſe whereof cannot ſtand without the help of temporal commodities; if all men be taught of nature to wiſh, and as much as in them lieth to procure the perpetuity of good things; if for that very cauſe we honour admire their wiſdom, who having been founders of commonweals, could deviſe how to make the benefit they left behind them durable; if, eſpecially in this reſpect, we prefer *Lycurgus* before *Solon*, and the *Spartan* before the *Athenian* polity, it muſt needs follow, that as we do unto God very acceptable ſervice in honouring him with our ſubſtance, ſo our ſervice that way is then moſt acceptable, when it tendeth to perpetuity. The firſt permament donations of honour in this kind are temples. Which works do ſo much ſet forward the exerciſe of religion, that while the world was in love with religion, it gave to no ſort greater reverence than to whom it could point and ſay, *Theſe are the men that have built us ſynagogues.* But of churches we have ſpoken ſufficiently heretofore. The next things to churches are the ornaments of churches; memorials which men's devotion hath added to remain in the treaſure of God's houſe, not only for uſes wherein the exerciſe of religion preſently needeth them, but alſo partly for ſupply of future caſual neceſſities, whereunto the church is on earth ſubject, and partly to the end that while they are kept, they may continually ſerve as teſtimonies, giving all men to underſtand that God hath in every age and nati-

Purum, pro-bum, profa-num, ſacrum, Feſt. L. 14.

ñation fuch as think it no burden to honour him with their fubftance. The riches
firft of the tabernacle of God, and then of the temple of *Jerufalem*, arifing out of
voluntary gifts and donations, were, as we commonly fpeak, a *Nemo fcit* , the value
of them above that which any man would imagine. After that the tabernacle was
made, furnifhed with all neceffaries, and fet up, although in the wildernefs their
ability could not poffibly be great, the very metal of thofe veffels , which the prin-
Numb. 7. 85,
86. ces of the twelve tribes gave to God for their firft prefents, amounted even to two
thoufand and four hundred fhekels of filver, an hundred and twenty fhekels of gold,
every fhekel weighing half an ounce. What was given to the temple which *Solo-*
1 Chron. 29.
Exod. 25. 28. *mon* erected we may partly conjecture, when over and befides wood, marble, iron,
& 37. 24. brafs, veftments, precious ftones and money, the fum which *David* delivered into
Ezra 2. 68, *Solomon's* hands for that purpofe was of gold in mafs eight thoufand, and of filver fe-
69.
Hag. 2. 4. venteen thoufand cichars, every cichar containing a thoufand and eight hundred
Ezra 8. 24. fhekels, which rifeth to nine hundred ounces in every one cichar, whereas the whole
charge of the tabernacle did not amount unto thirty fhekels. After their return out
of *Babylon*, they were not prefently in cafe to make their fecond temple of equal
magnificence and glory with that which the enemy had deftroyed. Notwithftanding
what they could they did. Infomuch that the buildings finifhed, there remained in
the coffers of the church to uphold the fabrick thereof, fix hundred and fifty cichars
of filver, one hundred of gold. Whereunto was added by *Nehemias* of his own gift
Nehem. 7. 70. a thoufand drams of gold, fifty veffels of filver, five hundred and thirty priefts veftments; by other the princes of the fathers twenty thoufand drams of gold, two thoufand and two hundred pieces of filver; by the reft of the people twenty thoufand of
gold, two thoufand of filver, threefcore and feven attires of priefts. And they furthermore bound themfelves towards other charges to give by the pole, in what part of
the world foever they fhould dwell, the third of a fhekel, that is to fay, the fixth
Neh. 10. 32. part of an ounce yearly. ª This out of foreign provinces they always fent in gold.
Whereof ᵇ *Mithridates* is faid to have taken up by the way before it could pafs to
ª Cic. orat. *Jerufalem* from *Afia*, in one adventure, eight hundred talents , *Craffus* after that to
pro L. Flac. have borrowed of the temple it felf eight thoufand ; at which time *Eleazar* having
Cum aurum both many other rich ornaments, and all the tapiftry of the temple under his cuftody,
Judæorum no-
minequotannis thought it the fafeft way to grow unto fome compofition ; and fo to redeem the refi-
ex Italia & due by parting with a certain beam of gold about feven hundred and an half weight,
ex omnibus vo- a prey fufficient for one man, as he thought, who had never bargained with *Craffus*
ftris Provinciis
Hierofolymam till then, and therefore upon the confidence of a folemn oath that no more fhould
exportari fole- be looked for, he fimply delivered up a large morfel, whereby the value of that
ret, Flaccus which remained was betrayed , and the whole loft. Such being the cafualties where-
fanxit edicto ;
ne ex Afia ex- unto moveable treafures are fubject , the law of *Mofes* did both require eight and
portari liceret. twenty cities, together with their fields and whole territories in the land of *Jewry*,
ᵇ Jofeph. An- to be referved for God himfelf, and not only provide for the liberty of farther addi-
tiq. l. 4. c. 12.
ᶜ Every ta- tions , if men of their own accord fhould think good, but alfo for the fafe pre-
lent in va- fervation thereof unto all pofterities, that no man's avarice or fraud, by defeating fo
lue 600
Crowns. virtuous intents, might difcourage from like purpofes. God's third endowment did
Num. 35. therefore of old confift in lands. Furthermore, fome caufe no doubt there is why
Levit. 25.34. befides fundry other more rare donations of uncertain rate, the tenth fhould be
& 27. 38. thought a revenue fo natural to be allotted out unto God. For of the fpoils which
Abraham had taken in war, he delivered unto *Melchifedeck* the tythes. The vow of
Gen. 14. 20. *Jacob*, at fuch time as he took his journey towards *Haran*, was , *If God will be*
Gen. 28. 20. *with me, and will keep me in this voyage which I am to go, and will give me*
bread to eat, and cloaths to put on, fo that I may return to my father's houfe in
fafety , then fhall the Lord be my God; and this ftone which I have fet up as a
pillar, the fame fhall be God's houfe ; and of all thou fhalt give me I will give unto
thee the tithe. And as *Abraham* gave voluntarily, as *Jacob* vowed to give God
Deut. 14. 22. tithes, fo the law of *Mofes* did require at the hands of all men the felf-fame kind
of tribute, the tenth of their corn, wine, oil, fruit, cattle, and whatfoever increafe
Plin. hift. nat. his heavenly providence fhould fend. Infomuch that *Paynims* being heretofore fol-
l. 12. c. 14. lowers of their fteps, paid tithes likewife : Imagine we that this was for no caufe
done , or that there was not fome fpecial inducement to judge the tenth of our
worldly profits the moft convenient for God's portion ? Are not all things by him
created in fuch fort, that the forms which give them their diftinction are number,
their operations meafure, and their matter weight ? *Three* being the myftical number
of God's unfearchable perfection within himfelf; *Seven* the number whereby our

own perfections through grace are most ordered; and ten the number of natures perfections (for the beauty of nature is order; and the foundation of order, number; and of number, ten the highest we can rise unto without iteration of numbers under it) could nature better acknowledge the power of the God of nature, than by assigning unto him that quantity which is the continent of all she possesseth? There are in *Philo* the *Jew*, many arguments to shew the great congruity and fitness of this number in things consecrated unto God. But because over-nice and curious speculations become not the earnestness of holy things, I omit what might be farther observed, as well out of others, as out of him, touching the quantity of this general sacred tribute; whereby it cometh to pass that the meanest and the very poorest amongst men yielding unto God as much in proportion as the greatest, and many times in affection more, have this as a sensible token always assuring their minds, that in his sight, from whom all good is expected, they are concerning acceptation, protection, divine privileges and pre-eminences whatsoever, equals and peers with them unto whom they are otherwise in earthly respects inferiors; being furthermore well assured, that the top as it were thus presented to God, is neither lost, nor unfruitfully bestowed, but doth sanctify to them again the whole mass, and that he by receiving a little undertaketh to bless all. In which consideration the *Jews* were accustomed to name their tithes, the *hedge* of their riches. Albeit a hedge do only fence and preserve that which is contained, whereas their tithes and offerings did more, because they procured increase of the heap out of which they were taken. God demanded no such debt for his own need, but for their only benefit that owe it. Wherefore detaining the same, they hurt not him whom they wrong; and themselves whom they think they relieve, they wound; except men will haply affirm, that God did by fair speeches and large promises, delude the world in saying, *Bring ye all the tithes into the store-house, that there may be meat in mine house,* (deal truly, defraud not God of his due, but bring all) *and prove if I will not open unto you the windows of heaven, and pour down upon you an immeasurable blessing.* That which St. *James* hath concerning the effect of our prayers unto God, is for the most part of like moment in our gifts: We pray and obtain not, because he which knoweth our hearts, doth know our desires are evil. In like manner we give, and we are not the more accepted, because he beholdeth how unwisely we spill our gifts in the bringing. It is to him which needeth nothing, all one whether any thing or nothing be given him. But for our own good, it always behoveth that whatsoever we offer up into his hands, we bring it seasoned with this cogitation, *Thou Lord art worthy of all honour.* With the church of Christ, touching these matters, it standeth as it did with the whole world before *Moses.* Whereupon for many years men being desirous to honour God in the same manner as other virtuous and holy personages before had done, both during the time of their life, and if farther ability did serve, by such device as might cause their works of piety to remain always, it came by these means to pass that the church from time to time had treasure, proportionable unto the poorer or wealthier estate of christian men. And assoon as the state of the church could admit thereof, they easily condescended to think it most natural and most fit that God should receive, as before, of all men his ancient accustomed revenues of tithes. Thus therefore both God and nature have taught to convert things temporal to eternal uses, and to provide for the perpetuity of religion, even by that which is most transitory. For to the end that in worth and value there might be no abatement of any thing once assigned to such purposes, the law requireth precisely the best of what we possess; and to prevent all damages by way of commutation, where instead of natural commodities or other rights the price of them might be taken, the law of *Moses* determined their rates, and the payments to be always made by the sicle of the sanctuary, wherein there was great advantage of weight above the ordinary currant sicle. The truest and surest way for God to have always his own, is by making him payment in kind out of the very self-same riches which through his gracious benediction the earth doth continually yield. This, where it may be without inconvenience, is for every man's conscience sake. That which cometh from God to us, by the natural course of his providence, which we know to be innocent and pure, is perhaps best accepted, because least spotted with the stain of unlawful or indirect procurement. Besides, whereas prices daily change, nature which commonly is one, must needs be the most indifferent and permanent standard between God and man. But the main foundation of all, whereupon the security of these things dependeth, as far as any thing may be ascertained amongst men, is that the title

and

[marginal notes:]

Δεκὰς ἀριθμῶν τῶν ἀπὸ μονάδ᾽ὦ τῶ πᾶσι περιέχων. Philo de Ἀπία.

Massoreth sepes est legis; divitiarum sepes decima. R. Aquiba in Pirk. Aboth.

Mal. 3.

Nemo libenter debet quod non accepit sed extpressit. Sen. de Benef. l. 1. c. 1.

Levit. 27. 25.

and right which man had in every of them before donation, doth by the act, and from the time of any such donation, dedication, or grant, remain the proper possession of God till the world's end, unless himself renounce or relinquish it. For if equity have taught us, that every one ought to enjoy his own; that what is ours, no other can alienate from us, but with our [a] own [b] deliberate consent; finally, that no man having past his consent or deed, may [c] change it to the prejudice of any other, should we presume to deal with God worse than God hath allowed any man to deal with us? Albeit therefore we be now free from the law of *Moses*, and consequently not thereby bound to the payment of tithes; yet because nature hath taught men to honour God with their substance, and scripture hath left us an example of that particular proportion, which for moral considerations hath been thought fittest by him whose wisdom could best judge; furthermore, seeing that the church of Christ hath long sithence entred into like obligation, it seemeth in these days a question altogether vain and superfluous, whether tithes be a matter of divine right: because howsoever at the first it might have been thought doubtful, our case is clearly the same now with theirs unto whom St. *Peter* sometime spake, saying, *While it was whole, it was whole thine.* When our tithes might have probably seemed our own, we had colour of liberty to use them as we our selves saw good. But having made them his whose they are, let us be warned by other men's example what it is ρωτοῖοι-δαι, to wash or clip that coin which hath on it the mark of God. For that all these are his possessions, and that he doth himself so reckon them, appeareth by the form of his own speeches. Touching gifts and oblations, *Thou shalt give them me*; touching oratories and churches, *My house* shall be called the house of prayer; touching tithes, *Will a man spoil God?* Yet behold, even me your God ye have *spoiled*, notwithstanding ye ask wherein, as though ye were ignorant what injury there hath been offered in tithes: ye are heavily accursed, because with a kind of publick consent ye have joined your selves in one to rob me, imagining the commonness of your offence to be every man's particular justification. Touching lands, *Ye shall offer to the Lord a sacred portion of ground, and that sacred portion shall belong to the priests.* Neither did God only thus ordain amongst the *Jews*, but the very purpose, intent, and meaning of all that have honoured him with their substance, was to invest him with the property of those benefits, the use whereof must needs be committed to the hands of men. In which respect the stile of ancient grants and charters is, *We have given unto God both for us and our heirs for ever.* Yea, *We know*, saith *Charles* the great, that *the goods of the church are the sacred endowments of God, to the Lord our God we offer and dedicate whatsoever we deliver unto his church.* Whereupon the laws imperial do likewise divide all things in such sort, that they make some to belong by right of nature indifferently unto every man, some to be the certain goods and possessions of commonweals, some to appertain unto several corporations and companies of men, some to be privately men's own in particular, and some to be separated quite [d] from all men; which last branch compriseth things sacred and holy, because thereof God alone is owner. The sequel of which received opinion, as well without as within the walls of the house of God touching such possessions, is, as hath been ever, that there is not an act more honourable than by all means to amplify and to defend the patrimony of religion, not any more [e] impious and hateful than to impair those possessions which men in former times, when they gave unto holy uses, were wont at the altar of God and in the presence of their ghostly superiors, to make as they thought inviolable by words of fearful execration, saying, *These things we offer to God, from whom if any take them away (which we hope no man will attempt to do) but if any shall, let his account be without favour in the last day, when he cometh to receive the doom which is due for sacrilege against that Lord and God unto whom we dedicate the same.* The best and most renowned prelates of the church of Christ have in this consideration rather sustained the wrath, than yielded to satisfy the hard desire of their greatest commanders on earth, coveting with ill advice and counsel that which they willingly should have suffered God to enjoy. There are of martyrs, whom posterity doth much honour, for that having under their hands the custody of such [f] treasures, they could by virtuous delusion invent how to save them from prey, even when the safety of their own lives they gladly neglected; as one, sometime an archdeacon under *Xistus* the bishop of *Rome*, did, whom when his judge understood

to

Lib. 11. *de Reg. Jur.*
[b] *Cujus per errorem dati repetitio est, ejus consulto dati donatio est,* l. 1. D. de cond. indeb. This is the ground of *Confideration* in alienations from man to man.
[c] *Nemo potest mutare confilium fuum in alterius prajudicium,* l. 75. de Reg. Jur. Acts 5. 4. Exod. 22. 28, 30. Matth. 21. 13. Mal. 3. 8.

Non videntur rem amittere quibus propria non fuit, l. 38. de Reg. Jur. Esech. 45. 1, 2.

Mag. char. c. 1.

Capit. Carol. l. 6. c. 284.

[d] *Nullius autem funt res facra & religiosa & fancta. Quod enim divini juris est, id nullius in bonis est.* Inftit. l. 2. tit. 1.
[e] *Soli cum diis facrilegi pugnant,* Curt. l. 7. *Sacrum facrove commendatum qui demferit rapferitve, parricida esto.* Leg. 12. tab. Capit. Carol. l. 6. c. 285.
[f] *deposita pietatis.* Terrul. Apologet. Prudent. Perisiteph.

to be one of the church stewards, thirst of blood began to slake, and another humour to work, which first by a favourable countenance, and then by quiet speech did thus calmly disclose it self; *You that profess the christian religion, make great complaint of the wonderful truelty we shew towards you. Neither peradventure altogether without cause. But for my self, I am far from any such bloody purpose. Ye are not so willing to live, as I unwilling that out of these lips should proceed any capital sentence against you. Your bishops are said to have rich vessels of gold and silver, which they use in the exercise of their religion; besides the fame is, that numbers sell away their lands and livings, the huge prices whereof are brought to your church coffers; by which means the devotion, that maketh them and their whole posterity poor, must needs mightily enrich you, whose God we know was no coiner of money, but left behind him many wholesome and good precepts, as namely, that Cæsar should have of you the things that are fit for, and due to Cæsar. His wars are costly and chargeable unto him. That which you suffer to rust in corners, the affairs of the commonwealth do need. Your profession is not to make account of things transitory. And yet if ye can be contented but to forego that which ye care not for, I dare undertake to warrant you both safety of life, and freedom of using your conscience, a thing more acceptable to you than wealth.* Which fair parley the happy martyr quietly hearing, and perceiving it necessary to make some shift for the safe concealment of that which being now desired, was not unlikely to be more narrowly afterwards sought, he craved respite for three days to gather the riches of the church together, in which space against the time the governor should come to the doors of the temple, big with hope to receive his prey, a miserable rank of poor, lame and impotent persons was provided, their names delivered him up in writing as a true inventory of the churches goods, and some few words used to signify how proud the church was of these treasures. If men did not naturally abhor sacrilege, to resist or to defeat so impious attempts would deserve small praise. But such is the general detestation of rapine in this kind, that whereas nothing doth either in peace or war more uphold men's reputation than prosperous success, because in common construction, unless notorious improbity be joined with prosperity, it seemeth to argue favour with God; they which once have stained their hands with these odious spoils, do thereby fasten unto all their actions an eternal prejudice, in respect whereof, for that it passeth through the world as an undoubted rule and principle that sacrilege is open defiance to God, whatsoever afterwards they undertake, if they prosper in it, men reckon it but *Dionysius* his navigation; and if any thing befal them otherwise, it is not, as commonly, so in them ascribed to the great uncertainty of casual events, wherein the providence of God doth controul the purposes of men oftentimes, much more for their good than if all things did answer fully their hearts desire, but the censure of the world is ever directly against them both [a] bitter and peremptory. To make such actions therefore less odious, and to mitigate the envy of them, many coloured shifts and inventions have been used, as if the world did hate only wolves, and think the fox a goodly creature. The [b] time it may be will come, when they that either violently have spoiled, or thus smoothly defrauded God, shall find they did but deceive themselves. In the mean while there will be always some skilful persons, which can teach a way how to grind treatably the church with

[a] *Novimus multa regna, & reges eorum, propterea cecidisse; quia Ecclesias spoliaverunt, resque earum vastaverunt, alienaverunt vel diripuerunt, Episcopisque & Sacerdotibus, atque, quod majus est, Ecclesiis eorum abstulerunt, & pugnantibus dederunt. Quapropter nec fortes in bello nec in fide stabiles fuerunt, nec victores extiterunt; sed terga multi vulnerati, & plures interfecti ceciderunt, vegnaque & regiones, & , quod pejus est, regna cælestia perdiderunt, atque propriis hereditatibus caruerunt, & hactenus carent.* Verba Corol. Ma. in Capitu. Carol. l. 7. cap. 104.

[b] *Turno tempus erit magno cum optaverit emptum Intactum Pallanta, & cum spolia ista diemque Oderit.* Virg. Æn. lib. 10.

jaws that shall scarce move, and yet devour in the end more than they that come ravening with open mouth, as if they would worry the whole in an instant; others also, who having wastfully eaten out their own patrimony, would be glad to repair, if they might, decayed estates with the ruin they care not of what nor of whom, so the spoil were theirs; whereof in some part if they happen to speed, yet commonly they are men born under that constellation which maketh them, I know not how, as unapt to enrich themselves as they are ready to impoverish others; it is their lot to sustain during life, both the misery of beggers and the infamy of robbers. But though no other [Greek text] plague and revenge should follow sacrilegious violations of holy things, the natural [Greek text] secret disgrace and ignominy, the very turpitude of such actions in the eye of a wise [Greek text] understanding heart, is it self a heavy punishment. Men of virtuous quality are by [Greek text] this sufficiently moved to beware how they answer and require the mercies of God with [Greek text]

Pp   in-

injuries, whether openly or indirectly offered. I will not absolutely say concerning the goods of the church, that they may in no case be seized on by men, or that no obligation, commerce and bargain made between man and man, can ever be of force to alienate the property which God hath in them. Certain cases I grant there are, wherein it is not so dark what God himself doth warrant, but that we may safely presume him as willing to forego for our benefit, as always to use and convert to our benefit whatsoever our religion hath honoured him withal. But surely under the name of that which may be, many things that should not be are often done. By means whereof the church most commonly for gold hath flatnel; and whereas the usual saw of old was *Glaucus his change*, the proverb is now, *A Church-Bargain*. And for fear left covetousness alone should linger our time too much, and not be able to make havock of the house of God with that expedition which the mortal enemy thereof did vehemently wish, he hath by certain strong enchantments so deeply bewitcht religion it self, as to make it in the end an earnest sollicitor, and an eloquent persuader of sacrilege, urging confidently that the very best service which men of power can do to Christ, is without any more ceremony to sweep all, and to leave the church as bare as in the day it was first born; that fulnefs of bread having made the children of the houshold wanton, it is without any scruple to be taken away from them, and thrown to dogs; that they which laid the prices of their lands as offerings at the apostles feet, did but fow the seeds of superstition; that they which endowed churches with lands, poisoned religion; that tithes and obligations are now in the sight of God as the sacrificed blood of goats; that if we give him our hearts and affections, our goods are better bestowed otherwise; that *Irenæus Polycarp's* disciple should not have said, *We offer unto God our goods as tokens of thankfulnefs for that we receive*; neither *Origen*, *He which worshippeth God, must by gifts and obligations acknowledge him the Lord of all*; in a word, that to give unto God is error; reformation of error, to take from the church that which the blindness of former ages did unwisely give. By these or the like suggestions, received with all joy, and with like sedulity practised in certain parts of the christian world, they have brought so pass, that as *David* doth say of man, so it is in hazard to be verified concerning the whole religion and service of God; *The time thereof may peradventure fall out to be threescore and ten years, or if strength do serve unto fourscore, what followeth, is likely to be small joy for them whatsoever they be that behold it.* Thus have the best things been overthrown, not so much by puissance and might of adversaries, as through defect of counsel in them that should have upheld and defended the same.

Pœnam non dico legum quas sæpe per-rumpunt, sed ipsius turpitu-dinis quæ acer-bissima est non vident. Cic. Offic. l. 3.

Impunita tu credes esse quæ invisa sunt? aut ullum sup-plicium gravi-us existimas publico odio? Sen. de Be-nef. l. 3. c. 17.
Iren. l. 4. c. 34.
Orig. in 18.
Num. hom. 11.

80. There are in a minister of God these four things to be considered, his Ordination which giveth him power to meddle with things sacred; the charge or portion of the church allotted unto him for exercise of his office; the performance of his duty, according to the exigence of his charge; and lastly, the maintenance which in that respect he receiveth. All ecclesiastical laws and canons which either concern the bestowing or the using of the power of ministerial order, have relation to these four. Of the first we have spoken before at large. Concerning the next, for more convenient discharge of ecclesiastical duties, as the body of the people must needs be severed by divers precincts, so the clergy likewise accordingly distributed. Whereas therefore religion did first take place in cities, and in that respect was a cause why the name of pagans, which properly signifieth a countrey people, came to be used in common speech for the same that infidels and unbelievers were; it followed thereupon that all such cities had their ecclesiastical colleges, consisting of deacons and of presbyters, whom first the apostles or their delegates the evangelists did both ordain and govern. Such were the colleges of *Jerusalem, Antioch, Ephesus, Rome, Corinth*, and the rest, where the apostles are known to have planted our faith and Religion. Now because religion and the cure of souls was their general charge in common over all that were near about them, neither had any one presbyter his several cure apart, till *Evaristus* bishop in the fee of *Rome* about the year 112. began to assign precincts unto every church or title which the christians held, and to appoint unto each presbyter a certain compass whereof himself should take charge alone, the commodiousness of this invention caused all parts of *Christendom* to follow it, and at the length among the rest our own churches about the year 636. became divided in like manner. But other distinction of. churches there doth not appear any in the apostles writings, save only, according to those cities wherein they planted the gospel of Christ, and erected

Of ordinations lawful without ti-tle, and with-out any po-pular electi-on preceedent, but in no case with-out regard of due infor-mation what their qua lity is, that enter into holy orders.

4

eccle-

ecclefiaftical colleges.   Wherefore to ordain *κατα πόλιν* throughout every city , and Tit. 1. 5.
κατα ὅκκλησίαν throughout every church, do in them fignify the fame thing. Churches Acts 14. 23.
then neither were, nor could be in fo convenient fort limited as now they are ; firft,
by the bounds of each ftate , and then within each ftate by more particular precincts, till at the length we defcend unto feveral congregations, termed *Parifhes;*
with far narrower reftraint than this name at the firft was ufed.   And from hence
hath grown their error, who as oft as they read of the duty which ecclefiaftical perfons are now to perform towards the church , their manner is always to
underftand by that church, fome particular congregation or parifh church.   They
fuppofe that there fhould now be no man of ecclefiaftical order, which is not
tied to fome certain parifh.   Becaufe the names of all church-officers are words
of relation , becaufe a fhepherd muft have his flock, a teacher his fcholars, a minifter his company which he miniftreth unto , therefore it feemeth a thing in
their eyes abfurd and unreafonable, that any man fhould be ordained a minifter,
otherwife than only for fome particular congregation.   Perceive they not how
by this means they make it unlawful for the church to employ men at all in converting nations ? For if fo be the church may not lawfully admit to an ecclefiaftical
function, unlefs it tie the party admitted unto fome particular parifh, then furely a
thanklefs labour it is, whereby men feek the converfion of infidels, which know not
Chrift, and therefore cannot be as yet divided into their fpecial congregations and
flocks.   But to the end it may appear how much this one thing among many more
hath been miftaken , there is firft no precept requiring that presbyters and deacons be
made in fuch fort, and not otherwife.   Albeit therefore the apoftles did make them
in that order, yet is not their example fuch a law , as without all exception bindeth to make them in no other order but that.   Again, if we will confider that which
the apoftles themfelves did, furely no man can juftly fay , that herein we practife
any thing repugnant to their example.   For by them there was ordained only in each
chriftian city a college of presbyters and deacons to adminifter holy things.   *Evari-*
ftus did a hundred years after the birth of our Saviour Chrift, begin the diftinction
of the church into parifhes.   Presbyters and deacons having been ordained before to
exercife ecclefiaftical functions in the church of *Rome* promifcuoufly, he was the
firft that tied them each one to his own ftation.   So that of the two , indefinite
ordination of presbyters and deacons doth come more near the apoftles example, and
the tying of them to be made only for particular congregations, may more juftly ground
it felf upon the example of *Evariftus*, than of any apoftle of Chrift.   It hath been
the opinion of wife and good men heretofore , that nothing was ever devifed more
fingularly beneficial unto God's church, than this which our honourable predeceffors
have to their endlefs praife found out, by the erecting of fuch houfes of ftudy , as
thofe two moft famous univerfities do contain, and providing that choice wits,
after reafonable time fpent in contemplation , may at the length either enter into
that holy vocation for which they have been fo long nourifhed and brought up, or
elfe give place and fuffer others to fucceed in their rooms, that fo the church may
be always furnifhed with a number of men, whofe abilities being firft known by publick trial in church-labours there where men can beft judge of them, their calling afterwards unto particular charge abroad may be accordingly.   All this is fruftrate,
thofe worthy foundations we muft diffolve, their whole device and religious purpofe
which did erect them is made void, their orders and ftatutes are to be cancelled and difannulled, in cafe the church be forbidden to grant any power of order, unlefs it be
with reftraint to the party ordained unto fome particular parifh or congregation.   Nay,
might we not rather affirm of presbyters and of deacons, that the very nature of
their ordination is unto neceffary local reftraint a thing oppofite and repugnant ? The
emperor *Juftinian* doth fay of tutors, *Certæ rei vel caufæ tutor dari non poteft,* Juft. l. 1. tit.
quia perfonæ, non caufæ vel rei, tutor datur.   He that fhould grant a tutorfhip, re- 14. fect. 4.
ftraining his grant to fome one certain thing or caufe, fhould do but idlely, becaufe
tutors are given for perfonal defenfe generally, and not for managing of a few particular things or caufes.   So he that ordaining a presbyter or a deacon fhould, in the
form of ordination, reftrain the one or the other to a certain place, might with
much more reafon be thought to ufe a vain and a frivolous addition , than they reafonably to require fuch local reftraint, as a thing which muft of neceffity concur
evermore with all lawful ordination.   Presbyters and deacons are not by ordination confecrated unto places , but unto functions.   In which refpect, and in no other
it is, that fith they are by virtue thereof bequeathed unto God, fevered and fancti-

fied

fied to be employed in his service, which is the highest advancement that mortal creatures on earth can be raised unto, the church of Christ hath not been acquainted in former ages with any such prophane and unnatural custom, as doth hallow men with ecclesiastical functions of order only for a time, and then dismiss them again to the common affairs of the world. Whereas, contrariwise from the place or charge where that power hath been exercised, we may be by sundry good and lawful occasions translated, retaining nevertheless the self-same power which was first given. It is some grief to spend thus much labour in refuting a thing that hath so little ground to uphold it, especially sith they themselves that teach it, do not seem to give thereto any credit, if we may judge their minds by their actions. There are amongst them that have done the work of ecclesiastical persons, sometime in the Families of noblemen, sometime in much more publick and frequent congregations; there are that have successively gone through perhaps seven or eight particular churches after this sort; yea, some that at one and the same time have been, some which at this present hour are, in real obligation of ecclesiastical duty, and possession of commodity thereto belonging, even in sundry particular churches within the land; some there are amongst them which will not so much abridge their liberty, as to be fastned or tied unto any place; some which have bound themselves to one place, only for a time, and that time being once expired, have afterwards voluntarily given other places the like experience and trial of them. All this I presume they would not do, if their persuasion were as strict as their words pretend. But for the avoiding of these and such other the like confusions, as are incident unto the cause and question whereof we presently treat, there is not any thing more material, than first to separate exactly the nature of the ministry from the use and exercise thereof: secondly, to know that the only true and proper act of ordination is, to invest men with that power which doth make them ministers, by consecrating their persons to God and his service in holy things, during term of life, whether they exercise that power or no; thirdly, that to give them a title or charge where to use their ministry, concerneth not the making, but the placing of God's ministers; and therefore the laws which concern only their election or admission unto place of charge, are not appliable to enfringe any way their ordination; fourthly, that as oft as any ancient constitution, law, or canon is alledged concerning either ordinations or elections, we forget not to examine whether the present case be the same which the ancient was, or else do contain some just reason for which it cannot admit altogether the same rules which former affairs of the church, now altered, did then require. In the question of making ministers without title, which to do, they say is a thing unlawful, they should at the very first have considered what the name of *Title* doth imply, and what affinity or coherence ordinations have with titles; which thing observed would plainly have shewed them their own error. They are not ignorant, that when they speak of a title, they handle that which belongeth to the placing of a minister in some charge, that the place of charge wherein a minister doth execute his office, requireth some house of God for the people to resort unto, some definite number of souls unto whom he there administreth holy things, and some certain allowance whereby to sustain life; that the fathers at the first named *Oratories*, and houses of prayer titles; thereby signifying how God was interessed in them, and held them as his own possessions. But because they know that the church had ministers before christian temples and oratories were, therefore some of them understand by a title, *a definite congregation* of people only, and so deny that any ordination is lawful, which maketh ministers that have no certain flock to attend: forgetting how the seventy whom Christ himself did ordain ministers, had their calling in that manner, whereas yet no certain charge could be given them. Others referring the name of a title especially to the maintenance of the minister, infringe all ordination made, except they which receive orders be first entituled to a competent ecclesiastical benefice, and (which is most ridiculously strange) except besides their present title to some such benefice, they have likewise some other title of annual rent or pension, whereby they may be relieved, in case

Unlawful to ordain a minister without a title, *Abstra.* p. 243. & pag. 246. The law requireth, that every one admitted unto orders having for his present relief some ecclesiastical benefice, should also have some other title unto some annual rent or pension, whereby he might be relieved, in case he were not able through infirmity, sickness, or other lawful impediment, to execute his ecclesiastical office and Function.

through infirmity, sickness, or other lawful impediment they grow unable to execute their ecclesiastical function. So that every man lawfully ordained must bring a bow which hath two strings, a title of present right, and another to provide for future poffibility or chance. Into thefe abfurdities and follies they flide, by mif-conceiving the true purpofe of certain canons, which indeed have forbidden to ordain a minifter without a title; not that fimply it is unlawful fo to ordain, but becaufe it might grow to an inconveniency, if the church did not fomewhat reftrain that liberty. For feeing they which have once received ordination, cannot again return into the world, it behoveth them which ordain to forefee how fuch fhall be afterwards able to live, left their poverty and deftitution fhould redound to the difgrace and difcredit of their calling. Which evil prevented, thofe very laws which in that refpect forbid, do exprefly admit ordinations to be made at large, and without title; namely, if the party fo ordained have of his own for the fuftenance of this life; or if the bifhop which giveth him orders, will find him competent allowance, till fome place of mi-niftration, from whence his maintenance may arife, be provided for him; or if any other fit and fufficient means be had againft the danger before-mentioned. Abfolute-ly therefore it is not true, that any ancient canon of the church, which is, or ought to be with us in force, doth make ordinations at large unlawful, and as the ftate of the church doth ftand, they are moft neceffary. If there be any confcience in men touching that which they write or fpeak, let them confider as well what the pre-fent condition of all things doth now fuffer, as what the ordinances of former ages did appoint; as well the weight of thofe caufes for which our affairs have altered, as the reafons in regard whereof our fathers and predeceffors did fometime ftrictly and feverely keep that, which for us to obferve now is neither meet, nor always poffi-ble. In this our prefent caufe and controverfy, whether any not having title of right to a benefice, may be lawfully ordained a minifter, is it not manifeft in the eyes of all men, that whereas the name of a benefice doth fignify fome ftanding ecclefiafti-cal revenue, taken out of the treafure of God, and allotted to a fpiritual perfon, to the end he may ufe the fame, and enjoy it as his own for term of life, unlefs his default caufe deprivation: the clergy for many years after Chrift, had no other bene-fices, but only their canonical portions, or monthly dividends allowed them, accord-ing to their feveral degrees and qualities, out of the common ftock of fuch gifts, oblations and tithes, as the fervour of chriftian piety did then yield. Yea, that even when minifters had their churches and flocks affigned unto them in feveral; yet for maintenance of life, their former kind of allowance continued, till fuch time as bi-fhops, and churches cathedral being fufficiently endowed with lands, other presbyters enjoyed, inftead of their firft benefices, the tithes and profits of their own congrega-tions whole to themfelves. Is it not manifeft, that in this realm, and fo in other the like dominions, where the tenure of lands is altogether grounded on military laws, and held as in fee under princes which are not made heads of the people by force or voluntary election, but born the fovereign Lords of thofe whole and entire territo-ries, which territories their famous progenitors obtaining by way of conqueft, re-tained what they would in their own hands, and divided the reft to others with re-fervation of foveraignty and capital intereft; the building of churches, and confe-quently the affigning of either parifhes or benefices, was a thing impoffible without confent of fuch as were principal owners of land; in which confideration, for their more encouragement hereunto, they which did fo far benefit the church, had by com-mon confent granted (as great equity and reafon was) a right for them and their heirs till the world's end, to nominate in thofe benefices men whofe quality the bi-fhop allowing might admit them thereunto? Is it not manifeft, that from hence ine-vitably fuch inequality of parifhes hath grown, as caufeth fome, through the multi-tude of people which have refort unto one church, to be more than any one man can wield, and fome to be of that nature by reafon of chapels annexed, that they which are incumbents fhould wrong the church, if fo be they had not certain fti-pendiaries under them, becaufe where the corps of the profit or benefice is but one, the title can be but one mans, and yet the charge may require more? Not to men-tion therefore any other reafon, whereby it may clearly appear how expedient it is, and profitable for the church to admit ordinations without title, this little may fuf-fice to declare, how impertinent their allegations againft it are out of ancient canons; how untrue their confident affeverations, that only through negligence of popifh pre-lates, the cuftom of making fuch kind of minifters hath prevailed in the church of *Rome* againft their canons, and that with us it is exprefly againft the laws of our own government, when a minifter doth ferve as a ftipendiary curate, which kind of fervice neverthelefs the greateft rabbins of that part do altogether follow. For how-foever they are loth peradventure to be named curates, ftipendiaries they are,

and

and the labour they beftow is in other mens cures; a thing not unlawful for them to do, yet unfeemly for them to condemn which practife it. I might here difcover the like over-fight throughout all their difcourfes, made in behalf of the peoples pretended right to elect their minifters, before the bifhop may lawfully ordain. But becaufe we have otherwhere at large difputed of popular elections, and of the right of patronage, wherein is drowned whatfoever the people under any pretence of colour may feem to challenge, about admiffion and choice of the paftors that fhall feed their fouls, I cannot fee what one duty there is which always ought to go before ordination, but only care of the parties worthinefs as well for integrity and virtue, as knowledge; yea for virtue more: in as much as defect of knowledge may fundry ways be fupplied, but the fcandal of vicious and wicked life is a deadly evil.

Of the learning that fhould be in minifters, their refidence, and the number of their livings.

81. The truth is, that of all things hitherto mentioned, the greateft is that threefold blot or blemifh of notable ignorance, unconfcionable abfence from the cures whereof men have taken charge, and unfatiable hunting after fpiritual preferments, without either care or confcience of the publick good. Whereof, to the end that we may confider, as in God's own fight and prefence with all uprightnefs, fincerity and truth, let us particularly weigh and examine in every of them, firft, how far forth they are reproveable by reafons and maxims of common right; fecondly, whether that which our laws do permit, be repugnant to thofe maxims, and with what equity we ought to judge of things practifed in this cafe, neither on the one hand defending that which muft be acknowledged out of fquare, nor on the other fide condemning rafhly whom we lift for whatfoever we difallow. Touching arguments therefore taken from the principles of common right, to prove that minifters fhould [a] be learned, that they ought to be [b] refident upon their livings, and that [c] more than one only benefice or fpiritual living may not be granted unto one man; the firft, becaufe St. *Paul* requireth in a minifter ability to teach, to convince, to diftribute the word rightly; becaufe alfo the Lord himfelf hath protefted they fhall be no priefts to him which have rejected knowledge, and becaufe if the blind lead the blind, they muft both needs fall into the pit; the fecond, becaufe teachers are fhepherds, whofe flocks can be no time fecure from danger; they are watchmen whom the enemy doth always befiege; their labours in the word and facraments admit no intermiffion; their duty requireth inftruction and conference with men in private; they are the living oracles of God, to whom the people muft refort for counfel; they are commanded to be patterns of holinefs, leaders, feeders, fupervifors amongft their own; it fhould be their grief, as it was the apoftles, to be abfent, though neceffarily, from them over whom they have taken charge; finally, the laft, becaufe plurality and refidence are oppofite; becaufe the placing of one clark in two churches is a point of merchandize and filthy gain; becaufe no man can ferve two mafters; becaufe every one fhould remain in that vocation whereunto he is called; what conclude they of all this? Againft ignorance, againft non-refidence, and againft plurality of livings, is there any man fo raw and dull, but that the volumes which have been written both of old and of late, may make him in fo plentiful a caufe eloquent? For if by that which is generally juft and requifite, we meafure what knowledge there fhould be in a minifter of the gofpel of Chrift; the arguments which light of nature offereth; the laws and ftatutes which fcripture hath; the canons that are taken out of ancient fynods; the decrees and conftitutions of fincereft times; the fentences of all antiquity; and in a word, even every man's full confent and confcience is againft ignorance in them that have charge and cure of fouls. Again, what availeth it if we be learned and not faithful? Or what benefit hath the church of Chrift, if there be in us fufficiency without endeavour or care to do that good which our place exacteth? Touching the pains and induftry therefore, wherewith men are in confcience bound to attend the work of their heavenly calling, even as much as in them lyeth bending thereunto their whole endeavour, without either fraud, fophiftication, or guile; I fee not what more effectual obligation or bond of duty there fhould be urged, than their own only vow and promife made unto God himfelf at the time of their ordination. The work which they have undertaken requireth both care and fear. Their floth that negligently perform it, maketh them fubject to malediction. Befides, we alfo know that the fruit of our pains in this function, is life both to our felves and others. And do we yet need incitements to labour? Shall we ftop our ears both againft thofe conjuring

exhor-

[a] *T. C. l. 1. p. 70.*   [b] *66.*   [c] *69.* 1 Tim. 3. 2. Titus 1. 9. 2 Tim. 2. 15. Hofea 4. 6. Matth. 15. 14. Luke 2. 8. Acts 20. 2. 1 Sam. 1. 19. 1 Tim. 4. 12. John 10. 4. 1 Pet. 5. 2. Acts 20. 28. 1 Theff. 2. 17. *Concil. Nic. Cap.* 15. Matth. 6. 24. 1 Cor. 7. 24.

exhortations which apostles, and against the fearful comminations which prophets have uttered out of the mouth of God, the one for prevention, the other for reformation of our sluggishness in this behalf? St. *Paul, Attend to your selves, and to all* Acts 20. 27. *the flock, whereof the Holy Ghost hath made you over-seers, to feed the church of God, which he hath purchased with his own blood.* Again, *I charge thee before God, and the Lord Jesus Christ, which shall judge the quick and the dead at his coming, preach the word; be instant.* Jeremiah, *Wo unto the pastors that destroy and* Jer. 23. 2. *scatter the sheep of my pasture; I will visit you for the wickedness of your works, saith the Lord; the remnant of my sheep I will gather together out of all countries, and will bring them again to their folds, they shall grow and increase, and I will set up shepherds over them, which shall feed them.* Ezekiel, *Should not the shep-* Ezek. 34. 2. *herds, should they not feed the flocks? Ye eat the fat, and ye cloath your selves with the wooll, but the weak ye have not strengthned, the sick ye have not cured, neither have ye bound up the broken, nor brought home again that which was driven away? Ye have not enquired after that which was lost, but with cruelty and rigor have ruled.* And verse 8. *Wherefore, as I live, I will require,* &c. Nor let us think to excuse our selves, if haply we labour, though it be at random, and sit not altogether idle abroad. For we are bound to attend that part of the flock of Christ, whereof the Holy Ghost hath made us over-seers. The residence of ministers upon their own peculiar charge, is by so much the rather necessary, for that absenting themselves from the place where they ought to labour, they neither can do the good which is looked for at their hands, nor reap the comfort which sweetneth life to them that spend it in these travels upon their own. For it is in this as in all things else, which are through private interest dearer, than what concerneth either others wholly, or us but in part, and according to the rate of a general regard. As for plurality, it hath not only the same inconveniencies which are observed to grow by absence; but over and besides, at the least in common construction, a shew of that worldly humour which men do think should not reign so high. Now from hence their collections are as followeth; first, a repugnancy or contradiction between the principles of common right, and that which our laws in special considerations have allowed: secondly, a nullity or fruition of all such acts as are by them supposed opposite to those principles, an invalidity in all ordinations of men unable to preach, and in all dispensations which mitigate the law of common right for the other two: And why so? Forsooth, because whatever we do in these three cases, and not by Abstract, p. virtue of common right, we must yield it of necessity done by warrant of peculiar 117. right or privilege. Now a privilege is said to be that, that for favour of certain persons cometh forth against common right; things prohibited are dispensed with, because things permitted are dispatched by common right, but things forbidden require dispensations. By which descriptions of a privilege and dispensation it is (they say) apparent, that a privilege must license and authorize the same which the law against ignorance, non-residence, and plurality doth infringe; and so be a law contrariant or repugnant to the law of nature and the law of God, because all the reasons whereupon the positive law of man against these three was first established, are taken and drawn from the law of nature, and the law of God. For answer whereunto, we will but lead them to answer themselves. First therefore, if they will grant (as they must) that all direct oppositions of speech require one and the self-same subject to be meant on both parts, where opposition is pretended, it will follow that either the maxims of common right do inforce *the very same things* not to be good which we say are good, grounding our selves on the reasons by virtue whereof our privileges are established; or if the one do not reach unto that particular subject for which the other have provided, then is there no contradiction between them. In all contradictions, if the one part be true, the other eternally must be false. And therefore if the principles of common right do at any time truly inforce *that particular* not to be good, which privileges make good, it argueth invincibly that such privileges have been grounded upon some error. But to say, that every privilege is opposite unto the principles of common right, because it dispenseth with that which common right doth prohibit, hath gross absurdity. For the voice of equity and justice is, that a general law doth never derogate from a special privilege; whereas if the one were contrary to the other, a general law being in force should always dissolve a privilege. The reason why many are deceived by imagining that so it should do, and why men of better insight conclude directly it should not, doth rest in the *subject* or *matter* it self; which matter *indefinitely* considered in laws of common right, is in privileges

consi-

confidered as *befet and limited with fpecial circumftances*; by means whereof to
them which refpect it but by way of generality, it feemeth one and the fame in both,
although it be not the fame, if once we defcend to particular confideration thereof.
Precepts do always propofe perfection, not fuch as none can attain unto, for then in
vain fhould we afk or require it at the hands of men, but fuch perfection as all men
muft aim at; to the end that as largely as human providence and care can extend it,
it may take place. Moral laws are the rules of politick; thofe politick, which are
made to order the whole church of God, rules unto all particular churches; and the
laws of every particular church, rules unto every particular man within the body of
the fame church. Now becaufe the higher we afcend in thefe rules, the further ftill
we remove from thofe fpecialties, which being proper to the fubject whereupon our
actions muft work, are therefore chiefly confidered by us, by them leaft thought upon, that wade altogether in the two firft kinds of general directions, their judgment
cannot be exact and found concerning either laws of churches, or actions of men in
particular, becaufe they determine of effects by a part of the caufes only out of
which they grow; they judge conclufions by demi-premifes, and half principles;
they lay them in the balance ftript from thofe neceffary material circumftances which
fhould give them weight; and by fhew of falling uneven with the fcale of moft univerfal and abftracted rules, they pronounce that too light which is not, if they had
the fkill to weigh it. This is the reafon why men altogether converfant in ftudy, do
know how to teach, but not how to govern; men experienced contrariwife govern
well, yet know not which way to fet down orderly the precepts and reafons of that
they do. He that will therefore judge rightly of things done, muft join with
his forms and conceits of general fpeculation, the matter wherein our actions
are converfant. For by this fhall appear what equity there is in thofe privileges and
peculiar grants or favours, which otherwife will feem repugnant to juftice,
and becaufe in themfelves confidered, they have a fhew of repugnancy, this deceiveth thofe great clerks, which hearing a privilege defined to be *an efpecial right brought in by their power and authority, that make it for fome publick
benefit, againft the general courfe of reafon*, are not able to comprehend how the word
againft doth import *exception* without any *oppofition* at all. For inafmuch as the
hand of juftice muft diftribute to every particular what is due, and judge what is due
with refpect had no lefs of particular circumftances, than of general rules and axioms;
it cannot fit all forts with one meafure, the wills, counfels, qualities and ftates of
men being divers. For example, the law of common right bindeth all men to keep
their promifes, perform their compacts, and anfwer the faith they have given either
for themfelves or others. Notwithftanding he which bargaineth with one under years,
can have no benefit by this allegation, becaufe he bringeth it againft a perfon which
is exempt from the common rule. Shall we then conclude, that thus to exempt
certain men from the law of common right is againft God, againft nature, againft
whatfoever may avail to ftrengthen and juftify that law before alledged; or elfe acknowledge (as the truth is) that fpecial caufes are to be ordered by fpecial rules;
that if men grown unto ripe age difadvantage themfelves by bargaining, yet what
they have wittingly done is ftrong and in force againft them, becaufe they are able
to difpofe and manage their own affairs; whereas youth for lack of experience and
judgment, being eafily fubject to circumvention, is therefore juftly exempt from the
law of common right, whereunto the reft are juftly fubject? This plain inequality
between men of years, and under years, is a caufe why equity and juftice cannot apply equally the fame general rule to both, but ordereth the one by common right,
and granteth to the other a fpecial privilege. Privileges are either tranfitory or permanent: Tranfitory, fuch as ferve only fome one turn, or at the moft extend no
farther than to this or that man, with the end of whofe natural life they expire; permanent, fuch as the ufe whereof doth continue ftill, for that they belong unto certain kinds of men and caufes which never dye. Of this nature are all immunities
and preeminencies, which for juft confiderations one fort of men enjoyeth above another, both in the church and commonwealth, no man fufpecting them of contrariety to any branch of thofe laws or reafons whereupon the general right is grounded.
Now there being general laws and rules, whereby it cannot be denied but the church
of God ftandeth bound to provide that the miniftry may be learned, that they which
have charge may refide upon it, and that it may not be free for them in fcandalous
manner to multiply ecclefiaftical livings; it remaineth in the next place to be examined, what the laws of the church of *England* do admit, which may be thought

Jus fingulare eft, quod contra tenorem ratio-nis propter ali-quam utilita-tem authoritate conftituentium introductum eft. Paulus ff. de leg!b.

Privilegium perfonale cum perfona extin-guitur, & pri-vilegium da-tum actioni tranfit cum actione. Op. de Regulis. q. 1. 227.

2   repug-

repugnant to any thing hitherto alledged, and in what special consideration they seem to admit the same. Considering therefore, that to furnish all places of cure in this realm, it is not an army of twelve thousand learned men that would suffice, nor two universities that can always furnish as many as decay in so great a number, nor a fourth part of the living with cure, that when they fall are able to yield sufficient maintenance for learned men, is it not plain that unless the greatest part of the people should be left utterly without the publick use and exercise of religion, there is no remedy but to take into the ecclesiastical order a number of men meanly qualified in respect of learning? For whatsoever we may imagine in our private closets, or talk for communication sake at our boards, yea, or write in our books through a notional conceit of things needful for performance of each man's duty, if once we come from the theory of learning, to take out so many learned men, let them be diligently viewed out of whom the choice shall be made, and thereby an estimate made what degree of skill we must either admit, or else leave numbers utterly destitute of guides, and I doubt not but that men endued with sense of common equity will soon discern, that, besides eminent and competent knowledge, we are to descend to a lower step, receiving knowledge in that degree which is but tolerable. When we commend any man for learning, our speech importeth him to be more than meanly qualified that way; but when laws do require learning as a quality, which maketh capable of any function, our measure to judge a learned man by, must be some certain degree of learning, beneath which we can hold no man so qualified. And if every man that listeth may set that degree himself, how shall we ever know when laws are broken, when kept, seeing one man may think a lower degree sufficient, another may judge them unsufficient, that are not qualified in some higher degree. Wherefore of necessity either we must have some judge, in whose conscience they that are thought and pronounced sufficient, are to be so accepted and taken, or else the law it self is to set down the very lowest degree of fitness that shall be allowable in this kind. So that the question doth grow to this issue. St. *Paul* requireth learning in presbyters, yea such learning as doth inable them to exhort in doctrine which is sound, and to disprove them that gain-say it. What measure of ability in such things, shall serve to make men capable of that kind of office, he doth not himself precisely determine, but referreth it to the conscience of *Titus*, and others which Tit. 1. 9. had to deal in ordering presbyters. We must therefore of necessity make this demand, whether the church, lacking such as the apostle would have chosen, may with good conscience take out of such as it hath in a meaner degree of fitness, them that may serve to perform the service of publick prayer, to minister the sacraments unto the people, to solemnize marriage, to visit the sick, and bury the dead, to instruct by reading, although by preaching they be not as yet so able to benefit and feed Christ's flock. We constantly hold, that in this case the apostles law is not broken. He requireth more in presbyters, than there is found in many whom the church of *England* alloweth. But no man being tied unto impossibilities, to do that we cannot, we are not bound. It is but a stratagem of theirs therefore, and a very indirect practice, when they publish large declamations to prove that learning is required in the ministry, and to make the silly people believe that the contrary is maintained by the bishops, and upheld by the laws of the land; whereas the question in truth is not, whether learning be required, but whether a church, wherein there is not sufficient store of learned men to furnish all congregations, should do better to let thousands of souls grow savage, to let them live without any publick service of God, to let their children dye unbaptized, to with-hold the benefit of the other sacrament from them, to let them depart this world like pagans, without any thing so much as read unto them concerning the way of life, than, as it doth in this necessity, to make such presbyters as are so far forth sufficient, although they want that ability of preaching which some others have. In this point therefore we obey necessity, and of two evils we take the less; in the rest a publick utility is sought, and in regard thereof some certain inconveniencies tolerated, because they are recompenced with greater good. The law giveth liberty of non-residence for a time to such as will live in universities, if they faithfully there labour to grow in knowledge, that so they may afterwards the more edify, and the better instruct their congregations. The church in their absence is not destitute, the peoples salvation not neglected for the present time, the time of their absence is in the intendment of law bestowed to the churches great advantage and benefit; those necessary helps are procured by it, which turn by many degrees more to the peoples comfort in time to come, than if their pastors had continually abidden with

them.

thém. So that the law doth hereby provide in some part to remedy and help that
evil, which the former necessity hath imposed upon the church. For compare two
men of equal meanness, the one perpetually resident, the other absent for a space in
such sort as the law permitteth. Allot unto both some nine years continuance with
cure of souls. And must not three years absence, in all probability and likelihood,
make the one more profitable than the other unto God's church, by so much as the
increase of his knowledge, gotten in those three years, may add unto six years travel following? For the greater ability there is added to the instrument, wherewith it
pleaseth God to save souls, the more facility and expedition it hath to work that
which is otherwise hardlier effected. As much may be said touching absence granted
to them that attend in the families of bishops, which schools of gravity, discretion
and wisdom, preparing men against the time that they come to reside abroad, are, in
my poor opinion, even the fittest places that any ingenious mind can wish to enter
into, between departure from private study, and access to a more publick charge of
souls; yea no less expedient, for men of the best sufficiency and most maturity in
knowledge, than the very universities themselves are for the ripening of such as be
raw. Employment in the families of noblemen, or in princes courts, hath another
end for which the self-same leave is given, not without great respect to the good of
the whole church. For assuredly, whosoever doth well observe how much all inferior things depend upon the orderly courses and motions of those great orbs, will
hardly judge it either meet or good, that the angels assisting them should be driven to
betake themselves to other stations, although by nature they were not tyed where
they now are, but had charge also elsewhere, as long as their absence from beneath
might but tolerably be supplied, and by descending their rooms above should become
vacant. For we are not to dream in this case of any platform which bringeth equally high and low unto parish-churches, nor of any constraint to maintain at their
own charge men sufficient for that purpose; the one so repugnant to the majesty and
greatness of *English* nobility, the other so improbable and unlikely to take effect,
that they which mention either of both, seem not indeed to have conceived what
either is. But the eye of the law is the eye of Gód, it looketh into the hearts and
secret dispositions of men, it beholdeth how far one star differeth from another in
glory, and as mens several degrees require, accordingly it guideth them; granting unto principal personages privileges correspondent to their high estates, and that not
only in civil, but even in spiritual affairs, to the end they may love that religion the
more, which no way seeketh to make them vulgar, no way diminishes their dignity
and greatness, but to do them good doth them honour also, and by such extraordinary favours teacheth them to be in the church of God, the same which the church of
God esteemeth them, more worth than thousands. It appeareth therefore in what
respect the laws of this realm have given liberty of non-residence to some, that their
knowledge may be increased, and their labours by that means be made afterwards the
more profitable to others, lest the houses of great-men should want that daily exercise
of religion, wherein their example availeth as much, yea many times peradventure
more than the laws themselves with the common sort. A third thing respected both
in permitting absence, and also in granting to some that liberty of addition or plurality, which necessarily inforceth their absence, is a mere both just and conscionable
regard, that as men are in quality, and as their services are in weight for the publick
good, so likewise their rewards and encouragements by special privilege of law,
might somewhat declare how the state it self doth accept their pains, much abhorring from their bestial and savage rudeness, which think that oxen should only labour, and asses feed. Thus to readers in universities, whose very paper and book-
expences, their ancient allowances and stipends at this day do either not, or hardly
sustain; to governors of colleges, lest the great over-plus of charges necessarily inforced upon them, by reason of their place, and very slenderly supplied, by means
of that charge in the present condition of things, which their founders could not
foresee; to men called away from their cures, and employed in weightier business, either of the church or common-wealth, because to impose upon them a burden which requireth their absence, and not to release them from the duty of residence, were a kind of cruel and barbarous injustice; to residents in cathedral
churches, or upon dignities ecclesiastical, forasmuch as these being rooms of
greater hospitality, places of more respect and consequence than the rest, they
are the rather to be furnished with men of best quality, and the men for
their qualities sake to be favoured above others: I say, unto all these in
regard

regard of their worth and merit, the law hath therefore given leave, while themselves bear weightier burdens, to supply inferior by deputation, and in like consideration partly, partly also by way of honour to learning, nobility and authority, permitteth, that men which have taken theological degrees in schools, the suffragans of bishops, the houshold-chaplains of men of honour, or in great offices, the brethren and sons of Lords temporal, or of knights, if God shall move the hearts of such to enter at any time into holy orders, may obtain to themselves a faculty or licence to hold two ecclesiastical livings, though having cure ; any spiritual person of the queen's council, three such livings ; her chaplains, what number of promotions her self in her own princely wisdom thinketh good to bestow upon them. But, as it fareth in such cases, the gap which for just considerations we open unto some, letteth in others through corrupt practices, to whom such favours were neither meant, nor should be communicated. The greatness of the harvest, and the scarcity of able workmen hath made it necessary, that law should yield to admit numbers of men but slenderly and meanly qualified. Hereupon, because whom all other worldly hopes have forsaken, they commonly reserve ministerial vocation as their last and surest refuge, ever open to forlorn men ; the church that should nourish them whose service she needeth, hath obtruded upon her their service that know not otherwise how to live and sustain themselves. These finding nothing more easy than means to procure the writing of a few lines to some one or other which hath authority ; and nothing more usual than too much facility in condescending unto such requests ; are often received into that vocation, whereunto their unworthiness is no small disgrace. Did any thing more aggravate the crime of *Jeroboam's* prophane apostasy, than that he chose to have his clergy the scum and refuse of his whole land ? Let no man spare to tell it them, that they are not faithful towards God, that burden wilfully his church with such swarms of unworthy creatures. I will not say of all degrees in the ministry, that which St. *Chrysostom* doth of the highest, *He that will undertake so weighty a charge, had need to be a man of great understanding, rarely assisted with divine grace, for integrity of manners, purity of life, and for all other virtues, to have in him more than a man :* But surely this I will say with *Chrysostom, We need not doubt whether God be highly displeased with us, or what the cause of his anger is, if things of so great fear and holiness as are the least and lowest duties of his service, be thrown wilfully on them whose not only mean, but bad and scandalous quality doth defile whatsoever they handle.* These eye-sores and blemishes in continual attendants about the service of God's sanctuary, do make them every day fewer that willingly resort unto it, till at length all affection and zeal towards God be extinct in them, through a wearisom contempt of their persons, which for a time only live by religion, and are for recompence, in fine, the death of the nurse that feedeth them. It is not obscure, how incommodious the church hath found both this abuse of the liberty which law is enforced to grant ; and not only this, but the like abuse of that favour also, which law in other considerations already mentioned affordeth, touching residence and plurality of spiritual livings. Now that which is practised corruptly to the detriment and hurt of the church, against the purpose of those very laws, which notwithstanding are pretended in defence and justification thereof, we must needs acknowledge no less repugnant to the grounds and principles of common right, than the fraudulent proceedings of tyrants to the principles of just sovereignty. Howbeit not so those special privileges which are but instruments wrested and forced to serve malice. There is in the patriarch of heathen philosophers this precept, [a] *Let no husbandman, nor no handycraftsman be a priest.* The reason whereupon he groundeth, is a maxim in the law of nature ; it importeth greatly the good *of all men that God be reverenced,* with whose honour it standeth not that they which are publickly employed in his service, should live of base and manuary trades. Now compare herewith the apostles words, [b] *Ye know that these hands have ministred to my necessities, and them that are with me.* What think we ? Did the apostle any thing opposite herein, or repugnant to the rules and maxims of the law of nature ? The self-same reasons that accord his actions with the law of nature, shall declare our privileges and his laws no less consonant. Thus therefore we see, that although they urge very colourably the apostles own sentences, requiring that a minister should be able to divide rightly the word of God, that they who are placed in charge should attend unto it themselves, which in absence they cannot do, and that they which have divers cures, must of necessity be absent from some, whereby the law apostolick seemeth apparently broken, which law requiring attendance, cannot otherwise be understood

than

Chrysost. de Sacerd. l. 3. c. 15.

[a] ἐπὶ γεωργὸν ἢ βάναυσον ἱερέα μὴ ποιεῖν. τοῦτο. ὑπὲρ ᾧ ᾧ φίλον τιμᾶν, τῆς θεῶν τιμᾶσθαι τοὺς θεούς. Arist. Po. 7.

[b] Acts 20. 34. 1 Cor. 4. 12. 1 Thess. 1. 9. [a] 2 Thess. 3. 8.

than so as to charge them with perpetual residence: Again, though in every of these causes they indefinitely heap up the sentences of fathers, the decrees of popes, the ancient edicts of imperial authority, our own national laws and ordinances prohibiting the same, and grounding evermore their prohibitions partly on the laws of God, and partly on reasons drawn from the light of nature, yet hereby to gather and infer contradiction between those laws which forbid indefinitely, and ours which in certain cases have allowed the ordaining of sundry ministers, whose sufficiency for learning is but mean; again, the licensing of some to be absent from their flocks, and of others to hold more than one only living which hath cure of souls; I say, to conclude repugnancy between these especial permissions, and the former general prohibitions which set not down their own limits, is erroneous, and the manifest cause thereof ignorance in differences of matter which both sorts of law concern. If then the considerations be reasonable, just and good, whereupon we ground whatsoever our laws have by special right permitted, if only the effects of abused privileges be repugnant to the maxims of common right, this main foundation of repugnancy being broken, whatsoever they have built thereupon, falleth necessarily to the ground. Whereas therefore, upon surmise, or vain supposal of opposition between our special and the principles of common right, they gather that such as are with us ordained ministers, before they can preach, be neither lawful, because the laws already mentioned forbid generally to create such, neither are they indeed ministers, although we commonly so name them, but whatsoever they execute by virtue of such their pretended vocation is void; that all our grants and tolerations as well of this as the rest, are frustrate and of no effect; the persons that enjoy them possess them wrongfully, and are deprivable at all hours; finally, that other just and sufficient remedy of evils there can be none, besides the utter abrogations of these our mitigations, and the strict establishment of former ordinances to be absolutely executed whatsoever follow: Albeit the answer already made, in discovery of the weak and unsound foundation, whereupon they have built these erroneous collections, may be thought sufficient; yet because our desire is rather to satisfy, if it be possible, than to shake them off, we are with very good will contented to declare the causes of all particulars more formally and largely, than the equity of our own defence doth require.

There is crept into the minds of men, at this day, a secret pernicious and pestilent conceit, that the greatest perfection of a christian man doth consist in discovery of other mens faults, and in wit to discourse of our own profession. When the world most abounded with just, righteous and perfect men, their chiefest study was the exercise of piety, wherein for their safest direction, they reverently hearkned to the readings of the law of God, they kept in mind the oracles and aphorisms of wisdom, which tended unto virtuous life; if any scruple of conscience did trouble them for matter of actions which they took in hand, nothing was attempted before counsel and advice were had, for fear lest rashly they might offend. We are now more confident, not that our knowledge and judgment is riper, but because our desires are another way.

Their scope was obedience, ours is skill; their endeavour was reformation of life, [a] our virtue nothing but to hear gladly the reproof of vice; they in the practise of their religion wearied chiefly their knees and hands, we especially our ears and tongues. We are grown as in many things else, so in this, to a kind of intemperancy, which (only sermons excepted) hath almost brought all other duties of religion out of taste. At the least they are not in that account and reputation which they should be. Now, because men bring all religion in a manner to the only office of hearing sermons, if it chance that they who are thus conceited, do embrace any special opinion different from other men, the sermons that relish not that opinion, can in no wise please their appetite. Such therefore as preach unto them, but hit not the string they look for, are respected as unprofitable, the rest as unlawful; and indeed no ministers, if the faculty of sermons want. For why? A minister of the word should, they say, be able rightly to *divide* the word. Which apostolick canon many think they do well observe, when in opening the sentences of holy scripture, they draw all things favourably spoken unto one side; but whatsoever is reprehensive, severe and sharp, they have others on the contrary part, whom that must always concern; by which their over-partial and un-indifferent proceeding, while they thus labour amongst the people to divide the word, they make the

word

[a] 'Αλλ' ἢ πολλοὶ ταῦτα μὲν ὑ πράττουσι, ἐπὶ ἢ τὸν λόγον καταφεύγοντες οἴονται φιλοσοφεῖν, κ' ὅπως ἔσεσθαι σπουδαῖοι· ὁμοίον τι ποιοῦντες τοῖς κάμνουσιν, οἳ τῶν ἰατρῶν ἀκούωσι μὲν ἐπιμελῶς, ποιοῦσι δ' ὀδὲν τῶν προστατομένων. ὥσπερ ὅν ὀδὲ ἐκεῖνοι ἕξουσι τὸ σῶμα ὅτω θεραπευόμενοι, ὀδὲ ὅτω τοῦ φιλοσοφῶν. Arist. Eth. l. 2. c. 5.

word a mean to divide and diſtract the people. Op꒱ꝋ꒱ꝋ, *to divide aright*, doth note in the apoſtles writings ſoundneſs of doctrine only ; and in meaning ſtandeth oppoſite to ꒱ꝋꝋ, *the broaching of new opinions againſt that which is received*. For queſtionleſs the firſt things delivered to the church of Chriſt, were pure and ſincere truth. Which whoſoever did afterwards oppugn, could not chuſe but divide the church into two moieties; in which diviſion, ſuch as taught what was firſt believed, held the truer part; the contrary ſide, in that they were teachers of novelty, erred. For prevention of which evil there are in this church many ſingular and well deviſed remedies ; as namely the uſe of ſubſcribing to the articles of religion before admiſſion to degrees of learning, or to any eccleſiaſtical living : the cuſtom of reading the ſame articles, and of approving them in publick aſſemblies, whereſoever men have benefices with cure of ſouls ; the order of teſtifying under their hands allowance of the book of Common-prayer, and the book of ordaining miniſters ; finally, the diſcipline and moderate ſeverity which is uſed, either in otherwiſe correcting or ſilencing them that trouble and diſturb the church with doctrines which tend unto innovation; it being better that the church ſhould want altogether the benefit of ſuch men's labours, than endure the miſchief of their inconformity to good laws; in which caſe, if any repine at the courſe and proceedings of juſtice, they muſt learn to content themſelves with the anſwer of *M. Curius*, which had ſometime occaſion to cut off one from the body Valer.L 6, of the commonwealth; in whoſe behalf becauſe it might have been pleaded, that the ꝏ. 3· party was a man ſerviceable, he therefore began his judicial ſentence with this preamble, *Non eſſe opus Reip. eo cive qui parere neſciret* ; *The commonwealth needeth men of quality, yet never thoſe men which have not learned how to obey*. But the ways which the church of *England* hath taken to provide, that they who are teachers of others may do it ſoundly, that the purity and unity as well of ancient diſcipline as doctrine may be upheld, that avoiding ſingularities we may all glorify God with one heart and one tongue, they of all men do leaſt approve, that do moſt urge the apoſtles rule and canon. For which cauſe they alledge it not ſo much to that purpoſe, as to prove that unpreaching miniſters (for ſo they term them) can have no true nor lawful calling in the church of God. St. *Auguſtin* hath ſaid of the will of man, that *ſimply to will proceedeth from nature, but our well-willing is from grace*. We ſay as much of the miniſter of God ; *publickly to teach and inſtruct the church, is neceſſary in every eccleſiaſtical miniſter ; but ability to teach by ſermons, is a grace which God doth beſtow on them, whom he maketh ſufficient for the commendable diſcharge of their duty*. That therefore wherein a miniſter differeth from other chriſtian men is not, as ſome have Ox. man. p· childiſhly imagined, the *ſound preaching of the word of God* ; but as they are lawfully 21. and truly governors, to whom authority of regiment is given in the commonwealth, according to the order which polity hath ſet, ſo canonical ordination in the church of Chriſt, is that which maketh a lawful miniſter, *as touching the validity of any act which appertaineth to that vocation*. The cauſe why St. *Paul* willed *Timothy* not to be over-haſty in ordaining miniſters, was (as we very well may conjecture) becauſe impoſition of hands doth conſecrate and make them miniſters, whether they have gifts and qualities fit for the laudable diſcharge of their duties or no. If want of learning and ſkill to preach, did fruſtrate their vocation, miniſters ordained before they be grown unto that maturity, ſhould receive new ordination, whenſoever it chanceth that ſtudy and induſtry doth make them afterwards more able to perform the office ; than which what conceit can be more abſurd? Was not St. *Auguſtine* himſelf contented to admit an aſſiſtant in his own church, a man of ſmall erudition, conſidering that what he wanted in knowledge, was ſupplied by thoſe virtues which made his life a better orator, than more learning could make others, whoſe converſation was leſs holy ? Were the prieſts ſithence *Moſes* all able and ſufficient men, learnedly to interpret the law of God? Or was it ever imagined that this defect ſhould fruſtrate what they executed, and deprive them of right unto any thing they claimed by virtue of their prieſthood ? Surely, as in magiſtrates the want of thoſe gifts which their office needeth, is cauſe of juſt imputation of blame in them that wittingly chuſe unſufficient and unfit men, when they might do otherwiſe, and yet therefore is not their choice void, nor every action of magiſtracy fruſtrate in that reſpect ; ſo whether it were of neceſſity, or even of very careleſneſs, that men unable to preach ſhould be taken in paſtors rooms, nevertheleſs it ſeemeth to be an error in them which think, the lack of any ſuch perfection defeateth utterly the calling. To wiſh that all men were qualified as their places and dignities require,to hate all ſiniſter and corrupt dealings which hereunto are any let, to covet ſpeedy redreſs of thoſe things whatſoever, whereby the church ſuſtaineth detriment, theſe good and virtuous defires cannot offend any but ungodly minds. Notwithftanding, fome in the true vehemency and others under the fair pretence of thefe defires, have adventured that which is ftrange, that which is violent and unjuft. There are which in confidence of their general allegation concerning the knowledge, the refidence and the fingle livings of minifters, prefume not only to annihilate the folemn ordinations of fuch as the church muft of force admit, but alfo to urge a kind of univerfal profcription againft them, to fet down articles, to draw commiffions, and almoft to name themfelves of the *Quorum*, for enquiry into men's eftates and dealings, whom at their pleafure they would deprive and make obnoxious to what punifhment themfelves lift, and that not for any violation of laws either fpiritual or civil, but becaufe men have trufted the laws too far, becaufe they have held and enjoyed the liberty which law granteth, becaufe they had not the wit to conceive as thefe men do, that laws were made to entrap the fimple, by permitting thofe things in fhew and appearance, which indeed fhould nevet take effect, for as much as they were but granted with a fecret condition to be put in practice, *If they fhould be profitable and agreeable with the word of God*; which condition failing in all minifters that cannot preach, in all that are abfent from their livings, and in all that have divers livings (for fo it muft be prefumed, though never as yet proved) therefore as men which have broken the law of God and nature, they are depriveable at all hours. Is this the juftice of that difcipline whereunto all chriftian churches muft ftoop and fubmit themfelves? Is this the equity wherewith they labour to reform the world? I will no way diminifh the force of thofe arguments whereupon they ground. But if it pleafe them to behold the vifage of thefe collections in another glafs, there are civil as well as ecclefiaftical unfufficiencies, non-refidences, and pluralities; yea, the reafons which light of nature hath miniftred againft both are of fuch affinity, that much lefs they cannot enforce in the one than in the other. When they that bear great offices be perfons of mean worth, the contempt

[a] Μεγάλων κλοποι κρατοῦντες ἐν ἀτελεῖς ἔπι μεγάλα βλάπ-ζουσι. Ariftot. Polit. 2. c. 11.

[b] *Nec ignoro maximos honores ad parum dignos penuria meliorum folere deferri.* Mamertin. paneg. ad Julian.
[c] *Neque enim aquum vifum eft abfentem Reipub. caufa Inter reos referri, dum Reipub. operatur.* Ulpian. l. 15. *Si maritus ad legem* Julian. de adulter.
[d] *Arift. Polit. l. 2. c. 11.* See the like preamble framed by the author of the *abftract*, where he fancieth a bifhop depofing one unapt to preach, whom himfelf had before ordained.

whereinto their Authority groweth, [a] weakneth the finews of the whole ftate. Notwithftanding, where many governors are needful, and they not many whom their quality can commend, [b] the penury of worthier muft needs make the meaner fort of men capable. Cities, in the abfcence of their governors, are as fhips wanting pilots at fea: But were it therefore [c] juftice to punifh whom fuperior authority pleafeth to call from home, or alloweth to be employed elfe-where? In committing [d] many offices to one

man, there are apparently thefe inconveniences; the commonwealth doth lofe the benefit of ferviceable men, which might be trained up in thofe rooms; it is not eafy for one man to difcharge many men's duties well; in fervice of warfare and navigation, were it not the overthrow of whatfoever is undertaken, if one or two fhould ingrofs fuch offices, as being now divided into many hands, are difcharged with admirable both perfection and expedition? Neverthelefs, be it far from the mind of any reafonable man to imagine, that in thefe confiderations princes either ought of duty to revoke all fuch kind of grants, though made with very fpecial refpect to the extraordinary merit of certain men, or might in honour demand of them the refignation of their offices with fpeech to this or the like effect; *For as much as you* A B *by the fpace of many years have done us that faithful fervice in moft important affairs, for which we always judging you worthy of much honour, have therefore committed unto you from time to time very great and weighty offices, which hitherto you quietly enjoy: We are now given to underftand, that certain grave and learned men have found in the books of ancient philofophers, divers arguments drawn from the common light of nature, and declaring the wonderful difcommodities which ufe to grow by dignities thus heaped together in one; for which caufe, at this prefent, moved in confcience and tender care for the publick good, we have fummoned you hither to difpoffefs you of thofe places, and to depofe you from thofe rooms whereof, indeed by virtue of our own grant, yet againft reafon, you are poffeffed. Neither ought you, or any other, to think us rafh, light, or inconftant, in fo doing: For we tell you plain, that herein we will both fay and do that thing which the noble and wife emperor fometime both faid and did in a matter of far lefs weight than this:* Quod inconfulto fecimus, confulto revocamus, *That which we unadvifedly have done, we advifedly will revoke and undo.* Now for mine own part, the greateft harm I would wifh them who think that this

were

were confonant with equity and right, is, that they might but live where all things are with fuch kind of juftice ordered, till experience have taught them to fee their error. As for the laft thing which is incident into the caufe whereof we fpeak, namely, what courfe were the beft and fafeft, whereby to remedy fuch evils as the church of God may fuftain, where the prefent liberty of the law is turned to great abufe, fome light we may receive from abroad, not unprofitable for direction of God's own facred houfe and family. The *Romans* being a people full of generofity, and by nature courteous, did no way more fhew their gentle difpofition, than by eafy condefcending to fet their bondmen at liberty. Which benefit in the happier and better times of the commonwealth, was beftowed for the moft part as an ordinary reward of virtue; fome few now and then alfo purchafing freedom with that which their juft labours could gain, and their honeft frugality fave. But as the empire daily grew up, fo the manners and conditions of men decayed, wealth was honoured, and virtue not cared for; neither did any thing feem opprobrious, out of which there might arife commodity and profit, fo that it could be no marvel in a ftate thus far degenerated, if when the more ingenuous fort were become bafe, the bafer laying afide all fhame and face of honefty, did fome by robberies, burglaries, and proftitution of their bodies, gather wherewith to redeem liberty; others obtain the fame at the hands of their lords, by ferving them as vile inftruments in thofe attempts, which had been worthy to be revenged with ten thoufand deaths. A learned, judicious, and polite hiftorian, having mentioned fo foul diforders, giveth his judgment and cenfure of them in this fort: *Such eye-fores in the commonwealth have occafioned many virtuous minds to condemn* Dionvf. Hal. *altogether the cuftom of granting liberty to any bond flave, for as much as it feemed a* car. Rom. *thing abfurd, that a people which commands all the world, fhould confift of fo vile re-* antiq. l. 4. *fufe. But neither is this the only cuftom wherein the profitable inventions of former are depraved by latter ages; and for my felf I am not of their opinion, that wifh the abrogation of fo grofly ufed cuftoms, which abrogation might peradventure be caufe of greater inconveniences enfuing: but as much as may be, I would rather advife that redrefs were fought through the careful providence of chief rulers and overfeers of the commonwealth, by whom a yearly furvey being made of all that are manumifed, they which feem worthy might be taken and divided into tribes with other citizens, the reft difperfed into colonies abroad, or otherwife difpofed of, that the commonwealth might fuftain neither harm nor difgrace by them.* The ways to meet with diforders growing by abufe of laws, are not fo intricate and fecret, efpecially in our cafe, that men fhould need either much advertifement, or long time for the fearch thereof. And if counfel to that purpofe may feem needful, this church (God be thanked) is not deftitute of men endued with ripe judgment, whenfoever any fuch thing fhall be thought neceffary. For which end, at this prefent, to propofe any fpecial inventions of my own, might argue in a man of my place and calling more prefumption perhaps than wit. I will therefore leave it entire unto graver confideration, ending now with requeft only and moft earneft fuit, firft, that they which give ordination would, as they tender the very honour of Jefus Chrift, the fafety of men, and the endlefs good of their own fouls, take heed left unneceffarily, and through their default the church be found worfe or lefs furnifhed than it might be: Secondly, that they which by right of patronage have power to prefent unto fpiritual livings, and may in that refpect much damnify the church of God, would, for the eafe of their own account in the dreadful day, fomewhat confider what it is to betray for gain the fouls which Chrift hath redeemed with blood, what to violate the facred bond of fidelity and folemn promife given at the firft to God and his church by them, from whofe original intereft, together with the felf-fame title of right, the fame obligation of duty likewife is defcended: Thirdly, that they unto whom the granting of difpenfations is committed, or which otherwife have any ftroke in the difpofition of fuch preferments as appertain unto learned men, would bethink themfelves what it is to refpect any thing either above or befide merit; confidering how hardly the world taketh it, when to men of commendable note and quality there is fo little refpect had, or fo great unto them whofe deferts are very mean; that nothing doth feem more ftrange than the one fort, becaufe they are not accounted of, and the other becaufe they are; it being every man's hope and expectation in the church of God, efpecially that the only purchafe of greater rewards fhould be always greater deferts, and that nothing fhould ever be able to plant a thorn where a vine ought to grow: Fourthly, that honourable perfonages, and they who by virtue of any principal office in the commonwealth, are enabled to qualify a certain number, and make them capable of favours or faculties above others, fuffer not their names to be abufed,

4

con-

contrary to the true intent and meaning of wholsome laws, by men in whom there is nothing notable besides covetousness and ambition : Fifthly, that the graver and wiser sort in both universities, or whosoever they be, with whose approbation the marks and recognizances of all learning are bestowed, would think the apostles caution against unadvised ordinations, not impertinent or unnecessary to be born in mind, even when they grant those degrees of schools, which degrees are not *gratiæ gratis datæ*, kindnesses bestowed by way of humanity, but they are *gratiæ gratum facientes*, favours which always imply a testimony given to the church and commonwealth concerning men's sufficiency for manners and knowledge : A testimony upon the credit whereof sundry statutes of the realm are built ; a testimony so far available, that nothing is more respected for the warrant of divers men's abilities to serve in the affairs of the realm; a testimony wherein if they violate that religion wherewith it ought to be always given, and do thereby induce into error such as deem it a thing uncivil to call the credit thereof in question, let them look that God shall return back upon their heads, and cause them in the state of their own corporations to feel, either one way or other, the punishment of those harms which the church through their negligence doth sustain in that behalf : Finally , and to conclude , that they who enjoy the benefit of any special indulgence or favour, which the laws permit, would as well remember what in duty towards the church, and in conscience towards God they ought to do, as what they may do by using to their own advantage whatsoever they see tolerated; no man being ignorant, that the cause why absence in some cases hath been yielded unto, and in equity thought sufferable , is the hope of greater fruit through industry elsewhere; the reason likewise wherefore pluralities are allowed unto men of note, a very sovereign and special care, that as fathers in the ancient world did declare the preheminence of priority in birth, by doubling the worldly portions of their first-born ; so the church by a course not unlike, in assigning men's rewards, might testify an estimation had proportionably of their virtues, according to the ancient rule apostolick,

For the main hypothesis or foundation of these conclusions, let that before set down in the 9th, be read together with this last the 81st paragraph. *They which excel in labour, ought to excel in honour* ; and therefore unless they answer faithfully the expectation of the church herein, unless sincerely they bend their wits day and night, both to sow because they reap, and to sow so much more abundantly as they reap more abundantly than other men , whereunto by their very acceptance of such benignities they formally bind themselves, let them be well assured, that the honey which they eat with fraud, shall turn in the end into true gall, for as much as laws are the sacred image of his wisdom, who most severely punisheth those colourable and subtil crimes, that seldom are taken within the walk of human justice. I therefore conclude, that the grounds and maxims of common right, whereupon ordinations of ministers unable to preach, tolerations of absence from their cures, and the multiplications of their spiritual livings, are disproved, do but indefinitely enforce them unlawful, not unlawful universally and without exception ; that the laws which indefinitely are against all these things, and the privileges which make for them in certain cases, are not the one repugnant to the other ; that the laws of God and nature are violated through the effects of abused privileges; that neither our ordinations of men unable to make sermons, nor our dispensations for the rest, can be justly proved frustrate, by virtue of any such surmised opposition between the special laws of this church, which have permitted, and those general which are alledged to disprove the same; that when privileges by abuse are grown incommodious, there must be redress; that for remedy of such evils, there is no necessity the church should abrogate either in whole or in part the specialities before-mentioned ; and that the most to be desired, were a voluntary reformation thereof on all hands, which may give passage unto any abuse.

2

OF THE

L A W S

OF

Ecclefiaftical Polity.

BOOK VI.

Containing their fifth Affertion, That our laws are corrupt and repugnant to the laws of God, in matter belonging to the power of ecclefiaftical jurifdiction, in that we have not throughout all churches certain lay-elders, eftablifhed for the exercife of that power.

THE fame men which in heat of contention, do hardly either fpeak or give ear to reafon, being after fharp and bitter conflicts retired to a calm remembrance of all their former proceedings; the caufes that brought them into quarrel, the courfe which their ftriving affections have follow-ed, and the iffue whereunto they are come, may peradventure as trou-bled waters, in fmall time of their own accord, by certain eafy degrees fettle them-felves again; and fo recover that clearnefs of well advifed judgment, whereby they fhall ftand at the length indifferent both to yield and admit any reafonable fatisfaction, where before they could not endure with patience to be gain-faid. Neither will I defpair of the like fuccefs in thefe unpleafant controverfies touching ecclefiaftical po-lity; the time of filence which both parts have willingly taken to breathe, feeming now as it were a pledge of all men's quiet contentment to hear with more indifferency the weightieft and laft remains of that caufe, jurifdiction, dignity, dominion ecclefiafti-cal. For, let not any imagine that the bare and naked difference of a few ceremonies, could either have kindled fo much fire, or have caufed it to flame fo long; but that the parties which herein laboured mightily for change, and (as they fay) for reformation, had fomewhat more than this mark whereat to aim.

The queftion between us, Whether all congregati-ons, or pa-rifhes ought to have lay-elders invefl-ed with pow-er of jurif-diction in fpiritual caufes.

Lib. 6.
Lib. 7.
Lib. 8.

Having therefore drawn out a compleat form, as they fuppofe, of publick fervice to be done to God, and fet down their plot for the office of the miniftry in that behalf; they very well knew how little their labours, fo far forth beftowed, would avail them in the end, without a claim of jurifdiction to uphold the fabrick which they had erect-ed; and this neither likely to be obtained but by the ftrong hand of the people, nor the people unlikely to favour it; the more, if overture were made of their own in-tereft, right and title thereunto. Whereupon there are many which have conjectured this to be the caufe, why in all their projects of their difcipline (it being manfeft that their drift is to wreft the key of fpiritual authority out of the hands of former gover-nors, and equally to poffefs therewith the paftors of all feveral congregations) the peo-ple firft for furer accomplifhment, and then for better defenfe thereof, are pretended neceffary actors in thofe things, whereunto their ability for the moft part is as flender, as their title and challenge unjuft.

Not-

Notwithstanding (whether they saw it necessary for them to persuade the people, without whose help they could do nothing, or else (which I rather think) the affection which they bear towards this new form of government, made them to imagin it God's own ordinance,) their doctrine is, that by the law of God, there must be for ever in all congregations certain lay-elders, ministers of ecclesiastical jurisdiction, in as much as our Lord and Saviour by testament (for so they presume) hath left all ministers or pastors in the church executors equally to the whole power of spiritual jurisdiction, and with them hath joined the people as colleagues. By maintenance of which assertion there is unto that part apparently gained a twofold advantage, both because the people in this respect are much more easily drawn to favour it, as a matter of their own interest ; and for that, if they chance to be crossed by such as oppose against them, the colour of divine authority, assumed for the grace and countenance of that power in the vulgar sort, furnisheth their leaders with great abundance of matter, behoveful for their encouragement to proceed always with hope of fortunate success in the end, considering their cause to be as *David*'s was, a just defense of power given them from above, and consequently their adversaries quarrel the same with *Saul*'s, by whom the ordinance of God was withstood.

Now, on the contrary side, if their surmise prove false ; if such, as in justification whereof no evidence sufficient either hath been or can be alledged (as I hope it shall clearly appear after due examination and trial) let them then consider, whether those

Numb. 16.   words of *Corah*, *Dathan*, and *Abiram*, against *Moses* and against *Aaron*, *It is too much that ye take upon you, seeing all the congregation is holy*, be not the very true abstract and abridgment of all their published admonitions, demonstrations, supplications, and treatises whatsoever, whereby they have laboured to avoid the rooms of their spiritual superiors before authorized, and to advance the new fansied scepter of lay-presbyterial power.

The nature of spiritual jurisdiction.

BUT before there can be any settled dretmination, whether truth do rest on their part or on ours, touching lay-elders ; we are to prepare the way thereunto, by explication of some things requisite and very needful to be considered ; as first, how besides that spiritual power which is of order, and was instituted for performance of those duties whereof there hath been speech already had, there is in the church no less necessary a second kind, which we call the power of jurisdiction. When the apostle doth speak of ruling the church of God, and of receiving accusations, his words have evident reference to the power of jurisdiction. Our Saviour's words to the power of or-

Acts 20. 21. der, when he giveth his disciples charge, saying, *Preach, baptize: do this in remem-*
1 Tim. 5. 19. *brance of me.* Τίμα μὲν τ̄ Θεὸν ὡς αἴτιον τ̄ ὅλων, ᾗ κύριον, Ἐπίσκοπον, ἢ ὡς ἀρχιερέα Θεῦ
Mark 6. 15.
Mat 28. 19. εἰκόνα φέροντα, κατὰ μὲν τὸ ἄρχειν Θεῦ, κατὰ ᾗ τὸ ἱερατεύειν Χριστῦ.   *Epist. ad Smyrn.*
1 Cor. 11. 24. A bishop (saith *Ignatius*) doth bear the image of God and of Christ ; of God in ruling, of Christ in administring holy things. By this therefore we see a manifest difference acknowledged between the power of ecclesiastical order, and the power of jurisdiction ecclesiastical.

The spiritual power of the church being such as neither can be challenged by right of nature, nor could by human authority be instituted, because the forces and effects thereof are supernatural and divine, we are to make no doubt or question but that from him which is the head, it hath descended unto us that are the body now invested therewith. He gave it for the benefit and good of souls, as a mean to keep them in the path which leadeth unto endless felicity, a bridle to hold them within their due and convenient bounds, and, if they do go astray, a forceable help to reclaim them. Now although there be no kind of spiritual power, for which our Lord Jesus Christ did not give both commission to exercise, and direction how to use the same, although his laws in that behalf, recorded by the holy evangelists, be the only ground and foundation, whereupon the practice of the church must sustain it self ; yet, as all multitudes once grown to the form of societies, are even thereby naturally warranted to enforce upon their own subjects particularly those things which publick wisdom shall judge expedient for the common good ; so it were absurd to imagine the church it self, the most glorious amongst them, abridged of this liberty, or to think that no law, constitution or canon, can be further made either for limitation or amplification in the practice of our Saviour's ordinances, whatsoever occasion be offered through variety of times and things, during the state of this inconstant world, which bringeth forth daily such new evils
and

as muſt of neceſſity by new remedies be redreſs'd, did both of old enforce our venerable predeceſſors, and will always conſtrain others, ſometime to make, ſometime to augment, and again to abridge ſometime; in ſum, often to vary, alter and change cuſtoms incident unto the manner of exerciſing that power, which doth it ſelf continue always one and the ſame. I therefore conclude, that ſpiritual authority is a power which Chriſt hath given to be uſed over them which are ſubject unto it for the eternal good of their ſouls, according to his own moſt ſacred laws, and the wholeſome poſitive conſtitutions of his church.

In doctrine referred unto action and practice, as this is which concerns ſpiritual juriſdiction, the firſt ſound and perfect underſtanding is the knowledge of the end, becauſe thereby both uſe doth frame, and contemplation judge all things.

Of penitency, the chiefeſt end propounded by ſpiritual juriſdiction. Two kinds of penitency, the one a private duty toward God, the other a duty of external diſcipline. Of the virtue of repentance from which the former duty proceedeth: And of contrition, the firſt part of that duty.

SEeing that the chiefeſt cauſe of ſpiritual juriſdiction is, to provide for the health and ſafety of men's ſouls, by bringing them to ſee and repent their grievous offences committed againſt God, as alſo to reform all injuries offered with the breach of chriſtian love and charity toward their brethren in matters of eccleſiaſtical cognizance; the uſe of this power ſhall by ſo much the plainlier appear, if firſt the nature of repentance it ſelf be known.

We are by repentance to appeaſe whom we offend by ſin. For which cauſe, whereas all ſin deprives us of the favour of Almighty God, our way of reconciliation with him is the inward ſecret repentance of the heart; which inward repentance alone ſufficeth, unleſs ſome ſpecial thing, in the quality of ſin committed, or in the party that hath done amiſs, require more. For beſides our ſubmiſſion in God's ſight, repentance muſt not only proceed to the private contentation of men, if the ſin be a crime injurious; but alſo farther, where the wholeſome diſcipline of God's church exacteth a more exemplary and open ſatisfaction. Now the church being ſatisfied with outward repentance, as God is with inward, it ſhall not be amiſs for more perſpicuity to term this latter always the virtue, the former the diſcipline of repentance; which diſcipline hath two ſorts of penitents to work upon, in as much as it hath been accuſtomed to lay the offices of repentance on ſome ſeeking, others ſhunning them; on ſome at their own voluntary requeſt, on others altogether againſt their wills, as ſhall hereafter appear by ſtore of ancient examples. Repentance being therefore either in the ſight of God alone, or elſe with the notice alſo of Men: without the one, ſometime throughly performed, but always practiſed more or leſs in our daily devotions and prayers, we can have no remedy for any fault. Whereas the other is only required in ſins of a certain degree and quality; the one neceſſary for ever, the other ſo far forth as the laws and order of God's church ſhall make it requiſite. The nature, parts and effects of the one always the ſame; the other limited, extended and varied by infinite occaſions.

Poenitentiae ſecundae, & unius, quanto in actu negotium eſt, tanto potior probatio eſt, ut non ſolâ conſcientiâ proferatur, ſed aliquo etiam actu adminiſtretur. Second penitency, following that before baptiſm, and being not more than once admitted in one man, requireth by ſo

much the greater labour to make it manifeſt, for that it is not a work which can come again in trial, but muſt be therefore with ſome open ſolemnity executed, and not to be diſcharged with the privity of conſcience alone, Tertul. de paen.

The virtue of repentance in the heart of man is God's handy-work, a fruit or effect of divine grace, which grace continually offereth it ſelf even unto them that have forſaken it, as may appear by the words of Chriſt in St. *John's* revelation, *I ſtand at the door and knock:* Nor doth he only knock without, but alſo within aſſiſt to open, whereby acceſs and entrance is given to the heavenly preſence of that ſaving power, which maketh man a repaired temple for God's good ſpirit again to inhabit. And albeit the whole train of vertues, which are implied in the name of grace, be infuſed at one inſtant; yet becauſe when they meet and concur unto any effect in man, they have their diſtinct operations riſing orderly one from another, it is no unneceſſary thing that we note the way or method of the Holy Ghoſt, in framing man's ſinful heart to repentance. A work, the firſt foundation whereof is laid by opening and illuminating the eye of faith, becauſe by faith are diſcovered the principles of this action, whereunto unleſs the underſtanding do firſt aſſent, there can follow in the will towards penitency no inclination at all. Contrariwiſe, the reſurrection of the dead, the judgment of the world to come, and the endleſs miſery of ſinners being apprehended,

ded,

ed, this worketh fear ; fuch as theirs was, who feeling their own diftrefs and perplexity, in that paffion befought our Lord's apoftles earneftly to give them counfel what
they fhould do. For fear, impotent and unable to advife it felf, yet this good it
hath, that men are thereby made defirous to prevent, if poffibly they may, whatfoever evil they dread. The firft thing that wrought the *Ninivites* repentance, was fear of
deftruction within forty days. Signs and miraculous works of God, being extraordinary
reprefentations of divine power, are commonly wont to ftir any the moft wicked with
terror, left the fame power fhould bend it felf againft them. And becaufe tractable
minds, though guilty of much fin, are hereby moved to forfake thofe evil ways which
make his power in fuch fort their aftonifhment and fear, therefore our Saviour denounced his curfe againft *Chorazin* and *Bethfaida* ; faying, That if *Tyre* and *Sidon*
had feen that which they did, thofe figns which prevailed little with the one, would have
brought the others to repentance. As the like thereunto did in the men given to curious arts, of whom the apoftolick hiftory faith, that *fear came upon them , and many
which had followed vain fciences, burnt openly the very books out of which they had
learned the fame.* As fear of contumely and difgrace amongft men , together with
other civil punifhments, are a bridle to reftrain from any heinous acts, whereinto men's
outrage would otherwife break ; fo the fear of divine revenge and punifhment, where
it takes place, doth make men defirous to be rid likewife from that inward guiltinefs of
fin, wherein they would elfe fecurely continue. Howbeit, when faith hath wrought
a fear of the event of fin, yet repentance hereupon enfueth not, unlefs our belief conceive both the poffibility and means to avert evil : The poffibility, in as much as God is
merciful, and moft willing to have fin cured : The means, becaufe he hath plainly
taught what is requifite, and fhall fuffice unto that purpofe. The nature of all wicked
men is, for fear of revenge to hate whom they moft wrong ; the nature of hatred, to
wifh that deftroyed which it cannot brook : and from hence arifeth the furious endeavours of godlefs and obdurate finners to extinguifh in themfelves the opinion of God,
becaufe they would not have him to be, whom execution of endlefs wo doth not fuffer them to love.

Every fin againft God abateth, and continuance in fin extinguifheth our love towards
him. It was once faid to the angel of *Ephefus* having finned, *Thou art fallen
away from thy firft love* ; fo that, as we never decay in love till we fin , in like
fort neither can we poffibly forfake fin, unlefs we firft begin again to love. What
is love towards God, but a defire of union with God ? And fhall we imagine a finner converting himfelf to God, in whom there is no defire of union with God
prefuppofed ? I therefore conclude, that fear worketh no man's inclination to repentance, till fomewhat elfe have wrought in us love alfo ; our love and defire of union
with God arifeth from the ftrong conceit which we have of his admirable goodnefs : The goodnefs of God which particularly moveth unto repentance , is his mercy towards mankind, notwithftanding fin : For, let it once fink deeply into the mind
of man, that howfoever we have injured God, his very nature is averfe from revenge,
except unto fin we add obftinacy, otherwife always ready to accept our fubmiffion, as
a full difcharge or recompence for all wrongs ; and can we chufe but begin to love
him whom we have offended, or can we but begin to grieve that we have offended
him whom we love ? Repentance confidereth fin as a breach of the law of God , an
act obnoxious to that revenge, which notwithftanding may be prevented, if we pacify
God in time.

The root and beginning of penitency therefore, is the confideration of our own fin,
as a caufe which hath procured the wrath, and a fubject which doth need the mercy
of God. For unto man's underftanding there being prefented, on the one fide, tribulation and anguifh upon every foul that doth evil ; on the other, eternal life unto them
which by continuance in well-doing feek glory, and honour, and immortality ;
on the one hand a curfe to the children of difobedience ; on the other, to lovers of righteoufnefs all grace and benediction : Yet between thefe extremes,that eternal God, from
whofe unfpotted juftice and undeferved mercy the lot of each inheritance proceedeth,
Caffia. Col.
20. c. 4. is fo inclinable rather to fhew compaffion than to take revenge, that all his fpeeches in
holy fcripture are almoft nothing elfe but intreaties of men to prevent deftruction by
amendment of their wicked lives ; all the works of his providence little other than
mere allurements of the juft to continue ftedfaft, and of the unrighteous to change their
courfe ; all his dealings and proceedings towards true converts, as have even filled the
grave writings of holy men with thefe and the like moft fweet fentences : repentance
(if I may fo fpeak) ftoppeth God in his way, when being provoked by crimes paft, he

cometh

cometh to revenge them with moſt juſt puniſhments; yea, it tyeth as it were the hands of the avenger, and doth not ſuffer him to have his will. Again,

The merciful eye of God towards men hath no power to withſtand penitency, at what time ſoever it comes in preſence. And again,

God doth not take it ſo in evil part, though we wound that which he hath required us to keep whole, as that after we have taken hurt, there ſhould be in us no deſire to receive his help. Finally, leſt I be carried too far in ſo large a ſea, there was never any man condemned of God but for negleƈt; nor juſtified, except he had care of repentance.

From theſe conſiderations, ſetting before our eyes our inexcuſable both unthankfulneſs in diſobeying ſo merciful, fooliſhneſs in provoking ſo powerful a God; there ariſeth neceſſarily a penſive and corroſive deſire that we had done otherwiſe; a deſire which ſuffereth us to foreſlow no time, to feel no quietneſs within our ſelves, to take neither ſleep nor food with contentment, never to give over ſupplications, confeſſions, and other penitent duties, till the light of God's reconciled favour ſhine in our darkned ſoul.

ᵃ *Fulgentius* asking the queſtion why *David's* confeſſion ſhould be held for effeƈtual penitence, and not *Saul's*; anſwereth, that the one hated ſin, the other feared only puniſhment in this world; *Saul's* acknowledgment of Sin, was fear; *David's* both fear and alſo love.

This was the fountain of *Peter's* tears, this the life and ſpirit of *David's* eloquence, in thoſe moſt admirable hymns intituled *Penitential*, where the words of ſorrow for ſin do melt the very bowels of God remitting it; and the comforts of grace in remitting ſin, carry him which ſorrowed, rapt as it were into heaven, with ecſtaſies of joy and gladneſs. The firſt motive of the *Ninevites* unto repentance, was their belief in a ſermon of fear; but the next and moſt immediate, an axiom of love; *Who can tell whether God will turn away his fierce wrath, that we periſh not?* No concluſion ſuch as theirs, Let every man turn from his evil way, but one of the premiſes ſuch as theirs were, fear and love. Wherefore the well-ſpring of repentance is faith; firſt breeding fear, and then love; which love cauſes hope, hope reſolution of attempt; *I will go to my father, and ſay, I have ſinned againſt heaven, and againſt thee*; that is to ſay, I will do what the duty of a convert requireth.

Now in a penitent's or convert's duty there are included, firſt the averſion of the will from ſin; ſecondly, the ſubmiſſion of our ſelves to God by ſupplication and prayer; thirdly, the purpoſe of a new life, teſtified with preſent works of amendment: Which three things do very well ſeem to be compriſed in one definition by them which handle repentance, as a virtue that hateth, bewaileth, and ſheweth a purpoſe to amend ſin: we offend God in thought, word, and deed, to the firſt of which three they make contrition; to the ſecond, confeſſion; and to the laſt, our works of ſatisfaƈtion, anſwerable.

Contrition doth not here import thoſe ſudden pangs and convulſions of the mind, which cauſe ſometimes the moſt forſaken of God to retraƈt their own doings; it is no natural paſſion, or anguiſh, which riſeth in us againſt our wills; but a deliberate averſion of the will of man from ſin, which being always accompanied with grief; and grief oftentimes partly with tears, partly with other external ſigns; it hath been thought, that in theſe things contrition doth chiefly conſiſt: Whereas the chiefeſt thing in contrition is that alteration whereby the will, which was before delighted with ſin, doth now abhor and ſhun nothing more. But foraſmuch as we cannot hate ſin in our ſelves without heavineſs and grief, that there ſhould be in us a thing of ſuch hateful quality, the will averted from ſin, muſt needs make the affeƈtion ſuitable; yea, there's great reaſon why it ſhould ſo do: For ſince the will by conceiving ſin hath deprived the ſoul of life; and of life there is no recovery without repentance, the death of ſin; repentance not able to kill ſin, but by withdrawing the will from it; the will unpoſſible to be withdrawn, unleſs it concur with a contrary affeƈtion to that which accompanied it before in evil: Is it not clear, that as an inordinate delight did firſt begin ſin, ſo repentance muſt begin with a juſt ſorrow, a ſorrow of heart, and ſuch a ſorrow as renteth the heart; neither a feigned nor ſlight ſorrow; not feigned, leſt it increaſe ſin; nor ſlight, leſt the pleaſures of ſin over-match it.

Wherefore of grace, the higheſt cauſe from which man's penitency doth proceed; of faith, fear, love, hope, what force and efficacy they have in repentance; of parts and duties thereunto belonging, comprehended in the ſchool-mens definitions; finally, of the firſt among thoſe duties, contrition, which diſliketh and bewaileth iniquity, let this ſuffice.

And becauſe God will have offences by repentance, not only abhorred within our ſelves, but alſo with humble ſupplication diſplayed before him; and a teſtimony of amendment to be given, even by preſent works worthy repentance, in that they are contrary

trary to thofe we renounce and difclaim; although the virtue of repentance do require that her other two parts, confeffion and farisfaction, fhould here follow; yet feeing they belong as well to the difcipline, as to the virtue of repentance, and only differ, for that in the one they are performed to man, in the other to God alone; I had rather diftinguifh them in joynt-handling, than handle them apart, becaufe in quality and manner of practice they are diftinct.

Of the difcipline of repentance inftituted by Chrift, practifed by the fathers, converted by the fchool-men into a facrament; and of confeffion, that which belongeth to the virtue of repentance, that which was ufed among the Jews, that which papacy imagineth a facrament, and that which ancient difcipline practifed.

1. OUR Lord and Saviour, in the fixteenth of St. *Matthew's* Gofpel, giveth his apoftles regiment in general over God's church. For they that have the keys of the kingdom of heaven, are thereby fignified to be ftewards of the houfe of God, under whom they guide, command, judge and correct his family. The fouls of men are God's treafure, committed to the truft and fidelity of fuch as muft render a ftrict account for the very leaft which is under their cuftody. God hath not invefted them with power to make a revenue thereof, but to ufe it for the good of them whom Jefus Chrift hath moft dearly bought.

And becaufe their office therein confifteth of fundry functions, fome belonging to doctrine, fome to difcipline, all contained in the name of the keys, they have for matters of difcipline, as well litigious as criminal, their courts and confiftories erected by the
heavenly authority of his moft facred voice, who hath faid *Dic Ecclefiæ*, tell the church; againft rebellious and contumacious perfons, which refufe to obey their fentence, armed they are with power to eject fuch out of the church, to deprive them of the honours, rights and privileges of chriftian men, to make them as Heathens and Publicans, with whom fociety was hateful.

Furthermore, left their acts fhould be flenderly accounted of, or had in contempt;
1 Cor. 5. 3.
2 Cor. 2. 6.
1 Tim. 1. 20.
whether they admit to the fellowfhip of faints, or feclude from it, whether they bind offenders, or fet them again at liberty, whether they remit or retain fins, whatfoever is done by way of orderly and lawful proceeding, the Lord himfelf hath promifed to ratify. This is that grand original warrant, by force whereof the guides and prelates in God's church, firft his apoftles, and afterwards others following them fucceffively, did both ufe and uphold that difcipline, the end whereof is to heal mens confciences, to cure their fins, to reclaim offenders from iniquity, and to make them by repentance juft.

Neither hath it of ancient time, for any other refpect, been accuftomed to bind by ecclefiaftical cenfures, to retain fo bound till tokens of manifeft repentance appeared, and upon apparent repentance to releafe, faving only becaufe this was received as a moft expedient method for the cure of fin.

The courfe of difcipline in former ages reformed open tranfgreffors, by putting them into offices of open penitence, efpecially confeffion, whereby they declared their own crimes in the hearing of the whole church, and were not from the time of their firft convention, capable of the holy myfteries of Chrift, till they had folemnly difcharged this duty.

Offenders in fecret knowing themfelves altogether as unworthy to be admitted to the Lord's table, as the other which were with-held; being alfo perfuaded, that if the church did direct them in the offices of their penitency, and affift them with publick prayers, they fhould more eafily obtain that they fought, than by trufting wholly to their own endeavours; finally, having no impediment to ftay them from it but bafhfulnefs, which countervailed not the former inducements; and befides, was greatly eafed by the good conftruction, which the charity of thofe times gave to fuch actions, wherein mens piety and voluntary care to be reconciled to God, did purchafe them much more love than their faults (the teftimonies of common frailty) were able to procure difgrace, they made it not nice to ufe fome one of the minifters of God, by whom the reft might take notice of their faults, prefcribe them convenient remedies, and in the end after publick confeffion, all join in Prayer unto God for them.

The firft beginner of this cuftom had the more followers, by means of that fpecial favour which always was with good confideration fhewed towards voluntary penitents above the reft.

But as profeſſors of chriſtian belief grew more in number, ſo they waxed worſe; when kings and princes had ſubmitted their dominions unto the ſcepter of Jeſus Chriſt, by means whereof perſecution ceaſing, the church immediately became ſubject to thoſe evils which peace and ſecurity bringeth forth; there was not now that love which before kept all things in tune, but every where ſchiſms, diſcords, diſſenſions amongſt men, conventicles of hereticks, bent more vehemently againſt the ſounder and better ſort than very infidels and heathens themſelves; faults not corrected in charity, but noted with delight, and kept for malice to uſe when the deadlieſt opportunities ſhould be offered.

Whereupon, foraſmuch as publick confeſſions became dangerous and prejudicial to the ſafety of well-minded men, and in divers reſpects advantageous to the enemies of God's church; it ſeemed firſt unto ſome, and afterwards generally requiſite, that voluntary penitents ſhould ſurceaſe from open confeſſion.

Inſtead whereof, when once private and ſecret confeſſion had taken place with the *Latins*, it continued as a profitable ordinance, till the *Lateran* council had decreed, that all men once in a year at the leaſt, ſhould confeſs themſelves to the prieſt.

So that being a thing thus made both general and alſo neceſſary, the next degree of eſtimation whereunto it grew, was to be honoured and lifted up to the nature of a ſacrament; that as Chriſt did inſtitute baptiſm to give life, and the euchariſt to nouriſh life, ſo penitence might be thought a ſacrament ordained to recover life, and confeſſion a part of the ſacrament.

They define therefore their private penitency to be a ſacrament of remitting ſins after baptiſm: The virtue of repentance, a deteſtation of wickedneſs, with full purpoſe to amend the ſame, and with hope to obtain pardon at God's hands. *Soto in 4. ſent. d. 14. q. 1. art. 1. In ead. diſt.*

Whereſoever the prophets cry *repent*, and in the goſpel St. *Peter* maketh the ſame exhortation to the *Jews* as yet unbaptized, they would have the virtue of repentance only to be underſtood; the ſacrament, where he adviſeth *Simon Magus* to repent, becauſe the ſin of *Simon Magus* was after baptiſm. *q. 1. art. 1.*

Now although they have only external repentance for a ſacrament, internal for a vertue, yet make they ſacramental repentance nevertheleſs to be compoſed of three parts, contrition, confeſſion, and ſatisfaction. Which is abſurd; becauſe contrition being an inward thing, belongeth to the virtue, and not to the ſacrament of repentance, which muſt conſiſt of external parts, if the nature thereof be external. Beſides, which is more abſurd, they leave out abſolution, whereas ſome of their ſchool divines, handling penance in the nature of a ſacrament, and being not able to eſpy the leaſt reſemblance of a ſacrament, ſave only in abſolution (for a ſacrament by their doctrine muſt both ſignify, and alſo confer or beſtow ſome ſpecial divine grace) reſolved themſelves, that the duties of the penitent could be but meer preparations to the ſacrament, and that the ſacrament it ſelf was wholly in abſolution. And albeit *Thomas*, with his followers, have thought it ſafer to maintain, as well the ſervices of the penitent, as the words of the miniſter neceſſary unto the eſſence of their ſacrament; the ſervices of the penitent, as a cauſe material; the words of abſolution, as a formal; for that by them all things are perfected to the taking away of ſin; which opinion now reigneth in all their ſchools, ſince the time that the council of *Trent* gave it ſolemn approbation, ſeeing they all make abſolution, if not the whole eſſence, yet the very form whereunto they aſcribe chiefly the whole force and operation of their ſacrament; ſurely to admit the matter as a part, and not to admit the form, hath ſmall congruity with reaſon. *Scot. ſent. l. 4. d. 14. q. 4. Sect. 14. e. 3. Docet Sancta Synodus Sacramenti poenitentiæ formam, in qua præcipue ipſius vis ſita eſt, in illis miniſtri verbis poſitam eſſe, ego te abſolvo. Sunt autem quaſi materia hujus ſacramenti, ipſius poenitentis actus, nempe contritio, confeſſio, & ſatisfactio.*

Again, foraſmuch as a ſacrament is compleat, having the matter and form which it ought, what ſhould lead them to ſet down any other parts of ſacramental repentance, than confeſſion and abſolution, as *Durandus* hath done?

For touching ſatisfaction, the end thereof, as they underſtand it, is a further matter which reſteth after the ſacrament adminiſtred, and therefore can be no part of the ſacrament.

Will they draw in contrition with ſatisfaction, which are no parts, and exclude abſolution (a principal part) yea, the very complement, form and perfection of the reſt, as themſelves account it? But for their breach of precepts in art, it ſkilleth not, if their doctrine otherwiſe concerning penitency, and in penitency touching confeſſion, might be found true.

We ſay, let no man look for pardon, which doth ſmother and conceal ſin, where in duty it ſhould be revealed.

The cauſe why God requireth confeſſion to be made to him is, that thereby teſtifying a deep hatred of our own iniquity, the only cauſe of his hatred and wrath towards us, we might, becauſe we are humble, be ſo much the more capable of that compaſſion and tender mercy, which knoweth not how to condemn ſinners that condemn themſelves.

If

Luke 7. 47. If it be our Saviour's own principle, that the conceit we have of our debt forgiven, proportioneth our thankfulnefs and love to him, at whofe hands we receive pardon ; doth not God forefee, that they which with ill-advifed modefty feek to hide their fin like *Adam*, that they which rake it up under afhes, and confefs it not, are very unlikely to require with offices of love afterwards, the grace which they fhew themfelves unwilling to prize at the very time when they fue for it ; inafmuch as their not confefing what crimes they have committed, is a plain fignification how loth they are that the benefit of God's moft gracious pardon fhould feem great ? Nothing more true than that of *Tertullian, confeffion doth as much abate the weight of mens offences, as concealment doth make them heavier.* For which confeffeth, hath purpofe to appeafe God ; he, a determination to perfift and continue obftinate, which keeps them fecret to himfelf. St. *Chryfoftome* almoft in the fame words, *Wickednefs is by being acknowledged leffened, and doth but grow by being hid.* If men, having done amifs, let it flip, as though they knew no fuch matter, what is there to ftay them from falling into one and the fame evil ? To call our felves finners availeth nothing, except we lay our faults in the ballance, and take the weight of them one by one. Confefs thy crimes to God, difclofe thy tranfgreffions before thy judge, by way of humble fupplication and fuit, if not with tongue, at the leaft with heart, and in this fort feek mercy. A general perfuafion that thou art a finner, will neither fo humble, nor bridle thy foul, as if the catalogue of thy fins examined feverally, be continually kept in mind.

'Tantum relevat confeffio derelictorum, quantum diffimulatio exaggerat. Confeffio autem fatisfactionis confilium eft, diffimulatio contumaciæ. Tert. de pœn. Chryf. hom. 30. in. Epift. ad Heb.

This fhall make thee lowly in thine own eyes ; this fhall preferve thy feet from falling, and fharpen thy defires towards all good things. The mind, I know, doth hardlp admit fuch unpleafant remembrances ; but we muft force it ; we muft conftrain it thereunto.

It is fafer now to be bitten with the memory, than hereafter with the torment of fin.

Levit. 16. 21. The *Jews*, with whom no repentance for fin is available without confeffion, either conceived in mind or uttered (which latter kind they call ufually ידוי confeffion delivered by word of mouth) had firft that general confeffion which once every year was made, both feverally by each of the people for himfelf upon the day of expiation, and by the prieft for them all. On the day of expiation, the high prieft maketh three exprefs confeffions, acknowledging unto God the manifold tranfgreffions of the whole nation, his own perfonal offences likewife, together with the fins as well of his family, as of the reft of his rank and order.

All *Ifrael* is bound on the day of expiation to re-pent and confefs. R. Mof. in lib. Mitfworth haggadol. par. 2. præ. 16.

They had again their voluntary confeffions, at the times and feafons when men bethinking themfelves of their wicked converfation paft, were refolved to change their courfe, the beginning of which alteration was ftill confeffion of fins.

Thirdly, over and befides thefe, the law impofed upon them alfo that fpecial confeffion, which they in their book called כי יחזר ודוי על עיד confeffion of that particular fault for which they namely feek pardon at God's hands.

Num. 5. 6. The words of the law concerning confeffion in this kind, are as followeth : When a man or woman fhall commit any fin that men commit, and tranfgrefs againft the Lord, their fin which they have done (that is to fay, the very deed it felf in particular) they fhall acknowledge.

Lev. 5. 5. In *Leviticus*, after certain tranfgreffions there mentioned, we read the like : When a man hath finned in any one of thefe things, he fhall then confefs, how in that thing he hath offended. For fuch kind of fpecial fins, they had alfo fpecial facrifices ; wherein the manner was, that the offender fhould lay his hands on the head of the facrifice which he brought, and fhould there make confeffion to God, faying, *Now, O Lord, that I have offended, committed fin, and done wickedly in thy fight, this or this being my fault ; behold I repent me, and am utterly afhamed of my doings ; my purpofe is, never to return more to the fame crime.*

Mifne Tora Tractatu Tefhuba cap. 1. & R. M. in lib. Mifhoth. par 2. chap. 6.

None of them, whom either the houfe of judgment had condemned to die, or of them which are to be punifhed with ftripes, can be clear by being executed or fcourged, till they repent and confefs their faults.

Mof. in Mifnoth, par. 2. præ. 16.

Finally, there was no man amongft them at any time, either condemned ;to fuffer death, or corrected, or chaftized with ftripes, none ever fick and near his end, but they called upon him to repent and confefs his fins.

To him which is fick, and draweth towards death, they fay, Confefs. Idem.

Of malefactors convict by witneffes, and thereupon either adjudged to die, or otherwife chaftifed, their cuftom was to exact, as *Jofhua* did of *Achan*, open confeffion ; *My fon, now give glory to the Lord God of Ifrael, confefs unto him, and declare unto me what thou haft committed, conceal it not from me.* Jof. 7. 19.

Concerning injuries and trefpaffes which happen between men, they highly commend fuch as will acknowledge before many.

4

It

It is in him which repenteth accepted as an high facrifice, if he will confefs before many, make them acquainted with his over-fights, and reveal the tranfgreffions which have paffed between him and any of his brethren; faying, I have verily offended this man, thus and thus I have done unto him, but behold I do now repent and am forry. Contrariwife, whofoever is proud, and will not be known of his faults, but cloaketh them, is not yet come to perfect repentance; for fo it is written, *He that hides his fins fhall not profper:* Which words of *Solomon* they do not farther extend, than only to fins committed againft men, which are in that refpect meet before men to be acknowledged particularly. But in fins between man and God, there is no neceffity that man fhould himfelf make any fuch open and particular recital of them; to God they are known, and of us it is required that we caft not the memory of them carelefly and loofly behind our backs, but keep in mind, as near as we can, both our own debt, and his grace which remitteth the fame.

Wherefore to let pafs *Jewifh* confeffion, and to come unto them which hold confeffion in the ear of the prieft commanded; yea, commanded in the nature of a facrament, and thereby fo neceffary that fin without it cannot be pardoned; let them find fuch a commandment in holy fcripture, and we ask no more.

John the *Baptift* was an extraordinary perfon, his birth, his actions of life, his office extraordinary.

It is therefore recorded for the ftrangenefs of the act, but not to fet down as an everlafting law for the world, *That to him Jerufalem and all Judea made confeffion of their fins;* Mat. 3. 6. Befides, at the time of this confeffion, their pretended facrament of repentance as they grant, was not yet inftituted; neither was it fin after baptifm which penitents did there confefs; when that which befel the feven fons of *Sceva* for ufing the name of our Lord Jefus Chrift in their conjurations, was notified to *Jews* and *Grecians* in *Ephefus,* it brought Acts 19. 18. an univerfal fear upon them, infomuch that divers of them which had believed before, but not obeyed the laws of Chrift as they fhould have done, being terrified by this example, came to the apoftle, and confeffed their wicked deeds.

Which good and virtuous act, no wife man, as I fuppofe, will difallow, but commend highly in them, whom God's good fpirit fhall move to do the like when need requireth.

Yet neither hath this example the force of any general commandment, or law to make it neceffary for every man to pour into the ears of the prieft whatfoever hath been done amifs, or elfe to remain everlaftingly culpable and guilty of fin; in a word, it proveth confeffion practifed as a vertuous act but not commanded as a facrament.

Now concerning St. *James* his exhortation, whether the former branch be confidered, James 5. 16. which faith, *Is any fick among you; let him call for the antients of the church, and let them make their prayers for him;* or the latter, which ftirreth up all chriftian men unto mutual acknowledgment of faults amongft themfelves; *Lay open your minds, make your confeffions one to another;* is it not plain, that the one hath relation to that gift of healing, which our Saviour promifed his church, faying, *They fhall lay their hands on the* Mat. 16. 18. *fick, and the fick fhall recover health?* Relation to that gift of healing, whereby the Apoftle impofed his hands on the father of *Publius,* and made him miraculoufly a found man; relation finally to that gift of healing, which fo long continued in practice after the Apo- Acts 28. 8. ftles times, that whereas the *Novatianifts* denyed the power of the church of God in curing fin after baptifm, St. *Ambrofe* asked them again, *Why it might not as well prevail* Amb. de pœn. *with God for fpiritual, as for corporal and bodily health; yea wherefore* (faith he) *do ye* l. 1. c. 7. *your felves lay hands on the difeafed, and believe it to be a work of benediction or prayer, if haply the fick perfon be reftored to his former fafety?* And of the other member which toucheth mutual confeffion, do not fome of themfelves, as namely *Cajetan,* deny, that any other confeffion is meant, than only that *which feeketh either affociation of prayers,* Annot. Rhem. *or reconciliation; or pardon of wrongs?* Is it not confeffed by the greateft part of their own in Jac. 5. retinue, that we cannot certainly affirm facramental confeffion to have been meant or fpoken of in this place? Howbeit, *Bellarmine,* delighted to run a courfe by himfelf where colourable fhifts of wit will but make the way paffable, ftandeth as formally for this place, and not lefs for that in St. *John,* than for this: St. *John* faith, *If we confefs our fins, God* 1 John 1. 9. *is faithful and juft to forgive us our fins, and to cleanfe us from all unrighteoufnefs;* doth St. *John* fay, if we confefs to the prieft, God is righteous to forgive; and if not, that our fins are unpardonable? No, but the titles of God *juft* and *righteous* do import that he pardoneth fin only for his promife fake; *And there is not* (they fay) *any promife of forgivenefs upon confeffion made to God without the prieft;* not any promife, but with this condition, and yet this condition no where expreft.

Is it not ftrange, that the fcripture fpeaking fo much of repentance and of the feveral duties which appertain thereunto, fhould ever mean, and no where mention that one condition, without which all the reft is utterly of none effect; or will they fay, becaufe our

Saviour hath said to his minifters, *Whofe fins ye retain*, &c. and becaufe they can remit no more than what the offenders have confeft, that therefore by the vertue of his promife, It ftandeth with the righteoufnefs of God to take away no man's fins until by auricular confeffion they be opened unto the prieft?

They are men that would feem to honour antiquity, and none more to depend upon the reverend judgment thereof. I dare boldly affirm, that for many hundred years after Chrift the fathers held no fuch opinion : they did not gather by our Saviour's words any fuch neceffity of feeking the prieft's abfolution from fin, by fecret and (as they now term it) facramental confeffion. Publick confeffion they thought neceffary by way of difcipline, not private confeffion, as in the nature of a facrament, neceffary.

For to begin with the pureft times, it is unto them which read and judge without partiality a thing moft clear, that the antient ἐξομολογήσις or confeffion, defigned by *Tertullian* to be a difcipline of humiliation and fubmiffion, framing men's behaviour in fuch fort as may be fitteft to move pity ; the confeffion which they ufe to fpeak of in the exercife of repentance was made openly in the hearing of the whole, both ecclefiaftical, confiftory, and affembly.

Plerofq; hoc opus ut publicationem fui aut fuffugere, aut de die in diem differre, præfumo pu-doris magis memores quam falutis, velut illi qui in partibus verecundiori-bus corporis contracta vexatione confci-entiam medentium vitant & ita cum e-rubefcentia fua pereunt. *Terr. de pæn.* This is the reafon wherefore he perceiving that divers were better content their fores fhould fecretly fefter and eat inward, than be laid fo open to the eyes of many, blameth greatly their unwife bafhfulnefs; and to reform the fame, perfuadeth with them, faying, *Amongft thy brethren and fellow fervants which are partakers with thee, of one and the fame nature, fear, joy, grief, fufferings (for of one common Lord and Father we have all received one fpirit) why fhouldeft thou not think with thy felf, that they are but thine own felf ? wherefore doft thou avoid them, as likely to infult over thee, whom thou knoweft fubject to the fame haps ? At that which grieveth any one part, the whole body cannot rejoyce, it muft needs be that the whole will labour and ftrive to help that wherewith a part of it felf is molefted.*

Qui neceffita-tem facrifi-candi pecunia apud Magi-ftratum redi-mebant, ac-cepta fecurita-tis Syngrapha libellatici dice-bantur. St. *Cyprian* being grieved with the dealings of them, who in time of perfecution had thro' fear betrayed their faith, and notwithftanding thought by fhift to avoid in that cafe the neceffary difcipline of the church, wrote for their better inftruction the book intituled *De lapfis* ; a treatife concerning fuch as had openly forfaken their religion and yet were loth o-penly to confefs their fault in fuch manner as they fhould have done : in which book he compareth with this fort of men, certain others which had but a purpofe only to have departed from the faith ; and yet could not quiet their minds, till this very fecret and hidden fault was confeft, *How much both greater in faith* (faith St. *Cyprian*) *and alfo as touching their fear, better are thofe men who altho' neither facrifice, nor libel could be objected againft them, yet becaufe they thought to have done that which they fhould not, even this their intent they dolefully open unto God's priefts ? They confefs that whereof their confci-ence accufeth them, the burthen that preffeth their minds they difcover ; they forflow not of fmaller and flighter evils, to feek remedy.* He faith they declared their fault, not to one only man in private, but revealed it to God's priefts ; they confeft it before the whole confiftory of God's minifters.

Hom. 1. de initio quarag. defin. *Salvianus* (for I willingly embrace their conjecture, who afcribe thofe homilies to him which have hitherto by common error paft under the counterfeit name of *Eufebius Emcfenus*) I fay, *Salvianus* tho' coming long after *Cyprian* in time, giveth neverthelefs the fame evidence for this truth, in a cafe very little different from that before alledged ; his words are thefe, *Whereas (moft dearly beloved) we fee that penance oftentimes is fought and fued for by holy fouls, which even from their youth have bequeathed themfelves a precious treafure unto God, let us know that the infpiration of God's good Spirit moveth them fo to do for the benefit of his church, and let fuch as are wounded learn to enquire for that remedy whereunto the very foundeft do thus offer and obtrude as it were themfelves, that if the virtuous do bewail fmall offences, the other ceafe not to lament great.* And furely, when a man that hath lefs need, performeth *fub oculis Ecclefiæ*, in the view, fight and beholding of the whole church, an office worthy of his faith and compunction for fin, the good which others thereby reap is his own harveft, the heap of his rewards groweth by that which another gaineth, and thro' a kind of fpiritual ufury from that amendment of life which o-thers learn by him, there returneth lucre into his coffers.

Hom. 10. ad Monachos. The fame *Salvianus* in another of his homilies, *If faults haply be not great and grievous (for example, if a man have offended in word, or in defire, worthy of reproof, if in the wantonnefs of his eye, or the vanity of his heart) the ftains of words and thoughts are by daily prayer to be cleanfed, and by private compunction to be fcoured out : But if any man examining inwardly his own confcience, have committed fome high and capital offence, as if by bearing falfe witnefs he have quelled and betrayed his faith, and by rafhnefs of perjury have violated the facred name of truth ; if with the mire of luftful uncleannefs he have* fullied

2

ſullied the veil of baptiſm and the gorgeous robe of virginity ; if by being the cauſe of any man's death, he hath been the death of the new man within himſelf ; if by conference with ſooth-ſayers, wizards and charmers, he hath enthralled himſelf to Satan ; theſe and ſuch like committed crimes, cannot thoroughly be taken away with ordinary, moderate, and ſecret ſatisfaction ; but greater cauſes do require greater and ſharper remedies, they need ſuch remedies as are not only ſharp, but ſolemn, open, and publick. Again, *Let that ſoul* (ſaith he) *anſwer me, which thro' pernicious ſhamefacedneſs is now ſo abaſht to acknowledge his ſin in* conſpectu fratrum, *before his brethren, as he ſhould have been abaſht to commit the ſame, what will he do in the preſence of that divine tribunal where he is to ſtand arraign'd in the aſſembly of a glorious and celeſtial hoſt ?* I will hereunto add but St. *Ambroſe's* teſtimony : For the places which I might alledge are more than the cauſe it ſelf needeth : *There are many* (ſaith he) *who, fearing the judgment that is to come, and feeling inward remorſe of conſcience, when they have offered themſelves unto penitency, and are enjoyned what they ſhall do ; give back for the only ſkar which they think that publick ſupplication will put them unto.*

Graviores, & actiores, & publicas curas requirunt, Hom. 8. ad Monach.

He ſpeaketh of them which ſought voluntarily to be penanced, and yet withdrew themſelves from open confeſſion, which they that are penitents for publick crimes could not poſſibly have done, and therefore it cannot be ſaid he meaneth any other than ſecret ſinners in that place. *Gennadius,* a presbyter of *Marſeilles,* in his book touching eccleſiaſtical aſſertions, maketh but two kinds of confeſſion neceſſary, the one in private to God alone for ſmaller offences ; the other open, when crimes committed are heinous and great : *Altho'* (ſaith he) *a man be bitten with conſcience of ſin, let his will be from thenceforward to ſin no more ; let him before he communicate, ſatisfy with tears and prayers, and then putting his truſt in the mercy of almighty God* (whoſe wont is to yield godly confeſſion) *let him boldly receive the ſacrament. But I ſpeak this of ſuch as have not burthened themſelves with capital ſins. Them I exhort to ſatisfy, firſt by publick penance, that ſo being reconciled by the ſentence of the prieſt, they may communicate ſafely with others.* Thus ſtill we hear of publick confeſſions, altho' the crimes themſelves diſcover'd were not publick ; we hear that the cauſe of ſuch confeſſions was not the openneſs, but the greatneſs of mens offences ; finally, we hear that the ſame being now held by the church of *Rome* to be ſacramental, were the only penitential confeſſions uſed in the church for a long time, and eſteemed as neceſſary remedies againſt ſin.

Lib. 2. de pœn. cap. 9.

They which will find auricular confeſſions in *Cyprian,* therefore, muſt ſeek out ſome other paſſage, than that which *Bellarmine* alledgeth, *Whereas in ſmaller faults which are not committed againſt the Lord himſelf, there is a competent time aſſigned unto penitency ; and that confeſſion is made, after that obſervation and tryal had been had of the penitents behaviour, neither may any communicate till the biſhop and clergy have laid their hands upon him ; how much more ought all things to be warily and ſtavedly obſerved, according to the diſcipline of the Lord, in theſe moſt grievous and extream crimes ?* St. *Cyprian's* ſpeech is againſt raſhneſs in admitting idolaters to the holy communion, before they had ſhew'd ſufficient repentance, conſidering that other offenders were forced to ſtay out their time, and that they made not their publick confeſſion, which was the laſt act of penitency, till their life and converſation had been ſeen into, not with the eye of auricular ſcrutiny, but of paſtoral obſervation, according to that in the council of *Nice,* where thirteen years being ſet for the penitency of certain offenders, the ſeverity of this degree is mitigated with ſpecial caution : *That in all ſuch caſes, the mind of the penitent and the manner of his repentance is to be noted, that as many as with fear, and tears, and meekneſs, and the exerciſe of good works, declared themſelves to be converts indeed, and not in outward appearance only, towards them the biſhop at his diſcretion might uſe more lenity.* If the council of *Nice* ſuffice not, let *Gracian* the founder of the canon law expound *Cyprian,* who ſheweth that the ſtint of time in penitency is either to be abridged, or enlarged, as the penitent's faith and behaviour ſhall give occaſion : *I have eaſilier found out men* (ſaith St. *Ambroſe*) *able to keep themſelves free from crimes than conformable to the rules which in penitency they ſhould obſerve.* St. *Gregory* biſhop of *Niſſe* complaineth and inveigheth bitterly againſt them, who in the time of their penitency lived even as they had done always before ; *Their countenance as chearful, their attire as neat, their diet as coſtly, and their ſleep as ſecure as ever, their worldly buſineſs purpoſely followed, to exile penſive thoughts for their minds repentance pretended, but indeed nothing leſs expreſt :* Theſe were the inſpections of life, whereunto St. *Cyprian* alludeth ; as for auricular examinations he knew them not.

Cypr. Epiſt. 12.
Inſpecta vita ejus qui agit pœnitentiam.
Con. Nic. par. 1. c. 11.
Pro fide & converſatione Pœnitentium.
De pœn. diſt. 1. cap. menſuram Ambr.
de pœn. lib. 2. c. 10. Greg. Niſſ. Orat. In eos qui alios ſcerbe judicant.

Were the Fathers then without uſe of private confeſſion as long as publick was in uſe ? I affirm no ſuch thing. The firſt and ancienteſt that mentioneth this confeſſion is *Origen,* by whom it may ſeem that men being loth to preſent raſhly themſelves and their faults unto the view of the whole church, thought it beſt to unfold firſt their minds to ſome one ſpecial

man

man of the clergy, which might either help them himself, or refer them to an higher
court if need were. *Be therefore circumspect* (faith *Origen*) *in making choice of the party,
to whom thou meanest to confess thy sin; know thy physician before thou use him; if he
find thy malady such as needeth to be made publick, that others may be the better by it and
thy self sooner help, his counsel must be obeyed.* That which moved sinners thus voluntarily to detect themselves both in private and in publick, was fear to receive with other christian men the mysteries of heavenly grace, till God's appointed stewards and ministers did
judge them worthy. It is in this respect that St. *Ambrose* findeth fault with certain men
which fought imposition of penance, and were not willing to wait their time, but would be
presently admitted communicants. *Such people* (faith he) *do seek by so rash and preposterous
desires, rather to bring the priest into bonds than to loose themselves.* In this respect it is
that St. *Augustine* hath likewise said, *When the wound of sin is so wide, and the disease
so far gone that the medicinable body and blood of our Lord may not be touched, men are by
the bishop's authority to sequester themselves from the altar, till such time as they have repented, and be after reconciled by the same authority.*

Furthermore, because the knowledge how to handle our own sores is no vulgar and
common art, but we either carry towards our selves for the most part an over soft and gentle hand, fearful of touching too near the quick; or else, endeavouring not to be partial,
we fall into timorous scrupulosities, and sometime into those extream discomforts of mind,
from which we hardly do ever lift up our heads again, men thought it the safest way to dif-
close their secret faults, and to crave imposition of penance from them whom our Lord Jesus Christ hath left in his church to be spiritual and ghostly physicians, the guides and pastors of redeemed souls, whose office doth not only consist in general persuasions unto
amendment of life, but also in private particular cure of diseased minds.

Howsoever the *Novatianists* presume to plead against the church (faith *Salvianus*) *that
every man ought to be his own penitentiary, and that it is a part of our duty to exercise, but
not of the church's authority to impose or prescribe repentance;* the truth is otherwise, the
best and strongest of us may need, in such cases, direction: *What doth the church in giving
penance, but shew the remedies which sin requireth? or what do we in receiving the same
but fulfil her precept? what else but sue unto God with tears, and fasts, that his merciful
ears may be opened?* St. *Augustine's* exhortation is directly to the same purpose; *Let every
man whilst he hath time judge himself, and change his life of his own accord, and when this
is resolved, let him from the disposers of the holy sacraments, learn in what manner he is to
pacify God's displeasure.* But the greatest thing which made men forward and willing upon
their knees to confess whatsoever they had committed against God, and in no wise to be with-
held from the same with any fear of disgrace, contempt, or obloquy, which might ensue, was
their fervent desire to be helped and assisted with the prayers of God's faints. Wherein,
as St. *James* doth exhort unto mutual confession; alledging this only for a reason, *that just
mens devout prayers are of great avail with God;* so it hath been heretofore the use of penitents for that intent to unburthen their minds, even to private persons; and to crave their
Prayers. Whereunto, *Cassianus* alluding, counselleth, *That if men possest with dulness of
spirit be themselves unapt to do that which is required, they should in meek affection seek
health at the least by good and vertuous mens prayers unto God for them.* And to the same
effect *Gregory* bishop of *Nisse*, humble thy self, and take unto thee such of thy brethren as
are of one mind, and do bear kind affection towards thee, that they may together mourn and
labour for thy deliverance. Shew me thy bitter and abundant tears, that I may blend my
own with them.

But because of all men there is or should be none in that respect more fit for troubled
and distressed minds to repair unto than God's Ministers, he proceedeth further, *Make the
priest, as a father, partaker of thy affliction and grief; be bold to impart unto him the
things that are most secret, he will have care both of thy safety and of thy credit.*

Confession (faith *Leo*) *is first to be offered to God, and then to the priest, as to one which
maketh supplication for the sins of penitent offenders.* Suppose we, that men would ever
have been easily drawn, much less of their own accord have come unto publick confession,
whereby they know they should found the trumpet of their own disgrace; would they willingly have done this, which naturally all men are loth to do, but for the singular trust and confidence which they had in the publick prayers of God's church? *Let thy mother the church
weep for thee* (faith *Ambrose*) *let her wash and bathe thy faults with her tears: our Lord
doth love that many should become suppliant for one.* In like sort, long before him *Tertullian*,
*some few assembled make a church; and the church is as Christ himself; when thou dost
therefore put forth thy hands to the knees of thy brethren, thou touchest Christ, it is Christ
unto whom thou art a supplicant; so when they pour out tears over them, it is even Christ
that taketh compassion; Christ which prayeth when they pray: neither can that easily be denied, for which the Son is himself contented to become a suiter.*   Where-

Side notes:
Orig. in Psal. 37.
Ambr. l. 2. de pœn. c. 9.
Si non tam se folvere cupi-unt quam fa-cerdotem li-gare. Aug. in pom. de pœn.
Hom. de pœn. Niniv.
Aug. hom. de pœn. citatur a Grat. dist. 1. c. judices. A præpositis Sacramento-rum accipiat satisfactionis suæ modum.
Jam. 5. 16.
Caffia col. 20. c. 8. Greg. Niff. oratione in eos qui alios acerbe judi-cant.
Leo 1. Ep. 78. ad Epist. Cam-pan. citat. a Grat. de pœn. d. 1. c. fufficit.
Ambr. l. 2. de pœn. c. 10. Tertul. de pœn.

Whereas in thefe confiderations therefore, voluntary penitents had been long accuftomed for great and grievous crimes, tho' fecret, yet openly both to repent and confefs, as the canons of antient difcipline required ; the *Greek* church firft, and in procefs of time the *Latin* altered this order, judging it fufficient and more convenient that fuch offenders fhould do penance and make confeffion in private only. The caufe why the *Latins* did, *Leo* declar-Leo. 1. Ep.78. eth, faying, *Altho' that ripenefs of faith be commendable, which for the fear of God doth not fear to incur fhame before all men, yet becaufe every ones crimes are not fuch, that it can be free and fafe for them to make publication of all things wherein repentance is neceffary ; let a cuftom, fo unfit to be kept, be abrogated, left many forbear to ufe remedies of penitency, whilft they either blufh or are afraid to acquaint their enemies with thofe acts for which the laws may take hold upon them. Befides, it fhall win the more to repentance, if the confciences of finners be not emptied into the peoples ears.* And to this only caufe doth *Sozomen* impute the change which the *Grecians* made, by ordaining throughout all churches certain *penitentiaries* to take the confeffions, and appoint the penances of fecret offenders. *Socrates* (for this alfo may be true that more inducements than one did fet forward an alteration fo generally made) affirmeth the *Grecians* (and not unlikely) to have fpecially refpected therein the occafion which the *Novatianifts* took at the multitude of publick penitents to infult over the difcipline of the church, againft which they ftill cried out wherefoever they had time and place, *He that fheweth finners favour, doth but teach the innocent to fin*: And therefore they themfelves admitted no man to their communion upon any repentance which once was known to have offended after baptifm, making finners thereby not the fewer, but the clofer, and the more obdurate, how fair foever their pretence might feem.

The *Grecians* canon for fome one presbyter in every church to undertake the charge of penitency, and to receive their voluntary confeffions which had finned after baptifm, continued in force for the fpace of above fome hundred years, till *Nectarius*, and the bifhops of churches under him begun a fecond alteration, abolifhing even that confeffion which their *penitentiaries* took in private. There came to the *penitentiary* of the church of *Conftantinople* a certain gentlewoman, and to him fhe made particular confeffion of her faults committed after baptifm, whom thereupon he advifed to continue in fafting and prayer, that as with tongue fhe had acknowledged her fins, fo there might appear likewife in her fome work worthy of repentance : But the gentlewoman goeth forward, and detecteth her felf of a crime, whereby they were forced to difrobe an ecclefiaftical perfon, that is, to degrade a deacon of the fame church. When the matter by this mean came to publick notice, the people were in a kind of tumult offended, not only at that which was done, but much more, becaufe the church fhould thereby endure open infamy and fcorn. The clergy was perplexed and altogether doubtful what way to take, till one *Eudæmon* born in *Alexandria*, but at that time a prieft in the church of *Conftantinople*, confidering that the caufes of voluntary confeffion, whether publick or private, was efpecially to feek the church's aid, as hath been before declared, left men fhould either not communicate with others, or wittingly hazard their fouls if fo be they did communicate, and that the inconvenience which grew to the whole church, was otherwife exceeding great, but efpecially grievous by means of fo manifold offenfive detections, which muft needs be continually more, as the world did it felf wax continually worfe ; for antiquity together with the gravity and feverity thereof (faith *Sozomen*) had already begun by little and little to degenerate into loofe and carelefs living, whereas before offences were lefs, partly through bafhfulnefs in them which open their own faults, and partly by means of their great aufterity which fate as judges in this bufinefs ; thefe things *Eudemon* having weighed with himfelf, refolved eafily the mind of *Nectarius*, that the *penitentiary's* office muft be taken away, and for participation in God's holy myfteries every man be left to his own confcience, which was, as he thought, the only means to free the church from danger of obloquy and difgrace. *Thus much* (faith *Socrates*) *I am the bolder to relate, becaufe I received it from Eudæmon's own mouth, to whom mine anfwer was at that time ; whether your counfel, Sir, have been for the church's good, or otherwife, God knoweth. But I fee, you have given occafion, whereby we fhall not now any more reprehend one another's faults, nor obferve that apoftolick precept, which faith, have no fellowfhip with the unfruitful works of darknefs, but rather be ye alfo reprovers of them.* With *Socrates, Sozomen* both agreeth in the occafion of abolifhing *penitentiaries* ; and moreover teftifieth alfo, that in his time living with the younger *Theodofius*, the fame abolition did ftill continue, and that the bifhops had in a manner every where followed the example given them by *Nectarius*.

Wherefore to implead the truth of this hiftory, cardinal *Baronius* alledgeth that *Socrates, Sozomen*, and *Eudæmon* were all *Novatianifts* ; and that they falfify in faying (for fo they report) that as many as held the confubftantial being of Chrift, gave their affent to

the

Tanta hæc Socrati teſtanti præſtanda eſt fides, quanta cæteris hæreticis de ſuis dogmatibus tractantibus; quippe Novatianus, ſect. cum fuerit, quam vere ac ſincere hæc ſcripſerit adverſus pœnitentiam in Eccleſia adminiſtrari ſolitam, quemlibet credo poſſe facile judicare. *Baron. 1. an. Chr. 56.*

Sozomenum eandem prorſus cauſam foviſſe certum eſt. Nec Eudæmonem illum alium quam Novatienæ ſectæ hominem fuiſſe credendum eſt. *Ibidem.*

Sacerdos ille merito à Nectario eſt gradu amotus officioque depoſitus, quo facto Novatiani (ut mos eſt hæreticorum) quamcunque licet levem, ut ſinceris dogmatibus detrahant, accipere auſi occaſionem, non tantum Presbyterum Pœnitentiarium in ordinem redactum, ſed & Pœnitentiam ipſam unà cum eo fuiſſe proſcriptam, calumnioſe admodum conclamarunt, cum tamen illa potius Theatralis fieri interdum ſolita peccatorum fuerit abrogata. *Ibidem.*

the abrogation of the fore-rehearſed canon. The ſum is, he would have taken it for a fable, and the world to be perſuaded that *Nectarius* did never any ſuch thing. Why then ſhould *Socrates* firſt, and afterwards *Sozomen* publiſh it? to pleaſe their pew fellows, the diſciples of *Novatian?* A poor gratification, and they very ſilly friends that would take lies for good turns. For the more acceptable the matter was, being deemed true, the leſs they muſt needs (when they found the contrary) either credit, or affect him which had deceived them. Notwithſtanding, we know that joy and gladneſs riſing from falſe information, do not only make men ſo forward to believe that which they firſt hear, but alſo apt to ſcholie upon it, and to report as true whatſoever they wiſh were true. But, ſo far is *Socrates* from any ſuch purpoſe, that the fact of *Nectarius*, which others did both like

and follow, he doth diſallow and reprove. His ſpeech to *Eudæmon* before ſet down, is proof ſufficient that he writeth nothing but what was famouſly known to all, and what himſelf did wiſh had been otherwiſe. As for *Sozomen* his correſpondency with hereticks, having ſhewed to what end the church did firſt ordain *penitentiaries*, he addeth immediately, that *Novatianiſts* which had no care of repentance could have no need of this office. Are theſe the words of a friend or enemy? Beſides, in the entrance of that who'e narration ; *Not to ſin* (ſaith he) *at all, would require a nature more divine than ours is : But, God hath commanded to pardon ſinners; yea, although they tranſgreſs and offend often.* Could there be any thing ſpoken more directly oppoſite to the doctrine of *Novatian?* *Eudæmon* was presbyter under *Nectarius.*

To *Novatianiſts* the emperor gave liberty of uſing their religion quietly by themſelves, under a biſhop of their own, even within the city, for that they ſtood with the church in defence of the catholick faith againſt all other hereticks beſides. Had therefore *Eudæmon* favoured their hereſy, their camps were not pitched ſo far off but he might at all times have found eaſy acceſs unto them. Is there any man that hath lived with him, and hath touched him that way? if not, why ſuſpect we him more than *Nectarius?* Their report touching *Grecian* catholick biſhops, who gave approbation to that which was done, and did alſo the like themſelves in their own churches, we have no reaſon to diſcredit without ſome manifeſt and clear evidence brought againſt it. For of catholick biſhops, no likelihood but that their greateſt reſpect to *Nectarius*, a man honoured in thoſe parts no leſs than the biſhop of *Rome* himſelf in the weſtern churches, brought them both eaſily and ſpeedily unto conformity with him ; *Arians, Eunomians, Apollinarians,* and the reſt that ſtood divided from the church, held their *penitentiaries* as before. *Novatianiſts* from the beginning had never any, becauſe their opinion touching penitency was againſt the practice of the church therein, and a cauſe why they ſevered themſelves from the church ; ſo that the very ſtate of things, as they then ſtood, giveth great ſhew of probability to his ſpeech who hath affirmed, *That them only which held the Son conſubſtantial with the Father, and Novatianiſts which joined with them in the ſame opinion, had no penitentiaries in their churches, the reſt retained them.* By this it appeareth therefore how *Baronius* finding the people relation plain, that *Nectarius* did aboliſh even thoſe private ſecret confeſſions which the had been before accuſtomed to make him that was *penitentiary*, laboureth what he may to diſcredit the authors of the report, and leave it imprinted in mens minds, that whereas *Nectarius* did but abrogate publick confeſſion, *Novatianiſts* have maliciouſly forged the abolition of private, as if the odds between theſe two were ſo great in the balance of their judgment which equally hated or contemned both; or, as if it were not more clear than light, that the firſt alteration which eſtabliſhed *penitentiaries* took away the burthen of publick confeſſion in that kind of penitents; and therefore the ſecond muſt either abrogate private, or nothing.

Cardinal *Bellarmine* therefore finding that againſt the writers of the hiſtory it is but in vain to ſtand upon ſo doubtful terms, and exceptions, endeavoureth mightily to prove, even by their report, no other confeſſion taken away than publick which *penitentiaries* uſed in private to impoſe upon publick offenders ; *For why! It is* (ſaith he) *very certain that the name of penitents in the fathers writings ſignifieth only publick penitents ; certain, that to hear the confeſſions of the reſt was more than one could poſſibly have done ; certain, that Sozomen, to ſhew how the Latin church retained in his time what the Greek had clean caſt off, declareth the whole order of publick penitency uſed in the church of*

Rome,

Rome, *but of private he maketh no mention.* And, in thefe confiderations, *Bellarmine* will have it the meaning both of *Socrates* and *Sozomen,* that the former epifcopal confti-tution which firft did erect *penitentiaries;* could not concern any other offenders than fuch, as publickly had finned after baptifm.   That only they were prohibited to come to the holy communion, except they did firft in fecret confefs all their fins to the *penitentiary,* by his appointment openly acknowledge their open crimes, and do publick penance for them :   That whereas before *Novatian's* uprifing, no man was conftrainable to confefs pub-lickly any fin, this canon enforced publick offenders thereunto, till fuch time as *Nectarius* thought good to extinguifh the practice thereof.

Let us examine therefore thefe fubtle and fine conjectures, whether they be able to hold τὰς ἐπὶ τὴς the touch. *It feemeth good* (faith *Socrates*) *to put down the office of thefe priefts which had* περτανίος ἐ-*charge of penitency*; *what charge that was, the kinds of penitency then ufual muft make* ἐλλ᾽ κρα-*manifeft.*   There is often fpeech in the fathers writings, in their books frequent mention of penitency, exercifed within the chambers of our heart, and feen of God and not com-municated to any other, is the whole charge of which penitency is impofed of God, and doth reft upon the finner himfelf.   But if penitents in fecret, being guilty of crimes whereby they knew they had made themfelves unfit guefts for the table of our Lord, did feek direc-tion for their better performance of that which fhould fet them clear ; it was in this cafe the *penitentiary's* office to take their confeffions, to advife them the beft way he could for their fouls good, to admonifh them, to counfel them, but not to lay upon them more than private *penance.*   As for notorious wicked perfons whofe crimes were known, to con-vict, judge, and punifh them was the office of the ecclefiaftical confiftory ; *penitentia-ries* had their inftitution to another end.   But unlefs we imagine that the antient time knew no other repentance than publick, or that they had little occafion to fpeak of any other repentance, or elfe that in fpeaking thereof they ufed continually fome other name, and not the name of repentance whereby to exprefs private penitency, how ftandeth it with reafon, that whenfoever they write of penitents, it fhould be thought they meant only publick penitents?   The truth is, they handle all three kinds, but private and volun-tary repentance much oftner, as being of far more general ufe ; whereas publick was but incident unto few, and not oftner than once incident unto any.   Howbeit becaufe they do not diftinguifh one kind of penitency from another by difference of names, our fafe-eft way for conftruction, is to follow circumftance of matter, which in this narration will not yield it felf appliable only unto publick penance, do what they can that would fo ex-pound it.

They boldly and confidently affirm, that no man being compellable to confefs publick-ly any fin before *Novatius's* time, the end of inftituting *penitentiaries* afterwards in the church was, that by them men might be conftrained unto publick confeffion.   Is there any record in the world which doth teftify this to be true? There is that teftify the plain contrary ; for *Sozomen,* declaring purpofely the caufe of their inftitution, faith, *That where-as men openly craving pardon at God's hands* (*for publick confeffion, the laft act of peni-tency, was always made in the form of a contrite prayer unto God,*) *it could not be avoid-ed, but they muft withal confefs what their offences were.*   This, in the opinion of their prelate, feemed from the firft beginning (as we may probably think) to be fomewhat bur-thenfom ; that men, whofe crimes were unknown, fhould blaze their own faults, as it were on the ftage, acquainting all the people with whatfoever they had done amifs.   And therefore to remedy this inconvenience they laid the charge upon one only prieft, chofen out of fuch as were of beft converfation, a filent and a difcreet man, to whom they which had offended might refort and lay open their lives.   He, according to the quality of every one's tranfgreffions, appointed what they fhould do or fuffer, and left them to execute it upon themfelves.   Can we wifh a more direct and evident teftimony, that the office here fpoken of, was to eafe voluntary penitents from the burthen of publick confeffions, and not to conftrain notorious offenders thereunto? That fuch offenders were not compellable to open confeffions till *Novatian's* time, that is to fay, till after the days of perfecution under *Decius* the Emperor; they, of all men, fhould not fo peremptorily avouch: with whom, if *Fabian* bifhop of *Rome,* who fuffered martyrdom in the firft year of *Decius,* be of any authority and credit, it muft inforce them to reverfe their fentence ; his words are fo plain and clear againft them.   *For fuch as commit thofe crimes, whereof the Apo-ftle hath faid, they that do them fhall never inherit the kingdom of heaven, muft* (faith Fab. Decret. he) *be forced unto amendment, becaufe they flip down to hell, if ecclefiaftical authority* Ep. 1. Tom. i. *ftay them not.*   Their conceit of impoffibility that one man fhould fuffice to take the ge- Conc. p. 318. neral charge of penitency in fuch a church as *Conftantinople,* hath rifen from a mere erro-neous fuppofal, that the antient manner of private confeffion was like the fhrift at this day ufual in the church of *Rome,* which tieth all men at one certain time to make confeffion ; whereas

whereas confession was then neither looked for till men did offer it, nor offered for the most part by any other than such as were guilty of heinous transgressions, nor to them any time appointed for that purpose. Finally, the drift which *Sozomen* had in relating the discipline of *Rome*, and the form of publick penitency there retained even till his time, is not to signify that only publick confession was abrogated by *Nectarius*, but that the west or *Latin* church held still one and the same order from the very beginning, and had not, as the *Greek*, first cut off publick voluntary confession by ordaining, and then private by removing *penitentiaries*. Wherefore, to conclude, it standeth, I hope, very plain and clear, first against the one cardinal, that *Nectarius*, did truly abrogate confession in such sort as the ecclesiastical history hath reported; and, secondly, as clear against them both, that it was not publick confession only which *Nectarius* did abolish.

Necest quod fibi blandian- tur illi de facto Nectarii, cum id potius secre- torum pecca- torum confes- fionem com- probet, & non aliud quam presbyterum poenitentialem illo officio suo moverit; uti amplissime deducit D. Jo- hannes Haffe- lus Paniel. in Nectarius. The paradox, in maintenance whereof *Hessels* wrote purposely a book touching this argument, to shew that *Nectarius* did but put the *penitentiary* from his office, and not take away the office it self, is repugnant to the whole advice which *Eudaemon* gave, of leaving the people from that time forwards to their own consciences, repugnant to the con- ference between *Socrates* and *Eudaemon* wherein complaint is made of some inconvenience which the want of office would breed; finally, repugnant to that which the history de- clareth concerning other churches, which did as *Nectarius* had done before them, not in deposing the same man (for that was impossible) but in removing the same office out of their churches, which *Nectarius* had banished from his. For which cause, *Bellarmine* doth well reject the opinion of *Hessels*, howsoever it please *Pamelius* to admire it as a wonderful happy invention. But in sum, they are all gravelled, no one of them able to go smoothly away, and to satisfy either others or himself with his own conceit concerning *Nectarius*.

Cypr. lib. de annot. 98. & in lib. Tertul. de poen. an- not. i. Only in this they are stiff, that auricular confession *Nectarius* did not abrogate, left if so much should be acknowledged, it might enforce them to grant that the *Greek* church at that time held not confession, as the *Latin* now doth, to be the part of a sacrament insti- tuted by our Saviour Jesus Christ, which therefore the church till the worlds end hath no power to alter. Yet seeing that as long as publick voluntary confession of private crimes did continue in either church (as in the one it remained not much above 200 years, in the other about 400) the only acts of such repentance were; first, the offenders intimation of those crimes to some one presbyter, for which imposition of penance was sought; second- ly, the undertaking of penance imposed by the bishop; thirdly, after the same performed and ended, open confession to God in the hearing of the whole church; whereupon, fourthly, ensued the prayer of the church; fifthly, then the bishop's imposition of hands; and so sixthly, the parties reconciliation or restitution to his former right in the holy sacra- ment. I would gladly know of them which make only private confession a part of their sacrament of penance, how it could be so in those times? For where the sacrament of penance is ministred, they hold that confession to be sacramental which he receiveth who must absolve; whereas during the fore-rehearsed manner of penance, it can no where be shewed, that the priest to whom secret information was given did reconcile or absolve any; for how could he, when publick confession was to go before reconciliation, and reconcilia- tion likewise in publick thereupon to ensue? So that if they did account any confession sa- cramental, it was surely publick, which is now abolished in the church of *Rome*, and as for that which the church of *Rome* doth esteem, the antients neither had it in such esti- mation, nor thought it to be of so absolute necessity for the taking away of sin, but (for any thing that I could ever observe out of them) although not only in crimes open and notorious, which made men unworthy and uncapable of holy mysteries, their discipline re- quired first publick penance, and then granted that which St. *Hierom* mentioneth, saying,

Sacerdos im- ponit manum subjecto, redi- tum spiritus Sancti invocat, atque ita eum qui traditus fuerat Satanæ in interitum carnis, ut Spi- ritus salvus fie- ret indicis in populum ora- tione altari re- conciliat. Hier. adverf. Lucif. Ambr. de poen.l.2.c.10. *The priest layeth his hand upon the penitent, and by invocation intreateth that the holy Ghost may return to him again; and so after having enjoined solemnly all the people to pray for him, reconcileth to the altar him who was delivered to Satan for the destruction of his flesh, that his spirit might be safe in the day of the Lord.* Altho' I say not only in such offences being famously known to the world, but also, if the same were commit- ted secretly, it was the customs of those times both that private intimation should be gi- ven and publick confession made thereof; in which respect whereas all men did willingly the one, but would as willingly have withdrawn themselves from the other had they known how; *Is it tolerable* (saith St. *Ambrose*) *that to sue to God thou shouldest be ashamed, which blushest not to seek and sue unto man? should it grieve thee to be a suppli- ant to him from whom thou canst not possibly hide thy self; when to open thy sins to him, from whom, if thou wouldest, thou mightest conceal them, it doth not any thing at all trouble thee? This thou art loth to do in the church, where, all being sinners, nothing is more opprobrious indeed than concealment of sin, the most humble the best thought of, and* the

2

the lowliest accounted the justest. All this notwithstanding, we should do them very great wrong to father any such opinion upon them, as if they did teach it a thing impossible for any sinner to reconcile himself unto God without confession unto the priest.

Would *Chrysostom* thus perswaded have said, *Let the enquiry and punishment of thy offences be made in thy own thoughts; let the tribunal whereat thou arraignest thy self be without witness; let God, and only God, see thee and thy confession?* Chryf. Hom. Πηι μετανοιας η ιξομολογησεως παρα του

λογισμω γνωθι των πεπλημμελημενων η εξεταισις, αμαρτημι εσω το διακτιμ, ο Θεος ιρατω μον@ εξομολογουμενων.

Would *Cassianus* so believing have given counsel, *That if any were with-held with bashfulness from discovering their faults to men, they should be so much the more instant and constant in opening them by supplication to God himself, whose wont is to help without publication of mens shame, and not to upbraid them when he pardoneth?* Caffian. Collat. 20. c. 8.

Finally, would *Prosper* settled in his opinion have made it, as touching reconciliation to God, a matter indifferent, *Whether men of ecclesiastical order did detect their crimes by confession, or leaving the world ignorant thereof, would separate voluntarily themselves, for a time from the altar, tho' not in affection, yet in execution of their ministry, and so bewail their corrupt life? Would he have willed them as he doth to make bold of it, that the favour of God being either way recovered by fruits of forcible repentance, they should not only receive whatsoever they had lost by sin, but also after this their new enfranchisement, aspire to endless joys of that supernal city?* Prosper. de vita contempl. l. 3. c. 7. To conclude, we every where find the use of confession, especially publick, allowed of and commended by the fathers; but that extream and rigorous necessity of auricular and private confession, which is at this day so mightily upheld by the church of *Rome*, we find not. First, it was not then the faith and doctrine of God's church, as of the papacy at this present. Secondly, that the only remedy for sin after baptism, is sacramental penitency. Thirdly, that confession in secret, is an essential part thereof. Fourthly, that God himself cannot now forgive sin without the priest. That, because forgiveness at the hands of the priest must arise from confession in the offenders, therefore to confess unto him, is a matter of such necessity as being not either in deed, or at the least in desire performed, excludeth utterly from all pardon, and must consequently in scripture be commanded wheresoever any promise or forgiveness is made. No, no; these opinions have youth in their countenance, antiquity knew them not, it never thought nor dreamed of them.

But to let pass the papacy. For as much as repentance doth import alteration within the mind of a sinful man, whereby, thro' the power of God's most gracious and blessed Spirit, he seeth, and with unfeigned sorrow acknowledgeth former offences committed against God; hath them in utter detestation, seeking pardon for them in such' sort as a christian should do, and with a resolute purpose settleth himself to avoid them; leading, as near as God should assist him, for ever after an unspotted life; and in the order (which christian religion hath taught for procurement of God's mercy towards sinners) confession is acknowledged a principal duty, yea, in some cases, confession to man, not to God only; it is not in reformed churches denied by the learneder sort of divines, but that even this confession, cleared from all errors, is both lawful and behoveful for God's people. Calv. Inft. l. 3. c. 4. fect. 7.

Confession by man being either private or publick; private confession to the minister alone touching secret crimes, or absolution thereupon ensuing, as the one, so the other is neither practised by the *French* discipline, nor used in any of those churches which have been cast by the *French* mould. Open confession to be made in the face of the whole congregation by notorious malefactors they hold necessary; howbeit not necessary towards the remission of sins; but only in some sort to content the church, and that one man's repentance may seem to strengthen many, which before have been weaken'd by one man's fall. Sed tantum ut ecclesiæ fit aliqua ratione fatisfactum, & omnes unius pœnitentia confirmentur.

Saxonians and *Bohemians* in their discipline constrain no man to open confession. Their doctrine is, that whose faults have been publick, and thereby scandalous unto the world, such, when God giveth them the spirit of repentance, ought as solemnly to return as they have openly gone astray. First, for the better testimony of their own unfeigned conversion unto God. Secondly, the more to notify their reconcilement unto the church. And lastly, that others may make benefit of their example. qui fuerant unius peccatis & fcandalis vulnerati. Sa-deel. in Pfal. 32.v.ς. Harm. Conf. Sect. 8. ex ς. cap. confeff. Bohem.

But concerning confession in private, the churches of *Germany*, as well the rest as *Lutherans* agree, that all men should at certain times confess their offences to God in the hearing of God's ministers, thereby to shew how their sins displease them; to receive instruction for the warier carriage of themselves hereafter; to be soundly resolved, if any scruple or snare of conscience do entangle their minds; and which is most material, to the end that men may at God's hand seek every one his own particular pardon, through the power of those

T t

those keys which the minister of God using according to our blessed Saviour's institution in that case it is their part to accept the benefit thereof, as God's most merciful ordinance for their good, · and without any distrust or doubt to embrace joyfully his grace so given them according to the word of our Lord, which hath said, *Whose sins ye remit they are remitted.* So that grounding upon this assured belief, they are to rest with minds encouraged and persuaded concerning the forgiveness of all their sins, as out of Christ's own word and power by the ministry of the keys.

Cap. 5. Confess. Bohem.

It standeth with us in the church of *England,* as touching publick confession thus:

First, seeing day by day we in our church begin our publick prayers to almighty God with publick acknowledgment of our sins, in which confession every man, prostrate as it were before his glorious Majesty, crieth against himself, and the minister with one sentence pronounceth universally all clear whose acknowledgment so made hath proceeded from a true penitent mind; what reason is there every man should not, under the general terms of confession, represent to himself his own particulars whatsoever, and adjoining thereunto that affection which a contrite spirit worketh, embrace to as full effect the words of divine grace, as if the same were severally and particularly uttered with addition of prayers, imposition of hands, or all the ceremonies and solemnities that might be used for the strengthning of men's affiance in God's peculiar mercy towards them? such compliments are helps to support our weakness, and not causes that serve to procure or produce his gifts, as *David* speaketh. The difference of general and particular forms in confession and absolution is not so material that any man's safety or ghostly good should depend upon it. And for private confession and absolution it standeth thus with us:

As for private confession, abuses and errors set apart, we condemn it not, but leave it at liberty.
Jewel, defen. part 156.

The minister's power to absolve is publickly taught and professed, the church not denied to have authority either of abridging or enlarging the use and exercise of that power, upon the people no such necessity imposed of opening their transgression unto men, as if remission of sins otherwise were impossible; neither any such opinion had of the thing it self, as though it were either unlawful or unprofitable, save only for these inconveniences which the world hath by experience observed in it heretofore. And in regard thereof, the church of *England* hath hitherto thought it the safer way to refer mens hidden crimes unto God and themselves only; howbeit, not without special caution for the admonition of such as come to the holy sacrament, and for the comfort of such as are ready to depart the world. First, because there are but few that consider how much that part of divine service, which consists in partaking the holy eucharist, doth import their souls; what they lose by neglect thereof, and what by devout practice they might attain unto: Therefore, lest carelesness of general confession should, as commonly it doth, extinguish all remorse of men's particular enormous crimes, our custom (whensoever men present themselves at the Lord's table) is, solemnly to give themselves fearful admonition, what woes are perpendicularly hanging over the heads of such as dare adventure to put forth their unworthy hands to those admirable mysteries of life, which have by rare examples been proved conduits of irremediable death to impenitent receivers; whom therefore, as we repel being known, so being not known, we cannot but terrify. Yet, with us, the ministers of God's most holy word and sacraments, being all put in trust with the custody and dispensation of those mysteries wherein our communion is, and hath been ever accounted the highest grace that men on earth are admitted unto, have therefore all equally the same power to with-hold that sacred mystical food from notorious evil-livers, from such as have any way wronged their neighbours, and from parties between whom there doth open hatred and malice appear, till the first sort have reformed their wicked lives, the second recompensed them unto whom they were injurious, and the last condescended unto some course of christian reconciliation whereupon their mutual accord may ensue. In which cases for the first branch of wicked life; and the last, which is open enmity, there can arise no great difficulty about the exercise of his power: In the second, concerning wrongs, they may, if men shall presume to define or measure injuries according to their own conceits, be depraved oftentimes as well by error, as partiality, and that no less to the minister himself, than in another of the people under him.

The knowledge therefore which he taketh of wrongs must rise, as it doth in the other two, not from his own opinion or conscience, but from the evidence of the fact which is committed; yea, from such evidence as neither doth admit denial nor defence. For if the offender, having either color of law to uphold, or any other pretence to excuse his own uncharitable and wrongful dealings, shall wilfully stand in defence thereof, it serveth as bar

Nos à communione quenquam prohibere non possumus. Quamvis hæc prohibitio nondum sit mortalis, sed medicinalis, nisi aut sponte confessum, aut aliquo sive seculari, sive ecclesiastico judicio accusarum atque convictum. Quis enim sibi utrumque audet assumere, ut cuiquam ipse sit & accusator & judex?

to the power of the minister in this kind. Because (as it is observed by men of very good judgment

+

judgment in thefe affairs) although in this fort our feparating of them be not to ftrike them with the mottal wound of excommunication, but to ftay them rather from running defperately headlong into their own harm; yet it is not in us to fever from the holy communion but fuch as are either found culpable by their own confeffion, or have been convicted in fome publick, fecular or ecclefiaftical court. For, who is he, that dares take upon him to be any man's both accufer and judge? evil perfons are not rafhly, and (as we lift) to be thruft from communion with the church. Infomuch that if we cannot proceed againft them by any orderly courfe of judgment, they rather are to be fuffered for the time than molefted. Many there are reclaimed, as *Peter*; many, as *Judas*, known well enough, and yet tolerated; many which muft remain undefcried till the day of appearance, by whom the fecret corners of darknefs fhall be brought into open light.

Non enim temere, & quodammodo libet, fed propter judicium, ab ecclefiæ communione feparandi funt mali, ut fi propter judicium auferri non poffint, tolerentur potiùs, velut palex cum tritico. Multi corriguntur, ut Petrus; multi tolerantur, ut Judas; multi nefciuntur, donec veniat dominus, & illuminabit abfcondita tenebrarum. Rhenan. admonit. de dogmat. Tertul.

Leaving therefore unto his judgment them, whom we cannot ftay from cafting their own fouls into fo great hazard, we have, in the other part of penitential jurifdiction in our power and authority to releafe fin, joy on all fides, without trouble or moleftation unto any. And, if to give, be a thing more bleffed than to receive, are we not infinitely happier in being authorized to beftow the treafure of God, than when neceffity doth conftrain to withdraw the fame?

They which, during life and health, are never deftitute of ways to delude repentance, do notwithftanding oftentimes when their laft hour draweth on both feel that fting which before lay dead in them, and alfo thirft after fuch helps as have been always, till then, unfavory. St. *Ambrofe*'s words touching late repentance are fomewhat hard, *If a man be peni- tent and receive abfolution (which cannot in that cafe be denied him) even at the very point of death, and fo depart, I dare not affirm he goeth out of the world well; I will counfel man to truft to this, becaufe I am loth to deceive any man, feeing I know not what no to think of it. Shall I judge fuch a one a caft away? Neither will I avouch him fafe: All I am able to fay, is, let his eftate be left to the will and pleafure of almighty God. Wilt thou be therefore delivered of all doubt? Repent while yet thou art healthy and ftrong. If thou defer it till time give no longer poffibility of finning, thou canft not be thought to have left fin, but rather fin to have forfaken thee.* Such admonitions may in their time and place be neceffary, but in no wife prejudicial to the generality of God's heavenly promife, *Whenfoever a finner doth repent from the bottom of his heart, I will put out all his iniquity.* And of this, altho' it hath pleafed God not to leave to the world any multitude of examples, left the carelefs fhould too far prefume, yet one he hath given and that moft memorable, to withhold from defpair in the mercies of God, at what inftant foever man's unfeigned converfion be wrought. Yea, becaufe to countervail the fault of delay, there are in the lateft repentance oftentimes the fureft tokens of fincere dealing; therefore upon fpecial confeffion made to the minifter of God, he prefently abfolveth in this cafe the fick party from all fins by that authority which Jefus Chrift hath committed unto him, knowing that God refpecteth not fo much what time is fpent, as what truth is fhewed in repentance.

Lib. 3. de pœn.

In fome, when the offence doth ftand only between God and man's confcience, the counfel is good, which St. *Chryfoftom* giveth, *I wifh thee not to bewray thy felf publickly, nor to accufe thy felf before others. I wifh thee to obey the prophet, who faith, difclofe thy way unto the Lord, confefs thy fins before him; tell thy fins to him that he may blot them out. If thou be abafhed to tell unto any other, wherein thou haft offended, rehearfe them every day between thee and thy foul. I wifh thee not to confefs them to thy fellow fervant, who may upbraid thee with them; tell them to God, who will cure them; there is no need for thee in the prefence of witneffes to acknowledge them; let God alone fee thee at thy confeffion. I pray and befeech you, that you would more often than you*

Non dico tibi, ut te prodas in publicum, neque ut te apud alios accufes, fed obedire te volo prophetæ dicenti, revela Domino viam tuam. Ante Deum confitere peccata tua; peccata tus dicito ut ea deleat; fi confunderis alicui dicere quæ peccafti, dicito ea quotidie in anima: Non dico ut confitearis confervo qui exprobret; Deo dicito qui ea curat; non neceffe eft præfentibus teftibus confiteri, folus te Deus confitentem videat. Rogo & oro ut crebrius Deo immortali confiteamini, & enumeratis veftris delictis veniam petatis. Non te in theatrum confervorum duco, non hominibus peccata tua conor detegere. Repete coram Deo confcientiam tuam, te explica, oftende medico præftantiffimo vulnera tua, & pete ab eo medicamentum. Chrifoft. hom. 31. ad Hebr. & in Pfal. 59. hom. de pœn. & confeff. & hom. 5. de incarn. Del natura, homil. itemque de Lazaro.

do, *confefs to God eternal, and reckoning up your trefpaffes, defire his pardon. I carry you not into a theatre or open court of many of your fellow fervants, I feek not to detect your crimes before men; difclofe your confcience before God, unfold your felves to him, lay forth your wounds before him the beft phyfician that is, and defire of him falve for them.* If hereupon it follow, as it did with *David, I thought, I will confefs againft my felf my wickednefs unto thee, O Lord, and thou forgaveft me the plague of my fin,* we have our defire,

fire, and there remaineth only thankfulnefs accompanied with perpetuity of care to avoid that, which being not avoided, we know we cannot remedy without new perplexity and grief. Contrariwife, if peace with God do not follow the pains we have taken in feeking after it, if we continue difquieted and not delivered from anguifh, miftrufting whether that we do be fufficient ; it argueth that our fore doth exceed the power of our own skill, and that the wifdom of the paftor muft bind up thofe parts, which being bruifed are not able to be recured of themfelves.

Of Satisfaction.

THere refteth now fatisfaction only to be confidered ; a point which the fathers do often touch, albeit they never afpire to fuch myfteries as the papacy hath found enwrapped within the folds and plaits thereof. And it is happy for the church of God, that we have the writings of the fathers to fhew what their meaning was. The name of fatisfaction, as the antient fathers mean it, containeth whatfoever a penitent fhould do in the humbling himfelf unto God, and teftifying by deeds of contrition the fame which confef-
Tert. de pœn. fion in words pretendeth ; *He which by repentance for fins* (faith *Tertullian*, fpeaking of fickle minded men) *had a purpofe to fatisfy the Lord, will now by repenting his repentance, make Satan fatisfaction ; and be fo much the more hateful to God, as he is unto God's enemy more acceptable.* Is it not plain, that fatisfaction doth here include the whole work of penitency, and that God is fatisfied when we are reftored through fin into favour
Chryfoft. in 1 Cor. hom. 8. τις Θεον ιλασαι αυτου. by repentance ? *How canft thou* (faith *Chryfoftom*) *move God to pity thee, when thou wilt not feem as much as to know that thou haft offended ?* By appeafing, pacifying, and mo-
Cypr. ep. 8. & ep. 26. fent. l. 4. diff. 16. ving God to pity, St. *Chryfoftom* meaneth the very fame with the *Latin* fathers, when they fpeak of fatisfying God. *We feel* (faith *Cyprian*) *the bitter fmart of his rod and fcourge, becaufe there is in us neither care to pleafe him without good deeds, nor to fatisfy him for our evil.* Again, *Let the eyes which have looked on idols, fpunge out their unlawful acts with thofe forrowful tears, which have power to fatisfy God.* The mafter of fentences alledgeth out of St. *Auguftine*, that which is plain enough to this purpofe : *Three things there are in perfect penitency, compunction, confeffion, and fatisfaction ; that as we three ways offend God, namely in heart, word and deed ; fo by three duties we may fatisfy God.*

Satisfaction, as a part, comprehended only that which the papifts meant by *worthy of repentance* ; and if we fpeak of the whole work of repentance it felf, we may in the phrafe of antiquity, term it very well *fatisfaction*.

Satisfaction is a work which juftice requireth to be done for contentment of perfons injured : neither is it in the eye of juftice a fufficient fatisfaction, unlefs it fully equal the injury for which we fatisfy. Seeing then that fin againft God eternal and infinite, muft needs be an infinite wrong ; juftice, in regard thereof, doth neceffarily exact an infinite recompence, or elfe inflict upon the offender infinite punifhment. Now, becaufe God was thus to be fatisfied, and man not able to make fatisfaction ; in fuch fort his unfpeakable love and inclination to fave mankind from eternal death, ordained in our behalf a mediator, to do that which had been for any other impoffible. Wherefore all fin is remitted in the only faith of Chrift's paffion, and no man without belief thereof juftified ; *Bonavent. in fentent.* 4. *dift.* 15. 9. 9. Faith alone maketh Chrift's fatisfaction ours, howbeit that faith alone which after fin maketh us by converfion his.

For in as much as God will have the benefit of Chrift's fatisfaction both thankfully acknowledged, and duly efteemed of all fuch as enjoy the fame, he therefore imparteth fo high a treafure unto no man, whofe faith hath not made him willing by repentance to do even that which of it felf, how unavailable foever, yet being required and accepted with God, we are in Chrift thereby made capable and fit veffels to receive the fruits of his fatisfaction : yea, we fo far pleafe and content God, that becaufe when we have offended he looked but for repentance at our hands ; our repentance and the works thereof are therefore termed fatisfactory, not for that fo much is thereby done as the juftice of God can exact, but becaufe fuch actions of grief and humility in man after fin, are *illices divinæ mifericordiæ* (as *Tertullian* fpeaketh of them) they draw that pity of God towards us, wherein he is for Chrift's fake contented, upon our fubmiffion, to pardon our rebellion againft him ; and when that little which his law appointeth is faithfully executed, it pleafeth him in tender compaffion and mercy to require no more.

Repentance is a name which noteth the habit and operation of a certain grace or virtue in us: Satisfaction, the effect which it hath, either with God or man. And it is not in this refpect faid amifs, the fatisfaction importeth acceptation, reconciliation, and amity ;

amity; becaufe that, through fatisfaction on the one part made, and allowed on the other, they which before did reject are now content to receive; they to be won again which were loft; and they to love unto whom juft caufe of hatred was given. We fatisfy therefore in doing that which is fufficient to this effect; and they towards whom we do it are fatisfied, if they accept it as fufficient, and require no more : Otherwife we fatisfy not, although we do fatisfy. For fo between man and man it oftentimes falleth out, but between man and God never. It is therefore true, that our Lord Jefus Chrift by one moft precious and propitiatory facrifice, which was his body, a gift of infinite worth, offered for the fins of the whole world, hath thereby once reconciled us to God, purchafed his general free pardon, and turned divine indignation from mankind. But we are not for that caufe to think any office of penitence either needlefs or fruitlefs, on our own behalf. For then would not God require any fuch Duties at our hands; Chrift doth remain everlaftingly a gracious interceffor, even for every penitent. Let this affure us, that God, how highly foever difpleafed and incenfed with our fins, is notwithftanding, for his fake, by our tears, pacified, taking that for fatisfaction, which is done by us, becaufe Chrift hath by his fatisfaction made it acceptable. For, as he is the high prieft of **[Apoc. 1. 6.]** our falvation, fo he hath made us priefts likewife under him, to the end we might offer unto God praife and thankfulnefs while we continue in the way of life; and when we fin, the fatisfactory or propitiatory facrifice of a broken and contrite heart. There is not any thing that we do, that could pacify God and clear us in his fight from fin, if the goodnefs and mercy of our Lord Jefus Chrift were not; whereas now beholding the **[Caffis col. 10. c. 8.]** poor offer of our religious endeavours, meekly to fubmit our felves as often as we have offended, he regardeth with infinite mercy thofe fervices which are as nothing, and with words of comfort reviveth our afflicted minds, faying, *It is I, even I, that taketh away thine iniquities for mine own fake.* Thus doth repentance fatisfy God, changing his wrath and indignation unto mercy.

Anger and mercy are in us paffions; but in him not fo.

God (faith St. *Bafil*) *is no ways paffionate, but becaufe the punifhments which his judgment doth inflict are like effects of indignation fevere and grievous to fuch as fuffer them, therefore we term the revenge which he taketh upon finners, anger; and the withdrawing of his plagues, mercy. His wrath* (faith St. *Auguftine*) *is not as ours, the trouble of a mind difturbed and difquieted with things amifs, but a calm, unpaffionate, and juft affignation of dreadful punifhment to be their portion which have difobeyed; his mercy a free determination of all felicity and happinefs unto men, except their fins remain as a bar betwixt it and them.* So that when God doth ceafe to be angry with finful men, when he receiveth them into favour, when he pardoneth their offences, and remembreth their iniquities no more (for all thefe fignify but one thing) it muft needs follow, that all punifhments before due in revenge of fin, whether they be temporal or eternal, are remitted.

[Basil. hom. in Psalm. 37. ... Cum Deus irascitur, non ejus significatur perturbatio qualis est in animo irascentis hominis; sed ex humanis moribus translato vocabulo dicta ejus, quae non nisi justa est, irae nomen accepit. Aug.]

For how fhould God's indignation import only man's punifhment, and yet fome punifhment remain unto them towards whom there is now in God no indignation remaining? *God* (faith *Tertullian*) *takes penitency at mens hands; and men at his, in lieu thereof, receive impunity*; which notwithftanding doth not prejudice the chaftifements which God, after pardon, hath laid upon fome offenders, as on [a] the people of *Ifrael*, on [b] *Mofes*, on [c] *Miriam*, on [d] *David*, either for their own [e] more found amendment, or for [f] example unto others in this prefent world (for in the world to come, punifhments have unto thefe intents no ufe, the dead being not in cafe to be better by correction, nor to take warning by executions of God's juftice there feen) but affuredly to whomfoever he remitteth fin, their very pardon is in it felf a full, abfolute, and perfect difcharge for revengeful punifhment, which God doth now here threaten but with purpofe of revocation if men repent, no where inflict but on them whom impenitency maketh obdurate.

[Tom. 3. Ench. cap. 33. Pœnitentiæ communi redimendam punitatem proponit impunitatem Deus. Tert. de pœniten. [a] Numb. 14. [b] Numb. 20. 12. [c] Num. 12.14.]

[a] 2 Sam. 12. 14. [b] Cui Deus verè propitius eft non folum condonat peccata ne noceant ad futurum feculum, fed etiam caftigat, ne femper peccare delectet. *Aug.* in *Pfal.* 98. [f] Plectuntur quidam quo cæteri corrigantur; exempla funt ominum, tormenta paucorum. *Cypr.* de lapfis. *Ezek.* 33. 14. *Rom.* 2. 5. *Ifa.* 1. 18.

Of the one therefore it is faid, *Tho' I tell the wicked, thou fhalt dye the death, yet if he turneth from his fin, and do that which is lawful and right, he fhall furely live and not dye.* Of the other, *Thou, according to thine hardnefs and heart that will not repent, treafureft up to thy felf wrath againft the day of wrath, and evident appearance of the judgment of God.* If God be fatisfied and do pardon fin, our juftification reftored is as perfect as it was at the firft beftowed. For fo the prophet *Ifaiah* witneffeth, *Tho' your fins were as crimfon, they fhall be made as white as fnow; though they were as fcarlet, they fhall be as white as wool.* And can we doubt concerning the punifhment of revenge, which was due to fin, but that if God be fatisfied and have forgotten his wrath, it muft be, even as St.
Auguftine

3

* Si texit Deus peccata, noluit advertere ; fi noluit advertere, noluit animadvertere. *Aug.* de pecc. mer. & rem. lib 2. cap. 34. Mirandum non est, & mortem corporis non fuisse eventuram homini, nisi præcessisset peccatum, cujus etiam talis pœna consequeretur, & post remissionem peccatorum eam fidelibus evenire, ut ejus timorem vincendo exerceretur fortitudo justitiæ. Sic & mortem corporis propter hoc peccatum Deus homini inflixit, & post peccatorum remissionem propter exercendam justitiam non ademit. Ante remissionem esse illa supplicia peccatorum, post remissionem autem certamina, exercitationesque justorum. *Cypr.* epist. 53.

Augustine reasoneth, ª *What God hath covered, he will not observe, and what he observeth not, he will not punish.* The truth of which doctrine is not to be shifted off by restraining it unto eternal punishment alone. For then would not *David* have said, *They are blessed to whom God imputeth not sin;* blessedness having no part or fellowship at all with malediction? Whereas to be subject to revenge for sin, although the punishment be but temporal, is to be under the curse of the law: wherefore, as one and the same fire consumeth stubble and refineth gold, so if it please God to lay punishment on them whose sins he hath forgiven; yet is not this done for any destructive end of wasting and eating them out, as in plagues inflicted upon the impenitent, neither is the punishment of the one as of the other proportioned by the greatness of sin past, but according to that future purpose whereunto the goodness of God referreth it, and wherein there is nothing meant to the sufferer but furtherance of all happiness, now in grace, and hereafter in glory. St. *Augustine*, to stop the mouths of *Pelagians* arguing, *That if God had imposed death upon* Adam, *and* Adam's *posterity, as a punishment of sin, death should have ceased when God procured sinners their pardon ;* answereth, first, *It is no marvel, either that bodily death should not have happened to the first man, unless he had first sinned (death as punishment following his sin) or that after sin is forgiven, death notwithstanding befalleth the faithful ; to the end that the strength of righteousness might be exercised by overcoming the fear thereof.* So that justly God did inflict bodily death on man for committing sin, and yet after sin forgiven took it not away, that his righteousness might still have whereby to be exercised. He fortifieth this with *David's* example, whose sin he forgave, and yet afflicted him for exercise and tryal of his humility. Briefly, a general axiom he hath for all such chastisements, *Before forgiveness, they are the punishment of sinners ; and after forgiveness, they are exercises and tryals of righteous men.* Which kind of proceeding is so agreeable with God's nature and man's comfort, that it seemeth even injurious to both, if we should admit those surmised reservations of temporal wrath in God appeased towards reconciled sinners. As a father he delights in his childrens conversion, neither doth he threaten the penitent with wrath, or them with punishment which already mourn ; but by promise assureth such of indulgence and mercy ; yea, even of plenary pardon, which taketh away all, both faults and penalties: there being no reason, why we should think him the less just, because he sheweth himself thus merciful; when they, which before were obstinate, labour to appease his wrath with the pensive meditation of contrition, the meek humility which confession expresseth, and the deeds wherewith repentance declareth it self to be an amendment as well of the rotten fruit, as the dried leaves, and withered root of the tree. For with these duties by us performed, and presented unto God in heaven by Jesus Christ, whose blood is a continual sacrifice of propitiation for us, we content, please, and satisfy God. Repentance therefore, even the sole virtue of repentance, without either purpose of shift or desire of absolution from the priest ; repentance, the secret conversion of the heart, in that it consisteth of these three, and doth by these three pacify God, may be without hyperbolical terms most truly magnified, as a recovery of the soul of man from deadly sickness, a restitution of glorious light to his darken'd mind, a comfortable reconciliation with God, a spiritual nativity, a rising from the dead, a day-spring from the depth of obscurity, a redemption from more than *Egyptian* thraldom, a grinding of the old *Adam* even into dust and powder, a deliverance out of the prisons of hell, a full restoration of the seat of grace, and throne of glory, a triumph over sin, and a saving victory.

Amongst the works of satisfaction, the most respected have been always these three, *prayers, fasts,* and *alms-deeds*; by prayer we lift up our souls to him from whom sin and iniquity hath withdrawn them ; by *fasting,* we reduce the body from thraldom under vain delights, and make it serviceable for parts of virtuous conversation ; by *alms,* we dedicate to charity those worldly goods and possessions, which unrighteousness doth neither get, nor bestow well: the first, a token of piety intended towards God ; the second, a pledge of moderation and sobriety in the carriage of our own persons : the last, a testimony of our meaning to do good to all men. In which three, the apostle, by way of abridgment, comprehendeth whatsoever may appertain to sanctimony, holiness, and good life: as contrariwise, the very mass of general corruption throughout the world, what is it but only forgetfulness of God, carnal pleasure, immoderate desire after worldly things, prophaneß, licentiousneß, covetousneß? All offices to repentance have these two properties ; there is in performance of them painfulneß, and in their nature a ₂ Cor. 7. 11. contrariety unto sin. The one consideration, causeth them both in holy scripture and elsewhere

where to be termed judgment or revenges taken voluntarily on our selves, and to be fur-*Ῥᾷ ἡμᾶς ἀυ-*
thermore also preservatives from future evils, in as much as we commonly use to keep with *τῶν ἧκαν λα-*
the greater care that which with pain we have recovered. And they are in the other respect *βωμεν, ἡμῶν*
contrary to sin committed; contrition, contrary to the pleasure; confession, to the error, *τηρούμεν ἀ-*
which is the mother of sin, and to the deeds of sin, the works of satisfaction contrary; *τυς ἧξιλαυ-*
therefore they are the more effectual to cure the evil habit thereof. Hereunto it was that *Chryf.*
St. *Cyprian* referred his earnest and vehement exhortation, *That they which had fallen, should* *hom. 30. in*
be instant in prayer, reject bodily ornaments when once they had stripped themselves out of *Ep. ad Heb.*
Christ's attire, abhor all food after Satan's morsels tasted, follow works of righteousness *Cypr. de lapsu.*
which was away sin, and be plentiful in alms-deeds wherewith souls are delivered from
death. Not, as if God did, according to the manner of corrupt judges, take some money
to abate so much in the punishment of malefactors. These duties must be offered (faith Sal- *Salv. ad Eccl.*
vianus) not in confidence to redeem or buy out sin, but as tokens of meek submission; neither *cath. lib. 1.*
are they with God accepted, because of their value, but for our affection sake which doth
thereby shew it self. Wherefore, concerning satisfaction made to God by Christ only;
and of the manner how repentance generally; particularly also, how certain special works
of penitency, both are by the fathers, in their ordinary phrase of speech, called satisfactory,
and may be by us very well so acknowledged, enough hath been spoken.

Our offences sometimes are of such nature as requireth that particular men be satisfied,
or else repentance to be utterly void and of none effect. For if either through open rapine, or crooked fraud; if through injurious, or unconscionable dealing, a man have
wittingly wronged others to enrich himself; the first thing evermore in this case required
(ability serving) is restitution. For let no man deceive himself, from such offences we are
not discharged, neither can be, till recompence and restitution to man, accompany the
penitent confession we have made to almighty God. In which case, the law of *Moses* was *Levit. 6. 2.*
direct and plain: *If any sin and commit a trespass against the Lord, and deny unto his*
neighbour that which was given him to keep, or that which was put unto him of trust; or
doth by robbery, or by violence oppress his neighbour; or hath found that which was lost,
and denieth it, and swears falsly: for any of these things that a man doth wherein he sin-
neth, he that doth thus offend and trespass, shall restore the robbery that he hath taken, or
the thing he hath got by violence, or that which was delivered him to keep, or the lost
thing which he found; and for whatsoever he hath sworn falsly, adding perjury to injury,
he shall both restore the whole sum, and shall add thereunto a fifth part more, and deliver
it unto him, unto whom it belongeth, the same day wherein he offereth for his trespass.
Now, because men are commonly over-slack to perform this duty, and do therefore defer
it sometime, till God hath taken the party wronged out of the world; the law providing
that trespassers might not under such pretence gain the restitution which they ought to make,
appointeth the kindred surviving to receive what the dead should, if they had continued.
But (saith *Moses*) *if the party wronged have no kinsman to whom this damage may be re-* *Num. 5. 8.*
stored, it shall then be rendred to the Lord himself for the priest's use. The whole order
of proceeding herein, is in sundry traditional writings set down by their great interpreters
and scribes, which taught them that a trespass between a man and his neighbour can never
be forgiven till the offender have by restitution made recompence for wrongs done; yea,
they hold it necessary that he appease the party grieved by submitting himself unto him;
or, if that will not serve, by using the help and mediation of others; *In this case* (say they)
for any man to shew himself unappeasable and cruel, were a sin most grievous, considering
that the people of God should be easy to relent, as Joseph *was towards his brethren;* finally, if so it fall out, that the death of him that was injured, prevent his submission which
did offend, let him then (for so they determine that he ought) go accompanied with ten
others unto the sepulchre of the dead, and there make confession of the fault, saying, *I* *Quamdiu e-*
have sinned against the Lord of Israel, and against this man, to whom I have done *nim res prop-*
such or such injury; and if money be due, let it be restored to his heirs, or in case he have *ter quam pec-*
none known, leave it with the house of judgment: That is to say, with the senators, an- *redditur, si*
tients, and guides of *Israel.* We hold not christian people tied unto *Jewish* orders for the *non agitur*
manner of restitution; but surely, restitution we must hold necessary, as well in our own *poenitentia,*
repentance as theirs, for sins of wilful oppression and wrong. *sed fingitur.*
Sent. 4. d. 15.

Now, altho' it suffices, that the offices wherewith we pacify God or private men be
secretly done; yet in cases where the church must be also satisfied, it was not to this end
and purpose unnecessary, that the antient discipline did farther require outward signs of
contrition to be shewed, confession of sins to be made openly, and those works to be ap- *Cypr. ep. l. 52.*
parent which served as testimonies for conversion before men. Wherein, if either hypocrisy did at any time delude their judgment, they knew that God is he whom masks and
mockeries cannot blind, that he which seeth mens hearts would judge them according

unto

unto his own evidence, and, as Lòrd, correct the sentence of his servants concerning matters beyond their reach ; or, if such as ought to have kept the rules of canonical satisfaction would by sinister means and practices undermine the same, obtruding presumptuously themselves to the participation of Chrift's moft sacred mysteries before they were orderly re-admitted thereunto, the church for contempt of holy things held them incapable of that grace, which God in the sacrament doth impart to devout communicants; and no doubt but he himself did retain bound, whom the church in those cases refused to loose.

The fathers, as may appear by sundry decrees and canons of the primitive church, were (in matter especially of publick scandal) provident that too much facility of pardoning might not be shewed. *He that casteth off his lawful Wife* (saith St. *Bafil*) *and doth* Bafil. ep. ad Amphi. c. 26. *take another, is adjudged an adulterer by the verdict of our Lord himself; and by our fathers it is canonically ordained, that such for the space of a year shall mourn, for two years space hear, three years be proftrate, the seventh year assemble with the faithful in prayer, and after that be admitted to communicate, if with tears they bewail their fault.*

Of them which had fallen from their faith in the time of the emperor *Licinius*, and Concil. Nicean, can. 11. were not thereunto forced by any extream usage, the *Nicene* synod under *Conftantine* ordained, *That earneftly repenting, they should continue three years hearers, seven years be proftrate, and two years communicate with the people in prayer, before they came to receive the oblation.* Which rigour sometimes they tempered neverthelefs with lenity, the felf-same synod having likewise defined, *That whatfoever the cause were, any man defirous at the time of departure out of this life to receive the euchariff, might (with examination and tryal) have it granted him by the bifhop.* Yea, befides this cafe of special commiseration, there is a canon more large, which giveth always liberty to abridge, or extend out the time, as the party's meek or sturdy difpofition should require.

Καθόλου ἢ ΄ ἐπι· ΄ πὶ πάντ῾ τὸ τοῖς ἐξελίνουσ῾ ἀληθῖν῾ μετιχῖσαν Ἔξα· δὲ ις, ὸ ἐπι· τασι῾ ἀ῾ ΄ ὅπιμθαίνωσ῾ μεθωδώνση τ῾ προσ῾ φοραῖς. Can. 13. ΄ ΄ Ɛιπμωσίας, id ett, manifettis indiciis deprehenfa peccatoris feria converfione ad Deum. Can. 12. By means of which discipline the church having power to hold them many years in suspence, there was bred in the minds of the penitents, through long and daily practice of fubmiffion, a contrary habit unto that which before had been their ruin, and for ever afterwards warinefs not to fall into those fnares out of which they knew they could not eafily wind themfelves. Notwithstanding, becaufe there was likewise hope and poffibility of shortning the time, this made them in all the parts and offices of their repentance the more fervent. In the firft ftation, while they only beheld others paffing towards the temple of God, whereunto for themfelves to approach it was not lawful, they ftood as miferable forlorn men, the very patterns of perplexity and woe. In the fecond, when they had the favour to wait at the doors of God, where the found of his comfortable word might be heard, none received it with attention like to theirs: thirdly, being taken and admitted to the next degree of proftrates at the feet, yet behind the back of that angel reprefenting God, whom the reft faw face to face, their tears and entreaties both of paftor and people were fuch as no man could refift. After the fourth ftep, which gave them liberty to hear and pray with the reft of the people, being fo near the haven, no diligence was then flacken'd which might haften admiffion to the heavenly table of Chrift, their laft defire. It is not therefore a thing to be marvelled at, tho' St. *Cyprian* took it in very ill part, when both backfliders from the faith and sacred religion of Chrift laboured by finister practice to procure from imprifoned faints those requefts for prefent absolution which the church could neither yield unto with fafety of difcipline nor in honour of martyrdom eafily deny. For, what would thereby enfue they needed not to conjecture, when they faw how every man which came fo commended to the church by letters thought that now he needed not to crave, but might challenge of duty his peace ; taking the matter very highly, if but any little forbearance or fmall delay was ufed. *He which is overthrown* (faith Jacens ftancibus, & integris vulneratus, minatur. Ex. 12. 31. Jer. 7. 15. Ezek. 14. 14. *Cyprian) menaceth them that ftand, they wounded them that were never toucht : and becaufe prefently he hath not the body of our Lord in his foul imbrued hands, nor the blood within his polluted lips, the mifcreant fumeth at God's priefts; such is thy madnefs, O thou furious man, thou art angry with him which laboureth to turn away God's anger from thee; him thou threatneft, which fueth unto God for grace, and mercy on thy behalf.*

Touching martyrs, he anfwereth, *That it ought not in this cafe to feem offenfive, tho' they were denied, feeing God himself did refufe to yield to the piety of his own righteous faints, making fuit for obdurate Jews.*

As for the parties, in whofe behalf fuch fhifts were ufed ; to have their defire was, in very truth, the way to make them the more guilty: Such peace granted contrary to the rigour of the gofpel, contrary to the law of our Lord and God, doth but under colour of merciful relaxation deceive finners, and by foft handling deftroy them. a grace dangerous for the giver; and to him which receiveth it nothing at all valuable. The patient expecta-

4

tion

tion that bringeth health is, by this means, not regarded; recovery of soundness not sought for by the only medicine available, which is satisfaction; penitency thrown but of mens hearts; the remembrance of that heaviest and last judgment clean banish'd; the wounds of dying men, which should be healed, are covered; the stroke of death, which hath gone as deep as any bowels are to receive it, is overcast with the slight shew of a cloudy look. From the altar of Satan to the holy table of the Lord, men are not afraid to come, even belching, in a manner, the sacrificed morsels they have eaten; yea, their jaws yet breathing out the irksome savour of their former contagious wickedness, they seize upon the blessed body of our Lord, nothing terrified with that dreadful commination, which saith, *Whosoever eateth and drinketh unworthily, is guilty of the body and* 1 Cor. 11.27. *blood of Christ.* They vainly think it to be peace, which is gotten before they be purged of their faults, before their crime be solemnly confest, before their conscience be cleared by the sacrifice and imposition of the priest's hands, and before they have pacified the indignation of God. Why term they that a favour, which is an injury? Wherefore cloak they impiety with the name of charitable indulgence? Such facility giveth not, but rather taketh away peace; and is it self another fresh persecution or trial, whereby that fraudulent enemy maketh a secret havock of such as before he had overthrown; and now, to the end that he may clean swallow them, he casteth sorrow into a dead sleep, putteth grief to silence, wipeth away the memory of faults newly done, smothereth the signs that should rise from a contrite spirit, drieth up eyes which ought to send forth rivers of tears, and permitteth not God to be pacified with full repentance, whom heinous and enormous crimes have displeased.

By this then we see, that in St. *Cyprian's* judgment, all absolutions are void, frustrate, The end of satisfaction. and of no effect, without sufficient repentance first shewed; whereas contrariwise, if true and full satisfaction have gone before, the sentence of man here given is ratified of God in heaven, according to our Saviour's own sacred testimony, *Whose sins ye remit, they are remitted.*

By what works in the vertue, and by what in the discipline of repentance we are said to satisfy either God or men, cannot now be thought obscure. As for the inventers of sacramental satisfaction, they have both alter'd the natural order heretofore kept in the church, by bringing in a strange preposterous course to absolve before satisfaction be made, and moreover by this their misordered practice, are grown into sundry errors concerning the end whereunto it is referred.

They imagine, beyond all conceit of antiquity, that when God doth remit sin, and the punishment eternal thereunto belonging, he reserveth the torments of hell-fire to be neverthelesse endured for a time, either shorter or longer, according to the quality of mens crimes. Yet so, that there is between God and man, a certain composition (as it were) or contract, by vertue whereof works assigned by the priests to be done after absolution, shall satisfy God as touching the punishment, which he otherwise would inflict for sin pardoned and forgiven.

Now, because they cannot assure any man, that if he performeth what the priest ap-The way of satisfying by others. pointeth it shall suffice; this (I say) because they cannot do, inasmuch as the priest hath no power to determine or define of equivalency between sins and satisfactions; and yet if a penitent depart this life, the debt of satisfaction being either in whole or in part undischarged, they stedfastly hold that the soul must remain in unspeakable torment till all be paid: therefore, for help and mitigation in this case, they advise men to set certain copes-mates on work, whose prayers and sacrifices may satisfy God for such souls as depart in debt. Hence have arisen the infinite pensions of their priests, the building of so many altars and tombs, the enriching of so many churches with so many glorious and costly gifts, the bequeathing of lands and ample possessions to religious companies, even with utter forgetfulness of friends, parents, wife and children, all natural affection giving place unto that desire which men, doubtful of their own estate, have to deliver their souls from torment after death.

Yet, behold even this being done, how far forth it shall avail they are not sure; and therefore the last up-shot unto their former inventions is, that as every action of Christ did both merit for himself, and satisfy partly for the eternal, and partly for the temporal punishment due unto men for sin; so his saints have obtained the like privilege of grace, making every good work they do, not only meritorious in their own behalf, but satisfactory too for the benefit of others. Or if, having at any time grievously sinned, they do more to satisfy God than he in justice can expect or look for at their hands; the surplusage runneth to a common stock, out of which treasury containing whatsoever Christ did by way of satisfaction for temporal punishment, together with the satisfactory force which resideth in all the vertuous works of saints,

and

and in their satisfactions whatsoever doth abound, (I say) *From hence they hold God satisfied for such arrearages as men behind in accompt discharge not by other means; and for disposition hereof, as it is their doctrine that Christ remitteth not eternal death without the priest's absolution, so without the grant of the pope they cannot but teach it alike unpossible, that souls in hell should receive any temporal release of pain. The sacrament of pardon from him being to this effect no less necessary, than the priest's absolution to the other.* So that by this postern-gate cometh in the whole mark of papal indulgences, a gain unestimable to him, to others a spoil; a scorn both to God and man. So many works of satisfaction pretended to be done by Christ, by saints, and martyrs; so many virtuous acts possessed with satisfactory force and virtue; so many supererogations in satisfying beyond the exigence of their own necessity; and this that the pope might make a monopoly of all, turning all to his own gain, or at least to the gain of those which are his own. Such facility they have to convert a pretended sacrament into a revenue.

Of Absolution of Penitents.

SIN is not helped but by being assecured of pardon. It resteth therefore to be considered, what warrant we have concerning forgiveness, when the sentence of man absolveth us from sin committed against God. At the words of our Saviour, saying to the sick of the palsy, *Son, thy sins are forgiven thee,* exception was taken by the Scribes, who secretly reasoned against him, *Is any able to forgive sins, but God only?* Whereupon they condemn his speech as blasphemy; the rest, which believed him to be a Prophet sent from God, saw no cause wherefore he might not as lawfully say, and as truly, to whomsoever amongst them, *God hath taken away thy sins,* as *Nathan* (they all knew) had used the very like speech; to whom *David* did not therefore impute blasphemy, but embraced, as became him, the words of truth with joy and reverence.

(marginal note: Mat. 9. 2. Mark 2. 7. Luke 5. 21.)

Now there is no controversion, but as God in that special case did authorize *Nathan,* so Christ more generally, his apostles and the ministers of his word, in his name, to absolve sinners. Their power being equal, all the difference between them can be but only in this, that whereas the one had prophetical evidence, the other have the certainty partly of faith, and partly of human experience, whereupon to ground their sentence; faith, to assure them of God's most gracious pardon in heaven unto all penitents, and touching the sincerity of each particular parties repentance as much, as outward sensible tokens or signs can warrant.

It is not to be marvelled, that so great a difference appeareth between the doctrine of *Rome* and ours, when we teach repentance. They imply in the name of repentance much more than we do. We stand chiefly upon the due inward conversion of the heart; they more upon works of eternal shew. We teach, above all things, that repentance which is one and the same from the beginning to the world's end; they a sacramental penance, of their own devising and shaping. We labour to instruct men in such sort, that every soul which is wounded with sin may learn the way how to cure it self; they clean contrary, would make all sores seem incurable, unless the priests have a hand in them.

(marginal note: Ipsius penitentis actio non est pars sacramenti, nisi quatenus potestati sacerdotali sub jicitur, & à ministro sacerdote dirigitur vel judetur. Bell. de Poen. l. 1. c. 16. Christus instituit sacerdotes judices super terram cum ea potestate, ut sine ipsorum sententia, nemo post baptismum lapsus reconciliari possit.)

Touching the force of whose absolution they strangely hold, that whatsoever the penitent doth, his contrition, confession, and satisfaction have no place of right to stand as material parts in this sacrament, nor consequently any such force as to make them available for the taking away of sin, in that they proceed from the penitent himself, without the privity of the minister, but only as they are enjoined by the minister's authority and power. So that no contrition or grief of heart, till the priest exact it; no acknowledgments of sins, but that which he doth demand; no praying, no fasting, no alms, no repentance or restitution for whatsoever we have done, can help, except by him it be first imposed. It is the chain of their own doctrine, no remedy for mortal sin committed after baptism, but the sacrament of penance only; no sacrament of penance, if either matter or form be wanting; no ways to make those duties a material part of the sacrament, unless we consider them as required and exacted by the priest.' Our Lord and Saviour, they say, hath ordained his priests judges in such sort, that no man which sinneth after baptism can be reconciled unto God, but by their sentence. For why? If there were any other way of reconciliation, the very promise of Christ should be false, in saying, *Whatsoever ye bind on earth, shall be bound in heaven, and whose sins soever ye retain, they are retained.* Except therefore the

I　　　　　　　priest

prieſt be willing, God hath by promiſe hampred himſelf ſo, that it is not now in his own power to pardon any man. Let him who hath offended crave as the publican did, *Lord, be thou merciful unto me a ſinner*, let him, as *David*, make a thouſand times his ſupplication, *Have mercy upon me, O God, according to thy loving kindneſs; according to the multitude of thy compaſſions, put away mine iniquities*; all this doth not help, till ſuch time as the pleaſure of the prieſt be known, till he have ſigned us a pardon, and given us our *quietus eſt*. God himſelf hath no anſwer to make, but ſuch as that of the angel unto *Lot*, I can do nothing. poſſit. Bell. l. 3. c. 1. de Poenit. Quod ſi poſſient ſi ſine ſupplication, cerdotum ſententia abſolvi, non effet vera Chriſti promiſſio, Quæcunque, &c. Bellarm. ibid.

It is true, that our Saviour by theſe words, *Whoſe ſins ye remit, they are remitted*, did ordain judges over our ſinful ſouls, gave them authority to abſolve from ſin, and promiſe to ratify in heaven whatſoever they ſhould do on earth in execution of this their office; to the end that hereby, as well his miniſters might take encouragement to do their duty with all faithfulneſs, as alſo his peoples admonition, gladly with all reverence to be ordered by them; both parts knowing that the functions of the one towards the other have his perpetual aſſiſtance and approbation. Howbeit all this with two reſtraints, which every juriſdiction in the world hath; the one, that the practice thereof proceed in due order; the other, that it do not extend it ſelf beyond due bounds; which bounds or limits have ſo confined penitential juriſdiction, that although there be given unto it power of remitting ſin, yet no ſuch ſovereignty of power that no ſin ſhould be pardonable in man without it. Thus to enforce our Saviour's words, is as though we ſhould gather, that becauſe whatſoever *Joſeph* did command in the land of *Egypt*, *Pharaoh*'s grant is, it ſhould be done; therefore he granteth that nothing ſhould be done in the land of *Egypt* but what *Joſeph* did command, and ſo conſequently, by enabling his ſervant *Joſeph* to command under him, diſableth himſelf to command any thing without *Joſeph*. Chriſtus ordinariam ſuam poteſtatem in Apoſtolos tranſtulit; extraordinariam ſibi reſervavit.

But by this we ſee how the papacy maketh all ſin unpardonable, which hath not the prieſt's abſolution; except peradventure in ſome extraordinary caſe, where albeit abſolution be not had, yet it muſt be deſired. Ordinaria e-nim remedia in Eccleſia ad remittenda

peccata ſunt ab eo inſtituta, ſacramenta: ſine quibus peccata remittere Chriſtus poteſt, ſed extraordinarie & multo rarius hoc facit, quam per ſacramenta. Noluit igitur eos extraordinariis remiſſionis peccatorum conſidere, quæ, & rara ſunt & incerta: ſed ordinaria, ut ita dicam, viſibilia ſacramentorum quærere remedia. Maldon. in Matt. 16. 19.

What is then the force of abſolution? What is it which the act of abſolution worketh in a ſinful man? Doth it by any operation derived from it ſelf alter the ſtate of the ſoul? Doth it really take away ſin, or but aſcertain us of God's moſt gracious and merciful pardon? The latter of which two is our aſſertion, the former theirs.

At the words of our Lord and Saviour Jeſus Chriſt, ſaying unto the ſick of the palſy, *Son, thy ſins are forgiven thee*, the Phariſees which knew him not to be *Son of the living God*, took ſecret exception, and fell to reaſoning with themſelves againſt him; *Is any able to forgive ſin but God only? The ſins* (ſaith St. *Cyprian*) *that are committed againſt him, he alone hath power to forgive, which took upon him our ſins, he which ſorrowed and ſuffered for us, he whom the Father delivered unto death for our offences.* Whereunto may be added, that which *Clemens Alexandrinus* hath. *Our Lord is profitable every way, every way beneficial, whether we reſpect him as man, or as God; as God for-giving, as man inſtructing, and learning how to avoid ſin.* * *For it is I, even I that putteth away thine iniquities for mine own ſake, and will not remember thy ſins, ſaith the Lord.* Matt. 9. 2. Mark 2. 7. Luke 5. 21. Cypr. de Lapſ. c. 4. Clem. Alex. Pædag. l. 1. Πᾶν ὄνιμον — * Eſa. 43. 25.

λῶ, ὡς ὁ ἀνθρωπῷ, ὡς ὁ Θεὸς. Τὰ μὲν ἁμαρτήματα ὡς Θεὸς ἀφιεὶς, εἰς δὲ τὸ μὴ ἐξαμαρτάνειν παιδαγωγῶν ὡς ἄνθρωπῷ.

Now, albeit we willingly confeſs with St. *Cyprian*, *The ſins which are committed againſt him, he only hath power to forgive, which hath taken upon him our ſins, he which hath ſorrowed and ſuffered for us, he, whom God hath given for our offences.* Yet neither did St. *Cyprian* intend to deny the power of the miniſter, otherwiſe than if he preſume beyond his commiſſion to remit ſin, where God's own will is it ſhould be retained; for, againſt ſuch abſolutions he ſpeaketh (which being granted to whom they ought to have been denied, or of no validity;) and, if rightly it be conſidered how higher cauſes in operation uſe to concur with inferior means, his grace with our miniſtry, God really performing the ſame which man is authorized to act as in his name, there ſhall need for deciſion of this point no great labour. Veniam peccatis quæ in ipſum cummiſſa ſunt ſolus po-teſt ille largiri, qui peccata no-ſtra portavit, qui pro nobis doluit, quem Deus tradidit pro peccatis noſtris.

To remiſſion of ſins there are two things neceſſary; grace, as the only cauſe which taketh away iniquity; and repentance, as a duty or condition required in us. To make repentance ſuch as it ſhould be, what doth God demand but inward ſincerity joined with fit and convenient offices for that purpoſe, the one referred wholly to our own conſciences, the other beſt diſcerned by them whom God hath appointed judges in this court. So that having firſt the promiſes of God for pardon generally unto all offenders penitent; and Victor. de perſe-cut. Vand.

and particularly for our own unfeigned meaning, the unfallible teſtimony of a good conſcience, the ſentence of God's appointed officer and vicegerent to approve with unpartial
judgment the quality of that we have done, and as from his tribunal in that reſpect, to
aſſoil us of any crime; I ſee no cauſe but by the rules of our faith and religion we may
reſt our ſelves very well aſſured touching God's moſt merciful pardon and grace; who,
eſpecially for the ſtrengthning of weak, timorous and fearful minds, hath ſo far indued his
church with power to abſolve ſinners. It pleaſed God that men ſometimes ſhould, by
miſſing this help, perceive how much they ſtand bound to him for ſo precious a benefit
enjoyed. And ſurely, ſo long as the world lived in any awe or fear of falling away from
God, ſo dear were his miniſters to the people, chiefly in this reſpect, that being through
tyranny and perſecution deprived of paſtors, the doleful rehearſal of their loſt felicities
hath not any thing more eminent, than that ſinners diſtreſt ſhould not know how or where
to unload their burthens. Strange it were unto me, that the Fathers, who ſo much every
where extol the grace of Jeſus Chriſt, in leaving unto his church this heavenly and divine
power, ſhould as men, whoſe ſimplicity had univerſally been abuſed, agree all to admire
and magnify a needleſs office.

The ſentence therefore of miniſterial abſolution, hath two effects: touching ſin, it
only declareth us freed from the guiltineſs thereof, and reſtored into God's favour; but
concerning right in ſacred and divine myſteries, whereof through ſin we were made
unworthy, as the power of the church did before effectually bind and retain us from acceſs unto them, ſo upon our apparent repentance it truly reſtoreth our liberty, looſeth
the chains wherewith we were tied, remitteth all whatſoever is paſt, and accepteth us no
leſs returned than if we had never gone aſtray.

For, inaſmuch as the power which our Saviour gave to his church, is of two kinds;
the one to be exerciſed over voluntary penitents only, the other over ſuch as are to be
brought to amendment by eccleſiaſtical cenſures, the words wherein he hath given this
authority muſt be ſo underſtood, as the ſubject or matter whereupon it worketh will permit. It doth not permit that in the former kind, (that is to ſay, in the uſe of power
over voluntary converts) to bind or looſe, remit or retain, ſhould ſignify any other than
only to pronounce of ſinners according to that which may be gathered by outward ſigns;
becauſe really to effect the removal or continuance of ſin in the ſoul of any offender, is
no prieſtly act, but a work which far exceedeth their ability. Contrariwiſe, in the latter
kind of ſpiritual Juriſdiction, which by cenſures conſtraineth men to amend their lives;
it is true, that the miniſter of God doth then more declare and ſignify what God hath
wrought. And this power, true it is, that the church hath inveſted in it.

Howbeit, as other truths, ſo this hath by error been oppugned and depraved through
abuſe. The firſt of name that openly in writing withſtood the church's authority and
power to remit ſin, was *Tertullian,* after he had combined himſelf with *Montaniſts,*
drawn to the liking of their hereſy through the very ſourneſs of his own nature, which
neither his incredible ſkill and knowledge otherwiſe, nor the doctrine of the goſpel it ſelf,
could but ſo much alter, as to make him favour any thing which carried with it the taſte
of lenity. A ſpunge ſteeped in wormwood and gall, a man through too much ſeverity
mercileſs, and neither able to endure nor be endured of any. His book entituled concerning chaſtity, and written profeſſedly againſt the diſcipline of the church, hath many
fretful and angry ſentences, declaring a mind very much offended with ſuch as would not
perſuade themſelves, that of ſins, ſome be pardonable by the keys of the church, ſome
uncapable of forgiveneſs; that middle and moderate offences, having received chaſtiſement, may by ſpiritual authority afterwards be remitted: but, greater tranſgreſſions muſt
(as touching indulgence) be left to the only pleaſure of almighty God in the world to
come: that as idolatry and bloodſhed, ſo likewiſe fornication and ſinful luſt, are of this
nature; that they, which ſo far have fallen from God, ought to continue for ever after
barred from acceſs unto his ſanctuary, condemned to perpetual profuſion of tears, deprived of all expectation and hope to receive any thing at the church's hands, but pub-
Securitas de- lication of their ſhame. *For,* (ſaith he) *who will fear to waſte out that which he hopeth*
licti, etiam li- *he may recover? Who will be careful for ever to hold that, which he knoweth cannot for*
bido eſt ejus. *ever be withheld from him? He which ſlackneth the bridle to ſin, doth thereby give it*
even the ſpur alſo. Take away fear, and that which preſently ſucceedeth inſtead thereof,
is licentious deſire. Greater offences therefore are puniſhable, but not pardonable by the
church. If any prophet or apoſtle be found to have remitted ſuch tranſgreſſions, they
did it not by the ordinary courſe of diſcipline, but by extraordinary power. For they all
raiſed the dead, which none but God is able to do; they reſtored the impotent and
lame man, a work peculiar to Jeſus Chriſt; yea, that which Chriſt would not do, becauſe executions of ſuch ſeverity beſeemed not him who came to ſave and redeem the

       world

world by his sufferings, they by their power struck *Elymas* and *Ananias*, the one blind, and the other dead. Approve first your selves to be, as they were, apostles or prophets, and then take upon you to pardon all men. But, if the authority you have be only ministerial, and no way sovereign, over-reach not the limits which God hath set you, know that to pardon capital sin, is beyond your commission.

Howbeit, as oftentimes the vices of wicked men do cause other their commendable qualities to be abhorred, so the honour of great mens virtues is easily a cloak of their errors. In which respect, *Tertullian* hath past with much less obloquy and reprehension than *Novatian*; who, broaching afterwards the same opinion, had not otherwise wherewith to countervail the offence he gave, and to procure it the like toleration. *Novatian*, at the first, a stoical philosopher (which kind of men hath always accounted stupidity the highest top of wisdom, and commiseration the deadliest sin) became by institution and study, the very same which the other had been before, through a secret natural distemper, upon his conversion to the christian faith, and recovery from sickness, which moved him to receive the sacrament of baptism in his bed. The bishops, contrary to the canons of ^{Concil. Novat-} the church, would needs, in special love towards him, ordain him presbyter, which fa-^{tur. c. 11.} vour satisfied not him who thought himself worthy of greater place and dignity. He closed therefore with a number of well-minded men and not suspicious what his secret purposes were, and having made them sure unto him by fraud, procureth his own consecration to be their bishop. His prelacy now was able, as he thought, to countenance what he intended to publish, and therefore his letters went presently abroad to sundry churches, advising them never to admit to the fellowship of holy mysteries, such as had after baptism offered sacrifice to idols.

There was present at the council of *Nice*, together with other bishops, one *Acesius* a ^{Socra. l. 4. c.} *Novatianist*, touching whose diversity in opinion from the church, the emperor desirous ^{23.}_{Concil. Nicen.} to hear some reason, ask'd of him certain questions: for answer whereunto, *Acesius* weav-_{c. 30.} eth out a long history of things that happen'd in the persecution under *Decius*; and of ^{Socra. l.1.c.7.} men, which to save life, forsook faith. But in the end was a certain bitter canon, framed in their own school. *That men which fall into deadly sin after holy baptism, ought never to be again admitted to the communion of divine mysteries: that they are to be exhorted unto repentance; howbeit not to be put in hope that pardon can be had at the priest's hands, but with God, which hath sovereign power and authority in himself to remit sin, it may be in the end they shall find mercy.* These followers of *Novatian*, which gave themselves the title of καθαροί, clean, pure, and unspotted men, had one point of *Montanism* more than their master did profess; for amongst sins unpardonable, they reckoned second marriages, of which opinion *Tertullian* making (as his usual manner was) a salt apology, *Such is* (saith he) *our stony hardness, that defaming our Comforter with a kind of enormity in discipline, we dam up the doors of the church, no less against twice-married men, than against adulterers and fornicators.* Of this sort therefore it was ordained by the *Nicene* synod, that if any such did return to the catholick and apostolick unity, they should in writing bind themselves to observe the orders of the church, and communicate as well with them which had been often married, or had fallen in time of persecution, as with other sort of christian people. But further to relate, or at all to refel the error of mis-believing men concerning this point, is not now to our present purpose greatly necessary.

The church may receive no small detriment by corrupt practice, even there where doctrine concerning the substance of things practised is free from any great or dangerous corruption. If therefore that which the papacy doth in matter of confessions and absolution be offensive, if it palpably serve in the use of the keys, howsoever, that which it teacheth in general concerning the church's power to retain and forgive sins, be admitted true, have they not on the one side as much whereat to be abasht, as on the other wherein to rejoice?

They bind all men, upon pain of everlasting condemnation and death, to make confessions to their ghostly fathers, of every great offence they know, and can remember, that they have committed against God. Hath Christ in his gospel so delivered the doctrine of repentance unto the world? Did his apostles so preach it to nations? Have the fathers so believed, or so taught? Surely *Novatian* was not so merciless in depriving the church of power to absolve some certain offenders, as they in imposing upon all a necessity thus to confess. *Novatian* would not deny but God might remit that which the church could not, whereas in the papacy it is maintained, that what we conceal from men, God himself shall never pardon. By which oversight, as they have here surcharged the world with multitude, but much abated the weight of confessions, so the careless manner of their absolution hath made discipline, for the most part, amongst them a bare formality: yea, ra-

ther

ther a means of emboldening unto vicious and wicked life, than either any help to prevent future, or medicine to remedy prefent evils in the foul of man. The fathers
were flow and always fearful to abfolve any before very manifeft tokens given of a true
penitent and contrite fpirit. It was not their cuftom to remit fin firft, and then to impofe
works of fatisfaction, as the fafhion of *Rome* is now; infomuch that this their prepofte-
rous courfe, and mifordered practices hath bred alfo in them an error concerning the end
and purpofe of thefe works. For againft the guiltinefs of fin, and the danger of everlafting condemnation thereby incurred, confeffion and abfolution fucceeding the fame,
are, as they take it, a remedy fufficient: and therefore what their penitentiaries do think to
enjoy farther, whether it be a number of *Ave-Maries* daily to be fcored up, a journey
of pilgrimage to be undertaken, fome few difhes of ordinary diet to be exchanged, offerings to be made at the fhrines of faints, or a little to be fcraped off from mens fuper-
fluities for relief of poor people, all is in lieu or exchange with God, whofe juftice, notwithftanding our pardon, yet oweth us ftill fome temporal punifhment, either in this or
in the life to come, except we quit it our felves here with works of the former kind,
and continued till the balance of God's moft ftrict feverity fhall find the pains we have
taken equivalent with the plagues which we fhould endure, or elfe the mercy of the
pope relieve us. And at this poftern-gate cometh in the whole mart of papal indulgen-
cies fo infinitely ftrewed, that the pardon of fin, which heretofore was obtained hardly,
and by much fuit, is with them become now almoft impoffible to be efcaped.

In peccato, tria
funt; actio ma-
la, interior ma-
cula, & fequela.
Bon. fent. l. 4.
d. 17. q. 3.
1 John 3. 4. To fet down then the force of this fentence in abfolving penitents; there are in fin
thefe three things: the act which paffeth away and vanifheth: the pollution wherewith
it leaveth the foul defiled; and the punifhment whereunto they are made fubject that
have committed it. The act of fin is every deed, word and thought againft the law of
God. *For fin is the transgreffion of the law*; and although the deed it felf do not continue, yet is that bad quality permanent, whereby it maketh the foul unrighteous and deformed in God's fight. *From the heart come evil cogitations, murthers, adulteries, for-*
Matth. 15. 19.*nications, thefts, falfe teftimonies, flanders; thefe are things which defile a man.* They
do not only, as effects of impurity, argue the neft to be unclean, out of which they
came, but as caufes they ftrengthen that difpofition unto wickednefs which brought
them forth; they are both fruits and feeds of uncleannefs, they nourifh the root out of
which they grow; they breed that iniquity which bred them. The blot therefore of fin
abideth, though the act be tranfitory. And out of both arifeth a prefent debt, to endure
what punifhment foever the evil which we have done deferveth; an obligation, in the
chains whereof finners, by the juftice of almighty God, continue bound till repentance
Acts 8. 22. loofe them. *Repent this thy wickednefs* (faith *Peter*) unto *Simon Magus*, befeech *God,*
that if it be poffible the thought of thine heart may be pardoned; for I fee thou art in the
Prov. 5. 22.*gall of bitternefs, and in the bond of iniquity.* In like manner *Solomon: The wicked*
fhall be held faft in the cords of his own fin.

Nor doth God only bind finners hand and foot by the dreadful determination of his
Sacerdotes o-
pus juftitiæ
exercent in
peccatores
cum eos jufta
pœna ligant; own unfearchable judgment againft them; but fometimes alfo the church bindeth by the
cenfures of her difcipline. So that when offenders upon their repentance are by the fame
difcipline abfolved, the church loofeth but her own bonds, the chains wherein fhe had
tied them before.

opus miferi-
cordiæ cum de ea aliquod relaxant, vel facramentorum communioni conciliant; alia opera in peccatores exercere nequeunt. Sent. l. 4.
dif. 18.

Acts 7. 60.
Mic. 7. 19.
1 Cor. vi. 11.
Tit. 3. 5.
Luke 12. 5.
Matt. 10. 28. The act of fin God alone remitteth, in that his purpofe is never to call it to account,
or to lay it unto men's charge; the ftain he wafheth out by the fanctifying grace of his
Spirit; and concerning the punifhment of fin, as none elfe hath power to caft body and
foul into hell fire, fo none have power to deliver either, befides him.

As for the minifterial fentence of private abfolution, it can be no more than a declaration what God hath done; it hath but the force of the prophet *Nathan's* abfoluti-
2 Sam. 12. 13.
Luke 7. 17.
Malach. 3. 15.on, *God hath taken away thy fin:* than which conftruction, efpecially of words judicial, there is not any thing more vulgar. For example, the publicans are faid in the
gofpel to have juftified God; the *Jews* in *Malachi* to have bleffed proud men, which
fin and profper; not that the one did make God righteous, or the other the wicked
happy: but to blefs, to juftify, and to abfolve, are as commonly ufed for words of judg-
Sent. l. 4. dif.
18.ment, or declaration, as of true and real efficacy; yea even by the opinion of the mafter of fentences. It may be foundly affirmed and thought that God alone doth remit
and retain fins, although he have given power to the church to do both; but he one way,
and the church another. He only by himfelf forgiveth fin, who cleanfeth the foul from
inward blemifh, and loofeth the debt of eternal death. So great a privilege he hath not
given

4
given

given unto his priests, who notwithstanding are authorized to loose and bind, that is to say, declare who are bound, and who are loosed. For albeit a man be already cleared before God, yet he is not in the church of God so taken, but by the vertue of the priest's sentence; who likewise may be said to bind by imposing satisfaction, and to loose by admitting to the holy communion.

Saint *Hierom* also, whom the master of the sentences alledgeth for more countenance of his own opinion, doth no less plainly and directly affirm; *That as the priests of the law could only discern, and neither cause nor remove leprosies; so the ministers of the gospel, when they retain or remit sin, do but in the one judge how long we continue guilty, and in the other declare when we are clear or free.* For there is nothing more apparent, than that the discipline of repentance, both publick and private, was ordained as an outward means to bring men to the vertue of inward conversion: so that when this by manifest tokens did seem effected, absolution ensuing (which could not make) served only to declare men innocent.

But the cause wherefore they are so stiff, and have forsaken their own master in this point is, for that they hold the private discipline of penitency to a sacrament; absolution an external sign in this sacrament; the signs external of all sacraments in the new testament, to be both causes of that which they signify, and signs of that which they truly cause.

To this opinion concerning sacraments, they are now ty'd by expounding a canon in the *Florentine* council according to the former ecclesiastical invention received from *Thomas.* For his deceit it was, that the mercy of God, which useth sacraments as instruments whereby to work, endueth them at the time of their administration with supernatural force and ability to induce grace into the souls of men; even as the axe and saw doth seem to bring timber into that fashion which the mind of the artificer intendeth. His conceit, *Scotus, Occam, Petrus Alliacensis,* with sundry others, do most earnestly and strongly impugn, shewing very good reason wherefore no sacrament of the new law can either by vertue which it self hath, or by force supernatural given it, be properly a cause to work grace; but sacraments are therefore said to work or confer grace, because the will of almighty God is, altho' not to give them such efficacy, yet himself to be present in the ministry of the working that effect, which proceedeth wholly from him, without any real operation of theirs, such as can enter into men's souls.

In which construction, seeing that our books and writings have made it known to the world how we join with them, it seemeth very hard and injurious dealing, that *Bellarmine* throughout the whole course of his second book [a] *De sacramentis in genere,* should so boldly face down his adversaries, as if their opinion were, that sacraments are naked, empty, and ineffectual signs; wherein there is no other force than only such, as in pictures to stir up the mind, that so by theory and speculation of things represented, faith may grow. Finally, that all the operations which sacraments have, is a sensible and divine institution. But had it pleased him not to hood-wink his own knowledge, I nothing doubt but he fully saw how to answer himself; it being a matter very strange and incredible, that one which with so great diligence hath winnowed [b] his adversaries writings, should be ignorant of their minds. For, even as in the person of our Lord Jesus Christ, both God and man, when his human nature is by it self considered, we may not attribute that unto him, which we do and must ascribe as oft as respect is had unto both natures combined; so because in sacraments there are two things distinctly to be considered, the outward sign, and the secret concurrence of God's most blessed Spirit, in which respect our Saviour hath taught that water and the holy Ghost are combined to work the mystery of new birth; sacraments therefore, as signs, have only those effects before mentioned; but of sacraments, in that by God's own will and ordinance they are signs assisted always with the power of the holy Ghost, we acknowledge whatsoever either the places of the scripture, or the authority of councils and fathers, or the proofs and arguments of reason which he alledgeth, can shew to be wrought by them. The elements and words have power of infallible significations, for which they are called seals of God's truth; the spirit affixed unto those elements and words, power of operation within the soul, most admirable, divine, and impossible to be exprest. For so God hath instituted and ordained, that, together with due administration and receipt of

[a] *Lutherani* de hac re interdum ita scribunt, ut videantur à catholicis non dissentire; interdum autem apertissime scribunt contraria: at semper in eadem sententia manent, sacramenta non habere immediate illam efficientiam respectu gratiæ, sed esse nuda signa, tamen mediate aliquid efficere quatenus excitant & alunt fidem, quod ipsum non faciunt nisi repræsentando, ut sacramenta per visum excitent fidem, quemadmodum prædicatio verbi per auditum. *Bellarm.* de sacr. in genere, l. 2. c. 2.

Quædam signa sunt theorica, non ad alium finem instituta, quam ad significandum; alia ad significandum & efficiendum, quæ ob id practica dici possunt. Controversia est inter nos & hæreticos, quod illi faciunt sacramenta signa prioris generis, Quare si ostendere poterimus esse signa posterioris generis, obtinuimus causam. cap. 8.

[b] Semper memoria repetendum est sacramenta nihil aliud quam instrumentales esse conferendæ nobis gratiæ causas. *Calv.* in Ant. con. Frid. fe 7. c. 5. Si qui sint qui negent sacramentis contineri gratiam quam figurant, illos improbamus. Ibid. cap. 6.

of

of facramental figns, there fhall proceed from himfelf, grace effectual, to fanctify, to cure, to comfort, and whatfoever elfe is for the good of the fouls of men. Howbeit *this opinion *Thomas* rejecteth, under pretence that it maketh facramental words and elements to be in themfelves no more than figns, whereas they ought to be held as caufes of that they fignify. He therefore reformeth it with this addition, that the very fenfible parts of the facraments do inftrumentally effect and produce, not grace, (for the fchoolmen both of thefe times, and long after did, for the moft part, maintain it untrue, and fome of them unpoffible, that fanctifying grace fhould efficiently proceed but from God alone, and that by immediate creation, as the fubftance of the foul doth) but the phantafy which *Thomas* had was, that fenfible things, thro' Chrift's and the prieft's benediction, receive a certain fupernatural tranfitory force, which leaveth behind it a kind of preparative quality or beauty within the foul, whereupon immediately from God doth enfue the grace that juftifieth.

Act. 3. *Albac.* in quart. fent. 9. 1 Capr. in 4. d. 1. q. 1. Palud. Tom. Ferrar. lib. 4. cont. Gent. c. 57. Neceffe eft ponere aliquam virtutem fupernaturalem in facramentis. Sent. 4. d. 1. q. 1. Act. 4. Sacramentum confequitur fpiritualem virtutem cum benedictione Chrifti, & applicatione miniftri ad ufum facramenti. part. 3. q. 62. art. 4. Concil. Victus facramentalis habet effe tranfiens ex uno in aliud & incompletum. Ibidem   Ex facramentis duo confequuntur in anima, unum eft character, five aliquis ornatus; aliud, eft gratia. Refpectu primo, facramenta funt caufae aliquo modo efficientes; refpectu fecundo, funt difponentes. Sacramenta caufant difpofitionem ad formam ultimam, fed ultimam perfectionem non inducunt. Sent. 4. d. 1. q. 1. art. 4.

Now they which pretend to follow *Thomas*, differ from him in two points. For firft, they make grace an immediate effect of the outward fign, which he for the dignity and excellency thereof was afraid to do. *Secondly*, Whereas he, to produce but a preparative quality in the foul, did imagine God to create in the inftrument a fupernatural gift or hability; they confefs, that nothing is created, infufed, or any way inherent either in the word or in the elements; nothing that giveth them inftrumental efficacy, but God's meer motion or application. Are they able to explain unto us, or themfelves to conceive, what they mean when they thus fpeak? For example, let them teach us, in the facrament of baptifm, what it is for water to be moved till it bring forth grace. The application thereof by the minifter is plain to fenfe; the force which it hath in the mind, as a moral inftrument of information, or inftruction, we know by reafon; and by faith, we underftand how God doth affift it with his Spirit: whereupon enfueth the grace which faint *Cyprian* did in himfelf obferve, faying, *After the bath of regeneration, having fcowred out the ftained foulnefs of former life, fupernatural light had entrance into the breaft which was purified and cleanfed for it: after that a fecond nativity had made another man, by inward receipt of the Spirit from heaven; things doubtful began in marvellous manner to appear certain, that to be open which lay hid, darknefs to fhine like a clear light, former hardnefs to be made facility, impoffibility eafinefs: infomuch as it might be difcerned how that earthly, which before had been carnally bred and lived, given over unto fins; that now God's own which the holy Ghoft did quicken.*

Our opinion is therefore plain unto every man's underftanding. We take it for a very good fpeech which *Bonaventure* hath uttered in faying, *Heed muft be taken that while we affign too much to the bodily figns in way of their commendation, we withdraw not the honour which is due to the caufe which worketh in them, and the foul which receiveth them. Whereunto we conformably teach, that the outward fign applied, hath of it felf no natural efficacy towards grace, neither doth God put into it any fupernatural inherent Virtue.* And as I think, we thus far avouch no more than they themfelves confefs to be very true.

If any thing difpleafe them, it is becaufe we add to thefe promifes another affertion; that, with the outward fign, God joineth his holy Spirit; and fo the whole inftrument of God bringeth that to pafs, whereunto the bafer and meaner part could not extend. As for operations through the motion of figns, they are dark, intricate and obfcure; perhaps poffible, howbeit, not proved either true or likely, by alledging, that the touch of our Saviour's garment reftored health, clay fight, when he applied it. Although ten thoufand fuch examples fhould be brought, they overthrow not this one principle; that, where the inftrument is without inherent, the effect muft neceffarily proceed from the only agent's adherent power.

It paffeth a man's conceit how water fhould be carried into the foul with any force of divine motion, or grace proceed but meerly from the influence of God's Spirit. Notwithftanding, if God himfelf teach his church in this cafe to believe that which he hath not given us capacity to comprehend, how incredible foever it may feem, yet our wits fhould fubmit themfelves, and reafon give place unto faith therein. But they yield it to be no queftion of faith, how grace doth proceed from facraments;

2   craments;

Solus Deus efficit gratiam conficit, adeo quod nec ingelis, qui funt nobiliores fenfibilibus creaturis, hoc communicetur. Sent. 4. d. 1. q. 1. art. 4. Eph. 2.

Cavendum e nim ne dum nimis damus corporalibus fignis ad laudem, fubtrahamus honorem caufae cuenti & animae fufcipienti.

Luke 18. 9. John 9.

Bel. de facr. in gen. l. 2. c. 1.

craments; if in general they be acknowledged true inftrumental caufes, by the miniftry whereof men receive divine grace. And that they which impute grace to the only operation of God himfelf, concurring with the external fign, do no lefs acknowledge the true efficacy of the facrament, than they that afcribe the fame to the quality of the fign apply'd, or to the motion of God applying, and fo far carrying it, till grace be not created, but extracted, out of the natural poffibility of the foul. Neverthelefs, this laft philofophical imagination (if I may call it philofophical, which ufeth the terms, but overthroweth the rules of philofophy, and hath no article of faith to fupport it; but whofoever it be) they follow it in a manner all; they caft off the firft opinion, wherein is moft perfpicuity and ftrongeft evidence of certain truth.

Dicimus gratiam non creari à Deo, fed produci ex aptitudine & potentia naturali animæ, ficut cætera omnia quæ producuntur in fubjectis tapibus quæ funt apta nata ad fufcipiendum accidentia. Allen de facr. in gen.

The council of _Florence_ and _Trent_ defining, that facraments contain and confer grace, the fenfe whereof (if it liked them) might fo eafily conform it felf with the fame opinion which they drew without any juft caufe, quite and clean the other way, making grace the iffue of bare words, in fuch facraments as they have framed deftitute of any vifible element, and holding it the offspring as well of elements as of words in thofe facraments where both are; but in no facrament acknowledging grace to be the fruit of the holy Ghoft working with the outward fign, and not by it, in fuch fort as _Thomas_ himfelf teacheth; that the apoftles impofition of hands caufed not the coming of the holy Ghoft, which notwithftanding was beftowed together with the exercife of that ceremony; yea, by it, (faith the evangelift) to wit, as by a mean, which came between the true agent and the effect; but not otherwife.

_c. 37._

Tho. de Verit. q. 27. art. 3. refp. ad 16. Acts 8. 18.

Many of the antient fathers, prefuppofing that the faithful before Chrift had not, till the time of his coming, that perfect life and falvation which they looked for and we poffefs, thought likewife their facraments to be but prefigurations of that which ours in prefent do exhibit. For which caufe the _Florentine_ council, comparing the one with the other, faith, _That the old did only fhadow grace, which was afterward to be given through the paffion of Jefus Chrift._ But the after-wit of latter days hath found out another more exquifite diftinction, that evangelical facraments are caufes to effect grace, through motions of figns legal, according to the fame fignification and fenfe wherein evangelical facraments are held by us to be God's inftruments for that purpofe. For howfoever _Bellarmine_ hath fhrunk up the _Lutherans_ finews, and cut off our doctrine by the skirts; _Allen_, although he terms us hereticks, according to the ufual bitter venom of his firft ftyle, doth yet ingenuoufly confefs, that the old fchoolmen's doctrine and ours is one concerning facramental efficacy, derived from God himfelf, affifting by promife thofe outward figns of elements and words, out of which their fchool-men of the newer mint are fo defirous to hatch grace. Where God doth work and ufe thefe outward means, wherein he neither findeth nor planteth force and aptnefs towards his intended purpofe; fuch means are but figns to bring men to the confideration of his omnipotent power, which, without the ufe of things fenfible, would not be marked.

Quod ad circumcifionem fequebatur miffio, fiebat ratione rei adjunctæ & ratione pacti divini, eodem plane modo quo non folum hæretici, fed etiam aliquot vetuftiores fcholaftici voluerunt nova facramenta conferre gratiam. Allen de facr. in gen. c. 39. Bonaventura, Scotus, Durandus, Richardus, Occamus, Marcilius, Gabriel.

volunt folum Deum producere gratiam ad præfentiam facramentorum. Bellarm. de facr. in gen. lib. 2. cap. 11. Puto longe probabiliorem & tutiorem fententiam quæ dat facramentis veram efficientiam. Primò quia doctores paffim docent, facramenta non agere nifi priùs à Deo virtutem feu benedictionem feu fanctificationem accipiant, & referunt effectum facramentorum ad omnipotentiam Dei, & conferunt cum veris caufis efficientibus. Secundò, quia non effet differentia inter modum agendi facramentorum, & fignorum magicorum. Tertiò, quia tunc non effe homo Dei minifter in ipfa actione facramenti, fed homo præberet fignum actione fua, & Deus fua actione vifa eo figno infunderet gratiam, ut cum unus oftendit fyngrapham mercatori, & ille dat pecunias. At fcripturæ docent, quod Deus baptizat per hominem. Bellarm. lib 2. cap. 1.

At the time therefore when he giveth his heavenly grace, he applieth, by the hands of his minifters, that which betokeneth the fame; not only betokeneth, but, being alfo accompanied for ever with fuch power as doth truly work, is in that refpect termed God's inftrument, a true efficient caufe of grace; a caufe not in it felf, but only by connexion of that which is in it felf a caufe, namely, God's own ftrength and power. Sacraments, that is to fay, the outward figns in facraments, work nothing till they be bleffed and fanctified by God.

But what is God's heavenly benediction and fanctification, faving only the affociation of his Spirit? Shall we fay that facraments are like magical figns, if thus they have their effect? Is it magick for God to manifeft by things fenfible what he doth, and to do by his moft glorious Spirit really what he manifefteth in his facraments? The delivery and adminiftration whereof remaineth in the hands of mortal men, by whom, as by perfonal inftruments, God doth apply figns, and with figns

I   X x   infeparably

Inseparably join his Spirit, and through the power of his Spirit work grace. The first is by way of concomitance and consequence to deliver the rest also that either accompany or ensue.

It is not here, as in cases of mutual commerce, where divers persons have divers acts to be performed in their own behalf; a creditor to shew his bill, and a debtor to pay his money. But God and man do here meet in one action upon a third, in whom, as it is the work of God to create grace, so it is his work by the hand of the ministry to apply a sign which should betoken, and his work to annex that Spirit which shall effect it. The action therefore is but one, God the author thereof, and man a co-partner, by him assigned to work for, with, and under him. God the giver of grace by the outward ministry of man, so far forth as he authorizeth man to apply the sacraments of grace in the soul, which he alone worketh, without either instrument or co-agent.

Whereas therefore with us the remissions of sin is ascrib'd unto God, as a thing which proceedeth from him only, and presently followeth upon the vertue of true repentance appearing in man; that which we attribute to the vertue, they do not only impute to the sacrament of repentance; but, having made repentance a sacrament, and thinking of sacraments as they do, they are enforced to make the ministry of the priest, and their absolution, a cause of that which the sole omnipotency of God worketh.

And yet, for my own part, I am not able well to conceive how their doctrine, that human absolution is really a cause out of which our deliverance from sin doth ensue, Conc. Trid. can cleave with the council of *Trent*, defining, *That contrition perfected with cha-* Seff. 14. c. 4. *rity, doth at all times it self reconcile offenders to God, before they come to receive* *actually the sacrament of penance.* How can it stand with those discourses of the Bellarm. de learned Rabbies, which grant, *That whosoever turneth unto God with his whole* Poenit. l. 2. c. *heart, hath immediately his sins taken away;* That if a man be truly converted, his 13. *pardon can neither be denied nor delayed;* it doth not stay for the priest's absolution, but presently followeth: *Surely if every contrite sinner, in whom there is charity, and* *a sincere conversion of heart, have remission of sins given him before he seek it at the* *priest's hands;* if reconciliation to God be a present, and immediate sequel upon every *such conversion or change: it must of necessity follow, seeing no man can be a true pe-* *nitent, or contrite, which doth not both love God, and sincerely abhor sin, that there-* *fore they all before absolution attain forgiveness;* whereunto notwithstanding absolu-* *tion is pretended a cause so necessary, that sin without it, except in some rare extra-* *ordinary case, cannot possibly be remitted.* Shall absolution be a cause producing and working that effect which is always brought forth without it, and had, before absolution be thought of? But when they which are thus before hand pardoned of God, shall come to be also assoiled by the priest, I would know what force his absolution hath in this case? Are they able to say here, that the priest doth remit any thing? Yet, when any of ours ascribeth the work of remission to God, and interpreteth the priest's sentence to be but a solemn declaration of that which God himself hath already performed, they scorn at it; they urge against it, that if this were true, our Saviour Christ should rather have said, *What is loosed in heaven, ye shall loose on earth,* than as he doth, *Whatsoever ye loose on earth, shall in heaven be loosed.* As if he were to learn of us how to place his words, and not we to crave rather of him a sound and right understanding, left to his dishonour and our own hurt we mis-expound them. It sufficeth, I think, both against their constructions to have proved that they ground an untruth on his speech; and, in behalf of our own, that his words, without any such transposition, do very well admit the sense we give them; which is, that he taketh to himself the lawful proceedings of authority in his name, and that the act of spiritual authority in Hæc expositio,this case, is by sentence to acquit or pronounce them free from sin whom they judge ego te absolvo,to be sincerely and truly penitent; which interpretation they themselves do acknow- id est, absolu-ledge, though not sufficient, yet very true. tum ostendo,
partim qui-
dem vera est, non tamen perfecta. Sacramenta quippe novæ legis non solum significant, sed efficiunt quod significant. Sent. sent.
l. 4. dist. 14. q. 1. art. 3.

Absolution, they say, declareth indeed; but this is not all, for it likewise maketh innocent; which addition being an untruth proved, our truth granted hath, I hope, sufficiency without it; and consequently our opinion therein neither to be challenged as untrue, nor as sufficient.

To

To rid themselves out of these briars, and to make remission of sins an effect of absolution, notwithstanding that which hitherto hath been said, they have two shifts. As first, that in many penitents there is but attrition of heart, which attrition they define to be grief proceeding from fear without love; and to these, they say, absolution doth give that contrition whereby men are really purged from sin. Secondly, that even where contrition or inward repentance doth cleanse without absolution; the reason why it cometh so to pass is, because such contrites intend and desire absolution, though they have it not. Which two things granted: the one, that absolution given maketh them contrite that are not; the other, even in them which are contrite, the cause why God remitteth sin is the purpose or desire they have to receive absolution; we are not to stand against a sequel so clear and manifest as this, that always remission of sin proceedeth from absolution either had or desired.

Attritio solum dicit dolorem propter poenas inferni; dum quis accedit attritus per gratiam sacramentalem, fit contritus. Sotò sent. 4. dist. 14. q. 1. art. 1.

Dum accedit vere contritus propter Deum, illa etiam contritio non est contritio, nisi quatenus prius natura informetur gratia per sacramentum in voto. Sotò sent. 4. dist. 14. q. 1. art. 1.

Legitima contritio votum sacramenti pro suo tempore debet inducere, atque adeò in virtute futuri sacramenti peccata remittit. Id. art. 3.

But should a reasonable man give credit to their bare conceit, and because their positions have driven them to imagine absolving of unsufficiently disposed penitents to be a real creating of further virtue in them, must all other men think it due? Let them cancel henceforward and blot out of all their books those old cautions touching necessity of wisdom, lest priests should inconsiderately absolve any man in whom there were not apparent tokens of true repentance; which to do, was, in saint Cyprian's judgment, *pestilent deceit and flattery, not only not avoidable, but hurtful to them that had transgrest: a frivolous, frustrate, and false peace, such as caused the unrighteous to trust to a lye, and destroyed them unto whom it promised safety.* What needeth observation whether penitents have worthiness and bring contrition, if the words of absolution do infuse contrition? Have they both us all this while in hand that contrition is a part of the matter of their sacraments; a condition or preparation of the mind towards grace to be received by absolution in the form of their sacraments? And must we now believe, that the form doth give the matter? That absolution bestoweth contrition, and that the words do make presently of *Saul, David; of Judas, Peter?* For what was the penitency of *Saul* and *Judas,* but plain attrition; horror of sin thro' fear of punishment, without any long sense, or taste of God's mercy?

Tunc sententia sacerdotis judicio Dei & totius coelestis curiae approbatur, & confirmatur, cum ita ex discretione procedit, ut reorum merita non contradicant. Sent. l. 4. d. 18.

Non est periculosum sacerdoti dicere, ego te absolvo, illis in quibus signa contritionis videt, quae sunt dolor de praeteritis, &. propositum de caetero, non peccandi; aliàs, absolvere non debet. Tho. Opusc. 22. Cypr. de lapsis.

Their other fiction, imputing remission of sin to desire of absolution from the priest, even in them which are truly contrite, is an evasion somewhat more witty, but no whit more possible for them to prove. Belief of the world and judgment to come, faith in the promises and sufferings of Christ for mankind, fear of his majesty, love of his mercy, grief for sin, hope for pardon, suit for grace, these we know to be elements of true contrition: Suppose that besides all this, God did also command that every penitent should seek his absolution at the priest's hands; where so many causes are concurring unto one effect, have they any reason to impute the whole effect unto one; any reason in the choice of that one, to pass by faith, fear, love, humility, hope, prayer, whatsoever else, and to enthronize above them all, a desire of absolution from the priest, as if in the whole work of man's repentance God did regard and accept nothing, but for and in consideration of this? Why do the *Tridentine* council impute it to charity, *that contrites are reconciled in God's sight before they receive the sacrament of penance;* if desired absolution be the true cause?

But let this pass how it will; seeing the question is not, what virtue God may accept in penitent sinners, but what Grace absolution actually given doth really bestow upon them.

If it were, as they would have it, that God regarding the humiliation of a contrite spirit, because there is joyned therewith a lowly desire of the sacrament of priestly absolution, pardoneth immediately and forgiveth all offences; doth this any thing help to prove that absolution received afterward from the priest, can more than declare him already pardoned which did desire it? To desire absolution, presupposing it commanded, is obedience: and obedience in that case is a branch of the virtue of repentance, which virtue being thereby made effectual to the taking away of sins

without

without the facrament of repentance, is not an argument that the facrament of abfolution hath here no efficacy, but the virtue of contrition worketh all? For how fhould any
effect enfue from caufes which actually are not? The facrament muft be applied wherefoever any grace doth proceed from it. *So that where it is but defired only, whatfoever*

A reatu mortis æternæ abfolvitur homo à Deo per contri-
tionem; manet autem reatus ad quandam pœnam temporalem;
& minifter ecclefiæ quicunque virtute clavium tollit reatum
cujufdam partis pœnæ illius. *Abul.* in defenf. p. 1. c. 7.

may follow upon God's acceptation of this defire, the
facrament, afterwards received, can be no caufe
thereof. Therefore the further we wade, the better
we fee it ftill appears, that the prieft doth never in

abfolution, no not fo much as by way of fervice and miniftry, really either forgive them,
take away the uncleannefs, or remove the punifhment of fin; but if the party penitent
come contrite, he hath, by their own grant, abfolution before abfolution; if not contrite,
although the prieft fhould feem a thoufand times to abfolve him, all were in vain. For
which caufe the antients and better fort of their fchool divines, *Abulenfis, Alexander
Hales,* and *Bonaventure,* afcribe *the real abolition of fin, and eternal punifhment,* to

Signum hujus
facramenti
eit caufa effe-
ctiva gratiæ
five remiffio-
nis peccato-
rum, non fim-
pliciter, ficut
ipfa prima
pœnitentia,
fed fecundum
quid; quia eft

*the meer pardon of almighty God, without dependency upon the prieft's abfolution, as a
caufe to effect the fame.* His abfolution hath in their doctrine certain other effects fpecified, but this denied. Wherefore having hitherto fpoken of the virtue of repentance
required; of the difcipline of repentance which Chrift did eftablifh; and of the facrament of repentance invented fithence, againft the pretended force of human abfolution in
facramental penitency; *let it fuffice thus far to have fhewed how God alone doth truly
give, the virtue of repentance alone procure, and private minifterial abfolution but declare remiffion of fins.*

caufa efficaciæ gratiæ quâ fit remiffio peccati, quantum ad aliquem effectum in pœnitente, ad minus quantum ad remiffionem fequelæ
ipfius peccati, fcilicet pœnæ, *Alex.* p. 4. q. 14. memb. 2. Poteftas clavium propriè loquendo non fe extendit fupra culpam; ad illud
quod objicitur. To. 22. Quorum remiferitis peccata: dicendum, quod vel illud de remiffione dicitur quantum ad offenfionem, vel folum
quantum ad pœnam, *Bon.* fent. l. 1. d. 18. q. 1. Ab æterna pœna nullo modo folvit facerdos, fed à purgatorio; neque hoc per fe, fed per
accidens, quod cum in pœnitente, virtute clavium, minuitur debitum pœnæ temporalis, non ità acriter punietur in purgatorio, ficut
fi non effet abfolutus. Sent. l. 4. d. 18. q. 2.

Now the laft and fometimes hardeft to be fatisfied by repentance, are our minds; and
our minds we have then fatisfied, when the confcience is of guilty become clear. For,
as long as we are in our felves privy to our moft heinous crimes, but without fenfe of
God's mercy and grace towards us, unlefs the heart be either brutifh for want of knowledge, or altogether hardned by wilful atheifm; the remorfe of fin is in it, as the deadly fting of the ferpent. Which point fince very infidels and heathens have obferved in
the nature of fin, (for the difeafe they felt, tho' they knew no remedy to help it) we are
not rafhly to defpife thofe fentences which are the teftimonies of their experience touching
this point. They knew that the eye of a man's own confcience is more to be feared by
evil doers than the prefence of a thoufand witneffes, in as much as the mouths of other
accufers are many ways ftopt, the ears of the accufed not always fubject to glowing
with contumely and exprobation; whereas a guilty mind being forced to be ftill both a
martyr and a tyrant in it felf, muft of neceffity endure perpetual anguifh and grief; for,
as the body is rent with ftripes, fo the mind with guiltinefs of cruelty, luft, and wicked
refolutions. Which furies brought the emperor *Tiberius* fometimes into fuch perplexity,
that writing to the fenate, his wonted art of diffimulation failed him utterly in this cafe;
and whereas it had been ever his peculiar delight fo to fpeak that no man might be able
to found his meaning, he had not the power to conceal what he felt thro' the fecret fcourge
of an evil confcience, tho' no neceffity did now enforce him to difclofe the fame. *What
to write, or how to write, at this prefent, if I know* (faith *Tiberius*) *let the Gods and
Goddeffes, who thus continually eat me, only be worfe to me than they are.* It was not
his imperial dignity and power that could provide a way to protect him againft himfelf; the
fears and fufpicions which improbity had bred, being ftrengthened by every occafion, and
thofe virtues clean banifhed which are the only foundation of found tranquillity of mind.
For which caufe it hath been truly faid, and agreeably with all men's experience, that if the
virtuous did excel in no other privilege, yet far happier they are than the contrary fort of
men, for that their hopes be always better.

Neither are we to marvel, that thefe things, known unto all, do ftay fo few from being authors of their own woe.

For we fee by the antient example of *Jofeph's* unkind brethren, how it cometh to remembrance eafily when crimes are once paft, what the difference is of good from evil, and
of right from wrong: but fuch confiderations, when they fhould have prevented fin, were
over-match'd by inordinate defires. Are we not bound then with all thankfulnefs to acknowledge his infinite goodnefs and mercy, which hath revealed unto us the way how to
rid our felves of thefe mazes; the way how to fhake off that yoke, which no flefh is able
to bear; the way how to change moft grifly horror into a comfortable apprehenfion of heavenly joy?   Whereunto

Whereunto there are many which labour with so much the greater difficulty, because imbecillity of mind doth not suffer them to censure rightly their own doings. Some fearful left the enormity of their crimes be so unpardonable that no repentance can do them good; some left the imperfection of their repentance make it uneffectual to the taking away of sin. The one drive all things to this issue, whether they be not men that have sinned against the holy Ghost; the other to this, what repentance is sufficient to clear sinners, and to assure them that they are delivered.

Such as by error charge themselves of unpardonable sin must think, it may be, they deem that unpardonable, which is not.

Our Saviour speaketh indeed of blasphemy which shall never be forgiven: but have they any sure and infallible knowledge what that blasphemy is? If not, why are they unjust and cruel to their own souls, imagining certainty of guiltiness in a crime concerning the very nature whereof they are uncertain? For mine own part, altho' where this blasphemy is mention'd, the cause why our Saviour spake thereof, was the Pharisees blasphemy, which was not afraid to say, *he had an unclean spirit, and did cast out spirits by the power of Beelze-* *Mat. 11. 31.* *bub*; nevertheless I dare not precisely deny, but that even the Pharisees themselves might *Mar. 3. 30.* have repented and been forgiven, and that our Lord Jesus Christ peradventure might but take occasion at their blasphemy, which, as yet, was pardonable, to tell them further of an unpardonable blasphemy, whereinto he foresaw that the Jews would fall. For it is plain, that many thousands, at the first, professing christian religion, became afterwards wilful apostates, moved with no other cause of revolt, but meer indignation that the Gentiles should enjoy the benefit of the gospel as much as they, and yet not be burthened with the yoke of *Moses* his law.

The apostles by preaching had won them to Christ, in whose name they embraced with great alacrity the full remission of their former sins and iniquities; they received by the imposition of the apostles hands *that grace and power of the holy Ghost* whereby they cured *Act. 2. 38.* diseases, prophesied, spake with tongues; and yet in the end, after all this, they fell utterly away, renounced the mysteries of christian faith, blasphemed in their formal abjurations that most glorious and blessed Spirit, the gifts whereof themselves had possest; and by this means sunk their souls in the gulf of that unpardonable sin; whereof, as our Lord JESUS CHRIST had told them before-hand, so the apostle at the first appearance of such their revolt, putteth them in mind again, that falling now to their former blasphemies, their salvation was irrecoverably gone. It was for them in this case impossible to be *Heb. 6. 6.* renewed by any repentance; because they were now in the state of Satan and his angels; the judge of quick and dead had passed his irrevocable sentence against them.

So great difference there is between infidels unconverted, and backsliders in this manner fallen away, that always we have hope to reclaim the one which only hate whom they never knew; but to the other which know and blaspheme, to them that with more than infernal malice accurse both the seen brightness of glory which is in him, and in themselves the tasted goodness of divine grace, as those execrable miscreants did, who first received in extraordinary miraculous manner, and then in outrageous sort blasphemed the *holy Ghost*, abusing *both it and the whole religion*, which God by it did confirm and mag-*Heb. 10. 26.* nify; to such as wilfully thus sin, after so great light of the truth, and gifts of the Spirit, there remaineth justly no fruit or benefit to be expected by Christ's sacrifice.

For all other offenders, without exception or stint, whether they be strangers that seek access, or followers that will make return unto God; upon the tender of their repentance, the grant of his grace standeth everlastingly signed with his blood in the book of eternal life. That which in this case over-terrifieth fearful souls is, a misconceit whereby they imagine every act which they do, knowing that they do amiss, and every wilful breach or transgression of God's law to be meer sin against the holy Ghost: forgetting that the law of *Moses* it self ordain'd sacrifices of expiation, as well for faults presumptuously committed, as things wherein men offend by error.

Now, there are on the contrary sides others, who, doubting not of God's mercy towards all that perfectly repent, remain notwithstanding scrupulous and troubled with continual fear, left defects in their own repentance be a bar against them.

These cast themselves into very great, and peradventure needless agonies thro' mis-con-*Jer 6. 26.* struction of things spoken about proportioning our griefs to our sins, for which they never *Mic. 1. 8. 9.* think they have wept and mourned enough; yea, if they have not always a stream of tears *Lament. 2. 18.* at command, they take it for a heart congealed and hardned in sin; when to keep the *Quam magna* wound of contrition bleeding, they unfold the circumstances of their transgressions, and *deliquimus, tam granditer* endeavour to leave nothing which may be heavy against themselves. *defleamus.* *Alto vulneri*

diligens & longa medicina non desit; poenitentia crimine minor non sit. *Cypr.* de lapsis. Non levi agendum est contritione, ut debita illa redimantur, quibus mors aeterna debetur; nec transitoria opus est satisfactione pro malis illis, propter quae paratus est ignis aeternus. *Eusеb.* Emissenus, vel potius salv. t. 106.   I.   Yet,

Yet, do what they can, they are still fearful, lest herein also they do not that which they ought and might. Come to prayer, their coldness taketh all heart and courage from them; with fasting, albeit their flesh should be withered, and their blood clean dried up, would they ever the less object, what is this to *David's* humiliation, whereNotwithstanding there was not any thing more than necessary? In works of charity and alms-deed; it is not all the world can persuade them they did ever reach the poor bounty of the widows two mites, or by many millions of leagues come near to the mark which *Cornelius* touched; so far they are off from the proud surmise of any penitential supererogation in miserable wretched worms of the earth.

Psal. 6. 6.
Matth. 12, 42.
Acts 10. 31.

Notwithstanding, for as much as they wrong themselves with over rigorous and extreme exactions, by means whereof they fall sometimes into such perplexities as can hardly be allayed; it hath therefore pleased almighty God, in tender commiseration over these imbecillities of Men, to ordain for their spiritual and ghostly comfort consecrated persons, which by sentence of power and authority given from above, may, as it were, out of his very mouth ascertain timorous and doubtful minds in their own particular; ease them of all their scrupulosities; leave them settled in peace; and satisfied touching the mercy of God towards them. To use the benefit of this help for the better satisfaction in such cases is so natural, that it can be forbidden no man; but yet not so necessary, that all men should be in case to need it.

They are, of the two, the happier therefore that can content and satisfy themselves, by judging discreetly what they perform, and soundly what God doth require of them. For having, that which is most material, the substance of penitency rightly bred; touching signs and tokens thereof, we may affirm that they do boldly, which imagine for every offence a certain proportionable degree in the passions and griefs of mind, whereunto whosoever aspireth not, repenteth in vain.

That to frustrate men's confession and considerations of sin, except every circumstance which may aggravate the same, be unript and laid in the balance, is a merciless extremity; although it be true, that as near as we can such wounds must be searched to the very bottom. Last of all, to set down the like stint, and to shut up the doors of mercy against penitents which come short thereof in the devotion of their prayers; in the continuance of their fasts; in the largeness and bounty of their alms, or in the course of any other such like duties; is more than God himself hath thought meet; and consequently more than mortal men should presume to do.

Jer. 20. 31.
Joel 2. 12.

That which God doth chiefly respect in men's penitency is their hearts. *The heart is it which maketh repentance sincere,* sincerity that which findeth favour in God's sight, and the favour of God that which supplieth by gracious acceptation whatsoever may seem defective in the faithful, hearty, and true officers of his servants.

Chrys. de repar. lapf. lib. ad Theodor.
Deposit. diß. 3. c. Talis.

Take it (saith *Chrysostom*) upon my credit, *such is God's merciful inclination towards men, that repentance offered with a single and sincere mind he never refuseth;* no, *not although we come to the very top of iniquity.* If there be a will and desire to return, he receiveth, embraceth, and omitteth nothing which may restore us to former happiness; yea, that which is above all the rest, albeit we cannot in the duty of satisfying him, attain what we ought, and would, but come far behind our mark, he taketh nevertheless in good worth that little which we do; be it never so mean, we lose not our labour therein.

Aug. in Psal. 138.

The least and lowest step of repentance in saint *Chrysostom's* judgment serveth and setteth us above them that perish in their sin: I therefore will end with saint *Augustine's* conclusion: *Lord, in thy book and volume of life all shall be written, as well the least of thy saints, as the chiefest.* Let not therefore the unperfect fear: let them only proceed and go forward.

2

O F

OF THE

L A W S

O F

Ecclesiastical Polity.

B O O K VII.

Their sixth Assertion, That there ought not to be in the Church,
Bishops endued with such Authority and Honour as ours are.

The Matter contained in this seventh Book.

15. Concerning

15. *Concerning the civil power and authority which our bishops have.*
16. *The arguments answered, whereby they would prove, that the law of God, and the judgment of the best in all ages condemneth the ruling superiority of one minister over another.*
17. *The second malicious thing wherein the state of bishops suffereth obloquy, is their honour.*
18. *What good doth publickly grow from the prelacy.*
19. *What kind of honour be due unto bishops.*
20. *Honour in title, place, ornament, attendance, and privilege.*
21. *Honour by endowments of lands and livings.*
22. *That of ecclesiastical goods, and consequently of the lands and livings which bishops enjoy, the propriety belongs unto God alone.*
23. *That ecclesiastical persons are receivers of God's rents, and that the honour of prelates is to be thereof his chief receivers, not without liberty from him granted of converting the same unto their own use, even in large manner.*
24. *That for their unworthiness to deprive both them and their successors of such goods, and to convey the same unto men of secular callings, is now extreme sacrilegious injustice.*

The state of bishops although some time oppugned, and that by such as therein would most seem to please God, yet by his providence upheld hitherto, whose glory it is to maintain that, whereof himself is the author.
I Have heard that a famous kingdom in the world being solicited to reform such disorders as all men saw the church exceedingly burthened with, when of each degree great multitudes thereunto inclined, and the number of them did every day so encrease that this intended work was likely to take no other effect than all good men did wish and labour for; a principal actor herein (for zeal and boldness of spirit) thought it good to shew them betimes what it was which must be effected, or else that there could be no work of perfect reformation accomplished. To this purpose, in a solemn sermon, and in a great assembly, he described unto them the present quality of their publick estate, by the parable of a tree, huge, and goodly to look upon, but without that fruit which it should and might bring forth; affirming, that the only way of redress was a full and perfect establishment of Christ's discipline (for so their manner is to entitle a thing hammered out upon the forge of their own invention) and that to make way of entrance for it, there must be three great limbs cut off from the body of that stately tree of the kingdom. Those three limbs, were three sorts of men: nobles, whose high estate would make them otherwise disdain to put their necks under that yoke: lawyers, whose courts being not pulled down, the new church consistories were not like to flourish: finally, prelates, whose ancient dignity, and the simplicity of their intended church-discipline, could not possibly stand together. The proposition of which device being plausible to active spirits, restless through desire of innovation, whom commonly nothing doth more offend than a change which goeth fearfully on by slow and suspicious paces; the heavier and more experienc'd sort began presently thereat to pluck back their feet again, and exceedingly to fear the stratagem of reformation for ever after. Whereupon ensued those extreme conflicts of the one part with the other; which continuing and encreasing to this very day, have now made the state of that flourishing kingdom even such, as whereunto we may most fitly apply those words of the prophet *Jeremiah, Thy breach is great like the sea, who can heal thee?* Whether this were done in truth, according to the constant affirmation of some avouching the same, I take not upon me to examine; that which I note therein is, how with us that policy hath been corrected. For to the authors of pretended reformation with us, it hath not seem'd expedient to offer the edge of the ax unto all three boughs at once, but rather to single them, and strike at the weakest first, making shew that the lop of that one shall draw the more abundance of sap to the other two, that they may thereby the better prosper. All prosperity, felicity and peace, we wish multiplied on each estate, as far as their own hearts desire is; but let men know that there is a God, whose eye beholdeth them in all their ways; a God, the usual and ordinary course of whose justice, is to return upon the head of malice the same devices which it contriveth against others. The foul practices which have been used for the overthrow of bishops, may perhaps wax bold in process of time to give the like assault even there, from whence at this present they are most seconded. Nor let it over-dismay them who suffer such things at the hands of this most unkind world, to see that heavenly estate and dignity thus conculcated, in regard whereof so many their predecessors were no less esteemed than if they had not been men, but angels amongst men. With former bishops it was as with *Job* in

the

the days of that prosperity which at large he deſcribeth, ſaying, *Unto me men gave ear, they waited and held their tongue at my counſel, after my words they replied not, I appointed out their way and did ſit as chief, I dwelt as it had been a king in an army.* At this day, the caſe is otherwiſe with them; and yet no otherwiſe than with the ſelf ſame *Job* at what time the alteration of his eſtate wreſted theſe contrary ſpeeches from him, *But now they that are younger than I mock at me, the children of fools, and off-ſpring of ſlaves, creatures more baſe than the earth they tread on; ſuch as if they did ſhew their heads, young and old would ſhout at them and chaſe them through the ſtreet with a cry, their ſong I am, I am a theme for them to talk on.* An injury leſs grievous if it were not offered by them whom Satan hath thro' his fraud and ſubtilty ſo far beguiled as to make them imagine herein they do unto God a part of moſt faithful ſervice. Whereas the Lord in truth, whom they ſerve herein is, as St. *Cyprian* telleth them, like not Chriſt (for he it is that doth appoint and protect biſhops) but rather Chriſt's adverſary and enemy of his church. *Cyp. l. 1. ep. 3.* A thouſand five hundred years and upward the church of Chriſt hath now continued under the ſacred regiment of biſhops. Neither for ſo long hath chriſtianity been ever planted in any kingdom throughout the world but with this kind of government alone; which to have been ordained of God, I am from mine own part even as reſolutely perſuaded, as that any other kind of government in the world whatſoever is of God. In this realm of *England*, before *Normans*, yea before *Saxons*, there being chriſtians, the chief paſtors of their ſouls were biſhops. This order from about the firſt eſtabliſhment of chriſtian religion, which was publickly begun through the virtuous diſpoſition of king *Lucius*, not fully two hundred years after Chriſt, continued till the coming in of the *Saxons*; by whom paganiſm being every where elſe replanted, only one part of the iſland, whereinto the antient, natural inhabitants the *Britains* were driven, retained conſtantly the faith of Chriſt; together with the ſame form of ſpiritual regiment, which their fathers had before received. Wherefore in the hiſtories of the church we find very antient mention made of our own biſhops. At the council of *Ariminum*, about the year 359, *Britain* had three of her biſhops preſent. At the arrival of *Auguſtine* the *Sulpit. Sever. l. 2.* monk, whom *Gregory* ſent hither to reclaim the *Saxons* from gentility about ſix hundred years after Chriſt, the *Britains* he found obſervers ſtill of the ſelf ſame govern- *Bæda eccl. hiſt. l. 2. c. 2.* ment by biſhops over the reſt of the clergy; under this form chriſtianity took root again, where it had been exiled. Under the ſelf ſame form it remained till the days of the [a] *Norman* conqueror. By him and his ſucceſſors thereunto [b] ſworn, it hath from that time till now, by the ſpace of five hundred years more, been upheld. O [a] *An. 1066.* nation utterly without knowledge, without ſenſe! We are not through error of mind [b] *Alfred. Ebo. racenſis archi- epiſcopus Galielmum cognomento Nathum ſpirantem adhuc minarum & cædis in populum, mitem reddidit; & religioſis pro conſervanda repub. tuen- daque eccleſi- aſt. diſc. ſacramento aſtringi- tur. Nubrig. l. 1. c. 1.* deceived, but ſome wicked thing hath undoubtedly bewitched us, if we forſake that government, the uſe whereof univerſal experience hath for ſo many years approved, and betake our ſelves unto a regiment neither appointed of God himſelf, as they who favour it pretend, nor till yeſterday ever heard of among men. By the *Jews*, *Feſtus* was much complained of, as being a governor marvellous corrupt, and almoſt intolerable: ſuch notwithſtanding were they who came after him, that men which thought the publick condition moſt afflicted under *Feſtus*, began to wiſh they had him again, and to eſteem him a ruler commendable. Great things are hoped for at the hands of theſe new preſidents, whom reformation would bring in: notwithſtanding the time may come, when biſhops, whoſe regiment doth now ſeem a yoke ſo heavy to bear, will be longed for again, even by them that are the readieſt to have it taken off their necks. But in the hands of divine Providence we leave the ordering of all ſuch events; and come now to the queſtion it ſelf which is raiſed concerning biſhops. For the better underſtanding whereof, we muſt beforehand ſet down what is meant, when in this queſtion we name a biſhop.

II. For whatſoever we bring from antiquity by way of defence in this cauſe of biſhops, *What a biſhop it is caſt off as impertinent matter; all is wiped away with an odd kind of ſhifting anſwer; is, what his That the biſhops which now are, be not like unto them which were.* We therefore beſeech *name doth im-* all indifferent judges to weigh ſincerely with themſelves how the caſe doth ſtand. If it *doth belong to* ſhould be at this day a controverſy whether kingly regiment were lawful or no; peradven- *his office as he* ture in defence thereof, the long continuance which it hath had ſithence the firſt begin- *is a biſhop.* ning might be alledged; mention perhaps might be made what kings there were of old even in *Abraham's* time, what ſovereign princes both before and after. Suppoſe that herein ſome man purpoſely bending his wit againſt ſovereignty, ſhould think to elude all ſuch allegations by making ample diſcovery through a number of particularities; wherein the kings that are, do differ from thoſe that have been, and ſhould therefore in the end conclude, that ſuch antient examples are no convenient proofs of that royalty which is now in ufe. Surely for decifion of truth in this cafe there were no remedy, but only to fhew the nature of fovereignty ; to fever it from accidental properties ; to make it clear that antient and prefent regality are one and the fame in fubftance, how great odds foever otherwife may feem to be between them. In like manner, whereas a queftion of late hath grown, whether ecclefiaftical regiment by bifhops be lawful in the church of Chrift or no: in which queftion, they that hold the negative, being preffed with that generally received order, accordingly whereunto the moft renowned lights of the chriftian world have governed the fame in every age as bifhops ; feeing their manner is to reply, that fuch bifhops as thofe antient were, ours are not ; there is no remedy but to fhew, that to be a bifhop is now the felf fame thing which it hath been ; that one definition agreeth fully and truly as well to thofe elder, as to thefe latter Bifhops. Sundry diffimilitudes we grant there are, which notwithftanding are not fuch that they caufe any equivocation in the name, whereby we fhould think a bifhop in thofe times to have had a clean other definition than doth rightly agree unto bifhops as they are now. Many things there are in the ftate of bifhops, which the times have changed ; many a parfonage at this day is larger than fome antient bifhopricks were ; many an antient bifhop poorer than at this day fundry under them in degree. The fimple hereupon, lacking judgment and knowledge to difcern between the nature of things which changeth not, and thefe outward variable accidents, are made believe that a bifhop heretofore and now are things in their very nature fo diftinct that they cannot be judged the fame. Yet to men that have any part of fkill, what more evident and plain in bifhops, than that augmentation or diminution in their precincts, allowances, privileges, and fuch like, do make a difference indeed ; but no effential difference between one bifhop and another ? As for thofe things in regard whereof we ufe properly to term them bifhops ; thofe things whereby they effentially differ from other paftors ; thofe things which the natural definition of a bifhop muft contain ; what one of them is there more or lefs appliable unto bifhops now than of old ? The name bifhop hath been borrowed from the [a] *Grecians,* with whom it fignifieth, one which hath principal charge to guide and overfee others. The fame word in ecclefiaftical writings being applied unto church governors, at the firft unto [b] all and not unto the chiefeft only, grew in fhort time peculiar and proper to fignify fuch epifcopal authority alone, as the chiefeft governors exercifed over the reft ; for with all names this is ufual, that in as much as they are not given till the things whereunto they are given, have been fometime firft obferved ; therefore generally, [c] things are antienter than the names whereby they are called.

[a] Οἱ παρ᾽ Ἀθηναίοις εἰς τὰς ἀπαύλους πόλεις ἐπισπουδάζοντες τὰ καθ᾽ ἑαυτοὺς πραγματικὸν Ἐπισκόπους καὶ φύλακας ἐκαλοῦντο ὥς οἱ Ἀθήνας ἀργυρολόγας λέγει. Suid. Καλῆφιν τε ἐφ᾽ ἑκάστοις τῶν πλάγιος ἀρχθέντα ἐπίσκοπόν τε καὶ ἄρχοντα ἢ ἰδίας μοίρας. *Dionyf.* Halicar. de Numa Pompilio, antiq. lib. 2. Vult me *Pompeius* effe quem tota hæc campania & maritima ora habeat Ἐπίσκοπον, ad quem delectus & negotii fumma referatur. *Cic.* ad artic. lib. 7. epift. 11. [b] *Act.* 20. *Phil.* 1. 1. [c] And God brought them unto *Adam,* that *Adam* might fee or confider what name it was meet he fhould give unto them, *Gen.* 2. 19.

Again, fith the firft things that grow into general obfervation, and do thereby give men occafion to find name for them, are thofe which being in many fubjects are thereby the eafier, the oftener, and the more univerfally noted ; it followeth, that names impofed to fignify common qualities of operations are antienter, than is the reftraint of thofe names, to note an excellency of fuch qualities and operations in fome one or few amongft others. For example, the name difciple being invented to fignify generally a learner, it cannot chufe but in that fignification be more antient than when it fignifies, as it were

So alfo the name defcon a minifter appropriated to ufe of minifters. by a kind of appropriation, thofe learners who being taught of Chrift, were in that refpect termed difciples by an excellency. The like is to be feen in the name apoftle, the ufe whereof to fignify a meffenger, muft needs be more antient than that ufe which reftraineth it unto meffengers fent concerning evangelical affairs ; yea this ufe more antient than that whereby the fame word is yet reftrained farther to fignify only thofe whom our Saviour himfelf immediately did fend. After the fame manner the title or name of a bifhop having been ufed of old to fignify both an ecclefiaftical overfeer in general, and more particularly alfo a principal ecclefiaftical overfeer ; it followeth, that this latter reftrained fignification is not fo antient as the former, being more common. Yet becaufe

The name likewife of a minifter was common to divers degrees, which now is peculiarly amongft our felves given only to paftors and not as antiently to deacons alfo. the things themfelves are always antienter than their names ; therefore that thing which the reftrained ufe of the word doth import, is likewife antienter than the reftraint of the word is ; and confequently that power of chief ecclefiaftical overfeers, which the term of a bifhop doth import, was before the reftrained ufe of the name which doth import it. Wherefore a lame and impotent kind of reafoning it is, when men go about to prove that in the apoftles times there was no fuch thing as the reftrained name of a bifhop doth now fignify ; becaufe in their writings there is found no reftraint of that name, but only a general ufe whereby it reacheth unto all fpiritual governors and overfeers.

✠

                                              But

But to let go the name, and come to the very nature of that thing which is thereby signified. In all kinds of regiment, whether ecclesiastical or civil, as there are sundry operations publick, so likewise great inequality there is in the same operations, some being of principal respect, and therefore not fit to be dealt in by every one to whom publick actions, and those of good importance, are notwithstanding well and fitly enough committed. From hence have grown those different degrees of magistrates or publick persons, even ecclesiastical as well as civil. Amongst ecclesiastical persons therefore bishops being chief ones, a bishop's function must be defined by that wherein his chiefty consisteth. A bishop is a minister of God, unto whom with permanent continuance, there is given not only power of administring the word and sacraments; which power other presbyters have; but also a further power to ordain ecclesiastical persons, and a power of chiefty in government over presbyters as well as lay-men, a power to be by way of jurisdiction a pastor even to pastors themselves. So that this office, as he is a presbyter or pastor, consisteth in those things which are common unto him with other pastors, as in ministring the word and sacraments; but those things incident unto his office, which do properly make him a bishop, cannot be common unto him with other pastors. Now even as pastors, so likewise bishops being principal pastors are either at large or else with restraint. At large, when the subject of their regiment is indefinite, and not tied to any certain place. Bishops with restraint, are they whose regiment over the church is contained within some definite, local compass, beyond which compass their jurisdiction reacheth not. Such therefore we always mean when we speak of that regiment by bishops which we hold a thing most lawful, divine, and holy, in the church of Christ.

III. In our present regiment by bishops two things are complain'd of: the one their great authority, and the other their great honour. Touching the authority of our bishops, the first thing which therein displeaseth their adversaries, is the superiority which bishops have over other ministers. They which cannot brook the superiority which bishops have, do notwithstanding themselves admit that some kind of difference and inequality there may be lawfully amongst ministers. Inequality as touching gifts and graces they grant, because this is so plain that no mist in the world can be cast before men's eyes so thick, but that they must needs discern thorough it, that one minister of the gospel may be more learned, holier and wiser; better able to instruct, more apt to rule and guide them than another: unless thus much were confest, those men should lose their fame and glory whom they themselves do entitle the lights and grand worthies of this present age. Again, a priority of order they deny not, but that there may be; yea such a priority as maketh one man amongst many a principal actor in those things whereunto sundry of them must necessarily concur, so that the same be admitted only during the time of such actions and no longer; that is to say just so much superiority, and neither more nor less may be liked of, than it hath pleased them in their own kind of regiment to set down. The inequality which they complain of is, *That one minister of the word and sacraments should have a permanent superiority above another, or in any sort a superiority of power mandatory, judicial, and coercive over other ministers.* By us, on the contrary side, *inequality, even such inequality as unto bishops being ministers of the word and sacraments granteth a superiority permanent above ministers, yea a permanent superiority of power mandatory, judicial, and coercive over them,* is maintained a thing allowable, lawful and good. For, superiority of power may be either above them or upon them, in regard of whom it is termed superiority. One pastor hath superiority of power above another, when either some are authorised to do things worthier than are permitted unto all; some are preferred to be principal agents, the rest agents with dependency and subordination. The former of these two kinds of superiority is such as the high-priest had above other priests of the law, in being appointed to enter once a year the holy place, which the rest of the priests might not do. The latter superiority, such as presidents have in those actions which are done by others with them, they nevertheless being principal and chief therein. One pastor hath superiority of power, not only above, but upon another, when some are subject unto others commandment and judicial controlment by virtue of publick jurisdiction. Superiority in this last kind is utterly denied to be allowable; in the rest it is only denied that the lasting continuance and settled permanency thereof is lawful. So that if we prove at all the lawfulness of superiority in this last kind, where the same is simply denied, and of permanent superiority in the rest where some kind of superiority is granted, but with restraint to the term and continuance of certain actions, with which the same must, as they say, expire and cease; if we can shew these two things maintainable, we bear up sufficiently that which the adverse party endeavoureth to overthrow. Our desire therefore is, that this issue may be strictly observed, and those things accordingly judged of, which we are to alledge. This

[margin: In bishops two things traduced; of which two the one their authority; and in it, the first thing condemned, their superiority over other ministers. What kind of superiority in ministers it is which the one part holdeth, and the other denieth lawful.]

we

we boldly therefore fet down as a moft infallible truth, *That the church of Chrift is at this day lawfully, and fo hath been fithence the firft beginning, governed by bifhops, having permanent fuperiority, and ruling power over other minifters of the word and facraments.*

For the plainer explication whereof, let us briefly declare firft the birth and original of the fame power, whence, and by what occafion it grew. Secondly, what manner of power antiquity doth witnefs bifhops to have had more than presbyters which were no bifhops. Thirdly, after what fort bifhops together with presbyters have ufed to govern the churches under them, according to the like teftimonial evidence of antiquity. Fourthly, how far the fame episcopal power hath ufually extended; unto what number of persons it hath reached; what bounds and limits of place it hath had. This done, we may afterwards defcend unto thofe by whom the fame either hath been heretofore, or is at this prefent hour gainfaid.

From whence it hath grown that the church is govern'd by bifhops.
Meminiffe di- accori debent, quoufam apo- ftolos, id eft e- pifcopos & præpofitos Dominus ele- git. Cypr. l. 3. ep. 9.
IV. The firft bifhops in the church of Chrift were his bleffed apoftles. For the office whereunto *Matthias* was chofen, the facred hiftory doth term 'Ἐπισκοπήν an episcopal office. Which being fpoken exprefly of one, agreeth no lefs unto them all than unto him. For which caufe St. *Cyprian* fpeaking generally of them all doth call them bifhops. They which were termed apoftles, as being fent of Chrift to publifh his gofpel throughout the world, and were named likewife bifhops, in that the care of government was also commit- ted unto them, did no lefs perform the offices of their episcopal authority by governing, than of their apoftolical by teaching. The word 'Ἐπισκοπὴ expreffing that part of their of- fice which did confift in regiment, proveth not (I grant) their chiefty in regiment over others, becaufe as then that name was common unto the function of their inferiors, and not peculiar unto theirs. But the hiftory of their actions fheweth plainly enough how the thing it felf which that name appropriated importeth, that is to fay, even fuch fpiri- tual chiefty as we have already defined to be properly episcopal was in the holy apoftles of Chrift. Bifhops therefore they were at large. But was it lawful for any of them to be a bifhop with reftraint? True it is their charge was indefinite, yet fo, that in cafe they did all, whether feverally or jointly difcharge the office of proclaiming every where the

Rom.1.14,15 1 Cor. 9. 16. Joh.11.15,16.
gofpel, and of guiding the church of Chrift, none of them cafting off his part in their burthen which was laid upon them, there doth appear no impediment but that they having received their common charge indefinitely, might in the execution thereof not- withftanding reftrain themfelves, or at leaftwife be reftrained by the after commandment of the Spirit, without contradiction or repugnancy unto that charge more indefinite and general before given them: efpecially if it feem'd at any time requifite, and for the greater good of the church, that they fhould in fuch fort take themfelves unto fome fpecial part of the flock of Jefus Chrift, guiding the fame in feveral as bifhops. For firft, notwithftand-

Gal. 2. 8.
ing our Saviour's commandment unto them all, to go and preach unto all nations; yet fome reftraint we fee there was made, when by agreement between *Paul* and *Peter*, moved with thofe effects of their labours which the providence of God brought forth; the one betook himfelf unto the *Gentiles*; the other unto the *Jews*, for the exercife of that office of every where preaching. A further reftraint of their apoftolical labours as yet there was alfo made, when they divided themfelves into feveral parts of the world;

a Him Eufebius governor of the churches in Afia. lib. 3. hift. ecclef. c. 16. Tertullian calleth the fame churches St. John's fofter daugh- ters. lib. 3. adverf. Mar- cion. b Jacobus qui appellatur frater Domini cognomento Juftus poft paffionem Do- mini ftatim ab apoftolis, Hie- rofolymorum epifcopus ordinatus eft. Hieron.defcrip. ecclef. Eodem
* *John* for his charge taking *Afia*, and fo the refidue, other quarters to labour in. If never- thelefs it feem very hard that we fhould admit a reftraint fo particular, as after that general charge received to make any apoftle notwithftanding the bifhop of fome one church; what think we of the bifhop of *Jerufalem*, b *James*, whofe confecration unto that mother fee of the world, becaufe it was not meet that it fhould at any time be left void of fome apoftle, doth feem to have been the very caufe of St. *Paul's* miraculous vocation to make up the c number of the twelve again, for the gathering of nations abroad, even as the d martyrdom of the other *James*, the reafon why *Barnabas* in his ftead was called. Fi- nally, apoftles whether they did fettle in any one certain place, as *James*, or elfe did otherwife as the apoftle *Paul*; episcopal authority either at large or with reftraint they had and exercifed. Their episcopal power they fometimes gave unto others to exercife as agents only in their ftead, and as it were by commiffion from them. Thus e *Titus*, and thus *Timothy* at the firft, tho' f afterwards indued with apoftolical power of their own. For in procefs of time the apoftles gave episcopal authority, and that to continue always with them which had it. g *We are able to number up them,* faith Irenæus, *who by the apoftles were made bifhops.* In *Rome* he affirmeth that the apoftles themfelves made *Linus* the firft bifhop. Again of *Polycarp* he faith likewife, that the apoftles made him bifhop of the church of *Smyrna*. Of *Antioch* they made *Evodius* bifhop, as h *Ignatius* witneffeth; exhorting that

tempore Jacobum primum fedem episcopalem ecclefiæ quæ eft Hierofolymis obtinuiffe memoriæ traditur. Eufeb. hift. ecclefiaft. lib. 2. cap. 1. The fame feemeth to be intimated Aûs 15. 13. and Aûs 21. 18. c Acts 12.1. d Acts 13. 2. e Tit. 1. 5. f This appeareth by thofe fubfcriptions which are fet after the epiftle to Titus, and the fecond to Timothy, and by Eufeb. ecclef. hift. l. 3. c. 4. g Iren. l. 3 c. 3. h In ep. ad Antioch.

church

church to tread in his holy steps, and to follow his virtuous example. The apostles therefore were the first which had such authority, and all others who have it after them in orderly sort are their lawful successors, whether they succeed in any particular church, where before them some apostle hath been seated, as *Simon* succeeded *James* in *Jerusalem*; or else
be otherwise endued with the same kind of bishoply power altho' it be not where any apostle before hath been. For to succeed them, is after them to have that episcopal kind of
power which was first given to them. *All bishops are*, saith *Jerome*, *the apostles successors*. [Hieron. ep. 81,]
In like sort *Cyprian* doth term bishops, *Præpositos qui apostolis vicaria ordinatione succe-* [Cypr. ep. ad Florent.]
dunt. From hence it may happily seem to have grown, that they whom we now call bi-
shops a were usually termed at the first apostles, and so did carry their very names in whose [a Thess. 2.]
rooms of spiritual authority they succeeded. Such as deny apostles to have b any succes- [1 Tim. 3.]
sors at all in the office of their apostleship, may hold that opinion without contradiction to [b Ipsius apo-stolatus nulla]
this of ours, if they well explain themselves in declaring what truly and properly apostle- [successio. Fi-]
ship is. In some things every presbyter, in some things only bishops, in some things nei- [nitur enim]
ther the one not the other are the apostles successors. The apostles were sent as special cho- [legatio cum legato, nec ad]
sen c eye-witnesses of Jesus Christ, from whom d immediately they receiv'd their whole [successores ip-sius transit.]
embassage and their commission to be the principal e first founders of an house of God [c Stapl. doct.]
consisting as well of f *Gentiles* as of *Jews*. In this there are not after them any other [Prin. l. 6. c. 7.]
like unto them: and yet the apostles have now their successors upon earth, their true [d Acts 1. 21,]
successors, if not in the largeness, surely in the kind of that episcopal function, whereby [e John 1. 3.]
they had power to sit as spiritual ordinary judges, both over laity and over clergy where [f Gal. 1. 1.]
christian churches were establish'd. [Apo. 21. 14. f Mat. 28. 19.]

V. The apostles of our Lord did, according unto those directions which were given them [The time and]
from above, erect churches in all such cities as received the word of truth, the gospel of [cause of insti-tuting every]
God. All churches by them erected, receiv'd from them the same faith, the same sacra- [where bishops]
ments, the same form of publick regiment. The form of regiment by them establish'd at [with restraint.]
first was, *That the laity of people should be subject unto a college of ecclesiastical persons,*
which were in every such city appointed for that purpose. These in their writings they term
sometime presbyters, sometime bishops. To take one church out of a number for a pattern [Act.20.36,37,]
what the rest were; the presbyters of *Ephesus*, as it is in the history of their departure from
the apostle *Paul* at *Miletum*, are said to have wept abundantly all, which speech doth shew
them to have been many. And by the apostles exhortation it may appear, that they had
not each his several flock to feed, but were in common appointed to feed that one flock the
church of *Ephesus*; for which cause the phrase of his speech is this, g *Attendite gregi*, look [g Acts 20. 29,]
all to that one flock over which the holy Ghost hath made you bishops. These persons eccle- [30.]
siastical being term'd as then, presbyters and bishops both, were all subject unto *Paul*, as to an
higher governor appointed of God to be over them. But forasmuch as the apostles could not [h As appeareth]
themselves be present in all churches, and as the apostle h St. *Paul* foretold the presbyters of [both by his sending to call]
the *Ephesians*, that *there would rise up from amongst their own selves, men speaking perverse* [the presbyters]
things to draw disciples after them; there did grow in short time amongst the governors of [of *Ephesus* be-fore him as far]
each church, those emulations, strifes and contentions, whereof there could be no sufficient [as to *Miletum*.]
remedy provided, except, according unto the order of *Jerusalem* already begun, some one [i Acts 20. 17.]
were indued with episcopal authority over the rest, which one being resident might keep [which was al-most 50 miles,]
them in order, and have preheminence or principality in those things, wherein the equality [and by his lea-]
of many agents was the cause of disorder and trouble. This one president or governor, [ving *Timothy*]
amongst the rest had his known authority establish'd a long time before that settled diffe- [in his place with his au-]
rence of name, and title took place, whereby such alone were named bishops. And there- [thority and in-]
fore in the book of St. *John's revelation* we find that they are entituled i angels. It will [structions for]
perhaps be answer'd, that the angels of those churches were only in every church a [ordaining of a ministers]
minister of sacraments: But then we ask, is it probable that in every of these churches, [there, 1 Tim.]
even in *Ephesus* it self, where many such ministers were long before, as hath been [5. 22. and for proportioning]
proved; there was but one such, when *John* directed his speech to the angel of that [their mainte-]
church? If there were many, surely St. *John* in naming but only one of them an angel, [nance,v.17,18 and for judici-]
did behold in that one somewhat above the rest. Nor was this order peculiar unto some [al hearing of]
few churches, but the whole world universally became subject thereunto; insomuch as [accusations brought a-]
they did not account it to be a church which was not subject unto a bishop. It was the [gainst them. v.]
general received persuasion of the antient christian world, that k *ecclesia est in episcopo*, the [19. and for holding them]
outward being of a church consisted in the having of a bishop. That where colleges of [in an unifor-]
presbyters were, there was at the first equality amongst them, St. *Jerome* l thinketh it a mat- [mity of doc-]
ter clear: but when the rest were thus equal, so that no one of them could command any [trine,c 1. v.3.]
other as inferior unto him, they all were controlable by the apostles, who had that episco- [k Revel. 2.]
pal authority, abiding at the first in themselves, which they afterwards derived unto others. [Cypr.l.4.epist.9.]
The i [l Hieron. ep. ad i Evagr.]

3

The cause wherefore they under themselves appointed such bishops as were not every where at the first, is said to have been those strifes and contentions; for remedy whereof whether the apostles alone did conclude of such a regiment, or else they together with the whole church judging it a fit and needful policy did agree to receive it for a custom; no doubt but being establish'd by them on whom the holy Ghost was poured in so abundant measure for the ordering of Christ's church, it had either divine appointment beforehand, or divine approbation afterwards, and is in that respect to be acknowledg'd the ordinance *Exod. 18. 19.* of God, no less than that antient *Jewish* regiment, whereof tho' *Jethro* were the deviser, yet after that God had allowed it, all men were subject unto it, as to the polity of God, and not of *Jethro*. That so the antient fathers did think of episcopal regiment; that they held this order as a thing received from the blessed apostles themselves, and authoriz'd even from Heaven, we may perhaps more easily prove, than obtain that they all shall *Ep. ad Januar.* grant it who see it prov'd. St. *Augustine* setteth it down for a principle, that whatsoever positive order the whole church every where doth observe, the same it must needs have receiv'd from the very apostles themselves, unless perhaps some general council were the authors of it. And he saw that the ruling superiority of bishops was a thing universally establish'd not by the force of any council, (for councils do all presuppose bishops, nor can there any council be named so antient, either general, or so much as provincial, sithence the apostles own times, but we can shew that bishops had their authority before it, and not from it.) Wherefore St. *Augustine* knowing this, could not chuse but reverence the authority of bishops, as a thing to him apparently and most clearly apostolical. But it will be perhaps objected, that regiment by bishops was not so universal nor antient as we pretend; and that an argument hereof may be *Jerome's* own testimony, who living at the very same time with St. *Augustine*, noteth this kind of regiment as being no where antient, saving only in *Alexandria*; his words are these, *It was for a remedy of schism that one was afterwards chosen to be placed above the rest; lest every man's pulling unto himself, should rend asunder the church of Christ.* For (that which also may serve for an argument *Ep. ad Evang. or token hereof*) at Alexandria *from* Mark *the* evangelist, *unto* Heraclas *and* Dionysius; *the T. C. 2. p. 82. presbyters always chose one of themselves, whom they placed in higher degree, and gave It is to be ob- unto him the title of bishop.* Now St. *Jerome* they say would never have picked out that served that one church from amongst so many, and have noted that in it there had been bishops from *Jerome* faith, it the time that St. *Mark* liv'd, if so be the self same order were of like antiquity every where; wasso in Alex-andria; signi- his words therefore must be thus scholied; in the church of *Alexandria* presbyters in-fying that in deed had even from the time of St. *Mark* the evangelist always a bishop to rule over them other churches for a remedy against divisions, factions and schisms: not so in other churches, nei-it was not so, ther in that very church any longer than *usque ad Heraclam & Dionysium*, till *Heraclas* and his successor *Dionysius* were bishops. But this construction doth bereave the words construed partly of wit, and partly of truth; it maketh them both absurd and false. For if the meaning be that episcopal government in that church was then expired, it must have expired with the end of some one, and not of two several bishops days, unless perhaps it fell sick under *Heraclas*, and with *Dionysius* gave up the ghost. Besides, it is clearly untrue that the presbyters of that church did then cease to be under a bishop. Who doth not know that after *Dionysius*, *Maximus* was bishop of *Alexandria*, after him *Theonas*, after him *Peter*, after him *Achillas*, after him *Alexander*, of whom *Socrates* in this sort *Socrat. l. 1. c. 3.* writeth? It fortuned on a certain time that this *Alexander*, in the presence of the presbyters which were under him, and of the rest of the clergy there, discoursed somewhat curiously and subtilly of the holy Trinity, bringing high philosophical proofs, that there is in the Trinity an unity. Whereupon *Arius* one of the presbyters which were placed in that degree under *Alexander*, opposed eagerly himself against those things which were uttered by the bishop. So that thus long bishops continued even in the church of *Alexandria*. Nor did their regiment here cease, but these also had others their successors till St. *Jerome's* own time, who living long after *Heraclas* and *Dionysius* had ended their days, did not yet live himself to see the presbyters of *Alexandria* otherwise than subject unto a bishop. So that we cannot, with any truth, so interpret his words as to mean, that in the church of *Alexandria* there had been bishops indued with superiority over presbyters from St. *Mark's* time only till the time of *Heraclas* and of *Dionysius*. Wherefore that St. *Jerome* may receive a more probable interpretation than this, we answer, that generally, of regiment by bishops, and what term of continuance it had in the church of *Alexandria*, it was no part of his mind to speak, but to note one only circumstance belonging to the manner of their e-lection, which circumstance is, that in *Alexandria* they used to chuse their bishops alto-gether out of the college of their own presbyters, and neither from abroad nor out of † *Unto Igna-* any other inferior order of the clergy; whereas oftentimes † elsewhere the use was to *tius bishop of* chuse as well from abroad as at home, as well inferior unto presbyters, as presbyters *Antioch, here a* when

3

when they faw occafion. This cuftom, faith he, the church of *Alexandria* did always keep, till in *Heraclas* and *Dionyfius* they began to do otherwife. Thefe two were the very firft not chofe out of their college of presbyters.

deacon there was made fucceffor. *Chryfoftom* being a presbyter of *Antioch* was chofen to fucceed *Nectarius* in the bifhoprick of *Conftantinople.*

The drift and purpofe of St. *Jerome's* fpeech doth plainly fhew what his meaning was; for whereas fome did over extol the office of the deacon in the church of *Rome*; where deacons being grown great, thro' wealth, challeng'd place above presbyters: St. *Jerome*, to abate this infolency, writing to *Evagrius*, diminifheth by all means the deacons eftimation, and lifteth up presbyters as far as poffible the truth might bear. *An attendant,* faith he, *upon tables and windows proudly to exalt himfelf above them at whofe prayers is made the body and blood of Chrift; above them, between whom and bifhops there was at the firft for a time no difference neither in authority nor in title. And whereas after fchifms and contentions made it neceffary, that fome one fhould be placed over them, by which occafion the title of bifhop became proper unto that one, yet was that one chofen out of the presbyters, as being the chiefeft, the higheft, the worthieft degree of the clergy, and not out of deacons: in which confideration alfo it feemeth that in* Alexandria, *even from St.* Mark *to* Heraclas *and* Dionyfius *bifhops there, the presbyters evermore have chofen one of themfelves, and not a deacon at any time to be their bifhop. Nor let any man think that Chrift hath one church in* Rome, *and another in the reft of the world; that in* Rome *he alloweth deacons to be honoured above presbyters, and otherwife will have them to be in the next degree to the bifhop. If it be deemed that abroad where bifhops are poorer, the presbyters under them may be the next unto them in honour; but at* Rome *where the bifhop hath ample revenues, the deacons whofe eftate is neareft for wealth, may be alfo for eftimation the next unto him; we muft know that a bifhop in the meaneft city is no lefs a bifhop than he who is feated in the greateft; the countenance of a rich, and the meannefs of a poor eftate doth make no odds between bifhops; and therefore if a presbyter at* Eugubium *be the next in degree to a bifhop, furely, even at* Rome *it ought in reafon to be fo likewife, and not a deacon for wealth's fake only to be above, who by order fhould be, and elfewhere is, underneath a presbyter. But ye will fay, that according to the cuftom of* Rome *a deacon prefenteth unto the bifhop him which ftandeth to be ordained presbyter, and upon the deacon's teftimony given concerning his fitnefs, he receiveth at the bifhop's hands ordination: fo that in* Rome *the deacons have this fpecial preheminence, the presbyter ought there to give place unto him. Wherefore is the cuftom of one city brought againft the practice of the whole world? The paucity of deacons in the church of* Rome *hath gotten the credit; as unto presbyters their multitude hath been caufe of contempt: howbeit even in the church of* Rome, *presbyters fit and deacons ftand: an argument as ftrong againft the fuperiority of deacons, as the fore-alledged reafon doth feem for it. Befides, whofoever is promoted muft needs be raifed from a lower degree to an higher; wherefore either let him which is presbyter be made a deacon, that fo the deacon may appear to be the greater; or if of deacons presbyters be made, let them know themfelves to be in regard of deacons, tho' below in gain, yet above in office. And to the end we may underftand that thofe apoftolick orders are taken out of the old teftament, what* Aaron *and his fons and the levites were in the temple, the fame in the church may bifhops, and presbyters, and deacons challenge unto themfelves.* This is the very drift and fubftance; this the true conftruction and fenfe of St. *Jerome's* whole difcourfe in that epiftle: which I have therefore endeavoured the more at large to explain, becaufe one thing is lefs effectual, or more ufual to be alledged againft the antient authority of bifhops; concerning whofe government St. *Jerome's* own words other where are fufficient to fhew his opinion; that this order was not only in *Alexandria* fo antient, but even as antient in other churches. We have before alledged his teftimony touching *James* the bifhop of *Jerufalem.* As for bifhops in other churches, on the firft of the epiftle to *Titus* thus he fpeaketh, *Till thro' inftinct of the devil there grew in the church factions, and among the people it began to be profeft,* I am of *Paul,* I of *Apollos,* and I of *Cephas, churches were governed by the common advice of presbyters; but when every one began to reckon thofe whom himfelf had baptized, his own and not Chrift's, it was decreed IN THE WHOLE WORLD, that one chofen out of the presbyters, fhould be placed above the reft, to whom all care of the church fhould belong, and fo the feeds of fchifm be removed.* If it be fo, that by St. *Jerome's* own confeffion this order was not then begun when people in the apoftles abfence began to be divided into factions by their teachers, and to rehearfe, I am of *Paul*; but that even at the very firft appointment thereof was agreed upon and received throughout the world: how fhall a man be perfuaded that the fame *Jerome* thought it fo antient no where faving in *Alexandria*, one only church of the whole world? A fentence there is indeed of St. *Jerome's*, which being not throughly confider'd and weighed, may caufe his meaning fo to be taken, as if he judg'd epifcopal regiment to have been the church's invention longer after, and not the apoftle's own inftitution; as namely, when

he

he admonisheth bishops in this manner; *as therefore presbyters do know that the custom* [*]Bishops he *of the church makes them subject to the bishop which is set over them; so let* [*] *bishops know,* meaneth by re- *that custom rather than the truth of any ordinance of the Lord maketh them greater than* straint; for *the rest, and that with common advice they ought to govern the church.* To clear the sense episcopal of these words therefore, as we have done already the former: laws which the church front power was always in the beginning universally hath observ'd were some delivered by Christ himself, with a charge the beginning to keep them to the world's end, as the law of baptizing and administring the holy eu- church insti- tuted by charist; some brought in afterwards by the apostles, yet not without the special direction Christ himself, the apostles be- of the holy Ghost, as occasions did arise; of this sort are those apostolical orders and laws, ing in govern- ment bishops whereby deacons, widows, virgins were first appointed in the church. at large, as no

Man will deny, having received from Christ himself that episcopal authority. For which cause *Cyprian* hath said of them. Meminisse dia-coni debent quoniam apostolos, id est, episcopos & præpositos Dominus elegit: Diaconos autem post ascensum Domini in cœlos apostoli sibi constituerunt, episcopatus sui & ecclesiæ ministros. lib. 3. ep. 9.

This answer to St. *Jerom* seemeth dangerous; I have qualified it as I may by addition of some words of restraint: yet I satisfy not my self, in my judgment it would be altered, *Now whereas* Jerom *doth term the government of bishops by restraint, an apostolical tra-dition, acknowledging thereby the same to have been of the apostles own institution, it may be demanded, how these two will stand together;* namely, that the apostles by divine in-*stinct, should be as* Jerom *confesseth the authors of that regiment; and yet the custom of the church be accounted (for so by* Jerom *it may seem to be in this place accounted) the chiefest prop that upholdeth the same?* To this we answer, *that forasmuch as the whole body of the church hath power to alter, with general consent and upon necessary occasions, even the positive law of the apostles, if there be no command to the contrary; and it ma-nifestly appears to her, that change of times have clearly taken away the very reason of God's first institution, as by sundry examples may be most clearly proved; what laws the universal church might change, and doth not; if they have long continued without any alteration; it seemeth that St.* Jerom *ascribeth continuance of such positive laws, tho' in-stituted by God himself, to the judgment of the church. For they which might abrogate a law and do not, are properly said to uphold, to establish it, and to give it being. The regi-ment therefore whereof* Jerom *speaketh being positive, and consequently not absolutely ne-cessary but of a changeable nature, because there is no divine voice which in express words forbiddeth it to be changed;* he might imagine both that it came by the apostles by very di-*vine appointment at the first, and notwithstanding be, after a sort, said to stand in force, rather by the custom of the church, choosing to continue in it, than by the necessary constraint of any commandment from the word requiring perpetual continuance thereof.* , So that St. Jerom's admonition is reasonable, sensible, and plain, being contrived to this effect; the ruling superiority of one bishop over many presbyters in each church, is an order descended from Christ to the apostles, who were themselves bishops at large; and from the apostles to those whom they in their steads appointed bishops over particular countries and cities; and even from those antient times universally establish'd, thus many years it hath continued, throughout the world; for which cause presbyters must not grudge to continue subject un-to their bishops, unless they will proudly oppose themselves against that which God himself ordain'd by his apostles, and the whole church of Christ approveth and judgeth most conve-nient.　On the other side bishops, albeit they may avouch, with conformity of truth, that their authority had thus descended even from the very apostles themselves, yet the absolute and everlasting continuance of it they cannot say that any commandment of the Lord doth injoin; *And therefore must acknowledge that the church hath power by universal con-sent upon urgent cause to take it away, if thereunto she be constrained thro' the proud, tyran-nical, and unreformable dealings of her bishops, whose regiment she hath thus long delighted in, because she hath found it good and requisite to be so governed. Wherefore lest bishops forget themselves, as if none on earth had authority to touch their states, let them conti-nually bear in mind, that it is rather the force of custom, whereby the church having so long found it good to continue under the regiment of her virtuous bishops, doth still uphold, maintain, and honour them in that respect; than that any such true and heavenly law can be shewed, by the evidence whereof it may of a truth appear that the Lord himself hath appointed presbyters for ever to be under the regiment of bishops, in what sort soever they behave themselves.* Let this consideration be a bridle unto them. let it teach them not to disdain the advice of their presbyters, but to use their authority with so much the greater humility and moderation, as a sword which the church hath power to take from them. In all this there is no let why St. *Jerom* might not think the authors of episcopal regiment to have been the very blessed apostles themselves, directed therein by the special motion of the holy Ghost, which the antients all before, and besides him and himself also elsewhere be-ment

ing known to hold, we are not without better evidence than this, to think him in judgment divided both from himfelf and from them.   Another argument that the regiment
of churches by one bifhop over many presbyters, hath been always held apoftolical, may
be this.   We find that throughout all thofe cities where the apoftles did plant chriftianity,
the hiftory of times hath noted fucceffion of paftors in the feat of one, not of many,
(there being in every fuch church evermore many paftors,) and the firft one in every rank
of fucceffion we find to have been, if not fome apoftle, yet fome apoftle's difciple.   By
Epiphanius the bifhops of *Jerufalem* are reckoned down from *James* to *Hilarion* then Lib. 2. to 2.
bifhop.   Of them which boafted that they held the fame things which they received of Hæref. 66.
fuch as lived with the apoftles themfelves, *Tertullian* fpeaketh after this fort; let them adverf. hæret.
therefore fhew the beginnings of their churches, let them recite their bifhops one by one,
each in fuch fort fucceeding other, that the firft bifhop of them have had for his author
and predeceffor fome apoftle, or at leaft fome apoftolical perfon who perfevered with the
apoftles.   For fo apoftolical churches are wont to bring forth the evidence of their eftates.
So doth the church of *Smyrna*, having *Polycarp* whom *John* did confecrate.   Catalogues
of bifhops in a number of other churches (bifhops and fucceeding one another) from the
very apoftles times are by *Eufebius* and *Socrates* collected; whereby it appeareth fo clear,
as nothing in the world more, that under them, and by their appointment, this order began, which maketh many presbyters fubject unto the regiment of fome one bifhop.   For
as in *Rome*, while the civil ordering of the commonwealth was jointly and equally in the
hands of two confuls, *hiftorical* records concerning them did evermore mention them
both, and note which two, as collegues, fucceeded from time to time.   So, there is
no doubt but ecclefiaftical antiquity had done the very like, had not one paftor's place
and calling been always fo eminent above the reft in the fame church.   And what need
we to feek far for proofs that the apoftles who began this order of regiment by bifhops,
did it not but by divine inftinct, when without fuch direction things of far lefs weight
and moment they attended not?   *Paul* and *Barnabas* did not open their mouths to the Acts 13.
Gentiles, till the Spirit had faid, *Separate me* Paul *and* Barnabas *for the work whereunto
I have fent them.*   The *eunuch*, by *Philip* was neither baptis'd nor inftructed, before the Acts 8.
angel of God was fent to give him notice that fo it pleafed the moft High.   In *Afia*,
Paul and the reft were filent, becaufe the Spirit forbad them to fpeak.   When they in- Acts 16.
tended to have feen *Bythinia* they ftay'd their journey, the Spirit not giving them leave
to go.   Before *Timothy* was imploy'd in thofe epifcopal affairs of the church, about which 1 Tim. 1. 18.
the apoftle St. *Paul* ufed him, the holy Ghoft gave fpecial charge for his ordination and
prophetical intelligence more than once, what fuccefs the fame would have.   And fhall
we think that *James* was made bifhop of *Jerufalem*, *Evodius* bifhop of the church of
Antioch, the angels in the churches of *Afia* bifhops, that bifhops every where were appointed to take away factions, contentions and fchifms without fome like divine inftiga-
tion and direction of the holy Ghoft?   Wherefore let us not fear to be herein bold and
peremptory, that if any thing in the church's government, furely the firft inftitution of
bifhops was from heaven, was even of God; the holy Ghoft was the author of it.

     VI. A bifhop, faith St. *Augustine*, is a presbyter's fuperior: but the queftion is now, What manner
wherein that fuperiority did confift.   The bifhop's preheminence we fay therefore was two- of power bi-
fold.   Firft, he excelled in latitude of power of order; fecondly, in that kind of power firft beginning
which belongeth unto jurifdiction.   Priefts in the law had authority and power to do have had.
greater things than *Levites*; the high prieft greater than inferior priefts might do, there- *Aug.* Ep. 19.
fore *Levites* were beneath priefts, and priefts inferior to the high prieft, by reafon of the hæref. 53.
very degree of dignity, and of worthinefs in the nature of thofe functions which they did
execute; and not only, for that the one had power to command and controul the other.
In like fort, presbyters having a weightier and worthier charge than deacons had, the
deacon was in this fort the presbyter's inferior, and where we fay that a bifhop was likewife ever accounted a presbyter's fuperior, even according unto his very power of order,
we muft of neceffity declare what principal duties belonging unto that kind of power a bifhop might perform, and not a presbyter.   The cuftom of the primitive church in con-
fecrating holy virgins and widows unto the fervice of God and his church, is a thing not obfcure, but eafy to be known *both by that which* St. Paul *himfelf concerning them hath, and* 1 Cor. 7. 25.
by the latter confonant evidence of other mens writings.   Now a part of the preheminence 1 Tim. 5. 9.
which bifhops had in their power of order was, that by them only fuch were confecrated. Tertul. de vel.
Again, the power of ordaining both deacons and presbyters, the power to give the power virg.
of order unto others, this alfo hath been always peculiar unto bifhops.   It hath not been
heard of, that inferior presbyters were ever authorized to ordain.   And concerning ordination fo great force and dignity it hath, that whereas presbyters by fuch power as they

                            Z z   have

have received for administration of the sacraments are able only to beget children unto God, bishops having power to ordain, do by vertue thereof create fathers to the people *Epiph. 3. l. 10.* of God, as *Epiphanius* fitly disputeth. There are which hold, that between a bishop and *1. Hær. 73.* a presbyter, touching power of order, there is no difference. The reason of which conceit is, for that they see presbyters no less than bishops, authorized to offer up the prayers of the church, to preach the gospel, to baptize, to administer the holy eucharist; but they considered not withal, as they should, that the presbyter's authority to do these things is derived from the bishop which doth ordain him thereunto: so that even in those things which are common unto both, yet the power of the one is as it were a certain light *Acts 14. 23.* borrowed from the other's lamp. The apostles being bishops at large, ordained every *Tit. 1. 5.* where presbyters. *Titus* and *Timothy* having received episcopal power, as apostolick *1 Tim. 5. 22.* ambassadors or legates, the one in *Greece*, the other in *Ephesus*, they both did, by vertue *Apud Ægypt-* thereof, likewise ordain throughout all churches, deacons, and presbyters within the cir-*rum presbyteri cuits* allotted unto them. As for bishops by restraint, their power this way incommunica-*confirmant si praesens non sit* ble unto presbyters, which of the ancients do not acknowledge? I make not *confirmation Episcopus.* any part of that power, which hath always belonged only unto bishops; because in some *Com. q. vulgo* places the custom was, that presbyters might also confirm in the absence of a bishop; *Amb. dic. in 4.* *Ep. ad Ephef.* albeit for the most part, none but only bishops were thereof the allowed ministers.

Here it will perhaps be objected, that the power of ordination it self was not every where peculiar and proper unto bishops, as may be seen by a council of *Carthage*, which sheweth their church's order to have been, That presbyters should, together with the bishop, lay hands upon the ordained. But the answer hereunto is easy; for doth it hereupon follow that the power of ordination was not principally and originally in the bishop? Our Saviour hath said unto his apostles, *With me ye shall sit and judge the twelve tribes of Israel*; yet we know that to him alone it belongeth to judge the world, and that to him all judgment is given. With us, even at this day, presbyters are licensed to do as much as that council speaketh of, if any be present. Yet will not any man thereby conclude that in this church others than bishops are allow'd to ordain. The association of presbyters is no sufficient proof that the power of ordination is in them; but rather that it never was in them we may hereby understand; for that no man is able to shew either deacon or presbyter ordain'd by presbyters only, and his ordination accounted lawful in any ancient part of the church; every where examples being found both of deacons and presbyters ordain'd by bishops alone oftentimes, neither even in that respect thought sufficient. Touching that other chiefly, which is of jurisdiction; amongst the Jews he which was highest through the worthiest of peculiar duties incident unto his function in the legal service of God, did bear always in ecclesiastical jurisdiction the chiefest sway. As long as the glory of the temple of God did last, there were in it sundry orders of men consecrated unto the service thereof; one sort of them inferior unto another in dignity and degree; the nathiners subordinate unto the levites, the levites unto the priests, the rest of the priests to those twenty four which were chief priests, and they all to the high priest. If any man surmise that the difference between them was only by distinction in the former kind of power, and not in this latter of jurisdiction, are not the words of the law manifest which *Numb. 3. 32.* made *Eleazar* the son of *Aaron* the priest chief captain of the levites, and overseer of them, unto whom the charge of the sanctuary was committed? Again, at the commandment of *Numb. 4. 27.* *Aaron* and his sons, are not the *Gersonites* themselves required to do all their service in the whole charge belonging unto the *Gersonites*, being inferior priests, as *Aaron* and his *2 Chr. 19. 11.* sons were high priests? Did not *Jehoshaphat* appoint *Amazias* the priest to be chief over *Joseph.* them who were judges for the cause of the Lord in *Jerusalem*? *Priests*, saith *Josephus*, *Antiq. lib.* *worship God continually, and the eldest of the stock are governors over the rest. He doth sa-* *p. 612.* *crifice unto God before others, he hath care of the laws, judgeth controversies, correcteth of-* *fenders, and whosoever obeyeth him not, is convict of impiety against God.* But unto this they answer, that the reason thereof was because the high priest did prefigure Christ, and represent to the people that chiefty of our Saviour which was to come; so that Christ being now come, there is no cause why such preheminence should be given unto any one. Which fancy pleaseth so well the humour of all sorts of rebellious spirits, that they all seek to shroud themselves under it. Tell the *Anabaptist*, which holdeth the use of the sword unlawful for a christian man, that God himself did allow his people to make wars; they have their answer round and ready, *Those ancient wars were figures of the spiritual wars of Christ.* Tell the *Barrowist* what sway *David*, and others the kings of *Israel*, did bear in the ordering of spiritual affairs, the same answer again serveth, namely, *That David, and the rest of the kings of* Israel, *prefigured Christ.* Tell the *Martinist* of the high priest's great authority and jurisdiction among the *Jews*, what other thing doth serve his turn but the self-same shift; *By the power of the high priest the universal supreme authority of our Lord Jesus*
Christ

Chrift was fhadowed. The thing is true, that indeed high-priefts were figures of Chrift; yet this was in things belonging unto their power of order; they figured Chrift by entring into the holy place, by offering for the fins of all the people once a year, and by other the like duties: But, that to govern and maintain order amongft thofe that were fubject to them, is an office figurative and abrogated by Chrift coming into the miniftry; that their exercife of jurifdiction was figurative, yea, figurative in fuch fort, that it had no other caufe of being inftituted, but only to ferve as a reprefentation of fomewhat to come, and that herein the church of Chrift ought not to follow them; this article is fuch as muft be confirmed, if any way by miracle, otherwife it will hardly enter into the heads of reafonable men, why the high-prieft fhould more figure Chrift in being a judge, than in being whatfoever he might be befides. St. *Cyprian* deemed it no wrefting of fcripture, to challenge as much for chriftian bifhops, as was given to the high prieft among the *Jews,* and to urge the law of *Mofes* as being moft effectual to prove it. St. *Jerom* likewife thought it an argument fufficient to ground the authority of bifhops upon. *To the end, faith he, we may underftand apoftolical traditions to have been taken from the old teftament; that which Aaron, and his fons, and the Levites were in the temple; bifhops, and presbyters, and deacons in the church, may lawfully challenge to themfelves.* In the office of a bifhop, *Ignatius* obferveth thefe two functions, ἱερατεύειν ἢ ἄρχειν. Concerning the one, fuch is the preheminence of a bifhop, that he only hath the heavenly myfteries of God committed originally unto him, fo that otherwife than by his ordination, and by authority received from him, others befides him are not licenfed therein to deal as ordinary minifters of God's church. And touching the other part of their facred function, wherein the power of their jurifdiction doth appear, firft how the apoftles themfelves, and fecondly how *Titus* and *Timothy* had rule and jurifdiction over presbyters, no man is ignorant. And had not chriftian bifhops afterward the like power? *Ignatius* bifhop of *Antioch* being ready by bleffed martyrdom to end his life, writeth unto his presbyters, the paftors under him, in this fort: Οἱ πρεσβύτεροι ποιμάνετε τὸ ἐν ὑμῖν ποίμνιον, ἕως ἄν ἀναδείξῃ ὁ Θεὸς τὸν μέλλοντα ἄρχειν ὑμῶν. Ἐγὼ γὰρ ἤδη σπένδομαι. After the death of *Fabian* bifhop of *Rome,* there growing fome trouble about the receiving of fuch perfons into the church as had fallen away in perfecution, and did now repent their fall, the presbyters and deacons of the fame church advertifed St. *Cyprian* thereof, fignifying, *That they muft of neceffity defer to deal in that caufe till God did fend them a new bifhop which might moderate all things.* Much we read, of extraordinary fafting ufually in the church; and in this appeareth alfo fomewhat concerning the chiefty of bifhops. The cuftom is, faith *Tertullian,* that bifhops do appoint when the people fhall all faft. Yea, it is not a matter left to our own free choice, whether bifhops fhall rule or no, but the will of our Lord and Saviour is, faith *Cyprian,* that every act of the church be governed by her bifhops. An Argument it is of the bifhops high preheminence, rule, and government over all the reft of the clergy; even that the fword of perfecution did ftrike efpecially, always at the bifhop as at the head, the reft, by reafon of their lower eftate, being more fecure, as the felf fame *Cyprian* noteth; the very manner of whofe fpeech unto his own both deacons and presbyters who remained fafe, when himfelf then bifhop was driven into exile, argueth likewife his eminent authority and rule over them. *By thefe letters,* faith he, *I both exhort and* command *that ye whofe prefence there is not envied at, nor fo much befet with dangers, fupply my room in daing thofe things which the exercife of religion doth require.* Unto the fame purpofe ferve moft directly thofe comparifons, than which nothing is more familiar in the books of the ancient fathers, who as oft as they fpeak of the feveral degrees in God's clergy, if they chance to compare presbyters with *Levitical* priefts of the law, the bifhop they compare unto *Aaron* the high-prieft; if they compare the one with the apoftles, the other they compare (although in a lower proportion) fometime to Chrift, and fometime to God himfelf, evermore fhewing that they placed the bifhop in an eminent degree of ruling authority and power above other presbyters. *Ignatius* comparing bifhops with deacons, and with fuch minifters of the word and facraments as were but presbyters, and had no authority over presbyters; *What is,* faith he, *the bifhop, but one which hath all principality and power over all, fo far forth as man may have it, being to his power a follower even af God's own Chrift?* Mr. *Calvin* himfelf, tho' an enemy unto regiment by bifhops, doth notwithftanding confefs, that in old time the minifters which had charge to teach, chofe of their company one in every city, to whom they appropriated the title of bifhop, left equality fhould breed diffention. He addeth farther, that look what duty the *Roman* confuls did execute in propofing matters unto the fenate, and asking their opinions, in directing them by advice, admonition, exhortation in guiding actions by their authority, and in feeing that perform-ed which was with common confent agreed on, the like charge had the bifhop in the affembly

Marginal notes (right):

Cypr. l.3.Ep.9.
ad Regenianum.

Hier. Ep.85.

Concern- Ep. ad Smyr.

1 Tim. 5. 19.
Againft a presbyter receive no accufation under two or three witneffes.
Ignat. Epift. ad Antioch.
Apud Cypr. Ep. 1. Ep. 7.

Tertul. adverf. Pfychic. Epifcopi univerfe plebi mandare jejunia affolent. Cypr. Ep. 27.

Cypr. Ep. 39.
Vide Ignat. ad Magnef.

Quod Aaron & filios ejus, hocepifcopum & presbyteros effe noveri-mus. Hier. Ep. 2. ad Nepotia-num.
Ita eftut in Epifcopis hemi-nem,in presby-teris apoftolos recognofcas. Auctor. opufc. de ordinib. Eccl. inter opera Hieron.
Ignat. Ep ad Tra.
Inftit. l. 4. cap. 4. fect. 2.

fembly

3

fembly of other minifters. Thus much *Calvin* being forced by the evidence of truth to grant, doth yet deny the bifhops to have been fo in authority at the firft as to bear rule over other minifters: wherein what rule he doth mean, I know not. But if the bifhops were fo far in dignity above other minifters, as the confuls of *Rome* for their year above other fenators, it is as much as we require. And undoubtedly, if as the confuls of *Rome*, fo the bifhops in the church of Chrift, had fuch authority, as both to direct other minifters, and to fee that every of them fhould obferve that which their common confent had agreed on, how this could be done by the bifhop not bearing rule over them, for mine own part I muft acknowledge that my poor conceit is not able to comprehend. One objection there is of fome force to make againft that which we have hitherto endeavoured to

Hieron. Ep. ad Evagr. 85. prove, if they miftake it not who alledge it. St. *Jerom* comparing other presbyters with him, unto whom the name of bifhop was then appropriate, asketh, *What a bifhop, by vertue of his place and calling, may do more than a presbyter, except it be only to ordain?*

Chryf. 10. in 1 *Tim.* 3. In like fort *Chryfoftom* having moved a queftion, wherefore St. *Paul* would give *Timothy* precept concerning the quality of bifhops, and defcend from them to deacons, omitting the order of presbyters between, he maketh thereunto this anfwer, *What things he fpake concerning bifhops, the fame are alfo meet for presbyters, whom bifhops feem not to excel in any thing but only in the power of ordination.* Wherefore feeing this doth import no ruling fuperiotity, it follows that bifhops were as then no rulers over that part of the clergy of God. Whereunto we anfwer, that both St. *Jerom* and St. *Chryfoftom* had in thofe their fpeeches an eye no farther than only to that function for which presbyters and bifhops were confecrated unto God. Now we know that their confecration had reference to nothing but only that which they did by force and vertue of the power of order, wherein fith bifhops received their charge, only by that one degree, to fpeak of, more ample than presbyters did theirs, it might be well enough faid that presbyters were that way authorized to do, in a manner, even as much as bifhops could do, if we confider what each of them did by vertue of folemn confecration; for as concerning power of regiment and jurifdiction, it was a thing withal added unto bifhops for the neceffary ufe of fuch certain perfons and people as fhould be thereunto fubject in thofe particular churches whereof they were bifhops, and belonging to them only, as bifhops of fuch or fuch a church; whereas the other kind of power had relation indefinitely unto any of the whole fociety of chriftian men, on whom they fhould chance to exercife the fame, and belonging to them abfolutely, as they were bifhops, wherefoever they lived. St. *Jerom's* conclufion thereof is, *That feeing in the one kind of power there is no greater difference between a presbyter and a bifhop, bifhops fhould not becaufe of their preheminence in the other, too much lift up themfelves above the presbyters under them.* St. *Chryfoftom's* collection, *That where the apoftle doth fet down the qualities, whereof regard fhould be had in the confecration of bifhops, there was no need to make a feveral difcourfe how presbyters ought to be qualified when they are ordained; becaufe there being fo little difference in the functions, whereunto the one and the other receive ordination, the fame precepts might well ferve for both; at leaftwife by the vertues required in the greater, what fhould need in the lefs might be eafily underftood.* As for the difference of jurifdiction, the truth is, the apoftles yet living, and themfelves where they were refident, exercifing the jurifdiction in their own perfons, it was not every where eftablifhed in bifhops. When the apoftles prefcribed thofe laws, and when *Chryfoftom* thus fpake concerning them, it was not by him at all refpected, but his eye was the fame way with *Jerom's*; his cogitation was wholly fixed on that power which by confecration is given to bifhops, more than to presbyters, and not on that which they have over presbyters by force of their particular acceffary jurifdiction. Wherein if any man fuppofe that *Jerom* and *Chryfoftom* knew no difference at all between a presbyter and a bifhop, let him weigh but one or two of their fentences. The pride of infolent bifhops hath not a fharper enemy than *Jerom*, for which caufe he taketh often occafions moft feverely to inveigh againft them, fometimes

ᵃ'Ve'ut in aliquo fublimi fpecula conftituti vix dignantur vi-dere mortales fervos fuos. In for ᵃ fhewing difdain and contempt of the clergy under them; fometimes for not ᵇ fuffering themfelves to be told of their faults, and admonifhed of their duty by inferiors; fometimes for not ᶜ admitting their presbyters to teach, if fo be themfelves were in prefence; fometimes for not vouchfafing to ufe any conference with them, or to take any counfel of them. Howbeit never doth he, in fuch wife, bend himfelf againft their dif-

4. c. Epift. ad Nepotian. Gal. ᵈ Nemo pec-cantibus epif-copis audet orders as to deny their rule and authority over presbyters. Of *Vigilantius* being a pref-byter he thus writeth, ᵈ *Miror fanctum epifcopum in cujus parochia presbyter effe dicitur, acquiefcere furori ejus, & non virga apoftolica virgaq; ferrea confringere vas inutile. I*

contradicere: nemo audet accufare majorem, propterea quafi fancti & beati & in præceptis Domini ambulantes augent peccata peccatis. Difficilis eft accufatio in epifcopum. Si enim peccaverit, non creditur, & fi convictus fuerit, non punitur. In cap. 8. *Ecclefiaft.* ᶜ Peffima confuetudinis eft, in quibufdam ecclefiis tacere presbyteros & præfentibus epifcopis non loqui; quafi aut invideant aut non dignentur audire. Ep. 2. ad *Nepotian.*   ᵉ Ep. 54. ad *Ripar.*

marvel

marvel that the holy bishop under whom Vigilantius *is said to be a presbyter, doth yield to his fury, and not break that unprofitable vessel with his apostolick and iron rod.* With [Hier. ad Nepot.] this agreeth most fitly the grave advice he gave to [No bishop may be a lord,] ᵃ *Nepotian, Be thou subject unto thy bishop, and receive him as the father of thy soul.* ᵇ *This also I say, that bishops should* [in reference unto the pres-] *know themselves to be priests, and not lords, that they ought to honour the clergy as becometh* [byters which are under him,] *the clergy to be honoured, to the end their clergy may yield them the honour* [if we take that] *which, as bishops, they ought to have.* That of the orator *Domitius* is famous, *Where-* [name in the] *fore should I esteem of thee as of a prince, when thou makest not of me that reckoning,* [worse part, as] *which should in reason be made of a senator? Let us know the bishop and his presbyters* [Jerom here] *to be the same which* Aaron *sometimes and his sons were.* Finally, writing against the he- [shop is to rule] reticks which were named *Luciferians, The very safety of the church,* saith he, *dependeth* [his presbyters,] *on the dignity of the chief priest, to whom, unless men grant an exceeding and an eminent* [not as lords do their slaves,] *power, there will grow in churches even as many schisms as there are persons which have* [but as fathers do their chil-] *authority.* [dren.]

Touching *Chrysostom,* to shew that by him there was also acknowledged a ruling superiority of bishops over presbyters, both then usual, and in no respect unlawful: what need we alledge his words and sentences, when the history of his own episcopal actions in that very kind, is till this day extant for all men to read that will? For St. *Chrysostom,* of [In vita Chrysf.] a presbyter in *Antioch,* grew to be afterwards bishop of *Constantinople,* and in process of [per Cassiod. Sm.] time, when the emperor's heavy displeasure had, thro' the practice of a powerful faction against him, effected his banishment, *Innocent* the bishop of *Rome* understanding thereof, wrote his letters unto the clergy of that church, *That no successor ought to be chosen in* Chrysostom's *room: nec ejus clerum alii parere pontifici, nor his clergy OBEY any other bishop than him.* A fond kind of speech, if so be there had been, as then, in bishops no ruling superiority over presbyters. When two of *Chrysostom's* presbyters had joined [Pallad. in vita] themselves to the faction of his mortal enemy *Theophilus,* patriarch in the church of [Chrysf.] *Alexandria;* the same *Theophilus,* and other bishops which were of his conventicle, having sent those two, amongst others, to cite *Chrysostom* their lawful bishop, and to bring him into publick judgment, he taketh against this one thing special exception, as being contrary to all order, that those presbyters should come as messengers, and call him to judgment, who were a part of that clergy, whereof himself was ruler and judge. So that bishops to have had in those times a ruling superiority over presbyters, neither could *Jerom* nor *Chrysostom* be ignorant; and therefore, hereupon it were superfluous that we should any longer stand.

VII. Touching the next point, how bishops, together with presbyters, have used to [After what sort] govern the churches which were under them. It is by *Zonaras* somewhat plainly and at [bishops, toge-] large declared, that the bishop had his seat on high in the church, above the residue which [byters, have u-] were present; that a number of presbyters did always there assist him; and that in the [fed to govern] oversight of the people those presbyters were ᶜ after a sort the bishop's coadjutors. The [the churches which were] bishops and presbyters, who, together with him, governed the church, are, for the most [under them.] part, by *Ignatius* jointly mentioned. In the epistle to them of *Trallis,* he saith of pres- [ᶜ Ὅτινες εἰσὶ-] byters, that they are σύμβελοι ἡ συνεδροτα] τῇ ἐπισκόπῳ, *counsellors and assistants of the* [ποι λόγον τῷ] *bishop;* and concludeth in the end, *He that should disobey these, were a plain atheist,* [ἱερατείαν. Zon.] *and an irreligious person, and one that did set Christ himself and his own ordinances at* [in can. apost.] *naught.* Which orders making presbyters or priests the bishop's assistants, doth not import that they were of equal authority with him, but rather so adjoined, that they also were subject, as hath been proved. In the writings of St. *Cyprian* nothing is more usual, [Cum episcopo] than to make mention of the college of presbyters subject unto the bishop; although in [presbyteri fa-cerdotali hono-] handling the common affairs of the church they assisted him. But of all other places [re conjuncti.] which open the ancient order of episcopal presbyters, the most clear is that epistle of *Cy-* [Ep. 28. Ego &] prian unto *Cornelius,* concerning certain *Novatian* hereticks, received again upon their [compresbyteri nostri qui no-] conversion into the unity of the church. *After that* Urbanus *and* Sidonius, *confessors,* [bis adsidebant.] *had come and signified unto our presbyters, that* Maximus, *a confessor and presbyter, did,* [Ep. 27.] *together with them, desire to return into the church, it seemed meet to hear from their own mouths and confessions, that which by message they had delivered. When they were come, and had been called to account by the presbyters, touching those things they had committed; their answer was, That they had been deceived; and did request, that such things as there they were charged with might be forgotten. It being brought unto me what was done, I took order that the presbytery might be assembled. There were also present five bishops, that, upon settled advice, it might be, with consent of all, determined what should be done about their persons.* Thus far St. *Cyprian.* Wherein it may be, peradventure, demanded, whether he, and other bishops, did thus proceed with advice of

their

their presbyters in all such publick affairs of the church, as being thereunto bound by ecclesiastical canons, or else that they voluntarily so did, because they judged it in discretion as then most convenient. Surely the words of *Cyprian* are plain, that of his own
accord he chose this way of proceeding. *Unto that*, saith he, *which* Donatus, *and* For-
tunatus, *and* Novatus, *and* Gordius *our com-presbyters have written, I could by my self
alone make no reason, forasmuch as at the very first entrance into my bishoprick I resolutely
determined not to do any thing of mine own private judgment, without your counsel, and
the peoples consent.* The reason whereof he rendreth in the same epistle, saying, *When
by the grace of God, my self shall come unto you,* (for St. *Cyprian* was now in exile) *of
things which either have been, or must be done we will consider,* sicut honor mutuus poscit,
as the law of courtesy which one doth owe to another of us requireth. And at this very
mark doth St. *Jerom* evermore aim, in telling bishops, that presbyters were at the first
their equals; that, in some churches, for a long time no bishop was made, but only such
as the presbyters did chuse out amongst themselves, and therefore no cause why the bishop
should disdain to consult with them, and in weighty affairs of the church to use their
advice; sometime to countenance their own actions; or to repress the boldness of proud
and insolent spirits, that which bishops had in themselves sufficient authority and power
to have done, notwithstanding they would not do alone, but craved therein the aid and
assistance of other bishops, as in the case of those *Novatian* hereticks, before alledged,
Cyprian himself did. And in *Cyprian* we find of others the like practice. *Rogatian,* a
bishop, having been used contumeliously by a deacon of his own church, wrote thereof
his complaint unto *Cyprian* and other bishops. In which case their answer was, *That altho', in his own cause, he did of humility rather shew his grievance, than himself
take revenge, which by the rigour of his apostolical office, and the authority of his chair,
he might have presently done, without any further delay;* yet if the party should do
again, as before their judgments were, *fungaris circa eum potestate honoris tui, & eum
vel deponas vel abstineas;* use on him that power which the honour of thy place giveth
thee, either to depose him, or exclude him from access unto holy things. The bishop,
for his assistance and ease, had under him, to guide and direct deacons in their charge,
his arch-deacon; so termed in respect of care over deacons, albeit himself were not deacon, but presbyter. For the guidance of presbyters in their function, the bishop had
likewise under him one of the self same order with them, but above them in authority,
one whom the ancients termed usually an [a] arch-presbyter, we at this day name him dean.
For, most certain truth it is, that churches-cathedral, and the bishops of them, are as
glasses, wherein the face and very countenance of apostolical antiquity remaineth even as
yet to be seen, notwithstanding the alterations which tract of time, and the course of
the world hath brought. For defence and maintenance of them we are most earnestly
bound to strive, even as the *Jews* were for their temple and the high-priest of God therein: the overthrow and ruin of the one, if ever the sacrilegious avarice of atheists should
prevail so far, which God of his infinite mercy forbid, ought no otherwise to move us,
than the people of God were moved, when having beheld the sack and combustion of
his sanctuary in most lamentable manner flaming before their eyes, they uttered from the
bottom of their grieved spirits, those voices of doleful supplication, *Exsurge, Domine, &
miserearis Sion, servi tui diligunt lapides ejus, pulveris ejus miseret eos.*

Cyr. Ep. 93.

Cyr. Ep. 38.

[a] Such a one
was that *Peter*
whom *Cassio-
dor,* writing
the life of *Chry-*
sostom, doth call
the arch-pres-
byter of the
church of *A-*
lexandria, un-
der *Theophilus,*
at that time bi-
shop.

Psal. 141.

VIII. How far the power which bishops had did reach, what number of persons was
subject unto them at the first, and how large their territories were, it is not for the question we have in hand a thing very greatly material to know. For if we prove that bishops
have lawfully of old ruled over other ministers, it is enough, how few soever those ministers have been, how small soever the circuit of place which hath contained them. Yet hereof somewhat, to the end we may so far forth illustrate church antiquities. A law imperial
there is, which sheweth that there was great care had to provide for every christian city
a bishop, as near as might be, and that each city had some territory belonging unto it,
which territory was also under the bishop of the same city; that because it was not universally thus, but in some countries one bishop had subject unto him many cities, and their
territories, the law which provided for establishment of the other orders, should not prejudice those churches wherein this contrary custom had before prevailed. Unto the bishop of every such city, not only the presbyters of the same city, but also of the territory thereunto belonging, were from the first beginning subject. For we must note, that
when as yet there were in cities no parish churches, but only colleges of presbyters under

How far the
power of bi-
shops hath
reached from
the beginning,
in respect of
territory or
local compass.
L. 36. c. E-
pisc. ad Cler.
Ἑκάστη πόλει
bi-
shops had did
ἱερέων ἢ καὶ
ἂν Sola; ἀλ-
γραφὰς τῶν μέ-
εν τὶς ἀφελίας,
πόλιν τῶν ἰδίαι.
πρεσβύτερον ἢ τῆς
shop of every
such city, not
ἢ τοῖς ἄλλοις λ-

τρεπέτω. Ἐξήρηται δ' ὁ τρόπων Σαϊλία; πόλεις. Ὁ δ' ἱερέων· αὐτὸς ἦ τὸν λαὸν ἱερῷ· Καὶ ἡ λειτουργία ἱερέως ἐπὶ τὸ ἐπίσκοπον ἱερ-
ἱσωτάτω. Besides, *Cyr. Ep. 52.* Cum jampridem per omnes provincias & per urbes singulas ordinarii sunt episcopi. [b] Ubi
ecclesiastici ordinis non est consessus, & offert & tingit sacerdos qui est ibi solus. *Tert. exhort. ad castit.*

their

their bishops regiment, yet smaller congregations and churches there were even then abroad, in which churches there was but some one only presbyter to perform among them divine duties. Towns and villages abroad receiving the faith of Christ from cities whereunto they were adjacent, did as spiritual and heavenly colonies, by their subjection, honour those ancient mother churches out of which they grew. And in the christian cities themselves, when the mighty increase of believers made it necessary to have them divided into certain several companies, and over every of those companies one only pastor to be appointed for the ministry of holy things; between the first, and the rest after it, there could not be but a natural inequality, even as between the temple and synagogues in *Jerusalem*. The clergy of cities were termed *Urbici*, to shew a difference between them and the clergies of towns, of villages, of castles abroad. And how many soever these *Cypr. Ep. 25.* parishes or congregations were in number, which did depend on any one principal city-church, unto the bishop of that one church they and their several sole presbyters were all subject.

For if so be, as some imagine, every petty congregation or hamlet had had his own *Hierm. adversf.* particular bishop, what sense could there be in those words of *Jerom* concerning castles, *Lucifer.* villages, and other places abroad, which having only presbyters to teach them, and to minister unto them the sacraments, were resorted unto by bishops for the administration of that wherewith their presbyters were not licensed to meddle. To note a difference of that one church where the bishop hath his seat, and the rest which depend upon it, that one hath usually been termed cathedral, according to the same sense wherein *Ignatius* speaking of the church of *Antioch*, termeth it his throne; and *Cyprian* mak-*Cypr. Ep. 49.* ing mention of *Euaristus* who had been bishop, and was now deposed, termeth him *Cathedræ extorrem*, one that was thrust besides his chair. The church where the bishop is set with his college of presbyters about him, we call a see; the local compass of his authority, we term a diocese. Unto a bishop within the compass of his own both see *a* Conc. Antioch. and diocese, it hath by right of his place evermore appertained *a* to ordain presbyters,⸱ *cap. 9. Ἀκολ-* to make deacons, and with judgment to dispose of all things of weight. The apostle *τὸς & ἱερωσί-* St. *Paul* had episcopal authority, but so at large, that we cannot assign unto him any *συντίποις λοιμ-* one certain diocese. His *b* positive orders and constitutions churches every where did *b* *τὸ μὴ κεῖσθαι* obey. Yea, a charge and a care, saith he, I *c* have even of all the churches. The walks *c* *λοῦ ᾖ τινα ἐλ-* of *Titus* and *Timothy* were limited within the bounds of a narrow precinct. As for *λοιν οἰκονομίας* other bishops, that which *Chrysostom* hath concerning them, *If they be evil, could not* *ληλωνωσμενας.* *possibly agree unto them, unless their authority had reached farther than to some one only* *Conc. Const.* *congregation.* The danger being so great, as it is, to him that scandalizeth one soul, *χεἰγκαν διὰ τῆς* What shall he, saith *Chrysostom*, speaking of a bishop, what shall he deserve, by whom *ἐλευθίρας, &c.* so many souls, yea, even whole cities and people, men, women and children, citizens, *lib. 5. cap. 8.* peasants, inhabitants, both of his own city, and of other towns subject unto it, are of-*I have ordain-* fended? A thing so unusual as it was for a bishop not to have ample jurisdiction, that *ed in the* *Theophilus*, patriarch of *Alexandria*, for making one a bishop of a small town, is noted *churches of* a proud despiser of the commendable orders of the church with this censure, such no-*Galatia, the* velties *d* *Theophilus* presumed every where to begin, taking upon him, as it had been an-*fo.* other *Moses*. Whereby is discovered also their error, who think, that such as in eccle-*d Chryf. in 1. ad* siastical writings they find termed *Chorepiscopos*, were the same in the country, which *Tit.* the bishop was in the city: whereas the old *Chorepiscopi* are they that were appointed of *Chryf.* the bishops to have, as his vicegerents, some oversight of those churches abroad, which were subject unto his see: in which churches they had also power to make sub-deacons, readers, and such like petty church officers. With which power so stinted, they not contenting themselves, but adventuring at the length, to ordain even deacons and presbyters also, as the bishop himself did, their presumption herein was controuled and stayed by *Conc. Antioch.* the ancient edict of councils. For example, that of *Antioch*, it hath seemed good to *can. 10.* the holy synod, that in such towns and countries as are called *Chorepiscopi* do know their limits, and govern the churches under them, contenting themselves with the charge thereof, and with authority to make readers, sub-deacons, exorcists, and to be leaders or guiders of them; but not to meddle with the ordination either of a presbyter or of a deacon, without the bishop of that city, whereunto the *Chorepiscopos* and his territory also is subject. The same synod appointed likewise that those *Chorepiscopi* shall be made by none but the bishop of that city under which they are. Much might hereunto be added, if it were further needful to prove, that the local compass of a bishop's authority and power was never so straitly lifted, as some men would have the world to imagine. But to go forward; degrees of these are, and have been of old, even amongst bishops also themselves; one sort of bishops being superiors unto presbyters only, another sort having preheminence also above bishops. It cometh here to be considered in what respect

4   spect

spect inequality of bishops was thought at the first a thing expedient for the church, and what odds there hath been between them, by how much the power of one hath been larger, higher and greater than of another. Touching the causes for which it hath been esteemed meet that bishops themselves should not every way be equals; they are the same for which the wisdom both of God and man hath evermore approved it as most requisite, that where many governors must of necessity concur, for the ordering of the same affairs, of what nature soever they be, one should have some kind of sway or stroke more than all the residue. For where number is, there must be order, or else of force there will be confusion. Let there be divers agents, of whom each hath his private inducements with resolute purpose to follow them, (as each may have;) unless in this case some had preheminence above the rest, a chance it were, if ever any thing should be either begun, proceeded in, or brought unto any conclusion by them; deliberations and counsels would seldom go forward, their meetings would always be in danger to break up with jars and contradictions. In an army, a number of captains, all of equal power, without some higher to over-sway them; what good would they do? In all nations where a number are to draw any one way, there must be some one principal mover. Let the practice of our very adversaries themselves herein be considered; are the presbyters able to determine of church-affairs, unless their pastors do strike the chiefest stroke, and have power above the rest? Can their pastoral synod do any thing, unless they have some president amongst them? In synods, they are forced to give one pastor preheminence and superiority above the rest. But they answer, That he, who being a pastor according to their discipline, is for the time, some little deal mightier than his brethren, doth not continue so longer than only during the synod. Which answer serveth not to help them out of the briars: for, by their practice they confirm our principle, touching the necessity of one man's preheminence, wheresoever a concurrency of many is required unto any one solemn action: this nature teacheth, and this they cannot chuse but acknowledge. As for the change of his person to whom they give this preheminence, if they think it expedient to make for every synod a new superior, there is no law of God which bindeth them so to do; neither any that telleth them, that they might suffer one and the same man being made president, even to continue so during life, and to leave his preheminence unto his successors after him, as by the ancient order of the church archbishops, president amongst bishops, have used to do. The ground therefore of their preheminence above bishops, is the necessity of often concurrency of many bishops about the publick affairs of the church; as consecrations of bishops, consultations of remedy of general disorders, audience judicial, when the actions of any bishop should be called in question, or appeals are made from his sentence by such as think themselves wronged. These, and the like affairs, usually requiring that many bishops should orderly assemble, begin, and conclude somewhat; it hath seemed, in the eyes of reverend antiquity, a thing most requisite, that the church should not only have bishops, but even amongst bishops some to be in authority chiefest. Unto which purpose, the very state of the whole world, immediately before christianity took place, doth seem by the special providence of God to have been prepared. For we must know, that the countries where the gospel was first planted, were for the most part subject to the *Roman* empire. The *Romans* use was commonly, when by war they had subdued foreign nations, to make them provinces, that is to place over them *Roman* governors, such as might order them according to the laws and customs of *Rome*. And to the end that all things might be the more easily and orderly done, a whole country being divided into sundry parts, there was in each part some one city, whereinto they about did resort for justice. Every such

* Cic. Fam. Ep. part was termed a *diocese*. Howbeit the name *diocese* is sometime so generally taken, 53. lib. 13. Si quid habebis cum aliquo Hellespontio controversiæ ut in illam λ. ἀἰκηστι. The suit which Tully maketh was this, that the party in whose behalf he wrote to the proprætor, might have his causes put over to that court which was held in the diocese of *Hellespont*, where the man did abide, and not to his trouble be forced to follow them at *Ephesus*, which was the chiefest court in that province. that it containeth not only more such parts of providence, but even more provinces also than one; as the diocese of *Asia* containing eight; the diocese of *Africa* seven. Touching dioceses according unto a stricter sense, whereby they are taken for a part of a province, the words of *Livy* do plainly shew what orders the *Romans* did observe in them. For at what time they had brought the *Macedonians* into subjection, the *Roman* governor, by order from the senate of *Rome*, gave charge that *Macedonia* should be divided into four regions or dioceses. *Capita regionum ubi concilia fierent, primæ sedis* Amphipolim, *secundæ* Thessalonicen, *tertiæ* Pellam, *quartæ* Pelagoniam *fecit. Eo, concilia sua cujusque regionis indici, pecuniam conferri, ibi magistratus creari jussit.* This before the days of the emperors, by their appointment *Thessalonica* was afterwards the chiefest, and in it the highest governor of *Macedonia* had his seat. Whereupon the other three dioceses were in that respect inferior unto it, as daughters unto a mother

city; for not unto every town of justice was that title given, but was peculiar unto those cities wherein principal courts were kept. Thus in *Macedonia* the mother city was *Thessalonica*; in *Asia*, *Ephesus*; in *Africa*, *Carthage*; for so [b] *Justinian* in his time made it. The governors, officers, and inhabitants of those mother-cities were termed for difference-sake *metropolites*, that is to say, *mother-city men*; than which nothing could possibly have been devised more fit to suit with the nature of that form of spiritual regiment, under which afterwards the church should live. Wherefore if the prophet saw cause to acknowledge unto the Lord, that the light of his gracious providence did shine no where more apparently to the eye, than in preparing the land of *Canaan* to be a receptacle for that church which was of old, *Thou hast brought a vine out of Egypt, thou hast cast out the heathen and planted* [Psal. 30. 8, 9] *it, thou madest room for it, and when it had taken root it filled the land*; how much more ought we to wonder at the handy-work of almighty God, who, to settle the kingdom of his dear Son, did not cast out any one people, but directed in such sort the politick counsels of them who ruled far and wide over all, that they throughout all nations, people and countries upon earth, should unwittingly prepare the field wherein the vine which God did intend, that is to say, the church of his dearly beloved Son, was to take root? For unto nothing else can we attribute it, saving only unto the very incomprehensible force of divine providence, that the world was in so marvellous fit sort divided, levelled, and laid out beforehand. Whose work could it be but his alone to make such provision for the direct implantation of his church? Wherefore inequality of bishops being found a thing convenient for the church of God, in such consideration as hath been shewed; when it came secondly in question, which bishops should be higher and which lower, [Concil. Antiochen. c. 9.] it seemed herein not to the civil monarch only, but to the most, expedient that the dignity and celebrity of mother-cities should be respected. They which dream, that if civil authority had not given such pre-eminence unto one city more than another, there had never grown an inequality among bishops, are deceived. Superiority of one bishop over another would be requisite in the church, although that civil distinction were abolished. Other causes having made it necessary, even amongst bishops, to have some in degree higher than the rest, the civil dignity of place was considered only as a reason wherefore this bishop should be preferred before that: Which deliberation had been likely enough to have raised no small trouble, but that such was the circumstance of place, as being followed in that choice, besides the manifest conveniency thereof, took away all shew of partiality, prevented secret emulations, and gave no man occasion to think his person disgraced, in that another was preferred before him.

Thus we see upon what occasion metropolitan bishops became archbishops. Now while the whole christian world, in a manner, still continued under the civil government, there being oftentimes within some one more large territory, divers and sundry mother-churches, the metropolitans whereof were archbishops, as for order's sake, it grew hereupon expedient, there should be a difference also among them; so no way seemed, in those times, more fit than to give pre-eminence unto them whose metropolitan sees were of special desert or dignity. For which cause these, as being bishops in the chiefest mother churches, were termed primates, and at the length, by way of excellency, *patriarchs*. For, ignorant we are not, how sometimes the title of *patriarch* is generally given to all metropolitan bishops. They are mightily therefore to blame which are so bold and confident, as to affirm that, for the space of above [Vilerius de statu primitivæ ecclesiæ.] four hundred and thirty years after Christ, all metropolitan bishops were in every respect equals, till the second council of *Constantinople* exalted certain metropolitans above the rest. True it is, they were equals as touching the exercise of spiritual power within their diocefes, when they dealt with their own flock. For what is it that one of them might do within the compass of his own precinct, but another within his might do the same? but that there was no subordination at all, of one of them unto another; that when they all, or sundry of them, were to deal in the same causes, there was no difference of first and second in degree, no distinction of higher and lower in authority acknowledged amongst them is most untrue. The great council of *Nice* was after our Saviour Christ but three hundred twenty four years, and in that council certain metropolitans are said even then to have had antient preheminence and dignity above the rest; namely, the primate of *Alexandria*, of *Rome*, and of *Antioch*. Threescore years after this, there were synods under [Socr. l. 3. c. 8.] the emperor *Theodosius*, which synod was the first at *Constantinople*, whereat one hundred and fifty bishops were assembled: at which council it was decreed, that the bishop of *Constantinople* should not only be added unto the former primates, but also that his place should be

[margin notes:]
[a] *Cic. ad Attic. lib. 5. Ep. 13. Item. l. observ. D. de officio proconfulis & legati.*
[b] *Lib. 1. Tit. 27. l. 1. sect. 1. & 2. Sancimus ut sicut oriens atque Illyricum, ita & Africa prætoriana maxima potestate speculariter a nostra clementia decoretur. Cujus sedem jubemus esse Carthaginem & ab ea, auxiliante Deo, septem proqvinciæ cum suis judicibus disponantur.*

Can. 28.

Can. 39.

Novel. 113.
22.

Conc.Nic.c.6.

Ejufd. Conc.
c. 7.

be fecond amongft them, the next to the bifhop of *Rome* in dignity. The fame decree again renewed concerning *Conftantinople*, and the reafon thereof laid open in the council of *Chalcedon*. At the length came that fecond of *Conftantinople*, whereat were fix hundred and thirty bifhops for a third confirmation thereof. Laws imperial there are likewife extant to the fame effect. Herewith the bifhop of *Conftantinople* being over much puffed up, not only could not endure that fee to be in eftimation higher, whereunto his own had preferment to be the next, but he challenged more than ever any chriftian bifhop in the world before either had, or with reafon could have. What he challenged, and was therein as then refufed by the bifhop of *Rome*, the fame bifhop of *Rome* in procefs of time obtained for himfelf, and having gotten it by bad means, hath both upheld and augmented it, and upholdeth it by acts and practices much worfe. But primates, according to their firft inftitution, were all in relation unto archbifhops, the fame by prerogative, which archbifhops were, being compared unto bifhops. Before the council of *Nice*, albeit there were both metropolitans and primates, yet could not this be a means forcible enough to procure the peace of the church ; but all things were wonderful tumultuous and troublefome, by reafon of one fpecial practice common unto the hereticks of thofe times ; which was that when they had been condemned and caft out of the church by the fentence of their own bifhops, they, contrary to the antient received orders of the church, had a cuftom to wander up and down, and to infinuate themfelves into favour where they were not known ; imagining themfelves to be fafe enough, and not to be clean cut off from the body of the church, if they could any where find a bifhop which was content to communicate with them : whereupon enfued, as in that cafe there needs muft, every day quarrels and jars unappeafable amongft bifhops. The *Nicene* council, for redrefs hereof, confidered the bounds of every archbifhop's ecclefiaftical jurifdictions, what they had been in former times ; and accordingly appointed unto each grand part of the chriftian world fome one primate, from whofe judgment no man living within his territory might appeal, unlefs it were to a council general of all bifhops. The drift and purport of which order was, that neither any man oppreft by his own particular bifhop might be deftitute of a remedy, thro' appeal unto the more indifferent fentence of fome other ordinary judge ; nor yet every man be left to fuch liberty, as before, to fhift himfelf out of their hands for whom it was moft meet to have the hearing and determining of his caufe. The evil, for remedy whereof this order was taken, annoyed at that prefent, efpecially the church of *Alexandria* in *Egypt*, where *Arianifm* begun. For which caufe the ftate of that church is in the *Nicene* canons concerning this matter mentioned before the reft. The words of their facred edict are thefe, let thofe cuftoms remain in force which have been of old the cuftoms of *Egypt* and *Libya*, and *Pentapolis* ; by which cuftoms the bifhop of *Alexandria* hath authority over all thefe ; the rather, for that this hath alfo been the ufe of the bifhop of *Rome*, yea, the fame hath been kept in *Antioch*, and in other Provinces. Now, becaufe the cuftom likewife had been, that great honour fhould be done to the bifhop of *Ælia* or *Jerufalem* ; therefore left their decree concerning the primate of *Antioch*, fhould any whit prejudice the dignity and honour of that fee, fpecial provifion is made, that altho' it were inferior in degree, not only unto *Antioch* the chief of the *Eaft*, but even unto *Cefaria* too ; yet fuch preheminence it fhould retain as belonged to a mother-city, and enjoy whatfoever fpecial prerogative or privilege it had befides. Let men therefore hereby judge of what continuance this order which upholdeth degrees of bifhops muft needs have been, when a general council of three hundred and eighteen bifhops, living themfelves within three hundred years after Chrift, doth reverence the fame for antiquities fake, as a thing which had been even then of old obferved in the moft renowned parts of the chriftian world. Wherefore needlefs altogether are thofe vain and wanton demands, no mention of an archbifhop in *Theophilus* bifhop of *Antioch* ? none in *Ignatius* ? none in *Clemens* of *Alexandria* ? none in *Juftin Martyr, Irenæus, Tertullian, Cyprian* ? none in all thofe old hiftoriographers, out of which *Eufebius* gathereth his ftory ? none till the time of the council of *Nice* three hundred and twenty years after Chrift ? As if the mention, which is thereof made in that very council where fo many bifhops acknowledge archiepifcopal dignity even then antient, were not of far more weight and value than if every of thofe fathers had written large difcourfes thereof. But what is it which they will blufh at who dare fo confidently fet it down, that in the council of *Nice* fome bifhops being termed metropolitans, no more difference is thereby meant to have been between

T. C. l. 1. 91. What ? no mention of him in *Theophilus*, bifhop of *Antioch* ? none in *Clemens Alexandrinus* ? none in *Ignatius* ? none in *Juftin Martyr* ? In *Irenæus*, in *Tertullian*, in *Origen*, in *Cyprian* ? In thofe old hiftoriographers, out of which *Eufebius* gathered his ftory ? Was it for his baffnefs and fmallnefs that he could not be feen amongft the bifhops, elders and deacons, being the chief and principal of them all ? Can the Cedar of *Lebanon* be hidden amongft the box-trees ? T. C. l. 1. *ubi fupra*. A metropolitan bifhop was nothing elfe but a bifhop of that place which it pleafed the emperor or magiftrate to make the chief of the diocefe or fhire ; and as for this name it makes no more difference between a bifhop and a bifhop, than when I fay a minifter of *London*, and a minifter of *Newington*.

tween

tween one bishop and another than is shewed between one minister and another, when we say such a one is a minister in the city of *London*, and such a one a minister in the town of *Newington*. So that, to be termed a metropolitan bishop did, in their conceit, import no more preheminence above other bishops, than we mean, that a girdler hath over others of the same trade, if we term him which doth inhabit some mother-city for difference-sake a metropolitan girdler. But the truth is too manifest to be eluded; a bishop at that time had power in his own diocese over all other ministers there, and a metropolitan bishop sundry preheminences above other bishops, one of which preheminences was, in the ordination of bishops to have κύϱᾳ τῶν γι- ᵛᵒᵐⁱⁿᵉ, the chief power of ordering all things done. Which preheminence that council it self doth mention, as also a greater belonging unto the patriarch or primate of *Alexandria*, concerning whom it is there likewise said, that to him did belong Ἐξουσία, authority and power over all Egypt, Pentapolis, and Lybia: within which compass sundry metropolitan sees to have been, there is no man ignorant, which in those antiquities have any knowledge. Certain prerogatives there are wherein metropolitans excelled other bishops, certain also wherein primates excelled other metropolitans. Archiepiscopal or metropolitan prerogatives are those mentioned in the old imperial constitutions, to a convocate the holy bishops under them, within the compass of their own provinces, when need required their meeting together for inquisition and redress of publick disorders; b to grant unto bishops under them leave and faculty of absence from their own dioceses, when it seemed necessary that they should other where converse for some reasonable while; c to give notice unto bishops under them of things commanded by supreme authority; d to have the hearing and first determining of such causes as any man had against a bishop; e to receive the appeals of the inferior clergy, in case they found themselves over-born by the bishop, their immediate judge. And left haply it should be imagined that canons ecclesiastical we want to make the self-same thing manifest; in the council of *Antioch* it was thus decreed, f *The bishop in every province must know, that he which is bishop in the mother-city, hath not only charge of his own parish or diocese, but even of the whole province also.* Again, *It hath seemed good, that other bishops, without him, should do nothing more than only that which concerns each one's parish, and the places underneath it.* Further, by the self-same council all council provincial are reckoned void and frustrate, unless the bishop of the mother-city within that province where such councils should be, were present at them. So that the want of his presence, and, in canons for church-government, want of his approbation also, did disannul them. Not so the want of any others. Finally, concerning election of bishops, the council of *Nice* hath this general rule, that the chief ordering of all things here, is in every province committed to the metropolitan. Touching them, who amongst metropolitans were also primates, and had of sundry united provinces, the chiefest metropolitan see, of such that canon in the council of *Carthage* was eminent, whereby a bishop is forbidden to go beyond seas without the licence of the highest chair within the same bishop's own country; and of such which beareth the name apostolical, is that antient canon likewise, which chargeth the bishop of each NATION to know him which is FIRST amongst them, and to esteem of him as an head, and to do no extraordinary thing but with his leave. The chief primates of the christian world were the bishops of *Rome*, *Alexandria*, and *Antioch*. To whom the bishop of *Constantinople*, being afterwards added, St. *Chrysostom* the bishop of that see is in that respect said, to have had the care and charge, not only of the city of *Constantinople*, sed etiam totius Thraciæ quæ sex præfecturis est divisa, & Asiæ totius quæ ab undecim præsidibus regitur. The rest of the east was under *Antioch*, the south under *Alexandria*, and the west under *Rome*. Whereas therefore *John* the bishop of *Jerusalem* being noted of heresy, had written an apology for himself unto the bishop of *Alexandria*, named *Theophilus*; St. *Jerome* reproveth his breach of the order of the church herein, saying, Tu qui regulas quæris ecclesiasticas, & Niceni concilii canonibus uteris, responde mihi, ad Alexandrinum episcopum Palæstina quid pertinet? Ni fallor, hoc ibi decernitur ut Palæstinæ metropolis Cæsarea sit, & totius orientis Antiochia. Aut igitur ad Cæsariensem episcopum referre debueras, aut si procul expetendum judicium erat, Antiochiam potius literæ dirigendæ. Thus much concerning that local compass which was antiently set out to bishops; within the bounds and limits whereof we find, that they did accordingly exercise that episcopal authority and power which they had over the church of Christ.

IX. The first whom we read to have bent themselves against the superiority of bishops

---

Marginal notes:

γι- Conc. Nicen.
c. 6. Illud autem omnino manifestum, quod siquis absque metropolitani sententia factus sit episc. hunc. magna synodus definivit episc. esse non oportere.
Can. 4.
a Novel. 123;
can. 10.
Nov. 123.
b can. 9.
c Nov. 79.
can. 2.
d Nov. 123;
can. 22.
e Nov. 123;
can. 23.

f Can. 9.

Can. 16;

Can. 4. τὸ πίσα τὸν γνμῖσ-λον.

Cassiod. in vita Chrysost.

Hieron. ep. 9;

---

shops were *Aerius* and his followers. *Aerius* seeking to be made a bishop, could not brook that *Euſtathius* was thereunto preferred before him. Whereas therefore he saw himself unable to rise to that greatneſs which his ambitious pride did affect, his way of revenge was to try what wit, being ſharpned with envy and malice, could do, in raiſing a new ſeditious opinion that the ſuperiority which biſhops had, was a thing which they ſhould not have; that a biſhop might not ordain; and that a biſhop ought not any way to be diſtinguiſhed from a presbyter. For ſo doth St. *Auguſtine* deliver the opinion of *Aerius*: *Epiphanius* not ſo plainly, nor ſo directly, but after a more rhetorical ſort. His ſpeech was rather furious than convenient for man to uſe, *What is*, ſaith he, *a biſhop more than a presbyter? The one doth differ from the other nothing. For their order is one, their honour one, one their dignity. A biſhop impoſeth his hands, ſo doth a presbyter. A biſhop baptizeth, the like doth a presbyter. The biſhop is a miniſter of divine ſervice, a presbyter the ſame. The biſhop ſitteth as a judge in a throne, even the presbyter ſitteth alſo. A presbyter therefore doing thus far the ſelf-ſame thing which a biſhop did, it was by* Aerius *inforced, that they ought not in any thing to differ.* Are we to think *Aerius* had wrong in being judged an heretick for holding this opinion? Surely if hereſy be an error falſly fathered upon ſcriptures, but indeed repugnant to the truth of the word of God, and by the conſent of the univerſal church in the councils, or in her contrary uniform practice throughout the whole world, declared to be ſuch; and the opinion of *Aerius* in this point be a plain error of that nature, there is no remedy, but *Aerius* ſo ſchiſmatically, and ſtiffly maintaining it, muſt even ſtand where *Epiphanius* and *Auguſtin* have placed him. An error repugnant unto the truth of the word of God is held by them, whoſoever they be, that ſtand in defence of any concluſion drawn erroneouſly out of ſcripture, and untruly thereon fathered. The opinion of *Aerius* therefore being falſly collected out of ſcripture, muſt needs be acknowledged an error repugnant unto the truth of the word of God. His opinion was, that there ought not to be any difference between a biſhop and a presbyter. His grounds and reaſons for his opinion were ſentences of ſcripture. Under pretence of which ſentences, whereby it ſeemed that biſhops and presbyters at the firſt did not differ, it was concluded by *Aerius*, that the church did ill in permitting any difference to be made. The anſwer which *Epiphanius* maketh unto ſome part of the proofs by *Aerius* alledged, was not greatly ſtudied or laboured; for through a contempt of ſo baſe an error, for this himſelf did perceive and profeſs, yieldeth he thereof expreſly this reaſon; men that have wit do evidently ſee that all this is meer fooliſhneſs. But how vain and ridiculous ſoever his opinion ſeemed

Τὸ τύτο πολ- λὰς ὑ πάντες.   unto wiſe men; with it *Aerius* deceived many, for which cauſe ſomewhat was convenient to be ſaid againſt it. And in that very extemporal ſlightneſs which *Epiphanius* there uſeth, albeit the anſwer made to *Aerius* be [a] in part

[a] As in that he ſaith, the apoſtle doth name ſometimes presbyters and not biſhops, 1 *Tim.* 4. 14. ſometime biſhops and not presbyters, *Phil.* 1. 1. becauſe all churches had not both, for want of able and ſufficient men. In ſuch churches therefore as had but the one, the apoſtle could not mention the other. Which anſwer is nothing to the latter place abovementioned: For that the church of *Philippi* ſhould have more biſhops than one, and want a few able men to be presbyters under the regiment of one biſhop, how ſhall we think it probable or likely?

     but raw, yet ought not hereby the truth to find any leſs favour than in other cauſes it doth, where we do not therefore judge hereſy to have the better, becauſe now and then it alledgeth that for it ſelf, which defenders of the truth do not always ſo fully anſwer. Let it therefore ſuffice, that *Aerius* did bring nothing unanſwerable. The weak ſolutions which the one doth give, are to us no prejudice againſt the cauſe, as long as the others oppoſitions are of no greater ſtrength and validity. Did not *Aerius*, trow ye, deſerve to be eſteemed as a new *Apollos*, mighty and powerful in the word, which could for maintenance of his cauſe bring forth ſo plain divine authorities, to prove by the apoſtles own writings that biſhops ought not in any thing to differ from other presbyters? for example, where it is ſaid that presbyters made *Timothy* biſhop, is it not clear that a biſhop ſhould not differ from a presbyter by having power of ordination? again, if a biſhop might by order be diſtinguiſhed from

[b] 1 *Tim.* 4. 14. with the impoſition of the hands. Of which presbytery St. *Paul* was chief, 2 *Tim.* 1. 6. And I think no man will deny that St. *Paul* had more than a ſimple presbyter's authority, *Phil.* 1. 1. To all the ſaints at *Philippi*, with the biſhops and deacons. For as yet in the church of *Philippi*, there was no one which had authority beſides the apoſtles, but their presbyters or biſhops were all both in title and in power equal.

     a presbyter, would the apoſtle have given [b] as he doth unto presbyters, the title of biſhops? Theſe were the invincible demonſtrations wherewith *Aerius* did ſo fiercely aſſault biſhops. But the ſentence of *Aerius* perhaps was only, that the difference between a biſhop and a presbyter hath grown by the order and cuſtom of the church, the word of God not appointing that any ſuch difference ſhould be. Well, let *Aerius* then find the favour to have his ſentence ſo conſtrued; yet his fault in condemning the order of the church, his not ſubmitting himſelf unto that order, the ſchiſm which he cauſed in the church about it, who can excuſe? No, the truth is, that theſe things did even neceſſarily enſue, by force of the very opinion which he and his followers did hold. His

                                                     concluſion

conclusion was, that there ought to be no difference between a presbyter and a bishop. His proofs, those scripture sentences which make mention of bishops and presbyters without any such distinction or difference. So that if between his conclusion and the proofs whereby he laboured to strengthen the same, there be any shew of coherence at all, we must of necessity confess, that when *Aerius* did plead, there is by the word of God no difference between a presbyter and a bishop ; his meaning was, not only that the word of God it self appointeth not, but that it enforceth on us the duty of not appointing, or allowing, that any such difference should be made.

X. And of the self same mind are the enemies of government by bishops, even at this present day. They hold, as *Aerius* did, that if Christ and his apostles were obeyed, a bishop should not be permitted to ordain ; that between a presbyter and a bishop the word of God alloweth not any inequality or difference to be made ; that their order, their authority, their power ought to be one ; that it is but by usurpation and corruption, that the one sort are suffered to have rule over the other, or to be any way superior unto them. Which opinion having now so many defenders, shall never be able while the world doth stand to find in some, believing antiquity, as much as one which hath given it countenance, or born any friendly affection towards it. Touching these men therefore, whose desire is to have all equal, three ways there are whereby they usually oppugn the received order of the church of 'Christ. First, by disgracing the inequality of pastors, as a new and meer human invention, a thing which was never drawn out of scripture, where all pastors are found (they say) to have one and the same power both of order and jurisdiction. Secondly, by gathering together the differences between that power which we give to bishops, and that which was given them of old in the church : so that, albeit even the antient took more than was warrantable ; yet so far they swerved not as ours have done. Thirdly, by endeavouring to prove, that the scripture directly forbiddeth, and that the judgment of the wisest, the holiest, the best in all ages, condemneth utterly the inequality which we allow.

In what respect episcopal regiment is gainsaid by the authors of present reformation at this day.

XI. That inequality of pastors is a meer human invention, a thing not found in the word of God, they prove thus :

1. *All the places of scripture where the word* bishop *is used, or any other derived of that name, signify an oversight in respect of some particular congregation only, and never in regard of pastors committed unto his oversight. For which cause the names of bishops, and presbyters, or pastoral elders, are used indifferently, to signify one and the self same thing. Which so indifferent and common use of these words for one and the self same office, so constantly and perpetually in all places, declareth that the word* bishop *in the apostle's writing importeth not a pastor of higher power and authority over other pastors.*

Their arguments in disgrace of regiment by bishops, as being 'a meer invention of man, and not found in scripture, answered.

2. *All pastors are called to their office by the same means of proceeding ; the scripture maketh no difference in the manner of their tryal, election, ordination : which proveth their office and power to be by scripture all one.*

1 *Tim.* 3. 5. *Phil.* 1. 1.

3. *The apostles were all of equal power, and all pastors do alike succeed the apostles in their ministry and power, the commission and authority whereby they succeed being in scripture but one and the same that was committed to the apostles, without any difference of committing to one pastor more, or to another less.*

1 *Pet.* 5. 1, 2.

4. *The power of the censures and keys of the church, and of ordaining and ordering ministers (in which two points especially this superiority is challenged) is not committed to any one pastor of the church, more than to another ; but the same is committed as a thing to be carried equally in the guidance of the church. Whereby it appeareth, that scripture maketh all pastors, not only in the ministry of the word and sacraments, but also in all ecclesiastical jurisdiction and authority, equal.*

5. *The council of Nice doth attribute this difference, not unto any ordination of God, but to an antient custom used in former times, which judgment is also followed afterward by other councils,* Concil. Antioch. cap. 9.

6. Upon these premises, their summary collection and conclusion is, *That the ministry of the gospel, and the functions thereof, ought to be from heaven and of God,* Joh. 1. 23. *that if they be of God, and from heaven, then are they set down in the word of God ; that the ministry if they be not in the word of God (as by the premises it doth appear* (they say) *that our kinds of bishops are not) it followeth, that they are invented by the brain of men, and are of the earth, and that consequently they can do no good in the church of Christ, but harm.*

T.C.l.1. p. 13. So that it appeareth that the ministry of the gospel, and the functions thereof ought to be from heaven :

From heaven, I say, and heavenly, because although it be executed by earthly men, and ministers are chosen also by men like unto themselves, yet because it is done by the word and institution of God, it may well be accounted to come from heaven and from God.

Our answer hereunto is, first, that their proofs are unavailable to shew that scripture affordeth no evidence for the inequality of pastors. Secondly, that albeit the scripture

Answ.

I

scripture did no way infinuate the fame to be God's ordinance, and the apoftles to have brought it in, albeit the church were acknowledged by all men to have been the firft beginner thereof a long time after the apoftles were gone; yet is not the authority of bifhops hereby difannulled, it is not hereby proved unfit, or unprofitable for the church.

1. That the word of God doth acknowledge no inequality of power amongft paftors of the church, neither doth it appear by the fignification of this word *bifhop*, nor by the indifferent ufe thereof. For, concerning fignification, firft it is clearly untrue that no other thing is thereby fignified but only an overfight in refpeft of a particular church and congregation. For, I befeech you, of what parifh or particular congrega-

Acts 1. 20. tion was *Matthias* bifhop? His office fcripture doth term epifcopal: which being no other than was common unto all the apoftles of Chrift; forafmuch as in that number there is not any to whom the overfight of many paftors did not belong by force and virtue of that office; it followeth that the very word doth fometimes, even in fcripture, fignify an overfight fuch as includeth charge over paftors themfelves. And if we look to the ufe of the word, being applied with reference unto fome one church, as *Ephefus*, *Philippi*, and fuch like, albeit the guides of thofe churches be interchangeably in fcripture termed fometime bifhops, fometime prebyters, to fignify men having overfight and charge, without relation at all unto other than the chriftian laity alone; yet this doth not hinder, but that fcripture may in fome place have other names, whereby certain of thofe prebyters or bifhops are noted to have the overfight and charge of pa-

Rev. 2. 1. ftors, as out of all peradventure they had whom St. *John* doth intitle angels.

2. As for thofe things which the apoftle hath fet down concerning tryal, election, and ordination of paftors, that he maketh no difference in the manner of their calling, this alfo is but a filly argument to prove their office and their power equal by the fcripture. The form of admitting each fort unto their offices, needed no particular inftruction. There was no fear, but that fuch matters of courfe would eafily enough be obferved. The apoftle therefore toucheth thofe things wherein judgment, wifdom, and confcience is required; he carefully admonifheth of what quality ecclefiaftical perfons fhould be, that their dealing might not be fcandalous in the church. And forafmuch as thofe things are general, we fee that of deacons there are delivered, in a manner, the felf-fame precepts which are given concerning paftors, fo far as concerneth their tryal, election, and ordination. Yet who doth hereby collect that fcripture maketh deacons and paftors equal? If notwithftanding it be yet demanded, *Wherefore he which teacheth what kind of perfons deacons and presbyters fhould be, hath nothing in particular about the quality of chief presbyters, whom we call bifhops?* I anfwer briefly, that there it was no fit place for any fuch difcourfe to be made, inafmuch as the apoftle wrote unto *Timothy* and *Titus*, who having by commiffion epifcopal authority, were to exercife the fame in ordaining, not bifhops (the apoftles themfelves yet living, and retaining that power in their own hands) but presbyters, fuch as the apoftles at the firft did create throughout all churches. Bifhops by reftraint (only *James* at *Jerufalem* excepted) were not yet in being.

3. About equality amongft the apoftles there is by us no controverfy moved. If in the rooms of the apoftles, which were of equal authority, all paftors do by fcripture fucceed alike, where fhall we find a commiffion in fcripture which they fpeak of, which appointed all to fucceed in the felf-fame equality of power; except that commiffion which doth authorize to preach and baptize, fhould be alledged, which maketh nothing to the purpofe; for in fuch things, all paftors are ftill equal? We muft, I fear me, wait very long before any other will be fhewed. For howfoever the apoftles were equals amongft themfelves, all other paftors were not equals with the apoftles while they lived, neither are they any where appointed to be afterward each other's equals. Apoftles had, as we know, authority over all fuch as were no apoftles; by force of which their authority they might both command and judge. It was for the fingular good and benefit of thofe difciples whom Chrift left behind him, and of the paftors which were afterwards chofen; for the great good, I fay, of all forts, that the apoftles were in power above them. Every day brought forth fomewhat wherein they faw by experience, how much it ftood them in ftead to be under controlment of thofe fuperiors and higher governors of God's houfe. Was it a thing fo behoveful that paftors fhould be fubject unto paftors in the apoftles own times? and is there any commandment that this fubjection fhould ceafe with them? and that the paftors of the fucceeding ages fhould be all equals? No, no, this ftrange and abfurd conceit of equality amongft paftors (the mother of fchifm, and of confufion) is but a dream newly brought forth, and feen never in the church before.

4. Power of cenfure and ordination appeareth even by fcripture marvellous probable to have been derived from Chrift to his church, without this furmifed equality in them

to

to whom he hath committed the same. For I would know, whether *Timothy* and *Titus* were commanded by St. *Paul* to do any thing, more than Christ hath authorized pastors to do; and to the one it is scripture which saith, *Against a presbyter receive thou no accusation,* ⟨t Tim. 5. 19.⟩ *saving under two or three witnesses*: Scripture which likewise hath said to the other, *for this very cause left I THEE in Crete, that THOU shouldst redress the things that re-* ⟨Tit. 1. 5.⟩ *main, and shouldst ORDAIN presbyters in every city, as I appointed THEE.* In the former place the power of censure is spoken of, and the power of ordination in the latter. Will they say that every pastor there was equal to *Timothy* and *Titus* in these things ? If they do, the apostle himself is against it, who saith, that of their two very persons he had made choice, and appointed in those places them for performances of those duties ; whereas, if the same had belonged unto others no less than to them, and not principally unto them above others, it had been fit for the apostle accordingly to have directed his letters concerning these things in general unto them all which had equal interest in them ; even as it had been likewise fit to have written those epistles in St. *John*'s revelation, unto whole ecclesiastical senates, rather than unto the angels of each church, had not some one been above the rest in authority to order the affairs of the church. Scripture therefore doth most probably make for the inequality of pastors, even in all ecclesiastical affairs, and by very express mention, as well in censures as ordinations.

5. In the *Nicene* council there are confirmed certain prerogatives and dignities belonging unto primates or archbishops, and of them it is said, that the antient custom of the church had been to give them such pre-eminence, but no syllable whereby any man should conjecture that those fathers did not honour the superiority which bishops had over other pastors only upon antient custom, and not as true apostolical heavenly and divine ordinance.

6. Now, altho' we should leave the general received persuasion held from the first beginning that the apostles themselves left bishops invested with power above other pastors ; although, I say, we would give over this opinion, and embrace that other conjecture ⟨They of Wal-den, Aen. Syl.⟩ which so many have thought good to follow, and which my self did sometimes judge a ⟨hist. Boem.⟩ great deal more probable than now I do, merely that after the apostles were deceased, ⟨Marsilius de-⟩ churches did agree amongst themselves, for preservation of peace and order, to make ⟨fenf. pac. Nicl.⟩ one presbyter in each city, chief over the rest, and to translate into him that power by ⟨Thomas Wald. c. 1. l. 2. c. 60.⟩ force and virtue whereof the apostles, while they were alive, did preserve and uphold or- ⟨Calvin. Com.⟩ der in the church, exercising spiritual jurisdiction, partly by themselves, and partly by ⟨in 1. ad Tit. Bullenger,⟩ evangelists, because they could not always every where themselves be present : this order ⟨Dewd. 1. Ser.⟩ taken by the church it self (for so let us suppose, that the apostles did neither by word ⟨3. Jucl. Def. apol. par. 2.⟩ nor deed appoint it) were notwithstanding more warrantable, than that it should give ⟨c. 9. Di. 1.⟩ place and be abrogated, because the ministry of the gospel, and functions thereof ought ⟨Fulk answ. to the Test.⟩ to be from heaven. There came chief priests and elders unto our Saviour Christ as ⟨Tit. 1. 5.⟩ he was teaching in the temple, and the question which they moved unto him was this, ⟨John 1. 25.⟩ *By what authority dost thou these things, and who gave thee this authority ?* their question ⟨Mat. 21. 23.⟩ he repelled with a counter-demand, *The baptism of* John *whence was it, from heaven, or of men ?* Hereat they paused, secretly disputing within themselves, *If we should say from heaven, he will ask, wherefore did ye not then believe him ? and if we say of men, we fear the people, for all hold* John *a prophet.* What is it now which hereupon these men would infer ? that all functions ecclesiastical ought in such sort to be from heaven, as the function of *John* was ? no such matter here contained. Nay, doth not the contrary rather appear most plainly by that which is here set down ? For when our Saviour doth ask concerning the *baptism,* that is to say, the whole spiritual function of *John, whether it were from heaven or of men,* he giveth clearly to understand that Men give authority unto some, and some God himself from heaven doth authorize. Nor is it said, or in any sort signified, that none have lawful authority which have it not in such manner as *John,* from heaven. Again, when the priests and elders were loth to say, that *John* had his calling *from men,* the reason was not because they thought that so *John* should not have any good or lawful calling, but because they saw that by this means they should somewhat embase the calling of *John* ; whom all men knew to have been sent from God, according to the manner of prophets by a meer celestial vocation. So that out of the evidence here alledged, these things we may directly conclude, first that whoso doth exercise any kind of function in the church, he cannot lawfully so do, except authority be given him : Secondly, that if authority be not given him from men, as the authority of teaching was given unto scribes and pharisees, it must be given him from heaven, as authority was given unto *Christ, Elias, John Baptist,* and the prophets. For these two only ways there are to have authority. But a strange conclusion it is, God himself did, from heaven, authorize *John* to bear witness of the light, to prepare a way for the promised *Messiah,* to publish the

᛭

nearness

nearnefs of the kingdom of God, to preach repentance, and to baptize (for by this part which was in the function of *John*, moft noted, all the reft are together fignified ;) therefore the church of God hath no power upon new occurrences to appoint, to ordain an ecclefiaftical function, as *Mofes* did upon *Jethro's* advice devife a civil. All things we grant which are in the church ought to be of God. But, forafmuch as they may be two ways accounted fuch : one, if they be of his own inftitution, and not of ours; another if they be of ours, and yet with his approbation ; this latter way there is no impediment, but that the fame thing which is of men, may be alfo juftly and truly faid to be of God, the fame thing from heaven which is from earth. Of all good things God himfelf is author, and confequently an approver of them. The rule to difcern when the actions of men are good, when they are fuch as they ought to be, is more ample and large than the law which God hath fet particular down in his holy word, the fcripture is but a part of that rule as hath been heretofore at large declared. If therefore all things be of God which are well done; and if all things be well done, which are according to the rule of well-doing ; and, if the rule of well-doing be more ample than the fcripture ; what neceffity is there, that every thing which is of God, fhould be fet down in holy fcripture? true it is in things of fome one kind, true it is, that what we are now of neceffity for ever bound to believe or: obferve in the fpecial myfteries of falvation, fcripture muft needs give notice of it unto the world ; yet true it cannot be, touching all things that are of God. Sufficient it is for the proof of lawfulnefs in any thing done, if we can fhew that God approveth it. And of his approbation, the evidence is fufficient, if either himfelf have by revelation in his word warranted it, or we by fome difcourfe of reafon find it good of it felf, and unrepugnant unto any of his revealed laws and ordinances. Wherefore injurious we are unto God, the author and giver of human capacity, judgment and wit, when, becaufe of fome things wherein he precifely forbiddeth men to ufe their own inventions, we take occafion to dif-authorize and difgrace the works which he doth produce by the hand either of nature, or of grace in them. We offer contumely, even unto him, when we fcornfully reject what we lift, without any other exception than this, *The brain of man hath devifed it.* Whether we look into the church or common-weal, as well in the one as in the other, both the ordination of officers, and the very inftitution of their offices, may be truly derived from God, and approved of him, although they be not always of him in fuch fort as thofe things are which are in fcripture. Doth not the apoftle term the law of nature even as the evangelift doth the law of fcripture, δικαίωμα τȣ̃ Θεȣ̃· God's own righteous ordinance? the law of nature then being his law, that muft needs be of him which it hath directed men unto. Great odds, I grant, there is between things devifed by men, although agreeable with the law of nature, and things in fcripture fet down by the finger of the holy Ghoft. Howbeit the dignity of thefe is no hindrance, but that thofe be alfo reverently accounted of in their place. Thus much they very well faw, who altho' not living themfelves under this kind of church polity, yet being thro' fome experience, more moderate, grave, and circumfpect in their judgment, have given hereof their founder and better advifed fentence. That which the holy fathers (faith *Zanchius*) have by common confent, without contradiction of fcripture, received ; for my part, I neither will, nor dare with good confcience difallow. And what more certain, than that the ordering of ecclefiaftical perfons, one in authority above another, was received into the church by the common confent of the chriftian world? What am I, that I fhould take upon me to controul the whole church of Chrift in that which is fo well known to have been lawfully, religioufly, and to notable purpofe inftituted? *Calvin* maketh mention even of primates that have authority above bifhops, *It was*, faith he, *the inftitution of the antient church, to the end that the bifhops might by this bond of concord, continued the fafter linked amongft themfelves.* And, left any man fhould think that as well he might allow the papacy it felf ; to prevent this he addeth, *Aliud eft moderatum gerere & honorem, quam totum terrarum orbem immenfo imperio complecti.* Thefe things ftanding as they do, we may conclude, that, albeit the offices which bifhops execute, had been committed unto them only by the church, and that the fuperiority which they have over other paftors were not firft by Chrift himfelf given to the apoftles, and from them defcended to others, but afterwards in fuch confideration brought in and agreed upon, as is pretended; yet could not this be a juft or lawful exception againft it.

Lib. 1.

Rom. 1. 32.
Luke 1. 6.

Confef. 169.

Epift. 190.

The argu-
ments to prove
there was no
neceffity of in-
ftituting bi-
fhops in the
church.

XII. But they will fay, *There was no neceffity of inftituting bifhops, the church might have ftood well enough without them, they are as thofe fuperfluous things, which neither while they continue do good, nor do harm when they are removed, becaufe there is not any profitable ufe whereunto they fhould ferve. For firft, in the primitive church their paftors were all equal, the bifhops of thofe days were the very fame which paftors of parifh*

churches

churches at this day are with us, no one at commandment or controulment by any others authority amongst them. The church therefore may stand and flourish without bishops: if they be necessary, wherefore were they not sooner instituted? 2. Again, if any such thing were needful for the church, Christ would have set it down in scripture, as he did all kind of officers needful for jewish regiment. He which prescribed unto the Jews so particularly the least thing pertinent unto their temple, would not have left so weighty offices undetermined of in scripture, but that he knew the church could never have any profitable use of them. 3. Furthermore it is the judgment of Cyprian, *that equality re-* Ep. 3. lib. 1. *quireth every man's cause to be heard, where the fault he is charged with was committed. And the reason he alledged is, forasmuch as there they may have both accusers and witnesses in their cause. Sith therefore every man's cause is meetest to be handled at home by the judges of his own parish, to what purpose serveth their device, which have appointed bishops, unto whom such causes may be brought, and archbishops to whom they may be also from thence removed?*

XIII. What things have necessary use in the church, they of all others are the most un- *The fore-*fit to judge, who bend themselves purposely against whatsoever the church useth, except *alledged ar-guments an-*it please themselves to give it the grace and countenance of their favourable approbation; *swered.*which they willingly do not yield unto any part of church polity, in the forehead whereof there is not the mark of that new devised stamp. But howsoever men like or dislike, whether they judge things necessary or needless in the house of God, a conscience they should have, touching that which they boldly affirm or deny. 1. *In the primitive church no bishops, no pastor having power over other pastors, but all equals, every man supreme commander and ruler within the kingdom of his own congregation or parish? The bishops that are spoken of in the time of the primitive church, all such as parsons or rectors of parishes are with us?* If thus it have been in the prime of the church, the question is how far they will have that prime to extend? and where the latter spring of that new-supposed disorder to begin ? That primitive church wherein they hold that amongst the fathers, all which had pastoral charge were equal, they must of necessity so far enlarge as to contain some hundred of years, because for proof hereof they alledge boldly and confidently St. *Cyprian,* who T.C.l.1.p.99, suffered martyrdom about two hundred and threescore years after our blessed Lord's incar- &100. The nation. A bishop, they say, such as *Cyprian* doth speak of, had only a church or congre- *Cyprian speak-*gation, such as the ministers and pastors with us, which are appointed unto several towns. *eth of, is no-*Every bishop in *Cyprian's* time was pastor of one only congregation, assembled in one place *such as we call*to be taught of one man. A thing impertinent, altho' it were true. For the question is *pastor, or as the*about personal inequality amongst governors of the church. Now to shew there was no *common name*such thing in the church at such time as *Cyprian* lived, what bring they forth ? Forsooth *son ; and his*that bishops had then but a small circuit of place for the exercise of their authority. Be *church where-*it supposed, that no one bishop had more than one only town to govern, one only con- *is neither dio-*gregation to rule : doth it by *Cyprian* appear, that in any such town or congregation, be- *cese nor pro-*ing under the cure and charge of some one bishop, there were not, besides that one bi- *vince, but a*shop, others also ministers of the word and sacraments, yet subject to the power of the *which met to-*same bishop? If this appear not, how can *Cyprian* be alledged for a witness that in those *gether in one*times there were no bishops which did differ from other ministers, as being above them in *place, and to be*degree of ecclesiastical power? But a gross and a palpable untruth it is, *that bishops with* *man.* Cyprian *were as ministers are with us in parish churches; and that each of them did guide some parish without any other pastors under him.* St. *Cyprian's* own person may serve for a manifest disproof hereof. *Pontius* being deacon under *Cyprian,* noteth, that his admirable vertues caused him to be bishop with the soonest; which advancement thereof himself endeavoured for a while to avoid. It seemed in his own eyes, too soon for him to take the title of so great honour, in regard whereof a bishop is termed *pontifex, sacerdos, antistes Dei.* Yet such was his quality, that whereas others did hardly perform that duty, whereunto the discipline of their order, together with the religion of the oath they took at their entrance into the office even constrained them; him the chair did not make, but receive such a one, as behoved that a bishop should be. But soon after followed that prescription, whereby being driven into exile, and continuing in that estate for the space of some two years, he ceased not by letters to deal with his clergy, and to direct them about the publick affairs of the church. They unto whom these * epistles were' Etsi fratres pro dilectione

sua cupidi sunt ad conveniendum & visitandum confessores bonos, quos illustravit jam gloriosis initiis divina dignatio; tamen caute hoc, & non glomeratim nec per multitudinem simul junctam, puto esse faciendum, ne ex hoc ipso invidia concitetur, & introeundi aditus denegetur, & dum insatiabiles multum volumus, totum perdamus; consulite ergo & providete ut cum temperamento hoc agi tutius possit. Ita ut presbyteri quoque qui illic apud confessores offerunt singuli cum singulis diaconis per vices accersant, quia & mutatio personarum, & vicissitudo convenientium minuit invidiam. Ep. 5.

written, he commonly entitled the presbyters and deacons of that church. If any man doubt whether those presbyters of *Carthage* were ministers of the word and sacraments or no, let him consider but that one only place of *Cyprian*, where he giveth them this careful advice, how to deal with circumspection in the perilous times of the church, that neither they which were for the truth's sake imprisoned might want those ghostly comforts which they ought to have, nor the church by ministring the same unto them incur unnecessary danger and peril. In which epistle it doth expresly appear, that the presbyters of whom he speaketh, did offer, that is to say, administer the eucharist; and that many there were of them in the church of *Carthage*, so as they might have every day change for performance of that duty. Nor will any man of sound judgment, I think, deny, that *Cyprian* was in authority and power above the clergy of that church, above those presbyters unto whom he gave direction. It is apparently therefore untrue, that in *Cyprian's* time ministers of the word and sacraments were all equal, and that no one of them had either title more excellent than the rest, or authority and government over the rest. *Cyprian* being bishop of *Carthage*, was clearly superior unto all other ministers there: Yea, *Cyprian* was, by reason of the dignity of his see, an archbishop, and so consequently superior unto bishops. Bishops, we say, there have been always, even as long as the church of Christ it self hath been. The apostles who planted it, did themselves rule as bishops over it; neither could they so well have kept things in order during their own times, but that episcopal authority was given them from above, to exercise far and wide over all other guides and pastors of God's church. The church indeed for a time continued without bishops by restraint, every where established in christian cities. But shall we thereby conclude that the church hath no use of them, that without them it may stand and flourish? No, the cause wherefore they were so soon universally appointed was, for that it plainly appeared, that without them the church could not have continued long. It was by the special providence of God, no doubt, so disposed, that the evil whereof this did serve for remedy, might first be felt, and so the reverend authority of bishops be made by so much the more effectual, when our general experience had taught men what it was for churches to want them. Good laws are never esteemed so good, nor acknowledged so necessary, as when precedent crimes are as seeds out of which they grow. Episcopal authority was even in a manner sanctified unto the church of Christ by that little bitter experience which it first had of the pestilent evil of schisms. Again, when this very thing was proposed as a remedy, yet a more suspicious and fearful acceptance it must needs have found, if the self-same provident wisdom of almighty God had not also given beforehand sufficient trial thereof in the regiment of *Jerusalem*, a mother-church, which having received the same order even at the first, was by it most peaceably govern'd, when other churches without it had trouble. So that by all means, the necessary use of episcopal government is confirmed, yea strengthned it is, and ratified, even by the not establishment thereof in all churches every where at the first. 2. When they further dispute, *That if any such thing were needful, Christ would in scripture have set down particular statutes and laws, appointing that bishops should be made, and prescribing in what order, even as the law doth for all kind of officers which were needful in the jewish regiment*; might not a man that would bend his wit to maintain the fury of the *Petrobrusian* hereticks, in pulling down oratories, use the self-same argument with as much countenance of reason? *If it were needful that we should assemble our selves in churches, would that God which taught the Jews so exactly the frame of their sumptuous temple; leave us no particular instructions in writing, no not so much as which way to lay any one stone?* Surely such kind of argumentation doth not so strengthen the sinews of their cause, as weaken the credit of their judgment which are led therewith. 3. And whereas thirdly, in disproof of that use which episcopal authority hath in judgment of spiritual causes, they bring forth the verdict of *Cyprian*, who saith, *that equity requireth every man's cause to be heard, where the fault he was charged with was committed, forasmuch as there they may have both accusers and witnesses in the cause.* This argument grounding it self on principles no less true in civil than in ecclesiastical causes, unless it be qualified with some exceptions or limitations, over-turneth the highest tribunal seats both in church and commonwealth; it taketh utterly away all appeals; it secretly condemneth even the blessed apostle himself, as having transgressed the law of equity, by his appeal from the court of *Judea* unto those higher which were in *Rome*. The generality of such kind of axioms deceiveth, unless it be construed with such cautions as the matter whereunto they are appliable doth require. An usual and ordinary transportation of causes out of *Africa* into *Italy*, out of one kingdom into another, as discontented persons list, which was the thing which *Cyprian* disalloweth, may be unequal and unmeet; and yet not therefore a thing unnecessary to have the courts erected in higher places, and judgment

Cypr. lib. 1.
Ep. 3.

Act. 25.

ment committed unto greater persons, to whom the meaner may bring their causes either by way of appeal or otherwise, to be determined according to the order of justice; which hath been always observed every where in civil states: and is no less requisite also for the state of the church of God. The reasons which teach it to be expedient for the one, will shew it to be for the other, at leastwise not unnecessary. Inequality of pastors is an ordinance both divine and profitable. Their exceptions against it in these two reasons, we have shewed to be altogether causeless, unreasonable and unjust.

XIV. The next thing which they upbraided us with, is the difference between that inequality of pastors which hath been of old, and which now is. For at length they grant, *That the superiority of bishops and of archbishops is somewhat ancient, but no such kind of superiority as ours have.* By the laws of our discipline, a bishop may ordain without asking the people's consent, a bishop may excommunicate and release alone, a bishop may imprison, a bishop may bear civil office in the realm, a bishop may be a counsellor of state; those things ancient bishops neither did nor might do. Be it granted, that ordinarily neither in elections nor deprivations, neither in excommunicating nor in releasing the excommunicate; in none of the weighty affairs of government, bishops of old were wont to do any thing without consultation with their clergy, and consent of the people under them; be it granted, that the same bishops did neither touch any man with corporal punishment, nor meddle with secular affairs and offices, the whole clergy of God being then tied by the strict and severe canons of the church, to use no other than ghostly power, to attend no other business than heavenly. *Tarquinus* was in the *Roman* commonwealth deservedly hated, of whose unorderly proceedings the history speaketh thus. *Hic regum primus traditum a prioribus morem de omnibus senatum consulendi solvit; domesticis consiliis rempub. administravit; bellum, pacem, fœdera, societates, per seipsum, cum quibus voluit injussu populi ac senatus, fecit diremitque.* Against bishops the like is objected, *That they are invaders of other mens rights, and by intolerable usurpation take upon them to do that alone, wherein ancient laws have appointed that others, not they only, should bear sway.* Let the case of bishops be put, not in such sort as it is, but even as their very heaviest adversaries would devise it. Suppose that bishops at the first had encroached upon the church; that by slights and cunning practices they had appropriated ecclesiastical, as *Augustus* did imperial power; that they had taken the advantage of mens inclinable affections, which did not suffer them for revenue sake to be suspected of ambition; that in the mean while their usurpation had gone forward by certain easy and insensible degrees; that being not discerned in the growth, when it was thus far grown, as we now see it hath proceeded, the world at length perceiving there was just cause of complaint, but no place of remedy left, had assented unto it by a general secret agreement to bear it now as an helpless evil: all this supposed for certain and true, yet surely a thing of this nature, as for the superior to do that alone, unto which of right the consent of some other inferiors should have been required by them; tho' it had an indirect entrance at the first, must needs thro' continuance of so many ages as this hath stood, be made now a thing more natural to the church, than that it should be oppress'd with the mention of contrary orders worn so many ages since quite and clean out of ure. But with bishops the case is otherwise; for in doing that by themselves, which others together with them have been accustomed to do, they do not any thing, but that whereunto they have been upon just occasions authorized by orderly means. All things natural, have in them naturally, more or less, the power of providing for their own safety: and as each particular man hath this power, so every politick society of men must needs have the same, that thereby the whole may provide for the good of all parts therein. For other benefit we have not any, by sorting our selves into politick societies, saving only that by this means each part hath that relief, which the virtue of the whole is able to yield it. The church therefore being a politick society or body, cannot possibly want the power of providing for it self: and the chiefest part of that power consisteth in the authority of making laws. Now, forasmuch as corporations are perpetual, the law of the ancienter church cannot chuse but bind the latter, while they are in force. But we must note withal, that because the body of the church continueth the same, it hath the same authority still, and may abrogate old laws, or make new, as need shall require. Wherefore vainly are the ancient canons and constitutions objected as laws, when once they are either let secretly to die by disusage, or are openly abrogated by contrary laws. The ancients had cause to do no otherwise than they did; and yet so strictly they judged not themselves in conscience bound to observe those orders, but that in sundry cases they easily dispensed therewith, which I suppose they would never have done, had they esteemed them as things whereunto everlasting, immurable, and indispensible observation did belong.

An answer unto those things which are objected, concerning the difference between that power which bishops now have, and that which ancient bishops had, more than other presbyters.

belong. The bishop usually promoted none which were not first allowed as fit by conference had with the rest of his clergy and with the people. Notwithstanding, in the case of *Aurelius*, St. *Cyprian* did otherwise. In matters of deliberation and counsel, for disposing of that which belongeth generally to the whole body of the church, or which being more particular, is nevertheless of so great consequence, that it needeth the force of many judgments conferred; in such things the common saying must necessarily take place, *An eye cannot see that which eyes can.* As for clerical ordinations, there are no such reasons alledged against the order which is, but that it may be esteemed as good in every respect, as that which hath been; and in some considerations better, at least-wise (which is sufficient to our purpose) it may be held in the church of Christ without transgressing any law, either ancient or late, divine or human, which we ought to observe and keep. The form of making ecclesiastical offices hath sundry parts, neither are they all of equal moment. When deacons having not been before in the church of Christ, the apostles saw it needful to have such ordained, they, first assemble the multitude, and shew them how needful it is that deacons be made. Secondly, they name unto them what number they judge convenient, what quality the men must be of, and to the people they commit the care of finding such out. Thirdly, the people hereunto assenting, make their choice of *Stephen* and the rest; those chosen men they bring and present before the apostles, howbeit, all this doth not endue them with any ecclesiastical power. But when so much was done, the apostles finding no cause to take exception, did with prayer and imposition of hands make them deacons. This was it which gave them their very being; all other things besides were only preparations unto this. Touching the form of making presbyters, altho' it be not wholly of purpose any where set down in the apostles writings, yet sundry speeches there are which insinuate the chief-est things that belong unto that action: as when *Paul* and *Barnabas* are said to have
Acts 14.23. *fasted, prayed,* and made presbyters: when *Timothy* is willed *to lay hands suddenly on*
1 Tim. 5.22. *no man,* for fear of participating with other mens sins. For this cause the order of the primitive church was, between choice and ordination to have some space for such prohibition and trial as the apostle doth mention in deacons, saying, *Let them first be proved, then minister, if so be they be found blameless.*

Lamprid. in Alex. Sever. *Alexander Severus* beholding in his time how careful the church of Christ was, especially for this point; how, after the choice of their pastors, they used to publish the names of the parties chosen, and not give them the usual act of approbation, till they saw whether any lett or impediment would be alledged; he gave commandment, that the like should also be done in his own imperial elections, adding this as a reason wherefore he so required, namely, *For that both Christians and Jews being so wary about the ordination of the priests, it seemed very unequal for him not to be in like sort circumspect, to whom he committed the government of provinces, containing power over mens both estates and*
Deca quando Epis. lect. Igitur. *lives.* This the canon it self doth provide for, requiring before ordination, scrutiny: *Let them diligently be examined three days together before the sabbath, and on the sabbath, let them be presented unto the bishop.* And even this in effect also is the very use of the church of *England,* at all solemn ordaining of ministers; and if all ordaining were solemn, I must confess it were much the better.

The pretended disorder of the church of *England* is, that bishops ordain them, to whose election the people give no voices, and so the bishops make them alone; that is to say, they give ordination without popular election going before, which ancient bishops neither did, nor might do. Now in very truth, if the multitude have hereunto a right, which right can never be translated from them for any cause, then is there no remedy but we must yield, that unto the lawful making of ministers the voice of the people is
Eccl. Discipl. p. 34. required; and that, according to the adverse party's assertion, such as make ministers without asking the peoples consent, do but exercise a certain tyranny.

At the first erection of the commonwealth of *Rome,* the people (for so it was then fit-est) determined of all affairs: afterwards, this growing troublesome, their senators did that for them, which themselves before had done: in the end all came to one man's hands; and the emperor alone was instead of many senators.

In these things, the experience of time may breed both civil and ecclesiastical change from that which hath been before received; neither do latter things always violently exclude former; but the one growing less convenient than it hath been, giveth place to that which is now become more. That which was fit for the people themselves to do at the first, might afterwards be more convenient for them to do by some other: which other is not hereby proved a tyrant because he alone doth that which a multitude were wont to do, unless by violence he take that authority upon him, against the order of law, and without any publick appointment; as with us, if any did, it should (I suppose) not long be safe for him so to do.   ı   This

This anſwer (I hope) will ſeem to be ſo much the more reaſonable, in that themſelves, who ſtand againſt us, have furniſh'd us therewith. For, whereas againſt the making of miniſters by biſhops alone, their uſe hath been to object, what ſway the people did bear when *Stephen* and the reſt were ordained deacons: they begin to eſpy how their own platform ſwerveth not a little from that example wherewith they controul the practices of others. For, touching the form of the peoples concurrence in that action, they obſerve it not; no, they plainly profeſs, that they are not in this point bound to be followers of the apoſtles. The apoſtles ordained whom the people had firſt choſen. They hold, that their eccleſiaſtical ſenate ought both to chuſe, and alſo to ordain. Do not themſelves then take away that which the apoſtles gave the people, namely, the privilege of chuſing eccleſiaſtical officers? They do. But behold in what ſort they anſwer it.

By the ſixth and the fourteenth of the Acts (ſay they) *it doth appear, that the people* **Eccl. Diſcipl.** *had the chiefeſt power of chuſing. Howbeit that, as unto me it ſeemeth, was done upon* fol. 41. *ſpecial cauſe which doth not ſo much concern us, neither ought it to be drawn unto the ordinary and perpetual form of governing the church. For, as in eſtabliſhing commonweals, not only if they be popular, but even being ſuch as are ordered by the power of a few the chiefeſt, or as by the ſole authority of one, till the ſame be eſtabliſhed, the whole ſway is in the peoples hands, who voluntarily appoint thoſe magiſtrates by whoſe authority they may be governed; ſo that afterward not the multitude it ſelf, but thoſe magiſtrates which are choſen by the multitude, have the ordering of publick affairs. After the ſelf-ſame manner it fared in eſtabliſhing alſo the church: when there was not as yet any placed over the people, all authority was in them all; but when they all had choſen certain to whom the regiment of the church was committed, this power is not now any longer in the hands of the whole multitude, but wholly in theirs who are appointed guides of the church. Beſides, in the choice of deacons, there was alſo another ſpecial cauſe wherefore the whole church at that time ſhould chuſe them. For inaſmuch as the* Grecians *murmured againſt the* Hebrews, *and complained that in the daily diſtribution which was made for relief of the poor, they were not indifferently reſpected, nor ſuch regard had of their widows as was meet; this made it neceſſary that they all ſhould have to deal in the choice of thoſe unto whom that care was afterwards to be committed, to the end that all occaſion of jealouſies and complaints might be removed. Wherefore that which was done by the people for certain cauſes, before the church was fully ſettled, may not be drawn out and applied unto a conſtant and perpetual form of ordering the church.*

Let them caſt the diſcipline of the church of *England* into the ſame ſcales where they weigh their own, let them give us the ſame meaſure which here they take, and our ſtrifes ſhall ſoon be brought to a quiet end. When they urge the apoſtles as precedents; when they condemn us of tyranny, becauſe we do not in making miniſters the ſame which the apoſtles did; when they plead, *that with us one alone doth ordain, and that our ordinations are without the peoples knowledge, contrary to that example which the bleſſed apoſtles gave;* we do not requeſt at their hands allowance as much as of one word we ſpeak in our own defence, if that which we ſpeak be of our own; but that which themſelves ſpeak, they muſt be content to liſten unto. To exempt themſelves from being over far preſt with the apoſtles example, they can anſwer, *that which was done by the people once upon ſpecial cauſes, when the church was not yet eſtabliſhed, is not to be made a rule for the conſtant and continual ordering of the church.* In defence of their own election, altho' they do not therein depend on the people ſo much as the apoſtles in the choice of deacons, they think it a very ſufficient apology, that there were ſpecial conſiderations why deacons at that time ſhould be choſen by the whole church, but not ſo now. In excuſe of diſſimilitudes between their own and the apoſtles diſcipline, they are contented to uſe this anſwer, *that many things were done in the apoſtles times, before the ſettling of the church, which afterward the church was not tied to obſerve.* For countenance of their own proceedings, wherein their governors do more than the apoſtles, and their people leſs than under the apoſtles the firſt churches are found to have done at the making of eccleſiaſtical officers, they deem it a marvelous reaſonable kind of pleading, to ſay, *that even as in commonweals, when the multitude have once choſen many, or one to rule over them, the right which was at the firſt in the whole body of the people, is now derived into thoſe many, or that one which is ſo choſen; and that this being done, it is not the whole multitude, to whom the adminiſtration of ſuch publick affairs any longer appertaineth, but that which they did, their rulers may now do lawfully without them: after the ſelf-ſame manner it ſtandeth with the church alſo.*

How eaſy and plain might we make our defence? how clear and allowable even unto them, if we could but obtain of them to admit the ſame things conſonant unto equity in our mouths, which they require to be ſo taken from their own? If that which is truth,

being

being uttered in maintenance of *Scotland* and *Geneva*, do not ceafe to be truth when the church of *England* once alledgeth it, this great crime of tyranny wherewith we are charged, hath a plain and an eafy defence. Yea, but we do not all ask the peoples approbation, which they do, whereby they fhew themfelves more indifferent and more free from taking away the peoples right. Indeed, when their lay-elders have chofen whom they think good, the peoples confent thereunto is asked, and if they give their approbation, the thing ftandeth warranted for found and good. But if not, is the former choice overthrown? No, but the people is to yield to reafon ; and if they which have made the choice, do fo like the peoples reafon, as to reverfe their own deed at the hearing of it, then a new election to be made ; otherwise the former to ftand, notwithftanding

Eccl. Difcip. the peoples negative and diflike.
P. 41. What is this elfe but to deal with the people, as thofe nurfes do with infants, whofe mouths they befmear with the backfide of the fpoon, as tho' they had fed them, when they themfelves do devour the food? They cry in the ears of the people, that all mens confent fhould be had unto that which concerns all ; they make the people believe we wrong them, and deprive them of their right in making minifters, whereas with us the people have commonly far more fway and force than with them. For inafmuch as there are but two main things obferved in every ecclefiaftical function, power to exercife the duty it felf, and fome charge of people whereon to exercife the fame ; the former of thefe is received at the hands of the whole vifible catholick church. For it is not any one particular multitude that can give power, the force whereof may reach far and wide indefinitely, as the power of order doth, which whofo hath once received, there is no action which belongeth thereunto, but he may exercife effectually the fame in any part of the world without iterated ordination. They whom the whole church hath from the beginning ufed as her agents in conferring this power, are not either one or mo of the laity, and therefore it hath not been heard of that ever any fuch were allowed to ordain minifters : only perfons ecclefiaftical, and they, in place of calling, fuperiors both unto deacons, and unto presbyters ; only fuch perfons ecclefiaftical have been authorized to ordain both, and give them the power of order, in the name of

Neque enim fu erat aut licebat ut inferior ordinaret majorem : Comment. q. Ambrof. induuntur, in 1Tim. 3. the whole church. Such were the apoftles, fuch was *Timothy*, fuch was *Titus*, fuch are bifhops. Not that there is between thefe no difference, but that they all agree in preheminence of place above both presbyters and deacons, whom they otherwife might not ordain. Now whereas hereupon fome do infer, that no ordination can ftand but only fuch as is made by bifhops, which have had their ordination likewife by other bifhops before them, till we come to the very apoftles of Chrift themfelves. In which refpect it was demanded of *Beza* at *Poiffie*, *By what authority he could adminifter the holy facraments, being not thereunto ordained by any other than* Calvin, *or by fuch as to whom the power of ordination did not belong, according to the ancient order and cuftoms of the church ; fith* Calvin, *and they who joined with him in that action, were no bifhops*: and *Athanafius* maintaineth the fact of *Macarius* a presbyter, which overthrew the holy table whereat one *Ifchyras* would have miniftred the bleffed facrament, having not been confecrated thereunto by laying on of fome bifhops hands, according to the ecclefiaftical ca-

'Εκκεκαυτός χειροτοννήσαι, nons ; as alfo *Epiphanius* inveigheth fharply againft divers for doing the like, when they had no episcopal ordination. To this we anfwer, that there may be fometimes very juft and fufficient reafon to allow ordination made without a bifhop. The whole church vifible being the true original fubject of all power, it hath not ordinarily allowed any other than bifhops alone to ordain : Howbeit, as the ordinary courfe is ordinarily in all things to be obferved, fo it may be in fome cafes not unneceffary that we decline from the ordinary ways. Men may be extraordinarily, yet allowably two ways admitted into fpiritual function in the church. One is, when God himfelf doth of himfelf raife up any, whofe labour he ufeth without requiring that men fhould authorife them. But then he doth ratify their calling by manifeft figns and tokens himfelf from heaven. And thus even fuch as believed not our Saviour's teaching, did yet acknowledge him a lawful teacher fent from God : *Thou art a teacher fent from God, otherwife none could do thofe things which thou doft do. Luther* did but reafonably therefore, in declaring that the fenate of *Melheufe* fhould do well to ask of *Muncer*, from whence he received power to teach ? who it was that had called him? And if his anfwer were, that God had given him his charge, then to require at his hands fome evident fign thereof for mens fatisfaction : becaufe fo God is wont, when he himfelf is the author of any extraordinary calling. Another extraordinary kind of vocation is, when the exigence of neceffity doth conftrain to leave the ufual ways of the church, which otherwife we would willingly keep : where the church muft needs have fome ordained, and neither hath, nor can have poffibly a bifhop to ordain ; in cafe of fuch neceffity, the ordinary inftitution of God hath given oftentimes, and may give place. And therefore we are not, fimply without exception, to urge a
lineal

lineal defcent of power from the apoftles by continued fucceffion of bifhops in every effectual ordination. Thefe cafes of inevitable neceffity excepted, none may ordain but only
bifhops: by the impofition of their hands it is, that the church giveth power of order,
both unto presbyters and deacons. Now, when that power fo received is once to have
any certain fubject whereon it may work, and whereunto it is to be tied, *here cometh in
the peoples confent, and not before.* The power of order I may lawfully receive, without
asking leave of any multitude; but that power I cannot exercife upon any one certain people utterly againft their wills; neither is there in the church of *England* any man, by order
of law, poffeffed with paftoral charge over any parifh, but the people in effect do chufe
him thereunto. For, albeit they chufe not by giving every man perfonally his particular
voice, yet can they not fay, that they have their paftors violently obtruded upon them, inafmuch as their ancient and original intereft therein, hath been by orderly means derived
into the patron who chufeth for them. And if any man be defirous to know how patrons
came to have fuch intereft, we are to confider, that at the firft erection of churches, it feemed but reafonable in the eyes of the whole chriftian world, to pafs that right to them and
their fucceffors, on whofe foil, and at whofe charge the fame were founded. This all men
gladly and willingly did, both in honour of fo great piety, and for encouragement of many
others unto the like, who peradventure elfe, would have been as flow to erect churches, or
to endow them, as we are forward both to fpoil them, and to pull them down.

It's no true affertion therefore, in fuch fort as the pretended reformers mean it, *That all
minifters of God's word ought to be made by confent of many, that is to fay, by the peoples
fuffrages; that ancient bifhops neither did nor might ordain otherwife; and that ours do
herein ufurp a far greater power than was, or then lawfully could have been granted unto bifhops which were of old.* Furthermore, as touching fpiritual jurifdiction, our bifhops, they fay, do that which of all things is moft intolerable, and which the ancient
never did, *Our bifhops excommunicate and releafe alone, whereas the cenfures of the church
neither ought, nor were wont to be adminiftred otherwife, than by confent of many.* Their
meaning here when they fpeak of many, is not as before it was: when they hold that
minifters fhould be made with confent of many, they underftand by *many,* the multitude,
or common people; but in requiring that many fhould evermore join with the bifhop in
the adminiftration of church-cenfures, they mean by many, a few lay-elders, chofen out
of the reft of the people to that purpofe. This, they fay, is ratified by ancient councils,Concil. *Car-*
by ancient bifhops this was practifed. And the reafon hereof, as *Beza* fuppofeth, was,*that.* 4. c. 23.
*Becaufe if the power of ecclefiaftical cenfures did belong unto any one, there would this*Cypr. l. 3. Ep.
*great inconvenience follow; ecclefiaftical regiment fhould be changed into meer tyranny,*Ep. 8.
*or elfe into a civil royalty: therefore no one, either bifhop or presbyter, fhould or can
alone exercife that power, but with his ecclefiaftical confiftory he ought to do it, as may
appear by the old difcipline.*

And is it poffible, that one fo grave and judicious fhould think it in earneft tyranny
for a bifhop to excommunicate, whom law and order hath authorized fo to do? or be perfuaded, that ecclefiaftical regiment degenerateth into civil regality, when one is allowed
to do that which hath been at any time the deed of mo? Surely, far meaner witted men
than the world accounteth Mr. *Beza,* do eafily perceive, that tyranny is power violently
exercifed againft order, againft law; and that the difference of thefe two regiments, ecclefiaftical and civil, confifteth in the matter about which the actions of each are converfant; and not in this, that civil royalty admitteth but one, ecclefiaftical government requireth many fupreme correctors. Which allegation, were it true, would prove no more
than only, that fome certain number is neceffary for the affiftance of the bifhop. But
that a number of fuch as they do require is neceffary, how doth it prove? Wherefore
albeit bifhops fhould now do the very fame which the ancients did, ufing the college of
presbyters under them as their affiftants, when they adminifter church-cenfures, yet fhould
they ftill fwerve utterly from that which thefe men fo bufily labour for, becaufe the agents
whom they require to affift in thofe cafes, are a fort of lay-elders, fuch as no ancient bifhop ever was affifted with.

Shall thefe fruitlefs jars and janglings never ceafe? fhall we never fee end of them? How
much happier were the world if thofe eager task-mafters, whofe eyes are fo curious and
fharp in difcerning what fhould be done by many, and what by few, were all changed into
painful doers of that which every good chriftian man ought either only or chiefly to do,
and to be found therein doing when that great and glorious judge of all men's both
deeds and words fhall appear? In the mean while, be it one that hath this charge, or be
they many that be his affiftants, let there be careful provifion that juftice may be adminiftred, and in this fhall our God be glorified more than by fuch contentious difputes.

Concerning
the civil power
and authority
which our bi-
fhops have. XV. Of which nature that alfo is, wherein bifhops are, over and befides all this, accufed *to have much more exceffive power than the ancient, inafmuch as unto their ecclefiaftical authority, the civil magiftrate for the better repreffing of fuch as contemn ecclefiaftical cenfures, hath for divers ages annexed civil.* The crime of bifhops herein is divided into *thefe two feveral branches, the one that in caufes ecclefiaftical, they ftrike with the fword of fecular punifhments; the other, that offices are granted them, by vertue whereof they meddle with civil affairs.* Touching the one, it reacheth no farther than only unto reftraint of liberty by imprifonment (which yet is not done but by the laws of the land, and by vertue of authority derived from the prince.) A thing which being allowable in priefts amongft the Jews, muft needs have received fome ftrange alteration in nature fince, if it be now fo pernicious and venomous to be coupled with a fpiritual vocation in any man which Jer. 29. 26. beareth office in the church of Chrift. *Shemaia* writing to the college of priefts which were in *Jerufalem,* and to *Zephaniah* the principal of them, told them they were appointed of God, *that they might be officers in the houfe of the Lord, for every man which raved, and did make himfelf a prophet,* to the end that they might, by the force of this their authority, *put fuch in prifon, and in the ftocks.* His malice is reproved, for that he provoketh them to fhew their power againft the innocent. But furely, when any man juftly punifhable had been brought before them, it could be no unjuft thing for them even in fuch fort then to have punifhed. As for offices, by vertue whereof bifhops have to deal in civil affairs, we muft confider that civil affairs are of divers kinds; and as they be not all fit for ecclefiaftical perfons to meddle with, fo neither is it neceffary, nor at this day haply convenient, that from meddling with any fuch thing at all they all fhould without exception be fecluded. I will therefore fet down fome few caufes, wherein it cannot but clearly appear unto reafonable men, that civil and ecclefiaftical functions may be lawfully united in one and the fame perfon.

Firft therefore, in cafe a chriftian fociety be planted amongft their profeffed enemies, or by toleration do live under fome certain ftate, whereinto they are not incorporated, whom fhall we judge the meeteft men to have the hearing and determining of fuch mere civil controverfies as are every day wont to grow between man and man? 1 Cor. 6. Such being the ftate of the church of *Corinth,* the apoftle giveth them this direction, *Dare any of you, having bufinefs againft another, be judged by the unjuft, and not under faints? Do ye not know that the faints fhall judge the world? If the world then fhall be judged by you, are ye unworthy to judge the fmalleft matters? Know ye not that we fhall judge the angels? how much more things that appertain to this life? If then ye have judgment of things pertaining to this life, fet up them which are leaft efteemed in the church. I fpeak it to your fhame; is it fo, that there is not a wife man amongft you? no not one that can judge between his brethren, but a brother goeth to law with a brother, and that under the infidels? Now therefore there is utterly a fault among you, becaufe ye go to law one with another; why rather fuffer ye not wrong, why rather fuftain ye not harm?* In which fpeech there are thefe degrees; better to fuffer and to put up injuries, than to contend; better to end contention by arbitrement, than by judgment; better by judgment before the wifeft of their own, than before the fimpler; better before the fimpleft of their own, than the wifeft of them without: fo that if judgment Vide *Barnab.*
Briffon. antiq.
Jur.l.40.c.16. of fecular affairs fhould be committed unto wife men, unto men of chiefeft credit and account amongft them, when the paftors of their fouls are fuch, who more fit to be alfo their judges for the ending of ftrifes? The wifeft in things divine, may be alfo in things human the moft fkilful. At leaftwife they are by likelihood commonly more able Aug. de oper.
Monarch.c.29. to know right from wrong, than the common unlettered fort. And what St. *Auguftin* did hereby gather, his own words do fufficiently fhew. *I call God to witnefs upon my foul,* faith he, *that according to the order which is kept in well ordered monafteries, I could wifh to have every day my hours of labouring with my hands, my hours of reading, and of praying, rather than to endure thefe moft tumultuous perplexities of other men's caufes, which I am forced to bear while I travel in fecular bufineffes, either by judging to difcufs them, or to cut them off by intreaty: unto which toils that apoftle, who himfelf fuftained them not, for any thing we read, hath notwithftanding tied us not of his own accord, but being thereunto directed by that Spirit which fpeaks in him. His own apoftlefhip, which drew him to travel up and down, fuffered him not to be any where fettled to this purpofe; wherefore the wife, faithful and holy men which were feated here and there, and not them which travelled up and down to preach, he made examiners of fuch bufineffes. Whereupon of him it is no where written, that he had leifure to attend thefe things, from which we cannot excufe our felves although we be fimple: becaufe even fuch he requireth, if wife men cannot be had, rather than that the affairs of chriftians fhould be brought into publick judgment. Howbeit, not without comfort in our Lord are thefe travels un-*

+   .   *dertaken*

dertaken by us, for the hope's fake of eternal life, to the end that with patience we may reap the fruit. So far is St. *Augustine* from thinking it unlawful for paſtors in ſuch ſort to judge civil cauſes, that he plainly colleƈteth out of the apoſtle's words, a neceſſity to un-dertake that duty; yea himſelf he comforteth with the hope of a bleſſed reward, in lieu of travel that they ſuſtained.

Again, even where whole chriſtian kingdoms are, how troubleſome were it for uni-verſities, and other great collegiate ſocieties, ereƈted to ſerve as nurſeries unto the church of Chriſt, if every thing which civilly doth concern them were to be carried from their own peculiar governors, becauſe for the moſt part they are (as fitteſt it is they ſhould be) perſons of eccleſiaſtical calling? It was by the wiſdom of our famous predeceſſors foreſeen how unfit this would be, and hereupon provided by grant of ſpecial charters, that it might be, as now it is in the univerſities; where their vice-chancellors being for the moſt part profeſſors of divinity, are neverthelefs civil judges over them in the moſt of their ordinary cauſes.

And to go yet ſome degrees further, a thing impoſſible it is not, neither altogether un-uſual for ſome who are of royal blood to be conſecrated unto the miniſtry of Jeſus Chriſt, and ſo to be the nurſes of God's church, not only as the prophet did foretel, but alſo as the apoſtle St. *Paul* was. Now in caſe the crown ſhould by this means deſcend unto ſuch perſons, perhaps when they are the very laſt, or perhaps the very beſt of their race, ſo that a greater benefit they are not able to beſtow upon a kingdom, than by accepting their right therein; ſhall the ſanƈtity of their order deprive them of that honour whereunto they have by right blood? or ſhall it be a bar to ſhut out the publick good that may grow by their virtuous regiment? If not, then muſt they caſt off the office which they receiv-ed by divine impoſition of hands; or, if they carry a more religious opinion concern-ing that heavenly funƈtion, it followeth, that being inveſted as well with the one as the other, they remain God's lawful anointed both ways. With men of ſkill and mature judgment there is of this ſo little doubt, that concerning ſuch as at this day are under the archbiſhops of *Ments*, *Colen*, and *Trevers*, being both archbiſhops and princes of the empire; yea, ſuch as live within the pope's own civil territories, there is no cauſe why any ſhould deny to yield them civil obedience in any thing which they command, not repugnant to chriſtian piety; yea, even that civilly, for ſuch as are under them, not to obey them, were the part of ſeditious perſons: howbeit for perſons eccleſiaſtical, thus to exerciſe civil dominion of their own, is more than when they only ſuſtain ſome publick office, or deal in ſome buſineſs civil, being thereunto even by ſupreme authority required. As nature doth not any thing in vain, ſo neither grace. Wherefore, if it pleaſe God to bleſs ſome principal attendants on his own ſanƈtuary, and to endue them with extraordi-nary parts of excellency, ſome in one kind, ſome in another, ſurely a great derogation it were to the very honour of him who beſtowed ſo precious graces, except they on whom he hath beſtowed them ſhould accordingly be imployed, that the fruit of thoſe heavenly gifts might extend it ſelf unto the body of the commonwealth wherein they live; which being of purpoſe inſtituted (for ſo all commonwealths are) to the end that all might enjoy whatſoever good it pleaſeth the Almighty to endue each one with, muſt needs ſuffer loſs, when it hath not the gain which eminent civil hability in eccleſiaſti-cal perſons is now and then found apt to afford. Shall we then diſcommend the people of *Milan* for uſing *Ambroſe* their biſhop as an ambaſſador about their publick and politick affairs; the *Jews* for electing their prieſts ſometimes to be leaders in war; *David* for making the high-prieſt his chiefeſt counſellor of ſtate: finally, all chriſtian kings and princes which have appointed unto like ſervices, biſhops or other of the clergy under them? No, they have done in this reſpeƈt that which moſt ſincere and religious wiſdom alloweth. Neither is it allowable only, when either a kind of neceſſity doth caſt civil offi-ces upon them, or when they are thereunto preferred in regard of ſome extraordinary fitneſs; but further alſo, when there are even of right annexed unto ſome of their places or of courſe impoſed upon certain of their perſons, funƈtions of dignity and account in the commonwealth; albeit no other conſideration be had therein ſave this, that their credit and countenance may by ſuch means be augmented. A thing, if ever to be re-ſpeƈted, ſurely moſt of all now, when God himſelf is for his own ſake generally no where honoured, religion almoſt no where, no where religiouſly adored, the miniſtry of the word and ſacraments of Chriſt a very cauſe of diſgrace in the eyes both of high and low, where it hath not ſomewhat beſides it ſelf to be countenanced with. For unto this very paſs are things come, that the glory of God is conſtrained even to ſtand upon borrow-ed credit, which yet were ſomewhat the more tolerable, if there were not that to diſſuade to lend it him. No praƈtice ſo vile, but pretended holineſs is made ſometimes a cloak to hide it.

Zanch. p. 214. obſerv. incon-ſeſ.

The *French* king *Philip Valois*, in his time made an ordinance, that all prelates and bishops should be clean excluded from parliaments, where the affairs of the kingdom were handled; pretending that a king, with good conscience, cannot draw pastors, having cure of souls, from so weighty a business, to trouble their heads with consultations of state. But irreligious intents are not able to hide themselves, no not when holiness is made their cloak. This is plain and simple truth, that the counsels of wicked men hate always the presence of them whose virtue, though it should not be able to prevail against their purposes, would notwithstanding be unto their minds a secret controversy; and therefore, till either by one shift or another they can bring all things to their own hands alone, they are not secure. Ordinances holier and better there stand as yet in force by the grace of almighty God and the works of his providence, amongst us. Let not envy so far prevail, as to make us account that a blemish, which if there be in us any spark of sound judgment or of religious conscience, we must of necessity acknowledge to be one of the chiefest ornaments unto this Land: by the antient laws whereof, the clergy being held for the chief of those three estates, which together make up the entire body of this commonwealth, under one supreme head and governor; it hath all this time ever born a sway proportionable in the weighty affairs of the land; wise and virtuous kings condescending most willingly thereunto, even of reverence to the most high; with the flower of whose sanctified inheritance, as it were with a kind of divine presence, unless their chiefest civil assemblies were so far forth beautified as might be without any notable impediment unto their heavenly functions, they could not satisfy themselves, as having shewed towards God an affection most dutiful.

Thus, first, in defect of the civil magistrates; secondly, for the ease and quietness of scholastical societies; thirdly, by way of political necessity; fourthly, in regard of quality, care, and extraordinary; fifthly, for countenance unto the ministry; and lastly, even of devotion and reverence towards God himself, there may be admitted at leastwise in some particulars well and lawful enough a conjunction of civil and ecclesiastical power, except there be some such law or reason to the contrary, as may prove it to be a thing simply in it self naught.

Against it many things are objected, as first, *That the matters which are noted in the holy scriptures to have belonged unto the ordinary office of any ministers of God's holy word and sacraments, are these which follow, with such like, and no other; namely, the watch of the sanctuary, the business of God, the ministry of the word and sacraments, oversight of the house of God, watching over his flock, prophesy, prayer, dispensations of the mysteries of God, charge and care of mens souls.* If a man would shew what the offices and duties of a surgeon or physician are; I suppose it were not his part, so much as to mention any thing belonging to the one or the other, in case either should be also a soldier or a merchant, or an house-keeper, or a magistrate; because the functions of these are different from those of the former, albeit one and the same man may happily be both. The case is like, when the scripture teacheth what duties are required in an ecclesiastical minister; in describing of whose office, to teach any other thing than such as properly and directly toucheth his office that way, were impertinent.

Yea, *but in the old testament the two powers civil and ecclesiastical were distinguished, not only in nature, but also in person; the one committed unto* Moses, *and the magistrates joined with him; the other to* Aaron, *and his sons.* Jehosaphat *in his reformation doth not only distinguish causes ecclesiastical from civil, and erecteth divers courts for them, but appointeth also divers judges.* With the *Jews* these two powers were not so distinguished, but that sometimes they might, and did concur in one and the same person. Was not *Eli* both priest and judge? After their return from captivity, *Esdras* a priest, and the same their chief governor even in civil affairs also? These men which urge the necessity of making always a personal distinction of these two powers, as if by *Jehosaphat's* example the same person ought not to deal in both causes, yet are not scrupulous to make men of civil place and calling presbyters and ministers of spiritual jurisdiction in their own spiritual consistories.

If it be against the *Jewish* precedents for us to give civil power unto such as have ecclesiastical; is it not as much against the same for them to give ecclesiastical power unto such as have civil? They will answer perhaps, that their position is only against conjunction of ecclesiastical power of order, and the power of civil jurisdiction in one person. But this answer will not stand with their proofs, which make no less against the power of civil and ecclesiastical jurisdiction in one person; for of these two powers *Jehosaphat's* example is: besides, the contrary example of *Eli*, and of *Ezra*, by us alledged, do plainly shew, that among the *Jews* even the power of order ecclesiastical and civil jurisdiction were sometimes lawfully united in one and the same person. Pressed further we

are

are with our Lord and Saviour's example, who *denieth his kingdom to be of this world, and therefore as not standing with his calling refused to be made a King, to give sentence in a criminal cause of adultery, and in a civil of dividing an inheritance.*

The *Jews*, imagining that their Messiah should be a potent monarch upon earth, no marvel, tho' when they did otherwise wonder at Christ's greatness, they sought forthwith to have him invested with that kind of dignity, to the end he might presently begin to reign. Others of the *Jews*, which likewise had the same imagination of the Messiah, and did somewhat incline to think that peradventure this might be he, thought good to try whether he would take upon him that which he might do, being a king, such as they supposed their true Messiah should be. But Christ refused to be a King over them, because it was no part of the office of their Messiah, as they did falsly conceive; and to intermeddle in those acts of civil judgment he refused also, because he had no such jurisdiction in that commonwealth, being, in regard of his civil person, a man of mean and low calling. As for repugnancy between ecclesiastical and civil power, or any inconvenience that these two powers should be united, it doth not appear, that this was the cause of his resistance either to reign, or else to judge.

What say we then to the blessed apostles who teach, *That soldiers intangle not them-*[^1] *selves with the businesses of this life, but leave them, to the end they may please him who hath chosen them to serve; and that so the good soldiers of Christ ought to do?*

The apostles which taught this, did never take upon them any place or office of civil power. No, they gave over the ecclesiastical care of the poor, that they might wholly attend upon the word and prayer. St. *Paul* indeed doth exhort *Timothy* after this manner, *Suffer thou evil as a noble soldier of Jesus Christ: No man warring is entangled with the affairs of life, because he must serve such as have pressed him unto warfare*, the sense and meaning whereof is plain, that soldiers may not be nice and tender, that they must be able to endure hardness, that no man betaking himself unto wars continueth entangled with such kind of businesses, as tend only unto the ease and quiet felicity of this life; but if the service of him who hath taken them under his banner require the hazard, yea, the loss of their lives, to please him; they must be content and willing with any difficulty, any peril, be it never so much against the natural desire which they have to live in safety. And at this point the clergy of God must always stand; thus it behoved them to be affected as oft as their Lord and captain leadeth them into the field, whatsoever conflicts, perils, or evils they are to endure. Which duty being not such, but that therewith the civil dignities, which ecclesiastical persons amongst us do enjoy, may well enough stand; the exhortation of *Paul* to *Timothy* is but a slender allegation against them. As well might we gather out of this place, that men having children or wives, are not fit to be ministers; (which also hath been collected, and that by sundry of the antient) and that it is requisite the clergy be utterly forbidden marriage. For, as the burthen of civil regiment doth make them who bear it the less able to attend their ecclesiastical charge; even so St. *Paul* doth say, that the married are careful for the world, the unmarried freer to give themselves wholly to the service of God. Howbeit, both experience hath found it safer, that the clergy should bear the care of honest marriage, than be subject to the inconveniences which single life, imposed upon them, would draw after it; and as many as are of sound judgment know it to be far better for this present age, that the detriment be born which haply may grow through the lessening of some few mens spiritual labours, than that the clergy and commonwealth should lack the benefit which both the one and the other may reap through their dealing in civil affairs. In which consideration, that men consecrated unto the spiritual service of God be licensed so far forth to meddle with the secular affairs of the world, as doth seem for some special good cause requisite, and may be without any grievous prejudice unto the church; surely, there is not in the apostles words, being rightly understood, any lett. That no apostle did ever bear office may it not be a wonder, considering the great devotion of the age wherein they liv'd, and the zeal of *Herod*, of *Nero* the great commander of the known world, and of other kings of the earth at that time, to advance by all means christian religion? their deriving unto others that smaller charge of distributing of the goods which are laid at their feet, and of making provision for the poor, which charge, being in part civil, themselves had before (as I suppose, lawfully) undertaken, and their following of that which was weightier, may serve as a marvellous good example for the dividing of one man's office into divers slips, and the subordinating of inferiors to discharge some part of the same, when by reason of multitude increasing, that labour waxeth great and troublesome, which before was easy and light: but very small force it hath to infer a perpetual divorce between ecclesiastical and civil power in the same persons. The most that can be said in this case is, *That sundry eminent canons, bearing the name of apostolical, and divers councils likewise there are, which have forbid-*

[^1]: 1 Tim. 2. 4.

Convenit hujusmodi eligi
& ordinari
sacerdotes,
quibus nec licere sint nec
nepotes. Et-
enim fieri vix
potest ut va-
cans hujus vitæ
quotidianæ cu-
ris quas liberi
creant parenti-
bus maxime,
omne studium
omnemque
cogitationem
circa divinam
liturgiam &
res ecclesiasti-
cas consumat.
lib. 42. sect. 1.
c. de episc. &
cler.

den

den the clergy to bear any secular office; and having enjoyn'd them to attend altogether upon reading, preaching, and prayer: whereupon the most of the antient fathers have
shewed great dislikes that these two powers should be united in one person.

For a full and final answer whereunto, I would first demand, whether commension
and separation of these two powers be a matter of meer positive law, or else a thing
simply with or against the law immutable of God and nature? That which is simply
against this latter law can at no time be allowable in any person, more than adultery,
blasphemy, sacrilege, and the like. But conjunction of power ecclesiastical and civil,
what law is there which hath not at some time or other allowed as a thing convenient and meet? In the law of God we have examples sundry, whereby it doth most
manifestly appear, how of him the same hath oftentime been approved. No kingdom or nation in the world, but hath been thereunto accustomed without inconvenience and hurt. In the prime of the world, kings
and civil rulers were priests for the most part all.
The [a] *Romans* note it is a thing beneficial in their
own commonwealth, and even to [b] them apparently forcible for the strengthening of the *Jews* regiment under *Moses* and *Samuel*. I deny not, but
sometime there may be, and hath been perhaps
just cause to ordain otherwise. Wherefore we are
not to urge those things which heretofore have
been either ordered or done as thereby to prejudice
those orders, which, upon contrary occasion, and
the exigence of the present time, by like authority
have been established. For, what is there which
doth let, but that from contrary occasions, contrary laws may grow, and each be reasoned and dis-

[a] Cum multa divinitus pontifices, à majoribus nostris
inventa atq; instituta sunt, tum nihil præclarius quam quod
vos eosdem & religionibus deorum immortalium, & sum-
mæ reipub. præesse voluerunt. *Cic. pro domo sua ad pontiff.*
[b] Honor sacerdotii firmamentum potentiæ assumebatur. *Ta-
cit. hist. lib. 5.* He sheweth the reason wherefore their rulers were also priests. The joyning of these two powers,
as now, so then likewise profitable for the publick State,
but in respect clean opposite and contrary. For, whereas
then divine things being more esteemed, were used as
helps for the countenance of secular power; the case in
these latter ages is turned upside down, earth hath now
brought heaven under foot, and in the course of the world,
hath of the two the greater credit. Priesthood was then a
strengthning to kings, which now is forced to take strength
and credit from far meaner degrees of civil authority. Hic
mos apud Judæos fuit, ut eosdem reges & sacerdotes haberent, quorum justitia religioni permixta incredibile quantum
evaluêre. *Just. hist. l. 36. lib. 41. sect. 21. c. de epist.*

puted for by such as are subject thereunto, during the time they are in force; and yet
neither so opposite to other, but that both may laudably continue, as long as the
ages which keep them do see no necessary cause which may draw them unto alteration? Wherefore in these things, canons, constitutions, and laws which have been at
one time meet, do not prove that the church should always be bound to follow
them. Ecclesiastical persons were by antient order forbidden to be executors of any
man's testament, or to undertake the wardship of children. Bishops, by the imperial
law, are forbidden to bequeath by testament, or otherwise to alienate any thing
grown unto them after they were made bishops. Is there no remedy but that these,
or the like orders, must therefore every where still be observed? the reason is not always evident, why former orders have been repealed and other established in their
room. Herein therefore we must remember the axiom used in the civil laws, *That
the prince is always presumed to do that with reason, which is not against reason being
done, although no reason of his deed be exprest.* Which being in every respect as true
of the church, and her divine authority in making laws, it should be some bridle unto
those malapert and proud spirits, whose wits not conceiving the reason of laws that are
established, they adore their own private fancy as the supreme law of all, and accordingly take upon them to judge that whereby they should be judged. But why
labour we thus in vain? for even to change that which now is, and to establish instead
thereof that which themselves would acknowledge the very self same which hath been,
to what purpose were it, sith they protest, *That they utterly condemn as well that which*
T.C.l.r.p.116 *hath been, as that which is; as well the antient, as the present superiority, authority,
and power of ecclesiastical persons?*

The argu-   XVI. Now there they lastly alledge, *That the law of our Lord Jesus Christ, and the*
ments answer-*judgment of the best in all ages, condemn all ruling superiority of ministers over ministers;*
ed, whereby they are in this, as in the rest, more bold to affirm, than able to prove the things which they
they would
prove that the bring for support of their weak and feeble cause. *The bearing of dominion, or the exercising*
law of God, *of authority* (they say) *is that wherein the civil magistrate is severed from the ecclesiasti-*
and the judg-*cal officer, according to the words of our Lord and Saviour,* kings of nations bear rule over
ment of the
best in all ages, them, but it shall not be so with you: *Therefore bearing of dominion doth not agree to one*
condemneth *minister over another.* This place hath been, and still is, altho' falsly, yet with far greater
the ruling su-
periority of shew and likelihood of truth brought forth by the anabaptists, to prove that the church
one minister of Christ ought to have no civil magistrates, but be ordered only by Christ. Where-
over another.
T C l: p.22.fore they urge the opposition between heathens, and them unto whom our Saviour
speaketh. For, sith the apostles were opposite to heathens, not in that they were apo-
I   stles,

ftles, but in that they were chriftians; the anabaptifts inference, is, *That Chrift doth here give a law, to be for ever obferved by all true chriftian men, between whom and heathens there muft be always this difference, that whereas heathens have kings and princes to rule, chriftians ought not in this thing to be like unto them.* Wherein their conftruction hath the more fhew, becaufe that which Chrift doth fpeak to his apoftles, is not found always agreeable unto them as apoftles, or as paftors of men's fouls, but oftentimes it toucheth them in generality, as they are chriftians; fo that chriftianity being common unto them with all believers, fuch fpeeches muft be fo taken that they may be applied unto all, and not only unto them. They which confent with us, in rejecting fuch collections as the anabaptift maketh with more probability, muft give us leave to reject fuch as themfelves have made with lefs; for a great deal lefs likely it is, that our Lord fhould here eftablifh an everlafting difference, not between his church and pagans, but between the paftors of his Church and civil governors. For if herein they muft always differ, that the one may not bear rule, the other may; how did the apoftles themfelves obferve this difference, the exercife of whofe authority, both in commanding and in controling others, the fcripture hath made fo manifeft that no glofs can over-fhadow it? Again, it being, as they would have it, our Saviour's purpofe to with-hold his apoftles, and in them all other paftors from bearing rule, why fhould kingly dominion be mentioned, which occafions men to gather, and not all dominion and rule, but this one only form was prohibited, and that authority was permitted them, fo it were not regal? Furthermore, in cafe it had been his purpofe to with-hold paftors altogether from bearing rule, why fhould kings of nations be mentioned, as if they were not forbidden to exercife, no not regal dominion it felf, but only fuch regal dominion as heathen kings do exercife? The very truth is, our Lord and Saviour did aim at a far other mark than thefe men feem to obferve. The end of his fpeech was to reform their particular mifperfuafion to whom he fpake: and their mif-perfuafion was that which was alfo the common fancy of the *Jews* at that time, that their Lord being the *Meffias* of the world, fhould reftore unto *Ifrael* that kingdom, whereof the *Romans* had as then bereaved them ; they imagined that he fhould not only deliver the ftate of *Ifrael*, but himfelf reign as king in the throne of *David* with all fecular pomp and dignity; that he fhould fubdue the reft of the world, and make *Jerufalem* the feat of univerfal monarchy. Seeing therefore they had forfaken all to follow him, being now in fo mean condition, they did not think, but that together with him they alfo fhould rife in ftate; that they fhould be the firft and the moft advanced by him.

Of this conceit it came, that the mother of the fons of *Zebedee* fued for her childrens preferment, and of this conceit it grew, that the apoftles began to queftion amongft themfelves which of them fhould be greateft: and in controlment of this conceit, it was, that our Lord fo plainly told them, *that the thoughts of their hearts were vain.* The kings of nations have indeed their large and ample dominions, they reign far and wide, and their fervants they advance unto honour in the world, they beftow upon them large and ample fecular preferments, in which refpect they are alfo termed many of them benefactors, becaufe of the liberal hand which they ufe in rewarding fuch as have done them fervice: but, was it the meaning of the antient prophets of God that the Meffias the king of *Ifrael* fhould be like unto thefe kings, and his retinue grow in fuch as theirs? Wherefore ye are not to look for at my hands fuch preferment as kings of nations are wont to beftow upon their attendants, *With you not fo.* Your reward in heaven fhall be moft ample, on earth your chiefeft honour muft be to fuffer perfecution for righteoufnefs fake; fubmiffion, humility and meeknefs are things fitter for you to inure your minds withal, than thefe afpiring cogitations: if any amongft you be greater than other, let him fhew himfelf greateft in being lowlieft; let him be above them in being under them, even as a fervant for their good. Thefe are affections which you muft put on; as for degrees of preferment and honour in this world, if ye expect any fuch thing at my hands ye deceive your felves, for in the world your portion is rather the clear contrary. Wherefore they who alledge this place againft epifcopal authority abufe it, they many ways deprave and wreft it clear from the true underftanding wherein our Saviour himfelf did utter it.

For firft, whereas he by way of meer negation had faid, *With you it fhall not be fo,* foretelling them only that it fhould not fo come to pafs as they vainly furmifed; thefe men take his words in a plain nature of a prohibition, as if Chrift had thereby forbidden all inequality of ecclefiaftical power. Secondly, whereas he did but cut off their idle hope of fecular advancements; all ftanding fuperiority amongft perfons ecclefiaftical thefe men would rafe off with the edge of his fpeech. Thirdly, whereas he in abating their hope even of fecular advancements fpeaks but only with relation unto himfelf, informing them that he would be no fuch munificent Lord unto them in their temporal dignity and ho-

nour

nor, as they did erroneously suppose; so that any apostle might afterwards have grown by means of others to be even emperors of *Rome* for any thing in those words to the contrary; these men removing quite and clean the hedge of all such restraints, enlarge so far the bounds of his meaning, as if his very precise intent and purpose had been not to reform the error of his apostles, conceived as touching him, and to teach what himself would not be towards them; but to prescribe a special law both to them and their successor for ever; a law determining what they should not be in relation of one to another; a law forbidding that any such title should be given to any minister as might import or argue in him a superiority over other ministers. Being thus defeated of that succour which they thought their cause might have had out of the words of our Saviour Christ, they try their adventure in seeking what aid man's testimony will yield them : Cyprian *objecteth it to* Florentinus *as a proud thing, that by believing evil report, and mis-judging of* Cyprian, *he made himself bishop of a bishop, and judge over him whom God had for the time appointed to be judge,* lib. 4. cp. 9. *The endeavour of godly men to strike at these insolent names may appear in the council of* Carthage: *where it was decreed, that the bishop of the chief see should not be entituled the exarch of priests, or the highest priest, or any other thing of like sense, but only the bishop of the chiefest see ; whereby are shut out the name of archbishop, and all other such haughty titles.* In these allegations it fareth as in broken reports snatch'd out of the author's mouth, and broached before they be half either told on the one part, or on the other understood. The matter which Cyprian complaineth of in *Florentinus* was thus : *Novatus* misliking the easiness of Cyprian to admit men into the fellowship of believers after they had fallen away from the bold and constant confession of christian faith, took thereby occasion to separate himself from the church ; and being united with certain excommunicate persons, they joyned their Wits together, and drew out against *Cyprian* their lawful bishop sundry grievous accusations ; the crimes such, as being true, had made him uncapable of that office whereof he was six years as then possessed, They went to *Rome,* and to other places, accusing him every where as guilty of those faults of which themselves had lewdly condemned him ; pretending that twenty five *African* bishops (a thing most false) had heard and examined his cause in a solemn assembly, and that they all had given their sentence against him, holding his election by the canons of the church void. The same factious and seditious persons coming also unto *Florentinus,* who was at that time a man imprisoned for the testimony of Jesus Christ, but yet a favourer of the error of *Novatus,* their malicious accusations he over-willingly hearkned unto, gave them credit, concurred with them, and unto *Cyprian* in fine wrote his letters against *Cyprian* : which letters he justly taketh in marvellous evil part, and therefore severely controleth his so great presumption in making himself a judge of a judge ; and, as it were, a bishop's bishop, to receive accusations against him, as one that had been his ordinary. *What height of pride is this,* saith Cyprian, *what arrogancy of spirit, what a puffing up of mind, to call guides and priests to be examined and sifted before him ? so that unless we shall be cleared in your court, and absolved by your sentence, behold for these six years space neither shall the brotherhood have had a bishop, nor the people a guide, nor the flock a shepherd, nor the church a governor, nor Christ a prelate, nor God a priest.* This is the pride which Cyprian condemneth in *Florentinus,* and not the title or name of archbishop; about which matter there was not at that time so much as the dream of any controversy at all between them. A silly collection it is, that because Cyprian reproveth *Florentinus* for lightness of belief, and presumptuous rashness of judgment, therefore he held the title of archbishop to be a vain and proud name. Archbishops were chief amongst bishops, yet archbishops had not over bishops that full authority which every bishop had over his own particular clergy. Bishops were not subject unto their archbishops as an ordinary, by whom at all times they were to be judged, according to the manner of inferior pastors, within the compass of each diocese. A bishop might suspend, excommunicate, depose such as were of his own clergy, without any other bishop's assistance ; not so an archbishop the bishops that were in his own province, above whom divers prerogatives were given him, howbeit no such authority and power, as alone to be judge over them. For as a bishop could not be ordained, so neither might he be judg'd by any one only bishop, albeit that bishop were his metropolitan. Wherefore Cyprian, concerning the liberty and freedom which every bishop had, spake in the council of *Carthage,* whereat fourscore and seven bishops were present, saying, *It resteth that every of us declare what we think of this matter, neither judging nor severing from the right of communion any that shall think otherwise: for of us there is not any which maketh himself a bishop of bishops, or with tyrannical fear constraineth his collegues unto the necessity of obedience, inasmuch as every bishop, according to the reach of his*

                                                      liberty

T.C.l.1.p.10. pag. 95.

Concil. Carthag. de hær. baptizandis.

liberty and power, hath his own free judgment, and can have no more another his judge, *than himself to be judge to another.* Whereby it appeareth, that among the *African* bi-^{Lib. 1. ep. G} shops none did use such authority over any, as the bishop of *Rome* did afterwards claim over all, forcing upon them opinions by main and absolute power. Wherefore unto the bishop of *Rome* the same *Cyprian* also writeth concerning his opinion about baptism : *These things we present unto your conscience, most dear brother, as well for common honour's sake, as of single and sincere love, trusting that as you are truly your self religious and faithful, so those things which agree with religion and faith will be acceptable unto you : howbeit we know, that what some have over-drunk in, they will not let go, neither easily change their mind, but with care of preserving whole amongst their brethren the bond of peace and concord, retaining still to themselves certain their own opinions wherewith they have been inured : wherein we neither use force, nor prescribe a law unto any, knowing that in the government of the church every ruler hath his own voluntary free judgment, and of that which he doth shall render unto the Lord himself an account.* As for the council of *Carthage,* doth not the very first canon thereof establish with most effectual terms all things which were before agreed on in the council of *Nice ?* and that the council of *Nice* did ratify the preheminence of metropolitan bishops, who is igno-^{Oετι, τα ετη} rant ? The name of an archbishop importeth only, a bishop having chiefly of certain pre-^{Νικαιαν συ-} rogatives above his brethren of the same order. Which thing, since the council of^{ιδη ηκούσαι} *Nice* doth allow, it cannot be that the other of *Carthage* should condemn it, inasmuch^{των τριων} as this doth yield unto that a christian unrestrained approbation.^{σιτιαι}

The thing provided for by the synod of *Carthage* can be no other therefore, than only that the chiefest metropolitan, where many archbishops were within any greater province, should not be termed by those names, as to import the power of an ordinary jurisdiction belonging in such degree and manner unto him over the rest of the bishops and archbishops as did belong unto every bishop over other pastors under him. But much more absurd it is to affirm, that both *Cyprian* and the council of *Carthage* condemn even such superiority^{T. C. l. 1. p.} also of bishops themselves, over pastors their inferiors, as the words of *Ignatius* imply, in^{113.} terming the bishop, *a prince of priests.* Bishops to be termed arch-priests, in regard of their superiority over priests, is in the writings of the antient fathers a thing so usu-al and familiar, as almost no one thing more. At the council of *Nice,* saith *Theodoret,*^{Theod. hist.} three hundred and eighteen arch-priests were present. Were it the meaning of the coun-^{λεγαφις,} cil of *Carthage,* that the title of chief-priests and such like, ought not in any sort at all^{Hieronymus} to be given unto any christian bishop, what excuse would we make for so many antient^{Salutem eccle-} both fathers, and synods of fathers, as have generally applied the title of arch-priest unto^{siæ pendere} every bishop's office ? High time I think it is, to give over the obstinate defence of this^{dicit à summi} most miserable forsaken cause; in the favour whereof neither God, nor amongst^{sonitate, id est,} many wise and virtuous men as antiquity hath brought forth, any one can be found to have^{episcopi. Idem} hitherto directly spoken. Irksome confusion must of necessity be the end whereunto all^{mo summus} such vain and ungrounded confidence doth bring, as hath nothing to bear it out but only^{sacerdos quod} an excessive measure of bold and peremptoty words, holpen by the start of a little time,^{Carthaginensi} before they came to be examined. In the writings of the antient fathers, there is not any^{concilio. Vide} thing with more serious asseveration inculcated, than that it is God which maketh bishops,^{C. omnes 38} that their authority hath divine allowance, that the bishop is the priest of God, that he is^{pontifices 12.} judge in Christ's stead, that, according to God's own law, the whole christian fraternity^{q. 3. Item. C.} standeth bound to obey him. Of this there was not in the christian world of old any doubt^{seq. dist. 5.} or controversy made; it was a thing universally every where agreed upon. What should move men to judge that, now so unlawful and naught, which then was so reverently esteemed? surely no other cause but this, men were in those times meek, lowly, tractable, willing to live in dutiful awe and subjection unto the pastors of their souls : now, we imagine our selves so able every man to teach and direct all others, that none of us can brook it to have superiors; and for a mask to hide our pride, we pretend falsly the law of Christ, as if we did seek the execution of his will, when in truth we labour for the meer satisfaction of our own against his.

XVII. The chiefest cause of disdain and murmur against bishops in the church of *Eng-*^{The second} *land* is, that evil-affected eye wherewith the world looked upon them since the time that^{main thing} irreligious prophaneness, beholding the due and just advancements of God's clergy, hath^{state of bishops} under pretence of enmity unto ambition and pride proceeded so far, that the contumely^{suffereth oblo-} of old offered unto *Aaron* in the like quarrel may seem very moderate and quiet dealing,^{honour.} if we compare it with the fury of our own times. The ground and original of both their proceedings one and the same; in declaration of their grievances they differ not; the complaints as well of the one as the other are, *Wherefore lift ye up your selves thus far*^{Numb. 16. 3.}
above

3

above the congregation of the Lord? It is too much which you take upon you, too much power, and too much honour. Wherefore, as we have shewed, that there is not in their power any thing unjust or unlawful, so it resteth that in their honour also the like be done. The labour we take unto this purpose is by so much the harder, in that we are forced to wrestle with the stream of obstinate affection, mightily carried by a wilful prejudice, the dominion whereof is so powerful over them in whom it reigneth, that it giveth them no leave, no not so much as patiently to hearken unto any speech which doth not profess to feed them in this their bitter humour. Notwithstanding, for as much as I am persuaded that against God they will not strive, if they perceive once that in truth it is he against whom they open their mouths, my hope is their own confession will be at the length, *Behold we have done exceeding foolishly, it was the Lord, and we knew it not ; him in his ministers we have despised, we have in their honour impugned his.* But the alteration of men's hearts must be his good and gracious work, whose most omnipotent power framed them. Wherefore to come to our present purpose, honour is no where due, saving only unto such as have in them that whereby they are found, or at the least presumed voluntarily beneficial unto them of whom they are honoured. Wheresoever nature seeth the-countenance of a man, it still presumeth that there is in him a mind willing to do good, if need require, inasmuch as by nature so it should be ; for which cause men unto men do honour, even for very humanity sake. And unto whom we deny all honour, we seem plainly to take from them all opinion of human dignity, to make no account or reckoning of them, to think them so utterly without virtue, as if no good thing in the world could be looked for at their hands. Seeing therefore it seemeth hard, that we should so hardly think of any man, the precept of St. *Peter* is, *Honour all men.* Which duty of every man towards all, doth vary according to the several degrees whereby they are more and less beneficial, whom we do honour. *Honour thy physician,* saith the wiseman: the reason why, because for necessity's sake, God created him. Again, *Thou shalt rise up before the hoary head, and honour the person of the aged:* the reason why, because the younger sort have great benefit by their gravity, experience, and wisdom, for which cause, these things the wiseman termeth the crown or diadem of the aged. Honour is due to parents: the reason why, because we have our beginning from them ; *Obey the father that hath begotten thee, the mother that bare thee despise thou not.* Honour is due unto kings and governors: the reason why, because God hath set them *for the punishment of evil doers, and for the praise of them that do well.* Thus we see by every of these particulars, that there is always some kind of virtue beneficial, wherein they excel who receive honour; and that degrees of honour are distinguished according to the value of those effects which the same beneficial virtue doth produce.

1 Pet. 2. 17.
Ecclus. 38. 1.
Lev. 19. 32.
Ecclus. 25. 6.
Prov. 23. 22.
1 Pet. 2. 14.

Nor is honour only an inward estimation, whereby they are reverenced and well thought of in the minds of men ; but honour, whereof we now speak, is defined to be an external sign, by which we give a sensible testification that we acknowledge the beneficial virtue of others. *Sarah* honoured her husband *Abraham*; this appeareth by the title she gave him. The brethren of *Joseph* did him honour in the land of *Egypt*; their lowly and humble gesture sheweth it. Parents will hardly persuade themselves that this intentional honour, which reacheth no farther than the inward conception only, is the honour which their children owe them.

Touching that honour which mystically agreeing unto Christ, was yielded literally and really unto *Solomon*; the words of the *Psalmist* concerning it are, *Unto him they shall give of the gold of* Sheba, *they shall pray for him continually, and daily bless him.* Weigh these things in themselves, titles, gestures, presents, other the like external signs wherein honour doth consist, and they are matters of no great moment. Howbeit, take them away, let them cease to be required, and they are not things of small importance, which that surcease were likely to draw after it. Let the lord mayor of *London,* or any other unto whose office honour belongeth, be deprived but of that title which in it self is a matter of nothing ; and suppose we that it would be a small maim unto the credit, force and countenance of his office? It hath not without the singular wisdom of God been provided, that the ordinary outward tokens of honour should for the most part be in themselves things of mean account; for to the end they might easily follow as faithful testimonies of that beneficial virtue whereunto they are due, it behoved them to be of such nature, that to himself no man might over-eagerly challenge them, without blushing ; nor any man where they are due withold them, but with manifest appearance of too great malice or pride. Now, forasmuch as, according to the antient orders and customs of this land, as of the kingdom of *Israel,* and of all christian kingdoms through the world, the next in degree of honour unto the chief sovereign, are the chief prelates of God's church ; what the reason hereof may be, it resteth next to be enquired.

Psal. 72. 15.

XVIII. Other

XVIII. Other reason there is not any, wherefore such honour hath been judged due, saving only that publick good which the prelates of God's clergy are authors of. For I would know which of these things it is whereof we make any question, either that the favour of God is the chiefest pillar to bear up kingdoms and states; or, that true religion publickly exercised, is the principal mean to retain the favour of God; or, that the prelates of the church are they, without whom the exercise of true religion cannot well and long continue. If these three be granted, then cannot the publick benefit of prelacy be dissembled. And of the first or second of these I look not for any profest denial: the world at this will blush, not to grant, at the leastwise in word, as much as ª heathens themselves have of old with most earnest asseveration acknowledged, concerning the force of divine grace in upholding kingdoms. Again, tho' his mercy doth so far strive with men's ingratitude, that all kind of publick iniquities deserving his indignation, their safety is thro' his gracious providence many times nevertheless continued, to the end that amendment might, if it were possible, avert their envy; so that as well commonweals as particular persons, both may and do endure much longer, when they are careful, as they should be, to use the most effectual means of procuring his favour on whom their continuance principally dependeth: yet this point no man will stand to argue, no man will openly arm himself to enter into set disputation against the emperors *Theodosius* and *Valentinian*, for making unto their laws concerning religion, this preface, ᵇ *Decere arbitramur nostrum imperium, subditos nostros de religione commonefacere. Ita enim & pleniorem acquiri Dei ac salvatoris nostri Jesu Christi benignitatem possibile existimamus, si quando & nos pro viribus ipsi placere studuerimus, & nostros subditos ad eam rem instituerimus:* or against the emperor *Justinian*, for that he also maketh the like profession, ᶜ *Per sanctissimas ecclesias & nostrum imperium sustineri, & communes res clementissimi Dei gratia muniri, credimus.* And in another place, ᵈ *Certissime credimus, quia sacerdotum puritas & decus, & Dominum Deum ac salvatorem nostrum Jesum Christum fervor, & ab ipsis missæ perpetuæ preces, multum favorem nostræ reipublicæ & incrementum præbent.*

ᵃ What good doth publickly grow from the prelacy. Quis est tam vecors, qui aut cumsuspexerit in cœlum Deos esse non sentiat, & ea quæ tanta mente fiunt ut vix quisquam arte ulla ordinem rerum ac vicissitudinem persequi possit, casu fieri putet, aut, cum Deos esse intellexerit, non intelligat eorum numine hoc tam rum imperium tentum? *Cic.* ᵈ *Oras. de Harusp. resp.* ᵇ *Tit. 1. l. 3. C. de summa trinit.* ᶜ *L. 3. C. de episc. & cler.* ᵈ *L. 34. C. de episc. audiend.*

Wherefore only the last point is that which men will boldly require us to prove; for no man feareth now to make it a question, *Whether the prelacy of the church be any thing available or no, to effect the good and long continuance of true religion?* Amongst the principal blessings wherewith God enriched *Israel*, the prophet in the psalm acknowledgeth especially this for one, *Thou didst lead thy people like sheep by the hands of Moses and Aaron.* That which sheep are, if pastors be wanting; the same are the people of God, if so be they want governors: and that which the principal civil governors are, in comparison of regents under them; the same are the prelates of the church, being compared with the rest of God's clergy.

Wherefore inasmuch as amongst the Jews, the benefit of civil government grew principally from *Moses*, he being their principal civil governor; even so the benefit of spiritual regiment grew from *Aaron* principally, he being in the other kind their principal rector, altho' even herein subject to the sovereign dominion of *Moses.* For which cause, these two alone are named as the heads and well-springs of all. As for the good which others did in service either in the commonwealth or of the sanctuary, the chiefest glory thereof did belong to the chiefest governors of the one sort and of the other, whose vigilant care and oversight kept them in their due order. Bishops are now as high-priests were then, in regard of power over other priests, and in respect of subjection unto high priests. What priests were then, the same now presbyters are, by way of their place under bishops. The one's authority therefore being so profitable, how should the other's be thought unnecessary. Is there any man professing christian religion which holdeth it not as a maxim, that the church of Jesus Christ did reap a singular benefit by apostolical regiment, not only for other respect, but even in regard of that prelacy whereby they had and exercised power of jurisdiction over lower guides of the church? Prelates are herein the apostles successors, as hath been proved.

ᵉ Psal. 77. 20. Qui sacerdotes in veteri testamento vocabantur, hi sunt qui nunc presbyteri appellantur: & qui tunc princeps sacerdotum, nunc episcopus vocatur. *Raba. Maur. de instit. cler. l. 3. c. 6.*

Thus we see, that prelacy must needs be acknowledged exceedingly beneficial in the church: and yet for more perspicuity's sake, it shall not be pains superfluously taken, if the manner how, be also declared at large. For this one thing not understood by the vulgar sort, causeth all contempt to be offered unto higher powers, not only ecclesiastical, but civil: whom when proud men have disgraced, and are therefore reproved by such as carry some dutiful affection of mind, the usual apologies which they make for themselves, are these: *What more vertue in these great ones, than in others? we see no such eminent good which they do above other men.* We grant indeed, that the good which higher governors

D d d   vernors

vernors do, is not fo immediate and near unto every of us, as many times the meaner labours of others under them, and this doth make it to be lefs efteemed.

But we muft note, that it is in this cafe as in a fhip; he that fitteth at the ftern is quiet, he moveth not, he feemeth in a manner to do little or nothing, in comparifon of them that fweat about other toil, yet that which he doth is in value and force more than all the labours of the refidue laid together. The influence of the heavens above worketh infinitely more to our good, and yet appeareth not half fo fenfible as the force doth of things below. We confider not what it is which we reap by the authority of our chiefeft fpiritual governors, nor are likely to enter into any confideration thereof, till we want them; and that is the caufe why they are at our hands fo unthankfully rewarded. Authority is a conftraining power; which power were needlefs if we were all fuch as we fhould be, willing to do the things we ought to do without conftraint. But, becaufe generally we are otherwife, therefore we all reap fingular benefit by that authority which permitteth no men, though they would, to flack their duty. It doth not fuffice, that the lord of an houfhold appoint labourers what they fhould do, unlefs he fet over them fome chief workman to fee they do it. Conftitutions and canons made, for the ordering of church affairs, are dead taskmafters. The due execution of laws fpiritual, dependeth moft upon the vigilant care of the chiefeft fpiritual governors, whofe charge is to fee that fuch laws be kept by the clergy and people under them: with thofe duties which the law of God, and the ecclefiaftical canons require in the clergy; lay-governors are neither for the moft part fo well acquainted, nor fo deeply and nearly touched. Requifite therefore it is, that ecclefiaftical perfons have authority in fuch things. Which kind of authority maketh them that have it prelates. If then it be a thing confeft, as by all good men it needs muft be, to have prayers read in all churches, to have the facraments of God adminiftred, to have the myfteries of falvation plainly taught, to have God every where devoutly worfhiped, and all this perpetually, and with quietnefs bringeth unto the whole church, and unto every member thereof ineftimable good; how can that authority, which hath been proved the ordinance of God for prefervation of thefe duties in the church, how can it chufe but deferve to be held a thing publickly moft beneficial? It were to be wifhed, and is to be laboured for, as much as can be, that they who are fet in fuch rooms may be furnifhed with honourable qualities and graces every way fit for their calling. But, be they otherwife, howfoever fo long as they were in authority, all men reap fome good by them, albeit not fo much good as if they were abler men. There is not any amongft us all, but is a great deal more apt to exact another man's duty, than the beft of us is to difcharge exactly his own; and therefore prelates, although neglecting many ways their duty unto God and men, do notwithftanding by their authority great good, in that they keep others, at the leaftwife, in fome awe under them.

It is our duty therefore, in this confideration, to honour them that rule as prelates, 1 Tim. 5. 17. which office if they difcharge well, the apoftle's own verdict is, that the honour they have they be worthy of, yea, tho' it were double. And if their government be otherwife, the judgment of fage men hath ever been this, that albeit the dealings of governors be culpable, yet honourable they muft be, in refpect of that authority by which they govern. Great caution muft be ufed that we neither be emboldned to follow them in evil, whom for authority's fake we honour, nor induced in authority to difhonour them, whom as examples we may not follow. In a word, not to diflike fin, tho' it fhould be in the higheft, were unrighteous mecknefs, and proud righteoufnefs it is to contemn or difhonour highnefs, tho' it fhould be in the finfulleft men that live. But fo hard it is to obtain at our hands, efpecially as now things ftand, the yielding of honour to whom honour in this cafe belongeth, that by a brief declaration only what the duties of men are Rom. 13. 7. towards the principal guides and paftors of their fouls, we cannot greatly hope to prevail, partly for the malice of their open adverfaries, and partly for the cunning of fuch as in a facrilegious intent work their difhonour under covert, by more myftical and fecret means. Wherefore requifite, and in a manner neceffary it is, that by particular inftances we make it even palpably manifeft what fingular benefit and publick ufe the nature of prelates is apt to yield.

Firft, no man doubteth, but that unto the happy condition of commonweals it is a principal help and furtherance, when in the eye of foreign ftates their eftimation and credit is great. In which refpect, the lord himfelf commending his own laws unto his people, mentioneth this as a thing not meanly to be accounted of, that their careful obedience yielded thereunto fhould purchafe them a great good opinion abroad, and make Deut. 4. 6. them every where famous for wifdom. Fame and reputation groweth efpecially by the virtue, not of common ordinary perfons, but of them which are in each eftate moft eminent by occafion of their higher place and calling. The mean man's actions, be they

+

good

good or evil, they reach not far, they are not greatly enquired into, except perhaps by such as dwell at the next door; whereas men of more ample dignity are as cities on the tops of hills, their lives are viewed afar off; so that the more there are which observe aloof *Mat. 5. 13.* what they do, the greater glory by their well-doing they purchase both unto God whom they serve, and to the state wherein they live. Wherefore if the clergy be a beautifying unto the body of this commonweal in the eyes of foreign beholders, and if in the clergy the prelacy be most exposed unto the world's eye, what publick benefit doth grow from that order, in regard of reputation thereby gotten to the land from abroad, we may soon conjecture. Amongst the *Jews* (their kings excepted) who so renowned throughout the world as their high-priest? Who so much or so often spoke of as their prelates?

2. Which order is not for the present only the most in sight, but for that very cause also the most commended unto posterity. For if we search those records wherein there hath descended from age to age whatsoever notice and intelligence we have of those things which were before us, is there any thing almost else, surely not any thing so much kept in memory, as the successions, doings, sufferings and affairs of prelates. So that either there is not any publick use of that light which the church doth receive from antiquity; or if this be absurd to think, then must we necessarily acknowledge our selves beholden more unto prelates than unto others their inferiors, for that good of direction which ecclesiastical actions recorded do always bring.

3. But to call home our cogitations, and more inwardly to weigh with our selves, what principal commodity that order yieldeth, or at leastwise is of its own disposition and nature apt to yield kings and princes, partly for information of their own consciences, partly for instruction what they have to do in a number of most weighty affairs, entangled with the cause of religion, having, as all men know, so usual occasion of often consultations and conferences with their clergy; suppose we, that no publick detriment would follow upon the want of honourable personages ecclesiastical to be used in those cases? It will be haply said, *That the highest might learn to stoop, and not to disdain the advice of some circumspect, wise, and virtuous minister of God, albeit the ministry were not by such degrees distinguished.* What princes in that case might or should do, it is not material. Such difference being presupposed therefore, as we have proved already to have been the ordinance of God, there is no judicious man will ever make any question or doubt, but that fit and direct it is for the highest and chiefest order in God's clergy to be employed before others, about so near and necessary offices as the sacred estate of the greatest on earth doth require. For this cause *Joshua* had *Eleazer*; *David, Abiathar*; *Constantine, Hosius* bishop of *Corduba*; other emperors and kings their prelates, by whom in private (for with princes this is the most effectual way of doing good) to be admonished, counselled, comforted, and, if need were, reproved.

Whensoever sovereign rulers are willing to admit these so necessary private conferences for their spiritual and ghostly good, inasmuch as they do for the time while they take advice, grant a kind of superiority unto them of whom they receive it, albeit haply they can be contented even so far to bend to the gravest and chiefest persons in the order of God's clergy, yet this of the very best being rarely and hardly obtained, now that there are whose greater and higher callings do somewhat more proportion them unto that ample conceit and spirit wherewith the mind of so powerful persons are possessed; what should we look for in case God himself not authorizing any by miraculous means, as of old he did his prophets, the equal meanness of all did leave, in respect of calling, no more place of decency for one than for another to be admitted? Let unexperienced wits imagine what pleaseth them, in having to deal with so great personages, these personal differences are so necessary that there must be regard had of them.

4. Kingdoms being principally (next unto God's almightiness, and the sovereignty of the highest under God) upheld by wisdom and by valour, as by the chiefest human means to cause continuance in safety with honour (for the labours of them who attend the service of God, we reckon as means divine, to procure our protection from heaven;) from hence it riseth, that men excelling in either of these, or descending from such, as for excellency either way have been ennobled, or possessing howsoever the rooms of such as should be in politick wisdom, or in martial prowess eminent, are had in singular recommendation. Notwithstanding, because they are by the state of nobility great, but not thereby made inclinable to good things; such they oftentimes prove, even under the best princes, as under *David* certain of the *Jewish* nobility were. In polity and council the world had not *Achitophel's* equal, nor hell his equal in deadly malice. *Joab* the general of the host of *Israel*, valiant, industrious, fortunate in war, but withal headstrong, cruel, treacherous, void of piety towards God; in a word, so conditioned, that easy it is not to define, whether it were for *David* harder to miss the benefit of his war-

like hability, or to bear the enormity of his other crimes. As well for the cherishing of those vertues therefore, wherein if nobility do chance to flourish, they are both an ornament and a stay to the commonwealth wherein they live; as also for the bridling of those disorders, which if they loosly run into, they are by reason of their greatness dangerous; what help could there ever have been invented more divine, than the forting of the clergy into such degrees, that the chiefest of the prelacy being matched in a kind of equal yoke, as it were, with the higher, the next with the lower degree of nobility, the reverend authority of the one, might be to the other as a courteous bridle, a mean to keep them lovingly in awe that are exorbitant, and to correct such excesses in them, as whereunto their courage, state, and dignity maketh them over-prone? O that there were for encouragement of prelates herein, that inclination of all christian kings and princes towards them, which sometime a famous king of this land either had, or pretended to have, for the countenancing of a principal prelate under him in the actions of spiritual authority.

Par. Blesens.
Ep. 5.   *Let my lord archbishop know,* (saith he) *that if a bishop, or earl, or any other great person, yea, if my own chosen son, shall presume to withstand, or to hinder his will and disposition, whereby he may be with-held from performing the work of the embassage committed unto him; such a one shall find, that of his contempt I will shew my self no less a persecutor and revenger, than if treason were committed against mine own very crown and dignity.* Sith therefore by the fathers and first founders of this commonweal, it hath, upon great experience and forecast, been judged most for the good of all forts, that as the whole body politick wherein we live, should be for strength's sake a threefold cable, consisting of the king as a supreme head over all, of peers and nobles under him, and of the people under them; so likewise, that in this conjunction of states, the second wreath of that cable should, for important respects, consist as well of Lords spiritual as temporal. Nobility and prelacy being by this mean twined together, how can it possibly be avoided, but that the tearing away of the one, must needs exceedingly weaken the other, and by consequence impair greatly the good of all?

5. The force of which detriment there is no doubt, but that the common fort of men would feel to their helpless wo, how goodly a thing foever they now surmise it to be, that themselves and their godly teachers did all alone without controlment of their prelate. For if the manifold jeopardies whereto a people destitute of pastors is subject, be unavoidably without government; and if the benefit of government, whether it be ecclesiastical or civil, do grow principally from them who are principal therein, as hath been proved out of the prophet, who albeit the people of *Israel* had fundry inferior governors, ascribeth not unto them the publick benefit of government, but maketh mention of *Moses* and *Aaron* only, the chief prince and chief prelate, because they were the well-spring of all the good which others under them did; may we not boldly conclude, that to take from the people their prelate, is to leave them in effect without guides; at leastwise, without those guides which are the strongest hands that God doth direct them

Psal. 77. 20.   by? *Thou didst lead thy people like sheep,* saith the prophet, *by the hands of Moses and Aaron.*

If now there arise any matter of grievance between the pastor and the people that are under him, they have their ordinary, a judge indifferent to determine their causes, and to end their strife. But in case there were no such appointed to fit, and to hear both, what would then be the end of their quarrels? They will answer, perhaps, *that for such purposes their synods shall serve.* Which is, as if in the commonwealth, the higher magistrates being removed, every township should be a state, altogether free and independent; and the controversies which they cannot end speedily within themselves, to the contentment of both parties, should be all determined by solemn parliaments. Merciful God! where is the light of wit and judgment, which this age doth so much vaunt of and glory in, when unto these such odd imaginations, so great not only assent, but also applause is yielded?

6. As for those in the clergy, whose place and calling is lower; were it not that their eyes are blinded, left they should see the thing that of all others is for their good most effectual; somewhat they might confider the benefit which they enjoy by having such in authority over them as are of the self-same profession, society, and body with them; such as have trodden the same steps before; such as know by their own experience, the manifold intolerable contempts and indignities which faithful pastors, intermingled with the multitude, are constrained every day to suffer in the exercise of their spiritual charge and function; unless their superiors, taking their causes even to heart, be, by a kind of sympathy, drawn to relieve and aid them in their virtuous proceedings, no less effectually, than loving parents their dear children.

+

Thus

Thus therefore prelacy being unto all forts fo beneficial, ought accordingly to receive honour at the hands of all, but we have juft caufe exceedingly to fear that thofe miferable times of confufion are drawing on, wherein *the people fhall be oppreffed one of another*; Ifai. 3. 5; inafmuch as already that which prepareth the way thereunto is come to pafs, *children prefume againft the ancient, and the vile againft the honourable*. Prelacy, the temperature of exceffes in all eftates, the glue and foder of the publick-weal, the ligament which tieth and connecteth the limbs of this body politick each to other, hath inftead of deferved honour, all extremity of difgrace. The foolifh every where plead, that unto the wife in heart they owe neither fervice, fubjection, nor honour.

XIX. Now that we have laid open the caufes for which honour is due unto prelates, What kinds of the next thing we are to confider is, what kinds of honour be due. The good govern- honour be due ment either of the church or the commonwealth, dependeth fcarcely on any one ex- unto bifhops. ternal thing fo much as on the publick marks and tokens whereby the eftimation that governors are in is made manifeft to the eyes of men. True it is, that governors are to be efteemed according to the excellency of their virtues; the more virtuous they are, the more they ought to be honoured, if refpect be had unto that which every man fhould voluntarily perform unto his fuperiors. But the queftion is now, of that honour which publick order doth appoint unto church-governors, in that they are governours; the end whereof is, to give open fenfible teftimony, that the place which they hold is judged publickly in fuch degree beneficial, as the marks of their excellency, the honours appointed to be done unto them do import. Wherefore this honour we are to do them, without prefuming our felves to examine how worthy they are: and withdrawing it, if by us they be thought unworthy. It is a note of that publick judgment which is given of them; and therefore not tolerable, that men in private fhould by refufal to do them fuch honour, reverfe, as much as in them lieth, the publick judgment. If it deferve fuch grievous punifhment, when any particular perfon adventureth to deface thofe marks whereby is fignified what value fome fmall piece of coin is publickly efteemed at; it is fufferable that honours, the character of that eftimation which publickly is had of publick eftates and callings in the church or commonwealth, fhould at every man's pleafure be cancelled? Let us not think that without moft neceffary caufe, the fame hath been thought expedient. The firft authors thereof were wife and judicious men; they knew it a thing altogether impoffible, for each particular in the multitude to judge what benefit doth grow unto them from their prelates, and thereupon uniformly to yield them convenient honour. Wherefore that all forts might be kept in obedience and awe, doing that unto their fuperiors of every degree, not which every man's fpecial fancy fhould think meet, but which being beforehand agreed upon as meet, by publick fentence and decifion might afterwards ftand as a rule for each in particular to follow; they found that nothing was more neceffary than to allot unto all degrees their certain honour, as marks of publick judgment concerning the dignity of their places; which mark, when the multitude fhould behold, they might be thereby given to know, that of fuch or fuch eftimation their governors are, and in token thereof do carry thofe notes of excellency. Hence it groweth, that the different notes and figns of honour, do leave a correfpondent impreffion in the minds of common beholders. Let the people be asked, who are the chiefeft in any kind of calling? who moft to be liftned unto? who of greateft account and reputation? and fee if the very difcourfe of their minds lead them not unto thofe fenfible marks, according to the difference whereof they give their fuitable judgment, efteeming them the worthieft perfons who carry the principal note and publick mark of worthinefs. If therefore they fee in other eftates a number of tokens fenfible, whereby teftimony is given what account there is publickly made of them, but no fuch thing in the clergy; what will they hereby, or what can they elfe conclude, but that where they behold this, furely in that commonwealth religion, and they that are converfant about it, are not efteemed greatly beneficial? Whereupon in time, the open contempt of God and godlinefs muft needs enfue: *Qui bona fide Deus colit, amat & facer-* Præf. l. 5. Silv. *dotes.* faith *Papinius.* In vain doth that kindom or commonwealth pretend zeal to the honour of God, which doth not provide that his clergy alfo may have honour. Now if all that are imployed in the fervice of God fhould have one kind of honour, what more confufed, abfurd and unfeemly? Wherefore in the honour which hath been allotted unto God's clergy, we are to obferve, how not only the kinds thereof, but alfo in every particular kind, the degrees do differ. The honour which the clergy of God hath hitherto enjoyed confifteth efpecially in the preheminence of title, place, ornament, attendance, privilege, endowment. In every of which it hath been evermore judged meet, that there fhould be no fmall odds between prelates, and the inferior clergy.

XX. Con-

Honour is ti-
tle, place, orna-
ments, atten-
dancy and pri-
vilege.
XX. Concerning title, albeit even as under the law, all they whom God hath fevered to offer him facrifice were generally termed priefts; fo likewife the name of paftor or presbyter be now common unto all that ferve him in the miniftry of the gofpel of Jefus Chrift, yet both then and now, the higher orders, as well of the one fort as of the other, have by one and the fame congruity of reafon their different titles of honour, wherewith we find them in the phrafe of ordinary fpeech exalted above others. Thus the heads of the twenty four companies of priefts, are in fcripture termed arch-priefts; *Aaron*
'Αρχιερεῖς.
and the fucceffors of *Aaron* being above thofe arch-priefts; themfelves are in that refpect further intituled high and great. After what fort antiquity hath ufed to ftile chriftian bifhops, and to yield them in that kind honour more than was meet for inferior paftors, I may the better omit to declare both becaufe others have fufficiently done it already, and in fo flight a thing, it were but a lofs of time to beftow further travel. The allegation of Chrift's prerogative to be named an arch-paftor fimply, in regard of his abfolute excellency over all, is no impediment but that the like title in an unlike fignification may be granted unto others befides him, to note a more limited fuperiority, whereof men are capable enough without derogation from his glory, than which nothing is more fovereign. To quarrel at fyllables, and to take fo poor exceptions at the firft four letters in the name of an archbifhop, as if they were manifeftly ftoln goods, whereof reftitution ought to be made to the civil magiftrate, toucheth no more the prelates that now are, than it doth the very bleffed apoftle, who giveth unto himfelf the title of an arch-builder.

As for our Saviour's words alledged againft the ftile of *lordſhip* and *grace*, we have before fufficiently opened how far they are drawn from their natural meaning, to boulfter up a caufe which they nothing at all concern. Bifhop *Theodoret* entituled moft honourable. Emperors writing unto bifhops, have not difdained to give them their appellations of ho- nour, *your holineſs, your bleſſedneſs, your amplitude, your highneſs*, and the like: fuch as purpofely have done otherwife, are noted of infolent fingularity and pride.

Lib. 5. c. 8.
Hift. Ecclef.
L. 7. C. de
fumma trinit.
L. 33. C. de Epifc. & Cler. & L. 16. C. de Sacrof. Ecclef. *Matth.* 23. 6, 7. They love to have the chief feats in the affemblies, and to be called of men, Rabbi.

Honour done by giving preheminence of place unto one fort before another, is for decency, order, and quietnefs-fake fo needful, that both imperial laws, and canons ecclefiaftical have made their fpecial provifions for it. Our Saviour's invective againft the vain affectation of fuperiority, whether in title, or in place, may not hinder thefe feemly differences ufual in giving and taking honour, either according to the one or the other.

Something there is even in the ornaments of honour alfo: otherwife idle it had been for the wife man, fpeaking of *Aaron*, to ftand fo much upon the circumftance of his prieftly attire, and to urge it as an argument of fuch dignity and greatnefs in him: *An*
Ecclus. 45. 7.
everlaſting covenant God made with Aaron, and gave him the prieſthood among the people, and made him bleſſed through his comely ornament, and cloathed him with the garment of honour. The robes of a judge do not add to his virtue; the chiefeft ornaments of kings is juftice; holinefs and purity of converfation doth much more adorn a bifhop, than his peculiar form of cloathing. Notwithftanding both judges, thro' the garments of judicial authority, and thro' the ornaments of fovereignty, princes; yea, bifhops thro' the very attire of bifhops are made bleffed, that is to fay, marked and manifefted they are to be fuch as God hath poured his bleffing upon, by advancing them above others, and placing them where they may do him principal good fervice. Thus to be called, is to be bleffed, and therefore to be honoured with the figns of fuch a calling, muft needs be in part a bleffing alfo; for of good things even the figns are good.

Of honour, another part is attendancy; and therefore in the vifions of the glory of God, angels are fpoken of as his attendants. In fetting out the honour of that myftical queen, the prophet mentioneth the virgin ladies which waited on her. Amongft the tokens of *Solomon's* honourable condition, his fervants and waiters the facred hiftory omitteth not. This doth prove attendants a part of honour: but this as yet doth not fhew with what attendancy prelates are to be honoured. Of the high-prieft's retinue amongft the *Jews*, fomewhat the gofpel it felf doth intimate. And, albeit our Saviour came to minifter, and not, as the *Jews* did imagine their meffias fhould, to be miniftred unto in this world, yet attended on he was by his bleffed apoftles, who followed him not only as fcholars, but even as fervants about him. After that he had fent them, as himfelf was fent of God, in the midft of that hatred and extreme contempt which they fuftained at the world's hands, by faints and believers this part of honour was moft plentifully done unto them. Attendants they had provided in all places where they went;

+

which

which custom of the church was still continued in bishops their successors, as by *Ignatius* it is plain to be seen. And from hence no doubt those *Acolyths* took their beginning, of whom so frequent mention is made; the bishop's attendants, his followers they were: in regard of which service, the name of *Acolyths* seemeth plainly to have been given. The custom for bishops to be attended upon by many is, as *Justinian* doth shew, ancient: Novel 6. The affairs of regiment, wherein prelates are employed, make it necessary that they always have many about them whom they may command, altho' no such thing did by way of honour belong unto them.

Some mens judgment is, that if clerks, students, and religious persons were more, common serving-men and lay-retainers fewer than they are, in bishops palaces, the use and the honour thereof would be much more suitable than now. But these things, concerning the number and quality of persons fit to attend on prelates, either for necessity, or for honour's sake, are rather in particular discretion to be ordered, than to be argued of by disputes. As for the vain imagination of some, who reach the original hereof to have been a preposterous imagination of *Maximinus* the emperor, who being addicted unto idolatry, chose of the choicest magistrates to be priests, and to the end they might be in great estimation, gave unto each of them a train of followers: and that christian emperors, thinking the same would promote christianity, which promoted superstition, endeavoured to make their bishops encounter and match with those idolatrous priests; such frivolous conceits having no other ground than conceit, we weigh not so much as to frame any answer unto them: our declaration of the true original of ancient attendancy on bishops being sufficient. Now, if that which the light of sound reason doth teach to be fit, have upon like inducements reasonable, allowable, and good, approved it self in such wise as to be accepted, not only of us, but of pagans and infidels also, doth conformity with them that are evil, in that which is good, make that thing which is good, evil? We have not herein followed the heathens, nor the heathens us, but both we and they one and the self same divine rule, the light of a true and sound understanding; which sheweth what honour is fit for prelates, and what attendancy convenient to be a part of their honour.

Touching privileges granted for honour's sake, partly in general unto the clergy, and partly unto prelates, the chiefest persons ecclesiastical in particular: of such quality and number they are, that to make but rehearsal of them we scarce think it safe, lest the very entrails of some of our godly brethren, as they term themselves, should thereat haply burst in sunder.

[margin: T. C. l. 3. p. 126. out of Jul. l. 8. c. 15.]

[margin: L. 11. C. de sacr. Eccl. l. 5. C. de sacr. Eccl. l 2. C de Epist. & Cler. l. 10. C. de Epist. & Cler.]

XXI. And yet of all these things rehearsed, it may be there never would have grown any question, had bishops honoured only thus far forth. But the honouring of the clergy with wealth, this is in the eyes of them which pretend to seek nothing but mere reformation of abuses, a sin that can never be remitted.

[margin: Honour by endowment with lands and livings.]

How soon, O how soon might the church be perfect, even without any spot or wrinkle, if publick authority would at the length say *Amen* unto the holy and devout requests of those godly brethren, who as yet with outstretched necks groan in the pangs of their zeal to see the houses of bishops rifled, and their so long desired livings gloriously divided amongst the righteous. But there is an impediment, a lett, which somewhat hindreth those good mens prayers from taking effect: they, in whose hands the sovereignty of power and dominion over this church doth rest, are persuaded there is a God; for undoubtedly either the name of godhead is but a feigned thing; or, if in heaven there be a God, the sacrilegious intention of church-robbers, which lurketh under this plausible name of reformation, is in his sight a thousand times more hateful than the plain professed malice of those very miscreants who threw their vomit in the open face of our blessed Saviour.

They are not words of persuasion by which true men can hold their own when they are over-beset with thieves. And therefore to speak in this cause at all, were but labour lost, saving only in respect of them, who being as yet unjoined unto this conspiracy, may be haply somewhat stayed, when they shall know betimes what it is to see thieves, and to run on with them, as the prophet in the psalm speaketh, *When thou sawest a thief,* Psal. 50. 18. *then thou consentedst with him, and hast been partaker with adulterers.*

For the better information therefore of men which carry true, honest, and indifferent minds, these things we will endeavour to make most clearly manifest.

First, That in goods and livings of the church, none hath propriety but God himself.

Secondly,

Secondly, that the honour which the clergy therein hath, is to be, as it were, God's receivers; the honour of prelates, to be his chief and principal receivers.

Thirdly, That from him they have right, not only to receive, but also to use such goods, the lower fort in smaller, and the higher in larger measure.

Fourthly, That in case they be thought, yea, or found to abuse the same, yet may not such honour be therefore lawfully taken from them, and be given away unto persons of other calling.

That of ec-
clefiaftical
goods, and
confequently
of the lands
and livings
which bifhops
enjoy, the
propriety be-
longeth unto
God alone.
* Hof. 2. 5.
* Pf. 50. 10.
* Job 1. 21.

Mal. 3. 10.

XXII. Poffeffions, lands, and livings spiritual, the wealth of the clergy, the goods of the church, are in such fort the Lord's own, that man can challenge no propriety in them. His they are, and not ours; all things are his, in that from him they have their being, *My corn, and my wine, and mine oil*, faith the Lord. All things his, in that he hath absolute power to dispose of them at his pleasure. b *Mine*, faith he, *are the sheep and oxen of a thousand hills.* All things his, in that when we have them, we may say with *Job*, c *God hath given*; and when we are deprived of them, *The Lord*, whose they are, hath likewise *taken them* away again. But these sacred poffeffions are his by another tenure: his, because those men who first received them from him, have unto him returned them again, by way of religious gift, or oblation. And in this respect it is, that the Lord doth term those houses, wherein such gifts and oblations were laid, *his treasuries.*

Prov. 3. 9.

Seneca.

The ground whereupon men have resigned their own interest in things temporal, and given over the same unto God, is that precept which *Solomon* borroweth from the law of nature, *Honour the Lord out of thy subflance, and of the chiefest of all thy reve-nue: so shall thy barns be filled with plenty, and with new wine the fat of thy press shall overflow.* For altho' it be by one most fitly spoken against those superstitious per-sons, who only are scrupulous in external rites; *Wilt thou win the favour of God? Be vertuous. They best worship him, that are his followers.* It is not the bowing of your knees, but of your hearts; it is not the number of your oblations, but the integrity of your lives; not your incense, but your obedience, which God is delighted to be honoured by: nevertheless, we must beware, lest simply understanding this, which comparatively is meant; that is to say, whereas the meaning is, that God doth chiefly respect the in-ward disposition of the heart, we must take heed we do not hereupon so worship him in spirit, that outwardly we take all worship, reverence, and honour from him.

Our God will be glorified both of us himself, and for us by others: to others because our hearts are known, and yet our example is required for their good; therefore it is not sufficient to carry religion in our hearts, as fire is carried in flint-stones, but we are outwardly, visibly, apparently to serve and honour the living God; yea, to employ that way, as not only for our souls, but our bodies; so not only our bodies, but our goods; yea, the choice, the flower, the chiefest of all thy revenue, faith *Solomon.* If thou haft any thing in all thy poffeffions, of more value and price than other, to what use shouldest thou convert it, rather than to this? *Samuel* was dear unto *Hannah* his mother: the child that *Hannah* did so much esteem, she could not chuse but greatly wish to ad-vance; and her religious conceit was, that the honouring of God with it, was the advancing of it unto honour. The chiefest of the offspring of men, are the males which be first born: and, for this cause, in the ancient world they all were by right of their birth priests of the most High. By these and the like precedents, it plainly enough appeareth, that in what heart soever doth dwell unfeigned religion, in the same there resteth also a willing-ness to bestow upon God that soonest, which is most dear. Amongst us the law is, that fith gold is the chiefest of metals, if it be any where found in the bowels of the earth, it belongeth in right of honour, as all men know, to the king: whence hath this custom grown, but only from a natural persuasion, whereby men judge it decent, for the highest persons always to be honoured with the choicest things? *If ye offer unto God the blind,* faith the prophet *Malachi, is it not evil; if the lame and sick, is it good enough? Present it unto thy prince, and see if he will content himself, or accept thy person, faith the Lord of hofts.* When *Abel* presented God with an offering, it was the fattest of all the lambs in his whole flock; he honoured God not only out of his subflance, but out of the very chiefest therein, whereby we may somewhat judge how religiously they stand affected towards God, who grudge that any thing worth the having should be his. Long it were to reckon up particularly, what God was owner of under the law; for of this fort 'was all which they spent in legal sacrifices; of this fort, their usual oblations and offerings; of this fort, tythes and firft-fruits; of this fort, that which by extraordinary occasions they vowed unto God; of this fort, all that they gave to the building of the tabernacle; of this fort, all that which was gathered amongst them for erecting of the

Mal. 1. 8.

temple,

temple, and the ᵃ adorning of it erected; of this fort, whatfoever their corban contained, *Becaufe (faith David) I have a delight in the houfe of my God, therefore I have given thereunto of my own both gold and filver to adorn it* wherein that bleffed widow's deodate was laid up.　Now either this kind of honour was prefiguratively altogether ceremonial, and then our Saviour accepteth it not; or, if we find that to him alfo it hath been done, and that with divine approbation given for encouragement of the world, to fhew, by fuch kind of fervice, their dutiful hearts towards Chrift; there will be no place left for men to make any queftion at all whether herein they do well or no. *with. 1 Chron.*

Wherefore to defcend from the fynagogue, unto the church of Chrift, albeit facrifices, wherewith fometimes God was highly honoured, be not accepted as heretofore at the hands ᵃ·⁵· of men: yet, forafmuch as *honour God with thy riches*, is an edict of the infeparable law of nature, fo far forth as men are therein required by fuch kind of homage to teftify their thankful minds; this facrifice God doth accept ftill.　Wherefore as it was faid of Chrift, *that all kings fhall worfhip him, and all nations do him fervice*; fo this very kind of worfhip or fervice was likewife mentioned, left we fhould think that our Lord and Saviour would allow of no fuch thing.　*The kings of Tarfhifh, and of the Ifles, fhall bring prefents, the kings of Sheba and Seba fhall bring gifts.*　And, as it maketh not a little to the praife of thofe fages mentioned in the gofpel, that the firft amongft men which did folemnly honour our Saviour on earth were they; fo it founded no lefs to the dignity of this particular kind, that the reft by it were prevented; *They fell down and worfhiped him, and opened their treafures, and prefented unto him gifts; gold, incenfe, and myrrh.* *Pf. 50. 13, 14.* *Phil. 4. 18.* *Pfal. 72. 11.* *Matth. 2. 11.*

Of all thofe things which were done to the honour of Chrift in his life-time, there is not one whereof he fpake in fuch fort, as when *Mary*, to teftify the largenefs of her affection, feemed to wafte away a gift upon him, the price of which gift might, as they thought who faw it, much better have been fpent in works of mercy towards the poor, *Verily I fay unto you, wherefoever this gofpel fhould be preached throughout all the world, there fhall alfo this that fhe hath done be fpoken of, for memorial of her.*　Of fervice to God, the beft works are they which continue longeft: and, for permanency, what like donation, whereby things are unto him for ever dedicated? That the ancient lands and livings of the church were all in fuch fort given into the hands of God, by the juft lords and owners of them, that unto him they paffed over their whole intereft and right therein, the form of fundry the faid donations, as yet extant, moft plainly fheweth. And where time hath left no fuch evidence as now remaining to be feen, yet the fame intention is prefumed in all donors, unlefs the contrary be apparent. But to the end it may yet more plainly appear unto all men, under what title the feveral kinds of ecclefiaftical poffeffions are held, *Our Lord himfelf* (faith St. *Auguftine*) *had coffers to keep thofe things which the faithful OFFERED unto him. Then was the form of the church-treafury firft inftituted, to the end that withal we might underftand, that in forbidding that for to morrow, his purpofe was not to bar his faints from keeping money, but to withdraw them from doing God fervice for wealth's fake, and from forfaking righteoufnefs thro' fear of lofing their wealth.* *Matth. 26. 13.* *John 15. 16.* *Aug. cap. 15. de mendu.*

The firft gifts confecrated unto Chrift after his departure out of the world, were fums of money, in procefs of time other moveables were added, and at length goods unmoveable; churches and oratories hallowed to the honour of his glorious name; houfes and lands for perpetuity conveyed unto him; inheritance given to remain his as long as the world fhould endure.　*The apoftles* (faith *Melchiades*) *they forefaw that God would have his church amongft the Gentiles, and for that caufe in* Judea *they took no lands, but price of lands fold.*　This he conjectureth to have been the caufe why the apoftles did that which the hiftory reporteth of them. *C. 12. p. 1. cap. 15. & 16.*

The truth is, that fo the ftate of thofe times did require, as well other where as in *Judea.*　Wherefore, when afterwards it did appear much more commodious for the church to dedicate fuch inheritances; then, the value and price of them being fold, the former cuftom was changed for this, as for the better.　The devotion of *Conftantine* herein, all the world, even till this very day, admireth.　They that lived in the prime of the chriftian world, thought no teftament chriftianly made, nor any thing therein well bequeathed, unlefs fomething were thereby added unto Chrift's patrimony. Touching which men, what judgment that the world doth now give, I know not; perhaps we deem them to have been herein but blind and fuperftitious perfons. Nay, we in thefe cogitations are blind; they contrariwife did with *Solomon* plainly know and perfuade themfelves, that thus to diminifh their wealth was, not to diminifh but to augment it; according to that which God doth promife to his own people by the prophet *Malachi*, and which they by their own particular experience found true. If *Wickliff* therefore were of that opinion which his adverfaries afcribe unto him, (whether truly, or of purpofe to make him odious, I cannot tell, for in his writings I do not find it) namely, *That Conftantine, and others* *Prov. 3. 10.* *Mal. 3. 10.* *1 Chr. 31. 10.* *following*

Th. Wald. tom.
1. lib. 4. c. 39.

Gen. 28. 20. *following his steps did evil, as having no sufficient ground whereby they might gather,
that such donations are acceptable to Jesus Christ*; it was in *Wickliff* a palpable error.
I will use but one only argument, to stand in the stead of many. *Jacob* taking his journey unto *Haran*, made in this sort his solemn vow, *If God will be with me, and will
keep me in this journey which I go, and will give me bread to eat, and cloaths to put on,
so that I come again to my father's house in safety; then shall the Lord be my God, and
this stone which I have set up a pillar shall be the house of God, and of all that thou
shalt give me will I give the tenth unto thee.* May a christian man desire as great things
as *Jacob* did at the hands of God? May he desire them in as earnest manner? May he
promise as great thankfulness in acknowledging the goodness of God? May he vow any
certain kind of publick acknowledgment beforehand? Or, tho' he vow it not, perform it
after, in such sort that men may see he is persuaded how the Lord hath been his God?
Are these particular kinds of testifying thankfulness to God, the erecting of oratories,
the dedicating of lands and goods to maintain them, forbidden any where? Let any
mortal man living shew but one reason wherefore in this point to follow *Jacob's* example, should not be a thing both acceptable unto God, and in the eyes of the world for
ever most highly commendable. Concerning goods of this nature, goods, whereof when
we speak, we term them, τὰ τῷ Θεῷ ἀφιερωθέντα, the goods that are consecrated unto
God; and, as *Tertullian* speaketh, *deposita pietatis*, things which piety and devotion
hath laid up as it were in the bosom of God: touching such goods, the law civil, following mere light of nature, defineth them to be no man's, because no mortal man, or
community of men, hath right of propriety in them.

That ecclesiastical persons are receivers of God's rents and that the honour of pre-lates is, to be chief receivers, not without liberty from him granted, of converting the same unto their own use, their own use, even in large manner.

* *Numb.* 18. 24.
b — 18. 28.
c — 31.
d *Heb.* 7. 3.
e *Acts* 4. 34.

2 *Cor.* 8. 5.

Acts 11. 30.
— 11. 10.
& 12. 17. XXIII. Persons ecclesiastical are God's stewards, not only for that he hath set them
over his family, as the ministers of ghostly food, but even for this very cause also, that they
are to receive and dispose his temporal revenues, the gifts and oblations which men bring
him. Of the *Jews* it is plain that their tithes they offered unto the Lord, and those a offerings the Lord bestowed upon the *Levites*. When the *Levites* gave the tenth of their
tithes, this their gift the law doth term the Lord's heave-offering, and b appoint that
thereof his the high-priest should receive the same. c Of spoils taken in war, that part which they
were accustomed to separate unto God, they brought it before the priest of the Lord,
by whom it was laid up in the tabernacle of the congregation, for a memorial of their
thankfulness towards God, and his goodness towards them in fighting for them against
their enemies. As therefore the apostle magnifieth the honour of *Melchisedech*, in that
he being an high-priest, did receive at the hands of *Abraham*, the tithes which *Abraham*
did honour God with; so it argueth in the apostles themselves great honour, that at their
feet the price of those possessions was laid, which men thought good to bestow on
Christ. St. *Paul*, commending the churches which were in *Macedonia*, for their exceeding liberality this way, saith of them, that he himself would bear record, they had
declared their forward minds according to their power, yea, beyond their power, and
had so much exceeded his expectation of them, *that they seemed as it were even to
give away themselves first to the Lord*, saith the apostle, *and then by the will of God
unto us*: to him, as the owner of such gifts; to us, as his appointed receivers and
dispensers. The gift of the church of *Antioch*, bestowed unto the use of distressed
brethren which were in *Judea*, *Paul* and *Barnabas* did deliver unto the presbyters of
Jerusalem; and the head of those presbyters was *James*, he therefore the chiefest disposer thereof.

Can. 41. &
Conc. Antioch.
c. 25. Ἑαυτὸν μὲν εἰχεν τὰ ἐκκλησιαστικὰ πράγματα μετὰ κρίσεως ἰδίας οἰκονομεῖν, μάρτυρα ἔχοντα τὸν Θεόν. Amongst those canons which are entituled apostolical, one is this, *We appoint that the
bishop have care of those things which belong to the church*; the meaning is, of churchgoods, as the reason following sheweth: *For if the precious souls of men must be committed unto him of trust, much more it behoveth the charge of money to be given him, that
by his authority the presbyters and deacons may administer all things to them that stand
in need*. So that he which hath done them the honour to be, as it were, his treasurers, hath
left them also authority and power to use these treasures, both otherwise, and for the maintenance even of their own estate; the lower sort of the clergy, according unto a meaner,
the higher, after a larger proportion. The use of spiritual goods and possessions hath been
a matter much disputed of; grievous complaints there are usually made against the evil
and unlawful usage of them, but with no certain determination hitherto on what things
and persons, with what proportion and measure they being bestowed, do retain their
lawful use. Some men condemn it as idle, superfluous, and altogether vain, that any
part of the treasure of God should be spent upon costly ornaments appertaining unto
John 4. 24. his service: who being best worshiped, when he is served in spirit and truth, hath
not for want of pomp and magnificence, rejected at any time those who with faithful

hearts

hearts have adored him.   Whereupon the hereticks, termed *Henriciani* and *Petrobuſiani*, threw down temples and houſes of prayer, erected with marvellous great charge, as be-ing in that reſpect not fit for Chriſt by us to be honoured in.   We deny not, but that they who ſometimes wandred as pilgrims on earth, and had no temples, but made caves and dens to pray in, did God ſuch honour as was moſt acceptable in his ſight ; God did not reject them for their poverty and nakedneſs ſake ; their ſacraments were not abhorred for want of veſſels of gold. `Heb. 11.38,`

Howbeit, let them who thus delight to plead anſwer me.   When *Moſes* firſt, and after-wards *David*, exhorted the people of *Iſrael* unto matter of charge about the ſervice of God ; ſuppoſe we it had been allowable in them to have thus pleaded, *Our fathers in E-gypt ſerved God devoutly, God was with them in all their afflictions, he heard their prayers, pitied their caſe, and delivered them from the tyranny of their oppreſſors ; what houſe, tabernacle, or temple had they ?*   Such argumentations are childiſh and fond ; God doth not refuſe to be honoured at all where there lacketh wealth ; but where abundance and ſtore is, he there requireth the flower thereof, being beſtowed on him, to be employ-ed even unto the ornament of his ſervice.   In *Egypt* the ſtate of his people was ſervi-tude, and therefore his ſervice was accordingly.   In the deſart they had no ſooner ought of their own, but a tabernacle is required ; and in the land of *Canaan* a temple.   In the eyes of *David* it ſeemed a thing not fit, a thing not decent, that himſelf ſhould be more richly ſeated than God.

But concerning the uſe of eccleſiaſtical goods beſtowed this way, there is not ſo much contention amongſt us, as what meaſure of allowance is fit for eccleſiaſtical perſons to be maintained with.   A better rule in this caſe to judge things by we cannot poſſibly have, than the wiſdom of God himſelf ; by conſidering what he thought meet for each degree of the clergy to enjoy in time of the law ; what for levites, what for prieſts, and what for high-prieſts, ſomewhat we ſhall be the more able to diſcern rightly what may be fit, convenient, and right for the chriſtian clergy likewiſe.   Prieſts for their maintenance had thoſe firſt-fruits of [e] cattle, [f] corn, wine, oil, and [g] other commodities of the earth, which the *Jews* were accuſtomed yearly to preſent God with.   They had [h] the price which was appointed for men to pay in lieu of the firſt-born of their children, and the [i] price of the firſt-born alſo amongſt cattle which were unclean : they had the vowed gifts of the people, or [k] the prices, if they were redeemable by the donors after vow, as ſome things were : they had the free and unvowed oblations of men : they had the remainder of things ſacrificed : with tithes the levites were maintained; and with the tithe of their tithes the high-prieſt. `*Numb. 18.` `ᶠNumb. 11.` `Numb. 13` `*Verſe 15.` `ᵛVerſe 8.` `*Lev.27.11,` `Numb. 18.8.` `Verſe 8,9,11,` `28.`

In a word, if the quality of that which God did aſſign to his clergy be conſidered, and their manner of receiving it, without labour, expence, or charge, it will appear, that the tribe of *Levi*, being but the twelfth part of *Iſrael*, had in effect as good as four twelfth parts of all ſuch goods as the holy land did yield : ſo that their worldly eſtate was four times as good as any other tribes in *Iſrael* beſides.   But the high-prieſts condi-tion, how ample ?   to whom belonged the tenth of all the tribe of this land, eſpeci-ally the law providing alſo, that as the people did bring the beſt of all things unto the prieſts and levites, ſo the levite ſhould deliver the choice and flower of all their com-modities to the high-prieſt, and ſo his tenth-part by that means be made the very beſt part amongſt ten : by which proportion, if the levites were ordinarily in all not above thirty thouſand men (whereas when *David* numbred them, he found almoſt thirty eight thouſand above the age of thirty years) the high-prieſt after this very reckoning, had as much as three or four thouſand others of the clergy to live upon.   Over and beſides all this, left the prieſts of *Egypt* holding lands, ſhould ſeem in that reſpect better pro-vided for than the prieſts of the true God, it pleaſed him further to appoint unto them forty and eight whole cities with territories of land adjoyning, to hold as their own free inheritance for ever.   For to the end they might have all kind of encouragement, not only to do what they ought, but to take pleaſure in that they did ; albeit they were ex-preſly forbidden to have any part of the land of *Canaan* laid out whole to themſelves, by themſelves, in ſuch ſort as the reſt of the tribes had ; foraſmuch as the will of God was rather that they ſhould throughout all tribes be diſperſed, for the eaſier acceſs of the peo-ple unto knowledge : yet were they not barred altogether to hold land, nor yet other-wiſe the worſt provided for, in reſpect of that former reſtraint ; for God, by way of ſpe-cial preheminence, undertook to feed them at his own table, and out of his own proper treaſury to maintain them, that want and penury they might never feel, except God himſelf did firſt receive injury.   A thing moſt worthy our conſideration is the wiſdom of God herein ; for the common ſort being prone unto envy and murmur little con-ſidereth of what neceſſity, uſe and importance, the ſacred duties of the clergy are, and `1 Chron. 1. 3;` `Gen. 47. 22.` `Numb. 35. 7;` `Joſh. 14.4.` `Deut. 18.8.` `Lev. 25. 33,` `34.`

for

for that caufe hardly yieldeth them any fuch honour without repining and grudging thereat; they cannot brook it, that when they have laboured and come to reap, there fhould fo great a portion go out of the fruit of their labours, and be yielded up unto fuch as fweat not for it. But when the Lord doth challenge this as his own due, and require it to be done by way of homage unto him, whofe meer liberality and goodnefs had raifed them from a poor and fervile eftate, to place them where they had all thofe ample and rich poffeffions; they muft be worfe than brute beafts, if they would ftorm at any thing which he did receive at their hands. And for him to beftow his own on his own fervants (which liberty is not denied unto the meaneft of men) what man liveth that can think it other than moft reafonable? Wherefore no caufe there was, why that which the clergy had, fhould in any man's eye feem too much, unlefs God himfelf were thought to be of an over-having difpofition.

Deut. 10. 9.
Jofh. 13. 14.
Numb.18.24. This is the mark whereat all thofe fpeeches drive, *Levi hath no part nor inheritance with his brethren, the Lord is his inheritance*; again, *To the tribe of Levi he gave no inheritance, the facrifices of the Lord God of Ifrael are an inheritance of Levi*; again, *The tithes of the which they fhall offer as an offering unto the Lord, I have given* Verfe 19. *the Levites for an inheritance*; and again, *All the heave-offerings of the holy things which the children of Ifrael fhall offer unto the Lord, I have given thee, and thy fons, and thy daughters with thee, to be a duty for ever; it is a perpetual covenant of falt before the Lord.* Now that, if fuch provifion be poffible to be made, the chriftian clergy ought not herein to be inferior unto the *Jewifh*, what founder proof 1 Cor. 9. 13. than the apoftle's own kind of argument? *Do ye not know, that they which minifter about the holy things, eat of the things of the temple? and they which partake of the altar, are partakers with the altar?* (even *S O*,) *hath the Lord ordained, that they which preach the gofpel, fhould live of the gofpel.* Upon which words I thus conclude, that if the people of God do abound, and abounding can fo far forth find in their hearts to fhew themfelves towards Chrift their Saviour thankful as to honour him with their riches, (which no law of God or nature forbiddeth) no lefs than the ancient *Jewifh* people did honour God; the plain ordinance of Chrift appointeth as large and as ample proportion out of his own treafure unto them that ferve him in the gofpel, as ever the priefts of the law did enjoy? What further proof can we defire? It is the bleffed apoftle's teftimony, That *even fo the Lord hath ordained.* Yea, I know not whether it be found to in- 1 Tim. 5. 17.
2 Cor. 3. 8.
Vide 11.q.77.
art. 1. terpret the apoftle otherwife than that, whereas he judgeth the presbyters *which rule well in the church of Chrift to be worthy of double honour*, he means double unto that which the priefts of the law received; *for if that miniftry which was of the letter were fo glorious, how fhall not the miniftry of the Spirit be more glorious?* If the teachers of the law of *Mofes*, which God delivered written with letters in tables of ftone, were thought worthy of fo great honour, how fhall not the teachers of the gofpel of Chrift be in his fight moft worthy, the holy Ghoft being fent from heaven to ingrave the gofpel on their hearts, who firft taught it, and whofe fucceffors they that teach it at this day are? So that according to the ordinance of God himfelf, their eftate for worldly maintenance ought to be no worfe that is granted unto other forts of men, each according to that degree they were placed in. Neither are we fo to judge of their worldly condition as if they were fervants of men, and at mens hands did receive thofe earthly benefits by way of ftipend in lieu of pains whereunto they are hired; nay that which is paid unto them is homage and tribute due unto the Lord Chrift. His fervants they are, and from him they receive fuch goods by way of ftipend. Not fo from men: for at the hands of men, he himfelf being honoured with fuch things, hath appointed his fervants therewith according to their feveral degrees and places to be maintained. And for their greater encouragement who are his labourers, he hath to their comfort affured them for ever, that 1 Tim. 5. 18. they are, in his eftimation, *worthy the hire* which he alloweth them; and therefore if men fhould withdraw from him the ftore, which thofe his fervants that labour in his work are maintained with, yet he in his word fhall be found everlaftingly true, their labour in the Lord fhall not be forgotten; the hire he accounteth them worthy of, they fhall furely have either one way or other anfwered.

Acts 4. 35. In the prime of the chriftian world, that which was brought and laid down at the apoftles feet, they difpofed of by diftribution according to the exigence of each man's need. Neither can we think that they, who, out of Chrift's treafury made provifion for all others, were carelefs to furnifh the clergy with all things fit and convenient for their eftate: and as themfelves were chiefeft in place of authority and calling, fo no man doubteth but that proportionally they had power to ufe the fame for their own decent maintenance.¹ The apoftles, with the reft of the clergy in *Jerufalem*, lived at that time according to the manner of a fellowfhip, for collegiate fociety, maintaining themfelves and the

I   power

power of the church with a common purse, the reft of the faithful keeping that purfe continually ftored. And in that fenfe it is, that the facred hiftory faith, *All which be-* **Acts 2. 44.** *lieved were in one place, and had all things common.* In the hiftories of the church, and in the writings of the ancient fathers for fome hundred of years after, we find no other way for the maintenance of the clergy but only this, the treafury of Jefus Chrift furnifhed through mens devotion, beftowing fometimes goods, fometimes lands that way, and out of his treafury the charge of the fervice of God was defrayed, the bifhop and the clergy under him maintained, the poor in their neceflity miniftred unto. For which purpofe, every bifhop had fome one of the presbyters under him to be a treafurer of the **a Difp. Profp.** church, to receive, keep, and deliver all; which office in churches, cathedral remaineth **de vita con-** even till this day, albeit the ufe thereof be not altogether fo large now as heretofore. The **Oecon. l. 14.** difpofition of thefe goods was by the appointment of the bifhop.   Wherefore b *Profper* **C, de facra.** fpeaking of the bifhop's care herein, faith, *It was neceffary for one to be troubled there-* **Ecclef. & No-** *with, to the end that the reft under him might be freer to attend quietly their fpiritual* **cip.** *bufineffes.* And left any man fhould imagine, that bifhops by this means were hindred **c Profp. de vi-** themfelves from attending the fervice of God, *Even herein,* faith he, *they do God fer-* **ta Contemp. l,** *vice; for if thofe things which are beftowed on the church be God's; he doth the work* *of God, who, not of a covetous mind, but with purpofe of moft faithful adminiftra-* *tion, taketh care of things confecrated unto God.* And forafmuch as the presbyters of every church could not all live with the bifhop, partly for that their number was great, and partly becaufe the people being once divided into parifhes, fuch presbyters as had feverally charge of them were by that mean more conveniently to live in the midft each of his own particular flock, therefore a competent number being fed at the fame c table **c Cypr. l. 4. Ep.** with the bifhop, the reft had their whole allowance apart, which feveral allowances were **f. Presbyterii** called *Sportulæ,* and they who received them, *Sportulantes fratres.* Touching the bifhop, **fignaffe nos il-** as his place and eftate was higher, fo likewife the proportion of his charges about him- **lia jam fciatis** felf being for that caufe in all equity and reafon greater; yet, forafmuch as his ftint here- **eifdem cum** in was no other than it pleafed him to fet, the reft (as the manner of inferiors is to think **Presbyteris** that they which are over them always have too much) grudged many times at the mea- **divifione** fure of the bifhops private expence, perhaps not without caufe. Howfoever, by this occa- **menfuratas æ-** fion there grew amongft them great heart-burning, quarrel, and ftrife: where the bifhops **quatis quanti-** were found culpable, as eating too much beyond their tether, and drawing more to their **antur, fenfuri** own private maintenance than the proportion of Chrift's patrimony, being not greatly **nobifcum pro-** abundant, could bear; fundry conftitutions hereupon were made to moderate the fame, **roboratis annis** according to the churches condition in thofe times. Some before they were made bifhops, **fuis. Which** having been owners of ample poffeffions, fold them and gave them away to the poor: **prian do fhew,** Thus did *Paulinus, Hillary, Cyprian,* and fundry others. Hereupon they, who entring **that every** into the fame fpiritual and high funcftion held their fecular poffeffions ftill, were hardly **presbyter had** thought of: and even when the cafe was fully refolved, that fo to do was not unlawful, **allowance** yet it grew a queftion, *Whether they lawfully might then take any thing out of the pub-* **out of the** *lick treafury of Chrift?* a queftion, *Whether bifhops, holding by civil title fufficient to* **ry; that be-** *live of their own, were bound in confcience to leave the goods of the church altogether* **fides the fame** *to the ufe of others?* Of contentions about thefe matters there was no end, neither **allowance cal-** appeared there any poffible way for quietnefs, otherwife than by making partition of **fome alfo had** church-revenues according to the feveral ends and ufes for which they did ferve, that **in that divi-** fo the bifhop's part might be certain. Such partition being made, the bifhop enjoy- **dend which** ed his portion feveral to himfelf; the reft of the clergy likewife theirs, a third part **was the re-** was fevered to the furnifhing and upholding of the church; a fourth to the erecftion **very months** and maintenance of houfes wherein the poor might have relief. After which fepa- **expence;** ration made, lands and livings began every day to be dedicated unto each ufe feveral- **thirdly, that** ly, by means whereof every of them became in fhort time much greater than they **byters under** had been for worldly maintenance; the fervent devotion of men being glad that **him, the bi-** this new opportunity was given, of fhewing zeal to the houfe of God in more cer- **had a certain** tain order. **number of the**

lived and commoned always with him.   e **Profp. de vita contempl. l. 2. c. 9. Pont. Diacon. in vita Cypr.**

By thefe things it plainly appeareth what proportion of maintenance hath been ever thought reafonable for a bifhop; fith in that very partition agreed on to bring him unto his certain ftint, as much is allowed unto him alone as unto all the clergy under him, namely, a fourth part of the whole yearly rents and revenues of the church. Nor is it likely, that, before thofe temporalities, which now are fuch eye-fores, were added unto the honour of bifhops, their ftate was fo mean as fome imagine. For if we had no other evidence than the covetous and ambitious humour of hereticks, whofe impotent defires

of

of afpiring thereunto, and extream difcontentment as oft as they were defeated, even this doth fhew that the ftate of bifhops was not a few degrees advanced above the reft. Wherefore of grand apoftates which were in the very prime of the primitive church, thus *Lactantius* above thirteen hundred years fithence teftified, *Men of a flippery faith they were, who feigning that they knew and worfhipped God, but feeking only that they might grow in WEALTH and honour, affected the place of the HIGHEST PRIEST-HOOD* ; *whereunto, when their betters were chofen before them, they thought it better to leave the church, and to draw their favourers with them, than to endure thofe men their governors, whom themfelves defire to govern.* Now, whereas againft the prefent eftate of bifhops, and the greatnefs of their port, and the largenefs of their expences at this day, there is not any thing more commonly objected than thofe ancient canons, whereby they are reftrained unto a far more fparing life ; their houfes, their retinue, their diet limited within a far more narrow compafs than is now kept ; we muft know, that thofe laws, and ordets were made when bifhops lived of the fame purfe which ferved as well for a number of others as them, and yet all at their difpofing ? So that convenient it was to provide that there might be a moderate ftint appointed to meafure their expences by, left others fhould be injured by their waftfulnefs. Contrariwife, there is now no caufe wherefore any fuch law fhould be injured, when bifhops live only of that which hath been peculiarly allotted unto them. They having therefore temporalities and other revenues to beftow for their own private ufe, according to that which their ftate requireth, and no other having with them any fuch common intereft therein, their own difcretion is to be their law for this matter ; neither are they to be preffed with the rigour of fuch ancient canons as were framed for other times, much lefs fo odioufly to be upbraided with unconformity unto the pattern of our Lord and Saviour's eftate, in fuch circumftances as himfelf did never mind to require that the reft of the world fhould of neceffity be like him. Thus againft the wealth of the clergy they alledge how meanly Chrift himfelf was provided for ; againft bifhops palaces, his want of a hole to hide his head in ; againft the fervice done unto them, that *he came to minifter, not to be miniftred unto in the world.* Which things, as they are not unfit to controul covetous, proud or ambitious defires of the minifters of Chrift, and even of all chriftians, whatfoever they be ; and to teach men contentment of mind, how mean foever their eftate is, confidering that they are but fervants to him, whofe condition was far more abafed than theirs is, or can be ; fo to prove fuch difference in ftate between us and him unlawfully, they are of no force or ftrength at all. If one convented before their confiftories, when he ftandeth to make this anfwer, fhould break out into invectives againft their authority, and tell them that Chrift, when he was on earth, did not fit to judge, but ftand to be judged ; would they hereupon think it requifite to diffolve their elderfhip, and to permit no tribunals, no judges at all, for fear of fwerving from our Saviour's example ? If thofe men, who have nothing in their mouths more ufual than the poverty of Jefus Chrift and his apoftles, alledge not this as *Julian* fometime did, *beati pauperes,* unto chriftians, when his meaning was to fpoil them of that they had ; our hope is then, that as they ferioufly and fincerely wifh, that our Saviour Chrift in this point may be followed, and to that end only propofe his bleffed example ; fo, at our hands again, they will be content to hear with like willingnefs the holy apoftle's exhortation made unto them of the laity alfo, *Be ye followers of us, even as we are of Chrift ; let us be your example, even as the Lord Jefus Chrift is ours, that we may all proceed by one and the fame rule.*

That for their unworthinefs to deprive both them and their fucceffors of fuch goods, and to convey the fame unto men of fecular calling, were extream facrilegious injuftice.

XXIV. But beware we of following Chrift as thieves follow true men, to take their goods by violence from them. Be it that bifhops were all unworthy, not only of livings, but even of life, yet what hath our Lord Jefus Chrift deferved, for which men fhould judge him worthy to have the things that are his given away from him unto others that have no right unto them ? For at this mark it is that the head lay-reformers do all aim. Muft thefe unworthy prelates give place ? What then ! Shall better fucceed in their rooms ? Is this defired, to the end that others may enjoy their honours which fhall do Chrift more faithful fervice than they have done ? Bifhops are the worft men living upon earth ; therefore let their fanctified poffeffions be divided : Amongft whom ? O bleffed reformation ! O happy men, that put to their helping hands for the furtherance of fo good and glorious a work ! Wherefore, albeit the whole world at this day do alrea-dy perceive, and pofterity be like hereafter a great deal more plainly to difcern ; not that the clergy of God is thus heaved at becaufe they are wicked, but that means are ufed to put it into the heads of the fimple multitude that they are fuch indeed, to the end that thofe who thirft for the fpoil of fpiritual poffeffions may, till fuch time as they have their purpofe, be thought to covet nothing but only the juft extinguifhment of un-reformable

I

Laft. de vera fup. l. 5. c. 30.

1 Cor. 11. 1. Phil. 3. 16.

reformable perfons; fo that in regard of fuch mens intentions, practices, and machina-
tions againft them, the pare that fuffereth thefe things may moft fitly pray with *David*,
Judge thou me, O Lord, according to my righteoufnefs, and according unto mine inno- Pfal. 7. 8.
cency: O let the malice of the wicked come to an end, and be thou the guide of the juft.
Notwithftanding, forafmuch as it doth not ftand with chriftian humility otherwife to
think, than that this violent outrage of men is a rod in the ireful hands of the Lord our
God, the fmart whereof we deferve to feel: let it not feem grievous in the eyes of my
reverend L L. the bifhops, if to their good confideration I offer a view of thofe fores
which are in the kind of their heavenly function moft apt to breed, and which, being
not in time cured, may procure at the length that which God of his infinite mercy avert.
Of bifhops in his time St. *Jerom* complaineth, that they took it in great difdain to have
any fault, great or fmall, found with them. *Epiphanius* likewife, before *Jerom*, noteth Epiph. contra
their impatiency this way to have been the very caufe of a fchifm in the church of Chrift; hæref. l. 3. to.
at what time one *Audius*, a man of great integrity of life, full of faith, and zeal towards 1. hær. 70.
God, beholding thofe things which were corruptly done in the church, told the B. B.
and presbyters their faults, in fuch fort as thofe men are wont, who love the truth from
their hearts, and walk in the paths of a moft exact life. Whether it were covetoufnefs,
or fenfuality in their lives; abfurdity or error in their teaching; any breach of the laws
and canons of the church wherein he efpied them faulty, certain and fure they were to be
thereof moft plainly told. Which thing, they whofe dealings were juftly culpable, could
not bear; but inftead of amending their faults, bent their hatred againft him who fought
their amendment, till at length they drove him, by extremity of infeftation, thro' wearinefs of ftriving againft their injuries, to leave both them, and with them the church.
Amongft the manifold accufations, either generally intended againft the bifhops of this
our church, or laid particularly to the charge of any of them, I cannot find that hitherto
their fpitefulleft adverfaries have been able to fay juftly, that any man for telling them
their perfonal faults in good and chriftian fort, hath fuftained in that refpect much perfecution. Wherefore, notwithftanding mine own inferior ftate and calling in God's church,
the confideration whereof affureth me, that in this kind the fweeteft facrifice which I can
offer unto Chrift is meek obedience, reverence and awe unto the prelates which he hath
placed in feats of higher authority over me, which I am, fo far as may conveniently
ftand with that duty of humble fubjection, meekly to crave my good L L. your favourable pardon, if it fhall feem a fault thus far to prefume; or, if otherwife, your wonted
courteous acceptation.

> ——*Smite hæc haud mollia fata*   *Æneid.* l. 12,
> *Sublatis aperire dolis.*

  In government, be it of what kind foever, but efpecially if it be fuch kind of government as prelates have over the church, there is not one thing publickly more hurtful, than
that an hard opinion fhould be conceived of governors at the firft: and a good opinion
how fhould the world ever conceive of them for their after-proceeding in regiment, whofe
firft accefs and entrance thereunto giveth juft occafion to think them corrupt men, which
fear not that God in whofe name they are to rule? Wherefore a fcandalous thing it is
to the church of God, and to the actors themfelves dangerous, to have afpired unto rooms
of prelacy by wicked means. We are not at this day troubled much with that tumultuous kind of ambition, wherewith the elections of *Damafus* in St. *Jerom*'s age, and* Ammian.
of *Maximus* in *Gregory*'s time, and of others, were long fithence ftained, Our greateft Marcel. l. 27.
fear is rather the evil which *Leo* and *Anthemius* did by imperial conftitution endeavour Greg. Naz.
as much as in them lay, to prevent. He which granteth, or he which receiveth the of- Nemo gra-
fice and dignity of a bifhop, otherwife than befeemeth a thing divine and moft holy; he pretii venali-
which beftoweth, and he which obtaineth it after any other fort than were honeft and tate mercetur;
lawful to ufe, if our Lord Jefus Chrift were prefent himfelf on earth to beftow it even quantum quif-
with his own hands, finneth a fin by fo much more grievous than the fin of *Belfhazar*, non quotum
by how much offices and functions heavenly are more precious than the meaneft orna- dare fufficiat,
ments or implements which thereunto appertain. If it be, as the apoftle faith, that the Profecto enim,
holy Ghoft doth make bifhops, and that the whole action of making them is God's own quis locus tu-
deed, men being therein but his agents, what fpark of the fear of God can there poffibly fa effe poterit
remain in their hearts, who reprefenting the perfon of God, in naming worthy men to excufats, fi veneranda Dei

templa pecuniis expugnentur? Quem murum integritatis aut vallum providebimus fi auri facra fames in penetralia veneranda proferpat?
quid denique crutum effe poterit aut fecurum, fi fanctitas incorrupta corrumpatur? Ceffet altaribus imminere profanus ardor avaritiæ,
& à facris adytis repellatur piaculare flagitium. Itaque caftus & humilis noftris temporibus eligatur epifcopus, ut quocunque locorum
pervenerit, omnia vitæ propriæ integritate purificet, Nec pretio fed precibus ordinetur antiftes. l. 31. C. de epifc. & cler.

ecclefiaftical

ecclefiaftical charge, do fell that which in his name they are to beftow; or who, ftanding as it were at the throne of the living God, do bargain for that which at his hands they are to receive? Wo worth fuch impious and irreligious prophanations. The church of Chrift hath been hereby made, not *a den of thieves*, but in a manner the very dwelling-place of foul fpirits; for undoubtedly fuch a number of them have been in all ages who thus have climbed into the feat of epifcopal regiment.

2. Men may by orderly means be invefted with fpiritual authority, and yet do harm, by reafon of ignorance how to ufe it to the good of the church. *It is*, faith *Chryfoftom*, πολλῶ μὼ ἀξιώματᾷ δύσκολον δὲ ἐπισκοπῶν; *a thing highly to be accounted of, but a hard thing to be that which a bifhop fhould be.* Yea, a hard and a toilfom thing it is for a bifhop to know the things that belong unto a bifhop. A right good man may be a very unfit magiftrate. And for difcharge of a bifhop's office, to be well minded is not enough, no, nor to be well learned alfo. Skill to inftruct is a thing neceffary, skill to govern much more neceffary in a bifhop. It is not fafe for the church of Chrift, when bifhops learn what belongeth unto government, as empericks learn phyfick by killing of the fick. Bifhops were wont to be men of great learning in the laws, both civil, and of the church; and while they were fo, the wifeft men in the land for counfel and government, were bifhops.

3. Know we never fo well what belongeth unto a charge of fo great moment, yet can we not therein proceed, but with hazard of publick detriment, if we rely on our felves alone, and ufe not the benefit of conference with others. A fingular mean to unity and concord amongft themfelves, a marvelous help unto uniformity in their dealings, no fmall addition of weight and credit unto that which they do, a ftrong bridle unto fuch as watch for occafions to ftir againft them; finally, a very great ftay unto all that are under their government, it could not chufe but be foon found, if bifhops did often and ferioufly ufe the help of mutual confultation. Thefe three rehearfed are things only preparatory unto the courfe of epifcopal proceedings. But the hurt is more manifeftly feen which doth grow to the church of God, by faults inherent in their feveral actions; as when they carelefly ordain; when they inftitute negligently; when corruptly they beftow church livings, benefices, prebends, and rooms efpecially of jurifdictions; when they vifit for gain fake, rather than with ferious intent to do good; when their courts erected for the maintenance of good order, are difordered; when they regard not the clergy under them; when neither clergy nor laity are kept in that awe for which this authority fhould ferve; when any thing appeareth in them rather than a fatherly affection towards the flock of Chrift; when they have no refpect to pofterity; and finally, when they neglect the true and requifite means whereby their authority fhould be upheld. Surely the hurt which groweth out of thefe defects muft needs be exceeding great. In a minifter ignorance and difability to teach is a maim; nor is it held a thing allowable, to ordain fuch, were it not for the avoiding of a greater evil which the church muft needs fuftain; if in fo great fcarcity of able men, and infufficiency of moft parifhes throughout the land to maintain them, both publick prayer and the adminiftration of facraments fhould rather want, than any man thereunto be admitted lacking dexterity and skill to perform that which otherwife was moft requifite. Wherefore the neceffity of ordaining fuch, is no excufe for the rafh and carelefs ordaining of every one that hath but a friend to beftow fome two or three words of ordinary commendation in his behalf. By reafon whereof the church groweth burdened with filly creatures more than need, whofe noted bafenefs and infufficiency bringeth their very order it felf into contempt.

It may be that the fear of a *quare impedit* doth caufe inftitutions to pafs more eafily than otherwife they would. And to fpeak plainly the very truth, it may be that writs of *quare non impedit* were for thefe times moft neceffary in the other's place: yet where law will not fuffer men to follow their own judgment, to fhew their judgment they are not hindred. And I doubt not but that even confciencelefs and wicked patrons, of which fort the fwarms are too great in the church of *England*, are the more emboldened to prefent unto bifhops any reffufe, by finding fo eafy acceptation thereof. Somewhat they might redrefs this fore, notwithftanding fo ftrong impediments, if it did plainly appear that they took it indeed to heart, and were not in a manner contented with it.

Shall we look for care in admitting whom others prefent, if that which fome of your felves confer be at any time corruptly beftowed? A foul and an ugly kind of deformity it hath, if a man do but think what it is for a bifhop to draw commodity and gain from thofe things whereof he is left a free beftower, and that in truft, without any other obligation than his facred order only, and that religious integrity which hath been prefumed on in him. Simoniacal corruption I may not for honour's fake fufpect to be amongft men of fo great place. So often they do not, I truft, offend by fale, as by unadvifed

vifed gift of fuch preferments, wherein that ancient canon fhould fpecially be remem-Can Apoſt. 6.
bred, which forbiddeth a bifhop to be led by human affe
ction, in beſtowing the things
of God.   A fault no where fo hurtful, as in beſtowing places of jurifdiction, and in furnifhing cathedral churches, the prebendaries and other dignities whereof are the very
true fucceffors of thofe ancient presbyters which were at the firſt as counfellors unto bifhops.   A foul abufe it is, that any one man fhould be loaded, as fome are, with livings
in this kind, yea, fome even of them who condemn utterly the granting of any two benefices unto the fame man, whereas the other is in truth a matter of far greater fequel,
as experience would foon fhew, if churches cathedral being furnifhed with the refidence of a competent number of vertuous, grave, wife and learned divines, the reſt of
the prebends of every fuch church were given within the diocefe, unto men of worthieſt
defert, for their better encouragement unto induſtry and travel; unlefs it feem alfo convenient to extend the benefit of them unto the learned in univerfities, and men of fpecial
employment otherwife in the affairs of the church of God.   But howfoever, furely with
the publick good of the church it will hardly ſtand, that in any one perfon fuch favours
be more multiplied than law permitteth in thofe livings which are with cure.

Touching bifhops vifitations, the firſt inſtitution of them was profitable, to the end
that the ſtate and condition of churches being known, there might be for evils growing, convenient remedies provided in due time.   The obfervation of church laws, the
correction of faults in the fervice of God, and manners of men, thefe are things that
vifitors fhould feek.   When thefe things are enquired of formally, and but for cuſtom
fake, fees and penfions being the only thing which is fought, and little elfe done by vifitations; we are not to marvel if the bafenefs of the end doth make the action it felf
loathfom.   The good which bifhops may do, not only by thefe vifitations belonging
ordinarily to their office, but alfo in refpect of that power which the founders of colleges have given them of fpecial truſt, charging even fearfully their confciences therewith:
the good, I fay, which they might do by this their authority, both within their own diocefe, and in the well-fprings themfelves, the univerfities, is plainly fuch as cannot chufe
but add weight to their heavy accounts in that dreadful day, if they do it not.

In their courts, where nothing but fingular integrity and juſtice fhould prevail, if palpable and grofs corruptions be found, by reafon of offices fo often granted unto men who
feek nothing but their own gain, and make no account what difgrace doth grow by their
unjuſt dealings unto them under whom they deal, the evil hereof fhall work more than
they which procure it do perhaps imagine.

At the hands of a bifhop, the firſt thing looked for is a care of the clergy under him,
a care, that in doing good they may have whatfoever comforts and encouragements his
countenance, authority, and place may yield.   Otherwife what heart fhall they have to
proceed in their painful courfe, all forts of men befides being fo ready to malign, defpife,
and every way opprefs them?   Let them find nothing but difdain in bifhops; in the enemies of prefent government, if that way they liſt to betake themfelves, all kind of favourable and friendly help; unto which part think we it likely that men having wit, courage,
and ſtomach will incline?

As great a fault is the want of feverity when need requireth, as of kindnefs and courtefy in bifhops.   But touching this, what with ill ufage of their power among the meaner,
and what with difufage amongſt the higher fort, they are in the eyes of both forts as bees
having loſt their ſting.   It is a long time fithence any great one hath felt, or almoſt any
one much feared the edge of that ecclefiaſtical feverity, which fometime held lords and
dukes in a more religious awe than now the meaneſt are able to be kept.

A bifhop, in whom there did plainly appear the marks and tokens of a fatherly affection towards them that are under his charge, what good might he do ten thoufand ways
more than any man knows how to fet down?   But the fouls of men are not loved; that
which Chriſt fhed his blood for is not eſteemed precious.   This is the very root, the
fountain of all negligence in church government.

Moſt wretched are the terms of mens eſtate, when once they are at a point of wretch-
lefnefs fo extreme, that they bend not their wits any farther than only to fhift out the
prefent time, never regarding what fhall become of their fucceffors after them.   Had our
predeceffors fo loofely caſt off from them all care and refpect to poſterity, a church
chriſtian there had not been, about the regiment whereof we fhould need at this day
to ſtrive.   It was the barbarous affection of *Nero*, that the ruin of his own imperial
feat he could have been well enough contented to fee, in cafe he might alfo have feen it
accompanied with the fall of the whole world: an affection not more intolerable than
theirs, who care not to overthrow all poſterity, fo they may purchafe a few days of ignominious fafety unto themfelves and their prefent eſtates; if it may be termed a fafety

F f f   which

which tendeth fo faft unto their very overthrow that are the purchafers of it in fo vile and bafe manner.

Men whom it ftandeth upon to uphold a reverend eftimation of themfelves in the minds of others, without which the very beft things they do are hardly able to efcape difgrace, muft, before it be over-late, remember how much eafier it is to retain credit, once gotten, than to recover it, being loft. The executors of bifhops are fued, if their manfion-houfe be fuffered to go to decay: but whom fhall their fucceffors fue for the dilapidations which they make of that credit, the unrepaired diminutions whereof will in time bring to pafs, that they which would moft do good in that calling, fhall not be able, by rea-fon of prejudice generally fettled in the minds of all forts againft them? By what means *Egifip. l. 2. c.* their eftimation hath hitherto decayed, it is no hard thing to difcern. *Herod* and *Ar-* *12.* *chelaus* are noted to have fought out purpofely the dulleft and moft ignoble that could be found amongft the people, preferring fuch to the high-prieft's office, thereby to abate the great opinion which the multitude had of that order, and to procure a more expedite courfe for their own wicked counfels, whereunto they faw the high-priefts were no fmall impediment, as long as the common fort did much depend upon them. It may be there hath been partly fome fhew and juft fufpicion of like practice in fome, in procuring the undeferved preferments of fome unworthy perfons, the very caufe of whofe advance-ment hath been principally their unworthinefs to be advanced. But neither could this be done altogether without the inexcufable fault of fome preferred before, and fo oft we cannot imagine it to have been done, that either only or chiefly from thence this decay of their eftimation may be thought to grow. Somewhat it is that the malice of their cun-ning adverfaries, but much more which themfelves have effected againft themfelves. A bifhop's eftimation doth grow from the excellency of virtues fuitable unto his place. Unto the place of a bifhop thofe high divine virtues are judged fuitable, which virtues being not eafily found in other forts of great men, do make him appear fo much the greater, in whom they are found.

Devotion, and the feeling fenfe of religion, are not ufual in the nobleft, wifeft, and chiefeft perfonages of ftate, by reafon their wits are fo much employed another way, and their minds fo feldom converfant in heavenly things. If therefore wherein themfelves are defective they fee that bifhops do bleffedly excel, it frameth fecretly their hearts to a ftooping kind of difpofition, clean oppofite to contempt: the very countenance of *Mofes* was glorious, after that God had conferred with him. And where bifhops are, the powers and faculties of whofe fouls God hath poffeft, thofe very actions, the kind whereof is common unto them with other men, have notwithftanding in them a more high and heavenly form, which draweth correfpondent eftimation unto it, by virtue of that celeftial impreffion which deep meditation of holy things, and as it were con-verfation with God, doth leave in their minds. So that bifhops which will be efteemed of as they ought, muft frame themfelves to that very pattern from whence thofe *Afian* bifhops unto whom St. *John* writeth, were denominated, even fo far forth as this our frailty will permit; fhine they muft, as angels of God in the midft of perverfe men. They are not to look that the world fhould always carry the affection of *Conftantine*, to bury that which might derogate from them, and to cover their imbecillities. More than high time it is, that they bethink themfelves of the apoftle's admonition, *attende tibi, have a vigi-lant eye to thy felf.* They err if they do not perfuade themfelves, that wherefoever they walk or fit, be it in their churches or in their confiftories, abroad or at home, at their ta-bles or in their clofets, they are in the midft of fnares laid for them. Wherefore, as they are, with the prophet, every one of them to make it their hourly prayer unto God, *Lead me, O Lord, in thy righteoufnefs, becaufe of enemies*; fo it is not fafe for them, no not for a moment, to flacken their induftry in feeking every way that eftimation which may fur-ther their labours unto the church's good. Abfurdity, though but in words, muft needs be this way a maim, where nothing but wifdom, gravity, and judgment is looked for. That which the fon of *Syrach* hath concerning the writings of the old fages, *wife fen-tences are found in them*, fhould be the proper mark and character of bifhops fpeeches, whofe lips, as doors, are not to be opened, but for egrefs of inftruction and found know-ledge. If bafe fervility and dejection of mind be ever efpied in them, how fhould men efteem them as worthy the rooms of the great ambaffadors of God? A wretched defire to gain by bad and unfeemly means, ftandeth not with a mean man's credit, much lefs with that reputation which fathers of the church fhould be in. But if befides all this there be alfo coldnefs in works of piety and charity, utter contempt even of learning it felf, no care to further it by any fuch helps as they eafily might and ought to afford, no not as much as that due refpect unto their very families about them, which all men that are of account do order, as near as they can, in fuch fort that no grievous offenfive defor-

I.   mity

mity be therein noted; if there ftill continue in that moft reverend order fuch as by fo
many engines work day and night to pull down the whole frame of their own eftimation amongft men, fome of the reft fecretly alfo permitting others their induftrious op-
pofites every day more to feduce the multitude, how fhould the church of God hope for
great good at their hands?

What we have fpoken concerning thefe things, let not malicious accufers think themfelves therewith juftified, no more than *Shimei* was by his fovereign's moft humble and
meek acknowledgment even of that very crime which fo impudent a caitiff's tongue upbraided him withal; the one in the virulent rancour of a canker'd affection took that
delight for the prefent which in the end did turn to his own more tormenting wo, the
other in the contrite patience even of deferved malediction, had yet this comfort, *It may* 2 Sam. 16. 12
be the Lord will look on mine affliction, and do me good for his curfing this day. As for us,
over whom Chrift hath placed them to be the chiefeft guides and paftors of our fouls, our
common fault is, that we look for much more in our governors than a tolerable fufficiency can yield, and bear much lefs than humanity and reafon do require we fhould. Too
much perfection over-rigoroufly exacted in them, cannot but breed in us perpetual difcontentment, and on both parts caufe all things to be unpleafant. It is exceedingly worth
the noting, which *Plato* hath about the means whereby men fall into an utter diflike of
all men with whom they converfe: *This fournefs of mind which maketh every man's* Plat. in Phæd.
dealings unfavory in our tafte, entereth by unskilful over-weaning, which at the firft we
have of one, and fo of another, in whom we afterwards find our felves to have been de-
ceived, they declaring themfelves in the end to be frail men, whom we judged demi-gods:
when we have oftentimes been thus beguiled, and that far befides expectation, we grow
at the length to this plain conclufion, That there is nothing at all found in any man.
Which bitter conceit is unfeemly, and plain to have rifen from lack of mature judgment in
human affairs: which if fo be we did handle with art, we would not enter into dealings
with men, otherwife than being beforehand grounded in this perfuafion, that the number of
perfons notably good or bad is but very fmall; that the moft part of good have fome evil,
and of evil men, fome good in them. So true our experience doth find thofe aphorifms of
Mercurius Trifmegiftus, Ἀδύνατὸν τὸ ἀγαθὸν ἐνθάδε καθαρεύειν ἢ κακίας, to purge goodnefs
quite and clean from all mixture of evil here, is a thing impoffible. Again, Τὸ μὴ λίαν M. Dif. in pῖ
κακὸν ἐνθάδε τὸ ἀγαθὸν ἐςι. When in this world we term a thing good, we cannot by mandro.dial.6,
exact construction have any other true meaning, than that the faid thing fo termed is
not noted to be a thing exceeding evil. And again, Μῆνον ὦ Ἀσκλήπιε τὸ ὄνομα
τῇ ἀγαθῇ ἐν ἀνθρώποις, τὸ δὲ ἔργον οὐδαμῖ. Amongft men, O *Efclapius*, the name
of that which is good we find, but no where the very true thing it felf. When we
cenfure the deeds and dealings of our fuperiors, to bring with us a fore-conceit thus qualified fhall be as well on our part as theirs a thing available unto quietnefs. But howfoever the cafe doth ftand with mens either good or bad quality, the verdict which our
Lord and Saviour hath given fhould continue for ever fure. *Quæ Dei funt, Deo*, let Mat. 3. 8.
men bear the burthren of their own iniquity; as for thofe things which are God's, let not Act. 5. 2,
God be deprived of them. For if only to with-hold that which fhould be given, be no
better than to rob God, if to withdraw any mite of that which is but in purpofe only
bequeathed, though as yet undelivered into the facred treafure of God, be a fin for which
Ananias and *Sapphyra* felt fo heavily the dreadful hand of divine revenge; quite and clean
to take that away which we never gave, and that after God hath for fo many ages therewith been poffeffed, and that without any other fhew of caufe, faving only that it feemeth in their eyes who feek it, too much for them which have it in their hands, can we
term it or think it lefs than moft impious injuftice, moft heinous facrilege? Such was
the religious affection of *Jofeph*, that it fuffered him not to take that advantage, no Gen. 47. 22,
not againft the very idolatrous priefts of *Egypt*, which he took for the purchafing of
other mens lands to the king; but he confidered, that albeit their idolatry deferved hatred, yet for the honour's fake due unto priefthood, better it was the king himfelf fhould
yield them relief in publick extremity, than permit that the fame neceffity fhould conftrain alfo them to do as the reft of the people did. But it may be, men have now found
out, that God hath propofed the chriftian clergy, as a prey for all men freely to feize
upon; that God hath left them as the fifhes of the fea, which every man that lifteth
to gather into his net may; or that there is no God in heaven to pity them, and to regard the injuries which man doth lay upon them: yet the publick good of this church
and commonwealth, doth, I hope, weigh fomewhat in the hearts of all honeftly difpofed
men. Unto the publick good no one thing is more directly available, than that fuch as
are in place, whether it be of civil or of ecclefiaftical authority, be fo much the more
largely furnifhed even with external helps and ornaments of this life, how much more

highly

highly they are in power and calling advanc'd above others. For nature is not contented with bare fufficiency unto the fuftenance of man, but doth evermore covet a decency proportionable unto the place which man hath in the body or fociety of others. For according unto the greatnefs of mens calling, the meafure of all their actions doth grow in every man's fecret expectation, fo that great men do always know that great things are at their hands expected. In a bifhop great liberality, great hofpitality, actions in every kind great are look'd for: And for actions which muft be great, mean inftruments will not ferve. Men are but men, what room foever amongft men they hold. If therefore the meafure of their worldly habilities be beneath that proportion which their calling doth make to be look'd for at their hands, a ftronger inducement it is than perhaps men are aware of unto evil and corrupt dealings for fupply of that defect. For which caufe we muft needs think it a thing neceffary unto the common good of the church, that great jurifdiction being granted unto bifhops over others, a ftate of wealth proportionable fhould likewife be provided for them. Where wealth is had in fo great admiration, as generally in this golden age it is, that without it angelical perfections are not able to deliver from extream contempt, furely to make bifhops poorer than they are, were to make them of lefs account and eftimation than they fhould be. Wherefore if detriment and difhonour do grow to religion, to God, to his church, when the publick account which is made of the chief of the clergy decayeth, how fhould it be, but in this refpect, for the good of religion, of God, of his church, that the wealth of bifhops be carefully preferved from the further diminution? The travels and croffes wherewith prelacy is never unaccompanied, they which feel them know how heavy and how great they are: Unlefs fuch difficulties therefore annexed unto that eftate be temper'd, by co-annexing thereunto things efteem'd of in this world, how fhould we hope that the minds of men, fhunning naturally the burthens of each function, will be drawn to undertake the burthen of epifcopal care, and labour in the church of Chrift? Wherefore if long we defire to enjoy the peace, quietnefs, order and ftability of religion, which prelacy (as hath been declared) caufeth, then muft we neceffarily, even in favour of the publick good, uphold thofe things, the hope whereof being taken away, it is not the meer goodnefs of the charge, and the divine acceptation thereof, that will be able to invite many thereunto. What fhall become of that commonwealth or church in the end, which hath not the eye of learning to beautify, guide, and direct it? At the length, what fhall become of that learning, which hath not wherewith any more to encourage her induftrious followers? And finally, what fhall become of that courage to follow learning, which hath already fo much failed through the only diminution of her chiefeft rewards, bifhopricks? Surely, wherefoever this wicked intendment of overthrowing cathedral churches, or of taking away thofe livings, lands, and poffeffions, which bifhops hitherto have enjoyed, fhall once prevail, the hand-maids attending thereupon will be paganifm and extreme barbarity. In the law of *Mofes*, how careful provifion is made that goods of this kind

Numb. 18.32. might remain to the church for ever: *Te fhall not make common the holy things of the children of Ifrael, left ye dye, faith the Lord.* Touching the fields annexed unto levitical cities, the law was plain, they might not be fold; and the reafon of the law this, *for*
Lev. 25. *it was their poffeffion for ever.* He which was Lord and owner of it, his will and pleafure was, that from the Levites it fhould never pafs to be enjoyned by any other. The Lord's own portion, without his own commiffion and grant, how fhould any man juftly
Ezek. 48. 14. hold? They which hold it by his appointment, had it plainly with this condition, *They fhall not fell of it, neither change it, nor alienate the firft-fruits of the land; for it is*
Habak. 2. 17. *holy unto the Lord.* It falleth fometimes out, as the prophet *Habakkuk* noteth, that the very *prey of favage beafts becometh dreadful unto themfelves.* It did fo in *Judas, Acham, Nebuchadnezzar*; their evil purchafed goods were their fnare, and their prey their own
Mal. 3. 9. terror; a thing no where fo likely to follow, as in thofe goods and poffeffions, which being laid where they fhould not reft, have by the Lord's own teftimony his moft bitter curfe; their undividable companion. Thefe perfuafions we ufe for other mens caufe, not for theirs with whom God and religion are parts of the abrogated law of ceremonies. Wherefore not to continue longer in the cure of a fore defperate, there was a time when the clergy had almoft as little as thefe good people wifh. But the kings of this realm and others, whom God had bleft, confidered devoutly with themfelves, as *Da-*
Prov. 3. 9. *vid* in like cafe fometimes had done, *It is meet that we at the hands of God fhould enjoy all kinds of abundance, and God's clergy fuffer want?* They confidered that of *Solomon, honour God with thy fubftance, and the chiefeft of all thy revenue; fo fhall thy barns be filled with corn, and thy veffels fhall run over with new wine.* They confidered how
2 Chron. 9. chap 19. the care which *Jehofaphat* had, in providing that the Levites might have encouragement to do the work of the Lord chearfully, was left of God as a fit pattern to be followed

in

in the church for ever. They confider'd what promife our Lord and Saviour had made unto them, at whofe hands his prophets fhould receive but the leaft part of the meaneft kind of friendlinefs, though it were but a draught of water: which promife feemeth not to be taken, as if Chrift had made them of any higher courtefy uncapable, and had promifed reward unto fuch as give them but that, but unto fuch as leave them but that. They confidered how earneft the apoftle is, that if the minifters of the law were fo amply provided for, lefs care then ought not to be had of them, who under the gofpel of Jefus Chrift poffeft correfpondent rooms in the church. They confidered how needful it is, that they who provoke all others unto works of mercy and charity, fhould efpecially have wherewith to be examples of fuch things, and by fuch means to win them, with whom other means, without thofe, do commonly take very fmall effect.

In thefe and the like confiderations, the church-revenues were in ancient times augmented, our Lord thereby performing manifeftly the promife made to his fervants, that they which did *leave either father, or mother, or lands, or goods for his fake, fhould receive even in this world an hundred fold.* For fome hundred of years together, they which joyned themfelves to the church, were fain to relinquifh all worldly emoluments, and to endure the hardnefs of an afflicted eftate. Afterward the Lord gave reft to his church, kings and princes became as fathers thereunto, the hearts of all men inclined towards it, and by his providence there grew unto it every day earthly poffeffions in more and more abundance, till the greatnefs thereof bred envy, which no diminutions are able to fatisfy. For, as thofe ancient nurfing fathers thought they did never beftow enough; even fo in the eye of this prefent age, as long as any thing remaineth, it feemeth to be too much. Our fathers we imitate *in perverfum,* as *Tertullian* fpeaketh; like them we are, by being in equal degree the contrary unto that which they were. Unto thofe earthly bleffings which God as then did with fo great abundance pour down upon the ecclefiaftical ftate, we may in regard of moft near refemblance, apply the felf fame words which the prophet hath, *God bleffed them exceedingly; and, by this very mean, turned the* $^{Pf.105.24.25}$ *hearts of their own brethren to hate them, and to deal politickly with his fervants.* Computations are made, and there are huge fums fet down for princes, to fee how much they may amplify and enlarge their own treafure; how many publick burthens they may eafe; what prefent means they have to reward their fervants about them, if they pleafe but to grant their affent, and to accept of the fpoil of bifhops, by whom church-goods are but abufed unto pomp and vanity. Thus albeit they deal with one, whofe princely vertue giveth them fmall hope to prevail in impious and facrilegious motions; yet fhame they not to move her royal majefty even with a fuit not much unlike unto that wherewith the *Jewifh* high-prieft tried *Judas,* whom they folicited unto treafon againft his mafter, and propofed unto him a number of filver pence in lieu of fo vertuous and honeft a fervice. But her facred majefty difpofed to be always like her felf, her heart fo far eftranged from willingnefs to gain by pillage of that eftate, the only awe whereof under God fhe hath been unto this prefent hour, as of all other parts of this noble commonwealth, whereof fhe hath vowed her felf a protector till the end of her days on earth, which if nature could permit, we wifh, as good caufe we have, endlefs: this her gracious inclination is more than a feven times fealed warrant, upon the fame affurance whereof touching time and action, fo difhonourable as this, we are on her part moft fecure, not doubting but that unto all pofterity it fhall for ever appear, that from the firft to the very laft of her fovereign proceedings there hath not been one authorized deed other than confonant with that *Symmachus* faith, *Fifcus bonorum principum, non facerdotum* $^{Lib.10.ep.54.}_{DDD. Valent.}$ *damnis fed hoftium fpoliis augeatur;* confonant with the imperial law, *Ea quæ ad bea-* $^{Theodof. \&}$ *tiffimæ ecclefiæ jura pertinent, tanquam ipfam facrofanctam & religiofam ecclefiam intacta* $^{Archad.l. 14.}$ *convenit venerabiliter cuftodiri; ut ficut ipfa religionis & fidei mater perpetua eft, ita* $^{c. de facrof.}_{ecclef.}$ *ejus patrimonium jugiter ferveter illæfum.* As for the cafe of publick burthens, let any politician living make it appear, that by confifcation of bifhops livings, and their utter diffolution at once, the commonwealth fhall ever have half that relief and eafe which it receiveth by their continuance as now they are, and it fhall give us fome caufe to think, that albeit we fee they are impioufly and irreligioufly minded, yet we may efteem them at leaft to be tolerable commonwealths men. But the cafe is too clear and manifeft, the world doth but too plainly fee it, that no one order of fubjects whatfoever within this land doth bear the feventh part of that proportion which the clergy beareth in the burthens of the commonwealth: no revenue of the crown like unto it, either for certainty or for greatnefs. Let the good which this way hath grown to the commonwealth by the diffolution of religious houfes, teach men what eafe unto publick burthens there is like to grow by the overthrow of the clergy. My meaning is not hereby to make the ftate

of

L

of biſhopricks, and of thoſe diſſolved companies alike the one no leſs unlawful to be removed than the other. For thoſe religious perſons were men which followed only a ſpecial kind of contemplative life in the commonwealth, they were properly no portion of
God's clergy (only ſuch amongſt them excepted, as were alſo prieſts, their goods (that
excepted, which they unjuſtly held through the pope's uſurped power of appropriating
eccleſiaſtical livings unto them) may in part ſeem to be of the nature of civil poſſeſſions,
held by other kinds of corporations, ſuch as the city of *London* hath divers. Wherefore,
as their inſtitution was human, and their end for the moſt part ſuperſtitious, they had
not therein merely that holy and divine intereſt which belongeth unto biſhops, who being
employed by Chriſt in the principal ſervice of his church, are receivers and diſpoſers of
his patrimony, as hath been ſhewed, which whoſoever ſhall with-hold or withdraw at
any time from them, he undoubtedly robbeth God himſelf. If they abuſe the goods of
the church unto pomp and vanity, ſuch faults we do not excuſe in them. Only we wiſh
it to be conſider'd whether ſuch faults be verily in them, or elſe but objeſted againſt
them by ſuch as gape after ſpoil, and therefore are no competent judges what is moderate and what exceſſive in them, whom under this pretence they would ſpoil. But the
accuſation may be juſt. In plenty and fulneſs it may be we are of God more forgetful
than were requiſite. Notwithſtanding men ſhould remember how not to the clergy alone
it was ſaid by *Moſes* in *Deuteronomy,* *Ne cum manducaveris & biberis & domos optimas*
ædificaveris: If the remedy preſcrib'd for this diſeaſe be good, let it impartially be applied. *Intereſt reip. ut re ſua QUISQUE bene utatur.* Let all ſtates be put to their moderate penſions, let their livings and lands be taken away from them whoſoever they be,
in whom ſuch ample poſſeſſions are found to have been matters of grievous abuſe: were
this juſt, would noble families think this reaſonable? The title which biſhops have to
their livings is as good as the title of any ſort of men unto whatſoever we account to be
moſt juſtly held by them; yea, in this one thing the claim of *B. B.* hath preheminence
above all ſecular titles of right, in that God's own intereſt is the tenure whereby they
hold, even as alſo it was to the prieſts of the law an aſſurance of their ſpiritual goods
and poſſeſſions, whereupon though they many times abuſed greatly the goods of the
church, yet was not God's patrimony therefore taken away from them, and made ſale-
able unto other tribes. To rob God, to ranſack the church, to overthrow the whole
order of chriſtian biſhops, and to turn them out of land and living, out of houſe
and home, what man of common honeſty can think it for any manner of abuſe to be a
remedy lawful or juſt? We muſt confeſs that God is righteous in taking away that which
men abuſe: but doth that excuſe the violence of thieves and robbers? Complain we

* Pudet dicere, will not with St. *Jerome,* * *That the hands of men are ſo ſtraitly tied, and their liberal*
ſacerdotes ido-
lorum aurigæ; *minds ſo much bridled and held back from doing good by augmentation of the church-pa-*
mimi & icorta *trimony.* For we confeſs that herein mediocrity may be and hath been ſometime exceed-
hæreditates ca-
piunt,ſolis cle- ed. There did want heretofore a *Moſes* to temper mens liberality, to ſay unto them who
ricis & mena- enrich'd the church *ſufficit*, ſtay your hands left fervor of zeal do cauſe you to empty
chis, id lege your ſelves too far. It may be the largeneſs of mens hearts being then more moderate,
prohibetur, &
prohibetur had been after more durable; and one ſtate by too much over-growing the reſt, had not
non à perſe- given occaſion unto the reſt to undermine it. That evil is now ſufficiently cur'd: the
cutoribus ſed church-treaſury, if then it were over full, hath ſince been reaſonably well emptied.
principibus
chriſtianis. That which *Moſes* ſpake unto givers, we muſt now inculcate unto takers away from the
Nec de lege church, let there be ſome ſtay, ſome ſtint in ſpoiling. ᵇ *If grape gatherers came unto*
conqueror, ſed
dolco quod *them,* ſaith the prophet, *would they not leave ſome remnant behind?* But it hath far'd
meruerimus with the wealth of the church as with a tower, which being built at the firſt with the
hanc legem.
Ad Nepot. 7. higheſt, overthroweth it ſelf after by its own greatneſs; neither doth the ruin thereof
ᵇ Obad.verſ.5. ceaſe with the only fall of that which hath exceeded mediocrity, but one part beareth
down another, till the whole be laid proſtrate. For although the ſtate eccleſiaſtical
both others and even biſhops themſelves, be now fallen to ſo low an ebb, as all the world
at this day doth ſee; yet becauſe there remaineth ſtill ſomewhat which unſatiable minds
can thirſt for, therefore we ſeem not to have hitherto ſufficiently wronged. Touching
that which hath been taken from the church in appropriations known to amount to the
value of one hundred twenty ſix thouſand pounds yearly, we reſt contentedly and quietly without it, till it ſhall pleaſe God to touch the hearts of men, of their own voluntary
accord to reſtore it to him again; judging thereof no otherwiſe than ſome others did of thoſe
goods which were by *Sylla* taken away from the citizens of *Rome,* that albeit they were
in truth *male capta,* unconſcionably taken away from the right owners at the firſt, ne-
Flor lib. 3. vertheleſs ſeeing that ſuch as were after poſſeſſed of them held them not without ſome
c. 13. title, which law did after a ſort make good, *repetitio eorum proculdubio labefactabat com-*
poſitam civitatem. What hath been taken away as dedicated unto uſes ſuperſtitious, and
conſequently not given unto God, or at the leaſtwiſe not ſo rightly given, we repine at

I　　　　　　　　　　　　　　　　　　　　　　　　　　　　　thereat.

thereat. That which hath gone by means secret and indirect, through corrupt compositions or compacts we cannot help. What the hardness of mens hearts doth make them loth to have exacted, though being due by law, even thereof the want we do also bear. Out of that which after all these deductions cometh clearly unto our hands, I hope it will not be said that towards the publick charge we disburse nothing. And doth the residue seem yet excessive? The ways whereby temporal men provide for themselves and their families, are fore-closed unto us. All that we have to sustain our miserable life with, is but a remnant of God's own treasure, so far already diminished and clipt, that if there were any sense of common humanity left in this hard-hearted world, the impoverished estate of the clergy of God, would at the length even of very commiseration be spared. The mean gentleman that hath but an hundred pound land to live on, would not be hasty to change his wordly estate and condition with many of these so over-abounding prelates; a common artisan or tradesman of the city, with ordinary pastors of the church. It is our hard and heavy lot, that no other sort of men being grudged at, how little benefit soever the publick weal reap by them, no state complained of for holding that which hath grown unto them by lawful means; only the governors of our souls, they that study day and night so to guide us, that both in this world we may have comfort, and in the world to come endless felicity and joy, (for even such is the very scope of all their endeavours; this they wish, for this they labour, how hardly soever we use to construe of their intents;) hard, that only they should be thus continually lifted at for possessing but that whereunto they have, by law both of God and man, most just title. If there should be no other remedy, but that the violence of men, in the end, must needs bereave them of all succour, further than the inclinations of others shall vouchsafe to cast upon them, as it were by way of alms, for their relief but from hour to hour; better they are not than their fathers, who have been contented with as hard a portion at the world's hands: let the light of the sun and moon, the common benefit of heaven and earth, be taken away from *B. B.* if the question were, whether God should lose his glory, and the safety of his church be hazarded, or they relinquish the right and interest which they have in the things of this world. But sith the question in truth is, whether *Levi* shall be deprived of the portion of God or no, to the end that *Simeon* or *Reuben* may devour it as their spoil, the comfort of the one, in sustaining the injuries which the other would offer, must be that prayer poured out by *Moses* the prince of prophets, in most tender affection to *Levi, Bless, O Lord, his substance, accept thou the work of his* bands; *smite through the loyns of them that rise up against him, and of them which hate him, that they rise no more.*

[margin: Deut. 33. 10]

OF THE

L A W S

OF

Ecclefiaftical Polity.

BOOK VIII.

Containing their feventh affertion, that to no civil Prince or Governor, there may be given fuch power of ecclefia-ftical dominion, as by the laws of this land belongeth unto the fupreme regent thereof.

WE come now to the laſt thing whereof there is controverſy moved, namely, *The power of fupreme jurifdiction*; which for diſtinction fake we call, *The power of ecclefiaftical dominion.* It was not thought fit in the *Jews commonwealth*, that the exercife of *fupremacy ecclefiaftical* ſhould be de-
Maccab. 14. nied unto him, to whom the exercife of *chiefly civil* did appertain; and therefore their kings were inveſted with both. This power they gave unto *Simon*, when they confented that he ſhould be their prince, not only to fet men over their works, and coun-
try, and weapons, but alfo to provide for the holy things; and that he ſhould be obeyed of every man, and that the writings of the country ſhould be made in his name, and that it ſhould not be lawful for any of the people, or prieſts, to withſtand his words, or to call any congregation in the country without him. And if haply it be furmifed, that thus much was given to *Simon*, as being both prince and high-
prieſt; which otherwife (being their *civil governor*) he could not lawfully have en-
joyed; we muſt note, that all this is no more than the ancient kings of that people had, being kings, and not prieſts. By this power *David*, *Afa*, *Jehofhaphat*, *Jofias*, and the reſt, made thofe laws and orders which facred hiſtory ſpeaketh of, concerning

matters

i

matters of meer religion, the affairs of the temple, and service of God. Finally, had it not been by the virtue of this power, how should it possibly have come to pass, that the piety or impiety of the kings did always accordingly change the publick face of religion, which things the prophets by themselves never did, nor at any time could hinder from being done? Had the priests alone been possest of all power in spiritual affairs, how should any thing concerning matter of religion have been made but only by them? In them it had been, and not in the king, to change the face of religion at any time; the altering of religion, the making of ecclesiastical laws, with other the like actions belonging unto the power of dominion, are still termed *the deeds of the king*; to shew, that in him was placed the supremacy of power in this kind over all, and that unto their priests the same was never committed, saving only at such times as the priests were also kings and princes over them. According to the pattern of which example the like power in causes ecclesiastical is by the laws of this realm annexed unto the crown; and there are which do imagine, that kings being meer lay persons, do by this means exceed the lawful bounds of their callings; which thing to the end that they may persuade, they first make a necessary separation perpetual and personal between *the church* and *the commonwealth*. Secondly, they so tie all kind of *power ecclesiastical* unto the church, as if it were in every degree their only right, who are by proper spiritual functions termed church-governors, and might not unto christian princes in any wise appertain. To lurk under shifting ambiguities, and equivocations of words in matter of principal weight, is childish. A church and a commonwealth we grant are things in nature one distinguished from the other. A commonwealth is one way, and a church another way defined. in their opinions the church and commonwealth are corporations, not distinguished only in nature and definition, but in substance perpetually severed; so that they which are of the one can neither appoint nor execute in whole nor in part the duties which belong to them which are of the other, without open breach of the law of God which hath divided them, and doth require that so being divided they should distinctly or severally work, as depending both upon God, and not hanging one upon the other's approbation for that which either hath to do. We say that the care of religion being common to all societies politick, such societies as do embrace the true religion have the name of the church given unto every one of them for distinction from the rest; so that every body politick hath some religion, but the church that religion which is only true. Truth of religion is the proper difference whereby a church is distinguished from other politick societies of men; we here mean true religion in gross, and not according to every particular. For they which in some particular points of religion do sever from the truth, may nevertheless truly (if we compare them to men of an heathenish religion) be said to hold and profess that religion which is true. For which cause there being of old so many politick societies established through the world, only the commonwealth of *Israel* which had the truth of religion was in that respect the church of God: and the church of Jesus Christ is every such politick society of men as doth in religion hold that truth which is proper to christianity. As a politick society it doth maintain religion, as a church that religion which God hath revealed by Jesus Christ. With us therefore the name of a church importeth only a society of men, first united into some publick form of regiment, and secondly distinguished from other societies by the exercise of religion. With them on the other side the name of the church in this present question importeth not only a multitude of men so united and so distinguished, but also further the same divided necessarily and perpetually from the body of the commonwealth; so that even in such a politick society as consisteth of none but christians, yet the church and commonwealth are two corporations, independently subsisting by it self.

We hold, that seeing there is not any man of the church of *England* but the same man is also a member of the commonwealth, nor any member of the commonwealth which is not also of the church of *England*, therefore as in a figure triangle the base doth differ from the sides thereof, and yet one and the self same line is both a base and also a side; a side simply, a base if it chance to be the bottom and underlye the rest: so albeit properties and actions of one do cause the name of a commonwealth, qualities and functions of another sort the name of the church to be given to a multitude, yet one and the self same multitude may in such sort be both. Nay, it is so with us, that no person appertaining to the one can be denied also to be of the other: contrariwise, unless they against us should hold, that the church and the commonwealth are two, both distinct and separate societies; of which two one comprehendeth always persons not belonging to the other, (that which they do) they could not conclude out of the difference between the church and the commonwealth, namely that the bishops may not meddle with the

affairs

affairs of the commonwealth becaufe they are governors of another corporation, which is the church; nor kings, with making laws for the church, becaufe they have government not of this corporation, but of another divided from it; the commonwealth and the walls of feparation between thefe two, muft for ever be upheld: they hold the neceffity of perfonal feparation which clean excludeth the power of one man's dealing with both; we of natural, but that one and the fame perfon may in both bear principal fway.

The caufes of common received errors in this point feem to have been efpecially two: one, that they who embrace true religion living in fuch commonwealths as are oppofite thereunto; and in other publick affairs, retaining civil communion with fuch as are conftrained for the exercife of their religion, to have a feveral communion with thofe who are of the fame religion with them. This was the ftate of the *Jewifh* church both in *E-gypt* and *Babylon*, the ftate of chriftian churches a long time after Chrift. And in this cafe, becaufe the proper affairs and actions of the church, as it is the church, hath no dependance on the laws, or upon the government of the civil ftate; an opinion hath thereby grown, that even fo it fhould be always. This was it which deceived *Allen* in the writing of his apology: *The apoftles* (faith he) *did govern the church in* Rome, *when* Nero *bare rule, even as at this day in all the church's dominions. The church hath a fpiritual regiment without dependance, and fo ought fhe to have amongft heathens, or with chriftians.* Another occafion of which mifconceit is, that things appertaining to religion are both diftinguifhed from other affairs, and have always had in the church fpiritual perfons chofen to be exercifed about them. By which diftinction of fpiritual affairs, and perfons therein employed from temporal, the error of perfonal feparation always neceffary between the church and commonwealth hath ftrengthen'd it felf. For of every poli-

Arift. Pol. l. 3.
cap. 16.
Maccab. 7. tick fociety that being true which *Ariftotle* faith, namely, *That the fcope thereof is not fimply to live, nor the duty fo much to provide for the life, as for the means of living well:* And that even as the foul is the worthier part of man, fo human focieties are much more to care for that which tendeth properly to the foul's eftate, than for fuch temporal things which the life hath need of. Other proof there needeth none to fhew that as by all men the kingdom of God is to be fought firft, fo in all commonwealths things fpiritual ought above temporal to be fought for; and of things fpiritual, the chiefeft is religion. For this caufe, perfons and things employ'd peculiarly about the affairs of religion are by an excellency term'd fpiritual. The heathens themfelves had their fpiritual laws, and caufes, and affairs always fever'd from their temporal; neither did this make two indepen-

Arift. Pol. l. 3.
cap. 20.
Liv. lib. 1. dent eftates among them. God by revealing true religion doth make them that receive it his church. Unto the *Jews* he fo reveal'd the truth of religion, that he gave them in fpecial confiderations laws, not only for the adminiftration of things fpiritual, but alfo temporal. The Lord himfelf appointing both the one and the other in that commonwealth, did not thereby diftract it into feveral independent communities, but inftitute feveral functions of one and the felf-fame community. Some reafons therefore muft there be alledg'd why it fhould be otherwife in the church of Chrift.

Three kinds of their proofs are taken from the difference of affairs and offices. I fhall not need to fpend any great ftore of words in anfwering that which is brought out of the holy fcripture to fhew that fecular and ecclefiaftical affairs and offices are diftinguifhed; neither that which hath been borrowed from antiquity, ufing by phrafe of fpeech to oppofe the commonweal to the church of Chrift; neither yet their reafons which are wont to be brought forth as witneffes, that the church and commonweal were always diftinct. For whether a church or commonweal do differ, is not the queftion we ftrive for; but our controverfy is concerning the kind of diftinction, whereby they are fever'd the one from the other; whether as under heathen kings the church did deal with her own affairs within her felf without depending at all upon any in civil authority; and the commonweal in hers, altogether without the privity of the church, fo it ought to continue ftill even in fuch commonweals as have now publickly embrac'd the truth of chriftian religion; whether they ought evermore to be two focieties in fuch fort, feveral and diftinct. I ask therefore what fociety was that in *Rome*, whereunto the apoftle did give the name of the church of *Rome* in his time? If they anfwer (as needs they muft) that the church of *Rome* in thofe days was that whole fociety of men which in *Rome* profeffed the name of Chrift, and not that religion which the laws of the commonweal did then authorize; we fay as much, and therefore grant that the commonweal of *Rome* was one fociety, and the church of *Rome* another, in fuch fort that there was between them no natural dependance. But when whole *Rome* became chriftian when they all embraced the gofpel, and made laws in defence thereof, if it be held that the church and commonweal of *Rome* did then remain as before; there is no way how this could be poffible, fave only one, and that is, they muft reftrain the name of a

church

church in a christian commonweal to the clergy, excluding all the rest of believers, both prince and people. For if all that believe be contained in the name of the church, how should the church remain by personal subsistence divided from the commonweal, when the whole commonweal doth believe? The church and the commonweal are in this case therefore personally one society, which society being termed commonweal as it liveth under whatsoever form of secular law and regiment; a church as it liveth under the spiritual law of Christ; forsomuch as these two laws contain so many and different offices, there must of necessity be appointed in it some to one charge, and some to another, yet without dividing the whole and making it two several impaled societies.

The difference therefore either of affairs or offices ecclesiastical from secular is no argument that the church and commonweal are always separate and independent the one on the other; which thing even *Allain* himself considering somewhat better, doth in this point a little correct his former judgment beforementioned, and confesseth in his defence of *English* catholicks, that the power political hath her princes, laws, tribunals; the spiritual, her prelates, canons, councils, judgments, and those (when the temporal princes were pagans) wholly separate; but in christian commonweals joyned though not confounded. Howbeit afterwards his former sting appeareth again; for in a commonwealth he holdeth, that the church ought not to depend at all upon the authority of any civil person whatsoever, as in *England* he saith it doth.

It will be objected, that the fathers do oftentimes mention the commonweal and the church of God by way of opposition. Can the same thing be opposed to it self? If one and the same society be both church and commonwealth, what sense can there be in that speech; *That they suffer and flourish together?* What sense is that which maketh one thing to be adjudg'd to the church, and another to the commonweal? Finally in that which putteth a difference between the causes of the province and the church, doth it not hereby appear that the church and the commonweal are things evermore personally separate? No, it doth not hereby appear that there is perpetually any such separation; we speak of them as two, we may sever the rights and the causes of the one well enough from the other, in regard of that difference which we grant is between them, albeit we make no personal difference. For the truth is, that the church and the commonwealth are names which import things really different: but those things are accidents, and such accidents as may and always should lovingly dwell together in one subject. Wherefore the real difference between the accidents signified by these names, doth not prove different subjects for them always to reside in. For albeit the subjects wherein they be resident be sometimes different, as when the people of God have their residence among infidels; yet the nature of them is not such, but that their subject may be one, and therefore it is but a changeable accident, in those accidents they are to be divers. There can be no error in our own conceit concerning this point, if we remember still what accident that is for which a society hath the name of a commonwealth, and what accident that which doth cause it to be termed a church. A commonwealth we name it simply in regard of some regiment or policy under which men live; a church for the truth of that religion which they profess. Now names betokening accidents inabstracted, betoken not only the accidents themselves, but also together with them subjects whereunto they cleave. As when we name a schoolmaster and a physician, those names do not only betoken two accidents, teaching and curing, but also some person or persons in whom those accidents are. For there is no impediment but both may be in one man, as well as they are for the most part in divers. The commonweal and church therefore being such names, they do not only betoken these accidents of civil government and christian religion which we have mention'd, but also together with them such multitudes as are the subjects of those accidents. Again, their nature being such as they may well enough dwell together in one subject, it followeth that their names though always implying difference of accidents that hath been set down, yet do not always imply different subjects also. When we oppose therefore the church and commonwealth in christian society, we mean by the commonwealth that society with relation to all the publick affairs thereof, only the matter of true religion excepted; by the church, the same society with only reference unto the matter of true religion, without any affairs. Besides, when that society which is both a church and a commonwealth doth flourish in those things which belong unto it as a commonwealth, we then say, the commonwealth doth flourish; when in both them, we then say, the church and commonwealth do flourish together.

The prophet *Esay* to note corruptions in the commonwealth complaineth, *That where justice and judgment had lodged, now were murtherers; princes were become companions of thieves, every one loved gifts and rewards, but the fatherless was not judged, neither did*

G g g 2   *the*

Mal. 1. 8. *the widows caufe come before them.* To fhew abufes in the church, *Malachy* doth make his complaint, *Te offer unclean bread upon mine altar: if ye offer the blind for facrifice, it is not evil as ye think; if the lame and the fick, nothing is amifs.* The treafure 1 Chron.29.3. which *David* beſtowed upon the temple did argue the love which he bore unto the Nehem.1.27. church: the pains which *Nehemiah* took for building the walls of the city are tokens of his care for the commonwealth. Caufes of the commonwealth, or province, are fuch as *Gallio* was content to be judge of. *If it were a matter of wrong, or an evil deed, (O ye Jews) I would according to reafon maintain you.* Caufes of the church are fuch as Acts 18. 14. *Gallio* there reciteth; *If it be a queſtion of your law, look ye to it, I will be no judge thereof.* In refpect of this difference therefore the church and the commonwealth may in fpeech be compared or oppofed aptly enough the one to the other; yet this is no argument that they are two independent focieties.

3. Taken from the effect of punifhment inflicted by the one or the other. Some other reafons there are which feem a little more nearly to make for the purpofe, as long as they are but heard and not fifted. For what though a man being fever'd by excommunication from the church be not thereby deprived of freedom in the city, or being there difcommoned, is not therefore forthwith excommunicated and excluded the church: what though the church be bound to receive them upon repentance, whom the commonweal may refufe again to admit: if it chance the fame man to be fhut out of both, divifion of the church and commonweal which they contended for will very hardly hereupon follow. For we muſt note, that members of a chriſtian commonweal have a triple ſtate; a natural, a civil, and a fpiritual. No man's natural eſtate is cut off otherwife than by that capital execution. After which he that is none of the body of the commonwealth doth not I think remain fit in the body of that vifible church. And concerning man's civil eſtate, the fame is fubject partly to inferior abatements of liberty, and partly to diminution in the higheſt degree, fuch as baniſhment is; fith it cafteth out quite and clean from the body of the commonweal, it muſt needs alfo confequently caſt the baniſhed party even out of the very church he was of before, becaufe that church and the commonweal he was of were both one and the fame fociety: fo that whatfoever doth utterly feparate a man's perfon from the one it feparateth from the other alfo. As for fuch abatements of civil eſtate as take away only fome privilege, dignity, or other benefit which a man enjoyeth in the commonweal, they reach only to our dealing with publick affairs, from which what may let but that men may be excluded and thereunto reftored again without diminiſhing or augmenting the number of perfons in whom either church or commonwealth confiſteth? He that by way of puniſhment lofeth his voice in a publick election of magiſtrates, ceafeth not thereby to be a citizen. A man disfranchiſed may notwithſtanding enjoy as a fubject the common benefit of protection under laws and magiſtrates. So that thefe inferior diminutions which touch men civilly, but neither do clean extinguiſh their eſtates as they belong to the commonwealth, nor impair a whit their condition as they are of the church of God: thefe, I fay, do clearly prove a difference of the one from the other, but fuch a difference as maketh nothing for their furmife of diſtracted focieties.

And concerning excommunication, it cutteth off indeed from the church, and yet not from the commonwealth; howbeit fo, that the party excommunicate is not thereby fever'd from one body which fubfiſteth in it felf, and retain'd by another in like fort fubfiſting; but he which before had fellowſhip with that fociety whereof he was a member, as well touching things fpiritual as civil, is now by force of excommunication, although not fever'd from the body in civil affairs, neverthelefs for the time cut off from it as touching communion in thofe things which belong to the fame body as it is the church. A man which having been both excommunicated by the church, and depriv'd of civil dignity in the commonwealth, is upon his repentance neceſſarily reunited into the one, but not of neceſſity into the other. What then? That which he is admitted unto is a communion in things divine, whereof both parts are partakers; that from which he is with-held is the benefit of fome human privilege or right which other citizens happily enjoy. But are not thefe faints and citizens one and the fame people? Are they not one and the fame fociety? Doth it hereby appear that the church which received an excommunicate, can have no dependancy on any perfon which hath chief authority and power of thefe things in the commonwealth whereunto the fame party is not admitted? Wherefore to end this point, I conclude; firſt, that under the dominions of infidels the church of Chriſt and their commonwealth were two focieties independent. Secondly, that in thofe commonwealths where the biſhop of *Rome* beareth fway, one fociety is both the church and the commonwealth: but the biſhop of *Rome* doth divide the body into two divers bodies, and doth not fuffer the church to depend upon the power of any civil prince and potentate. Thirdly, that within this realm of *England* the cafe is neither as in the

one,

one, nor as in the other of the former two: but from the state of pagans we differ, in that with us one society is both the church and commonwealth, which with them it was not; as also from the state of those nations which subjected themselves to the bishop of *Rome*, in that our church hath dependance from the chief in our commonwealth, which it hath not when he is suffered to rule. In a word, our state is according to the pattern of God's own ancient elect people, which people was not part of them the commonwealth, and part of them the church of God; but the self-same people whole and entire were both under one chief governor on whose supream authority they did all depend. Now the drift of all that hath been alledged to prove perpetual separation and independency between the church and the commonwealth is, that this being held necessary, it might consequently be thought fit, that in a christian kingdom he whose power is greatest over the commonwealth, may not lawfully have supremacy of power also over the church, that is to say, so far as to order thereby and to dispose of spiritual affairs, so far as the highest uncommanded commander in them. Whereupon it is grown a question, whether government ecclesiastical, and power of dominion in such degrees as the laws of this land do grant unto the sovereign governor thereof, may by the said supream governor lawfully be enjoy'd and held. For resolution wherein, we are, first, to define what the power of dominion is. Secondly, then to shew by what right. Thirdly, after what sort. Fourthly, in what measure. Fifthly, in what inconveniency. According to whose example christian kings may have it. And when these generals are opened, to examine afterwards how lawful that is which we in regard of dominion do attribute unto our own: namely, the title of headship over the church, so far as the bounds of this kingdom do reach. Secondly, the prerogative of calling and dissolving great assemblies, about spiritual affairs publick. Thirdly, the right of assenting unto all those orders concerning religion, which must after be in force as law. Fourthly, the advancement of principal church governors to their rooms of prelacy. Fifthly, judicial authority higher than others are capable of. And sixthly, exemption from being punishable with such kind of censures as the platform of reformation doth teach, that they ought to be subject unto.

What the power of Dominion is.

Without order there is no living in publick society, because the want thereof is the mother of confusion, whereupon division of necessity followeth; and out of division destruction. The apostle therefore giving instruction to publick societies, requireth that all things be orderly done. Order can have no place in things, except it be settled, a-mongst the persons that shall by office be conversant about them. And if things and persons be ordered, this doth imply that they are distinguished by degrees. For order is a gradual disposition. The whole world consisting of parts so many, so different, is by this only thing upheld; he which framed them, hath set them in order. The very deity it self both keepeth and requireth for ever this to be kept as a law, that wheresoever there is a coagmentation of many, the lowest be knit unto the highest by that which being interjacent may cause each to cleave to the other, and so all to continue one. This order of things and persons in publick societies is the work of policy, and the proper instrument thereof in every degree is power; power being that hability which we have of our selves, or receive from others for performance of any action. If the action which we have to perform be conversant about matters of meer religion, the power of performing it is then spiritual; and if that power be such as hath not any other to over-rule it, we term it dominion, or power supream, so far as the bounds thereof extend. When therefore christian kings are said to have spiritual dominion or supream power in ecclesiastical affairs and causes, the meaning is, that within their own precincts and territories they have an authority and power to command even in matters of christian religion, and that there is no higher nor greater than can in those cases over-command them, where they are placed to reign as kings. But withal we must likewise note that their power is termed supremacy, as being the highest, not simply without exception of any thing. For what man is so brain-sick, as not to except in such speeches God himself the king of all dominion? Who doubteth but that the king who receiveth it must hold it of and under the law, according to that old axiom, *Attribuat rex legi, quod lex attribuit ei potestatem:* and again, *rex non debet esse sub homine, sed sub Deo & lege.* Thirdly, whereas it is altogether without reason, *That kings are judged to have by virtue of their dominion, altho' greater power than any, yet not than all the state of those societies conjoyned, wherein such sovereign rule is*

Luke 14.
1 Cor. 14.

given

given them; there is not any thing hereunto to the contrary by us affirm'd, no not when we grant supream authority unto kings, becaufe fupremacy is not otherwife intended or meant to exclude partly foreign powers, and partly the power which belongeth in feveral unto others, contain'd as parts in that politick body over which thofe kings have fupremacy: *Where the king hath power of dominion, or fupream power, there no foreign ftate, or potentate, no ftate or potentate domeftical, whether it confifteth of one or many, can poffibly have in the fame affairs and caufes authority higher than the king.* Power of fpiritual dominion therefore is in caufes ecclefiaftical that ruling authority which neither any foreign ftate nor yet any part of that politick body at home, wherein the fame is eftablifh'd, can lawfully over-rule. It hath been declar'd already in general how *the beft eftablifh'd dominion is where the law doth moft rule the king ;* the true effect whereof particularly is found as well in ecclefiaftical as civil affairs. In thefe the king, thro' his fupream power, may do fundry great things himfelf, both appertaining to peace and war, both at home, and by command, and by commerce with ftates abroad, becaufe the law doth fo much permit. Sometimes, on the other fide, *The king alone hath no right to do without confent of his lords and commons in parliament: the king himfelf cannot change the nature of pleas, nor courts, no not fo much as reftore blood,* becaufe the law is a bar unto him ; the pofitive laws of the realm have a privilege therein, and reftrain the king's power ; which pofitive laws, whether by cuftom or otherwife eftablifh'd without repugnancy to the laws of God and nature, ought not lefs to be in force even in fupernatural affairs of the church; whether in regard of ecclefiaftical laws, we willingly embrace that of *Ambrofe, imperator bonus intra ecclefiam, non fupra ecclefiam eft, Kings have dominion to exercife in ecclefiaftical caufes, but according to the laws of the church ;* whether it be therefore the nature of courts, or the form of pleas, or the kind of governors, or the order of proceeding in whatfoever bufinefs, for the receiv'd laws and liberty of the church *the king hath fupream authority and power, but againft them never.* What fuch pofitive laws hath appointed to be done by others than the king, or by others with the king, and in what form they have appointed the doing of it, the fame of neceffity muft be kept; neither is the king's fole authority to alter it ; yet, as it were a thing unreafonable, if in civil affairs the king, albeit the whole univerfal body did joyn with him, fhould do any thing by their abfolute power for the ordering of their ftate at home, in prejudice of thofe ancient laws of nations which are of force throughout all the world, becaufe the neceffary commerce of kingdoms dependeth on them: fo in principal matters belonging to chriftian religion a thing very fcandalous and offenfive it muft needs be thought if either kings or laws fhould difpofe of the law of God, without any refpect had unto that which of old hath been reverently thought of throughout the world, and wherein there is no law of God which forceth us to fwerve from the ways wherein fo many and holy ages have gone. Wherefore not without good confideration the very law it felf hath provided, *That judges ecclefiaftical appointed under the king's commiffion fhall not adjudge for herefy any thing but that which heretofore hath been adjudged by the authority of the canonical fcriptures, or by the firft four general councils, or by fome other general council wherein the fame hath been declared herefy by the expreft words of the faid canonical fcriptures, or fuch as hereafter fhall be determin'd to be herefy by the high court of parliament of this realm, with the affent of the clergy in the convocation, an.* 1. *reg. Eliz.* By which words of the law who doth not plainly fee, how that in one branch of proceeding by virtue of the king's fupream authority, the credit which thofe four firft general councils have throughout all churches, and evermore had, was judg'd by the making of the aforefaid act a juft caufe wherefore they fhould be mention'd in that cafe, as a requifite part of that rule wherewith dominion was to be limited? But of this we fhall further confider when we come unto that which fovereign power may do in making ecclefiaftical laws.

Unto which fupream power in kings two kinds of adverfaries there are which have oppofed themfelves: one fort defending, *That fupream power in caufes ecclefiaftical throughout the world appertaineth of divine right to the bifhop of* Rome : another fort, *That the faid power belongeth in every national church unto the clergy thereof affembled.* We

The right which men g ve, God ra. tifies.

which defend as well againft the one as againft the other, *That kings within their own precincts may have it,* muft fhew by what right it muft come unto them. Firft unto me it feemeth almoft out of doubt and controverfy, that every independent multitude before any certain form of regiment eftablifh'd, hath under God fupream authority, full dominion over it felf, even as a man not tied with the band of fubjection as yet unto any other, hath over himfelf the like power. God creating mankind did endue it naturally with power to guide it felf in what kind of fociety foever he fhould chufe to live. A man which is born lord of of himfelf may be made another fervant.   And that power which naturally whole focie-ties have, may be derived unto many, few, or one, under whom the reft fhall then live in fubjection.   Some multitudes are brought into fubjection by force, as they who being fub-dued are fain to fubmit their necks unto what yoke it pleafeth their conquerors to lay upon them, which conquerors by juft and lawful wars do hold their power over fuch multitudes as a thing defcending unto them, divine providence it felf fo difpofing.   For it is God who giveth victory in the day of war, and unto whom dominion in this fort is derived, the fame they enjoy according to the law of nations, which law authorizeth conquerors to reign as abfolute lords over them whom they vanquifh.   Sometimes it pleafeth God himfelf by fpecial appointment to chufe out and nominate fuch as to whom dominion fhall be given, which thing he did often in the commonwealth of *Ifrael.* ^{Corona eft po-teftas delegata à Deo.Bracton.} They which in this fort receive power immediately from God, have it by meer divine right, they by human on whom the fame is beftowed according to mens difcretion, when they are left freely by God to make choice of their own governors.   By which of thefe means foever it happen that kings or governors be advanced unto their eftates, we muft acknowledge both their lawful choice to be approved of God, and themfelves to be God's lieutenants, and confefs their power which they have to be his.   As for fu-pream power in ecclefiaftical affairs, the word of God doth no where appoint that all kings fhould have it, neither that any fhould not have it; for which caufe it feemeth to ftand altogether by human right, that unto chriftian kings there is fuch dominion given.

Again, on whom the fame is beftowed at men's difcretions, they likewife do hold it by divine right.   If God in his revealed word hath appointed fuch power to be, although himfelf extraordinarily beftow it not, but leave the appointment of perfons to men ; yea, albeit God do neither appoint nor affign the perfon, neverthelefs when men have affign-ed and eftablifhed both, who doth doubt but that fundry duties and affairs depending thereupon are prefcribed by the word of God, and confequently by that very right to be exacted ?   For example fake, the power which *Roman* emperors had over foreign provin-ces was not a thing which the law of God did ever inftitute ; neither was *Tiberius Cæfar* by efpecial commiffion from heaven therewith invefted, and yet payment of tribute unto *Cæfar* being now made emperor is the plain law of Jefus Chrift ; unto kings by hu-man right, honour by very divine right, is due ; man's ordinances are many times propo-fed as grounds in the ftatutes of God.   And therefore of what kind foever the means be whereby governors are lawfully advanced to their ftates, as we by the laws of God ftand bound meekly to acknowledge them for God's lieutenants, and to confefs their power his, fo by the fame law they are both authoriz'd and required to ufe that power as far as it may be in any ftate available to his honour.   The law appointeth no man to be a huf-band, but if a man hath betaken himfelf unto that condition, it giveth him power and au-thority over his own wife.   That the chriftian world fhould be ordered by the kingly regiment, the law of God doth not any where command ; and yet the law of God doth give them which once are exalted unto that place of eftate right to exact at the hands of their fubjects general obedience in whatfoever affairs their power may ferve to command, and God doth ratify works of that fovereign authority which kings have received by men. This is therefore the right whereby kings do hold their power ; but yet in what fort the fame doth reft and abide in them it fomewhat behoveth farther to fearch, where that we be not enforced to make over large difcourfes about the different conditions of fovereign or fupream power, that which we fpeak of kings fhall be in refpect of the ftate, and accord-ing to the nature of this kingdom, where the people are in no fubjection, but fuch as willing-ly themfelves have condefcended unto for their own moft behoof and fecurity.   In kingdoms therefore of this quality the higheft governor hath indeed univerfal dominion, but with dependency upon that whole entire body, over the feveral parts whereof he hath domi-nion ; fo that it ftandeth for an axiom in this cafe, the king is *major fingulis, univerfis mi-nor.*   The king's dependency we do not conftrue as fome have done, who are of opinion that no man's birth can make him a king, but every particular perfon advanced to fuch au-thority hath at his entrance into his reign the fame beftowed on him as an eftate in con-dition by the voluntary deed of the people, in whom it doth lie to put by any one, and to prefer fome other before him better liked of, or judged fitter for the place, and that the party fo rejected hath no injury done unto him, no, although the fame be done in a place where the crown doth go διὰ γένος, by fucceffion, and to a perfon which is capital, and hath apparently, if blood be refpected, the neareft right.   They plainly af-firm in all well appointed kingdoms, the cuftom evermore hath been and is, that children fucceed not their parents till the people after a fort have created them anew, neither that they grow to their fathers as natural and proper heirs, but are then to be reckoned for

kings

V. . . Bodin, kings when at the hands of such as represent the king's majesty, they have by scepter and
Vindic. p. 83 a diadem received as it were the investiture of a kingly power. Their very words are,
*That where such power is settled into a family or kindred, the stock it self is thereby
chosen, but not the twig that springeth of it. The next of the stock unto him that*
pag. 85. *reigneth are not through nearness of blood made kings, but rather set forth to stand for
the kingdom. Where regal dominion is hereditary, it is notwithstanding (if we look to
the persons which have it) altogether elective.* To this purpose are selected heaps of
scriptures concerning the solemn coronation or inauguration of *Saul,* of *David,* of *Solomon,* and others, by the nobles, ancients, and people of the commonweal of *Israel;* as
if these solemnities were a kind of deed, whereby the right of dominion is given.
Which strange, untrue, and unnatural conceits, set abroad by seeds-men of rebellion, only
to animate unquiet spirits, and to feed them with possibility of aspiring to thrones, if they
can win the hearts of the people, what hereditary title soever any other before them may
have: I say unjust and insolent positions I would not mention, were it not thereby to
make the countenance of truth more orient; for unless we will openly proclaim defiance
unto all law, equity, and reason, we must (there is no remedy) acknowledge, that in
kingdoms hereditary birth giveth right unto sovereign dominion; and the death of the
predecessor putteth the successor by blood in seisin. Those publick solemnities before specified do but serve for an open testification of the inheritor's right, or belonging unto the
form of inducting him into possession of that thing he hath right unto: therefore in case
it doth happen that without right of blood a man in such wise be possessed, all these new
elections and investings are utterly void, they make him no indefeasible estate, the inheritor
by blood may dispossess him as an usurper. The case thus standing, albeit we judge it a
thing most true, that kings, even inheritors, do hold their right in the power of dominion,
with dependency upon the whole body politick over which they have rule as kings; yet so
it may not be understood as if such dependency did grow, for that every supream governor
doth personally take from thence his power by way of gift, bestowed of their own free
accord upon him at the time of his entrance into the said place of his sovereign government: but the case of dependency is that first original conveyance, when power was
derived from the whole into one; to pass from him unto them, whom out of him nature
by lawful births should produce, and no natural or legal inability make uncapable.
Tully de Of. *Neither can any man with reason think, but that the first institution of kings, a sufficient consideration wherefore their power should always depend on that from which it always flows by original influence of power, from the body unto the king, is the cause of
kings dependency in power upon the body.* By dependency we mean subordination and
subjection. A manifest token of which dependency may be this; as there is no more
certain argument that lands are held under any as lords, than if we see that such lands in
defect of heirs fall unto them by escheat: In like manner it doth follow rightly, that
seeing dominion when there is none to inherit it returneth unto the body, therefore they
which before were inheritors thereof did hold it with dependency upon the body, so that
by comparing the body with the head, as touching power, it seemeth always to reside
in both, fundamentally and radically in the one, in the other derivatively; in one the
habit, in the other the act of power. May a body politick then at all times withdraw in
whole or in part the influence of dominion which passeth from it, if inconveniencies do
grow thereby? It must be presumed, that supream governors will not in such case oppose themselves, and be stiff in detaining that, the use whereof is with publick detriment:
but surely without their consent I see not how the body by any just means should be
able to help it self, saving when dominion doth escheat; such things therefore must be
thought upon beforehand, that power may be limited e're it be granted, which is the
next thing we are to consider.

In what Measure.

IN power of dominion, all kings have not an equal latitude. Kings by conquest make
their own charter; so, that how large their power, either civil or spiritual is, we
cannot with any certainty define further, than only to set them in the line of the law of
God and nature for bounds. Kings by God's own special appointment have also that
largeness of power which he doth assign or permit with approbation. Touching kings
which were first instituted by agreement and composition made with them, over whom they
reign, and how far their power may extend, the articles of compact between them is to

                                                                          shew:

shew: not only the articles of compact at the first beginning, which for the most part are either clean worn out of knowledge, or else known to very few, but whatsoever hath been after in free and voluntary manner condescended unto, whether by express consent, (whereof positive laws are witnesses,) or else by silent allowance, famously notified through custom, reaching beyond the memory of man. By which means of after-agreement, it cometh many times to pass in kingdoms, that they whose ancient predecessors were by violence and force made subject, do by little and little grow into that sweet form of kingly government which philosophers define, *regency willingly sustained,* Arist. Pol. lib. *and indued with chiefty of power in the greatest things.* Many of the ancients, in their 3. cap. 1. writings, do speak of kings with such high and ample terms, as if universality of power, even in regard of things, and not of persons, did appertain to the very being of a king. The reason is, because their speech concerning kings they frame according to the state of those monarchs to whom unlimited authority was given ; which some not observing, imagine that all kings, even in that they are kings, ought to have whatsoever power they judge any sovereign ruler lawfully to have enjoyed. But the most judicious philo- *Pythagoras al* sopher, whose eye scarce any thing did escape, which was to be found in the bosom *pud Erdant.* of nature, he considering how far the power of one sovereign ruler may be different *de regno.* from another regal authority, noteth in *Spartan* kings, *That of all others they were most tied to law, and so the most restrained power.* A king which hath not supreme power in the greatest things, rather intituled a king, than invested with real sovereignty. We cannot properly term him a king, of whom it may not be said, at the leastwise, as touching certain the chiefest affairs of the state, ἄρχειν ἄρχεσθαι ὑπὸ οὐδενὸς, his right in them is to have rule, not subject to any other predominancy. I am not of opinion that simply in kings the most, but the best limited power is best both for them and the people : the most limited is that which may deal in fewest things, the best that which in dealing is tied unto the soundest, perfectest, and most indifferent rule, which rule is the law : I mean not only the law of nature, and of God ; but the national law consonant thereunto. *Happier that people whose law is their king in the greatest things, than that whose king is himself their law. Where the king doth guide the state, and the law the king, that commonwealth is like an harp or melodious instrument, the strings whereof are tuned and handled all by one hand, following as laws the rules and canons of musical science.* Most divinely therefore *Archytas* maketh unto publick felicity these four steps and degrees, every of which doth spring from the former, as from another cause, ὁ δὲ βασιλεὺς νόμιμος, ὁ δὲ ἄρχων ἀκόλουθος, ὁ δὲ ἀρχόμενος ἀπόλυτος, ἡ δὲ ὅλη κοινωνία εὐδαίμων, *The king ruling by law, the magistrate following, the subject free, and the whole society happy.* Adding on the contrary side, that where this order is not, it cometh by transgression thereof to pass that a king groweth a tyrant ; he that ruleth under him abhorreth to be guided by him, or commanded ; the people subject unto both, have freedom under neither, and the whole community is wretched. In which respect, I cannot chuse but commend highly their wisdom, by whom the foundation of the commonwealth hath been laid ; wherein though no manner of person or cause be unsubject unto the king's power, yet so is the power of the king over all, and in all limited, that unto all his proceedings the law it self is a rule. The axioms of our regal government are these, *Lex facit regem:* the king's grant of any favour made contrary to the law is void ; *Rex nihil potest nisi quod jure potest.* Our kings therefore, when they are to take possession of the crown, they are called unto, have it pointed out before their eyes, even by the very solemnities and rites of their inauguration, to what affairs, by the same law, their supreme power and authority reacheth ; crowned we see they are, enthronized and anointed ; the crown a sign of a military dominion ; the throne of sedentary or judicial ; the oil of religious and sacred power. It is not on any side denied, that kings may have authority in secular affairs. The question then is, *What power they may lawfully have, and exercise in causes of God. A prince, or magistrate,* Stapl. de Do. *or a community,* (saith Doctor *Stapleton,*) *may have power to lay corporal punishment on* Pr n-ip. l. 3. *them which are teachers of perverse things ; power to make laws for the peace of the* c. 17. *church ; power to proclaim, to defend, and even by revenge to preserve* dogmata *the very articles of religion themselves from violation.* Others, in affection no less devoted unto the papacy, do likewise yield, that the civil magistrate may by his edicts and laws keep all ecclesiastical persons within the bounds of their duties, and constrain them to observe the canons of the church, to follow the rule of ancient discipline. That if *Joash* was commended for his care and provision concerning so small a part of religion, as the church-treasure ; it must needs be both unto christian kings themselves greater honour, and to christianity a larger benefit, when the custody of religion, and the worship of God in general is their charge. If therefore all these things mentioned be most properly the affairs of God's ecclesiastical causes ; if the actions specified be works of power ; and if that power

H h h   be be such as kings may use of themselves, without the fear of any other power superior in the same thing; it followeth necessarily, that kings may have supreme power, not only in civil, but also in ecclesiastical affairs, and consequently that they may withstand what bishop or pope soever shall, under the pretended claim of higher spiritual authority, oppose themselves against their proceedings. But they which have made us the former grant, will never hereunto condescend; what they yield that princes may do, it is with secret exception always understood, if the bishop of *Rome* give leave, if he interpose no prohibition; wherefore, somewhat it is in shew, in truth nothing, which they grant. Our own reformers do the very like, when they make their discourse in general concerning the authority which magistrates may have, a man would think them to be far from withdrawing any jot of that which with reason may be thought due, *The prince*

T. C. l. 1. p. 191. *and civil magistrate* (saith one of them) *hath to see the laws of God touching his worship, and touching all matters, and all orders of the church to be executed, and duly observed; and to see every ecclesiastical person do that office whereunto he is appointed;*

Former's def. of the godly magistrate. *and to punish those which fail in their office accordingly.* Another acknowledgeth, *That the magistrate may lawfully uphold all truth by his sword, punish all persons, enforce all to their duties towards God and men; maintain by his laws every point of God's word, punish all vice in all men; see into all causes, visit the ecclesiastical estate, and correct the abuses thereof: finally, to look to his subjects, that under him they may lead their*

Humble motion, p. 163. *lives in all godliness and honesty.* A third more frankly professeth, *That in case their church-discipline were established, so little it shortneth the arms of sovereign dominion, in causes ecclesiastical, that her gracious majesty, for any thing they teach or hold to the contrary, may no less than now remain still over all persons, in all things supreme governess, even with that full and royal authority, superiority, and preheminence, supremacy and prerogative, which the laws already established do give her, and her majesty's injunctions, and the articles of the convocation-house, and other writings apologetical of her royal authority, and supreme dignity, do declare and explain.* *Possidonius* was wont to

Cicero, lib. 1. de nat. deor. say of the epicure, *That he thought there were no gods, but that those things which he spake concerning the gods, were only given out for fear of growing odious amongst men; and therefore that in words he left gods remaining, but in very deed overthrew them, insomuch as he gave them no kind of action.* After the very self-same manner, when we come unto those particular effects, prerogatives of dominion which the laws of this land do grant unto the kings thereof, it will appear how these men, notwithstanding their large and liberal speeches, abate such parcels out of the afore-alledged grant and flourishing shew; that a man comparing the one with the other, may half stand in doubt, left their opinion in very truth be against that authority which by their speeches they seem mightily to uphold, partly for the avoiding of publick obloquy, envy, and hatred; partly to the intent they may both in the end by the establishment of their discipline, extinguish the force of supreme power which princes have, and yet, in the mean while, by giving forth these smooth discourses, obtain that their favourers may have somewhat to alledge for them by way of apology, and that such words only sound towards all kind of fulness of power. But for my self, I had rather construe such their contradictions in the better part, and impute their general acknowledgment of the lawfulness of kingly power unto the force of truth, presenting it self before them sometimes above their particular contrarieties, oppositions, denials, unto that error which having so fully possest their minds, casteth things inconvenient upon them; of which things in their due place. Touching that which is now in hand, we are on all sides fully agreed, first, that there is not any restraint or limitation of matter for regal authority and power to be conversant in, but of religion only; and of whatsoever cause thereunto appertaineth, kings may lawfully have charge, they lawfully may therein exercise dominion, and use the temporal sword. Secondly,

Kinds. that some kind of actions conversant about such affairs are denied unto kings: as namely, actions of power and order, and of spiritual jurisdiction, which hath with it inseparably joined power to administer the word and sacraments, power to ordain, to judge as an or-

By what rule. dinary, to bind and loose, to excommunicate, and such like. Thirdly, that even in those very actions which are proper unto dominion, there must be some certain rule, whereunto kings in all their proceedings ought to be strictly tied; which rule for proceeding in ecclesiastical affairs and causes by regal power, hath not hitherto been agreed upon with that uniform consent, and certainty, as might be wished. The different sentences of men herein I will now go about to examine, but it shall be enough to propose what rule doth seem in this case most reasonable.

The case of deriving supreme power from a whole intire multitude into some special part thereof; as partly the necessity of expedition in publick affairs, partly the inconvenience of confusion and trouble, where a multitude of equals dealeth; and partly the diffi-

pation

pation which muſt needs enſue, in companies where every man wholly ſeeketh his own particular (as we all would do, even with other mens hurts) and haply the very overthrow of themſelves, in the end alſo, if for the procurement of the common good of all men, by keeping every ſeveral man in order, ſome were not inveſted with authority over all, and encouraged with prerogative-honour to ſuſtain the weighty burthen of that charge. The good which is proper unto each man, belongeth to the common good of all, as part to the whole perfection ; but theſe two are things different ; for men by that which is proper, are ſevered ; united they are by that which is common.   Wherefore, beſides that which moveth each man in particular to ſeek his own private good, there muſt be of neceſſity in all publick ſocieties alſo a general mover directing unto common good, and framing every man's particular unto it.   The end whereunto all government was inſtituted, was *bonum publicum*, the *univerſal* or *common good*.   Our queſtion is of domi nion, for that end and purpoſe derived into one ; ſuch as all in one publick ſtate have agreed, that the ſupreme charge of all things ſhould be committed unto one: they, I ſay, conſidering what inconveniency may grow where ſtates are ſubject unto ſundry ſupreme authorities, have for fear of theſe inconveniences withdrawn from liking to eſtabliſh many ; ἐκ ἀγαθὸν πολυκοιρανὶη ; the multitude of ſupreme commanders is troubleſome. *No man* (ſaith our Saviour) *can ſerve two maſters* ; ſurely two ſupreme maſters would make any ones ſervice ſomewhat uneaſy in ſuch caſes as might fall out.   Suppoſe that to morrow the power which hath dominion in juſtice require thee at the court ; that which in war, at the field ; that which in religion, at the temple ; all have equal authority over thee, and impoſſible it is, that then in ſuch caſe thou ſhouldſt be obedient unto all: by chuſing any one whom thou wilt obey, certain thou art for thy diſobedience to incur the diſpleaſure of the other two.

Ob utilitatem publicam reip. per unum conſuli oportere, docent. *L. C.* prudentiſſimi 11. F. de origine juris civilis.

But there is nothing for which ſome comparable reaſon or other may not be found. Are we able to ſhew any commendable ſtate of government, which by experience and practiſe hath felt the benefit of being in all cauſes ſubject unto the ſupreme authority of one ?   Againſt the policy of the *Iſraelites*, I hope there will no man except, where *Moſes* deriving ſo great a part of his burthen in government unto others, did notwithſtanding retain to himſelf univerſal ſupremacy ; *Jehoſhaphat* appointing one to be choſen in the affairs of God, and another in the king's affairs, did this as having dominion over them in both.   If therefore from approbation of heaven, the kings of God's own choſen people had in the affairs of jewiſh religion ſupreme power, why not chriſtian kings the like alſo in chriſtian religion ?   Firſt, unleſs men will anſwer, as ſome have done, *That the* Jews *religion was of far leſs perfection and dignity than ours, ours being that truth whereof theirs was but a ſhadowiſh prefigurative reſemblance.*   Secondly, *That all parts of their religion, their laws, their ſacrifices, and their rites and ceremonies, being fully ſet down to their hands, and needing no more, but only to be put in execution, the kings might well have higheſt authority to ſee that done ; whereas with us there are a number of myſteries even in belief, which were not ſo generally for them, as for us neceſſary to be with ſound expreſs acknowledgment underſtood.   A number of things belonging to external government, and our manner of ſerving God, not ſet down by particular ordinances, and delivered to us in writing, for which cauſe the ſtate of the church doth now require that the ſpiritual authority of eccleſiaſtical perſons be large, abſolute, and not ſubordinate to regal power.*   Thirdly, *That whereas God armeth religion* jewiſh *as* chriſtian *with the temporal ſword ; but of ſpiritual puniſhment, the one with power to impriſon, to ſcourge, to put to death ; the other with bare authority to cenſure and excommunicate: there is no reaſon that the church, which hath no viſible ſword, ſhould in regiment be ſubject unto any other power, than only unto theirs which have authority to bind and looſe.*   Fourthly, *That albeit whilſt the church was reſtrained unto one people, it ſeemed not incommodious to grant their king the general chiefty of power ; yet now the church having ſpread it ſelf over all nations, great inconveniences muſt thereby grow, if every chriſtian king in his ſeveral territory ſhall have the like power.*   Of all theſe differences, there is not one which doth prove it a thing repugnant to the law either of God, or of nature, that all ſupremacy of external power be in chriſtian kingdoms granted unto kings thereof, for preſervation of quietneſs, unity, order, and peace, in ſuch manner as hath been ſhewed.

According to what example.

Stapl. de prin. Doct. p. 197.

Stapl. ib.

Idem. ib.

Of the Title of Headship.

FOR the title or ſtate it ſelf, although the laws of this land have annexed it to the crown, yet ſo far we ſhould not ſtrive, if ſo be men were nice and ſcrupulous in this behalf only; becauſe they do wiſh that for reverence to Chriſt Jeſus the civil magiſtrate did rather uſe ſome other form of ſpeech, wherewith to expreſs that ſovereign authority which he lawfully hath over all, both perſons and cauſes of the church. But I ſee that hitherto they which condemn utterly the name ſo applied, do it becauſe they miſlike that ſuch power ſhould be given to civil governors. The great exception that Sir Rafienfis epift. *Thomas Moor* took againſt that title, who ſuffered death for denial of it, was *for that it* p. 517. Perf. *maketh a lay, a ſecular perſon, the head of the ſtate ſpiritual or eccleſiaſtical*; as tho' Cent. 7. Calvin God himſelf did not name *Saul* the head of all the tribes of *Iſrael*; and conſequently of in com. 7. that tribe alſo among the reſt, whereunto the ſtate ſpiritual or eccleſiaſtical belonged. Amos 7. 13. When the authors of the centuries reprove it in kings and civil governors, the reaſon is, *iſtis non competit iſte primatus*; ſuch kind of power is too high for them, they fit it not. In excuſe of Mr. *Calvin*, by whom this realm is condemned of blaſphemy, for intituling *H. 8. Supreme head of this church, under Chriſt*, a charitable conjecture is made, that he ſpake by miſinformation; howbeit, as he profeſſeth utter diſlike of that name, ſo whether the name be uſed or no, the very power it ſelf which we give unto civil magiſtrates, he much complaineth of, and proteſteth, *That their power over all things was it, which had ever wounded him deeply: that unadviſed perſons had made them too ſpiritual, that throughout* Germany *this fault did reign; that in thoſe very parts where* Calvin *himſelf was, it prevailed more than was to be wiſhed; that rulers by imagining themſelves ſo ſpiritual, have taken away eccleſiaſtical government; that they think they cannot reign unleſs they aboliſh all the authority of the church, and be themſelves the chief judges, as well in doctrine, as in the whole ſpiritual regency.* So that, in truth, the queſtion is, whether the magiſtrate, by being head in ſuch ſenſe as we term him, do uſe or exerciſe any part of that authority, not which belongeth unto Chriſt, but which other men ought to have.

These things being firſt conſidered thus, it will be eaſier to judge concerning our own eſtate, whether by force of eccleſiaſtical government kings have any other kind of prerogative than they may lawfully hold and enjoy. It is, as ſome do imagine, too much that kings of *England* ſhould be termed heads, in relation of the church. That which we do underſtand by headſhip is, their only ſupreme power in eccleſiaſtical affairs and cauſes. That which lawful princes are, what ſhould make it unlawful for men in ſpiritual ſtiles or titles to ſignify? If the having of ſupreme power be allowed, why is the expreſſing thereof by the title of *head*, condemned? They ſeem in words (at leaſtwiſe ſome of them) now at length to acknowledge, that kings may have dominion or ſupreme government, even over all, both perſons and cauſes. We, in terming our princes *heads of the church*, do but teſtify that we acknowledge them ſuch governors. Again, to this it will peradven-

T. C. l. 2. p. 4. ture be reply'd, *That howſoever we interpret our ſelves, it is not fit for a mortal man,* 11. *and therefore not fit for a civil magiſtrate to be intituled the head of the church, which was given to our Saviour Chriſt, to lift him above all powers, rules, dominions, titles, in heaven or in earth. Where, if this title belong alſo to civil magiſtrates, then it is manifeſt that there is a power in earth, whereunto our Saviour Chriſt is not in this point ſuperior. Again, if the civil magiſtrate may have this title, he may be termed alſo the firſt-begotten of all creatures, the firſt-begotten of all the dead, yea, the redeemer of his people. For theſe are alike given him, as dignities whereby he is lifted up above all crea-* Eph 1. 21. *tures. Beſides this, the whole argument of the apoſtle, in both places, doth lead to ſhew* Col. 1. 18. *that this title,* head of the church, *cannot be ſaid of any creature. And further, the very demonſtrative articles amongſt* the Hebrews, *eſpecially whom* St. Paul *doth follow, ſerveth to tie that which is verified of one, unto himſelf alone: ſo that when the apoſtle doth ſay that Chriſt is* κεφαλὴ, *the head; it is as if he ſhould ſay,* Chriſt, *and none other, is* the head of the church. Thus have we againſt the entituling of the higheſt magiſtrate, *head*, with relation unto the church, four ſeveral arguments gathered, by ſtrong ſurmiſe, out of words marvellouſly unlikely to have been written to any ſuch purpoſe, as that where- Eph. 1. 20, 21. unto they are now uſed and urged. To the *Epheſians* the apoſtle writeth, *That Chriſt,* 22, 23. *God had ſet on his right hand in the heavenly places above all the regency and authority, and power and dominion, and whatſoever name is named, not in this world only, but in that which ſhall be alſo: and hath under his feet ſet all things, and hath given him head* Col. 1. 18. *above all things unto the church, which is his body, even the fulneſs of him which ac-* compliſheth all in all. To the *Coloſſians*, in like manner, *That he is the head of the body*

+

of

of the church, who is a *first-born regency out of the dead, to the end he might be made amongst them all such an one as hath the chiefty*: he meaneth, amongst all them whom he mentioned before, saying, *By him all things that are, were made; the things in the* Col. 1. 16. *heavens, and the things in the earth, the things that are visible, and the things that are invisible, whether they be thrones or dominions, or regencies*, &c. Unto the fore-alledged arguments therefore we answer: first, that it is not simply the title of *head*, in such sort understood, as the apostle himself meant it; so that the same being imparted in another sense unto others, doth not any ways make those others his equals; inasmuch as diversity of things is usually to be understood, even when of words there is no diversity; and it is only the adding of one and the same thing unto divers persons, which doth argue equality in them. If I term Christ and *Cæsar* Lords, yet this is no equalizing *Cæsar* with Christ, because it is not thereby intended: *To term the emperor lord*, (saith *Tertullian*) *I, for my part, will not refuse, so that I be not required to call him lord in the same sense that God is so termed.* Neither doth it follow, which is objected in the second place, that if the civil magistrate may be intituled a *head*, he may as well be termed, *the first begotten of all creatures, the first begotten of the dead, and the redeemer of his people.* For albeit the former dignity doth lift him up no less than these, yet these terms are not appliable, and apt to signify any other inferior dignity, as the former term of *head* was. The argument of matter which the apostle followeth hath small evidence or proof, that his meaning was to appropriate unto Christ that the aforesaid title; otherwise than only in such sense as doth make it, being so understood, too high to be given to any creature.

As for the force of the article where our Lord and Saviour is called the *head*, it serveth to tie that unto him by way of excellency, which in meaner degrees is common to others; it doth not exclude any other utterly from being termed *head*, but from being intituled as Christ is, *the head*, by way of the very highest degree of excellency: not in the communication of names, but in the confusion of things, there is error. Howbeit, if *head* were a name that could not well be, nor never had been used to signify that which a magistrate may be in relation to some church, but were by continual use of speech appropriated unto the only thing it signifieth; being applied unto Jesus Christ then, altho' we must carry in our selves a right understanding, yet ought we otherwise rather to speak, unless we interpret our own meaning by some clause of plain speech, because we are all else in manifest danger to be understood according to that construction and sense, wherein such words are personally spoken. But here the rarest construction, and most removed from common sense, is that which the word doth import being applied unto Christ; that which we signify by it in giving to the magistrate, it is a great deal more familiar in the common conceit of men.

The word is so fit to signify all kinds of superiority, preheminence, and chiefty, that Esai. 7. 9. *Pekah* nothing is more ordinary than to use it in vulgar speech, and in common understanding is termed the so to take it. If therefore christian kings may have any preheminence or chiefty above all *ria.* head of *Sama-* others, altho' it be less than that which *Theodore Beza* giveth, who placeth kings amongst the principal members whereunto publick function in the church belongeth; and denieth not, but that of them which have publick function, the civil magistrate's power hath all the rest at command, in regard of that part of his office, which is to procure that peace and good order be especially kept in things concerning the first table; if even hereupon they term him *the head of the church*, which is *his kingdom*, it should not seem so unfit a thing; which title surely we could not communicate to any other, no not altho' it should at our hands be exacted with torments, but that our meaning herein is made known to the world, so that no man which will understand can easily be ignorant that we do not impart unto kings, when we term them *heads*, the honour which is properly given to our Lord and Saviour Christ, when the blessed apostle in scripture doth term him the *head of the church.*

The power which we signify in that name, differeth in three things plainly from that which Christ doth challenge.

First, it differeth in order, because God hath given to his church for the head, ὑπὲρ αὐτὰ ὑπεράνω πάσης ἀρχῆς, *far above all principalities, and powers, and might, and do-* Eph. 1. 21. *minion, and every name that is named, not in this world only, but also in that which is to come:* whereas the power which others have, is subordinate unto his.

Secondly, again, as he differeth in order, so in measure of power also; because God Psal. 2. 8. hath given unto him the ends of the earth for his possession; unto him, dominion from sea to sea, unto him all power both in heaven and earth, unto him such sovereignty, as doth not only reach over all places, persons, and things, but doth rest in his own only person, and is not by any succession continued; he reigneth as head and king, nor is
                                                                                                    there

there any kind of law which tieth him, but his own proper will and wifdom, his power is abfolute, the fame jointly over all, which it is feverally over each: not fo the power of any other headfhip. How kings are reftrained, and how their power is limited, we have fhewed before; fo that unto him is given by the title of *headfhip over the church*, that largenefs of power, wherein neither man nor angel, can be matched nor compared with him.

Thirdly, the laft and greateft difference between him and them, is in the very kind of their power. The head being, of all other parts of the body, moft divine, hath dominion over all the reft; it is the fountain of fenfe, of motion; the throne where the guide of the foul doth reign; the court from whence direction of all things- human proceedeth. Why Chrift is called *the head of the church*, thefe caufes themfelves do yield. As the head is the chiefeft part of a man, above which there is none, always joined wit hthe body; fo Chrift the higheft in his church, is always knit to it. Again, as the head giveth fenfe and motion unto all the body, fo he quickneth us, and, together with underftanding of heavenly things, giveth ftrength to walk therein. Seeing therefore that they cannot affirm Chrift fenfibly prefent, or always vifibly joined unto his body the church which is on earth, inafmuch as his corporal refidence is in heaven. Again, feeing they do not affirm (it were intolerable if they fhould) that Chrift doth perfonally adminifter the external regiment of outward actions in the church, but, by the fecret inward influence of his grace, giveth fpiritual life, and the ftrength of ghoftly motions thereunto: impoffible it is, that they fhould fo clofe up their eyes, as not to difcern what odds there is between that kind of operation which we imply in the *headfhip* of princes, and that which agreeth to our Saviour's dominion over the church. The *headfhip* which we give unto kings, is altogether vifibly exercifed, and ordereth only the external frame of the church-affairs here amongft us; fo that it plainly differeth from Chrift's, even in very nature and kind. To be in fuch fort united unto the church as he is; to work as he worketh, either on the whole church, or upon any particular affembly, or in any one man, doth neither agree, nor hath any poffibility of agreeing unto any one befides him.

T. C. l. 2.
p. 411.

Againft the firft diftinction or difference, it is to be objected, *That to entitle a magiftrate head of the church, although it be under Chrift, is abfurd. For Chrift hath a twofold fuperiority; over his, and over kingdoms: according to the one, he hath a fuperior, which is his Father; according to the other, none but immediate authority with his Father; that is to fay, of the church he is head and governor only as the fon of man; head and governor of kingdoms only as the Son of God. In the church, as man, he hath officers under him, which officers are ecclefiaftical perfons. As for the civil magiftrate, his office belongeth unto kingdoms, and to commonwealths, neither is he there an under or fubordinate head, confidering that his authority cometh from God, fimply and immediately, even as our Saviour Chrift's doth.* Whereunto the fum of our anfwer is, firft, that as Chrift being Lord or Head over all, doth by vertue of that fovereignty rule all; fo he hath no more a fuperior in governing his church, than in exercifing fovereign dominion upon the reft of the world befides. Secondly, that all authority, as well civil as ecclefiaftical, is fubordinate unto him. And thirdly, the civil magiftrate being termed head, by reafon of that authority in ecclefiaftical affairs which hath been already declared that themfelves do acknowledge to be lawful; it followeth, that he is a head even fubordinated of Chrift, and to Chrift. For more plain explication whereof, unto God we acknowledge daily, that kingdom, power, and glory, are his; that he is the immortal and invifible king of ages; as well the future which fhall be, as the prefent which now is. That which the Father doth work as Lord and King over all, he worketh not without, but by the Son, who thro' coeternal generation received of the Father that power which the Father hath of himfelf. And for that caufe our Saviour's words concerning his own dominion are, *to me all power both in heaven and earth is given.* The Father by the Son did create, and doth guide all; wherefore Chrift hath fupreme dominion over the whole univerfal world. Chrift is God. Chrift is Λόγος, the confubftantial Word of God, Chrift is alfo that confubftantial Word which made man. As God, he faith of himfelf, *I am alpha and omega, the beginning and the end: he which was, and which is, and which is to come; even the very Omnipotent.* As the confubftantial Word of God, he hath with God, before the beginning of the world, that glory, which, as he was man, he requireth to have; *Father, glorify thy Son with that glory which with thee be enjoyed before the world was.* Further, it is not neceffary, that all things fpoken of Chrift fhould agree to him either as God, or elfe as man; but fome things as he is the confubftantial Word of God, fome things as he is that Word incarnate. The works of fupreme dominion which have been fince the firft beginning wrought by the power of the Son of God, are now moft properly and truly the works of the Son of man: the Word made flefh doth fit for

T. C. l. 2.
p. 418.

Apoc. 1. 8.

John 17. 5.

+   ever

ever, and reign as sovereign Lord over all. Dominion belongeth unto the kingly office of Christ, as propitiation and mediation unto his priestly; instruction, unto his pastoral and prophetical office. His works of dominion are, in sundry degrees and kinds, according to the different conditions of them that are subject unto it: he presently doth govern, and hereafter shall judge the world, intire and wholly; and therefore his regal power cannot be with truth restrained unto a proportion of the world only. Notwithstanding, forasmuch as all do not shew and acknowledge, with dutiful submission, that obedience which they owe unto him; therefore such as do, their Lord he is termed by way of excellency, no otherwise than the apostle doth term God the Saviour generally of all, but especially of the faithful; these being brought to the obedience of faith, are every where spoken of as men translated into that kingdom, wherein whosoever is comprehended, Christ is the author of eternal salvation unto them; they have a high and ghostly fellowship with God, and Christ, and saints; or, as the apostle in more ample manner speaketh, *Heb.* 12. 22] *Aggregated they are unto mount Sion, and to the city of the living God; the celestial Jerusalem, and to the company of innumerable angels, and to the congregation of the first born, which are written in heaven, and to God the judge of all; and to the spirits of just and perfect men, and to Jesus the Mediator of the new testament.* In a word, they are of that mystical body, which we term the church of Christ. As for the rest, we account them *aliens from the commonwealth of Israel, and that live in the kingdom of darkness, and that are in this present world without God.* Our Saviour's dominion is therefore over these, as over rebels; over them, as over dutiful and loving subjects. Which things being in holy scriptures so plain, I somewhat muse at that strange position, that Christ in the government of his church, and superiority over the officers of it, hath himself a superior, which is the Father; but in governing of kingdoms and commonwealths, and in the superiority which he hath over kingdoms, no superior.

Again, *That the civil magistrate's authority cometh from God immediately, as Christ's doth,* T. C. l. 4. *and is subordinate unto Christ.* In what evangelist, apostle, or prophet, is it found, that P. 411. Christ (supreme governor of the church) should be so unequal to himself, as he is supreme governor of kingdoms? The works of his providence for the preservation of mankind by upholding kingdoms, not only obedient unto, but also obstinate and rebellious against him, are such as proceed from divine power; and are not the works of his providence for safety of God's elect, by gathering, inspiring, comforting, and every way preserving his church, such as proceed from the same power likewise. Surely, if Christ, as God and man, hath ordained certain means for the gathering and keeping of his church, seeing this doth belong to the government of that church; it must in reason follow, I think, that as God and man he worketh in church regiment; and consequently hath no more there any superiors, than in the government of the commonwealth. Again, to *be in the midst of his, wheresoever they are assembled in his name,* and to be *with them to the world's end,* are comforts which Christ doth perform to his church as Lord and Governor; yea, such as he cannot perform, but by that very power wherein he hath no superior. Wherefore, unless it can be proved, that all the works of our Saviour's government in the church are done by the mere and only force of his human nature, there is no remedy but to acknowledge it a manifest error, that Christ in the government of the world is equal to the Father, but not in the government of the church. Indeed, to the honour of this dominion, it cannot be said, that God did exalt him otherwise than only according to that human nature wherein he was made low. For, as the Son of God, there could no advancement or exaltation grow unto him: and yet the dominion whereunto he was in his human nature lifted up, is not without divine power exercised. It is by divine power, that the Son of man, who sitteth in heaven, doth work as King and Lord upon us which are on earth. The exercise of his dominion over the church militant cannot chuse but cease, when there is no longer any militant church in the world. And therefore, as generals of armies when they have not finished the work, are wont to yield up such commissions as were given for that purpose, and to remain in the state of subjects, and not as lords, as concerning their former authority; even so, when the end of all things is come, the Son of man (who till then reigneth) shall do the like, as touching regiment over the militant church on the earth. So that between the Son of man and his brethren, over whom he reigneth now in this their warfare, there shall be then, as touching the exercise of that regiment, no such difference; they not warfaring any longer under him, but he together with them, under God, receiving the joys of everlasting triumph, that so God may be in all; all misery in all the wicked, thro' his justice; in all the righteous, thro' his love, all felicity and bliss. In the mean while he reigneth over the world as king, and doth those things wherein none is superior unto him, whether we respect the works of his providence and kingdom, or of his regiment over the church. The cause of error in this point doth seem to have been a misconceit,

ceit, that Chrift, as Mediator, being inferior to his Father, doth, as Mediator, all works of regiment over the church; when, in truth, regiment doth belong to his kingly office, mediatorſhip to his prieſtly.   For, as the high-prieſt both offered ſacrifices for expiation of the peoples ſins, and entred into the holy place, there to make interceſſion for them: ſo, Chriſt having finiſhed upon the croſs that part of his prieſtly office, which wrought the propitiation for our ſins, did afterwards enter into very heaven, and doth there, as Mediator of the new teſtament, appear in the ſight of God for us.   A like ſleight of judgment it is, when they hold, that civil authority is from God, but not immediately thro' Chriſt, nor with any ſubordination to God, nor doth any thing from God, but by the hands of our Lord Jeſus Chriſt.   They deny it not to be ſaid of Chriſt in the old teſtament, *By me princes rule, and the nobles, and all the judges of the earth.*   In the new as much is taught, *That Chriſt is the Prince of the kings of the earth.*   Wherefore, to the end it may more plainly appear, how all authority of man is derived from God through Chriſt, and muſt by chriſtian men be acknowledged to be no otherwiſe held than of, and under him; we are to note, that, becauſe whatſoever hath neceſſary being, the Son of God doth cauſe it to be, and thoſe things without which the world cannot well continue, have neceſſary being in the world; a thing of ſo great uſe as government cannot chuſe but be originally from him.   Touching that authority which civil magiſtrates have in eccleſiaſtical affairs, it being from God by Chriſt, as all other good things are, cannot chuſe but be held as a thing received at his hands; and becauſe ſuch power is of neceſſity for the ordering of religion, wherein the eſſence and very being of the church conſiſteth, can no otherwiſe flow from him, than according to that ſpecial care which he hath to govern and guide his own people; it followeth, that the ſaid authority is of and under him after a more ſpecial manner, in that *he is head of the church*, and not in reſpect of his general regency over the world.   *All things* (ſaith the apoſtle, ſpeaking unto the church) *are yours, and ye are Chriſt's, and Chriſt is God's.*   Kings are Chriſt's as ſaints, becauſe they are of the church, if not collectively, yet diviſively underſtood.   It is over each particular perſon within that church where they are kings: ſurely, authority reaching both unto all mens perſons, and to all kinds of cauſes alſo, it is not denied but that they may have and lawfully exerciſe it; ſuch authority it is, for which, and for no other in the world, we term them heads; ſuch authority they have under Chriſt, becauſe he in all things is Lord over all; and even of Chriſt it is that they have received ſuch authority, inaſmuch as of him all lawful powers are; therefore the civil magiſtrate is, in regard of this power, an under and ſubordinate head of Chriſt's people.

It is but idle where they ſpeak, *That altho', for ſeveral companies of men, there may be ſeveral heads or governors, differing in the meaſure of their authority from the chiefeſt, who is head over all; yet it cannot be in the church, for that the reaſon why head-magiſtrates appoint others for ſuch ſeveral places is, becauſe they cannot be preſent every where to perform the office of an head.   But Chriſt is never from his body, nor from any part of it, and therefore needeth not to ſubſtitute any, which may be heads, ſome over one church, and ſome over another.*   Indeed the conſideration of man's imbecility, which maketh many heads neceſſary where the burthen is too great for one, moved *Jethro* to be a perſuader of *Moſes*, that a number of heads or rulers might be inſtituted for diſcharge of that duty by parts, which in whole he ſaw was troubleſome.   Now although there be not in Chriſt any ſuch defect or weakneſs, yet other cauſes there be divers, more than we are able to ſearch into, wherefore it might ſeem unto him expedient to divide his kingdom into many provinces, and place many heads over it, that the power which each of them hath in particular with reſtraint, might illuſtrate the greatneſs of his unlimited authority.   Beſides, howſoever Chriſt be ſpiritually always united unto every part of his body, which is the church; nevertheleſs, we do all know, and they themſelves who alledge this, will, I doubt not, confeſs alſo, that from every church here viſible, Chriſt, touching viſible and corporal preſence, is removed as far as heaven from the earth is diſtant.   Viſible government is a thing neceſſary for the church; and it doth not appear, how the exerciſe of viſible government over ſuch multitudes every where diſperſed throughout the world, ſhould conſiſt without ſundry viſible governors; whoſe power being the greateſt in that kind, ſo far as it reacheth, they are in conſideration thereof termed ſo far heads.   Wherefore, notwithſtanding the perpetual conjunction, by vertue whereof our Saviour always remaineth ſpiritually united unto the parts of his myſtical body; heads indeed with ſupreme power, extending to a certain compaſs, are for the exerciſe of a viſible regiment not unneceſſary.   Some other reaſons there are belonging unto this branch which ſeem to have been objected, rather for the exerciſe of mens wits in diſſolving ſophiſms, than that the authors of them could think in likelihood thereby to ſtrengthen their cauſe.   For example, *If the magiſtrate be head of*

of

T. C. l. 2.
of. 419.
Ut Hm. 8.6.9;

of the church within his own dominion, then is he none of the church: for all that are *of the church make the body of Christ, and every one of the church fulfilleth the place of one member of the body.* *By making the magistrate therefore head, we do exclude him from being a member subject to the head, and so leave him no place in the church.* By which reason, the name of a body politick is suppofed to be always taken of the inferior fort alone, excluding the principal guides and governors, contrary to all mens customs of speech. The error arifeth by misconceiving of some fcripture-fentences, where Chrift as the head, and the church as the body, are compared or oppofed the one to the other. And becaufe in fuch comparifons or oppofitions, the body is taken for thofe only parts which are fubject unto the head, they imagine that whofo is the head of any church, he is therefore even excluded from being a part of that church; that the magiftrate can be none of the church, if fo we make him the head of the church in his own dominions: a chief and principal part of the church therefore, next this, is furely a ftrange conclufion. A church doth indeed make the body of Chrift, being wholly taken together; and every one in the fame church fulfilleth the place of a member in the body, but not the place of an inferior member, the which hath fupreme authority and power over all the reft. Wherefore, by making the magiftrate head in his own dominions, we exclude him from being a member fubject unto any other perfon which may vifibly there rule in a place of a fuperior or head over him ; but fo far are we off from leaving him by this means no place in the church, that we do grant him the chief place. Indeed the heads of thofe vifible bodies, which are many, can be but parts inferior in that fpiritual body which is but one; yea, they may from this be excluded clean, who notwithftanding ought to be honoured, as poffeffing in order the higheft rooms: but for the magiftrate to be termed, in his dominions, an head, doth not bar him from being any way a part or member of the church of God.

As little to the purpofe are thofe other cavils: *A church which hath the magistrate for head, is perfect man without Christ.* So that the knitting of our Saviour thereunto fhould be an addition of that which is too much. Again, *If the church be the body of Christ and of the civil magistrate, it shall have two heads, which being monstrous, is to the great dishonour of Christ and his church.* Thirdly, *If the church be planted in a popular estate, then, forasmuch as all govern in common, and all have authority, all shall be heads there, and no body at all; which is another monster.* It might be feared what this birth of fo many monfters together might portend, but that we know how things, natural enough in themfelves, may feem monftrous, thro' mifconceit; which error of mind is indeed a monfter: and the fkilful in nature's myfteries have ufed to term it the womb of monfters; if any be, it is that troubled underftanding, wherein, becaufe things lie confufedly mixt together, what they are it appeareth not. A church perfect without Chrift, I know not how a man fhall imagine; unlefs there may be either chriftianity without Chrift, or elfe a church without chriftianity. If magiftrates be heads of the church, they are of neceffity chriftians, then is their head Chrift. The adding of Chrift, univerfal head over all, unto magiftrates particular headfhip, is no more fuperfluous in any church than in other focieties; each is to be both feverally fubject unto fome head, and to have a head alfo general for them all to be fubject unto. For fo in armies, in civil corporations, we fee it fareth. A body politick, in fuch refpects, is not like a natural body; in this, more heads than one is fuperfluous; in that not. It is neither monftrous, nor yet uncomely for a church to have different heads: for if chriftian churches be in number many, and every of them a perfect body by it felf, Chrift being Lord and Head over all; why fhould we judge it a thing more monftrous for one body to have two heads, than one head fo many bodies? Him that God hath made the fupreme head of the whole church; the head, not only of that myftical body which the eye of man is not able to difcern, but even of every chriftian politick fociety, of every vifible church in the world? And whereas, laftly, it is thought fo ftrange, that in popular ftates a multitude, to it felf, fhould be both body and head, all this wonderment doth grow from a little over-fight, in deeming that the fubject wherein headfhip ought to refide, fhould be evermore fome one perfon; which thing is not neceffary. For in the collective body that have not derived as yet the principality of power into fome one or few, the whole of neceffity muft be head over each part; otherwife it could not have power poffibly to make any one certain perfon head; inafmuch as the very power of making a head belongeth unto headfhip. Thefe fuppofed *monsters* we fee therefore are no fuch *giants,* as that there fhould need any *Hercules* to tame them.

The laft difference which we have between the title of head when we give it unto Chrift, and when we give it to other governors is, that the kind of dominion which it importeth is not the fame in both. Chrift is head, as being the fountain of life and ghoftly nutri-

ment

ment, the well-fpring of fpiritual bleflings poured into the body of the church; they heads, as being the principal inftruments for the church's outward government; he head, as founder of the houfe; they, as his chiefeft overfeers. Againft this is exception efpecially taken, and our purveyors are herein faid to have their provifion from the popifh fhambles: for by *Pighius* and *Harding*, to prove that Chrift alone is not head of the church, this diftinction, they fay, is brought, that according to the inward influence of grace, Chrift only is head; but according to the outward government, the being head is a thing common to him with others.   To raife up falfhoods of old condemned, and bring it for confirmation of any thing doubtful, which already hath fufficiently been proved an error, and is worthily fo taken, this would juftly deferve cenfuring.   But fhall manifeft truth therefore be reproached, becaufe men convicted in fome things of manifeft untruth have at any time thought or alledged it?   If too much eagernefs againft their adverfaries had not made them forget themfelves, they might remember, where being charged as maintainers of thofe very things, for which others before them had been condemn'd of herefy, yet, left the name of any fuch heretick holding the fame which they do, fhould C.l.3.p.168.make them odious; they ftick not frankly to confefs, *That they are not afraid to confent in fome points with* Jews *and* Turks.   Which defence, for all that, were a very weak buckler for fuch as fhould confent with *Jews* and *Turks* in that which they have been abhorred and hated for in the church.   But as for this diftinction of headfhip, fpiritual and myftical of Jefus Chrift, minifterial and outward in others befides Chrift; what caufe is there to miflike either *Harding* or *Pighius*, or any other befides for it?   That which they have been reprov'd for, is, not becaufe they did therein utter an untruth, but fuch a truth as was not fufficient to bear up the caufe which they did thereby feek to maintain.   By this diftinction, they have both truly and fufficiently proved that the name of *head* importing power and dominion over the church might be given to others befides Chrift, without prejudice to any part of his honour.   That which they fhould have made manifeft was, the name of *head*, importing the power of univerfal dominion over the whole church of Chrift militant, doth, and that by divine right, appertain to the pope of *Rome*.   They did prove it lawful to grant unto others befides Chrift, the power of headfhip in a different kind from his; but they fhould have proved it lawful to challenge, as they did to the bifhop of *Rome*, a power univerfal in that different kind.   Their fault was therefore in exacting wrongfully fo great power as they challenged in that kind, and not in making two kinds of power, unlefs fome reafons can be fhewed for which this diftinction of power fhould be thought erroneous and falfe.   A little they ftir, (altho' in vain) to prove that we cannot with truth make fuch diftinction of power, whereof the one kind fhould agree C.l.2.p.415.unto Chrift only, and the other be further communicated.   Thus therefore they argue, *If there be no head but Chrift, in refpect of fpiritual government, there is no head but he in refpect of the word, facraments, and difcipline adminiftred by thofe whom he hath appointed, for as much alfo as it is his fpiritual government.*   Their meaning is, that whereas we make two kinds of power, of which two, the one being fpiritual, is proper unto Chrift; the other, men are capable of, becaufe it is vifible and external: we do amifs altogether in diftinguifhing, they think, for as much as the vifible and external power of regiment over the church, is only in relation unto the word, facraments, and difcipline, adminiftred by fuch as Chrift hath appointed thereunto, and the exercife of this power is alfo his fpiritual government: therefore we do but vainly imagine a vifible and external power in the church differing from his fpiritual power.   Such difputes as this, do fomewhat refemble the practifing of well-willers upon their friends in the pangs of death; whofe manner is, even then, to put fmoak in their noftrils, and fo to fetch them again, although they know it a matter impoffible to keep them living.   The kind of affection which the favourers of this labouring caufe bear towards it will not fuffer them to fee it dye, although by what means they fhould make it live, they do not fee.   But they may fee that thefe wreftlings will not help.   Can they be ignorant how little it booteth to overcaft fo clear a light with fome mift of ambiguity in the name of fpiritual regiment?   to make things therefore fo plain, that henceforward a child's capacity may ferve rightly to conceive our meaning, we make the fpiritual regiment of Chrift to be generally that whereby his church is ruled and governed in things fpiritual.   Of this general we make two diftinct kinds; the one in vifible, exercifed by Chrift himfelf in his own perfon; the other outwardly adminiftred by them whom Chrift doth allow to be rulers and guiders of his church.   Touching the former of thefe two kinds, we teach that Chrift, in regard thereof, is particularly term'd *the head of the church of God*; neither can any other creature, in that fenfe and meaning, be termed head befides him, becaufe it importeth the conduct and government of our fouls by the hand of that bleffed Spirit wherewith we are fealed and marked, as being peculiarly his.   Him only therefore do we acknowledge to be the

s   Lord,

Lord, which dwelleth, liveth, and reigneth in our hearts; him only to be that head, which giveth falvation and life unto his body ; him only to be that fountain from whence the influence of heavenly graces diftilleth, and is deriv'd into all parts, whether the word, or the facraments, or difcipline, or whatfoever be the means whereby it floweth. As for the power of adminiftring thefe things in the church of Chrift, which power we call the power of order, it is indeed both fpiritual and his; fpiritual, becaufe fuch properly concerns the fpirit : his, becaufe by him it was inftituted. Howbeit, neither fpiritual, as that which is inwardly and invifibly exercifed; nor his, as that which he himfelf in perfon doth exercife. Again, that power of dominion, which is indeed the point of this controverfy, and doth alfo belong to this fecond kind of fpiritual government, namely, unto that regiment which is external and vifible; this likewife being fpiritual in regard of the manner about which it dealeth ; and being his, in as much as he approveth whatfoever is done by it, muft notwithftanding be diftinguifhed alfo from that power whereby he himfelf in perfon adminiftreth the former kind of his own fpiritual regiment, becaufe he himfelf in perfon doth not adminifter this ; we do not therefore vainly imagine, but truly and rightly difcern a power external and vifible in the church exercifed by men, and fevered in nature from that fpiritual power of Chrift's own regiment: which power is termed fpiritual, becaufe it worketh fecretly, inwardly, and invifibly : his, becaufe none doth, nor can it perfonally exercife, either befides or together with him ; feeing that him only we may name our head, in regard of his; and yet, in regard of that other power from this, term others alfo, befides him heads, without any contradiction at all. Which thing may very well ferve for anfwer unto that alfo which they further alledge againft the aforefaid diftinction, namely, *That even the outward focieties and affemblies of the* T.C.l.1.p.415. *church, where one or two are gathered together in his name, either for hearing of the word, or for prayer, or any other church exercife, our Saviour Chrift being in the midft of them as mediator, muft be their head: and if he be not there idle, but doing the office of a head fully, it followeth, that even in the outward focieties and meetings of the church, no meer man can be called the head of it, feeing that our Saviour Chrift doing the whole office of the head himfelf alone, leaveth nothing to men, by doing whereof they may obtain that title.* Which objection I take as being made for nothing but only to maintain argument. For they are not fo far gone as to argue this in footh and right good earneft. *God ftandeth* (faith the *Pfalmift*) *in the midft of Gods*; if God be there prefent, he muft undoubtedly be prefent as God ; if he be not there idle, but doing the office of a God fully, it followeth, that God himfelf alone doing the whole office of a God, leaveth nothing in fuch affemblies to any other, by doing whereof they may obtain fo high a name. The *Pfalmift* therefore hath fpoken amifs, and doth ill to call judges, Gods. Not fo ; for as God hath this office differing from theirs, and doth fully dif- T.C.l.1.p.413: charge it even in the midft of them, fo they are not hereby excluded from all kind of duty, for which that name fhould be given unto them alfo, but in that duty for which it was given them they are encouraged religioufly and carefully to order themfelves after the felf-fame manner. Our Lord and Saviour being in the midft of his church as head is our comfort, without the abridgment of any one duty ; for performance whereof others are termed heads in another kind than he is. If there be of the ancient fathers, which fay, *That there is but one head of the church, Chrift; and that the minifter that baptizeth cannot be the head of him that is baptized, becaufe Chrift is the head of the whole church: and that Paul could not be head of the church which he planted, becaufe Chrift is the head of the whole body*; they underftand the name of head in fuch fort as we grant, that it is not applicable to any other, no not in relation, to the leaft part of the whole church ; he which baptizeth, baptizeth into Chrift ; he which converteth, converteth into Chrift ; he which ruleth, ruleth for Chrift. The whole church can have but one to be head as lord and owner of all ; wherefore if Chrift be head in that kind, it followeth, that no other befides can be fo either to the whole or to any part.

To call and diffolve all folemn Affemblies about the publick affairs of the Church.

Amongft fundry prerogatives of *Simon's* dominion over the *Jews* there is reckoned, as not the leaft, *That no man might gather any great affembly in the land without him.* For fo the manner of *Jewifh* regiment had always been, that whether the caufe for which men aſſembled themſelves in peaceable, good, and orderly ſort were ec-cleſiaſtical, or civil, ſupream authority ſhould aſſemble them. *David* gather'd all *Iſrael* together unto *Jeruſalem*; when the ark was to be remov'd, he aſſembled the ſons of *Aaron* and the *Levites*. *Solomon* did the like at ſuch time as the temple was to be dedicated; when the church was to be reform'd *Aſa* in its time did the ſame. The ſame upon like occaſions was done afterwards by *Joaſh*, *Hezekias*, *Joſia*, and others.

Polyb. l. 6. de milit. ac do-meſt Rom. diſcipl. The conſuls of *Rome*, *Polybius* affirmeth to have had a kind of regal authority, in that they might call together the ſenate and people whenſoever it pleaſed them. Seeing there-fore the affairs of the church and chriſtian religion are publick affairs, for the order-ing whereof more ſolemn aſſemblies ſometimes are of as great importance and uſe, as they are for ſecular affairs; it ſeemeth no leſs an act of ſupream authority to call the one, than the other. Wherefore the clergy, in ſuch wiſe gathered together, is an eccleſiaſtical ſe-nate, which with us, as in former times, the chiefeſt prelate at his diſcretion did uſe to aſ-ſemble; ſo that afterwards in ſuch conſiderations as have been before ſpecified, it ſeemed more meet to annex the ſaid prerogative to the crown. The plot of reform'd diſcipline not liking thereof ſo well, taketh order that every former aſſembly before it breaketh up

Lib. 1. de col. illicit. & de conventiculis, cap. de epiſc. & presbyt. ſhould it ſelf appoint both the time and place of their after-meeting again. But becauſe I find not any thing on that ſide particularly alledged againſt us herein, a longer diſputa-tion about ſo plain a cauſe ſhall not need. The ancient imperial law forbiddeth ſuch aſ-ſemblies as the emperor's authority did not cauſe to be made. Before emperors became chriſtians, the church had never any general ſynod; their greateſt meeting conſiſting of biſhops and other the graveſt in each province. As for the civil governor's authority,

Hierarch.lib.6. cap. 1. it ſuffered them only as things not regarded, or not accounted of at ſuch times as it did ſuffer them. So that what right a chriſtian king hath as touching aſſemblies of that kind, we are not able to judge till we come to later times, when religion had won the hearts

Conſtant. con-cil.àTheodoſio. Sardicen con-cil. à Con. Hieron. contr. Ruffinum l. 1. of the higheſt powers. *Conſtantine* (as *Pighius* doth grant) was not only the firſt that ever did call any general council together, but even the firſt that deviſed the calling of them for conſultation about the buſineſſes of God. After he had once given the example, his ſucceſſors a long time follow'd the ſame; in ſo much that St. *Hierom* to diſprove the au-thority of a ſynod which was pretended to be general, uſeth this as a forcible argument, *Dic, quis imperator hanc ſynodum juſſerit convocari?* Their anſwer hereunto is no an-ſwer, which ſay, *That the emperors did not this without conference had with the biſhops*: for to our purpoſe it is enough, if the clergy alone did it not otherwiſe than by the leave

Sozomen l. 6. cap. 7. Ambroſ. epiſt. 32. and appointment of their ſovereign lords and kings. Whereas therefore it is on the con-trary ſide alledg'd, that *Valentinian* the elder being requeſted by catholick biſhops to grant that there might be a ſynod for the ordering of matters call'd in queſtion by the *Arians*, an-ſwered, that he being one of the laity might not meddle with ſuch matters; and there-upon willed, that the prieſts and biſhops to whom the care of thoſe things belongeth, ſhould meet and conſult together by themſelves where they thought good. We muſt, with the emperor's ſpeech, weigh the occaſion and drift thereof. *Valentinian* and *Valens*, the one a *catholick* and the other an *Arian*, were emperors together: *Valens*, the governor of the *eaſt*, and *Valentinian* of the *weſt* empire. *Valentinian* therefore taking his journey from the *eaſt* unto the *weſt* parts, and paſſing for that intent thro' *Thracia*, there the bi-ſhops which held the ſoundneſs of chriſtian belief, becauſe they knew that *Valens* was their profeſſed enemy, and therefore if the other was once departed out of thoſe quarters, the catholick cauſe was like to find very ſmall favour, moved preſently *Valentinian* about a council to be aſſembled under the countenance of his authority; who by likelihood conſidering what inconvenience might grow thereby, inaſmuch as it could not be but a means to incenſe *Valens* the more againſt them, refuſed himſelf to be author of, or preſent at any ſuch aſſembly; and of this his denial gave them a colourable reaſon, to wit, that he was, although an emperor, yet a ſecular perſon, and therefore not able in matters of ſo great obſcurity to ſit as competent judge: but if they which were biſhops and learned men, did think good to conſult thereof together, they might. Whereupon, when they could not obtain that which they moſt deſired, yet that which he granted unto them they took and forthwith had a council. *Valentinian* went on towards *Rome*, they remaining in conſultation till *Valens* which accompanied him returned back; ſo that now there was no remedy, but either to incur a manifeſt contempt, or elſe at the hands of *Valens* him-ſelf to ſeek approbation of that they had done. To him therefore they became ſuitors: his anſwer was ſhort, *Either Arianiſm, or exile, which they would*; whereupon their ba-niſhment enſued. Let reaſonable men now therefore be judges, how much this example of *Valentinian* doth make againſt the authority, which we ſay that ſovereign rulers may lawfully have as concerning ſynods and meetings eccleſiaſtical.

Of the authority of making Laws.

THere are which wonder that we should account any statute a law, which the high court of *parliament* in *England* hath establish'd about the matters of *church-regiment*; the prince and court of parliament having (as they suppose) no more lawful means to give order to the church and clergy in those things, than they have to make laws for the hierarchies of angels in heaven; that the parliament being a meer temporal court, can neither by the law of nature, nor of God, have competent power to define of such matters: That supremacy in this kind cannot belong unto kings, as kings, because pagan emperors, whose princely power was true sovereignty, never challenged so much over the church; that power, in this kind, cannot be the right of an earthly crown, prince, or state, in that they be christians, forasmuch as if they be christians, they all owe subjection to the pastors of their souls; that the prince therefore not having it himself, cannot communicate it to the parliament, and consequently cannot make laws here, or determine of the church's regiment by himself, parliament, or any other court subjected unto him.

The parliament of *England*, together with the convocation annexed thereunto, is that whereupon the very essence of all government within this kingdom doth depend; it is even the body of the whole realm: it consisteth of the king, and of all that within the land are subject unto him. The parliament is a court, not so merely temporal as if it might meddle with nothing but only leather and wool. Those days of queen *Mary* are not yet forgotten, wherein the realm did submit it self unto the legate of pope *Julius*, at which time, had they been persuaded, as this man seemeth now to be, had they thought that there is no more force in laws made by parliament concerning church-affairs, than if men should take upon them to make orders for their hierarchies of angels in heaven, they might have taken all former statutes of that kind as cancelled, and by reason of nullity, abrogated.   What need was there that they should bargain with the cardinal, and purchase their pardon by promise made beforehand, that what laws they had made, assented unto, or executed, against the bishop of *Rome*'s supremacy, the same they would, in that present parliament, effectually abrogate and repeal? had they power to repeal laws made, and none to make laws concerning the regiment of the church? Again, when they had by suit obtained his confirmation for such foundations of bishopricks, cathedral churches, hospitals, colleges, and schools; for such marriages before made, for such institutions into livings ecclesiastical, and for all such judicial processes, as having been ordered according to the laws before in force, but contrary unto the canons and orders of the church of *Rome*, were in that respect thought defective, although the cardinal in his Letters of dispensation did give validity unto those acts, even *Apostolicæ firmitatis robur*, the very strength of apostolical solidity; what had all these been without those grave authentical words? *Be it enacted by the authority of this present parliament, that all and singular* An. 1 & 2. *articles and clauses contained in the said dispensation, shall remain and be reputed and taken* Phil. & Mar. *to all intents and constructions in the laws of this realm, lawful, good, and effectual, to* cap. 8. *be alledged and pleaded in all courts ecclesiastical and temporal, for good and sufficient matter either for the plantiff or defendant, without any allegation or objection to be made against the validity of them, by pretence of any general council, canon, or decree to the contrary.* Somewhat belike they thought there was in this meer temporal court, without which the pope's own mere ecclesiastical legat's dispensation had taken small effect in the church of *England*; neither did they, or the cardinal imagine any thing committed against the law of nature, or of God, because they took order for the church's affairs, and that even in the court of parliament. The most natural and religious course in making laws is, that the matter of them be taken from the judgment of the wisest in those things which they are to concern. In matters of God, to set down a form of prayer, a solemn confession of the articles of the christian faith, and ceremonies meet for the exercise of religion: it were unnatural not to think the pastors and bishops of our souls a great deal more fit, than men of secular trades, and callings: howbeit, when all which the wisdom of all sorts can do, is done for the devising of laws in the church, it is the general consent of all that giveth them the form and vigour of laws, without which they could be no more unto us than, the counsel of physicians to the sick. Well might they seem as wholsom admonitions and instructions; but laws could they never be, without the consent of the whole church, to be guided by them; whereunto both nature and the practice of the church of God set down in scripture, is found every way so fully consonant, that God himself would

not

not impose his own laws upon his people by the hand of *Moses*, without their free and open consent. Wherefore, to define and determine, even of the church's affairs by way of assent and approbation, as laws are defined in that right of power, which doth give them the force of laws; thus to define of our own church's regiment, the parliament of *England* hath competent authority.

Touching that supremacy of power which our kings have in the case of making laws, it resteth principally in the strength of a negative voice; which not to give them, were to deny them that, without which they were kings but by a meer title and not in exercise of dominion. Be it in regiment-popular, aristocratical, or regal, principality resteth in that person, or those persons unto whom is given right of excluding any kind of law whatsoever it be before establishment. This doth belong unto kings as kings; pagan emperors, even *Nero* himself had no less; but much more than this in the laws of his own empire. That he challeng'd not any interest of giving voice in the laws of the church, I hope no man will so construe, as if the cause were conscience and fear to encroach upon

Item quod principi placuit, legis habet vigorem. Inst. de J.N.G.&C.

the apostles right. If then it be demanded, by what right from *Constantine* downward, the christian emperors did so far intermeddle with the church's affairs, either we must herein condemn them, as being over presumptuously bold, or else judge that, by a law, which is term'd *regia*, that is to say, regal; the people having deriv'd unto their emperors their whole power for making of laws, and by that means his edicts being made laws, what matter soever they did concern, as imperial dignity endow'd them with competent authority and power to make laws for religion, so they were thought by christianity to use their power, being christians, unto the benefit of the church of Christ. Was there any christian bishop in the world which did then judge this repugnant unto the dutiful subjection which christians do owe to the pastors of their souls; to whom, in respect of their sacred order, it is not by us, neither may be denied, that kings and princes are as much as the very meanest that liveth under them, bound in conscience to shew themselves gladly and willingly obedient; receiving the seals of salvation, the blessed sacraments at their hands, as at the hands of our Lord Jesus Christ, with all reverence, not disdaining to be taught and admonish'd by them, nor with-holding from them as much as the least part of their due and decent honour? All which, for any thing that hath been alledged, may stand very well without resignation of supremacy of power in making laws, even laws concerning the most spiritual affairs of the church; which laws being made amongst us, are not by any of us so taken or interpreted, as if they did receive their force from power which the prince doth communicate unto the parliament or unto any other court under him, but from power which the whole body of the realm being naturally possest with, hath by free and deliberate assent derived unto him that ruleth over them, so far forth as hath been declared. So that our laws made concerning religion, do take originally their essence from the power of the whole realm and church of *England*, than which, nothing can be more consonant unto the law of nature and the will of our Lord Jesus Christ.

T.C.l.1.p.92.

To let these go, and return to our own men; *ecclesiastical governors*, they say, *may not meddle with making of civil laws, and of laws for the commonwealth; nor the civil magistrate, high or low, with making of orders for the church.* It seemeth unto me very strange, that these men, which are in no cause more vehement and fierce than where they plead, that ecclesiastical persons may not κρατεῖν, be lords, should hold that the power of making ecclesiastical laws, which thing of all other is most proper unto dominion, belongeth to none but ecclesiastical persons only. Their over-sight groweth herein for want of exact observation, what it is to make a law. *Tully*, speaking of the law of nature, saith, *That thereof God himself was* inventor, disceptator, lator, *the deviser, the discusser, and deliverer:* wherein he plainly alludeth unto the chiefest parts which then did appertain to his publick action. For when laws were made, the first thing was to have them devised; the second to sift them with as much exactness of judgment as any way might be used; the next by solemn voice of sovereign authority to pass them, and give them the force of laws. It cannot in any reason seem otherwise than most fit, that unto ecclesiastical persons the care of devising ecclesiastical laws be committed, even as the care of civil unto them which are in those affairs most skilful. This taketh not away from ecclesiastical persons all right of giving voice with others, when civil laws are proposed for regiment of the commonwealth, whereof themselves, though now the world would have them annihilated, are notwithstanding as yet a part; much less doth it cut off that part of the power of princes, whereby, as they claim, so we know no reasonable cause wherefore we may not grant them, without offence to almighty God, so much authority in making all manner of laws within their own dominions, that neither civil nor ecclesiastical do pass without their royal assent.

‡

In

In devising and discussing of laws, wisdom especially is required; but that which establisheth them and maketh them, is power, even power of dominion; the chiefty whereof (amongst us) resteth in the person of the king. Is there any law of Christ's which forbiddeth kings and rulers of the earth to have such sovereign and supream power in the making of laws either civil or ecclesiastical? If there be, our controversy hath an end. Christ, in his church, hath not appointed any such law concerning temporal power, as God did of old unto the commonwealth of *Israel*; but leaving that to be at the world's free choice, his chiefest care is, that the spiritual law of the gospel might be published far and wide. They that received the law of Christ, were, for a long time, people scattered in sundry kingdoms, christianity not exempting them from the laws which they had been subject unto, saving only in such cases as those laws did injoyn that which the religion of Christ did forbid. Hereupon grew their manifold persecutions throughout all places where they lived; as oft as it thus came to pass, there was no possibility that the emperors and kings under whom they lived, should meddle any whit at all with making laws for the church. From Christ, therefore, having received power; who doubteth, but as they did, so they might bind them to such orders as seemed fittest for the maintenance of their religion, without the leave of high or low in the commonwealth; forasmuch as in religion it was divided utterly from them, and they from it. But when the mightiest began to like of the christian faith; by their means, whole free states and kingdoms became obedient unto Christ. Now the question is, whether kings, by embracing christianity, do thereby receive any such law as taketh from them the weightiest part of that sovereignty which they had even when they were heathens: whether, being infidels, they might do more in causes of religion, than now they can by the laws of God, being true believers. For, whereas in regal states, the king, or supream head of the commonwealth, had before christianity a supream stroak in making of laws for religion; he must by embracing christian religion utterly deprive himself thereof, and in such causes become subject unto his subjects, having even within his own dominions them whose commandment he must obey; unless his power be placed in the head of some foreign spiritual potentate: so that either a foreign or domestick commander upon earth, he must admit more now, than before he had, and that in the chiefest things whereupon commonwealths do stand. But apparent it is unto all men which are not strangers unto the doctrine of Jesus Christ, that no state of the world receiving christianity, is by any law therein contained bound to resign the power which they lawfully held before: but over what persons, and in what causes soever the same hath been in force, it may so remain and continue still. That which, as kings, they might do in matters of religion, and did in matter of false religion, being idolatrous and superstitious kings, the same they are now even in every respect fully authorized to do in all affairs pertinent to the state of true christian religion. And, concerning the supream power of making laws for all persons, in all causes to be guided by, it is not to be let pass, that the head enemies of this head-ship are constrained to acknowledge the king endued even with this very power, so that he may and ought to exercise the same, taking order for the church and her affairs, of what nature or kind soever, in case of necessity: as when, there is no lawful ministry, which they interpret then to be (and this surely is a point very remarkable,) wheresoever the ministry is wicked. A wicked ministry is no lawful ministry; and in such sort no lawful ministry, that, what doth belong unto them as ministers by right of their calling, the same to be annihilated in respect of their bad qualities; their wickedness in it self a deprivation of right to deal in the affairs of the church, and a warrant for others to deal in them which are held to be of a clean other society, the members whereof have been before so peremptorily for ever excluded from power of dealing for ever with affairs of the church. They which once have learn'd throughly this lesson, will quickly be capable perhaps of another equivalent unto it. For the wickedness of the ministry transfers their right unto the king; in case the king be as wicked as they, to whom then shall the right descend? There is no remedy, all must come by devolution at length, even as the family of *Brown* will have it, unto the godly among the people, for confusion unto the wife and the great by the poor and the simple; some *Kniperdoling*, with his retinue, must take this work of the Lord in hand; and the making of church-laws and orders must prove to be their right in the end. If not for love of the truth, yet for shame of gross absurdities, let these contentions and trifling fancies be abandoned. The cause which moved them for a time to hold a wicked ministry no lawful ministry; and in this defect of a lawful ministry, authorized kings to make laws and orders for the affairs of the church, till it were well established, is surely this: first, they see that whereas the continual dealing of the kings of *Israel* in the affairs of the church doth make now very strong against them, the burthen whereof they shall in time well enough shake off, if it may be obtained, that it is

indeed

T.C.L.3.p.51.

indeed lawful for kings to follow thefe hóly examples; howbeit no longer than during the cafe of neceffity, while the wickednefs, arid in refpect theteof, the unlawfulnefs of the miniftry doth continue.   Secondly, They perceive right well, that unlefs they fhould yield authority unto kings in cafe of fuch fuppofed neceffity, the difcipline they urge were clean excluded, as long as the clergy of *England* doth thereunto remain oppofite. To open therefore a door for her entrance, there is no reafon but the tenet muft be this: that now, when the miniftry of *England* is univerfally wicked, and in that refpect hath loft all authority, and is become no lawful miniftry, no fuch miniftry as hath the right, which otherwife fhould belong unto them, if they were virtuous and godly, as their ad-verfaries are; in this neceffity the king may do fomewhat for the church: that which we do imply in the name of headfhip, he may both have and exercife till they be entered which will disburthen and eafe him of it: till they come, the king is licenfed to hold that power which we call headfhip.   But what afterwards?   In a church ordered, that

T. C. l. 1. which the fupreme magiftrate hath to do, is to fee that the laws of God, touching his
P. 192. worfhip, and touching all matters and orders of the church, be executed and duly ob-ferved; to fee that every ecclefiaftical perfon do that office whereunto he is appointed;

Apol. 1. fol. 40. to punifh thofe that fail in their office.   In a word, that which *Allain* himfelf acknow-
P. 2. ledged unto the earthly power which God hath given him it doth belong to defend the laws of the church, to caufe them to be executed, and to punifh rebels and tranfgreffors of the fame; on all fides therefore it is confeft, that to the king belongeth power of maintaining the laws made for church-regiment, and of caufing them to be obferved; but principality of power in making them, which is the thing we attribute unto kings, this both the one fort and the other do withftand.

Power to com-   Touching the king's fuper-eminent authority in commanding, and in judging of caufes
mand all per-   ecclefiaftical; firft, to explain therein our meaning, it hath been taken as if we did hold,
fons, and to be   that kings may prefcribe what themfelves think good to be done in the fervice of God:
over all judges   how the word fhall be taught, how the facraments adminiftred; that kings may perfonally
in caufes eccle-   fit in the confiftory where the bifhops do, hearing and determining what caufes foever
fiaftical.   do appertain unto the church; that kings and queens, in their own proper perfons, are by judicial fentence to decide the queftions which do arife about matters of faith and chriftian religion; that kings may excommunicate: finally, that kings may do whatfo-ever is incident unto the office and duty of an ecclefiaftical judge.   Which opinion, be-caufe we account as abfurd as they who have fathered the fame upon us, we do them to wit, that this is our meaning, and no otherwife: there is not within this realm an ec-clefiaftical officer, that may by the authority of his own place, command univerfally throughout the king's dominions: but they of this people whom one may command, are to another's commandment unfubject.   Only the king's royal power is of fo large compafs, that no man commanded by him according to the order of law, can plead him-felf to be without the bounds and limits of that authority; I fay, according to order of law, becaufe with us the higheft have thereunto fo tied themfelves, that otherwife than fo, they take not upon them to command any.   And, that kings fhould be in fuch fort fupreme commanders over all men, we hold it requifite, as well for the ordering of fpi-ritual as civil affairs; inafmuch as without univerfal authority in this kind, they fhould

1 Chron. 24. not be able when need is, to do as virtuous kings have done.   *Jofiah, purpofing to renew*
5, 6, 7, 8, 9. *the houfe of the Lord, affembled the priefts and Levites; and when they were together, gave them their charge, faying: Go out unto the cities of Judah, and gather of Ifrael money to repair the houfe of the Lord from year to year, and hafte the things: but the Levites haftened not.   Therefore the king commanded Jehoiada, the chief prieft, and faid unto him; why haft thou not required of the Levites, to bring in out of Judah and Jerufalem, the tax of Mofes, the fervant of the Lord, and of the congregation of If-rael, for the tabernacle of the teftimony?   For wicked Athaliah, and her children, brake up the houfe of the Lord God, and all the things that were dedicated for the houfe of*

Chap. 6. 30. *the Lord, did they beftow upon Balaam.   Therefore the king commanded, and they made*
6. *a cheft, and fet it at the gate of the houfe of the Lord without, and they made a proclamation through Judah and Jerufalem, to bring unto the Lord, the tax of Mofes the fervant of the Lord, laid upon Ifrael in the wildernefs.*   Could either he have done this, or after him *Ezekias* the like concerning the celebration of the paffover, but that all forts of men in all things did owe unto thefe their fovereign rulers the fame obedi-

Jofh. 1. 18. ence which fometimes *Jofhua* had them by vow and promife bound unto?   *Whofoever fhall rebel againft thy commandments, and will not obey thy words in all thou com-mandeft him, let him be put to death: only be ftrong and of a good courage.*   Further-more, judgment ecclefiaftical we fay is neceffary for decifion of controverfies rifing be-tween man and man, and for correction of faults committed in the affairs of God:

unto the due execution whereof there are three things neceffary, laws, judges, and fupream governors of judgments.   What courts there fhall be, and what caufes fhall belong
unto each court, and what judges fhall determine of every caufe, and what order in all
judgments fhall be kept: of thefe things the laws have fufficiently difpofed, fo that his duty
who fitteth in any fuch court, is to judge, not of, but after the fame law. *Imprimis illud ob-* Juft. de offic.
fervare debet judex, nè aliter judicet quàm legibus, conftitutionibus, aut moribus proditum jud.
eft, ut imperator Juftinianus; which laws (for we mean the pofitive laws of our realm concerning ecclefiaftical affairs) if they otherwife difpofe of any fuch thing, than according to
the law of reafon, and of God, we muft both acknowledge them to be amifs, and endeavour to have them reform'd: but touching that point, what may be objected fhall after appear.   Our judges in caufes ecclefiaftical, are either ordinary, or commiffionary: ordinary, thofe whom we term ordinaries; and fuch, by the laws of this land, are none but prelates only, whofe power to do that which they do, is in themfelves, and belonging to the
nature of their ecclefiaftical calling.   In fpiritual caufes, a lay-perfon may be no ordinary;
a commiffionary judge there is no let but that he may be; and that our laws do evermore refer the ordinary judgment of fpiritual caufes unto fpiritual perfons, fuch as are
termed ordinaries, no man which knoweth any thing of the practice of this realm can
eafily be ignorant.   Now, befides them which are authorized to judge in feveral territories, there is required an univerfal power which reacheth over all, imparting fupream
authority of government over all courts, all judges, all caufes; the operation of which
power is as well to ftrengthen, maintain, and uphold particular jurifdictions, which haply might elfe be of fmall effect; as alfo to remedy that which they are not able to help,
and to redrefs that wherein they at any time do otherwife than they ought to do.   This
power being fometime in the bifhop of *Rome,* who by finifter practices had drawn it into his hands, was for juft confiderations by publick confent annexed unto the king's royal feat and crown; from thence the authors of reformation would tranflate it into their
national affemblies or fynods; which fynods are the only helps which they think lawful
to ufe againft fuch evils in the church, as particular jurifdictions are not fufficient to redrefs.   In which caufe, our laws have provided, that the king's fupereminent authority 1 Eliz. cap. 1.
and power fhall ferve: As namely, when the whole ecclefiaftical ftate, or the principal
perfons therein, do need vifitation and reformation; when in any part of the church
errors, fchifms, herefies, abufes, offences, contempts, enormities, are grown; which
men in their feveral jurifdictions either do not, or cannot help.   Whatfoever any fpiritual authority and power (fuch as legates from the fee of *Rome* did fometimes exercife)
hath done or might heretofore have done for the remedies of thofe evils in lawful fort,
(that is to fay, without the violation of the laws of God or nature in the deed done) as
much in every degree our laws have fully granted that the king for ever may do, not
only by fetting ecclefiaftical fynods on work, that the thing may be their act and the
king their motioner unto it, for fo much perhaps the mafters of the reformation will
grant; but by commiffions few or many, who having the king's letters patents, may in the
vertue thereof execute the premifes as agents in the right, not of their own peculiar and
ordinary, but of his fupereminent power.   When men are wronged by inferior judges, or
have any juft caufe to take exception againft them; their way for redrefs is to make their
appeal; an appeal is a prefent delivery of him which maketh it out of the hands of their
power and jurifdictions from whence it is made.   Pope *Alexander* having fometimes the
king of *England* at advantage, caufed him, amongft other things, to agree, that as many
of his fubjects as would, might have appeal to the court of *Rome, And thus* (faith one) Machiavel.
that whereunto a mean perfon at this day would fcorn to fubmit himfelf, fo great a king lib. 1. hift. Florent.
was content to be fubject to.   Notwithftanding, even when the pope (faith he) *had fo*
great authority amongft princes which were far off, the Romans *he could not frame to*
obedience, nor was able to obtain that himfelf might abide at Rome, *though promifing*
not to meddle with other than ecclefiaftical affairs.   So much are things that terrify more
feared by fuch as behold them aloof off than at hand.   Reformers I doubt not in fome 25 Hen. 8.
caufes will admit appeals, but appeals made to their fynods; even as the church of *Rome* c. 19.
doth allow of them fo they be made to the bifhop of *Rome.*   As for that kind of appeal
which the *Englifh* laws do approve from the judge of any certain particular court unto the
king, as the only fupream governor on earth, who by his delegates may give a final definitive fentence, from which no farther appeal can be made; will their platform allow of this?
Surely, forafmuch as in that eftate which they all dream of, the whole church muft be divided into parifhes, in which none can have greater or lefs authority and power than another; again, the king himfelf muft be a common member in the body of his own parifh,
and the caufes of that only parifh, muft be by the officers thereof determinable; in cafe
the king had fo much favour or preferment, as to be made one of thofe officers (for other-

wife by their positions he were not to meddle any more than the meaneft amongft his fubjects with the judgment of any ecclefiaftical caufe) how is it poffible they fhould allow of appeals to be made from any other abroad to the king? To receive appeals from all other judges, belongeth to the higheft in power of all, and to be in power over all (as touching judgment in ecclefiaftical caufes) this, as they think, belongeth only to fynods. Whereas therefore, with us kings do exercife over all things, perfons, and caufes, fupreme power, both of voluntary and litigious jurifdictions; fo that according to the one they incite, reform, and command; according to the other, they judge univerfally, doing both in far other fort than fuch as have ordinary fpiritual power; oppugned we are herein by fome colourable fhew of argument, as if to grant thus

T. C. l. 3.
p. 154.
a Chr. 19
Heb. 5. 1.

much to any fecular perfon it were unreafonable: *For fith it is* (fay they) *apparent out of the chronicles, that judgment in church-matters pertaineth to God; feeing likewife it is evident out of the apoftles, that the high-prieft is fet over thofe matters in God's behalf; it muft needs follow, that the principality or direction of the judgment of them is, by God's ordinance, appertaining to the high-prieft, and confequently to the miniftry of the church; and if it be by God's ordinance appertaining unto them, how can it be tranflated from them to the civil magiftrate?* Which argument, briefly drawn into form, lieth thus: that which belongeth unto God, may not be tranflated unto any other but whom he hath appointed to have it in his behalf; but principality of judgment in church-matters appertaineth unto God, which hath appointed the high-prieft, and confequently the miniftry of the church alone to have it in his behalf; *ergo*, it may not from them be tranflated to the civil magiftrate. The firft of which propofitions we grant, as alfo in the fecond branch which afcribeth unto God principality in church-matters. But, that either he did appoint none but only the high-prieft to exercife the faid principality for him; or that the miniftry of the church may in reafon from thence be concluded to have alone the fame principality by his appointment, thefe two points we deny utterly. For, concerning the high prieft, there is,

Heb. 5. 1.

firft, no fuch ordinance of God to be found; *Every high-prieft* (faith the apoftle) *is taken from amongft men, and is ordained for men in things pertaining to God*; whereupon it may well be gathered, that the prieft was indeed ordained of God to have power in things appertaining unto God. For the apoftle doth there mention the power of offering gifts and facrifices for fin; which kind of power, was not only given of God unto priefts, but reftrained unto priefts only. The power of jurifdiction and ruling authority, this alfo God gave them, but not them alone. For it is held, as all men know, that others of the laity were herein joined by the law with them. But, concerning principality in church-affairs, (for of this our queftion is, and of no other) the prieft neither had it alone, nor at all, but in fpiritual or church-affairs, (as hath been already fhewed) it was the royal prerogative of kings only. Again, though it were fo, that God had appointed the high-prieft to have the faid principality of government in thofe matters; yet how can they who alledge this, enforce thereby, that confequently the miniftry of the church, and no other, ought to have the fame, when they are fo far off from allowing fo much to the miniftry of the gofpel, as the priefthood of the law had by God's appointment: that we by collecting thereout a difference in authority and jurifdiction amongft the clergy, to be for the polity of the church not inconvenient; they forthwith think to clofe up our mouths by anfwering, *That the jewifh high-prieft had authority above the reft, only in that they prefigured the fovereignty of Jefus Chrift; as for the minifters of the gofpel, it is altogether unlawful to give them as much as the leaft title, any fyllable whereof may found to principality.* And of the regency which may be granted, they hold others even of the laity no lefs capable than the paftors themfelves. How fhall thefe things cleave together? The truth is, that they have fome reafon to think it not at all of the fitteft for kings to fit as ordinary judges in matters of faith and religion. An ordinary judge muft be of the quality which in a fupreme judge is not neceffary: becaufe the perfon of the one is charged with that which the other authority difchargeth, without imploying perfonally himfelf therein. It is an error to think, that the king's authority can have no force nor power in the doing of that which himfelf may not perfonally do. For firft, impoffible it is that at one and the fame time, the king in perfon fhould order fo many, and fo different affairs, as by his own power every where prefent, are wont to be ordered both in peace and war, at home and abroad. Again, the king in regard of his nonage or minority, may be unable to perform that thing wherein years of difcretion are requifite for perfonal action; and yet his authority even then be of force. For which caufe we fay, that the king's authority dieth not, but is, and worketh always alike. Sundry confiderations there may be effectual to with-hold the king's perfon from being a doer of that which notwithftanding his power muft give force unto, even

in

in civil affairs; where nothing doth more either concern the duty, or better befeem the majefty of kings, than perfonally to adminifter juftice to their people (as moft famous princes have done); yet if it be in cafe of felony or treafon, the learned in the law of this realm do affirm, that well may the king commit his authority to another to judge between him and the offender; but the king being himfelf there a party, he cannot perfonally fit to give judgment.

As therefore the perfon of the king may, for juft confiderations, even where the caufe *Stamf. pleas of the crown l. 2. c. 3.* is civil, be notwithftanding withdrawn from occupying the feat of judgment, and others under his authority be fit, he unfit himfelf to judge; fo the confiderations for which it were haply not convenient for kings to fit and give fentence in fpiritual courts, where caufes ecclefiaftical are ufually debated, can be no bar to that force and efficacy which their fovereign power hath over thofe very confiftories, and for which we hold, without any exception, that all courts are the king's: All men are not for all things fufficient, and therefore publick affairs being divided, fuch perfons muft be authorized judges in each kind, as common reafon may prefume to be moft fit : which cannot of kings and princes ordinarily be prefumed in caufes merely ecclefiaftical; fo that even common fenfe doth rather adjudge this burthen unto other men. We fee it hereby a thing neceffary, to put a difference, as well between that ordinary jurifdiction which belongeth unto the clergy alone, and that commiffionary wherein others are for juft confiderations appointed to join with them, as alfo between both thefe jurifdictions; and a third, whereby the king hath tranfcendent authority, and that in all caufes over both. Why this may not lawfully be granted unto him there is no reafon. A time there was when kings were not capable of any fuch power, as namely, when they profeffed themfelves open enemies unto Chrift and chriftianity. A time there followed, when they, being capable, took fometimes more, fometimes lefs to themfelves, as feemed beft in their own eyes, becaufe no certainty, touching their right, was as yet determined. The bifhops, who alone were before accuftomed to have the ordering of fuch affairs, faw very juft caufe of grief, when the higheft, favouring herefy, withftood, by the ftrength of fovereign authority, religious proceedings. Whereupon they oftentimes, againft this unrefiftible power, pleaded the ufe and cuftom which had been to the contrary; namely, that the affairs of the church fhould be dealt in by the clergy, and by no other; unto which purpofe the fentences that then were uttered in defence of unabolifhed orders and laws, againft fuch as did of their own heads contrary thereunto, are now altogether impertinently brought in oppofition againft them, who ufe but that power which laws have given them, unlefs men can fhew that there is in thofe laws fome manifeft iniquity or injuftice. Whereas therefore againft the force judicial and imperial, which fupream au-*T.C.l.3.p.155.* thority hath, it is alledged, how *Conftantine* termeth *church-officers, overfeers within the church*; himfelf, *of thofe without the church*: how *Auguftine* witneffeth, that the em-*Eufeb. de vita* peror not daring to judge of the bifhop's caufe, committed it to the bifhops; and was to *Conftant. l. 4. ep. 161, 166.* crave pardon of the bifhops, for that by the *Donatifts* importunity, which made no end of appealing unto him, he was, being weary of them, drawn to give fentence in a matter of theirs; how *Hillary* befeecheth the emperor *Conftance* to provide that the governors of his provinces fhould not prefume to take upon them the judgment of ecclefiaftical caufes, to whom only commonwealth matters belonged; how *Ambrofe* affirmeth, that *Lib. 5. ep. 33.* *palaces* belong unto the *emperor*; *churches to the miniftry*; that the emperor hath the authority over the common walls of the city, and not in holy things; for which caufe he never would yield to have the caufes of the church debated in the prince's confiftories, but excufed himfelf to the emperor *Valentinian*, for that being convented to anfwer concerning church matters in a civil court, he came not. We may by thefe teftimonies drawn from antiquity, if we lift to confider them, difcern how requifite it is that authority fhould always follow received laws in the manner of proceeding. For, inafmuch as there was at the firft no certain law determining what force the principal civil magiftrate's authority fhould be of, how far it fhould reach, and what order it fhould obferve; but chriftian emperors from time to time did what themfelves thought moft reafonable in thofe affairs; by this means it cometh to pafs that they in their practice vary, and are not uniform. Virtuous emperors, fuch as *Conftantine* the great was, made confcience to fwerve unneceffarily from the cuftom which had been ufed in the church, even when it lived under infidels; *Conftantine*, of reverence to bifhops and their fpiritual authority, rather abftained from that which himfelf might lawfully do, than was willing to claim a power not fit or decent for him to exercife. The order which hath been before he ratifieth, exhorting the bifhops to look to the church, and promifing that he would do the office of a bifhop over the commonwealth; which very *Conftantine* notwithftanding, did not thereby fo renounce all authority in judging of fpecial caufes, but that fometime he he took, as St. *Augustine* witnesseth, even personal cognition of them; howbeit, whether as purposing to give them judicially any sentence, I stand in doubt. For if the other of whom St. *Augustine* elsewhere speaketh, did in such sort judge, surely there was cause why he should excuse it as a thing not usually done. Otherwise there is no let, but that any such great person may hear those causes to and fro debated, and deliver in the end his own opinion of them, declaring on which side himself doth judge that the truth is. But this kind of sentence bindeth no side to stand thereunto; it is a sentence of private persuasion, and not of solemn jurisdiction, albeit a king, or an emperor pronounce it. Again, on the contrary part, when governors infected with heresy were possessed of the highest power, they thought they might use it as pleased themselves to further by all means that opinion which they desired should prevail; they not respecting at all what was meet, presumed to command and judge all men, in all causes, without either care of orderly proceeding, or regard to such laws and customs as the church had been wont to observe. So that the one sort feared to do even that which they might; and that which the other ought not, they boldly presumed upon; the one sort, of modestly excused themselves where they scarce needed; the other, though doing that which is inexcusable, bear it out with main power, not enduring to be told by any man how far they roved beyond their bounds. So great odds was between them whom before we mentioned, and such as the younger *Valentinian*, by whom St. *Ambrose* being commanded to yield up one of the churches under him unto the *Arians*, whereas they which were sent on his message alledged, that the emperor did but use his own right, forasmuch as all things were in his power; the answer which the holy bishop gave them was, *That the church is the house of God, and that those things that are God's are not to be yielded up, and disposed of at the emperor's will and pleasure; his palaces he might grant to whomsoever he pleaseth, but God's own habitation not so.* A cause why many times emperors do more by their absolute authority than could very well stand with reason, was the overgreat importunity of wicked hereticks, who being enemies to peace and quietness, cannot otherwise than by violent means be supported.

In this respect therefore we must needs think the state of our own church much better setled than theirs was; because our laws have with far more certainty prescribed bounds unto each kind of power. All decision of things doubtful, and correction of things amiss are proceeded in by order of law, what person soever he be unto whom the administration of judgment belongeth. It is neither permitted unto prelates nor prince to judge and determine at their own discretion, but law hath prescribed what both shall do. What power the king hath, he hath it by law, the bounds and limits of it are known; the intire community giveth general order by law, how all things publickly are to be done, and the king, as the head thereof, the highest in authority over all, causeth, according to the same law, every particular to be framed and ordered thereby. The whole body politick maketh laws, which laws gave power unto the king; and the king having bound himself to use according unto law that power, it so falleth out, that the execution of the one is accomplished by the other in most religious and peaceable sort. There is no cause given unto any to make supplication, as *Hilary* did, that civil governors, to whom commonwealth matters only belong, may not presume to take upon them the judgment of ecclesiastical causes. If the cause be spiritual, secular courts do not meddle with it, we need not excuse our selves with *Ambrose*, but boldly and lawfully we may refuse to answer before any civil judge in a matter which is not civil, so that we do not mistake either the nature of the cause or of the court, as we easily may do both, without some better direction than can be by the rules of this new-found discipline. But of this most certain we are, that our laws do neither suffer a * spiritual court to entertain in those causes which by the law are civil; nor yet, if the matter be indeed spiritual, a meer civil court to give judgment of it. Touching supream power therefore to command all men, and in all manner of causes of judgment to be highest, let thus much suffice as well for declaration of our own meaning, as for defence of the truth therein.

* See the statute of *Ed.* 1. and *Ed.* 2. and *Nat. Brev.* touching prohibition. See also in *Bracton* these sentences l. 5. c. 2.

Est jurisdictio ordinaria quædam delegata, quæ pertinet ad sacerdotium, & forum ecclesiasticum, sicut in causis spiritualibus & spiritualitati annexis. Est etiam alia jurisdictio ordinaria vel delegata quæ pertinet ad coronam, & dignitatem regis, & ad regnum in causis & placitis rerum temporalium in foro seculari. *Again*, Cum diversæ sint hinc inde jurisdictiones, & diversi judices, & diversæ causæ, debet quilibet ipsorum imprimis æstimare, an sua sit jurisdictio, ne falcem videatur ponere in messem alienam. *Again*, Non pertinet ad regem injungere pœnitentias, nec ad judicem secularem, nec etiam ad eos pertinet cognoscere de iis quæ sunt spiritualibus annexa, sicut de decimis & aliis ecclesiæ proventionibus. *Again*, Non est laicus conveniendus coram judice ecclesiastico de aliquo quod in foro seculari terminari possit & debeat.

The cause is not like when such assemblies are gathered together by supream authority concerning other affairs of the church, and when they meet about the making of

ecclesiastical

ecclefiaftical laws or ftatutes. For in the one they are only to advife, in the other to decree. The perfons which are of the one, the king doth voluntarily affemble, as being in refpect of quality fit to confult withal; them which are of the other, he calleth by prefcript of law, as having right to be thereunto called. Finally, the one are but themfelves, and their fentence hath but the weight of their own judgment; the other reprefent the whole clergy, and their voices are as much as if all did give perfonal verdict. Now the queftion is, whether the clergy alone fo affembled, ought to have the whole power of making ecclefiaftical laws, or elfe confent of the laity may thereunto be made neceffary, and the king's affent fo neceffary, that his fole denial may be of force to ftay them from being laws.

If they with whom we difpute were uniform, ftrong and conftant in that which they say, we fhould not need to trouble our felves about their perfons, to whom the power of making laws for the church belongs. For they are fometime very vehement in contention, that from the greateft thing unto the leaft about the church, all muft needs be immediately from God. And to this they apply the pattern of the ancient tabernacle which God delivered unto *Mofes*, and was therein fo exact, that there was not left as much as the leaft pin for the wit of man to devife in the framing of it. To this they alfo apply that ftreight and fevere charge which God fo often gave concerning his own law, *Whatfoever I command you, take heed ye do it; thou fhalt put nothing thereto, thou fhalt take nothing from it;* nothing, whether it be great or fmall. Yet fometimes be-thinking themfelves better, they fpeak as acknowledging that it doth fuffice to have received in fuch fort the principal things from God, and that for other matters the church had fufficient authority to make laws. Whereupon they now have made it a queftion, what perfons they are whofe right it is to take order for the church's affairs, when the inftitution of any new thing therein is requifite. Law may be requifite to be made, either concerning things that are only to be known and believed in, or elfe touching that which is to be done by the church of God. The law of nature, and the law of God, are fufficient for declaration in both what belongeth unto each man feparately, as his foul is the fpoufe of Chrift; yea, fo fufficient, that they plainly and fully fhew whatfoever God doth require by way of neceffary introduction unto the ftate of everlafting blifs. But as a man liveth joined with others in common fociety, and belongeth to the outward politick body of the church, albeit the fame law of nature and fcripture have in this refpect alfo made manifeft the things that are of greateft neceffity; neverthelefs, by reafon of new occafions ftill arifing, which the church, having care of fouls, muft take order for as need requireth; hereby it cometh to pafs, that there is, and ever will be, fo great ufe even of human laws and ordinances, deducted by way of difcourfe as a conclufion from the former divine and natural, ferving as principals thereunto. No man doubteth, but that for matters of action and practice in the affairs of God, for manner in divine fervice, for order in ecclefiaftical proceedings about the regiment of the church, there may be oftentimes caufe very urgent to have laws made: but the reafon is not fo plain, wherefore human laws fhould appoint men what to believe. Wherefore in this we muft note two things: 1, That in matters of opinion, the law doth not make that to be truth which before was not, as in matter of action it caufeth that to be a duty which was not before; but manifefteth only and giveth men notice of that to be truth, the contrary whereunto they ought not before to have believed. 2. That opinions do cleave to the underftanding, and are in heart affented unto, it is not in the power of any human law to command them, becaufe to prefcribe what men fhall think belongeth only unto God: *Corde creditur, ore fit confeffio,* faith the apoftle. As opinions are either fit or inconvenient to be profefs'd, fo man's laws hath to determine of them. It may for publick unity's fake require mens profeffed affent, or prohibit their contradiction to fpecial articles, wherein, as there haply hath been controverfy what is true, fo the fame were like to continue ftill, not without grievous detriment unto a number of fouls, except law, to remedy that evil, fhould fet down a certainty which no man afterwards is to gainfay. Wherefore, as in regard of divine laws, which the church receiveth from God, we may unto every man apply thofe words of wifdom in *Solomon, My fon, keep thou thy father's precepts; Conferva, fili mi, præcepta patris tui:* even fo concerning the ftatutes and ordinances which the church it felf makes, we may add thereunto the words that follow, *Et ne dimittas legem matris tuæ, And forfake thou not thy mother's law.*

It is a thing even undoubtedly natural, that all free and *independent* focieties fhould themfelves make their own laws, and that this power fhould belong to the whole, not to any certain part of a politick body, tho' haply fome one part may have greater fway in that action than the reft; which thing being generally fit and expedient in the making

What laws may be made for the affairs of the church, and to whom the power of making them appertaineth.

Deut. 12. 32. and 4. 2. Jofh. 1. 7.

Rom. 1. 2. queft. 108. Art. 2.

Prov. 6.

2   of

of all laws, we fee no caufe why to think otherwife in laws concerning the fervice of God, which in all well-ordered ftates and commonwealths is the ª firft thing that law hath care to provide for. When we fpeak of the right which naturally belongeth to a commonwealth, we fpeak of that which muft needs belong to the church of God. For if the commonwealth be chriftian, if the people which are of it do publickly embrace the true religion, this very thing doth make it the church, as hath been fhewed. So that unlefs the verity and purity of religion do take from them which embrace it that power wherewith otherwife they are poffeffed; look what authority, as touching laws for religion, a commonwealth hath fimply, it muft of neceffity retain the fame, being of the chriftian religion.

ᵃ Δεῖ τ νέμειν τὰ God, Θεοῖς, ἥ Δαίμοσιν ἡ γέ-νει, ἢ ἰδίᾳ τὰ μαλιᾶ ἡ τιμία, πρῶ τὰ τίμια. Δεύτερον ᵇ τὰ Συμφέροντα, τὰ γὰρ μείρω τὰ μείζονα ἀναλο- γοῦντα ᵇᵉ Ῥ. Ἀριστ. de leg. & infra. That is; it behov- eth the law firft to eftablish or fettle thofe things which belong to the gods, and divine powers, and to our parents, and univerfally thofe things which be vertuous and honourable. In the fecond place, thofe things that be convenient and profitable; for it is fit that matters of the lefs weight fhould come after the greater.

It will be therefore perhaps alledged, that a part of the verity of chriftian religion is to hold the power of making ecclefiaftical laws a thing appropriated unto the clergy in their fynods; and whatfoever is by their only voices agreed upon, it needeth no further approbation to give unto it the ftrength of a law, as may plainly appear by the canons of that firft moft venerable affembly: where thofe things the apoftles and *James* had con-cluded, were afterwards publifhed and impofed upon the churches of the Gentiles abroad as laws, the records thereof remaining ftill in the book of God for a teftimony, that the power of making ecclefiaftical laws belongeth to the fucceffors of the apoftles, the bifhops and prelates of the church of God.

To this we anfwer, that the council of *Jerufalem* is no argument for the power of the clergy to make laws. For firft, there has not been fithence any council of like au-thority to that in *Jerufalem*. Secondly, The caufe why that was of fuch authority, came by a fpecial accident. Thirdly, the reafon why other councils being not like un-to that in nature, the clergy in them fhould have no power to make laws by themfelves alone, is in truth fo forcible, that except fome commandment of God to the contrary can be fhewed, it ought notwithftanding the aforefaid example to prevail.

The decrees of the council of *Jerufalem* were not as the canons of other ecclefiafti-cal affemblies, human, but very divine ordinances: for which caufe the churches were far and wide commanded every where to fee them kept, no otherwife than if Chrift him-felf had perfonally on earth been the author of them. The caufe why that council was of fo great authority and credit above all others which have been fithence is exprefs'd in thofe words of principal obfervation, *Unto the holy Ghoft, and to us it hath feemed good:* which form of fpeech, tho' other councils have likewife ufed, yet neither could they themfelves mean, nor may we fo underftand them, as if both were in equal fort af-fifted with the power of the holy Ghoft; but the latter had the favour of that general affiftance and prefence which Chrift doth promife unto all his, according to the quality of their feveral eftates and callings; the former, the grace of fpecial, miraculous, rare and extraordinary illumination, in relation whereunto the apoftle comparing the old tefta-ment and the new together, termeth the one a teftament of the letter, for that God de-livered it written in ftone; the other a teftament of the Spirit, becaufe God imprinted it in the hearts, and declared it by the tongues of his chofen apoftles, thro' the power of the holy Ghoft, feigning both their conceits and fpeeches in moft divine and incompre-henfible manner. Wherefore, inafmuch as the council of *Jerufalem* did chance to con-fift of men fo enlightned, it had authority greater than were meet for any other council befides to challenge, wherein fuch kind of perfons are, as now the ftate of the church doth ftand; kings being not then that which now they are, and the clergy not now that which then they were. Till it be proved that fome fpecial law of Chrift hath for ever annexed unto the clergy alone the power to make ecclefiaftical laws, we are to hold it a thing moft confonant with equity and reafon, that no ecclefiaftical laws be made in a chriftian commonwealth, without confent as well of the laity as of the clergy, but leaft of all without confent of the higheft power.

For of this thing no man doubteth, namely, that in all focieties, companies, and cor-porations, what feverally each fhall be bound unto, it muft be with all their affents ra-tified. Againft all equity it were, that a man fhould fuffer detriment at the hands of men, for not obferving that which he never did, either by himfelf or by others, medi-ately or immediately, agree unto. Much more then a king fhould conftrain all others to the ftrict obfervation of any fuch human ordinance as paffeth without his own approba-tion, in this cafe therefore efpecially, that vulgar axiom is of force, *Quod omnes tangit, ab omnibus tractari & approbari debet*. Whereupon pope *Nicholas*, altho' otherwife not

Acts 15. 7. 13, 23.

v. 4.

Matth. 16. Chap. ult.

2 Cor. 3.

Cap. delict. de excefi. prælator L. per fundum ruſticor. præd. & fect. religiofum de rerum divif. Glofſ. dict. 96. c. ubinam.

2   not

not admitting lay-perfons, no not emperors themfelves, to be prefent at fynods, doth notwithstanding feem to allow of their prefence, when matters of faith are determined whereunto all men muft ftand bound: *Ubinam legiftis imperatores anteceffores veftros, fynodalibus conventibus interfuiffe; nifi forfitan in quibus de fide tractatum eft, quæ non folum ad clericos, verum etiam ad laicos & omnes pertinet chriftianos?* A law, be it civil or ecclefiaftical, is a publick obligation, wherein, feeing that the whole ftandeth charged, no reafon it fhould pafs without his privity and will, whom principally the whole doth depend upon. *Sicut laici jurifdictionem clericorum perturbare, ita clerici jurifdictionem laicorum non debent minuere,* faith *Innocentius, Extra de judic. novit. As the laity fhould not hinder the clergy's jurifdiction, fo neither is it reafon that the laity's right fhould be abridged by the clergy,* faith pope *Innocent.* But were it fo that the clergy alone might give laws unto all the reft, forafmuch as every eftate doth defire to enlarge the bounds of their own liberties, is it not eafy to fee how injurious this might prove to men of other conditions? Peace and juftice are maintained by pre- ferving unto every order their right, and by keeping all eftates, as it were in an even balance. Which thing is no way better done, than if the king, their common pa- rent, whofe care is prefumed to extend moft indifferently over all, do bear the chiefeft fway in making laws which all muft be ordered by. Wherefore of them which in this point attribute moft to the clergy, I would demand, what evidence there is where- by it may clearly be fhew'd that in ancient kingdoms chriftian, any canon devifed by the clergy alone in their fynods, whether provincial, national, or general, hath, by mere force of their agreement, taken place as a law, making all men conftrainable to be obe- dient thereunto, without any other approbation from the king, before or afterwards re- quired in that behalf. But what fpeak we of ancient kingdoms, when at this day, even the papacy it felf, the very *Tridental* council hath not every where as yet ob- tained to have in all points the ftrength of ecclefiaftical laws; did not *Philip* king of *Spain,* publishing that council in the low countries, add thereunto an exprefs claufe of fpecial provifion, that the fame fhould in no wife prejudice, hurt, or diminifh any kind of privilege which the king or his vaffals afore-time had enjoyed, touching either poffeffory judgments of ecclefiaftical livings, or concerning nominations thereunto, or belonging to whatfoever right they had elfe in fuch affairs? If therefore the king's ex- ception, taken againft fome part of the canons contained in that council, were a fuf- ficient bar to make them of none effect within his territories; it follows that the like exception againft any other part had been alfo of like efficacy; and fo confequently that no part thereof had obtained the ftrength of a law, if he which excepted againft a part, had fo done againft the whole. As, what reafon was there, but that the fame authority which limited, might quite and clean have refufed that council? Whofo al- loweth the faid act of the catholick king's for good and lawful, muft grant that the canons, even of general councils, have but the face of wife mens opinions concerning that whereof they treat, till they be publickly affented unto, where they are to take place as laws; and that, in giving fuch publick affent as maketh a chriftian kingdom fubject unto thofe laws, the king's authority is the chiefeft. That which an univerfity of men, a company, a corporation, doth without confent of their rector is as nothing. Except therefore we make the king's authority over the clergy lefs in the greateft things, than the power of the meaneft governor is in all things over the college, or fociety which is under him; how fhould we think it a matter decent, that the clergy fhould impofe laws, the fupreme governor's affent not afked?

Yea, that which is more, the laws thus made, God himfelf doth in fuch fort autho- rize, that to defpife them, is to defpife in them, him. It is a loofe and licentious opinion, which the *Anabaptifts* have embraced, holding that a chriftian man's liberty is loft, and the foul which Chrift hath redeemed unto himfelf injurioufly drawn into fervitude under the yoke of human power, if any law be now impofed befides the gofpel of Chrift; in obe- dience whereunto the Spirit of God, and not the conftraint of men, is to lead us, accord- ing to that of the bleffed apoftle, *Such as are led by the Spirit of God, they are the fons of God, and not fuch as live in thraldom* unto men. Their judgment is therefore, that the church of Chrift fhould admit of no law-makers but the evangelifts, no courts but presbyters, no punifhments but ecclefiaftical cenfures. Againft this fort, we are to main- tain the ufe of human laws, and the continual neceffity of making them from time to time, as long as this prefent world doth laft; fo likewife the authority of laws fo made doth need much more by us to be ftrengthned againft another fort; who, although they do utterly condemn the making of laws in the church, yet make they a deal lefs account of them than they fhould do. There are which think fimply of human laws, that they

can

Boet. Epod. heroic. quæft. l. 1. fect. 28,

can in no fort touch the confcience. That to break and tranfgrefs them, cannot make men in the fight of God culpable, as fin doth; only when we violate fuch laws, we do thereby make our felves obnoxious unto external punifhment in this world, fo that the magiftrate may, in regard of fuch offence committed, juftly correct the offender, and caufe him, without injury, to endure fuch pains as law doth appoint, but further it reacheth not. For firft, the confcience is the proper court of God, the guiltinefs thereof is fin, and the punifhment eternal death; men are not able to make any law that fhall command the heart, it is not in them to make inward conceit a crime, or to appoint for any crime other punifhment than corporal; their laws therefore can have no power over the foul, neither can the heart of man be polluted by tranfgreffing them. St. *Auftin* rightly defineth fin to be that which is fpoken, done, or defired, not againft any laws, but againft the law of the living God. The law of God is propofed unto man, as a glafs wherein to behold the ftains and the fpots of their finful fouls. By it they are to judge themfelves, and when they feel themfelves to have tranfgreffed againft it, then to bewail their offences with *David*, *Againft thee only, O Lord, have I finned, and done wickedly in thy fight*; that fo our prefent tears may extinguifh the flames, which otherwife we are to feel, and which God in that day fhall condemn the wicked unto, when they fhall render account of the evil which they have done, not by violating ftatute-laws and canons, but by difobedience unto his law and his word.

For our better inftruction therefore concerning this point, firft we muft note, that the law of God it felf doth require at our hands, fubjection. *Be ye fubject*, faith St. *Peter*; and St. *Paul*, *Let every foul be fubject*; *fubject all unto fuch powers as are fet over us*. For if fuch as are not fet over us require our fubjection, we by denying it are not difobedient to the law of God, or unduriful unto higher powers; becaufe, though they be fuch in regard of them over whom they have lawful dominion, yet having not fo over us, unto us they are not fuch. Subjection therefore we owe, and that by the law of God; we are in confcience bound to yield it even unto every of them that hold the feats of authority and power in relation unto us. Howbeit, not all kinds of fubjection unto every fuch kind of power. Concerning *Scribes* and *Pharifees*, our Saviour's precept was, *Whatfoever they fhall tell ye, do it*: Was it his meaning, that if they fhould at any time enjoin the people to levy any army, or to fell their lands and goods for the furtherance of fo great an enterprize; and, in a word, that fimply whatfoever they did command, they ought, without any exception, forthwith to be obeyed? No, but whatfoever they fhall tell you, muft be underftood *in pertinentibus ad cathedram*, it muft be conftrued with limitation, and reftrained unto things of that kind which did belong to their place and power. For they had not power general, abfolutely given them to command all things. The reafon why we are bound in confcience to be fubject unto all fuch power, is, becaufe *all powers are of God*.

They are of God either inftituting or permitting them. Power is then of divine inftitution, when either God himfelf doth deliver, or men by light of nature find out the kind thereof. So that the power of parents over children, and of hufbands over their wives, the power of all forts of fuperiors, made by confent of commonwealths within themfelves, or grown from agreement amongft nations, fuch power is of God's own inftitution in refpect of the kind thereof. Again, if refpect be had unto thofe particular perfons to whom the fame is derived, if they either receive it immediately from God, as *Mofes* and *Aaron* did; or from nature, as parents do; or from men by a natural and orderly courfe, as every governor appointed in any commonwealth, by the order thereof, doth; then is not the kind of their power only of God's inftituting, but the derivation thereof alfo, into their perfons is from him. He hath placed them in their rooms, and doth term them his minifters; fubjection therefore is due unto all fuch powers, inafmuch as they are of God's own inftitution, even then when they are of man's creation, *Omni humanæ creaturæ*: which things the heathens themfelves do acknowledge.

ΣκηπίȣχΘ. Βασιλεὺς ὅτι Ζεὺς κῦδΘ. ἔδωκεν.

As for them that exercife power altogether againft order, although the kind of power which they have may be of God, yet is their exercife thereof againft God, and therefore not of God, otherwife than by *permiffion*, as all injuftice is.

Touching fuch acts as are done by that power which is according to his inftitution, that God in like fort doth authorize them, and account them to be his; though it were not confeffed, it might be proved undeniably. For if that be accounted our deed, which others do, whom we have appointed to be our agents, how fhould God but approve thofe deeds, even as his own, which are done by virtue of that commiffion and power which

I   he

Margin notes:

Verum ac proprium civis à peregrino diferimen eſt, quòd alter imperio ac poteſtate civili obligatur, alter juſſa principis alieni refpuere poteſt. Illum law of God; princeps ab hoſtium æque ac civium injuria tueri tenetur, hunc non item niſi rogatus & humanitatis officiis impulfus, faith *Bodin. de* rep.l.1.c.6.non multum à fine p.61. edit. Lugd. B. in fol. 1586.

Hom. Il. l. 2.
A fcepter fwaying king, to whom even *Jupiter* himfelf hath given honour and command mandment.

he hath given. *Take heed* (faith *Jehofaphat* unto his judges) *be careful and circumfpect what ye do, ye do not execute the judgments of man, but of the Lord,* 2 Chron. 19. 6. The authority of *Cæfar* over the *Jews*, from whence was it? Had it any other ground than the law of nations, which maketh kingdoms, fubdued by juft war, to be fubject unto their conquerors? By this power *Cæfar* exacting tribute, our Saviour confeffeth it to be his right, a right which could not be with-held without injury, yea difobedience herein unto him, and even rebellion againft God. Ufurpers of power, whereby we do not mean them that by violence have afpired unto places of higheft authority, but them that ufe more authority than they did ever receive in form and manner beforementioned; (for fo they may do, whofe title to the rooms of authority which they poffefs, no man can deny to be juft and lawful: even as contrariwife fome mens proceedings in government have been very orderly, who notwithftanding did not attain to be made governors without great violence and diforder) fuch ufurpers thereof, as in the exercife of their power do more than they have been authorized to do, cannot in confcience bind any man unto obedience.

That fubjection which we owe unto lawful powers, doth not only import that we fhould be under them by order of our ftate, but that we fhew all fubmiffion towards them both by honour and obedience. He that refifteth them, refifteth God: and refift-ed they be, if either the authority it felf which they exercife be denied, as by anabaptifts all fecular jurifdictions; or if refiftance be made but only fo far forth as doth touch their perfons which are invefted with power; (for they which faid, *Nolumus hunc regnare,* did not utterly exclude regiment; nor did they wifh all kind of government clearly remo-ved, which would not at the firft have *David* to govern) or if that which they do by vir-tue of their power, namely, their laws, edicts, fervices, or other acts of jurifdiction, be not fuffered to take effect, contrary to the bleffed apoftle's moft holy rule, *Obey them who have the overfight of you,* Heb. 13. 17. or if they do take effect, yet is not the will of God thereby fatisfied neither, as long as that which we do is contemptuoufly, or repi-ningly done, becaufe we can do no otherwife. In fuch fort the *Ifraelites* in the defart obeyed *Mofes,* and were notwithftanding defervedly plagued for difobedience. The apo-ftle's precept therefore is, *Be fubject even for God's caufe; be fubject, not for fear, but of meer confcience, knowing, that he which refifteth them, purchafeth to himfelf con-demnation.* Difobedience therefore unto laws which are made by them, is not a thing of fo fmall account as fome would make it.

Howbeit too rigorous it were, that the breach of every human law fhould be held a deadly fin: a mean there is between thefe extremities, if fo be we can find it out.

TO THE

READER.

THE pleasures of thy spacious walks in Mr. Hooker's temple-garden (not unfitly so called, both for the temple whereof he was master, and the subject, Ecclesiastical Polity) do promise acceptance to these flowers, planted and watered by the same hand, and, for thy sake composed into this posy. Sufficiently are they commended by their fragrant smell, in the dogmatical truth ; by their beautiful colours, in the accurate style ; by their medicinable virtue, against some diseases in our neighbour churches, now proving epidemical, and threatning farther infection ; by their streight feature and spreading nature, growing from the root of faith (which, as here is proved, can never be rooted up) and extending the branches of charity to the covering of Noah's nakedness ; opening the windows of hope to men's misty conceits of their bemisted fore-fathers. Thus, and more than thus, do the works commend themselves ; the workman needs a better workman to commend him ; (Alexander's picture requires Apelles his pencil) nay, he needs it not, His own works commend him in the gates ; and, being dead he yet speaketh ; the syllables of that memorable name Mr. Richard Hooker, proclaiming more, than if I should here stile him, a painful student, a profound scholar, a judicious writer, with other due titles of his honour. Receive then this posthume orphan for his own, yea, for thine own sake ; and if the printer hath with overmuch haste, like Mephibosheth's nurse, lamed the child with slips and falls, yet be thou of David's mind, shew kindness to him for his father Jonathan's sake. God grant, that the rest of his brethren be not more than lamed, and that as Saul's three sons died the same day with him, so those three promised to perfect his Polity, with other issues of that learned brain, be not buried in the grave with their renowned father. Farewel.

W. S.

The Contents of the Treatises following.

A
SUPPLICATION

Made to the

COUNCIL

B Y

Mafter Walter Travers.

Right Honourable,

THE manifold benefits which all the fubjects within this dominion do at this prefent, and have many years enjoyed, under her majefty's moft happy and profperous reign, by your godly wifdom and careful watching over this eftate night and day, I truly and unfeignedly acknowledge from the bottom of my heart, ought worthily to bind us all to pray continually to almighty God for the continuance and increafe of the life and good eftate of your honours, and to be ready, with all good duties, to fatisfy and ferve the fame to our power. Befides publick benefits common unto all, I muft needs, and do willingly confefs my felf to ftand bound by moft fpecial obligation, to ferve and honour you more than any other, for the honourable favour it hath pleafed you to vouchfafe both oftentimes heretofore, and alfo now of late, in a matter more dear unto me than my earthly commodity, that is, the upholding and furthering of my fervice in the miniftring of the gofpel of Jefus Chrift. For which caufe, as I have been always careful fo to carry my felf as I might by no means give occafion to be thought unworthy of fo great a benefit, fo do I ftill, next unto her majefty's gracious countenance, hold nothing more dear and precious to me, than that I may always remain in your honours favour, which hath oftentimes been helpful and comfortable unto me in my miniftry, and to all fuch as reaped any fruit of my fimple and faithful labour. In which dutiful regard I humbly befeech your honours to vouchfafe to do me this grace, to conceive nothing of me otherwife than according to the duty wherein I ought to live, by any information againft me, before your honours have heard my anfwer, and been throughly informed of the matter. Which, altho' it be a thing that your wifdoms, not in favour, but in juftice, yield to all men, yet the ftate of the calling into the miniftry, whereunto it hath pleafed God of his goodnefs to call me, though unworthieft of all, is fo fubject to mifinformation, as, except we may find

this

this favour with your honours, we cannot look for any other, but that our unindifferent parties may eafily procure us to be hardly efteemed of; and that we fhall be made like the poor fifher-boats in the fea, which every fwelling wave and billow raketh and runeth over. Wherein my eftate is yet harder than any others of my rank and calling, who are indeed to fight againft flefh and blood in what part foever of the Lord's hoft and field they fhall ftand marfhalled to ferve, yet many of them deal with it naked, and unfurnifhed of weapons: but my fervice was in a place where I was to encounter with it well appointed and armed with fkill and with authority, whereof as I have always thus deferved, and therefore have been careful by all good means to entertain ftill your honours favourable refpect of me, fo have I fpecial caufe at this prefent, wherein mifinformation to the lord archbifhop of *Canterbury*, and other of the high commiffion hath been able fo far to prevail againft me, that by their letter they have inhibited me to preach, or execute any act of miniftry, in the *Temple* or elfewhere, having never once called me before them, to underftand by mine anfwer the truth of fuch things as had been informed againft me. We have a ftory in our books, wherein the *Pharifees* proceeding againft our Saviour Chrift, without having heard him, are reproved by an honourable councellor (as the evangelift doth term him) faying, *Doth our law judge a man before it hear him, and know what he hath done?* Which I do not mention, to the end that by an indirect and covert fpeech I might fo compare thofe who have, without ever hearing me, pronounced a heavy fentence againft me; for notwithftanding fuch proceedings, I purpofe by God's grace to carry my felf towards them in all feeming duty, agreeable to their places: much lefs do I prefume to liken my caufe to our Saviour Chrift's, who hold it my chiefeft honour and happinefs to ferve him, tho' it be but among the hinds and hired fervants, that ferve him in the bafeft corners of his houfe: but my purpofe in mentioning it is, to fhew by the judgment of a prince and great man in *Ifrael*, that fuch proceeding ftandeth not with the law of God, and in a princely pattern to fhew it to be a noble part of an honourable councellor, not to allow of indirect dealings, but to allow and affect fuch a courfe in juftice as is agreeable to the law of God. We have alfo a plain rule in the word of God, not to proceed any otherwife againft any elder of the church; much lefs againft one that laboureth in the word, and in teaching. Which rule is delivered with this moft earneft charge and obteftation, *I befeech and charge thee in the fight of God, and the Lord Jefus Chrift, and the elect angels, that thou keep thofe [rules] without preferring one before another, doing nothing of partiality, or inclining to either part*; which apoftolical and moft earneft charge, I refer to your honours wifdom how it hath been regarded in fo heavy a judgment againft me, without ever hearing my caufe; and whether, as having God before their eyes, and the Lord Jefus, by whom all former judgments fhall be tried again; and, as in the prefence of the elect angels, witneffes and obfervers of the regiment of the church, they have proceeded thus to fuch a fentence. They alledge indeed two reafons in their letters, whereupon they reftrain my miniftry; which, if they were as ftrong againft me as they are fuppofed, yet I refer to your honours wifdoms, whether the quality of fuch an offence as they charge me with, which is in effect but an indifcretion, deferve fo grievous a punifhment both to the church and me, in taking away my miniftry, and that poor little commodity which it yieldeth for the neceffary maintenance of my life; if fo unequal a balancing of faults and punifhments fhould have place in the commonwealth, furely we fhould fhortly have no actions upon the cafe, nor of trefpafs, but all fhould be pleas of the crown, nor any man amerced, or fined, but for every light offence put to his ranfom. I have credibly heard, that fome of the miniftry have been committed for grievous tranfgreffions of the laws of God and men, being of no ability to do other fervice in the church than to read, yet hath it been thought charitable, and ftanding with chriftian moderation and temperance, not to deprive fuch of miniftry and beneficence, but to inflict fome more tolerable punifhment. Which I write, not becaufe fuch, as I think, were to be favoured, but to fhew how unlike their dealing is with me, being through the goodnefs of God not to be touched with any fuch blame; and one, who, according to the meafure of the gift of God, have laboured now fome years painfully, in regard of the weak eftate of my body, in preaching the gofpel, and, as I hope, not altogether unprofitably, in refpect of the church. But I befeech your honour's to give me leave briefly to declare the particular reafons of their letter, and what anfwer I have to make to it.

The firft is, that, as they fay, *I am not lawfully called to the function of the miniftry, nor allowed to preach, according to the laws of the church of* England.

For

For anfwer to this, I had need to divide the points. And firft to make anfwer to the former; wherein leaving to fhew what by the holy fcriptures is required in a lawful calling, and that all this is to be found in mine, that I be not too long for your weighty affairs, I reft.

I thus anfwer. My calling to the miniftry was fuch as, in the calling of any thereunto, is appointed to be ufed by the orders agreed upon in the national fynods of the Low-countries, for the direction and guidance of their churches ; which orders are the fame with thofe whereby the *French* and *Scotifh* churches are governed ; whereof I have fhewed fuch fufficient teftimonial to my lord the archbifhop of *Canterbury*, as is requifite in fuch a matter : whereby it muft needs fall out, if any man be lawfully called to the miniftry in thofe churches, then is my calling, being the fame with theirs, alfo lawful. But I fuppofe, notwithftanding they ufe this general fpeech, they mean only, my calling is not fufficient to deal in the miniftry within this land, becaufe I was not made minifter according to that order, which in this cafe is ordained by our laws. Whereunto I befeech your honours to confider throughly of mine anfwer, becaufe exception now again is taken to my miniftry, whereas having been heretofore called in queftion for it, I fo anfwered the matter, as I continued in my miniftry, and, for any thing I difcerned, looked to hear that no more would be objected unto me. The communion of faints (which every chriftian man profeffeth to believe) is fuch, as that the acts which are done in any true church of Chrift's according to his word, are held as lawful, being done in one church as in another. Which, as it holdeth in other acts of miniftry, as baptifm, marriage, and fuch like, fo doth it in the calling to the miniftry ; by reafon whereof, all churches do acknowledge and receive him for a minifter of the word, who hath been lawfully called thereunto in any church of the fame profeffion. A doctor created in any univerfity of Chriftendom, is acknowledged fufficiently qualified to teach in any country. The church of *Rome* it felf, and the canon-law holdeth it, that being ordered in *Spain*, they may execute that belongeth to their order in *Italy*, or in any other place. And the churches of the gofpel never made any queftion of it ; which if they fhall now begin to make doubt of, and deny fuch to be lawfully called to the miniftry, as are called by another order than our own ; then may it well be looked for, that other churches will do the like : and if a minifter called in the Low-countries be not lawfully called in *England*, then may they fay to our preachers which are there, that being made of another order than theirs, they cannot fuffer them to execute any act of miniftry amongft them ; which in the end muft needs breed a fchifm, and dangerous divifions in the churches. Further, I have heard of thofe that are learned in the laws of this land, that by exprefs ftatute to that purpofe, *Anno* 13. upon fubfcription to the articles agreed upon, *Anno* 62. that they who pretend to have been ordered by another order than that which is now eftablifhed, are of like capacity to enjoy any place of miniftry within the land, as they which have been ordered according to that which is now by law in this eftablifhed. Which comprehending manifeftly all, even fuch as were made priefts according to the order of the church of *Rome*, it muft needs be, that the law of a chriftian land, profeffing the gofpel, fhould be as favourable for a minifter of the word, as for a popifh prieft ; which alfo was fo found in Mr. *Whittingham's* cafe, who notwithftanding fuch replies againft him, enjoyed ftill the benefit he had by his miniftry, and might have done until this day, if God had fpared him life fo long ; which, if it be underftood fo, and practifed in others, why fhould the change of the perfon alter the right which the law giveth to all others ?

The place of miniftry whereunto I was called, was not prefentative : and if it had been fo, furely they would never have prefented any man whom they never knew ; and the order of this church is agreeable herein to the word of God, and the ancient and beft canons, that no man fhould be made a minifter *fine titulo :* therefore having none, I could not by the orders of this church have entred into the miniftry, before I had a charge to tend upon. When I was at *Antwerp*, and to take a place of miniftry among the people of that nation, I fee no caufe why I fhould have returned again over the feas for orders here ; nor how I could have done it, without difallowing the orders of the churches provided in the country where I was to live. Whereby I hope it appeareth, that my calling to the miniftry is lawful, and maketh me, by our law, of capacity to enjoy any benefit or commodity, that any other, by reafon of his miniftry, may enjoy. But my caufe is yet more eafy, who reaped no benefit of my miniftry by law, receiving only a benevolence and voluntary contribution ; and the miniftry I dealt with, being preaching only, which every deacon here may do, being licenfed, and certain that are neither minifters nor deacons. Thus I anfwer the former of thefe two points, whereof, if there be yet any doubt, I humbly defire, for a final end thereof, that fome

competent

competent judges in law may determine of it; whereunto I refer and submit my self with all reverence and duty.

The second is, *That I preached without licence.* Whereunto, this is my answer; I have not presumed, upon the calling I had to the ministry abroad, to preach or deal with any part of the ministry within this church, without the consent and allowance of such as were to allow me unto it. My allowance was from the bishop of *London*, testified by his two several letters to the *Inner Temple*, who without such testimony would by no means rest satisfied in it: which letters being by me produced, I refer it to your honours wisdom, whether I have taken upon me to preach, without being allowed (as they charge) according to the orders of the realm. Thus having answered the second point also, I have done with the objection, *Of dealing without calling or licence.*

The other reason they alledge, is, concerning a late action, wherein I had to deal with Mr. *Hooker*, master of the *Temple*. In the handling of which cause, they charge me with an indiscretion, and want of duty, *in that I inveighed* (as they say) *against certain points of doctrine taught by him, as erroneous, not conferring with him, nor complaining of it to them.* My answer hereunto standeth, in declaring to your honours the whole course and carriage of that cause, and the degrees of proceeding in it, which I will do as briefly as I can, and according to the truth, God be my witness, as near as my best memory, and notes of remembrance, may serve me thereunto. After that I have taken away that which seemed to have moved them to think me not charitably minded to Mr. *Hooker*; which is, because he was brought into Mr. *Alvey's* place, wherein this church desired that I might have succeeded: which place, if I would have made suit to have obtained, or if I had ambitiously affected and sought, I would not have refused to have satisfied, by subscription, such as the matter then seemed to depend upon: whereas contrariwise, notwithstanding I would not hinder the church to do that they thought to be most for their edification and comfort, yet did I, neither by speech nor letter, make suit to any for the obtaining of it, following herein that resolution, which I judge to be most agreeable to the word and will of God; that is, that labouring and suing for places and charges in the church is not lawful. Further, whereas at the suit of the church, some of your honours entertained the cause, and brought it to a near issue, that there seemed nothing to remain, but the commendation of my Lord the archbishop of *Canterbury*, when as he could not be satisfied, but by my subscribing to his late articles; and that my answer agreeing to subscribe according to any law, and to the statute provided in that case, but praying to be respited for subscribing to any other, which I could not in conscience do, either for the *Temple* (which otherwise he said he would not commend me to) nor for any other place in the church, did so little please my lord archbishop as he resolved that otherwise I should not be commended to it. I had utterly here no cause of offence against Mr. *Hooker*, whom I did in no sort esteem to have prevented or undermined me, but that God disposed of me as it pleased him, by such means and occasions as I have declared.

Moreover, as I have taken no cause of offence at Mr. *Hooker* for being preferred, so there were many witnesses, that I was glad that the place was given him, hoping to live in all godly peace and comfort with him, both for acquaintance and goodwill which hath been between us, and for some kind of affinity in the marriage of his nearest kindred and mine. Since his coming, I have so carefully endeavoured to entertain all good correspondence and agreement with him, as I think he himself will bear me witness of many earnest disputations and conferences with him about the matter; the rather, because that, contrary to my expectation, he inclined from the beginning but finally thereunto, but joined rather with such as had always opposed themselves in this charge, and made themselves to be brought indisposed to his present state and proceedings. For, both knowing that God's commandment charged me with such duty, and discerning how much our peace might further the good service of God and his church, and the mutual comfort of us both, I had resolved constantly to seek for peace; and though it should fly from me (as I saw it did by means of some, who little desired to see the good of our church) yet according to the rule of God's word, to follow after it. Which being so (as hereof I take God to witness, who searcheth the heart and reins, and who by his Son will judge the world, both quick and dead) I hope no charitable judgment can suppose me to have stood evil-affected towards him for his place, or desirous to fall into any controversy with him.

Which my resolution I pursued, that, whereas I discovered sundry unsound matters in his doctrine (as many of his sermons tasted some sour leaven or other) yet thus I

2   carried

catried my felf towards him. Matters of fmaller weight, and fo covertly difcovered, that no great offence to the church was to be feared in them, I wholly paffed by, as one that difcerned nothing of them, or had been unfurnifhed of replies; for others of great moment, and fo openly delivered, as there was juft caufe of fear left the truth and church of God fhould be prejudiced and perilled by it, and fuch as the confeience of my duty and calling would not fuffer me altogether to pafs over, this was my courfe, to deliver, when I fhould have juft caufe by my text, the truth of fuch doctrine as he had other-wife taught, in general fpeeches, without touch of his perfon in any fort; and further at convenient opportunity to confer with him in fuch points.

According to which determination, whereas he had taught certain things concerning predeftination otherwife than the word of God doth, as it is underftood by all churches profeffing the gofpel, and not unlike that wherewith *Coranus* fometimes troubled his church, I both delivered the truth of fuch points in a general doctrine, without any touch of him in particular, and conferred with him alfo privately upon fuch articles. In which conference, I remember, when I urged the confent of all churches and good writers againft him that I knew; and defired, if it were otherwife, what authors he had feen of fuch doctrine: he anfwered me, that his beft author was his own reafon; which I wifhed him to take heed of, as a matter ftanding with chriftian modefty and wifdom in a doctrine not received by the church, not to truft to his own judgment fo far as to publifh it before he had conferred with others of his profeffion labouring by daily prayer and ftudy to know the will of God, as he did, to fee how they underftood fuch doctrine. Notwith-ftanding, he, with wavering, replied, that he would fome other time deal more largely in the matter. I wifhed him, and prayed him not fo to do, for the peace of the church, which, by fuch means, might be hazarded; feeing he could not but think, that men, who make any confcience of their miniftry, will judge it a neceffary duty in them, to teach the truth, and to convince the contrary.

Another time, upon like occafion of this doctrine of his, *That the affurance of that we believe by the word, is not fo certain, as of that we perceive by fenfe*; I both taught the doctine otherwife, namely, the affurance of faith to be greater, which affured both of things above, and contrary to all fenfe and human underftanding, and dealt with him alfo privately upon that point: according to which courfe of late, when as he had taught, *That the church of* Rome *is a true church of Chrift, and a fanctified church by profeffion of that truth, which God hath revealed unto us by his Son, tho' not a pure and perfect church;* and further, *That he doubted not, but that thoufands of the fathers, which li-ved and died in the fuperftitions of that church, were faved, becaufe of their ignorance, which excufeth them;* mif-alledging to that end a text of fcripture to prove it: the mat-[1 Tim. 1. 13] ter being of fet purpofe openly and at large handled by him, and of that moment, that might prejudice the faith of Chrift, encourage the ill-affected to continue ftill in their damnable ways, and others weak in faith to fuffer themfelves eafily to be feduced to the deftruction of their fouls; I thought it my moft bounden duty to God and to his church, whilft I might have opportunity to fpeak with him, to teach the truth in a general fpeech in fuch points of doctrine.

At which time I taught, *That fuch as dye, or have died at any time in the church of* Rome, *holding in their ignorance that faith which is taught in it, and namely, juftifica-tion in part by works, could not be faid by the fcriptures to be faved.* In which matter, forefeeing that if I waded not warily in it, I fhould be in danger to be reported, (as hath fallen out fince notwithftanding) to condemn all the fathers, I faid directly and plainly to all mens underftanding, *That it was not indeed to be doubted, but many of the fathers were faved; but the means* (faid I) *was not their ignorance, which excufeth no man with God, but their knowledge and faith of the truth, which it appeareth God vouchfafed them, by many notable monuments and records extant in all ages.* Which being the laft point in all my fermon, rifing fo naturally from the text I then propounded, as would have occafion'd me to have deliver'd fuch matter, notwithftanding the former doctrine had been found; and being dealt in by a general fpeech, without touch of his particular; I looked not that a matter of controverfy would have been made of it, no more than had been of my like dealing in former time. But, far otherwife than I looked for, Mr. *Hooker* fhewing no grief of offence taken at my fpeech all the week long, the next fabbath, leaving to pro-ceed upon his ordinary text, profeffed to preach again that he had done the day before, for fome queftion that his doctrine was drawn into, which he defired might be examined with all feverity.

So proceeding, he beftowed his whole time in that difcourfe, concerning his former doctrine, and anfwering the places of fcripture which I had alledged to prove that a man dying in the church of *Rome* is not to be judged by the fcriptures to be faved.

In which long fpeech, and utterly impertinent to his text, under colour of anfwering for himfelf, he impugned directly and openly to all mens underftanding, the true doctrine which I had delivered; and, adding to his former points fome other like (as willingly one error follows another) that is, *That the* Galatians *joining with faith in Chrift's circumcifion, as neceffary to falvation, might not be faved: and that they of the church of* Rome, *may be faved by fuch a faith of Chrift as they had, with a general repentance of all their errors, notwithftanding their opinion of juftification in part by their works and merits:* I was neceffarily, though not willingly, drawn to fay fomething to the points he objected againft found doctrine; which I did in a fhort fpeech in the end of my fermon, with proteftation of fo doing not of any finifter affection to any man, but to bear witnefs to the truth according to my calling; and wifhed, if the matter fhould needs farther be dealt in, fome other more convenient way might be taken for it. Wherein, I hope, my dealing was manifeft to the confciences of all indifferent hearers of me that day, to have been according to peace, and without any uncharitablenefs, being duly confidered.

For that I conferred with him the firft day, I have fhewed that the caufe requiring of me the duty, at the leaft not to be altogether filent in it, being a matter of fuch confequence, that the time alfo being fhort wherein I was to preach after him, the hope of the fruit of our communication being fmall upon experience of former conferences, my expectation being that the church fhould be no further troubled with it, upon the motion I made of taking fome other courfe of dealing: I fuppofe my deferring to fpeak with him till fome fit opportunity, cannot in charity be judged uncharitable.

The fecond day, his unlookt for oppofition with the former reafons, made it to be a matter that required of neceffity fome publick anfwer; which being fo temperate as I have fhewed, if notwithftanding it be cenfured as uncharitable, and punifhed fo grievoufly as it is, what fhould have been my punifhment, (if without all fuch cautions and refpects as qualified my fpeech) I had before all, and in the underftanding of all, fo reproved him offending openly, that others might have feared to do the like? Which yet, if I had done, might have been warranted by the rule and charge of the apoftle, *Them that offend openly, rebuke openly, that the reft may alfo fear*; and by his example, who, when *Peter* in this very cafe which is now between us, had (not in preaching) but in a matter of converfation, not gone with a right foot, as was fit for the truth of the gofpel, conferred not privately with him, but, as his own rule required, reproved him openly before all, that others might hear, and fear, and not dare to do the like. All which reafons together weighed, I hope, will fhew the manner of my dealing to have been charitable, and warrantable in every fort.

The next fabbath day after this, Mr. *Hooker* kept the way he had entered into before, and beftowed his whole hour and more only upon the queftions he had moved and maintained; wherein he fo fet forth the agreement of the church of *Rome* with us, and their difagreement from us, as if we had confented in the greateft and weightieft points, and differed only in certain fmaller matters: which agreement noted by him in two chief points, is not fuch as he would have made men believe. The one, in that he faid, *They acknowledge all men finners, even the bleffed virgin,* though fome freed her from fin, for the council of *Trent* holdeth, that fhe was free from fin. Another, in that he faid, *They teach Chrift's righteoufnefs to be the only meritorious caufe of taking away fin, and differ from us only in the applying of it:* for *Thomas Aquinas* their chief fchoolman, and archbifhop *Catherinus* teach, *That Chrift took away only original fin, and that the reft are to be taken away by our felves*; yea, the council of *Trent* teacheth, *That righteoufnefs whereby we are righteous in God's fight, is an inherent righteoufnefs;* which muft needs be of our own works, and cannot be underftood of the righteoufnefs inherent only in Chrift's perfon, and accounted unto us. Moreover he taught the fame time, *That neither the* Galatians, *nor the church of* Rome, *did directly overthrow the foundation of juftification by Chrift alone, but only by confequent, and therefore might well be faved; or elfe neither the churches of the* Lutherans, *nor any which hold any manner of error could be faved; becaufe* (faith he) *every error by confequent overthroweth the foundation.* In which difcourfes, and fuch like, he beftowed his whole time and more; which, if he had affected either the truth of God, or the peace of the church, he would truly not have done.

Whofe example could not draw me to leave the fcripture I took in hand, but ftanding about an hour to deliver the doctrine of it, in the end, upon juft occafion of the text, leaving fundry other his unfound fpeeches, and keeping me ftill to the principal, I confirmed the believing the doctrine of juftification by Chrift only, to be neceffary

to

to the juftification of all that fhould be faved, and that the church of *Rome* directly denieth, that a man is faved by Chrift, or by faith alone, without the works of the law. Which my anfwer, as it was moft neceffary for the fervice of God, and the church, fo was it without any immodeft or reproachful fpeech to Mr. *Hooker*; whofe unfound and wilful dealings in a caufe of fo great importance to the faith of Chrift, and falvation of the church, notwithftanding I knew well what fpeech it deferved, and what fome zealous earneft man of the fpirit of *John* and *James*, firnamed *Boaner-* Mark 3. 17. *ges*, fons of thunder, would have faid in fuch a cafe; yet I chofe rather to content my felf in exhorting him to re-vifit his doctrine, as *Nathan* the prophet did the device, 2 Sam. 7. 2, 3. which, without confulting with God, he had of himfelf given to *David*, concerning 4, 5. the building of the temple; and with *Peter* the apoftle, who endure to be withftood in Gal. 2. 11, 14. fuch a cafe, not unlike unto this. This in effect, was that which paffed between us con-cerning this matter, and the invectives I made againft him, wherewith I am charged. which rehearfal, I hope, may clear me (with all that fhall indifferently confider it) of the blames laid upon me for want of duty to Mr. *Hooker* in not conferring with him, whereof I have fpoken fufficiently already; and to the high commiffion, in not reveal-ing the matter to them, which yet now I am further to anfwer. My anfwer is, that I pro-teft, no contempt nor wilful neglect of any lawful authority, ftayed me from complaining unto them, but thefe reafons following:

Firft, I was in fome hope, that Mr. *Hooker*, notwithftanding he had been over-carried with a fhew of charity to prejudice the truth, yet when it fhould be fufficiently proved would have acknowledged it, or at the leaft induced with peace, that it might be offered without any offence to him, or to fuch as would receive it; either of which would have taken away any caufe of juft complaint. When neither of thefe fell out according to my expectation and defire, but that he replied to the truth, and objected againft it, I thought he might have fome doubts and fcruples in himfelf; which yet, if they were cleared, he would either embrace found doctrine, or at leaft fuffer it to have its courfe: which hope of him I nourifhed fo long, as the matter was not bitterly and immodeftly handled between us.

Another reafon was the caufe it felf, which, according to the parable of the tares (which are faid to be fown among the wheat) fprung up firft in his grafs: therefore, as the fervants in that place, are not faid to have come to complain to the Lord, till the tares came to fhew their fruits in their kind; fo, I thinking it yet but a time of difcovering of what it was, defired not their fickle to cut it down.

For further anfwer, It is to be confidered, that the confcience of my duty to God, and to his church, did bind me at the firft, to deliver found doctrine in fuch points as had been otherwife uttered in that place, where I had now fome years taught the truth; otherwife the rebuke of the prophet had fallen upon me, for not going up to the breach, Ezek. 22. 30. and ftanding in it, and the peril for anfwering the blood of the city, in whofe watch- Chap. 33. 6. tower I fate; if it had been furprized by my default. Moreover, my publick protefta-tion, in being unwilling, that if any were not yet fatisfied, fome other more convenient way might be taken for it. And laftly, that I had refolved (which I uttered before to fome, dealing with me about the matter) to have protefted the next fabbath day, that I would no more anfwer in that place, any objections to the doctrine taught by any means, but fome other way fatisfy fuch as fhould require it.

Thefe, I truft, may make it appear, that I failed not in duty to authority, notwith-ftanding I did not complain, nor give over fo foon dealing in the cafe. If I did, how is he clear, which can alledge none of all thefe for himfelf; who leaving the expounding of the fcriptures, and his ordinary calling, voluntarily difcourfed upon fchool-points and queftions, neither of edification, nor of truth? Who after all this, as promifing to him-felf, and to untruth, a victory by my filence, added yet in the next fabbath day, to the maintenance of his former opinions, thefe which follow:

That no additament taketh away the foundation, except it be a privitive; of which fort neither the works added to Chrift by the church of Rome, *nor circumcifion by the* Ga-latians *were: as one denieth him not to be a man, that faith, he is a righteous man, but he that faith he is a dead man:* whereby it might feem, that a man might, without hurt, add works to Chrift, and pray alfo that God and St. *Peter* would fave them.

That the Galatians *cafe is harder than the cafe of the church of* Rome, *becaufe the* Gala-tians *joyned circumcifion with Chrift, which God had forbidden and abolifh'd; but that which the church of* Rome *joyn'd with Chrift, were good works which God hath commanded.* Where-in he committed a double fault, one, in expounding all the queftions of the *Galatians*, and

confequently

confequently of the *Romans*, and other epiftles, of circumcifion only, and the ceremonies of the law (as they do, who anfwer for the church of *Rome* in their writings) contrary to the clear meaning of the apoftle, as may appear by many ftrong and fufficient
reafons: the other, in that he faid, *the addition of the church of* Rome *was of works
commanded of God*. Whereas the leaft part of the works whereby they looked to merit,
was of fuch works; and moft were works of fupererogation, and works which God
never commanded, but was highly difpleafed with, as of maffes, pilgrimages, pardons,
pains of purgatory, and fuch like: *That no one fequel urged by the apoftle againft the*
Galatians *for joyning circumcifion with Chrift, but might be as well enforced againft the*
Lutherans; *that is, that for their ubiquity it may be as well faid to them, if ye hold the
body of Chrift to be in all places, you are fallen from grace, you are under the curfe of
the law, faying,* Curfed be he that fulfilleth not all things written in this book, with
fuch like. He added yet farther, *That to a bifhop of the church of* Rome, *to a cardinal, yea, to the pope himfelf acknowledging Chrift to be the Saviour of the world, denying other errors, and being difcomforted for want of works whereby he might be juftified, he would not doubt, but ufe this fpeech; thou holdeft the foundation of chriftian
faith, though it be but by a flender thread; thou holdeft Chrift, though but by the
hem of his garment; why fhouldft thou not hope that virtue may pafs from Chrift to
fave thee? That which thou holdeft of juftification by thy works, overthroweth indeed by confequent the foundation of chriftian faith; but be of good chear, thou haft
not to do with a captious fophifter, but with a merciful God, who will juftify thee
for that thou holdeft, and not take the advantage of doubtful conftruction to condemn
thee. And if this,* faid he, *be an error, I hold it willingly; for it is the greateft comfort I have in the world, without which I would not wifh either to fpeak or live.* Thus
far, being not to be anfwered in it any more, he was bold to proceed, the abfurdity of
which fpeech I need not to ftand upon. I think the like to this, and other fuch in this
fermon, and the reft of this matter, hath not been heard in publick places within this
land fince queen *Mary*'s days. What confequence this doctrine may be of, if he be
not by authority ordered to revoke it, I befeech your H. H. as the truth of God
and his gofpel is dear and precious unto you, according to your godly wifdom to
confider.

I have been bold to offer to your H. H. a long and tedious difcourfe of thefe matters;
but fpeech being like to tapiftry, which if it be folded up, fheweth but part of that
which is wrought; and being unlapt and laid open, fheweth plainly to the eye all the
work that is in it; I thought it neceffary to unfold this tapiftry, and to hang up the
whole chamber of it in your moft honourable fenate, that fo you may the more eafily
difcern of all the pieces, and the fundry works and matters contained in it. Wherein
my hope is, your H. H. may fee I have not deferved fo great a punifhment as is laid upon the church for my fake, and alfo upon my felf, in taking from me the exercife of my
miniftry. Which punifhment, how heavy it may feem to the church, or fall out indeed
to be, I refer it to them to judge, and fpare to write what I fear, but to my felf it is exceeding grievous, for that it taketh from me the exercife of my calling. Which I do not
fay is dear unto me, as the means of that little benefit whereby I live (although this be
a lawful confideration, and to be regarded of me in due place, and of the authority
under whofe protection I moft willingly live, even by God's commandment both unto
them, and unto me:) which ought to be more precious unto me than my life, for the
love which I fhould bear to the glory and honour of almighty God, and to the edification and falvation of his church, for that my life cannot any other way be of like fervice to God, nor of fuch ufe and profit to men by any means. For which caufe, as I difcern how dear my miniftry ought to be unto me, fo it is my hearty defire, and moft humble requeft unto God, to your H. H. and to all the authority I live under, to whom any
dealing herein belongeth, that I may fpend my life according to his example, who in a
word of like found, of fuller fenfe, comparing by it the beftowing of his life to the offering poured out upon the facrifice of the faith of God's people, and efpecially of this
church, whereupon I have already poured out a great part thereof in the fame calling, from
which I ftand now reftrained. And if your H. H. fhall find it fo, that I have not deferv'd
fo great a punifhment, but rather performed the duty which a good and faithful fervant
ought, in fuch cafe, to do to his Lord and the people he putteth them in truft withal
carefully to keep; I am a moft humble fuitor by thefe prefents to your H. H. that, by
your godly wifdom, fome good courfe may be taken for the reftoring of me to my miniftry and place again. Which fo great a favour, fhall bind me yet in a greater obligation
of duty, which is already fo great, as it feemed nothing could be added unto it to make

it greater) to honour God daily for the continuance and encreafe of your good eftate, and to be ready with all the poor means God hath given me, to do your H. H. that faithful fervice I may poffibly perform. But if, notwithftanding my caufe be never fo good, your H. H. can by no means pacify fuch as are offended, nor reftore me again, then am I to reft in the good pleafure of God, and to commend to your H. H. protection, under her majefty's, my private life, while it fhall be led in duty; and the church to him, who hath redeemed to himfelf a people with his precious blood, and is making ready to come to judge both the quick and dead, to give to every one according as he hath done in this life, be it good or evil; to the wicked and unbelievers, juftice unto death; but to the faithful, and fuch as love his truth, mercy and grace to life everlafting.

Your Honour's moft bounden,

and moft humble Supplicant,

Walter Travers,

Minifter of the Gofpel.

M m m 2   Mr.

Mr. *HOOKER*'s
ANSWER
TO THE
SUPPLICATION
THAT
Mr. *TRAVERS*
Made to the
COUNCIL.

To my Lord of CANTERBURY his Grace.

MY duty in my moſt humble wiſe remembred. May it pleaſe your grace to underſtand, that whereas there hath been a late controverſy raiſed in the *Temple*, and purſued by Mr. *Travers*, upon conceit taken at ſome words by me uttered, with a moſt ſimple and harmleſs meaning. In the heat of which purſuit, after three publick invectives, ſilence being enjoined him by authority, he hath hereupon, for defence of his proceedings, both preſented the right honourable lords, and others of her majeſty's privy council with a writing; and alſo cauſed or ſuffered the ſame to be copied out, and ſpread thro' the hands of ſo many, that well nigh all ſorts of men have it in their boſoms. The matters wherewith I am therein charged, being of ſuch quality as they are, and my ſelf being better known to your grace than to any other of their honours beſides, I have choſen to offer to your grace's hand a plain declaration of my innocence in all thoſe things wherewith I am ſo hardly, and ſo heavily charged; left, if I ſtill remain ſilent, that which I do for quietneſs ſake, be taken as an argument, that I lack what to ſpeak truly and juſtly in mine own defence.

2. Firſt, becauſe Mr. *Travers* thinketh it an expedient to breed an opinion in mens minds, that the root of all inconvenient events which are now ſprung out, is the ſurly and unpeaceable diſpoſition of the man with whom he hath to do; therefore the firſt in the rank of accuſations laid againſt me, is, *my inconformity, which have ſo little inclined to ſo many, and ſo earneſt exhortations and conferences, as my ſelf*, he ſaith, *can witneſs, to have been ſpent upon me, for my better faſhioning unto good correſpondence and agreement.*

3. Indeed, when at the firſt, by means of ſpecial well-willers, without any ſuit of mine, as they very well know (although I do not think it had been a mortal ſin, in a reaſonable ſort, to have ſhewed a moderate deſire that way) yet when by their endeavour without inſtigation of mine, ſome reverend and honourable, favourably affecting me, had procured her majeſty's grant of the place; at the very point of my entring thereinto, the evening before I was firſt to preach, he came, and two other gentlemen join'd with him: the effect of his conference then was, *That he thought it his duty to advise me, not to enter with a ſtrong hand, but to change my purpoſe of preaching there the next day, and to ſtay till he had given notice of me to the congregation, that ſo their allowance might ſeal my calling.* The effect of my anſwer was, *That, as in a place where ſuch order is, I would not break; ſo here, where it never was, I might not, of my own head, take upon me to begin it:* but liking very well the motion of the opinion which I had of his good meaning who made it, requeſted him not to miſlike my anſwer, tho' it were not correſpondent to his mind.

4. When this had ſo diſpleaſed ſome, that whatſoever was afterwards done or ſpoken by me, it offended their taſte, angry informations were daily ſent out, intelligence given far and wide, what a dangerous enemy was crept in; the worſt that jealouſy could imagine was ſpoken and written to ſo many, that at the length ſome knowing me well, and perceiving how injurious the reports were, which grew daily more and more unto my diſcredit, wrought means to bring Mr. *Travers* and me to a ſecond conference. Wherein, when a common friend unto us both, had quietly requeſted him to utter thoſe things, wherewith he found himſelf any way griev'd: he firſt renew'd the memory of my entring into this charge, by virtue only of an human creature (for ſo the want of that formality of popular allowance was then cenſured) and unto this was annexed a catalogue, partly of cauſeleſs ſurmiſes, as, *That I had conſpired againſt him, and that I ſought ſuperiority over him*; and partly of faults, which to note, I ſhould have thought it a greater offence than to commit, if I did account them faults, and had heard them ſo curiouſly obſerved in any other than my ſelf, they are ſuch ſilly things, as, *praying in the entrance of my ſermon only, and not in the end, naming biſhops in my prayer, kneeling when I pray, and kneeling when I receive the communion,* with ſuch like, which I would be as loth to recite, as I was ſorry to hear them objected, if the rehearſal thereof were not by him thus wreſted from me. Theſe are the conferences wherewith I have been woed to entertain peace and good agreement. ^{A meer formality it had been to me in that place; where, as no man had ever uſed it before me, ſo it could neither further me if I did uſe it, nor hinder me if I did not.}

5. As for the vehement exhortations he ſpeaketh of, I would gladly know ſome reaſon wherefore he thought them needful to be us'd. Was there any thing found in my ſpeeches or dealings that gave them occaſion, who are ſtudious of peace, to think that I diſpoſed my ſelf with ſome unquiet kind of proceedings? Surely, the ſpecial providence of God I do now ſee it was, that the firſt words I ſpake in this place, ſhould make the firſt thing whereof I am accus'd, to appear not only untrue, but improbable, to as many as then heard me with indifferent ears; and do, I doubt not, in their conſciences clear me of this ſuſpicion. Howbeit, I grant this were nothing, if it might be ſhewed, that my deeds following were not ſuitable to my words. If I had ſpoken of peace at the firſt, and afterwards ſought to moleſt and grieve him, by croſſing him in his function, by ſtorming, if my pleaſure were not asked, and my will obeyed in the leaſt occurrences, by carping needleſly ſometimes at the manner of his teaching, ſometimes at this, ſometimes at that point of his doctrine: I might then with ſome likelihood have been blamed, as one diſdaining a peaceable hand when it had been offered. But if I be able (as I am) to prove that my ſelf hath now a full year together, born the continuance of ſuch dealings, not only without any manner of reſiſtance, but alſo without any ſuch complaint, as might let or hinder him in his courſe, I ſee no cauſe in the world why of this I ſhould be accuſed, unleſs it be, leſt I ſhould accuſe, which I meant not. If therefore I have given him occaſion to uſe conferences and exhortations to peace, if when they were beſtowed upon me I have deſpiſed them, it will not be hard to ſhew ſome one word or deed wherewith I have gone about to work diſturbance: one is not much, I require but one. Only, I require if any thing be ſhewed, it may be proved, and not objected only as this is, *That I have joined to ſuch as have always oppoſed to any good order in his church, and made themſelves to be thought indiſpoſed to the preſent eſtate and proceedings.* The words have reference, as it ſeemeth, unto ſome ſuch things as being attempted before my coming to the *Temple,* went not ſo effectually (perhaps) forward, as he that deviſed them would have wiſhed. An order, as I learn, there was tendred, that communicants ſhould neither kneel, as in moſt places of the realm; nor ſit, as in this place the cuſtom is; but walk to the one ſide of the table, and there ſtanding till they had received, paſs afterwards away round about by the other. Which being on a ſudden begun to be practiſed in the church, ſome ſate wondering
dering

dering what it ſhould mean, others deliberating what to do : till ſuch time as at length by name one of them being called openly thereunto, requeſted that they might do as they had been accuſtomed, which was granted ; and as Mr. *Travers* had miniſtred this way to the reſt, ſo a curate was ſent to miniſter to them after their way. Which un-proſperous beginning of a thing (ſaving only for the inconvenience of needleſs alterations otherwiſe harmleſs) did .ſo diſgrace that order, in their conceit who had to allow or diſallow it, that it took no place. For neither could they ever induce themſelves to think it good, and it ſo much offended Mr. *Travers*, who ſuppoſed it to be the beſt, that he ſince that time, although contented to receive it as they do, at the hands of others, yet hath not thought it meet they ſhould ever receive out of his, which would not admit that order of receiving it, and therefore in my time hath been always preſent not to mi-niſter, but only to be miniſtred unto.

6. Another order there was likewiſe deviſed, but an order of much more weight and importance. This ſoil in reſpect of certain immunities and other ſpecialties belong-ing unto it, ſeemed likely to bear that which in other places of the realm of *England* doth not take. For which cauſe, requeſt was made to her majeſty's privy council, that whereas it is provided by a ſtatute there ſhould be collectors and ſidemen in churches, which thing, or ſomewhat correſpondent unto it, this place did greatly want ; it would pleaſe their honours to motion ſuch a matter to the antients of the *Temple*. And ac-cording to their honourable manner of helping forward all motions ſo grounded, they wrote their letters, as I am informed, to that effect. Whereupon, although theſe houſes never had uſe of ſuch collectors and ſide men as are appointed in other places, yet they both erected a box and received mens devotions for the poor, appointing the treaſurer of both houſes to take care for beſtowing it where need was ; and granting farther, that if any could be entreated (as in the end ſomewhere) to undertake the labour of obſerving men's ſlackneſs in divine duties, they ſhould be allowed their complaints heard at all times, and the faults they complained of, if Mr. *Alvey's* private admonition did not ſerve, then by ſome other means to be redreſſed ; but according to the old received orders of both houſes. Whereby the ſubſtance of their honours letters were indeed fully ſatisfied. Yet becauſe Mr. *Travers* intended not this, but as it ſeemed, another thing ; therefore, notwithſtanding the orders which have been taken, and for any thing I know, do ſtand ſtill in as much force in this church now as at any time heretofore, he complaineth much of the good orders which he doth mean have been withſtood. Now it were hard, if as many as did any ways oppoſe unto theſe and the like orders, in his per-ſuaſion good, do thereby make themſelves diſlikers of the preſent ſtate and proceeding. If they, whom he aimeth at, have any other ways made themſelves to be thought ſuch, it is likely he doth know wherein, and will, I hope, diſcloſe wherein it appertaineth, both the perſons whom he thinketh, and the cauſes why he thinketh them ſo ill affected. But whatſoever the men be, do their faults make me faulty ? They do, if I joyn my ſelf with them. I beſeech him therefore to declare wherein I have joined with them. Other joyning than this with any man here, I cannot imagine : it may be I have talked, or walk-ed, or eaten, or interchangeably uſed the duties of common humanity with ſome ſuch as he is hardly perſuaded of. For I know no law of God or man, by force where-of they ſhould be as heathens and publicans unto me, that are not gracious in the eyes of another man, perhaps without cauſe, or if with cauſe, yet ſuch cauſe as he is privy unto, and not I. Could he, or any reaſonable man think it as a charitable courſe in me, to obſerve them that ſhew by external courteſies a favourable inclination toward him, and if I ſpy out any one amongſt them of whom I think not well, here-upon to draw ſuch an accuſation as this againſt him, and to offer it where he hath given up his againſt me : which notwithſtanding I will acknowledge to be juſt and reaſonable, if he or any man living ſhall ſhew that I uſe as much as the bare familiar company but of one, who by word or deed hath ever given me cauſe to ſuſpect or conjecture him ſuch as here they are termed with whom complaint is made that I joyn my ſelf. This being ſpoken therefore, and written without all poſſibility of proof, doth not Mr. *Travers* give me over-great cauſe to ſtand in ſome fear leſt he make too little conſcience how he uſeth his tongue or pen? Theſe things are not laid againſt me for nothing ; they are to ſome purpoſe if they take place. For in a mind perſuaded that I am, as he deciphereth me, one which refuſes to be at peace with ſuch as embrace the truth, and ſide my ſelf with men ſiniſterly affected thereunto, any thing that ſhall be ſpoken concerning the unſoundneſs of my doctrine cannot chuſe but be favourably entertained. This preſuppoſed, it will have likelihood enough which afterwards followeth, *that many of my ſermons have taſted of ſome four leaven or other, that in them he hath diſcover'd many un-ſound matters.* A thing much to be lamented, that ſuch a place as this, which might have

been

been so well provided for, hath fallen into the hands of one no better instructed in the truth. But what if in the end it be found, that he judgeth my words, as they do colours which look upon them with green spectacles, and think that which they see is green, when indeed that is green whereby they see?

7. Touching the first point of this discovery, which is about the matter of predestination, to set down that I spake (for I have it written) to declare and confirm the several branches thereof would be tedious now in this writing, where I have so many things to touch, that I can but touch them only. Neither is it herein so needful for me to justify my speech, when the very place and presence where I spake, doth it self speak sufficiently for my clearing. This matter was not broached in a blind alley, or uttered where none was to hear it that had skill with authority to controul; or covertly insinuated by some gliding sentence.

8. That which I taught was at *Paul's cross*; it was not hudled in amongst other matters, in such sort that it could pass without noting; it was opened, it was proved, it was some reasonable time stood upon. I see not which way my lord of *London*, who was present and heard it, can excuse so great a fault, as patiently, without rebuke or controulment afterwards, to hear any man there teach otherwise than the *word of God doth*; nor as it is understood by the private interpretation of some one or two men, or by a special construction received in some few books; but, as it is understood *by all churches professing the gospel*; by them all, and therefore even by our own also amongst others. A man that did mean to prove that he speaketh, would surely take the measure of his words shorter.

9. The next thing discovered, is an opinion about the assurance of men's persuasions in matters of faith. I have taught, he saith, *That the assurance of things which we believe by the word, is not so certain as of that we perceive by sense.* And, is it as certain? yea, I taught as he himself, I trust will not deny, that the things which God doth promise in his word are surer unto us than any thing which we touch, handle, or see. But are we so sure and certain of them? if we be, why doth God so often prove his promises unto us, as he doth by argument taken from our sensible experience? We must be surer of the proof, than of the thing proved, otherwise it is no proof. How is it, that if ten men do all look upon the moon, every one of them knoweth it is as certainly to be the moon as another; but many believing one and the same promise, all have not one and the same fulness of persuasion? How falleth it out, that men being assured of any thing by sense, can be no surer of it than they are; whereas the strongest in faith that liveth upon the earth, hath always need to labour and strive, and pray, that his assurance concerning heavenly and spiritual things, may grow, encrease, and be augmented?

10. The sermon wherein I have spoken somewhat largely of this point was, long before this late controversy rose between him and me, upon request of some of my friends, seen and read by many, and amongst many, some who are thought able to discern: and I never heard that any one of them hitherto hath condemned it as containing unsound matter. My case were very hard, if as oft as any thing I speak displeasing one man's taste, my doctrine upon his only word should be taken for four leaven.

11. The rest of this discovery is all about the matter now in question; wherein he hath two faults predominant would tire out any that should answer unto every point severally: unapt speaking of school-controversies, and of my words so untoward a reciting, that he which should promise to draw a man's countenance, and did indeed express the parts, at leastwise most of them, truly, but perversly place them, could not represent a more offensive visage, than unto me my own speech seemeth in some places, as he hath ordered it. For answer whereunto, that writing is sufficient, wherein I have set down both my words and meaning in such sort, that where this accusation doth deprave the one, and either misinterpret, or without just cause, mislike the other, it will appear so plainly, that I may spare very well to take upon me a new needless labour here.

12. Only at one thing which is there to be found, because Mr. *Travers* doth here seem to take such a special advantage, as if the matter were unanswerable, he constraineth me either to detect his oversight, or to confess mine own in it. In setling the question between the church of *Rome* and us, about grace and justification, lest I should give them an occasion to say, as commonly they do, that when we cannot refute their opinions, we propose to our selves such instead of theirs, as we can refute; I took it for the best and most perspicuous way of teaching, to declare first, how far we do agree, and then to shew our disagreement: not generally

(as

*His words be (as Mr. *Travers* his ª words would carry it, for the easier fastning that upon me where-
thefe, The next with, faving only by him, I was never in my life touched;) but about the matter only
fabbath-day at- of juftification: for further I had no caufe to meddle at this time. What was then my
ter this, Mr. *Hooker* kept offence in this cafe? I did, as he faith, fo fet it out as if we had confented in the great-
the way he en- eft and weightieft points, and differed only in fmaller matters. It will not be found,
tred into be- when it cometh to the balance, a light difference where we difagree, as I did acknow-
fore, and be- ledge that we do, about the very effence of the medicine whereby Chrift cureth our
ftowed his difeafe. Did I go about to make a fhew of agreement in the weightieft points, and
whole hour was I fo fond as not to conceal our difagreement about this? I do wifh that fome indif-
and more, on- ferency were ufed by them that have taken the weighing of my words.
ly upon the
queftions be
had moved
and maintain-
ed. Wherein he fo fet the agreement of the church of *Rome* with us, and their difagreement from us, as if we had confented in the
greateft and weightieft points, and differed only in certain fmaller matters. Which agreement noted by him, in two chief points, is
not fuch as he would have men believe: the one, in that he faid they acknowledged all men finners, even the bleffed virgin, though
fome of them freed her from fin: for the council of *Trent* holdeth, that fhe was free from fin. Another, in that he faid, They
teach Chrift's righteoufnefs to be the only meritorious caufe of taking away fin, and differ from us only in the applying of it. For
Thomas Aquinas, their chief fchoolman, and archbifhop *Catharinus*, teach, That Chrift took away only original fin, and that the reft are
to be taken away by our felves: yes, the council of *Trent* teacheth, That the righteoufnefs whereby we are righteous in God's fight,
is inherent righteoufnefs, which muft needs be of our own works, and cannot be underftood of the righteoufnefs inherent only in
Chrift's perfon, and accounted unto us.

13. Yea, but our agreement is not fuch in two of the chiefeft points, as I would
have men believe it is. And what are they? The one is, I faid, *They acknowledge all
men finners, even the bleffed virgin, though fome of them free her from fin.* Put the
cafe I had affirmed, that only fome of them free her from fin, and had delivered it as
the moft current opinion amongft them, that fhe was conceived in fin: doth not *Bonaventure* fay plainly, *omnes fere,* in a manner all men do hold this? doth he not bring
many reafons wherefore all men fhould hold it; were their voices fince that time ever
counted, and their number found fmaller which hold it, than theirs that hold the contrary? Let the queftion then be, whether I might fay, the moft of them *acknowledged
all men finners, even the bleffed virgin her felf.* To fhew, that their general received
opinion is the contrary, the *Tridentine* council is alledged, peradventure not altogether fo
confiderately. For if that council have by refolute determination freed her, if it hold,
as Mr. *Travers* faith it doth, that fhe was free from fin; then muft the church of *Rome*
needs condemn them that hold the contrary. For what that council holdeth, the fame
they all do and muft hold. But in the church of *Rome*, who knoweth not, that it is
a thing indifferent to think and defend the one or the other? So that, by this argument,
the council of *Trent* holdeth the virgin free from fin; *ergo,* it is plain that none of them
may, and therefore untrue, that moft of them do acknowledge her a finner, were forcible to overthrow my fuppofed affertion, if it were true that the council did hold this.
But to the end it may clearly appear, how it neither holdeth this nor the contrary, I will
open what many do conceive of the canon that concerneth this matter. The fathers of
Trent perceived, that if they fhould define of this matter, it would be dangerous howfoever it were determined. If they had freed her from her original fin, the reafons
againft them are unanfwerable, which *Bonaventure* and others do alledge, but efpecially
Thomas, whofe line, as much as may be, they follow. Again, if they did refolve the
other way, they fhould controul themfelves in another thing, which in no cafe might
be altered. For they profefs to keep no day holy in the honour of an unholy thing;
and the virgin's conception they honour with a

ᵇ This doth much trouble *Thomas*, holding her conception
ftained with the natural blemifh inherent in mortal feed.
And therefore he putteth it off with two anfwers; the
one, that the church of *Rome* doth not allow, but tolerate
the feaft, which anfwer now will not ferve. The other,
that being fure fhe was fanctify'd before birth, but unfure
how long a while after her conception, therefore under the
name of her conception-day, they honour the time of her
fanctification. So that befides this, they have now no foder
to make the certain allowance of their feaft, and their uncertain fentence concerning her fin, to cleave together.
Tom. 3. *part queft.* 27. *art.* 2. *ad* 2 *&* 3.

ᵇfeaft, which they could not abrogate without cancelling a conftitution of *Xyftus Quartus.* And, that
which is worfe, the world might perhaps fufpect,
that if the church of *Rome* did amifs before in this,
it is not impoffible for her to fail in other things.
In the end, they did wifely quote out their canon
by a middle thread, eftablifhing the feaft of the virgin's conception, and leaving the other queftion
doubtful as they found it; giving only a caveat, that
no man fhould take the decree which pronounceth all mankind originally finful, for a
definitive fentence concerning the bleffed virgin. This in my fight is plain by their own
Annot. in words, *Declarat hac ipfa fancta fynodus, &c.* wherefore our countrymen at *Rheims,*
Rom. 5. *fect.* 9. mentioning this point, are marvelous wary how they fpeak; they touch it as tho' it were
a hot coal: *Many godly devout men judge that our bleffed lady was neither born nor conceived in fin.* Is it their wont to fpeak nicely of things definitively fet down in that
council?

In

In like sort, we find that the rest, which have since the time of the *tridentine* synod written of original sin, are in this point, for the most part, either silent, or very sparing in speech: and, when they speak, either doubtful what to think, or whatsoever they think themselves, fearful to set down any certain determination. If I be thought to take the canon of that council otherwise than they themselves do, let him expound it whose sentence was neither last asked, nor his pen least occupied in setting it down; I mean *Andradius*, whom *Gregory* the thirteenth hath allowed plainly to confess, that it is a matter which neither express evidence of scripture, nor the tradition of the fathers, nor the sentence of the church hath determined; that they are too surly and self-willed, which defending their opinion, are displeased with them by whom the other is maintained: final-ly, that the fathers of *Trent* have not set down any certainty about this question, but left it doubtful and indifferent. ^{Lib. 5. defens. fidei.}

Now whereas my words, which I had set down in writing, before I uttered them, were indeed these, *Although they imagine, that the mother of our Lord Jesus Christ, were, for his honour, and by his special protection, preserved clean from all sin: yet concerning the rest, they teach as we do, that all have sinned.* Against my words they might, with more pretence, take exception, because so many of them think she had sin: which ex-ception notwithstanding, the proposition being indefinite, and the matter contingent, they cannot take, because they grant, that many whom they account grave and devout amongst them think, that she was clear from all sin. But, whether Mr. *Travers* did note my words himself, or take them upon the credit of some other man's noting, the tables were faulty wherein it was noted: *All men sinners, even the blessed virgin.* When my second speech was rather, *All men except the blessed virgin.* To leave this; another fault he findeth, that I said, *They teach Christ's righteousness to be the only meritorious cause of taking away sin, and differ from us only in the applying of it.* I did say so, and, *They teach as we do, that altho' Christ be the only meritorious cause of our justice, yet as a medi-cine which is made for health, doth not heal by being made, but by being applied: so, by the merits of Christ, there can be no life nor justification, without the application of his merits: but about the manner of applying Christ, about the number and power of means whereby he is applied, we dissent from them.* This of our dissenting from them is acknowledged.

14. Our agreement in the former is denied to be such as I pretend. Let their own words therefore and mine concerning them be compared, doth not *Andradius* plainly confess; *Our sins do shut, and only the merits of Christ open the entering unto blessedness?* And *Soto, It is put for a good ground, that all, since the fall of Adam, obtained salvation only by the passion of Christ: howbeit, as no cause can be effectual without applying, so neither can any man be saved to whom the suffering of Christ is not applied.* In a word, who not? When the council of *Trent*, reckoning up the causes of our first justification, doth name no end but God's glory, and our felicity; no efficient but his mercy; no instrumental but baptism; no meritorious but Christ; whom to have merited the taking away of no sin but original, is not their opinion: which himself will find, when he hath well examined his witnesses, *Ca-therinus* and *Thomas.* Their jesuites are marvellous angry with the men out of whose glean-ings Mr. *Travers* seemeth to have taken this; they openly disclaim it; they say plainly, *Of all the catholicks there is not one that did ever so teach;* they make solemn protestation, *We believe and profess, that Christ upon the cross hath altogether satisfied for all sins, as well original as actual.* Indeed they teach, that the merit of Christ doth not take away ac-tual sin in such sort as it doth original; wherein, if their doctrine had been understood, for my speech had never been accused. As for the council of *Trent*, concerning inherent righteousness, what doth it here? No man doubteth, but they make another formal cause of justification than we do. In respect whereof, I have shewed you already, that we dis-agree about the very essence of that which cureth our spiritual disease. Most true it is which the grand philosopher hath, *Every man judgeth well of that which he knoweth;* and therefore till we know the things throughly whereof we judge, it is a point of judgment to stay our judgment. ^{Orthod. lib. 3. In sent. dist. 1. quæst. 4. art.6,} ^{Bellarm. judic. de lib. concor. mendac. 18. Nemo catho-licorum ua-quam sie docu-it; sed credi-mus & profite-mur, Christum in cruce pro omnibus om-nino peccatis satisfecisse, tam originali-bus quam ac-tualibus.}

15. Thus much labour being spent in discovering the unsoundness of my doctrine, some pains he taketh further to open faults in the manner of my teaching, as that, *I be-stowed my whole hour and more, my time and more than my time, in discourses utterly im-pertinent to my text.* Which, if I had done, it might have past without complaining of to the privy council.

16. But I did worse, as he saith, *I left the expounding of the scriptures, and my ordi-nary calling, and discoursed upon school points and questions, neither of edification, nor of truth.* I read no lecture in the law, or in physick. And except the bounds of ordinary calling may be drawn like a purse, how are they so much wider unto him than to me, that he which in the limits of his ordinary calling, should reprove that in me, which he under-

stood

ftood not; and I labouring that both he and others might underſtand, could not do this without forſaking my calling? The matter whereof I ſpake was ſuch, as being at firſt by me but lightly touched, he had in that place openly contradicted, and ſolemnly taken upon him to diſprove. If therefore it were a ſchool-queſtion, and unfit to be diſcourſed of there, that which was in me but a propoſition only at the firſt, wherefore made he a problem of it? Why took he firſt upon him to maintain the negative of that which I had affirmatively ſpoken only to ſhew mine own opinion, little thinking that ever it would have been a queſtion? Of what nature ſoever the queſtion were, I could do no leſs than there explain my ſelf to them, unto whom I was accuſed of unſound doctrine; wherein if to ſhew what had been through ambiguity miſtaken in my words, or miſapplied by him in this cauſe againſt me, I uſed the diſtinction and helps of ſchools, I truſt that herein I have committed no unlawful thing. Theſe ſchool implements are acknowledged by grave and wiſe men not unprofitable to have been invented. The moſt approved for learning and judgment do uſe them without blame; the uſe of them hath been well liked in ſome that have taught even in this very place before me: the quality of my hearers is ſuch, that I could not but think them of capacity very ſufficient, for the moſt part to conceive harder than I uſed any; the cauſe I had in hand did in my judgment, neceſſarily require them which were then uſed: when my words ſpoken generally without diſtinctions had been perverted, what other way was there for me, but by diſtinctions to lay them open in their right meaning, that it might appear to all men whether they were conſonant to truth or no? And, although Mr. *Travers* be ſo inured with the city, that he thinketh it unmeet to uſe any ſpeech which favoureth of the ſchool, yet his opinion is no canon; though unto him, his mind being troubled, my ſpeech did ſeem like fetters and manacles, yet there might be ſome more calmly affected which thought otherwiſe; his private judgment will hardly warrant his bold words, that the things which I ſpake *were neither of edification nor truth.* They might edify ſome other, for any thing he knoweth, and be true for any thing he proveth to the contrary. For it is no proof to cry *abſurdities; the like whereunto have not been heard in publick places within this land ſince queen* Mary's *days!* If this came in earneſt from him, I am ſorry to ſee him ſo much offended without cauſe; more ſorry, that his fit ſhould be ſo extream, to make him ſpeak he knoweth not what. That I neither *affected the truth of God, nor the peace of the church; mihi pro minimo eſt,* it doth not much move me, when Mr. *Travers* doth ſay that, which I truſt a greater than Mr. *Travers* will gainſay.

Calv. inſt. l. 1. c. 6. ſect. 9.

17. Now let all this which hitherto he hath ſaid be granted him, let it be as he would have it, let my doctrine and manner of teaching be as much diſallowed by all mens judgments as by his, what is all this to his purpoſe? He alledgeth this to be the cauſe why he bringeth it in; the high commiſſioners *charge him with an indiſcretion and want of duty in that he inveigheth againſt certain points of doctrine, taught by me as erroneous, not conferring firſt with me, nor complaining of it to them.* Which faults, a ſea of ſuch matter as he hath hitherto waded in, will never be able to ſcour from him. For the avoiding of ſchiſm and diſturbance in the church, which muſt needs grow if all men might think what they liſt, and ſpeak openly what they think; therefore by a * decree agreed upon by the biſhops, and confirmed by her majeſty's authority, it was ordered that erroneous doctrine, if it were taught publickly, ſhould not be publickly refuted; but that notice thereof ſhould be given unto ſuch as are by her highneſs appointed to hear and to determine ſuch cauſes. For breach of which order, when he is charged with lack of duty, all the faults that can be heaped upon me will make but a weak defence for him. As ſurely his defence is not much ſtronger, when he alledges for himſelf, That *he was in ſome hope that his ſpeech in proving the truth, and clearing thoſe ſcruples which I had in my ſelf, might cauſe me either to embrace ſound doctrine, or ſuffer it to be embraced of others; which, if I did, he ſhould not need to complain: that it was meet he ſhould diſcover firſt what I had ſown, and make it manifeſt to be tares, and then deſire their ſcythe to cut it down: that, conſcience did bind him to do otherwiſe, than the foreſaid order requireth; that, he was unwilling to deal in that publick manner, and wiſhed a more convenient way were taken for it: that, he had reſolved to have proteſted the next ſabbath day, that he would ſome other way ſatisfy ſuch as ſhould require it, and not deal more in that place.* Be it imagined, [let me not be taken as if I did compare the offenders, when I do not, but their anſwers

I
only]

* In the advertiſements publiſhed in the ſeventh year of her majeſty's reign: If any preacher, or parſon, vicar, or curate ſo licenſed, ſhall fortune to preach any matter tending to diſſention, or to derogation of the religion and doctrine received, that the hearers denounce the ſame to the ordinary, or to the next biſhop of the ſame place, but not openly to contrary, or to impugn the ſame ſpeech ſo diſorderly uttered, whereby may grow offence, and diſquiet of the people, but ſhall be convinced and reproved by the ordinary, after ſuch agreeable order as ſhall be ſeen to him, according to the gravity of the offence: and that it be preſented within one month after the words ſpoken.

only] that a libeller did make this apology for himself, I am not ignorant that if I have juſt matter againſt any man the law is open, there are judges to hear it, and courts where it ought to be complained of; I have taken another courſe againſt ſuch or ſuch a man, yet without breach of duty; foraſmuch as I am able to yield a reaſon of my doing, I conceive ſome hope that a little diſcredit amongſt men would make him aſhamed of himſelf, and that his ſhame would work his amendment; which if it did, other accuſation there ſhould not need; could his anſwer be thought ſufficient, could it in the judgment of diſcreet men free him from all blame? No more can the hope Mr. *Travers* conceiv'd to reclaim me by publick ſpeech, juſtify his fault againſt the eſtabliſh'd order of the church.

18. His thinking it meet, *he ſhould firſt openly diſcover to the people the tares that had been ſown amongſt them, and then require the hand of authority to mow them down;* doth only make it a queſtion, whether his opinion that this was meet, may be a privilege or protection againſt the lawful conſtitution which had before determined of it as of a thing unmeet. Which queſtion I leave for them to diſcuſs whom it moſt concerneth. If the order be ſuch, that it cannot be kept without hazarding a thing ſo precious as a good conſcience, the peril whereof could be no greater to him, than it needs muſt be to all others whom it toucheth in like cauſes; then this is evident, it will be an effectual motive, not only for *England,* but alſo for other reform'd churches, even *Geneva* it ſelf [for they have the like] to change or take that away which cannot but with great inconvenience be obſerved. In the mean while the breach of it may, in ſuch conſideration, be pardon'd [which truly I wiſh howſoever it be] yet hardly defended as long as it ſtandeth in force uncancelled.

19. Now, whereas he confeſſeth another *way had been more convenient,* and that he found in himſelf ſecret unwillingneſs to do that which he did, doth he not ſay plainly, in effect, that the light of his own underſtanding proved the way that he took perverſe and crooked? Reaſon was ſo plain and pregnant againſt it, that his mind was alienated, his will averted to another courſe; yet ſomewhat there was that ſo far over-ruled, that it muſt needs be done even againſt the very ſtream, what doth it bewray? Finally, his purpoſed proteſtation, whereby he meant openly to make it known, that he did not allow this kind of proceeding, and therefore would ſatisfy men otherwiſe, *and deal no more in this place,* ſheweth his good mind in this, that he meant to ſtay himſelf from further offending; but it ſerveth not his turn. He is blamed becauſe the thing he hath done was amiſs, and his anſwer is, that which I would have done afterwards had been well, if ſo be I had done it.

20. But as in this he ſtandeth perſuaded, that he hath done nothing beſides duty, ſo he taketh it hardly, that the high commiſſioners ſhould charge him with indiſcretion. Wherefore, as if he could ſo waſh his hands, he maketh a long and a large declaration concerning the carriage of himſelf; how he waved in *matters of ſmaller weight,* and how in things of *greater moment* how warily he dealt; how *naturally he took his things riſing from the text;* how *cloſely he kept himſelf to the ſcriptures he took in hand;* how much *pains he took to confirm the neceſſity of believing juſtification by Chriſt only,* and to ſhew how *the church of* Rome *denieth that a man is ſaved by faith alone, without works of the law;* what *the ſons of thunder would have done,* if they had been in his caſe; that his *anſwer was very temperate, without immodeſt or reproachful ſpeech;* that when he might *before all have reproved me,* he did not, *but contented himſelf with exhorting me* before all, *to follow* Nathan's *example, and reviſit my doctrine;* when he might have followed St. *Paul's* example in *reproving* Peter, he did not, but exhorted me with *Peter,* to *endure to be withſtood.* This teſtimony of his diſcreet carrying himſelf in the handling of his matter, being more agreeably fram'd and given him by another than by himſelf, might make ſomewhat for the praiſe of his perſon; but for defence of his action, unto them by whom he is thought indiſcreet for not conferring privately before he ſpake, will it ſerve to anſwer, that when he ſpake, he did it conſiderately? He perceiveth it will not, and therefore addeth reaſons, ſuch as they are; as namely, how he purpoſed at the firſt to take another courſe, and that was this, *publickly to deliver the truth of ſuch doctrine as I had otherwiſe taught, and at convenient opportunity to confer with me upon ſuch points.* Is this the rule of Chriſt? If thy brother offend openly in his ſpeech, controul it firſt with contrary ſpeech openly, and confer with him afterwards upon it, when convenient opportunity ſerveth? Is there any law of God or man, whereupon to ground ſuch a reſolution? any church extant in the world, where teachers are allow'd thus to do, or to be done unto? He cannot but ſee how weak an allegation it is, when he bringeth in his following diſcourſe, firſt in one matter, and ſo afterwards in another, to approve himſelf now following it again. For if the purpoſe of doing of a thing ſo uncharitable be a fault, the deed is a greater fault; and doth the doing of it twice, make it the third time fit and allowable to be done? The weight of the cauſe, which is his third defence, relieveth him as little. The weightier it was, the more it required conſiderate advice and conſultation, the more it

ſtood

ſtood him upon to take good heed, that nothing were raſhly done or ſpoken in it. But he meaneth weighty, in regard of the wonderful danger, except he had preſently withſtood me without expecting a time of conference. *This cauſe being of ſuch moment that might prejudice the faith of Chriſt, encourage the ill-affected to continue ſtill in their damnable ways, and others weak in faith, to ſuffer themſelves to be ſeduced, to the deſtruction of their ſouls, he thought it his bounden duty to ſpeak before he talked with me.* A man that ſhould read this, and not know what I had ſpoken, might imagine that I had at the leaſt denied the divinity of Chriſt. But they which were preſent at my ſpeech, and can teſtify that nothing paſſed my lips more than is contained in their writings, whom, for ſoundneſs of doctrine, learning and judgment, Mr. *Travers* himſelf doth, I dare ſay, not only allow, but honour; they which heard, and do know, that the doctrine here ſignified in ſo fearful manner, the doctrine that was ſo dangerous to the faith of Chriſt, that was ſo likely to *encourage ill-affected men to continue ſtill in their damnable ways*; that gave ſo great cauſe to tremble for fear of the preſent *deſtruction of ſouls*, was only this, *I doubt not but God was merciful to ſave thouſands of our fathers, living heretofore in the popiſh ſuperſtition, inaſmuch as they ſinned ignorantly*; and this ſpoken in a ſermon, the greateſt part whereof was againſt popery, they will hardly be able to diſcern how *CHRISTIANITY* ſhould herewith be ſo grievouſly ſhaken.

21. Whereby his fourth excuſe is alſo taken from him. For what doth it boot him to ſay, *The time was ſhort wherein he was to preach after me*, when his preaching of this matter perhaps ought, ſurely might have been either very well omitted, or at leaſt more conveniently for a while deferred; even by their judgments that caſt the moſt favourable aſpect towards theſe his haſty proceedings. The poiſon which men had taken at my hands, was not ſo quick and ſtrong in operation, as in eight days to make them paſt cure; by eight days delay, there was no likelihood that the force and power of his ſpeech could die, longer meditation might bring better and ſtronger proofs to mind than extemporal dexterity could furniſh him with. And who doth know whether *time*, the only mother of ſound judgment and diſcreet dealing, might have given that action of his ſome better ripeneſs, which, by ſo great feſtination hath, as a thing born out of time, brought ſmall joy unto him that begat it? Doth he think it had not been better, that neither my ſpeech had ſeemed in his eyes as an arrow ſticking in a thigh of fleſh; nor his own as a child whereof he muſt needs be delivered by an hour? His laſt way of diſburthening himſelf is, by caſting his load upon my back, as if I had brought him by former conferences, out of hope, that any fruit ſhould ever come of conferring with me. Loth I am to rip up thoſe conferences, whereof he maketh but a ſlippery and looſe relation. In one of them, the queſtion between us was, whether the perſuaſion of faith concerning remiſſion of ſins, eternal life, and whatſoever God doth promiſe unto man, be as free from doubting, as the perſuaſion which we have by ſenſe concerning things taſted, felt, and ſeen? For the negative, I mentioned their example, whoſe faith in ſcripture is moſt commended, and the experience which all faithful men have continually had of themſelves. For proof of the affirmative, which he held, I deſiring to have ſome reaſon, heard nothing but *all good writers* oftentimes inculcated. At the length, upon requeſt to ſee ſome one of them, *Peter Martyr's* common places were brought, where the leaves were turned down, at a place ſounding to this effect, *That the goſpel doth make chriſtians more virtuous than moral philoſophy doth make heathens:* which came not near the queſtion by many miles.

22. In the other conference he queſtioned about the matter of reprobation, miſliking firſt, that I had termed God a permiſſive, and no poſitive cauſe of the evil which the ſchoolmen do call *malum culpæ*. Secondly, that to their objection, who ſay, *If I be elected, do what I will, I ſhall be ſaved;* I had anſwered, that the will of God in this thing is not abſolute, but conditional, to ſave his elect believing, fearing, and obediently ſerving him. Thirdly, that to ſtop the mouths of ſuch as grudge and repine againſt God for rejecting caſt-aways, I had taught that they are not rejected, no not in the purpoſe and counſel of God, without a foreſeen worthineſs of rejection going, tho' not in time, yet in order, before. For, if God's electing do in order (as needs it muſt) preſuppoſe the foreſight of their being that are elected, tho' they be elected before they be; nor only the poſitive foreſight of their being, but alſo the permiſſive of their being miſerable, becauſe election is through mercy, and mercy doth always preſuppoſe miſery: it followeth, that the very choſen of God acknowledge, to the praiſe of the riches of his exceeding free compaſſion, that when he in his ſecret determination ſet it down, *Thoſe ſhall live, and not die,* they lay as ugly ſpectacles before him, as lepers covered with dung and mire, as ulcers putrified in their fathers loins, miſerable, worthy to be had in deteſtation; and ſhall any forſaken creature be able to ſay unto God, thou didſt

plunge

plunge me into the depth, and affign me únto endlefs torments, only to fatisfy thine own will, finding nothing in me for which I could feem in thy fight fo well worthy to feel everlafting flames?

23. When I faw that Mr. *Travers* carped at thefe things, only becaufe they lay not open, I promifed at fome convenient time to make them clear as light, both to him and all others. Which, if they that reprove me will not grant me leave to do, they muft think that they are for fome caufe or other more defirous to have me reputed an unfound man, than willing that my fincere meaning fhould appear and be approved. When I was further asked what my grounds were? I anfwered, that St. *Paul's* words concerning this caufe were my grounds. His next demand, what author I did follow in expounding St. *Paul*, and gathering the doctrine out of his words, againft the judgment (he faith) *of all churches and all good writers.* I was well affured, that to controul this over-reaching fpeech, the fentences which I might have cited out of church-confeffions, together with the beft learned monuments of former times, and not the meaneft of our own, were more in number, than perhaps he would willingly have heard of: but what had this booted me? For, altho' he himfelf in generality do much ufe thofe formal fpeeches, *all churches,* and *all good writers,* yet as he holdeth it, in pulpir, lawful to fay in general, the *Paynims* think this, or the *Heathens* that, but utterly unlawful to cite any fentence of theirs that fay it; fo he gave me at that time great caufe to think, that my particular alledging of other mens words, to fhew their agreement with mine, would as much have difpleafed his mind, as the thing it felf for which it had been alledged; for he knoweth how often he hath in publick place bitten me for this, altho' I did never in any fermon ufe many of the fentences of other writers, and do make moft without any; having always thought it meeteft, neither to affect nor contemn the ufe of them.

24. He is not ignorant, that in the very entrance to the talk which we had privately at that time, to prove it unlawful altogether in preaching, either for confirmation, declaration, or otherwife, to cite any thing but mere canonical fcripture, he brought in, *The fcripture is given by infpiration, and is profitable to teach, improve,* &c. urging much the vigour of thefe two claufes, *The man of God,* and *every good work.* If therefore the work were good which he required at my hands, if privately to fhew why I thought the doctrine I had delivered to be according to St. *Paul's* meaning, were a good work, can they which take the place before alledged for a law, condemning every man of God, who in doing the work of preaching any other way ufeth human authority, like it in me, if in the work of ftrengthning that which I had preached, I fhould bring forth the teftimonies and the fayings of mortal men? I alledged therefore that which might under no pretence in the world be difallowed, namely reafons; not meaning thereby mine own reafon, as now it is reported, but true, found, divine reafon; reafon whereby thofe conclufions might be out of St. *Paul* demonftrated, and not probably difcourfed of only; reafon, proper to that fcience whereby the things of God are known; theological reafon, without principles in fcripture that are plain, foundly deduced more doubtful inferences, in fuch fort that being heard they cannot be denied, not any thing repugnant unto them received, but whatfoever was before otherwife by mifcollecting gathered out of dark places, is thereby forced to yield it felf, and the true confonant meaning of fentences not underftood is brought to light. This is the reafon which I intended. If it were poffible for me to efcape the ferula in any thing I do or fpeak, I had undoubtedly efcaped in this. In this I did that which by fome is enjoined as the only allowable, but granted by all as the moft fure and fafe way, whereby to refolve things doubted of in matters appertaining to faith and chriftian religion. So that Mr. *Travers* had here fmall caufe given him to be weary of conferring, unlefs it was in other refpects, than that poor one which is here pretended, that is to fay, the little hope he had of doing me any good by conference.

25. Yet behold his firft reafon of not complaining to the high-commiffion is, *That fith I offended only thro' an over-charitable inclination, he conceived good hope, when I fhould fee the truth cleared, and fome fcruples which were in my mind removed by his diligence, I would yield.* But what experience foever he had of former conferences, how fmall foever his hope was that fruit would come of it, if he fhould have conferred, will any man judge this a caufe fufficient, why to open his mouth in publick, without any one word privately fpoken? He might have confidered that men do fometimes reap, where they fow but with fmall hope; he might have confider'd, that altho' unto me (whereof he was not certain neither) but if to me his labour fhould be as water fpilt or poured into a torn difh, yet to him it could not be fruitlefs to do that which order in chriftian churches, that which charity amongft chriftian men, that which at many mens hands, even common humanity it felf, at his, many other things befides, did require. What fruit could there come of his open contradicting in fo great hafte, with fo fmall advice, but fuch as muft

needs

needs be unpleasant, and mingled with much acerbity? Surely, he which will take upon him to defend, that in this there was no oversight, must beware, lest by such defences he leave an opinion dwelling in the minds of men, that he is more stiff to maintain what he hath done, than careful to do nothing but that which may justly be maintained.

26. Thus have I, as near as I could, seriously answered things of weight: with smaller I have dealt, as I thought their quality did require. I take no joy in striving, I have not been nuzled or trained up in it. I would to Christ they which have at this present enforced me hereunto, had so ruled their hands in any reasonable time, that I might never have been constrained to strike so much as in mine own defence. Wherefore to prosecute this long and tedious contention no further, I shall wish that your grace, and their honours (unto whose intelligence the dutiful regard, which I have of their judgments, maketh me desirous, that as accusations have been brought against me, so that this my answer thereunto may likewise come) did both with one and the other, as *Constantine* with books containing querulous matter. Whether this be convenient to be wished or no, I cannot tell: but sith there can come nothing of contention, but the mutual wast of the parties contending, till a common enemy dance in the ashes of them both, I do wish heartily that the grave advice which *Constantine* gave for re-uniting of his clergy so many times, upon some small occasions, in so lamentable sort divided; or rather the strict commandment of Christ unto his, that they should not be divided at all; may at the length, if it be his blessed will, prevail so far, at least in this corner of the christian world, to the burying and quite forgetting of strife, together with the causes that have either bred it, or brought it up, that things of small moment never disjoin them, whom one God, one Lord, one faith, one spirit, one baptism, bands of so great force have linked; that a respective eye towards things wherewith we should not be disquieted, make us not, as through infirmity the very patriarchs themselves sometimes were, full gorged, unable to speak peaceably to their own brother. Finally, that no strife may ever be heard of again, but this, who shall hate strife most, who shall pursue peace and unity with swiftest paces.

TO THE

Christian Reader.

WHEREAS *many desirous of resolution in some points handled in this learned discourse, were earnest to have it copied out; to ease so many labours, it hath been thought most worthy and very necessary to be printed: that not only they might be satisfied, but the whole church also hereby edified. The rather, because it will free the author from the suspicion of some errors, which he hath been thought to have favoured. Who might well have answered with* Cremutius *in* Tacitus, Verba mea arguuntur, adeò factorum innocens sum. *Certainly the event of* Lib. 4. Ann. *that time wherein he lived, shewed that to be true, which the same author spake of a worse,* Cui deerat inimicus, per amicos oppressus, *and that there is not* minus periculum Lib. 1. Hist. ex magna fama, quàm ex mala. *But he hath so quit himself, that all may see how, as it was said of* Agricola, Simul suis virtutibus, simul vitiis aliorum, in ipsam gloriam In vita Agri-præceps agebatur. *Touching whom I will say no more, but that which my author said* colæ *of the same man,* Integritatem, &c. in tanto viro referre; injuria virtutum fuerit. *But as of all other his writings, so of this I will add that which* Velleius *spake in com-*Lib. 4. *mendation of* Piso, Nemo fuit, qui magis quæ agenda erant curaret, sine ulla ostentatione agendi. *So not doubting, good christian reader, of thy assent herein, but wishing thy favourable acceptance of this work, (which will be an inducement to set forth others of his learned labours,) I take my leave; from* Corpus Christi College *in* Oxford, *the sixth of* July, 1612.

Thine in Christ Jesus,

Henry Jackson.

A

A LEARNED

DISCOURSE

O F

Juſtification, Works,

And how the

Foundation of FAITH is Overthrown.

Habak. I. 4.

The wicked doth compaſs about the righteous: therefore per-
verſe judgment doth proceed.

1.
2.
3.

FOR the better manifeſtation of the prophet's meaning in this place, we are, firſt, to conſider *the wicked*, of whom he ſaith, that *they compaſs about the righteous*: ſecondly, *the righteous* that are compaſſed about by them: and, thirdly, that which is inferr'd; *therefore perverſe judgment proceedeth.* Touching the firſt, there are two kinds of wicked men, of whom in the fifth of the former to the *Corinthians*, the bleſſed apoſtle ſpeaketh thus: *Do ye not judge them that are within; but God judgeth them that are without.* There are wicked therefore whom the church may judge, and there are wicked whom God only judgeth: wicked *within*, and wicked *without* the walls of the church. If within the church, particular perſons be apparently ſuch, as cannot otherwiſe be reformed; the rule of the apoſtolical judgment is this, *Separate them from among you:* if whole aſſemblies, this, *Separate your ſelves from among them: for what ſociety hath light with darkneſs?* But the wicked, whom the prophet meaneth, were *Babylonians*, and therefore without. For which cauſe we have heard at large heretofore in what ſort he urgeth God to judge them.

2. Now concerning the righteous, there neither is, nor ever was any mere natural man abſolutely righteous in himſelf, that is to ſay, void of all unrighteouſneſs, of all ſin. We dare not except, no not the bleſſed virgin her ſelf, of whom altho' we ſay with St. *Auguſtine*, for the honour ſake which we owe to our Lord and Saviour Chriſt, we are not willing in this cauſe, to move any queſtion of his mother; yet foraſmuch as the ſchools of

1 Cor. 5. 13.

2 Cor. 6. 7.

1   *Rome*

Rome have made it a queſtion; we may anſwer with [a] *Euſebius Emiſſenus,* who ſpeak- _{Or whoſo-} eth of her, and to her, in this effect: *Thou didſt by ſpecial prerogative nine months* _{ever it be, that} *together entertain within the cloſet of thy fleſh, the hope of all the ends of the earth,* _{was the author} *the honour of the world, the common joy of men. He, from whom all things had their* _{lies that go un-} *beginning, had his beginning from thee; of thy body he took the blood which was to be* _{der his name.} *ſhed for the life of the world; of thee he took that which even for thee he paid. A pec-* *cati enim veteris nexu, per ſe non eſt immunis ipſa genitrix redemptoris:* the mother of _{Knowing how} the Redeemer himſelf, is not otherwiſe looſed from the bond of ancient ſin, than by _{the ſchoolmen} redemption. If Chriſt have paid a ranſom for all, even for her, it followeth, that all, _{tion, ſome cri-} without exception, were captives. If one have died for all, then all were dead in ſin; _{tical wits may} all ſinful therefore, none abſolutely righteous in themſelves; but we are abſolutely righ- _{ſpect that theſe} teous in Chriſt. The world then muſt ſhew a righteous man, otherwiſe it is not able _{two words, Per} to ſhew a man that is perfectly righteous: *Chriſt is made to us wiſdom, juſtice, ſancti-* _{But if the place} *fication, and redemption: wiſdom,* becauſe he hath revealed his Father's will: *juſtice,* be- _{which they} cauſe he hath offered up himſelf a ſacrifice for ſin: *ſanctification,* becauſe he hath given _{own, their} us his Spirit; *redemption,* becauſe he hath appointed a day to vindicate his children out _{ſenſe can be} of the bands of corruption into liberty which is glorious. How Chriſt is made *wiſdom,* _{than that} and how *redemption,* it may be declared, when occaſion ſerveth; but how Chriſt is made _{which I have} the *righteouſneſs* of men, we are now to declare. _{a paraphraſtical}

3. There is a glorifying righteouſneſs of men in the world to come: as there is a juſti- _{interpretation.} fying and ſanctifying righteouſneſs here. The righteouſneſs, wherewith we ſhall be cloathed in the world to come, is both perfect and inherent. That whereby here we are juſtified is perfect, but not inherent. That whereby we are ſanctified, is inherent, but not perfect. This openeth a way to the underſtanding of that grand queſtion, which hangeth yet in controverſy between us and the church of *Rome,* about the matter of juſti-fying righteouſneſs.

4. Firſt, although they imagine that the mother of our Lord and Saviour Jeſus Chriſt, _{They teach as} were for his honour, and by his ſpecial protection, preſerved clean from all ſin, yet _{we do, that} touching the reſt, they teach as we do, that infants, that never did actually offend, have _{tify the ſoul of} their natures defiled, deſtitute of juſtice, averted from God; that in making man righ- _{man alone,} teous, none do efficiently work with God, but God. They teach as we do, that unto _{en-effective} juſtice no man ever attained, but by the merits of Jeſus Chriſt. They teach as we do, _{cauſe of juſ-} that altho' Chriſt as God, be the efficient; as man, the meritorious cauſe of our juſtice; _{tice,} yet in us alſo there is ſomething required. God is the cauſe of our natural life, in him _{dio co-effecti-} we live: but he quickneth not the body without the ſoul in the body. Chriſt hath me- _{vo animam ju-} rited to make us juſt: but, as a medicine which is made for health, doth not heal by be- _{de quadripart.} ing made, but by being applied; ſo, by the merits of Chriſt there can be no juſtification, _{juſt. l. 6. c. i-} without the application of his merit. Thus far we join hands with the church of *Rome.* _{dem. l. 3. c. 9.}

5. Wherein then do we diſagree? We diſagree about the nature and eſſence of the me- _{The difference} dicine whereby Chriſt cureth our diſeaſe; about the manner of applying it; about the _{between the} number, and the power of means, which God requireth in us for the effectual applying _{papiſts and us} thereof to our ſoul's comfort. When they are required to ſhew what the righteouſneſs is _{tion.} whereby a chriſtian man is juſtified: they [b] anſwer,

that it is a divine ſpiritual quality; which quality re-ceived into the ſoul, doth firſt make it to be one of them who are born of God: and ſecondly, endue it with power to bring forth ſuch works, as they do that are born of him; even as the ſoul of man be-ing joined to his body, doth firſt make him to be of the number of reaſonable creatures; and ſecondly, enable him to perform the natural functions which are proper to his kind; that it maketh the ſoul amiable and gracious in the ſight of God, in regard whereof it is termed grace; that it purgeth, purifieth, and waſheth out all the ſtains and pollutions of ſins; that by it, thro' the merit of Chriſt we are deliver'd as from ſin, ſo from eternal death and condemnation, the reward of ſin. This grace they will have to be applied by infuſion; to the end, that as the body is warm by the heat which is in the body, ſo the ſoul might be righteous by inherent grace: which grace they make capable of increaſe; as the body may be more and more warm, ſo the ſoul more and more juſtified, according as grace ſhould be augmented; the augmentation whereof is merited by good works, as good works are made meritorious by it. Wherefore, the firſt receit of grace in their divinity is the firſt juſtification; the increaſe thereof, the ſecond juſtification. As grace may be increaſed by the merit of good works; ſo it may be di-miniſhed by the demerit of ſins venial; it may be loſt by mortal ſin. Inaſmuch therefore

[a] *Tho. Aquin.* 1 2. quæſt. 100. Gratia gratum faciens, id eſt, juſtificans eſt in anima quiddam reale & poſitivum, qua-litas quædam (art. 2. concl.) ſupernaturalis, non eadem cum virtute infuſa, ut magiſter; ſed magiſter (art. 3.) præter vir-tutes infuſas, fidem, ſpem, charitatem; habitudo, quædam (art. 3. ad 3.) quæ præſupponitur in virtutibus iſtis ſicut ea-rum principium & radix, eſſentiam animæ tanquam ſubjec-tum occupat, non potentias, ſed ab ipſa (art. 4. ad 1.) efflu-unt virtutes in potentias animæ, per quas potentiæ moven-tur ad actus; plur. vid. quæſt. 113. de juſtificatione.

as it is needful in the one cafe to repair, in the other to recover the lofs which is made: the infufion of grace hath her fundry after-meals; for the which caufe, they make many ways to apply the infufion of grace. It is applied to infants thro' baptifm, without either faith or works, and in them really it taketh away original fin, and the punifhment due unto it; it is applied to infidels and wicked men in the firft juftification, thro' baptifm without works, yet not without faith; and it taketh away both fins actual and original together, with all whatfoever punifhment, eternal or temporal, thereby deferved. Unto fuch as have attained the firft juftification, that is to fay, the firft receipt of grace, it is applied farther by good works to the increafe of former grace, which is the fecond juftification. If they work more and more, grace doth more increafe, and they are more and more juftified. To fuch as diminifh it by venial fins, it is applied by holy-water, *Ave Mary's*, croffings, papal falutations, and fuch like, which ferve for reparations of grace decayed. To fuch as have loft it thro' mortal fin, it is applied by the facrament (as they term it) of penance: which facrament hath force to confer grace anew, yet in fuch fort, that being fo conferred, it hath not altogether fo much power as at the firft. For it only cleanfeth out the ftain or guilt of fin committed, and changeth the punifhment eternal into a temporal fatisfactory punifhment here, if time do ferve; if not, hereafter to be endured, except it be lightned by maffes, works of charity, pilgrimages, fafts, and fuch like; or elfe fhortned by pardon for term, or by plenary pardon quite removed and taken away. This is the myftery of the man of fin. This maze the church of *Rome* doth caufe her followers to tread, when they afk her the way to juftification. I cannot ftand now to unrip this building, and fift it piece by piece; only I will pafs it by in few words, that that may befal *Babylon*, in the prefence of that which God hath builded, as hapned unto *Dagon* before the ark.

Phil. 2. 3.   6. Doubtlefs, faith the apoftle, *I have counted all things lofs, and judge them to be dung, that I may win Chrift; and to be found in him, not having my own righteoufnefs, but that which is through the faith of Chrift, the righteoufnefs which is of God through faith.* Whether they fpeak of the firft or fecond juftification, they make the effence of a divine quality inherent, they make it righteoufnefs which is in us. If it be in us, then is it ours, as our fouls are ours, tho' we have them from God, and can hold them no longer than pleafeth him; for if he withdraw the breath of our noftrils, we fall to duft: but the righteoufnefs wherein we muft be found, if we will be juftified, is not our own; therefore we cannot be juftified by any inherent quality. Chrift hath merited righteoufnefs for as many as are found in him. In him God findeth us, if we be faithful; for by faith we are incorporated into Chrift. Then, altho' in our felves we be altogether finful and unrighteous, yet even the man which is impious in himfelf, full of iniquity, full of fin; him being found in Chrift thro' faith, and having his fin remitted thro' repentance; him God upholdeth with a gracious eye, putteth away his fin by not imputing it, taketh quite away the punifhment due thereunto, by pardoning it, and accepteth him in Jefus Chrift, as perfectly righteous, as if he had fulfilled all that was commanded him in the law: fhall I fay more perfectly righteous than if himfelf had

2 Cor. 5. 21. fulfilled the whole law? I muft take heed what I fay: but the apoftle faith, *God made him to be fin for us, who knew no fin; that we might be made the righteoufnefs of God in him.* Such we are in the fight of God the Father, as is the very Son of God himfelf. Let it be counted folly or frenzy, or fury, whatfoever; it is our comfort, and our widom; we care for no knowledge in the world but this, that man hath finned, and God hath fuffered; that God hath made himfelf the fon of man, and that men are made the righteoufnefs of God. You fee therefore, that the church of *Rome*, in teaching juftification by inherent grace, doth pervert the truth of Chrift; and that by the hands of the apoftles we have received otherwife than fhe teacheth. Now concerning the righteoufnes of fanctification, we deny it not to be inherent: we grant, that unlefs we work, we have it not: only we diftinguifh it as a thing different in nature from the righteoufnefs of juftification: we are righteous the one way, by the faith of *Abraham*; the other way, except we do the

Rom. 4. 6. works of *Abraham*, we are not righteous. Of the one, St. *Paul, To him that worketh not, but believeth, faith is counted for righteoufnefs.* Of the other, St. *John, Qui facit juftitiam, juftus eft:* he is righteous which worketh righteoufnefs. Of the one, St. *Paul* doth prove by *Abraham's* example, that we have it of faith without works. Of the other, St. *James* by *Abraham's* example, that by works we have it, and not only by faith. St. *Paul* doth plainly fever thefe two parts of chriftian righteoufnefs one from the other.

Chap. 6.   For in the fixth to the *Romans*, thus he writeth, *Being freed from fin, and made fervants to God, ye have your fruit in holinefs, and the end everlafting life. Ye are made free from fin, and made fervants unto God;* this is the righteoufnefs of *juftification; Ye have your fruit in holinefs;* this is the righteoufnefs of fanctification. By the one we are interefted in the

right

right of inheriting; by the other we are brought to the actual poſſeſſion of eternal bliſs, and ſo the end of both is everlaſting life.

7. The prophet *Habakkuk* doth here term the Jews *righteous men*, not only becauſe being juſtified by faith they were free from ſin; but alſo becauſe they had their meaſure of fruits in holineſs. According to whoſe example of charitable judgment, which leaveth it to God to diſcern what we are, and ſpeaketh of them according to that which they do profeſs themſelves to be, although they be not holy men whom men do think, but whom God doth know indeed to be ſuch: yet let every chriſtian man know, that in chriſtian equity, he ſtandeth bound for to think and ſpeak of his brethren, as of men that have a meaſure in the fruit of holineſs, and a right unto the titles wherewith God, in token of ſpecial favour and mercy, vouchſafeth to honour his choſen ſervants. So we ſee the apoſtles of our Saviour Chriſt, do uſe every where the name of *ſaints*; ſo the prophet the name of *righteous*. But let us all be ſuch as we deſire to be termed: *Reatus impii eſt pium nomen*, ſaith *Salvianus*; godly names do not juſtify godleſs men. We are but upbraided, when we are honoured with names and titles whereunto our lives and manners are not ſuitable. If indeed we have our fruit in holineſs, notwithſtanding we muſt note, that the more we abound therein, the more need we have to crave that we may be ſtrengthned and ſupported. Our very virtues may be ſnares unto us. The enemy that waiteth for all occaſions to work our ruin, hath found it harder to overthrow an humble ſinner, than a proud ſaint. There is no man's caſe ſo dangerous, as his whom Satan hath perſuaded that his own righteouſneſs ſhall preſent him pure and blameleſs in the ſight of God. If we could ſay, we were not guilty of any thing at all in our conſciences (we know our ſelves far from this innocency; we cannot ſay, we know nothing by our ſelves; but if we could) ſhould we therefore plead not guilty before the preſence of our judge, that ſees further into our hearts than we our ſelves can do? If our hands did never offer violence to our brethren, a bloody thought doth prove us murderers before him: if we had never opened our mouth to utter any ſcandalous, offenſive, or hurtful word, the cry of our ſecret cogitations is heard in the ears of God. If we did not commit the ſins which daily and hourly, either in deed, word, or thoughts we do commit; yet in the good things which we do, how many defects are there intermingled! God, in that which is done, reſpecteth the mind and intention of the doer. Cut off then all thoſe things wherein we have regarded our own glory, thoſe things which men do to pleaſe men, and to ſatisfy our own liking, thoſe things which we do for any by-reſpect, not ſincerely and purely for the love of God, and a ſmall ſcore will ſerve for the number of our righteous deeds. Let the holieſt and beſt things which we do be conſidered. We are never better affected unto God than when we pray; yet when we pray, how are our affections many times diſtracted! how little reverence do we ſhew unto the grand majeſty of God, unto whom we ſpeak! how little remorſe of our own miſeries! how little taſte of the ſweet influence of his tender mercies do we feel! Are we not as unwilling many times to begin, and as glad to make an end, as if in ſaying, *Call upon me*, he had ſet us a very burdenſome task? It may ſeem ſomewhat extream, which I will ſpeak; therefore let every one judge of it, even as his own heart ſhall tell him, and no otherwiſe; I will but only make a demand: If God ſhould yield unto us, not as unto *Abraham*, if fifty, forty, thirty, twenty, yea, or if ten good perſons could be found in a city, for their ſakes this city ſhould not be deſtroyed: but, and if he ſhould make us an offer thus large; ſearch all the generations of men, ſithence the fall of our father *Adam*, find one man, that hath done one action, which hath paſt from him pure, without any ſtain or blemiſh at all; and for that one man's only action, neither man nor angel ſhall feel the torments which are prepared for both. Do you think that this ranſom, to deliver men and angels, could be found to be among the ſons of men? The beſt things which we do, have ſomewhat in them to be pardoned. How then can we do any thing meritorious, or worthy to be rewarded? Indeed, God doth liberally promiſe whatſoever appertaineth to a bleſſed life, to as many as ſincerely keep his law, tho' they be not exactly able to keep it. Wherefore we acknowledge a dutiful neceſſity of doing well, but the meritorious dignity of doing well we utterly renounce. We ſee how far we are from the perfect righteouſneſs of the law; the little fruit which we have in holineſs, it is, God knoweth, corrupt and unſound: we put no confidence at all in it, we challenge nothing in the world for it, we dare not call God to reckoning, as if we had him in our debt-books: our continual ſuit to him, is, and muſt be, to bear with our infirmities, and pardon our offences.

8. But the people of whom the prophet ſpeaketh, were they all, or were the moſt part of them ſuch as had care to walk uprightly? Did they thirſt after righteouſneſs? did they wiſh? did they long with the righteous prophet? *O that our ways were ſo direct that we might keep thy ſtatutes!* Did they lament with the righteous apoſtle? *O miſera-*

ble men, the good which we wifh and purpofe, and ftrive to do, we cannot? No, the words of the other prophet concerning this people, do fhew the contrary. How grievoufly hath *Efay* mourned over them! *O finful nation, laden with iniquity, wicked feed, corrupt children!* All which notwithftanding, fo wide are the bowels of his compaffion enlarged, that he denieth us not, no, not when we were laden with iniquity, leave to commune familiarly with him, liberty to crave, and intreat that what plagues foever we have deferved, we may not be in worfe cafe than unbelievers, that we may not be hemmed in by pagans and infidels. *Jerufalem* is a finful polluted city: but *Jerufalem* compared with *Babylon,* is righteous. And fhall the righteous be over-born? fhall they be compaffed about by the wicked? But the prophet doth not only complain, Lord, how cometh it to pafs, that thou handleft us fo hardly, of whom thy name is called, and beareft with the heathen nations that defpife thee? no, he breaketh out thro' extremity of grief, and inferreth violently, this *proceeding is perverfe,* the righteous are thus handled; *therefore perverfe judgment doth proceed.*

9. Which *dilation* containeth many things, whereof it were better much for you to hear, and me to fpeak, if neceffity did not draw me to another task. *Paul* and *Barnabas* being requefted to preach the fame things again which once they had preached, thought it their duty to fatisfy the godly defires of men fincerely affected to the truth. Nor may it feem burdenous for me, nor for you unprofitable, that I follow their example, the like occafion unto theirs being offered me. When we had laft the epiftle of St. *Paul* to the *Hebrews* in hand, and of that epiftle thefe words, *In thefe laft days he has fpoken to us by his Son;* after we had thence collected the nature of the vifible church of Chrift, and had defined it to be a community of men *fanctified through the profeffion of the truth which God hath taught the world by his Son; and had declared, that the fcope of chriftian doctrine is the comfort of them whofe hearts are over-charged with the burden of fin; and had proved that the doctrine profeffed in the church of *Rome,* doth bereave men of comfort, both in their lives, and in their deaths; the conclufion in the end, whereunto we came, was this, the church of *Rome,* being in faith fo corrupted as fhe is, and refufing to be reformed as fhe doth, we are to fever our felves from her; the example of our fathers may not retain us in communion with that church, under hope that we fo continuing, may be faved as well as they. God, I doubt not, was merciful to fave thoufands of them, though they lived in popifh fuperftitions, inafmuch as they finned ignorantly: but the truth is now laid before our eyes. The former part of this laft fentence, namely, thefe words, *I doubt not but God was merciful to fave thoufands of our fathers living in popifh fuperftitions, inafmuch as they finned ignorantly.* This fentence, I befeech you to mark, and to fift it with the feverity of aufere judgment, that if it be found to be gold, it may be fuitable to the precious foundation whereon it was then laid; for I proteft, that if it be hay or ftubble, my own hand fhall fet fire on it. Two queftions have rifen by this fpeech before alledged: the one, *Whether our fathers, infected with popifh errors and fuperftitions, may be faved?* the other, *Whether their ignorance be a reafonable inducement to make us think they might?* We are then to examine, firft, what poffibility; then, what probability there is, that God might be merciful unto fo many of our fathers.

10. So many of our fathers living in popifh fuperftitions, yet by the mercy of God be faved? No; this could not be: God hath fpoken by his angel from heaven, unto his people concerning *Babylon,* (by *Babylon,* we underftand the church of *Rome,*) *Go out of her, my people, that ye be not partakers of her plagues.* For anfwer whereunto, firft, I do not take the words to be meant only of temporal plagues, of the corporal death, forrow, famine and fire, whereunto God in his wrath had condemned *Babylon;* and that to fave his chofen people from thefe plagues, he faith, *Go out,* with like intent, as in the gofpel, fpeaking of *Jerufalem's* defolations, he faith, *Let them that are in Judea, fly unto the mountains, and them that are in the midft thereof depart out:* or as in the former times to *Lot, Arife, take thy wife and thy daughters which are there, left thou be deftroyed in the punifhment of the city:* but forafmuch as here it is faid, *Go out of Babylon;* we doubt, their everlafting deftruction, which are partakers therein, is either principally meant, or neceffarily implied in this fentence. How then was it poffible for fo many of our fathers to be faved, fince they were fo far from departing out of *Babylon,* that they took her for their mother, and in her bofom yielded up the ghoft?

11. Firft, for the plagues being threatned unto them that are partakers in the fins of *Babylon,* we can define nothing concerning our fathers out of this fentence: unlefs we fhew what the fins of *Babylon* be, and what they be which are fuch partakers of them that their everlafting plagues are inevitable. The fins which may be common both to them of the church of *Rome,* and to others departed thence, muft be fevered from this queftion. He which faith, *Depart out of Babylon, left ye be partakers of her fins;* sheweth

Acts 13. 43. 44.

Heb. 1. 2.

* By fanctification, I mean a feparation from others not profeffing as they do: for true holinefs confifteth not unto in profeffing, but in obeying the truth of Chrift.

Apoc. 18. 4.

Mat. 24. 16.

Gen. 19. 15.

sheweth plainly, that he meaneth such sins, as except we separate our selves, we have no power in the world to avoid; such impieties, as by their law they have established, and whereunto all that are among them, either do indeed assent, or else are, by powerful means, forced in shew and appearance to subject themselves. As for example, in the church of *Rome* it is maintained, that the same credit and reverence that we give to the scriptures of God, ought also to be given to unwritten verities; that the pope is supreme head ministerial over the universal church militant; that the bread in the eucharist is transubstantiated into Christ; that it is to be adored, and to be offered up unto God, as a sacrifice propitiatory for quick and dead; that images are to be worshiped, saints to be called upon as intercessors, and such like. Now, because some heresies do concern things only believed, as the transubstantiation of the sacramental elements in the eucharist; some concern things which are practised and put in ure, as the adoration of the elements transubstantiated: we must note, that *erroneously* the practice of that is sometime received, whereof the doctrine that teacheth it is not *heretically* maintained. They are all partakers of the maintenance of heresies, who by word or deed allow them, knowing them, altho' not knowing them to be heresies; as also they, and that most dangerously of all others, who knowing heresy to be heresy, do notwithstanding in worldly respects, make semblance of allowing that, which in heart and judgment they condemn: but heresy is heretically maintained, by such as obstinately hold it after wholesome admonition. Of the last sort, as of the next before, I make no doubt, but that their condemnation, without an actual repentance, is inevitable. Lest any man therefore should think, that in speaking of our fathers, I should speak indifferently of them all: let my words, I beseech you, be well marked, *I doubt not but God was merciful to save thousands of our fathers:* which thing, I will now, by God's assistance, set more plainly before your eyes.

12. Many are partakers of the error, which are not of the heresy of the church of *Rome.* The people, following the conduct of their guides, and observing as they did, exactly that which was prescribed, thought they did God good service, when indeed they did dishonour him. This was their error. But the heresy of the church of *Rome,* their dogmatical position opposite unto christian truth, what one man among ten thousand did ever understand? Of them which understand *Roman* heresies, and allow them, all are not alike partakers in the action of allowing. Some allow them as the first founders and establishers of them: which crime toucheth none but their popes and councils: the people are clear and free from this. Of them which maintain popish heresies, not as authors, but receivers of them from others, all maintain them not as masters. In this are not the people partakers neither, but only the predicant and schoolmen. Of them which have been partakers in this sin of teaching popish heresy, there is also a difference; for they have not all been teachers of all popish heresy. *Put a difference,* saith St. *Jude,* Verse 22. *have compassion upon some.* Shall we lap up all in one condition? Shall we cast them all headlong? Shall we plunge them all into that infernal and everlasting flaming lake? Them that have been partakers of the errors of *Babylon,* together with them which are in the heresy? them which have been the authors of heresy, with them that by terror and violence have been forced to receive it? them who have taught it, with them whose simplicity hath by flights and conveyances of false teachers been seduced to believe it? them which have been partakers in one, with them which have been partakers in many? them which in many, with them which in all?

13. Notwithstanding I grant, that although the condemnation of them be more tolerable than of these: yet from the man that laboureth at the plough, to him that sitteth in the vatican; to all partakers in the sins of *Babylon;* to our fathers, though they did but erroneously practise that which the guide heretically taught; to all without exception, plagues were due. The pit is ordinarily the end, as well of the guide, as of the guided in blindness. But wo worth the hour wherein we were born, except we might promise our selves better things; things which accompany man's salvation, even where we know that worse, and such as accompany condemnation are due. Then must we shew some way how possibly they might escape. What way is there that sinners can find to escape the judgment of God, but only by appealing to the seat of his saving mercy? Which mercy, with *Origen,* we do not extend to devils and damned spirits. God hath mercy upon thousands, but there be thousands also which he hardneth. Christ hath therefore set the bounds, he hath fixed the limits of his saving mercy within the compass of these terms: *God sent not his own Son to condemn the world, but that the world through him might be saved.* In the third of St. *John's* gospel, mercy is restrained to believers: *He that believeth shall not* John 3. 17. *be condemned; he that believeth not, is condemned already, because he believeth not in the Son of God.* In the second of the *Revelation,* mercy is restrained to the penitent. For of *Jezabel* and her sectaries, thus he speaketh: *I gave her space to repent, and she re-* Rev. 2. 21. *pented*

pented not. *Behold, I will cast her into a bed, and them that commit fornication with her into great affliction, except they repent them of their works, and I will kill her children with death.* Our hope therefore of the fathers is, if they were not altogether faithless and impenitent, that they are saved.

14. They are not all faithless that are weak in assenting to the truth, or stiff in maintaining things opposite to the truth of christian doctrine. But as many as hold the foundation which is precious, tho' they hold it but weakly, and as it were with a slender thread, altho' they frame many base and unsuitable things upon it, things that cannot abide the trial of the fire; yet shall they pass the fiery trial and be saved, which indeed have builded themselves upon the rock, which is the foundation of the church. If then our fathers did not hold the foundation of faith, there is no doubt but they were faithless. If many of them held it, then is therein no impediment but many of them might be sav'd. Then let us see what the foundation of faith is, and whether we may think that thousands of our fathers being in popish superstitions, did notwithstanding hold the foundation.

15. If the foundation of faith do import the general ground whereupon we rest when we do believe, the writings of the evangelists and the apostles are the foundation of the christian faith: *Credimus quia legimus,* saith St. *Jerome.* O that the church of *Rome* did ᵃ soundly interpret these fundamental writings whereupon we build our faith, as she doth willingly hold and embrace them!

ᵃ They misin-as terpret, noton-ly by making false and corrupt glosses upon the scripture, but also by forcing the old vulgar translation, as the only authentical. Howbeit, they refuse no book which is canonical, tho' they admit sundry which are not.

16. But if the name of *foundation* do note the principal thing which is believed: then is that the foundation of our faith which St. *Paul* hath to *Timothy*: *God manifested in the flesh, justified in the spirit,* &c. that of *Nathaniel, Thou art the Son of the living God: thou art the King of Israel:* that of the inhabitants of *Samaria, This is Christ the Saviour of the world*: he that directly denieth this, doth utterly raze the foundation of our faith. I have prov'd heretofore, that altho' the church of *Rome* hath plaid the harlot worse than ever did *Israel,* yet are they not, as now the synagogue of the *Jews* which plainly deny Christ Jesus, quite and clean excluded from the new covenant. But as *Samaria* compared with *Jerusalem,* is termed *Aholah,* a church or tabernacle of her own; contrariwise *Jerusalem Aholibah,* the resting place of the Lord: so, whatsoever we term the church of *Rome* when we compare her with reformed churches, still we put a difference, as then between *Babylon* and *Samaria,* so now between *Rome* and the heathenish assemblies: which opinion I must and will recal; I must grant and will, that the church of *Rome,* together with all her children, is clean excluded. There is no difference in the world between our fathers and *Saracens, Turks* and *Painims,* if they did directly deny Christ crucified for the salvation of the world.

17. But how many millions of them were known so to have ended their lives, that the drawing of their breath hath ceased with the uttering of this faith, *Christ my Saviour, my Redeemer Jesus?* Answer is made, that this they might unfeignedly confess, and yet be far enough from salvation. For behold, saith the apostle, *I Paul say unto you, that if ye be circumcised, Christ shall profit you nothing.* Christ, in the work of man's salvation, is alone: the *Galatians* were cast away by joining circumcision and the other rites of the law with Christ: the church of *Rome* doth teach her children to join other things likewise with him; therefore their faith, their belief doth not profit them any thing at all. It is true, that they do indeed join other things with Christ: but how? Not in the work of redemption it self, which they grant that Christ alone hath performed sufficiently for the salvation of the whole world; but in the application of this inestimable treasure, that it may be effectual to their salvation: how demurely soever they confess that they seek remission of sins no otherwise than by the blood of Christ, using humbly the means appointed by him to apply the benefit of his holy blood; they teach indeed so many things pernicious in christian faith, in setting down the means whereof they speak, that the very foundation of faith which they hold is thereby ᵇ plainly overthrown, and the force of the blood of Jesus Christ extinguish'd. We may therefore, disputing with them, urge 'em even with as dangerous sequels, as the apostle doth the *Galatians.* But I demand, if some of those *Galatians,* heartily embracing the gospel of Christ, sincere and sound in faith (this one only error excepted) had ended their lives before they were ever taught how perilous an opinion they held; shall we think that the danger of this error did so overweigh the benefit of their faith, that the mercy of God might not save them? I grant they oversee not that threw the foundation of faith by consequent; doth not that so likewise which the ᶜ *Lu-*

ᵇ Plainly in all mens sight of whose eyes God hath enlightned to behold his truth. For they which are in error, are in darkness, and which in light

ᶜ is plain, in that which they teach concerning the natures of Christ, they held the same with *Nestorius* fully, the same with *Eutyches* about the proprieties of his nature. The opinion of the *Lutherans,* tho' it be no direct denial of the foundation, may notwithstanding be damnable unto some; and I do not think but that in many respects it is less damnable, as at this day some maintain it, than it was in them which held it at first; as *Luther* and others, whom I had an eye unto in this speech. The question is not, whether an error with such and such circumstances; but simply, whether an error overthrowing the foundation, do exclude all possibility of salvation, if it be not recanted, and expresly repented of.

theran

theran churches do at this day so stiffly and so firmly maintain? For mine own part, I dare not here deny the possibility of their salvation, which have been the chiefest instruments of ours, albeit they carried to their graves a persuasion so greatly repugnant to the truth. Forasmuch therefore, as it may be said of the church of *Rome*, she hath yet a little strength, she doth not directly deny the foundation of christianity: I may, I trust, without offence, persuade my self that thousands of our fathers, in former times, living and dying within her walls, have found mercy at the hands of God.

18. What altho' they repented not of their errors? God forbid that I should open my mouth to gainsay that which Christ himself hath spoken: *Except ye repent, ye shall all perish*. And if they did not repent, they perished. But withal note, that we have the benefit of a double repentance: the least sin which we commit, in deed, thought or word, is death, without repentance. Yet how many things do escape in every of these, which we do not know? How many, which we do not observe to be sins? And without knowledge, without the observation of sin, there is no actual repentance. It cannot then be chosen, but that for as many as hold the foundation, and have holden all sins and errors in hatred, the blessing of repentance for unknown sins and errors is obtained at the hands of God, thro' the gracious meditation of Jesus Christ, for such suiters as cry with the prophet *David, Purge me, O Lord, from my secret sins.*

19. But we wash a wall of lome, we labour in vain, all this is nothing; it doth not prove; it cannot justify that which we go about to maintain. Infidels and heathen men are not so godless, but that they may, no doubt, cry God mercy, and desire in general to have their sins forgiven. To such as deny the foundation of faith, there can be no salvation (according to the ordinary course which God doth use in saving men) without a particular repentance of that error. The *Galatians* thinking that unless they were circumcis'd they could not be saved, overthrew the foundation of faith directly: therefore if any of them did die so persuaded, whether before or after they were told of their errors, their end is dreadful; there is no way with them but one, death and condemnation. For the apostle speaketh nothing of men departed, but saith generally of all, *If ye be circumcised, Christ shall profit you nothing. Ye are abolished from Christ, whosoever are justified by the law; ye are fallen from grace.* Gal. 5. Of them in the church of *Rome*, the reason is the same. For whom antichrist hath seduced, concerning them did not St. *Paul* speak long before, they received not the word of truth, that they might not be saved? Therefore God would *send them strong delusions to believe lies, that all they might be damned which believe not the truth, but had pleasure in unrighteousness.* And St. *John, All that dwell upon the earth shall worship him, whose names are not written in the book of life.* Apoc. 13. Indeed many in former times, as their books and writings do yet shew, held the foundation, to wit, salvation by Christ alone, and therefore might be saved. God hath always had a church amongst them, which firmly kept his saving truth. As for such as hold with the church of *Rome*, that we cannot be saved by Christ alone without works; they do not only by a circle of consequents, but directly deny the foundation of faith; they hold it not, no, not so much as by a thread.

20. This, to my remembrance, being all that hath been opposed with any countenance or shew of reason, I hope, if this be answered, the cause in question is at an end. Concerning general repentance therefore: What? a murtherer, a blasphemer, an unclean person, a Turk, a Jew, any sinner to escape the wrath of God by a general repentance, *God forgive me?* Truly, it never came within my heart, that a general repentance doth serve for all sins: it serveth only for the common over-sights of our sinful life, and for the faults which either we do not mark, or do not know that they are faults. Our fathers were actually penitent for sins, wherein they knew they displeased God: or else they fall not within the compass of my first speech. Again, that otherwise they could not be saved, than holding the foundation of christian faith, we have not only affirmed, but proved. Why is it not then confessed, that thousands of our fathers which lived in popish superstitions, might yet, by the mercy of God, be saved? First, if they had directly denied the very foundations of christianity, without repenting them particularly of that sin, he which saith, there could be no salvation for them, according to the ordinary course which God doth use in saving men, granteth plainly, or at the least, closely insinuateth, that an extraordinary privilege of mercy might deliver their souls from hell; which is more than I required. Secondly, if the foundation be denied, it is denied for fear of some heresy which the church of *Rome* maintaineth. But how many were there amongst our fathers, who being seduced by the common error of that church, never knew the meaning of her heresies? So that altho' all popish hereticks did perish; thousands of them which lived in popish superstitions might be saved. Thirdly, seeing all that held popish heresies did not hold all the heresies of the pope; why might not thousands which were infected

fected with other leven, die unfowred with this, and fo be faved? Fourthly, if they all held this herefy, many there were that held it, no doubt, but only in a general form of words which a favourable interpretation might expound in a fenfe differing far enough from the poifoned conceit of herefy. As for example; did they hold that we cannot be faved by Chrift without good works? We our felves do, I think, all fay as much, with this conftruction, falvation being taken as in that fentence, *Corde creditur ad juftitiam, ore fit confeffio ad falutem,* except infants and men, cut off upon the point of their converfion; of the reft none fhall fee God, but fuch as feek peace and holinefs, though not as a caufe of their falvation, yet as a way which they muft walk which will be faved. Did they hold, that without works we are not juftified? Take juftification fo as it may alfo imply fanctification, and St. *James* doth fay as much. For except there be an ambiguity in the fame term, St. *Paul* and St. *James* do contradict each the other: which cannot be. Now there is no ambiguity in the name either of faith, or of works, being meant by them both in one and the fame fenfe. Finding therefore, that juftification is fpoken of by St. *Paul* without implying fanctification, when he proveth that a man is juftified by faith without works; finding likewife that juftification doth fometime imply fanctification alfo with it: I fuppofe nothing to be more found, than fo to interpret St. *James* fpeaking not in that fenfe, but in this.

12. We have already fhewed, that there be two kinds of chriftian righteoufnefs: the one without us, which we have by imputation; the other in us, which confifteth of faith, hope, and charity, and other chriftian virtues: and St. *James* doth prove that *Abraham* had not only the one, becaufe the thing believed was imputed unto him for righteoufnefs; but alfo the other, becaufe he offered up his fon. God giveth us both the one juftice and the other; the one for accepting us for righteous in Chrift; the other by working chriftian righteoufnefs in us. The proper and moft immediate efficient caufe in us of this latter, is, the fpirit of adoption we have received into our hearts. That whereof it confifteth, whereof it is really and formally made, are thofe infufed virtues proper and peculiar unto faints; which the Spirit in the very moment when firft it is given of God, bringeth with it: the effects whereof are fuch actions as the apoftle doth call the fruits of works, the operations of the Spirit: the difference of the which operation from the root whereof they fpring, maketh it needful to put two kinds likewife of fanctifying righteoufnefs, *habitual,* and *actual. Habitual,* that holinefs, wherewith our fouls are inwardly indued, the fame inftant when firft we begin to be the temples of the holy Ghoft. *Actual,* that holinefs, which afterwards beautifieth all the parts and actions of our life, the holinefs for which *Enoch, Job, Zachary, Elizabeth,* and other faints, are in the fcriptures fo highly commended. If here it be demanded, which of thefe we do firft receive? I anfwer, that the Spirit, the virtue of the Spirit, the habitual juftice, which is ingrafted, the external juftice of Jefus Chrift, which is imputed; thefe we receive all at one and the fame time; whenfoever we have any of thefe, we have all; they go together: yet firh no man is juftified except he believe, and no man believeth except he has faith, and no man except he hath received the fpirit of adoption, hath faith: forafmuch as they do neceffarily infer juftification, and juftification doth of neceffity prefuppofe them: we muft needs hold that imputed righteoufnefs, in dignity being the chiefeft, is notwithftanding in order to the laft of all thefe: but *actual righteoufnefs,* which is the righteoufnefs of good works, fucceedeth all, followeth after all, both in order and time. Which being attentively marked, fheweth plainly how the faith of true believers cannot be divorced from hope and love; how faith is a part of fanctification, and yet unto juftification neceffary; how faith is perfected by good works, and not works of ours without faith: finally, how our fathers might hold, that we are juftified by faith alone, and yet hold truly that without works we are not juftified. Did they think that men do merit rewards in heaven by the works they perform on earth? The ancients ufe *meriting* for *obtaining,* and in that fenfe they of *Wittenberg* have in their confeffion; *We teach that good works commanded of God, are neceffarily to be done, and by the free kindnefs of God they merit their certain rewards.* Therefore fpeaking as our fathers did, and we taking their fpeech, in a found meaning, as we may take our fathers, and might, forafmuch as their meaning is doubtful, and charity doth always interpret doubtful things favourably; what fhould induce us to think that rather the damage of the worft conftruction did light upon them all, than that the bleffing of the better was granted unto thoufands? Fifthly, if in the worft conftruction that may be made, they had generally all embraced it living, might not many of them dying utterly renounce it? howfoever men when they fit at eafe, do vainly tickle their hearts with the vain conceit of I know not what proportionable correfpondence between their merits and their rewards, which in the trance of their high fpeculations they dream that God hath meafured, weighed, and laid up, as it were, in bundle for them: notwithftanding we

(marginal notes:) For this is the only thing alledged to prove the impoffibility of their falvation: the church of *Rome* joineth works with Chrift, which is a denial of the foundation; and unlefs we hold the foundation, we cannot be faved.

2   fee

fee by daily experience, in a number even of them, that when the hour of death approach-eth, when they fecretly hear themfelves fummoned forthwith to appear, and ftand at the bar of that judge, whofe brightnefs caufeth the eyes of the angels themfelves to dazle, all thefe idle imaginations do then begin to hide their faces; to name merits then, is to lay their fouls upon the rack, the memory of their own deeds is loathfome unto them, they forfake all things wherein they have put any truft or confidence; no ftaff to lean upon, no eafe, no reft, no comfort then, but only in Jefus Chrift.

22. Wherefore if this propofition were true: *to hold in fuch wife, as the church of* Rome *doth, that we cannot be faved by Chrift alone without works, is directly to deny the foundation of faith*; I fay, that if this propofition were true: neverthelefs fo many ways I have fhewed, whereby we may hope that thoufands of our fathers which lived in po-pifh fuperftition might be faved. But what if it be not true? What if neither that of the *Galatians*, concerning circumcifion; nor this of the church of *Rome* by works be any direct denial of the foundation as it is affirmed, that both are? I need not wade fo far as to difcufs this controverfy, the matter which was firft brought into queftion being fo clear, as I hope it is. Howbeit, becaufe I defire that the truth even in that al-fo fhould receive light, I will do mine endeavour to fet down fomewhat more plainly firft, the foundation of faith, what it is: fecondly, what is directly to deny the foun-dation: thirdly, whether they whom God hath chofen to be heirs of life, may fall fo far as directly to deny it: fourthly, whether the *Galatians* did fo by admitting the error about *circumcifion* and the *law*; laft of all, whether the church of *Rome* for this one opi-nion of works, may be thought to do the like, and thereupon to be no more a chriftian church, than are the affemblies of *Turks* and *Jews*.

They may ceafe to put any confidence in works and yet never think, living in popifh fu-perftition, they did amifs. Fig-bus died po-pifh, and yet denied popery in the article of juftification by workslongbe-fore his death.

23. This word foundation being figuratively ufed, hath always reference to fomewhat which refembleth a material building, as both that doctrine of *laws* and the community of chriftians do. By the mafters of civil policy nothing is fo much inculcated, as that *commonwealths are founded upon laws*; for that a multitude cannot be compacted into one body otherwife than by a common acception of laws, whereby they are to be kept in order. The ground of all civil laws is this: *No man ought to be hurt or injured by an-other*; take away this perfuafion, and ye take away all the laws; take away laws, and what fhall become of commonweals? So it is in our fpiritual chriftian community: I do not mean that body myftical, whereof Chrift is only the head, that building undifcernable by mortal eyes, wherein Chrift is the chief corner ftone: but I fpeak of the vifible church; the foundation whereof is the doctrine which the prophets and the apoftles profeft. The mark whereunto their doctrine tendeth, is pointed at in thefe words of *Pe-*ter unto Chrift, *Thou haft the words of eternal life:* in thofe words of *Paul* to *Timothy, The holy fcriptures are able to make thee wife unto falvation.* It is the demand of nature it felf, *What fhall we do to have eternal life?* The defire of immortality and the know-ledge of that, whereby it may be obtained, is fo natural unto all men, that even they who are not perfuaded that they fhall, do notwithftanding wifh that they might know a way how to fee no end of life. And becaufe natural means are not able ftill to refift the force of death, there is no people in the earth fo favage which hath not devifed fome fu-pernatural help or other to fly for aid and fuccour in extremities againft the enemies of the laws. A longing therefore to be fav'd, without underftanding the true way how, hath been the caufe of all the fuperftitions in the world. O that the miferable ftate of others, which wander in darknefs and wot not whither they go, could give us underftanding hearts, wor-thily to efteem the riches of the mercy of God towards us, before whofe eyes the doors of the kingdom of heaven are fet wide open! fhould we offer violence unto it? it offereth vio-lence unto us, and we gather ftrength to withftand it. But I am befides my purpofe when I fall to bewail the cold affection which we bear towards that whereby we fhould be faved; my purpofe being only to fet down what the ground of falvation is. The doctrine of the gofpel propofeth falvation as the end: and doth it not teach the way of attaining there-unto? Yet the damfel poffeft with a fpirit of divination fpake the truth: *Thefe men are the fervants of the moft high God, which fhew unto us the way of falvation: a new and living way which Chrift hath prepared for us, thro' the vail, that is, his flefh;* falvation purchafed by the death of Chrift. By this foundation the children of God, before the written law were diftinguifhed from the fons of men, the reverend patriarchs both poffeft it living, and fpake exprefly of it at the hour of their death. It comforted *Job* in the midft of grief; as it was afterwards the anchor-hold of all the righteous in *Ifrael*, from the writing of the law, to the time of grace. Every prophet making mention of it. It was famoufly fpoken of, about the time, when the coming of Chrift to accomplifh the pro-mifes, which were made long before it drew near, that the found thereof was heard even amongft the Gentiles. When he was come, as many as were his, acknowledged that he was

What the foundation of faith is: Vocata multitudinem qua molefcere in po-puli unius corpus nulla re præter-quam legibus poterat. Liv. de Rom. lib. 1.

Ephef. 1. 13. and 4. 15.

Ephef. 2. 20. John 6. 63. 2 Tim. 3. 15.

Acts 16. 17. Heb. 10. 20.

Gen. 49. Job 19.

their

P p p

Acts 4. 12. their falvation; he, that long expected hope of *Ifrael*; he, that *feed, in whom all the nations of the earth fhall be bleffed.* So that now he is a name of ruin, a name of death and condemnation, unto fuch as dream of a new *Meffias*, to as many as look for falvation by any other but by him. *For amongft men there is given no other name under heaven whereby we muft be faved.* Thus much St. *Mark* doth intimate by that which he doth put in the front of this book, making his entrance with thefe words: *The beginning of the gofpel of Jefus Chrift, the Son of God.* His doctrine he termeth the gofpel, becaufe he teacheth falvation; the gofpel of Jefus Chrift the Son of God, becaufe it teacheth falvation by him. This is then the foundation, whereupon the frame of the gofpel is erected; Luke 1. 28.
1 Cor. 3. that very *Jefus* whom the *Virgin* conceived of the holy Ghoft, whom *Simeon* embraced in his arms, whom *Pilate* condemned, whom the *Jews* crucified, whom the apoftles preached, he is Chrift, the Lord, the only Saviour of the world: *Other foundation can no man lay.* Thus I have briefly opened that principle in chriftianity, which we call the foundation of our faith. It followeth now that I declare unto you, what is directly to overthrow it. This will be better opened, if we underftand, what it is to hold the foundation of faith.

24. There are which defend, that many of the *Gentiles*, who never heard the name of Chrift, held the foundation of chriftianity, and why? they acknowledged many of them, the providence of God, his infinite wifdom, ftrength, power; his goodnefs, and his mercy towards the children of men; that God hath judgment in ftore for the wicked, but for the righteous which ferve him rewards, *&c.* In this which they confeffed, that lyeth covered which we believe; in the rudiments of their knowledge concerning God, the foundation of our faith concerning Chrift, lyeth fecretly wrapt up, and is virtually contained: therefore they held the foundation of faith, tho' they never had it. Might we not with as good a colour of reafon defend, that every plowman hath all the fciences, wherein philofophers have excelled? For no man is ignorant of their firft principles, which do virtually contain whatfoever by natural means is or can be known. Yea, might we not with as great reafon affirm, that a man might put three mighty oaks wherefoever three acorns may be put? For virtually an acorn is an oak. To avoid fuch paradoxes, we teach plainly, that to hold the foundation, is, in exprefs terms, to acknowledge it.

25. Now, becaufe the foundation is an affirmative pofition, they all overthrow it, who deny it; they directly overthrow it, who deny it directly; and they overthrow it by confequent, or indirectly, which hold any one affertion whatfoever, whereupon the direct denial thereof may be neceffarily concluded. What is the queftion between the *Gentiles* and us, but this, *Whether falvation be by Chrift?* What between the *Jews* and us, but this, *Whether by this Jefus, whom we call Chrift, yea or no?* This is to be the main point whereupon chriftianity ftandeth, it is clear by that one fentence of *Feftus* concerning *Paul's* accufers: *They brought no crime of fuch things as I fuppofed, but had certain queftions againft him of their fuperftitions, and of one Jefus which was dead, whom Paul affirmed to be alive.* Where we fee that Jefus, dead and raifed for the falvation of the world, is by *Jews* denied, defpifed by a *Gentile*, by a chriftian apoftle maintained. The fathers therefore in the primitive church when they wrote; *Tertullian*, the book which he called *Apologeticus*; *Minutius Fælix*, the book which he entituleth *Octavius*; *Arnobius*, the feven books againft the *Gentiles*; *Chryfoftom*, his orations againft the *Jews*; *Eufebius*, his ten books of *evangelical demonftration*: they ftand in defence of chriftianity againft them, by whom the foundation thereof was directly denied. But the writings of the fathers againft *Novatians*, *Pelagians*, and other hereticks of the like note, refel pofitions, whereby the foundation of chriftian faith was overthrown by confequent only. In the former fort of writings the foundation is proved; in the latter, it is alledged as a proof, which to men that had been known directly to deny, muft needs have feemed a very beggarly kind of difputing. All infidels therefore deny the foundation of faith directly; by confequent, many a chriftian man, yea whole chriftian churches denied it, and do deny it at this prefent day. Chriftian churches, the foundation of chriftianity? not directly, for then they ceafe to be chriftian churches; but by confequent, in refpect whereof we condemn them as erroneous, altho', for holding the foundation, we do and muft hold them chriftians.

26. We fee what it is to hold the foundation; what directly, and what by confequent to deny it. The next thing which followeth is, whether they whom God hath chofen to obtain the glory of our Lord Jefus Chrift, may, once effectually called, and thro' faith juftified truly, afterwards fall fo far, as directly to deny the foundation which their hearts have before imbraced with joy and comfort in the holy Ghoft; for fuch is the faith, which indeed doth juftify. Devils know the fame things which we believe, and the minds

of

of the moſt ungodly may be fully perſuaded of the truth; which knowledge in the one and in the other, is ſometimes termed faith, but equivocally, being indeed no ſuch faith as that whereby a chriſtian man is juſtified. It is the ſpirit of adoption which worketh faith in us, in them not: the things which we believe, are by us apprehended, not only as true, but alſo as good, and that to us: as good, they are not by them apprehended; as true they are. Whereupon followeth the third difference; the chriſtian man the more he encreaſeth in faith, the more his joy and comfort aboundeth: but they, the more ſure they are of the truth, the more they quake and tremble at it. This begetteth another effect, where the hearts of the one ſort have a different diſpoſition from the other. *Non ignoro pleroſque conſcientia meritorum, nihil ſe eſſe per mortem magis optare quam credere; malunt enim extingui penitus, quam ad ſupplicia reparari.* I am not ignorant ſaith *Minutius*, that there be many, who being conſcious what they are to look for, do rather wiſh that they might, than think that they ſhall ceaſe, when they ceaſe to live; becauſe they hold it better that death ſhould conſume them unto nothing, than God revive them unto puniſhment. So it is in other articles of faith, whereof wicked men think, no doubt, many times they are too true: on the contrary ſide, to the other, there is no grief or torment greater, than to feel their perſuaſion weak in things, whereof when they are perſuaded, they reap ſuch comfort and joy of ſpirit: ſuch is the faith whereby we are juſtified; ſuch, I mean, in reſpect of the quality. For touching the principal object of faith, longer than it holdeth the foundation whereof we have ſpoken, it neither juſtifieth, nor is, but ceaſeth to be faith; when it ceaſeth to believe, that Jeſus Chriſt is the only Saviour of the world. The cauſe of life ſpiritual in us, is Chriſt, not carnally or corporally inhabiting, but dwelling in the ſoul of man, as a thing which (when the mind apprehendeth it) is ſaid to inhabit or poſſeſs the mind. The mind conceiveth Chriſt by hearing the doctrine of chriſtianity, as the light of nature doth the mind to apprehend thoſe truths which are merely rational, ſo that ſaving truth, which is far above the reach of human reaſon, cannot otherwiſe, than by the Spirit of the Almighty, be conceived. All theſe are implied, whereſoever any of them is mentioned as the cauſe of the ſpiritual life: wherefore if we have read, that [a] *the Spirit is our life*; or, [b] *the word our life*; or, [c] *Chriſt our life:* we are in every of theſe to underſtand, that our life is Chriſt, by the hearing of the goſpel apprehended as a Saviour, and aſſented unto through the power of the holy Ghoſt. The firſt intellectual conceit and comprehenſion of Chriſt ſo embraced, St. *Peter* calleth *the ſeed whereof we be new born:* our firſt embracing of Chriſt, is our firſt reviving from the ſtate of death and condemnation. *He that hath the Son hath life,* ſaith St. *John, and he that hath not the Son of God, hath not life.* If therefore he which once hath the Son, may ceaſe to have the Son, though it be for a moment, he ceaſeth for that moment to have life. But the life of them which have the Son of God, is everlaſting *in the world to come.* But becauſe as Chriſt being raiſed from the dead died no more, death hath no more power over him: ſo juſtified man, being allied to God in Jeſus Chriſt our Lord doth as neceſſarily from that time forward always live, as Chriſt, by whom he hath life, liveth always. I might, if I had not otherwhere largely done it already, ſhew by many and ſundry manifeſt and clear proofs, how the motions and operations of life are ſometime ſo indiſcernable, and ſo ſecret, that they ſeem ſtone-dead, who notwithſtanding are ſtill alive unto God in Chriſt.

[a] Rom. 8. 10. Phil. 2. 16.
[b] Col. 3. 4.
[c] Pet. 1.
Epheſ. 2. 5.
1 John 5. 12.
Perpetuity of faith.
Rom. 6. 10.
John 14. 19.

For as long as that abideth in us, which animateth, quickneth, and giveth life, ſo long we live, and we know that the cauſe of our faith abideth in us for ever. If Chriſt, the fountain of life may flit, and leave the habitation, where once he dwelleth, what ſhall become of his promiſe, *I am with you to the world's end?* If the ſeed of God, which containeth Chriſt, may be firſt conceived and then caſt out: how doth St. *Peter* term it im*mortal?* How doth St *John* affirm *it abideth?* If the Spirit, which is given to cheriſh, and preſerve the ſeed of life, may be given and taken away, how is it the earneſt of our inheritance until redemption; how doth it continue with us for ever? If therefore the man which is once juſt by faith, ſhall live by faith, and live for ever, it followeth, that he which once doth believe the foundation, muſt needs believe the foundation for ever. If he believe it for ever, how can he ever directly deny it? Faith holding the direct affirmation; the direct negation, ſo long as faith continueth, is excluded.

1 Pet. 1. 23.
1 John 3. 9.
Epheſ. 1. 4, 5.
John 4. 14.

Object. But you will ſay, *That as he that is to day holy, may to morrow forſake his holineſs, and become impure, as a friend may change his mind, and be made an enemy; as hope may wither; ſo faith may dye in the heart of man, the Spirit may be quenched, grace may be extinguiſhed, they which believe may be quite turned away from the truth.*

Sol. The caſe is clear, long experience hath made this manifeſt, it needs no proof. I grant we are apt, prone, and ready to forſake God; but is God as ready to forſake us? Our minds are changeable; is his ſo likewiſe? Whom God hath juſtified hath not Chriſt

aſſured,

aſſured, that it is *his Father's will to give them a kingdom?* Notwithſtanding, it ſhall not be otherwiſe given them, than if they continue grounded and eſtabliſhed in the faith, and

Col. 1. 23. be not moved away from the hope of the goſpel; *if they abide in love and holineſs.* Our Saviour therefore, when he ſpake of the ſheep effectually called, and truly gathered into

1 Tim. 2. 15.
John 10. his fold, *I give unto them eternal life, and they ſhall never periſh, neither ſhall any pluck them out of my hands;* in promiſing to ſave them, he promiſed no doubt to preſerve them in that, without which there can be no ſalvation, as alſo from that whereby it is irrecoverably loſt. Every error in things appertaining unto God, is repugnant unto faith; every fearful cogitation, unto hope; unto love, every ſtragling inordinate deſire; unto holineſs, every blemiſh wherewith either the inward thoughts of our minds, or the outward actions of our lives are ſtained. But hereſy, ſuch as that of *Ebion, Cerinthus,* and others, againſt whom the apoſtles were forced to bend themſelves, both by word, and alſo by writing; that repining diſcouragement of heart which tempteth God, whereof we have *Iſrael* in the deſart for a pattern; coldneſs, ſuch as that in the angels of *Epheſus;* foul ſins, known to be expreſly againſt the firſt, or ſecond table of the law, ſuch as *Noah, Manaſſes, David, Solomon,* and *Peter* committed: theſe are each in their kind ſo oppoſite to the former virtues, that they leave no place for ſalvation without an actual repentance. But infidelity, extream deſpair, hatred of God and all goodneſs, obduration in ſin cannot ſtand where there is but the leaſt ſpark of faith, hope, love, and ſanctity: even as cold in the loweſt degree cannot be, where heat in the higheſt degree is found. Whereupon I conclude, that although in the firſt kind, no man liveth which ſinneth not; and in the ſecond, as perfect as any do live, may ſin: yet ſith the man which is born of God,

1 John 3. 9. hath a promiſe, that in him the *ſeed of God ſhall abide;* which ſeed is a ſure preſervative againſt the ſins that are of the third ſuit: greater and clearer aſſurance we cannot have of any thing, than of this, that from ſuch ſins God ſhall preſerve the righteous, as the apple of his eye for ever. Directly to deny the foundation of faith, is plain infidelity; where faith is entered, there infidelity is for ever excluded: therefore by him which hath once ſincerely believed in Chriſt, the foundation of chriſtian faith can never be directly denied. Did not *Peter?* Did not *Marcellinus?* Did not others both directly deny Chriſt, after that they had believed; and again believe, after they had denied? No doubt, as they confeſs in words, whoſe condemnation is nevertheleſs their not believing: (for example we have *Judas:*) ſo likewiſe, they may believe in heart, whoſe condemnation, without repentance, is their not confeſſing. Although therefore, *Peter* and the reſt, for whoſe faith Chriſt hath prayed that it might not fail, did not by denial, ſin the ſin of infidelity, which is an inward abnegation of Chriſt; (for if they had done this, their faith had clearly failed:) yet, becauſe they ſinned notoriouſly and grievouſly, committing that which they knew to be expreſly forbidden by the law, which ſaith, *Thou ſhalt worſhip the Lord thy God, and him only ſhalt thou ſerve;* neceſſary it was, that he which purpoſed to ſave their ſouls ſhould, as he did, touch their hearts with true unfeigned repentance, that his mercy might reſtore them again to life, whom ſin had made the children of death and condemnation. Touching the point therefore, I hope I may ſafely ſet down, that if the juſtified err, as he may, and never come to underſtand his error, God doth ſave him through general repentance: but if he fall into hereſy, he calleth him at one time or other by actual repentance; but from infidelity, which is an inward direct denial of the foundation, he preſerveth him by ſpecial providence for ever. Whereby we may eaſily know, what to think of thoſe *Galatians* whoſe hearts were ſo poſſeſt with the love of the truth, that, if it had been poſſible, they would have pluckt out their eyes to beſtow upon

* Howſoever their teachers. It is true, that they were greatly * changed both in perſuaſion and af-
men be chan- fection: ſo that the *Galatians,* when St. *Paul* wrote unto them, were not now the *Gala-*
ged (for chan- *tians* which they had been in former time, for that through error they wandred, al-
ged they may though they were his ſheep. I do not deny, but that I ſhould deny that they were his
be, even the men) if they ſheep, if I ſhould grant, that through error they periſhed. It was a perilous opinion
beſt amongſt that they held; perilous even in them that held it only as an error, becauſe it overthrow-
men) if they eth the foundation by conſequent. But in them which obſtinately maintain it, I cannot
that have re- think it leſs than a damnable hereſy. We muſt therefore put a difference between them
ceived, as it which err of ignorance, retaining nevertheleſs a mind deſirous to be inſtructed in truth,
ſeemeth ſome- and them, which after the truth is laid open, perſiſt in the ſtubborn defence of their blind-
of the *Gala-* neſs. Heretical defenders, froward and ſtiff-necked teachers of circumciſion, the bleſ-
ans which fell
into error, had
received the
giftsandgraces
of God which
are called

ἀπερραμμένα, ſuch as faith, hope, and charity are, which God doth never take away from him to whom they are given, as if it reported him to have given them; if ſuch might be ſo far changed by error, as that the very root of faith ſhould be quite extinguiſhed in them, and ſo their ſalvation utterly loſt; it would ſhake the hearts of the ſtrongeſt, and ſhorteſt of us all. See the contrary in *Beza* his obſervations upon the harmony of confeſſions.

fed apoſtle calls dogs. Silly men, who were ſeduced to think they taught the truth, he pitieth, he taketh up in his arms, he lovingly embraceth, he kiſſeth, and with more than fatherly tenderneſs doth ſo temper, qualify, and correct the ſpeech he uſeth towards them, that a man cannot eaſily diſcern whether did moſt abound, the love which he bare to their godly affection, or the grief which the danger of their opinion bred him. Their opinion was dangerous; was not theirs alſo, who thought the kingdom of Chriſt ſhould be earthly? Was not theirs, which thought the goſpel only ſhould be preached to the *Jews:* what more oppoſite to prophetical doctrine, concerning the coming of Chriſt, than the one? concerning the catholick church, than the other? Yet they which had theſe fancies, even when they had them, were not the worſt men in the world. The hereſy of *free-will* was a mill-ſtone about the *Pelagians* neck, ſhall we therefore give ſentence of death inevitably againſt all thoſe fathers in the *Greek* church, which being miſ-perſuaded, died in the error of *free-will?* Of theſe *Galatians* therefore, which firſt were juſtified, and then deceived, as I can ſee no cauſe why as many as died before admonition might not by mercy be received, even in error; ſo I make no doubt, but as many as lived till they were admoniſhed, found the mercy of God effectual in converting them from their [a] error, leſt any one that is Chriſt's ſhould periſh. Of this I take it, there is no controverſy: only againſt the ſalvation of them that died, though before admonition, yet in error, it is objected, that their opinion was a very plain direct denial of the foundation. If *Paul* and *Barnabas* had been ſo perſuaded, they would haply have uſed the terms otherwiſe, ſpeaking of the maſters themſelves who did firſt ſet that error abroach, [b] certain of the ſect of the phariſees which believed. What difference was there between theſe phariſees and other phariſees, from whom by a ſpecial deſcription they are diſtinguiſhed, but this? Theſe which came to *Antioch*, teaching the neceſſity of circumciſion were chriſtians; the other, enemies of chriſtianity. Why then ſhould theſe be termed ſo diſtinctly believers, if they did directly deny the foundation of our belief; beſides which, there was no other thing, that made the reſt to be no believers? We need go no further than St. *Paul's* very reaſoning againſt them for proof of this matter: ſeeing you know God, or rather are known of God; how turn you again to impotent rudiments? The [c] law engendereth ſervants, her children are in bondage: [d] they which are begotten by the goſpel, are free. [e] Brethren, we are not children of the ſervant but of the free woman, and will ye yet be under the law? That they thought it unto ſalvation neceſſary, for the church of Chriſt to [f] obſerve days, and months, and times, and years, to keep the ceremonies and ſacraments of the law, this was their error. Yet he [f] which condemneth their error, confeſſeth that, notwithſtanding, they knew God, and were known of him; he taketh not the honour from them to be termed ſons, begotten of the immortal ſeed of the goſpel. Let the heavieſt words which he uſeth be weighed; conſider the drift of thoſe dreadful concluſions: *If ye be circumciſed, Chriſt ſhall profit you nothing: as many as are juſtified by the law, are fallen from grace.* It had been to no purpoſe in the world ſo to urge them, had not the apoſtle been perſuaded, that at the hearing of ſuch ſequels, *No benefit by Chriſt, a defection from Chriſt,* their hearts would tremble and quake within them: and why? Becauſe that they knew, that in Chriſt, and in grace, their ſalvation lay, which is a plain direct acknowledgment of the foundation. Leſt I ſhould herein ſeem to hold that which no one learned or godly hath done, let theſe words be conſidered, which import as much as I affirm. Surely thoſe brethren, which in ſaint *Paul's* time, thought that God did lay a neceſſity upon them to make choice of days and meats, ſpake as they believed, and could not but in words condemn the liberty, which they ſuppoſed to be brought in againſt the authority of divine ſcripture. Otherwiſe it had been needleſs for St. *Paul* to admoniſh them, not to condemn ſuch as eat without ſcrupuloſity, whatſoever was ſet before them. This error, if you weigh what it is of it ſelf, did at once overthrow all ſcriptures, whereby we are taught ſalvation by faith in Chriſt, all that ever the prophets did foretel, all that ever the apoſtles did preach of Chriſt, it drew with it the denial of Chriſt utterly: inſomuch, that St. *Paul* complaineth, that his labour was loſt upon the *Galatians,* unto whom this error is obtruded, affirming that Chriſt, if ſo be they were circumciſed, ſhould not profit them any thing at all. Yet ſo far was St. *Paul* from ſtriking their names out of Chriſt's book, that he commandeth others to entertain them, to accept with ſingular humanity, to uſe them like brethren; he knew man's imbecility, he had a feeling of our blindneſs, which are mortal men, how great it is, and being ſure that they are the ſons of God, whoſoever be endued with his fear, would not have them counted enemies of that whereunto they could not as yet frame themſelves to be friends, but did, ever upon a very religious affection to the truth, willingly reject the truth. They acknowledged Chriſt to be their only and perfect Saviour, but ſaw not how repugnant their believing the neceſſity of *Moſaical* ceremonies

Marginal notes:
[a] Error convicted, and afterwards maintained, is more than error; for alltho' opinion be the ſame it be the ſame it was, in which reſpect I ſtill call it error; yet they are not now the ſame they were when they taught what the truth is, and plainly taught.

[b] Acts 15. 5.
[c] Gal. 4. 5, 6.
[d] Verſe 23.
[e] Verſe 31.
[f] Verſe 10.

Bucer de unit. ecclef. ſervanda.

was to their faith in Jefus Chrift. Hereupon a reply is made, that if they had not directly denied the foundation, they might have been faved; but faved they could not be, therefore their opinion was, not only by confequent, but directly a denial of the foundation. When the queftion was about the poffibility of their falvation, their denying of the foundation was brought to prove that they could not be faved: now, that the queftion is about their denial of the foundation, the impoffibility of their falvation is alledged to prove they denied the foundation. Is there nothing which excludeth men from falvation, but only the foundation of faith denied? I fhould have thought, that befides this, many other things are death to as many as underftanding that to cleave thereun'o was to fall from Chrift, did notwithftanding cleave unto them. But of this enough. Wherefore I come to the laft queftion, *Whether that the doctrine of the church of* Rome, *concerning the neceffity of works unto falvation, be a direct denial of our faith.*

27. I feek not to obtrude unto you any private opinion of my own. The beft learned in our profeffion are of this judgment, that all the corruptions of the church of *Rome* do not prove her to deny the foundation directly; if they did, they fhould grant her fimply to be no chriftian church. *But, I fuppofe,* faith one, *that in the papacy fome church remaineth, a church crazed, or, if you will, broken quite in pieces, forlorn, mifhapen, yet fome church:* his reafon is this, *antichrift muft fit in the temple of God.* Left any man fhould think fuch fentences as thefe to be true only in regard of them whom that church is fuppofed to have kept by the fpecial providence of God, as it were, in the fecret corners of his bofom, free from infection, and found in the faith; as we truft, by his mercy, we our felves are; I permit it to your wife confiderations, whether it be more likely, that as frenzy, tho' it take away the ufe of reafon, doth notwithftanding prove them reafonable creatures which have it, becaufe none can be frantick but they; fo antichriftianity being the bane and overthrow of chriftianity, may neverthelefs argue the church where antichrift fitteth to be chriftian. Neither have I hitherto heard or read any one word alledged of force to warrant that God doth otherwife, than fo as in the two next queftions before hath been declared, bind himfelf to keep his elect from worfhiping the beaft and from receiving his mark in their foreheads: but he hath preferved, and will preferve them from receiving any deadly wound at the hands of the man of fin, whofe deceit hath prevailed over none unto death, but only unto fuch as never loved the truth, fuch as took pleafure in unrighteoufnefs. They in all ages, whofe hearts have delighted in the principal truth, and whofe fouls have thirfted after righteoufnefs, if they received the mark of error; the mercy of God, even erring, and dangeroufly erring, might fave them; if they received the mark of herefy, the fame mercy, did, I doubt not, convert them. How far *Romifh* herefies may prevail over God's elect, how many God hath kept from falling into them, how many have been converted from them, is not the queftion now in hand. For if heaven had not received any one of that coat for thefe thoufand years, it may ftill be true, that the doctrine which this day they do profefs doth not directly deny the foundation, and fo prove them fimply to be no chriftian church. One I have alledged, whofe words, in my ears, found that way. Shall I add another, whofe fpeech is plain? *I deny her not the name of a church,* faith another, *no more than to a man the name of a man, as long as he liveth, what ficknefs foever he hath.* His reafon is this, *falvation in Jefus Chrift, which is the mark which joineth the head with the body, Jefus Chrift with the church, is fo cut off by many merits, by the merits of faints, by the pope's pardons, and fuch other wickednefs that the life of the church holdeth by a very thread,* yet ftill the life of the church holdeth. A third hath thefe words, *I acknowledge the church of* Rome, *even at this prefent day, for a church of Chrift, fuch a church as* Ifrael *did* Jeroboam, *yet a church.* His reafon is this, *every man feeth, except he willingly hood-wink himfelf, that as always, fo now, the church of* Rome *holdeth firmly and ftedfaftly the doctrine of truth concerning Chrift; and baptizeth in the name of the Father, the Son, and the holy Ghoft; confeffeth and avoucheth Chrift to be the only Redeemer of the world, and the judge that fhall fit upon quick and dead, receiving true believers into endlefs joy, faithlefs and godlefs men being caft with fatan and his angels into flames unquenchable.*

28. I may, and will rein the queftion fhorter than they do. Let the pope take down his top, and captivate no more men's fouls by his papal jurifdictions; let him no longer count himfelf *lord paramount* over the princes of the world, no longer hold kings as his fervants *paravaile;* let his ftately fenate fubmit their necks to the yoke of Chrift, and ceafe to dye their garments, like *Edom,* in blood; let them from the higheft to the loweft hate and forfake their idolatry, abjure all their errors and herefies, wherewith they have any way perverted the truth; let them ftrip their church, till they leave no poliuted rag, but only this one about her, *By Chrift alone without works we cannot*

Calv. ep. 104.

Morn. de ecclef.

Zanch. præfat. de relig.

I   not

not be saved: it is enough for me, if I shew, that the holding of this one thing doth not prove the foundation of faith directly denied in the church of *Rome.*

29. Works are an addition: be it so, what then? the foundation is not subverted by every kind of addition. Simply to add unto those fundamental words is not to mingle wine with water, heaven and earth; things polluted with the sanctified blood of Christ: of which crime indict them which attribute those operations in whole or in part to any creature, which in the work of our salvation wholly are peculiar unto Christ; and if I open my mouth to speak in their defence; if I hold my peace, and plead not against them as long as breath is within my body, let me be guilty of all the dishonour that ever hath been done to the Son of God. But the more dreadful a thing it is to deny salvation by Christ alone, the more slow and fearful I am, except it be too manifest, to lay a thing so grievous to any man's charge. Let us beware, lest if we make too many ways of denying Christ, we scarce leave any way for our selves truly and soundly to confess him. Salvation only by Christ is the true foundation whereupon indeed christianity standeth. But what if I say, you cannot be saved only by Christ, without this addition, Christ believed in heart, confessed with mouth, obeyed in life and conversation? Because I add, do I therefore deny that which I did directly affirm? There may be an additament of explication, which overthroweth not, but proveth and concludeth the proposition, whereunto it is annexed. He which saith, *Peter* was a chief apostle, doth prove that *Peter* was an apostle: he which saith, our salvation is of the Lord through sanctification of the Spirit, and faith of the truth, proveth that our salvation is of the Lord. But if that which is added be such a privation, as taketh away the very essence of that whereunto it is added, then by the sequel it overthroweth it. He which saith, *Judas* is a dead man, tho' in a word, he granteth *Judas* to be a man, yet in effect he proveth him by that very speech no man, because death depriveth him of being. In like sort, he that should say, our election is of grace for our works sake, should grant in sound of words, but indeed Rom. 11. 6, by consequence deny, that our election is of grace; for the grace which electeth us is no grace, if it elect us for our works sake.

30. Now whereas the church of *Rome* addeth works, we must note further, that the adding of * works is not like the adding of circumcision unto Christ. Christ came not [a] I deny not to abrogate and put away good works: he did to change circumcision; for we see that but that the in place thereof he hath substituted holy baptism. To say, ye cannot be saved by Christ, *Rome* requireth except ye be circumcised, is to add a thing excluded, a thing not only not necessary to some kinds of works which be kept, but necessary not to be kept by them that will be saved. On the other side, to he ought not say, ye cannot be saved by Christ without works, is to add things not only not excluded, to require at but commanded, as being in their place and in their kind necessary, and therefore subor-mens hands. dinated unto Christ by Christ himself, by whom the web of salvation is spun: [b] *Except* tion is gene-*your righteousness exceed the righteousness of the Scribes and Pharisees, ye shall not enter* ral about the adding of *into the kingdom of heaven.* They were [c] rigorous exacters of things not utterly to be good works, neglected and left undone, washing and tithing, &c. As they were in these, so must we not whether be in judgment and the love of God. Christ, in works ceremonial, giveth more liberty, in such or such works be [c] moral, much less, than they did. Works of righteousness therefore are added in the one good. In this comparison it proposition; as in the other, circumcision is. is enough to touch so much

of the matter in question between St. *Paul* and the *Galatians,* as inferreth those conclusions, *Ye are fallen from grace, Christ can profit you nothing:* Which conclusions will follow circumcision and rights of the law ceremonial, if they be required as things necessary to salvation. This only was alledged against me: and need I touch more than was alledged? [c] Matth. v. 20. [b] Luke 11. 39. [c] Matth. 5. 21.

31. But we say, our salvation is by Christ alone; therefore howsoever, or whatsoever we add unto Christ in the matter of salvation, we overthrow Christ. Our case were very hard, if this argument, so universally meant as it is supposed, were found and good. We our selves do not teach Christ alone, excluding our own faith, unto justification; Christ alone, excluding our own works, unto sanctification; Christ alone, excluding the one or the other unnecessary unto salvation. It is a childish cavil, wherewith in the matter of justification, our adversaries do so greatly please themselves, exclaiming, that we tread all christian virtues under our feet, and require nothing in christians but faith, be-cause we teach that faith alone justifieth; whereas by this speech we never meant to exclude either hope or charity from being always joined as inseparable mates with faith in the man that is justified; or works from being added as necessary duties, required at the hands of every justified man: but to shew that faith is the only hand which putteth on Christ unto justification; and Christ the only garment, which being so put on, covereth the shame of our defiled natures, hideth the imperfection of our works, pre-serveth us blameless in the sight of God, before whom otherwise, the weakness of our
faith

faith were cause sufficient to make us culpable, yea, to shut us from the kingdom of heaven, where nothing that is not absolute can enter. That our dealing with them be not as childish as theirs with us: when we hear of salvation by Christ alone, considering that [*alone*] as an exclusive particle, we are to note what it doth exclude, and where. If I say, *Such a judge only ought to determine such a case,* all things incident to the determination thereof, besides the person of the judge, as laws, depositions, evidences, &c. are not hereby excluded; persons are not excluded from witnessing herein, or assisting, but only from determining and giving sentence. How then is our salvation wrought by Christ alone? is it our meaning, that nothing is requisite to man's salvation, but Christ to save, and he to be saved quietly without any more ado? No, we acknowledge no such foundation. As we have received, so we teach, that besides the bare and naked work, wherein Christ without any other associate finished all the parts of our redemption, and purchased salvation himself alone; for conveyance of this eminent blessing unto us, many things are of necessity required, as, to be known and chosen of God before the foundation of the world; in the world to be called, justified, sanctified; after we have left the world, to be received unto glory; Christ in every of these hath somewhat which he work-
Eph. 1. 11. eth alone. Thro' him, according to the eternal purpose of God before the foundation of the world, born, crucified, buried, raised, &c. we were in a gracious acceptation known unto God long before we were seen of men: God knew us, loved us, was kind to us in Jesus Christ, in him we were elected to be heirs of life. Thus far God through Christ hath wrought in such sort alone, that our selves are meer patients, working no more than dead and senseless matter, wood, stone, or iron, doth in the artificers hands; no more than clay, when the potter appointeth it to be framed for an honourable use; nay, not so much. For the matter whereupon the crafts-man worketh he chuseth, being moved by the fitness which is in it to serve his turn; in us no such thing. Touching the rest which is laid for the foundation of our faith, it importeth farther, that by him we are called, that we have redemption, remission of sins through his blood, health by his stripes; justice by him; that he doth sanctify his church, and make it glorious to himself, that entrance into joy shall be given us by him; yea, all things by him alone. Howbeit, not so by him alone, as if in us to our vocation, the hearing of the gospel; to our justification, faith; to our sanctification, the fruits of the Spirit; to our entrance into rest, perseverance in hope, in faith, in holiness, were not necessary.

32. Then what is the fault of the church of *Rome?* Not that she requireth works at their hands which will be saved: but that she attributeth unto works a power of satisfying God for sin; yea, a virtue to merit both grace here, and in heaven glory. That this overthroweth the foundation of faith, I grant willingly; that it is a direct denial thereof, I utterly deny. What it is to hold, and what directly to deny the foundation of faith, I have already opened. Apply it particularly to this cause, and there needs no more ado. The thing which is handled, if the form under which it is handled be added thereunto, it sheweth the foundation of any doctrine whatsoever. Christ is the matter whereof the doctrine of the gospel treateth; and it treateth of Christ as of a Saviour. Salvation therefore by Christ is the foundation of christianity: as for works, they are a thing subordinate, no otherwise than because our sanctification cannot be accomplished without them. The doctrine concerning them is a thing builded upon the foundation; therefore the doctrine which addeth unto them the power of satisfying, or of meriting, addeth unto a thing subordinated, builded upon the foundation, not to the very foundation it self; yet is the foundation by this addition consequently overthrown, forasmuch as out of this addition it may be negatively concluded, he which maketh any work good and acceptable in the sight of God, to proceed from the natural freedom of our will; he which giveth unto any good works of ours the force of satisfying the wrath of God for sin, the power of meriting either earthly or heavenly rewards; he which holdeth works going before our vocation, incongruity to merit our vocation; works following our first, to merit our second justification, and by condignity our last reward in the kingdom of heaven, pulleth up the doctrine of faith by the roots; for out of every of these the plain direct denial thereof may be necessarily concluded. Not this only, but what other heresy is there that doth not raze the very foundation of faith by consequent? Howbeit, we make a difference of heresies; accounting them in the next degree to infidelity, which directly deny any one thing to be, which is expresly acknow-
Hæc ratio ec-
clesiastici sa-
cramenti & ca-ledged in the articles of our belief; for out of any one article so denied the very foundation it self is straitway deferred. As for example, if a man should say, *There is no*

tholicæ fidei est, ut qui partem divini sacramenti negat, partem non valeat confiteri. Ita enim sibi connexa & concorporata sunt omnia, ut aliud sine alio stare non possit, & qui unum ex omnibus denegaverit, alia ei omnia credidisse non profit. *Cassian.* lib. 6. de incarnat. Dom. If he obstinately stand in the denial, pag. 193.

2

catholick

catholick church, it followeth immediately thereupon, that this *Jesus* whom we call the Saviour, is not the Saviour of the world ; because all the prophets bear witness, that the true *Messias* should *shew light unto the Gentiles* ; that is to say, gather such a church as is catholick, not restrained any longer unto one circumcised nation.   In the second rank we place them, out of whose positions the denial of any the foresaid articles may be with like facility concluded : such as are they which have denied, with *Hebion,* or with *Marcion,* his humanity ; an example whereof may be that of *Cassianus* defending the incarnation of the Son of God against *Nestorius* bishop of *Antioch,* who held, that the virgin, when she brought forth Christ, did not bring forth the Son of God, but a sole and meer man. Out of which heresy the denial of the articles of the christian faith he deduceth thus, *If* [Acts 16. 13.] [Lib. 9. de in-] [car. Dom. cap.] *thou dost deny our Lord Jesus Christ, in denying the Son, thou canst not chuse but deny the Father ; for, according to the voice of the Father himself,* He that hath not the Son, hath [16.] not the Father.   *Wherefore denying him which is begotten, thou deniest him which doth beget.   Again, denying the Son of God to have been born in the flesh, how canst thou believe him to have suffered ? believing not his passion, what remaineth, but that thou deny his resurrection ?   For we believe him not raised, except we first believe him dead : neither can the reason of his rising from the dead stand, without the faith of his death going before. The denial of his death and passion inferreth the denial of his rising from the depth.   Whereupon it followeth, that thou also deny his ascension into heaven.   The apostle affirmeth,* That he which ascended, did first descend ; so that, as much as lieth in thee, our Lord *Jesus* Christ hath neither risen from the depth, nor is ascended into heaven, nor sitteth on the right hand of God the Father, neither shall he come at the day of the final account which is looked for, nor shall judge the quick and dead. And darest thou yet set foot in the church ? Canst thou think thy self a bishop, when thou hast denied all those things whereby thou dost obtain a bishoply calling ? *Nestorius* confessed all the articles of the creed, but his opinion did imply the denial of every part of his confession.   Heresies there are of the third sort, such as the church of *Rome* maintaineth, which be removed by a greater distance from the foundation, altho' indeed they overthrow it.   Yet because of that weakness, which the philosopher noteth in mens capacities when he saith, that the common sort cannot see things which follow in reason, when they follow, as it were, afar off by many deductions ; therefore the repugnancy of such heresy and the foundation is not so quickly, or so easily found, but that an heretick of this, sooner than of the former kind, may directly grant, and consequently nevertheless deny the foundation of faith.

33. If reason be suspected, tryal will shew that the church of *Rome* doth no otherwise, by teaching the doctrine she doth teach concerning good works.   Offer them the very fundamental words, and what man is there that will refuse to subscribe unto them ?   Can they directly grant, and directly deny, one and the very self-same thing ?   Our own proceedings in disputing against their works satisfactory and meritorious do shew, not only that they hold, but that we acknowledge them to hold the foundation, notwithstanding their opinion.   For are not these our arguments against them ? *Christ alone hath satisfied and appeased his Father's wrath : Christ hath merited salvation alone.*   We should so fondly to use such disputes, neither could we think to prevail by them, if that whereupon we ground, were a thing which we know they do not hold, which we are assured they will not grant.   Their very answers to all such reasons, as are in this controversy brought against them, will not permit us to doubt whether they hold the foundation or no.   Can any man, that hath read their books concerning this matter, be ignorant how they draw all their answers unto these heads ? *That the remission of all our sins, the pardon of all whatsoever punishments thereby deserved, the rewards which God hath laid up in heaven, are by the blood of our Lord Jesus Christ purchased, and obtained sufficiently for all men : but for no man effectually for his benefit in particular, except the blood of Christ be applied particularly to him by such means as God hath appointed that to work by. That those means of themselves, being but dead things, only the blood of Christ is that which putteth life, force, and efficacy in them to work, and to be available, each in his kind, to our salvation. Finally, that grace being purchased for us by the blood of Christ, and freely without any merit or desert at the first bestowed upon us, the good things which we do, after grace received, be thereby made satisfactory and meritorious.*   Some of their sentences to this [Lewis of Gra-] effect I must alledge for mine own warrant.   If we desire to hear foreign judgments, we find [nada. med. cap.] [laft. 3.] in one this confession, *He that could reckon how many the virtues and merits of our Saviour Jesus Christ hath been, might likewise understand how many the benefits have been that are to come to us by him, for so much as men are made partakers of them all by means of his passion : by him is given unto us remission of our sins, grace, glory, liberty, praise, salvation, redemption, justification, justice, satisfaction, sacraments, merits, and all other things which we had, and were behoveful for our salvation.*   In another we have these [Paulgarda. let;] oppositions[11]

oppositions and anfwers made unto them: *All grace is given by Chrift Jefus. True, but not except Chrift Jefus be applied. He is the propitiation for our fin; by his ftripes we are healed, he hath offered himfelf up for us: all this is true, but apply it. We put all fatisfaction in the blood of Jefus Chrift; but we hold, that the means, which Chrift hath appointed for us in the cafe to apply it, are our penal works.* Our countrymen in *Rheims* make the like anfwer, that they feek falvation no other way than by the blood of Chrift; and that humbly they do ufe prayers, faftings, alms, faith, charity, facrifice, facraments, priefts, only as the means appointed by Chrift, to apply the benefit of his holy blood unto them: touching our good works, that in their own natures they are not meritorious, nor anfwerable to the joys of heaven: it cometh by the grace of Chrift, and not of the work it felf, that we have by well-doing a right to heaven, and deferve it worthily. If any man think that I feek to varnifh their opinions, to fet the better foot of a lame horfe foremoft; let him know, that fince I began throughly to underftand their meaning, I have found their halting greater than perhaps it feemeth to them which know not the deepnefs of Satan, as the bleffed divine fpeaketh. For, altho' this be proof fufficient, that they do not directly deny the foundation of faith; yet, if there were no other leaven in the lump of their doctrine but this, this were fufficient to prove, that their doctrine is not agreeable to the foundation of chriftian faith. The *Pelagians* being over-great friends unto nature, made themfelves enemies unto grace, for all their confeffing, that men have their fonls, and all the faculties thereof, their wills, and all the ability of their wills from God. And is not the church of *Rome* ftill an adverfary to Chrift's merits, becaufe of her acknowledging, that we have received the power of meriting by the blood of Chrift? Sir *Thomas More* fetteth down the odds between us and the church of *Rome* in the matter of works thus. *Like as we grant them, that no good work of man is rewardable in heaven of its own nature, but thro' the meer goodnefs of God, that lifts to fet fo high a price upon fo poor a thing; and that this price God fetteth thro' Chrift's paffion, and for that alfo they be his own works with us; for good works to God-ward worketh no man, without God work in him: and as we grant them alfo, that no man may be proud of his works, for his imperfect working; and for that in all that man may do, he can do God no good, but is a fervant unprofitable, and doth but his bare duty: as we, I fay, grant unto them thefe things, fo this one thing or twain do they grant us again, that men are bound to work good works, if they have time and power; and that whofo worketh in true faith moft, fhall be moft rewarded, but then fet they thereto, that all his rewards fhall be given him for his faith alone, and nothing for his works at all, becaufe his faith is the thing, they fay, that forceth him to work well.* I fee by this of Sir *Thomas More,* how eafy is it for men of the greateft capacity to miftake things written, or fpoken as well on the one fide as on the other. Their doctrine, as he thought, maketh the work of man rewardable in the world to come thro' the goodnefs of God, whom it pleafed to fet fo high a price upon fo poor a thing: and ours, that a man doth receive that eternal and high reward, not for his works, but for his faith's fake, by which he worketh; whereas in truth our doctrine is no other than that we have learned at the feet of Chrift; namely, that God doth juftify the believing man, yet not for the worthinefs of his belief, but for the worthinefs of him which is believed; God rewardeth abundantly every one which worketh, yet not for any meritorious dignity which is, or can be in the work, but thro' his meer mercy, by whofe commandment he worketh. Contrariwife, their doctrine is, that as pure water of it felf hath no favour, but if it pafs thro' a fweet pipe, it taketh a pleafant fmell of the pipe through which it paffeth: fo, altho' before grace received, our works do neither fatisfy nor merit; yet after, they do both the one and the other. Every virtuous action hath then power in fuch to fatisfy; that if we our felves commit no mortal fin, no hainous crime, whereupon to fpend this treafure of fatisfaction in our own behalf, it turneth to the benefit of other mens releafe, on whom it fhould pleafe the fteward of the houfe of God to beftow it; fo that we may fatisfy for our felves and others; but merit only for our felves. In meriting, our actions do work with two hands; with one, they get their morning ftipend, the increafe of grace; with the other, their evening hire, the everlafting crown of glory. Indeed they teach, that our good works do not thefe things as they come from us, but as they come from grace in us, which grace in us is another thing in their divinity, than is the meer goodnefs of God's mercy towards us in Chrift Jefus.

34. If it were not a long deluded fpirit which hath poffeffion of their hearts; were it poffible but that they fhould fee how plainly they do herein gainfay the very ground of apoftolick faith? Is this that falvation by grace, whereof fo plentiful mention is made in the fcriptures of God? was this their meaning, which firft taught the world to look for falvation only by Chrift? By grace the apoftle faith, and by grace in fuch fort as a gift: a thing that cometh not of our felves, nor of our works, left any man fhould

Marginal notes:

Annot. in 1 John 1.

In his book of confolation.

Works of fupererogation.

boaft

boast, and say, *I have wrought out my own salvation.* By grace they confess; but by grace in such sort, that as many as wear the diadem of bliss, they wear nothing but what they have won. The apostle, as if he had foreseen how the church of *Rome* would abuse the world in time by ambiguous terms, to declare in what sense the name of grace must be taken, when we make it the cause of our salvation, saith, *He saved us according to his mercy:* which mercy, altho' it exclude not the washing of our new birth, the renewing of our hearts by the holy Ghost, the means, the virtues, the duties which God requireth of our hands which shall be saved; yet it is so repugnant unto merits, that to say, we are saved for the worthiness of any thing which is ours, is to deny we are saved by grace. Grace bestoweth freely; and therefore justly requireth the glory of that which is bestowed. We deny the grace of our Lord Jesus Christ; we abuse, disannul, and annihilate the benefit of his bitter passion, if we rest in these proud imaginations, that life is deservedly ours, that we merit it, and that we are worthy of it.

35. Howbeit, considering how many virtuous and just men, how many saints, how many martyrs, how many of the antient fathers of the church, have had their sundry perilous opinions; and amongst sundry of their opinions this, that they hoped to make God some part of amends for their sins, by the voluntary punishment which they laid upon themselves, because by a consequent it may follow hereupon, that they were injurious unto Christ; shall we therefore make such deadly epitaphs, and set them upon their graves, *They denied the foundation of faith directly, they are damned, there is no salvation for them?* Saint *Austin* saith of himself, *Errare possum, hæreticus esse nolo.* And, except we put a difference between them that err, and them that obstinately persist in error, how is it possible that ever any man should hope to be saved? Surely, in this case, I have no respect of any person either alive or dead. Give me a man, of what estate or condition soever, yea, a cardinal or a pope, whom in the extream point of his life, affliction hath made to know himself; whose heart God hath touched with true sorrow for all his sins, and filled with love towards the gospel of Christ, whose eyes are opened to see the truth, and his mouth to renounce all heresy and error, any wise opposite thereunto; this one opinion of merits excepted, he thinketh God will require at his hands, and because he wanteth, therefore trembleth, and is discouraged; it may be I am forgetful, and unskilful, not furnished with things new and old, as a wise and learned scribe should be, nor able to alledge that, whereunto, if it were alledged, he doth bear a mind most willing to yield, and so to be recalled, as well from this, as from other errors; and shall I think, because of this only error, that such a man toucheth not so much as the hem of Christ's garment? If he do, wherefore should not I have hope, that virtue might proceed from Christ to save him? Because his error doth by consequent overthrow his faith, shall I therefore cast him off, as one that hath utterly cast off Christ? One that holdeth not so much as by a slender thread? No, I will not be afraid to say unto a pope or cardinal in this plight, be of good comfort, we have to do with a merciful God, ready to make the best of a little which we hold well, and not with a captious sophister, which gathereth the worst out of every thing wherein we err. Is there any reason, that I should be suspected, or you offended for this speech? Is it a dangerous thing to imagine, that such men may find mercy? The hour may come, when we shall think it a blessed thing to hear, that if our sins were the sins of the pope and cardinals, the bowels of the mercy of God are larger. I do not propose unto you a Let all affecti-pope with the neck of an emperor under his feet; a cardinal, riding his horse to the on be laid aside, bridle in the blood of saints; but a pope or a cardinal sorrowful, penitent, dis-robed, indifferently stript, not only of usurped power, but also delivered and recalled from error and anti-be considered. christ, converted and lying prostrate at the foot of Christ; and shall I think that Christ shall spurn at him? And shall I cross and gainsay the merciful promises of God, generally made unto penitent sinners, by opposing the name of a pope or cardinal? What difference is there in the world between a pope and a cardinal, and *John a Style* in this case; if we think it impossible for them, if they be once come within that rank, to be afterwards touched with any such remorse? Let that be granted, the apostle saith, *If I, or an angel from heaven preach unto,* &c. Let it be as likely, that St. *Paul,* or an angel from heaven should preach heresy, as that a *pope* or *cardinal* should be brought so far forth to acknowledge the truth; yet if a *pope* or *cardinal* should, what find we in their persons why they might not be saved? It is not the persons, you will say, but the error, wherein I suppose them to die which excludeth them from the hope of mercy; the opinion of merits doth take away all possibility of salvation from them. What if they hold it only as an error? Although they hold the truth truly and sincerely in all other parts of christian faith: Although they have in some mea-

sure

sure all the virtues and graces of the Spirit, all other tokens of God's elect children in them: Although they be far from having any proud presumptuous opinion, that they shall be saved by the worthiness of their deed: although the only thing which troubleth and molesteth them, be but a little too much dejection, somewhat too great a fear, rising from an erroneous conceit that God would require a worthiness in them, which they are grieved to find wanting in themselves: Although they be not obstinate in this persuasion: Although they be willing, and would be glad to forsake it, if any one reason were brought sufficient to disprove it: Although the only let, why they do not forsake it e're they dye, be the ignorance of the means, by which it might be disproved: Although the cause, why the ignorance in this point is not removed, be the want of knowledge in such as should be able, and are not, to remove it. Let me dye, if ever it be proved, that simply an error doth exclude a pope or a cardinal in such a case, utterly from hope of life. Surely, I must confess unto you, if it be an error, that God may be merciful to save men even when they err, my greatest comfort is my error; were it not for the love I bear unto this error, I would never wish to speak, nor to live.

36. Wherefore to resume that mother sentence, whereof I little thought that so much trouble would have grown, *I doubt not but God was merciful to save thousands of our fathers, living in popish superstition, inasmuch as they sinned ignorantly.* Alas! what bloody matter is there contained in this sentence, that it should be an occasion of so many hard censures? Did I say, That *thousands of our fathers might be saved?* I have shewed which way it cannot be denied. Did I say, *I doubt not but that they were saved?* I see no impiety in this persuasion, tho' I had no reason for it. Did I say, *Their ignorance did make me hope they did find mercy, and so were saved?* What hindreth salvation but sin? Sins are not equal; and ignorance, tho' it doth not make sin to be no sin, yet seeing it did make their sin the less, why should it not make our hope concerning their life the greater? We pity the most, and doubt not but God hath most compassion over them that sin for want of understanding. As much is confessed by sundry others, almost in the self-same words which I have used. It is but only my evil hap, that the same sentences which favour verity,in other mens books, should seem to bolster heresy when they are once by me recited. If I be deceived in this point, not they, but the blessed apostle hath deceived me. What I said of others, the same he said of himself, *I obtained mercy, for I did it ignorantly.* Construe his words, and you cannot misconstrue mine. I speak no otherwise, I mean no otherwise, than he did.

37. Thus have I brought the question concerning our fathers at length unto an end. Of whose estate, upon so fit an occasion as was offered me, handling the weighty causes of separation between the church of *Rome* and us, and the weak motives which are commonly brought to retain men in that society; amongst which motives the examples of our fathers deceased is one; altho' I saw it convenient to utter the sentence which I did, to the end that all men might thereby understand, how untruly we are said to condemn as many as have been before us otherwise persuaded than we our selves are; yet more than that one sentence, I did not think it expedient to utter, judging it a great deal meeter for us to have regard to our own estate, than to sift over-curiously what is become of other men. And fearing, lest that such questions as these, if voluntarily they should be too far waded in, might seem worthy of that rebuke which our Saviour thought needful in a case not unlike, *What is this unto thee?* When I was forced, much beside my expectation, to render a reason of my speech, I could not but yield at the call of others, and proceed so far as duty bound me, for the fuller satisfying of minds. Wherein I have walked, as with reverence, so with fear: with reverence in regard of our fathers, which lived in former times: not without fear, considering them that are alive.

38. I am not ignorant, how ready men are to feed and sooth up themselves in evil. Shall I (will the man say, that loveth the present world, more than he loveth Christ) shall I incur the highest displeasure of the mightiest upon earth? Shall I hazard my goods, endanger my estate, put my self into jeopardy, rather than to yield to that which so many of my fathers embraced, and yet found favour in the sight of God? *Curse ye Meroz,* saith the Lord, *curse her inhabitants, because they helped not the Lord, they helped him not against the mighty.* If I should not only not help the Lord against the mighty, but help to strengthen them that are mighty against the Lord; worthily might I fall under the burthen of that curse,worthy I were to bear my own judgment: But, if the doctrine which I teach be a flower gathered in the garden of the Lord; a part of the saving truth of the gospel, from whence notwithstanding poysonous creatures do suck venom; I can but wish it were otherwise, and content my self with the lot that hath befallen me, the rather, because it hath not befallen me alone. Saint *Paul* taught a truth, and a comfortable truth,

3

truth, when he taught, that the greater our mifery is, in refpect of our iniquities, the readier is the mercy of God for our releafe, if we feek unto him; the more we have finned, the more praife, and glory, and honour, unto him that pardoneth our fin. But mark what lewd collections were made hereupon by fome: *Why then am I condemned for a finner?* And the apoftle (as we are blamed, and as fome affirm that we fay, *Why do we not evil that good may come of it?*) he was accufed to teach that which ill-difpofed people did gather by his teaching, though it were clean not only befides, but againft his meaning. The apoftle addeth, *Their condemnation* (which thus do) *is juft.* I am not hafty to apply fentences of condemnation: I wifh from my heart their converfion, whofoever are thus perverfly affected. For I muft needs fay, their cafe is fearful, their eftate dangerous, which harden themfelves, prefuming on the mercy of God towards others. It is true, that God is merciful, but let us beware of prefumptuous fins. God delivered *Jonah* from the bottom of the fea; will you therefore caft your felves headlong from the tops of rocks, and fay in your hearts, God fhall deliver us? He pitieth the blind that would gladly fee; but will he pity him that may fee, and hardneth himfelf in blindnefs? no, Chrift hath fpoken too much unto you, to claim the privilege of your fathers.

39. As for us that have handled this caufe concerning the condition of our fathers, whether it be this thing or any other which we bring unto you, the counfel is good, which the wife man giveth, *Stand thou faft in thy fure underftanding, in the way and knowledge of the Lord, and have but one manner of word, and follow the word of peace and righteoufnefs.* As a loofe tooth is a grief to him that eateth: fo doth a wavering and unftable word in fpeech, that tendeth to inftruction, offend. *Shall a wife man fpeak words for the wind,* faith *Eliphaz,* light, unconftant, unftable words? Surely the wifeft may fpeak words of the wind: fuch is the untoward conftitution of our nature, that we do neither fo perfectly underftand the way and knowledge of the Lord, nor fo fteadfaftly embrace it when it is underftood; nor fo gracioufly utter it, when it is embraced; nor fo peaceably maintain it, when it is uttered; but that the beft of us are over-taken fometimes thro' blindnefs, fometimes thro' haftinefs, fometimes thro' impatience, fometimes thro' other paffions of the mind, whereunto (God doth know) we are too fubject. We muft therefore be contented both to pardon others, and to crave that others may pardon us for fuch things. Let no man, that fpeaketh as a man, think himfelf, while he liveth, always freed from fcapes and over-fights in his fpeech. The things themfelves which I have fpoken unto you are found, howfoever they have feemed otherwife unto fome: at whofe hands I have, in that refpect, received injury, I willingly forget it: altho' indeed, confidering the benefit which I have reaped by this neceffary fpeech of truth, I rather incline to that of the apoftle, *They have not injured me at all.* I have caufe to wifh them as many bleffings in the kingdom of heaven, as they have forced me to utter words and fyllables in this caufe; wherein I could not be more fparing of my fpeech than I have been. *It becometh no man,* faith St. *Jerome, to be patient in the crime of herefy.* Patient, as I take it, we fhould be always, tho' the crime of herefy were intended; but filent in a thing of fo great confequence I could not, beloved, I durft not be; efpecially the love, which I bear to the truth of Chrift Jefus, being hereby fomewhat called in queftion. Whereof I befeech them in the meeknefs of Chrift, that have been the firft original caufe, to confider that a watch-man may cry (*an enemy,*) when indeed a friend cometh. In which caufe, as I deem fuch a watch-man more worthy to be loved for his care than mifliked for his error; fo I have judged it my own part in this, as much as in me lyeth, to take away all fufpicion of any unfriendly intent or meaning againft the truth, from which, God doth know my heart is free.

40. Now to you, beloved, which have heard thefe things, I will ufe no other words of admonition, than thofe that are offered me by St. *James, My brethren, have not the faith of our glorious Lord Jefus in refpect of perfons.* Ye are not now to learn, that as of itfelf it is not hurtful, fo neither fhould it be to any, fcandalous and offenfive in doubtful cafes, to hear the indifferent judgments of men. Be it that *Cephas* hath one interpretation, and *Apollos* hath another; that *Paul* is of this mind, and *Barnabas* of that; if this offend you, the fault is yours. Carry peaceable minds, and you may have comfort by this variety.

Now the God of peace, give you peaceable minds, and turn it to your everlafting comfort.

A

A LEARNED

SERMON

O F

The Nature of PRIDE.

HABAK. II. 4.

His mind swelleth, and is not right in him: But the just by
Faith shall live.

THE nature of man being much more delighted to be led than drawn, doth many times stubbornly resist authority, when to persuasion it easily yieldeth. Whereupon the wisest law-makers have endeavoured always that those laws might seem most reasonable, which they would have most inviolably kept. A law simply commanding or forbidding, is but dead in comparison of that which expresseth the reason wherefore it doth the one or the other. And surely, even in the laws of God, altho' that he hath given commandment be in it self a reason sufficient to exact all obedience at the hands of men; yet a forceable inducement it is to obey with greater alacrity and chearfulness of mind, when we see plainly that nothing is imposed more than we must needs yield unto, except we will be unreasonable. In a word, whatsoever be taught, be it precept for direction of our manners; or article for instruction of our faith; or document any way for information of our minds, it then taketh root and abideth, when we conceive not only what God doth speak, but why. Neither is it a small thing which we derogate as well from the honour of his truth, as from the comfort, joy and delight which we our selves should take by it, when we loosly slide over his speech as tho' it were as our own is, commonly vulgar and trivial. Whereas he uttereth nothing but it hath, besides the substance of doctrine delivered, a depth of wisdom, in the very choice and frame of words to deliver it in. The reason whereof being not perceived, but by greater intention of brain than our nice minds for the most part can well away with, fain would we bring the world, if we might, to think it but a needless curiosity to rip up any thing further than extemporal readiness of wit doth serve to reach unto. Which course, if here we did list to follow, we might tell you, that in the first branch of this sentence God doth condemn the *Babylonian*'s pride; and in the second, teach what happiness of state shall grow to the righteous by the constancy of their faith, notwithstanding the troubles which now they suffer; and after certain notes of wholesome instruction hereupon collected, pass over without detaining your minds in any further removed speculation. But, as I take it, there is a difference between the talk that beseemeth nurses among children, and that which men of capacity and judgment do, or should receive instruction by.

The mind of the prophet being erected with that which hath been hitherto spoken, receiveth here for full satisfaction a short abridgment of that which is afterwards more particularly unfolded. Wherefore as the question before disputed of doth concern two sorts

+

of

of men, the wicked flourishing as the bay, and the righteous like the withered grass, the one full of pride, the other cast down with utter discouragement; so the answer which God doth make for resolution of doubts hereupon arisen, hath reference unto both sorts, and this present sentence containing a brief abstract thereof, comprehendeth summarily as well the fearful estate of iniquity over-exalted, as the hope laid up for righteousness oppress. In the former branch of which sentence, let us first examine what this rectitude or streightness importeth which God denieth to be in the mind of the *Babylonian*. All things which God did create he made them at the first true, good, and right. True, in respect of correspondence unto that pattern of their Being, which was eternally drawn in the counsel of God's fore-knowledge; good, in regard of the use and benefit which each thing yieldeth unto other; right, by an apt conformity of all parts with that end which is outwardly proposed for each thing to tend unto. Other things have ends proposed, but have not the faculty to know, judge, and esteem of them; and therefore as they tend thereunto wittingly, so likewise in the means whereby they acquire their appointed ends, they are by necessity so held that they cannot divert from them. The ends why the heavens do move, the heavens themselves know not, and their motions they cannot but continue. Only men in all their actions know what it is which they seek for, neither are they by any such necessity tied naturally unto any certain determinate mean to obtain their end by, but that they may, if they will, forsake it. And therefore in the whole world, no creature but only man, which hath the last end of his actions proposed as a recompence and reward whereunto his mind directly bending it self, is termed right or strait, otherwise perverse.

To make this somewhat more plain, we must note, that as they, which travel from city to city, enquire ever for the streightest way, because the streightest is that which soonest bringeth them to their journey's end; so we, *having here*, as the apostle speaketh, *no abiding city*, but being always in travel towards that place of joy, immortality, and rest, cannot but in every of our deeds, words, and thoughts, think that to be best, which with most expedition leadeth us thereunto, and is for that very cause termed right. That sovereign good, which is the eternal fruition of all good, being our last and chiefest felicity, there is no desperate despiser of God and godliness living, which doth not wish for. The difference between right and crooked minds, is in the means which the one or the other eschew or follow. Certain it is, that all particular things which are naturally desired in the world, as food, raiment, honour, wealth, pleasure, knowledge, they are subordinated in such wise unto that future good which we look for in the world to come, that even in them there lyeth a direct way tending unto this. Otherwise we must think, that God making promises of good things in this life, did seek to pervert them, and to lead them from their right minds. Where is then the obliquity of the mind of man? his mind is perverse and crooked, not when it bendeth it self unto any of these things, but when it bendeth so that it swerveth either to the right hand or to the left, by excess or defect, from the exact rule whereby human actions are measured. The rule to measure and judge them by, is the law of God. For this cause the prophet doth make so often and so earnest suit, *O direct me in the way of thy commandments: as long as I have respect to thy statutes, I am sure not to tread amiss*. Under the name of the law we must comprehend not only that which God hath written in tables and leaves, but that which nature also hath engraven in the hearts of men. Else how should those heathens which never had books, but heaven and earth to look upon, be convicted of perverseness? *But the Gentiles which had not the law in books, had*, saith the apostle, *the effect of the law written in their hearts*.

Then seeing that the heart of man is not right exactly, unless it be found in all parts such, that God examining and calling it unto account with all severity of rigor, be not able once to charge it with declining or swerving aside (which absolute perfection when did God ever find in the sons of mere mortal men?) doth it not follow, that all flesh must of necessity fall down and confess, we are not dust and ashes, but worse; our minds from the highest to the lowest are not right; if not right, then undoubtedly not capable of that blessedness which we naturally seek, but subject unto that which we most abhor, anguish, tribulation, death, woe, endless misery. For whatsoever misseth the way of life, the issue thereof cannot be but perdition. By which reason, all being wrapped up in sin, and made thereby the children of death, the minds of all men being plainly convicted not to be right; shall we think that God hath indued them with so many excellencies more, not only than any, but than all the creatures in the world besides, to leave them in such estate, that they had been happier if they had never been? Here cometh necessarily in a new way unto salvation, so that they which were in the other perverse, may in this be found streight and righteous. That the way of nature,
this

this the way of grace. The end of that way, falvation merited, prefuppofing the righ-teoufnefs of mens works; their righteoufnefs, a natural hability to do them; that ha-bility, the goodnefs of God which created them in fuch perfection; but the end of this way, falvation beftowed upon men as a gift, prefuppofing not their rightcoufnefs, but the forgivenefs of their unrighteoufnefs, juftification; their juftification, not their natural ability to do good, but their hearty forrow for their not doing, and unfeign-ed belief in him, for whofe fake not-doers are accepted, which is their vocation, their vocation, the election of God, taking them out from the number of loft chil-dren; their election, a Mediator in whom to be elect; this mediation, inexplicable mercy; his mercy, their mifery, for whom he vouchfafed to make himfelf a Mediator. The want of exact diftinguifhing between thefe two ways, and obferving what they have common, what peculiar, hath been the caufe of the greateft part of that con-fufion whereof chriftianity at this day laboureth. The lack of diligence in fearching, laying down, and inuring mens minds with thofe hidden grounds of reafon, where-upon the leaft particular in each of thefe are moft firmly and ftrongly builded, is the only reafon of all thofe fcruples and uncertainties, wherewith we are in fuch fort in-tangled, that a number defpair of ever difcerning what is right or wrong in any thing. But we will let this matter reft, whereinto we ftepped to fearch out a way, how fome minds may be, and are right truly, even in the fight of God, tho' they be fimply in themfelves not right.

Howbeit, there is not only this difference between the juft and impious, that the mind of the one is right in the fight of God, becaufe his obliquity is not imputed; the other perverfe, · becaufe his fin is unrepented of; but even as lines that are drawn with a trembling hand, but yet to the point which they fhould, are thought ragged and uneven, neverthelefs direct in comparifon of them which run clean another way; fo there is no incongruity in terming them right minded men, whom tho' God may charge with many things amifs, yet they are not as hideous and ugly monfters, in whom, becaufe there is nothing but wilful oppofition of mind againft God, a more than tolerable de-formity is noted in them, by faying, that their minds are not right. The angel of the church of *Thyatira*, unto whom the Son of God fendeth thus greeting, *I know thy works, and thy love, and thy fervice, and faith; notwithftanding, I have a few things againft thee*, was not as he, unto whom St. *Peter, Thou haft no fellowfhip in this bufinefs; for thy heart is not right in the fight of God.* So that whereas the orderly difpofition of the mind of man fhould be this, perturbation and fenfual appetites all kept in awe by a mode-rate and fober will, in all things framed by reafon; reafon directed by the law of God and nature; this *Babylonian* had his mind, as it were, turned upfide down. In him un-reafonable cecity and blindnefs trampled all laws, both of God and nature, under feet; wilfulnefs tyrannized over reafon; and brutifh fenfuality over will: an evident token that his out-rage would work his overthrow, and procure his fpeedy ruin. The mother whereof was that which the prophet in thefe words fignified, *His mind doth fwell.*

Immoderate fwelling, a token of very eminent breach, and of inevitable deftruction. pride, a vice which cleaveth fo faft unto the hearts of men, that if we were to ftrip our felves of all faults one by one, we fhould undoubtedly find it the very laft and hardeft to put off. But I am not here to touch the fecret itching humour of vanity wherewith men are generally touched. It was a thing more than meanly inordinate, wherewith the *Ba-bylonian* did fwell. Which that we may both the better conceive, and the more eafily reap profit by the nature of this vice, which fetteth the whole world out of courfe, and hath put fo many even of the wifeft befides themfelves, is firft of all to be enquired into: fe-condly, the danger to be difcovered which it draweth inevitably after it, being not cured: and laft of all, the way to cure it.

Whether we look upon the gifts of nature, or of grace, or whatfoever is in the world admired as a part of man's excellency, adorning his body, beautifying his mind, or ex-ternally any way commending him in the account and opinion of men, there is in every kind fomewhat poffible which no man hath, and fomewhat had which few men can at-tain unto. By occafion whereof, there groweth difparagement neceffarily; and by occa-fion of difparagement, pride thro' mens ignorance. Firft therefore, altho' men be not proud of any thing which is not, at leaft in opinion, good; yet every good thing they are not proud of, but only of that which neither is common unto many, and being de-fired of all, caufeth them which have it to be honoured above the reft. Now there is no man fo void of brain, as to fuppofe that pride confifteth in the bare poffeffion of fuch things; for then to have virtue were a vice, and they fhould be the happieft men who are moft wretched, becaufe they have leaft of that which they would have. And tho' in fpeech we do intimate a kind of vanity to be in them of whom we fay, *They are wife*
men

men, and they know it ; yet this doth not prove, that every wife man is proud which doth not think himfelf to be blockifh. What we may have, and know that we have it without offence, do we then make offenfive when we take joy and delight in having it? What difference between men enriched with all abundance of earthly and heavenly bleffings, and idols gorgeoufly attired, but this, *the one takes pleafure in that which they have, the other none?* If we may be poffeft with beauty, ftrength, riches, power, knowledge, if we may be privy to what we are every way, if glad and joyful for our own welfare, and in all this remain unblameable; neverthelefs, fome there are, who granting thus much, doubt whether it may ftand with humility to accept thofe teftimonies of praife and commendation, thofe titles, rooms, and other honours which the world yieldeth, as acknowledgments of fome mens excellencies above others. For, inafmuch as Chrift hath faid unto thofe that are his, *The kings of the gentiles reign over them, and they that bear rule over them, are called gracious lords*; *be ye not fo*: the anabaptift hereupon urgeth equality amongft chriftians, as if all exercife of authority were nothing elfe but heathenifh pride. Our Lord and Saviour had no fuch meaning. But his difciples feeding themfelves with a vain imagination for the time, that the Meffias of the world fhould in *Jerufalem* erect his throne, and exercife dominion with great pomp and outward ftatelinefs, advanced in honour and terrene power above all the princes of the earth, began to think, how with their Lord's condition their own would alfo rife; that having left and forfaken all to follow him, their place about him fhould not be mean; and becaufe they were many, it troubled them much, which of them fhould be the greateft man. When fuit was made for two by name, that of them *one might fit at his right hand, and the other at his left*, the reft began to ftomach, each taking it grievoufly that any fhould have what all did affect; their Lord and Mafter, to correct this humour, turneth afide their cogitations from thefe vain and fanciful conceits, giving them plainly to underftand that they did but deceive themfelves: his coming was not to purchafe an earthly, but to beftow an heavenly kingdom, wherein they (if any) fhall be greateft whom unfeigned humility maketh in this world loweft, and leaft amongft others: *Ye are they which have continued with me in my temptations, therefore I leave unto you a kingdom, as my Father hath appointed me, that ye may eat and drink at my table in my kingdom, and fit on feats, and judge the twelve tribes of Ifrael.* But my kingdom is no fuch kingdom as ye dream of. And therefore thefe hungry ambitious contentions are feemlier in heathens than in you. Wherefore, from Chrift's intent and purpofe nothing is farther removed, than diflike of diftinction in titles and callings, annexed for order's fake unto authority, whether it be ecclefiaftical or civil. And when we have examined throughly, what the nature of this vice is, no man knowing it can be fo fimple as not to fee an ugly fhape thereof apparent many times in rejecting honours offered, more than in the very exacting of them at the hands of men. For as *Judas* his care for the poor was meer covetoufnefs; and that frank-hearted waftefulnefs fpoken of in the gofpel, thrift; fo, there is no doubt, but that going in rags may be pride, and thrones be clothed with unfeigned humility.

We muft go farther therefore, and enter fomewhat deeper, before we can come to the clofet wherein this poifon lieth. There is in the heart of every proud man, firft, an error of underftanding, a vain opinion whereby he thinketh his own excellency, and by reafon thereof his worthinefs of eftimation, regard and honour, to be greater than in truth it is. This maketh him in all his affections accordingly to raife up himfelf; and by his inward affections his outward acts are fafhioned. Which, if you lift to have exemplified, you may, either by calling to mind things fpoken of them whom God himfelf hath in fcripture efpecially noted with this fault; or by prefenting to your fecret cogitations that which you daily behold in the odious lives and manners of high-minded men. It were too long to gather together fo plentiful an harveft of examples in this kind as the facred fcripture affordeth. That which we drink in at our ears, doth not fo piercingly enter, as that which the mind doth conceive by fight. Is there any thing written concerning the *Affyrian* monarch, in the tenth of *Ifaiah*, of his fwelling mind, his haughty looks, his great and prefumptuous taunts; *By the power of mine own hand I have done all things, and by mine own wifdom I have fubdued the world?* Any thing concerning the dames of *Sion*, in the third of the prophet *Ifaiah*, of their ftretched out necks, their immodeft eyes, their pageant-like, ftately and pompous gate? Any thing concerning the practices of *Corah*, *Dathan* and *Abiram*, of their impatience to live in fubjection, their mutinies, repining at lawful authority, their grudging againft their fuperiors ecclefiaftical and civil? Any thing concerning pride in any fort of fect, which the prefent face of the world doth not, as in a glafs, reprefent to the view of all mens beholding? So that if books, both profane and holy, were all loft, as long as

R r r the

the manners of men retain the eſtate they are in; for him that obſerveth, how that when men have once conceived an over-weening of themſelves, it maketh them in all their affections to ſwell; how deadly their hatred, how heavy their diſpleaſure, how un-appeaſable their indignation and wrath is above other mens, in what manner they com-poſe themſelves to be as *Heteroclites*, without the compaſs of all ſuch rules as the com-mon ſort are meaſured by; how the oaths which religious hearts do tremble at, they af-fect as principal graces of ſpeech; what felicity they take to ſee the enormity of their crimes above the reach of laws and puniſhments; how much it delighteth them when they are able to appale with the cloudineſs of their looks; how far they exceed the terms wherewith man's nature ſhould be limited; how high they bear their heads over others; how they brow-beat all men which do not receive their ſentences as oracles, with marvelous applauſe and approbation; how they look upon no man, but with an indirect countenance, nor hear any thing, ſaving their own praiſe, with patience, nor ſpeak with-out ſtornfulneſs and diſdain; how they uſe their ſervants, as if they were beaſts, their in-feriors as ſervants, their equals as inferiors, and as for ſuperiors they acknowledge none; how they admire themſelves as venerable, puiſſant, wiſe, circumſpect, provident, every way great, taking all men beſides themſelves for cyphers, poor, inglorious, ſilly creatures, needleſs burthens of the earth, off-ſcourings, nothing: in a word, for him which mark-eth how irregular and exorbitant they are in all things, it can be no hard thing hereby to gather, that pride is nothing but an inordinate elation of the mind, proceeding from a falſe conceit of mens excellency in things honoured, which accordingly frameth alſo their deeds and behaviour, unleſs they be cunning to conceal it; for a foul ſcar may be covered with a fair cloth; and as proud as *Lucifer*, may be in outward appearance lowly.

No man expecteth grapes of thiſtles; nor from a thing of ſo bad a nature, can other than ſuitable fruits be looked for. What harm ſoever in private families there groweth by diſobedience of children, ſtubbornneſs of ſervants, untractableneſs in them, who although they otherwiſe may rule, yet ſhould in conſideration of the imparity of their ſex, be alſo ſubject; whatſoever, by ſtrife amongſt men combined in the fellow-ſhip of greater ſocieties, by tyranny of potentates, ambition of nobles, rebellion of ſub-jects in civil ſtates; by hereſies, ſchiſms, diviſions in the church; naming pride, we name the mother which brought them forth, and the only nurſe that feedeth them. Give me the hearts of all men humbled, and what is there that can overthrow or di-ſturb the peace of the world, wherein many things are the cauſe of much evil, but pride of all?

To declaim of the ſwarms of evils iſſuing out of pride, is an eaſy labour. I rather wiſh that I could exactly preſcribe and perſuade effectually the remedies, whereby a ſore ſo grievous might be cured, and the means how the pride of ſwelling minds might be taken down. Whereunto ſo much we have already gained, that the evidence of the cauſe which breedeth it pointeth directly unto the likelieſt and fitteſt helps to take it away. Diſeaſes that come of fulneſs, emptineſs muſt remove. Pride is not cured but by abating the error which cauſeth the mind to ſwell. Then ſeeing that they ſwell by miſ-conceit of their own excellency; for this cauſe, all tends to the beating down of their pride, whether it be advertiſement from men, or from God himſelf chaſtiſement; it then maketh them ceaſe to be proud, when it cauſeth them to ſee their error in over-ſeeing the thing they were proud of. At this mark *Job*, in his apology unto his elo-quent friends, aimeth: For perceiving how much they delighted to hear themſelves talk, as if they had given their poor afflicted familiar a ſchooling of marvellous deep and rare inſtruction, as if they had taught him more than all the world beſides could acquaint him with; his anſwer was to this effect: ye ſwell, as tho' ye had conceived ſome great matter; but as for that which ye are delivered of, who knoweth it not? is any man ignorant of theſe things? At the ſame mark the bleſſed apoſtle driveth: *Te abound in all things, ye are rich, ye reign, and would to Chriſt we did reign with you: but boaſt not.* For what have ye, or are ye of your ſelves? To this mark all thoſe humble confeſſions are referred, which have been always frequent in the mouths of ſaints truly wading in the trial of themſelves: as that of the prophet's, *We are nothing but ſoreneſs and feſtered corruption:* our very light is darkneſs, and our righteouſneſs it ſelf unrigh-teouſneſs: that of *Gregory, Let no man ever put confidence in his own deſerts; ſordet in conſpectu judicis, quod fulget in conſpectu operantis,* in the ſight of the dreadful judge, it is noiſome, which in the doer's maketh a beautiful ſhew: that of *Anſelm, I adore thee, I bleſs thee, Lord God of heaven, Redeemer of the world, with all the power, ability, and ſtrength of my heart and ſoul, for thy goodneſs ſo unmeaſurably extended; not in regard of my merits, whereunto only torments were due, but of thy mere unprocured*

2

benignity.

benignity. If thefe fathers fhould be raifed again from the duft, and have the books laid open before them wherein fuch fentences are found as this: *Works no other than the value, defert, price, and worth of the joys of the kingdom of heaven; heaven, in relation to our works, as the very ftipend, which the hired labourer covenanteth to have of him whofe work he doth, as a thing equally and juftly anfwering unto the time and weight of his travels, rather than to a voluntary or bountiful gift.* If, I fay, thofe reverend fore-rehcarfed fathers, whofe books are fo full of fentences witneffing their chriftian humility, fhould be raifed from the dead, and behold with their eyes fuch things written; would they not plainly pronounce of the authors of fuch writs, that they were fuller of *Lucifer,* than of Chrift; that they were proud-hearted men, and carried more fwelling minds than fincerely and feelingly known chriftianity can tolerate.

But as unruly children, with whom wholefome admonition prevaileth little, are notwithftanding brought to fear that ever after, which they have once well fmarted for; fo the mind which falleth not with inftruction, yet under the rod of divine chaftifement ceafeth to fwell. If therefore the prophet *David,* inftructed by good experience, have acknowledged; Lord, I was even at the point of clean forgetting my felf, and fo ftraying from my right mind; but thy rod was my reformer; it *hath been good for me,* even as much as my foul is worth, *that I have been with forrow troubled.* If the bleffed apoftle did need the corrofive of fharp and bitter ftrokes, left his heart fhould fwell with too great *abundance of heavenly revelations,* furely, upon us whatfoever God in this world doth or fhall inflict, it cannot feem more than our pride doth exact, not only by way of revenge, but of remedy. So hard it is to cure a fore of fuch quality as pride is, inafmuch as that which rooteth out other vices, caufeth this; and (which is even above all conceit) if we were clean from all fpot and blemifh both of other faults, of pride, the fall of angels doth make it almoft a queftion, whether we might not need a prefervative ftill, left we fhould haply wax proud, that we are not proud. What is virtue, but a medicine, and vice, but a wound? Yet we have fo often deeply wounded our felves with medicine; that God hath been fain to make wounds medicinable; to cure by vice where virtue hath ftrucken; to fuffer the juft man to fall, that being raifed, he may be taught what power it was which upheld him ftanding. I am not afraid to affirm it boldly with St. *Auguftine,* that men puffed up thro' a proud opinion of their own fanctity and holinefs, receive a benefit at the hands of God, and are affifted with his grace, when with his grace they are not affifted, but permitted, and that grievoufly to tranfgrefs; whereby, as they were in over-great liking of themfelves fupplanted, fo the diflike of that which did fupplant them, may eftablifh them afterwards the furer. Ask the very foul of *Peter,* and it fhall undoubtedly make you it felf this anfwer; my eager proteftations, made in the glory of my ghoftly ftrength, I am afhamed of; but thofe cryftal tears wherewith my fin and weaknefs was bewailed, have procured my endlefs joy; my ftrength hath been my ruin, and my fall my ftay.

A

A
R E M E D Y

A G A I N S T

Sorrow and Fear.

D E L I V E R E D   I N   A

F U N E R A L   S E R M O N.

J O H N XIV. 27.

Let not your hearts be troubled, nor fear.

THE holy apoſtles having gathered themſelves together by the ſpecial appointment of Chriſt, and being in expectation to receive from him ſuch inſtruction as they had been accuſtomed with, were told that which they leaſt looked for, namely, that the time of his departure out of the world was now come.
Whereupon they fell into conſideration, firſt, of the manifold benefits which his abſence
ſhould bereave them of; and, ſecondly, of the ſundry evils which themſelves ſhould be
ſubject unto, being once bereaved of ſo gracious a maſter and patron. The one conſideration overwhelmed their ſouls with heavineſs, the other with fear. Their Lord and
Saviour, whoſe words had caſt down their hearts, raiſeth them preſently again with choſen ſentences of ſweet encouragement. My dear, it is for your own ſakes I leave the
world; I know the affections of your hearts are tender, but if your love were directed
with that adviſed and ſtaid judgment which ſhould be in you, my ſpeech of leaving the
world, and going unto my Father, would not a little augment your joy. Deſolate and
comfortleſs I will not leave you; in ſpirit I am with you to the world's end. Whether
I be preſent or abſent, nothing ſhall ever take you out of theſe hands. My going is to
take poſſeſſion of that, in your names, which is not only for me, but alſo for you prepared; where I am, you ſhall be. In the mean while, *my peace I give, not as the
world giveth, give I unto you: let not your hearts be troubled, nor fear.* The former
part of which ſentence having otherwhere already been ſpoken of, this unacceptable occaſion to open the latter part thereof here, I did not look for. But ſo God diſpoſeth the
ways of men. Him I heartily beſeech, that the thing which he hath thus ordered by his
providence, may thro' his gracious goodneſs turn unto your comfort.

Our nature coveteth for preſervation from things hurtful. Hurtful things being preſent, do breed heavineſs; being future, do cauſe fear. Our Saviour, to abate the one,
ſpeaketh thus unto his diſciples, *Let not your hearts be troubled*; and to moderate the
other, addeth, *Fear not.* Grief and heavineſs in the preſence of ſenſible evils, cannot
but trouble the minds of men. It may therefore ſeem that Chriſt required a thing im-

poſſible.

poſſible. Be not troubled. Why, how could they chuſe? But we muſt note this being natural, and therefore ſimply not reprovable, is in us good or bad, according to the cauſes for which we are grieved, or the meaſure of our grief. It is not my meaning to ſpeak ſo largely of this affection, or to go over all the particulars whereby men do one way or other offend in it, but to teach it ſo far only, as it may cauſe the very apoſtles equal to ſwerve. Our grief and heavineſs therefore is reprovable, ſometime in reſpect of the cauſe from whence, ſometime in regard of the meaſure whereunto it groweth.

When Chriſt, the life of the world, was led unto cruel death, there followed a number of people and women, which women bewailed much his heavy caſe. It was a natural compaſſion which cauſed them, where they ſaw undeſerved miſeries, there to pour forth unreſtrained tears. Nor was this reproved. But in ſuch readineſs to lament where they leſs needed, their blindneſs in not diſcerning that for which they ought much rather to have mourned; this our Saviour a little toucheth, putting them in mind that the tears which were waſted for him, might better have been ſpent upon themſelves; *Daughters of Jeruſalem, weep not for me, weep for your ſelves and for your children.* It is not, as the ſtoicks have imagined, a thing unſeemly for a wiſe man to be touched with grief of mind: but to be ſorrowful when we leaſt ſhould, and where we ſhould lament, there to laugh, this argueth our ſmall wiſdom. Again, when the prophet *David* confeſſeth this of himſelf, *I grieved to ſee the great proſperity of godleſs men, how they flouriſh and go untoucht.* Pſal. 73. Himſelf hereby openeth both our common, and his peculiar imperfection, whom this cauſe ſhould not have made ſo penſive. To grieve at this, is to grieve where we ſhould not, becauſe this grief doth riſe from error. We err, when we grieve at wicked mens impunity and proſperity; becauſe, their eſtate being rightly diſcerned, they neither proſper, nor go unpuniſhed. It may ſeem a paradox, it is truth, that no wicked man's eſtate is proſperous, fortunate or happy. For what tho' they bleſs themſelves, and think their happineſs great? Have not frantick perſons many times a great opinion of their own wiſdom? It may be that ſuch as they think themſelves, others alſo do account them. But what others? Surely ſuch as themſelves are. Truth and reaſon diſcerneth far otherwiſe of them. Unto whom the Jews wiſh all proſperity, unto them the phraſe of their ſpeech is to wiſh peace. Seeing then the name of peace containeth in it all parts of true happineſs, when the prophet ſaith plainly, *That the wicked have no peace*; how can we think them to have any part of other than vainly imagined felicity? What wiſe man did ever account fools happy? If wicked men were wiſe, they would ceaſe to be wicked. Their iniquity therefore proving their folly, how can we ſtand in doubt of their miſery? They abound in thoſe things which all men deſire. A poor happineſs, to have good things in poſſeſſion, *A man to whom God hath given riches,* Eccleſ. 6. 2 *and treaſures, and honour, ſo that he wanteth nothing for his ſoul, of all that it deſireth, but yet God giveth him not the power to eat thereof;* ſuch a felicity Solomon eſteemeth but as vanity, a thing of nothing. If ſuch things add nothing to mens happineſs, where they are not uſed, ſurely wicked men that uſe them ill, the more they have, the more wretched. Of their proſperity therefore, we ſee what we are to think. Touching their impunity, the ſame is likewiſe but ſuppoſed. They are oftner plagued than we are aware of. The pangs they feel, are not always written in their forehead. Tho' wickedneſs be ſugar in their mouths, and wantonneſs as oil to make them look with chearful countenances; nevertheleſs, if their hearts were diſcloſed, perhaps their glittering ſtate would not greatly be envied. The voices that have broken out from ſome of them, *O that God had given me a heart ſenſleſs, like the flints in the rocks of ſtone!* which as it can taſte no pleaſure, ſo it feeleth no woe: theſe and the like ſpeeches, are ſurely tokens of the curſe which *Zophar*, in the book of *Job*, poureth upon the head of the impious man, *He ſhall ſuck the gall of aſps, and the viper's tongue ſhall ſlay him.* If this ſeem light, becauſe it is ſecret, ſhall we think they go unpuniſhed, becauſe no apparent plague is preſently ſeen upon them? The judgments of God do not always follow crimes, as thunder doth lightning; but ſometimes the ſpace of many ages coming between. When the ſun hath ſhined fair the ſpace of ſix hours upon their tabernacle, we know not what clouds the ſeventh may bring. And when their puniſhment doth come, let them make their account in the greatneſs of their ſuffering, to pay the intereſt of that reſpite which hath been given them. Or if they chance to eſcape clearly in this world, which they ſeldom do; in the day when the heavens ſhall ſhrivel as a ſcroul, and the mountains move as frighted men out of their places, what cave ſhall receive them? What mountain or rock ſhall they get by intreaty to fall upon them? What covert to hide them from that wrath, which they ſhall neither be able to abide or avoid? No man's miſery therefore being greater than theirs whoſe impiety is moſt fortunate; much more cauſe there is for them to bewail their own infelicity, than for others to be troubled with their proſperous

        and

and happy eſtate, as if the hand of the Almighty did not, or would not touch them; For theſe cauſes, and the like unto theſe, therefore *be not troubled.*

Now, tho' the cauſe of our heavineſs be juſt, yet may not your affections herein be yielded unto with too much indulgency and favour. The grief of compaſſion, whereby we are touched with the feeling of other mens woes, is of all other leaſt dangerous: yet this is a let unto ſundry duties; by this we are apt to ſpare ſometimes where we ought to ſtrike. The grief which our own ſufferings do bring, what temptations have not riſen from it? What great advantage Satan hath taken even by the godly grief of hearty contrition for ſins committed againſt God, the near approaching of ſo many afflicted ſouls, whom the conſcience of ſin hath brought unto the very brink of extream deſpair, doth but too abundantly ſhew. Theſe things, whereſoever they fall, cannot but trouble and moleſt the mind. Whether we be therefore moved vainly with that which ſeemeth hurtful, and is not; or have juſt cauſe of grief, being preſſed indeed with thoſe things which are grievous, our Saviour's leſſon is touching the one, be not troubled; nor over-troubled for the other. For, tho' to have no feeling of that which merely concerneth us were ſtupidity, nevertheleſs, ſeeing that as the author of our ſalvation was himſelf conſecrated by affliction, ſo the way which we are to follow him by, is not ſtrewed with ruſhes, but ſet with thorns; be it never ſo hard to learn, we muſt learn to ſuffer with patience, even that which ſeemeth almoſt impoſſible to be ſuffered; that in the hour when God ſhall call us unto our trial, and turn his honey of peace and pleaſure wherewith we ſwell, into that gall and bitterneſs which fleſh doth ſhrink to taſte of, nothing may cauſe us in the troubles of our ſouls to ſtorm, and grudge, and repine at God; but every heart be enabled with divine inſpired courage to inculcate unto it ſelf, *be not troubled;* and in thoſe laſt and greateſt conflicts to remember, that nothing may be ſo ſharp and bitter to be ſuffered, but that ſtill we our ſelves may give our ſelves this encouragement, *even learn alſo patience, O my ſoul.*

Naming patience, I name that virtue which only hath power to ſtay our ſouls from being over-exceſſively troubled. A virtue, wherein if ever any, ſurely that ſoul had good experience, which extremity of pains having chaſed out of the tabernacle of this fleſh, angels, I nothing doubt, have carried into the boſom of her father *Abraham.* The death of the ſaints of God is precious in his ſight. And ſhall it ſeem unto us ſuperfluous at ſuch times as theſe are, to hear in what manner they have ended their lives? The Lord himſelf hath not diſdained ſo exactly to regiſter in the book of life, after what ſort his ſervants have cloſed up their days on earth, that he deſcendeth even to their very meaneſt actions; what meat they have longed for in their ſickneſs, what they have ſpoken unto their children, kinsfolks, and friends, where they have willed their dead carkaſſes to be laid, how they have framed their wills and teſtaments; yea, the very turning of their faces to this ſide or that, the ſetting of their eyes, the degrees whereby their natural heat hath departed from them, their cries, their groans, their pantings, breathings, and laſt gaſpings he hath moſt ſolemnly commended unto the memory of all generations. The care of the living both to live and die well muſt needs be ſomewhat encreaſed, when they know that their departure ſhall not be folded up in ſilence, but the ears of many be made acquainted with it. Again, when they hear how mercifully God hath dealt with others in the hour of their laſt need, beſides the praiſe which they give to God, and the joy which they have, or ſhould have by reaſon of their fellowſhip and communion of ſaints, is not their hope alſo much confirmed againſt the day of their diſſolution? Finally, the ſound of theſe things doth not ſo paſs the ears of them that are moſt looſe and diſſolute of life, but it cauſeth them ſome time or other to wiſh in their hearts, *Oh, that we might die the death of the righteous, and that our end might be like his!* Howbeit, becauſe to ſpend herein many words, would be to ſtrike even as many wounds into their minds, whom I rather wiſh to comfort: therefore concerning this virtuous gentlewoman only this little I ſpeak, and that of knowledge, *ſhe lived a dove, and died a lamb.* And if amongſt ſo many virtues, hearty devotion towards God, towards poverty tender compaſſion, motherly affection towards ſervants, toward friends even ſerviceable kindneſs, mild behaviour, and harmleſs meaning towards all; if, where ſo many virtues were eminent, any be worthy of ſpecial mention, I wiſh her deareſt friends of that ſex, to be her neareſt followers in two things; *ſilence,* ſaving only where duty did exact ſpeech; and *patience,* even then when extremity of pains did enforce grief. *Bleſſed are they that die in the Lord.* And concerning the dead which are bleſſed, let not the hearts of any living be over-charged, with grief over-troubled.

Touching the latter affection of fear, which reſpecteth evil to come, as the other which we have ſpoken of doth preſent evils; firſt, in the nature thereof it is plain, that we are not of every future evil afraid. Perceive we not how they, whoſe tenderneſs

ſhrinketh

shrinketh at the least tast of a needle's point, do kis the sword that pierceth their souls quite thorow? If every evil did cause fear, sin, because it is sin, would be feared; whereas properly sin is not feared as sin, but only as having some kind of harm annexed. To teach men to avoid sin, it had been sufficient for the apostle to say, *Fly it:* but to make them afraid of committing sin, because the naming of sin sufficed not, therefore he addeth further, that it is a *serpent which stingeth the soul.* Again, be it that some nocive or hurtful thing be towards us, must fear of necessity follow hereupon? Not except that hurtful thing do threaten us either with destruction or vexation, and that such, as we have neither a conceit of ability to resist, nor of utter impossibility to avoid. That which we know our selves able to withstand, we fear not; and that which we know we are unable to defer or diminish, or any way avoid, we cease to fear; we give our selves over to bear and sustain it. The evil therefore which is feared, must be in our persuasion unable to be resisted when it cometh, yet not utterly impossible for a time in whole or in part to be shunned. Neither do we much fear such evils, except they be imminent and near at hand; nor if they be near, except we have an opinion that they be so. When we have once conceived an opinion, or apprehended an imagination of such evils prest, and ready to invade us; because they are hurtful unto our nature, we feel in our selves a kind of abhorring; because they are thought near, yet not present, our nature seeketh forthwith how to shift and provide for it self; because they are evils which cannot be resisted, therefore she doth not provide to withstand, but to shun and avoid. Hence it is, that in extreme fear, the mother of life contracting her self, avoiding as much as may be the reach of evil, and drawing the heat together with the spirits of the body to her, leaveth the outward parts cold, pale, weak, feeble, unapt to perform the functions of life; as we see in the fear of *Balthasar* king of *Babel.* By this it appeareth, that fear is nothing else but a perturbation of the mind, thro' an opinion of some imminent evil, threatning the destruction, or great annoyance of our nature, which to shun it doth contract and deject it self.

Now because, not in this place only, but otherwise often we hear it repeated, *Fear not,* it is by some made a question, *Whether a man may fear destruction or vexation, without sinning.* First, the reproof wherewith Christ checketh his disciples more than once, *O men of little faith, wherefore are ye afraid?* Secondly, the punishment threatned in *Rev.* 21. *viz.* the lake, and fire, and brimstone, not only to murtherers, unclean persons, sorcerers, idolaters, liars, but also to the fearful and faint-hearted: this seemeth to argue, that fearfulness cannot but be sin. On the contrary side we see, that he which never felt motion unto sin, had of this affection more than a slight feeling. How clear is the evidence of the Spirit, that *in the days of his flesh he offered up prayers and supplications, with strong cries and tears, unto him that was able to save him from death, and was also heard in that which he feared?* Heb. 5. 7. Whereupon it followeth, that fear in it self is not sinful. For, is not fear a thing natural, and for mens preservation necessary, implanted in us by the provident and most gracious giver of all good things, to the end that we might not run headlong upon those mischiefs wherewith we are not able to encounter, but use the remedy of shunning those evils which we have not ability to withstand? Let that people therefore which receive a benefit by the length of their prince's days, the father or mother which rejoiceth to see the off-spring of their flesh grow like green and pleasant plants, let those children that would have their parents, those men that would gladly have their friends and brethrens days prolonged on earth (as there is no natural-hearted man but gladly would) let them bless the Father of lights, as in other things, so even in this, that he hath given man a fearful heart, and settled naturally that affection in him, which is a preservation against so many ways of death. Fear then, in it self, being mere nature, cannot in it self be sin, which sin is not nature, but therefore an accessary deprivation.

But in the matter of fear we may sin, and do, two ways. If any man's danger be great, theirs is greatest that have put the fear of danger farthest from them. Is there any estate more fearful than that *Babylonian* strumpet's that sitteth upon the tops of seven hills, glorying and vaunting, *I am a queen,* &c. *Rev.* 18. 7.? How much better and happier are they, whose estate hath been always as his, who speaketh after this sort of himself, *Lord, from my youth have I born thy yoke?* They which sit at continual ease, and are settled in the lees of their security, look upon them, view their countenance, their speech, their gesture, their deeds: *Put them in fear, O God,* saith the prophet, *that so they may know themselves to be but men;* worms of earth, dust and ashes, frail, corruptible, feeble things. To shake off security therefore, and to breed fear in the hearts of mortal men, so many admonitions are used concerning the power of evils which beset them, so many threatnings of calamities, so many descriptions of things threatned, and those so lively,

to

to the end they may leave behind them a deep impreſſion of ſuch as have force to keep the heart continually waking. All which do ſhew, that we are to ſtand in fear of nothing more than the extremity of not fearing.

When fear hath delivered us from that pit, wherein they are ſunk that have put far from them the evil day, that have made a league with death, and have ſaid, *Tuſh, we ſhall feel no harm;* it ſtandeth us upon to take heed it caſt us not into that, wherein ſouls deſtitute of all hope are plunged. For our direction, to avoid, as much as may be, both extremities, that we may know, as a ſhip-maſter by his card, how far we are wide, either on the one ſide, or on the other, we muſt note, that in a chriſtian man there is, firſt, nature: ſecondly, corruption perverting nature: thirdly, grace correcting and amending corruption. In fear all theſe have their ſeveral operations: nature teacheth ſimply, to wiſh preſervation, and avoidance of things dreadful; for which cauſe our Saviour himſelf prayeth, and that often, *Father, if it be poſſible.* In which caſes, corrupt nature's ſuggeſtions are, for the ſafety of temporal life not to ſtick at things excluding from eternal; wherein how far even the beſt may be led, the chiefeſt apoſtle's frailty teacheth. Were it not therefore for ſuch cogitations as, on the contrary ſide, grace and faith miniſtreth, ſuch as that of *Job, Though God kill me;* that of *Paul, Scio cui credidi,* I know him on whom I do rely; ſmall evils would ſoon be able to overthrow even the beſt of us. *A wiſe man,* ſaith *Solomon, doth ſee a plague coming, and hideth himſelf.* It is *nature* which teacheth a wiſe man in fear to hide himſelf, but *grace* and *faith* doth teach him *where.* Fools care not to hide their heads: but where ſhall a wiſe man hide himſelf when he feareth a plague coming? Where ſhould the frighted child hide his head, but in the boſom of his loving father? where a chriſtian, but under the ſhadow of the wings of Chriſt his Saviour? *Come, my people,* ſaith God in the prophet, *enter into thy chamber, hide thy ſelf,* &c. Iſai. 26. But becauſe we are in danger, like chaſed birds, like doves, that ſeek and cannot ſee the reſting holes that are right before them; therefore our Saviour giveth his diſciples theſe encouragements beforehand, that fear might never ſo amaze them, but that always they might remember, that whatſoever evils at any time did befet them, to him they ſhould ſtill repair for comfort, counſel and ſuccour. For their aſſurance whereof, his *peace he gave them, his peace he left unto them, not ſuch peace as the world offereth,* by whom his name is never ſo much pretended, as when deepeſt treachery is meant; but *peace which paſſeth all underſtanding, peace* that bringeth with it all happineſs, *peace* that continueth for ever and ever with them that have it.

This peace God the Father grant, for his Son's ſake; unto whom, with the holy Ghoſt, three perſons, one eternal and everlaſting God, be all honour, and glory, and praiſe, now and for ever. Amen.   2

A

A Learned and Comfortable

S E R M O N

O F

The Certainty and Perpetuity of F A I T H in the E L E C T :

Efpecially of the Prophet *HABAKKUK*'s F A I T H.

H A B A K. I. 4.

Whether the Prophet Habakkuk, *by admitting this cogitati-on into his mind,* the Law doth fail, *did thereby fhew himfelf an unbeliever.*

WE have feen in the opening of this claufe, which concerneth the weaknefs of the prophet's faith, firft, what things they are, whereunto the faith of found believers doth affent : fecondly, wherefore all men affent not there-unto : and thirdly, why they that do, do it many times with fmall affurance. Now, becaufe nothing can be fo truly fpoken, but thro' mifunderftanding it may be de-praved ; therefore to prevent, if it be poffible, all mifconftruction in this caufe, where a fmall error cannot rife but with great danger ; it is perhaps needful e're we come to the fourth point, that fomething be added to that which hath been already fpoken concerning the third.

That meer natural men do neither know nor acknowledge the things of God, we do not marvel, becaufe they are fpiritually to be difcerned : but they in whofe hearts the light of grace doth fhine, they that are taught of God, why are they fo weak in faith ? why is their affenting to the law fo fcrupulous ? fo much mingled with fear and wavering ? It feemeth ftrange that ever they fhould imagine the law to fail. It cannot feem ftrange if we weigh the reafon. If the things which we believe be confidered in themfelves, it may truly be faid that faith is more certain than any fcience. That which we know either by fenfe, or by infallible demonftration, is not fo certain as the principles, articles and con-clufions of chriftian faith. Concerning which we muft note, that there is a *certainty* of *evidence*, and a *certainty* of *adherence*. *Certainty* of *evidence* we call that, when the mind doth affent to this or that, not becaufe it is true in it felf, but becaufe the truth is clear, becaufe it is manifeft unto us. Of things in themfelves moft certain, except they be alfo moft evident, our perfuafion is not fo affured as it is of things more evident, altho' in them-felves they be lefs certain. It is as fure, if not furer, that there be fpirits, as that there be men ; but we be more affured of thefe than of them, becaufe thefe are more evident. The truth of fome things are fo evident, that no man which heareth them can doubt of them : as when we hear that *a part of any thing is lefs than the whole,* the mind is con-ftrained to fay, this is true. If it were fo in matters of faith, then, as all men have equal certainty of this, fo no believer fhould be more fcrupulous and doubtful than another. But we find the contrary. The angels and fpirits of the righteous in heaven have certainty moft evident of things fpiritual : but this they have by the light of glory. That which

S f f

we

we see by the light of grace, tho' it be indeed more certain; yet it is not to us so evidently certain, as that which sense or the light of nature will not suffer a man to doubt of. Proofs are vain and frivolous, except they be more certain than is the thing proved. And do we not see how the Spirit every where in the scripture proving matters of faith, laboureth to confirm us in the things which we believe by things whereof we have sensible knowledge? I conclude therefore that we have less *certainty* of *evidence* concerning things believed, than concerning sensible or naturally perceived. Of those who doth doubt at any time? Of them at sometime who doubteth not? I will not here alledge the sundry confessions of the perfectest that have lived upon earth, concerning their great imperfections this way; which if I did, I should dwell too long upon a matter sufficiently known by every faithful man that doth know himself.

The other, which we call the *certainty* of *adherence* is, when the heart doth cleave and stick unto that which it doth believe. This certainty is greater in us than the other. The reason is this, the faith of a christian doth apprehend the words of the law, the promises of God, not only as true, but also as good; and therefore even then, when the evidence which he hath of the truth is so small, that it grieveth him to feel his weakness in assenting thereto, yet is there in him such a sure adherence unto that which he doth but faintly and fearfully believe, that his spirit having once truly tasted the heavenly sweetness thereof, all the world is not able to quite and clean remove him from it: but he striveth with himself to hope against all reason of believing, being setled with *Job* upon this immoveable resolution, *Tho' God kill me, I will not give over trusting in him.* For why? this lesson remaineth for ever imprinted in him, *It is good for me to cleave unto God, Psal.* 37.

Now the minds of all men being so darkned as they are with the foggy damp of original corruption, it cannot be that any man's heart living should be either so enlightned in the knowledge, or so establisht in the love of that wherein his salvation standeth, as to be perfect, neither doubting nor shrinking at all. If any such were, what doth let why that man should not be justified by his own inherent righteousness? For righteousness inherent, being perfect, will justify. And perfect faith is a part of perfect righteousness inherent; yea, a principal part, the root and the mother of all the rest: so that if the fruit of every tree be such as the root is, faith being perfect as it is, if it be not at all mingled with distrust and fear, what is there to exclude other christian virtues from the like perfections? And then what need we the righteousness of Christ? His garment is superfluous: we may be honourably cloathed with our own robes, if it be thus. But let them beware, who challenge to themselves strength which they have not, lest they lose the comfortable support of that weakness which indeed they have.

Some shew, altho' no soundness of ground, there is, which may be alledged for defence of this supposed perfection in certainty touching matters of our faith; as first, that *Abraham* did believe, and doubted not: secondly, that the Spirit, which God hath given us to no other end, but only to assure us that we are the sons of God; to embolden us to call upon him as our Father; to open our eyes, and to make the truth of things believed evident unto our minds, is much mightier in operation than the common light of nature, whereby we discern sensible things: wherefore we must needs be more sure of that we believe, than of that we see; we must needs be more certain of the mercies of God in Christ Jesus, than we are of the light of the sun when it shineth upon our faces. To that of *Abraham, He did not doubt*; I answer, that this *negation* doth not exclude all fear, all doubting, but only that which cannot stand with true faith. It freeth *Abraham* from doubting thro' infidelity, not from doubting thro' infirmity; from the doubting of unbelievers, not of weak believers; from such a doubting as that whereof the prince of *Samaria* is attainted, who hearing the promise of sudden plenty in the midst of extream dearth, answered, *Tho' the Lord would make windows in heaven, were it possible so to come to pass?* But that *Abraham* was not void of all doubtings, what need we any other proof, than the plain evidence of his own words? *Gen.* 17. 17. The reason which is taken from the power of the Spirit were effectual, if God did work like a natural agent, as the fire doth inflame, and the sun enlighten, according to the uttermost ability which they have to bring forth their effects: But the incomprehensible wisdom of God doth limit the effects of his power to such a measure as it seemeth best to himself wherefore he worketh that certainty in all, which sufficeth abundantly to their salvation in the life to come; but in none so great as attaineth in this life unto perfection. Even so, O Lord, it hath pleased thee; even so it is best and fittest for us, that feeling still our own infirmities, we may no longer breath than pray *Adjuva, Domine, Help, Lord, our incredulity.* Of the third question, this I hope will suffice, being added unto that which hath been thereof already spoken. The fourth question resteth, and so an end of this point.

3

That

That which cometh laſt of all in this firſt branch to be conſidered concerning the weakneſs of the prophet's faith is, *Whether he did by this very thought* [The law doth fail] *quench the Spirit, fall from faith, and ſhew himſelf an unbeliever, or no ?* The queſtion is of moment ; the repoſe and tranquillity of infinite ſouls doth depend upon it. The prophet's caſe is the caſe of many ; which way ſoever we caſt for him, the ſame way it paſſeth for all others. If in him this cogitation did extinguiſh grace, why the like thoughts in us ſhould not take the like effects, there is no cauſe. Foraſmuch therefore as the matter is weighty, dear and precious, which we have in hand, it behoveth us with ſo much the greater charineſs to wade thro' it, taking ſpecial heed both what we build, and whereon we build, that if our building be pearl, our foundation be not ſtubble ; if the doctrine we teach be full of comfort and conſolation, the ground whereupon we gather it be ſure : otherwiſe we ſhall not ſave, but deceive both our ſelves and others. In this we know we are not deceived, neither can we deceive you, when we teach that the faith whereby ye are ſanctified cannot fail ; it did not in the prophet, it ſhall not in you. If it be ſo, let the difference be ſhewed between the condition of unbelievers, and his in this, or in the like imbecility or weakneſs. There was in *Habakkuk* that which St. *John* doth call the *ſeed of God,* meaning thereby the *firſt grace* which God poureth into the hearts of them that are incorporated into Chriſt ; which having received, if becauſe it is an adverſary to ſin we do therefore think we ſin not both otherwiſe, and alſo by diſtruſtful and doubtful apprehending of that which we ought ſtedfaſtly to believe, ſurely we do but deceive our ſelves. Yet they which are of God do not ſin either in this, or in any thing, any ſuch ſin as doth quite extinguiſh grace, clean cut them off from Chriſt Jeſus ; *becauſe the ſeed of God abideth* in them, and doth ſhield them from receiving any irremediable wound. Their faith, when it is at ſtrongeſt, is but weak ; yet even then, when it is at the weakeſt, ſo ſtrong, that utterly it never faileth, it never periſheth altogether, no not in them who think it, extinguiſhed in themſelves. There are, for whoſe ſakes I dare not deal ſlightly in this cauſe, ſparing that labour which muſt be beſtowed to make plain. Men in like agonies unto this of the prophet *Habakkuk's,* are thro' the extremity of grief, many times in judgment ſo confounded, that they find not themſelves in themſelves. For that which dwelleth in their hearts they ſeek, they make diligent ſearch and enquiry. It abideth, it worketh in them, yet ſtill they ask, where? Still they lament as for a thing which is paſt finding : they mourn as *Rachel,* and refuſe to be comforted, as if that were not, which indeed is ; and as if that, which is not, were ; as if they did not believe when they do ; and, as if they did deſpair when they do not. Which in ſome, I grant, is but a melancholy paſſion, proceeding only from that dejection of mind, the cauſe whereof is the body, and by bodily means can be taken away. But where there is no ſuch bodily cauſe, the mind is not lightly in this mood, but by ſome of theſe three occaſions : One, that judging by compariſon either with other men, or with themſelves at ſome other time more ſtrong, they think imperfection to be a plain deprivation, weakneſs to be utter want of faith. Another cauſe is, they often miſtake one thing for another. St. *Paul* wiſhing well to the church of *Rome,* prayeth for them after this ſort : *The God of hope fill you with all joy of believing.* Hence an error groweth, when men in heavineſs of ſpirit ſuppoſe they lack faith, becauſe they find not the ſugred joy and delight which indeed doth accompany faith, but ſo as a ſeparable accident, as a thing that may be removed from it ; yea, there is a cauſe why it ſhould be removed. The light would never be ſo acceptable, were it not for that uſual intercourſe of darkneſs. Too much honey doth turn to gall, and too much joy, even ſpiritual, would make us wantons. Happier a great deal is that man's caſe, whoſe ſoul by inward deſolation is humbled, than he whoſe heart is thro' abundance of ſpiritual delight lifted up and exalted above meaſure. Better it is ſometimes to go down into the pit with him, who beholding darkneſs, and bewailing the loſs of inward joy and conſolation, crieth from the bottom of the loweſt hell, *My God, my God, why haſt thou forſaken me?* than continually to walk arm in arm with angels, to ſit as it were in *Abraham's* boſom, and to have no thought, no cogitation, but *I thank my God it is not with me as it is with other men.* No, God will never let them that ſhall walk in light to feel now and then what it is to ſit in the ſhadow of death. A grieved ſpirit therefore is no argument of a faithleſs mind. A third occaſion of men's misjudging themſelves, as if they were faithleſs when they are not, is, they faſten their cogitations upon the diſtruſtful ſuggeſtions of the fleſh, whereof finding great abundance in themſelves, they gather thereby, ſurely unbelief hath full dominion, it hath taken plenary poſſeſſion of me ; if I were faithful it could not be thus. Not marking the motions of the Spirit and of faith, becauſe they lye buried and overwhelmed with the contrary : when notwithſtanding, as the bleſſed apoſtle doth acknowledge, that the *ſpirit groaneth,* and that God heareth when we do not ; ſo there is no doubt but that our faith may have, and hath her private operations ſecret to us, yet known to

him

him by whom they are. Tell this to a man that hath a mind deceived by too hard an opinion of himself, and it doth but augment his grief: he hath his answer ready, will you make me think otherwise than I find, than I feel in my self? I have throughly considered, and exquisitely sifted all the corners of my heart, and I see what there is; never seek to persuade me against my knowledge, *I do not, I know, I do not believe.* Well, to favour them a little in their weakness, let that be granted which they do imagine, be it that they be faithless and without belief. But are they not grieved for their unbelief? They are. Do they not wish it might, and also strive that it may be otherwise? We know they do. Whence cometh this, but from a secret love and liking which they have of those things that are believed? No man can love things which in his own opinion are not. And if they think those things to be, which they shew that they love when they desire to believe them; then must it needs be, that by desiring to believe, they prove themselves true believers. For without faith no man thinketh that things believed are. Which argument all the subtilty of infernal powers will never be able to dissolve. The faith therefore of true believers, tho' it hath many and grievous downfals, yet doth it still continue invincible; it conquereth and recovereth it self in the end. The dangerous conflicts whereunto it is subject, are not able to prevail against it. The prophet *Habakkuk* remained faithful in weakness, tho' weak in faith. It is true, such is our weak and wavering nature, we have no sooner received grace, but we are ready to fall from it. We have no sooner given our assent to the law that it cannot fail, but the next conceit which we are ready to embrace is, that it may, and that it doth fail. Tho' we find in our selves a most willing heart to cleave unseparably unto God, even so far as to think unfeignedly with *Peter, Lord, I am ready to go with thee into prison and to death;* yet how soon, and how easily, upon how small occasions are we changed, if we be but a while let alone, and left unto our selves? The *Galatians* to day, for their sakes which teach them the truth of Christ, are content, if need were, to pluck out their own eyes, and the next day, ready to pluck out theirs which taught them. The love of the angel of the church of *Ephesus*, how greatly enflamed, and how quickly slacked: the higher we flow, the nearer we are unto an ebb, if men be respected as meer men, according to the wonted course of their alterable inclination, without the heavenly support of the Spirit. Again, the desire of our ghostly enemy is so incredible, and his means so forcible to overthrow our faith, that whom the blessed apostle knew betrothed and made hand-fast unto Christ, to them he could not write but with great trembling. *I am jealous over you with a godly jealousy, for I have prepared you to one husband, to present you a pure virgin unto Christ: but I fear, lest as the serpent beguiled Eve through his subtilty, so your minds should be corrupted from the simplicity which is in Christ.* The simplicity of faith which is in Christ taketh the naked promise of God, his bare word, and on that it resteth. This simplicity the serpent laboureth continually to pervert, corrupting the mind with many imaginations of repugnancy and contrariety between the promise of God and those things which sense or experience, or some other fore-conceived persuasion hath imprinted. The word of the promise of God unto his people is, *I will not leave thee nor forsake thee:* upon this the simplicity of faith resteth, and is not afraid of famine. But mark how the subtilty of Satan did corrupt the minds of that rebellious generation, whose spirits were not faithful unto God. They beheld the desolate state of the desart in which they were, and by the wisdom of their sense concluded the promise of God to be but folly: *Can God prepare a table in the wilderness?* The word of the promise to *Sarah* was, *Thou shalt bear a son.* Faith is simple, and doubteth not of it: but Satan, to corrupt this simplicity of faith, entangleth the mind of the woman with an argument drawn from common experience, to the contrary, *A woman that is old;* Sarah *now to be acquainted with forgotten passions again of youth!* The word of the promise of God by *Moses* and the prophets, made the Saviour of the world so apparent unto *Philip*, that his simplicity could conceive no other Messias than *Jesus* of *Nazareth*, the son of *Joseph*. But to stay *Nathaniel*, left being invited to come and see, he should also believe, and so be saved, the subtilty of Satan casteth a mist before his eyes, putteth in his head against this the common conceived persuasion of all men concerning *Nazareth, Is it possible that any good thing should come from thence?* This stratagem he doth use with so great dexterity, that the minds of all men are so strangely bewitched with it, that it bereaveth them, for the time, of all perceivance of that which should relieve them, and be their comfort; yea, it taketh all remembrance from them, even of things wherewith they are most familiarly acquainted. The people of *Israel* could not be ignorant, that he which led them thro' the sea was able to feed them in the desart: but this was obliterated, and put out by the sense of their present want. Feeling the hand of God against them in their food, they remember not his hand in the

day

day that he delivered them from the hand of the oppreſſor. *Sarah* was not then to learn, that *with God all things were poſſible.* Had *Nathaniel never* noted how *God doth chuſe the baſe things of this world to diſgrace them that are moſt honourably eſteemed?* The prophet *Habakkuk* knew that the promiſes of grace, protection and favour which God in the law doth make unto his people, do not grant them any ſuch immunity as can free and exempt them from all chaſtiſements: he knew that, as God ſaid, *I will continue for ever my mercy towards them;* ſo he likewiſe ſaid, *Their tranſgreſſions I will puniſh with a rod:* he knew that it could not ſtand with any reaſon we ſhould ſet the meaſure of our own puniſhments, and preſcribe unto God how great, or how long our ſufferings ſhall be: he knew that we were blind, and altogether ignorant what is beſt for us; that we ſue for many things very unwiſely againſt our ſelves, thinking we *ask fiſh,* when indeed we crave *a ſerpent:* he knew that when the thing we ask is good, and yet God ſeemeth ſlow to grant it, he doth not deny but defer our petitions, to the end we might learn to deſire great things greatly; all this he knew. But beholding the land which God had ſevered for his own people, and ſeeing it abandoned unto heathen nations; viewing how reproachfully they did tread it down, and wholly make havock of it at their pleaſure; beholding the Lord's own royal ſeat made an heap of ſtones, his temple de-filed, the carcaſſes of his ſervants caſt out for the fowls of the air to devour, and the fleſh of his meek ones for the beaſts of the field to feed upon; being conſcious to himſelf how long and how earneſtly he had cried, *Succour us, O God of our welfare, for the glory of thine own name;* and feeling that their ſore was ſtill increaſed; the conceit of repugnancy between this which was objected to his eyes, and that which faith upon pro-miſe of the law did look for, made ſo deep an impreſſion, and ſo ſtrong, that he diſ-puteth not the matter, but without any further inquiry or ſearch, inferreth as we ſee, *The law doth fail.*

Of us who is here, which cannot very ſoberly adviſe his brother? Sir, you muſt learn to ſtrengthen your faith by that experience which heretofore you have had of God's great goodneſs towards you, *Per ea quæ agnoſcas præſtita, diſcas ſperare promiſſa,* by thoſe things which you have known performed, learn to hope for thoſe things which are promiſed. Do you acknowledge to have received much? let that make you cer-tain to receive more: *Habenti dabitur; to him that hath, more ſhall be given.* When you doubt what you ſhall have, ſearch what you have had at God's hands. Make this reckoning, that the benefits which he hath beſtowed are bills obligatory and ſuffi-cient ſureties, that he will beſtow further. His preſent mercy is ſtill a warrant of his future love, becauſe *whom he loveth, he loveth to the end.* Is it not thus? Yet if we could reckon up as many evident, clear, undoubted ſigns of God's reconciled love to-wards us as there are years, yea days, yea hours paſt over our heads; all theſe ſet toge-ther have no ſuch force to confirm our faith, as the loſs, and ſometimes the only fear of loſing a little tranſitory goods, credit, honour, or favour of men, a ſmall calamity, a matter of nothing, to breed a conceit, and ſuch a conceit as is not eaſily again removed, that we are clean croſs'd out of God's book, that he regards us not, that he looketh up-on others, but paſſeth by us like a ſtranger, to whom we are not known. Then we think, looking upon others, and comparing them with our ſelves, their tables are furniſh-ed day by day; earth and aſhes are our bread: they ſing to the lute, and they ſee their children dance before them; our hearts are heavy in our bodies as lead, our ſighs beat as thick as a ſwift pulſe, our tears do waſh the bed whereon we lie: the ſun ſhineth fair up-on their foreheads; we are hang'd up like bottles in the ſmoak, caſt into corners like the ſherds of a broken pot: tell not us of the promiſes of God's favour, tell ſuch as do reap the fruit of them; they belong not to us, they are made to others. The Lord be mer-ciful to our weakneſs, but thus it is. Well, let the frailty of our nature, the ſubtilty of Satan, the force of our deceiveable imaginations be, as we cannot deny but they are, things that threaten every moment the utter ſubverſion of our faith; faith notwithſtanding is not hazarded by theſe things, that which one ſometimes told the ſenators of *Rome, Ego ſic exiſtimabam,* P. C. *uti patrem ſæpe meum prædicantem audiveram, qui veſtram amicitiam diligenter colerent, eos multum laborem ſuſcipere, cæterùm ex omnibus maximè tutos eſſe,* as I have often heard my father acknowledge, ſo I my ſelf did ever think, that the friends and favourers of this ſtate charged themſelves with great labour, but no man's condition ſo ſafe as theirs; the ſame we may ſay a great deal more juſtly in this caſe: our fathers and pro-phets, our Lord and Maſter hath full often ſpoken, by long experience we have found it true, as many as have entred their names in the myſtical book of life, *eos maximum la-borem ſuſcipere,* they have taken upon them a labourſome, a toilſome, a painful profeſſion, *ſed omnium maximè tutos eſſe,* but no man's ſecurity like to theirs. *Simon, Simon, Satan hath deſired to winnow thee as wheat;* here is our toil: *but I have prayed for thee, that thy*

3

faith

faith fail not, this is our fafety. No man's condition fo fure as ours: the prayer of Chrift is more than fufficient both to ftrengthen us, be we never fo weak; and to overthrow all adverfary power, be it never fo ftrong and potent. His prayer muft not exclude our labour: their thoughts are vain, who think that their *watching* can preferve the *city,* which God himfelf is not willing to *keep.* And are not theirs as vain, who think that *God will keep the city,* for which they themfelves are not careful to *watch?* The husbandman may not therefore burn his plough, nor the merchant forfake his trade, becaufe God hath promifed *I will not forfake thee.* And do the promifes of God concerning our ftability, think you, make it a matter indifferent for us to ufe, or not to ufe the means whereby to attend, or not to attend to reading? To pray, or not to *pray, that* we *fall not into temptations?* Surely, if we look to ftand in the faith of the fons of God, we muft hourly, continually be providing and fetting our felves to ftrive. It was not the meaning of our Lord and Saviour in faying, *Father, keep them in thy name,* that we fhould be carelefs to keep our felves. To our own fafety, our own fedulity is required. And then bleffed for ever and ever be that mother's child, whofe faith hath made him the child of God. The earth may fhake, the pillars of the world may tremble under us; the countenance of the heaven may be appaled, the fun may lofe his light, the moon her beauty, the ftars their glory; but concerning the man that trufteth in God, if the fire have proclaimed it felf unable as much as to finge a hair of his head; if lyons, beafts ravenous by nature, and keen with hunger, being fet to devour, have as it were religioufly adored the very flefh of the faithful man; what is there in the world that fhall change his heart, overthrow his faith, alter his affection towards God, or the affection of God to him? If I be of this note, who fhall make a *feparation* between me and my God? *Shall tribulation, or anguifh, or perfecution, or famine, or nakednefs, or peril, or fword? no; I am perfuaded, that neither tribulation, nor anguifh, nor perfecution, nor famine, nor nakednefs, nor peril, nor fword, nor death, nor life, nor angels, nor principalities, nor powers, nor things prefent, nor things to come, nor height, nor depth, nor any other creature fhall ever* prevail fo far over me. *I know in whom I have believed;* I am not ignorant whofe precious blood hath been fhed for me; I have a fhepherd full of kindnefs, full of care, and full of power, unto him I commit my felf; his own finger hath engraven this fentence in the tables of my heart, *Satan hath defired to winnow thee as wheat, but I have prayed that thy faith fail not:* therefore the affurance of my hope I will labour to keep as a jewel, unto the end; and by labour, thro' the gracious mediation of his prayer, I fhall keep it.   I

To the WORSHIPFUL

Mr. GEORGE SUMMASTER,

Principal of *Broad-Gates Hall* in *Oxford*,

HENRY JACKSON Wifheth all Happinefs.

SIR,

YOUR *kind acceptance of a former teftification of that refpeɛt I owe you, hath made me venture to fhew the world thefe godly fermons under your name. In which, as every point is worth obfervation, fo fome efpecially are to be noted; the firft, that as the fpirit of prophecy is from God himfelf, who doth inwardly heat and enlighten the hearts and minds of his holy pen-men, (which if fome would diligently confider, they would not puzzle themfelves with the contentions of* Scot, *and* Thomas, *Whether God only, or his miniftring fpirits, do infufe into mens minds prophetical revelations, per fpecies intelligibiles) fo God framed their words alfo. Whence the holy father St.* Auguftine *religioufly obferveth, That all thofe who underftand* Lib. 4. cap. 6. *the facred writers, will alfo perceive, that they ought not to ufe other words than they* de doɛt. chr. *did, in expreffing thofe heavenly myfteries which their hearts* conceived, *as the bleffed virgin did our Saviour, by the holy Ghoft. The greater is* Caftellio *his offence, who hath laboured to teach the prophets to fpeak otherwife than they have already. Much like to that impious King of* Spain, Alphonfus *the tenth, who found fault with God's work: Si, inquit,* creationi affuiffem, mundum melius ordinaffem; *if he had been with* Rob.Tolet.l.4. *God at the creation of the world, the world had gone better than now it doth. As this* c. 5. *man found fault with God's works, fo did the other with God's words; but, becaufe we have a moft fure word of the prophets, to which we muft take heed, I will let his words* 2 Pet. 1. *pafs with the wind, having elfewhere fpoken to you more largely of his errors, whom* Pref in Orat. *notwithftanding for his other excellent parts, I much refpeɛt.* D. Rainold.

You fhall moreover from hence underftand, how chriftianity confifts not in formal and feeming purity, (under which who knows not notorious villany to mask?) but in the heart root. Whence the author truly teacheth, that mockers, which ufe religion as a cloak, to put off and on, as the weather ferveth, are worfe than Pagans *and* Infidels. *Where I cannot omit to fhew how juftly this kind of men hath been reproved by that renowned martyr of* Jefus Chrift, Bifhop Latimer, *both becaufe it will be appofite to this* Parfons in *purpofe, and alfo free that chriftian worthy from the flanderous reproaches of him, who* 3 converf. *was, if ever any, a mocker of God, religion, and all good men. But firft I muft defire you, and in you all readers, not to think light of that excellent man for ufing this and the like witty fimilitudes in his fermons. For whofoever will call to mind with what riff-raff God's people were fed in thofe days, when their priefts, whofe lips fhould have* Mal. 2. 7. *preferved knowledge, preached nothing elfe but dreams and falfe miracles of counterfeit faints, enrolled in that fottifh legend, coined and amplified by a drowfy head between fleep-* Canus locor. *ing and waking. He that will confider this, and alfo how the people were delighted with* l. 11. c. 6. Di-*fuch toys (God fending them ftrong delufions that they fhould beleve lies) and how hard* ves, lib. 2. de *it would have been for any man, wholly, and upon the fudden, to draw their minds to* corrupt. art. *another bent, will eafily perceive, both how neceffary it was to fhew fymbolical difcourfe,* Hard. lib. 4. *and how wifely and moderately it was applied by the religious father, to the end he might lead their underftanding fo far, till it were fo convinced, informed, and fettled, that it might forget the means and way by which it was led, and think only of that it had acquired. For in all fuch myftical fpeeches, who knows not that the end for which they are ufed is only to be thought upon?*

This then being firft confidered, let us hear the ftory, as it is related by Mr. Fox: Pag. 1903.
" Mr. Latimer (*faith he*) in his fermon gave the people certain cards out of the fifth, edit. 1570.
" fixth, and feventh chapters of Matthew. For the chief triumph in the cards he li-
" mited the heart, as the principal thing that they fhould ferve God withal, whereby he
" quite overthrew all hypocritical and external ceremonies, not tending to the neceffary
" furtherance of God's holy word and facraments. By this he exhorted all men to ferve
" the Lord with inward heart, and true affeɛtion, and not with outward ceremonies;
" adding

a adding moreover to the praiſe of that triumph, that tho' it were never ſo ſmall, yet it
" would take up the beſt coat card beſide in the bunch, yea, though it were the king of
" clubs, &c. meaning thereby, how the Lord would be worſhiped and ſerved in ſimplicity
" of the heart, and verity, wherein conſiſteth the true chriſtian religion, &c." Thus
Mr. Fox.

By which it appears, that the holy man's intention was to lift up the peoples hearts
to God, and not that he made a ſermon of playing at cards, and taught them how to
play at triumph, and plaid (himſelf) at cards in the pulpit, as that baſe companion [a] Parſons reports the matter, in his wonted ſcurrilous vein of railing; whence he calleth it a
[b] Chriſtmas ſermon. Now he that will think ill of ſuch alluſions, may, out of the abundance of his folly, jeſt at [c] Demoſthenes, for his ſtory of the ſheep, wolves, and dogs:
and [d] Menenius, for his fiction of the belly. But, hinc illæ lachrymæ, the good biſhop
meant that the Romiſh religion came not from the heart, but conſiſted in outward ceremonies: which ſorely grieved Parſons, who never had the leaſt warmth or ſpark of honeſty. Whether Bp. Latimer compared the biſhops to the knave of clubs, as the fellow
interprets him, I know not: I am ſure Parſons, of all others, deſerved thoſe colours;
and ſo I leave him. We ſee then, what inward purity is required of all chriſtians,
which if they have, then in prayer, and all other chriſtian duties, they ſhall lift up
pure hands, as the [e] apoſtle ſpeaks, not as [f] Baronius would have it, waſhed from ſins
with holy water; but pure, that is, holy, free from the pollution of ſin, as the Greek
word δσιας does ſignify.

You may ſee alſo here refuted thoſe calumnies of the papiſts, that we abandon all religious rites, and godly duties; as alſo the confirmation of our doctrine touching certainty
of faith (and ſo of ſalvation) which is ſo ſtrongly denied by ſome of that faction, that
they have told the world, [g] St. Paul himſelf was uncertain of his own ſalvation. What
then ſhall we ſay, but pronounce a woe to the moſt ſtrict obſervers of St. Francis's rules,
and his canonical diſcipline (tho' they make him even [h] equal with Chriſt) and the moſt
meritorious monk that ever was regiſtred in their kalender of ſaints? But we, for our
comfort, are otherwiſe taught out of the holy ſcripture, and therefore exhorted to build
our ſelves in our moſt holy faith, that ſo, [i] When our earthly houſe of this tabernacle
ſhall be deſtroyed, we may have a building given of God, a houſe not made with hands,
but eternal in the heavens.

[margin notes:]
[a] In the third part of the three converſions of *England*.
[b] in the exami-nation of *Fox's* ſaints, c. 14.
ſect. 53. 54.
p. 215.
Sect. 55.
[c] Plut. in De-noſth.
[d] Liv. dec. 1. l.2.an.V.C.60.

[e] 1 Tim. 1. 8.
[f] Annal.tom. 1. an. 57. n.109, 110.& tom.1. an. 132. num.

[g] S. Paulus deſua ſalute in-certus *Xichem*, Jeſuit l.2.c.12.
Idolat.huguen. p.119.inmarg. edit. Lat. Mo-terpret. Mar-cel. Bomper, Jeſuits.
[h] Witneſs the verſes of *Horatius* a Jeſuit, recited by *Poſſ. Biblioth. ſelect.* part 2. l. 17. c. 19. Exue franciſcum tunicâ laceroque cucullo. Qui fran-ciſcus erat, jam tibi Chriſtus erit. Franciſci exuviis (ſi quâ licet) indue Chriſtum: jam franciſcus erit, qui modo Chriſtus erat. The like hath *Bencius* another Jeſuit.
[i] 2 Cor. 5. 1.

This is that which is moſt piouſly and feelingly taught in theſe few leaves, ſo that
you ſhall read nothing here, but what I perſuade my ſelf you have long practiſed in the
conſtant courſe of your life. It remaineth only that you accept of theſe labours tendred
to you by him, who wiſheth you the long joys of this world, and the eternal of that
which is to come.

Oxon, from *Corp. Chriſti College*,
this 13ᵗʰ of *January*, 1613.

TWO

Two SERMONS

Upon Part of St. *JUDE's* Epiſtle.

SERMON I.

Epiſt. JUDE, ver. 17, 18, 19, 20, 21.

But ye, beloved, remember the words which were ſpoken before of the
apoſtles of our Lord Jeſus Chriſt:
How that they told you, that there ſhould be mockers in the laſt time, which
ſhould walk after their own ungodly luſts.
Theſe are makers of ſects, fleſhly, having not the Spirit.
But ye, beloved, edify your ſelves in your moſt holy faith, praying in the
holy Ghoſt.
And keep your ſelves in the love of God, looking for the mercy of our
Lord Jeſus Chriſt unto eternal life.

THE occaſion whereupon, together with the end wherefore this epiſtle was written, is opened in the front and entry of the ſame. There were then, as there
are now, many evil and wickedly diſpoſed perſons, not of the myſtical body,
yet within the viſible bounds of the church, *men which were of old ordained*
to condemnation, ungodly men, which turned the grace of our God into wantonneſs, and
denied the Lord Jeſus. For this cauſe the Spirit of the Lord is in the hand of *Jude the*
ſervant of Jeſus and brother of James, to exhort them that are called, and ſanctified
of God the Father, that they would earneſtly *contend to maintain the faith, which was*
once delivered to the ſaints. Which faith, becauſe we cannot maintain, except we
know perfectly, firſt, againſt whom; ſecondly, in what ſort it muſt be maintained; therefore in the former three verſes of that parcel of ſcripture which I have read, the enemies
of the croſs of Chriſt are plainly deſcribed; and in the latter two, they that love the
Lord Jeſus have a ſweet leſſon given them how to ſtrengthen and ſtabliſh themſelves in
the faith. Let us firſt therefore examine the deſcription of theſe reprobates concerning
faith ; and afterwards come to the exhortation, wherein chriſtians are taught how to reſt
their hearts on God's eternal and everlaſting truth. The deſcription of theſe godleſs perſons is twofold, *general* and *ſpecial.* The *general* doth point them out, and ſhew what
manner of men they ſhould be. The *particular* pointeth at them, and ſaith plainly,
theſe are they. In the *general* deſcription we have to conſider of theſe things; *Firſt,*
when they were deſcribed, *They were told of before.* Secondly, the men by whom they
were deſcribed, *They were ſpoken of by the apoſtles of our Lord Jeſus Chriſt.* Thirdly,
the days when they ſhould be manifeſt unto the world, they told you, *they ſhould be in*
the laſt time. Fourthly, their diſpoſition and whole demeanour, *Mockers, and walkers*
after their own ungodly luſts.

2. In the third to the *Philippians,* the apoſtle deſcribeth certain; *They are men* (ſaith
he) *of whom I have told you often, and now with tears I tell you of them, their god is*
their belly, their glory and rejoicing is in their own ſhame, they mind earthly things.

Theſe were enemies to the croſs of Chriſt, enemies whom he ſaw, and his eyes guſht
out with tears to behold them. But we are taught in this place, how the apoſtle ſpake
alſo of enemies, whom as yet they had not ſeen, deſcrib'd a family of men as yet unheard of, a generation reſerved for the end of the world, and for the laſt time; they
had not only declared what they heard and ſaw in the days wherein they lived, but they
have propheſied alſo of men in time to come. And *you do well* (ſaith St. *Peter*) *in*
that you take heed to the words of prophecy, ſo that ye firſt know this, that no prophecy
in the ſcripture cometh of any man's own reſolution. No prophecy in ſcripture cometh of any man's reſolution ; for all prophecy which is in ſcripture, came by the
ſecret inſpiration of God. But there are prophecies which are no ſcripture ; yea, there
are prophecies againſt the ſcripture : my brethren, beware of ſuch prophecies, and take

heed

heed you heed them not. Remember the things that were fpoken of before; but fpoken of before by the apoftles of our Lord and Saviour Jefus Chrift. Take heed to prophecies, but to prophecies which are in fcripture; for both the manner and matter of thofe prophecies do fhew plainly that they are of God.

Of the fpirit of prophecy received from God himfelf. 3. Touching the manner how men by the fpirit of prophecy in holy fcripture, have fpoken and written of things to come, we muft underftand, that as the knowledge of that they fpake, fo likewife the utterance of that they knew, came not by thefe ufual and ordinary means whereby we are brought to underftand the myfteries of our falvation, and are wont to inftruct others in the fame. For whatfoever we know, we have it by the hands and miniftry of men, which lead us along like children from a letter to a fyllable, from a fyllable to a word, from a word to a line, from a line to a fentence, from a fentence to a fide, and fo turn over. But God himfelf was their inftructor, he himfelf taught them, partly by dreams and vifions in the night, partly by revelations in the day, taking them afide from amongft their brethren, and talking with them as a man would talk with his neighbour in the way. Thus they became acquainted even with the fecret and hidden counfels of God, they faw things which themfelves were not able to utter; they beheld that whereat men and angels are aftonifhed, they underftood in the beginning, what fhould come to pafs in the laft days.

Of the prophets manner of fpeech. 4. God, which lightned thus the eyes of their underftanding, giving them knowledge by unufual and extraordinary means, did alfo miraculoufly himfelf frame and fafhion their words and writings, infomuch that a greater difference there feemeth not to be between the manner of their knowledge, than there is between the manner of their fpeech and others. When we have conceived a thing in our hearts, and throughly underftand it, as we think within our felves, e're we can utter in fuch fort, that our brethren may receive inftruction or comfort at our mouths, how great, how long, how earneft meditation are we forced to ufe? And after much travel and much pains, when we open our lips to fpeak of the wonderful works of God, our tongues do faulter within our mou hs, yea, many times we difgrace the dreadful myfteries of our faith, and grieve the fpirit of our hearers by words unfavory, and unfeemly fpeeches: *Shall* **Job 15. 2, 3.** *a wife man fill his belly with the eaftern wind,* faith *Eliphaz? Shall a wife man difpute with words not comely? or with talk that is not profitable?* Yet behold, even they that are wifeft amongft us living, compared with the prophets, feem no otherwife to talk of God, than as if the children which are carried in arms fhould fpeak of the greateft matters of ftate. They whofe words do moft fhew forth their wife underftanding, and whofe lips do utter the pureft knowledge, fo long as they underftand and fpeak as men, are they not fain fundry ways to excufe themfelves? fometimes acknowledging with the wife man, *Hardly can we difcern the things that are on earth, and with great labour find we out the things that are before us. Who can then feek out the things that are in heaven?* Sometimes confeffing with *Job* the righteous, in treating of things too wonderful for us, we have fpoken we wift not what: fometimes ending their talk, as do the hiftory of *Maccabees*; if we have done well, and as the caufe required, it is that we defire; if we have fpoken flenderly and barely, we have done what we could. But *God* **Efai. 49. 2.** *hath made my mouth like a fword,* faith *Ifaiah.* And *we have received,* faith the apoftle, *not the fpirit of the world, but the Spirit which is of God, that we might know the things that are given to us of God, which things alfo we fpeak, not in words which man's wifdom teacheth, but which the holy Ghoft doth teach.* This is that which the prophets mean by thofe books written full within and without; which books were fo often delivered them to eat, not becaufe God fed them with ink and paper, but to teach us, that fo oft as he employ'd them in this heavenly work, they neither fpake nor wrote any word of their own, but uttered fyllable by fyllable, as the Spirit put it into their mouths, no otherwife than the harp or the lute doth give a found, according to the difcretion of his hands that holdeth and ftriketh it with fkill. The difference is only this; an inftrument, whether it be a pipe or harp, maketh a diftinction in the times and founds, which diftinction is well perceived of the hearer, the inftrument it felf underftandeth **Ezekiel 3.** not what is piped or harped. The prophets and holy men of God not fo: *I opened my mouth,* faith *Ezekiel, and God reached me a fcrowl, faying, Son of man, caufe thy belly to eat, and fill thy bowels with this I give thee; I ate it, and it was fweet in my mouth as honey,* faith the prophet; yea, fweeter, I am perfuaded, than either honey or the honey-comb. For herein they were not like harps or lutes, but they felt, they felt the power and ftrength of their own words. When they fpake of our peace, every corner of their hearts was filled with joy. When they prophefied of mourning, lamentations, and woes to fall upon us, they wept in the bitternefs and indignation of fpirit, the arm of the Lord being mighty and ftrong upon them.

5. On this manner were all the prophecies of holy fcripture. Which prophecies although they contain nothing which is not profitable for our inftruction; yet as one ftar

differeth

diffeneth from another in glory, fo every word of prophecy hath a treafure of matter in it: but all matters are not of like importance, as all treafures are not of equal price; the chief and principal matter of prophecy is the promife of righteoufnefs, peace, holinefs, glory, victory, immortality, unto *every foul which believeth that Jefus is Chrift, of the Jew firft, and of the Gentile.* Now confirue the doctrine of falvation to be looked for by faith in him, who was in outward appearance as it had been a man forfaken of God; in him, who was numbred, judged, and condemned with the wicked; in him, whom men did fee buffeted on the face, fcoffed at by the foldiers, fcourged by tormentors, hanged on the crofs, pierced to the heart; in him, whom the eyes of many witneffes did behold, when the anguifh of his foul enforced him to roar, as if his heart had rent in funder, *O my God, my God, why haft thou forfaken me ?* I fay, becaufe the doctrine of falvation by him, is a thing improbable to a natural man, that whether we preach to the *Gentile,* or to the *Jew,* the one condemneth our faith as madnefs, the other as blafphemy; therefore to eftablifh and confirm the certainty of this faving truth in the hearts of men, the Lord, together with their preachings whom he fent immediately from himfelf to reveal thefe things unto the world, mingled prophecies of things, both civil and ecclefiaftical, which were to come in every age, from time to time, till the very laft of the latter days, that by thofe things, wherein we fee daily their words fulfilled and done, we might have ftrong confolation in the hope of things which are not feen, becaufe they have revealed as well the one as the other. For when many things are fpoken of before in fcripture, whereof we fee firft one thing accomplifhed, and then another, and fo a third, perceive we not plainly, that God doth nothing elfe but lead us along by the hand, till he have fettled us upon the rock of an affured hope, that not one jot or tittle of his word fhall pafs, till all be fulfilled ? It is not therefore faid in vain that thefe godlefs wicked ones *were fpoken of before.*

6. But by whom? By them, whofe words, if men or angels from heaven gainfay, they are accurfed; by them, whom whofoever defpifeth, *defpifeth not them but me,* faith Chrift. If any man therefore doth love the Lord Jefus, (and wo worth him that ᴬ ⁿᵃᵗᵘʳᵃˡ ᵐᵃⁿ loveth not the Lord Jefus!) hereby we may know that he loveth him indeed, if he de-ᵖᵉʳᶜᵉⁱᵛᵉᵗʰ ⁿᵒᵗ fpife not the things that are fpoken of by his apoftles, whom many have defpifed, even ʰᵉᵃᵛᵉⁿˡʸ for the bafenefs and fimplenefs of their perfons. For it is the property of flefhly and carnal men to honour and difhonour, credit and difcredit the words and deeds of every man, according to that he wanteth or hath without. *If a man of gorgeous apparel* ᴶᵃᵐᵉˢ ²; *come amongft us,* altho' he be a thief or a murtherer, (for there are thieves and murtherers in gorgeous apparel,) be his heart whatfoever, if his coat be of purple or velvet, or tiffue, every one rifeth up, and all the reverend folemnities we can ufe are too little. But the man that ferveth God, is contemned and defpifed amongft us for his poverty. *Herod* fpeaketh in judgment, and the people cry out, *The voice of God, and not of* ᴬᶜᵗˢ ¹²; *man.* *Paul* preacheth Chrift, they term him a *trifler.* Hearken, beloved, *hath not God* ᶜʰᵃᵖ. ¹⁷. *chofen the poor of this world, that they fhould be rich in faith ?* Hath he not chofen the refufe of the world to be heirs of his kingdom, which he hath promifed to them that love him ? Hath he not chofen the off-fcourings of men to be the lights of the world, and the apoftles of Jefus Chrift ? Men unlearned, yet how fully replenifhed with underftanding ? Few in number, yet how great in power ? Contemptible in fhew, yet in fpirit how ftrong ? how wonderful ? *I would fain learn the myftery of the eternal generation of the Son of God,* faith *Hillary.* Whom fhall I feek ? Shall I get me to the fchools of the *Grecians ?* Why, I have read, *Ubi fapiens ? ubi fcriba ? ubi conquifitor hujus feculi ?* Thefe wife men in the world muft needs be dumb in this, becaufe they have rejected the wifdom of God. Shall I befeech the fcribes and interpreters of the law to become my teachers ? How can they know this, fith they are offended at the crofs of Chrift ? It is death for me to be ignorant of the unfearchable myftery of the Son of God; of which myftery notwithftanding I fhould have been ignorant, but that a poor fifher-man, unknown, unlearned, new-come from his boat, with his cloaths wringing wet, hath opened his mouth and taught me, *In the beginning was the Word, and the Word was with God, and the Word was God.* Thefe poor filly creatures have made us rich in the knowledge of the myfteries of Chrift.

7. Remember therefore that which is fpoken of by the apoftles; whofe words if the children of this world do not regard, is it any marvel ? They are the apoftles of our Lord Jefus; not of their Lord, but of ours. It is true which one hath faid in a certain place, *apoftolicam fidem feculi homo non capit,* a man fworn to the world is not capable of that faith which the apoftles do teach. What mean the children of this world then to tread in the courts of our God ? What fhould your bodies do at *Bethel,* whofe hearts are at *Bethaven ?* The god of this world, whom ye ferve, hath provided apoftles and teachers for you, *chaldeans, wizards, footh-fayers, aftrologers,* and fuch like; hear them. ᵂᵉ ᵐᵘˢᵗ ⁿᵒᵗ Tell not us that ye will facrifice to the Lord our God, if ye will facrifice to *Afhtoreth* or ʰᵃˡᵗ ᵇᵉᵗʷᵉᵉⁿ ᵗʷᵒ ᵒᵖⁱⁿⁱᵒⁿˢ.

Melcom; that ye will read our fcriptures, if we will liften to your traditions; that if ye may have a mafs by permiffion, we fhall have a communion with good leave and liking; that ye will admir the things that are fpoken of by the apoftles of our Lord Jefus, if your Lord and Mafter may have his ordinances obferved, and his ftatutes kept. *Solomon* took it (as he well might) for an evident proof, that fhe did not bear a motherly affection to her child, which yielded to have it cut in divers parts. He cannot love the Lord Jefus with his heart, which lendeth one ear to his apoftles, and another to falfe apoftles; which can brook to fee a mingle-mangle of religion and fuperftition, minifters and maffing-priefts, light and darknefs, truth and error, traditions and fcriptures. No, we have no Lord, but Jefus; no doctrine, but the gofpel; no teachers, but his apoftles. Were it reafon to require at the hand of an *Englifh* fubject, obedience to the laws and edicts of the *Spaniards*? I do marvel, that any man bearing the name of a fervant of the fervants of Jefus Chrift, will go about to draw us from our allegiance. We are his fworn fubjects; it is not lawful for us to hear the things that are not told us by his apoftles. They have told us, that *in the laft days there fhall be mockers*, therefore we believe it; *Credimus quia legimus*, we are fo perfuaded, becaufe we read it muft be fo. If we did not read it, we would not teach it: *Nam quæ libro legis non continentur, ea nec noffe decemus*, faith *Hillary*; Thofe things that are not written in the book of the law, we ought not fo much as to be acquainted with them. *Remember the words, which were fpoken of before by the apoftles of our Lord Jefus Chrift.*

Mockers in the laft time. 8. The third thing to be confidered in the defcription of thefe men, of whom we fpeak, is the time wherein they fhould be manifefted to the world. They told you *there fhould be mockers in the laft time*. *Noah*, at the commandment of God, built an ark, and there were in it beafts of all forts, clean and unclean. A husbandman planteth a vineyard, and looketh for grapes, but when they come to the gathering, behold, together with grapes, there are found alfo wild grapes. A rich man prepareth a great fupper, and biddeth many, but when he fitteth him down, he findeth amongft his friends here and there a man whom he knoweth not. This hath been the ftate of the church fithence the beginning. God always hath mingled his faints with faithlefs and godlefs perfons, as it were the clean with the unclean, grapes with fower grapes, his friends and children with aliens and ftrangers. Marvel not then, if *in the laft days* alfo ye fee the men with whom you live and walk arm in arm, laugh at your religion, and blafpheme that glorious name whereof you are called. Thus it was in the days of the patriarchs and prophets, and are we better than our fathers? Albeit we fuppofe that the bleffed apoftles, in forefhewing what manner of men were fet out for the laft days, meant to note a calamity fpecial and peculiar to the ages and generations which were to come. As if he fhould have faid, as God hath appointed a time of feed for the fower, and a time of harveft for him that reapeth; as he hath given unto every herb and every tree his own fruit, and his own feafon, not the feafon nor the fruit of another (for no man looketh to gather figs in the winter, becaufe the fummer is the feafon for them; not grapes of thiftles, becaufe grapes are the fruit of the vine:) fo the fame God hath appointed fundry for every generation of men, other men for other times, and for the laft times the worft men, as may appear by their properties; which is the fourth point to be confidered of in this defcription.

Mockers. 9. They told you that there fhould be *mockers*: he meaneth men that fhall ufe religion as a cloak, to put off and on as the weather ferveth; fuch as fhall, with *Herod*, hear the preaching of *John Baptift* to day, and to morrow condefcend to have him beheaded; or with the other *Herod* fay they will worfhip Chrift, when they purpofe a maffacre in their hearts; kifs Chrift with *Judas*, and betray Chrift with *Judas*. Thefe are mockers. For *Ifhmael* the Son of *Hagar* laughed at *Ifaac*, which was heir of the promife: fo fhall thefe men laugh at you as the maddeft people under the fun, if ye be like *Mofes*, chufing rather to fuffer affliction with the people of God, than to enjoy the pleafures of fin for a feafon, and why? God hath not given them eyes to fee, nor hearts to conceive that exceeding recompence of your reward. The promifes of falvation made to you, are matters wherein they can take no pleafure, even as *Ifhmael* took no pleafure in that promife wherein God had faid unto *Abraham, In Ifaac fhall thy feed be called*; becaufe the promife concerned not him, but *Ifaac*. They are termed for their impiety towards God, *mockers*; and for the impurity of their life and converfation, *walkers after their own ungodly lufts*. St. *Peter*, in his fecond epiftle, and third chapter, foundeth the very depth of their impiety; fhewing firft, how they fhall not fhame at the length to profefs themfelves profane and irreligious, by flat denying the gofpel of Jefus Chrift, and deriding the fweet and comfortable promifes of his appearing. Secondly, that they fhall not be only deriders of all religion, but alfo difputers againft God, ufing truth to fubvert the truth; yea, fcriptures themfelves, to difprove fcriptures. Being in this fort mockers, they muft needs be alfo followers of *their own ungodly lufts*. Being atheifts in perfuafion, can they chufe but be beafts in converfation? For why remove

they

they quite from them the fear of God? Why take they such pains to abandon and put out from their hearts all sense, all taste, all feeling of religion? But only to this end and purpose, that they may without inward remorse and grudging of conscience, give over themselves to all uncleanness. Surely the state of these men is more lamentable than *Mockers worse* is the condition of *Pagans* and *Turks*. For at the bare beholding of heaven and earth *than Pagans and Infidels.* the infidel's heart by and by doth give him, that there is an eternal, infinite, immortal, and ever-living God, whose hands have fashioned and framed the world; he knoweth that every house is builded of some man, tho' he see not the man which built the house; and he considereth that it must be God which hath built and created all things, altho' because the number of his days be few, he could not see when God disposed his works of old; when he caused the light of his clouds first to shine, when he laid the corner-stone of the earth, and swaddled it with bands of water and darkness, when he caused the morning star to know his place, and made bars and doors to shut up the sea within his house, saying, *Hitherto shalt thou come, but no further.* He hath no eye-witness of these things; yet the light of natural reason hath put this wisdom in his reins, and hath given his heart thus much understanding. Bring a *Pagan* to the schools of the prophets of God; prophesy to an infidel, rebuke him, lay the judgments of God before him, make the secret sins of his heart manifest, and he shall fall down and worship God. They that crucified the Lord of glory, were not so far past recovery, but that the preaching of the apostles was able to move their hearts, and to bring them to this, *Men and brethren, what shall we do? Agrippa*, that sate in judgment against *Paul* for preaching, yielding notwithstanding thus far unto him; *Almost thou persuadest me to become a christian.* Altho' the *Jews*, for want of knowledge, have not submitted themselves to the righteousness of God; yet *I bear them record*, saith the apostle, *that they have a zeal.* The *Athenians*, a people having neither zeal nor knowledge, yet of them also the same apostle beareth witness, *Ye men of Athens, I perceive ye are* δεισι- Rom. 10. δαιμονίςεροι, some way religious, but mockers walking after their own ungodly lusts, they have smothered every spark of that heavenly light, they have trifled away their very natural understanding. O Lord, thy mercy is over all thy works, thou savest man and beast; yet a happy case it had been for these men, if they had never been born: and so I leave them.

10. Saint *Jude* having his mind exercised in the doctrine of the apostles of Jesus *Judas vir sapi-* Christ, concerning things to come in the last time, became a man of wise and staid *ens & certi ju-dicii.* judgment. Grieved he was to see the departure of many, and their falling away from the faith which before they did profess; grieved, but not *dismayed.* With the simpler and weaker sort it was otherwise: their countenance began by and by to change, they were half in doubt they had deceived themselves in giving credit to the gospel of Jesus Christ.

St. *Jude*, to comfort and refresh these silly babes, taketh them up in his arms, and sheweth them the men at whom they were offended. Look upon them that forsake this blessed profession wherein you stand: they are now before your eyes, view them, mark them, are they not carnal? are they not like to noisome carrion cast out upon the earth? is there that spirit in them which crieth *Abba Father* in your bosoms? Why should any man be discomforted? Have you not heard that there should be *mockers in the last time?* These verily are they that now do separate themselves.

11. For your better understanding what this severing and separating of themselves doth mean, we must know that the multitude of them which truly believe (howsoever they be dispersed far and wide each from other) is all *one body*, whereof the head is Christ; *one building*, whereof he is corner-stone, in whom they, as the members of the body, being knit, and as the stones of the building, being coupled, grow up to a man of perfect stature, and rise to an holy temple in the Lord. That which linketh Christ to us, is his mere mercy and love towards us. That which tieth us to him, is our faith in the promised salvation revealed in the word of truth. That which uniteth and joineth us amongst our selves, in such sort that we are now as if we had but one heart and one soul, is our love; who be inwardly in heart the lively members of this body, and the polished stones of this building, coupled and joined to Christ, as flesh of his flesh, and bones of his bones, by the mutual bond of his unspeakable love towards them, and their unfeigned faith in him, thus linked and fastned each to other, by a spiritual, sincere, and hearty affection of love, without any manner of simulation; who be *Jews* within, and what their names be, none can tell, save he whose eyes do behold the secret dispositions of all mens hearts. We, whose eyes are too dim to behold the inward man, must leave the secret judgment of every servant to his own Lord, accounting and using all men as brethren, both near and dear unto us, supposing Christ to love them tenderly, so as they keep the profession of the gospel, and join in the outward communion of saints. Whereof the one doth warrantize unto us their faith, the other

their

their love, till they fall away, and forsake either the one, or the other, or both; and then it is no injury to term them as they are. When they separate themselves, they are αὐτοκατάκριτοι, not judged by us, but by their own doings. Men do separate themselves either by heresy, schism, or apostacy. If they loose the bond of faith, which then they are justly supposed to do when they frowardly oppugn any principal point of christian doctrine, this is to separate themselves by *heresy*. If they break the bond of unity, whereby the body of the church is coupled and knit in one, as they do which wilfully forsake all external communion with saints in holy exercises purely and orderly established in the church, this is to separate themselves by *schism*. If they willingly cast off, and utterly forsake both profession of Christ and communion with christians, taking their leave of all religion, this is to separate themselves by plain *apostacy*. And St. *Jude*, to express the manner of their departure, which by *apostacy* fell away from the faith of Christ, saith, *They separated themselves*; noting thereby, that it was not constraint of others, which forced them to depart, it was not infirmity and weakness in themselves; it was not fear of persecution to come upon, whereat their hearts did fail; it was not grief of torment, whereof they had tasted, and were not able any longer to endure them: no, they voluntarily did separate themselves with a fully settled, and altogether determined purpose, never to name the Lord Jesus any more, nor to have any fellowship with his saints, but to bend all their counsel, and all their strength, to raze out their memorial from amongst them.

Threefold separation.

1. Heresy.

2. Schism.

3. Apostacy.

12. Now, because that by such examples, not only the hearts of infidels were hardned against the truth, but the minds of weak brethren also much troubled, the holy Ghost hath given sentence of these backsliders, that they were carnal men, and had not the Spirit of Christ Jesus, lest any man having an over-weening of their persons should be over much amazed and offended at their fall. For simple men, not able to discern their spirits, were brought, by their apostacy, thus to reason with themselves: If Christ be the Son of the living God, if he have the words of eternal life, if he be able to bring salvation to all men that come unto him, what meaneth this apostacy and unconstrained departure? Why do his servants so willingly forsake him? Babes, be not deceived, his servants forsake him not. They that separate themselves were amongst his servants, but if they had been of his servants, they had not separated themselves. *They were amongst us, not of us*, saith St. *John*; and St. *Jude* proveth it, because they were carnal, and had not the Spirit. Will you judge of wheat by chaff, which the wind hath scattered from amongst it? Have the children no bread, because the dogs have not tasted it? Are christians deceived of that salvation they look for, because they were denied the joys of the life to come which were no christians? What if they seemed to be pillars and principal upholders of our faith? What is that to us, which know that angels have fallen from heaven? Altho' if these men had been of us indeed (O the blessedness of a christian man's estate!) they had stood surer than the angels that had never departed from their place: whereas now we marvel not at their departure at all, neither are we prejudiced by their falling away; because they were not of us, sith they are fleshly, and have not the Spirit. Children abide in the house for ever; they are bond-men and bond-women which are cast out.

Infallible evidence in the faithful, that they are God's children.

13. It behoveth you therefore greatly, every man to examine his own estate, and to try whether you be bond or free, children or no children. I have told you already, that we must beware we presume not to sit as gods in judgment upon others; and rashly, as our conceit and fancy doth lead us, so to determine of this man, he is sincere; or of that man, he is an hypocrite; except by their falling away they make it manifest and known that they are. For who art thou that takest upon thee to judge another before the time? judge thy self. God hath left us infallible evidence, whereby we may at any time give true and righteous sentence upon our selves. We cannot examine the hearts of other men, we may our own. That we have passed from death to life, we know it, saith St. *John*, because we love the brethren: *And know ye not your own selves, how that Jesus Christ is in you, except you be reprobates?* I trust, beloved, we know that we are not reprobates, because our spirit doth bear us record, that the faith of our Lord Jesus Christ is in us.

14. It is as easy a matter for the spirit within you to tell whose ye are, as for the eyes of your body to judge where you sit, or in what place you stand. For what saith the scripture? *Ye which were in times past strangers and enemies, because your minds were set on evil works, Christ hath now reconciled in the body of his flesh through death, to make you holy, and unblameable, and without fault in his sight; if you continue grounded and established in the faith, and be not moved away from the hope of the gospel*, Coloss. 1. And in the third to the *Colossians*, *Ye know, that of the Lord ye shall receive the reward of that inheritance; for ye serve the Lord Christ.* If we can make this account with our selves, I was in times past dead in trespasses and sins, I

walked after the prince that ruleth in the air, and after the fpirit that worketh in the children of difobedience; but God, who is rich in mercy, through his great love, wherewith he loved me, even when I was dead, hath quickned me in Chrift. I was fierce, heady, proud, high-minded; but God hath made me like the child that is newly weaned. I loved pleafures more than God, I followed greedily the joys of this prefent world; I efteemed him that erected a ftage or theatre, more than *Solomon*, which built a temple to the Lord; the harp, viol, timbrel, and pipe, men fingers and womenfingers were at my feaft; it was my felicity to fee my children dance before me; I faid of every kind of vanity, O how fweet art thou in my foul! All which things now are crucified to me, and I to them: now I hate the pride of life, and pomp of this world; now *I take as great delight in the way of thy teftimonies, O Lord, as in all riches*; now I find more joy of heart in my Lord and Saviour, than the worldly-minded man, when *his wheat and oil do much abound:* now I tafte nothing fweet but the *bread which came down from heaven, to give life unto the world*; now mine eyes fee nothing but Jefus rifing from the dead; now my ears refufe all kind of melody, to hear the fong of them that have gotten victory of the beaft, and of his image, and of his mark, and of the number of his name, that ftand on the fea of glafs, *having the harps of God, and finging the fong of Mofes the fervant of God, and the fong of the Lamb, faying, Great and marvellous are thy works, Lord God Almighty, juft and true are thy ways, O King of faints*. Surely, if the Spirit have been thus effectual in the fecret work of our regeneration unto newnefs of life; if we endeavour thus to frame our felves anew; when we fay boldly with the bleffed apoftle, in the tenth to the *Hebrews*, *We are not of them which withdraw our felves to perdition, but which follow faith to the confervation of the foul*. For they which fall away from the grace of God, and feparate themfelves unto perdition, they are flefhly and carnal, they have not God's holy Spirit. But unto you, *becaufe ye are fons, God hath fent forth the Spirit of his Son into your hearts*, to the end ye might know that Chrift hath built you upon a rock unmoveable; that he hath regiftred your names in the book of life; that he hath bound himfelf in a fure and everlafting covenant to be your God, and the God of your children after you; that he hath fuffered as much, groaned as oft, prayed as heartily for you, as for *Peter, O Father, keep them in thy name, O righteous Father, the world hath not known thee, but I have known thee, and thefe have known that thou haft fent me. I have declared thy name unto them, and will declare it, that the love, wherewith thou haft loved them, may be in me, and I in them*. The Lord of his infinite mercy give us hearts plentifully fraught with the treafure of this bleffed affurance of faith unto the end.

15. Here I muft advertife all men that have the teftimony of God's holy fear within their breafts to confider, how unkindly and injurioufly our own countrymen and brethren have dealt with us by the fpace of twenty four years, from time to time, as if we were the men of whom St. *Jude* here fpeaketh, never ceafing to charge us, fome with *fchifm*, fome with *herefy*, fome with plain and manifeft *apoftacy*, as if we had clean feparated our felves from Chrift, utterly forfaken God, quite abjured heaven, and trampled all truth and religion under our feet. Againft this third fort, God himfelf fhall plead our caufe in that day, when they fhall anfwer us for thefe words, not we them. To others, by whom we are accufed for fchifm and herefy, we have often made our reafonable, and, in the fight of God, I truft, allowable anfwers. For in the way which they call *Herefy*, we worfhip the God of our fathers, believing all things which are written in the law and the prophets. That which they call *fchifm*, we know to be our reafonable fervice unto God, and obedience to his voice, which cryeth fhrill in our ears, *Go out of Babylon, my people, that you be not partakers of her fins, and that ye receive not of her plagues*. And therefore when they rife up againft us, having no quarrel but this, we need not feek any farther for our apology, than the words of *Abiah* to *Jeroboam* and his army, 2 *Chron.* 13. O *Jeroboam and Ifrael, hear you me: ought you not to know, that the Lord God of Ifrael hath given the kingdom over Ifrael to David for ever, even to him, and to his fons, by a covenant of falt?* that is to fay, an everlafting covenant. Jefuits and papifts, hear ye me: ought you not to know, that the Father hath given all power unto the Son, and hath made him the only head over his church, wherein he dwelleth as an hufbandman in the midft of his vineyard, manuring it with the fweat of his own brows, not letting it forth to others? For, as it is in the *Canticles*, *Solomon had a vineyard in Baalhamon, he gave the vineyard unto keepers, every one bringing for the fruit thereof a thoufand pieces of filver*; but my vineyard, which is mine, is before me, faith Chrift. It is true, this is meant of the myftical head fet over the body, which is not feen. But as he hath referved the myftical adminiftration of the church invifible unto himfelf; fo he hath committed the myftical government of congregations vifible to the fons of *David*, by the fame covenant; whofe fons
they

The papifts falfly accufe us of herefy and apoftafy.

Acts 15.

Apoc. 18.

Cant. 8. 11.

they are in the governing of the flock of Chrift, whomfoever the holy Ghoft hath fet over them, to go before them, and to lead them in feveral paftures, one in this congregation, another in that; as it is written, *Take heed unto your felves, and to all the flock whereof the holy Ghoft hath made you overfeers, to feed the church of God, which he hath purchafed with his own blood.* Neither will ever any pope or papift under the cope of heaven, be able to prove the *Romifh* bifhop's ufurped fupremacy over all churches by any one word of the covenant of falt, which is the fcripture. For the children in our ftreets do now laugh them to fcorn, when they force [*Thou art Peter*] to this purpofe. The pope hath no more reafon to draw the charter of his univerfal authority from hence, than his brethren had to gather by the words of Chrift in the laft of St. *John*, that the difciple which Jefus loved fhould not die. *If I will that he tarry till I come, what is that to thee?* faith Chrift. Straitways a report was raifed amongft the brethren, that this difciple fhould not die. *Yet Jefus faid not unto him, He fhall not die; but, if I will that he tarry till I come, what is that to thee?* Chrift hath faid in the xvi[th] of St. *Matthew's* gofpel to *Simon* the fon of *Jonas, I fay to thee, Thou art Peter.* Hence an opinion is held in the world, that the pope is univerfal head of all churches. Yet Jefus faid not, the pope is univerfal head of all churches; but, *Tu es Petrus,* Thou art *Peter.* Howbeit, as *Jeroboam,* the fon of *Nebat,* the fervant of *Solomon,* rofe up and rebelled againft his lord, and there were gathered unto him vain men and wicked, which made themfelves ftrong againft *Roboam* the fon of *Solomon,* becaufe *Roboam* was but a child and tender-hearted, and could not refift them; fo the fon of perdition and man of fin, (being not able to brook the words of our Lord and Saviour Jefus Chrift, which forbad his difciples to be like princes of nations, *They bear rule that are called gracious, it fhall not be fo with you,*) hath rifen up and rebelled againft his Lord; and to ftrengthen his arm, he hath crept into the houfes almoft of all the nobleft families round about him, and taken their children from the cradle to be his cardinals; he hath fawned upon the kings and princes of the earth, and by fpiritual cozenage hath made them fell their lawful authority and jurifdiction for titles of *Catholicus, Chriftianiffimus, Defenfor Fidei,* and fuch like; he hath proclaimed fale of pardons to inveigle the ignorant; built feminaries to allure young men defirous of learning; erected ftews to gather the diffolute unto him. This is the rock whereupon his church is built. Hereby the man is grown huge and ftrong, like the cedars which are not fhaken with the wind, becaufe princes have been as children, over-tender-hearted, and could not refift.

Hereby it is come to pafs, as you fee this day, that the man of fin doth war againft us, not by men of a language which we cannot underftand, but he cometh as *Jeroboam* againft *Judah,* and bringeth the fruit of our own bodies to eat up, that the bowels of the child may be made the mother's grave; and hath caufed no fmall number of our brethren to forfake their native country, and with all difloyalty to caft off the yoak of their allegiance to our dread fovereign, whom God in mercy hath fet over them; for whofe fafeguard, if they carried not the hearts of tygers in the bofoms of men, they would think the deareft blood in their bodies well fpent. But now faith *Abiah* to *Jeroboam,* ye think ye be able to refift the kingdom of the Lord, which is in the hands of the fons of *David.* Ye be a great multitude, the golden calves are with you, which *Jeroboam* made you for gods: have ye not driven away the priefts of the Lord, the fons of *Aaron,* and the *Levites,* and have made you priefts like the people of nations? whofoever cometh with a young bullock, and feven rams, the fame may be a prieft of them that are no gods. If I fhould follow the comparifon, and here uncover the cup of thofe deadly and ugly abominations, wherewith this *Jeroboam,* of whom we fpeak, hath made the earth fo drunk that it hath reeled under us, I know your godly hearts would loath to fee them. For my own part, I delight not to rake in fuch filth, I had rather take a garment upon my fhoulders, and go with my face from them to cover them. The Lord open their eyes, and caufe them, if it be poffible, at the length to fee how they are wretched, and miferable, and poor, and blind, and naked. Put it, O Lord, in their hearts, to feek white raiment, and to cover themfelves, that their filthy nakednefs may no longer appear. For, beloved in Chrift, we bow our knees, and lift up our hands to heaven in our chambers fecretly, and openly in our churches we pray heartily and hourly, even for them alfo: tho' the pope hath given out as a judge in a folemn declaratory fentence of *excommunication* againft this land, that our gracious lady hath quite abolifhed *prayer* within her realm: and his fcholars, whom he hath taken from the midft of us, have in their publifhed writings charged us, not only not to have any holy affemblies unto the Lord for prayer, but to hold a common fchool of fin and flattery; to hold facrilege to be God's fervice; unfaithfulnefs and breach of promife to God, to give it to a ftrumpet to be a vertue; to abandon fafting; to abhor confeffion; to miflike with penance; to like well of ufury; to charge none with reftitution; to find no good before God in fingle life; not in no well-working; that all men, as they fall to us, are much worfe,

2   and

Side notes (left margin):

Acts 20.

The pope's ufurped fupremacy.

Conc. delect. Card. Laur. Surius Com. de reb. geft Pio 5. Franciſc. Sanſovin. de gubern. rerum. pub. l. 11. cap. de Jud. Mareſcal. & Sold.

and more than afore, corrupted. I do not add one word or fyllable unto that which Mr. *Briftow*, a man both born and fworn amongft us, hath taught his hand to deliver to the view of all. I appeal to the confcience of every foul, that hath been truly converted by us, whether his heart were never raifed up to God by our preaching ; whether the words of our exhortation never wrung any tear of a penitent heart from his eyes ; whether his foul never reaped any joy and comfort, any confolation in Chrift Jefus by our facraments, and prayers, and pfalms, and thankfgiving ; whether he were never bettered, but always worfe by us.

O merciful God! If heaven and earth in this cafe do not witnefs with us, and againft them, let us be rázed out from the land of the living! Let the earth on which we ftand, fwallow us quick, as it hath done *Corab*, *Dathan*, and *Abiram*! But if we belong unto the Lord our God, and have not forfaken him ; if our priefts, the fons of *Aaron*, minifter unto the Lord, and the *Levites* in their office ; if we offer unto the Lord every morning and every evening the burnt-offerings, and fweet incenfe of prayers, and thankfgiving ; if the bread be fet in order upon the pure table, and the candleftick of gold, with the ² Chron. 13. lamps thereof, burn every morning ; that is to fay, if amongft us God's bleffed facraments be duly adminiftred, his holy word fincerely and daily preached ; if we keep the watch of the Lord our God, and if ye have forfaken him ; then doubt ye not, this God is with us as a captain, his priefts with founding trumpets muft cry alarm againft you ; *O ye* Ver. 18. *children of Ifrael, fight not againft the Lord God of your fathers, for ye fhall not profper.*

S E R M O N II.

Epift. J U D E, ver. 17, 18, 19, 20, 21.

But ye, beloved, remember the words which were fpoken before of the apoftles of our Lord Jefus Chrift:
How that they told you, that there fhould be mockers in the laft time, which fhould walk after their own ungodly lufts.
Thefe are makers of fects, flefhly, having not the Spirit.
But ye, beloved, edify your felves in your moft holy faith, praying in the holy Ghoft.
And keep your felves in the love of God, looking for the mercy of our Lord Jefus Chrift unto eternal life.

Having otherwhere fpoken of the words of St. *Jude*, going next before, concerning *mockers* which fhould come in the laft time, and back-fliders which even then fhould fall away from the faith of our Lord and Saviour Jefus Chrift ; I am now by the aid of Almighty God, and thro' the affiftance of his good Spirit, to lay before you the words of exhortation which I have read.

2. Wherein firft of all, whofoever hath an eye to fee let him open it, and he fhall well perceive how careful the Lord is for his children, how defirous to fee them profit and grow up to a manly ftature in Chrift, how loth to have them any way mifled, either by the examples of the wicked, or by inticements of the world, and by provocation of the flefh, or by any other means forceable to deceive them, and likely to eftrange their hearts from God. For God is not at that point with us, that he careth not whether we fink or fwim. No, he hath written our names in the palm of his hand, in the fignet upon his finger are we graven ; In fentences not only of mercy, but of judgment alfo we are remembred, he never denounceth judgments againft the wicked, but he maketh fome *provifo* for his children, as it were for fome certain privileged perfons, *Touch not mine anointed, do my prophets no harm : hurt not the earth, nor the fea, nor the trees, till we have fealed the fervants of God in their foreheads.* He never fpeaketh of godlefs men, but he adjoyneth words of comfort, or admonition, or exhortation, whereby we are moved to reft and fettle our hearts on him. In the fecond to *Timothy*, the third chapter, *Evil men* (faith the apoftle) *and deceivers fhall wax worfe and worfe, deceiving and being deceived. But continue thou in the things which thou haft learned.* And in the firft to *Timothy*, the fixth chapter, *Some men lufting after money, have*

erred

erred *from the faith, and pierced themselves thro' with many sorrows: but thou, O man of God, fly these things, and follow after righteousness, godliness, faith, love, patience, meekness.* In the second to the *Thessalonians*, the second chapter, *they have not received the love of the truth, that they might be saved, God shall send them strong delusions that they may believe lyes.* But *we ought to give thanks alway to God for you, brethren, beloved of the Lord, because God hath from the beginning chosen you to salvation, thro' sanctification of the Spirit, and faith in the truth.* And in this epistle of St. *Jude, There shall come mockers in the last times, walking after their own ungodly lusts.* But *beloved, edify ye your selves in your most holy faith.*

3. These sweet exhortations, which God putteth every where in the mouths of the prophets and apostles of Jesus Christ, are evident tokens that God sitteth not in heaven careless and unmindful of our estate. Can a mother forget her child? Surely a mother will hardly forget her child. But if a mother be haply found unnatural, and do forget the fruit of her own womb; yet God's judgments shew plainly that he cannot forget the man whose heart he hath framed and fashioned anew in simplicity and truth to serve and fear him. For when the wickedness of man was so great, and the earth so filled with cruelties, that it could not stand with the righteousness of God any longer to forbear,

Gen. 6. 3. and wrathful sentences brake out from him, like wine from a vessel that hath no vent: *My Spirit*
13. (saith he) *can struggle and strive no longer, an end of all flesh is come before me.* Yet
Chap. 6.8. and then did *Noah* find grace in the eyes of the Lord: *I will establish my covenant with thee,*
18. (saith God) *thou shalt go into the ark, thou, and thy sons, and thy wife, and thy sons wives with thee.*

4. Do we not see what shift God doth make for *Lot* and for his family, in the nineteenth of *Genesis,* left the fiery destruction of the wicked should overtake him? Overnight the angels make enquiry what sons and daughters, or sons in law, what wealth and
Chap. 19. 12. substance he had. They charged him to carry out all, *Whatsoever thou hast in the city, bring it out.* God seemed to stand in a kind of fear, left something or other would be left behind. And his will was, that nothing of that which he had, not an hoof of any beast, nor a thread of any garment should be singed with that fire. In the morning the
Chap. 19. 15. angels fail not to call him up, and to hasten him forward, *Arise, take thy wife and thy daughters which are here, that they be not destroyed in the punishment of the city.* The angels having spoken again and again, *Lot* for all this lingreth out the time still, till at
Verse 16. the length they were forced to take *both him, his wife, and his daughters by the arms, (the Lord being merciful unto him) and to carry them forth, and set them without the city.*

5. Was there ever any father thus careful to save his child from the flame? A man would think, that now being spoken unto to escape for his life, and not to look behind him, nor to tarry in the plain, but to hasten to the mountain, and there to save himself, he should do it gladly. Yet behold, now he is so far off from a chearful and willing heart to do whatsoever is commanded him for his own weal, that he beginneth to reason the matter, as if God had mistaken one place for another, sending him to the hill, when salvation was in the city. *Not so, my Lord, I beseech thee, behold, thy servant hath found grace in thy sight, and thou hast magnified thy mercy, which thou hast shewed unto me in saving my life. I cannot escape in the mountain, left some evil take me, and I dye. Here is a city hard by, a small thing ; O, let me escape thither (is it not a small thing ?) and my soul shall live.* Well, God is contented to yield to any conditions: *Behold, I have received thy request concerning this thing also, I will spare this city for which thou hast spoken ; haste thee, save thee there ; For I can do nothing till thou come thither.*

6. He could do nothing! Not because of the weakness of his strength (for who is like unto the Lord in power?) but because of the greatness of his mercy, which would not suffer him to lift up his arm against that city, nor to pour out his wrath upon that place, where his righteous servant had a fancy to remain, and a desire to dwell. O the depth of the riches of the mercy and love of God! God is afraid to offend us, who are not afraid to displease him. God can do nothing till he have saved us, who can find in our hearts rather to do any thing than to serve him. It contenteth him not to exempt us, when the pit is digged for the wicked ; to comfort us at every mention which is made of reprobates and godless men; to save us as the apple of his own eye, when fire cometh down from heaven to consume the inhabitants of the earth ; except every prophet, and every apostle, and every servant whom he sendeth forth, do come loaden with these or the like exhortations, *O beloved, edify your selves in your most holy faith ; give your selves to prayer in the spirit ; keep your selves in the love of God ; look for the mercy of our Lord Jesus Christ unto eternal life.*

7. *Edify your selves.* The speech is borrowed from material builders, and must be
2　　　　　　　　　　　　　　　　　　　　　　　　　　　spiritually

spiritually underſtood. It appears in the ſixth of St. *John's* goſpel, by the *Jews*, that their mouths did water too much for bodily food, *Our fathers, ſay they, did eat manna in the deſart, as it is written, he gave them bread from heaven to eat ; Lord, evermore give us of this bread.* Our Saviour, to turn their appetite another way, maketh them this anſwer, *I am the bread of life ; he that cometh to me ſhall not hunger ; and he that believeth in me ſhall never thirſt.*

8. An uſual practice it is of Satan, to caſt heaps of worldly baggage in our way, that whilſt we deſire to heap up gold as duſt, we may be brought at the length to eſteem vilely that ſpiritual bliſs. Chriſt in *Mat.* 6. to correct this evil affection, putteth us in mind to lay up treaſure for our ſelves in heaven. The apoſtle, 1 *Tim.* 3. miſliking the vanity of thoſe women who attired themſelves more coſtly than beſeemed the heavenly calling of ſuch as profeſſed the fear of God, willeth them to cloath themſelves with ſhamefacedneſs and modeſty, and to put on the apparel of good works. *Taliter pigmentatæ, Deum habebitis amatorem,* ſaith *Tertullian.* Put on righteouſneſs as a garment; inſtead of civet have faith which may cauſe a ſavour of life to iſſue from you, and God ſhall be enamoured, he ſhall be raviſhed with your beauty. Theſe are the ornaments, bracelets, and jewels which inflame the love of Chriſt, and ſet his heart on fire upon his Spouſe. We ſee how he breaketh out in the *Canticles* at the beholding of this attire, *How fair art thou, and how pleaſant art thou, O my love, in theſe pleaſures !*

9. And perhaps St. *Jude* exhorteth us here not to build our houſes, but our ſelves, foreſeeing by the Spirit of the Almighty which was with him, that there ſhould be men in the laſt days like to thoſe in the firſt, who ſhould encourage and ſtir up each other to make brick, and to burn it in the fire, to build houſes huge as cities, and towns as high as heaven, thereby to get them a name upon earth; men that ſhould turn out the poor, and the fatherleſs, and the widow, to build places of reſt for dogs and ſwine in their rooms ; men that ſhould lay houſes of prayer even with the ground, and make them ſtables where God's people have worſhipped before the Lord. Surely this is a vanity of all vanities, and it is much amongſt men ; and a ſpecial ſickneſs of this age. What it ſhould mean I know not, except God hath ſet them on work to provide fuel againſt that day, when the Lord Jeſus ſhall ſhew himſelf from heaven with his mighty angels in flaming fire. What good cometh unto the owners of theſe things, ſaith *Solomon,* but only the beholding thereof with their eyes ? *Martha, Martha, thou buſieſt thy ſelf about many things ; one thing is neceſſary,* Ye are too buſy, my brethren, with timber and brick ; they have choſen the better part, they have taken a better courſe that build themſelves. *Ye are the temples of the living God, as God hath ſaid, I will dwell in them, and will walk in them ; and they ſhall be my people, and I will be their God.*

10. Which of you will gladly remain or abide in a miſhapen, or a ruinous, or a broken houſe ? And ſhall we ſuffer ſin and vanity to drop in at our eyes, and at our ears, and at every corner of our bodies, and of our ſouls, knowing that we are the temples of the holy Ghoſt ? Which of you receiveth a gueſt whom he honoureth, or whom he loveth, and doth not ſweep his chamber againſt his coming ? And ſhall we ſuffer the chambers of our hearts and conſciences to lie full of vomiting, full of filth, full of garbage, knowing that Chriſt hath ſaid, *I and my father will come and dwell with you ?* Is it meet for your oxen to lie in parlors, and your ſelves to lodge in cribs ? Or is it ſeemly for your ſelves to dwell in your cieled houſes, and the houſe of the Almighty to lie waſte, whoſe houſe ye are your ſelves ? Do not our eyes behold, how God every day overtaketh the wicked in their journeys? How ſuddenly they pop down into the pit ? How God's judgments for their crimes come ſo ſwiftly upon them, that they have not the leiſure to cry, alas ! How their life is cut off like a thread in a moment ? How they paſs like a ſhadow? How they open their mouths to ſpeak, and God taketh them even in the midſt of a vain or an idle word ? and dare we for all this lie down, and take our reſt, eat our meat ſecurely and careleſly in the midſt of ſo great and ſo many ruins ? Bleſſed and praiſed for ever and ever be his name, who perceiving of how ſenſeleſs and heavy metal we are made, hath inſtituted in his CHURCH a ſpiritual ſupper, and an holy communion to be celebrated often, The ſacrament that we might thereby be occaſioned often to examine theſe buildings of ours, in what caſe they ſtand. For ſith God doth not dwell in temples which are unclean, ſith a ſhrine cannot be a ſanctuary unto him ; and this ſupper is received as a ſeal unto us, that we are his houſe, and his ſanctuary ; that his Chriſt is as truly united to me, and I to him, as my arm is united and knit unto my ſhoulder ; that he dwelleth in me as verily as the elements of bread and wine abide within me ; which perſuaſion, by receiving theſe dreadful myſteries, we profeſs our ſelves to have : a due comfort, if truly ; and if in hypocriſy, then wo worth us. Therefore e'er we put forth our hands to take this bleſſed ſacrament, we are charged to examine and try our hearts whether God be in us of a truth or no : as if by faith and love unfeigned we be found the temples of the holy Ghoſt, then to judge whether we have had ſuch regard every one to our building, that the Spirit which dwelleth

of the Lord's ſupper

in us hath no way been vexed, molested and grieved: or if it had, as no doubt sometimes it hath by incredulity, sometimes by breach of charity, sometimes by want of zeal, sometimes by spots of life, even in the best and most perfect amongst us; (for who can say his heart is clean?) O then to fly unto God by unfeigned repentance, to fall down before him in the humility of our souls, begging of him whatsoever is needful to repair our decays, before we fall into that desolation, whereof the prophet speaketh, saying, *Thy breach is great like the sea, who can heal thee?*

Lam. 2. 13.

11. Receiving the sacrament of the supper of the Lord after this sort (you that are spiritual judge what I speak) is not all other wine like the water of *Marah*, being compared to the cup which we bless? Is not *Manna* like to gall, and our bread like to *Manna?* Is there not a taste, a taste of Christ Jesus in the heart of him that eateth? Doth not he which drinketh behold plainly in this cup, that his soul is bathed in the blood of the Lamb? O beloved in our Lord and Saviour Jesus Christ, if ye will taste how sweet the Lord is, if ye will receive the King of glory, *build your selves.*

12. *Young men,* I speak this to you, for ye are his house, because by faith ye are conquerors over Satan, and have overcome that evil. *Fathers,* I speak it also to you, ye are his house, because ye have known him, who is from the beginning. Sweet *babes,* I speak it even to you also, ye are his house, because your sins are forgiven you for his name sake. *Matrons* and *sisters,* I may not hold it from you, ye are also the Lord's building; and as St. *Peter* speaketh, *Heirs of the grace of life as well as we.* Tho' it be forbidden you to open your mouths in publick assemblies, yet ye must be inquisitive in things concerning this building which is of God, with your husbands and friends at home; not as *Dalilah* with *Sampson,* but as *Sarah* with *Abraham*; whose daughters ye are, whilst ye do well, and build your selves.

13. Having spoken thus far of the exhortation, as whereby we are called upon to edify and build our selves; it remaineth now, that we consider the things prescribed, namely, wherein we must be built. This prescription standeth also upon two points, the *thing* prescribed, and the *adjunct* of the *thing.* And that is, our most pure and *holy faith.*

14. The thing prescribed is *faith.* For, as in a chain which is made of many links, if you pull the first, you draw the rest; and as in a ladder of many staves, if you take away the lowest, all hope of ascending to the highest will be removed: so, because all the precepts and promises in the law and in the gospel do hang upon this, *believe;* and because the last of the graces of God doth so follow the first, that he glorifieth none, but whom he hath justified, not justifieth any, but whom he hath called to a true, effectual, and lively faith in Christ Jesus; therefore St. *Jude* exhorting us to *build our selves,* mentioneth here expresly only faith, as the thing wherein we must be edified; for that faith is the ground and the glory of all the welfare of this building.

Ephes. 1 2.

15. *Ye are strangers and foreigners, but citizens with the saints, and of the houshold of God,* (saith the apostle) *and are built upon the foundation of the prophets and apostles, Jesus Christ himself being the chief corner-stone, in whom all the building being coupled together, groweth unto an holy temple in the Lord, in whom ye also are built together to be the habitation of God by the Spirit.* And we are the habitation of God by the Spirit, if we believe, for it is written, *Whosoever confesseth that Jesus is the Son of God, in him God dwelleth, and he in God.* The strength of this habitation is great, it prevaileth against Satan, it conquereth sin, it hath death in derision; neither principalities nor powers can throw it down; it leadeth the world captive, and bringeth every enemy that riseth up against it to confusion and shame, and all by faith; for *this is the victory that overcometh the world, even our faith. Who is it that overcometh the world, but he which believeth that Jesus is the Son of God?*

1 John 4.
Chap. 5.

16. The strength of every building which is of God, standeth not in any man's arms or legs; it is only in our faith, as the valour of *Sampson* lay only in his hair. This is the reason, why we are so earnestly called upon to *edify our selves in faith.* Not as if this bare action of our minds, whereby we believe the gospel of Christ, were able in it self, as of it self, to make us unconquerable, and invincible, like stones, which abide in building for ever, and fall not out: No, it is not the worthiness of our believing, it is the virtue of him in whom we believe, by which we stand sure, as houses that are builded upon a rock. He is a wiseman which hath builded his house upon a rock; for he hath chosen a good foundation, and no doubt his house will stand; but how shall it stand? Verily, by the strength of the rock which beareth it, and by nothing else. Our fathers, whom God delivered out of the land of *Egypt,* were a people that had no peers amongst the nations of the earth, because they were built by faith upon the rock, which rock is Christ. *And the rock* (saith the apostle in the first to the *Corinthians,* the tenth chapter) *did follow them.* Whereby we learn not only this, that being built by faith on Christ, as on a rock, and grafted into him as into an olive, we receive all our strength and fatness from him; but also, that this strength and fatness of ours ought to be no cause, why we should be high-minded,

Matth. 7.

3
minded,

minded, and not work out our falvation with a reverent trembling, and holy fear. For if thou boafteft thy felf of thy faith, know this, that Chrift chofe his apoftles, his apoftles chofe not him ; that *Ifrael* followed not the rock, but the rock followed *Ifrael*; and that thou beareft not the root, but the root thee. So that every heart muft thus think, and every tongue muft thus fpeak, *Not unto us, O Lord, not unto us,* nor unto any thing Rom. 11. which is within us, but unto thy Name only, only to thy Name belongeth all the praife of all the treafures and riches of every temple which is of God. This excludeth all boafting and vaunting of our faith.

17. But this muft not make us carelefs to edify our felves in faith. It is the Lord that 1 John 5. delivereth mens fouls from death, but not except they put their truft in his mercy. It is God that hath given us eternal life, but no otherwife than thus, if we believe in the Name of the Son of God ; for he that hath not the Son of God, hath not life. It was the Spirit of the Lord which came upon *Sampfon,* and made him ftrong to tear a lyon, as a man would rend a kid; but his ftrength forfook him, and he became like other men, when the razor had touched his head. It is the power of God whereby the faithful *have fubdued kingdoms, wrought righteoufnefs, obtained the promifes, ftopped the mouths of lyons, quenched the violence of fire, efcaped the edge of the fword:* but take away their faith, and doth not their ftrength forfake them? Are they not like unto other men?

18. If ye defire yet further to know, how neceffary and needful it is that we edify and build up our felves in faith, mark the words of the bleffed apoftle, *Without faith it is impoffible to pleafe God.* If I offer to God all the fheep and oxen, that are in the world; if all the temples, that were builded fince the days of *Adam* till this hour, were of my foundation; if I break my very heart with calling upon God, and wear out my tongue with preaching; if I facrifice my body and foul unto him, *and have no faith,* all this availeth nothing. *Without faith it is impoffible to pleafe God.* Our Lord and Saviour No pleafing of therefore being asked in the fixth of St. *John's* gofpel, *What fhall we do that we might* God without *work the works of God?* maketh anfwer, *This is the work of God, that ye believe in him, whom he hath fent.* faith.

19. That no work of ours, no building of our felves in any thing can be available or profitable unto us, except we be edified and built in faith, what need we to feek about for long proof? Look upon *Ifrael,* once the very chofen and peculiar of God, to whom the adoption of the faithful, and the glory of cherubims, and the covenants of mercy, and the law of *Mofes,* and the fervice of God, and the promifes of Chrift were made impropriate, who not only were the off-fpring of *Abraham,* father unto all them which do believe, but Chrift their off-fpring, which is God to be bleffed for evermore.

20. Confider this people, and learn what it is *to build your felves in faith.* They were the Lord's vine: he brought it out of *Egypt,* he threw out the heathen from their places, that it might be planted; he made room for it, and caufed it to take root, till it had filled the earth; the mountains were covered with the fhadow of it, and the boughs thereof were as the goodly cedars; fhe ftretched out her branches to the fea, and her boughs unto the river. But, when God having fent both his fervants and his Son to vifit this vine, they neither fpared the one, nor received the other, but ftoned the prophets, and crucified the Lord of glory which came unto them; then began the curfe of God to come upon them, even the curfe whereof the prophet *David* hath fpoken, faying, *Let their table be* Pfal. 69. *made a fnare, and a net, and a ftumbling-block, even for a recompence unto them: let* Rom. 11. *their eyes be darkned, that they do not fee, bow down their backs for ever,* keep them down. And fithence the hour that the meafure of their infidelity was firft made up, they have been fpoiled with wars, eaten up with plagues, fpent with hunger and famine; they wander from place to place, and are become the moft bafe and contemptible people that are under the fun. *Ephraim,* which before was a terror unto nations, and they trembled at his voice, is now by infidelity fo vile, that he feemeth as a thing caft out to be trampled under mens feet. In the midft of thefe defolations they cry, *Return, we befeech thee, O* Pfal. 80. 14. *God of hofts, look down from heaven, behold and vifit this vine:* But their very prayers are turned into fin, and their cries are no better than the lowing of beafts before him. *Well,* faith the apoftle, *by their unbelief they are broken off, and thou doft ftand by thy faith:* Rom. 11. 10. *behold therefore the bountifulnefs, and feverity of God; towards them feverity, becaufe they have fallen, bountifulnefs towards thee, if thou continue in his bountifulnefs, or elfe* Verfe 22. *thou fhalt be cut off.* If they forfake their unbelief and be grafted in again, and we at any time for the hardnefs of our hearts be broken off, it will be fuch a judgment as will amaze all the powers and principalities which are above. Who hath fearched the counfel of God Hofea 1. 9. not concerning this fecret? And who doth not fee, that *infidelity* doth threaten *Lo-ammi* unto my people verfe 6. not the *Gentiles,* as it hath brought *Lo-ruchama* upon the *Jews?* It may be that thefe words obtaining feem dark unto you: but the words of the apoftle, in the eleventh to the *Romans,* are mercy. plain enough, *If God hath not fpared the natural branches, take heed, left he fpare not thee:* build thy felf in faith. Thus much of the thing which is prefcribed, and

wherein

wherein we are exhorted, *edify your selves.* Now confider the *condition* and *properties* which are in this place annexed unto faith. The former of them (for there are but two) is this, *Edify your selves in your faith.*

21. A ftrange, and a ftrong delufion it is wherewith the *man of fin* hath bewitched the world; a forceable fpirit of error it muft needs be, which hath brought men to fuch a fenfelefs and unreafonable perfuafion as this is, not only that men cloathed with mortality and fin, as we our felves are, can do God fo much fervice as fhall be able to make a full and perfect fatisfaction before the tribunal feat of God for our own fins, yea, a great deal more than is fufficient for themfelves; but alfo, that a man at the hands of a bifhop or a pope, for fuch or fuch a price, may buy the *overplus* of other mens merits, purchafe the fruits of other mens labours, and build his foul by another man's faith. Is not this man drowned in the gall of bitternefs? Is his heart right in the fight of God? Can he have any part or fellowfhip with *Peter*, and with the fucceffors of *Peter*, who thinketh fo vilely of building the precious temples of the holy Ghoft? Let his money perifh with him, and he with it, becaufe he judgeth that the gift of God may be fold for money.

22. But, beloved in the Lord, deceive not your felves, neither fuffer ye your felves to be deceived: ye can receive no more eafe nor comfort for your foul by another man's faith, than warmth for your bodies by another man's cloaths, or fuftenance by the bread which another man doth eat. The juft fhall live by his own faith. *Let a faint, yea a martyr, content himfelf that he hath cleanfed himfelf of his own fins,* faith *Tertullian:* No faint or martyr can cleanfe himfelf of his own fins. But if fo be a faint or a martyr can cleanfe himfelf of his own fins, it is fufficient that he can do it for himfelf. Did ever any man by his death deliver another man from death, except only the Son of God? He indeed was able to fafe conduct a thief from the crofs to paradife: for to this end he came, that being himfelf pure from fin, he might obey for finners. Thou which thinkeft to do the like, and fuppofeft that thou canft juftify another by thy righteoufnefs, if thou be without fin, then lay down thy life for thy brother; die for me. But if thou be a finner, even as I am a finner, how can the oyl of thy lamp be fufficient both for thee and for me? *Virgins* that are wife, get ye oyl, while ye have day, into your own lamps: for out of all peradventure, others, tho' they would, can neither give nor fell. Edify your felves in your own moft holy faith. And let this be obferved for the firft *property* of that wherein we ought to edify our felves.

23. Our faith being fuch is that indeed which St. *Jude* doth here term *faith*; namely, a thing moft *holy.* The reafon is this, we are juftified by *faith*: for *Abraham* believed, and this was imputed unto him for righteoufnefs. Being juftified, all our iniquities are covered; God beholdeth us in the righteoufnefs which is imputed, and not in the fins which we have committed.

24. It is true, we are full of fin, both *original* and *actual*; whofoever denieth it is a double finner, for he is both a finner and a lyar. To deny fin is moft plainly and clearly to prove it, becaue he that faith he hath no fin, lyeth, and by lying proveth that he hath fin.

25. But *imputation* of righteoufnefs hath covered the fins of every foul which believeth; God by pardoning our fin hath taken it away: fo that now, altho' our tranfgreffions be multiplied above the hairs of our head, yet being juftified, we are as free and as clear as if there were no one fpot or ftain of any uncleannefs in us. For it is God that juftifieth; *And who fhall lay any thing to the charge of God's chofen?* faith the apoftle in *Rom.* 8.

26. Now fin being taken away, we are made the righteoufnefs of God in Chrift: for *David* fpeaking of this righteoufnefs, faith, *Bleffed is the man whofe iniquities are forgiven.* No man is bleffed, but in the righteoufnefs of God: Every man whofe fin is taken away is bleffed, Therefore every man whofe fin is covered, is made the righteoufnefs of God in Chrift. This righteoufnefs doth make us to appear moft holy, moft pure, moft unblameable before him.

27. This then is the fum of that which I fay, faith doth juftify; juftification wafheth away fin; fin remov'd, we are cloath'd with the righteoufnefs which is of God; the righteoufnefs of God maketh us moft holy. Every of thefe I have proved by the teftimony of God's own mouth; therefore I conclude, that faith is that which maketh us moft holy, in confideration whereof, it is called in this place, *Our moft holy faith.*

28. To make a wicked and a finful man moft holy thro' his believing, is more than to create a world of nothing. Our faith moft holy! Surely, *Solomon* could not fhew the queen of *Sheba* fo much treafure in all his kingdom, as is lapt up in thefe words. O that our hearts were ftretched out like tents, and that the eyes of our underftanding were as bright as the fun, that we might throughly know the riches of the glorious inheritance of the faints, and what is the exceeding greatnefs of his power towards us, whom he accepteth for pure, and moft holy, through our believing! O that the Spirit of the Lord would give this doctrine entrance into the ftony and brazen heart of the *Jew*, which fol-

loweth the law of righteoufnefs, but cannot attain unto the righteoufnefs of the law! Wherefore, faith the apoftle, they feek righteoufnefs, and not by faith; wherefore they ftumble at Chrift, they are bruifed, fhivered to pieces, as a fhip that hath run her felf upon a rock. O that God would caft down the eyes of the proud, and humble the fouls of the high-minded! that they might at the length abhor the garments of their own flefh, which cannot hide their nakednefs, and put on the faith of Chrift Jefus, as he did put it on, who hath faid, *Doubtlefs I think all things but lofs, for the excellent knowledge fake of Chrift Jefus my Lord, for whom I have counted all things lofs, and do judge them to be dung, that I might win Chrift, and might be found in him, not having my own righteoufnefs, which is of the law; but that which is thro' the faith of Chrift, even the righteoufnefs which is of God thro' faith.* O that God would open the ark of mercy, wherein this doctrine lieth, and fet it wide before the eyes of poor afflicted confciences, which fly up and down upon the water of their afflictions, and can fee nothing but only the gulf and deluge of their fins, wherein there is no place for them to reft their feet. The God of pity and compaffion give you all ftrength and courage, every day, and every hour, and every moment, to build and edify yourfelves in this moft pure and holy faith. And thus much both of the thing profcribed in this exhortation, and alfo of the properties of the thing, *Build your felves in your moft holy faith.* I would come to the next branch, which is of prayer; but I cannot lay this matter out of my hands, till I have added fomewhat for the applying of it, both to others, and to our felves.

29. For your better underftanding of matters contained in this exhortation, *Build your felves,* you muft note, that every church and congregation doth confift of a multitude of believers, as every houfe is built of many ftones. And altho' the nature of the myftical body of the church be fuch, that it fuffereth no diftinction in the vifible members, but whether it be *Paul* or *Apollos,* prince or prophet, he that is taught, or he that teacheth, all are equally Chrift's, and Chrift is equally theirs: yet in the external adminiftration of the church of God, becaufe God is not the author of confufion, but of peace, it is neceffary, that in every congregation there be a diftinction, if not of inward dignity, yet of outward degree; fo that all are faints, or feem to be faints, and fhould be as they feem: but are all apoftles? If the whole body were an eye, where were then the hearing? God therefore hath given fome to be apoftles, and fome to be paftors, *&c.* for the edification of the body of Chrift. In which work, we are God's labourers (faith the apoftle) and ye are God's husbandry, and God's building.

30. The church, refpected with reference unto adminiftration ecclefiaftical, doth generally confift but of two forts of men, the *labourers* and the *building;* they which are miniftred unto, and they to whom the work of the miniftry is committed; *paftors* and the *flock* over whom the holy Ghoft hath made them overfeers. If the *guide* of a congregation, be his name or his degree whatfoever, be diligent in his vocation, feeding the flock of God which dependeth upon him, caring for it, *not by conftraint, but willingly; not for filthy lucre, but of a ready mind;* not as tho' he would tyrannize over God's heritage, but as a pattern unto the flock, wifely guiding them: if the people in their degree do yield themfelves framable to the truth, not like rough ftone or flint, refufing to be fmoothed and fquared for the building: if the magiftrate do carefully and diligently furvey the whole order of the work, providing by ftatutes and laws, and bodily punifhments, if need require, that all things might be done according to the rule which cannot deceive; even as *Mofes* proved, that all things might be done according to the pattern which he faw in the mount; there the words of this exhortation are truly and effectually heard. Of fuch a congregation every man will fay, *Behold a people that are wife, a people that walk in the ftatutes and ordinances of their God, a people full of knowledge and underftanding, a people that have skill in building themfelves.* Where it is otherwife, there, *as by flothfulnefs the roof doth decay;* and as by *idlenefs of hands the houfe droppeth thorow,* as it is in *Ecclef.* 10. 18. fo firft one piece, and then another of their building fhall fall away, till there be not a ftone left upon a ftone.

31. We fee how fruitlefs this exhortation hath been to fuch as bend all their travel only to build and manage a *papacy* upon earth, without any care in the world of building themfelves in their moft holy faith. God's people have enquired at their mouths, *What fhall we do to have eternal life?* Wherein fhall we build and edify our felves? And they have departed home from their prophets, and from their priefts, laden with doctrines which are precepts of men; they have been taught to tire out themfelves with bodily exercife: thofe things are enjoined them, which God did never require at their hands, and the things he doth require are kept from them; their eyes are fed with pictures, and ears are filled with melody, but their fouls do wither, and ftarve, and pine away; they cry for bread, and behold ftones are offered them; they ask for fifh, and fee they have fcorpions in their hands. Thou feeft, O Lord, that they build themfelves, but not in faith; they feed their children, but not with food: their rulers fay with fhame, bring, and not
build.

build. But God is righteous; their drunkennefs ftinketh, their abominations are known, their madnefs is manifeft, the wind hath bound them up in her wings, and they fhall be afhamed of their doings. *Ephraim,* faith the prophet, *is joined to idols, let him alone.* I will turn me therefore from the priefts, which do minifter unto idols, and apply this exhortation to them, whom God hath appointed to feed his chofen in *Ifrael.*

32. If there be any feeling of Chrift, any drop of heavenly dew, or any fpark of God's good Spirit within you, ftir it up, be careful to build and edify, firft your felves, and then your flocks in this moft holy faith.

33. I fay, *firft, your felves*; for, he which will fet the hearts of other men on fire with the love of Chrift, muft himfelf burn with love. It is want of faith in our felves, my bre-
* Carelefs. thren, which makes us * wretchlefs in building others. We forfake the Lord's inheritance, and feed it not. What is the reafon of this? Our own defires are fettled where they fhould not be. We our felves are like thofe women which have a longing to eat coals, and lime, and filth; we are fed, fome with honour, fome with eafe, fome with wealth; the gofpel waxeth loathfome and unpleafant in our tafte; how fhould we then have a care to feed others with that which we cannot fancy our felves? If *faith* wax cold and flender in the
Amos 8. 11, heart of the prophet, it will foon perifh from the ears of the people. The prophet *Amos*
12. fpeaketh of a famine, faying, *I will fend a famine in the land, not a famine of bread, nor a thirft of water, but of hearing the word of the Lord. Men fhall wander from fea to fea, and from the north unto the eaft fhall they run to and fro, to feek the word of the Lord, and*
1 Pet. 4. 17. *fhall not find it. Judgment muft begin at the houfe of God,* faith *Peter.* Yea, I fay, at the fanctuary of God this judgment muft begin. This famine muft begin at the heart of the prophet. He muft have darknefs for a vifion, he muft ftumble at noon-day, as at the twilight, and then truth fhall fall in the midft of the ftreets; then fhall the people wander from fea to fea, and from the north unto the eaft fhall they run to and fro, to feek the word of the Lord.

34. In the fecond of *Haggai, fpeak now,* faith God to his prophet, *fpeak now to* Zerubbabel, *the fon of* Shealtiel, *prince of* Judah, *and to* Jehofhua, *the fon of* Jehozadak *the high-prieft, and to the refidue of the people, faying, who is left among you that faw this houfe in her firft glory? and how do you fee it now? Is not this houfe in your eyes, in comparifon of it, as nothing?* The prophet would have all mens eyes turn'd to the view of themfelves, every fort brought to the confideration of their prefent ftate. This is no place to fhew what duty *Zerubbabel* or *Jehofhua* do owe unto God in this refpect. They have, I doubt not, fuch as put them hereof in remembrance, I ask of you, which are a part of the refidue of God's elect and chofen people, who is there amongft you that hath taken a furvey of the houfe of God, as it was in the days of the bleffed apoftles of Jefus Chrift? Who is there amongft you that hath feen and confidered this holy temple in her firft glory? And how do you fee it now? Is it not, in comparifon of the other, almoft as nothing? When you look upon them which have undertaken the charge of your fouls, and know how far thefe are, for the moft part, grown out of kind, how few there be that tread the fteps of their antient predeceffors, ye are eafily filled with indignation, eafily drawn unto thefe complaints, wherein the difference of prefent from former times is bewailed; eafily perfuaded to think of them that lived to enjoy the days which now are gone, that furely they were happy in comparifon of us that have fucceeded them: were not their bifhops men unreproveable, wife, righteous, holy, temperate, well reported of, even of thofe which were without? Were not their paftors, guides, and teachers, able and willing to exhort with wholefom doctrine, and to reprove thofe which gain-faid the truth? Had they priefts made of the refufe of the people? Were men, like to the children which were in *Nineveh,* unable to difcern between the right hand and the left, prefented to the charge of their congregations? Did their teachers leave their flocks, over which the holy Ghoft had made them overfeers? Did their prophets enter upon holy things as fpoils, without a reverend calling? Were their leaders fo unkindly affected towards them, that they could find in their hearts to fell them as fheep or oxen, not caring how they made them away? But beloved, deceive not your felves. Do the faults of your guides and paftors offend you? It is your fault if they be thus faulty. *Nullus, qui malum rectorem patitur, eum accufet: quia fui fuit meriti perverfi paftoris fubjacere ditioni,* faith St. *Gregory,* whofoever thou art, whom the inconvenience of an evil gover-
Jer. 3. 14. 15. nor doth prefs, accufe thy felf, and not him; his being fuch, is thy deferving. *O ye difobedient children, turn again,* faith the Lord, *and then will I give you paftors according to mine own heart, which fhall feed you with knowledge and underftanding.* So that the only way to repair all ruins, breaches, and offenfive decays in others, is to begin reformation at your felves. Which that we may all fincerely, ferioufly, and fpeedily do, God the Father grant for his Son our Saviour Jefus's fake, unto whom, with the holy Ghoft, three Perfons, one eternal and everlafting God, be honour, and glory, and praife, for ever. *Amen.*

F I N I S.

THE
INDEX.

Note, that the numeral letters refer to the *preface*, all the figures to the *book*; *a* denotes the top of the page, *b* about the middle, *c* towards the end.

INDEX.

I.

INDEX.

Y y y   Masses

INDEX.

TEXTS of SCRIPTURE explain'd, and particularly consider'd.

Lightning Source UK Ltd.
Milton Keynes UK
UKHW022223281122
413021UK00005B/88